W9-BRF-504

Trailer Life's

RV Travel Guide & Atlas

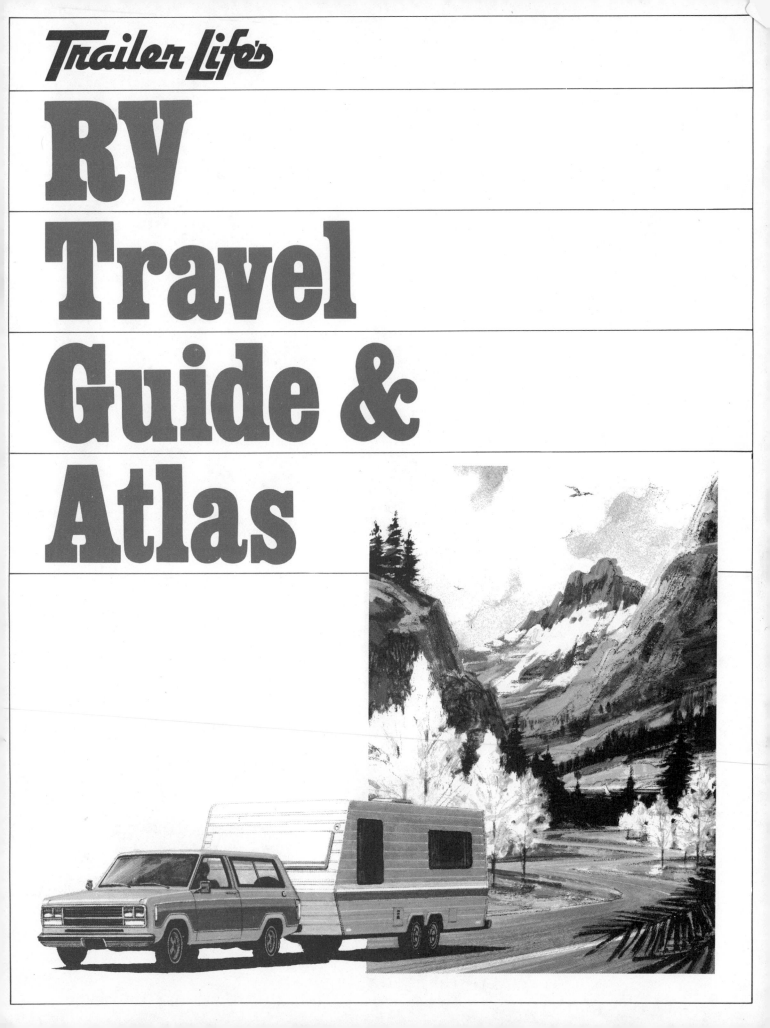

Trailer Life's

RV Travel Guide & Atlas

By Bob Longsdorf
and the Editors of Trailer Life

Editor in Charge: Patrick J. Flaherty

Published by TL Enterprises, Inc.
29901 Agoura Road, Agoura, California 91301

Book Division
TL Enterprises, Inc.

Art Rouse
Chairman of the Board

Richard Rouse
President

Denis Rouse
Executive Vice President/Publisher

Patrick J. Flaherty
Vice President/Editor-In-Chief

Dana Brown
Vice President/Production Director

Composition By:
Publisher's Typography
(A Division of TL Enterprises, Inc.)

Director: Pat Van Fleet

Book Design: Jim Doolan, Nan Kane
Illustrator: Ron McKee
Editorial Associate: Kim Mallon
Editorial Assistants: Tina Hill, Pat Kolb, Olga Markowitz

Published by TL Enterprises, Inc., 29901 Agoura Road, Agoura, California 91301. International Standard Book Number 0-934798-01-X. Library of Congress Catalog Card Number 79-66971. Printed and Bound in the United States of America by R.R. Donnelley & Sons Company.

Hours, admission fees and prices in the editorial content of this book are as of November, 1980.

Foreward

During my many years of traveling by RV, I've visited just about every part of this great country of ours. And to help make my trips more enjoyable, I've bought enough travel books, atlases and road maps to stock a small library.

But the one thing I continually searched for and could never find was a *single* book that could answer *all* of my RV travel questions.

Well, now there is such a book — the one you're holding in your hands. And, like the subtitle says, it really does tell you "everything you need to know to RV America."

Here is a book that combines the best features of an atlas with an astounding amount of useful and entertaining information that is of specific interest to the ardent RVer.

For example, within these pages you'll find special maps that will help you locate state and national parks and forests (including a complete listing of all monuments and historical sites), a complete listing of amusement parks (including admission fees, if any), plus a guide to America's most colorful festivals, pageants, fairs, rodeos, races and rallies.

But best of all, this book has been designed so that you can use it on a state, regional or national basis.

I'm sure you will find, as I have, that our *RV Travel Guide & Atlas* makes the perfect companion for *Trailer Life's RV Campground & Services Directory*.

So please use it . . . and enjoy it. And may your future RV travels give you as much pleasure as I have had in introducing this exceptional book to you.

Art Rouse
Chairman of the Board

Table of Contents

America's Legacy

Lush forests, awesome glaciers, spectacular waterfalls and underground caverns – this nation's bounty to generations of travelers from Yellowstone to Yosemite.

Discovery Tours

Discover America through its historical sites and museums, its native peoples, California's wine country and the continent's finest dining places.

Travel Adventures

Thrill to the joys of America's wild rivers; explore the backcountry; pan for gold; experience ranch life and fish America's rivers and lakes.

Practical RVing

Tried-and-true methods of enjoying worry-free hours of RVing and adding more smiles to the mile.

About This Book

". . . Light-hearted I take to the open road,
Healthy, free, the world before me,
The long brown path before me leading wherever I choose."

Walt Whitman — *Song of the Open Road*

But where to choose?

In Whitman's time, the choices were few. But today, his "brown paths" have given way to a complex network of superhighways, two-lane blacktops and meandering country lanes that put the entire North American continent — all 9,363,000 square miles of it — virtually at your doorstep.

There is the fiery spectacle of a New England autumn, the checkered green fields of the nation's heartland, the undulating grasslands of the Great Plains, the awesome splendor of the Grand Canyon, the breathtaking beauty of the Canadian Rockies and the astonishing ruins of Mexico's ancient Indian cultures. And there are so many things to do: Hike a quiet forest trail, plunge through the roaring white water of a rushing river, discover the Old World charm of New Orleans, fish a clear mountain stream, visit the quiet halls of a great museum, glide through the white silence of a winter landscape — the choices are as limitless as your imagination.

For these very reasons we have published *Trailer Life's RV Travel Guide & Atlas.* This unique book combines the best features of an atlas with a wealth of entertaining and useful information that will help you make the most of your travel experiences. Within these pages you will find more than 100 maps and a guide to state and national forests and parks. There are features to acquaint you with travel activities, historical sites, America's Indian cultures and California's wine country, plus a listing of amusement parks and a hunting and fishing section that includes details on all license fees for each state, Canada and Mexico. To make your journeys even more enjoyable, we have also included some general travel hints, a troubleshooting guide, winter travel suggestions and a Travel Adventure section that covers such activities as river running, backpacking, aero sports, bicycling, rockhounding and prospecting for gold.

In addition to all this, we have put together some surprises, too — for as Whitman said, "much unseen is also here," and we want to make sure that you don't miss any of it. Throughout the *RV Travel Guide & Atlas* you'll find *TL Highlights* and *Suggested TL Tours* that will point out unique attractions and guide you along a route that we think especially captures the essence of travel within a particular state. For each regional grouping of states, we have also included a seasonal breakdown of festivals, fairs and special events, including the dates of some of the more celebrated attractions, as well as a comprehensive listing of many colorful local events. For instance, we tell you the date of the swallows' return to California's Mission San Juan Capistrano — but we also tell you when the buzzards make their annual migration to Hinckley, Ohio. With this detailed list as a guide, you can plan to attend such diverse events as the National Hollerin' Contest at Spivey's Corner, North Carolina; Rhode Island's Gaspee Days; Sauerkraut Day in Wishek, North Dakota; Ontario's George Bernard Shaw Festival; the Valdez Winter Carnival in Valdez, Alaska; the Annual Native Dance Festival in Texcoco, Mexico — and hundreds more, scores of which are celebrated in your very own state.

So if you'd like to know where to go, when to go, what to see, how to get there and how to enjoy yourself en route . . . this is the RV book you've been waiting for.

— The Editors

NEW HAMPSHIRE
Great Stone Face
Flume Gorge
MASSACHUSETTS
Plymouth
RHODE ISLAND
Providence
Slater Mill

VERMONT
MAINE
CONNECTICUT
Guilford
Mystic

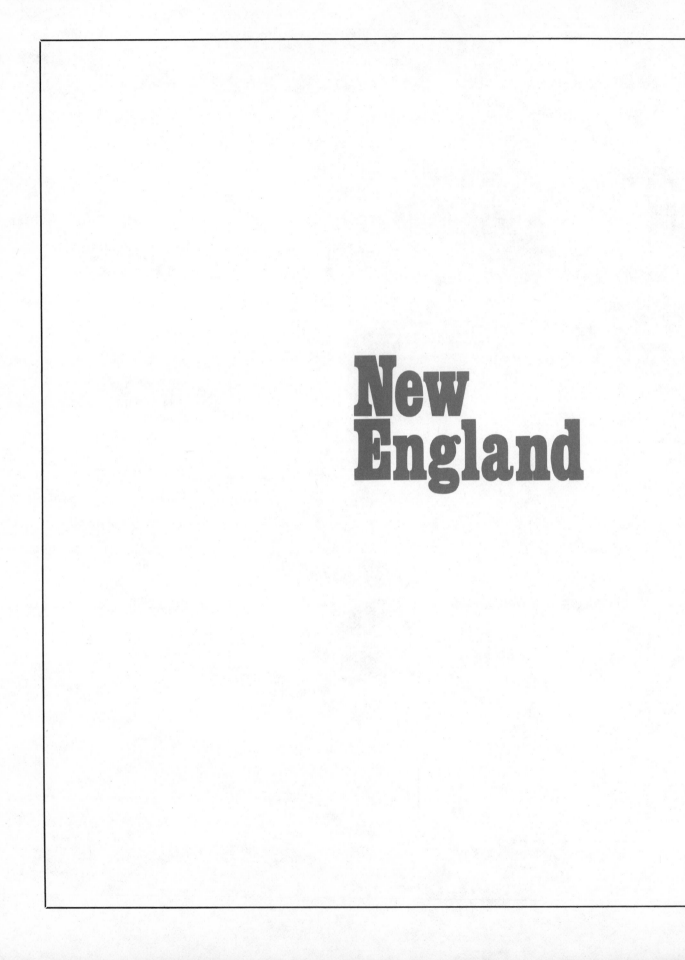

New England

For even the most provincial traveler, New England is no stranger. So much of the nation's history has come out of this region, along with countless photographs depicting its spectacular fall colors, peaceful wooded landscapes and quaint rural villages, that no one can really say he is a first-time visitor.

The colorful names of colonial America — the Old North Church, Plymouth Rock, the Boston Tea Party, Lexington and Concord — and the colorful figures so familiar to every school child — Myles Standish, Paul Revere, John Adams, Daniel Webster — are all a part of New England's heritage. Blessed with such a rich past, the region is doubly-blessed with an abundance of natural beauty: Maine's rugged coast, the sandy beaches of Cape Cod, sparkling glacial lakes, cascading streams, silvery rivers. Many of the farms claimed from the land with such hard labor by the early settlers have now been reclaimed by nature, so lush forests once again cover much of the land. Rising above the coastline and the lowland forests are the highlands, the rolling Connecticut hills, the Berkshires of Massachusetts, Vermont's Green Mountains and the White Mountains of New Hampshire, where the winds never seem to stop and gusts have been recorded as high as 321 miles per hour.

Of course, one can't overlook New England's most important resource — its people. For this is the seat of "good old Yankee know-how" — the inventive genius that gave us such diverse items as the first submarine, steel fishhooks and the first football tackling dummy. And we can't forget that dry Yankee wit preserved in stories like the one about the husband who chastised his wife for buying a book of useless home remedies by penning inside the flyleaf, "I cain't find no cure here for suckers."

Of such stuff is New England made, and it's yours to enjoy in the cities and on the backroads that make this region such a very special treat for travelers.

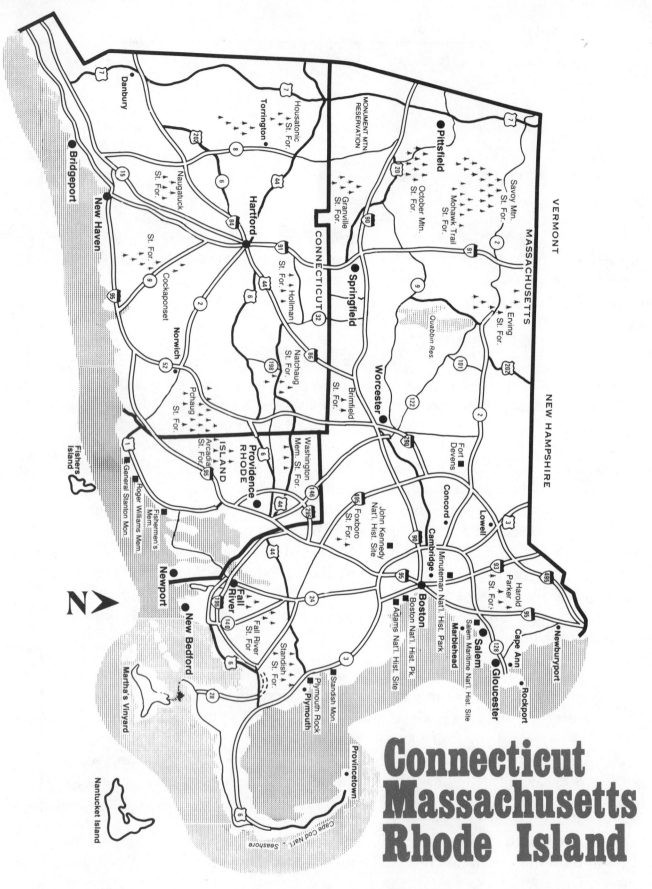

Connecticut Massachusetts Rhode Island

Map not to exact scale.

Connecticut

It wasn't easy to wrest a living from the rocky soil of Connecticut, so many of its early settlers formed cottage industries to supply the "Yankee peddlers" who traveled the countryside hawking pins, combs, clocks, kettles, pans and skillets. Some of the more enterprising peddlers even took to selling fake nutmegs, carved from wood, instead of the genuine spice; thus, Connecticut's sometime nickname, The Nutmeg State.

The state's history can be traced from its earliest inhabitants through later occupation by the Dutch and final settlement by the English. English settlements were established at Hartford and Saybrook in 1635, and the representatives of these and other communities united in 1639 to form the Connecticut colony — which adopted the "Fundamental Orders" that gave citizens the right to elect government officials and omitted the religious test for citizenship. This document later became a part of the model for the U.S. Constitution, and is considered to be the world's first written constitution. Later, the Connecticut colonists refused to surrender their charter to King James II; and to keep his governor from seizing it, they hid it in the legendary Charter Oak Tree.

With this early feeling for independence, it's not surprising that Connecticut took a leading role in the Revolutionary War, contributing such patriots as Nathan Hale and Governor Jonathan Trumbull, and serving as a major supply area for the Continental Army. Similarly, Connecticut's contribution to the Union cause in the Civil War was noteworthy, as five times the state's quota of men volunteered for service.

Beginning with the Civil War, the economic base of the state began to shift from agriculture to industry and the state became known as the "Arsenal of the Nation" because of pioneers like Samuel Colt, who invented the revolver, and Eli Whitney, who innovated mass production

Full name: State of Connecticut
Origin of name: Indian, Quinnehtukqut, meaning "Beside the Long Tidal River."
Motto: *Qui Transtulit Sustinet* (He Who Transplanted Still Sustains).
Nickname: Constitution State, Nutmeg State.
Capital: Hartford
Statehood: January 9, 1788, fifth state.
Population: 3,108,000 (ranks 24th).
Major Cities: Bridgeport (142,960), Hartford (138,152), New Haven (126,845).
Bird: Robin
Flower: Mountain laurel
Tree: White oak

Average daily temperatures by month

	Northern	Southern
Jan.	28.1 to 11.7	36.2 to 18.4
Feb.	30.0 to 12.5	38.6 to 20.3
Mar.	38.0 to 21.1	45.9 to 27.7
Apr.	52.5 to 32.5	58.6 to 36.7
May	64.5 to 42.6	68.6 to 45.6
Jun.	73.1 to 52.4	77.8 to 55.5
Jul.	77.6 to 57.3	82.7 to 61.0
Aug.	75.6 to 55.4	81.2 to 59.6
Sept.	68.3 to 48.7	74.5 to 52.5
Oct.	57.2 to 38.1	64.7 to 42.0
Nov.	44.1 to 29.0	52.0 to 33.3
Dec.	32.0 to 17.3	40.1 to 22.6
Year	53.4 to 34.9	60.1 to 39.6

Connecticut's Pick-Your-Own Farms

A number of farms throughout Connecticut offer visitors the opportunity to pick their own fresh fruits and vegetables during the harvest season — and these are a few of the many:

Strawberries	Eddie Draghi & John Berruti 183 Tryon Street S. Glastonbury 06073 (203) 633-7206/(203) 633-9187
Beans, peppers, tomatoes, eggplant	R. A. Futtner & Son 914 Silver Lane E. Hartford 06118 (203) 569-1365
Strawberries	Leo A. Grouten II Coppermine Road Farmington 06032 (203) 677-0422/(203) 678-0704
Strawberries	Hein Farms 303 Meadow Road Farmington 06032
Strawberries	Edwin A. Jarmoc 147 Abbe Road Enfield 06082
Pears, apples	Kensington Orchards 1435 Chamberlain Kensington 06037 (203) 828-5490
Strawberries	Larson's Farm Products 1379 Farmington Avenue Bristol 06010 (203) 583-4645
Strawberries	Lewis Farms 391 Belleview Avenue Southington 06489 (203) 628-9736
Apples	Midway Orchards Intersection Routes 364 & 71 Berlin 06037
Pears, apples	Mountain View Farm 3582 Hebron Avenue Glastonbury 06033 (203) 633-7024
Blueberries	Roxbury Blueberry Farm Chalybes Road Roxbury 06783 (203) 354-1188
Apples	Rumpf Orchard Mrs. S. W. Webster Old Mount Tom Road Bantam 06750 (203) 567-9188
Apples	Souza's Orchard South Road (Off Route 202) New Hartford 06057 (203) 561-0411
Apples	Terekook Farm Kielwasser Road New Preston 06777 (203) 868-2648
Sweet corn, eggplant, tomatoes, cucumbers, peppers, squash, melons, cole crops	West Valley Farms William C. Taff 148 Sycamore Avenue Woodbury 06798 (203) 263-4418
Strawberries	Pell Farm Town Line Road Plainville 06062 (203) 747-4531
Strawberries	Rose's Berry Farm Henry M. Rose 295 Matson Hill Road S. Glastonbury 06073 (203) 633-6001
Strawberries	Edward Thurz 219 Addison Street Glastonbury 06033 (203) 633-9562
Strawberries, peas, tomatoes, string beans, cucumbers, peppers, squash, lettuce, pumpkins	C. F. Woodford & Son Inc. 276 Nod Road Avon 06001 (203) 677-9552
Strawberries	Zeppa Farms 738 Birch Mountain Road Manchester 06040 (203) 643-6318

of firearms (and later invented the cotton gin which revolutionized the textile industry).

Today, Connecticut is a leader in the production of ball and roller bearings, helicopters, submarines, jet engines, chemicals, plastics, silverware and electronic goods. Hartford has become the insurance capital of the world, serving as headquarters for nearly 40 firms in that field, and in some areas the industrial base is beginning to shift from manufacturing with the establishment of headquarters for major companies such as Xerox, IBM, Pepsico and Union Carbide. The state is also the national leader in the utilization of nuclear power, with more than half of its electrical power coming from several nuclear generating plants.

State Offices

Tourism
Connecticut Department of Economic Development
210 Washington Street
Hartford, Connecticut 06106
(203) 566-3385

Connecticut Business and Industry Association
Suite 1202
60 Washington Street
Hartford, Connecticut 06106
(203) 547-1661

State Police
Department of Public Safety
Hartford, Connecticut 06101
(203) 566-3200

Radio Stations

Hartford
WTIC 1080 (AM)
WCCC 106.9 (FM)

New Haven
WPLR 99.1 (FM)
WELI 960 (AM)

Connecticut Points of Interest and Attractions

Barnes Memorial Nature Center. Self-guiding trails lead through 70-acre preserve. Variety of habitats with emphasis on stages of ecological succession. Interpretive buildings with displays. Closed major holidays and January. Free. Bristol, 175 Shrub Road, off State Route 69. (203) 589-6082.

Ferry Boat Ride across Connecticut River. Five-minute trip, a quaint and scenic way to get to the other side. Operates daily, April 1 to November 1. Fare: 25 cents for vehicle and driver, 5 cents for each additional passenger. Chester, on State Route 148. Harbor Cruises depart from submarine memorial. Groton, Thames Street and New London City Pier. For schedules and rates: (203) 536-0659, 448-1616.

Long Island Cruises. Cruises to Port Jefferson, Long Island, from Union Square Dock. Operates daily May through September, then weekends only to mid-October. Bridgeport, Interstate 95, exit 27. For schedules and rates: (203) 367-8571, 344-5993.

Submarines By Boat. Hour-long, seven-mile tour of historic Thames River and New London harbor includes U.S. submarine base, Groton Monument and U.S. Coast Guard Academy. Operates late May through mid-September. Adults $3, children $1.25. Groton, 86 Fairview Avenue. (203) 445-7401.

Thimble Islands Cruise. Sightseeing tours through the tiny Thimble Islands from Stony Creek Public Dock. Operates daily. Branford, Interstate 95, exit 56. For schedule and rates: (203) 488-9978, 481-3345.

Bushnell Park Carousel. A real old-time merry-go-round with period Wurlitzer and

48 intricately carved wooden horses, housed in an elegant pavilion. Hartford. May through September, Tuesday through Sunday; 10 cents a ride. (203) 525-1618.

Connecticut Yankee Energy Information Center. Located on the grounds of a nuclear power plant, the center features displays and films on nuclear power and alternate energy sources. July to August, Monday through Saturday 9 a.m. to 4 p.m., Sunday, noon to 5 p.m.; September 1 to June 30, Monday through Friday 9 a.m. to 4 p.m. Closed holidays. Free. (203) 267-9279. Haddam Neck, off State Route 151.

Elizabeth Park Rose Gardens. The first municipally-owned rose gardens in the country with 14,000 plants, 1,100 varieties. Peak bloom: late June. Features annual and perennial gardens, rock garden, picnic facilities, greenhouses. Open year-round. Hartford, Interstate 84, Prospect Avenue exit.

Larsen Sanctuary. Headquarters of the Connecticut Audubon Society, featuring displays of local wildlife, research library, organic garden and 6½ miles of trails in the 170-acre sanctuary. Open Tuesday through Saturday 9 a.m. to 5 p.m., Sunday noon to 5 p.m. Closed on major holidays. Adults $1, children 50 cents. (203) 259-6305. Fairfield, 2325 Burr Street (Interstate 95, exit 21).

Nature Center for Environmental Activities. 53-acre wildlife sanctuary with trails, museum, live animal shelter and gift shop. Monday through Saturday 9 a.m. to 5 p.m., Sunday 1 p.m. to 4 p.m. Adults 50 cents, children 25 cents. (203) 227-7253. Westport, 10 Woodside Lane (Interstate 95, exit 17; State Route 15, exit 41).

Roaring Brook Nature Center. Interpretive buildings with year-round nature exhibits, store, resource room, 115-acres of woods with many trails. Tuesday through Saturday 10 a.m. to 5 p.m., Sunday 1 p.m. to 5 p.m. Closed major holidays. Adults 50 cents, children 12 and under, 25 cents. (203) 693-0263. Ganton, 176 Gracey Road (off US-44).

U.S. Coast Guard Academy. Grounds open to visitors daily, 9 a.m. to sunset. Visitors center features displays and multi-media show. The 295-foot training bark *Eagle* may be boarded when in port. Guided campus tours during school year. Dress reviews and band concerts held throughout year. Free. (203) 443-8463. New London, Mohegan Avenue (Interstate 95, exit 83).

Yale University. Guided one-hour walking tours of the historic campus, including Connecticut Hall where Nathan Hale, William Howard Taft and Noah Webster studied. Open seven days a week. For schedule call (203) 436-8330. New Haven (Interstate 95, exit 47).

Free Touring Information

Touring and routing information is available from the oil companies listed below. When writing, give point of departure/destination and advise if you prefer a scenic or economic route.

Exxon Touring Service, PO Box 2180, Houston, Texas 77001.

Gulf Tourguide Bureau, PO Box 93, Versailles, Kentucky 40383.

Mobile Travel Service, PO Box 25, Versailles, Kentucky 40383.

Union Oil Company of California, Box 7600, Los Angeles, California 90051.

For more information on state parks and forests, contact: *Department of Environmental Protection, Parks and Recreation Unit, Hartford, Connecticut 06115, (203) 566-2304*

Connecticut State Parks

Park	Location	CAMPING	PICNICKING	CONCESSIONS	SWIMMING	HIKING	BOATING	FISHING	HUNTING	WINTER SPORTS
Black Rock	*Watertown, State Routes 6 and 22.*	•	•	•	•	•	•	•		
Bluff Point	*Groton, near junction of State Route 117 and Interstate 95.*					•		•		•
Bolton Notch	*Bolton, at Junction of US-6 and State Route 85.*					•				
Burr Pond	*Torrington, five miles north on State Route 8.3*	•	•	•	•	•		•		•
Chatfield Hollow	*Killingworth, off State Route 80.*				•	•		•		
Day Pond	*Colchester, five miles west on State Route 149.*		•		•	•		•		
Devil's Hopyard	*Colchester, five miles south on State Route 82.*	•	•			•		•		
Gay City	*Bolton, three miles south on State Route 85.*		•		•	•		•		•
Gilette Castle	*Hadlyme, off State Route 148.*		•	•		•		•		
Housatonic Meadows	*One mile north of Cornwall Bridge on State Route 7.*	•	•			•				
Indian Well	*Shelton, northwest on State Route 110.*		•	•	•	•		•		
John A. Minetto	*Drakeville, north on State Route 272.*		•			•		•		•
Kent Falls	*North Kent, north on US-7.*	•	•			•		•		
Kettletown	*Southbury, five miles south off Interstate 84.*	•	•		•	•				
Macedonia Brook	*Kent, off State Route 341.*	•	•			•		•		
Mashamoquet Brook	*Putnam, off U.S. Route 44.*	•	•	•	•	•		•		•
Mount Tom	*Torrington, southwest off State Route 202.*		•	•	•	•				
Penwood	*Simsbury, off State Route 185.*		•			•				•
Putnam Memorial	*Redding, at junction of State Routes 107 and 58.*		•			•		•		•
Quaddick	*Quaddick, three miles north of US-44.*		•	•	•			•		
Rocky Neck	*Niantic, three miles west off State Route 156.*	•	•	•	•	•		•		
Sleeping Giant	*Mount Carmel, north off State Route 10.*	•	•			•		•		
Southford Falls	*Southford, off State Route 67.*		•			•		•		
Squantz Pond	*New Fairfield, north off State Route 39.*		•	•	•	•	•	•		
Stratton Brook	*Simsbury, on State Route 309.*		•			•		•		
Talcott Mountain	*Bloomfield, three miles west on State Route 185.*		•			•				
Wharton Brook	*Wallingford, three miles south on US-5.*		•	•	•	•		•		

Connecticut State Forests

Forest	Location	CAMPING	PICNICKING	CONCESSIONS	SWIMMING	HIKING	BOATING	FISHING	HUNTING	WINTER SPORTS
American Legion	*Pleasant Valley, north off US-44.*	•				•		•	•	•
Cockaponset	*Chester, three miles west on State Route 148.*	•				•		•	•	•
Housatonic	*Covers large area of northwest corner of state, bisected by U.S. Route 7.*		•			•		•	•	•
Natchaug	*Phoenixville, four miles south on State Route 198.*	•	•			•		•	•	•
Naugatuck	*Beacon Falls, one mile north of State Route 8.*		•			•			•	•
Pachaug	*Voluntown, one mile south off State Route 49.*	•	•		•	•	•	•	•	•
Peoples	*Pleasant Valley, one mile north on East River Road.*		•			•		•	•	•
Topsmead	*Litchfield, east off State Route 118.*		•			•		•	•	•
Tunxis	*Robertsville, north off State Route 8.*		•			•		•	•	•

Massachusetts

History and culture: They are inescapable in Massachusetts. Plymouth Rock, the Boston Massacre, the Boston Tea Party, Lexington and Concord — all are a part of this state's glorious past. Then there is the Boston Symphony, the famed Boston Pops, Tanglewood and the Berkshire Festival, the opera company, the unique atmosphere of the Boston Common, the Museum of Fine Arts, and the homes of Emerson, Hawthorne and Thoreau. As if that weren't enough, Massachusetts also boasts the nation's oldest university, Harvard, founded in 1636, as well as some of the country's other distinguished centers of higher education — Massachusetts Institute of Technology, Amherst, Smith, Williams and Mount Holyoke.

It has been speculated that Leif Ericsson may have also been the first European to catch sight of Massachusetts, perhaps visiting its shores as early as 1000 A.D. But there's no doubt that the first indisputable record of a landing was that of the English explorer Bartholomew Gosnold in 1602. Later, Captain John Smith, immortalized in the Pocahontas legend, explored the region in 1614. Ironically, the landing of the Pilgrims at Plymouth six years later was purely accidental, as the *Mayflower's* intended destination was a point somewhere south of the Hudson River. Because this area was beyond the bounds of the sponsoring company in London, a provisional government was drawn up under the Mayflower Compact. This covenant of the Massachusetts Bay Colony later formed the very foundation of American democracy. It was not a very democratic document in the beginning, however, as it granted religious

Full name: Commonwealth of Massachusetts
Origin of name: Algonquian Indian, Massa-dchu-es-at, meaning "Great-Hill-Small-Place."
Motto: *Ense Petit Placidam Sub Liberstate Quietem* (By the Sword We Seek Peace, but Peace Only Under Liberty).
Nickname: Bay State
Capital: Boston
Statehood: February 6, 1788, sixth state.
Population: 5,782,000 (ranks 10th).
Major Cities: Boston (636,725), Worcester (171,566), Springfield (170,790).
Bird: Chickadee
Flower: Mayflower
Tree: American elm

Average daily temperatures by month

	Northwestern	Southwestern
Jan.	29.7 to 11.7	36.8 to 17.3
Feb.	31.9 to 12.9	38.9 to 19.2
Mar.	40.1 to 23.1	45.7 to 26.8
Apr.	54.5 to 33.9	57.8 to 35.1
May	66.4 to 42.3	68.3 to 44.1
Jun.	76.2 to 52.2	77.2 to 54.3
Jul.	80.7 to 56.6	82.0 to 60.2
Aug.	78.5 to 54.1	80.3 to 58.2
Sept.	71.0 to 47.5	73.1 to 50.8
Oct.	60.6 to 37.0	63.8 to 40.0
Nov.	46.2 to 29.3	51.7 to 31.9
Dec.	33.7 to 18.1	40.6 to 21.7
Year	55.8 to 34.9	59.7 to 38.3

freedom to the Puritans while denying it to others. Perhaps the most vivid example of this early Puritan oppression is illustrated by the infamous Salem Witch Trials, which resulted in the deaths of 20 persons.

Even before the American Revolution, Massachusetts experienced a good deal of turmoil, beginning with a war with the Pequot Indians in 1637, a later war with the Wampanoag Indians and a conflict with the French. After the hostilities of the Revolution ceased, the state was gripped by a severe depression, and a stable economy wasn't restored until the War of 1812 brought a manufacturing boom.

Today, Massachusetts remains a leading producer of machinery, electrical equipment, chemicals, rubber and plastics. Agriculture remains a thriving part of the economy in the western portion of the state, and the fishing industry — scallops, lobster, flounder, haddock, cod — flourishes all along the coast. In addition to all these products, tourism has an extremely important role in the commonwealth's livelihood.

BOSTON

Boston plays two roles. Officially, it is capital of the commonwealth of Massachusetts. Unofficially, it serves as capital of the six-state northeastern area Americans call "New England." Bostonians treasure their town for its place in America's history, pointing to the storied Freedom Trail — a rambling 1½-mile walk that leads visitors to the city's most famous landmarks.

Steeped in the past, Boston has a bright eye on the future. Its skyscraping Prudential Center — a towering office and shopping complex — and the striking Government Center rate high among the nation's best new architecture.

Intimate restaurants and cafes represent the cuisine and atmosphere of all the world's continents. The delicious seafood restaurants are Boston's own and the many specialty restaurants prepare the finest meals according to a great American tradition of culinary quality. Boston's many nightspots accommodate dancing and international entertainment to suit all ages.

State Offices

Division of Tourism
Massachusetts Department of Commerce and Development
100 Cambridge Street
Boston, Massachusetts 02202
(617) 727-3201

State Police
Department of Public Safety
Boston, Massachusetts 02215
(617) 566-4500

Radio Stations

Boston
WBCN 104.1 (FM)
WBZ 1030 (AM)
WRKO 680 (AM)
Springfield
WHYN 560 (AM)
WAQY 102.1 (FM)

Massachusetts Points of Interest and Attractions

Albert Schweitzer Friendship House. Features library of books and taped music by and about Dr. Schweitzer, on 41-acre site in Berkshires. Open Saturday and Sunday 10 a.m. to 5 p.m., Tuesday through Friday by appointment. Great Barrington, Hurlburt Road. (413) 528-3124.

Arnold Arboretum, Harvard University. A living collection of over 6,000 varieties of hardy trees and shrubs on 265 acres, scientific collections of plant materials, library, greenhouses, research laboratories. Jamaica Plain (Boston). (617) 524-1717.

Aquarium of the National Marine Fisheries Service. Open daily, including holidays, June 10 through September 11, 10 a.m. to 4:30 p.m. Woods Hole. (617) 548-5123.

Bartholomew's Cobble. A natural rock garden overlooking the Housantonic River, featuring a profusion of many types of rare ferns, flowers, Ashley Falls, in extreme southwest corner of state, on State Route 7A.

Basketball Hall of Fame. Commemorates the founder of basketball, Dr. James Naismith, who invented the game in 1891 in Springfield. Collections of memorabilia; movies shown hourly. Open daily, year-round (closed Thanksgiving, Christmas and New Year's day). Adults $2, children 6-12, 75 cents. Springfield, 460 Alden Street. (413) 781-6500.

Berkshire Garden Center. Beautiful gardens, trees, perennials, herbs, annuals, flowers, trial grain and vegetable plots, lily pond, wild flower area. Open daily, year-round. Free. Stockbridge, two miles west on State Routes 102 and 183. (413) 298-5530.

Boat Cruises. The *Arminda* and *Merrimac II*; half-hour narrated cruise around Plymouth Harbor. Adults $1.50, children under 12 75 cents. Plymouth, off State Pier. (617) 746-4762.

The *Mayflower II*, a replica of the ship that brought the Pilgrims to Plymouth in 1620, is moored at State Pier in Plymouth Harbor.

Hy-Line. Passenger ferry to Martha's Vineyard and Nantucket. Open May 1 through November 1. Adults $10, children under 15, $5. Hyannis, at Ocean Street Dock. (617) 775-7185.

Brandeis University. One of the most respected institutions of higher learning, named after Louis D. Brandeis, U.S. Supreme Court Justice. Features three chapels, Rapaporte Treasure Hall, Rose Art Museum. Open September through December and February through May, Monday through Saturday tours at 10:30 a.m., 1 and 3 p.m.; in January, June, July, August, tours conducted Monday through Friday 10:30 a.m., 1 and 3 p.m. Waltham, 415 South Street, off US-20. (617) 647-2000.

Bridge of Flowers. A 400-foot trolley bridge over the Deerfield River between Shelburne Falls and Buckland, converted into a garden by women of the town. The five-arch bridge is floodlighted nightly until 10:30 p.m. during summer. Admission: contributions expected. Shelburne Falls, off State Route 2.

Canoe Meadows Wildlife Sanctuary. Has 270 acres of open fields, woodlands, small streams, short hiking trails. Open dawn to dusk daily. Pittsfield, Holmes Road. (413) 637-0320.

Coleman Map Building. The largest revolving steel globe in the world, 28 feet in diameter, weighing 25 tons, is on display outside the building. Inside is a giant relief map of the U.S., 65 feet x 45 feet. Open daily, April 1 through October 31, 10 a.m. to 5 p.m.; November 1 through March 31, 2 p.m. to 5 p.m. Wellesley, Wellesley Avenue, on Babson College Campus, State Routes 9 to 16. (617) 235-1200, Extension 232.

Cranberry World Visitors Center. History of America's native berry from colonial times to the present. Indoor displays, antique and modern picking equipment, products, miniature diorama. Open daily; April 1 to late November, 10 a.m. to 5 p.m. Free. Plymouth, Water Street.

The draggers still come with their nets and the lobstermen still land their catches at Meneshma on Martha's Vineyard off the coast of Cape Cod.

Drumlin Farm Wildlife Sanctuary. Domestic animals found on a typical New England farm, as well as crops of grains and vegetables. Open Saturday and Sunday, 9 a.m. to 5 p.m. Adults $1.50, children 50 cents. Lincoln, south of State Route 2. (617) 259-9005.

Harvard University. During academic year, 45-minute walking tours of the nation's oldest university. Leave from Admissions Office, Byerly Hall, 8 Garden Street, at 11:15 a.m., 1:15 p.m. and 2:15 p.m. on weekdays. From mid-June to August 31, tours start at Information Center, Holyoke Center Arcade, 1350 Massachusetts Avenue, Monday through Saturday at 10 a.m., 11:15 a.m., 2 p.m. and 3:15 p.m. Cambridge. (617) 495-1573.

John Hancock Observatory. A 60th floor observatory, highest man-made attraction in New England. Audiovisual show, color films, skyline view of Boston. Open Monday through Saturday 9 a.m. to 10:15 p.m., Sunday noon to 11 p.m. Admission: Adults $1.50, children 75 cents, under 5 free. Boston, 200 Clarendon Street. (617) 247-1976.

Laughing Brook Education Center and Wildlife Sanctuary. Home and studio of the late children's author, Thornton W. Burgess. Live exhibits of animal characters, nature center, memorabilia, natural history exhibits, nature trails. Operated by the Massachusetts Audubon Society. Open Tuesday through Sunday 10 a.m. to 5 p.m. Admission: Adults $1.50, children under 12, 50 cents. Hampden, 789 Main Street. (413) 566-3571.

Millicent Library. Italian Renaissance architecture, many rare objects of art, original manuscripts, Mark Twain material. Open weekdays. Free. Fairhaven, 45 Center Street.

Moose Hill Wildlife Sanctuary. The oldest sanctuary operated by the Massachusetts Audubon Society. Beautiful vista from atop Firetower Trail. Open sunrise to sunset. Admission: $1 per vehicle; parking fee. Sharon, State Routes 95 and 27 (off Route 27). (617) 784-5691.

Robert S. Peabody Foundation for Archaeology. Exhibits concerning general anthropology and the evolution of man, and the archaeological development of New England and adjacent portions of Canada. Open Monday through Saturday, 9 a.m. to 4:15 p.m. Andover, 175 Main Street. (617) 475-0248.

Stony Brook Nature Center. Massachusetts Audubon Society project offering nature tours through Bristol-Blake Reservation. Open daily, sunrise to sunset. Norfolk, North Street, State Route 115. (617) 528-3140.

Worcester Science Center. Sixty-acre park includes science museum with natural and physical exhibits, Alden Omnisphere (multi-media planetarium), zoo featuring four endangered species, train, nature trails, picnic area. Open year-round, Monday through Saturday 10 a.m. to 5 p.m., Sunday noon to 5 p.m. Adults $2, children 16 and under $1. Worcester, Harrington Way. (617) 791-9211.

Massachusetts' Maple Sugar

Early spring is the sweetest — and the busiest — season in Pioneer Valley in western Massachusetts.

It's maple-sugarin' time!

From the middle of March through early April, farmers in nearly every hilltown village and hamlet honor an old New England tradition when they take to the woods with buckets and pails to gather sap from maple trees and boil it down to make syrup and sugar.

It's old-fashioned fun time, too.

Old Man Winter disappears in puffs of sweet smoke from weather-beaten sugarhouses and city folk take to country roads to witness these rustic rites of spring. It's time for the first taste of the liquid "fruit" of the maple tree poured over pancakes or waffles in a farm kitchen. Or, for hot syrup dribbled over a pan of clean snow to make a warm rich taffy, eaten wound-up on a fork or spoon.

Sugaring is a thriving retail business as well, and Pioneer Valley maple products find their way to tables across the land. Farmers mail syrup and sugar to all points of the compass — as far away as Africa.

The Maple Tree

Any recipe for making maple syrup would have to begin: "Find a grove of centuries-old sugar maples." This is not so difficult, for this leafy giant (*Acer saccharum*), from 75 to 100 feet tall, is a sturdy native of the Northeastern United States and was growing here in abundance long before the white man came.

The sugar maple is a majestic tree for all seasons. In summer, its broad three- to five-lobed leaves form a canopy of shade and a home for nesting birds. Its two-seeded, winged fruit ripens in late summer and lingers long on the branches, providing food for birds and squirrels.

The sugar tree is unrivaled queen of New England's autumn foliage, coloring the countryside yellow, orange and scarlet. The maple's gray bark, which forms dark plates and becomes flaky with age, is a sturdy overcoat for the rigors of a Yankee winter. In spring, the rugged tree trunk is a reservoir of sap, a colorless, watery, slightly sweet liquid.

Sugar Science

Scientists explain the magic of the sugar maple in terms of chemistry. In summer, each microscopic cell in a maple leaf is a busy factory. With sunlight providing the power, water from the soil, carbon dioxide from the air and chlorophyll in the leaf cells are combined to form a simple sugar — glucose. The sugar is then converted into starch and stored in the roots and trunk of the tree.

By springtime another chemical change has taken place and a more complicated sugar — sucrose — has been formed. Sap, the liquid that rises in the tree trunk during the warm sunny days of March, is made up of as little as one percent of this sugar. The rest is water with minute traces of organic compounds.

Thirty-five gallons of sap in a good season, to 60 in a poor one, will produce one gallon of syrup. It is the sugar farmer's job to boil away the water, to distill the sap into the amber gold of maple syrup.

This sounds an easy task. It isn't. It is a long process from tree juice to table syrup. Ask the city slicker who tried to boil-down sap on a kitchen stove and ended up steaming off the wallpaper all over the room and loosening the ceiling plaster.

One of the first of its kind, this water-powered grist mill still grinds grain at Saugus, Massachusetts.

Country Craft

Sugaring is country alchemy, an ancient and honorable craft handed down from father to son. Early colonists learned it from the Indians who collected sap in hollowed-out logs and steamed away the water by dropping in hot stones.

An old Indian legend says that maple syrup was discovered as the result of a quarrel between a squaw and her brave. The lady of the wigwam asked her husband to fill a cooking pot with water. "Ugh!" said the disgruntled brave, who left the tepee in a huff, put the pot near a maple tree and vented his wrath by slashing the bark with his tomahawk.

The next day the squaw found the pot filled with liquid. She took it back to her tent, boiled some venison in it — and made the first maple syrup.

Another Indian legend explains why maple-sugaring is such hard work. According to this tale, the old Earth mother, Nokomis, made the first syrup. All she had to do was bore a hole in a tree: The liquid which dripped out was not sap, but syrup. Her grandson, Manabush, thought this was too easy, that the redmen should work to get their syrup or they would become lazy and shiftless. He climbed to the top of a sugar maple and showered it with water, turning the syrup into sap. Syrup-making has been hard labor ever since.

Country Wizard

With all of the newfangled devices at his command, the sugar farmer must still rely largely on his own skill.

There is an aura of mystery and a special magic in watching this country wizard at work, moving like a phantom in the steamy mists of a sugarhouse.

Near the evaporator he stands, big wooden spoon in hand. Bending now over the boiling sea of sap to remove a bit of bark . . . now inserting a measuring rod or scanning a hydrometer gauge to see how much water has been steamed away. When the bubbling liquid looks as if it might spill over the sides of the pan, he is ready to dunk a piece of salt pork, or add a drop of cream to calm the churning sap.

He must know just when the sap has boiled long enough to become good syrup — the exact moment when the liquid has the right density. If overcooked, syrup will crystallize; if undercooked and thin, it will ferment and spoil.

The sugarman wears many hats. He is weatherman and woodcutter, trail-blazer and tree expert, transporter, pipe-fitter, cook and chemist, demonstrator, processor, packager and retail merchant.

Had sugar maples grown in the Garden of Eden, Adam and Eve would have been too busy to get into mischief.

Vera Lesure's Maple Syrup Recipes

Quick Maple Frosting

Bring one-half cup maple syrup to boil for one minute. Remove from heat and stir in tablespoon butter, add two cups confectionary sugar, continue stirring until consistency to spread. Frosting thickens as the syrup cools.

Bread Pudding

1 quart dry bread crumbs
½ cup maple syrup
½ cup raisins
Dash salt
Dash nutmeg
Dash cinnamon
1 cup milk
Steam 1 hour
Serve plain or with marshmallow fluff.

Graham Bread

4 cups graham flour
2 cups all purpose white flour
1 teaspoon salt
1 heaping teaspoon baking soda
3 cups buttermilk
1 cup maple syrup

Put graham flour in large bowl. Sift rest of dry ingredients and add to graham flour. Stir buttermilk and syrup into the combined dry ingredients. If batter seems too thick, add a little plain milk. Bake in slow oven until tester comes out clean. While hot, brush with butter. Makes two loaves.

Mincemeat

1½ quarts ground meat (I use beef)
4½ quarts chopped apples
1 quart water in which meat was cooked
1½ pounds raisins
1½ quarts maple syrup
10 teaspoons cinnamon
2 teaspoons pepper
2 teaspoons salt
8 teaspoons cloves
4 teaspoons nutmeg

Cook over very low heat until apples are soft and mixture is quite thick. Either can, freeze or make into 12 pies.

Jiffy Baked Beans

Buy your favorite brand of canned baked beans (without tomato sauce). Drain beans, add maple syrup to taste and bake until brown on top.

Maple Milk Shake

Blend one tablespoon maple syrup with glass of cold milk. For weight watchers — use skim or dried milk.

Courtesy of Pioneer Valley Association

Sandy grasslands mark the Atlantic coastline near the Marconi Interpretive Center at Cape Cod National Seashore. South Wellfleet, Massachusetts.

Massachusetts State Forests

Forest	Location	CAMPING	PICNICKING	CONCESSIONS	SWIMMING	HIKING	BOATING	FISHING	HUNTING	WINTER SPORTS
Bash Bish Falls	*Mt. Washington. Near junction of State Routes 23 and 41.*					•		•	•	•
Beartown	*Monterey. Off State Route 23.*	•	•		•	•	•	•	•	•
Brimfield	*Brimfield. Off US-20.*					•	•	•	•	•
Campbells Falls	*Southfield. Off State Route 272.*					•		•	•	•
Chester-Blanford	*Chester. Off US-20.*		•		•	•		•	•	•
D.A.R.	*Goshen. Off State Route 9.*	•	•		•	•	•	•	•	•
Douglas	*Douglas. Off State Route 100.*		•		•	•	•	•	•	•
Erving	*Erving. Off State Route 2.*	•	•		•	•	•	•	•	•
Granville	*Granville. Off State Route 57.*	•	•		•	•	•	•	•	•
Greylock Mountain	*Adams. Off State Routes 2 and 8.*	•	•			•		•	•	•
Harold Parker	*North Reading. Off State Route 125.*	•	•		•	•	•	•	•	•
Hawley	*Hawley. Off State Route 8A.*		•			•			•	•
Leominster	*Fitchburg. Off State Routes 2 and 31.*		•			•		•	•	•
Mohawk Trail	*Charlemont. Off State Route 2.*	•	•		•	•		•	•	•
Myles Standish	*South Carver. Off State Route 58, north 3 miles.*	•	•		•	•	•	•	•	•
October Mountain	*Lee and Lenox. Off US-20.*	•				•	•		•	•
Otter River	*Winchendon. Off State Route 202.*	•	•		•	•		•	•	•
Pittsfield	*Pittsfield. West on West Street 5 miles.*	•	•		•	•	•	•	•	•
Sandisfield	*Sandisfield. Off State Route 57.*		•		•	•	•	•	•	•
Savoy Mountain	*Florida. Off State Route 2.*	•	•		•	•	•	•	•	•
Tolland	*Otis. Off State Route 23.*	•	•		•	•	•	•	•	•
Wendell	*Wendell. Off State Route 2.*	•		•	•	•	•	•		•
Willard Brook	*Ashby. Off State Route 119.*	•	•		•	•		•	•	•
Willowdale	*Ipswich. Off Linebrook Road.*					•	•	•	•	•
Windsor	*West Cummington. Off State Route 9.*	•	•		•	•		•	•	•

Massachusetts State Reserves

Reserve	Location	CAMPING	PICNICKING	CONCESSIONS	SWIMMING	HIKING	BOATING	FISHING	HUNTING	WINTER SPORTS
Blue Hills	*Milton. Off State Route 138.*	•			•			•		
Breakheart	*Saugus. Off Lynfells Parkway.*	•	•		•			•		
Salisbury Beach	*Salisbury. Off State Route 1A.*	•			•			•		

Massachusetts State Parks

Park	Location	CAMPING	PICNICKING	CONCESSIONS	SWIMMING	HIKING	BOATING	FISHING	HUNTING	WINTER SPORTS
Ames-Nowell	*Abington. Near junction of State Routes 18 and 123.*		•			•	•	•		•
Ashland	*Ashland. Off State Route 135.*		•		•	•		•		•
Buffumville	*Oxford. Off State Route 12.*		•		•	•	•	•	•	•
Chicopee	*Chicopee. Off Massachusetts Turnpike at exit 6.*		•		•	•	•	•	•	•
Clarksburg	*Clarksburg. Off State Routes 2 and 8.*	•	•		•	•	•	•	•	•
Cochituate	*Cochituate. At junction of State Routes 30 and 27.*		•		•		•	•		
Demarest Lloyd	*South Dartmouth. 8 miles south of US-6.*		•		•	•	•	•		•
Gardner	*Huntington. Off State Route 112.*		•		•	•		•		•
Hampton Ponds	*Westfield. North off US-202.*		•		•		•	•		
Holland Pond	*Holland. North 2 miles.*				•			•	•	
Hopkinton	*Hopkinton. Off State Route 85.*		•		•	•		•		•
Lake Dennison	*Winchendon. South off US-202.*	•	•		•	•	•	•	•	•
Massasoit	*Taunton. At junction of State Routes 25 and 18, and US-44.*	•			•			•	•	
Pearl Hill	*Townsend. Off State Route 119.*	•	•		•	•		•	•	
R.C. Nickerson	*Brewster. Off State Route 6A.*	•	•		•	•	•	•		•
Rutland	*Rutland. Off State Route 122.*		•		•		•	•		
Wells	*Sturbridge. Near junction of State Route 49 and US-20.*	•			•	•	•	•		•

For more information on Massachusetts state parks, contact: *Department of Environmental Management, Division of Forests and Parks, 100 Cambridge Street, Boston, Massachusetts 02202, (617) 727-3180.*

Rhode Island

Rhode Islanders like to refer to their state as America's "first vacationland," claiming it earned that distinction in 1524 with the visit of Italian navigator Giovanni da Verrazano. Exploring North America for the King of France, Verrazano was said to be so captivated by the beauty of Narragansett Bay that he stayed a fortnight — originating the first "two-week vacation with pay." As a rich vacation area, and the nation's smallest state, the Rhode Island Tourist Division also likes to remind gas-conscious visitors that the state is only "four gallons long and three gallons wide."

Seeking an escape from Puritan oppression in Massachusetts — a place where "persons distressed for conscience" could go — Roger Williams founded Rhode Island's first settlement at Providence in 1636. Like most of the early settlements, the livelihood of the first colonists was dependent on agriculture, but that gave way to a thriving maritime trade as more and more of the colonial sons took to the sea. Rhode Island soon became one of the largest and busiest world trade centers in the early colonies, primarily because of its position in the "trade triangle" — ships carried rum from Newport to Africa, transported slaves from there to the West Indies, and took molasses from there to Newport, where it was, in turn, made into rum. This prosperity ended abruptly, however, when Rhode Island renounced slavery (1774) and prohibited the importation of slaves.

With such a firm foundation of political and religious freedom, the colony attracted settlers who were not always welcome elsewhere — so it's not surprising that

Full name: State of Rhode Island and Providence Plantations
Origin of name: In honor of the Isle of Rhodes.
Motto: Hope
Nickname: Little Rhody
Capital: Providence
Statehood: May 29, 1790, 13th state.
Population: 935,000 (ranks 39th).
Major cities: Providence (167,724), Warwick (85,875), Cranston (74,381).
Bird: Rhode Island Red
Flower: Violet
Tree: Red maple

Average daily temperatures by month

	Central	Block Island
Jan.	36.2 to 20.6	37.4 to 25.4
Feb.	37.6 to 21.2	37.2 to 25.3
Mar.	44.7 to 29.0	42.7 to 31.0
Apr.	56.7 to 37.8	51.7 to 38.8
May	66.8 to 46.9	60.4 to 47.2
Jun.	76.3 to 56.5	69.7 to 56.5
Jul.	81.1 to 63.0	75.6 to 63.3
Aug.	79.8 to 61.0	75.3 to 63.1
Sept.	73.1 to 53.6	69.8 to 57.7
Oct.	63.9 to 43.4	61.4 to 49.2
Nov.	52.0 to 34.6	51.8 to 40.1
Dec.	39.6 to 23.4	41.2 to 29.1
Year	59.0 to 40.9	56.2 to 43.9

Rhode Island developed a rebellious character. In 1769, Newport rebels scuttled the British ship *Liberty* and, in a later protest to British trade and navigation laws, a Providence group burned the English revenue ship *Gaspee* in the waters off Warwick.

Having lost its prominence as a maritime trade center after the war for independence, Rhode Island sparked another revolution — the Industrial Revolution — with the introduction of the factory system in 1790 at the Slater textile mill in Pawtucket. Now, nearly two centuries later, Slater Mill operates as a museum of American crafts and industry. Late in the 17th century, Newport became a fashionable summer residence for the wealthy, and many palatial mansions were built, some of which are now open to tourists. Today, Newport is probably best known as the nation's yachting capital and host to the America's Cup Race. One of Rhode Island's prime attractions is its section of the New England Heritage Trail, which stretches west to Providence and Little Compton, passing many of the state's historic and scenic attractions, recreation and resort areas, beaches, salt marshes and bird sanctuaries, amusement parks, Indian monuments, beautiful ocean vistas and scenic Narragansett Bay.

Rhode Island's economy now rests on a foundation of agricultural products, fishing and the manufacture of products like jewelry and silverware, electrical equipment, rubber, plastics and textiles. Visitors are especially welcome in Rhode Island, as the state is presently trying to broaden its economic base by expanding its tourist industry.

The Apples of Rhode Island

When the Yellow Sweeting was developed in Rhode Island in 1635, it gained distinction as the first name-variety apple in America and created a passion for apples in the state. While apples don't boast to be all things to all people, Rhode Islanders depend on apples for as many uses as there are varieties. Thirteen varieties actually originated in Rhode Island, and today seven varieties dominate the scene at most commercial orchards.

Traditional Rhode Island Apple Recipes

Rhode Island Apple Slump

Twelve large sour apples, pared and quartered and cored; three cupfuls of molasses; a little nutmeg and cinnamon.

Line the sides of a baking kettle with crust made from raised dough, or plain crust made light with soda or cream of tartar; allowing enough crust to fold over the top, put the apples in, sprinkle with the spice; then pour in the molasses; fold the crust from the sides, over the top and cook for half an hour over a moderate fire.

Fried Apple Pies

1 cup sugar
2 eggs
1 cup sour milk
1 level teaspoon baking soda
little salt
flour to roll

Roll about ¼-inch thickness and cut into circles with saucer. Put one tablespoon hot filling on one-half and fold over and press down, edges having been moistened, and fry in deep fat. Filling: Stew dried or evaporated apples until soft. Sweeten to taste and add a little cinnamon.

Apple Crisp Delight

6 to 8 unpeeled apples, sliced
½ cup butter or margarine
1 cup sugar
¾ cup flour
1 teaspoon cinnamon

Preheat oven to 350 degrees. Place sliced apples in a greased baking dish. Blend butter, sugar, flour and cinnamon in a bowl, mixing until crumbly; pack firmly over apples. Bake 45 to 60 minutes at 350 degrees. Garnish with raisins and chopped walnuts, if desired.

Cinnamon Apples

4 baking apples
½ cup sugar
1 cup water
¾ teaspoon cinnamon
¼ cup walnuts or ½ cup raisins

Pare and core apples without cutting through the stem end. In a saucepan, stir sugar, water and cinnamon until blended. Heat over a low flame. When mixture is warm, add apples, one at a time. Simmer until fruit is tender, then remove apples from syrup.

Tour Rhode Island Apple Country

Touring Rhode Island Apple Country is as delightful in the spring, when it's a wonderland of fragrantly blooming orchards, as in the fall, when the apple harvest is out. This marvelous region, scattered mostly throughout the northern part of the state, beckons you to venture and explore all that it has to offer.

Each spring, scores of Rhode Islanders flock to see the splendor of the apple blossoms. An Apple Blossom Festival serves to highlight this season, leaving all in anticipation of the rich harvest to follow. During the harvest, when the orchards actually yield their fruit, the menu reads McIntosh, Cortland, Rhode Island Greening and the like. There are apples galore at every roadside stand, pick-your-own, and churning cider mills pressing apples into cider, which is readily available too.

Helpful Apple Land Hints

While the orchards in Rhode Island Apple Country bloom on or around May 10, it is during the Mother's Day weekend that both the blossoms and the blossom watchers are usually at their peak. During the apple harvest the orchards become more than a pretty face as they bustle with the activity of apple picking, cider sipping; even a family picnic becomes a good idea. So whether you plan to buy by the bushel or the bag, pick your own or stop at your favorite stand, you're sure to find Apple Land to your liking.

State Offices

Tourism
Tourist Promotion Division
Department of Economic Development
One Weybossett Hill
Providence, Rhode Island 02903
(401) 277-2614

State Police
Department of Public Safety
PO Box 185
North Scituate, Rhode Island 02857
(401) 647-3311

Radio Stations

Providence
WPRO 630 (AM)
WPJB 105.1 (FM)

Rhode Island Points of Interest and Attractions

Blithewold Gardens and Arboretum. Thirty-three acres of landscaped grounds and gardens bordering Bristol Harbor. Originally the summer estate of Marjorie Van Wickle Lyon. Open May through October, 10 a.m. to 7 p.m.; closed Mondays and holidays. Adults $2, children $1. Bristol, Ferry Road. (401) 253-8714.

Brown University. Nation's seventh-oldest college, chartered in 1764. Guide service available at the admissions office, Prospect and Angell Streets. Open year-round, except during exam periods in January and May; Monday through Friday, 10 a.m., 11 a.m., 1 p.m., 3 p.m., and 4 p.m. October, November and December; Saturday, 10 a.m., 11 a.m. and noon. Providence.

Cliff Walk. Picturesque walk along Atlantic Ocean shoreline, passing in front of many famous Newport summer mansions. Designated a National Recreational Trail in 1975. Newport, Memorial Boulevard.

Diamond Hill. A striking face of veined quartz, a mile long, deposited by mineral-laden hot water flowing along a fracture in the earth's crust millions of years ago. Cumberland, off State Route 114.

Enchanted Forest. Fairyland theme park designed especially for children, ages 3 to 11. Open May to mid-June, weekends; mid-June through September 5, daily, 10 a.m. to 5 p.m.; weekends remainder of September. Admission: NA. Hopkinton, on State Route 3, between exits 2 and 3 off Interstate 95. (401) 539-7711.

Green Animals Topiary Gardens. Eighty sculptured trees and shrubs shaped in animal forms — giraffe, elephant, lion, etc. Espaliered fruit trees, rose arbor and formal flower beds. Open May 1 through September 30, daily, 10 a.m. to 5 p.m. Adults $1.50, children 6-15 75 cents. Portsmouth, Cory's Lane off State Route 114. (401) 847-1000.

Highland and Cider River Railroad. Train consisting of a tender, two open coaches, one covered coach and a caboose. The steam-powered locomotive, *I Wonda II,* is scaled three inches to a foot and modeled after Baldwin-built engines of 1870-75. There are also two paddlewheel riverboats and a carousel. Open May through November, Saturday and Sunday, noon to dusk; July through Labor Day, Monday to Friday, 1 p.m. to dusk. Admission: NA (nominal charge). Scituate, off State Route 101.

International Tennis Hall of Fame and Tennis Museum. Birthplace of national tennis tournaments. Site of Miller Hall of Fame Championships, July 9 to 15. Open year-round, May through November, 10 a.m. to 5 p.m.; November through May, 11 a.m. to 4 p.m. Adults $2, children 6-18 $1. Newport, 194 Bellevue Avenue. (401) 846-4567.

Norman Bird Sanctuary and Museum. Several wildlife habitats represented on a 450-acre refuge. Museum exhibit includes mounted species of birds. Open year-round, Wednesday to Sunday 1 p.m. to 4 p.m. Adults $1, children accompanied by adult free. Middletown, Third Beach Road. (401) 846-2577.

Point Judith Lighthouse. An octagonal brick building erected in 1816. Important beacon for mariners. A Coast Guard and tower beacon were maintained here during the American Revolution. Open year-round. Free. Narragansett, off State Route 1A.

Portsmouth Abbey. Benedictine Monastery and Preparatory School. Outstanding church in contemporary style designed by Pietro Belluschi. Noteworthy interior feature of the church is wire sculpture by Richard Lippold. Open year-round. Free. Portsmouth, Cory's Lane.

Prudence Island Vineyards. Tours of vineyards by appointment. Open year-round. Free. Portsmouth, Homestead Landing of Prudence Island Ferry, one-third mile up hill. (401) 683-2452.

Rocks, Minerals, Fossils Collection. University of Rhode Island, Department of Geology; collection of rocks, minerals and fossils found in Rhode Island and elsewhere. Display on first floor of Green Hall. Open year-round, Monday to Friday, 8:30 a.m. to 4:30 p.m. Free. Kingstown, off North Road or State Route 138. (401) 792-2265.

Sakonnet Vineyards. Tours include a vineyard walk, the winery facilities and complimentary wine tasting. Open May 30 through October 30, Wednesday and Saturday, 10 a.m. to 5 p.m., or by appointment. Free. Little Compton, on West Main Road. (401) 635-4356.

Step Stone Falls. View of unusual rock formations beneath and around stepped falls in a wooded setting. West Greenwich, at Beach Pond State Park, Escoheag Hill Road, off State Route 165.

Walk-About Trail. An 8.2-mile nature walk, created and named in 1965 by officers and crew of the Australian destroyer *HMS Perth*. Name describes nomadic habit of Australia's aborigines, who wander from place to place — a "walk-about." Glocester, George Washington Management Area, off US-44.

Rhode Island State Parks

Park	Location	CAMPING	PICNICKING	CONCESSIONS	SWIMMING	HIKING	BOATING	FISHING	HUNTING	WINTER SPORTS
Arcadia	*Richmond. Off State Route 165.*	•	•	•	•	•		•		
Beach Pond	*Exeter. Off State Route 165.*	•	•	•	•	•		•		
Burlingame	*Charlestown. Off US-1 and State Route 216.*	•	•	•	•		•	•		
Colt	*Bristol. Off State Route 114.*		•			•	•	•		
Diamond Hill	*Cumberland. Off State Route 114.*		•	•		•		•		
East Matunick	*South Kingstown. Off State Route 108.*		•	•	•			•		
Fisherman's Memorial	*Narragansett. Off State Route 1A.*	•	•							
Goddard	*Warwick. Off US-1.*		•	•	•	•	•	•		
Haines Memorial	*Barrington-East Providence. Off State Route 103.*		•	•			•			
Lincoln Woods	*Lincoln. Off State Route 123.*		•	•		•	•	•		
Pulaski Memorial	*Glocester. Off US-44.*		•	•	•	•		•		

There are no state forests in Rhode Island. For more information on Rhode Island state parks, contact: *Department of Natural Resources, Parks Division, 83 Park, Providence, Rhode Island 02903, (401) 277-2632.*

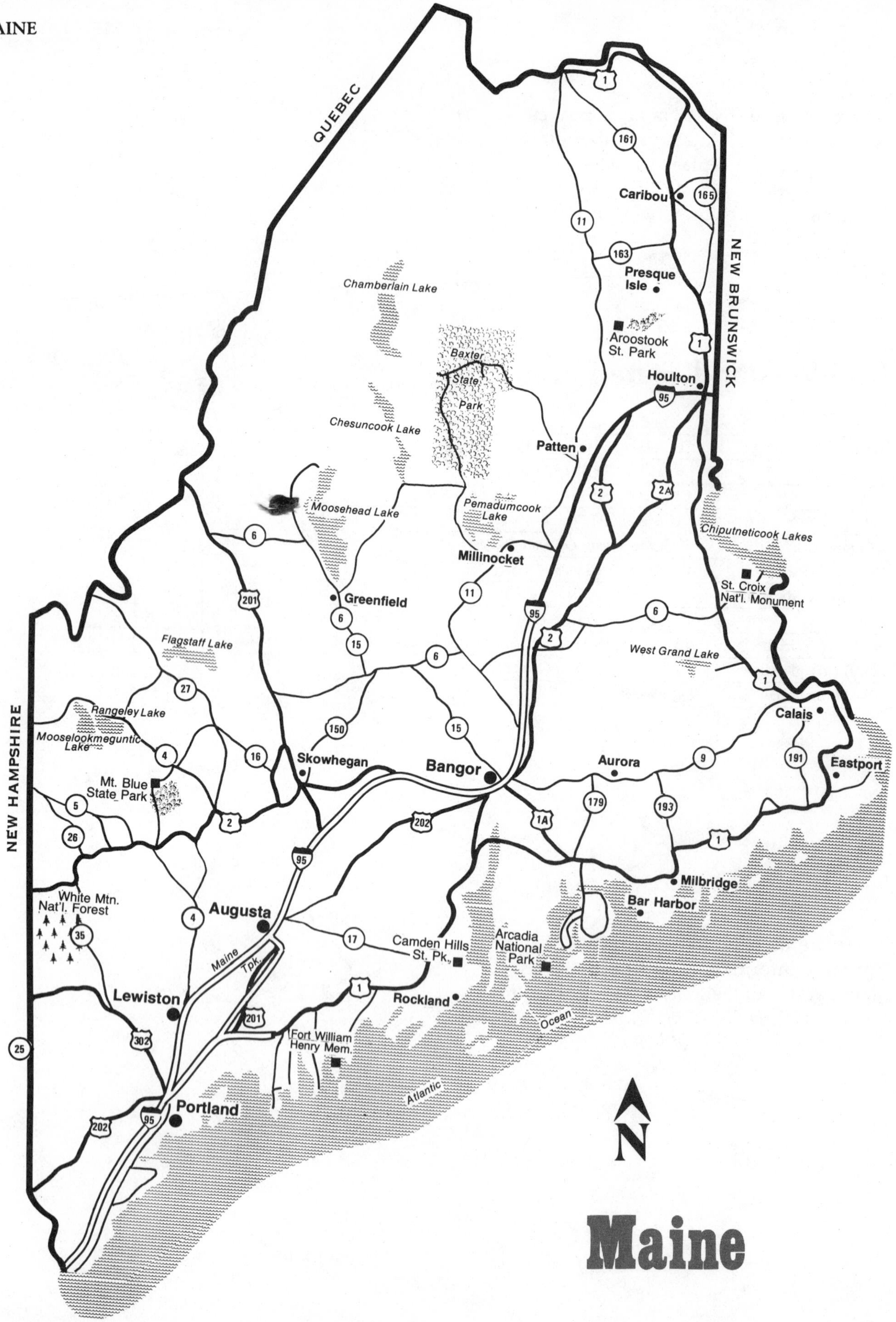

QUEBEC
NEW BRUNSWICK
NEW HAMPSHIRE
Caribou
Presque Isle
Aroostook St. Park
Houlton
Chamberlain Lake
Baxter State Park
Chesuncook Lake
Patten
Moosehead Lake
Pemadumcook Lake
Millinocket
Chiputneticook Lakes
St. Croix Nat'l. Monument
Greenfield
Flagstaff Lake
West Grand Lake
Rangeley Lake
Mooselookmeguntic Lake
Mt. Blue State Park
Skowhegan
Bangor
Aurora
Calais
Eastport
Milbridge
Bar Harbor
Augusta
White Mtn. Nat'l. Forest
Camden Hills St. Pk.
Arcadia National Park
Maine Tpk.
Rockland
Lewiston
Fort William Henry Mem.
Ocean
Atlantic
Portland
N

Maine

Map not to exact scale.

Maine

With 90% of its territory covered by vast stands of evergreens and hardwoods, Maine certainly deserves its reputation as a wilderness wonderland and an outdoorsman's paradise. Fishermen can choose from 5,000 rivers and 2,500 lakes and ponds, while campers, canoeists and skiers can pursue their activities in the Allagash Wilderness, on the 92-mile Allagash Wilderness Waterway or on one of the many mountains, including Mount Katahdin (5,268 feet), the state's highest peak. Framing the beauty of the interior is a craggy coastline with innumerable bays and harbors sheltering picturesque fishing villages. And south of Portland you'll find the more placid shores referred to as "Down East" by the natives.

It is believed that Maine may have first been sighted by Norse explorer Leif Ericsson as early as 1000 A.D., and John Cabot may also have briefly landed here in 1498. (The first explorer certainly known to have set foot in the state was Giovanni da Verrazano, in 1524.) The first settlement was established in 1622 with a land grant from the British Council for New England, and the first settlers coexisted peacefully with the thousands of Abnaki and Etchemin Indians through a succession of jurisdictional disputes, including an attempted takeover by the French.

Having established strong links with Massachusetts as a result of these earlier disputes, it is not surprising that Maine colonists followed the lead of Boston patriots and burned a supply of British Tea (York Tea Party, 1774) in their own protest of English rule. The first naval battle of the American Revolution took place off the Maine Coast when patriots captured the British ship *Margaretta*. Maine remained closely tied to Massachusetts following the revolution, until the Missouri Compromise called for its admission to the union as a free state to balance out Missouri's admission as a slave state.

As might be expected, Maine has an enormous wood-processing industry, and a thriving food-processing industry has grown significantly in recent years. Some of the state's agricultural products include

Full name: State of Maine
Origin of name: From name of ancient province in France.
Motto: *Dirigo* (I Guide).
Nickname: Pine Tree State
Capital: Augusta
Statehood: March 15, 1820, 23rd state.
Population: 1,085,000 (ranks 38th).
Major cities: Portland (59,857), Lewiston (41,045), Bangor (32,262).
Bird: Chickadee
Flower: White pine cone
Tree: White pine

Average daily temperatures by month

	Northern	Southern
Jan.	21.8 to 3.2	32.4 to 15.2
Feb.	25.0 to 4.4	33.4 to 15.7
Mar.	34.2 to 15.4	40.5 to 24.6
Apr.	47.2 to 28.4	51.9 to 33.7
May	62.4 to 39.0	63.3 to 42.4
Jun.	72.8 to 49.6	71.8 to 50.8
Jul.	77.3 to 54.5	76.8 to 58.4
Aug.	74.4 to 51.8	75.4 to 56.0
Sept.	66.2 to 44.5	68.0 to 49.9
Oct.	54.0 to 35.5	58.5 to 41.9
Nov.	39.0 to 25.0	47.2 to 32.6
Dec.	25.4 to 8.7	36.1 to 20.2
Year	50.0 to 30.0	54.6 to 36.6

A Suggested Tour

Acadia National Park

Within the boundaries of Acadia National Park, 47 miles southeast of Bangor, travelers will find a number of scenic routes that provide an excellent view of Maine's famed coastline.

Schoodic Point. A park road off State Route 186 follows the coastline of Schoodic Peninsula to Schoodic Point on the eastern side of Frenchman Bay. Beside the point, a magnificent rock headland rises some 400 feet — providing a sweeping view of the Bay of Fundy to the east and the Mount Desert Range to the west.

Ocean Drive. Offers access to several different sites: Great Head, one of the highest sheer Atlantic headlands in North America; Thunder Hole, a deep chasm cut by waves that produces booming reverberations when the waves and tide are right; Otter Cliffs, where a dense forest extends right to the edge; and Sand Beach, a beach that consists of shell fragments.

Park Loop Road. This road will take you to some of the deep-blue lakes that are shielded among the steep mountain slopes. At Beech Cliff, on the western side of the island, you'll find a superb view of the Echo Lake area.

potatoes, blueberries, and beet sugar; its fishing industry supplies lobsters and canned sardines. From the Maine mudflats come the nation's largest supply of bloodworms and sandworms — prime bait for saltwater sport fishing. Hydroelectric power supplies much of the state's energy, and a communications satellite station near Andover is part of the worldwide satellite communications that includes Telstar and Early Bird.

State Offices

Tourism
Maine State Development Office
State House
Augusta Maine 04333
(207) 289-2656

Maine State Police
Department of Public Safety
Augusta, Maine 04330
(207) 289-2155

Radio Stations

Bangor
WLBZ 620 (AM)
Portland
WGAN 560 (AM)

Maine Points of Interest and Attractions

Campobello Island. Summer home of President Franklin Delano Roosevelt, set in park operated jointly by U.S. and Canada. Lubec, off US-1 in extreme northeast corner of state.

Colonial Pemaquid Restoration. Extensive archaelogical dig where several foundations, thought to be 16th- and 17th-century settlements, have been unearthed. Bristol, off State Route 130, on extreme point of land near mouth of Pemaquid River.

Earth Station. Center for communications satellites. Andover, off State Route 120.

Easternmost Point of Contiguous 48 States. West Quoddy Head, off US-1, in extreme northeast corner of state bordering Canada.

Paper Mill Tours. Bucksport, off US-1, south of Bangor.

Paul Bunyan Statue. Thirty-one feet tall. Bangor, off Interstate 95, on Penobscot River.

Maine State Parks

Park	Location	CAMPING	PICNICKING	CONCESSIONS	SWIMMING	HIKING	BOATING	FISHING	HUNTING	WINTER SPORTS
Aroostok	*Presque Isle. Off US-1.*	•	•		•	•		•		•
Baxter	*Millinocket. North 16 miles (north-central Maine).*	•	•		•	•	•	•		
Bradbury Mountain	*Pownal. North on State Route 9.*	•	•			•				•
Camden Hills	*Camden. Two miles north off US-1.*	•	•			•				•
Cobscook Bay	*Dennysville. South on US-1.*	•	•				•	•		•
Crescent Beach	*Cape Elizabeth. At junction of State Routes 77 and 207.*		•	•	•					
Grafton Notch	*Grafton. Off State Route 26.*	•	•			•	•	•		
Lake St. George	*Liberty. On State Route 3.*	•	•		•	•	•	•		•
Lamoine	*Lamoine. Off State Route 184.*	•	•			•	•	•		
Lily Bay	*Greenville. North 12 miles.*	•	•		•		•	•		•
Mount Blue	*Weld. Off State Route 142.*	•	•		•	•	•	•		•
Peacock Beach	*Richmond. North on State Route 24.*		•		•					
Peaks-Kenny	*Dover-Foxcroft. North off State Route 153.*	•	•		•			•		•
Rangeley Lake	*Rangeley. Off State Route 17.*	•	•		•		•	•		
Reid	*Georgetown. Off State Route 127.*		•	•	•	•		•		
Sebago Lake	*Naples. South off State Route 35.*	•	•	•	•	•	•	•		•
Warren Island	*Islesboro. Entrance off US-1. Park reached by boat only.*	•	•			•		•		

There are no state forests in Maine. For further information on state parks contact: *Maine Department of Conservation, Bureau of Parks and Recreation, State House, Augusta, Maine 04333, (207) 289-3821.*

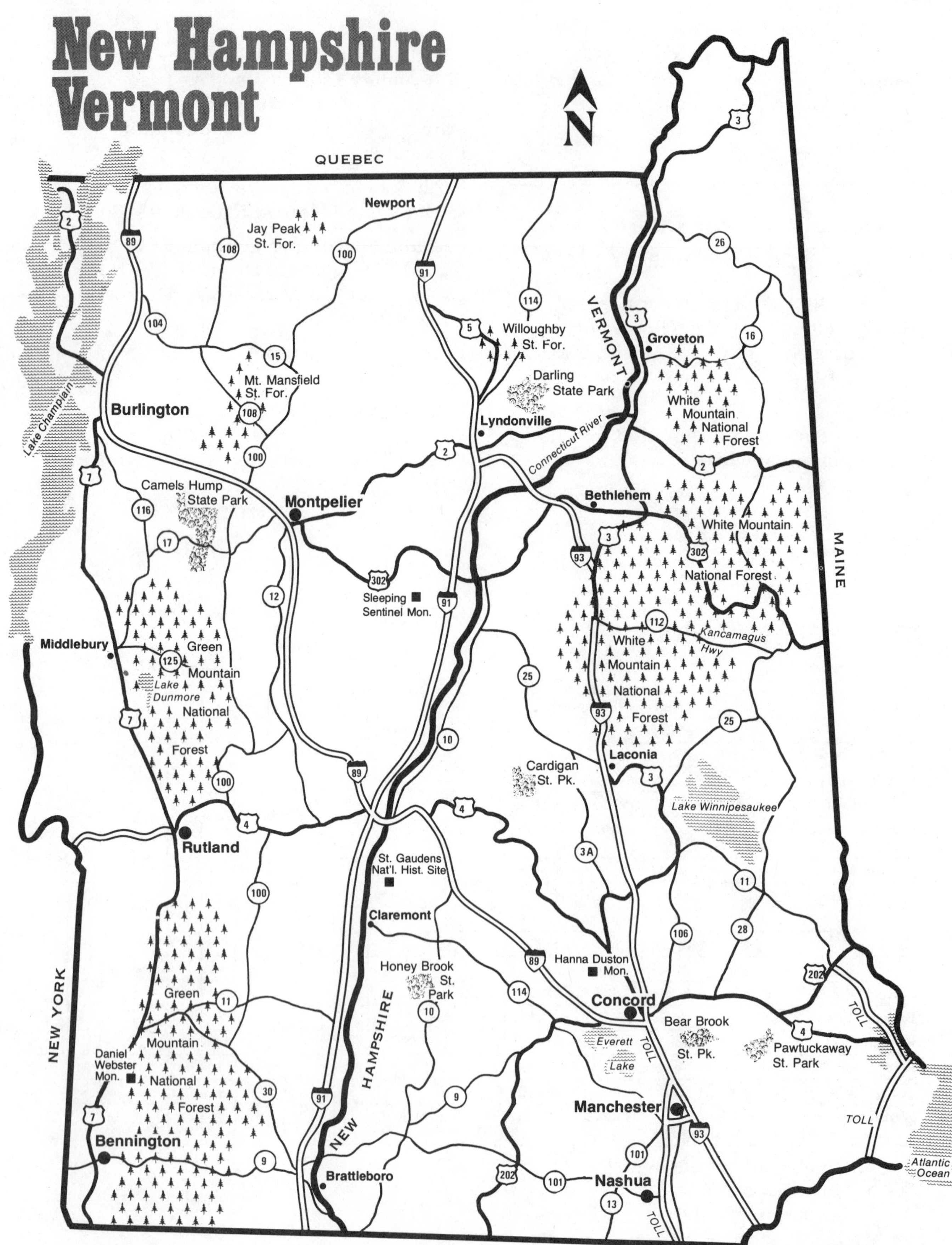

Map not to exact scale.

New Hampshire

"The Four Season State," "The Land of Scenic Splendor," "The Alps Around the Corner," "The Switzerland of America" — these descriptive phrases merely hint at what awaits the New Hampshire visitor.

More than anything, its rugged mountains have shaped the history and character of New Hampshire — for they kept the early colonists close to the 17.8-mile coastline (the shortest of any ocean-bordering state), and limited the location of future settlements to the river valleys, which were ideal sites for the mills that later became so important to the state's industrial development.

The first explorers to the area — Captain Martin Pring (1603), Samuel de Champlain (1605), and Captain John Smith (1614) — found about 5,000 peaceable Indians of various tribes living there. The colonists who came in 1623, under the authority of an English land grant, established New Hampshire's first settlement at what is now the seacoast town of Rye. New Hampshire has the distinction of being the first of the states to declare its independence from England, the first state to adopt its own constitution, and the ninth and deciding state to ratify the U.S. Constitution.

Full name: State of New Hampshire
Origin of name: From the English county of Hampshire.
Motto: Live Free or Die.
Nickname: Granite State.
Capital: Concord
Statehood: June 21, 1788, ninth state.
Population: 849,000 (ranks 42nd).
Major cities: Manchester (83,417), Nashua (61,000), Concord (29,321).
Bird: Purple finch
Flower: Purple lilac
Tree: White birch

Average daily temperatures by month

	North	South
Jan.	25.5 to 5.5	32.6 to 10.7
Feb.	28.9 to 7.3	36.0 to 13.2
Mar.	37.3 to 17.8	43.6 to 22.7
Apr.	50.8 to 29.8	58.3 to 32.7
May	64.3 to 40.2	70.2 to 42.1
Jun.	73.5 to 50.0	79.1 to 52.3
Jul.	77.3 to 54.4	83.5 to 56.5
Aug.	74.8 to 52.4	81.5 to 54.7
Sept.	67.6 to 45.3	73.9 to 47.6
Oct.	57.0 to 35.7	63.4 to 36.8
Nov.	41.9 to 25.7	48.1 to 28.9
Dec.	29.1 to 11.4	35.4 to 16.9
Year	52.3 to 31.3	58.8 to 34.6

With about one-third of its territory having an elevation of 2,000 feet or more, New Hampshire has also earned the distinction of being the most mountainous of the New England states. The 6,288-foot Mount Washington, the highest peak in the Northeast, has been aptly named "Misery Hill" because it is home to some of the most severe weather on the face of the earth. Winter temperatures on the mountain have plunged as low as -47 degrees F, and the peak still holds the record for the strongest wind ever measured on the earth's surface: 231 mph on April 12, 1934. Today, a toll road, a quaint old cog railway and a network of trails all stand ready to lead you to the barren summit and its spectacular views.

While Mount Washington may be known for its especially ornery weather, the opposite holds true for the remainder of New Hampshire. The state actually has

Highlight

Franconia Notch

Franconia Notch is probably the most famous mountain gap in the East. In this picturesque, heavily-forested gorge, which stretches for eight miles from the Kinsman Mountains to the peaks of the Franconia Range, you'll find a number of famous scenic attractions. Among them are the Old Man of the Mountains — a 40-foot-high head, carved out of Cannon Mountain by erosion — towering over Profile Lake; the Basin, a deep glacial pothole at the foot of a waterfall; and Echo Lake, completely enclosed by mountains and noted for its excellent swimming and fishing waters.

While you're in the area you should also plan to see the Flume, a chasm formed by a mountain stream thousands of years ago. This chasm extends along the flank of Mount Liberty for nearly 800 feet, with granite walls 60 to 90 feet high. Within the general area are a number of waterfalls. A solidly constructed boardwalk leads through the gorge. Open late-May through mid-October, daily, 9 a.m. to 5 p.m. Adults $1.75, children 6 to 12, $1.25. There is a free bus to the foot of the gorge.

Franconia Notch is traversed by US-3, southwest of Twin Mountain to Lincoln.

One of the man-made attractions in the area is Cannon Mountain Aerial Tram, which extends from Valley Station, one-half mile north of the Old Man, to the top of Cannon Mountain. The tram makes a vertical ascent of 2,022 feet in 7½ minutes. At the top of the mountain, an observation platform provides a spectacular view of the surrounding mountains and valleys. The tram is open from late-May through mid-October, daily, 9 a.m. to 5 p.m. Adults $3, children 6 to 12, $1.75, round-trip.

a relatively mild climate, ranging from a mean annual winter temperature of 17 degrees F in the north to pleasant summer temperatures that vary from an average of 75 degrees F in the mountains to 80 degrees F in other areas. Summers are cool and refreshing; and even on the warmest days, nights are likely to be fairly cool.

With forests covering 84% of the land, it's not surprising that lumber and paper products are an important part of New Hampshire's economy, along with the manufacture of electrical equipment, rubber, plastics and leather goods. Agricultural products include dairy products, eggs and apples; the narrow coastline supports a healthy fishing industry that supplies lobsters, cod and flounder to the world market. Tourism ranks among the state's most important sources of revenue, bringing in more than $500 million annually.

New Hampshire Points of Interest and Attractions

Abenaki Indian Shop. Indian artifacts and carvings. Open daily, June 15 through October 15; after Labor Day, weekends only, 9:30 a.m. to 5:30 p.m. Intervale, off Routes 16 and 302.

Arctic Circle Aviaries. Ornamental pheasants, dove, royal palm, wild turkeys, wild waterfowl; gift shop. Open June 18 through Labor Day. Free. Gorham, 84 Lancaster Road (Route 1). (603) 466-2379.

Bunthaus. Doll exhibits, miniature house, handcarved reproductions of antique furniture. Open June 26 through October 13, Tuesday through Saturday 9 a.m. to 5 p.m. Adults $1, children 50 cents. Swanzey, on Main Street. (603) 352-7751.

Busch Clydesdale Hamlet. Complimentary tours of Anheuser-Busch brewery, featuring famous eight-horse Clydesdale Budweiser hitch, oxen, tack room, carriage house, exhibits. Merrimack, Everett Turnpike (exit 8).

Cannon Mountain Aerial Tramway. Open May 26 through October 14. Adults $3, children $1.75. Franconia Notch State Park, Franconia, on State Route 116. (603) 823-5563.

Conway Scenic Railroad. One-hour train ride from century-old restored station; antique passenger coaches and open-air observation cars; 58-year-old steam locomotive or early diesel. Open May 5 through October 21, weekends only from May 5 through June 17, daily June 16 through October 21. Departures: 11 a.m., 1, 2:30 and 4 p.m. Adults $3, children 4-12 $1.75, under 4 free. North Conway, State Routes 16 and 302.

Frost Place. Poetry readings, musical programs. Open July 1 through Labor Day, Tuesday through Sunday, 1 p.m. to 5 p.m.; weekends through fall foliage (late September to late October). Adults $1.50, children 75 cents. Franconia, Ridge Road. (603) 823-5510.

Fuller Gardens. Two-acre formal flower gardens; roses, annuals, perennials, Japanese garden. Adults 50 cents, children 25 cents; children with adults, free. North Hampton, 10 Willow Avenue.

Hopkins Center. Center for creative and performing arts at Dartmouth College. Concerts, plays, films, art gallery shows, exhibitions, outdoor sculpture court, snack bar, social lounge. Events calendar free at box office. Hanover. (603) 646-2422.

Indian Village. Stage shows, Indian lore and dancing, wagon rides, live animals, picnic grove, trading post. Open June 23 through Labor Day, daily, 10 a.m. to 6 p.m. Adults $3, children over 4 $1.75. Weirs Beach, off US-3. (603) 366-4377.

Kellerhaus. See New Hampshire candies made and packed; make your own ice cream sundae; individual rooms featuring selection of cheeses, music boxes, candles; Christmas shop with sleeping Santa and working elves. Open May 8 through December 24, daily, 9 a.m. to 5 p.m.; Sunday 10 a.m. to 5 p.m. Free. Weirs, off US-3. (603) 366-4466.

Mt. Washington Auto Road. From Glen House on State Route 16, ride to scenic summit of state's highest point. Open mid-May through late October (weather permitting). Toll: $7 for RV and driver plus $2 for each passenger. (603) 466-3988.

Mt. Washington Cog Railway. Scenic ride to top of Mt. Washington. Open Memorial Day weekend to Columbus Day, from 9 a.m. and hourly as needed. Weekdays partial service and reduced rates. Full Season: June 23 to Labor Day, early bird 8 a.m. and hourly all day; last train three hours before sunset. Adults $13.95, children 6-15 $7, under 6 free if not using seat. Mt. Washington, off State Route 16. (603) 846-5404.

Polar Caves. Tours of caves; mineral collection; waterfowl collection; maple museum; picnic area. Open mid-May through October 8. Adults $3.25, children 6-12 $1.75. Plymouth, west on State Route 25, off Interstate 93 (exit 26). (603) 536-1888.

Ruggles Mine. Two-mile drive to mountains; mineral exhibits; oldest mica, feldspar and beryl mine in U.S.; mineral collecting permitted. Open weekends from May 19, daily June 20 through October 20. Adults $3.25, children $1. Grafton, just off US-4 on Isinglass Mountain.

White Mountain Vineyards, Inc. and Winery. Tours through vineyards, wine tasting and retail sales. Open year-round, Monday through Friday, 9:30 a.m. to 4 p.m.; Saturday by appointment; closed Sunday from June 1 to August 31. Free. Laconia, 2½ miles south, at intersection of Province Road and Durrell Mountain Road. (603) 524-0174.

Wildcat Mountain Gondola. Twenty-five minute ride (round trip) to mountain top; self-guided nature trails at base and summit; cafeteria; gift shop. Open May 26 through October 14. Adults $3.25, children 6-11 $1.75, under 6 free. Pinkham Notch, off State Route 16.

Wolfeboro Railroad Company. Twenty-four-mile scenic ride through countryside that is especially scenic during fall foliage season. Open weekends, April through mid-June and Labor Day to end of October; daily, mid-June through Labor Day. Admission: NA. Boarding at three stations: Wolfeboro, downtown; Wakefield, off State Route 16; Sanbornville, Main Street.

Yankee Notion Country Store. Unique old-time store featuring antiques. Open June 1 through October 15; later, weather permitting. Free. Jefferson, junction of US-2 and State Route 16.

For more information on New Hampshire state parks, contact: *Division of Parks, Concord, New Hampshire 03301, (603) 271-3556.*

State Offices

Tourism
New Hampshire Division of Economic Development
PO Box 856
Concord, New Hampshire 03301
(603) 271-2343

State Police
Department of Public Safety
Concord, New Hampshire 03301
(603) 271-3636

Radio Stations

Berlin
WBRL 1400 (AM)
WXLQ 104 (FM)
Concord
WKXL 1450 (AM)
102.3 (FM)
Manchester
WFEA 1370 (AM)
WKBR 1250 (AM)
WGIR 610 (AM)
101.1 (FM)
Nashua
WOTW 900 (AM)
106.3 (FM)

New Hampshire State Parks

Park	Location	CAMPING	PICNICKING	CONCESSIONS	SWIMMING	HIKING	BOATING	FISHING	HUNTING	WINTER SPORTS
Bear Brook	*Allenstown. Off State Route 28.*	•	•		•	•		•		
Cardigan	*Orange. Off State Route 118.*		•			•				
Clough	*Weare. Off State Routes 77 and 114.*		•		•					
Coleman	*Stewartstown. Off State Route 26.*	•	•					•		
Crawford Notch	*Willey House. Off US-302.*	•	•			•		•		
Echo Lake	*North Conway. Off US-302.*		•		•	•				
Franconia Notch	*Franconia. Five miles south on State Route 116.*	•	•		•	•		•		
Greenfield	*Greenfield. Off State Route 31.*	•	•		•					
Lake Francis	*Pittsburgh. Off US-3.*	•					•	•		
Milan Hill	*Milan. Off State Route 110B.*	•	•							
Monadnock	*Jaffrey. Off State Route 124.*	•	•			•				
Moose Brook	*Gorham. Off US-2.*	•	•	•				•		
Mt. Sunapee	*Newbury. Off State Route 103.*				•	•		•		•
Pawtuckaway	*Nottingham. Off State Route 101.*	•	•		•					
Wadleigh	*North Sutton. Off State Route 44.*		•		•					
White Lake	*Tamworth. Off State Route 25.*	•	•		•	•		•		

Vermont

Mention Vermont, the Green Mountain State, and most people think immediately of moonlight, quaint country landscapes, rustic towns and villages, brilliant fall foliage and maple syrup. As the only New England state without an ocean coastline, Vermont has enjoyed a certain insularity that has helped it retain a flavor of days gone by and has produced a people noted for their independent character. There's a good deal of truth to the old saying: "Vermonters will do nothing that you tell them to; most anything that you ask them to."

In all likelihood, the first European to visit the region was Samuel de Champlain (1609), who gave his name to the northern lake that borders New York state. The British established the first permanent settlement at Fort Dummer in 1724, and assumed full control of the entire territory at the close of the French and Indian War (1763). Later, Ethan Allen and his "Green Mountain Boys" gained fame as resistors of an attempted takeover by officers of the New York territory. Vermonters played a key role in the American Revolution, capturing Fort Ticonderoga and Crown Point. In 1777, Vermont proclaimed its independence and drew up the first state constitution, which outlawed slavery and granted universal manhood suffrage without property qualifications.

Lake Champlain ranks as one of the state's biggest attractions, and the highlight of any visit to the 107-mile-long lake is the northern loop drive that takes travelers across several islands, or the ferry boats that take visitors on scenic cruises to New York state. In the winter, Vermont's mountains offer some of the best skiing and winter sports activities in the East, and winter sport enthusiasts come from all parts of the nation to fill the many fine resorts. In early spring, just before the warm weather feeds the brooks with snowmelt and colorful wildflowers dot the landscape, sap buckets hang in the groves of sugar maples, drawing off the sap that will later become the sweet golden syrup for which Vermont is so famous.

Full name: State of Vermont
Origin of name: French, meaning "Green Mountain."
Motto: Freedom and Unity
Nickname: Green Mountain State
Capital: Montpelier
Statehood: March 4, 1791, 14th state.
Population: 483,000 (ranks 48th).
Major cities: Burlington (37,133), Rutland (19,019), Bennington (15,900).
Bird: Hermit thrush
Flower: Red clover
Tree: Sugar maple

Average daily temperatures by month

	Northern	Southern
Jan.	24.4 to 2.9	30.5 to 9.0
Feb.	28.3 to 4.4	33.5 to 10.1
Mar.	37.4 to 15.9	41.9 to 22.0
Apr.	51.2 to 29.0	55.6 to 33.2
May	64.9 to 40.0	68.2 to 42.2
Jun.	75.1 to 50.0	78.0 to 53.0
Jul.	79.2 to 54.5	82.8 to 57.4
Aug.	76.7 to 52.3	80.7 to 55.1
Sept.	69.1 to 45.1	72.9 to 48.1
Oct.	57.4 to 35.9	62.1 to 37.2
Nov.	41.7 to 26.0	46.9 to 28.9
Dec.	28.5 to 10.7	33.9 to 15.9
Year	52.8 to 30.6	57.3 to 34.3

Highlight
Vermont's Covered Bridges

Covered bridges scattered throughout the valleys of Vermont are among the most scenic and memorable attractions that can be found anywhere. Many were uncovered wooden bridges constructed years before they found it expedient to cover and protect them.

The fact that they are covered usually leads to the question, why? The answer is very simple: To protect from the elements and preserve the wooden trusses that make up the bridge. The covering usually does not contribute any strength to the bridge, but it does make it very picturesque. Actually, this was the only part of the construction in which the builder could show his ingenuity in the trimming of the portals and windows.

The earliest trusses were simple wooden Kingposts for short spans and Queenposts for longer spans. The Multiple Kingpost, Long, Paddleford, Burr Arch and Town Lattice trusses were developed next to span much larger rivers. The Howe truss (1840 Patent) revolutionized bridge building by utilizing iron rods with wood. This commercialized bridge building because the members could be pre-cut at a factory and shipped to be easily assembled for erection at the site. Because of the construction and use of bolted iron rods, the bridge could be tightened up and adjusted when necessary. There were other types of trusses made using one or more of the original designs, plus new truss designs that had limited use in their own region.

The first arches were of single planks usually attached to the trusses, but some were built into the trusses. The use of arches of laminated planks gained popularity as a means of strengthening older bridges and in new construction. As engineering developed, it was found that the arches built into the various new bridges were the main load support. The truss strengthened the arch, rather than the arch strengthening the truss, which some old bridge builders would find hard to accept.

The fact that so many covered bridges have been removed is hard to understand. Actually, there were some built that were poorly constructed in the beginning and nothing could be done to correct them. Others were not built strong enough to withstand modern loads. The main problem has been too little headroom or clearance for large vehicles. Actually, if our forefathers had known of these facts they could have built these features into the bridges and they would be more serviceable today. They did build many bridges that carried locomotives which had the necessary height and strength.

There are many things that one can look for in visiting covered bridges — for example, type of roof covering, style and color of covering, portal or entrance shape, window size and placement, river or stream condition, type of abutment or pier construction, size of timbers, cross bracing construction, trunnels or wooden pegs, type of arch (plain, laminated, built in, added), and, naturally, how well the bridge blends into the local landscape.

Vermont presently has 114 covered bridges of these various trusses:

Town Lattice	43	Pratt Arch	1
Queenpost	24	Howe	1
Kingpost	6	Paddleford	3
Multiple Kingpost	11	Haupt	1
Burr Arch	9	Stringer	9
Tied Arch	3	Railroad	3

Besides being the number one producer of maple syrup, Vermont produces other agricultural products that include dairy products, beef cattle, apples, hay and forest products. Vermont also leads the nation in the production of building stones (granite, limestone), and its other major industries are fabricated metals, paper products, printing and publishing, electrical equipment and glass products.

State Offices

Tourism
Agency of Development and Community Affairs
Vermont Travel Division
61 Elm Street
Montpelier, Vermont 05602
(802) 828-3236

State Police
Department of Public Safety
Montpelier, Vermont 05602
(802) 828-2115

Radio Stations

Burlington
WDOT 1400 (AM)
WJOY 1230 (AM)
WVMT 620 (AM)
WRUV 90.1 (FM)
WEZF 92.9 (FM)
Bennington
WBTN 1370 (AM)
Rutland
WSYB 1380 (AM)
WHWB 98.1 (FM)
WRUT 97.1 (FM)

Vermont Points of Interest and Attractions

Bromley Mountain Alpine Slide and Scenic Chairlift Ride. Exciting slide-ride nearly a mile long with hairpin turns, curves and straightaways. Round-trip scenic chairlift ride to summit lookout tower. Picnic area, gift shop, air-conditioned restaurant, cafeteria. Open late May to late October, daily 10 a.m. to dusk (weather permitting). Adult admission NA, children 6 and under ride free with adult. Manchester Center, north on State Routes 30 and 11.

Cabot Farmers' Co-operative. New England's largest and most modern manufacturer of cheddar cheese and butter. Large picture windows allow visitors to view the manufacture of famous "Cabot, Vermont Cheddar Cheese." Excellent buys on cheese and other dairy products. Open year-round, Monday to Friday, 8 a.m. to 4:30 p.m.; Saturday, 9 a.m. to 3:30 p.m. Free. Cabot, between US-2 and State Route 15.

Dewey's at Quechee Gorge. Located at Vermont's "Little Grand Canyon," the Dewey shops feature sportswear for men and women, gifts and maple sugar products. In the Red Barns you'll find outstanding woolens and easy-to-do kits. Restaurant. Open May to November, daily. Between Woodstock and White River junction, on US-4. (802) 295-3545.

Ferry Crossings. Save 50 to 85 miles between the Green Mountains of Vermont and the Adirondacks of New York with one of these three routes: Burlington, Vermont, to Port Kent New York; Grand Isle, Vermont, to Plattsburgh, New York; Charlotte, Vermont, to Essex, New York. Open April 1 to January 1. Burlington, Lake Champlain Transportation Company. (802) 864-9804 for rates and schedules.

Kennedy Brothers, Incorporated. Watch raw Vermont pine wood transformed into fine furniture and gift accessories. Open year-round. Two locations: Vergennes, on State Route 22A; Burlington, corner of College and Church Streets.

Killington Gondola Tramway. Ride the world's longest ski lift, 3½ miles, to the highest point reached by aerial lift in New England. Summit restaurant, observation decks, cocktail lounge, rest rooms, nature trail. Spectacular views of five states. Sunset dining and twilight rides. Open June 26 through September 3, and

September 25 through October 15; daily, except Monday. Killington, Killington Road. (802) 422-3333.

Maple Grove Honey Museum. Guided tours, live working bee display, maple syrup and confections produced; film, honey making, gift shop. Open year-round, daily, 8 a.m. to 5 p.m. Free. Wilmington, on State Route 9. (802) 748-5141.

Mt. Mansfield Resort. Gondola ride up Vermont's highest peak, Alpine slide, restaurants, shops. Open mid-June through fall foliage. Stowe, off Interstate 89 (exit 10). (802) 253-7311 for rates and schedules.

Rock of Ages Granite Quarries. Guided tours of world's largest granite quarry, 25-minute quarry train ride, exhibits. Open year-round, except July 4 to July 18; train ride, June 1 through August 31, 9:30 a.m. to 3:30 p.m.; quarry tours May 1 through October 31, daily, 8:30 a.m. to 5 p.m. Free; train ride, adults $1, children 25 cents. Barre, at junction of State Routes 62 and 14, and US-302.

St. Anne's Shrine. Religious and historical site which contains the famous statue of Samuel de Champlain sculpted at Canada's Expo '67. In heart of scenic Grand Isle country. Open year-round. Isle La Motte, off State Route 129.

Santa's Land USA. Charming Christmas village featuring unique Christmas decorations and gifts; exotic animals and birds; picnic areas; play parks; miniature railroad; antique German carousel; puppet, magic and cartoon shows; annual Christmas festival, held every Friday evening between Thanksgiving and Christmas. Open year-round, except Thanksgiving, Christmas, New Year's and Easter. Putney, US-5, off Interstate 91 (exits 4 and 5). (802) 387-5550.

Schooner Cruise. Unwind on a leisurely Lake Champlain windjammer cruise aboard the *Richard Robbins*, a historic sailing ship. Savor 19th-century schooner life, help to steer, coil halyards, plot a course, or just loaf, eat and swim. Deck is 58 feet, with 19-foot beam; sleeps 16 in seven cabins. Six-day cruises depart Burlington May 20 through October 20. Fare: $265 per person. Vergennes, Box 195. (802) 759-2411.

UVM Morgan Horse Farm. World famous home of the Morgan horse and national historic site. Statue of Justin Morgan; guided tours; slide-tape show; more than 60 registered horses; picnic tables. Open May 1 through November 1, 8 a.m. to 4 p.m., daily; from November 1 through May 1, closed Saturday afternoon and all day Sunday. Adult admission NA, children under 12 free. Middlebury, three miles north from junction of US-7 and State Route 125. (802) 388-2011.

Vermont Marble Exhibit. Collection of marble from all over the world. Color movie on how marble is discovered, quarried and processed; displays, sculptor at work; gift shop. Open May 26 through October, daily, 9 a.m. to 5:30 p.m. Adults $1, children under 12, 25 cents (admission charged to exhibit only). Proctor, off State Route 3.

Weston Bowl Mill. A southern Vermont landmark for more than 75 years, the Weston Bowl Mill features a magnificent collection of Vermont-made woodenware. Watch as bowls and wood products are made. Open year-round, daily, 8 a.m. to 5 p.m.; Sunday, 10 a.m. to 5 p.m. Weston, off State Route 100. (802) 824-6219.

Wilson Castle. An architectural masterpiece built in the mid-19th century, featuring unique European and Far East furnishings. Open mid-May through mid-October, daily, 8 a.m. to 6 p.m. Admission: NA. Proctor, off State Route 4 on West Proctor Road. (802) 773-3284.

Woolen Wonderland. Fine Vermont woolens, maple products, gifts, souvenirs, deerskin products. Open year-round, 8:30 a.m. to 8:30 p.m. (July through October); 9 a.m. to 5 p.m. (spring and late fall). White River Junction, on US-4 and 5, off Interstate 89 and Interstate 91.

Vermont State Parks

Park	Location	CAMPING	PICNICKING	CONCESSIONS	SWIMMING	HIKING	BOATING	FISHING	HUNTING	WINTER SPORTS
Allis	*Randolph. Off State Route 12.*	•	•							
Ascutney	*Windsor. Off Interstate 91 (exit 8) on Brownsville Road.*	•	•			•				
Bomossen	*Fair Haven. Off US-4 (exit 8).*	•	•	•	•	•	•	•		
Branbury	*Brandon. Off State Route 53.*	•	•	•	•	•	•	•		
Brighton	*Island Pond. Off State Route 105.*	•	•		•	•	•	•		
Burton Island	*St. Albans Bay. (Accessible only by boat.)*	•	•		•		•	•		
Button Bay	*Vergennes. Off State Route 22A.*	•	•		•		•	•		
Calvin Coolidge	*Plymouth. Off State Route 100A.*	•	•			•				•
Crystal Lake	*Barton. Off State Route 16.*		•		•					
D.A.R.	*Vergennes. Off State Route 17.*	•	•		•					
Darling	*East Burke. Off State Route 114.*	•	•							•
Elmore	*Lake Elmore. Off State Route 12.*	•	•	•	•	•	•	•		
Emerald Lake	*East Dorset. Off US-7.*	•	•	•	•	•	•	•		
Fort Dummer	*Brattleboro. Off US-5.*	•				•				
Gifford Woods	*Killington. Off State Route 100.*	•	•			•		•		
Grand Isle	*Grand Isle. Off US-2.*	•		•	•		•	•		
Jamaica	*Jamaica. Off State Route 30.*	•	•		•					
Knight Point	*North Hero. Off US-2.*		•		•		•	•		
Lake Carmi	*Enosburg Falls. Off State Route 105.*	•	•	•		•	•	•		
Lake St. Catherine	*Poultney. Off State Route 30.*	•	•	•	•	•	•	•		
Molly Stark	*Wilmington. Off State Route 9.*	•				•				
North Hero	*North Hero. Off US-2.*	•			•	•	•	•		
St. Albans Bay	*St. Albans Bay. Off State Route 36.*		•		•					
Sand Bar	*Milton. Off US-2.*		•	•	•		•	•		
Shaftsbury	*Shaftsbury. Off US-7.*	•	•	•	•	•	•	•		
Silver Lake	*Barnard. Off State Route 12.*	•	•		•		•	•		
Wilgus	*Ascutney. Off US-5.*	•	•			•	•	•		
Woodford	*Bennington. Off State Route 9.*	•	•		•	•	•	•		

Vermont State Forests

Forest	Location	CAMPING	PICNICKING	CONCESSIONS	SWIMMING	HIKING	BOATING	FISHING	HUNTING	WINTER SPORTS
Groton	*Montpelier. Off US-2.*	•	•		•	•	•	•		•
Maidstone	*Bloomfield. Off State Route 102.*	•	•		•	•	•	•		
Mount Mansfield	*Waterbury. Off Interstate 89 (exit 10).*	•	•		•	•	•	•		•
Thetford	*Thetford. Off State Route 113A.*	•	•							
Townshend	*Newfane. Off State Route 30.*	•	•		•	•				

For additional information on Vermont state parks and forests, contact:
Department of Forests, Parks, and Recreation, Montpelier, Vermont 05602, (802) 828-3375.

New England Calendar of Events

Spring
(March, April, May)

Connecticut

Shad Derby and Festival. Parade. May, Windsor.

Dogwood Festival, Greenfield Hill. May, Fairfield.

"Main Street USA." May, New Britain.

Antiques Festival, Village Center. May, Woodbridge.

Art Fair. May 26, Salisbury.

Maine

Old-Timers Weekend, Sugarloaf. First weekend in March, Kingfield.

Rangeley Lakes Sled Dog Race. March, Rangeley.

St. Patrick's Day Celebration. March 17, Camden.

Fisherman's Festival. March, Boothbay Harbor.

Family Alpine Race, Tube, Tub and Shovel Race — Sunday River Annual Spring Fling. All during April, Bethel.

Downhill Canoes-on-Snow Races, Squaw Mountain. April, Greenville.

YMCA Annual Maypole Festival, auditorium. May, Bangor.

Fort Western Days. May, Fort Western.

Massachusetts

Antique Show and Sale, Stoneleigh-Burnham School. March, Greenfield.

Spring Flower Show, Worcester County Horticultural Society. March, Worcester.

New England Spring Garden and Flower Show, Massachusetts Horticultural Society. March, Boston.

St. Patrick's Day Parade. March, Holyoke.

Annual Student Show. Exhibition of works by craft center students, Craft Center. April-May, Worcester.

White Water Races for canoes and kayaks, sponsored by Westfield Wild Water Canoe Club. April, Westfield.

National Exhibit, Springfield Art League, George Walter Smith Art Museum. April. Springfield.

The Hanging of Lanterns at the Old North Church. April, Boston.

Annual 26-mile Patriot's Day Marathon Race. April, Boston.

Antique Car Parade. April, Nantucket Island.

Gillette Castle, built as a private home in 1919 by actor William Gillette, is a popular spot for visitors to its hilltop location overlooking the Connecticut River.

Annual Panic Sale/Flea Market. Entire town joins in sale of used items, 10 a.m. to dusk, Town Hall parking lot. April, Ipswich.

Annual Cambridge River Festival. Citywide celebration of spring and the arts. May, Cambridge.

Annual Arts and Crafts Fair, Sherborn Library. May, Sherborn.

Trout Fishing Derby. Open to all ages with trophies for largest catches, Gardner Fish and Gun Club. May, Gardner.

Open House. All historic houses open to public, 10 a.m. to 5 p.m. May, Plymouth.

New Hampshire

Artisans Craft Fair. Exhibits by more than 70 craftspersons at New Hampshire Highway Hotel. April, Merrimack City.

Annual Easter Parade. March or April (at Easter), Peterborough.

Annual Contoocock River Canoe/Kayak Clinic. April, Peterborough.

Vermont

Orvis Fly Fishing Schools. Casting, coaching and lectures. The Orvis Company. April through August, Manchester.

Franklin County Maple Festival. Sugaring, pancake breakfasts. April, St. Albans.

Antique and Flea Market. May, Newfane.

Handmade Crafts Display. May, Saxton's River.

Summer
(June, July, August)

Connecticut

Sidewalk Exhibit, Museum of American Art. June, New Britain.

Greater Hartford Arts Festival. June, Hartford.

Yale-Harvard Regatta, Thames River. June, New London.

Jumping Frog Contest, Mark Twain Memorial. June, Hartford.

Branford Trolley Museum Parade and Pageant. June, East Haven.

P. T. Barnum Festival. June through early July, Bridgeport.

Rose/Arts Festival. June, Norwich.

Connecticut State Fair. July, Durham.

Sports Car Races. July Fourth, Lime Rock.

Open House Tour of Homes. July, Litchfield.

Country Antiques Festival. July, Riverton.

Outdoor Arts Festival. August, Mystic.

Bridgewater Country Fair. August, Bridgewater.

Oyster Festival. August, Milford.

Ancient Fife and Drum Corps Parade and Muster. August, Westbrook.

Annual Squam Lakes Fishing Derby. Fish for salmon and lake trout; prizes. May through end of June, Squam Lakes.

Saco River Down River Race. May, Conway.

Golden Age Olympics North. Thirty different events for those 55 and older — decathlon, dancing, hobbies, bridge, checkers, golf, swimming, rowing, etc.; Nashua Senior Center. May, Nashua.

Rhode Island

Annual Governor's Tennis Tournament, Court II Tennis Club. April, Lincoln.

Annual Northeast Feline Fanciers Cat Show. April, Warwick.

Woonsocket Heritage Fair, Woonsocket Historical Society. April, Woonsocket.

Annual Jaguar Motor Car Festival. April, Newport.

Annual Tulip Show, Roger Williams Park. April, Providence.

Annual Azalea and Rhododendron Show, Winsor Azalea Garden. April, Cranston.

Rolling Rhodies Antique Auto Post-Easter Parade. April, for locale call (401) 821-7298.

Annual Greyholme "Class B" Horse Show, Rocky Hill Fairgrounds. May, East Greenwich.

May Day Breakfasts. Unique events (originating in 1867) held throughout Rhode Island at various grange halls and private clubs. Most are open to the public. A list of places serving May Breakfasts is available through the state Tourist Promotion Division.

Annual Jaguar Motor Car Festival. May, Newport.

Wickford Yacht Club Regatta, Wickford Yacht Club. May, Wickford.

Connecticut Bluefish Tournament. August through October, Niantic.

Trolley Car Parade and Pageant, Branford Trolley Museum. August, East Haven.

Maine

Ellis River Canoe Marathon. Public supper and picnic. June, Andover.

Maine Children's Festival. June, Cape Elizabeth.

Power Boat Races, Chickawauki Lake. June, Rockland.

Maine Humorist Festival, Community Theater. June, Pittsfield.

Antique Show. Displays of china, silver, furniture. July, Camden.

Windjammer Days. Boat parade, lobster feast, dance. July, Boothbay Harbor.

Sloop Days. July, Friendship.

Seafoods Festival. August, Rockland.

Massachusetts

Band Concerts. June, Plymouth.

Sunday Evening Band Concerts, Harbor Square. June, Nantucket.

Annual Banjo Pickers Convention. Banjo players from throughout New England compete in various age groups for prize money and trophies. June, Cummington.

Gaelic Games at Castle Hill. Irish dancing, piping, drumming, athletic events. June, Ipswich.

Annual Strawberry Festival. Homemade pies, jams, tarts, cookies, teas, punch, ice cream, dips and shortcakes. June, Ipswich.

St. Peter's Fiesta. Three days of block dances, concerts, games, dory races, blessing of the fishing fleet. June, Gloucester.

Annual 50-Mile Arthur M. Longsjo Memorial Bicycle Race. July, Lunenburg.

Annual Independence Day Ball. July, Ipswich.

Whaling City Festival, Buttonwood Park. Craft show, art exhibits, music, athletic events, food, movies, flea market, auto and van shows. July, New Bedford.

Annual Billfish Tournament. July, Nantucket.

Yankee Homecoming. A tribute to New England with parades, exhibits, concerts, river cruises, sailboat and canoe races. July, Newburyport.

Yankee Ingenuity Crafts Fair. August, Winchendon.

Annual "Heritage Days" Weekend. Concerts, U.S. Coast Guard cutter open house, road race, arts and crafts, square dance, boat parade. August, Scituate.

Annual Ipswich Days. Week-long celebration and sale of arts and crafts. August, Ipswich.

Feast of the Fishermen, Madonna Del Soccorso. Colorful religious festival in the predominantly Italian North End section of Boston. August, Boston.

Berkshire Balloonfest. Giant hot-air balloons from throughout the East perform and compete in races and free flights. August, Cummington.

Bluefish Tournament, Merrimac Valley Striper Club. August, Newburyport.

New Hampshire

Saco Bound Mass Start Canoe Race, Saco River. June, Conway.

Market Square Day, Market Square. June, Portsmouth.

Annual Spring Horse Pull, Cheshire Fair Ice Arena. June, Keene.

American Motorcycle Association Laconia Classic, Bryar Motorsport Park. June, Loudon.

Annual Strawberry Festival. June, Fitzwilliam.

Annual Gilsum Rock Swap. Exhibits, tours of local mines, old-fashioned church supper. June, Gilsum.

Annual Old-Timers Fair. Parade, ox pulling. June, Etna.

Annual Arts and Crafts Festival, Proctor Academy. July, Andover.

Annual Muster, Old Fort #4. July, Charlestown.

Annual Antiques Show. July, Newcastle.

Sidewalk Carnival Days and Crafts Fair. July, Keene.

Quaint coastal villages and docks laden with nets and lobster traps are synonymous with Maine.

Canterbury Fair. Auction, antiques, chicken barbecue, crafts, country dancing. July, Canterbury Center.
Annual Art Show. July, Alton.
Annual Craftsmen's Fair, Sunapee State Park. Auction of craft items, daily entertainment. August, Newbury.
Annual Antiques Show. More than 70 dealers. August, Concord.
Annual White Mountains Old-Time and Bluegrass Music Festival. Over $2,000 in prizes for all areas of traditional old-time and bluegrass music. August, West Ossipee.
American Motorcycle Association Autumn Nationals, Bryar Motorsport. August, Loudon.

Rhode Island

Annual Children's Expo, Ceramic Show. June, Cumberland.
Annual Festival of the Towers, sponsored by the Narragansett Art Association. June, Narragansett.
Strawberry Festival. June, Warwick.
Diamond Hill Music Festival. June, Cumberland.
"Gaspee Days." Commemorates the June 9, 1772 burning of the British revenue schooner *HMS Gaspee* by Rhode Island patriots; parade, colonial muster, costume ball, clambake. June, Warwick.
Newport Music Festival. 19th-century romantic music in 19th-century mansions. July, Newport.
Newport Outdoor Festival. July, Newport.
Newport Jazz Festival. July, Newport.
Bristol County Fair. July, Warren.
Annual Providence County Kennel Club All-Breed Dog Show and Obedience Trial, Victory Field. July, Barrington.
Sundays-In-The-Park Concerts, Roger Williams Park. July, Providence.
Annual South County Heritage Festival. Antique cars, boat cruises, music; Marina Park. July, Wakefield.
Annual Blessing of the Fleet. July, Newport.
Annual Block Island Billfish Invitational Tournament. July, Block Island.
Washington County Fair. August, Richmond.
Children's Parade, Town Common. August, Bristol.
Newport Opera Festival. 18th- and 19th-century chamber operas and concerts. August, Newport.
Annual Beer Fest. August, Middletown.
Annual Craft Fair, Kimball Wildlife Refuge. August, Charlestown.
Annual Historic House Tour of Narragansett Historical Society. August, Narragansett.
Annual South Shore Bass and Bluefish Tournament. August, Galilee.

Vermont

Flower Festival. June, Woodstock.
Annual Fun-O-Rama. June, Barton.
Annual Country Fair. Rides, food, games, crafts, flower and cattle show. June, Milton.
Father's Day Kite Flying. June, East Burke.
Historical Day. Parade, exhibits, flea market. June, Concord.
Annual Antique Show and Sale. June, Swanton.

Dover Dunkers Drunken Sailors Race. Parade preceding race, food. July, Mount Snow.
Norwich Fair. Parades, rides, food, bands, ox pulling, crafts. July, Norwich.
Folk Festival and Traditional Craft Fair. Includes concerts, dances, afternoon workshops. July, West Brattleboro.
Peasant Market. Booths, food, crafts. July, Middlebury.
Annual Airshow. Featuring the Flying Farmer and Jim Parker; glider rides. July, Warren.
Community Summer Festival. Craft fair, theater, music, food, fireworks. July, Woodstock.
Annual Maple Sugar-On-Snow Supper, Church and Community House. July, Morgan.
Wooden Sap Bucket and Maple Sugar Making Demonstrations, New England Maple Museum. July, Pittsford.
Annual Children's Fair. July, South Wallingford.
Vermont Mozart Festival. July, Burlington.
Annual Carnival. Rides and games. July, Chester.
Annual Art and Craft Show. July, Brattleboro.
Annual Antiques Fair. July, Woodstock.
Annual Old-Time Fiddlers Contest. July, Craftsbury.
Annual Fun Fare Bazaar. Crafts, games, food, band concert, the Village Green. August, Bristol.
Annual Country Fair Bazaar. August, Wallingford.
Annual Horse Show. August, South Woodstock.
Annual Vermont Artisans Summer Festival and Country Revels. August, Strafford.
Bluegrass Festival. August, Stratton Mountain.
Village Fair. August, Thetford Hill.
St. Mark's Annual Antique Show and Sale. August, Burlington.
Marlboro Music Festival. August, Marlboro.
"Vermont Day." Demonstrations of old crafts and skills, food. August, Calais.

A granite portico protects Plymouth Rock where the Pilgrims stepped ashore on December 20, 1620.

Bazaar, Smorgasbord and Band Concert. August, South Royalton.
Vermont Square and Round Dance Mini-Convention. August, Randolph.
Antiques Show. August, Brandon.
Modern Woodmen of America Annual Carnival and Parade. August, Wells.
Annual Scottish Festival. August, Quechee.

Fall
(September, October, November)

Connecticut

Dixieland Band Cruise, Mystic River. September, Mystic.
North Haven Fair. September, North Haven.
Apple Harvest Festival. October, Southington.
Connecticut Antiques Show. October, Hartford.
Stratton Arts Festival. October, Stratton.

Maine

Fall Foliage Festival and Art Show. September-October, Sugarloaf Mountain.
Bridgton Arts Show. October, Bridgton.

Massachusetts

Annual Hilltown Fiddlers Convention. Fiddling competition for various age groups. September, Cummington.
Barrington County Fair. September, Great Barrington.

Annual Eastern States Exposition. Features agricultural, educational and industrial shows; famous name performers; championship horse show. September, West Springfield.
Annual Regatta, "Oktoberfest." September, Lowell.
Striped Bass and Bluefish Derby. September, Martha's Vineyard.
Annual Antique Show and Sale. September, Ipswich.
Fall Foliage Festival. September, North Adams.
Indian-Summer Days. September, Milton.
Massachusetts Cranberry Festival and Fair. October, South Carver.
Annual Bourne Bay Scallop Festival. October, Bourne.
Annual Harvest Day Festival. Games, contests, hayrides, baked goods. October, Hampden.
Fall Boat Regatta. River cruise up the Merrimack to Haverhill and return. October, Newburyport.
Rowing Regatta. World's largest one-day rowing event. October, Boston and Cambridge.
Annual Worcester Music Festival. October, Worcester.
Fall Foliage Season, Berkshire Hills. Mid-October viewing is usually best, but this can vary according to weather.

Mark Twain's Hartford, Connecticut, home, built in 1874, is completely restored with original Clemens family furnishings and the author's memorabilia.

Yankee Ingenuity Crafts Fair. November, Winchendon.
Annual Welcome to Santa Parade. November, Ipswich.
Thanksgiving Day Celebration. Spend Thanksgiving Day where the first Thanksgiving was celebrated in 1621. Historic houses open, and many serve cider and doughnuts to visitors. Restaurants in town feature special menus. November, Plymouth.

New Hampshire

Old Home Day. Flag raising, contests, pony wagon rides, dance, barbecue. September, Thornton.
Annual Folk and Square Fall Dance Camp. September, Troy.
Annual Tri-State Collectors Exhibition. Coins, stamps and other collectibles. October, Concord.
Annual Christmas Fair. November, Portsmouth.
Annual Square Dance Weekend. November, Troy.

Rhode Island

Annual Moosup Valley Grange Clambake. September, Foster.
Annual Fall Chowder Day. September, Warwick.
Annual Harvest Fair. Pony rides, haystack sliding, greased money pole. September, Bristol.
Oktoberfest. October, Jamestown.
Apple Festival. Greek music, dancing, booths, children's events. October, Pawtucket.
Anniversary of the Founding of the American Navy. Cannon firing and ceremony aboard Revolutionary War-era frigate. October, Newport.
Harvest Thanksgiving Ceremony and Dinner. November, Exeter.
Kimball Christmas Fair, Kimball Wildlife Refuge. November, Charlestown.

Vermont

Vermont State Fair. September, Rutland.
Antique and Classic Car Show. September, Bennington.

Stratton Arts Show. September-October, Stratton Mountain.
Oktoberfest. October, Sugarbush Valley.

Winter

(December, January, February)

Connecticut

Festival of Lights. November-January, Hartford.
Celebrations at Santa Claus Christmas Village. December, Torrington.

Maine

Children's Santa Claus Party. Santa enters the harbor on tugboat and rides horse-drawn wagon to Legion Hall. December, Boothbay Harbor.
Torchlight Parade, Pleasant Mountain. December, Bridgton.
Snow Bowl Winter Wonderland Carnival. January, Camden.
Annual Paul Bunyan International Snowmobile Open. January, Bangor.
Birthday Celebration. Old ski costumes, walk-up race, down over 50s race. February, Camden.
Annual Goose River Cross Country Race. February, Camden.
The Great Inner Tube Race, Pleasant Mountain. February, Bridgton.
Torchlight Parade. February, Bridgton.

New Hampshire

Annual Year End Square and Folk Dance Camp. December, Keene.
Winter Carnival with World Championship Sled Dog Race. February, Laconia.
Winter Carnival. February, Wolfeboro.
Dartmouth Winter Carnival. February, Hanover.

Rhode Island

Christmas in Newport. December, Newport.

Vermont

Winter Carnival. Ice show, snowshoe race, ski jumping. February, Middlebury.

Massachusetts

Annual Christmas Parade. December, Middleboro.
Annual Performance of *The Nutcracker* by the Boston Ballet Company, Music Hall. December, Boston.
Annual Christmas Displays on Taunton Green. December, Taunton.
Annual Christmas Market. Handmade gifts, wreaths, roasted chestnuts, carolers and Kris Kringle. December, Salem.
Anniversary of Boston Tea Party, Boston Tea Party Ship and Museum. Reenactment of historic event. December, Boston Harbor.

Trailing blinding white rooster tails, three entrants in the International Snowmobile Championship head for home at Briar Motorsport Park in Laconia, New Hampshire.

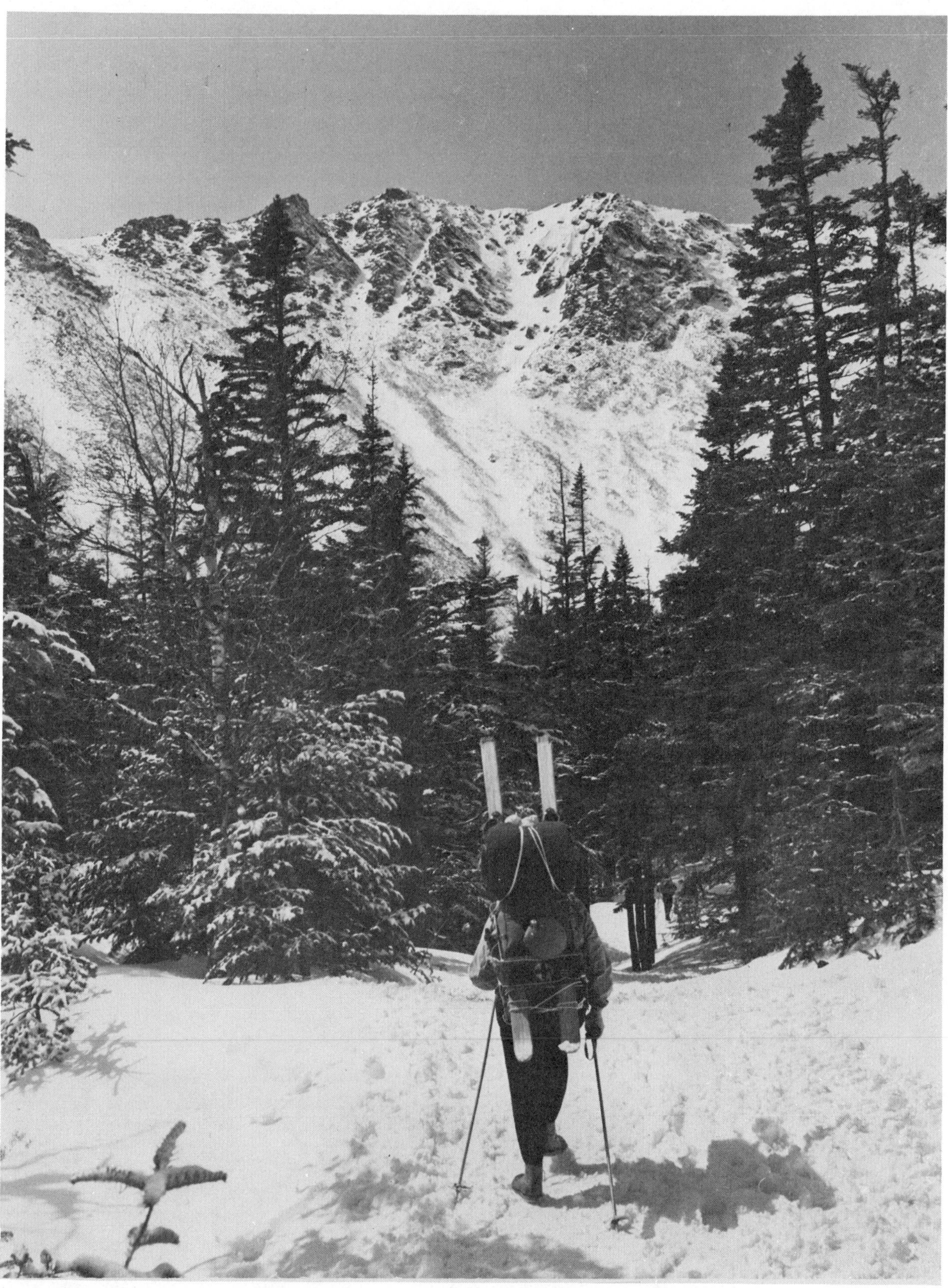

Some of the finest spring skiing in New Hampshire can be found here, in the massive snow bowl known as Tuckerman Ravine.

NEW YORK
Central Park Hansom Cab
Independence Hall – Philadelphia
PENNSYLVANIA
Betsy Ross House
Liberty Bell
Amish buggy
Amish boys

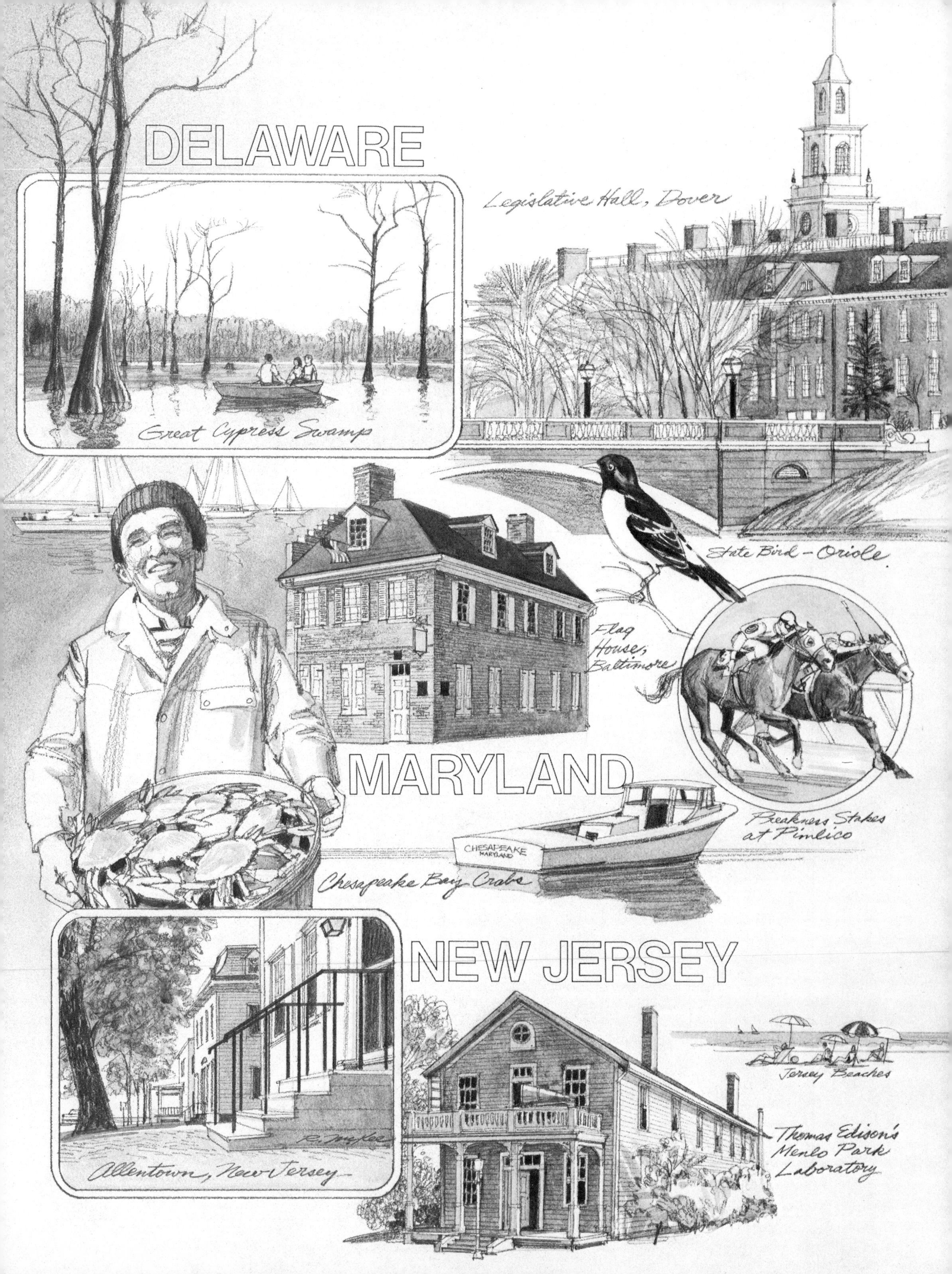

DELAWARE
Great Cypress Swamp
Legislative Hall, Dover
State Bird - Oriole
Flag House, Baltimore
MARYLAND
Preakness Stakes at Pimlico
CHESAPEAKE MARYLAND
Chesapeake Bay Crabs
NEW JERSEY
Jersey Beaches
Thomas Edison's Menlo Park Laboratory
Allentown, New Jersey

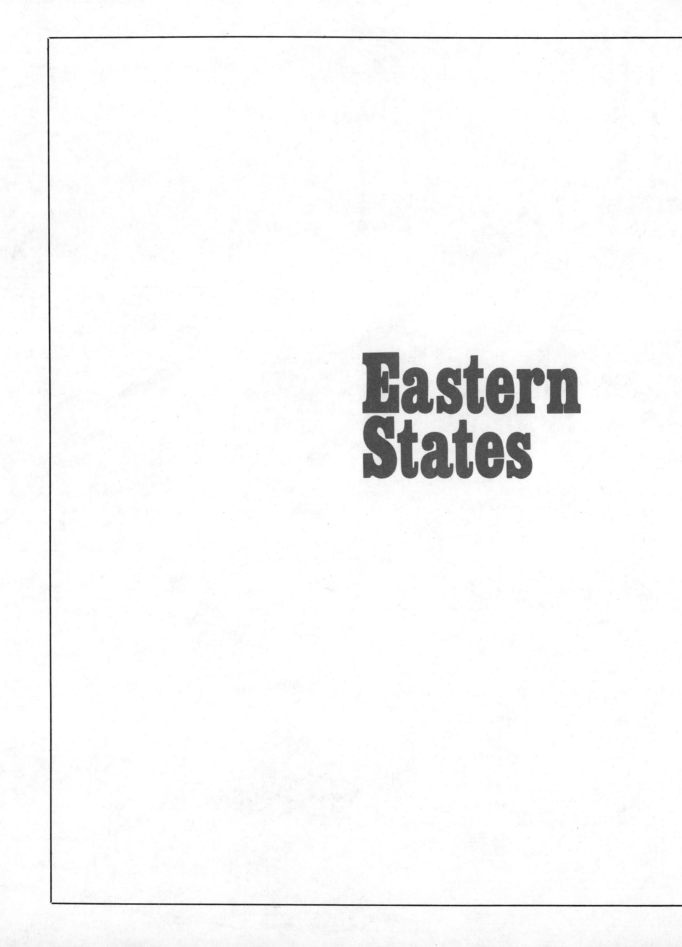

Eastern States

Bustling urban centers, contrasting sharply with relaxed country settings, are the most striking characteristics of the Eastern states. If you like big city excitement, you'll find it in abundance in New York, Philadelphia, Baltimore and other major cities of the East. If your tastes run more to the pastoral, there's a vast countryside to be explored — the Poconos, the Catskills, the Adirondacks, New Jersey's Pine Barrens and the unique farming country of Pennsylvania.

The land itself is one of the reasons why the East has such an appeal for the traveler, for few areas boast such a diversity of scene — or a history that can be so easily traced. It all begins with the great stretch of Atlantic coastal plain that gradually slopes upward to form the piedmont. The line where these two land masses meet — the fall line — became the ideal site for early settlements because energy could be found in the rivers and streams that spilled over the falls and rapids. As the settlements along this line grew to cities, the arteries that linked them also tended to follow its path. Thus, today, you can travel the historic fall line along Interstate 95.

If you were to search for the most apt description of the Eastern states, you need look no further than the words of Captain John Smith, who penned the following during his 1608 exploration of Delaware Bay: *"Here are the mountaines, hills, plaines, valleys, rivers and brookes all running most pleasantly into a faire bay compassed but for the mouth with fruitfull and delightsome land."*

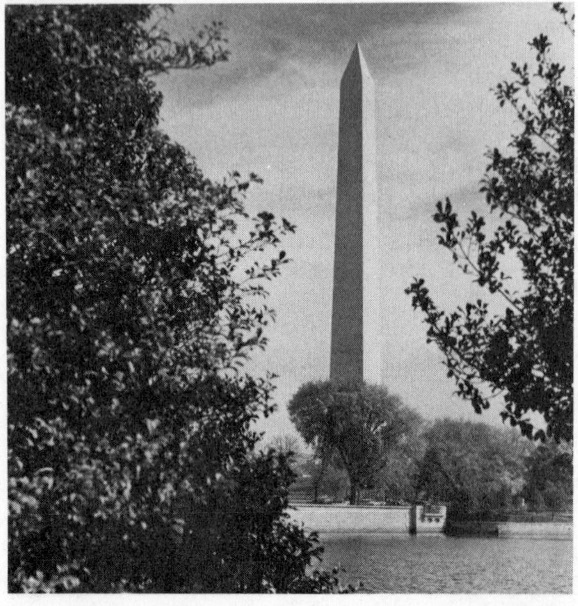

The supreme example of a government edifice, the U.S. Capitol Building (above) contains the chambers of the House and Senate, reflecting 150 years of architectural evolution. The Jefferson Memorial (top left) was dedicated in 1943 in memory of the author of the Declaration of Independence, Thomas Jefferson. (Bottom left) Distinguished as the tallest spire in the United States, the Washington Memorial rises above the capitol grounds in awesome simplicity.

District of Columbia

Carved out of the state of Maryland, Washington, D.C. is one of the leading tourist attractions in the United States. This well-planned city, which serves as the nation's capital, is situated at the edge of a coastal plain between the foothills of the Appalachians and the Atlantic Ocean. Located about equal distance from New England and Georgia, Washington serves as the gateway city to both the north and the south.

Washington was selected as the nation's capital after nearly seven years of congressional debate. The site, selected by George Washington, was originally a mosquito-infested swamp; but French engineer Pierre L'Enfant and American free black Benjamin Banneker, chief architects of the city, were able to envision a place of broad avenues, spacious circles and magnificent monuments.

The cornerstone of the Capitol Building was laid in 1793, and when the north wing was completed in 1800, Congress was moved from its temporary headquarters in Philadelphia. The President's House, which would later become known as the White House, was first occupied by John Adams. Other than the government buildings, the Federal City was originally composed of only a few cabins. The city was muddy and dusty, depending upon the season, and became the object of scornful jokes. In fact, the living conditions in early Washington were so deplorable that the officials assigned there received hardship pay.

The War of 1812 dealt a crippling blow to Washington's growth when about 5,000 British troops defeated the American defenders and entered and burned much of the city. Rebuilding began as soon as the war ended and the President's House, which survived, was painted white to cover the fire damage, thus earning the name "White House."

After the reconstruction period, Washington's growth was spurred by the addition of the Chesapeake and Ohio Canal railroads, so that by 1860, the population of the city had risen to about 75,000. With the outbreak of the Civil War, Washington was again threatened with invasion from Confederate forces; however, on the two occasions when Confederate forces approached Washington, their tactical blunders saved the city.

Full Name: Washington, District of Columbia.
Origin of Name: In honor of George Washington.
Population: City, 721,800; metropolitan area, 3,015,300.
Motto: *Justitia Omnibus* (Justice to All).
Bird: Wood thrush
Flower: American Beauty rose.

Average daily temperatures by month

	High	Low
January	44	30
February	46	29
March	54	36
April	66	46
May	76	56
June	83	65
July	87	69
August	85	68
September	79	61
October	68	50
November	57	39
December	46	31

The close of the Civil War was a major turning point for Washington when, in late May of 1865, more than 100,000 people flocked to the capital to witness the Grand Review of the victorious Union Army. For two days and nights, the people watched 150,000 Union soldiers parade up Pennsylvania Avenue. And when those visitors finally went home, they took stories with them of the sights to be seen in Washington. Soon, tourists started coming to see their capital city, and new businesses sprang up to meet their needs.

Washington underwent other periods of rapid expansion during World Wars I and II. In each case, new federal agencies, new buildings and thousands of civil servants appeared almost overnight. This population increase stimulated further business and many new hotels, shops and restaurants were constructed as a result.

Until recently, Washington, D.C. was a federal district governed by Congress and administered by a mayor-commissioner and a nine-member city council appointed by the President. Now, however, the voters of Washington elect their own mayor and city council.

As the capital of the United States, government is the city's major industry and accounts for much of the city's economic base. The leading private industry is tourism, with more than 15 million visitors coming to the city each year. Recently, many research and development companies in electronics, physics and other sciences have located in the Washington, D.C. area, and more and more light industry is expected to follow suit in the coming years. As Washington does not have any heavy industry, it is one of the cleanest cities in the country.

Washington offers an endless number of attractions that can fill an entire vacation. Some points of interest, like the famed Smithsonian Institution, are so extensive that it is almost impossible to see them all. Of course, you'll want to see the Washington Monument, the White House, the Lincoln Memorial and some of the city's other more prominent attractions, but be sure to save time for some of the cultural activities at the John F. Kennedy Center of the Performing Arts and for the many points of interest in neighboring Maryland and Virginia.

Washington, D.C. Points of Interest and Attractions

Anacostia Park. A 750-acre park that was once the site of the Indian village of Nacotchtank; now offering tennis courts, swimming pool, recreation center and skating rink. Open year-round, daily, 7:30 a.m. to 6 p.m. On the Anacostia River in northeast section of the city.

Blair House. Used as a guesthouse for visiting dignitaries, this was also the residence of the President during the renovation of the White House from 1948 to 1952. 1651 Pennsylvania Avenue, NW.

C & O Canal Barge Trips. Excursions on the canal depart daily at 11:30 a.m., 1:30, 3:30 and 5:30 p.m. from April through October. Adults $2, children under 13 $1. 1055 Thomas Jefferson Street, NW. (301) 299-2026.

Corcoran Gallery of Art. Houses an extensive collection of American paintings, drawings, sculptures and prints from the 18th and 19th centuries; frequently-changing exhibits of modern art. Open year-round, Tuesday to Sunday, 11 a.m. to 5 p.m. Adults $1.50, children over 12, 75 cents, senior citizens and children under 12, free. On 17th Street, between E Street and New York Avenue.

Dumbarton Oaks. This former estate of Mrs. Robert Woods Bliss now houses the Center for Byzantine Studies, which includes a comprehensive library and art of the Early Christian and Byzantine periods. Open year-round, daily, 2 p.m. to 5 p.m. Free. 1703 32nd Street, NW.

Explorers Hall, National Geographic Society. Contains exhibits of National Geographic expeditions and features the

The Lincoln Memorial, situated at the west end of the National Mall in Washington, D.C., is just across the Potomac River from the former home of Confederate commander Robert E. Lee.

Lincoln Memorial

"There is no new thing to be said about Lincoln. There is no new thing to be said of the mountains, or of the sea, or of the stars. But to the mountains and sea and stars men turn forever in unwearied homage. And thus with Lincoln."
— Homer Hoch, Kansas congressman.

Without a doubt, the Lincoln Memorial is the most inspiring of all the Washington sites. Within the depths of the memorial, the imposing 21-foot figure of Lincoln looks down upon visitors — and almost seems ready to speak. The structure is surrounded by 36 marble columns, one for each state in the Union at the time of the Great Emancipator's death. Fifty-six steps, one for every year of Lincoln's life, lead up to the inner chamber. Between the Lincoln Memorial and the Washington Monument lie two reflecting pools with a combined length of 2,292 feet. At night, the memorial shimmers in the waters of the reflecting pool, adding a new aspect to the beauty of the edifice. Open year-round, daily, 24 hours.

world's largest free-moving globe suspended over a reflecting pool; recorded narrations and films. Open year-round, daily, 9 a.m. to 5 p.m. Free. 17th and M Streets, NW.

Folger Shakespeare Library. Features a small theater in the style of the public theaters of Shakespeare's day, and offers lectures, poetry readings, art exhibits and concerts. Plays are presented nightly except Monday. Open year-round, daily, 10 a.m. to 4:30 p.m.; closed Sunday from Labor Day through April. Free (admission charged to plays). Second and East Capitol Streets.

J. Edgar Hoover FBI Building. Features photos and biographies of notorious criminals, as well as exhibits of firearms and FBI equipment; tours. Open year-round, Monday to Friday, 9 a.m. to 4 p.m. Free. On Pennsylvania Avenue, between Ninth and 10th Streets.

John F. Kennedy Center for the Performing Arts. Offers music, dramatic, dance and film productions from the U.S. and foreign countries. Box office open Monday to Saturday, 10 a.m. to 9 p.m.; Sunday, noon to 9 p.m. Restaurant open for lunch and dinner. Tours daily from 10 a.m. to 1:15 p.m. Parking fee $2.50. At the foot of New Hampshire Avenue. (202) 254-3600.

Lafayette Square. The most famous square in Washington, across Pennsylvania Avenue from the White House; a statue of Andrew Jackson is the central monument.

Library of Congress. A magnificent architectural showcase of Italian Renaissance architecture, this library contains more than 18 million books and pamphlets and more than 32 million manuscripts, as well as extensive files of films, photos, maps, prints and newspapers. Exhibits include Thomas Jefferson's rough draft of the Declaration of Independence and Lincoln's first and second drafts of the Gettysburg Address. Concerts and literary programs are presented Monday to Friday evenings, October through April. Open Monday to Friday, 8:30 a.m. to 9:30 p.m.; Saturday 8:30 a.m. to 5 p.m.; Sunday, 1 p.m. to 5 p.m. Free. Facing the Capitol, across East Capitol Street from the Supreme Court Building.

National Archives. This facility preserves government records and makes them

The historic Chesapeake & Ohio Canal, started in 1824, parallels the Potomac River and offers such spectacular scenery that it is probably the number one recreational attraction for Washington residents and visitors.

available for public use. It also houses the Declaration of Independence, the Constitution, the Bill of Rights and other important documents. Open year-round, Monday to Saturday, 9 a.m. to 6 p.m.; Sunday, 1 p.m. to 10 p.m. Free. On Constitution Avenue, between Seventh and Ninth Streets, NW.

Smithsonian Institution. The center for several national museums, art galleries, zoological gardens and research centers; visitor information center. Open year-round, daily, 10 a.m. to 5:30 p.m. On Jefferson Drive, between Ninth and 12th Streets, SW. (202) 737-8811.

Supreme Court Building. A distinguished white marble edifice that houses the country's highest judicial body; court opens at 9:30 a.m. on the days that court is in session. Open year-round, Monday to Friday, 9 a.m. to 4:30 p.m.; from October through June, Monday to Wednesday, 10 a.m. to noon and 1 p.m. to 3 p.m. Free. Facing the Capitol, between Maryland Avenue and East Capitol Street, NE.

Thomas Jefferson Memorial. A circular, domed structure surrounded by Ionic columns, containing a bronze statue of Jefferson and inscriptions from Jefferson's writings; tours. Open year-round, daily, 8:30 a.m. to 11:30 p.m. Free. On the southeast side of the Tidal Basin.

United States Botanical Gardens. Contains many rare plants and an outstanding collection of orchids; offers flower shows throughout the year. Open year-round, daily, 9 a.m. to 5 p.m. Free. At First Street and Maryland Avenue.

United States Capitol. Designed by Dr. William Thornton, the building is 751 feet long, 350 feet wide and contains some 540 rooms. The two wings house the Senate and House chambers and the central part of the building includes the Rotunda, Senate Chambers, the original Supreme Court and Statuary Hall. A 19½-foot statue of Freedom stands atop the Capitol Dome. Open year-round, daily, 9 a.m. to 10 p.m. On Capitol Hill.

United States National Arboretum. This 44-acre arboretum, established in 1927, contains a wide variety of plants including peonies, holly, magnolias, azaleas, camellias, native ferns, boxwood and daylilies; trails. The National Bonsai Collection was a gift of the Japanese people for the American bicentennial. Open year-round, daily, 8 a.m. to 5 p.m. Free. On New York Avenue, NE.

United States Naval Observatory. This facility determines correct standard time, investigates celestial bodies and publishes official Almanacs for astronomers and

Mount Vernon, George Washington's elegant plantation estate, is situated atop a knoll overlooking the Potomac River about 16 miles south of Washington, D.C. The 200-acre estate is completely restored and looks just as it did when the first president lived there.

navigators; guided tours. Open year-round, Monday to Friday; tours at 12:30 p.m. and 2 p.m. Free. 34th Street and Massachusetts Avenue, NW.

United States Treasury. Features exhibits and information relating to activities that fall under the jurisdiction of the Treasury Department. Open year-round, Tuesday to Saturday, 9:30 a.m. to 3:30 p.m. Free. At 15th Street and Pennsylvania Avenue.

Washington Cathedral. A fine example of Gothic architecture and one of the largest cathedrals in the world, offering magnificent stained glass windows and unique furnishings. Carillon concerts and organ recitals weekly. Open year-round, daily. Donation: $1. On Mount St. Alban at Massachusetts and Wisconsin Avenues, NW.

Washington Monument. One of the city's most famous landmarks, the monument is the tallest masonry structure in the world (555 feet) and took more than 40 years to complete. An elevator whisks visitors to the top in just 70 seconds. Open year-round, daily, 8 a.m. to midnight. Elevator 10 cents, children under 16 free. At the west end of the Mall, it's bordered by 14th and 17th Streets and Constitution and Independence Avenues.

White House. The home of every President except George Washington, the White House contains unique furnishings and antiques, as well as portraits of former occupants. Tours conducted year-round, Tuesday to Saturday, 10 a.m. to 12:45 p.m. 1600 Pennsylvania Avenue, NW.

District of Columbia Calendar of Events

Spring
(March, April, May)

Cherry Blossom Festival. March or April, coincident with the blooming of the Cherry Trees around the Tidal Basin.
Easter Egg Roll. On Easter Monday, on the south lawn of the White House.
Georgetown Garden Tour. April.
Georgetown House Tour. April.
White House Gardens and Grounds Tour. April.

Summer
(June, July, August)

President's Cup Regatta. June, Potomac River.
Fireworks Display. July, Washington Monument.

Fall
(September, October, November)

No major events.

Winter
(December, January, February)

Pageant of Peace. December. Festivities begin with the lighting of the national Christmas Tree on the Ellipse, south of the White House.
Presidential Inauguration. January, every four years.

Tourist Information

Washington Area Convention and Visitors Association
1129 20th Street, NW
Washington, D.C. 20036
(202) 857-5500

Delaware Maryland

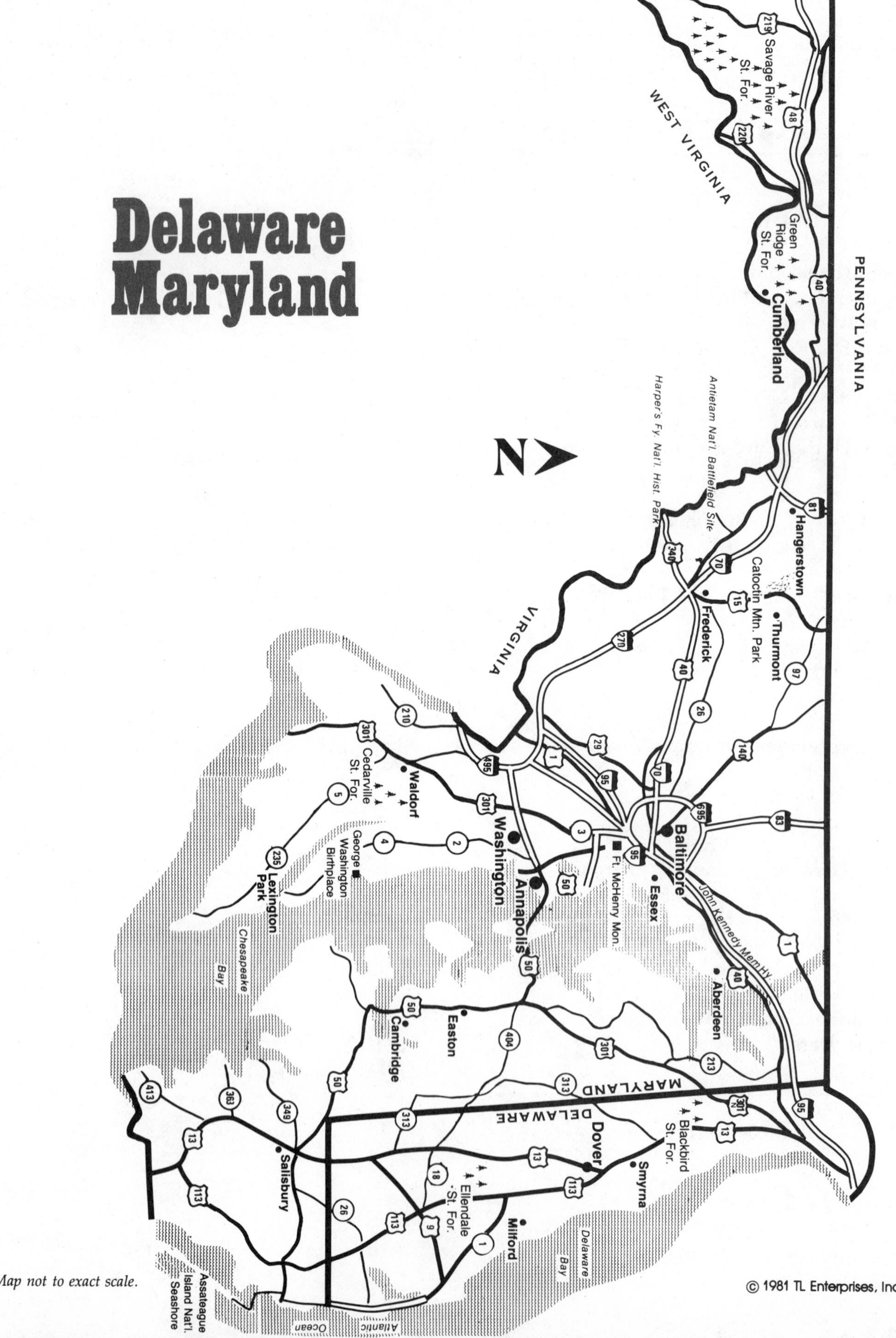

Map not to exact scale.

Delaware

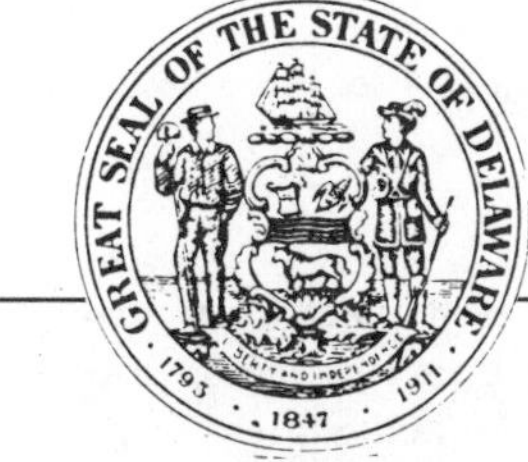

Delaware may be the second smallest state in terms of area, but its proximity to the major urban centers of New York, Philadelphia and Washington, D.C. has earned it a position of prominence in the nation. The state's location, combined with its favorable incorporation laws, have made it an important business center that serves as the home base for more than 70,000 corporations. That location has also created a sort of microcosm of the rest of the country within the borders of the state — and this is why pollsters often turn to Delaware when they want to take the pulse of the nation.

Delaware has an interesting history, in that it was under the control of three different nations before the American Revolution. The first colony, a Dutch settlement established in 1631 in the southern part of the region, was wiped out by Indians in its first year. Some six years later, a group of Swedish colonists landed on the banks of what is now the Christina River and named the territory New Sweden. In 1655, the Dutch returned under the rule of Peter Stuyvesant, reclaimed the territory by force, and remained in control until the English claimed the region in 1664. In 1682, King Charles II included Delaware in his grant to William Penn; however, Penn was mainly interested in governing the larger territory of Pennsylvania, so the tiny Delaware region broke away and became a crown colony in 1704. Delaware fought in the Revolution as a separate state, and later earned the distinction of being the first state to ratify the U.S. Constitution (1787), as well as the first state to be admitted to the Union.

Full name: State of Delaware
Origin of name: From Lord De La Warr, first governor of the Virginia colony.
Motto: Liberty and Independence.
Nicknames: Blue Hen State, Diamond State, First State.
Capital: Dover
Statehood: December 7, 1787, first state.
Population: 583,000 (ranks 47th).
Major Cities: Wilmington (76,152), Newark (26,645), Dover (22,480).
Bird: Blue hen chicken
Flower: Peach blossom
Tree: American holly

Average daily temperature by month

	Northern	Southern
Jan.	39.0 to 23.5	43.6 to 25.5
Feb.	41.3 to 24.9	46.2 to 26.7
Mar.	49.3 to 32.0	53.8 to 32.9
Apr.	61.9 to 41.8	66.0 to 42.2
May	71.5 to 51.0	75.2 to 51.5
Jun.	80.5 to 60.6	83.5 to 60.8
Jul.	84.6 to 65.6	87.1 to 65.4
Aug.	82.6 to 64.2	85.3 to 63.5
Sept.	76.5 to 57.5	79.5 to 56.9
Oct.	65.9 to 46.5	69.0 to 46.0
Nov.	53.3 to 36.6	57.7 to 36.5
Dec.	42.7 to 27.7	47.1 to 28.9
Year	62.4 to 44.3	66.2 to 44.7

The varied topography of Delaware contributes greatly to the state's diverse attractions. The northern part of the state consists of rolling hills, while the southern region is a nearly sea-level plain that includes a 30,000-acre swamp along its southern border. The lengthy Atlantic coastline includes many stretches of sandy

This Welsh Tract Church near Newark, Delaware, is the oldest Primitive Baptist church in the United States. Built in 1746, it is maintained in its original condition, so evidence still remains of damage incurred during the battle of Cooch's Bridge in 1777.

beach, as well as two large wildlife refuges; and on the sandy peninsula of Cape Henlope, an enormous sand dune rises 80 feet above the shore to form the highest dune between Cape Hatteras and Cape Cod. Numerous historical sites also await the visitor — including Lewes, the location of the original Dutch settlement.

Besides the production of chemicals and related products, Delaware is a manufacturing center for leather goods, textiles and machinery. Agriculture and fishing also contribute substantially to the state's economy, and Delaware has recently been mentioned as a prime site for a deepwater terminal, due to the fact that Delaware Bay contains a suitable natural channel and is convenient to major East Coast oil refineries.

No account of the history of Delaware would be complete without some mention of the Du Ponts, a family that has dominated much of the state's history since the early 17th century. Eleuthere Irenee Du Pont, the American progenitor of the family, established a gunpowder mill on the Brandywine River near Wilmington in 1802, and this business later became the foundation for the family's — and the state's — enormous chemical industry. Today, the Du Pont Chemical Corporation has earned the state its title as "chemical capital of the world," and the individual members of the Du Pont family continue to play important roles in Delaware's political and social structure.

Highlight
Longwood Gardens

Longwood is a magnificent gardens that encompasses woodlands, a formal gardens, picturesque fountains and two lakes. The green houses and conservatories are at their best from November to May, displaying a wide variety of colorful blooms. The Main Conservatory features some rare flowering plants. During the Christmas season, poinsettias are displayed throughout December.

In the summer, the outdoor gardens are especially beautiful, with tropical blooms and water lilies in abundance. The three spectacular fountains are located in the Italian Water Garden, on the stage of the Open-Air Theater and in front of the Main Conservatory. Throughout the summer, half-hour color displays are featured on Tuesday, Thursday and Saturday at 9:15 p.m. in the Main Conservatory. Organ recitals are also held in the conservatory from October through March, Sunday 2 p.m. to 3 p.m. Performances in the Open-Air Theater are scheduled from June through August.

Open year-round, daily, 9 a.m. to 5 p.m. Adults $2, children 6 to 14 $1. Wilmington, 13 miles north at the junction of US-1 and State Route 52.

Delaware Points of Interest and Attractions

Boardwalk. Host to a series of special events held throughout the summer on the beach. Complete information and schedules available from Rehoboth Beach Chamber of Commerce, 73 Rehoboth Avenue, Rehoboth Beach, Delaware 19971.

Bombay Hook National Wildlife Refuge. A 15,110-acre haven for migrating and wintering waterfowl. Auto tour routes, observation towers, trails and boardwalk. Open year-round, daily, sunrise to sunset. Free. Leipsic, off State Route 9. (302) 653-9345.

Brandywine Raceway. Pari-mutual night harness racing. Reserved seats, group rates and clubhouse dining available. Open April through September, post time 8 p.m., nightly except Mondays. Wilmington, off US-202N. (302) 478-1220.

Delaware Park. Site of thoroughbred racing. Open July through September, daily except Monday, 1:30 p.m. Wilmington, off State Route 7. (302) 994-2521.

Fenwick Island Lighthouse. Near the base is the first marker on the Delaware-Maryland boundary — a crownstone placed by surveyors in 1751, 12 years before Mason and Dixon were sent from England to survey the North-South line. At extreme southeast tip of state, at junction of State Routes 1 and 54.

Great Cypress Swamp. Contains the northernmost stand of bald cypress in the U.S.; follow directions from Trap Pond State Park. Trussum Pond, off State Route 24, west to Laurel.

Governor's House, Woodburn. Official residence of the governor, and an excellent example of middle-Georgian architecture. Once a station of the pre-Civil War underground railroad. Open year-round, Saturdays, 1:30 p.m. to 4:30 p.m. Free. Dover, on Kings Highway. (302) 678-5656.

Harrington Raceway. Harness racing. Open September through November, daily, weekday post time 8 p.m., Sunday post time 6:30 p.m. Harrington, off US-13. (302) 398-3269.

Longwood Gardens. Outdoor gardens, conservatories with seasonal displays of magnificent plantings, illuminated fountains and open-air theater. Open year-round, daily, 10 a.m. to 5 p.m. Adults $2, children 6 to 14 $1, under 5 admitted free. Kennet Square, Pennsylvania, on Delaware-Pennsylvania border, off State Route 52. (215) 388-7393.

Solar One. Nation's first solar-powered house; experimental building on University of Delaware campus uses sunlight for heat, air-conditioning and electricity. Open year-round; Wednesday evenings; 10 a.m. to noon, Saturday; and by appointment. Free. Newark, 190 South Chapel Street. (302) 995-7155.

Willington Square. Composed of six 18th-century houses; named after Thomas Willing who, in 1731, laid out the village that later became Wilmington. Group tours available through the Historical Society of Delaware. Wilmington, Market Street Mall. (302) 655-7161.

Wilmington and Western Steam Railroad. Authentic turn-of-the-century steam train; trips through beautiful Red Clay Valley. Open May through August, Saturday and Sunday; September through October, Sundays only; 12:30 p.m., 2 p.m. and 3:30 p.m. Adults $2.50, children 3 to 12 $1.25. Wilmington, Greenbank Station, on State Route 41 near junction with State Route 1. (302) 998-1930.

Woodland Ferry. A three-vehicle cable ferry that has operated sunup to sundown on the Nanticoke River since 1793. Free. Laurel, five miles northwest on Road 78.

State Offices

Tourism
Delaware Department of Community Affairs and Economic Development
630 State College Road
Dover, Delaware 19901
(302) 678-4254

State Police
Department of Public Safety
PO Box 430
Dover, Delaware 19901
(302) 734-5973

Radio Stations

Wilmington
WDEL 1150 (AM)

Delaware State Parks

Park	Location	CAMPING	PICNICKING	CONCESSIONS	SWIMMING	HIKING	BOATING	FISHING	HUNTING	WINTER SPORTS
Bellevue	*Arden. Off US-13.*		•					•		
Brandywine Creek	*Wilmington. Off US-202.*		•			•				
Delaware Seashore	*Rehoboth Beach. Off State Route 1.*	•	•	•	•		•	•		
Fort Delaware	*Pea Patch Island. Reached by boat only, off State Route 9.*		•			•				
Holts Landing	*Millville. Off State Route 26.*		•		•		•	•		
Killen Pond	*Felton. Off US-13.*	•	•		•		•	•		
Lums Pond	*Kirkwood. Off State Routes 896 and 71.*	•	•	•	•	•	•	•		
Trap Pond	*Laurel. Off State Route 24.*	•	•	•	•	•	•	•		
Walter S. Carpenter	*Newark. Off State Route 896.*		•			•				

Delaware State Forests

Forest	Location	CAMPING	PICNICKING	CONCESSIONS	SWIMMING	HIKING	BOATING	FISHING	HUNTING	WINTER SPORTS
Blackbird	*Forest. Off US-13.*	•							•	
Redden	*Georgetown. Off US-113.*		•						•	

For additional information on Delaware state parks and forests, contact:
Department of Natural Resources and Environmental Control, Edward Tatnall Building, Dover, Delaware 19901, (302) 687-4506.

Maryland

Bisected by the long arm of Chesapeake Bay, Maryland really has two identities. The western half of the state, influenced by the nearby cities of Philadelphia and Washington, D.C., is highly urbanized and dominated by the bustling industrial center of Baltimore, where more than half of the state's population is centered. The eastern Delmarva Peninsula, backed by the Chesapeake and lapped by the waters of the Atlantic in the southeast, has been traditionally rural in character, and many of the people there still make their living as farmers or fishermen.

Maryland was originally carved out of Virginia through a grant given by Charles I to George Calvert, first Baron Baltimore, in 1632. Calvert died before the grant had passed the royal seal, however, so the province was colonized under the leadership of his eldest son, Cecilius, second Baron Baltimore. In its initial days, the colony was developed primarily as an income source and a religious haven for Baltimore's fellow Catholics. When the Puritans gained control of the region in the 1650s, they resented the presence of a separate colony under Catholic leadership, and a brief civil war erupted in which the Puritans were victorious. A later compromise briefly restored the colony to Lord Baltimore, but Maryland finally became a British province in 1691. Later, Marylanders fought so well in the American Revolution that George Washington nicknamed Maryland "The Old Line State," in honor of its dependable "troops of the line." Though Maryland declared its independence and adopted its own constitution in 1776, it did not become a member of the Confederation of States until 1781, after Virginia had yielded all its claims to the territories in the Northwest. Maryland adopted the U.S. Constitution in 1788.

Attractions for the visitor include a wide variety of state parks and forests; Annapolis, the site of the U.S. Naval Academy; the beaches of the Assateague

Full name: State of Maryland
Origin of Name: From Queen Henrietta Maria of England, wife of Charles I.
Motto: *"Fatti maschi, parole femine"* (Manly deeds, womanly words).
Nickname: Old Line State
Capital: Annapolis
Statehood: April 28, 1788, seventh state.
Population: 4,139,000 (ranks 18th).
Major Cities: Baltimore (851,698), Rockville (44,300), Bowie (37,323).
Bird: Baltimore oriole
Flower: Blackeyed Susan
Tree: White oak

Average daily temperature by month

	Northern	Southern
Jan.	38.8 to 22.7	43.3 to 26.9
Feb.	41.3 to 23.8	46.0 to 28.8
Mar.	50.2 to 30.7	53.5 to 35.1
Apr.	63.4 to 41.0	65.5 to 45.3
May	72.5 to 49.8	74.9 to 54.5
Jun.	81.0 to 58.9	82.7 to 63.5
Jul.	84.9 to 63.5	86.7 to 68.2
Aug.	83.2 to 62.1	85.3 to 66.7
Sept.	76.8 to 55.4	79.7 to 60.0
Oct.	65.6 to 44.6	69.9 to 49.5
Nov.	52.8 to 35.0	57.9 to 39.3
Dec.	41.6 to 26.3	46.8 to 30.5
Year	62.7 to 42.8	66.0 to 47.4

National Seashore; boating on Chesapeake Bay; and the charm of colonial homes and buildings.

Maryland's economic base reflects the diversity of the state and its east-west division. In the west, the emphasis is on the manufacture of steel, copper smelting, shipbuilding, chemicals and food processing. The spillover of government agencies from Washington, D.C. also plays a key role in the activities of this area. Agricultural products include broiler chickens, dairy products, beef cattle, soybeans and tobacco, while the Chesapeake and the Atlantic yield vast quantities of oysters, crabs, clams and striped bass to Maryland's fishing industry.

State Offices

Tourism
Division of Tourist Development
Department of Economic and Community Development
1748 Forest Drive
Annapolis, Maryland 21401
(301) 269-2686

State Police
Department of Public Safety
Pikesville, Maryland 21208
(301) 391-0700

Radio Stations

Baltimore
WFBR 1300 (AM)
WCBM 630 (AM)

From colonial days, when the first settlers of the region arrived from Virginia in 1648, this area of Annapolis — the City Dock, on the Severn River — has been the focal point for commerce and pleasure. The dock is too small for modern steamers, but tourists crowd the area to watch the hundreds of sailing craft which make Annapolis a mecca for yachtsmen.

The Old Senate Chamber of the Maryland State House in Annapolis (left) is arranged as of December 1783, when George Washington resigned his commission to the Continental Congress. (Below) Fort Frederick, in Washington County, is the only fortress of the French and Indian War period still standing in the United States. Settlers brought their families here for refuge when French troops and their Indian allies set fire to their villages.

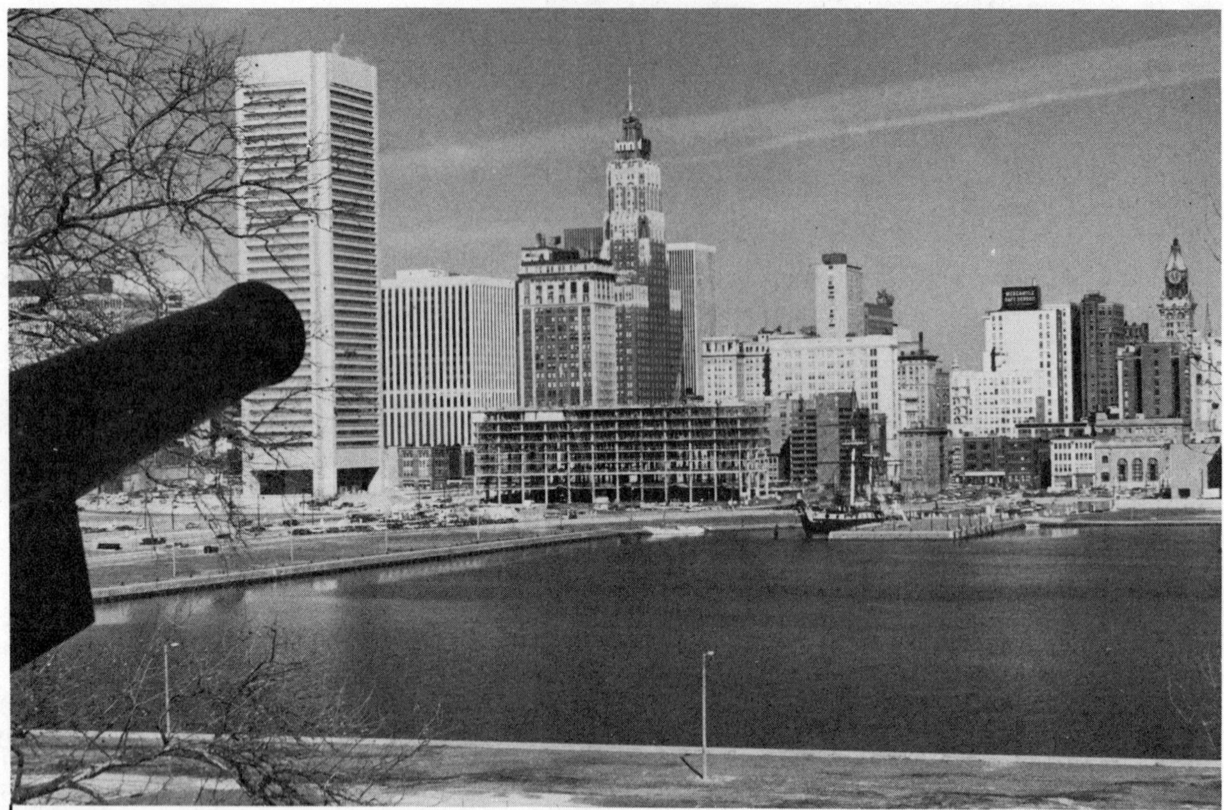

The ever-changing Baltimore skyline serves as a backdrop for the *Constellation* (right center), a 36-gun frigate that was launched in September 1797 and now has the honor of being the world's oldest ship continuously afloat.

Highlight

Baltimore

Founded in 1729 by an act of the Provincial Assembly, Baltimore has grown into Maryland's largest city (2,140,000) and its most important economic center. In Baltimore's early days the city was an important port and shipbuilding center.

During the War of 1812, Baltimore became a major objective of the British and they launched an attack on Fort McHenry, guardian of Baltimore's inner harbor, in an effort to capture this strategic port. Miraculously, Fort McHenry survived a 25-hour bombardment by the British and Baltimore was saved from occupation. It was during this siege that Francis Scott Key penned the national anthem as he watched the shelling from a boat anchored near the British fleet. Today, the fort has been restored to its pre-Civil War condition. From the fort's flagpole, the flag flies 24 hours a day by presidential proclamation. Fort McHenry is open year-round, daily, 9 a.m. to 5 p.m.; guided tours and special programs are offered in the summer. It's located off East Fort Avenue.

Other historical points of interest within Baltimore are the Mount Clare Station, the first passenger and freight railroad station in the country; the Basilica of the Assumption of the Blessed Virgin Mary, the oldest Catholic cathedral in the nation; and the Lloyd Street Synagogue, the first synagogue in Maryland, built in 1845.

Maryland Points of Interest and Attractions

Al Marah. World's largest Arabian horse breeding farm, featuring more than 300 purebred Arabian horses on 2,800 acres of rolling pasture. Open year-round. Barnesville, off State Route 109.

Babe Ruth Birthplace and Museum. Memorabilia, audio-visual presentation and wax figures commemorating baseball's greatest hero. Open year-round. Admission: NA. Baltimore, 216 Emory Street.

The Annapolitan II. Cruise on Chesapeake Bay to quaint St. Michaels and spend three hours there. Operates: Memorial Day through Labor Day, daily except Mondays; weekends only, May 1 through Labor Day, and Labor Day to September 30. Fare: Adults $15, children 12 and under half fare. Departs Annapolis City Dock 10 a.m., arrive St. Michaels, noon; depart St. Michaels 3 p.m., arrive Annapolis City 5 p.m. For reservations and further information contact: Chesapeake Marine Tours, PO Box 3323, Annapolis, Maryland 21403. (301) 268-7600.

The Harbor Queen. Forty-minute narrated tours daily of Chesapeake Bay. Operates: Memorial Day through Labor Day, daily; May 1 through Memorial Day, Labor Day to September 30, weekends only. Fare: Adults $2, children $1. Leaves Annapolis City Dock: noon, 2 p.m. and 4 p.m., weekdays; every hour on the hour, noon to 6 p.m., weekends and holidays. For further information contact: Chesapeake Marine Tours, PO Box 3323, Annapolis, Maryland 21403. (301) 268-7600.

The Lady Katie. Cruise the Chesapeake aboard the last working skipjack. The *Lady Katie* harvests oysters from November to March; from April through October, she is available for charter as a pleasure craft. Outfitted to accommodate six passengers plus crew. For further information contact: Capt. Stanley Larrimore, Tilghman, Maryland 21671. (301) 886-2630.

Smith Island Cruises. Cruise aboard the *Captain Tyler* to Smith Island and the villages of Ewell, Tylerton and Rhodes Point; four-hour and 45-minute trip. Operates: Memorial Day through September. Fares: NA. For further information contact: Captain Alan Tyler, Rhodes Point, Maryland 21858. (301) 425-2771.

College Park Airport. Oldest airport in continuous operation in the nation since 1909. (Our first military aviators trained here under the direction of Wilbur and Orville Wright.) College Park, off Interstate 95.

Goddard Space Flight Center. Center for all NASA tracking activities as well as the development of unmanned rockets. Two weeks advance reservation required for tours. Greenbelt, on Greenbelt Road.

U.S. Naval Academy. Center for training of U.S. Naval officers; academy chapel contains the tomb of John Paul Jones; museum has flags, weapons, models, portraits of naval heroes and other relics. Full-dress parades held each Wednesday during school term. Open year-round. Annapolis, on Severn River, off US-50 and State Route 665.

Maryland State Parks

Park	Location	CAMPING	PICNICKING	CONCESSIONS	SWIMMING	HIKING	BOATING	FISHING	HUNTING	WINTER SPORTS
Assateague	*Ocean City. Off State Route 611.*	•	•	•	•			•		
Big Run	*Bloomington. Off State Route 135.*	•					•	•		
Calvert Cliffs	*Prince Frederick. Off State Routes 2 and 4.*		•			•		•	•	
Casselman	*Grantsville. Off US-40.*	•								
Cedarville	*Cedarville. Off US-301.*	•	•			•		•	•	
Cunningham Falls	*Thurmont. Off US-15 and State Route 77.*	•	•	•	•	•	•	•	•	
Deep Creek Lake	*Thayerville. Off US-219.*	•	•	•	•	•	•	•	•	
Elk Neck	*North East. Off State Route 272.*	•	•	•	•	•	•	•	•	•
Fort Frederick	*Indian Springs. Off State Route 56.*	•	•	•		•	•	•		
Fort Tonoloway	*Hancock. Off US-114.*	•								
Gambrill	*Frederick. Off US-40.*	•	•			•		•		
Greenbrier	*Hagerstown. Off US-40.*	•	•	•	•	•	•	•		
Herrington Manor	*Oakland. Off State Route 20.*		•	•	•	•	•	•		
Janes Island	*Crisfield City. Off State Route 358.*	•	•		•	•	•	•	•	
Martinak	*Denton. Off State Route 404.*	•	•				•	•		
New Germany	*Grantsville. Off US-40.*	•	•	•	•	•	•	•		
Patapsco	*Baltimore City. Park has five separate areas off US-40 and State Route 1, and Interstate 70.*	•	•			•		•		
Pocomoke River	*Snow Hill. Off State Route 12.*	•	•	•	•		•	•		
Point Lookout	*Point Lookout. Off State Route 5.*	•	•		•	•	•	•	•	
Rocks	*Bel Air. Off State Route 24.*		•			•		•		•
Rocky Gap	*Cumberland. Off US-40.*	•	•	•	•	•	•	•	•	
Sandy Point	*Skidmore. Off US-50.*		•	•	•		•	•		
Seneca Creek	*Germantown. Off State Route 270.*								•	
Susquehanna	*Havre de Grace. Off State Route 155.*	•	•	•		•	•	•		
Swallow Falls	*Oakland. Off State Route 20.*	•	•					•		
Tuckahoe	*Queen Anne. Off State Route 480.*	•	•			•		•	•	
Washington Monument	*Boonsboro. Off alternate US-40.*	•	•			•				
Wye Oak	*Wye Mill. Off US-213.*		•							

Foxtail grass grows peacefully along the sunken road known as "Bloody Lane" at Antietam National Battlefield Site, near Sharpsburg, Maryland. On September 17, 1862, during the day-long Battle of Antietam, Confederate infantry contested this road point-blank with Union divisions — and 4,000 men fell here in less than three hours. Losses on both sides of this bloodiest single day of fighting in the Civil War were staggering: 12,410 Federals were killed or wounded, as were 10,700 Confederates.

Maryland State Forests

Forest	Location	CAMPING	PICNICKING	CONCESSIONS	SWIMMING	HIKING	BOATING	FISHING	HUNTING	WINTER SPORTS
Doncaster	*Doncaster. Off State Route 6.*					•		•	•	
Elk Neck	*Elkton. Off US-7.*	•				•			•	
Garrett	*Oakland. Off US-219.*			•					•	•
Green Ridge	*Cumberland. Off US-40.*	•				•		•	•	
Pocomoke	*Pocomoke City. Off US-13.*		•					•	•	
Potomac	*Tasker Corners. Off State Route 135.*					•			•	
Savage River	*Bloomington. Off State Route 495.*	•				•		•	•	•
Seth	*Easton. Off US-50.*								•	
Wicomico	*Pittsville. Off State Route 353.*								•	

For more information on Maryland's state parks and forests, contact: *Department of Natural Resources, Maryland State Park Service, Tawes State Office Building, Annapolis, Maryland 21401, (301) 269-3761.*

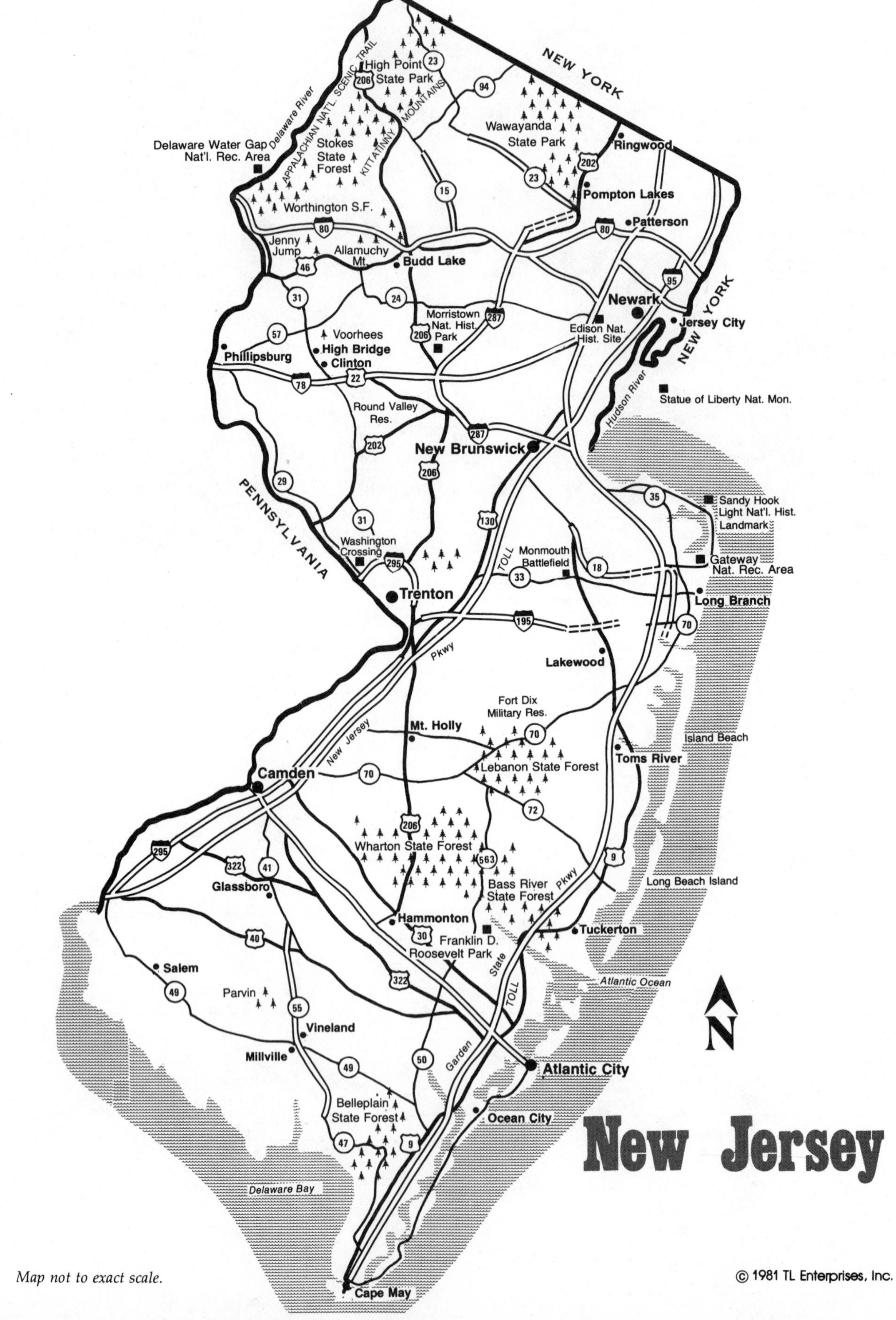
NEW YORK
High Point
State Park
APPALACHIAN NAT'L. SCENIC TRAIL
KITTATINNY MOUNTAINS
Delaware River
Delaware Water Gap
Nat'l. Rec. Area
Stokes
State
Forest
Wawayanda
State Park
Ringwood
Pompton Lakes
Worthington S.F.
Patterson
Jenny
Jump
Allamuchy
Mt.
Budd Lake
Newark
NEW YORK
Morristown
Nat. Hist.
Park
Edison Nat.
Hist. Site
Jersey City
Voorhees
High Bridge
Clinton
Phillipsburg
Hudson River
Statue of Liberty Nat. Mon.
Round Valley
Res.
New Brunswick
PENNSYLVANIA
Sandy Hook
Light Nat'l. Hist.
Landmark
Washington
Crossing
Monmouth
Battlefield
TOLL
Gateway
Nat. Rec. Area
Trenton
Long Branch
Pkwy
Lakewood
Fort Dix
Military Res.
Mt. Holly
New Jersey
Island Beach
Toms River
Camden
Lebanon State Forest
Wharton State Forest
Long Beach Island
Glassboro
Bass River
State Forest
Pkwy
Hammonton
Franklin D.
Roosevelt Park
Tuckerton
Salem
State
TOLL
Atlantic Ocean
Parvin
Vineland
Millville
Garden
Atlantic City
Belleplain
State Forest
Ocean City
New Jersey
Delaware Bay
Cape May
N

Map not to exact scale.

New Jersey

The people of this state invite you to "experience New Jersey." It's an experience that's bound to be enjoyable, too, because New Jersey has something to offer just about everyone — a mild climate, an abundance of history, arts and cultural activities, scenic parks, sandy beaches and a booming gambling resort city.

New Jersey's colonial history is closely tied to that of New York, of which it was a part until 1738, when a separate governor was appointed for the region. As the war with England loomed on the horizon, the then-governor, William Franklin, refused to send delegates to the Continental Congress, so the reigns of government were assumed by the committee-appointed Provincial Congress which elected the delegates, adopted a state constitution and declared the state independent on July 18, 1776. Because New Jersey was strategically located between New York City and Philadelphia, and stood in the path of the armies that were vying for control of the Hudson and Delaware Rivers, the state was the site of many of the most important battles (Trenton, Princeton, Monmouth) of the Revolution. New Jersey ratified the Federal Constitution in 1787, and was the third state to join the Union.

Today, New Jersey has the distinction of being the most densely populated of all the states (975 people per-square-mile), while it also boasts one of the most sparsely settled wilderness areas in the Eastern U.S., the 1,000 square-mile Pine Barrens. The south-central part of the state is made up of a fertile plain so rich that some 60 different varieties of vegetables are grown there. During the growing season, the state supplies much of the produce for both New York City and Philadelphia, proving that New Jersey richly deserves its nickname as the "Garden State."

If your preference is for outdoor activities, New Jersey offers some 50 beaches and beach resorts and a like number of state parks, in addition to a number of wildlife management areas. If you're looking for excitement, try the

Full name: State of New Jersey
Origin of name: From Channel Island of Jersey
Motto: Liberty and Prosperity
Nickname: Garden State
Capital: Trenton
Statehood: December 18, 1787, third state.
Population: 7,330,000 (ranks ninth).
Major Cities: Newark (339,568), Jersey City (243,756), Patterson (137,000).
Bird: Eastern goldfinch
Flower: Purple violet
Tree: Red oak

Average daily temperature by month

	Northern	Southern
Jan.	34.2 to 15.3	40.4 to 21.4
Feb.	36.7 to 17.2	43.2 to 23.3
Mar.	45.6 to 26.2	50.5 to 29.8
Apr.	59.7 to 36.3	63.4 to 38.6
May	70.2 to 44.7	73.4 to 47.6
Jun.	79.7 to 54.2	82.4 to 57.1
Jul.	84.4 to 58.7	86.2 to 62.0
Aug.	82.2 to 56.5	84.3 to 60.6
Sept.	75.3 to 49.1	78.2 to 53.6
Oct.	64.2 to 38.0	67.7 to 42.5
Nov.	50.4 to 30.5	55.4 to 33.6
Dec.	38.2 to 20.6	44.0 to 25.2
Year	60.1 to 37.3	64.1 to 41.3

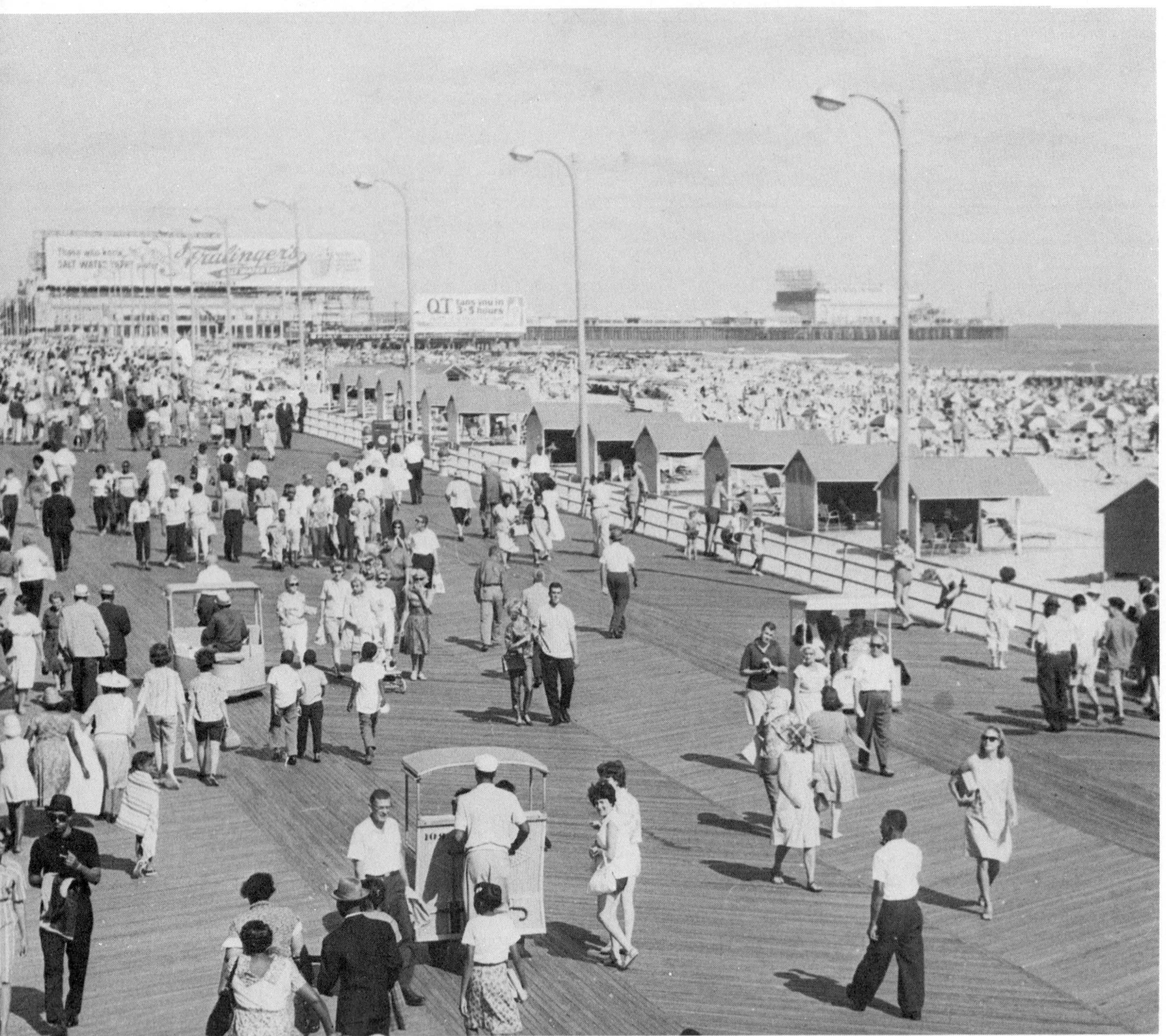

Atlantic City's famous boardwalk offers visitors the opportunity to soak up the sun along the coast, eat saltwater taffy and experience the carnival atmosphere of the popular resort area.

gaming tables in Atlantic City or one of the fine amusement areas, like Asbury Park or Wildwoods By-The-Sea. If you're a history buff, the selection is endless: Washington's headquarters at Morristown; the McKonkey Ferry House, near where Washington crossed the Delaware; the Monmouth Battlefield; and James Fenimore Cooper's birthplace, to name but a few.

Over the next few years, gambling and tourism should play an increasingly important role in New Jersey's economy, but other staples include the manufacturing of household appliances, transportation equipment, chemicals and drugs, as well as agricultural products and a flourishing fishing industry.

Highlight

Fall Foliage

TOUR 1. Essex, Morris, Sussex and Warren counties. Take Route 80 to Netcong and Route 206 to Andover. Then take Route 517 south to Route 611 and turn right to Tranquility. Return to Route 517 south and continue to Allamuchy where you turn right onto County Road 12 (Allamuchy Johnsonburg Road) into Johnsonburg. Turn left onto Route 519 to Jenny Jump Forest. Stop at the Forest Headquarters for extensive panoramas and display. Continue on Route 519 south to Hope and turn left at the Old Mill, over the mountain and past the Great Meadows to Route 46. You can stay on Route 46 for the trip home, or take Route 10, if you prefer.

TOUR 2. Essex, Morris, Warren, Sussex counties. Take Route 23 to Mountain View. Bear right onto Route 202 south through Lincoln Park, Towaco, Boonton to Parsippany; right turn on Route 46. In Dover, turn left onto Bergen Street and immediately bear right onto Clinton (Route 15) and continue through Wharton, Hurdtown, and Sparta to Newton. Take Route 206 to Ross Corner; turn left on 206 through Branchville to Normanock in Stokes State Forest where you may obtain a map of the forest. Proceed through forest, stopping at Tillman's Ravine, the most striking forest glen in the state. Continue down mountain and across Flatbrook to Wallpack Center. Turn right and drive through Peters Valley and Bevans to Route 206 at Tuttle's Corner; turn left on 206, continue through Hainesville to Route 653, bear right to Mashipong Road which merges with several other roads before junctioning with Sawmill Road. Turn left on Sawmill to Route 23 south for your return trip. If you happen to miss a turn, simply continue on Route 653. It'll take you to Route 23 a bit down the road.

TOUR 3. Essex, Morris, Passaic counties. Take Route 23 to Pompton Plains and Riverdale; Ringwood Avenue through Wanaque to Erskine R.R. Manor House. Also visit Skylands, about half a mile south. Retrace route to the Village of Ringwood Manor and take Route 511 to Hewitt, then left on Route 513 for West Milford and Newfoundland. Then, take Ridge Road into Berkshire Valley Road, following it to the end where you turn right onto Kenvil Avenue. When Kenvil ends at Main Street, turn left and continue through Mt. Freedom to Route 202. Turn right to Route 24 cast for the return home.

TOUR 4. Essex, Morris, Somerset, Union counties. Take Route 24 through Morristown to Ralston. Turn left at Roxiticus Road. Turn right at Jackson Avenue in Gladstone, go one block and turn left two blocks and make a right onto Route 512 (Pottersville Road) to Fairmont and Califon. Turn left on Route 513 through High Bridge to Route 31. Turn left on Route 31 for one-half mile then bear right to Clinton; take Route 123 to Annandale and Route 22 to Whitehouse and White House Station. Take Routes 523 and 517 to Oldwick. Backtrack to Route 523 and turn left to Lamington and Bedminster. Follow Route 206 south to Route 202, then to Washington Valley Road in Pluckemin where you turn left. Continue to Route 512 in Summit. Continue on 512 to Route 24 where you head for home.

New Jersey Points of Interest and Attractions

Absecon Lighthouse. Commissioned in 1857, this venerable structure guided seafarers for three-quarters of a century. Hammonton, in Wharton State Forest, off Atlantic City Expressway on State Route 585.

Barnegat Lighthouse. This lighthouse, commissioned in 1834, also served for nearly a century. Long Beach Island, Seaside Park, off State Route 72.

Boardwalk-Steel Pier. Famous Atlantic City landmarks. Atlantic City, off Atlantic City Expressway.

Jersey Cape. More than 1.5 million vacationers come to this area each year to enjoy swimming, fishing, camping, golf, tennis, bird watching and a host of other forms of recreation. The biggest attraction is the 30 miles of shore along the Atlantic Ocean that is said to be the finest and safest bathing beach in the world. The long, gentle surf is warmed to a delightful 76 degrees in the summer. Boats and small runabouts are available for charter, and there are a number of convenient launching ramps for trailered boats. For RVers, the Cape offers a choice of 40 individual camping areas, and over 6,000 individual sites from one end of the county to the other. Entertainment includes band concerts, amusement rides, nightclubs, boardwalk strolls and bicycle and horseback riding. Located on extreme southern tip of the state, between Delaware Bay and the Atlantic Ocean, off the Garden State Parkway.

Pine Barrens. No visit to New Jersey would be complete without a trip through the boggy beauty of the Pine Barrens of south Jersey. Despite the fact that more than 40 million people are within a few hours' drive of the Pine Barrens, the 1,000 square-mile region remains a virtual wilderness sparsely populated with fascinating people known as "Pineys." The million acres of the Pine Barrens are dotted with cranberry bogs, orchards, scrub trees and, here and there, a ghost town. "The woods are trellised by two-track sand roads," says noted writer John McPhee, who roamed the Pine Barrens in his youth, "cut through by charcoal burners and others years ago, and you can drive along for half an hour or so and then climb a hill . . . and look around. What you look out upon is 400 or so square miles of forest — virtually nothing visible made by man." Located in south-central New Jersey, the Barrens can be reached by US-206, or State Routes 563 and 539.

State Offices

Tourism
Division of Tourism and Promotion
Department of Labor and Industry
PO Box 400
Trenton, New Jersey 08625
(609) 292-2470

State Police
Department of Public Safety
West Trenton, New Jersey 08625
(609) 882-2000

Radio Stations

Newark
WVNJ 620 (AM)
Trenton
WPST 97.5 (FM)

New Jersey State Parks

Park	Location	CAMPING	PICNICKING	CONCESSIONS	SWIMMING	HIKING	BOATING	FISHING	HUNTING	WINTER SPORTS
Allaire	*Farmingdale. Off Garden State Parkway.*	•	•	•		•				
Allamuchy Mt.	*Hackettstown. Off US-206.*	•						•	•	
Cape May Point	*Cape May Point. Off US-9.*		•					•		•
Cheesequake	*Matawan. Off Garden State Parkway.*	•	•	•	•	•	•	•		•
Corson's Inlet	*Belleplain. Off Garden State Parkway.*				•	•	•	•	•	
Delaware and Raritan Canal Park	*Belle Mead. Off US-1.*	•	•				•	•		
Fort Mott	*Salem. Off State Route 9.*		•				•	•		
Hacklebarney	*Long Valley. Off US-206.*		•	•		•		•		
High Point	*Sussex. Off State Route 519.*	•	•	•	•	•	•	•	•	•
Hopatcong	*Landing. Off US-80.*		•		•		•	•		•
Liberty Park	*Jersey City. Off US-78.*		•	•	•			•		
Monmouth Battlefield	*Freehold. Off US-9.*		•	•						
Parvin	*Elmer. Off State Route 540.*	•	•	•	•		•	•		
Ringwood	*Ringwood. Off State Route 511.*	•	•			•		•	•	•
Round Valley	*Lebanon. Off US-78.*	•	•	•	•	•	•	•	•	•
Spruce Run	*Clinton. Off US-78.*	•	•	•	•	•	•	•	•	•
Swartswood	*Newton. Off State Route 94.*	•	•	•	•		•	•	•	•
Voorhees	*Glen Gardner. Off State Route 513.*	•	•		•			•	•	
Washington Crossing	*Titusville. Off State Route 29.*	•	•			•		•		•
Wawayanda	*Highland Lakes. Off State Route 94.*	•			•	•	•	•		

New Jersey State Forests

Forest	Location	CAMPING	PICNICKING	CONCESSIONS	SWIMMING	HIKING	BOATING	FISHING	HUNTING	WINTER SPORTS
Bass River	*New Gretna. Off Garden State Parkway.*	•	•	•	•	•	•	•	•	•
Belleplain	*Woodbine. Off State Route 47.*	•	•	•	•	•	•	•	•	•
Jenny Jump	*Hope. Off State Route 519.*	•	•			•				
Lebanon	*New Lisbon. Off State Routes 70 and 72.*	•	•		•	•			•	•
Stokes	*Branchville. Off US-206 and State Route 519.*	•	•	•	•	•	•	•	•	•
Wharton	*Hammonton. Off US-206.*	•	•	•	•	•	•	•		•
Worthington	*Colombia. Off US-80.*	•	•			•	•	•	•	•

For further information on New Jersey state parks and forests, contact:
Environmental Protection Department, John Fitch Plaza, Trenton, New Jersey 08625, (609) 292-2772.

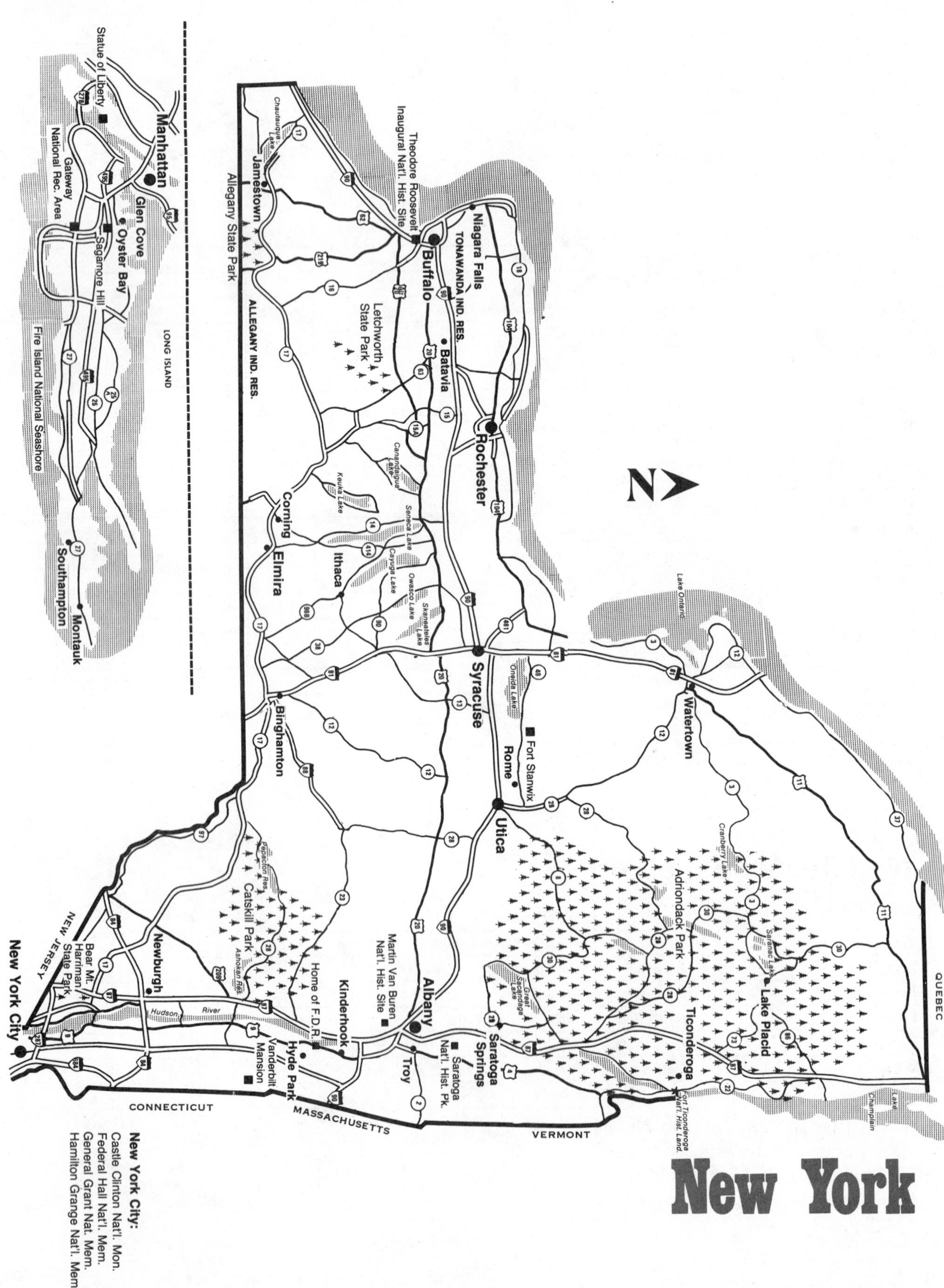
New York
N
Manhattan
Statue of Liberty
Glen Cove
Oyster Bay
Sagamore Hill
Gateway National Rec. Area
LONG ISLAND
Fire Island National Seashore
Southampton
Montauk
Jamestown
Chautauqua Lake
Allegany State Park
ALLEGANY IND. RES.
Theodore Roosevelt Inaugural Nat'l. Hist. Site
Niagara Falls
TONAWANDA IND. RES.
Buffalo
Batavia
Letchworth State Park
Rochester
Canandaigua Lake
Keuka Lake
Seneca Lake
Cayuga Lake
Owasco Lake
Skaneateles Lake
Corning
Elmira
Ithaca
Lake Ontario
Syracuse
Oneida Lake
Fort Stanwix
Rome
Watertown
Binghamton
Utica
Cranberry Lake
Adirondack Park
Saranac Lake
Lake Placid
Great Sacandaga Lake
Pepacton Res.
Catskill Park
Ashokan Res.
Home of F.D.R.
Kinderhook
Martin Van Buren Nat'l. Hist. Site
Albany
Troy
Saratoga Springs
Saratoga Nat'l. Hist. Pk.
Ticonderoga
Fort Ticonderoga Nat'l. Hist. Land.
Lake Champlain
QUEBEC
VERMONT
MASSACHUSETTS
CONNECTICUT
NEW JERSEY
Newburgh
Bear Mt. Harriman State Park
Hudson River
Hyde Park
Vanderbilt Mansion
New York City
New York City:
Castle Clinton Nat'l. Mon.
Federal Hall Nat'l. Mem.
General Grant Nat. Mem.
Hamilton Grange Nat'l. Mem.

Map not to exact scale.

New York

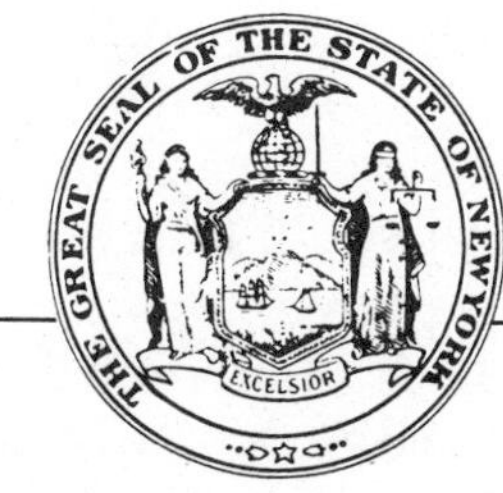

For most people, New York means only two things: the pulse-quickening excitement of midtown Manhattan, and the misty majesty of Niagara Falls. But New York is much more than this. It's thousands of islands, hundreds of lakes and streams, miles of sandy beaches and a countryside both vast and beautiful.

The Italian explorer Giovanni da Verrazano is thought to be the first European to have discovered New York (1524), but extensive exploration came nearly a century later, when Henry Hudson, an Englishman exploring for the Dutch West India Company, sailed up the river that now bears his name. Some 20 years later, the Dutch West India Company gave the region the name of New Netherlands and founded a settlement at Fort Orange (now Albany). Shortly after the establishment of this colony, Governor Peter Minuit made his legendary purchase of Manhattan Island for 60 guilders ($24) worth of trinkets, thus legalizing the occupation that had already begun.

The early years of the colony's development were marked by Indian troubles, mismanagement and disagreement among administrators of the company over exactly what direction the colony should take. Weakened by this internal strife, the province was overthrown in 1664 by a British invasion force and claimed for the Duke of York. A period of unrest followed the English takeover, including the French and Indian War, and it wasn't until the American Revolution that the area achieved some measure of stability. Prior to the actual outbreak of hostilities, there was a good deal of agitation from the colonists themselves, and state revolutionary committees finally took over the government of the colony. On July 9, 1776, the Provincial Congress of New York approved the Declaration of Independence, and New York was declared a free state the following day.

Full name: State of New York
Origin of Name: In honor of the Duke of York.
Motto: *Excelsior* (Ever Upward).
Nickname: Empire State
Capital: Albany
Statehood: July 26, 1788, 11th state.
Population: 17,924,000 (ranks second).
Major Cities: New York City (7,481,613), Buffalo (407,160), Rochester (267,173).
Bird: Bluebird
Flower: Rose
Tree: Sugar maple

Average daily temperature by month

	Eastern	Western
Jan.	28.9 to 11.7	31.4 to 15.2
Feb.	31.8 to 13.7	33.5 to 16.2
Mar.	40.1 to 23.2	41.5 to 23.9
Apr.	55.9 to 34.2	56.3 to 35.2
May	67.5 to 44.0	67.6 to 45.0
Jun.	76.6 to 53.6	77.6 to 54.8
Jul.	80.8 to 57.9	81.3 to 58.8
Aug.	78.6 to 56.0	79.3 to 57.1
Sept.	71.2 to 49.3	73.1 to 50.8
Oct.	60.6 to 39.3	62.5 to 41.2
Nov.	45.4 to 30.4	47.6 to 32.0
Dec.	33.0 to 18.4	35.6 to 21.1
Year	55.9 to 36.0	57.3 to 37.6

In recent years, New York has waged an extensive campaign to attract tourists and bolster regional pride with the slogan, "I Love New York." And love it you will, because it is a superb vacationland. In the northern region you'll find Albany, the seat of the state government, and a grand new attraction, the Empire State Plaza, which houses the State Museum. You can also visit Howes Cave, the Adirondacks, Lake Placid, Lake Champlain and the Thousand Islands. The central-western region boasts Niagara Falls, the Baseball Hall of Fame at Cooperstown, the Finger Lakes and 65,000-acre Allegany State Park. In the southern region, there's New York City, sometimes called the "tourist capital of the world," and the Statue of Liberty, Rockefeller Center, the United Nations and Long Island — New York's ocean oasis encompassing 1,723 square miles.

In recent years, New York City has had its problems; but the state is thriving on an economic base that includes the manufacturing of clothing, textiles, appliances, scientific instruments and electrical equipment. Agriculture, mining and fishing are other important activities, as are printing, publishing, advertising, banking and tourism.

A familiar New York sight is this view of Manhattan across the East River capturing the 39-story Secretariat office building of the United Nations as it casts a reflection on the waters. Empire State Building on the left and the Chrysler Building to the right loom imposingly in the background.

New York Points of Interest and Attractions

(Note: Refer to shaded map below for regional breakdown of New York State points of interest and attractions.)

Long Island

Bayard Cutting Arboretum. Walks through model plantings. Open year-round, Wednesday to Sunday, 10 a.m. to 5:30 p.m. Great River off State Route 27A.

Belmont Park Race Track. Thoroughbred racing. Seasons: May 23 through July 30 — August 29 through October 15; racing daily except Tuesday. Elmont, Hempstead Turnpike and Cross Parkway.

Bridgehampton Race Circuit. Automobile and motorcycle races. Season: April 15 through November 15, weekends only. Bridgehampton, on Millstone Road.

Hargrave Vineyards. Only winery on Long Island. Open year-round; daily, except Sunday, 10 a.m. to 5 p.m. Cutchogue, off State Route 25.

Muttontown Nature Center. Nature trails, study. Open year-round, daily, 9:30 a.m. to 4:30 p.m. Free. East Norwich, on Muttontown Lane.

Nassau Farmers' Market. Two-and-one-half acre market with 300 indoor booths, children's amusements. Open year-round, Friday and Saturday, 11 a.m. to 11 p.m. Bethpage, off State Route 107.

Planting Fields Arboretum. Labeled trees, shrubs, bulbs, plants, greenhouse displays. Open year-round, daily, 10 a.m. to 5 p.m. Oyster Bay, Planting Fields Road.

Roosevelt Raceway. Harness racing. Season: year-round, Monday to Saturday, post-time 8 p.m. Westbury, off Old Country Road.

Sands Point Park and Reserve. Nature trails, study, historic home built in 1923 by Captain Harry F. Guggenheim. Open May 15 through November 15, Wednesday to Sunday, 10 a.m. to 5 p.m.; closed on Election Day and Veteran's Day. Port Washington, off Middleneck Road.

Hudson Valley

Ancram Opera House and Gardens. Restoration of early 20th-century opera house. Open May 1 through August 31, Thursday to Sunday, 1 p.m. to 5 p.m.; September 1 through January 15, Saturday and Sunday, 1 p.m. to 5 p.m. Gardens closed to visitors during performances. Ancram, off Taconic State Parkway, on State Route 82.

Brotherhood Winery. America's oldest winery where guided wine-tasting tours last one hour and 20 minutes. Open April 30 through June 23; weekdays, noon to 3 p.m.; June 25 through September 3, weekdays, 10 a.m. to 4 p.m.; September 4 through November 9, weekdays, noon to 3 p.m.; closed Good Friday, Easter Sunday and Thanksgiving Day. Free. Washingtonville, off State Route 94 on North Street. (914) 496-9101.

Caramoor. A 180-acre estate built by financier Walter T. Rosen; house surrounding cloistered courtyards, art galleries, period rooms with art, sculpture and furnishing dating from the Middle Ages to the 18th century. Open April through late fall, Wednesday and Saturday, 10 a.m. to 4 p.m.; Tuesday, Thursday and Friday by appointment. Music festival, chamber music concerts and opera performances during summer. Katonah, off State Route 137. (914) 232-4206.

Crailo Gardens. More than 200 varieties of ornamental evergreen dwarfs, shrubs and trees. Open May through September, Sunday afternoons, or by appointment. Ancram, off Taconic State Parkway, on State Route 82. (518) 329-0601.

Culinary Institute of America. Seventy-five acre campus overlooking the Hudson River; restaurant. Open for tours every Wednesday by appointment. Hyde Park, off State Route 9. (914) 452-9600.

Hammond Museum and Oriental Stroll Gardens. Museum of the humanities, changing exhibits, lectures, documentary films, concerts, dramatic readings. Open (museum) late May through December, 11 a.m. to 5 p.m.; (gardens) late May through October, Wednesday to Sunday, 11 a.m. to 5 p.m. North Salem, off State Route 124, on Deveau Road.

Orange County Airport. Aircraft rides, air shows and air meet activities. Open April through October. Monroe, off State Route 211.

United States Military Academy (West Point). Founded in 1802 to school officers for the United States Army. Parades in the spring and fall; visitor information center; displays; hotel and restaurant on grounds. Open April through October, daily, 8:30 a.m. to 4:30 p.m.; November through April, Wednesday to Sunday, 8:30 a.m. to 4:30 p.m. West Point, off State Route 307. (914) 938-2638.

Wildcliff Crafts Center. Exhibits, demonstrations and classes in papermaking and blacksmithing. Also adult classes in etching, calligraphy, pottery, photography, art. Sunday activities for children; nature walks. Open year-round, Monday to Thursday 1 p.m. to 4:30 p.m.; Sunday 1 p.m. to 5 p.m. New Rochelle, 764 Pinebrook Boulevard. (914) 636-1537.

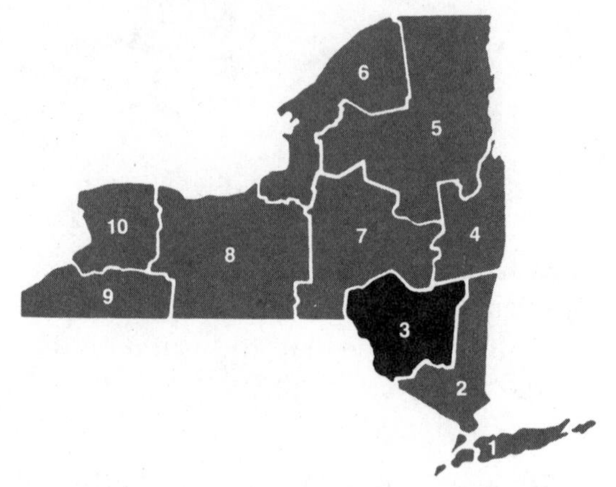

The Catskills

Cagnasso Winery. Tours, wine tasting. Open April through December, daily, 10 a.m. to 5 p.m. Marlboro, two miles north off State Route 9W. (914) 236-4630.

Hudson Valley Wine Village. Winery, vineyards, wine village, cellars, snack bar, picnic area; all on 325-acre estate. Open February 12 through November 26, Saturday 10 a.m. to 3 p.m., Sunday 11 a.m. to 6 p.m.; May, June and September through November, Monday to Friday, 11 a.m. to 3 p.m.; July and August, Monday to Friday, 10 a.m. to 4 p.m. Highland, off State Route 9W.

Monticello Raceway. Harness races. Season: spring, Monday to Saturday, 8 p.m.; summer, Monday to Saturday, 8:30 p.m., Sunday, 2:30 p.m. Monticello, at intersection of State Routes 17 and 17B.

Royal-Kedem Winery. Wine-tasting and film in Early American railway station; picnic area. Open May through November 30, Sunday to Friday, 11 a.m. to 5 p.m.; closed on Jewish holidays. Free. Milton, on Dock Road.

Widmark Farms. One of the largest comb honey producers in New York state; dancing bear performances. Open May through October 14, daily, 8 a.m. to 8 p.m.; bear performances on Saturday, 7 p.m. Free. Gardiner, two miles west. (914) 255-6400.

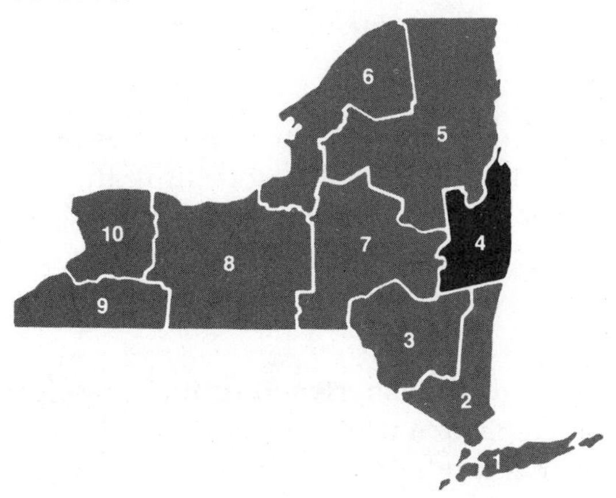

Capital-Saratoga

Albany. New York state's capital city; 2½-hour guided bus tour and 1½-hour self-guided walking tour of city, featuring unique architecture and restorations. Season: year-round, daily by appointment. Historic Albany Foundation, 300 Hudson Avenue, Albany 12210. (518) 463-0622.

Petrified Gardens. Reefs of ancient petrified plants (Cryptozoons); glacial crevices; outdoor sundial museum. Open June 2 through September 9, daily, 9 a.m. to 5 p.m. (National Natural Landmark). Saratoga Springs, off State Route 29.

Saratoga County Antiques Center. Open year-round. Rock City Falls, off State Route 29. (518) 885-7645.

Saratoga Harness. Harness racing. Season: spring through November, Monday to Saturday, 8:15 p.m.; 2:15 p.m. for holiday matinees and for Grand Circuit Week in July. Saratoga Springs, off Interstate 87, on State Route 29. (518) 584-2110.

The reconstructed walls of Fort Ticonderoga wear a look of Colonial authenticity. Cannon, guards and waving flags re-create the scene of the first aggressive action of the American Revolution in 1775 when Ethan Allen and his Green Mountain Boys took control in the name of the Continental Congress.

Uncle Sam's Grave. "Uncle Sam" Wilson, a local meat packer, supplied beef to the U.S. Army during the War of 1812. Soldiers interpreted government stamp, "U.S. Beef," to mean "Uncle Sam's Beef." Later, a caricature of Sam Wilson came to personify the United States. Troy, at junction of State Routes 2 and 7, in Oakwood Cemetery.

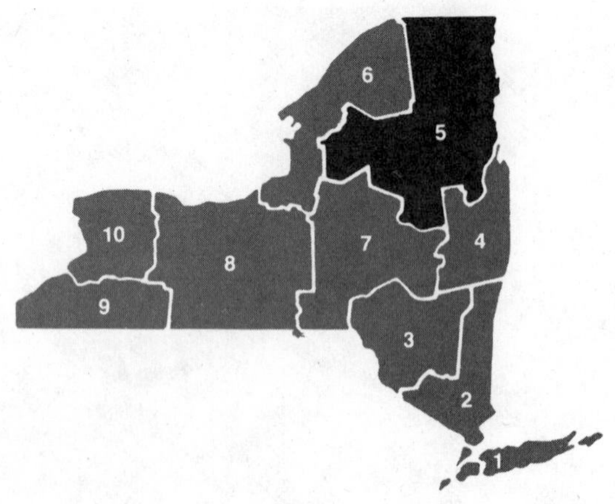

Adirondacks

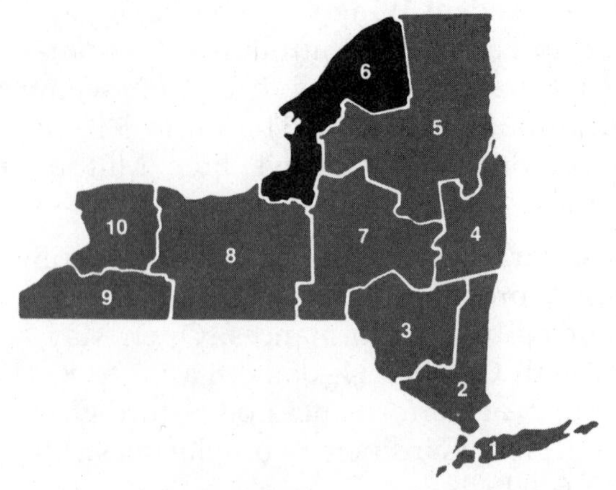

1000 Islands-Seaway

Ausable Chasm. Walking tour and boat ride through flume of 1½-mile scenic wonder. Season: May 19 through October 8, daily, 9 a.m. to 4 p.m.; July through August, 9 a.m. to 5 p.m.

Ausable Chasm Recreation Center. Auto museum, glass blower, leather and pottery shop. May 19 through June, September through October 8, weekends 10 a.m. to 5 p.m.; July through August, daily. Campground open, May 18 through October 8. Ausable Chasm, off Interstate 87 (exits 34 and 35), on State Route 9.

Natural Stone Bridge and Caves. Open May through October, daily, 8 a.m. to dark. Pottersville, 2½ miles north at Northway exit 26. (518) 494-2283.

Prospect Mountain Veterans Memorial Highway. A 5½-mile scenic drive, three overlooks, picnic tables, fireplace at summit. Season: July through fall foliage season, daily, 10 a.m. to dusk.

Santa's Workshop. Village home of Santa Claus, his helpers, storybook characters, live reindeer and other animals; children's rides, puppet theater; magic shows. Open May 27 through October 9, daily, 9:30 a.m. to 3:30 p.m.; July 1 through September 4, daily, 9 a.m. to 5 p.m. Wilmington, at North Pole, off State Route 86, on Whiteface Mountain Highway.

Boat Trips. Three-hour, 50-mile sight-seeing tours of Thousand Islands; stop at Boldt Castle. Season: June through September, daily, frequent departures; departures less often during other months. Clayton, off Interstate 81, on State Route 12.

Cape Vincent Fisheries Station. New York State Department of Environmental Conservation aquarium with Great Lakes fish; nature trails; displays. Open June through October, Monday to Friday, 9 a.m. to 4:30 p.m. Free. Cape Vincent, off Interstate 81, on State Route 12E.

Natural Bridge Caverns. Underground boat trip on Indian River; lessons in geology and natural history. Open June 20 through September 30, daily, 9 a.m. to 5:30 p.m.; June and October dates depend on water level. Natural Bridge, off State Route 3.

Nine Mile Point Energy Information Center. Sponsored by the state power authority and Niagara Mohawk Corporation, the center features exhibits and a three-part program portraying methods of producing and using energy today and in the future. Open March through November, Tuesday to Sunday, 10 a.m. to 5 p.m.; December through February, Monday to Friday, 10 a.m. to 5 p.m. Free. Oswego, on Lake Road.

THE NATIONAL BASEBALL HALL OF FAME

It started out as a small room of New York's Cooperstown Village Club, where Abner Doubleday's baseball was on display. The ball had been discovered in an attic trunk where it had apparently been stored for generations; and it was purchased in 1935 by Stephen C. Clark, a Cooperstown native, who wished to share this piece of baseball memorabilia with the townsfolk. The Baseball Hall of Fame was dedicated in 1939, and today baseball's famous showcase is undergoing a multi-million dollar expansion and renovation program which will provide display potential for almost the entire museum's collection of over 10,000 pieces of memorabilia, half of which have been in storage over the years due to space limitations. (The building program will double the size of the existing facility and provide a more complete, better organized and even more exciting review of baseball as the Hall of Fame celebrates its 41st anniversary.)

Upon entering, visitors will now enjoy browsing through the Cooperstown Room, containing an artifact and pictorial history both of the unique village going back to the James Fenimore Cooper days and of the origin of the game of baseball, believed by many to have been devised here by Abner Doubleday in 1839.

An exciting new feature certain to be well received is the Great Moments Room where baseball's most exciting games and feats are depicted through giant 8 x 10-foot blowups of historic photographs. Here fans will re-live Joe DiMaggio's 56 game hitting streak, Ruth's 60th home run, Maris' 61st and Hank Aaron's 715th, Ted Williams' batting .406, Jackie Robinson's debut, Lou Brock's 118th steal, Lou Gehrig's 2,130 consecutive games, Sandy Koufax' 4th no-hitter and perfect game, Bobby Thompson's dramatic 1951 home run, Harvey Haddix' perfect game loss, Johnny VanderMeer's double no-hitters, Don Drysdale's 58-2/3 scoreless innings and Bob Feller's no-hitters and shutouts.

Also on the first floor will be the traditional Hall of Fame Room containing the bronze plaques of the game's immortals.

Most of the second floor will be designed to portray the History of Baseball utilizing mementos and photographs, supplemented by original paintings. On display will be Hall of Famers' bats, uniforms, gloves, autographed baseballs, sliding pads, baseball cards, team sweaters, shoes, scorecards, ticket stubs, trophies, cups, awards and player contracts. Also in this section will be detailed displays showing the evolution of baseballs, bats, catchers' equipment, fielding gloves and player uniforms.

Black baseball going back to the early Negro leagues will be an integral part of the second floor exhibit, and Baseball's World Tours promise to make an unusual display. Finally, the second floor will contain the All-Star Game exhibit — a year-by-year collection of All-Star memorabilia going back to the initial contest in 1933.

Moving on to the third floor, the visitor will be entertained by two delightful collections — the Babe Ruth display and the Casey Stengel exhibit. Over 130 Babe Ruth items will surround his locker in the Babe Ruth Room. Fans will also get a special thrill from comparing ballparks in the Ballpark Room. The Polo Grounds, Ebbets Field, Shibe Park, Forbes Field and Crosley Field are represented here along with souvenirs from present-day stadia; and the actual lockers used by Walter Johnson, Honus Wagner, Hank Aaron, Joe DiMaggio, Lou Gehrig and Roberto

Clemente will be on display.

The World Series Room on the third floor will bring back October excitement. Beginning with the first World Series in 1903 between the Pittsburgh Pirates and the Boston Red Sox, fans will thrill to highlights of baseball's great championship games. Life-size figures of World Series' heroes will delight the young and old alike — Dizzy Dean, Al Gionfriddo, Jackie Robinson, Home Run Baker, Willie Mays, Babe Ruth, Don Larsen, Sandy Koufax, Reggie Jackson, Joe Rudi and Carlton Fisk are on display along with an abundance of World Series' memorabilia, including collections of World Series' tickets, press pins, programs and Championship rings.

The lower level of the Hall of Fame features Baseball Today exhibits, where each of the 26 teams are represented. The clubs' present-day uniforms provide a colorful contrast as today's stars receive their due. An elaborate and complete gift shop will accommodate the souvenir hunter and the adjacent Hall of Fame Library contains voluminous collections of books, photographs and clippings for research and reference.

The end result is a showcase worthy of its contents, where the famous heroes, the brilliant plays and the great games are preserved for all fans who can now enjoy the excitement of baseball today without missing the thrills of baseball past.

HOURS: The National Baseball Hall of Fame and Museum is open seven days a week the year-round, including all holidays except Thanksgiving, Christmas and New Year's. Summer: May 1 through October 31, 9 a.m. to 9 p.m. Winter: November 1 through April 30, 9 a.m. to 5 p.m.

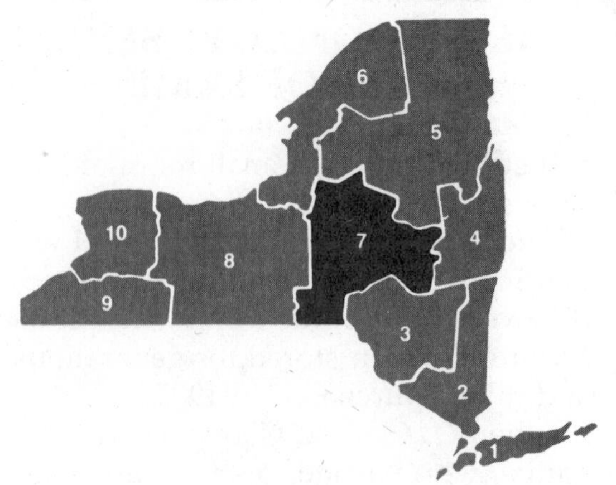

Central-Leatherstocking

Baseball Hall of Fame and Museum. Plaques honoring baseball's all-time greats, mememtos and displays that tell the history of America's national pastime. Open May 1 through October 31, daily, 9 a.m. to 9 p.m.; November 1 through April 30, daily, 9 a.m. to 5 p.m. Cooperstown, at junction of State Routes 28 and 80. (607) 547-9988

Colgate University. Open for tours September through May, Monday to Friday, 10 a.m. to 4:15 p.m.; June through August, Monday to Friday, 10 a.m. to 3 p.m. Hamilton, off State Route 12B. (315) 824-1000, extension 401.

Gates Hill Homestead. Horsedrawn sleigh and wagon rides, stagecoach tour of "The Eternal Hills" with meal. Open year-round, daily, by reservation. Brookfield, off State Routes 12 and 8. (315) 899-5837.

Gladding International Sport Fishing Museum. Open May 30 through September 1, Tuesday to Sunday, 10 a.m. to 5 p.m. South Otselic, off State Route 26.

Griffis Air Force Base. Home of Strategic Air Command's 416th Bombardment Wing. Open for tours June 1 through August 31, Monday to Saturday, 1 p.m. Rome, at junction of State Routes 365, 49 and 26.

Seeley's Doll Center. Antique and reproduction dolls, educational facilities. Open year-round, Monday to Saturday, 8:30 a.m. to 5 p.m. Oneonta, 35 Main Street.

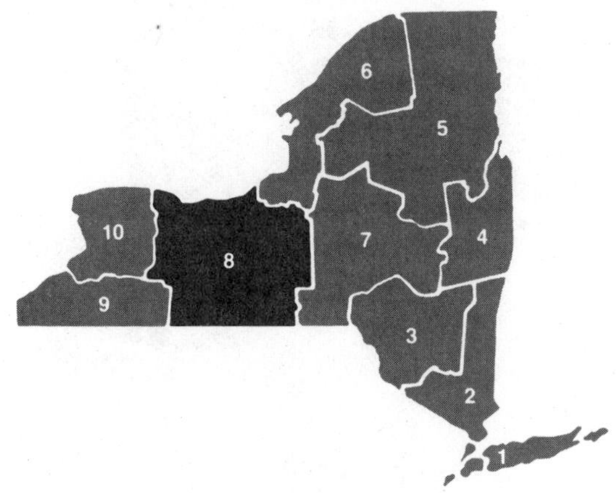

The Finger Lakes

Brookwood Science Information Center. Nuclear energy exhibits. Open year-round, Sunday to Thursday, 10 a.m. to 4 p.m. Ontario, off State Route 18, on Lake Road.

Corning Glass Center and Steuben Glass Factory. Museum with more than 16,000 glass objects; science hall; Steuben factory. Open year-round, daily, 9 a.m. to 5 p.m.; closed Thanksgiving, December 24 and 25, and January 1. Corning, off State Route 17.

F. Eberhardt Winery. Tours, wine-tasting. Open year-round, Monday to Saturday, 8:30 a.m. to 5 p.m. Williamson, 569 Tuckahoe Road.

The State Capitol Building in Albany, New York, is a massive castle-like structure that was built over a 30-year period at a cost of $25 million.

Glendora Wine Cellars. Tours, wine-tasting. Open year-round, by appointment only. Dundee, off State Route 14. (607) 243-7600.

Kodak Tours. Free guided tours of the famous Eastman Kodak facility, photo exhibits. Open year-round, Monday to Friday; tours 9:30 a.m. and 1:30 p.m.; children under 5 not admitted. Rochester, Kodak Park Division, 200 West Ridge Road.

Lollypop Farm. Live animals. Open year-round, daily, except Thanksgiving, Christmas and New Year's Day. Fairport, 99 Victory Road.

Silver Floss Food Plants Tour. Sauerkraut shredding. Open August 27 through September 14, Monday to Friday, 1 p.m. to 3 p.m. Phelps, off State Route 96, on Eagle Street.

Sonnenberg Gardens and Mansion. Fifty-acre turn-of-the-century estate; special events; tea room; gift shop. Open mid-May to mid-October, daily, 9:30 a.m. to 6 p.m. Canandaigua, off State Route 21 North, at 151 Charlotte Street. (716) 394-4922.

Tioga Gardens. Solar-domed conservatory, natural woods, handcrafted products. Owego, off State Route 17C.

Tioga Park. Quarterhorse racing. Season: June through August, Thursday to Saturday, 7:45 p.m.; Sunday, 2 p.m. Owego, off State Route 17 (exit 62). (607) 699-3511.

Watkins Glen Grand Prix Circuit. This famous 1,100-acre facility includes a 3.37-mile road racing track. Open June through October, daily. Watkins Glen, off State Route 414, at Montour and Townsend Road. (607) 535-7145.

Women's Hall of Fame. Honors women in art, athletics, business, education, government, humanities, philanthropy and science. Open year-round, daily, 10 a.m. to 4 p.m. Seneca Falls, 76 Fall Street. (315) 568-8060.

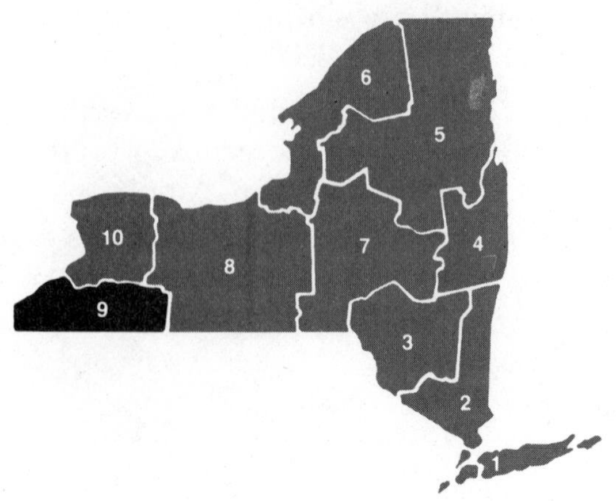

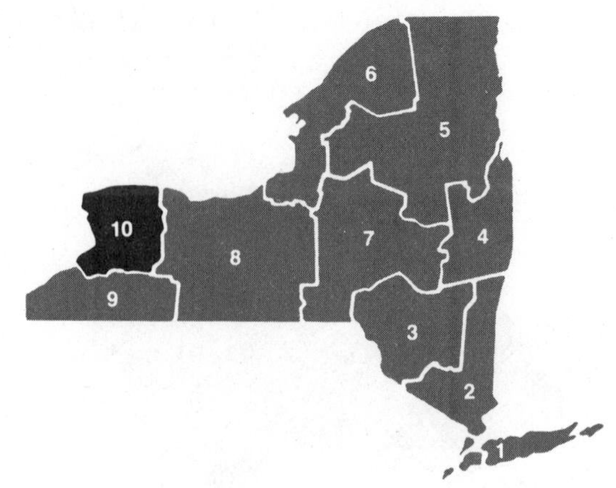

Chautauqua-Allegheny

Boat Rides. Aboard the yacht *Gadfly*, 1¼-hour cruises from Chautauqua Institution dock on Chautauqua Lake. Season: July through Ausut, Tuesday to Sunday, 2 p.m. and 3:30 p.m.; Wednesday, Friday to Sunday, 7 p.m. Special two-hour trips, Tuesday and Saturday, 10:30 a.m.; July Fourth trips, 2 p.m., 3 p.m. and 7 p.m., fireworks cruise at 9:30 p.m. Chautauqua, off State Route 17.

Johnson Estate Wines. Tours, wine-tastings, sales. Open July through August, Monday to Saturday, 9 a.m. to 5:30 p.m.; Sunday, noon to 5 p.m. Free. Tastings and sales year-round, 9:30 a.m. to 5 p.m. Westfield, off State Route 20, two miles west to West Main Road.

Old Northside Walking Tour. Tour of downtown Jamestown with fine examples of architecture spanning 75 years, from Gothic Revival to Art Deco. Also includes commercial and industrial buildings of late 1800s, churches, private buildings and residences. Similar tour titled **Old Southside Walking Tour.** Full information in brochures available at Fenton Historical Center. Jamestown, at junction of State Route 394 and US-62.

The Niagara Frontier

Arcade and Attica Railroad. Steam-train excursions, antique railroad equipment. Season: May 26 through October, weekends and holidays. Departures: noon, 2 p.m. and 4 p.m. Arcade, at junction of State Routes 98 and 39.

Broadway Market. "Old World Market" where farmers sell fresh field-grown products. Area surrounded by many low-priced ethnic restaurants featuring German, Polish and Balkan dishes. Open year-round, Monday and Tuesday, 8 a.m. to 4 p.m.; closed Wednesday; Thursday, 8 a.m. to 5 p.m.; Friday, 7 a.m. to 8 p.m.; Saturday, 6 a.m. to 5 p.m. Buffalo, 999 Broadway.

Lockport Cave Raceway Tour. Power tunnel once part of Erie Canal. Geological formations, waterpower equipment, early industrial ruins. Tour includes Erie Canal, locks 34 and 35, and lasts 1¼ hours. Open May 26 through September 5, daily, 10:30 a.m. to 5 p.m. Lockport, off State Route 78N, on Clinton Street.

Niagara Falls. Aquarium of Niagara Falls. Performing dolphins, sea life. Open June through September, Monday to Friday, 9 a.m. to 8 p.m., weekends, 9 a.m. to 9 p.m.; rest of year, weekdays, 9 a.m. to 5 p.m., weekends 9 a.m. to 7 p.m. Off US-701, on Whirlpool Street.

Boat Trip. *The Maid of the Mist.* On Niagara River to foot of the falls; departs every 20 minutes from Observation Tower. Open late May through October, daily, 10 a.m. to 5 p.m.; July and August, daily, 9:15 a.m. to 8 p.m.

Goat Island Heliport. Helicopter flights over falls. Open May through October (weather permitting), daily, 10:30 a.m. to dark. Parking Lot 3, Niagara Reservation.

Niagara Power Project. Power vista, energy exhibits, movies, history of Niagara power. Open June 27 through September 3, daily, 9 a.m. to 7:30 p.m.; rest of year, daily, 9 a.m. to 5 p.m. Free. Off State Route 104.

Shea's Buffalo Theater. A circa-1920 movie palace with pipe organ (on National Register of Historic Places). Open year-round, Saturday 10 a.m. to 1 p.m., by appointment only. Buffalo, 646 Main Street. (716) 847-0050.

South Park Botanical Gardens. Garden tours; tour guides available with advance notice. Open year-round, daily, 9 a.m. to 4 p.m. Free. Buffalo, South Park and McKinley Parkway. (716) 825-9816.

Studio Arena Theater. A professional equity theater; stage performances; seven plays a season. Open October through May, and various special events. Buffalo, 710 Main Street. Box Office information: (716) 856-5650 or (716) 856-8025.

The spectacular Niagara Falls has been thrilling millions of visitors and honeymooners since its discovery in 1678. The Falls may be viewed from the brink, the bottom, from observation decks, from boats and from helicopters for views like this looking toward Canada over the Prospect Point Observation Tower.

Highlight

Long Island

Long Island measures but 125 miles in length, yet it offers 250 miles of coastline indented with intriguing inlets and promising bays. Home to over two million people, it is host to more millions of annual visitors who come to enjoy the sea breezes, the surf fishing, the sandy beaches and the strong sense of history that pervades the island.

RVers will find much to see and do here, so let's take a quick tour of the atrractions awaiting you:

Today's fashionable Southampton village was a going concern in 1640, when it was purchased from the Shinnecock Indians by English settlers. Montauk was the first landfall after a transatlantic crossing and soon became cattle country for stock shipped from Europe.

"I hear America singing the varied carols I hear . . ." So wrote the good gray poet, Walt Whitman, whose home at West Hills is popular with literary buffs.

Smithtown was founded in 1665 by one Richard Smith — its parameters decided by the distance Mr. Smith could cover in one day on the back of a bull.

Raynham Hall, in Oyster Bay, was the headquarters of one of General Washington's spies, whose family graciously entertained unwitting English officers in the hope of learning military plans. A walk through this lovely restored colonial home today imparts a sense of intrigue.

Watch the Montauk fleet come in one morning and what you'll see is a glimpse of the pleasures that await visiting fishermen. Montauk is the home port for the largest fleet of charter and party boats in the entire Northeast. Sag Harbor and Shelter Island are not far behind. Catches include bluefish, striped bass, swordfish, tuna, marlin and shark. There are 28 world records for sport fish caught off Long Island.

Surf casters can try their luck at both north and south shore beaches, notably Jones Beach, Center Moriches and Bayville.

Billions of freshwater fish of varying species have been introduced into Long Island's inland waters by the Cold Spring Harbor Fish Hatchery.

Pier fishing is possible anywhere on the island but especially promising at Lindenhurst, Long Beach and Captree State Park.

For many people, beaches are the be-all and end-all of a Long Island holiday. Wide reaches of sand, allowing ample room for picnickers, sunbathers, ball games and strollers, lead smoothly from the shore inward to dunes marked by marsh grass and cattails. Depending on time and place, they may be filled with escaping weekenders or splendidly desolate. They may also be developed for recreational facilities or left largely untouched. Some are quite short; many are mile-long stretches.

Jones Beach is part of the state park of the same name. In addition to its six and one-half miles of sand beach, it offers a saltwater pool and a staggering selection of recreational facilities.

Jones Beach Marine Theater, a four-million-dollar extravaganza that is the largest of its kind in the country, offers theatrical spectaculars during the summer season.

The complete opposite in attraction is Hither Hills State Park, also on the South Shore but much closer to Montauk Point. There are facilities here for recreational vehicles, but the parkland consists largely of barren dunes.

The eating is good on Long Island. In addition to fresh fish on every restaurant's menu, there's a satisfying variety of local produce which doesn't have far to travel from the central farm belt of the island to your table. Long Island ducklings are hatched in enough numbers to satisfy fully 70% of the nation's market. Fresh fruit and strawberries, in particular, are a summer treat throughout the island, and are eagerly snatched up by Manhattanites in preference to southern and far-western produce.

There are more windmills on Long Island than in any other part of the country. Eleven in Suffolk County alone, including Hook Mill in East Hampton, which actually works. And including Pantigo Mill, the blades of which can be seen behind "Home, Sweet Home," the boyhood home of John Howard Payne.

Long Island's resort character is very much in evidence in its eastern end towns and villages where main streets feature dainty tea shops, pretty little boutiques, homey antique shops and quaint general stores with post offices. The community of Stony Brook has gone one step further in planned rehabilitation, and its center looks much as it did in the early 19th century.

There's even a full-fledged spa in Montauk. Its extensive facilities are international — Finnish saunas, Russian baths, Swedish and Oriental massages — but its setting is very much Long Island — high on a bluff overlooking 1,000 feet of wide, white sand beach.

—PJF

State Offices

Tourism
Travel Bureau
New York State Department of Commerce
99 Washington Avenue
Albany, New York 12245
(518) 474-4116

State Police
Department of Public Safety
Albany, New York 12226
(518) 457-6811

Radio Stations

Albany
- WPTR 1540 (AM)

Burlington
- WQCR 98.9 (FM)

New York
- WRVR 106.7 (FM)
- WNBC 660 (AM)
- WABC 770 (AM)
- WPLJ 95.5 (FM)
- WNEW 102.7 (FM)
- WPIX 101.9 (FM)

Rochester
- WHAM 1180 (AM)

Syracuse
- WKFM 104.7 (FM)
- WNDR 1260 (AM)

Utica
- WKCW 104.3 (FM)

The Catskill Mountains of New York state boast many well-stocked trout streams.

New York State Parks

NOTE: Due to the abundance of New York state parks, this listing has been broken into three regions — Northern, Central-Western and Southern.

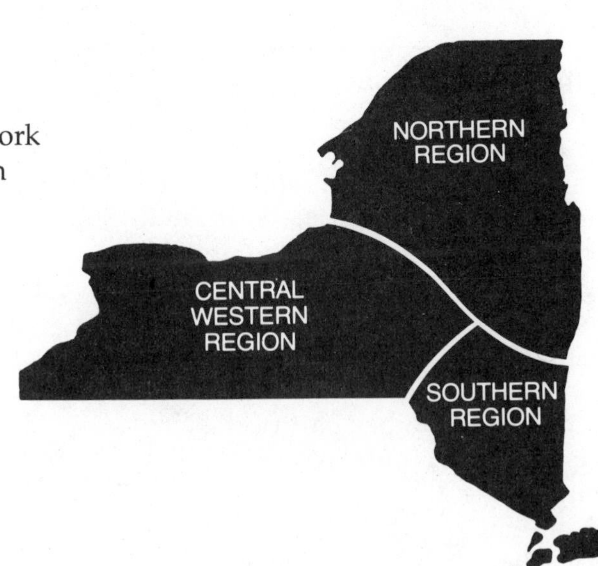

Central-Western Region

Park	Location	CAMPING	PICNICKING	CONCESSIONS	SWIMMING	HIKING	BOATING	FISHING	HUNTING	WINTER SPORTS
Allegany	*Salamanca. Off State Route 17.*	•	•	•	•	•	•	•		•
Bowman Lake	*Oxford. Off State Route 220.*	•	•	•	•	•	•	•		•
Cayuga Lake	*Seneca Falls. Off State Route 89.*	•	•	•	•		•	•		•
Chenango Valley	*Binghampton. Off State Route 369.*	•	•	•	•	•	•	•		•
Chittenango Falls	*Cazenovia. Off State Route 13.*	•	•			•	•	•		•
Darien Lakes	*Darien Center. Off US-20.*	•	•	•	•	•	•	•		•
Delta Lake	*Rome. Off State Route 46.*	•	•	•	•	•	•	•		•
Evangola	*Farnham. Off State Route 5.*	•	•		•					•
Fair Haven Beach	*Fair Haven. Off State Route 104A.*	•	•	•	•	•	•	•		•
Filmore Glen	*Moravia. Off State Route 38.*	•	•	•	•	•		•	•	•
Gilbert Lake	*Oneonta. Off State Routes 205 and 51.*	•	•	•	•	•	•	•		•
Glimmerglass	*East Springfield. Off US-20.*	•	•	•	•	•		•		•
Golden Hill	*Barker. Off State Route 269.*	•						•		•
Green Lakes	*Syracuse. Off State Routes 290 and 5.*	•	•	•	•	•	•	•		•
Hamlin Beach	*Hamlin. Off State Route 19, on Lake Ontario State Parkway.*	•	•	•	•	•		•		•
Keuka Lake	*Penn Yan. Off State Route 54A.*	•	•		•		•	•		•
Lake Erie	*Brocton. Off US-90.*	•	•	•	•	•		•		•
Lakeside Beach	*Albion. On Lake Ontario State Parkway.*	•		•		•		•	•	•
Letchworth	*Mount Morris. Off State Route 408.*	•	•	•	•	•		•	•	•
Long Point	*Aurora. Off State Route 34.*	•	•		•		•	•		
Pixley Falls	*Boonville. Off State Route 46.*	•	•					•	•	
Robert H. Treman	*Ithaca. Off State Route 13.*	•	•		•	•		•		•
Sampson	*Ovid. Off State Route 96A.*	•	•	•	•		•	•		•
Selkirk Shores	*Pulaski. Off State Route 3.*	•	•	•	•	•		•		•
Stony Brook	*Dansville. Off State Route 36.*	•	•	•	•	•		•		•
Taughannock Falls	*Ithaca. Off State Route 89.*	•	•	•	•	•	•	•		•
Verona Beach	*Oneida. Off State Route 13.*		•	•	•	•		•		•
Watkins Glen	*Watkins Glen. Entrance in village of Watkins Glen, off State Route 14.*	•	•	•	•	•		•		•

Northern Region

Park	Location	CAMPING	PICNICKING	CONCESSIONS	SWIMMING	HIKING	BOATING	FISHING	HUNTING	WINTER SPORTS
Burnham Point	*Cape Vincent. Off State Route 12 E.*	•	•	•	•		•	•		
Cedar Point	*Clayton. Off State Route 12 E.*	•	•		•		•	•		
Coles Creek	*Massena. Off State Route 37.*	•	•	•	•		•	•		
Cumberland Bay	*Plattsburgh. Off US-9.*	•	•	•	•			•	•	•
DeWolf Point	*Wellesley Island. Off State Route 81.*	•					•	•		
Eel Weir	*Ogdensburg. Off State Route 87S.*	•	•		•		•	•		
Grass Point	*Fishers Landing. Off State Route 12.*	•	•		•		•	•		
Higley Flow	*South Colton. Off State Route 56.*	•	•		•		•	•		
Jacques Cartier	*Morristown. Two miles south off River Road.*	•	•	•	•		•	•		
Keewaydin	*Alexandria Bay. Off State Route 12.*	•	•		•		•	•		
Kring Point	*Alexandria Bay. Off State Route 12.*	•	•	•	•		•	•		
Long Point	*Three Mile Bay. Off State Route 12E.*	•	•				•	•		
Robert Moses	*Massena. Off State Route 87.*	•	•	•	•	•	•	•		•
Southwick Beach	*Woodville. Off State Route 181.*	•	•	•	•	•		•		
Wellesley Island	*Wellesley Island. Two miles north of Thousand Islands bridge.*	•	•	•	•	•	•	•		•
Wescott Beach	*Sacketts Harbor. Off State Route 3.*	•	•	•	•		•	•		
Whetstone Gulf	*Lowville. Off State Route 12D.*	•	•	•	•	•				

Southern Region

Park	Location	CAMPING	PICNICKING	CONCESSIONS	SWIMMING	HIKING	BOATING	FISHING	HUNTING	WINTER SPORTS
Bear Mountain	*New York City. 45 miles north of Palisades Interstate Parkway.*		•	•	•	•	•	•		•
Clarence Fahnestock Memorial	*Peekskill. Off Taconic Parkway.*	•	•			•	•	•		•
Harriman	*New York City. 35 miles north of Palisades Interstate Parkway.*	•	•	•	•	•	•	•		•
Heckscher	*New York City. 50 miles east on Heckscher Parkway.*		•	•	•	•	•	•		•
Hither Hills	*Montauk. Off State Route 27.*	•	•	•	•			•		
James Baird	*Poughkeepsie. Off Taconic State Parkway and State Route 55.*		•	•	•		•			•
Lake Taghkanic	*Hudson. Off State Route 82.*	•	•	•	•	•	•	•		•
Margaret Lewis Norrie	*Hyde Park. Off US-9.*	•	•	•		•	•	•		•
Mine Kill	*Middleburgh. Off State Route 30.*		•	•	•	•	•	•		
Mohansic	*White Plains. Taconic State Parkway and US-202.*		•	•	•		•	•		•
Orient Beach	*Orient Point. 118 miles east of New York City, off City Route 25.*		•	•	•			•		
Robert Moses	*New York City. 49 miles east on Robert Moses Parkway.*		•	•	•			•	•	
Rockland Lake	*New York City. 18 miles north of US-9W.*		•	•	•	•	•	•		•
Taconic Copake Falls	*Copake Falls. Off State Route 22.*	•	•		•		•	•		•
Taconic Rudd Pond	*Millerton. Off State Route 22.*	•	•		•	•	•	•		•
Toe Path Mountain	*Middleburgh. Off State Route 30.*	•	•			•		•		

New York State Forests

Forest	Location	CAMPING	PICNICKING	CONCESSIONS	SWIMMING	HIKING	BOATING	FISHING	HUNTING	WINTER SPORTS
Allen Lake	*Allegany County*	•	•		•			•		•
Bear Swamp	*Cayuga County*	•	•			•				•
Beaver Creek	*Madison County*	•	•			•				•
Beaver Meadow	*Chenango County*	•	•			•				•
Big Brook	*Oneida County*	•	•	•		•				•
Birdseye Hollow	*Steuben County*	•	•	•		•				•
Bowman Creek	*Chenango County*	•	•			•				•
Brasher	*St. Lawrence County*	•	•			•				•
Burnt-Rossman Hills	*Schoharie County*	•	•			•				•
Cameron	*Steuben County*	•	•	•		•				•
Carlton Hill	*Wyoming County*	•	•			•				•
Charles E. Baker	*Madison County*	•	•	•		•				•
Coon Hollow	*Schuyler County*	•	•			•				•
Coyle Hill	*Allegany County*	•	•			•				•
Cuyler Hill	*Cortland County*	•	•			•				•
Danby	*Tompkins County*	•	•			•				•
Deer River	*Franklin County*	•	•			•				•
Fairlands	*Schoharie County*	•	•			•				•
Fall Brook	*Oneida County*	•	•			•				•
Five Streams	*Chenango County*	•	•	•		•				•
Frank E. Jadwin	*Lewis County*	•	•			•				•
Franklinville	*Cattaraugus County*	•	•			•				•
Geneganslet	*Chenango County*	•	•	•		•				•
Gillies Hill	*Allegany County*	•	•	•		•				•
Goundry Hill	*Schuyler County*	•	•			•				•
Griggs Gulf	*Cortland County*	•	•			•				•
Hammond Hill	*Tompkins County*	•	•			•				•
James D. Kennedy Memorial	*Cortland County*	•	•			•				•
Lassellsville	*Fulton County*	•	•			•				•
Long Pond	*Chenango County*	•	•			•				•
Lookout	*Lewis County*	•	•			•				•
Macomb Reservation	*Clinton County*	•	•			•				•
McCarthy Hill	*Cattaraugus County*	•	•	•		•				•
Mohawk Springs	*Lewis County*	•	•			•				•
Morgan Hill	*Cortland County*	•	•			•				•
Nine-Mile Creek	*Cattaraugus County*	•	•			•				•
North Harmony	*Chatauqua County*	•	•			•				•
Palmer Pond	*Allegany County*	•	•			•				•
Peck Hill	*Fulton County*	•	•			•				•
Rensselaerville	*Albany County*	•	•			•				•
Rock City	*Cattaraugus County*	•	•			•				•
Seacord Hill	*Cortland County*	•	•			•				•
South Hammond	*St. Lawrence County*	•	•			•				•
South Valley	*Cattaraugus County*	•	•			•				•

New York State Forests

Forest	Location	CAMPING	PICNICKING	CONCESSIONS	SWIMMING	HIKING	BOATING	FISHING	HUNTING	WINTER SPORTS
Summer Hill	*Cayuga County*	•	•			•				•
Swancott Hill	*Oneida County*	•	•			•				•
Tassell Hill	*Oneida County*	•	•			•				•
Terry Mountain	*Clinton County*	•	•	•		•				•
Titusville Mountain	*Franklin County*	•	•			•				•
Tug Hill	*Jefferson County*	•	•			•				•
Urbana	*Steuben County*	•	•			•				•
Vandermark	*Allegany County*	•	•			•				•
Whiskey Flats	*St. Lawrence County*	•	•			•				•
Winona	*Oswego County*	•	•			•				•
Wolf Lake	*St. Lawrence County*	•	•			•	•	•		•
Zoar Valley	*Cattaraugus County*	•	•			•				•

For additional information on New York state parks and forests, contact: ***Parks:*** *Parks and Recreation, Empire State Plaza, Albany, New York 12238, (518) 474-0456;* ***Forests:*** *Department of Environmental Conservation, Forestry Division, Albany, New York 12233, (518) 474-2121.*

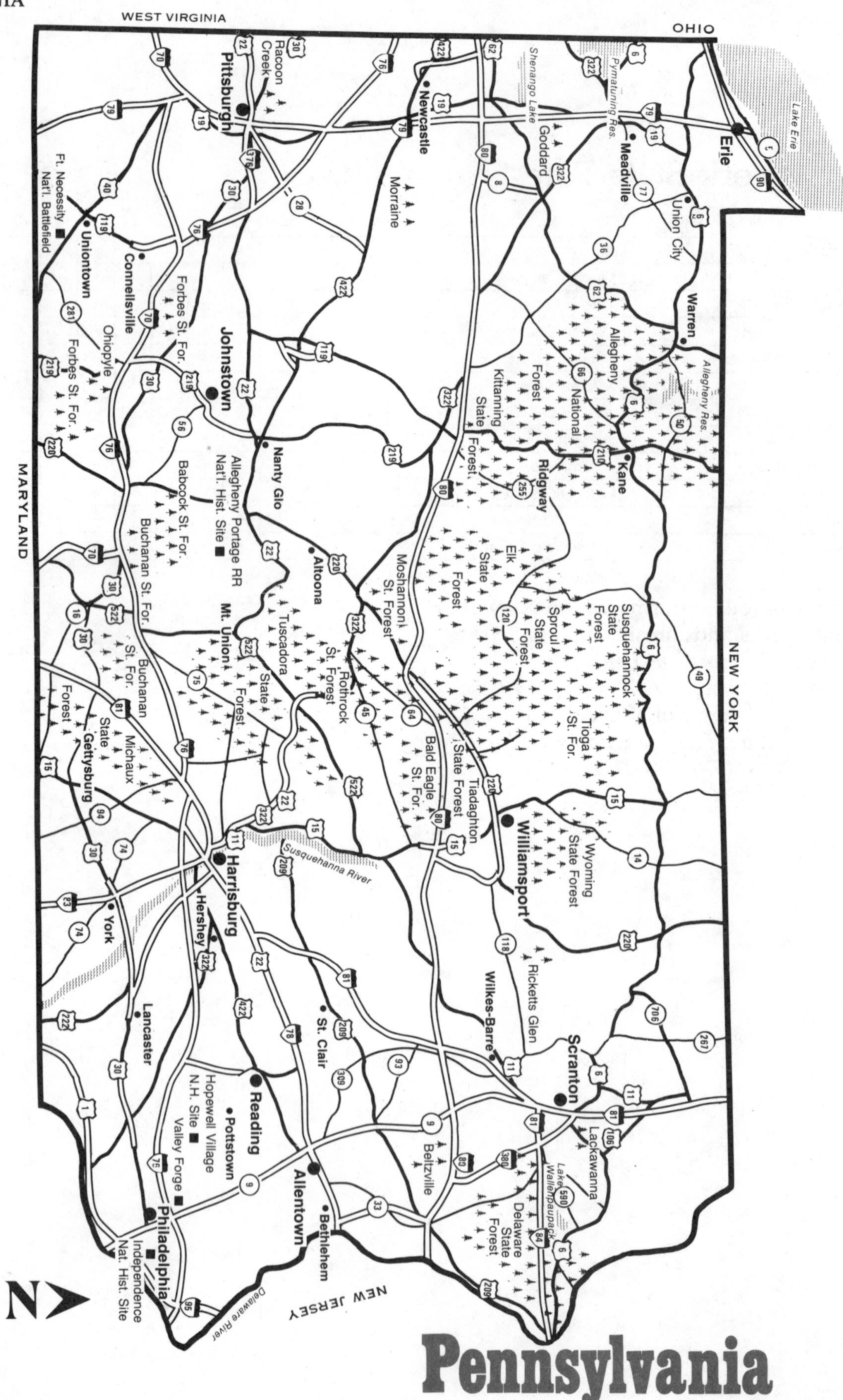

Map not to exact scale.

Pennsylvania

Pennsylvania earned the title "Keystone State" by virtue of its central location among the original 13 colonies. Today, as an important economic center and a vital link between the East and the states of the central U.S., it continues to live up to its nickname.

In the early 17th century, claim to the territory of Pennsylvania was disputed among the English, Dutch and Swedes. Henry Hudson established the Dutch claim, John Cabot, the English; and Peter Minuit, with the founding of Fort Christina, the Swedish. The Dutch briefly came to prominence in 1655 with the capture of Fort Christina, but they were forced to give way to the English with the fall of New Amsterdam in 1664. In less than two decades, the English once again relinquished control of the region when William Penn was given a grant to the territory in return for a debt of 16,000 pounds owed to his father by the British crown. Penn and his descendants remained in control of the area until 1776 when, despite a heavy Quaker population, the region was caught up in the events of the American Revolution — a war in which Pennsylvania played a pivotal role. The Declaration of Independence was signed at Independence Hall in Philadelphia; two Continental Congresses were also held there; Washington's army wintered at Valley Forge, and Betsy Ross is said to have crafted the nation's first flag in her Philadelphia home.

Given the importance of Pennsylvania in the founding of the nation, one would expect to find a lot of history here and, indeed, there are numerous reminders of the struggle for independence in and around the Philadelphia area. But there are also a great many other historical sites to be explored — Daniel Boone's Homestead; William Penn's home, Pennsbury Manor; Brandywine Battlefield, the site of one of Washington's worst defeats and the scene of the Civil War's bloodiest battle, Gettysburg. Certainly one of the most

Full name: Commonwealth of Pennsylvania
Origin of name: In honor of William Penn, father of the founder.
Motto: Virtue, Liberty and Independence.
Nickname: Keystone State
Capital: Harrisburg
Statehood: December 12, 1787, second state.
Population: 11,785,00 (ranks fourth).
Major Cities: Philadelphia (1,815,808), Pittsburgh (458,651), Erie (127,895).
Bird: Ruffed grouse
Flower: Mountain laurel
Tree: Hemlock

Average daily temperature by month

	Northwestern	Southeastern
Jan.	34.8 to 16.9	40.4 to 20.1
Feb.	36.7 to 16.9	43.2 to 21.9
Mar.	45.5 to 24.8	52.0 to 29.5
Apr.	59.9 to 35.2	65.1 to 38.9
May	70.5 to 44.0	75.0 to 48.3
Jun.	79.0 to 53.4	83.5 to 57.7
Jul.	82.8 to 57.5	87.5 to 62.3
Aug.	81.3 to 56.3	85.6 to 60.5
Sept.	75.0 to 49.8	79.1 to 53.9
Oct.	64.4 to 39.6	68.1 to 42.1
Nov.	49.8 to 31.6	55.2 to 33.3
Dec.	38.2 to 22.5	43.8 to 24.7
Year	59.8 to 37.4	64.9 to 41.1

fascinating areas of the state is the "Pennsylvania Dutch" country, where you'll encounter 19th-century farms, horsedrawn carriages and the plain lifestyle of the Amish. For those who enjoy outdoor activities, Pennsylvania has a number of outstanding state parks and forests that offer excellent camping facilities, hiking and backpacking trails, fishing and hunting and a host of winter pursuits.

Mining has long been one of the most important staples of the Pennsylvania economy, and it remains the nation's number-one producer of hard coal. The state also produces one-fourth of the country's steel, as well as other fabricated metals, chemicals and food products. Tourism also ranks as one of the state's most important activities.

State Offices

Tourism
Bureau of Travel Development
Pennsylvania Department of Commerce
431 South Office Building
Harrisburg, Pennsylvania 17120
(717) 787-3003

State Police
Department of Public Safety
1800 Elmerton Avenue
Harrisburg, Pennsylvania 17120
(717) 783-5599

Radio Stations

Philadelphia
WDAS 105.3 (FM)
WZZD 990 (AM)
WRCP 1540 (AM)

Pittsburgh
WPEZ 94.5 (FM)
WKTQ 1320 (AM)

An incongruous, but pleasant, sight in the 1980s is this horse-drawn buggy entering a covered bridge in Lancaster County, Pennsylvania.

Highlight

Pennsylvania's Chester County

Tucked in a quiet corner of Pennsylvania, Chester County's half-million acres are intersected with major highways such as the Pennsylvania Turnpike, U.S. Routes 1, 30, 202 and nearby Interstate 95. Regardless of the direction you're heading, a stop of a day or two in historic Chester County is convenient as well as rewarding.

Some areas of Chester County have not changed in the nearly 300 years since William Penn first named it in 1682. Other areas are totally modern, offering every type of tourist attraction imaginable. Yet this delightfully pleasant mixture of the old and the new is completely accessible via most major travel routes.

The diversity of Chester County attractions truly offers something for everyone. And the Chester County Tourist Bureau is anxious to provide you with all the information necessary to make your stay as enjoyable as possible.

Walking in the footsteps of the patriots at Valley Forge . . . enjoying the enriching experience of a fine art museum . . . or simply camping somewhere in the county's 1,300 acres of public parks . . . you'll find Chester County to be a tourist's dream. One of the few places in the Boston to Washington corridor that is still green, beautiful and inviting.

HISTORY. Step back in time to the major focal points of the Revolutionary War: The Battle of the Brandywine; the Paoli Massacre; the Battle of the Clouds; and Valley Forge where the American army faced its severest test. Hear again the echoing thunder of cannon produced in the furnaces of Hopewell and Warwick. Envision the sick and wounded brought together at the hospital at Yellow Springs. Visit the virtually unchanged farms that supplied the sustenance to keep the Revolution alive. For the interested traveler or the traveling scholar, Chester County is steeped in our nation's history.

CULTURE. Museums, art centers, theaters, horticultural displays and antique shops are but a few of the fascinating stops for the culturally-minded tourist in Chester County. Each one highlights the rich heritage of yesteryear or the cultural fullness of American life today. From Longwood Gardens, one of the world's most famous horticultural achievements, to quaint villages reflecting a quieter time, Chester County is an educational experience for the whole family.

NATURAL BEAUTY. For those who love the outdoors, Chester County has no equal. These half-million acres offer the tourist a year-round festival of outdoor activities. Skiing and tobogganing in the winter and camping, hiking or just plain sightseeing throughout the rest of the year. Chester County alone has more campgrounds than all other southeastern Pennsylvania counties combined.

On fields such as these at Gettysburg, Lee's Army of Northern Virginia met Meade's Army of the Potomac in three days of furious fighting that caused combined casualties of 37,500 men, and dealt a mortal blow to the Confederate cause.

GETTYSBURG NATIONAL MILITARY PARK

The three days of fighting at Gettysburg in 1863 are history. Much has been written and said about this, the greatest battle of the Civil War, and many are the treasured artifacts collected in museums here and across the country. But the most tangible link to Gettysburg's past is the battleground itself.

Upon these peacefully tilled Pennsylvania fields, more men fell than in any other battle fought in North America before or since. Many of the soldiers are buried here in the National Cemetery where Lincoln delivered that simple, poignant statement of purpose, the Gettysburg Address.

Come walk the sun-flooded fields and shaded groves of trees. Climb the knobby hills and the Round Tops and let Gettysburg Battlefield stir in you powerful visions of the past. The names and regimental numbers on hundreds of monuments in the park may be unfamiliar to us today. But these statues in stone and bronze still echo the sentiments of North and South, enobling the sacrifice of soldiers who gave what Lincoln called "the last full measure of devotion."

The Battle In Brief

In the spring of 1863, General Robert E. Lee reorganized the Army of Northern Virginia into three infantry corps and began marching westward from Fredericksburg, Virginia, through the gaps of the Blue Ridge, then northward into Maryland and Pennsylvania. For a second time in less than a year, Lee was carrying the war to Northern soil. His first invasion had been turned back at the Battle of Antietam.

President Lincoln, learning that Lee's army was moving again, ordered the

Army of the Potomac to follow. Lee was prevented from knowing precisely the enemy's whereabouts because his cavalry had gone on a brash raid around the Union Army and was unable to rejoin the others. Advance columns of Confederate troops were already at Carlisle and York when Lee finally learned that Major-General George G. Meade's entire force was close at hand. By chance the two armies touched at Gettysburg when a Confederate brigade sent there for supplies observed a forward column of Meade's cavalry.

The next day, **July 1**, the great battle opened with Confederate troops attacking Union troops on McPherson Ridge, west of town. Outnumbered, the Union forces managed to hold until afternoon when they were overpowered and driven back through town. In the confusion, thousands of Union soldiers were captured before they could rally on Cemetery Hill, south of town. Long into the night Union troops labored over their defenses while the bulk of Meade's army arrived and took positions.

On **July 2**, the battle lines were drawn up in two sweeping arcs. The main portions of both armies were nearly one mile apart on two parallel ridges, Union forces on Cemetery Ridge facing Confederate forces on Seminary Ridge to the west. Lee ordered an attack against both Union flanks. James Longstreet's thrust on the Union left broke through D. E. Sickles' advance lines at the Peach Orchard, left the Wheatfield strewn with dead and wounded, and turned the base of Little Round Top into a shambles. R. S. Ewell's attack proved futile against the entrenched Union right on East Cemetery Hill and Culp's Hill.

On **July 3**, Lee's artillery opened a bombardment that for a time engaged the massed guns of both sides in a thundering duel for supremacy, but did little to soften up the Union center on Cemetery Ridge. Then, in a desperate attempt to recapture the partial success of the preceding day, some 12,000 Confederate troops under George Pickett charged across the open field toward the Union center. Raked by artillery and rifle fire, Pickett's men reached but failed to break the Union line; only one in three retreated to safety.

The Confederate army that staggered back from the fight at Gettysburg was physically and spiritually exhausted. Lee would never again attempt an offensive operation of such proportions. Meade, though he was criticized for not immediately pursuing Lee's army, had carried the day in the battle that has become known as the High Water Mark of the Confederacy.

Exploring the Battlefield

An absorbing historical experience awaits those who want to tour the battlefield at their own pace. Both a one-hour walking tour leading to Meade's Headquarters and the High Water Mark and a two- to three-hour auto tour covering the entire park start from the visitor center. The text and map that follow describe the auto tour.

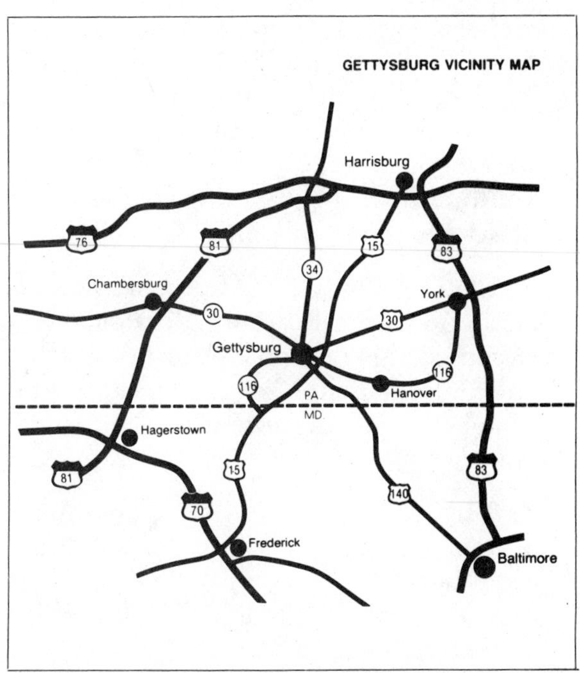

1. HIGH WATER MARK. Here at the Copse of Trees and The Angle, Pickett's Charge was halted on July 3. This was the climax at Gettysburg.

2. PENNSYLVANIA MEMORIAL. On a field noted for its monuments, this one is outstanding. Statues of officers and bronze nameplates call the roll of nearly 35,000 Pennsylvanians who fought here.

3. LITTLE ROUND TOP. Longstreet's attack on July 2 foundered on the rocky slopes of this hill. Quick action by Meade's chief engineer, General Gouverneur Warren, saved Little Round Top for the Union army and foiled hopes for early victory.

4. DEVIL'S DEN. Longstreet's July 2 attack cleared Union troops from these boulders. Confederate sharpshooters, one of whose barricades can still be seen, fired on Little Round Top from here.

5. THE WHEATFIELD. Diamonds, Maltese crosses, and trefoils on monuments mark this ground as the field of battle of three Union corps defending against Longstreet's onslaught.

6. THE PEACH ORCHARD. On July 2, General Sickles' Union salient extended from Devil's Den to here, then angled northward on the Emmitsburg Road. Federal batteries from the high ground here bombarded Confederates to the south and west before Longstreet's attack shattered this line.

7. PITZER WOODS. After a skirmish at noon on July 2, the Confederates occupied these woods. Four hours later they attacked and smashed Sickles' line along the road three-tenths of a mile to the east.

8. VIRGINIA MEMORIAL. General Lee watched the gallant charge of July 3 from here. And when it failed, he rode forward to the fields in front of you and rallied his men.

9. NORTH CAROLINA MEMORIAL. Along and in front of this ridge, Lee marshaled his forces, among them thousands of North Carolinians, for the supreme effort on July 3.

10. McPHERSON RIDGE. Just beyond McPherson's barn, the Battle of Gettysburg began early on July 1. General John F. Reynolds, whose Union infantry held this line, was killed in the woods to the left.

11. ETERNAL LIGHT PEACE MEMORIAL. This memorial was dedicated in 1938, 75th anniversary of the battle, to "Peace Eternal in a Nation United." Arrival of General Rodes' Confederate division on this hill at 1 p.m. on July 1 threatened Federal forces west and north of Gettysburg.

12. OAK RIDGE. Union troops here held stubbornly against Rodes' advance from Oak Hill to the north on the afternoon of July 1.

The Betsy Ross House is called the "Birthplace of Old Glory," for it is here that the Philadelphia seamstress is said to have made the first American flag.

13. BARLOW KNOLL. When Jubal Early's Confederates smashed Union defenders here on the afternoon of July 1, the Union line north of Gettysburg collapsed.

From Barlow Knoll, take US-15 toward Gettysburg to the point where it curves right. Just past the curve, turn left on Stratton Street. Continue to East Middle Street, then turn left and drive east one block to East Confederate Avenue (Liberty Street). Turn right on East Confederate Avenue and proceed to Culp's Hill.

14. CULP'S HILL. At dusk on July 2 Johnson's Confederates unsuccessfully attacked Union troops on Culp's Hill (ahead), advancing over the fields to your left.

15. SPANGLER'S SPRING. Though repulsed at Culp's Hill, the Confederates seized this spring and the Union earthworks north of it, only to lose them the next morning.

16. CEMETERY HILL. Here Union troops rallied late on July 1. The next evening they repelled a Confederate assault that reached the crest of the hill east of this road.

17. NATIONAL CEMETERY. Soldiers' National Monument, commemorating Union dead who fell here, stands on the spot where President Lincoln delivered his Gettysburg Address.

This concludes the auto tour except for the important site at *East Cavalry Battlefield,* three miles east of Gettysburg on Pa. 116. Here Union cavalry under General D. M. Gregg intercepted and defeated J. E. B. Stuart's cavalry.

You can help make your visit and the visit of those who come after you safe and enjoyable by observing the following rules: SPEED LIMIT is 25 mph (15 mph in crowded areas); PARK only on the avenues and in designated parking areas — please do not drive on the grass; DO NOT CLIMB on cannons and monuments; PICNIC only in designated areas; HELP PRESERVE all natural and historical features.

Gettysburg National Cemetery

Both armies marched away from Gettysburg in the rain, July 5, 1863. They left behind more than 51,000 killed, wounded and missing, a community in shambles — and a legend. Even before the dead could be interred in temporary graves, sightseers came to Gettysburg to view the carnage of the war's most devastating battle.

The hasty and inadequate burial of the dead particularly distressed Pennsylvania's governor, Andrew Curtin, and a local attorney, David Wills. Curtin authorized Wills to purchase battlefield land for a cemetery, and within six weeks reinterment had begun (on 17 acres that became Gettysburg National Cemetery).

Because of the epic proportions of the battle, it was thought fitting to consecrate the grounds with appropriate ceremonies. The choice of Edward Everett as principal speaker signaled an event of great dignity, for Everett was the outstanding orator of his day. He was invited well in advance of the date, November 19, to allow him time to prepare his address. President Abraham Lincoln and a number of other national figures were invited, too. And when those in charge of the ceremonies learned that Lincoln indeed would attend, Wills sent him a personal invitation, requesting that he dedicate the cemetery with "a few appropriate remarks."

Throngs filled the town the day before the ceremony, and the next morning thousands more poured in. The procession to the cemetery commenced at noon to the playing of funeral music. A prayer was offered. Then Everett arose, surveyed for a moment the distant South Mountain range, and for nearly two hours delivered a fine classical oration. President Lincoln next arose and spoke in two minutes the 10 sentences that stand as one of the nation's noblest utterances.

If Everett by a learned address, rich in historical and classical allusions, lent stateliness to the occasion, Lincoln by his few remarks came closer to the central idea. He asked his audience to remember not the soldiers' deeds in combat, but to recall the reasons for which they fought. The words of the Gettysburg Address captured the national spirit by giving meaning to the sacrifice of the dead and an inspiration to the living. —PJF

For additional information on Gettysburg and Gettysburg National Military Park, write:
Director,
Gettysburg Travel Council
(Information Center)
35 Carlisle Street
Gettysburg, Pennsylvania 17325
or
Superintendent
Gettysburg National Military Park
Gettysburg, Pennsylvania 17325

Pennsylvania Points of Interest and Attractions

(Note: Refer to shaded maps for regional location of points of interest and attractions.)

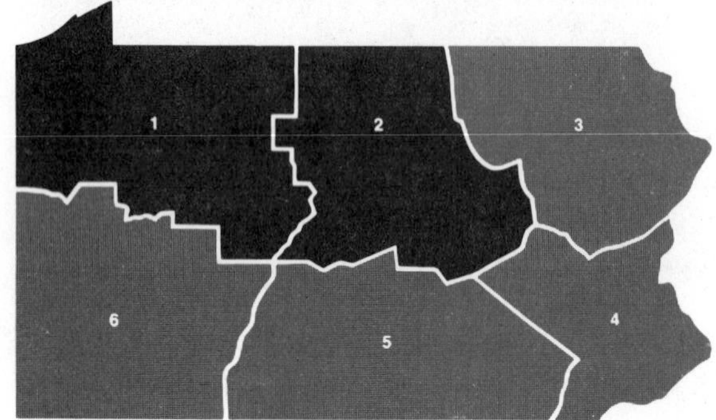

Region 1

Fairyland Forest. Hundreds of live animals; Mother Goose characters in picture-book setting. Open daily, Memorial Day through Labor Day; weekends, May and September through mid-October. Conneaut Lake Park, off US-6.

Region 2

Animaland. Hundreds of tame wild animals and exotic birds, plus a pit of rattlesnakes; herd of buffalo; mountain lions; elk; black bear; llamas. Gift shop and picnic area. Open April through October, 8 a.m. to dusk. Wellsboro, off State Route 660.

Clyde Peeling's Reptiland. Tour the fascinating world of reptiles with professional guides; gift shop; snack bar. Open May 15 through September 15; weekends, September 15 through October. Allenwood, off Interstate 80 (exit 30N), on US-15. (717) 538-1869.

Penn's Cave. America's only all-water cavern. Ride through colorful, well-lighted caverns onto Lake Nitanee on a 50-minute tour. Centre Hall, off Interstate 80, on State Route 192. (814) 364-1664.

Woodward Cave. Largest cavern in Pennsylvania, 400 million years old; two levels; miniature lake. Fall facility campground; gift shop; picnic area. Open year-round. Woodward, off Interstate 80 (exit 23), on State Route 45. (814) 349-5185.

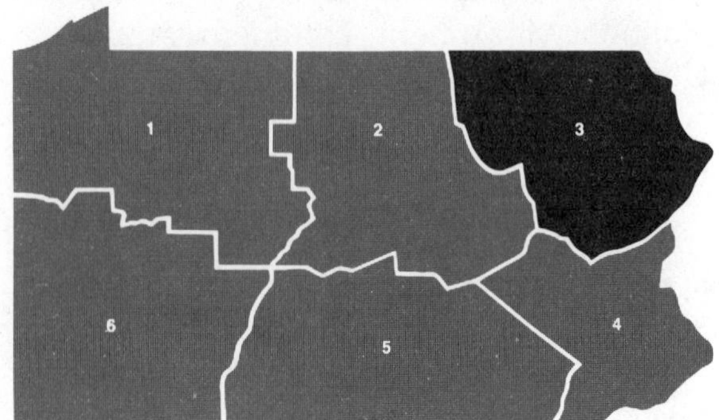

Region 3

Bushkill Falls. "The Niagara of Pennsylvania," famous for its natural beauty; marked nature trails, picnic grounds, boating, fishing; gift and craft shops; restaurant. Open April through November, 8 a.m. to dusk. Bushkill, off State Route 209.

Claws 'N Paws Wild Animal Park. More than 100 animals; bears, wolves, monkeys, etc. Wooded trails; animal petting area; picnic grounds. Open May through October, daily. Lake Wallenpaupack, off Interstate 84, on State Route 507. (717) 698-6154.

Memorytown, USA. Largest country store in the East; hex shop; wax museum; Christmas shop; restaurant; print shop. Open year-round. Mt. Pocono, between State Routes 611 and 940. (717) 839-7176.

Pennsylvania Dutch Farm. "Amish Life" program; tours of farm; Pennsylvania Dutch foods; jellies; gift shop. Open spring through fall, daily. Mt. Pocono, off US-81E. (717) 839-7960.

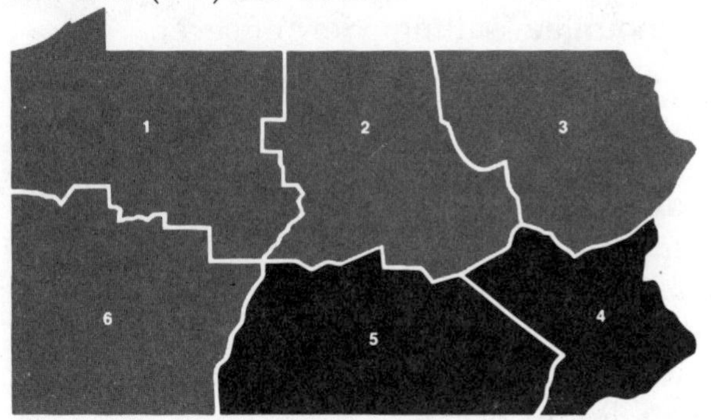

Region 4

Crystal Cave. Discovered in 1871, Crystal Cave is noted for its unique formations; guided tours; gift shop. Open Washington's Birthday to October 31, daily. Kutztown, off US-222.

Koziar's Christmas Village. An entire valley set aglow with Christmas lights; fairy-tale scenes; gift shop; musical walkways. Open year-round, nightly. Bernville, off Interstate 78. (215) 488-1110.

Roadside America. Largest miniature village of Americana; electrically lighted and operated. Open year-round. Shartlesville, off US-22.

Region 5

Amish Farm and House. Guided tour through 10-room Amish house, lecture on Amish way of life; complete farm operation. Open year-round, daily. Lancaster, off US-30, on Lincoln Highway, East.

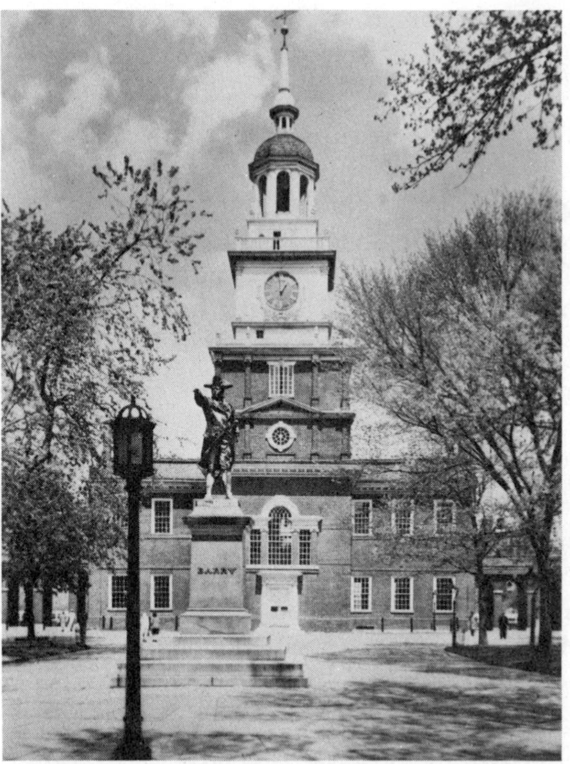

Based on a plan by Andrew Hamilton, Philadelphia's Independence Hall was originally constructed in 1732. It was here that the Declaration of Independence was adopted on July 4, 1976. After the war the hall became the site of the Constitutional Convention, which in 1787 hammered out the document under which the nation has been governed ever since.

Amish Homestead. Authentic farm actually occupied and farmed by an Old Order Amish family; gift shop. Open year-round, daily; summer, 9 a.m. to 8 p.m.; fall and winter, 9 a.m. to 5 p.m. Lancaster, three miles east off US-462.

Choo Choo Barn. Handcrafted model railroad and animated miniature Dutch village; 32 years in construction. Open May through October, daily; April and November, weekends. Strasburg, off State Route 741.

East Broad Top Railroad. Rides on the last operating narrow-gauge steam railroad east of the Mississippi. Open July through

August, daily; June, September, October, weekends. (Registered National Historic Landmark.) Oribsonia, off State Route 522.

Hershey. Tourist attractions abound in "Chocolate Town, USA," and these include Hersheypark, Hershey's Chocolate World, the Hershey Museum and the Hershey Rose Garden. For additional information, write: Hershey Information Center, Hershey, Pennsylvania 17033.

Indian Caverns. Scenic caverns, massive rock formations, Indian history. Open year-round, 9 a.m. to dusk. Spruce Creek, on State Route 45. (814) 632-7575.

Indian Echo Caverns. Magnificent crystal formations, cavern room where hermit Amos Wilson lived from 1802 to 1821, picnic area. Open April 1 through November 1, daily. Hummelston, at junction of US-322 and 422.

International Village. Sixty-six Old World shops; restaurants; theater; campground; recreation facilities, including boating, fishing, bicycling and tennis. Gettysburg, on State Route 15S. (717) 334-8383.

Lincoln Caverns. Two crystal caves; picnic area; gift shop. Open May 1 through October 31, daily; April and November, weekends. Huntingdon, on US-22. (717) 766-4714.

Pennsylvania Dutch Tourist Bureau. Visit historic Lancaster County; information on attractions, maps, exhibits. Open year-round, daily. Lancaster, 1800 Hempstead Road, on US-30.

Railroad Model Showcase. Displays of handcarved wooden trains; located adjacent to Dutch Haven shops. Tours and guides available. Open year-round, daily. Lancaster, eight miles east, on US-30. (717) 687-7611.

Strasburg Railroad. Ride America's oldest short-line railroad through Lancaster County's colorful Amish country. Open year-round; trains run daily, May through October; weekends, remainder of year. Strasburg, on State Route 741.

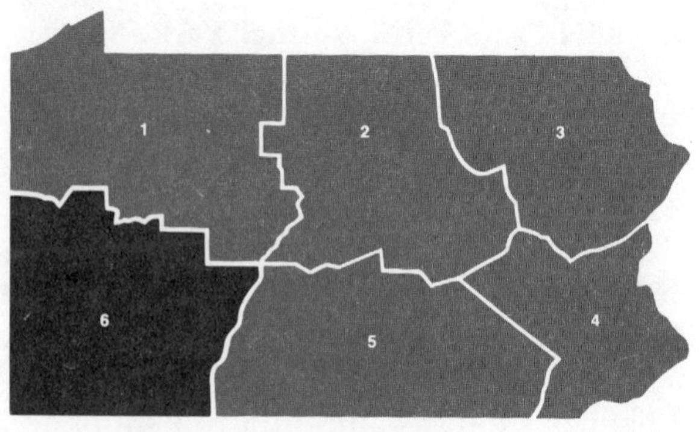

Region 6

Inclined Plane Railway. Ride up steep mountainside, view site of famous Johnstown flood from observation platform at top. Johnstown, off US-219.

Laurel Caverns. Large and colorful caverns in mountain setting; view of seven counties; trackless train ride; restaurant; gift shop. Open year-round, daily. Uniontown, on State Route 40.

Valley Mine. Soft coal mine open to visitors; ride electric cars to mine face deep under Allegheny Mountains. Open May 15 through September 30, daily; April and October, weekends only. Patton, on State Route 36.

NORTHWEST
NORTH CENTRAL
NORTH EAST
SOUTH WEST
SOUTH CENTRAL
SOUTH EAST

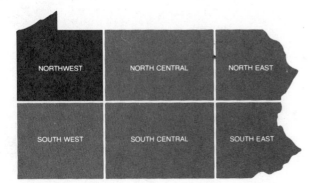

Pennsylvania State Parks
Northwest

Park	Location	CAMPING	PICNICKING	CONCESSIONS	SWIMMING	HIKING	BOATING	FISHING	HUNTING	WINTER SPORTS
Chapman	*Warren. Off US-6.*	•	•	•	•	•	•	•	•	•
Clear Creek	*Brookville. Off State Route 949.*	•	•	•	•	•		•	•	
Cook Forest	*Brookville. Off State Route 36.*	•	•	•	•	•		•	•	•
Maurice K. Goddard	*New Vernon. Off US-79.*		•	•			•	•	•	•
Moraine	*Prospect. At junction of US-422 and 79.*		•	•	•	•	•	•	•	•
Presque Isle	*Erie. Off US-79.*		•	•	•	•	•	•	•	•
Pymatuning	*Turnersville. Off US-322.*	•	•	•	•	•	•	•	•	•

Wearing a simple dress made of homespun flax, an Amish child learns to enjoy the spartan pleasures of farm life in Lancaster County, Pennsylvania, where the members of her sect first settled in 1727.

NORTHWEST
NORTH CENTRAL
NORTH EAST
SOUTH WEST
SOUTH CENTRAL
SOUTH EAST

Northcentral

Park	Location	CAMPING	PICNICKING	CONCESSIONS	SWIMMING	HIKING	BOATING	FISHING	HUNTING	WINTER SPORTS
Bald Eagle	*Howard. Off US-220.*	•	•			•	•	•	•	•
Bendigo	*Johnsonburg. Off US-219.*		•	•	•			•		
Cherry Springs	*Cherry Springs. At junction of State Route 44 and Lyman Road.*	•	•							•
Colton Point	*Ansonia. Off US-6.*	•	•			•				•
Curwensville	*Bloomington. Off State Route 879.*		•	•	•	•	•	•	•	
Denton Hill	*Walton. Off US-6.*		•	•		•			•	
Elk	*Johnsonburg. Off US-219.*	•	•			•	•	•	•	•
Hills Creek	*Mansfield. Off US-6.*	•	•	•	•	•	•	•		•
Hyner Run	*Hyner. Off State Route 120.*	•	•	•	•	•	•	•		•
Hyner View	*Renovo. Off State Route 120.*		•							•
Kettle Creek	*Renovo. Off State Route 120.*	•	•	•	•	•	•	•	•	
Leonard Harrison	*Wellsboro. Off State Route 660.*	•	•	•		•		•	•	
Little Pine	*Waterville. Off State Route 44.*	•	•		•	•	•	•	•	•
Ole Bull	*Oleona. Off State Route 144.*	•	•		•	•		•	•	
Parker Dam	*Penfield. Off State Route 153.*	•	•	•	•	•	•	•	•	•
Patterson	*Sweden Valley. Off US-6.*	•	•			•				
Prouty Place	*Sweden Valley. Off US-6.*	•	•			•		•		
S.B. Elliot	*Anderson Creek. Off Interstate 80 (exit 18).*	•	•			•				
Sinnemahoning	*Sinnemahoning. Off State Route 872.*	•	•		•	•	•	•	•	•
Sizerville	*Emporium. Off State Route 155.*	•	•	•	•	•			•	
World's End	*Forksville Off State Route 154.*	•	•	•	•	•		•	•	

Northeast

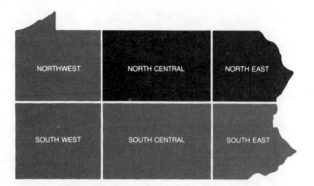

Park	Location	CAMPING	PICNICKING	CONCESSIONS	SWIMMING	HIKING	BOATING	FISHING	HUNTING	WINTER SPORTS
Bruce Lake	*Canadensis. Off State Route 390.*					•		•	•	
Frances Slocum	*Dallas. Off State Route 309.*		•	•	•	•	•	•		•
Hickory Run	*Hickory Run. Off Pennsylvania Turnpike (exit 35).*	•	•	•	•	•		•	•	•
Promised Land	*Canadensis. Off State Route 390.*	•	•	•	•	•	•	•	•	•
Ricketts Glen	*Red Rock. Off State Route 487.*	•	•	•	•	•	•	•	•	•
Tobyhanna	*Goludsboro. Off US-380.*	•	•	•	•	•	•	•	•	•

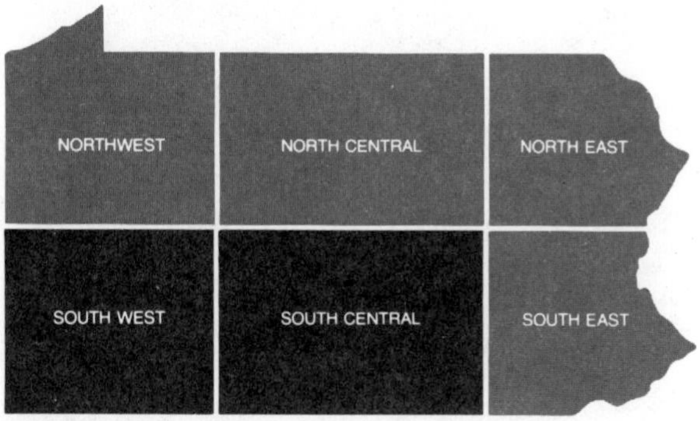

NORTHWEST
NORTH CENTRAL
NORTH EAST
SOUTH WEST
SOUTH CENTRAL
SOUTH EAST

Southwest

Park	Location	CAMPING	PICNICKING	CONCESSIONS	SWIMMING	HIKING	BOATING	FISHING	HUNTING	WINTER SPORTS
Crooked Creek	*Ford City. Off State Route 66.*	•	•	•	•	•	•	•	•	•
Keystone	*New Alexandria. Off State Route 981.*	•	•	•	•	•	•	•	•	•
Kooser	*Somerset. Off State Route 31.*	•	•	•	•	•		•		
Laurel Hill	*Trent. Off State Route 31.*	•	•	•	•	•	•	•	•	•
Laurel Mountain	*Jennerstown. Off US-30.*			•						•
Ohiopyle	*Ohiopyle. Off State Route 381.*	•	•	•		•		•	•	
Ryerson Station	*Waynesburg. Off State Route 31.*	•	•	•	•	•	•	•	•	•

Southcentral

Park	Location	CAMPING	PICNICKING	CONCESSIONS	SWIMMING	HIKING	BOATING	FISHING	HUNTING	WINTER SPORTS
Black Moshannon	*Philipsburg. Off State Route 504.*	•	•	•	•	•	•	•	•	•
Blue Knob	*Pavia. Off Blue King Road.*	•	•	•	•	•		•	•	•
Caledonia	*Caledonia. Off US-30.*	•	•	•	•	•		•		
Codorous	*Hanover. Off State Route 116.*	•	•	•	•	•	•	•	•	•
Colonel Denning	*Doubling Gap. Off State Route 233.*	•	•	•	•	•		•	•	•
Cowans Gap	*Knobsville. Off US-522.*	•	•	•	•	•	•	•	•	•
Fowlers Hollow	*Germantown. State Route 274.*	•	•			•		•		
Gifford Pinchot	*Rossville. Off State Route 177.*	•	•	•	•	•	•	•	•	•
Greenwood Furnace	*Greenwood Furnace. Off State Route 305.*	•	•	•	•	•		•		•
Penn Roosevelt	*Milroy. Off US-322.*	•	•			•		•		
Pine Grove Furnace	*Carlisle. Off State Route 233.*	•	•	•	•	•	•	•	•	•
Poe Paddy	*Potter Mills. Off US-322.*	•	•			•		•		
Poe Valley	*Lewistown. Off US-322.*	•	•	•	•	•	•	•	•	•
Prince Gallitzin	*Flinton. Off State Route 53.*	•	•	•	•	•	•	•	•	•
Shawnee	*Bedford. Off US-30.*	•	•	•	•	•	•	•	•	•
Trough Creek	*Marklesburg. Off State Route 994.*	•	•			•		•	•	

Southeast

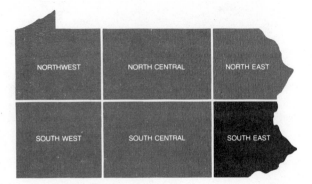

Park	Location	CAMPING	PICNICKING	CONCESSIONS	SWIMMING	HIKING	BOATING	FISHING	HUNTING	WINTER SPORTS
Beltzville	*Parryville. Off US-209.*		•	•	•	•	•	•	•	•
French Creek	*Birdsboro. Off State Route 422.*	•	•	•	•	•	•	•	•	•
Locust Lake	*Pottsville. Off Interstate 81.*	•			•	•	•	•	•	•
Nockamixon	*Quakertown. Off State Route 313.*		•	•		•	•	•	•	•
Tuscarora	*Barnesville. Off State Route 54.*		•	•	•	•	•	•	•	•

Pennsylvania state forests are integrated with the state parks. For additional information on Pennsylvania state parks and forests, contact: *Department of Environmental Resources, State Office Building, Harrisburg, Pennsylvania 17120, (717) 787-6640.*

Eastern Region Calendar of Events

Spring
(March, April, May)

Delaware

Spring peak of Canada geese and duck migration, Bombay Hook National Wildlife Refuge. March, Smyrna.

Gardens in bloom at Americana Museum. April, Winterthur.

Clothesline Art Fair. April, Wilmington.

Easter Promenade. April, Rehoboth Beach

Spring songbird migration, purple martins' return, Bombay Hook National Wildlife Refuge. April, Smyrna.

Old Dover Day. May, Dover.

Wilmington Flower Market. May, Wilmington.

Wilmington Garden Day. May, Wilmington.

Peak concentrations of shorebirds. Warbler migration, spring wildflowers. Bombay Hook National Wildlife Refuge. May, Smyrna.

Maryland

Maryland House and Garden Pilgrimage. April through May, Baltimore.

Maryland Hunt Cup. April, Glyndon.

Point to Point Steeplechase. April, Glyndon.

Tobacco Auctions. April through June, Upper Marlboro.

Preakness Festival Week. May, Baltimore.

Painters Mills Music Fair at Owings Mills. May through November, Baltimore.

Revolutionary War Days. May, Smallwood.

Heritage Day. May, Bowie.

New Jersey

Flower Show. March, Morristown.

Cherry Blossom Festival. April, Newark.

Cherry Blossom Festival. May, Cherry Hill.

Annual Fishing Contest, Water Works Park. May, Dover.

Flower Show, Boro Hall. May, Haddon Heights.

Loyalty Day Parade. May, Neptune.

Festival of Music. May, Ridgewood.

Marching Band Festival. May, Jackson.

Spring Craft Festival. May, Smithville.

Victorian Fair, Physik Estate. May, Cape May.

Annual Regatta. May, Ventnor.

Annual Fishing Tournament. May, Asbury Park.

New York

Snowmobile Grand Prix. March, Erie.

New York City Flower Show. March, New York City.

St. Patrick's Day Parade. March, New York City.

Antiques Fair. March, New York City.

Antiques Fair. April, White Plains.

Canoe Regatta. May, Bainbridge.

Lilac Time Festival. May, Rochester.

Tulip Festival. May, Albany.

Washington Square Arts Show. May through June, New York City.

Pennsylvania

Pocono Winter Carnival. Tobogganing, snow sculpture, cross-country scavenger hunt. March, Stroudsburg.

Pennsylvania Maple Festival. March, Meyersburg.
Cherry Blossom Festival. April, Wilkes-Barre.
Bach Music Festival, Packer Memorial Chapel, Lehigh University. May, Bethlehem.
Fine Arts Fiesta, Public Square. May, Wilkes-Barre.
National Pike Fiesta. Tours of historic homes, arts and crafts displays and sales. May, Washington.
Northern Appalachian Festival. May, Bedford.
Pittsburgh Folk Festival, Civic Arena. May, Pittsburgh.
Three Rivers Arts Festival. More than 150 theater performances, dance and music. May, Pittsburgh.

Summer
(June, July, August)

Delaware
Delmarva Chicken Festival. June, Salisbury.
Country Fair and Flea Market, Ross Mansion. June, Seaford.
Scottish Games. June, Fair Hill.
Folk Festival. June, Millsboro.
Fireworks and Boat Parade (week-long festival). July, Rehoboth.
Cape Henlopen Craft Fair. July, Lewes.
Delaware State Fair. July, Harrington.
Fort Delaware Pageant. July, Delaware City.
Antique Fair and Flea Market, Historical Complex. August, Lewes.
Arts and Craft Fair, Wilmington Market Street Mall. August, Wilmington.

Maryland
Bell and History Days. June, Frederick.
National Flag Day. June, Baltimore.
Jousting Tournament. August, Easton.
Maryland State Fair. August through September, Lutherville-Timonium.

New Jersey
Horseshoe Pitching Tournament. June, Warinacko Park, Union County.
Pops Concert. June, Ridgewood.
Festival Parade. June, Seaside Heights.
Annual Outdoor Art and Photo Show. June, Hackensack.
Publick Day. June, Mt. Olive Township.
Square Dance Festival, Deserted Village. June, Allaire State Park.
Polish Heritage Festival. June, Holmdel.
Flower Show, Music Pier. June, Ocean City.
Heritage Days Festival. June, Trenton.
Invitational Regatta. June, Stone Harbor.
Miss Seaside Beauty Contest. Ages 17-24. June, Seaside Heights.
International Folk Festival. June, Edison.
Annual Skimmer Weekend. June, Sea Isle City.
Founder's Day Street Fair. June, Toms River.
Irish Festival, Garden State Arts Center. June, Holmdel.
New Jersey Shakespeare Festival (through August). June, Madison.
Concerts Under the Stars. June, Flemington.
Fireworks Celebration, Hamilton Field. July, Dover.
Fireworks Display. July, Long Branch.
Opera in the Park, Thompson Park, Theater Barn. July, Lincroft.
Art Festival, Echo Lake Park. July, Westfield and Mountainside.
Bluefish Tournament. July, Margate.
Sand Sculpting Contest, 12th Street Beach. July, Ocean City.
Miss Cape May County Pageant, Music Pier. July, Ocean City.
Black Heritage Festival, Garden State Arts Center. July, Holmdel.
Spanish Fiesta. August, Long Branch.
Antique Show. August, Margate.
Senior Citizens Pageant. August, Long Branch.
Monmouth County Fair. August, Freehold.
White Marlin Invitational Tournament. August, Beach Haven.

Sailboat Regatta, Sunset Lake. August, Wildwood.

Diaper Changing Contest. August, Asbury Park.

Various Contests. Hermit tree crab race, sand sculpting, beauty pageant. August, Ocean City.

Miss Ocean City Pageant, Music Pier. August, Ocean City.

Annual Boardwalk Art Show. August, Cape May.

Baby Parade and Pageant. August, Asbury Park.

Miss Pigtail Contest, Garden Pier. August, Atlantic City.

Annual Clamshell Pitching Contest. August, Cape May.

Great Falls Festival. August, Paterson.

New York

Northeast Craft Fair. June, Rhinebeck.

Summer Festival of Arts. June, Erie.

Newport Jazz Festival. June, New York City and Saratoga Springs.

1000 Islands Open Skeet Shooting Championships. June, Alexandra Bay.

Old Whalers Festival. June, Sag Harbor.

Outdoor Arts Festival. June, White Plains.

Melody Fair. June through September, Buffalo.

Band Concerts, Canoe and Kayak Races. July, Freeport.

Lake George Opera Festival. July through August, Glen Falls.

Rodeos, every Friday night. July through August, Lake Luzerne.

I Love New York Horse Show. July, Lake Placid.

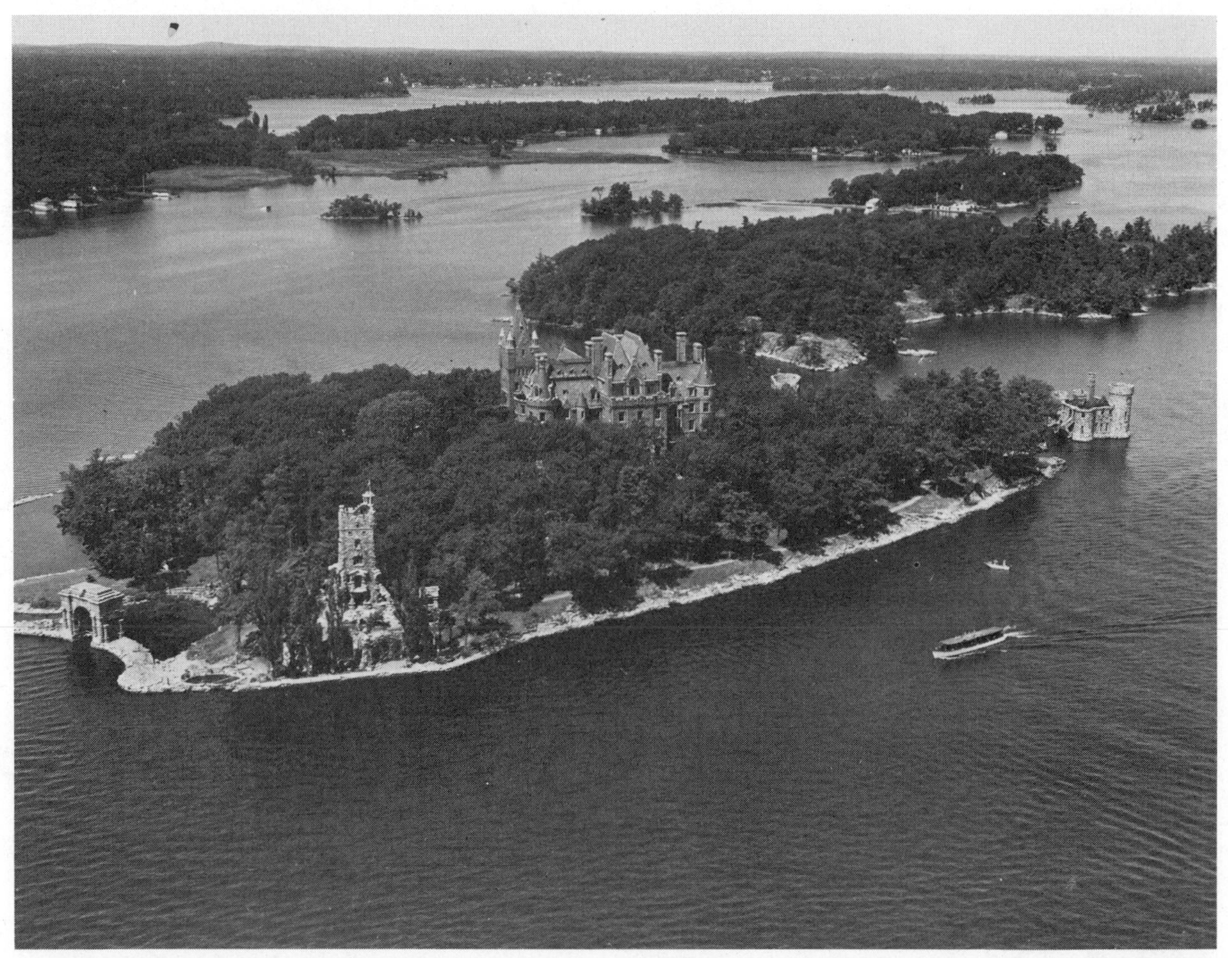

For 75 years, Boldt Castle on Heart Island in the Thousand Islands has been one of the region's most popular tourist attractions. The Thousand Islands-Seaway region of northern New York is noted for water sports including fishing and sightseeing trips on charter boats.

Annual French Festival. July, Cape Vincent.

International Seaway Festival. July, Ogdensburg.

Miss New York State Pageant. July, Buffalo.

Tuscarora Indian Nation Picnic. July, Niagara Falls.

Summer Ski Jump. July, Lake Placid.

Antique Boat Show. August, Clayton.

Central New York Scottish Games. August, Syracuse.

Sunshine Fair. August, Cobleskill.

New York Woodmen's Field Day. August, Boonville.

Dutchess County Fair. August, Rhinebeck.

Annual Country Fair. August, Broadalbin.

Annual Olde Home Daze. August, Caroga Lake.

Annual Barnestown Fair. August, Mayfield.

White Water Canoe and Kayak Race. August, Pulaski.

Alps Festival. August, Catskill.

Heritage Day, August, New Paltz.

Pennsylvania

Philadelphia In The Summer. Wide variety of free entertainment, jazz and pop groups, dancers, Mummers string bands. June, Philadelphia.

Kunstfest. Craft presentation of the early 19th century, demonstrations of cabinet making, candle making, cooking, shoemaking, spinning, weaving, lace making. June, Ambridge.

Pennsylvania State Laurel Festival. June, Wellsboro.

West Penn Laurel Festival. June, Brookville.

Freedom Week. Special events, ceremonies and activities honoring the birth of the nation. July, Philadelphia.

Bavarian Summer Festival. July, Barnesville.

Kutztown Folk Festival. Internationally famous exhibition of Pennsylvania Dutch crafts and arts; ethnic foods. July, Kutztown.

Observance of the Battle of Gettysburg. Activities include memorial services, parade, fireworks. July, Gettysburg.

Pennsylvania Dutch Days. Arts and crafts, quilting parties, spinning and weaving, candle dipping, glass blowing. August, Hershey.

Pennsylvania Guild of Craftsmen State Fair. August, Bedford.

Fall

(September, October, November)

Delaware

Brandywine Arts Festival, Josephine Gardens. September, Wilmington.

Maritime Days and Boat Races. September, Wilmington.

Harvest Festival. September, Milford.

Great Canoe Races. September, Milford.

Delaware Flower Show, Wilmington Mall. September, Wilmington.

Old Willington Days, Willington Square. October, Wilmington.

Winterthur Gardens in Autumn, Winterthur Museum. October, Winterthur.

Fall peak of migration of Canada geese, snow geese, and ducks, Bombay Hook National Wildlife Refuge. November, Smyrna.

Maryland

Blessing of the Fleet. September, St. Mary's City.

National Hard Crab Derby and Fair. September (Labor Day weekend), Crisfield.

Baltimore City Fair. September, Baltimore.

Fall Harvest Days. October, Westminster.

Mummers Parade. October, Hagerstown.

Catoctin Colorfest. October, Thurmont.

Octoberfest. October, Bowie.

New Jersey

Fall Flower Show, Trailside Nature and Science Center. September, Union County Park.

Pitch and Putt Tournament, Ash Brook Golf Course. September, Scotch Plains.
Renaissance Fair, City Park. September, Bridgeton.
Miss America Pageant, Convention Hall. September, Atlantic City.
Heritage Crafts Festival. September, Breille Park.
Hungarian Festival. September, Holmdel.
Scandinavian-American Festival. September, Holmdel.
Seafood Festival. September, Point Pleasant.
Square Dance Festival. September, Allaire State Park.
Championship Cat Show. September, Asbury Park.
Slovak Heritage Festival. September, Holmdel.
German Heritage Festival. September, Holmdel.
Miss Senior Citizen Contest, Convention Hall. September, Atlantic City.
Octoberfest. September, Wildwood.
Harvest Festival. October, Denville.
Harvest Jubilee. October, Clinton.
Colonial Fair. October, Califon.
Halloween Hullabaloo and Witch Hunt. October, Middletown.
Halloween Parade and Carnival. October, Red Bank.
Halloween Parade and Costume Contest. October, Bradley Beach.
Country Homes Tour. November, Sergeantville.
House Tour and Colonial Crafts Festival. November, Sergeantsville.
Annual Junior Miss Pageant. November, Cape May.

New York

Annual Salmon Fishing Festival. September, Pulaski.
Mayor's Cup Soccer Tournament. September, Oneonta.
Crafts Show. September, Cooperstown.
Oktoberfest. September, Rochester.
Figure Skating Operetta. September, Lake Placid.
Thanksgiving Day Parade. November, New York City.

Pennsylvania

Grand Irish Jubilee. Features Irish music and dancing. September, Mahonoy City.
American Ukrainian Festival. Polka bands, ethnic songs and dances. September, Nanticoke.
Polish Festival. Folk dances, Polish foods, exhibits, games, rides, polka bands. September, Doylestown.
Flax Scutching Festival. The art of making linen from flax. September, Stahlstown.
Ligonier Highland Games. Colorful Scottish pageant. September, Altoona.
Pennsylvania Dutch Farm Festival. September, Kempton.
Keystone Country Festival. September, Blair County, between Altoona and Holidaysburg.
McClure Bean Soup Festival. Unique festival started 90 years ago by Civil War veterans; thousands of gallons of bean soup prepared in 35-gallon iron kettles. September, McClure.
Covered Bridge Festival. September, Washington.
Apple Harvest Festival. October, Gettysburg.
Pennsylvania Flaming Foliage Festival. October, Renovo.
Autumn Leaf Festival. October, Clarion.
Fall Foliage Festival. October, Bedford.
Pennsylvania National Horse Show. Largest indoor show in America. October, Harrisburg.
Christmas Celebration. November (Thanksgiving through Christmas), Bethlehem.

Winter

(December, January, February)

Delaware

Christmas in Odessa. December, Odessa.
Red-tailed, marsh and rough-legged hawks in abundance at Bombay Hook National Wildlife Refuge. January, Smyrna.

Pintail duck migration, Bombay Hook National Wildlife Refuge. February, Smyrna.

New Jersey

Children's Christmas Show, Croydon Gym. December, Leonardo.

Christmas Festival. December, Long Branch.

Holly Trail Home Tour. December, Stanton.

Reenactment of the arrival of the Continental Army at Morristown. December, Morristown.

Annual Christmas Parade. More than 100 entries. December, Cape May.

Tree Lighting Ceremony. December, Farmingdale.

Christmas Pageant. December, Asbury Park.

Candlelight Tours, Liberty Village. December, Flemington.

Candlelight House Tours. December, Cape May.

New York

Tree Lighting Ceremony. December, New York City.

Winter Carnival. Snowmobile races, ice hockey. January, Saranac Lake.

Eastern States Speed Skating Championships. January, Saratoga Springs.

ISIA Figure Skating Competitions. January, Lake Placid.

Chinese New Year Celebration. January or February, New York City.

Malone Winter Carnival. February, Malone.

Bobsled Races. February, Lake Placid.

Westminster Kennel Club Show. February, New York City.

Pennsylvania

Army-Navy Football Classic, John F. Kennedy Stadium. December, Philadelphia.

Jaycee Christmas Boulevard. Mile-long display running through main street of town. December, Berwick.

Washington Crossing the Delaware Reenactment. Exact replicas of the Durham boats used by George Washington on Christmas night, 1776. December, Washington Crossing.

Mummers Parade. January (New Year's Day), Philadelphia.

Pennsylvania Farm Show. Annual event that is the showplace for the state's agriculture and agribusiness industry. January, Harrisburg.

U.S. Pro Indoor Tennis Championship. Largest indoor men's tournament in the world. January, Philadelphia.

Pottsville Winter Carnival. January, Pottsville.

Groundhog Day Festivities. The king of the weather prophets performs his annual weather forecasting duties. February, Gobblers Knob, Punxsutawney.

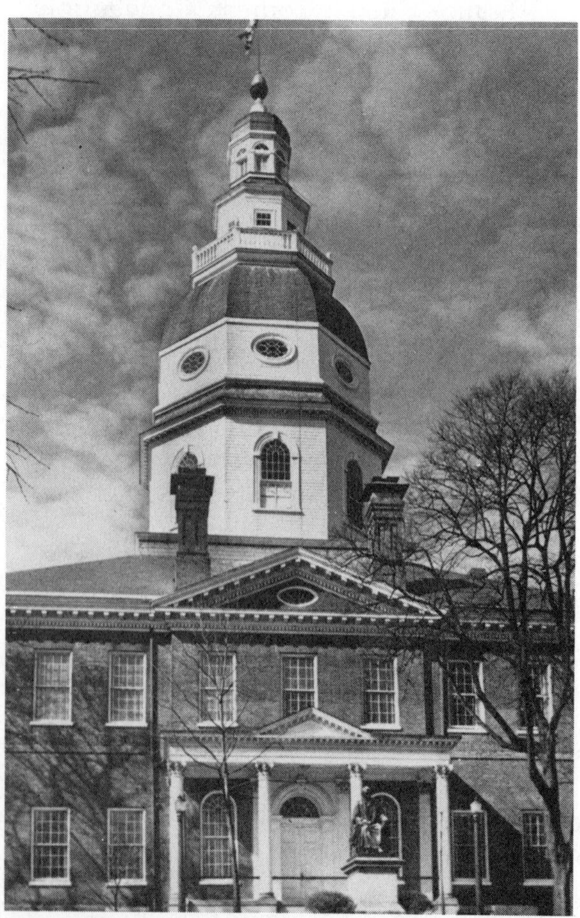

The State House of Maryland is the oldest State House in use and the only one in use that is a Registered National Historic Landmark.

Mt. Vernon
Monticello at Charlottesville
VIRGINIA
WEST VIRGINIA
Shepherdstown Mill
Harpers Ferry
Old Slave Mart
Charlestown
Charleston's Magnolia Gardens
SOUTH CAROLINA
NORTH CAROLINA
Pres. Polk's Birthplace
Pineville, N.C.
Penn Castle
Eureka Springs
U.S.S. North Carolina
Battleship Memorial
ARKANSAS
Ozarks Waterfall

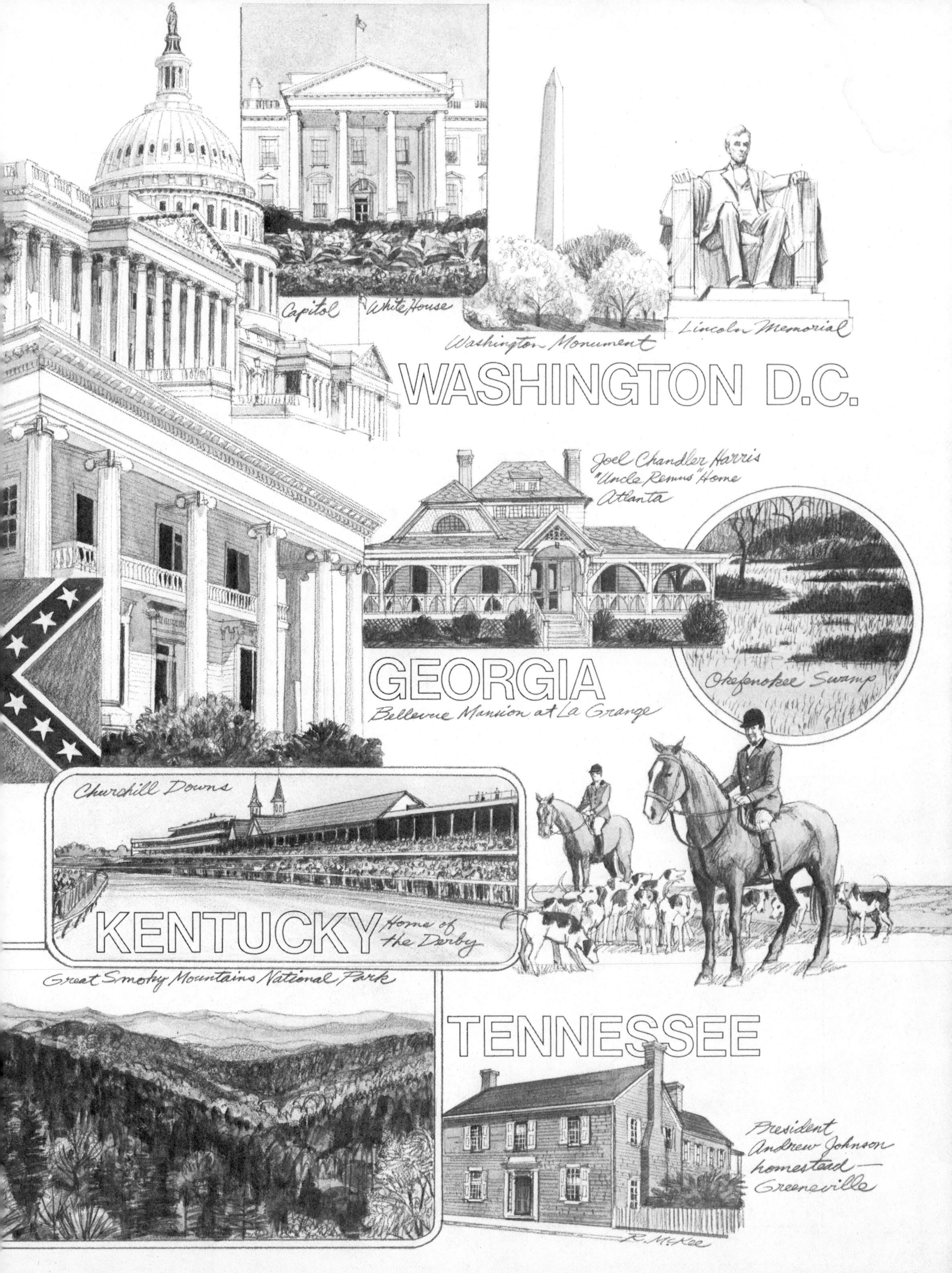

Capitol
White House
Washington Monument
Lincoln Memorial
WASHINGTON D.C.
Joel Chandler Harris
"Uncle Remus" Home
Atlanta
Okefenokee Swamp
GEORGIA
Bellevue Mansion at La Grange
Churchill Downs
KENTUCKY
Home of the Derby
Great Smoky Mountains National Park
TENNESSEE
President
Andrew Johnson
homestead—
Greeneville
R. McKee

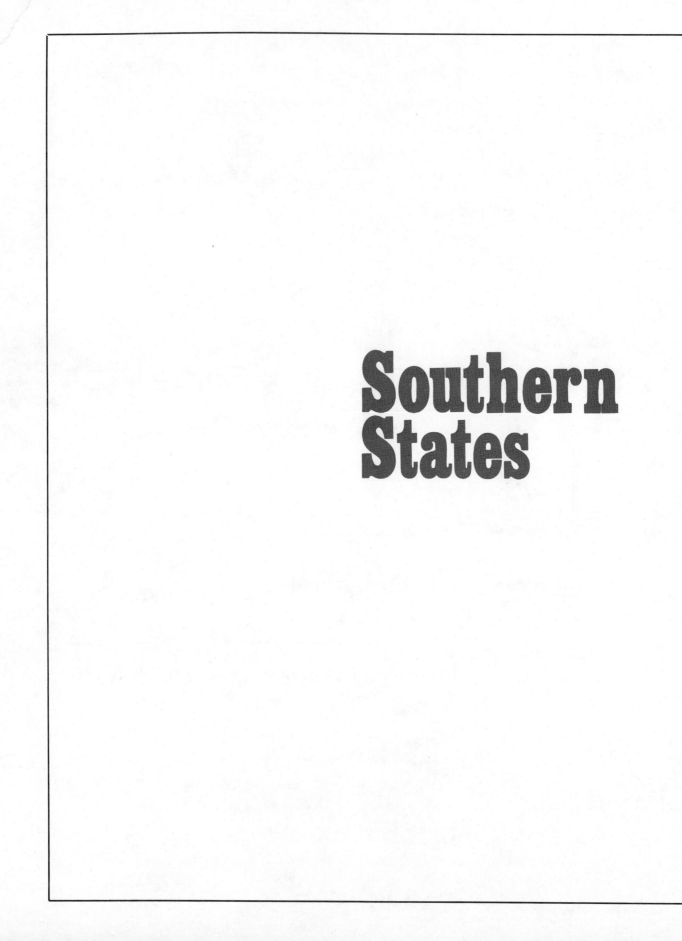

Southern States

The home of deep-rooted traditions, the Southern states are now a region in transition. Only a few years ago, there was a general population outflow; today, a diversified and flourishing industrial base has brought a new prosperity and spurred growth all across the South. But that doesn't mean the Old South of magnificent mansions, magnolias and colorful folklore can't still be found. Indeed, you won't have to travel far in any of the Southern states to take a tour of the antebellum homes that so vividly recall the South's glorious past. The South of old was also famous for its superb gardens, and this tradition remains strong throughout the region in numerous formal and informal gardens that feature bright displays of camellias, azaleas and other native flowers.

In the rural South and the "Hill Country," the old folkways, crafts and folklore are still very much alive. In fact, many of those traditions are celebrated throughout the year in colorful local events such as the Pioneer Crafts Festival at Rison, Arkansas; the Cotton Pickin' Antique Fair in Gay, Georgia; North Carolina's Old Quawk's Day; or the Annual National Hollerin' Contest held each June at Spivey's Corner, North Carolina. For those who want to take some of the local color back home, there are a number of arts and crafts fairs throughout the region where you can purchase handmade native artifacts.

Of course, there is also the Southern states' magnificent landscape: the Appalachians; the Great Smoky Mountains; awesome caverns and unique regional treasures like Mammoth Spring, which flows 200 million gallons of sparkling water each day; Tallulah Gorge, the oldest natural gorge on the continent; and Natural Bridge, towering 215 feet high — one of the seven natural wonders of the world.

Such are the scenic wonders that await you — and yours — in America's "New South."

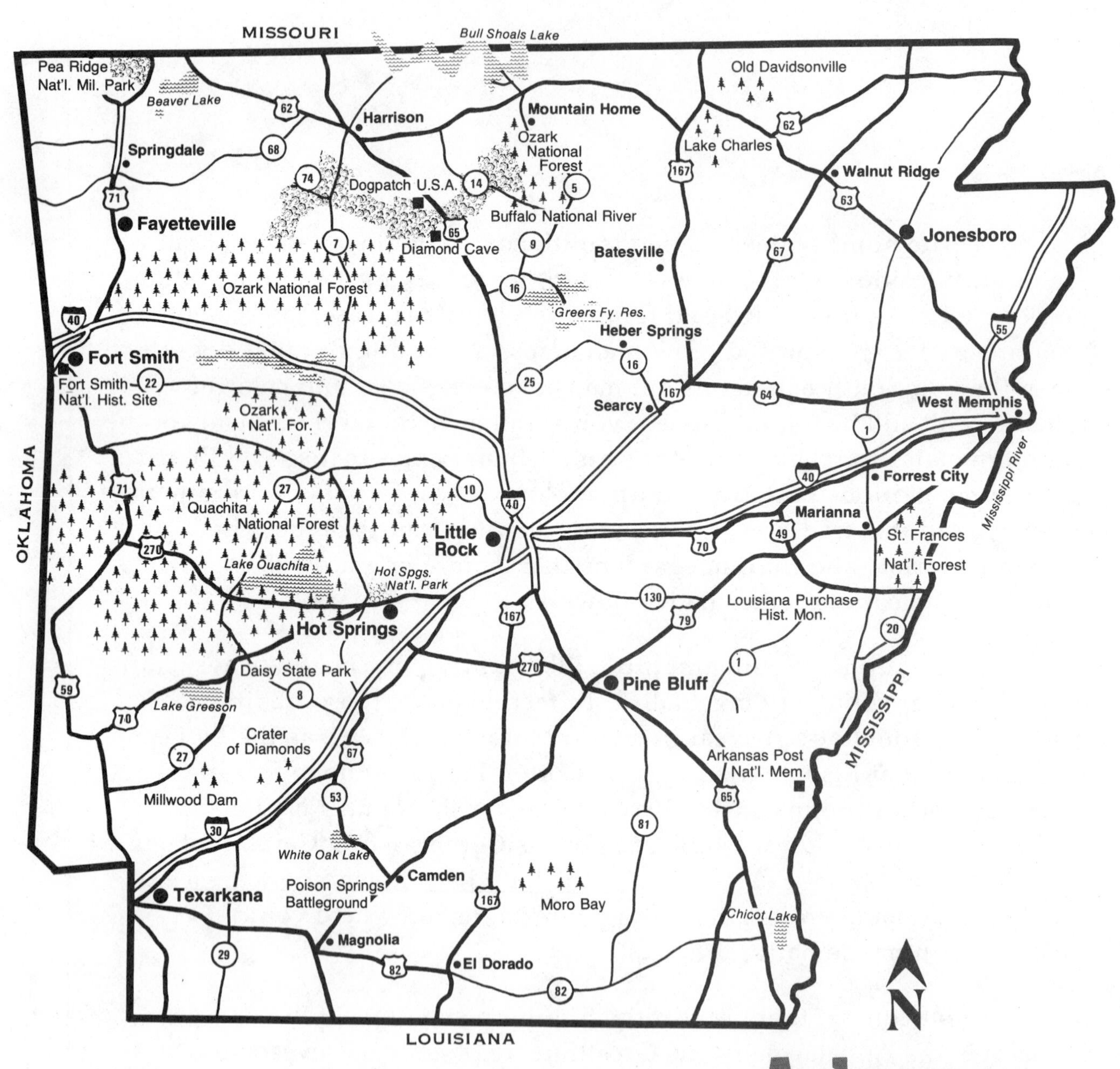

Arkansas

Map not to exact scale.

Arkansas

In just one visit to Arkansas you will take away many a memory — the view of sweeping valleys from the summit of the Ozark Mountains, the sound of Arkansas music played on old-fashioned instruments, the thrill of canoeing white water streams, the calm of quiet lakes and virgin forests, the taste of fresh trout and catfish cooked over an open fire.

Spanish explorers, led by Hernando De Soto, were the first Europeans to visit the area (1541), while French explorers, Marquette, Jolliet and LaSalle arrived more than a century later to lay claim to much of the territory. Following the explorations of the French, a grant was given to Henry de Tonti and the first settlement, Arkansas Post, was established in the Mississippi Valley. Much of the subsequent history of the territory is tied to Louisiana, of which Arkansas was a part until 1812, when it was attached to the Missouri Territory. The cotton boom of 1818 accelerated settlement of the area, and the separate Arkansas Territory was created in 1819. Arkansas achieved statehood in 1836, just as slavery was becoming a more and more divisive issue for the nation. As the Civil War threatened, the Arkansas Convention voted to remain in the Union, but later voted for secession when President Lincoln asked for troops to support the Northern cause. Loyalties remained divided within the state when two separate state governments were established from 1864-65: A Union one at Little Rock, and the Confederate at Washington, Arkansas. The state was the site of many battles during the Civil War, including the famous Union victory at Pea Ridge.

Full name: State of Arkansas
Origin of name: From Algonquian name of the Quapaw Indians.

Motto: *Regnat Populus* (The People Rule).
Capital: Little Rock
Statehood: June 15, 1836, 25th state.
Population: 2,144,000 (ranks 33rd).
Major Cities: Little Rock (141,143), Fort Smith (66,663), North Little Rock (61,768).
Bird: Mockingbird
Flower: Apple blossom
Tree: Pine

Average daily temperature by month

	Northern	Southern
Jan.	51.4 to 23.7	55.1 to 31.3
Feb.	55.2 to 27.1	59.6 to 34.2
Mar.	62.4 to 34.0	67.1 to 40.8
Apr.	74.0 to 45.4	76.8 to 51.3
May	80.7 to 52.8	83.6 to 59.1
Jun.	88.1 to 61.0	90.5 to 66.8
Jul.	92.2 to 64.7	93.6 to 70.2
Aug.	91.7 to 62.6	93.2 to 68.5
Sept.	85.3 to 56.0	87.9 to 62.0
Oct.	75.9 to 44.0	78.2 to 50.0
Nov.	62.6 to 33.8	66.1 to 39.4
Dec.	53.6 to 27.0	57.2 to 33.5
Year	72.8 to 44.3	75.7 to 50.6

The Hot Springs area is the most popular with tourists, as it features three sparkling lakes offering excellent fishing and swimming, thoroughbred racing at the Oaklawn Jockey Club, gourmet restaurants, a number of fine resorts and the famous hot mineral springs bath houses. Other noteworthy Arkansas attractions include: the Ouachita National

Forest; Crater of Diamonds State Park, where hundreds of gems are discovered every year; the lively theme park, Dogpatch USA; Blanchard Springs Caverns; and the scenic Buffalo National River.

Tourism and sport fishing are among the state's most important activities today, but it also enjoys a solid economic base made up of agricultural products like rice, cotton and beef cattle; mining; and manufacturing of electrical equipment, paper and wood products, chemicals and electrical equipment.

State Offices

Tourism
Arkansas Department of Parks and Tourism
149 State Capitol Building
Little Rock, Arkansas 72201
(501) 371-7777

State Police
Department of Public Safety
PO Box 4005
Little Rock, Arkansas 72214
(501) 371-2151

Radio Stations

Little Rock
KAAY 1090 (AM) KKYK 103.7 (FM)

Arkansas' capitol building is a massive structure made of Arkansas white marble and granite.

Highlight
Great River Road

Journey back in time through lands rich in Arkansas history along the Great River Road. Pilot wheel markers chart your route on Arkansas' link in a series of highways running parallel to the Mississippi River from Canada to the Gulf of Mexico.

Begin your journey in Blytheville — a bustling agricultural center surrounded by some of the richest cotton-growing land in the nation. You'll pass through Osceola, a major river port.

Take time to see Wilson . . . one of the largest cotton plantations in the South . . . built to resemble the architecture of an English Tudor village. Wilson borders Hampson Museum State Park. The museum itself exhibits the history of Mound Builder Indians including a collection of their artifacts.

Village Creek State Park, located between Forrest City and Wynne, is Arkansas' largest state park. When completed, the park will offer four lakes for fishing and water sports, campsites, a lodge and housekeeping cabins, an 18-hole golf course, marked nature trails and a 2,500-acre wilderness backpacking area.

From mid-May through mid-October, be prepared for speed when you reach West Memphis and the nationally known Southland Greyhound Park where the dogs follow "lady luck" to the finish line.

After an exciting visit to the track, relax in the St. Francis National Forest, located on the famed Crowley's Ridge (formed long ago by wind-blown silt and sand). Visitors may fish and swim in two excellent lakes formed on Bear and Storm Creeks. Hikers will enjoy the wilderness area where a variety of natural flora provides sanctuary for native small game and deer.

Driving due south takes you to Helena, a living monument to the charm of the Old South with dozens of stately, oak-shaded, antebellum homes. Once a steamboat port, it is now a major loading and off-loading point for sea-going barges. On high points throughout the modern city are markers and monuments recalling the times when Confederate forces battled with the Union for control of the entire area during the War Between the States.

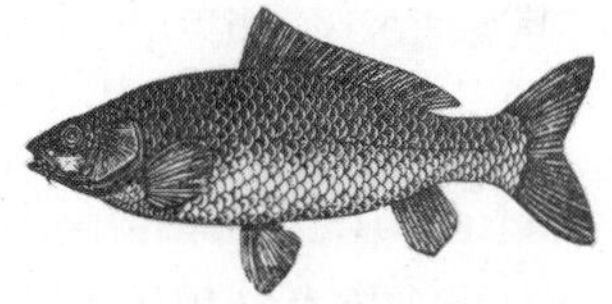

From Helena, the route passes through the wild, swampy White River Wildlife Refuge . . . over 113,000 acres of marshy delta land preserved in its natural state. Nearby is the Louisiana Purchase Marker, the base from which all surveys of the gigantic territory were made. A state park commemorates the site.

French explorers visited the area south of Helena during the 17th century and established the first white settlement, Arkansas Post. Though most of the town was destroyed during the Civil War, the nearby Arkansas Post County Museum has been built to remind visitors of the story of this national monument.

Your trek on Arkansas' Great River Road ends at Lake Village, entrance to Lake Chicot State Park. Oxbow-shaped Lake Chicot is the state's largest natural body of water. The state park provides housekeeping cottages, bait shop and marina, plus facilities for camping, swimming, boating and excellent fishing among tall cypress trees and colorful water lilies lining the lake.

Highlight

The Ozark Folk Center

YESTERYEAR REVISITED. Be prepared to see yesterday today when you visit Arkansas' new multi-million-dollar Ozark Folk Center at Mountain View. The Center is a living museum, where the people are the "displays." Situated on an 80-acre hillside site, the Center has been built to provide a home for the area's musicians and craftsmen.

You'll be surrounded by the sights and sounds of an earlier time — almost miraculously preserved. You'll see the old-time crafts operations performed as they have been for ages past, and hear the sometime plaintive, sometimes playful, often joyful tunes of the mountain musicians. Visit the folklore library or attend a special folklore workshop designed for you.

AUDITORIUM. The Ozark Folk Center features a 1,043-seat music auditorium, complete with rehearsal rooms, recording facilities, and an indoor-outdoor stage. On scheduled evenings, a program of mountain music is presented here typical of the tunes that are native to these hills. Native musicians of Stone County, Arkansas, perform on the dulcimer, the autoharp, the banjo, the fiddle, the pickin' bow, the guitar and the mandolin. Many of the instruments owned and played by the musicians are handmade by local craftsmen and have been handed down from father to son over the years. Jig and square dancing fills the stage with happy activity. Ancient ballads tell the stories of family sorrows, loves and haunting mysteries of these hills. Gospel songs express their faith.

CRAFTS FORUM. Beyond the auditorium is the Crafts Forum — numerous buildings and outdoor areas where craftsmen demonstrate their specialties. Here you'll watch quilts being made, wool yarn spun, wood carving that raises the whittler's skills to a fine art. There are demonstrations of leather work, wheel pottery, basketry, broom making, primitive furniture, doll making and performances of traditional Ozark music throughout the day. Sounds of the blacksmith's anvil and the aroma of smoked turkey and fried pies fill the Craft Forum, and a barbecue stand with covered picnic pavilion offers a cool spot for rest and a noon meal. At the sales shop on the grounds, visitors may purchase handmade crafts, books on Ozark life and recordings made at the Center.

RESTAURANT. When you're ready to take a break in your explorations, there's a 130-seat restaurant featuring the Ozark favorites — catfish or ham and beans with homemade pies and rolls, homemade biscuits and red-eye gravy with country ham for breakfast — all served by waitresses wearing long ginghams and pinafores. The glass-enclosed dining room overlooking a rocky, tree-covered bluff, adds peaceful beauty to your dining pleasure.

HILL FOLKLORE FAMILY STYLE. You and your children will become a part of the scene as you watch the bees working in their hive, pet the goat and encourage the baby ducks in their swimming lessons. Stop by the "School Yard" and learn to play "Fox and Geese," or accompany the naturalist on his guided hikes through the native Ozark woods. Ask the Indian historian to tell you about the Ozark's true original inhabitants. You'll learn lots about the hill country heritage and take with you an appreciation of its place in the past — and for the future.

JOIN IN. That's what the Ozark Folk Center is all about. Daily operation of the Center extends from Memorial Day through Labor Day, with limited operations in May, September, and October. For detailed schedules of the season's events and rates for lodging and admissions, write for "Calendar of Operations." The Ozark Folk Center also features unique folk festivals each spring and fall. Special concerts, films and workshops are scheduled periodically throughout the season. During months of operation, the Craft Forum is open from 10 a.m. until 6 p.m. daily with a folk music concert at 8 p.m. in the main auditorium (except on Sundays). Individual admission tickets, one-time-only immediate family tickets, and season tickets covering both crafts and music are available, with group rates offered for 20 or more by prior arrangement. Come join us — and take home warm memories of your visit to the Ozark Folk Center, "A People Place."

FOR ADDITIONAL INFORMATION. Write General Manager, Ozark Folk Center, Mountain View, Arkansas 72560; (501) 269-3851. Lodge reservations: (501) 269-3871.

Quilting is one of the 18 traditional craft demonstrations on display at Arkansas' unusual Ozark Folk Center.

Highlight

PEA RIDGE NATIONAL MILITARY PARK

Pea Ridge — the battle in Arkansas that saved Missouri for the Union — was a strange battle: one that saw Southern troops attacking from the north, and soldiers from Arkansas and Texas fighting alongside French-speaking Louisianans and Indian regiments serving under their own officers. Moreover, the Missouri State Guardsmen who fought for the Southern cause were not yet officially in the Confederate service. The Union soldiers came from Missouri, Iowa, Illinois, Indiana, and Ohio. And many spoke German as their first language.

Pea Ridge brought to an end a campaign that began on Christmas Day, 1861. On that day, Brig. Gen. Samuel R. Curtis assumed command of the Federal Southwestern District of Missouri, and, acting with more zeal than his predecessors, began pushing pro-Confederate forces out of the state. In mid-February 1862, the Missouri State Guard, commanded by Maj. Gen. Sterling Price, crossed into Arkansas.

In the Boston Mountains, south of Fayetteville, the Guardsmen joined forces with Brig. Gen. Ben McCulloch's Confederates. There, Maj. Gen. Earl Van Dorn took command of the combined force of 16,000 and on March 4 headed northward, intending to strike into Missouri. His goal: St. Louis. But between that city and Van Dorn stood Curtis with 10,500 English- and German-speaking soldiers.

As Van Dorn marched, Curtis' men were digging in on the bluffs overlooking Little Sugar Creek, not far from Elkhorn Tavern and nearby Pea Ridge.

Van Dorn, realizing that a frontal assault against the Little Sugar Creek position would be suicidal, swung north to come in behind the Federals. He scheduled his attack for dawn of March 7, but his troops, weary from a three-day march through difficult country, arrived hours behind schedule. The delay gave Curtis enough time to pull his men away from Little Sugar

Creek, face about, and prepare to receive the assault in the open.

To make up for lost time, Van Dorn decided not to consolidate his force and to launch a two-pronged assault. From west of Pea Ridge and the Round Top, his men drove down upon the village of Leetown. They ran into intensive fire that killed two generals, and the ranking colonel was captured. With their command structure practically destroyed, the Confederates scattered from the field. Some simply deserted. Most, however, regrouped and made their way toward Elkhorn Tavern about two miles to the east.

The other prong of the attack — Price's Missourians — fared considerably better. Attacking east of the ridge, they slowly but steadily pushed the Federals back until, at nightfall, they held Elkhorn Tavern and the crucial Telegraph and Huntsville Roads. During the night the survivors of the Leetown fight joined them.

On the morning of March 8 Curtis counterattacked in the tavern area. His massed artillery severely punished the Confederates and his concerted infantry and cavalry attacks began to crumple their defenses. Still, the Confederates held. But ammunition was running short. If the wagon train had moved up with the reserve ammunition, Van Dorn might have seized victory. Unaccountably, the wagons turned around and drove away from the battle. Van Dorn disengaged and marched eastward, down the Huntsville Road, away from Elkhorn Tavern. A few hundred stragglers pushed their way down Telegraph Road, and the Federals, believing them to be the main force, pursued them, allowing the bulk of Van Dorn's column to continue an orderly retreat. The battle of Pea Ridge was over. Missouri was safe in Union hands, and most of the Union and Confederate troops moved east of the Mississippi to fight in other campaigns.

—PJF

A TOUR OF THE PARK

After stopping at the Visitor Center, follow the arrows from the parking area to the Old Telegraph Road. This road is more than 150 years old. In 1858, the Butterfield Overland Mail Company routed its stagecoaches over it to Fort Smith and then westward to California. The road received its name in 1860, when a telegraph line was strung along it. The road was used before the Battle of Pea Ridge by both Confederate and Union armies.

ABOUT YOUR VISIT

Pea Ridge is 10 miles northeast of Rogers, Arkansas. Near the visitor center, open daily from 8 a.m. to 5 p.m. with extended hours during the summer, is a picnic area with tables, fireplaces and a water fountain. No camping is permitted in the park but facilities are available at Beaver Reservoir, 20 miles away. Federal regulations prohibit hunting, disturbing wildlife and removing relics.

For additional information on Pea Ridge National Military Park, contact: Superintendent, Pea Ridge, Arkansas 72751.

One of the country's most scenic highways, Arkansas 7, passes through some of Arkansas' most beautiful terrain as it approaches 13,400-acre DeGray Lake north of Arkadelphia.

Arkansas Points of Interest and Attractions

Blanchard Caverns. An intricate network of passages and huge subterranean cavities, with brilliant lighting and walkways developed by the National Forest Service. Open year-round. Mountain View, off State Route 87.

Diamond Mines. The only diamond mines in the United States, discovered in 1906 by John Huddleston. The mines have yielded many valuable diamonds over the years, including some of exceptional quality only recently. Open year-round. Murfreesburo, off State Route 301.

Louisiana Purchase Marker. The site where surveys were begun in 1815 of the newly acquired Louisiana Territory. The area is currently being developed from a swamp into a state park. Marvell, west of Helena off US-49.

Magnet Cove. A valley of only 5.1-square miles surrounded by low hills and containing one of the most remarkable assortments of minerals in the nation. More than 42 kinds of minerals have been discovered at this site by geologists. Central, off US-71.

Mammoth Spring. The largest spring in the world — flowing 200 million gallons of water each day. Also the source for the Spring River. Mammoth Spring, off US-63.

Mid-America Park. A unique 470-acre center combining industry, education and entertainment facilities; includes a museum on energy, matter and life; outdoor theater performed each evening, except Sunday, from mid-June through August. Hot Springs, off US-70 and 270.

Mystery Cave. Massive and spectacular rock formations, with rooms as much as 60 feet high and 60 feet in circumference. Open year-round. Marshall, 12 miles north off State Route 27.

Natural Bridge. A natural rock formation developed as a tourist attraction by the Ozark Forest Service. The bridge is a 130-foot natural span carved by the erosive action of a small stream; 12 feet wide and 25 feet high. The area also features several large rooms weathered out of rocky cliffs nearby. Deer, off State Route 16.

Scott and Bearskin Lake Railway. Rides on an original steam-powered train through the cotton fields of a working plantation. A nearby museum preserves the agricultural heritage of the area. Scott, off State Route 130.

Southland Greyhound Park. An active calendar of greyhound racing. Open throughout the summer. West Memphis, off US-70.

Sugarloaf Mountain. A mountain island in the middle of Greers Ferry Lake, accessible only by boat; well-developed nature trail and magnificent view of the island and lake from the summit. Heber, off State Routes 5 and 16.

Tontitown. An Italian community where wine grapes grow in abundance and an annual grape festival is celebrated in August; town also features a number of superb Italian restaurants. Fayetteville, west on State Route 68.

White River Wildlife Refuge. Encompassing 113,000 acres, including more than 100 small natural lakes, the region is one of the wildest areas in the state featuring winding, swamplike natural canals and dense underbrush. St. Charles, off State Route 1 (free ferry river crossing).

The Arkansas Territorial Restoration at Little Rock is a collection of 13 original structures dating from the early 1800s. Guided tours of the historic area are given daily and a nearby visitors center offers a gift shop and art gallery featuring local crafts (left). Music comes naturally to the hill people of the Ozarks who perform their traditional ballads, jig tunes and square dances in the 1,043-seat auditorium of the Ozark Folk Center (below).

The Falls Branch Hiking Trail at Arkansas' Lake Catherine State Park leads to this isolated waterfall in the beauty of the forest.

Arkansas State Parks

Park	Location	CAMPING	PICNICKING	CONCESSIONS	SWIMMING	HIKING	BOATING	FISHING	HUNTING	WINTER SPORTS
Bull Shoals	*Mountain Home. On State Route 178.*	•	•	•	•	•	•	•		
Crater of Diamonds	*Kimberly. Off State Route 301.*	•	•	•						
Crowley's Ridge	*Paragould. Off State Route 168.*	•	•	•	•	•		•		
Daisy	*Daisy. Off US-70.*	•	•			•		•		
DeGray	*Arkadelphia. Off Interstate 30 and State Route 7.*	•	•	•	•	•	•	•		
Devil's Den	*Winslow. Off State Routes 74 and 170.*	•	•	•	•	•		•		
Jacksonport	*Jacksonport. Off State Route 69.*		•			•		•		
Lake Catherine	*Malvern. Off State Route 171.*	•	•	•	•	•	•	•		
Lake Charles	*Powhatan. Off State Route 25.*	•	•	•	•	•	•	•		
Lake Chicot	*Lake Village. Off State Route 144.*	•	•		•	•	•	•		
Lake Dardanelle	*Russellville. Off State Route 326.*	•	•	•			•	•		
Lake Fort Smith	*Mountainburg. Off US-71.*	•	•	•	•	•	•	•		
Lake Frierson	*Jonesboro. Off State Route 141.*		•					•		
Lake Ouachita	*Mountain Pine. Off State Route 227.*	•	•	•	•	•	•	•		
Lake Poinsett	*Harrisburg. Off State Route 163.*	•	•			•	•	•		
Logoly	*Magnolia. Off US-79.*		•	•						
Mammoth Spring	*Mammoth Spring. Off US-63.*		•			•		•		
Millwood	*Ashdown. Off State Route 32.*	•	•		•	•	•	•		
Moro Bay	*El Dorado. Off State Route 15.*	•	•		•			•		
Mt. Nebo	*Dardanelle. Off State Route 155.*	•	•	•	•	•				
Old Davidsonville	*Pocahontas. Off State Route 166.*	•	•	•		•		•		
Ozark Folk Center	*Mt. View. Off State Route 9.*		•	•	•	•				
Petit Jean	*Morrilton. Off State Route 154.*	•	•	•	•	•		•		
Pinnacle Mountain	*Little Rock. Off State Route 300.*		•			•	•	•		
Queen Wilhelmina	*Mena. Off State Route 88.*	•	•	•		•				
Village Creek	*Wynne. Off State Route 284.*	•	•	•	•	•	•	•		
White Oak Lake	*Camden. Off State Routes 24 and 387.*	•	•	•	•	•	•	•		
Withrow Springs	*Huntsville. Off State Route 23.*	•	•		•	•		•		
Woolly Hollow	*Greenbrier. Off State Route 285.*	•	•	•	•	•	•	•		

Arkansas has no state forests. For additional information on Arkansas state parks, contact: *Arkansas Department of Parks and Tourism, 149 State Capitol, Little Rock, Arkansas 72201, (501) 371-1511.*

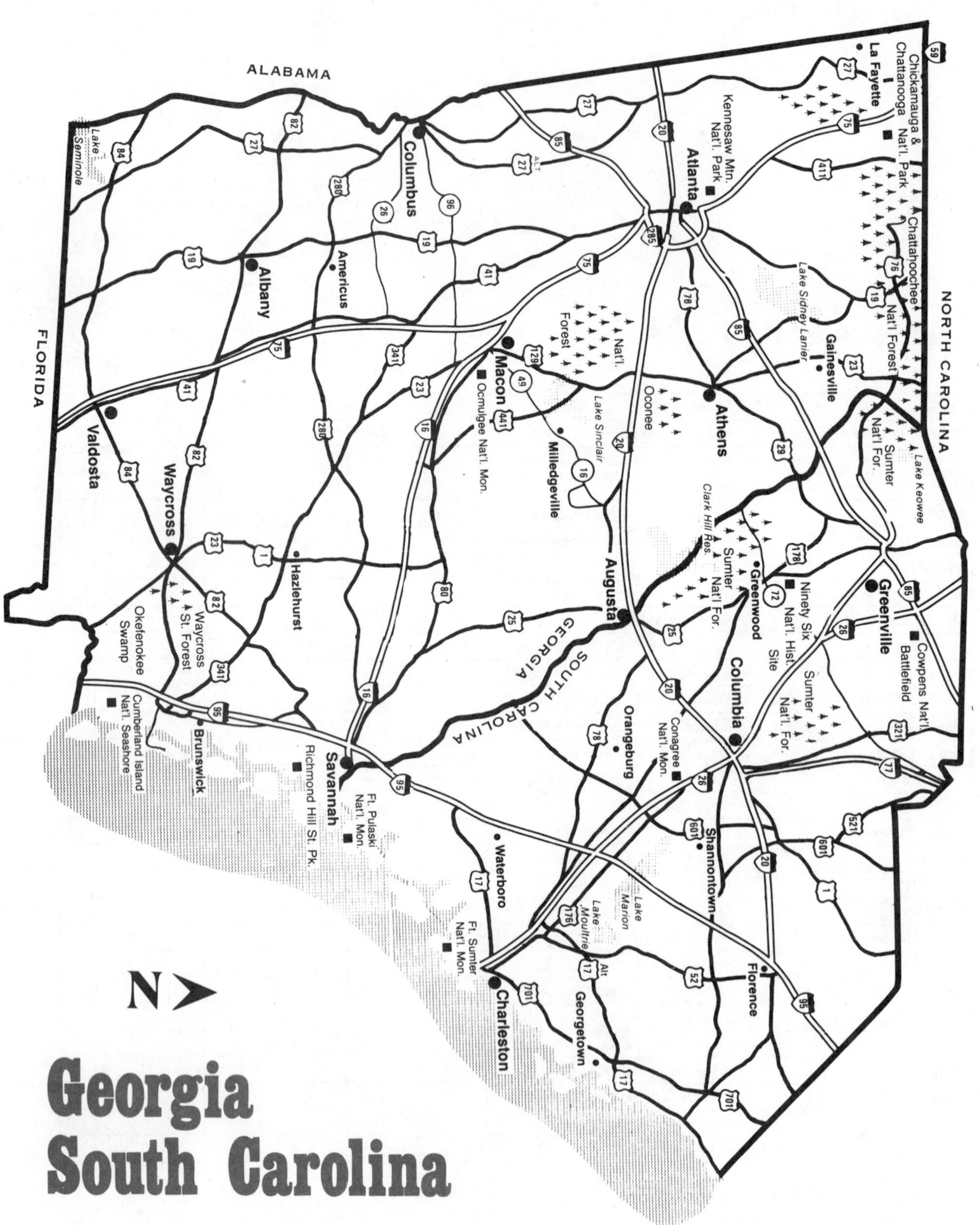

Map not to exact scale.

Georgia

Georgia, the largest state east of the Mississippi and the last of the original 13 colonies, is the nation's number-one producer of "Goober Peas" (peanuts), the number-one supplier of granite, the third-largest supplier of peaches, and, of course, the home state of Jimmy Carter, the 39th President of the United States. And Georgia is also the home of the moss-draped Sea Island, the Okefenokee Swamp, the Chattahoochee River of *Deliverance* fame and the colorful city of Atlanta.

Primitive mound-building Indians were the first known inhabitants of Georgia, followed by Creek and Cherokee Indians. Spanish explorers led by De Soto are thought to be the first Europeans to visit the area in 1540, but the British were the first to establish a settlement with the Savannah Colony of 1733. At first, the sale of rum and the introduction of slaves was prohibited in the colony, but by 1750 legislation was passed that ended these restrictions. As the American Revolution approached, Georgia was reluctant to join the agitation out of gratitude for the money England had supplied to the colony and out of fear of attack by English forces in Florida. Georgia was not represented at the Stamp Act Congress or the First Continental Congress, but did join the Revolution in time to be represented at the Second Continental Congress. Little serious fighting took place in the state until the British seized Savannah in 1778. The patriots later attempted an assault on Savannah without success, but eventually regained the city when losses elsewhere forced the British to evacuate. Georgia became the first Southern state to ratify the Federal Constitution in 1788. Strong feelings of state's rights and unfavorable Supreme Court decisions led to Georgia's secession on January 19, 1861. During most of the war, the state remained relatively free from conflict — until General Sherman made his famous march to the sea, leaving bitter feelings in his wake that rankle even today.

Full name: State of Georgia
Origin of Name: In honor of King George II of England.
Motto: Wisdom, Justice and Moderation
Nickname: Peach State
Capital: Atlanta
Statehood: January 2, 1788, fourth state.
Population: 5,048,000 (ranks 14th).
Major Cities: Atlanta (436,057), Columbus (159,352), Macon (121,157).
Bird: Brown thrasher
Flower: Cherokee rose
Tree: Live oak

Average daily temperature by month

	Northern	Southern
Jan.	50.5 to 31.6	63.1 to 39.9
Feb.	53.5 to 32.6	65.6 to 41.5
Mar.	60.9 to 38.7	72.0 to 47.3
Apr.	71.2 to 47.7	79.7 to 54.4
May	78.4 to 55.1	86.1 to 61.3
Jun.	84.1 to 61.6	90.1 to 66.9
Jul.	86.7 to 65.0	91.5 to 69.3
Aug.	86.2 to 64.5	91.6 to 69.1
Sept.	81.0 to 59.4	87.6 to 65.6
Oct.	71.9 to 48.4	80.3 to 55.4
Nov.	60.7 to 39.0	71.2 to 45.1
Dec.	52.0 to 33.3	64.7 to 40.1
Year	69.8 to 48.1	78.6 to 54.7

Plains Country

Plains Country is where rural Georgians take life easy, ignore the hectic pace of the big city in favor of wide open spaces, and in some cases, deliberately stop time.

The most famous small town in America is the focal point of Plains Country, and from there it is merely a few hours' drive to a number of other interesting attractions.

Time seems to stand still in the re-created 1850 frontier village of Westville, just 30 miles west of Plains in Lumpkin. A few miles farther is Providence Canyon, where time and weather play sand-sculptor with a colorful geological phenomenon.

To the southeast of Plains lie two more places that turn back the clock. At Chehaw Wild Animal Park near Albany, wild animals roam their natural preserves free of the shackles or cages of a modern zoo, and the Georgia Agrirama in Tifton, history comes alive in the form of a late 19th-century agricultural community.

More history can be found at Andersonville National Historic Site and in the beautifully restored homes of Columbus and Thomasville.

For the fisherman Plains Country offers a variety of lakes and ponds, and for the quail hunter there can be no better sports holiday than in Albany, the quail hunting capital of the world.

Now that the popularity of the Georgia-grown peanut and other local favorites is at an all-time high, perhaps you'll want to spend a few days learning all about their roots. This calls for a trip to rustic Plains Country, the Georgia vacation spot where life's simple pleasures have long been a way of life.

Risen from the ashes of the Civil War, Atlanta remains Georgia's dominant modern attraction, in addition to being one of the South's most strategic cities. Other points of interest include FDR's "Little White House" at Warm Springs, the Confederate Naval Museum at Columbus, the Chattahoochee and Oconee National Forests, Andersonville Prison Park and National Cemetry, and the tomb of Martin Luther King, Jr. in Atlanta.

Georgia's rich resources include a wealth of untapped hydroelectric power, valuable marble and gravel deposits and vast stands of hardwoods. Tourism is extremely important to the state, as is the manufacture of textiles, transportation equipment, chemicals, paper and wood products.

State Offices

Tourism
Tourist Division
Bureau of Industry and Trade
PO Box 38097
Atlanta, Georgia 30334
(404) 656-3590

State Police
Department of Public Safety
Atlanta, Georgia 30301
(404) 656-5890

Radio Stations

Atlanta
WKLS 96.1 (FM)
WKQI 790 (AM)
WSB 750 (AM)
WLTA 99.7 (FM)
Macon
WMAZ 940 (AM)
Savannah
WTOC 1290 (AM)

Georgia Points of Interest and Attractions

The following shaded map provides a regional breakdown of the various points of interest and attractions within the state of Georgia.

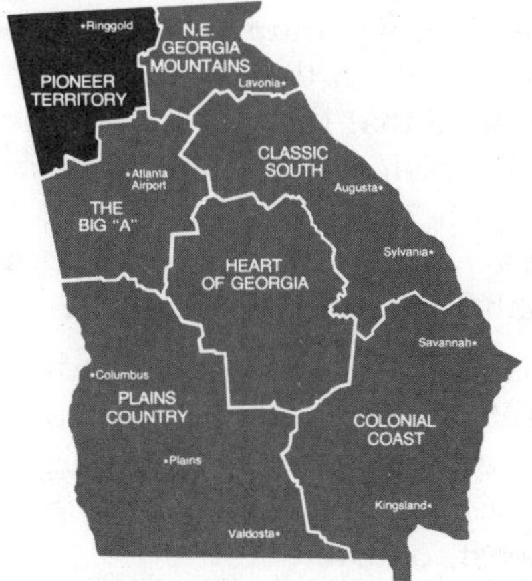

Pioneer Territory

Allatoona Beach. One-quarter mile sand beach, boating, amusement area, camping. Open late spring, summer and early fall. Cartersville, on Lake Allatoona, off Interstate 75 and State Route 20.

Carpet Capital of the World. More than 160 carpet mills are located in the city of Dalton; tours available. Open year-round. Dalton, off Interstate 75.

Capitoline Statue. Statue of Romulus and Remus presented to Rome, Georgia, by the governor of Rome, Italy, in 1929. Located in the municipal building downtown. Rome, on US-27.

Creative Arts Guild. A unique and well-equipped community center for visual and performing arts. Located in old firehouse. Open year-round, daily, 10 a.m. to 5 p.m.; Sunday from 2 p.m. to 5 p.m. Dalton, off Interstate 75, on Pentz Street.

Georgia Marble. An almost unlimited supply of Georgia Marble is found in the Long Swamp valley region of the state (marble from Georgia is used throughout the world for buildings and monuments). Georgia Marble Company offers tours. Open year-round, Monday through Friday. Tate, off State Route 53.

Glass Lake. A five-acre lake with excellent fishing for catfish, bass, bluegill and shell cracker. Calhoun, off Interstate 75, on State Route 53.

Rock City. A natural attraction with unique rock formations, sweeping panoramic views of the Appalachians, colorful native flowers and foliage; Fairyland Caverns; and Mother Goose Village. Open year-round, daily, 8:30 a.m. to sunset. Wildwood, north, atop Lookout Mountain, off Interstates 24, 59 and 75.

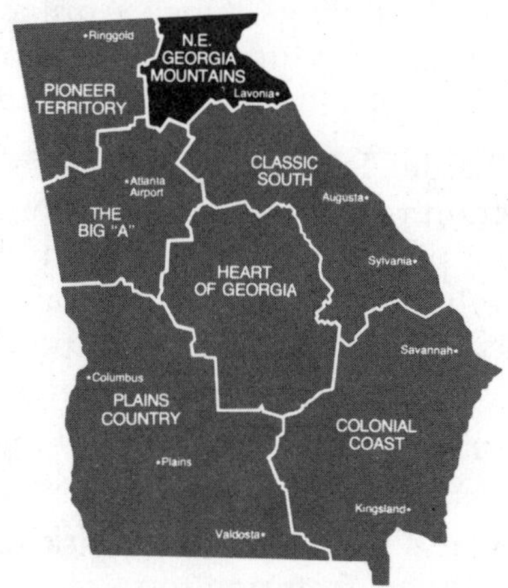

Northeast Georgia Mountains

Andy's Trout Farm. Offers rainbow trout fishing without a license; RV campground, trails and playgrounds. Open year-round. Dillard, five miles west on US-441.

Anna Ruby Falls. One of the area's most beautiful waterfalls within the boundaries of the Chattahoochee National Forest; fishing, hiking, picnicking. Helen, off State Route 75.

Appalachian Trail. This famous hiking route begins in Georgia and extends 2,000 miles to Maine. Dawsonville, Amicalola Falls State Park, off State Route 183.

Art and Cultural Center. The historical and creative center of the community of Dillard since its establishment in 1934. Features programs in weaving, pottery, dance, music, nature, creative writing, photography, painting and art history. Dillard, State Route 246.

Brasstown Bald. Highest point in Georgia, 4,784 feet; visitors center open May 1 through October 31. Blairsville, US-129 and US-19, east via State Route 180, then State Route 66.

Crisson's Gold Mine. Gold panning, picnic facilities, RV camping. Dahlonega, three miles north on Wimpy Mill Road.

Gold Hills of Dahlonega. Located on the site of mines that were in use during Dahlonega's gold rush; re-created gold mine town. Visitors may pan for gold and keep their findings. Open April and May, weekends only; June through September, daily; fall foliage season, weekends only.

Lake Lanier Islands. A 1,200-acre family recreation resort situated on a series of islands; picnicking, sandy beach, golf course, rental houseboats, rental sailboats, kayaks, canoes, fishing, trout ponds, riding stable and 430-foot water slide. Open year-round, daily, 24 hours. Buford, Lake Sidney Lanier, off State Route 347.

Lanierland Country Music Park. Country music shows featuring top country-western, Grand Ole Opry stars. Open May through October, every other Saturday night. Cumming, off State Route 306.

Memorial Tower. A fire observation station at the summit of Tower Mountain, built as a memorial to the men of the Forest Service killed in World War II. Open May 1 through November 1. Cornelia, off US-23.

Nacoochee Station. Restored state depot of the Gainesville Northwestern Railroad Line, now serving as an Information Center for attractions and facilities in the area, including RV campgrounds. Helen, off State Route 75.

Richard Russell Scenic Highway. Designated as Georgia Highway 348, the route stretches 14.1 miles through some of the state's most beautiful mountain areas. The Appalachian Trail crosses the highway at Tessnatee Gap, highest point on the highway. Elevations range from 1,600 to approximately 3,000 feet. Blairsville, eight miles southeast via State Route 180.

Tallulah Gorge. Believed to be the oldest natural gorge in North America; 1½ miles long with a maximum depth of 2,000 feet; five waterfalls in the bottom of the gorge. It was here that the late Karl Wallenda made his historic tightwire walk across the gorge on a 1,000-foot-long cable. A trail follows a portion of the gorge's rim. Tallulah Falls, off US-441.

Taccoa Falls. Spectacular falls dropping 186 feet; on grounds of the Toccoa Falls Institute. Open year-round, daily, 7:30 a.m. to 7:30 p.m. Toccoa, two miles northeast, off State Route 17.

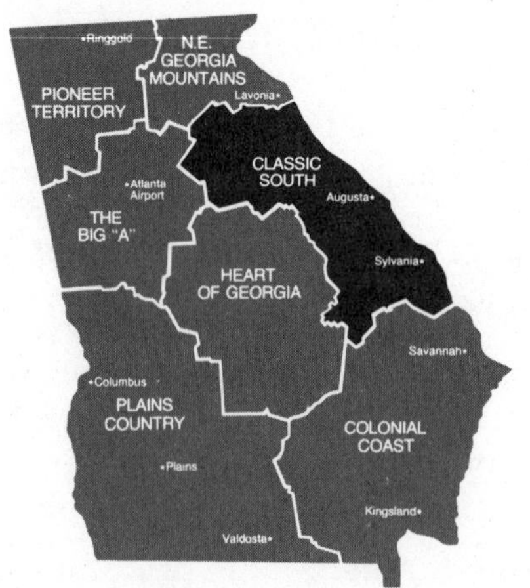

Classic South

Cotton Exchange Building. The center of cotton trading in the days when the streets were lined with bales being bought and sold. At one time, Augusta was the largest inland cotton market in the world. The building was constructed in 1886 and used continuously until 1964. Augusta, 775 Reynolds Street.

Double-Barreled Cannon. Located on city hall lawn in Athens, this cannon is the only one of its kind in the world. Invented in 1863 for use in the Civil War, it was to have fired two balls simultaneously,

The 220-acre Vogel State Park, near Blairsville, offers camping, picnicking, hiking and boating in a scenic setting.

connected by a chain. It failed to fire accurately, however, and was relegated to its present location as an object of curiosity. Athens, US-29 and State Route 72.

Founder's Memorial Garden. A memorial to the founders of the first garden club in the United States (12 ladies, 1891). Also serves as headquarters of the Garden Club of Georgia. Open year-round. Athen, Babcock Drive and Lumpkin Street.

Garden Center. A Greek revival, stucco-covered "Old Medical College," built in 1835. The first medical college in Georgia, now headquarters of the Augusta Council of Garden Clubs. Open year-round. Augusta, 598 Telfair Street.

Granite Center. Area furnishes one-third of the monumental granite used in the United States. Open May 15 through October 15, Monday to Friday; free tours of quarries and plants at 10 a.m. Elberton, State Routes 17 and 72.

National Fish Hatchery. Features a 26-tank aquarium that displays the fish raised by the hatchery plus a variety of other interesting species. Open year-round, daily, 9 a.m. to 5 p.m. Millen, off State Route 25.

New Savannah Bluff Lock and Dam. Fishing for shad, ocean striper, bream, yellow perch and jack; picnic facilities. Augusta, State Route 56, 12 miles south on Savannah River.

Tree That Owns Itself. The tree was deeded the land extending eight feet on all sides by an early University of Georgia professor who used to delight in the comfort of its shade. Athens, corner of Findley and Dearing Streets.

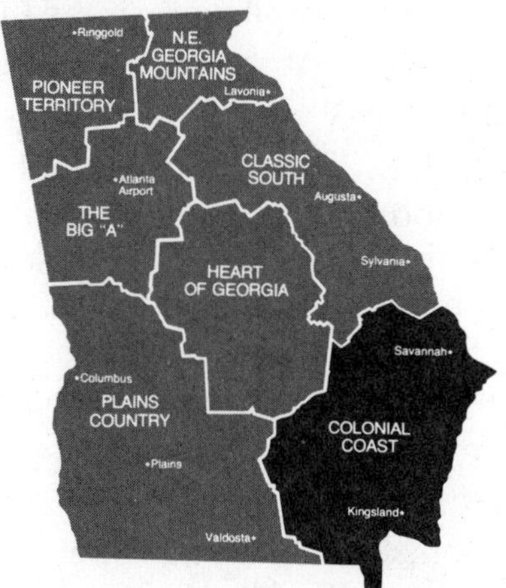

Colonial Coast

Aquarama. A center for convention and meeting activities, housing one of the largest heated indoor pools in the Southeastern United States. Open year-round. Brunswick, Jekyll Island, Beachview Drive.

Arabia Bay Game Management Area. Consists of 45,000 acres where hunters may take deer and small game in season. Regulated by the Department of Natural Resources. Pearson, seven miles south on US-441.

Edwin I. Hatch Nuclear Visitors Center. A showcase of nuclear power illustrated by animated exhibits, films and special effects. Open year-round, Monday to Friday, 9 a.m. to 5 p.m.; Sundays 1 p.m. to 5 p.m. Baxley, 10 miles north at US-1 crossing of Altamaha River.

Factor's Walk. A 19th-century meeting place for cotton merchants; bridgeways connect buildings to the bluffs; museums

Atlanta's Stone Mountain Park features this antebellum plantation.

and nightclubs capitalize on the Old World charm of the area. Savannah, Bay Street (along river bluff).

Forsyth Park. Beautiful park with spring-blooming azaleas, flowering trees and a large fountain dating back to 1858; Confederate monument honors Civil War dead. Savannah, Bull Street, between Gaston Street and Park Avenue.

John. P. Rousakis Riverfront Plaza. Restoration of riverfront bluff to preserve and stabilize the historic waterfront area; features nine-block concourse with parks ideal for strolling, picnicking and shipwatching; museums, shops, restaurants, pubs. Savannah, US-80.

Okefenokee Swamp Park. Wildlife shows, boat trips, interpretive center, exhibits. Open year-round, daily, 8 a.m. to sunset. Okefenokee National Wildlife Refuge. Fargo, Folkston, and Waycross, off State Route 177 and US-23.

The Rocks. Outstanding geological formations, caves, bluffs and camping area. Open year-round. Douglas, 17 miles north off State Route 107.

Sapelo Island. Long an exclusive preserve of scientists and millionaires, Sapelo may be visited each Saturday morning by the first 25 people to make reservations. Trip is a three-hour tour of the 9,250-acre island operated by the University of Georgia Marine Institute. Open year-round; for reservations telephone (912) 485-2449 or (912) 485-2242. Meridian, off State Route 99.

Heart of Georgia

Avenue of the Flags. Features the flag of each state, as well as the territorial flags of the United States. Macon, Poplar Street.

Brer Rabbit Statue. A colorful likeness of one of Uncle Remus' most famous creations; on courthouse lawn. Eatonton, off US-129.

Mark Smith Planetarium. The second largest planetarium in the Southeast; housed at the Macon Museum of Arts and Sciences. Open year-round, Monday to Friday, 9 a.m. to 5 p.m.; Friday nights, 7:30 p.m. to 10 p.m. Macon, 4182 Forsyth Road.

Peach Blossoms. The heart of Georgia's peach production area; blossoms at their best in mid-March; fruit available June through August. Fort Valley, along US-341 for best views.

Tobesofkee Recreation Area. RV camping, zoo, swimming, fishing, picnic areas, playgrounds; three parks. Open year-round. Macon, off Interstate 75 at Thomaston exit.

At Lake Lanier Islands, boaters may ride into numerous coves.

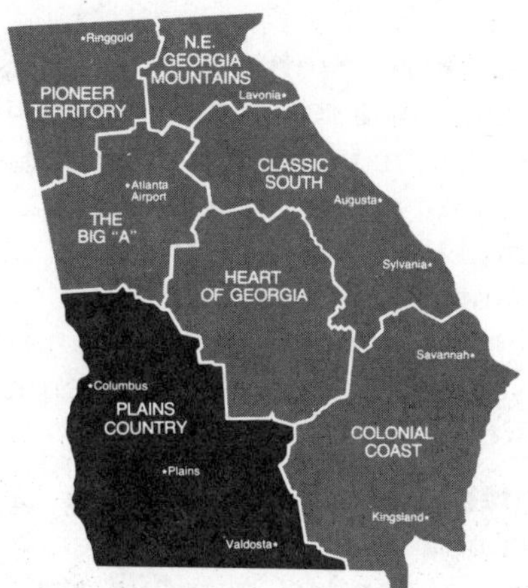

Plains Country

Andersonville Trail.
Seventy-five-mile-long trail that includes the headquarters of the American Camellia Society, river ferry, antebellum homes, Andersonville National Historic Site, historic windsor hotel, Victorian homes in Americus, Veterans Memorial State Park, Lake Blackshear, and Plains, Georgia. Andersonville, State Route 49.

Callaway Gardens. A 2,500-acre family resort famous for its wildflowers of the southern Appalachian; miles of scenic drives, trails, display greenhouses, fishing, skeet and trap shooting. Open year-round; beach open April through September. Pine Mountain, on US-27.

Camellia Gardens. An extensive camellia library and a Boehm porcelain collection, as well as vast gardens of camellias; blossoms at their best January 15 through March 15. Marchallville, at Masse Lane Farms, off Interstate 75, on State Route 49.

Confederate Flag Pole. The last remaining Confederate flag pole, erected in 1861. Blakely, off US-27 (on courthouse square).

Flint River Ferry. The ferry is a 50-foot flat steel barge, drawn by cable across the Flint River. Montezuma, eight miles north on State Route 127 at Flint River.

Little Theater. Features four plays annually in an authentically-restored pre-Civil War home. Albany, Pine Avenue.

Peanut Monument. Constant reminders that the area is one of the nation's largest producers of peanuts. Two locations: Blakely, Court House Square; Ashburn, off Interstate 75.

Plains. The small town made famous as the birthplace of Jimmy Carter. Points of interest include the home of the President, downtown area, old railroad depot, peanut warehouses and shops. On State Route 49.

Radium Springs. The largest natural spring in Georgia, maintains constant temperature of 68 degrees; swimming available. Albany, four miles south on State Route 3.

Rose Test Gardens. One of 25 gardens in the nation experimenting with development of new types of roses. Open mid-April through mid-November, Monday to Saturday, 8 a.m. to 5 p.m.; Sunday, 2 p.m. to 5 p.m. Thomasville, one mile east on US-84.

Thomasville Oak. Nearly 300-year-old tree has a limb spread of 155 feet and is 65 feet high and 22 feet in circumference. Thomasville, corner of East Monroe and North Crawford Streets.

East of coastal Savannah is Fort Pulaski, where Robert E. Lee carried out his first engineering assignment after graduating from West Point.

Mountain trails in Georgia's Chattahoochee and Oconee National Forests offer hikers scenic vistas of lush hardwood forests.

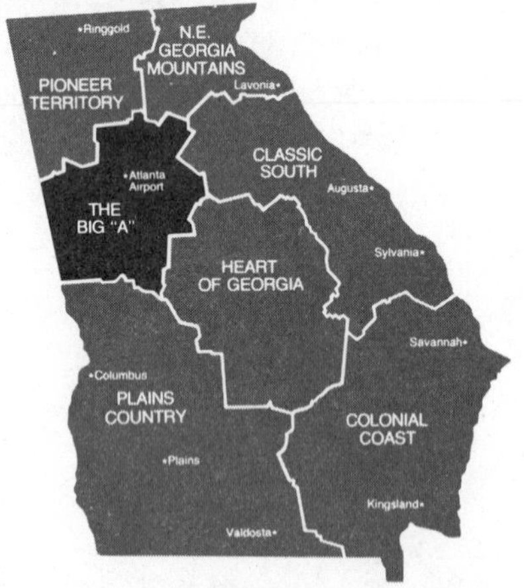

The Big "A"

Acworth Beach. Sand beach, bath house, snack bar, picnic facilities, foot trails. Open May through September, daily. Acworth, northeast off US-41, on State Route 92 (on Allatoona Lake).

Atlanta International Raceway. A 1½-mile paved oval featuring two major Grand National race events annually; NASCAR- and FIA-sanctioned. Hampton, two miles southwest on US-41.

Georgia Warm Springs. The waters found here maintain a constant temperature of 88 degrees and have been recognized for their healing properties since Indian days. Franklin D. Roosevelt came here for treatment of polio, and through his efforts the Georgia Warm Springs Foundation was established in 1927. Warm Springs, off State Route 85.

Margaret Mitchell Library. One of the most complete Civil War reference libraries, begun by *Gone With The Wind* author Margaret Mitchell. Open year-round. Fayetteville, between South Glynn Street and Lee Street, adjacent to site of original Fayatteville Academy.

Monastery of the Holy Ghost. Founded in 1944 by a group of monks who practice self-sufficiency, cultivating their own food and providing their necessities. Open year-round; winter, 10 a.m. to noon and 2:30 p.m. to 4:30 p.m.; summer, 3:30 p.m. to 5:30 p.m. (Only men inside monastery.)

Starr's Mill. One of the most scenic spots in the area, the old mill site is believed to date back more than 200 years. Starr's Mill, at intersection of State Routes 85 and 74.

Stone Mountain Park. A 3,200-acre family recreation park surrounding the world's largest granite monolith. Facilities include RV campground, motel, historic trails, fishing, canoe and sailboating. Open year-round, daily; summer hours 10 a.m. to 9 p.m.

Stone Mountain Memorial Carving. Figures of Confederate President Jefferson Davis, General Robert E. Lee and Stonewall Jackson carved from granite make this the world's largest work of sculptural art.

Underground Atlanta. A series of restored buildings now used as shops, restaurants, boutiques and quaint lounges. The buildings were left below street level when a system of viaducts were built in the 1920s. Open year-round, Monday to Saturday. Atlanta, Central Avenue and Old Alabama Street.

Georgia State Parks

Park	Location	CAMPING	PICNICKING	CONCESSIONS	SWIMMING	HIKING	BOATING	FISHING	HUNTING	WINTER SPORTS
A.H. Stephens	*Crawfordville. Off Interstate 20.*	•	•	•	•	•		•		
Amicalola Falls	*Dawsonville. Off State Route 183.*	•	•			•		•		
Black Rock Mountain	*Clayton. Off US-411.*	•	•	•		•		•		
Bobby Brown	*Elberton. off State Route 72.*	•	•		•	•	•	•		
Chattahoochee River	*Atlanta. Off US-41.*		•			•	•	•		
Cloudland Canyon	*Lafayette. Off State Route 143.*	•	•	•		•		•		
Crooked River	*Kingsland. Off State Route 40.*	•	•		•	•	•	•		
Elijah Clark	*Lincolnton. Off US-378.*	•	•		•	•	•	•		
Fort Mountain	*Chatsworth. Off US-76.*	•	•		•	•		•		
Fort Yargo	*Winder. Off State Route 81.*	•	•		•	•	•	•		
Franklin D. Roosevelt	*Pine Mountain. Off State Route 190.*	•	•	•	•	•	•	•		
General Coffee	*Douglas. Off State Route 32.*	•	•	•	•	•		•		
George T. Bagby	*Fort Gaines. Off State Route 39.*	•	•			•		•		
Georgia Veterans Memorial	*Cordele. Off US-280.*	•	•		•		•	•		
Hamburg	*Sandersville. Off State Route 248.*	•	•	•			•	•		
Hard Labor Creek	*Rutledge. Off US-278.*	•	•	•	•	•	•	•		
Hart	*Hartwell. Off US-29.*	•	•	•	•		•	•		
High Falls	*Forsyth. Off Interstate 75.*	•	•		•	•	•	•		
Indian Springs	*Jackson. On State Route 42.*	•	•		•	•	•	•		
James H. Floyd	*Summerville. Off US-27.*		•				•	•		
John Tanner	*Carrollton. Off State Route 16.*	•	•	•	•	•	•	•		
Kolomoki Mounds	*Blakely. Off US-27.*	•	•		•	•	•	•		
Laura S. Walker	*Waycross. Off State Route 48.*	•	•		•		•	•		
Little Ocmulgee	*McRae. Off US-319 and 441.*	•	•		•	•	•	•		
Magnolia Springs	*Millen. Off US-25.*	•	•		•	•	•	•		
Moccasin Creek	*Clayton. On State Route 197.*	•	•			•	•	•		
New Echota	*Calhoun. Off State Route 225.*		•							
Panola Mountain	*Atlanta. Off State Route 155.*		•			•				
Red Top Mountain	*Cartersville. Off Interstate 75.*	•	•	•	•	•	•	•		
Reed Bingham	*Adel. Off State Route 37.*	•	•	•	•	•	•	•		
Richmond Hill	*Richmond Hill. On State Route 144 spur.*	•	•			•	•	•		
Seminole	*Donalsonville. Off State Route 39.*	•	•		•		•	•		
Skidaway Island	*Savannah. Off State Route 26.*	•	•		•	•	•	•		
Stephen C. Foster	*Fargo. Off State Route 177.*	•	•	•		•	•	•		
Tugaloo	*Lavonia. Off State Route 328.*	•	•	•	•	•	•	•		
Unicoi	*Helen. Off State Route 356.*	•	•	•	•	•		•		
Victoria Bryant	*Royston. Off US-29.*	•	•		•	•		•		
Vogel	*Blairsville. Off US-19.*	•	•	•	•			•		
Watson Mill Bridge	*Comer. On State Route 22.*	•	•			•		•		

Georgia has no state forests. For additional information on Georgia state parks, contact: *Department of Natural Resources, Parks and Historical Sites Division, 270 Washington, SW, Atlanta, Georgia 30334, (404) 656-3530.*

South Carolina

South Carolinans have taken great pains to preserve their history, and more than 130 museums within this state will allow you to trace in detail the events of the past 200 years. By contrast, you'll also want to visit modern Hilton Head Island, home of 11 championship golf courses, and the site of many beautiful and unusual homes that have been built to strict standards in order to preserve the natural beauty of the area.

South Carolina was first explored by Spaniards in 1521, and temporarily settled by them under Aylion in 1526. The Spanish successfully thwarted attempts by the French to colonize the area, but the English later gained control of the Carolinas and South Carolina was included in the territory that Charles II granted to eight of his favorite noblemen. The first English settlement was established in 1670 along the Ashley River, but was later moved across the river to the present site of Charleston. The colony prospered due to the excellent harbor and an economy based on the cultivation of rice and indigo. The economy later proved unstable, however, and troubles with Indians, pirates and the management of the colony forced a takeover by England in 1719. Unhappy experiences with the methods of royal control and a desire for local self-government brought resistance to the Stamp Act and, finally, in July of 1774, a provincial congress elected delegates to the Continental Congress and practically assumed control of the colony. On September 15, 1775, the royal governor fled, and in the spring of the following year a state constitution was signed. During the hostilities of the Revolution, Charleston fell to the British. But sporadic

Full name: State of South Carolina
Origin of name: In honor of Charles I of England.
Mottoes: *Animus Opibusque Parati* (Prepared in Mind and Resources); *Dum Spiro, Spero* (While I Breathe, I Hope).
Nickname: Palmetto State
Capital: Columbia
Statehood: May 23, 1788, eighth state.
Population: 2,876,000 (ranks 26th).
Major Cities: Columbia (111,616), North Charlestown (58,544), Greenville (58,518).
Bird: Carolina wren
Flower: Yellow jessamine
Tree: Palmetto

Average daily temperatures by month

	Northern	Southern
Jan.	54.4 to 29.5	59.7 to 34.7
Feb.	57.7 to 31.6	62.5 to 37.0
Mar.	65.3 to 37.6	69.4 to 42.9
Apr.	75.4 to 47.0	77.8 to 50.9
May	82.3 to 55.4	84.5 to 58.3
Jun.	88.1 to 62.9	88.9 to 65.1
Jul.	90.8 to 66.9	91.1 to 68.7
Aug.	90.0 to 66.2	90.4 to 68.5
Sept.	84.9 to 60.1	85.6 to 63.4
Oct.	75.3 to 48.4	77.8 to 52.2
Nov.	65.3 to 37.6	69.2 to 41.8
Dec.	56.3 to 31.3	61.9 to 36.3
Year	73.8 to 47.9	76.6 to 51.7

attacks by patriots, and victories at King's Mountain and Cowpens, put pressure on the British and eventually forced their evacuation in 1782. South Carolina ratified the U.S. Constitution on May 23, 1788. State's rights became a major issue in

South Carolina during the years prior to the Civil War and the state ultimately became the first to secede from the Union. The Civil War began with Confederate artillery firing on Fort Sumter in Charleston Harbor, April 12, 1861. The South Carolina coast was the scene of a good deal of fighting during the war, and a Union blockade of Charleston Harbor severely crippled the state's economy. In 1865, General William T. Sherman led his troops across the state, destroying many plantations and burning Columbia.

Visitors to South Carolina won't want to miss the stately old homes that crowd Charleston's historic harbor area or the state's other attractions that include Magnolia and Cypress Gardens, Myrtle Beach, Fort Sumter National Monument and the scenic beauty of the Sumter National Forest and the Sand Hills State Forest.

Today, South Carolina is in the last stages of transition from an agrarian to an industrial economy. Agriculture and products such as tobacco, soybeans and cotton are still important to the state, but mining and the manufacture of textiles, chemicals, clothing, machinery, electrical equipment and wood products are becoming an increasingly significant part of the economic base.

Highlight

Charles Towne Landing

Three hundred years ago, brave men and women established the first permanent English settlement in South Carolina at Charles Towne Landing. Today, magnificent live oaks draped in the gray lace of Spanish moss reflect the same tranquility found by the early settler.

Aboard the full-scale replica 17th century trading vessel *Adventure,* visitors learn the important role the sea played in the development of the colony. Near the ship's wharf, the original fortified area is preserved for future archaeological discovery. Animals the settlers would have seen in South Carolina — wolves, pumas, bears, bison and alligators — roam in their own environment, uninhibited by the presence of man. Exhibits interpret the story of the first hundred years of the colony. Colonial buildings and tools permit visitors to experience settlers' life here during those early years.

Surrounding these historic areas are 80 acres of gardens alive with hundreds of varieties of plants and shrubbery offering a year-round array of color. Discover all of Charles Towne Landing

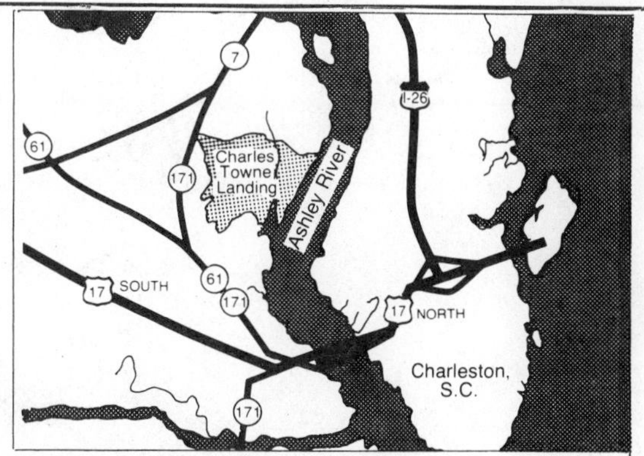

along miles of foot and bicycle paths or on tram tours. Charles Towne Landing is a place for fun and relaxation — a place to see, hear and learn of those who came before us.

Picnic tables are available for visitors. Explore the gardens on rented bicycles, kayaks or on tram tours. Special events, films and concerts are regularly scheduled for the visitors' enjoyment. Organized groups, companies and institutions use the landing's reserved picnic areas, the 10,000-square-foot Geodesic Dome, the Plaza and the Theater for special activities including outings, conventions, banquets and dances. Additional information may be obtained by writing: Charles Towne Landing, 1500 Old Town Road, Charleston, South Carolina 29407. (803) 556-4450.

The enchanting semi-tropical Hilton Head Island has been developed into one of South Carolina's most popular vacation spots.

Highlight

South Carolina's Beaches

South Carolina's beaches are nature's conspiracy of white sand and warm sun — long and wide and every one of their 281 miles filled with fun, excitement and mystery . . . lush sea islands and seashells . . . lazy alligators and graceful herons . . . a sub-tropical climate and the refreshing Atlantic . . . places like Calibogue Cay and Port Royal Sound and Bulls Bay.

Summer, winter, spring or fall, you'll find a full schedule of activities to make your visit a pleasant one because spring comes early to the coastal area and stays late.

Stroll one of South Carolina's beaches in the light of the first dawn and watch the sun rising slowly from the sea, bringing a blush to the morning sky. Relax among the sand dunes and sea oats in the early evening and watch the moonlight upon the sea. Watch the Spanish moss dancing eerily in the moonlight and listen to the sounds of the woodlands, far from the noise of the city. Or harvest your own oysters in one of the 20 public oyster beds set aside for you. The beds are in Georgetown, Charleston, Colleton, Beaufort and Jasper counties. (A free brochure listing the rules and giving the locations may be obtained by writing the South Carolina Wildlife and Marine Resources Department.)

Go crabbing in a tidal creek. All you need is string, a piece of meat and a net, or try your hand at fishing from one of the 13 piers strung along the coast. Do a little casting in the surf or rent a boat and fish in a river or inlet. If you like, you can take one of the "head boats" and go deep-sea fishing or even charter a boat and go out to the Gulf Stream.

Fishing piers are located in the areas of Cherry Grove Beach, Tilghman Beach, Crescent Beach, Windy Hill, Myrtle Beach, Myrtle Beach State Park, Isle of Palms and Folly Beach. A nominal fee is charged for fishing from the piers. You can use your own gear or rent what you need. You'll have plenty of company on the piers almost any time of the year, but two of the best months are September and October, from pier or surf.

At places like Little River, Murrells Inlet and Charleston, you can go deep-sea fishing on one of the "head boats." Some of these boats have half-day trips, which are great for the casual fisherman and his family or those who would just like to go to sea for a few hours. Some of the other boats leave early and return late, and you can bet the captains really try to find the fish. Rods, lines and bait are furnished. If you are a little squeamish, the crew will even bait your line and take your fish off the hook.

From these same ports, and at Georgetown and Hilton Head Island, you can charter a boat and go out to the gulf stream for big game fish. These boats usually carry four to six fishermen. Again, all equipment is furnished.

Trips on the "head boats" cost about $10 per person for a half-day to around $20 for the entire day. The charter boat prices start at around $250 a day. Arrangements for food aboard should be verified in making arrangements for the trips.

Normally a city of about 15,000 people, Myrtle Beach is the hub of the Grand Strand, the state's most popular resort area. This 55-mile stretch of beaches extends from Little River to Georgetown. In between are Cherry Grove, Crescent Beach, Ocean Drive, Atlantic Beach, Myrtle Beach, Surfside Beach, Garden City, Murrells Inlet, Litchfield Beach and Pawleys Island.

At the Grand Strand you can set your own pace — amusement parks; roller coasters; horses; bicycles; stock car races; nightclubs and top-flight entertainment; Brookgreen, an internationally acclaimed garden of sculpture; seafood restaurants; and golf courses. They're all at the Grand Strand. And if the beach itself is what you want, chair, umbrella and float rentals are always nearby.

To delight those who love beauty and history, old and historic Charleston graces South Carolina's southern coast. But there is more. There are marinas, fishing, golf and tennis. Nearby are the Isle of Palms, Sullivans Island and Folly Beach, all primarily residential islands; and Bulls Island, wild, desolate and a bird watcher's paradise — accessible only by a boat which departs and returns once a day at a cost of $5 per person. You can tour Charleston, which figured prominently in the Revolutionary War and Confederate War, in your RV, on bicycle or by walking, utilizing tour maps or cassette tapes available at the Charleston Visitor Information Center.

There are more than 9,000 campsites along the Grand Strand. Camping fees are generally in the $4.25 to $8 range.

State Offices

Tourism
Division of Tourism
South Carolina Department of Parks, Recreation and Tourism
1205 Pendleton Street
Columbia, South Carolina 29202
(803) 758-2536

State Police
Department of Public Safety
Columbia, South Carolina 29202
(803) 758-2815

Radio Stations

Columbia
WNOK 104.7 (FM)
Charleston
WCSC 1390 (AM)

South Carolina Points of Interest and Attractions

Aiken. This beautiful area is famed as a winter training area for race horses and as a polo grounds for some of the top polo ponies in the nation. Nearby, in Hopeland Gardens, is the Thoroughbred Racing Hall of Fame. Open year-round; Hall of Fame, November 15 through March 31. Free. Aiken, US-1, 78, and State Route 19.

African Village of Oyotunji. Oyotunji is a Yoruba African Village founded in 1970 by His Highness Oseijeman Adefunmi I. The community is composed of 125 black Americans who live in the same way that their Yoruban ancesters lived. The villagers live in primitive thatched huts, without electricity and other modern conveniences, and worship the African gods of the Yoruban religion. Open year-round, daily, 10 a.m. to dusk. Adults $1.50, children 50 cents. Yemassee, off US-17-21.

Brookgreen Gardens. On the site of four old rice plantations, the gardens contain more than 350 works representing the history of American sculpture from the 19th and 20th centuries; wildlife park. Open year-round, daily (except Christmas), 9:30 a.m. to 4:45 p.m. Adults $1.50, children 50 cents, children under six free. Myrtle Beach, 18 miles south on US-17.

Caesar's Head. Towering 3,277 feet above sea level, one of the state's most scenic views is provided from this outcropping said to resemble the head of Caesar; privately owned. Open year-round, daily. Adults 75 cents, children 35 cents. Caesar's Head, off State Scenic Route 11, on US-276.

Cape Romain Wildlife Refuge. One of the outstanding wildlife refuges along the East Coast, Cape Romain is an unspoiled primitive marsh and sea area located on an island served daily by boat. Visitors can collect shells, birdwatch or fish. Near McClellanville, off US-17-701. (803) 928-3368.

Castle Dracula. Meet Count Dracula and his scary friends on a spooky trip through the Count's castle. The realistic animated characters are only wax, but the sights and sounds here will almost certainly give you

Many beautiful homes and gardens preserve the rich history of Charleston, one of the nation's oldest cities.

chills. Open March through September, daily, 10 a.m. to midnight. Adults $2.50; children $1.50, under 6 admitted free. Myrtle Beach, 907 North Ocean Boulevard.

Charleston. Carriage Rides. Take a tour of Charleston in a picturesque horsedrawn carriage. Open year-round. Cost: $4. In White Point Gardens, 96 North Market Street.

Harbor Tour. Cruise along Charleston's historic waterfront, past antebellum homes and historic Fort Sumter. Open year-round, daily, departure times vary according to time of year. Adults $3.50, children under 11 $2, children under 6 free. At Gray Line Pier, on the Battery.

Charleston Naval Base. Generally, you'll find a destroyer, submarine, minesweeper and submarine tender here — all of which you can board and tour. Open year-round; tours Saturday and Sunday, 1 p.m. to 4 p.m. Off Interstate 26 at Spruill Avenue exit.

Port of Charleston. Some of the largest ships in the world can be viewed in this bustling harbor. Open year-round, daily. Free. At foot of Market Street, on Union Pier.

Cheraw National Fish Hatchery. This hatchery raises all warm-water fish native to South Carolina — largemouth bass, striped bass, bream and channel catfish. Children receive a free copy of *Fish Story for Children,* a booklet published by the Department of the Interior. Open year-round, Monday to Friday, 7 a.m. to 4 p.m. Free. Cheraw, five miles south, on US-1.

Cypress Gardens. Features centuries-old cypress trees; banks studded with flowers; displays of camellias, daffodils and azaleas. Boat or walking tours available; outdoor restaurant. Open February 1 through May 1, daily, 8 a.m. to sunset. Adults $3, children over 12 $1.25, under 12 free. Charleston, 24 miles north, off State Route 52.

Edisto Gardens. Tall cypress, crab apple and flowering dogwood, surrounded by plantings of azaleas which reach their peak in April; 9,500 rose bushes in 300 varieties. Open year-round, daily. Free. Orangeburg, on US-301.

Glencairn Gardens. A formal garden with terraced lawns, landscaped beds, fountain, reflection pool. Open year-round, daily, sunrise to sunset. Free. Rock Hill, at corner of Charlotte Avenue and Crest Street.

Grand Strand. A 55-mile stretch of beach with Myrtle Beach as its hub, offering 10,000 campsites, 28 golf courses, 150 tennis courts, historical sites, recreation facilities, fishing, unique shopping complexes, boutiques, fine restaurants, and, of course, the beach. Open year-round. Extends from Little River in north to Georgetown in south, off US-17.

Guinness Hall of World Records. In the Guinness Hall fantastic human and natural occurrences spring to life through video tapes, replicas and unique displays; three movie theaters, appearances by record holders during summer. Open March through November, daily, 10 a.m. to 11 p.m. Adults $2.50, children over 6 $1.50, under 6 free. Myrtle Beach, North Ocean Boulevard, between Ninth and 10th Avenues.

Healing Springs. Waters used by the Indians before the white settlers came are said to keep one youthful and cure many diseases. Open year-round, daily. Free. Blackville, three miles north, off State Route 3.

Highway 11. Extending from Gaffney in a 130-mile loop to Interstate 85 at Lake Hartwell, South Carolina Scenic Highway 11 winds through some of the most beautiful mountain terrain east of the Mississippi. The route is especially popular in the fall, when the mountain foliage bursts into a blaze of color.

Hilton Head Island. Located in the southeastern corner of the state, Hilton

Head Island is one of the largest sea islands on the Atlantic Coast, with 12 miles of unspoiled beaches. The island is the site of many beautiful plantations, historic sites, Sea Pines Forest Preserve, Whooping Crane Pond; tennis, golf, bike riding, horseback riding, fishing, sailing, restaurants, clubs, shopping centers. Open year-round. Bluffton, east on US-278.

Kalmia Gardens. A 12-acre arboretum featuring the kalmia latifolia, mountain laurel, as well as many Up-Country and Low-Country plants. Open year-round, daily, sunrise to sunset. Free. Hartsville, West Carolina Avenue.

Kiawah Island. A 10,000-acre island that was once the home of the Kiawah Indians. Its uncrowded beach is 10 miles long and 150 yards wide at various points; wildlife, tours available. Charleston, 20 miles south off State Route 700.

Magnolia Plantation and Gardens. In the gardens you'll find camellias so old that they are now trees, plus magnificent magnolias; petting zoo; walking tours; bicycle rentals; electric boats. Open year-round, daily, 8 a.m. to sunset. Adults $3, students 13-20 $2, students 4-12 $1, under 4 free; prices increase during March and April. Charleston, 10 miles north, on State Route 61.

Park Seed Company. Gardens of the Park Seed Company, one of the largest seed supply houses in the nation, feature stunning floral displays; guided tours of plant available. Open year-round, Monday to Friday, 8 a.m. to 4:30 p.m. Free. Greenwood, off US-178 and State Route 72.

Pretty Place. Located atop Standing Stone Mountain, this spot offers a view of range after range of the Blue Ridge Mountains; formally named Symmes Chapel, it has come to be known simply as the "Pretty Place." North of Greenville, off US-276.

Sassafras Mountain. From the summit of South Carolina's highest peak (3,548 feet), you can see into North Carolina, Tennessee and Georgia. A narrow paved road winds off US-178 to the U.S. Forestry Lookout Tower on top of the mountain. Open year-round, daily. Free. Rocky Bottom, about 45 miles north of Interstate 85. (If you want the lookout tower opened, call (803) 878-3415.)

Savannah National Wildlife Refuge. A 13,000-acre refuge teeming with wildfowl, deer, raccoons, alligators; principal winter species of wildfowl include green-winged teal, pintails, ring-necked ducks, wood ducks, black ducks, gadwalls, coots and common gallinules; nature drive; picnic areas. Open year-round, daily, sunrise to sunset. Free. Savannah, north off US-17.

Stumphouse Mountain Tunnel and Issaqueena Falls. Walk 1,600 feet into this lighted tunnel that was begun in 1852 as a planned rail line between the port city of Charleston and the Midwest. Picnic and camp at nearby park; visit Issaqueena Falls. Open year-round, daily, sunrise to sunset. Free. Walhalla, 35 miles off Interstate, on State Route 28.

Truluck Vineyards. Tour vineyards, fermentation room and aging cellar where wines are produced by European methods; wine-tasting, sales. Open year-round, Tuesday to Saturday, 10:30 a.m. to 5:30 p.m. Free. Lake City, on US-52.

Tunnelvision. A unique piece of art painted on the side of a building, it portrays a highway that leads through a tunnel. Painted on a flat brick wall, the artist's perspective and technique are combined to create a life-size illusion so real it tempts motorists to drive through. Free. Columbia, corner of Taylor and Marion Streets on Federal Land Bank Building.

USS Sequioa. The presidential yacht for 45 years. Open May through October, 10 a.m. to 10 p.m. for tours. Adults $2.50, children $1.50. North Myrtle Beach, Vereen's Inland Waterway Marina, on US-17.

Vagabond Cruise. Cruises around Calibogue Sound and nearby islands, including Hilton Head. Open mid-March through October, daily except Monday, departs 3 p.m.; sunset cruise at 7:30 p.m. during June and July. Adults $4.50, children $2.

Vertical Sundial. A 140-year-old sundial, believed to be the only one of its kind remaining in the country; keeps perfect time. Free. Barnwell, in front of the county courthouse on Main Street (on State Route 70, 10 miles west of US-301).

Walhalla National Fish Hatchery. Hatchery raises brook, rainbow and brown trout. Open year-round, daily, 8 a.m. to 4 p.m. Free. Walhalla, 21 miles north, off State Route 107.

Yorktown. Known as the "Fighting Lady," the aircraft carrier *Yorktown* is the only carrier ever made accessible to the public by the Navy. Now operated by the state of South Carolina, the *Yorktown* has been designated as a Naval and Maritime Museum; models, exhibits, movies, actual aircraft on board. Open year-round, daily, 9 a.m. to 6 p.m. Adults $2, children $1. Charleston, at east end of Cooper River Bridge in Mt. Pleasant, off US-17.

South Carolina State Parks

Park	Location	CAMPING	PICNICKING	CONCESSIONS	SWIMMING	HIKING	BOATING	FISHING	HUNTING	WINTER SPORTS
Aiken	*Aiken. Off US-78.*	•	•		•	•	•	•		
Andrew Jackson	*Lancaster. On US-521.*	•	•			•	•	•		
Baker Creek	*McCormick. On US-378.*	•	•		•	•	•	•		
Barnwell	*Barnwell. On State Route 3.*	•	•		•	•	•	•		
Cheraw	*Cheraw. On US-1.*	•	•		•	•	•	•		
Chester	*Chester. On State Route 72.*	•	•			•	•	•		
Colleton	*Walterboro. On US-15.*	•	•			•		•		
Croft	*Spartanburg. Off State Route 56.*	•	•		•	•	•	•		
Edisto Beach	*Charleston. On State Route 174.*	•	•		•	•		•		
Givhans Ferry	*Summerville. On State Route 61.*	•	•			•		•		
Greenwood	*Greenwood. On State Route 702.*	•	•	•	•	•	•	•		
Hamilton Branch	*McCormick. Off US-221.*	•	•				•	•		
Hickory Knob	*McCormick. On US-378.*	•	•			•	•	•		
Hunting Island	*Beaufort. On US-21.*	•	•	•	•	•	•	•		
Huntington Beach	*Murells Inlet. On US-17.*	•	•	•	•	•	•	•		
Kings Mountain	*York. On State Route 161.*	•	•	•	•	•	•	•		
Lee	*Bishopville. Off Interstate 20.*	•	•		•	•	•	•		
Little Pee Dee	*Dillon. Off State Route 57.*	•	•		•	•	•	•		
Myrtle Beach	*Myrtle Beach. On US-17.*	•	•	•	•	•	•	•		
Oconee	*Walhalla. On State Route 107.*	•	•	•	•	•	•	•		
Paris Mountain	*Greenville. Off US-25.*	•	•		•	•	•	•		
Pleasant Ridge	*Greenville. On State Route 11.*	•	•		•	•	•	•		
Poinsett	*Sumter. Off State Route 261.*	•	•		•	•	•	•		
Rivers Bridge	*Ehrhardt. On State Route 641.*	•	•		•		•	•		
Sadlers Creek	*Anderson. Off US-29.*	•	•		•	•	•	•		
Santee	*Santee. Off Interstate 95.*	•	•	•	•	•	•	•		
Sesquicentennial	*Columbia. Off US-1.*	•	•		•	•	•	•		
Table Rock	*Pickens. On State Route 11.*	•	•	•	•	•	•	•		

Huge oaks, draped in Spanish moss, add to the tranquil beauty of Middleton Place Gardens and Plantation at Charleston.

South Carolina State Forests

Forest	Location	CAMPING	PICNICKING	CONCESSIONS	SWIMMING	HIKING	BOATING	FISHING	HUNTING	WINTER SPORTS
Manchester	*Wedgefield. On State Route 261.*	•	•			•	•	•		
Sand Hills	*Patrick. On US-1.*	•	•			•	•	•		

For more information on South Carolina state parks and forests, contact: *South Carolina State Parks, PO Box 71, Columbia, South Carolina 29203, (803) 578-7507; State Commission of Forestry, PO Box 21707, Columbia, South Carolina 29221, (803) 758-2226.*

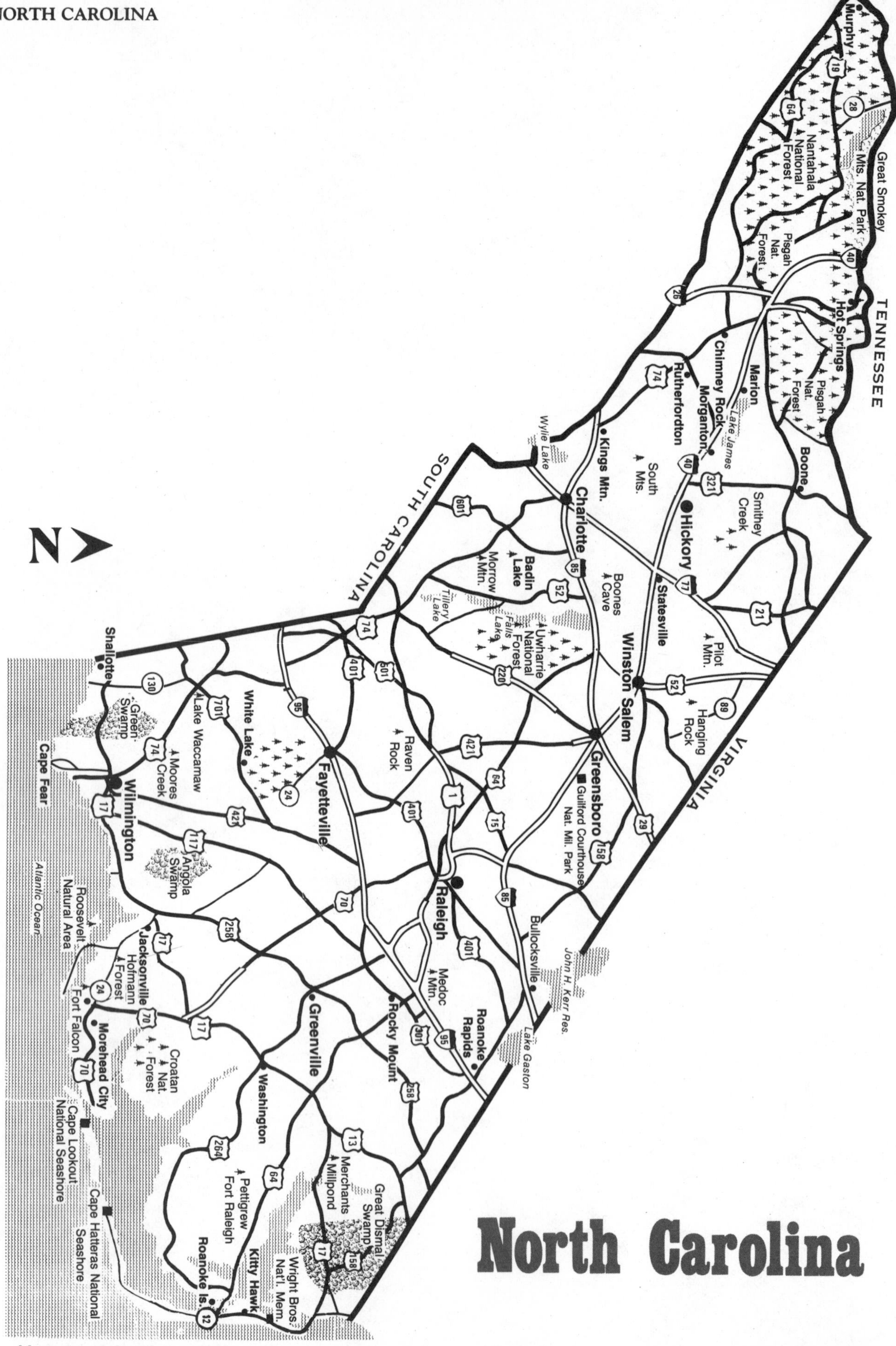

North Carolina

Map not to exact scale.

North Carolina

North Carolina has much to interest visitors. As one of the original 13 colonies, the state has roots deep in colonial America, yet it is also firmly tied to the traditions of the South. For natural wonders, there are the islands of the Outer Banks, the Blue Ridge Mountains or the scenic splendor of the Great Smokies. Then there's North Carolina's rich history, which stretches from the first English settlement in the New World, at Roanoke Island, to more recent events like the Wright Brothers' flight at Kitty Hawk.

The first English Colony in America was established on Roanoke Island in 1585, with Ralph Lane as governor and Sir Walter Raleigh as sponsor. This colony failed, as did another sent in 1587 which came to be known as the Lost Colony because all the members simply disappeared (among the missing was Virginia Dare, the first child of English parentage born in America). More than 50 years later, a group of Virginia settlers moved into the region and began to locate along the Albemarle Sound, near the state's present northeastern border. In 1663, Charles II transferred the charter of Carolina to eight lords and, later, the boundaries were firmly established. North Carolina grew slowly during its early years, primarily because its dangerous coast and inefficient management made other colonies more desirable. Finally, England made the region a royal colony and the area flourished. As the break with England drew near, North Carolina patriots openly resisted the Stamp Act, organized a boycott of British goods and chose delegates to the Continental Congress. During the Revolution, very little fighting took place on North Carolina soil, but troops from the state fought valiantly in other states. North Carolina rejected the Federal Constitution in 1788, but ratified it the following year, thus becoming the next to last state to accept

Full name: State of North Carolina
Origin of name: In honor of Charles I of England.
Motto: *Esse Quam Videri* (To Be Rather Than To Seem).
Nickname: Tar Heel State
Capital: Raleigh
Statehood: November 21, 1789, the 62th state.
Population: 5,525,000 (ranks 11th).
Major Cities: Charlotte (281,417), Greensboro (155,848), Winston-Salem (141,018).
Bird: Cardinal
Flower: Dogwood
Tree: Pine

Average daily temperature by month

	Eastern	Western
Jan.	54.6 to 34.0	46.3 to 24.4
Feb.	56.9 to 35.6	49.1 to 26.1
Mar.	63.0 to 41.6	57.0 to 32.2
Apr.	72.2 to 49.8	67.9 to 41.3
May	78.5 to 57.8	76.0 to 49.7
Jun.	84.0 to 65.7	82.1 to 57.3
Jul.	87.2 to 69.9	84.5 to 61.3
Aug.	86.6 to 69.6	84.0 to 60.2
Sept.	82.0 to 64.6	79.6 to 53.8
Oct.	74.3 to 54.8	69.5 to 42.1
Nov.	65.4 to 44.1	57.7 to 32.4
Dec.	57.7 to 36.2	49.1 to 26.7
Year	71.9 to 52.0	66.9 to 42.3

that document. North Carolina joined the Confederacy after the Civil War had begun, despite considerable pro-Union and antislavery sentiments within the state. During the war the port of Wilmington became a haven for Confederate blockade-runners.

Scenic Laurel Falls near Rosman are typical of the many natural wonders of the state.

Among the many attractions you'll find in North Carolina are the Cherokee Indian Reservation, home of the eastern band of the Cherokee Indians; Daniel Boone Native Gardens; Mystery Hill, including Mystery House where the law of gravity seems to be defied; Bentonville Battleground, site of the largest Civil War battle fought in North Carolina; the Thomas Wolfe Memorial and Carl Sandburg's Home. For the outdoor enthusiast, the state also has many fine state parks and forests, as well as several national forests and the Cape Lookout and Cape Hatteras National Seashores.

Both tourism and fishing are of major importance to the state's economy, which also rests on a foundation of textiles, tobacco products, furniture, electrical equipment and wood products.

State Offices

Tourism
Travel Department Section
North Carolina Department of Natural and Economic Resources
PO Box 27687
Raleigh, North Carolina 27611
(919) 733-4171

State Police
Department of Public Safety
Raleigh, North Carolina 27611
(919) 733-3911

Radio Stations

Charlotte
WBT 1110 (AM)
Durham
WDBS 107.4 (FM)
Greensboro
WCOG 1320 (AM)
WRQK 98.7 (FM)
Raleigh
WRAL 101.5 (FM)

North Carolina Points of Interest and Attractions

Airlie Gardens. Azaleas, camellias and huge live oaks form the backdrop for scenic lakeside drives. Open year-round, peak bloom in April. Free. Wilmington, off US-76.

Appalachian Trail. Some 200 miles of the wilderness route pass through North Carolina along the high ridges in the Pisgah and Nantahala National Forests and Great Smoky Mountains National Park. The trail crosses Fontana Dam, Newfound Gap Road and US-64.

Asheville. The hometown of North Carolina's famous native son, Thomas Wolfe, author of *Look Homeward Angel* and other works. Wolfe's home is open to visitors during the summer months. Asheville, off US-40 and 26.

A Suggested Tour

Winston-Salem

One of the South's most progressive cities, Winston-Salem is a combination of two communities; Salem, with the traditions of its Moravian founders and Winston, an industrial center.

Located here is one of the world's largest tobacco manufacturing centers, the R.J. Reynolds Tobacco Company, which offers free guided tours of its facilities.

The Joseph Schlitz Brewing Company in Winston-Salem is one of the largest plants under a single roof within the state. It has a production capacity of over four million barrels of beer annually. Tours are provided on weekdays at the plant which is located 5½ miles south of Interstate 40 just off US-52.

Reynolda House, home of the late Richard Joshua Reynolds, founder of the R.J. Reynolds Tobacco Company, was occupied in 1917. In 1965, it was opened to the public and dedicated to the advancement of education and the arts. Open daily, a small admission fee is charged.

Old Salem

Old Salem was founded in 1766 by Moravians, a devout Germanic people who brought to what was then the Carolina wilderness a strong faith, artisans' skills, a sense of order, a belief in the importance of education, an abhorrence of violence and a unique closely-knit way of life.

The spirit of these industrious people lives even today in the restored village. Visitors may see such buildings as the Salem Tavern, which once provided lodging for George Washington; the Single Brothers' House; the John Vogler House and the Boys' School. There is also the bakery, still in operation and craft shops.

Bethabara

Historic Bethabara is the site of the first Moravian settlement in North Carolina. Founded in 1753, Bethabara became a trading center where fine craft wares could be bought. The 1788 Church and Gemeinhaus has been restored and is one of the finest examples of Moravian architecture in America.

Tanglewood

Located on the Yadkin River, a few miles west of Winston-Salem, Tanglewood offers facilities and programs for individuals, family and group activities such as golf, tennis, family camping, vacation cottages, swimming, horseback riding and a summer theater. The excellent golf course here was the site of the 1974 Professional Golf Association Championship Tournament.

Hiddenite

West of Winston-Salem off Interstate 40 on NC-90 is the small community of Hiddenite, where rockhounds dig for emeralds, hiddenite and other gems and minerals.

Blowing Rock. The resort of Blowing Rock is named for its unique rock formations, where air currents from John's River Gorge return light objects to their point of departure. Blowing Rock, off US-321.

Bridal Veil Falls. This picturesque falls cascades over US-64, while cars drive under the 120-foot falls. Highlands.

Charlotte Motor Speedway. One and one-half mile banked asphalt track with seating for more than 50,000 in the grandstand and 35,000 in the infield. Open year-round. NASCAR-sanctioned stock car races in May *(World 600)* and October *(National 500)*. Charlotte, Interstate 85 and Interstate 77.

Clarendon Gardens. Over 300 varieties of holly; also camellias, azaleas, lake, nursery. Open year-round. Pinehurst, off State Route 211.

Coker Arboretum. Botanical garden on campus of University of North Carolina. Open year-round. Chapel Hill, off State Route 54 and 86.

Connestee Falls. Twin falls, each about 110 feet high; picnic grounds with fireplaces, shelters and spring water; walkway to base of falls. Open year-round. Admission fee. Brevard, six miles south on US-276.

Craggy Gardens. Recreation area in high altitude profusion of crimson-purple, rhododendrons; visitors center, picnic area, trails. Open year-round; peak bloom in mid-June. Busick, southwest on Blue Ridge Parkway.

Daniel Boone Native Gardens. Six different areas featuring native plants and rustic architecture. Boone, off State Route 194.

Elizabethan Gardens. Formal and informal plantings, with fine collection of antique garden ornaments. Roanoke Island, off US-64 and 264.

Flat Rock Playhouse. Designated North Carolina's state theater, this is the oldest professional summer theater in the state; Vagabond players stage productions. Open June through Labor Day. Flat Rock, off US-26. (704) 692-2281.

Golf Hall of Fame. Opened in 1974, this magnificent contemporary structure houses collections of photographs, gold artifacts, and the portraits of world golfing greats who have been inducted into the Golf Hall of Fame. Open year-round. Pinehurst, off US-15 and 501.

Grandfather Mountain. The highest peak (5,964 feet) in the Blue Ridge range. Mile-High Swinging Bridge connects two peaks accessible by privately built toll road; hiking trails, picnicking, camping. Open April through November. Linville, off US-221.

Great Dismal Swamp. A portion of the huge swamp shared by North Carolina and Virginia. Elizabeth City, along US-17 and 158.

Greenfield Gardens. A municipal park with five-mile azalea drive around Greenfield Lake; boat rides, playgrounds, zoo, amphitheater, extensive plantings of azaleas and other flowers, wide variety of native shrubs and trees. Wilmington, off US-74 and 76.

John C. Campbell Folk School. Crafts and recreation courses; famous for woodcarvings. Open year-round. Brasstown, off US-64.

Jumpoff Rock. Huge rock on Jumpoff Mountain overlooking Blue Ridge Areas. Hendersonville, off US-26.

Laurel Lake Gardens. Extensive plantings of camellias, sasanquas, and other ornamentals; picnic area, nursery. Open year-round; peak bloom period is November through April. Salemburg, off State Route 242.

Liggett and Myers, Incorporated. Manufacturing plant for L & M cigarettes. Open year-round, Monday to Friday; tours 8 a.m. to 11:30 a.m., 12:30 p.m. to 3 p.m. Durham, off Interstate 85. (919) 638-5521.

Linville Caverns. Stalactites and stalagmites along an underground river in well-lighted, marked passageways; picnic area on grounds. Open year-round. Linville, off US-221.

Linville Falls. Spectacular double-level falls and gorge, surrounded by Pisgah National Forest. Open year-round. Linville, just off Blue Ridge Parkway and US-221 and State Route 105.

Mystery Hill. Amazing natural phenomena with authentic mountain life exhibits. See Mystery House, where the law of gravity seems to be defied and where objects act the opposite of what is normally expected. Between Boone and Blowing Rock, off US-321 and Blue Ridge Parkway.

Nantahala Gorge. Spectacular canyon that follows the Nantahala River; Cherokee Indian name meaning "Land of the Noonday Sun." Between Bryson City and Topton, off US-19.

North Carolina Botanical Gardens. A 300-acre area of pine and deciduous woodlands, fields and streams with varied habitats where many species of native plants grow. Open year-round, daily. Chapel Hill, off State Route 86.

Research Triangle Park. A uniquely-planned area for industrial and governmental research; 4,600 acres in a triangle formed by Duke University, University of North Carolina and North Carolina State University. Open year-round. Durham, Chapel Hill and Raleigh, off US-70.

Santa's Land. See Santa in year-round workshop complete with blacksmith shop, toy shop and gift store. Open year-round. Cherokee, off US-19.

Sarah P. Duke Memorial Gardens. Formal and informal plantings of annuals, perennials, ornamental shrubs. Open year-round, peak bloom in April. Durham, on campus of Duke University, off Interstate 85.

Schlitz Brewery. The Joseph P. Schlitz brewery is the largest plant under one roof in North Carolina, producing four million barrels of beer annually. Open year-round, Monday to Friday, tours from 9 a.m. to 4 p.m. Free. Winston-Salem, off US-40. (919) 788-6710.

Tweetsie Railroad. Ride on a sightseeing train pulled by steam locomotive over a narrow gauge track; frontier village, sky lift and amusement park. Open June 1 through October. Blowing Rock, off US-321.

USS North Carolina Battleship Memorial. The 35,000-ton battleship is preserved as a war memorial; "Immortal Showboat" light and sound spectacular in summer; museum. Open year-round. Wilmington, off US-421, 74 and 76. (919) 762-1829.

Whitaker Park. Home of the R.J. Reynolds Tobacco Company plant. Open year-round, Monday to Friday, tours from 8 a.m. to 2:30 p.m. and 4:30 p.m. to 10 p.m. Winston-Salem, off US-40. (919) 748-2632.

Whitewater Falls. Two-level falls; upper falls cascades 411 feet and is believed to be the highest in Eastern U.S. Route to falls passes by four other falls. Oakland, between Cashiers and Lake Toxaway, off US-64.

North Carolina State Parks

Park	Location	CAMPING	PICNICKING	CONCESSIONS	SWIMMING	HIKING	BOATING	FISHING	HUNTING	WINTER SPORTS
Carolina Beach	*Carolina Beach. Off US-421.*	•	•			•		•		
Cliffs of the Neuse	*Seven Springs. Off State Route 111.*	•	•	•	•	•	•	•		
Crowder's Mountain	*Gastonia. Off Interstate 85.*		•			•		•		
Duke Power	*Troutman. Off Interstate 77.*	•	•	•	•	•		•		
Goose Creek	*Washington. US-264 and 17.*	•	•			•	•	•		
Hammocks Beach	*Swansboro. Off State Route 24.*		•	•	•	•		•		
Hanging Rock	*Danbury. Off State Route 89.*	•	•	•	•	•	•	•		
Jones Lake	*Ammon. Off State Route 242.*	•	•	•	•	•	•	•		
Medoc Mountain	*Hollister. Off Interstate 95 and US-301.*	•	•			•		•		
Merchants Millpond	*Sunbury. Off US-158.*					•	•	•		
Morrow Mountain	*Albemarle. Off State Route 740.*	•	•	•	•	•	•	•		
Mount Mitchell	*Burnsville. Off State Route 128.*	•	•	•		•				
Pettigrew	*Creswell. Off US-64.*	•	•		•	•	•	•		
Pilot Mountain	*Pinnacle. Off US-52.*		•			•				
Raven Rock	*Lillington. off US-421.*	•	•			•		•		
Singletary Lake	*Elizabethtown. Off State Route 53.*	•	•			•	•	•		
William B. Umstead	*Raleigh. Off US-70.*	•	•		•	•	•	•		

North Carolina State Forests

Forest	Location	CAMPING	PICNICKING	CONCESSIONS	SWIMMING	HIKING	BOATING	FISHING	HUNTING	WINTER SPORTS
Clemmons	*Clayton. Off US-70.*	•	•	•		•				
Holmes	*Hendersonville. Off US-64.*	•	•			•				
Tuttle	*Lenoir. Off State Route 18.*	•	•	•		•				

For more information on North Carolina state parks and forests, contact: *Division of Parks and Recreation, PO Box 27687, Raleigh, North Carolina 27687, (919) 733-5133.*

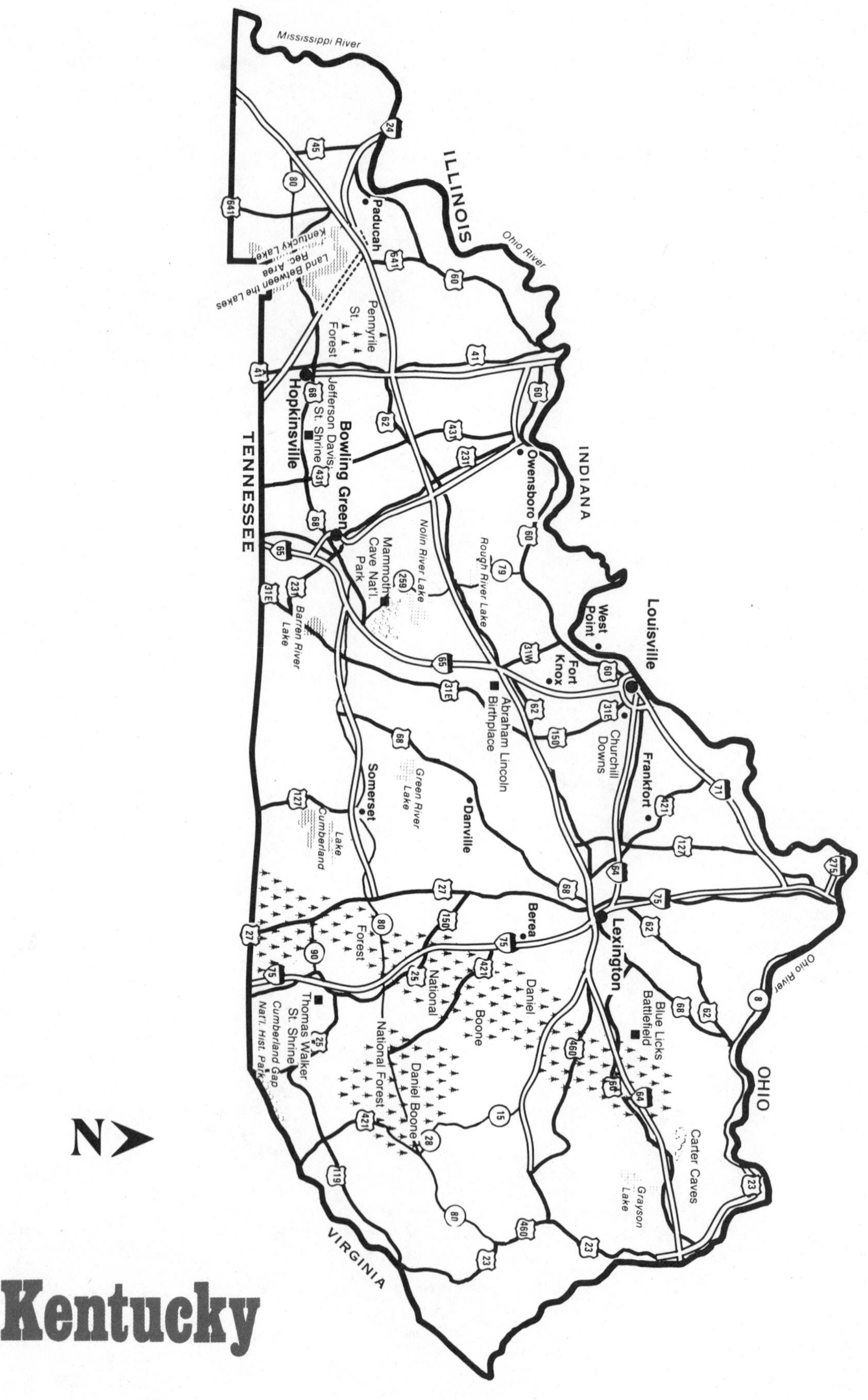

Kentucky

Map not to exact scale.

Kentucky

Fine tobacco, racehorses and whiskey are among the more notable distinctions of the "Bluegrass State." But Kentucky also boasts the world's longest cave system at Mammoth Cave National Park; a sprawling outdoor wonderland called "Land Between the Lakes"; the scenic Daniel Boone National Forest; colorful "mountain folk" and their rich folklore; and the cultural offerings of Louisville and Abraham Lincoln's birthplace at Hodgenville.

Indians may have lived in the forests of what is now western Kentucky some 15,000 years ago; but the first extensive exploration of the territory did not come until 1750, when Dr. Thomas Walker scouted the region for Loyal Land Company. A number of other explorers entered Kentucky over the next two decades, including Daniel Boone in 1769, but the first permanent settlements — Harrodstown, Boonesborough, McGary's Fort, St. Asaph — weren't established until 1775. From 1775 to 1785, Kentucky immigrants were continually menaced by Indian attacks, which persisted until General Anthony Wayne's victory in the Battle of Fallen Timbers, in Ohio, finally ended them. Kentucky became a member of the Union on June 1, 1792.

When the Civil War began, Kentucky was prospering in trade with both the North and South and attempted to remain neutral in the conflict. Later, the state was divided in its sentiments and supplied troops to both sides (30,000 to the South, 64,000 to the North). The war was brought briefly to Kentucky when it was invaded by Confederate armies seeking to rally the countryside to their cause.

Full name: Commonwealth of Kentucky
Origin of name: From Wyandot Indian name, Ken-tah-teh, meaning "Land of Tomorrow."
Motto: United We Stand, Divided We Fall.
Nickname: Bluegrass State
Capital: Frankfort
Statehood: June 1, 1792, 15th state.
Population: 3,458,000 (ranks 23rd).
Major Cities: Louisville (335,954), Lexington (186,048), Owensboro (50,788).
Bird: Cardinal
Flower: Goldenrod
Tree: Tulip poplar

Average daily temperature by month

	Eastern	Western
Jan.	45.1 to 23.6	45.1 to 25.5
Feb.	48.5 to 25.2	49.4 to 28.1
Mar.	57.4 to 33.0	58.1 to 35.8
Apr.	69.8 to 42.3	70.8 to 46.9
May	77.9 to 50.4	78.8 to 54.6
Jun.	84.7 to 58.4	86.2 to 62.6
Jul.	87.3 to 62.6	89.3 to 66.2
Aug.	86.4 to 61.1	88.6 to 64.1
Sept.	81.4 to 54.5	83.0 to 57.4
Oct.	71.2 to 42.5	72.6 to 45.8
Nov.	57.6 to 33.0	58.4 to 36.0
Dec.	48.0 to 27.0	48.2 to 29.2
Year	67.9 to 42.8	69.0 to 46.0

Visitors to Kentucky may want to time their trip to take in the Kentucky Derby Festival in May, and perhaps stay on for the National Coon Hunt in Paducah the following month. Other samples of Kentucky's offerings can be found at Boonesborough State Park, Cumberland Gap National Historic Park, Ohio River cruises on old stern-wheelers and hundreds of sprawling thoroughbred horse farms.

Spurred on by a renewed demand for coal, Kentucky's mines are once again active and the state's economy is also heavily industrialized with the manufacture of machinery, tobacco products, clothing, transportation equipment, chemicals, paper and paper products among the more important industries.

State Offices

Tourism
Division of Advertising and Travel Promotion
Capital Annex
Frankfort, Kentucky 40601
(502) 564-4270

State Police
Department of Public Safety
Frankfort, Kentucky 40601
(502) 227-2221

Radio Stations

Lexington
WLAP 630 (AM)
Louisville
WHAS 840 (AM)

Kentucky Points of Interest and Attractions

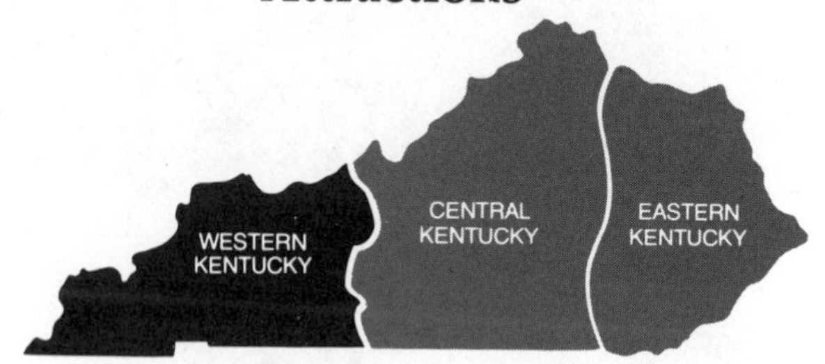

Western Kentucky

Beech Bend Park. A 1,000-acre park featuring RV campsites, indoor roller skating rink, free stage attractions, swimming pool, miniature golf, rides, free zoo, car racing, trampoline, ski lift, refreshment stands. Open year-round (campsites), June through Labor Day (concessions); daily. Bowling Green, three miles west off US-31W. (502) 842-8101.

Boat Rides. The *Belle of the Lakes.* A 150-passenger, diesel-powered excursion boat available for sightseeing above Kentucky Dam, through Barkley Canal and into Lake Barkley. Season: Summer. May, weekends only 1 p.m. and 4 p.m.; Memorial Day through July 4, daily, 1 p.m. and 4 p.m.; July 4 through Labor Day,

Golden ripe burley and tobacco barn. Tobacco is grown in almost every county in Kentucky, where it has been a major cash crop since pioneer days.

Churchill Downs, home of the fabulous Kentucky Derby. Its twin spires are a Louisville landmark.

daily, 1 p.m., 4 p.m., and 7 p.m.; Labor Day through end of September, daily, 1 p.m. and 4 p.m. Adults $3.50, children 3 to 12, $2.50, under 2, free. Benton, Kentucky Dam Marina, off US-641. (502) 527-8626. *The Princess.* Authentic side-wheeler takes travelers for rides on Kentucky Lake. Season: Memorial Day through Labor Day, daily, 11 a.m., 2 p.m. and 7:15 p.m.; September, two trips daily; October, by appointment only. Benton, Kenlake Marina, off US-68. (502) 354-6205.

Kentucky Lake Music Barn. A rustic barn offering square dancing and stage shows on Saturday nights, with entertainment provided by professional recording stars. Bluegrass and country music featured in a down-home atmosphere. Season: year-round, Friday and Saturday, 8:30 p.m. Adults $3, children $1.50. For square dance on Friday night, adults $2, children $1. Murray, 14 miles southeast, on State Route 121. (502) 436-8806.

Land Between the Lakes. A long narrow strip of land nearly surrounded by two man-made lakes and covered with a green, forested canopy. The 170,000-acre "peninsula" has been developed by the Tennessee Valley Authority as a national demonstration in outdoor recreation and environmental education; camping, boating, swimming, water-skiing, archery, slide show. Between Lake Barkley and Kentucky Lake, off US-62, 641 and 68, and State Routes 80 and The Trace. (502) 924-5602.

Midwest Harness Raceway. Two standard-bred harness meets a year; air-conditioned clubhouse seats 350, grandstand seating for 2,500. Seasons: end of April through June 29; after Labor Day through October; Monday through Saturday, 7:30 p.m. (10 races, Friday and Saturday). (502) 827-5641.

Highlight

KENTUCKY BOURBON

Legend has it that the creator of Kentucky bourbon was a Baptist minister at Georgetown, the Reverend Elijah Craig. In 1789, he is said to have produced a new taste in whiskey by using corn, rye and barley malt — the same ingredients that are used today.

The fundamental steps used by distillers are universal: grain handling and milling, mashing, fermentation, distillation, aging and bottling. However, the differences in taste among the bourbon brands can best be expressed by a quotation from National Distillers Products: "Like the celebrated chef who, having earned a reputation for unique, exotic and delicious dishes and sauces, carefully guards the secrets of his trade, so a distiller has production techniques and formulas which are confidential and cannot be disclosed."

This much, though, is certain: Corn, rye and barley malt are ground separately to a mealy substance. Then the corn, rye and limestone water, indigenous to Kentucky, are cooked together to form a starchy liquid.

The barley malt containing enzymes that break starch into sugar is added. The end result of this process is called mash, which is then transferred to large, sterilized vats into which yeast is introduced. A fermentation process takes on the appearance of a boiling action as the grain sugar is changed into alcohol and carbon dioxide is liberated into the air. Here, also, evidence is perceived of the flavoring components which give bourbon its taste and aroma.

To separate the alcohol from the fermented mash, the mixture is put into a large, chimney-like still. The alcohol is drawn off and the solids are compressed and dried, making a high-protein animal feed supplement. The bourbon industry is ecologically efficient; there is little or no waste in making the product.

The colorless, new bourbon is almost ready to be stored in new, charred oak barrels, but first the desired proof is obtained by adding demineralized water. Charring the barrels serves two purposes: It gives bourbon its color and adds to its flavor and bouquet. The aging process varies in the barrel before it can be "bottled in bond."

After the bourbon has matured, charcoal picked up from the barrels is screened out. More demineralized water is added to bring it down to the desired proof and then the Kentucky bourbon whiskey is bottled, put in cases and made ready for shipment.

Many distillers in Kentucky (including some in Frankfort, Owensboro, Louisville and Bardstown, as well as other places in the state) encourage visitors to walk through the process from grain milling to bottling.

The Mint Julep

The preparation of the quintessence of gentlemanly beverages can be described only in like terms. A mint julep is not the product of a formula. It is a ceremony and must be performed by a gentleman possessing a true sense of the artistic, a deep reverence for the ingredients and a proper appreciation of the occasion. It is a rite that must not be entrusted to a novice, a statistician nor a Yankee. It is a heritage of the old South, an emblem of hospitality and a vehicle in which noble minds can travel together upon the flower-strewn paths of happy and congenial thought.

So far as the mere mechanics of the operation are concerned, the procedure, stripped of its ceremonial embellishments, can be described as follows:

Go to a spring where cool, crystal-clear water bubbles from under a bank of dew-washed ferns. In a consecrated vessel, dip up a little water at the source. Follow the stream through its banks of green moss and wild flowers until it broadens and trickles through beds of mint growing in aromatic profusion and waving softly in the summer breeze. Gather sweetest and tenderest shoots and gently carry them to your rig. Go to the sideboard and select a decanter of Kentucky bourbon, distilled by a master hand, mellowed with age, yet still vigorous and inspiring. An ancestral sugar bowl, a row of silver goblets, some spoons and some ice and you are ready to start.

In a canvas bag, pound twice as much ice as you think you will need. Make it fine as snow, keep it dry and do not allow it to degenerate into slush.

In each goblet, put a slightly heaping teaspoonful of powdered sugar, barely cover this with spring water and slightly bruise one mint leaf into this, leaving the spoon in the goblet. Then pour elixir from the decanter until the goblets are about one-fourth full. Fill the goblets with snowy ice, sprinkling in a small amount of sugar as you fill. Wipe the outside of the goblets dry and embellish copiously with mint.

Then comes the important and delicate operation of frosting. By proper manipulation of the spoon, the ingredients are circulated and blended until Nature, wishing to take a further hand and add another of its beautiful phenomena, encrusts the whole in a glistening coat of white frost. Thus harmoniously blended by the deft touches of a skilled hand, you have a beverage eminently appropriate for honorable men and beautiful women.

When all is ready, assemble your guests on the veranda of your RV, where the aroma of the juleps will rise heavenward and make the birds sing. Propose a worthy toast, raise the goblet to your lips, bury your nose in the mint, inhale a deep breath of its fragrance and sip the nectar of the gods. — PJF

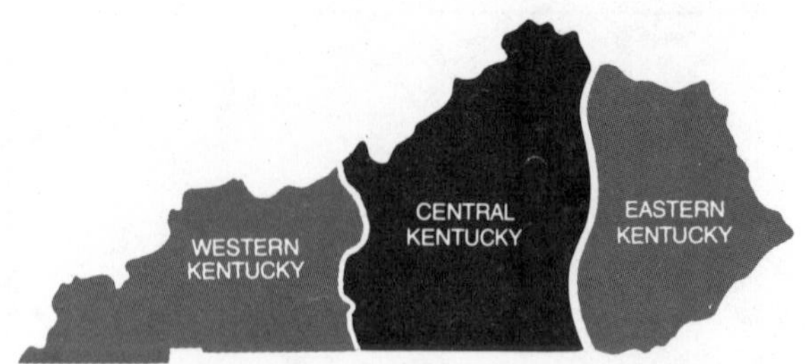

Central Kentucky

Ancient Age Distillery. The world's only one-barrel bonded whiskey warehouse, at one of the country's oldest and largest distilleries, producing over 60 million cases since the end of Prohibition. Located on the site of old Leestown, settled in 1773 by General George Rogers Clark, where the old Buffalo Trace crosses the Kentucky River. Open year-round. Frankfort, one mile north on US-421. (502) 223-7641.

Bakery Square. Cluster of 34 specialty shops and restaurants in heart of Louisville's oldest neighborhood, the German community of Butchertown; central brick courtyard and outdoor cafe. Open year-round, daily, 10 a.m. to 5 p.m.; Sunday, 12:30 p.m. to 5 p.m. Louisville, Butchertown, 1324 East Washington Street. (502) 584-7945.

Bernheim Forest. A 10,000-acre wildlife preserve and arboretum featuring nature museums, trails, scenic lakes and several picnic areas; display of 1,200 varieties of trees, shrubs and smaller plants in arboretum. Open March 15 through November 15. Free. Clermont, on State Route 245, off Interstate 65. (502) 543-2451.

Boat Rides. The *Dixie Belle.* A 150-passenger, double-deck, paddlewheel vessel that will take you on a tour of the Kentucky River while the captain recounts tall tales and explains the river's lock and dam system. Excellent views of Boonesborough Beach, fabled Lover's Leap and the Palisades of the Kentucky River. Season: May 1 through Labor Day, daily, 11 a.m., 1:30 p.m., 3 p.m., 4:30 p.m. and 6 p.m. (weather permitting). Fort Boonesborough State Park, South of Lexington on Interstate 75, on State Route 388.

Miss Green River II. A 63-foot twin-diesel cruiser built for comfort and sightseeing pleasure. Enjoy a ride through scenic areas and natural wildlife habitat along the Green River in Mammoth Cave National Park. Season: April through October, daily, four trips each day with additional tours added from Memorial Day to Labor Day. Adults $1.50, children under 12, 75 cents. Cave City, inside Mammoth Cave National Park, off Interstate 65. (502) 758-2243.

Brown-Forman Distilleries Corporation. The largest Kentucky-based distiller, with annual sales exceeding $300 million. Orientation center with displays showing how bourbon is produced, aged and bottled. Season: year-round, Monday to Friday, tours at 9 a.m., 10 a.m., 10:30 a.m., noon, 1 p.m., 2 p.m., 3:30 p.m. and 4 p.m. Free. Louisville, 850 Dixie Highway. (502) 778-5531.

Brown and Williamson Tobacco Corporation. The third-largest manufacturer of tobacco products in the United States, and one of the latest plants in Kentucky. Orientation center shows visitors how tobacco is cultivated, harvested, processed and packaged into cigarettes. Open year-round (except major holidays), Monday to Friday, 8 a.m. to 10:30 a.m.; noon to 4 p.m. Free. Louisville, 1600 West Hill Street. (502) 774-7475.

Capitol Building. One of the handsomest statehouses in America, Kentucky's capitol building is surrounded by an architectural stone terrace; face-work of oolitic limestone with Vermont granite base; 70 Ionic columns; walls and stairways of Georgian white marble; Italian marble floors. A giant 34-foot floral clock is on the grounds of the capitol annex. Open year-round, daily. Free. Frankfort, at south end of Capitol Avenue. (502) 564-3449.

Churchill Downs. Home of the world-famous Kentucky Derby, 80-day racing season. Museum has brief histories and silks of all Derby winners; 42,000 seats line the homestretch. Season: year-round, daily, 9:30 a.m. to 4:30 p.m.; during racing season gates open to general public at 11 a.m. Louisville, off Interstate 264 (at marked exit). (502) 634-3261.

Churchill Downs is the site of the famous Kentucky Derby on the first Saturday of every May.

Churchill Weavers. Beauty and softness are the hallmarks of Churchill handweavings; watch skilled artisans at work; complete selection of finished products for purchase. Open year-round. Berea, off Interstate 75, on US-25 and 421. (606) 986-3126.

Diamond Caverns. One of Kentucky's most beautiful caves, featuring projecting peaks, palatial underground rooms, large deposits of onyx and masses of stalactites and stalagmites — all explained by trained guides. Open year-round, daily, 8 a.m. to 8 p.m. (summer); 8 a.m. to 5 p.m. (winter). Adults $2.75, children under 12 $1.50, under 6 free. Park City, off Interstate 65, one mile north on State Route 255. (502) 749-2891.

Diners' Playhouse. Enjoy drinks and dinner while watching Broadway plays featuring top professional talent. Open year-round, Tuesday to Saturday, 6:30 p.m.; performance begins at 8:15 p.m. Rates: $10.50 to $12.50. Lexington, 434 Interstate Avenue. (606) 299-8407.

Gallery of Miniatures. Thirty-two rooms done in the scale of one to twelve inches; also there's a special exhibit of colonial tools and implements done in miniature on same scale. Open summer through fall; 8:30 a.m. to 9 p.m. Monday to Saturday; 1 p.m. to 5 p.m., Sunday. Adults $2.10, children $1.50. Cave City, at Interstate 65 interchange. (502) 773-2365.

Great Saltpetre Cave. An unusual cavern running through a spur of the Big Hill Range, with an opening on each side of the mountain. Many well-lighted rooms in cave; underground theater with near-perfect acoustics and seating for 2,000; remnants of works used to extract saltpetre for making of gunpowder during War of 1812, Mexican War and Civil War. Season: April through November, daily, 8:30 a.m. to 5 p.m. Adults $2, children over 6 $1. Livingston, off Interstate 75. (606) 256-4582.

Hadley Pottery. All of the designs on display were created by Mary Alice Hadley, one of the most respected names in stoneware, and painted by hand on each piece; display room where pottery may be bought. Open year-round, Monday to Friday, 8:30 a.m. to 4:30 p.m.; Saturday, 9 a.m. to 12:30 p.m. Free. Louisville, 1570 Story Avenue. (502) 584-2171.

Horse Cave Theater. A professional repertory theater in the renovated Thomas Opera House, built in 1911; three different plays on three succeeding nights throughout summer. Season: June through September, daily, 8 p.m. (weekdays); matinees only, 2 p.m., Saturday and Sunday. Horse Cave, off Interstate 65, at 107 Main Street. (502) 786-2177.

Located in Kentucky's 1,899-acre Natural Bridge State Park, this wonder of nature is 30 feet wide at the top, 40 feet thick at the center of the arch and 85 feet wide at the base opening.

Huckleberry Hill, Pixie World and Shark Tank. Huckleberry Hill craft center; ice-cream parlor; farm and cartoon characters that come to life via animation and sound; shark tank featuring a killer whale, a 17-foot white shark and other denizens of the deep. Open year-round (shops and most displays open summer season only); daily, 9 a.m. to 5 p.m. (winter); 8 a.m. to 10 p.m. (summer). Rates: from 50 cents to $1 depending upon attraction. Cave City, off Interstate 65, on State Route 70.

Jesse James Cave. Jesse James and his gang are reported to have hidden out in this cave overnight while they were being pursued by the law. The cave features several miles of charted passages below a surface area of only 1,200 square feet; an Indian burial ground was discovered in 1963. Open year-round, daily, tours at 9 a.m., 10:30 a.m., 12:30 p.m. and 2 p.m.; June 15 through Labor Day one night tour at 8 p.m. Adults $2, children $1. Park City, off Interstate 65, one mile west of US-31W. (502) 749-4101.

Keeneland Race Course. Thoroughbred racing; built on old Keene estate, with bluegrass countryside providing a picturesque backdrop. Open year-round; racing season, April and October. General admission: $1.25. Lexington, five miles west on US-60. (606) 254-3412.

Kentucky Horse Center. A new facility opened in May 1978, for the training, rehabilitation and sale of horses. Located on 270 acres, the center features two barns housing 600 stalls, a one-mile outdoor track, a 5/8-mile covered track, and a swimming pool for horses; gift shop. Open year-round, daily. Lexington, at the intersection of Paris Pike and Johnston Road.

Kentucky Horse Park. A park designed to honor the Thoroughbred, Saddlebred and Standardbred; visitors center, museum, restaurant, half-mile track, steeplechase course, polo field, and a memorial to the legendary Man O' War. Open year-round, daily. Adults $3.25, children 7 to 12 $2, 6 and under free. Lexington, off Interstate 75, on Iron Works Pike. (606) 233-4304.

"Legend of Daniel Boone." Play by award-winning playwright Jan Hartman affords an opportunity for audience to return to the days of Boone and his companions. Season: mid-June through August, daily, 8:30 p.m. Adults $5, children under 12 $3. Harrodsburg, at Old Fort Harrod State Park, off US-127. (606) 734-3346.

Maker's Mark Distillery. On the grounds of Star Hill Farm, nestled deep in the country on Hardin's Creek; demonstrations on the making of truly fine sour mash whiskey. Open year-round, Monday to Friday, tours hourly on the half-hour, 10:30 a.m. until 3:30 p.m. Loretto, off US-68, on State Route 52. (502) 865-2881.

Mammoth Onyx Cave. A cave of magnificent onyx formations discovered in 1799; crystal-clear underground pools. Open year-round, daily, 8 a.m. to 6 p.m. (summer); 8 a.m. to 5 p.m. (winter). Horse Cave, off Interstate 65 (exit 58).

Rauch Memorial Planetarium. Regular sky shows and special shows every month except August; special Christmas show. Open year-round, daily; shows 8 p.m. Fridays; Sundays 3 p.m. and 5 p.m.; Saturday children's shows at 2 p.m. Adults $1, children under 12 50 cents. Louisville, Belknap Campus, University of Louisville. (502) 588-6664.

Red Mile. Harness racing on the fastest trotting track in the world; home of the Kentucky Futurity, oldest harness race in North America. Season: April through July (spring meet), September through October (Grand Circuit Meet), November (fall meet). General admission: $1. Lexington, 847 South Broadway. (606) 255-0752.

Renfro Valley. A place where the pace of life is slow and nostalgia is the keynote. The old original music barn presents old-time and bluegrass music, while the "new" barn presents updated styles in country music; square dancing the fourth Friday of each month; Renfro Valley Barn Dance every Saturday night. Season: year-round, Saturday, 7:30 p.m. to 9:30 p.m.; Sunday Mornin' Gatherin', 8:30 a.m.; Friday, 8 p.m. Renfro Valley, off Interstate 75, 16 miles south of Berea, two miles north of Mount Vernon.

Stephen Foster Story. This lively and colorful outdoor drama is a living memorial to Stephen Foster. Enjoy such old favorites as *Camptown Races, Oh Susanna, Jeannie With the Light Brown Hair* and *Old Folks at Home.* Season: mid-June through Labor Day, nightly except Monday, 8:30 p.m. Adults $5, children 12 and under $2.50. Bardstown, at Old Kentucky Home State Park, off US-62.

Old Fitzgerald Distillery. The bourbon at this distillery is produced the "old-fashioned way" — without use of chemicals to speed the process and without the use of air-conditioned warehouses. Season: year-round, Monday to Friday, tours at 11 a.m., 1 p.m. and 2 p.m. Free. Louisville, Fitzgerald Road. (502) 448-2860.

Old Grand-Dad Distillery. Old Taylor and Old Crow are also produced by this firm that makes, bottles and warehouses fine bourbon whiskey. Season: year-round, Monday to Friday, 8:30 a.m. to 3:30 p.m. Free. Frankfort, north of US-460. (502) 223-8251.

Old Taylor Distillery. Castle built in 1887 by Colonel E. H. Taylor, Jr. as a distillery in which to make his bourbon whiskey; Old Taylor Hall of Fame Museum also on grounds. Season: year-round, Monday to Friday, 8:30 a.m. to 3:30 p.m. Frankfort, off US-60, south on Glenn's Creek Road. (502) 223-8251.

Philip Morris, Incorporated. Start with a 12-minute slide presentation on the firm, then follow the tobacco from the time the leaves are conditioned to the proper temperature and moisture, to the blending department where they are mixed for flavor. Season: year-round, Monday to Friday, 8 a.m. to 11 p.m. Free. Louisville, 1930 Maple Street. (502) 778-2761.

Wilderness Road. This saga of the Civil War tells the tale of brother pitted against brother; a full measure of drama, music, comedy and colorful pageantry; presented outdoors. Season: mid-June through Labor Day, nightly except Sunday, 8:30 p.m. Adults $5, $4, $2, children $3.50, $2.50, $1.25. Berea, Indian Fort Theater, south of Berea in College Forest, off Interstate 75.

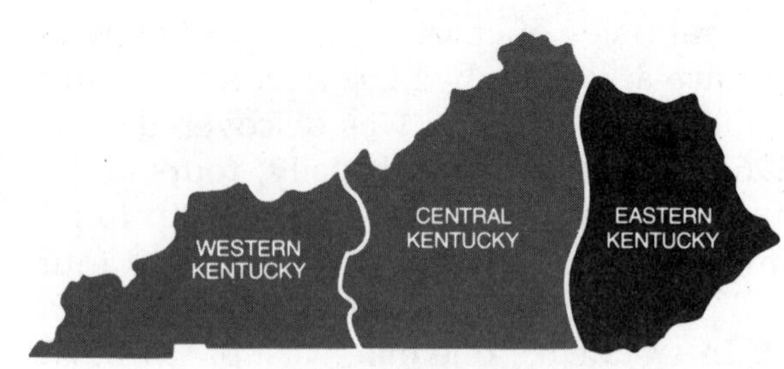

Eastern Kentucky

Cumberland Falls. "The Niagara of the South," surrounded by Daniel Boone National Forest, this awesome falls is the largest to be found east of the Rockies — except for Niagara. By night, when the moon is full, a mysterious moonbow appears in the mist from the 150-foot-wide falls which plummets 58 feet into the boulders of the Cumberland River. Season: year-round. Free. Corbin, off Interstate 75, 18 miles southwest on State Route 90.

The Little Shepherd of Kingdom Come. Drama based on the novel by John Fox, Jr.; the first American novel to sell one million copies. Story of the people of the Kentucky Hills. Season: late June through early September; Thursday, Friday and Saturday nights, 8:30 p.m. Adults $4, students $3.50, children 6 to 12, $2, children under 6, free. Whitesburg, five miles north on State Route 15.

Old Washington. The first town in the United States to be named for the first President. Guided tours of restored buildings; special events such as Frontier Christmas and Geranium Day. Season: May through Christmas, Tuesday to Friday 11 a.m. to 4:30 p.m.; weekends noon to 4:30 p.m. Maysville, three miles southwest at junction of US-62 and US-68.

Kentucky State Parks

Park	Location	CAMPING	PICNICKING	CONCESSIONS	SWIMMING	HIKING	BOATING	FISHING	HUNTING	WINTER SPORTS
Barren River Lake	*Lucas. Off US-31E.*	•	•	•	•	•	•	•		
Big Bone Lick	*Florence. Off State Routes 42 and 127.*	•	•							
Blue Licks Battlefield	*Off US-68.*	•	•	•	•					
Buckhorn Lake	*Buckhorn. Off State Route 28.*	•	•	•	•	•	•	•		
Carter Caves	*Olive Hill. Off Interstate 64.*	•	•	•	•	•	•	•		
Columbus-Belmont Battlefield	*Columbus. Off State Route 123.*	•	•	•		•				
Cumberland Falls	*Corbin. Off State Route 90.*	•	•	•	•	•		•		
E.P. "Tom" Sawyer	*Louisville. Off State Route 155.*		•		•					
Fort Boonesborough	*Boonesboro. Off Interstate 75.*	•	•	•	•		•	•		
Fort Hill	*Frankfort. Off Interstate 64.*		•							
General Burnside	*Burnside. Off US-27.*	•	•		•			•		
General Butler	*Carrollton. Off State Route 227.*	•	•	•	•	•	•	•		
Grayson Lake	*Grayson. Off State Route 79.*	•	•		•			•		
Greenbo Lake	*Greenup. Off State Route 1.*	•	•	•	•	•	•	•		
Jenny Wiley	*Prestonsburg. Off US-23.*	•	•	•	•	•	•	•		
John James Audubon	*Henderson. Off US-60.*	•	•	•	•	•	•	•		
Kenlake	*Hardin. Off US-68.*	•	•	•	•	•	•	•		
Kentucky Dam Village	*Gilbertsville. Off US-641.*	•	•	•	•	•	•	•		
Kincaid Lake	*Falmouth. Off State Route 159.*	•	•		•	•	•	•		
Lake Barkley	*Cadiz. Off US-68.*	•	•	•	•	•	•	•		
Lake Cumberland	*Jamestown. Off US-127.*	•	•	•	•	•	•	•		
Lake Malone	*Dunmor. Off State Route 973.*		•		•	•	•	•		
Levi Jackson	*London. Off US-25.*		•	•	•	•				
Lincoln Homestead	*Springfield. Off US-150.*		•	•						
My Old Kentucky Home	*Bardstown. Off US-62.*		•	•						
Natural Bridge	*Slade. Off State Route 11.*	•	•	•	•	•	•	•		
Pine Mountain	*Pineville. Off US-25E.*	•	•	•	•	•				
Rough River Dam	*Falls of Rough. Off State Route 79.*	•	•	•	•	•	•	•		

Kentucky State Forests

Forest	Location	CAMPING	PICNICKING	CONCESSIONS	SWIMMING	HIKING	BOATING	FISHING	HUNTING	WINTER SPORTS
Kentenia	*Harlan. Off US-421.*	•	•			•		•	•	
Kentucky Ridge	*Middlesboro. Off US-119.*	•	•	•		•		•	•	
Knob	*Bardstown. Off US-62.*	•	•	•		•		•	•	
Olympic	*Owingsville. Off Interstate 64.*	•	•			•		•	•	
Pennyrile	*Dawson Springs. Off State Route 109.*	•	•	•	•	•	•	•	•	

For more information on Kentucky state parks and forests, contact: *Department of Parks, Capital Plaza Office Tower, Frankfort, Kentucky 40601, (502) 564-5410.*

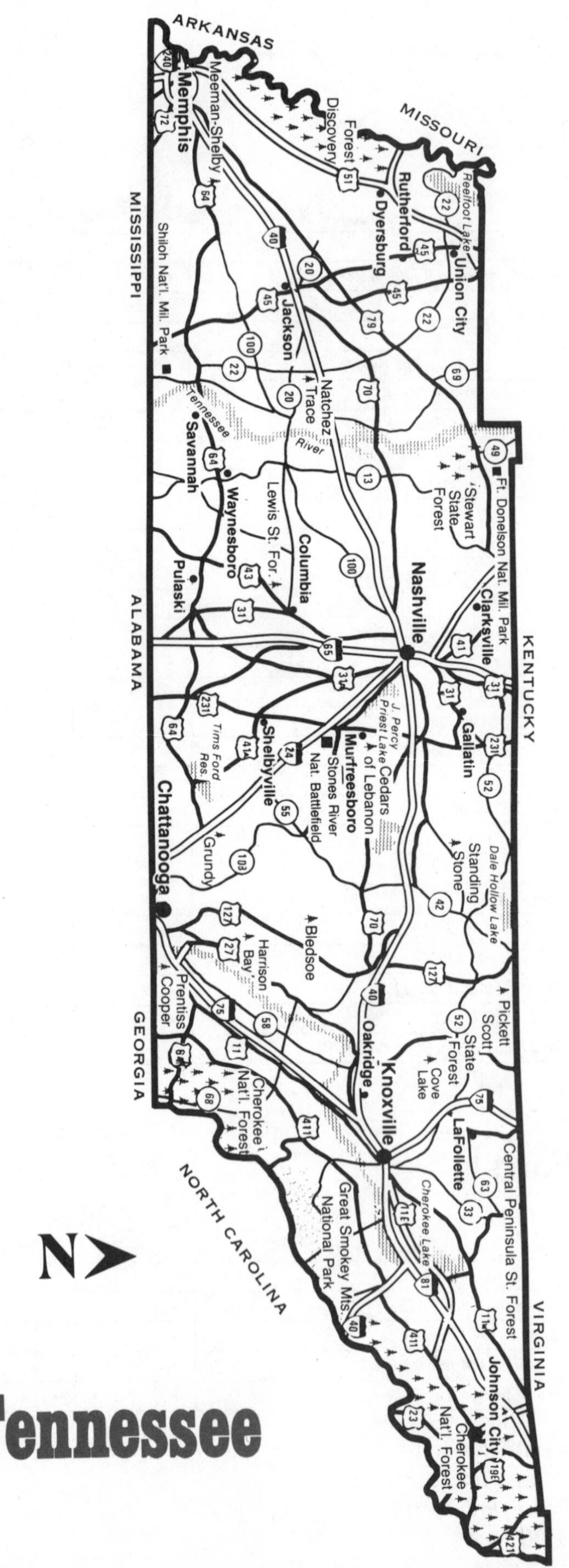

Tennessee

Map not to exact scale.

Tennessee

Tennessee is blessed with a varied and beautiful landscape, a generally mild climate and a hospitable people just waiting to welcome visitors. The state is known for its outdoor pleasures and these can be enjoyed in a host of state and national parks, forests, wilderness areas and game preserves. There's history here too — from prehistoric Indian sites to Civil War battlefields to such figures as Sam Houston, Andrew Jackson and Sergeant Alvin York. And no visitor will want to overlook Nashville, "Music City USA."

Spanish explorer Hernando De Soto is thought to be the first European to have entered the territory of Tennessee (in 1541). No attempt was made to develop the region, however, until French and English traders began to vie for the friendship of the Indian tribes which occupied the territory. Relations between the Europeans and the Indians remained cordial for many years until the two dominant tribes — Cherokee and Chickasaw — began to fight amongst themselves for control of the area. For the next 30 years, the conflicts continued — with the English siding with the Cherokee and the French supporting the rival Chickasaw. Lured by tales of hunters and scouts such as Daniel Boone, the first permanent settlers came in 1769 to settle along the Watauga, Nolichucky and Holston Rivers in the northeastern corner of the state. After a number of years of uncertainty over the region's boundaries, Tennessee was finally organized in 1790 as the "Territory South of the River Ohio," and admitted to the Union as a state on June 1, 1796. Despite its position as a slaveholding state, Tennessee was pro-Union in the years before the Civil War — but after Fort Sumter, the people voted for secession and Tennessee became the last of the Confederate states to secede.

Full name: State of Tennessee
Origin of name: From Tennese, name of leading Cherokee Indian town.
Motto: Agriculture and Commerce.
Nickname: Volunteer State. (During the Mexican War, a statewide call for 2,800 volunteers was answered by 30,000 men.)
Capital: Nashville
Statehood: June 1, 1796, 16th state.
Population: 4,299,000 (ranks 17th).
Major Cities: Memphis (661,319), Nashville (423,426, Knoxville (183,383).
Bird: Mockingbird
Flower: Iris
Tree: Tulip poplar

Average daily temperature by month

	Eastern	Western
Jan.	48.0 to 26.1	46.5 to 29.3
Feb.	51.6 to 28.4	50.7 to 32.7
Mar.	60.2 to 34.7	58.9 to 39.9
Apr.	72.0 to 44.3	71.1 to 51.0
May	79.6 to 52.6	80.2 to 59.3
Jun.	86.1 to 60.9	88.4 to 67.4
Jul.	88.9 to 64.6	90.5 to 70.4
Aug.	88.3 to 63.5	89.5 to 68.5
Sept.	83.7 to 57.4	83.5 to 61.9
Oct.	72.6 to 44.9	73.6 to 50.0
Nov.	59.7 to 34.3	59.6 to 39.4
Dec.	50.6 to 28.4	49.5 to 32.9
Year	70.1 to 45.0	70.2 to 50.2

The Great Smoky Mountains contain the highest peaks in eastern North America; 23 summits of the range rise more than 6,000 feet.

Today, Tennesseans view their state as three distinct regions: East, Middle and West. In the east, you'll find the small isolated farms of the Appalachians, the modern cities of Knoxville and Kingsport, and the "atomic city," Oak Ridge, where uranium was produced during World War II for the first atomic bombs. The state's mid-section is made up of rolling pasturelands, tobacco fields and antebellum plantations; while in the west you'll find cotton plantations, the bustling city of Memphis and the scenic bluffs that overlook the swampy lowlands of the Mississippi Valley.

Music and tourism play a key role in Tennessee's economy, but strip mining for coal is also of major importance, as are the manufacture of rubber products, chemicals, transportation equipment, clothing and machinery. Agricultural products include soybeans, tobacco, cotton, dairy products and beef cattle.

Highlight

Fall Creek Falls

Deep in the rugged Cumberland Mountains of East Tennessee near Pikeville, the highest waterfall in the eastern United States tumbles over a sheer cliff and drops 256 feet into a shallow pool on the floor of a canyon. Ninety feet higher than Niagara Falls, Fall Creek Falls is the focal point of a 16,000-acre Tennessee State Park.

Developed to preserve the mountain wilderness which has existed since the beginning of time, and to provide a place for visitors to explore a lifestyle outside the city, the park offers miles of hiking trails through native flora and fauna. One of them slopes steeply down a switchback trail into the Fall Creek Falls canyon which is blurred with the mist from the waterfall. Other trails lead to more waterfalls: Caney Creek, Piney Falls and the Cascades which provide the water for a popular swimming hole at its base. Additional trails lead to scenic overlooks along the bluffs of the four major canyons, some as deep as 600 feet.

A quiet lake in the heart of the park has been reserved for fishing where bream and bass fishing excel; the state record bream was landed at the lake in 1977. The marina has fishing boats, canoes and paddleboats for rent as well as other fishing needs on hand.

The Betty Dunn Nature Center near Caney Creek offers lectures and exhibits on the geologic structures of the park, its wildlife and the forest ecosystems of the area.

The park has taken special care to provide top-notch conditions for golfers, bicyclers and horseback riders, going even so far as renting bicycles and horses.

Fall Creek Falls in Tennessee's Fall Creek Falls State Park, is the highest waterfall east of the Rockies.

Highlight

Northeastern Tennessee

The folks up in northeastern Tennessee say the sun peeks over their mountains every morning, rests a bit to take in the sights, and then decides to smile for the rest of the day.

Lord knows there's plenty to smile about. Those rugged mountains and rolling hills are steeped with American heritage and blessed with an abundance of good living.

You can stroll through the streets of Jonesboro, the first town in Tennessee. Or visit the historic grounds of Rocky Mount, the original U.S. Territorial Capitol built way back in 1770.

You can slip through silent green forests, following the paths of Daniel Boone and Davy Crockett. Or try to trace the elusive trail of Colonel John Mosby, the Gray Ghost of the Confederacy.

History comes alive at the original Tipton-Haynes Farm, which has been carefully preserved to depict the life of the early Tennessee settlements.

Early morning golfers watch the mist rise from the first tee at any number of splendid golf courses. And ardent anglers cast for trout and bass in beautiful Watauga Lake.

Visitors often spend a whole day at Roan Mountain, viewing some of the most incredible scenery on this earth, or exploring the cool mysteries of some of the most magnificent caverns God ever hid under a mountain.

Such are the pleasures to be found in the friendly peaks and valleys of northeastern Tennessee — so do try to sample them the next time you find yourself headed south.

State Offices

Tourism
Tourist Development Division
1028 Andrew Jackson Building
Nashville, Tennessee
(615) 741-2158

State Police
Department of Public Safety
Nashville, Tennessee 37219
(615) 741-2925

Radio Stations

Chattanooga
WFLI 1070 (AM)
Knoxville
WBIR 103.5 (FM)
WNOX 990 (AM)
Nashville
WKDF 103.3 (FM)
WLAC 1510 (AM)
WSIX 980 (AM)

Tennessee Points of Interest and Attractions

American Museum of Atomic Energy. Exhibits on the uses of nuclear energy for research, agriculture, medicine and industry. Open year-round. Oak Ridge, off State Route 62, at Tulane and Illinois Avenues.

Chattanooga. Located in the southeastern corner of the state, Chattanooga sprawls at the foot of Lookout Mountain in the famous Moccasin Bend of the Tennessee River. The city's many attractions include:

Chattanooga Choo Choo. Once the Southern Railroad's terminal in Chattanooga, the old station has been restored and converted into a fascinating collection of Victorian-era shops, lounges and restaurants. A trolley car from the streets of New Orleans offers a complete tour of the complex. Open year-round.

Incline Railway. Carries passengers to the top of famous Lookout Mountain, reaching a grade of more than 70% near the top — which makes the Incline the world's steepest railway.

Point Park. On top of Lookout Mountain, Point Park was the site of the Civil War's "Battle Above the Clouds." The park, which offers some of the most photographed views in the South, is part of the Chickamauga-Chattanooga National Military Park, the nation's oldest, largest and most visited national military park.

Ruby Falls. Here's an impressive 145-foot-high waterfall deep within Lookout Mountain Caverns — the deepest commercially operated cave in the nation at 1,120 feet under the earth's surface.

Gatlinburg. Gateway to the Great Smoky Mountains National Park, Gatlinburg is a mountain village framed by mile-high peaks and laced with sparkling, fresh-flowing mountain streams. The village is nationally recognized as a center for mountain arts and crafts, and visitors are invited to browse in its numerous shops and studios and observe skilled artisans at work. The famous Arrowmont School of Arts and Crafts is located here.

Ober Gatlinburg Tramway. Carries passengers 2.2 miles to the slopes of the Gatlinburg Ski Resort and the old Heidelberg Castle, a colorful German restaurant complete with an Oom-Pah-Pah Band.

Jack Daniels Distillery. The oldest registered distillery in the United States. Open year-round, Monday to Friday. Winchester, north on State Route 55.

Memphis. Situated on a bluff overlooking the Mississippi River, Memphis is Tennessee's largest city — a city of fine old homes, abundant cultural activities and strong ties to the past. Stern-wheel riverboats still ply the waters of the Mississippi carrying visitors on cruises into another era of American life.

Graceland. Undoubtedly Memphis' most famous attraction, Graceland was the home of Elvis Presley and now stands as a shrine to his memory.

Nashville. In recent years, Nashville has come to be known as "Music City USA," a nickname earned by the city's devotion to country music. Among the city's music-oriented attractions are:

Grand Ole Opry. Originated in 1925 by WSM Radio, the Opry is the oldest continuously running radio program in the nation. The regular Friday and Saturday night broadcasts are heard by millions throughout most of the U.S. and Canada, and attended by more than 900,000 fans each year. Shows: Friday and Saturday nights for broadcast; Friday, Saturday and Sunday matinees are not broadcast. Reserved seats $6 (generally sold out weeks and months in advance); general admission $5, on sale each Tuesday prior to weekend shows.

Music Hall of Fame. Displays of musical instruments and costumes worn by many famous country music stars; simulated recording session; Elvis Presley's 1960 gold Cadillac occupies a special place of honor. On 16th Avenue South. Open year-round.

Music Row. A complex of recording studios and music publishing companies located along several blocks of 16th Avenue South. RCA's historic Studio B is open to the public.

Nashville Jubilee. A fast-paced 2½-hour live show originating from Nashville's War Memorial Auditorium, featuring many of the best known country music stars as well as talented new artists. Season: April through October, weekends. Admission: reserved seats $6, general admission $5.

Printers' Alley. Once the home of Nashville's three newspaper printing firms, the Alley is now filled with restaurants and clubs offering big-name entertainers and music that runs the gamut from rock to bluegrass.

Tennessee State Parks

Park	Location	CAMPING	PICNICKING	CONCESSIONS	SWIMMING	HIKING	BOATING	FISHING	HUNTING	WINTER SPORTS
Big Ridge	*Maynardville. Off State Route 61.*	•	•	•	•	•	•	•		
Bledsoe Creek	*Gallatin. Off State Route 25.*	•	•			•	•	•		
Booker T. Washington	*Chattanooga. Off State Route 58.*	•	•	•	•	•	•	•		
Cedars of Lebanon	*Lebanon. Off State Route 10 and US-231.*	•	•	•	•	•				
Chickasaw	*Henderson. Off State Route 100.*		•		•		•	•		
Cove Lake	*Carryville. Off US-25W and Interstate 75.*	•	•	•	•	•	•	•		
Cumberland Mountain	*Crossville. Off Interstate 40 on US-127.*	•	•		•		•	•		
David Crockett	*Lawrenceburg. Off US-64.*	•	•	•	•		•	•		
Edgar Evins	*Nashville. Off Interstate 40.*	•	•	•			•	•		
Fall Creek Falls	*Pikeville. Off State Route 30.*	•	•	•	•	•	•	•		
Harrison Bay	*Harrison. Off US-58.*	•	•	•	•		•	•		
Henry Horton	*Chapel Hill. Off US-31A.*	•	•	•	•					
Indian Mountain	*Jellico. Off Interstate 75.*	•			•	•	•	•		
Meeman Shelby	*Millington. Off US-51.*	•	•	•	•	•	•	•		
Montgomery Bell	*Burns. Off US-70.*	•	•	•	•	•	•	•		
Natchez Trace	*Wildersville. Off Interstate 40.*	•	•	•	•	•	•	•		
Nathan Bedford Forrest	*Eva. Off US-70.*	•	•							
Norris Dam	*Norris. Off US-441.*	•	•	•	•	•	•	•		
Panther Creek	*Morristown. Off US-11E.*	•	•		•	•	•	•		
Paris Landing	*Buchanan. Off US-79.*	•	•	•	•	•				
Pickett	*Jamestown. Off State Route 154.*	•	•	•		•	•	•		
Pickwick Landing	*Pickwick Dam. Off State Route 57.*	•	•	•	•					
Reelfoot Lake	*Tiptonville. Off State Route 21.*	•	•	•		•	•	•		
Roan Mountain	*Roan Mountain. Off State Route 143.*	•	•			•				
Rock Island	*Rock Island. Off US-70S.*	•	•		•		•	•		
Standing Stone	*Livingston. Off State Route 52.*	•	•	•			•	•		
Tims Ford	*Winchester. West on Mansford Road.*	•	•	•	•		•	•		
T.O. Fuller	*Memphis. Off US-61.*	•	•		•					
Warrior's Path	*Kingsport. Off US-23.*	•	•	•		•	•	•		

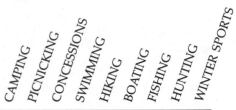

Tennessee State Forests

Forest	Location	CAMPING	PICNICKING	CONCESSIONS	SWIMMING	HIKING	BOATING	FISHING	HUNTING	WINTER SPORTS
Bledsoe	*Pikeville. Off State Route 101.*		•			•			•	
Chickasaw	*Henderson. Off US-100.*	•	•			•			•	
Chuck Swan	*Sharps Chapel. Off State Route 63.*		•			•			•	
Franklin	*Sewanee. Off State Route 56.*	•	•			•			•	
Lewis	*Hohenwald. Off State Route 48.*		•			•			•	
Lone Mountain	*Wartburg. Off State Route 116.*	•	•			•			•	
Picket	*Jamestown. Off State Route 154.*	•	•			•			•	
Prentice-Cooper	*Chattanooga. Off Interstate 24.*	•	•			•			•	
Scott	*Jamestown. Off US-27.*	•	•			•			•	
Standing Stone	*Livingston. Off State Route 136.*	•	•			•			•	

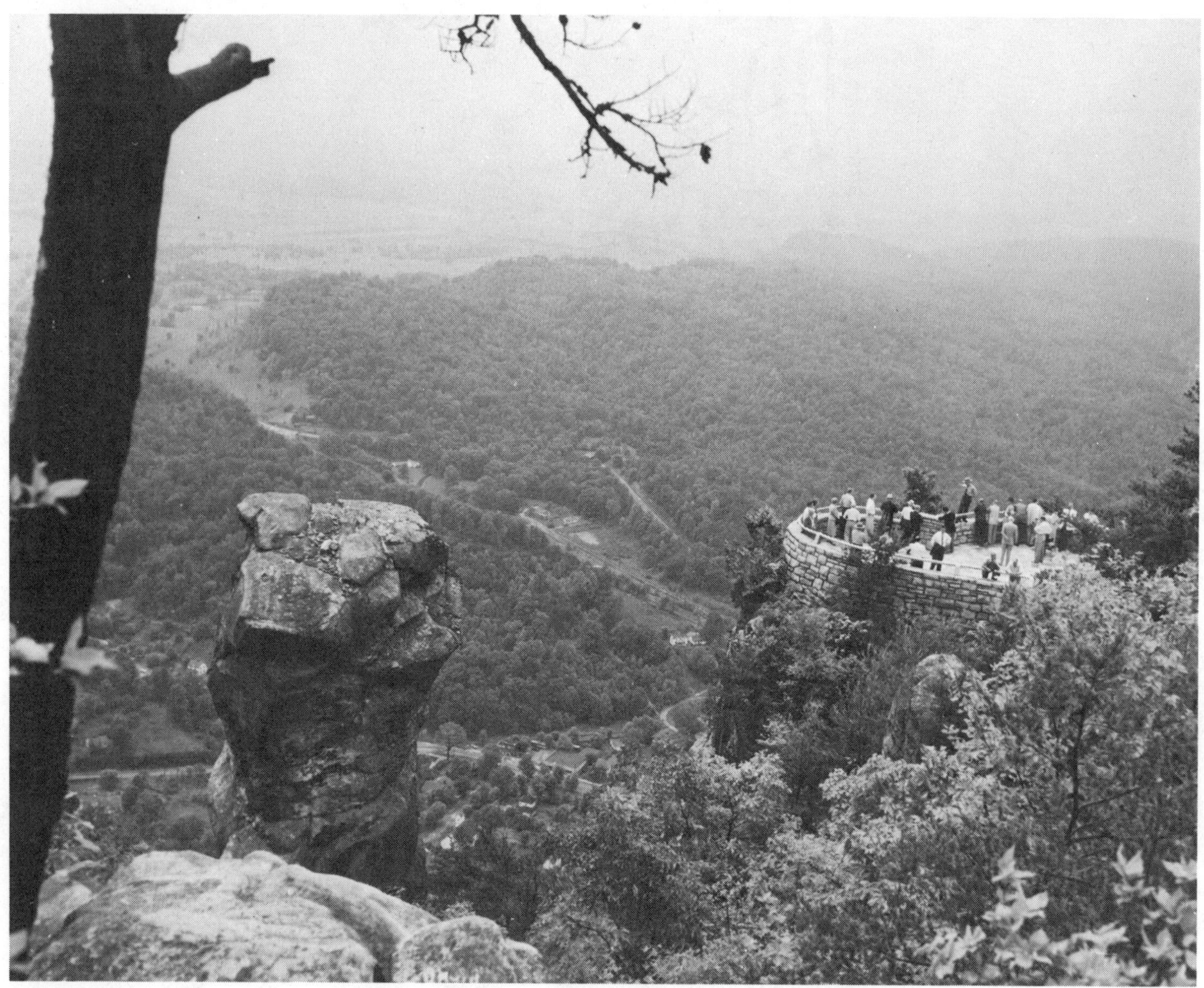

Shared by Kentucky, Tennessee and Virginia, the historic Cumberland Gap, blazed by Daniel Boone in 1775, was a strategic point during the Civil War.

For further information on Tennessee's state parks and forests, contact: *Department of Parks and Recreation, 2611 West End Avenue, Nashville, Tennessee 37203, (615) 741-3251.*

Virginia

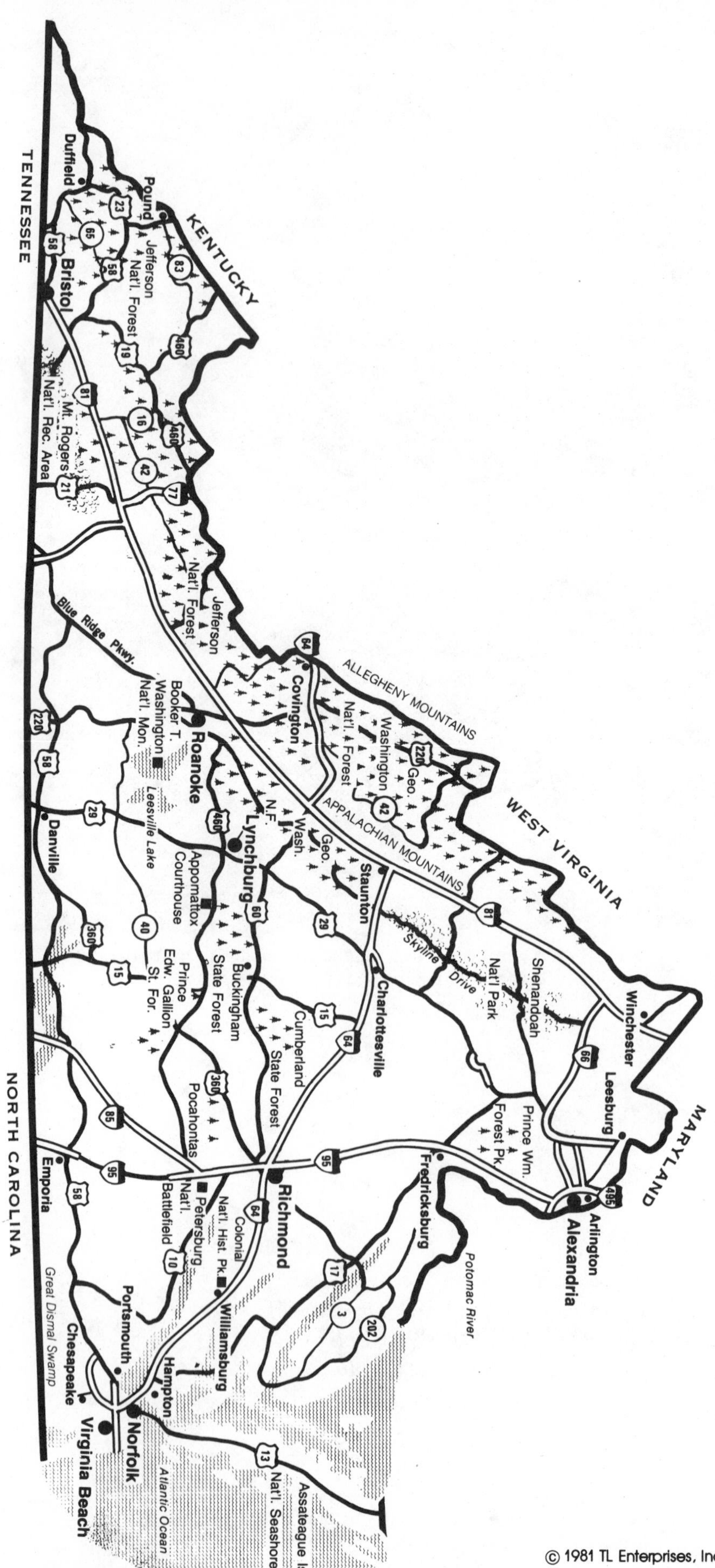

Map not to exact scale.

Virginia

Virginia, a state particularly rich in American history, is the home of the first successful English settlement in North America, Jamestown, established in 1607. Today, in the "historic triangle" of restored Jamestown, Williamsburg and Yorktown, visitors can immerse themselves in some of the sights and sounds of those early settlements. And in other areas of the state, you can discover a few of Virginia's other historic points of interest: Thomas Jefferson's home, Monticello; Washington's Mount Vernon; Manassas, the site of two major Civil War battles; and the Appomattox Court House, where General Lee surrendered to General Grant, ending the Civil War.

The settlement at Jamestown began happily but soon endured a number of hardships, such as malaria and attacks by Indians, that led to the deaths of several hundred settlers. The Virginia colony succeeded in spite of these setbacks, however, and in 1624 James I declared it a royal colony, England's first in the New World. From Virginia came a number of political philosophers who were largely responsible for the colonial attitude toward England that was to lead to the creation of independent states. Stirred by these philosophers and the passionate oratory of men like Patrick Henry, Virginians drafted a Declaration of Rights and adopted a state constitution on June 29, 1776, several days before the Continental Congress approved the Declaration of Independence. Virginia ratified the Federal Constitution on June 25, 1788, and became the 10th state to enter the Union. At the outbreak of the Civil War, Virginia's sympathies lay with the Confederacy and the state seceded from the Union on April 17, 1861. The western part of the state — which refused to secede — later became West Virginia. Virginia returned to the Union in 1870.

In speaking of his home state, Thomas Jefferson is said to have remarked, "I know nothing so charming as our own

Full name: Commonwealth of Virginia
Origin of name: In honor of Queen Elizabeth of England, the "Virgin Queen."
Motto: *Sic Semper Tyrannis* (Thus Ever to Tyrants).
Nickname: Old Dominion State
Capital: Richmond
Statehood: June 25, 1788, 10th state.
Population: 5,135,000 (ranks 13th).
Major Cities: Norfolk (286,694), Richmond (232,652), Virginia Beach (213,954).
Bird: Cardinal
Flower: American dogwood
Tree: American dogwood

Average daily temperature by month

	Eastern	Western
Jan.	48.4 to 25.8	41.8 to 21.7
Feb.	51.0 to 27.6	44.1 to 23.0
Mar.	59.1 to 34.0	52.2 to 29.1
Apr.	70.7 to 43.8	64.2 to 38.6
May	78.3 to 53.1	73.4 to 47.2
Jun.	85.2 to 61.5	79.8 to 54.6
Jul.	88.6 to 65.9	82.7 to 58.6
Aug.	87.0 to 64.9	81.4 to 58.0
Sept.	81.1 to 57.6	75.3 to 51.6
Oct.	71.3 to 45.8	65.4 to 41.2
Nov.	61.1 to 35.8	53.2 to 31.7
Dec.	50.5 to 28.2	43.4 to 24.5
Year	69.4 to 45.3	63.1 to 40.0

Located in Wakefield, near Washington's birthplace, is this reconstruction of a typical Virginia plantation.

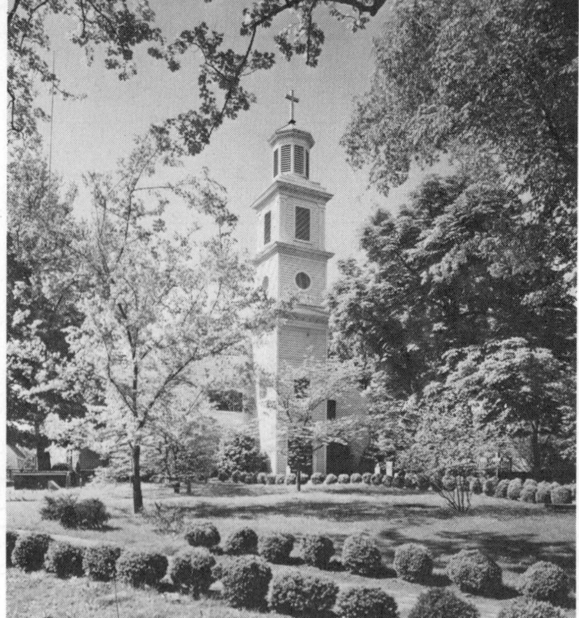

The walls of historic St. John's Church in Richmond echo the ringing challenge of Patrick Henry — "Give me liberty or give me death!"

country." Ever since, Virginians have taken great pains to show off their state. The Virginia State Travel Service now operates several travel information centers at key entry points to the state, and each is stocked with a wealth of tourist information to guide you to the state's varied attractions. Besides the numerous historical sites, Virginia has a number of excellent state parks and forests, as well as the George Washington and Jefferson National Forests and the scenic Shenandoah Valley. In the northern part of the state, near the Washington, D.C. border, you'll find Arlington National Cemetery, the site of the Tomb of the Unknown Soldier, and the Pentagon.

Virginia's Atlantic coast region supports a thriving fishing industry and the economy is further supported by agriculture, mining and the manufacturing of tobacco, textiles, chemicals and fabricated metals.

Highlight

Dismal Swamp

The vast Dismal Swamp sprawls across 223,000 acres of southeastern Virginia and northeastern North Carolina and harbors heavily forested peat bogs and dense scrub vegetation consisting of briars and vines. Throughout the region, there is a network of canals and ditches that often resembles green tunnels disappearing into the thick foliage.

Within the swamp is the 3,000-acre Lake Drummond, characterized by dark, coffee-colored water and a porous, sandy bottom. Because of the gnarled cypress trees, hanging moss and dense vegetation, the lake has a generally forbidding appearance. An unusual aspect of the lake is that it is not formed in a basin, but rests on a gently sloping hillside. Fishing is permitted on the lake. Wildlife in the area includes otters, black bears, bobcats, myriad small mammals and nearly 180 different species of birds.

The swamp was first surveyed in 1728 by Colonel William Byrd, who gave it the name of the Great Dismal. George Washington later explored the region in 1763 in an effort to exploit its rich timber resources. Washington did initiate drainage operations on the swamp and it was considerably reduced from its original size, which is estimated at some 2,200 square miles. Reached via US-58, US-13, US-17, or Interstate 64.

State Offices

Tourism
Virginia State Travel Service
6 North Sixth Street
Richmond, Virginia 23219
(804) 786-4484

State Police
Department of Public Safety
Richmond, Virginia 23261
(804) 272-1431

Radio Stations

Richmond
  WGOE 1590 (AM)
  WLEE 1480 (AM)
Roanoke
  WFIR 960 (AM)
Norfolk
  WQRK 104.5 (FM)

Virginia Points of Interest and Attractions

American Tobacco Company. One of the nation's major tobacco firms, American has been in continuous operation since 1890. Open year-round, Monday to Friday, tours available. Free. Richmond, at intersection of 26th and Cary Streets.

The restored Capitol Building in Williamsburg is Virginia's most important edifice.

Barter Theater. When Robert Porterfield came home to the mountains during the Depression, he brought with him Broadway artists who performed in return for food. Now Porterfield's "barter" theater is the State Theater of Virginia. Abingdon, off US-11 and 58.

Brown and Williamson Tobacco Company. Leading tobacco products firm, producing more than 50 billion cigarettes per year. Open year-round, Monday to Friday, tours available. Free. Petersburg, Brown and Perry Streets.

Charles C. Steirly Heron Rookery. Located in a dense swamp surrounded by timber, brush and briars. When visiting the area, which preserves one of the few remaining rookeries in the state, hip boots are recommended. Open year-round. Free. Waverly, five miles northeast off State Route 603.

Chincoteague. Famous pony roundup on Assateague Island and annual swim to Chincoteague on Pony Day. Chincoteague, off US-13, on State Route 175.

Gardens-By-The-Sea. Camellia, azalea and rhododendron bloom in brilliant display from spring through late summer. Open year-round. Norfolk, off US-60, adjoining airport.

Goshen Pass. One of Virginia's designated scenic byways; parallels the Maury River. Lexington, north along State Route 39.

Natural Bridge. This towering arch, one of the seven natural wonders of the world, is 215 feet high, and its 90-foot span joins two mountains carrying a major highway (US-11) over the chasm. Natural Bridge was surveyed by George Washington and was once owned by Thomas Jefferson. During the summer season, there is a nightly drama on the story of creation. A new attraction was added to the area recently with the opening of the Caverns of Natural Bridge. Near Natural Bridge, off Interstate 81, on US-11.

Skyline Drive and Blue Ridge Parkway. These roads meet at Afton Mountain to form a 320-mile scenic drive from Front Royal southward through Virginia. Access is provided to many attractions along the route and numerous overlooks offer frequent opportunities to enjoy the panoramic beauty of the mountains.

Virginia State Parks

Park	Location	CAMPING	PICNICKING	CONCESSIONS	SWIMMING	HIKING	BOATING	FISHING	HUNTING	WINTER SPORTS
Bear Creek Lane	*Cumberland. Off State Routes 622 and 629.*	•	•	•	•	•	•	•		
Chippokes Plantation	*Surry. On State Route 10.*		•							
Claytor Lake	*Dublin. Off Interstate 81 (exit 33).*	•	•	•	•	•	•	•		
Douthat	*Clifton Forge. Off US-60, on State Route 629.*	•	•	•	•	•	•	•		
Fairy Stone	*Bassett. Off State Routes 8 and 57.*	•	•	•	•	•	•			
Goodwin Lake	*.Burkeville. Off State Route 619.*	•	•		•	•	•	•		
Grayson Highlands	*Volney. Off US-58.*	•	•			•				
Holliday Lake	*Appomattox. Off State Routes 24, 626 and 692.*	•	•		•		•	•		
Hungry Mother	*Marion. Off Interstate 81 (exits 16 and 17), on State Route 16.*	•	•	•	•	•	•	•		
Natural Tunnel	*Clinchport. Off State Route 871.*	•	•							
Occoneechee	*Clarksville. On US-58.*	•	•				•	•		
Pocahontas	*Chesterfield. Off State Route 780.*	•	•		•	•	•	•		
Staunton River	*Scottsburg. Off US-58.*	•	•	•	•	•	•	•		
Westmoreland	*Montross. Off State Route 3.*	•	•	•	•	•	•	•		

Virginia state forests are incorporated with the following state parks: *Holliday Lake, Goodwin Lake, Bear Lake, and Pocahontas.*

For more information on Virginia state parks and forests, contact: *Virginia State Parks, 1201 State Office Building, Capitol Square, Richmond, Virginia 23219, (804) 786-2134.*

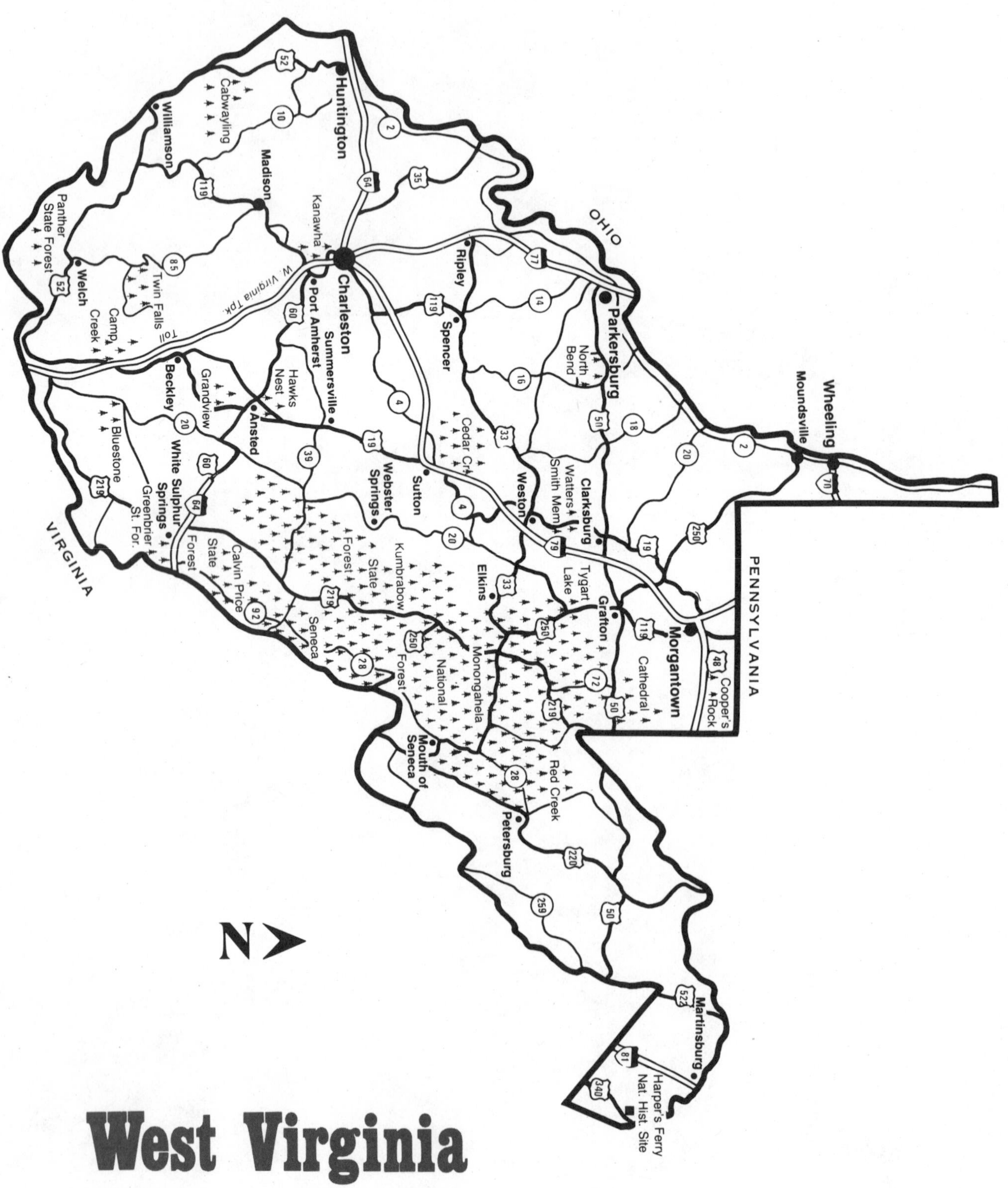

Map not to exact scale.

West Virginia

West Virginians bill their state as a "land of many moods" — exhilirating, reflective, tranquil, happy, artistic, progressive. And you can sample these many moods as you roll through its countryside — along mountain ridges, past sparkling rivers, through quiet valleys, and on into the commercial hubbub of the cities.

The first European settlement of record in what is now West Virginia was established in the eastern arm of the region by Morgan Morgan in 1731. These early settlers, many of whom were dissenters in church and state, tended to be very provincial in their politics. But following the War of 1812, the region developed a decided nationalism — a fact that ultimately led West Virginia to break away from Virginia when that state voted for secession from the Union at the outbreak of the Civil War.

Perhaps the most colorful event in the state's history is the famous feud between the Hatfields of West Virginia and the McCoys of neighboring Kentucky. The Hatfields and McCoys had long had their differences, but the feud began in earnest in 1880 when a Hatfield was accused of stealing a hog belonging to one Randolph McCoy. In 1882, three sons of Randolph were seized by a group of Hatfields and brutally murdered. This fueled the feud for many years — with the McCoys getting the worst of it — until Kentucky officers made several raids into West Virginia during 1888. At least two Hatfields were killed and nine more captured, two of whom were executed while the rest were sent to prison.

Full name: State of West Virginia
Origin of name: In honor of Queen Elizabeth of England, the "Virgin Queen."
Motto: *Montani Semper Liberi* (Mountaineers Are Always Free).
Nickname: Mountain State
Capital: Charleston
Statehood: June 20, 1863, 35th state.
Population: 1,859,000 (ranks 34th).
Major Cities: Huntington (68,811), Charleston (67,348), Wheeling (44,369).
Bird: Cardinal
Flower: Big rhododendron
Tree: Sugar maple

Average daily temperatures by month

	Northeastern	Southwestern
Jan.	41.7 to 18.1	44.2 to 24.1
Feb.	43.3 to 20.3	47.9 to 25.6
Mar.	51.6 to 28.0	56.8 to 32.5
Apr.	64.0 to 37.9	69.3 to 41.9
May	73.4 to 46.4	78.5 to 51.0
Jun.	81.5 to 54.9	85.5 to 59.8
Jul.	85.6 to 59.1	88.5 to 64.5
Aug.	84.3 to 57.4	87.5 to 63.6
Sept.	78.5 to 50.2	82.6 to 56.7
Oct.	67.9 to 38.8	71.5 to 44.4
Nov.	55.3 to 30.2	57.4 to 33.7
Dec.	44.4 to 22.0	47.2 to 27.7
Year	64.3 to 38.6	68.1 to 43.8

Today, along the Tug Fork River in the southwestern section of the state, you can visit the valley where much of the feuding took place. At one of the many fairs and festivals held annually throughout the state, you can learn more about the ways of West Virginia's mountain people through their tasty home cooking, lively music and beautiful arts and crafts. As one of the nation's most rugged and mountainous regions, West Virginia was made to order for outdoor enthusiasts; there are numerous state parks and forests, the Monongahela National Forest, miles of crystal clear rivers and white-water streams, and a number of excellent ski areas.

As the second-leading coal producer in the U.S., West Virginia has a largely mineral-based economy, but the Ohio and Kanawha valleys are important chemical producing centers. The manufacture of stone, clay and glass products, as well as machinery and electrical equipment, are also important. Tourism also ranks as one of the state's leading industries.

Highlight

West Virginia's Famous Glass

Glassmaking, a time-honored art, has become one of West Virginia's major industries and its decorative glass is in great demand. Indeed, exquisite West Virginia tableware graces homes around the world, including the home of the President of the United States.

Many of the factories have colorful display rooms where you can browse as long as you like or purchase pieces of sparkling glassware; choosing the one you want may be a very difficult decision. Visitors are encouraged to bring their cameras on their tour of a glass factory and record the exciting and educational story of glassmaking — from molten glass to finished product.

Visitors are invited to tour the state's major glass factories, each with its own unique characteristics, and watch the glassblowers at work from special observation decks. The working area of a factory is a beehive of purposeful activity. Artisans go about their tasks in much the same way their fathers and grandfathers did before them, using tools and techniques of centuries ago.

West Virginia Glass Companies

Bailey Glass Co., Inc., PO Box 1076, Morgantown, 26505, Phone: (304) 296-8388.

Blenko Glass Co., Inc., PO Box 67, Henry Road, Milton 25541, Phone: (304) 743-9081.

Brilliant Glass Co., PO Box 148, Weston 24652. Phone: (304) 269-1361.

Fenton Art Glass Co. (The), PO Box 156, Williamstown 26187. Phone: (304) 375-6122.

Fostoria Glass Co., 1200 First Street, Moundsville 26041. Phone: (304) 845-1050.

Gentile Glass Co., 425 Industrial Avenue, Star City 26505. Phone: (304) 599-2750.

Mid-Atlantic Glass Co., Ellenboro 26346. Phone: (304) 869-3351.

Pennsboro Glass Co., PO Box 487, Pennsboro 26415. Phone: (304) 659-2871.

Pilgrim Glass Corp. (The), PO Box 395, Ceredo 25507. Phone: (304) 453-3553.

Seneca Glass Co., Inc., PO Box 855, 709 Beechurst Avenue, Morgantown 26505. Phone: (304) 292-7121.

Viking Glass Co., Plant No. 1, PO Box 29, Parkway Street, New Martinsville 26155. Phone: (304) 455-2900.

Viking Glass Co., Plant No. 2, PO Box 9246, Huntington 25704. Phone: (304) 429-1321

WV Glass Specialty Co., Inc., PO Box 510, Weston 26452. Phone: (304) 269-2842.

Hamon Glass & Visitors Center, 102 Hamon Drive, Scott Depot 25560. Phone: (304) 755-3381 or 755-2025.

State Offices

Tourism
Travel Department Division
West Virginia Department of Commerce
1900 Washington Street, E.
Charleston, West Virginia 25305
(304) 348-2286

State Police
Department of Public Safety
South Charleston, West Virginia 25309
(304) 348-6370

Radio Stations

Charleston
WCAW 680 (AM)
Wheeling
WKWK 97.3 (FM)

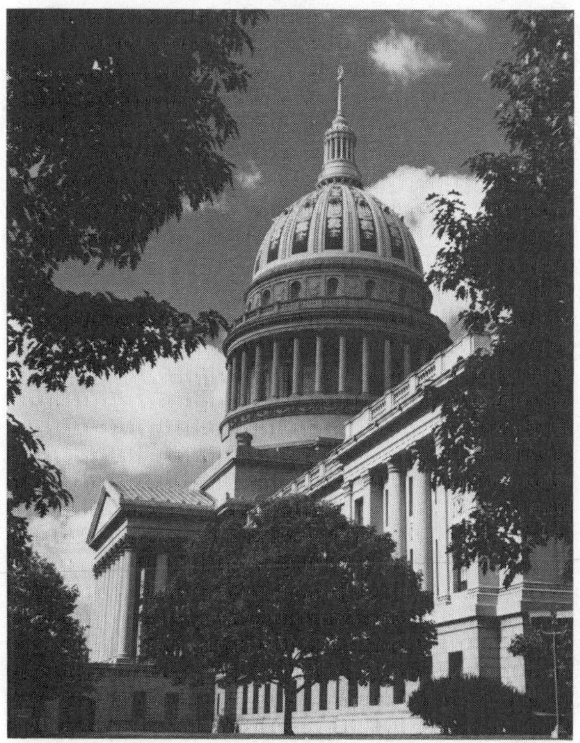

The stately West Virginia state capitol on the north bank of the Great Kanawha River in Charleston is known for its 300-foot blue and gold dome, its 3,000-piece Czechoslovakian crystal chandelier and Roman porticos and collonades. Daily tours are conducted through the various government offices.

West Virginia Points of Interest and Attractions

Berkeley Springs. Long before the first Europeans discovered the warm waters of Berkeley Springs, it was already famous among the Indians from Canada to the Carolinas. Advocated by George Washington and Lord Fairfax of Virginia, it soon became popular with the colonial elite. The mineral water that flows from the springs provides the medium for the various baths, treatments and health services offered. Massages and swimming are also available. Open year-round. Berkeley Springs, off US-522.

Big Bend Tunnels. Famous twin railroad tunnels, 6,500 feet long. The legend of John Henry was born here when he was victorious in a race with a steam drill in 1873. John Henry's statue overlooks the tunnels. Talcott, off State Route 3.

Cathedral Park. A 133-acre stand of majestic virgin timber that has been entered in the National Registry of Natural History Landmarks by the U.S. Department of Interior-National Park Service; picnicking, hiking. Aurora, off US-50.

Lost World Caverns. West Virginia's newest commercial cavern, designated by the U.S. Department of Interior as a registered National Landmark. Special features of this magnificent cave are rooms larger than a football field and an ancient beach more than 300,000 years old. Open year-round. Lewisburg, off Interstate 64.

Organ Cave. This cave contains evidence of its important role in the Civil War when General Robert E. Lee's troops made ammunition in the wooden hoppers that are still preserved in the cave. Lee is immortalized in a rock formation that is said to resemble him. The cave's focal point is a majestic organ, nearly 40 feet tall, that emits music when its limestone pipes are struck with a hammer. Caldwell, off US-60.

Seneca Caves. The legend of the beautiful Indian Princess Snow Bird is contained in one of this cave's rock formations, which is said to be a perfect profile of the princess with her long hair flowing down her back. (In the cave's Great Ballroom, the princess is supposed to have married the young brave who proved his love for her by climbing to the peak of the treacherous Seneca Rocks.) Open year-round. Riverton, off US-33.

Smoke Hole. This cave contains the world's longest ribbon stalactite and was first used by the Seneca Indians for smoking meat. During the Civil War, it served as a storage room for ammunition. A serenely quiet coral pool in the diamond-bright crystal cave is home for golden and rainbow trout. Open year-round. Jordan Run, off State Route 28.

Skyland's Ridge Runner. The shortest interstate railroad in the nation, crossing the West Virginia-Virginia state line four times on top of the East River Mountain. Bluefield, off US-460.

Stulting House. The renovated home of writer Pearl S. Buck, containing many of the furnishings that were there at the time of the famous author's birth; museum nearby. Open year-round. Hillsboro, off US-219.

Harper's Ferry, situated at the confluence of the Shenandoah and Potomac Rivers in West Virginia's Blue Ridge Mountains, is the site of John Brown's famous anti-slavery raid in 1859. The tiny village of 100 years ago has now grown into a major industrial community.

West Virginia State Parks

Park	Location	CAMPING	PICNICKING	CONCESSIONS	SWIMMING	HIKING	BOATING	FISHING	HUNTING	WINTER SPORTS
Audra	*Buckhannon. Off US-33.*	•	•	•	•	•		•		
Babcock	*Clifftop. Off State Route 41.*	•	•	•	•	•	•	•		
Blackwater Falls	*Davis. Off State Route 32.*	•	•	•	•	•	•	•		
Bluestone	*Hinton. Off State Route 20.*	•	•	•	•	•	•	•	•	
Cacapon	*Berkeley Springs. Off US-522.*		•	•	•	•	•	•		
Canaan Valley	*Davis. Off State Route 32.*	•		•	•	•	•	•		•
Cedar Creek	*Glenville. Off US-33.*	•	•		•	•		•		
Chief Logan	*Logan. Off US-119.*		•	•	•	•				
Grandview	*Beckley. Off State Route 41.*		•			•				
Hawks Nest	*Ansted. Off US-60.*		•	•	•	•	•	•		
Holly River	*Hacker Valley. Off State Route 20.*	•	•	•	•	•	•	•		
Lost River	*Mathias. Off State Route 259.*		•	•	•	•				
North Bend	*Cairo. Off US-50.*	•	•	•	•	•		•		
Pipestem	*Pipestem. Off State Route 20.*	•	•	•	•	•	•	•		
Tomlinson Run	*New Manchester. Off State Route 2.*		•		•	•	•	•		
Twin Falls	*Mullens. Off State Route 97.*		•	•	•	•				
Tygart Lake	*Grafton. Off US-119.*	•	•	•	•		•	•		
Valley Falls	*Fairmont. Off State Route 310.*		•							
Watoga	*Marlinton. Off US-219.*	•	•	•	•	•	•	•		

West Virginia State Forests

Forest	Location	CAMPING	PICNICKING	CONCESSIONS	SWIMMING	HIKING	BOATING	FISHING	HUNTING	WINTER SPORTS
Cabwaylingo	*Dunlow. Off State Route 152.*	•	•		•	•		•	•	
Calvin Price	*Dunmore. Off US-219.*	•				•		•	•	
Camp Creek	*Camp Creek. Off West Virginia Turnpike.*	•	•			•		•	•	
Coopers Rock	*Bruceton. Off US-48.*	•	•	•		•		•	•	•
Greenbrier	*Caldwell. Off Interstate 64.*	•	•	•	•	•	•	•	•	
Kanawha	*Charleston. Off US-119.*	•	•	•	•	•				
Kumbrabow	*Huttonsville. Off US-219.*	•	•			•		•	•	
Panther	*Panther. Off US-52.*	•	•		•	•		•	•	
Seneca	*Dunmore. Off State Route 28.*	•	•			•	•	•	•	

For more information on West Virginia state parks and forests, contact: *West Virginia Department of Natural Resources, Division of Parks and Recreation, State Capitol-SP, Charleston, West Virginia 25305, (304) 348-2764.*

Southern Region Calendar of Events

Spring
(March, April, May)

Arkansas

Annual Arkansas Marathon. Official AAU 26-mile race. March, Booneville.

T. A. G. Outdoor Art Show. Displays by members of the Traditional Art Guild. March, Hot Springs.

Jonquil Festival, Old Washington State Park. March, Washington.

Pioneer Crafts Festival. Parade, crafts demonstrations, sales, authentic string music. March, Rison.

Annual Forum On the Decorative Arts. March, Little Rock.

Shakespearean Festival. March, Beebe.

Rainbow Trout Tournament. March, Heber Springs.

Pinnacle Mountain Wildflower Weekend. Guided walks led by park naturalists, Pinnacle Mountain State Park. March, Roland.

Little Rock Air Force Base Open House and Air Show. April, Jacksonville.

Annual Burl Lynch Trail Ride. April, Booneville.

Newton County Dogwood Tours. April, Jasper.

Family Fun Festival, Lake Chicot State Park. April, Lake Village.

Tour of Iris Gardens. April, Hot Springs.

Annual Fairfield Bay Spring Festival. April, Fairfield Bay.

Arkansas All-Girl Rodeo. April, Little Rock.

Annual Hot Spring County Arts and Crafts Show and Sale. April, Malvern.

Lions Club Annual Pancake Breakfast. April, Hot Springs.

Spring Pilgrimage. Annual tour of antebellum homes and churches. April, Helena.

Annual Miss WestArk Pageant. April, Fort Smith.

Annual Spring Concert. April, Fort Smith.

Ozark Region Rodeo. April, Beebe.

Annual Spring Environmental Backpacking Workshop, Devil's Den State Park. April, West Fork.

Lake Catherine Wildflower Weekends, Lake Catherine State Park. April, Hot Springs.

Annual Arkansas Folk Festival. Craft demonstrations, exhibits, live music, folk dancing, parade, rodeo. April, Mountain View.

Spring Tour of Historic Homes. April, Eureka Springs.

Dogwood Arts and Crafts Fair. April, Siloam Springs.

Ouachita River Canoe Races. April, Mount Ida.

Annual Pioneer Days Celebration. Parade, square dancing, arts and crafts show and sale, Arkansas Champion Tobacco Spitting Contest. April, Monticello.

Southern Regional Mountain and Hammer Dulcimer Contest and Workshops, Ozark Folk Center. April, Mountain View.

Annual Saline County Craft Show and Sale. April, Benton.

Annual Iris Show. April, Hot Springs.

Bluegrass Festival. May, Crossett.

Annual Kiddies Fishing Rodeo, Lake Lou Emma. May, Van Buren.

Booneville Riding Club Spring Rodeo, fairgrounds. May, Booneville.

Annual Pioneer Day. Residents dress in old-time costumes; wide range of special events. May, Melbourne.

Annual "Back In the Hills" Antique Show and Collectors Fair. May, Hindsville.

Annual Mount Nebo Chicken Fry, Mount Nebo State Park. May, Dardanelle.

Annual Small Fry Fishing Derby, Oaklawn Park. May, Pine Bluff.

Annual Spring River Canoe Race. May, Hardy.

Civil War Day, Prairie Grove Battlefield State Park. Reenactment of battle that took place here, rifle demonstrations. May, Prairie Grove.

Annual Memorial Day Bass Tournament, Lake Dardanelle State Park. May, Russellville.

Georgia

Annual Musical Show, Grand Opera House. March, Macon.

Annual Azalea Bridge Tournament. March, Savannah.

Annual Rattlesnake Roundup. March, Claxton.

Spring Flower Show, Garden Center. March, Augusta.

Kite Flying Contest, Vallotton Park. March, Valdosta.

Tour of Homes and Gardens. March, Savannah.

Annual Savannah Needlework Exhibit. March, Savannah.

Dogwood Festival, Cracker Williams Recreation Center. March, Jesup.

Jazz Festival, Fine Arts Hall. April, Columbus.

Spring Festival. April, Lumpkin.

Bass Derby. April, Lula.

Helena is Arkansas' major Mississippi River port, an important destination along the Great River Road in eastern Arkansas. The town is famous for its outstanding collection of antebellum homes. During the annual Helena Pilgrimage in April, many of the homes are open to the public. Here, the Estevan Hall is typical of the town's gracious architecture.

Dogwood Week, Tullie Smith House. April, Atlanta.
Georgia Antique Fair, Lakewood Fairgrounds. April, Atlanta.
Glee Club Annual Spring Concert, Agnes Scott College. April, Decatur.
Annual Rose Festival. April, Thomasville.
Tour of Homes by candlelight. April, Thomasville.
Annual Spring Dance Concert, Agnes Scott College. April, Decatur.
Spring Arts and Crafts Festival, Hunter Park. April, Douglasville.
Annual Rose Sunday, Lapham-Patterson House. April, Thomasville.
Annual Forest Festival, Laura Walker State Park. May, Waycross.
Pine Tree Festival. May, Swainsboro.
Plantation Tours. May, Thomasville.
Arts and Crafts Festival. May, Forsyth.
Savannah Scottish Games. May, Savannah.
Cottin Pickin' Antique Fair. May, Gay.
Bluegrass Festival, Twin Oaks Park. May, Schlatterville.
Arts Festival of Atlanta, Piedmont Park. May, Atlanta.
Blessing of Shrimp Fleet. May, Brunswick.
Onion Festival. May, Vidalia.
Peach Harvest, Peach County. May, Fort Valley.
Savannah River Raft Race. May, Augusta.
Railroad Days Festival. May, Lula.

Kentucky

Tater Day. Parade, beauty pageant, arts and crafts; City Park on the Square. April, Benton.
Mountain Folk Festival, Berea College. April, Berea.
Mountain Dew Festival. Athletic events, dances, exhibits. April, Prestonsburg.
Kentucky Derby Festival. April and May, Louisville.
May Day Festival. Parade and pageant. May, Owingsville.
Annual Golden Age Day. May, Cave City.
Butchertown Spring Festival. May, Louisville.
Kentucky Mountain Laurel Festival. Parades, queen contest. May, Pineville.
Annual Village Craft Festival. May to June, Cave City.

North Carolina

Spring Arts and Crafts Show, Carolina Circle Mall. March, Greensboro.
Sundrop 500, Hickory Speedway. March, Hickory.
J. E. Mainer Memorial Old-Time Fiddlers and Bluegrass Music Convention. March, Denver.
Old Quawk's Day. Revival of legend of shipwrecked sailor who became known as the meanest man in Carteret County. March, Morehead City.
Annual Antiques Fair. March, Southern Pines.
Spring Festival of Arts and Crafts. March, Chapel Hill.
Miss National Teenager Pageant. March, Raleigh.
Annual Good Life Show, Civic Center. March, Charlotte.
Folk Music Festival, Louisburg College. March, Louisburg.
Annual Bass Tournament. $3,000 in cash prizes. March, Fontana Dam.
Annual North Carolina Artists Convention. April, Raleigh.
Storytelling Festival. April, Raleigh.
Greater Greensboro Open Golf Tournament, Forest Oaks Country Club. April, Greensboro.
North Carolina Azalea Festival. Coronation ball, fireworks, parade, tour of homes, garden tours. April, Wilmington.
Annual Senior Citizens Antique and Crafts Sale. April, Winston-Salem.
Annual Gardeners Sunday. April, New Bern.
Annual Fontana Fishing Contest. April, Fontana Dam.
Spring Art Show. April, Dallas.
Annual Stoneybrook Steeplechase Races. April, Southern Pines.
Spring Flower Hiking Week. April, Fontana Dam.
Shad Festival. Fishing contests, fish fry, canoe race, dancing, games, model airplane show. April, Grifton.

Celebrate Charlotte Festival. April, Charlotte.
Carolina Dogwood Festival. April, Statesville.
Springfest. Bavarian tradition of celebrating spring's arrival; German bands, dancers. April, Raleigh.
Annual Strawberry Festival. Golf, tennis, basketball tournaments, parade, dance, food, arts and crafts. April, Chadbourn.
Annual Bass Fishing Tournament. May, Roanoke Rapids.
Annual Spring Wildflower Pilgrimage. May, Asheville.
Annual Central Carolina Art Festival, Frazier Park. May, Asheboro.
Gliding Spectacular. Annual hang-gliding competition for distance. May, Nags Head.
Annual Outdoor Art Show. May, Rocky Mount.
Capitol Square Arts Festival. Music, dancing. May, Raleigh.
Pleasure Island Spring Festival. Parade, antique car show, flea market, moonlight musical. May, Carolina and Kure Beaches.
World 600, Charlotte Motor Speedway. May, Harrisburg.
Kemper Open Golf Tournament, Quail Hollow Country Club. May, Charlotte.
Rowan Rose Show. May, Salisbury.

South Carolina

Chattooga River Rafting Adventures. Shoot the rapids on a guided seven-hour raft trip. March, Portsmouth.
Garden Club of Charleston Walking House Tour. March, Charleston.
Annual St. Patrick's Day Fashion Show. March, Allendale.
Annual Coastal Carolina Diamond Classic. Baseball competition. March, Conway.
Annual Canadian-American Days Festival. March, Myrtle Beach and the Grand Strand.
Aiken Horse Trials. Spring debut of some of the nation's finest thoroughbreds. March, Aiken.
Annual Tour of Homes and Plantations. March, Beaufort.
Aiken Steeplechase and Hunt Meet. March, Aiken.
Walking Garden Tour. March, Charleston.
Annual Spring House Tours. March, Charleston.
Annual Carolina Cup Races. Steeplechase and flat racing. March, Camden.
Eshu Festival. Yoruban African village salutes the god of uncertainty. April, Sheldon.
Annual Grand Strand Fishing Rodeo and Fish of the Month Contest. April, Myrtle Beach.
Allendale County Spring Festival. April, Allendale.
Annual Spring Concert. April, Charleston.
Musical Garden Tour. Tour of several gardens with musical groups performing live. April, Columbia.
St. Thaddeus' Annual Spring House and Garden Tour. April, Aiken.
The Governor's Annual Frog Jumping Contest and International Egg Striking Contest. April, Springfield.
Annual Candlelight Tour of Homes. April, Charleston.
Purple Martin Festival. Honors the return of the purple martin. April, St. Matthews.
Annual Arts and Crafts Fair. May, Williamston.
South Carolina Festival of Roses. May, Orangeburg.
Hell Hole Swamp Festival. Colorful festival includes moonshine making, talent contest, snake show, leg contest, barbecue and chicken-bog dinners, crowning of Miss Hell Hole Swamp. May, Jamestown.
Annual Cross Trails Fair. Craft exhibits, square dancing. May, Laurens.
Rose Festival Road Run. May, Orangeburg.
Annual Batesburg-Leesville Sandlapper Festival. Miss Sandlapper pageant, pork and chicken barbecue. May, Batesburg-Leesville.
Annual Historic Camden Arts Festival. May, Camden.

Senior Citizens Saltwater Fishing Tournament. May, Myrtle Beach.

Tennessee

Knoxville International Festival, Deane Hill Country Club. March, Knoxville.

Nashville Antiques Exposition. March, Nashville.

Great Smoky Mountain Festival of Champions Square Dance, Civic Auditorium. March, Gatlinburg.

Dogwood Arts Festival. April, Knoxville.

Mule Day. Mule shows, auctions, races, pulling contests, crowning of "King Mule." April, Columbia.

Annual Celebration Rodeo. April, Shelbyville.

Reelfoot Lake Spring Art Show. April, Tiptonville.

Wildflower Pilgrimage. April, Gatlinburg.

Steam Train Excursion. Spring train ride through scenic countryside. April, Chattanooga.

Old Oak Festival. April, Tusculum.

Annual Open House and Arts and Crafts Sale. April, Kingsport.

Memphis in May International Festival. April through May, Memphis.

World's Biggest Fish Fry. Marks the beginning of fishing season, April, Paris.

Annual Opryland Festival. May, Nashville.

Old Mountain Crafts Fair. May, Chattanooga.

East Tennessee Strawberry Festival. May, Dayton.

Folk Music Festival. May, Jonesboro.

West Tennessee Strawberry Festival. May, Humboldt.

Rugby Spring Music and Crafts Festival. May, Rugby.

Nashville Rose Society Spring Show. May, Nashville.

Annual Spring Fun Show. First walking horse show of the season. May, Shelbyville.

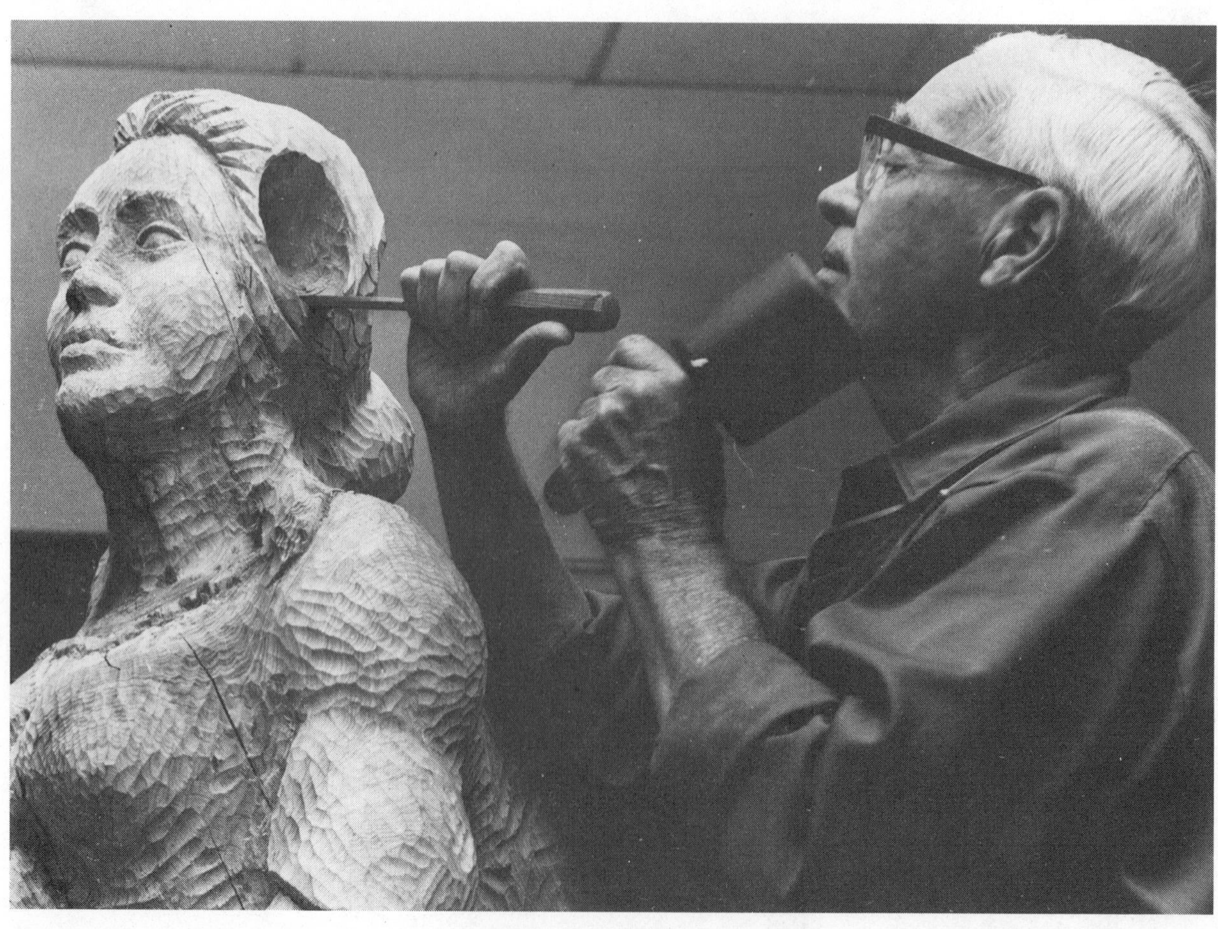

Soybean Festival. Beauty pageant, parades, horse show, carnival. May, Dyersburg.

Virginia

International Azalea Festival. April, Norfolk.
Garden Week in Virginia. April, Richmond.
Garden Symposium. April, Williamsburg.
Militia Muster. April through October, Williamsburg.
Bristol Country Music Days. April to May, Bristol.
Strawberry Hill Races. April, Richmond.
Dogwood Festival. April, Charlottesville.
Jamestown Day. May, Jamestown.
Annual Seawall Art Show. May, Portsmouth.
Festival In The Park. May, Danville.
Lonesome Pine Arts and Crafts Festival. May, Big Stone Gap.

West Virginia

Alpine Winter Festival, Canaan Valley. March, Davis.
Jazz Festival, Smith Recital Hall, Marshall University. March, Huntington.
State Swing Festival. March, Charleston.
Spring Showing, Old Stone House. March, Morgantown.
Annual Home Garden and Sport Show, White Palace, Wheeling Park. April, Wheeling.
Webster County Nature Tour, Camp Caesar. April, Webster Springs.
Annual House and Garden Tour. April, Berkeley and Jefferson Counties.
Guided Interpretive Nature Walks, Bunner Ridge Recreation Area. May, Fairmont.
Spring Nature Festival. May, Parkersburg.
West Virginia Wildflower Pilgrimage, Blackwater Falls State Park. May, Davis.
Annual Benefit Antiques Show and Sale. May, Huntington.
Strawberry Festival. May, Berkeley Springs.
Cheat Down River Races, Cheat River. May, Rowlesburg.
Marble Shooting Contest, North Bend State Park. May, Cairo.
West Virginia Strawberry Festival. May, Buckhannon.
Memorial Day Celebration, North Bend State Park. May, Cairo.

Summer
(June, July, August)

Arkansas

Annual Big Maumelle Canoe Race, Pinnacle Mountain State Park. June, Roland.
Annual National Buffalo River Canoe Race. June, Marshall.
Annual Pink Tomato Festival. Parade, all tomato lunch, beauty pageant, tomato eating contest — all to celebrate tomato harvest. June, Warren.
Annual IRA Championship Rodeo. June, Calico Rock.
Annual Minnow Festival, City Park. June, Lonoke.
Annual Arkansas Fun Festival. Arts and crafts, golf and tennis tournament, bowling, Miss Hot Springs Pageant, parade of boats. June, Hot Springs.
Annual Ozarks Arts and Crafts Seminar, War Eagle Mills Farm. June, Hindsville.
Ridiculous Day. Event got its name when local people said it was "ridiculous" to try to build a big city out in the hills. June, Horseshoe Bend.
Ding Dong Daddy Bass Tournament, Pendleton Marina. June, Dumas.
Annual Ozark Mountain Music Makers String Band and Fiddler Contest. June, Salem.
Annual Trout Derby. June, Calico Rock.
Annual Johnson County Peach Festival. Soapbox derby, terrapin race, horseshoe pitching, street dance, beauty pageants. June, Clarksville.
Annual Summer Music Festival, Arts Center of the Ozarks. July, Springdale.
Annual Rodeo of the Ozarks, Parsons Rodeo Arena. July, Springdale.
Annual Jonesboro Open Ski Tournament, Craighead Lake. July, Jonesboro.

Annual Fireworks Display. July, Fairfield Bay.

Fourth of July Rescue Squad Fish Fry and Fireworks Display. Proceeds from fish fry go to rescue squad. July, Diamond City.

Corning Annual Homecoming Picnic, Wynn Park. Carnival atmosphere, rides, games. July, Corning.

Fireworks Display, Lake Dardanelle State Park. July, Russellville.

Annual Madison County Arts and Crafts Festival. July, Huntsville.

Miss Arkansas Pageant, Convention Auditorium. July, Hot Springs.

Annual Celebrity Canoe Race. July, Fairfield Bay.

Annual Paragould Jaycee Rodeo. July, Paragould.

Frontier Days. Arts and crafts, talent show, pet show, parade. July, Prescott.

Annual Northwest Arkansas Bluegrass Festival. August, Harrison.

Annual White River Water Carnival and Beauty Contest. August, Batesville.

Wooten Bluegrass Festival. August, Morrilton.

Annual Old Soldiers Reunion, Spring Park. Parade, beauty pageant, carnival. August, Heber Springs.

Pine Tree Festival. Country music, pie baking, egg throwing, women's arm wrestling, bait casting, skillet throwing. August, Dierks.

Greers Ferry Lake Water Festival. August, Heber Springs.

Annual Hell's Valley Bluegrass Festival. August, Nashville.

Annual Tontitown Grape Festival. August, Springdale.

Annual Weekend with the Arts. August, Maumelle.

Watermelon Festival. August, Hope.

Annual Arkansas Prison Rodeo. Inmates and free-world entrants compete in events for more than $14,000 in prize money; Cummins Prison. August, Pine Bluff.

Annual St. Francis County Wildlife Association Barbecue. August, Forrest City.

Arkansas River Festival and Great Raft Race, Slackwater Harbor. August, Pine Bluff.

Georgia

Atlanta Jazz Festival. June, Atlanta.

Sunshine Festival. July, Simons Island.

Tobacco Auctions. July through September, Douglas.

Watermelon Festival. July, Cordele.

Sidewalk Art Show. July, LaGrange.

Western Week. July, Chatsworth.

Georgia Grassroots Music Festival. August, Atlanta.

Kentucky

Bluegrass Music Festival of the United States. June, Louisville.

Annual Rosine Arts and Crafts Spring Festival. June, Rosine.

Kentucky Folksong Festival. June, Grayson.

Daniel Boone Days. Horse show, fireworks, rodeo, Kentucky Longriflemen's show. July, Booneville.

Paducah Summer Festival. August, Paducah.

Sacajawea Festival. August, Cloverport.

Annual International Banana Festival. August, Fulton.

Kentucky Highlands Folk Festival. Annual event aimed at preserving the traditions and cultural heritage of the people of Appalachia. August, Prestonsburg.

Contestants in authentic mountainman garb test their skill with the long rifles at the Daniel Boone Days celebration held each July in Booneville, Kentucky.

North Carolina

Bluegrass and Old-Time Fiddlers Convention. June, Mount Airy.

Annual Bluegrass Fiddlers Convention, Eden Fairgrounds. June, Eden.

Festival on the Square. Arts and Crafts, jailhouse gallery. June, Morganton.

Annual Lions Club Horse Show, Franklin County Fairgrounds. June, Louisburg.

Children's Walking Tour. Tour of historic district for young people. June, Salisbury.

Annual Invitational Blue Marlin Tournament. June, Hatteras.

Annual North Carolina Corn Shuckin' Contest. June, Spivey's Corner.

Annual National Hollerin' Contest. Junior hollerin', Ladies Callin'; revives the almost lost art of hollerin'. June, Spivey's Corner.

Annual High Rock Lake Days. Bass fishing tournament, beauty pageant. June, Southmont.

Annual Highland Heritage Arts and Crafts Show. June, Asheville.

Annual Long Leaf Arts and Crafts Show. June, Wilmington.

Annual "Singin' on the Mountain," Grandfather Mountain. Modern and traditional gospel music. June, Linville.

Annual Mount Pilot Bluegrass Festival. June, Pinnacle.

Old Homes Tour. June, Beaufort.

Annual Antique Country Fair and Flea Market. June, Blowing Rock.

Blue Ridge Mountain Fair. Arts, crafts, canoe race, horse show, parade, outdoor drama. July, Sparta.

Annual Tar Heel Regatta, Lake Wheeler. July, Raleigh.

National Antiques Fair. July, Hendersonville.

Blue Ridge Wagon Train. July, Wilkesboro.

Old-fashioned Fourth of July, Town Hall. Parade, games, children's activities, fireworks, dancing. July, Carrboro.

Annual North Carolina State Pipe Smoking Contest. July, Chapel Hill.

Annual Lumber River Canoe Regatta. July, Wagram.

July Fourth Celebration, Tweetsie Railroad. July, Blowing Rock.

High Country Arts and Crafts Fair. July, Highlands.

Shindig-On-The-Green, City-County Plaza. July, Asheville.

Helen's Barn Square Dance Festival. July, Highlands.

North Carolina Shakespeare. July, High Point.

World Championship Drag Boat Races. July, High Point.

Annual Watermelon Seed Spitting Contest and Sidewalk Sale. July, Jacksonville.

Smoky Mountain Folk Festival. July, Waynesville.

Winston 300 Auto Race. August, Winston-Salem.

Mineral and Gem Festival. August, Spruce Pine.

Annual Mountain Dance and Folk Festival, Civic Center. August, Asheville.

Annual Village Art and Craft Fair. August, Asheville.

Fiddlers' Convention, Ashe County Park. August, West Jefferson.

Annual National Open Cribbage Tournament. August, Raleigh.

Shrimp Festival. Parade, shrimparoo, military displays, skydivers, music, rides, street dance. August, Sneads Ferry.

Festival of Outer Banks Folk Music. August, Atlantic Beach.

North Carolina Apple Festival. August, Hendersonville.

South Carolina

Annual Sun Fun Festival. Miss Sun Fun Pageant, Miss Bikini Wahine, parades, beach games, dances, band concerts, golf, arts and crafts. June, Myrtle Beach.

Annual Sun Fun Road Races. June, Myrtle Beach.

Summer Bird Count (statewide); contact Division of State Parks. June, Columbia.

Annual Gulf Stream Marina King Mackerel Tournament. June, Garden City.

Miss Hartsville Pageant. June, Hartsville.

Annual South Carolina Food Festival. June, Columbia.

Might Mo Day. Reunion for the men who fought on the *USS Cowpens* in World War II. June, Cowpens.

Honor America Days. Barbecue, parachute jumps, cake walk, square dance, fireworks. July, Landrum.

Lexington County Peach Festival. July, Gilbert.

Mountain Rest Hillbilly Day. July, Mountain Rest.

Annual Independence Day Celebration. July, Charleston.

Miss South Carolina Pageant. July, Greenville.

Gold Rush Day. July, McCormick.

Beaufort Water Festival. Spectacular week-long celebration with golf, tennis and fishing tournaments, talent contests, bicycle races, band concerts, supper featuring local dishes. July, Beaufort.

Park Seed's Annual Open House and Flower Day. July, Greenwood.

Lake City Tobacco Festival. July, Lake City.

Annual Toadfish Tournament. August, Hilton Head Island.

Grape Festival. Tours of vineyards, grape stomping, festival ball, parade, beauty pageant, art show. August. York.

Tractor Pull. August, Saluda.

Tennessee

Buffalo River Canoe Racing. June, Hohenwald.

Mill Spring Summer Jubilee of Folklife and Folk Arts. June, Jonesboro.

Walking Horse Spring Jubilee. June, Columbia.

Tullahoma Street Festival. June, Tullahoma.

Annual Dulcimer Competition. June, Crosby.

Summer Solstice. Outdoor multi-media celebration welcoming summer. June, Nashville.

Annual Rhododendron Festival, Roan Mountain. June, Johnson City.

Old-Time Fiddlers Jamboree and Crafts Festival. July, Smithville.

Craftsman Fair. July, Crossville.

Mid-Summer Craft Fair, Civic Auditorium. July, Gatlinburg.

Annual David Crockett Arts and Crafts Festival. August, Lawrenceburg.

Loretto Tractor Pull. August, Lawrenceburg.

David Crockett Days. August, Lawrenceburg.

Annual Rugby Pilgrimage. Open house of original homes and buildings. August, Rugby.

Okra Festival. August, Bells.

National Walking Horse Celebration. August, Shelbyville.

Annual Opryland Western Square Dance Festival. August, Nashville.

Annual Opryland Country Music and Crafts Festival. August, Nashville.

Virginia

The Common Glory. Spirit of '76 drama. June through August, Williamsburg.

Trail of the Lonesome Pine. Hill drama. June, Big Stone Gap.

Hampton Kool Jazz Festival. June, Newport News.

Virginia Scottish Games. July, Alexandria.

Happy Birthday USA. July, Staunton.

Shenandoah Valley Music Festival. July through August, Orkney Springs.

Virginia Highlands Arts and Crafts Festival. August. Abingdon.

Burley Tobacco Festival and Farm Show. August, Abingdon.

Boardwalk Art and Craft Show. August, Colonial Beach.

Jousting Tournament. August, Natural Chimneys.

West Virginia

Rhododendron State Outdoor Art and Crafts Festival. June, Charleston.

Mountain Heritage Art and Craft Festival. June, Harpers Ferry.

Annual Bluegrass Festival. June, Fairmont.

Annual Harpers Ferry Art Festival. June, Harpers Ferry.

Annual Performing Arts Workshop, Bethany College. June, Wheeling.

West Virginia Regatta Festival, Sutton Lake. June, Sutton.

Pearl S. Buck Birthday Celebration, Pearl S. Buck Birthplace Foundation. June, Hillsboro.
July Jamboree, Town Park. July, Fayetteville.
Fourth of July Celebration. July, Helvetia.
Franklin Firemen's Fourth of July Celebration. July, Franklin.
The Great Huntington Balloon Festival, Chesapeake Air Park. July, Huntington.

Flag-raising ceremony in James Fort within Jamestown Festival Park, Jamestown, Virginia. The fort dramatizes how the first permanent English settlers lived and protected themselves from the Indians and other wilderness hardships during the first years of the Virginia Colony. Jamestown Island and the park are open to visitors the year round, seven days a week. Both are near Williamsburg and Yorktown.

Department of Natural Resources Cranberry Glades Tour, Cranberry Information Center. July, Richwood.
Good Neighbor Days. July, Bruceton Mills.
Bridgeport Dolphin's Annual Water Show, Benedum Civic Center Pool. July, Bridgeport.
Huntington Square Dance and Festival. July, Huntington.
Annual Festival of Opera. July through August, Wheeling.
Lions Fall Festival. August, St. Marys.
Cherry River Festival. August, Richwood.
Annual Logan County Arts and Crafts, Logan Memorial Field House. August, Logan.
Mountain State Bluegrass Festival, Mountain State Park. August, Webster Springs.
Mineral Winfield District Fair. August, Fairmont.
Tri-County Fair. August, Petersburg.
Ohio River Festival, Ravenswood Riverfront Park. August, Ravenswood.
Square Dance Festival, North Bend State Park. August, Cairo.
State Fair of West Virginia. August, Fairlea.

Fall
(September, October, November)

Arkansas

Annual Air Show. September, Flippin.

Bluegrass Festival. September, Russellville.

United Way Raft Race, Arkansas River. September, Fort Smith.

Mid-America Banjo Rally. Formal performances, jam sessions, classes. September, Eureka Springs.

Fiddlers Contest, Pine Plaza Shopping Center. September, Arkadelphia.

Annual Festival of Two Rivers. September, Arkadelphia.

Annual Clothesline Fair. Arts and Crafts, old-time fiddlers contest, square dancing, chicken dinners. September, Prairie Grove.

Annual Pioneer Day. September, St. Paul.

Annual Parade of Harmony. September, Hot Springs.

Greene County Fair. September, Paragould.

Antique Car Festival. September, Eureka Springs.

Annual Benton County Fair. September, Bentonville.

Annual Grand Prairie Festival of the Arts. September, Stuttgart.

Annual Saunders Memorial Muzzle Shoot. Old-time muzzle-loading rifle and pistol matches with percussion and flintlock weapons. September, Berryville.

Arkansas Appreciation Day. September, Horseshoe Bend.

Arkansas State Fair and Livestock Show. September, Little Rock.

Fall Foliage Tours. October, Jasper.

Fall Rambles. Guided walks on park trails during height of autumn color change; Pinnacle Mountain State Park. October, Roland.

Arkansas Apple Festival. Street dance, Apple Harvest Queen contest, arts and crafts show, square dancing, apple core throwing, apple seed popping. October, Lincoln.

Wiederkehr's Oktoberfest, Wiederkehr's Winery. October, Altus.

Annual Crossbow Tournament, Withrow Springs State Park. October, Huntsville.

Annual Arkansas Oktoberfest, Convention Auditorium. October, Hot Springs.

Annual National Wild Turkey Calling Contest and Turkey Trot Festival. Free entertainment on town square. October, Yellville.

Annual Ozark Frontier Trail Festival and Craft Show. October, Heber Springs.

Annual Fall Environmental Backpacking Workshop, Devil's Den State Park. October, West Fork.

Ashley County Arts and Crafts Festival. October, Hamburg.

Annual Delta Art Exhibition, Arkansas Arts Center. October, Little Rock.

Annual Grant County Arts and Crafts Show and Sale. October, Sheridan.

Fall Arts and Crafts Show. November, Fort Smith.

Annual Frontier Days, Old Washington Historic State Park. November, Washington.

Annual Pancake Day. November, Malvern.

Annual World's Championship Duck Calling Contest and Annual Queen Mallard Contest. November, Stuttgart.

Georgia

Oaky Farms Arts and Crafts Show. September, Springfield.

Golden Isles Art Festival. October, Simons Island.

Coastal Empire Fair. October through November, Savannah.

Southeastern Arts and Crafts Festival. November, Macon.

Stock Car Races, Atlanta International Raceway. November, Atlanta.

Kentucky

Kentucky Highlands Folk Festival, Jenny Wiley State Resort Park. September, Prestonsburg.

Annual Rosine Arts and Crafts Festival. September, Rosine.

Harvest Festival. Three weeks of special events. September, Pleasant Hill.

Annual Tobacco Festival. September, Shelbyville.

Marigold Festival. September, Williamstown.

Annual Cave Country Artists and Craftsmen's Fair. September, Cave City.

Fall Festival. September, Paducah.

Daniel Boone Festival. October, Barbourville.

Logan County Tobacco Festival. October, Russellville.

Annual Kentucky Guild of Artists' and Craftsmen's Fall Fair. October, Berea.

Annual Kingdom Come Swappin' Meeting. Singing, dancing, folk arts demonstrations, flea market. October, Cumberland.

North Carolina

Soybean Festival. Carnival, fish fry, crafts. September, Clayton.

Old-Time Engine Day. Collection of antique railroad equipment. September, Blowing Rock.

Horse Show. Largest one-day horse show in the U.S. September, Enfield.

Cary Gourd Festival. September, Cary.

Country Music Championships, Haney's Blue Grass Music Park. September, Champ Springs.

Bright Leaf Festival. Crafts, music, food. September, Kinston.

Tractor Pull. September, Fuquay-Varina.

Mule Day Celebration. Oldest, youngest, ugliest mule contests; pulling contest; beauty pageant; street dance; square dance; parade; music; food. September, Benson.

Annual Masters of Hang-Gliding Championship. September, Grandfather Mountain, Linville.

Annual Fall Jubilee. September, Fontana.

October Tour. Takes in more than 12 sites in historic district. October, Salisburg.

Fall Street Fair. October, Chapel Hill.

Annual Durham First Marathon. A 10,000-meter run. October, Durham.

Cherokee Indian Fall Festival. Indian stickball, blowguns, archery, traditional dancing, arts, crafts, clogging. October, Cherokee.

Craft Bazaar and Tasting Party. October, Louisburg.

Oktoberfest, Civic Center. October, Raleigh.

Fall Festival. October, Asheboro.

Annual Any And All-Dog Show. October, Tryon.

Dudley Volunteer Fire Department Fire Prevention Parade and Show. October, Dudley.

Annual Autumn Leaves Festival. October, Mount Airy.

Autumn Glory Arts and Crafts Fair. October, Asheville.

Mullet Festival. Parade, mullet dinners, speedboat races, carnival, crafts, games, clowns, fireworks. October, Swansboro.

Festival of Champions Clog Dancing. October, Fontana.

Fall Colors Hiking Week. October, Fontana.

Mistletoe Show, Park Center. November, Charlotte.

Annual Oyster Festival. Parade, crafts, games, country store, roasted oysters. November, Newport.

North American Indian Festival and Fall Powwow. November, Gastonia.

Annual Holiday Parade. November, Jacksonville.

South Carolina

Annual South Carolina Apple Festival. September, Westminster and Long Creek.

Southern 500 Race and Southern 500 Festival. September, Darlington.

Aiken Whiskey Road Run. A 10,000-meter run. September. Aiken.

Annual Atalaya Arts and Crafts Festival. September, Murrells Inlet.

Annual Oktoberfest at Charles Towne Landing. September, Charleston.

Annual Gem and Mineral Show. September, Columbia.

Annual Foothills Festival. September, Easley.

Raylrode Daze Festival Road Race. September, Columbia.

Fall Foliage (statewide); contact Department of Parks and Recreation. October, Columbia.

Annual Arts and Crafts Show. October, Spartanburg.

Annual Governor's Cup Race. October, Columbia.

Gopher Hill Day. October, Ridgeland.

Annual Oconee Country Festival. October, Seneca.

Annual Catfish Festival. Boat races, raft drifts, game booths, gospel singing, parade, cake baking contest, catfish dinner. October, Hardeeville.

Fall Candlelight Tours. October, Charleston.

Annual Low-Country Bluegrass Jamboree. October, Holly Hill.

Autumn Leaves Special. October, Spartanburg.

Annual Southeastern Hobby Fair. November, Jackson.

Fall Clogging Festival. November, Walhalla.

Thanksgiving Week Celebration. November, Hilton Head Island.

Holiday Fiesta. Turkey shoots, community caroling, golf tournaments, Christmas concert, home tours. November, Myrtle Beach.

Annual Homecoming Parade. Procession of beauty queens, bands. November, Sumter.

Annual Christmas Parade. November, Hartsville.

Chitlins Strut. Chitlins, country music, dancing. November, Salley.

Tennessee

Italian Street Fair. September, Nashville.

Schlitz Memphis Music Heritage Festival. September, Memphis.

National Outboard Hydroplane Races, Kingston City Park. September, Kingston.

Annual Folk Festival of the Smokies. September, Cosby.

Annual Opryland Western Square Dance Festival. September, Nashville.

Tennessee Grassroots Days. September, Nashville.

Annual Tennessee State Fair. September, Nashville.

Signal Mountain Road Race. Jogging. September, Chattanooga.

National Hunting and Fishing Days. September, Chattanooga.

Annual Farmers Harvest Market. September, Knoxville.

Annual Reelfoot Lake Arts and Crafts Festival. September, Tiptonville.

Tuckaleechee Cover Arts, Crafts and Music Festival. September, Townsend.

Oktoberfest. September, Gatlinburg.

American Horticultural Society Annual Meeting. October, Nashville.

Annual Mid-South Craft Fair. October, Memphis.

National Storytelling Festival. October, Jonesboro.

Market Street Festival and Old-Time Courthouse Day. October, Nashville.

Harvest Festival of LaGrange. Tour of plantation, antebellum homes. October, LaGrange.

Oktoberfest, Mid-America Mall. October, Memphis.

Annual Crafts Festival. October, Silver Dollar City.

Autumn Leaf Special. Train trip through fall foliage country. October, Crossville to Chattanooga.

Majestic Middle Tennessee Tour of Homes. October, Columbia.

Fall Flower Show, Tennessee Botanical Gardens. October, Nashville.
Mountain Makins Festival. October, Morristown.
Halloween Arts Festival. October, Athens.
Annual Foothills Craft Guild Show and Sale. November, Oak Ridge.
Christmas Parade. Floats, bands, personalities. November, Nashville.
Fall Fair I. November, Nashville.

Virginia
Fredericksburg Agricultural Fair. September, Fredericksburg.
Virginia State Fair. September and October, Richmond.
Neptune Festival. September through October, Virginia Beach.
Yorktown Day. October, Yorktown.
National Tobacco Festival. October, Richmond.
Dog Mart. October, Fredericksburg.
Festival of Leaves. October, Front Royal.
Flying Circus Aerodrome Air Show. October, Bealeton.

West Virginia
Annual Ox Roast, Bunner Ridge. September, Fairmont.
Guided Interpretive Nature Walks, Bunner Ridge Recreation Area. September, Fairmont.
Hick Festival. September, Hendricks.
West Virginia Balloon Race. September, Charleston.
Annual Snowshoe Invitational Tennis Tournament. September, Slatyfork.
Heritage Week and King Coal Festival. September, Williamson.
Shinnston Frontier Days. September, Shinnston.
West Virginia Harvest Festival. September, Grafton.
Annual Harvest Moon Festival, City Park. September, Parkersburg.
Annual Ridge Heritage Days, Bunner Ridge. October, Fairmont.
Frontier Days. October, South Charleston.
Old-Fashioned Apple Harvest Festival. October, Burlington.
Mountain State Forest Festival. October, Elkins.
West Virginia Black Walnut Festival. October, Spencer.
Octoberfest, Heritage Village. October, Huntington.
West Virginia Turkey Festival. October, Mathias.
Decoration for Christmas. November, South Charleston.
Senior Citizen Thanksgiving Dinner. November, Dunbar.

Winter
(December, January, February)

Arkansas
Christmas Parade. December, El Dorado.
Christmas Parade. December, Jonesboro.
Arkansas Territorial Restoration Open House. December, Little Rock.
An Old-Fashioned Christmas. December, Eureka Springs.
Santa Claus Arrives By Decorated Barge, Lake Hamilton. December, Hot Springs.
Annual Christmas Concert. December, Hot Springs.
Colonial Christmas. December, Rison.
Annual Lighting Ceremony. December, Fairfield Bay.
Annual Christmas on the Mountain. December, Queen Wilhelmina State Park.
Annual Coon Supper. February, Cotter.
Beaux Arts Ball, Fine Arts Center. February, Hot Springs.
Thoroughbred Racing, Oaklawn Jockey Club. February, Hot Springs.
Degray Lodge Island Festival. February, Arkadelphia.
Annual Yell County Field Trials. Bird dogs. February, Centerville.
Annual Black History Series, Arkansas Art Center. February, Little Rock.

Georgia
Daily Plantation Tours. January, Thomasville.

First Saturday Festival. January, Savannah.
Eighth Annual Needlecraft School and Exhibit, Callaway Gardens. January, Pine Mountain.
Georgia Antique Fair. January, Atlanta.
Rattlesnake Roundup. January, Whigham.
Black History Month, Inner City Libraries. February, Savannah.
Annual Camellia Show. February, Savannah.
Georgia Day Birthday Celebration. February, Savannah.
Georgia Week Celebration. February, Savannah.
Georgia Antique Fair, Lakewood Park Fairgrounds. February, Atlanta.
Mardi Gras Ball, Country Club. February, Columbus.

North Carolina

Lake Norman Fiddlers Convention and Buck Dance Contest. December, Terrell.
Annual Christmas Parade. December, Cleveland.
18th-Century Christmas Outing. December, New Bern.
Christmas At Historic Halifax. December, Halifax.
Colonial Candlelighting Service. December, Gastonia.
Annual Bell-Ringing, historic bell tower. December, Salisbury.
Antique Show and Sale. January, Raleigh.
Southern Farm Show. February, Raleigh.
Annual Boat Show. February, Raleigh.

South Carolina

Elgin Catfish Stomp. Christmas parade, serving of catfish stew. December, Elgin.
Annual Marlborough Historical Society Antique Show. December, Bennettsville.
Blue Ridge Annual Show. Art exhibits and sales. December, Walhalla.
South Carolina's Junior Miss Pageant. December, Sumter.
Christmas Tree Lighting at Charles Towne Landing. December, Charleston.
Christmas Open House at Rose Hill. December, Union.
Christmas and New Year's Celebration. December, Hilton Head Island.
Reading of the Year. King of Oyotunji gives a psychic reading of the year's events, Yoruban African Village. January, Sheldon.
Baroque Festival. January, Spartanburg.
Polo Matches. February, Aiken.
Annual Sea Pines Jogging Holiday. Features many of America's top joggers. February, Hilton Head Island.
Annual Red Stockings Revue. Variety show. February, Columbia.
Carolina Capers Square and Round Dance Festival. February, Columbia.

Tennessee

Annual Christmas Parade. December, Tullahoma.
Twelve Days of Christmas. December, Gatlinburg.
"Christmas in a Country Kitchen." December, Kingsport.
Cowan Christmas Parade. December, Cowan.
Cheekwood's Tree of Christmas Exhibit, Tennessee Botanical Gardens. December, Nashville.
Exchange Place Yule Log and Caroling. December, Kingsport.
Antique Show and Sale. January, Chattanooga.
Lawn and Garden Fair. February, Nashville.
National Field Trial Championship, Ames Plantation. February, Grand Junction.

Virginia

Christmas Celebration. December, Williamsburg.
Colonial Weekends. December through February, Williamsburg.
Scottish Christmas Walk. December, Alexandria.

West Virginia

Heritage Village Old-Fashioned Yule Celebration. December, Huntington.
Annual Christmas Parade. December, Mullens.

Festival of Appalachian Christmas Traditions, Fort New Salem. December, Salem.
Old-Tyme Christmas. December, Harpers Ferry.
Winter Carnival. January, Parkersburg.
Civitan Pancake Festival. February, Parkersburg.
Snowmobile Race Weekend for Family Sleds. February, Davis.

LOUISIANA
Old Courthouse Museum
Vicksburg
Mardi Gras
Biloxi Lighthouse
DELTA QUEEN
SHRIMPER
SHRIMPER
MISSISSIPPI
June Shrimp Festival

Mobile's
Ante-bellum homes
ALABAMA
Fort Gaines
Mobile Bay
Space Center
Walt Disney World
FLORIDA
Cypress Gardens
St. Augustine
Ringling
Museum
Miami
R. McKee

Gulf States

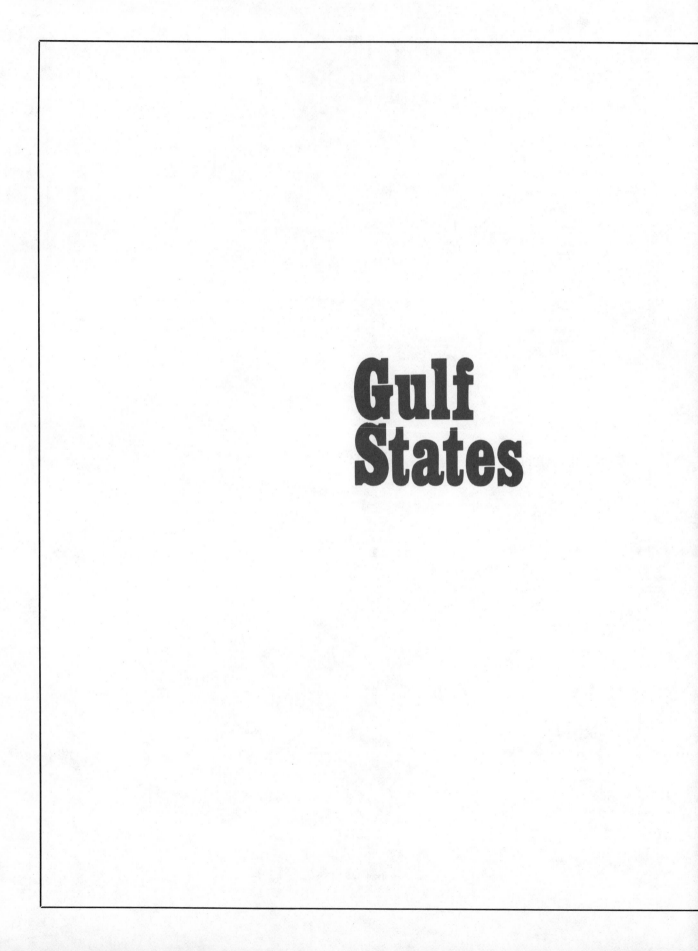

Few states are as colorful and fascinating as those which line the Gulf of Mexico. Louisiana's Spanish and French heritage have provided the region with some of the most stunning architecture to be found in the country, as well as a rich cultural mix that includes the backcountry Cajuns and the city-loving Creoles. In both Louisiana and Mississippi there is the mysterious bayou country, where the morning mist hangs heavy over swamps dotted with moss-draped cypress. In Alabama, you'll find plenty of reminders of the genteel antebellum days, but there are also a number of examples — space complexes, steel mills, chemical plants — of the South's growing industrial strength. And for sharp contrasts, there's Florida — where attractions range from the nation's leading launch pad at Cape Canaveral to bustling coastal resorts and the forbidding Everglades wilderness.

One of the Gulf states' most interesting areas is the Delta region, where the mighty Mississippi ends its 2,350-mile journey from its Minnesota source. Today, the Mississippi has been tamed for much of its length, but it continues the ageless process of carrying mud and sand deposits down to the Delta. It's this very process that built the land — some 1,000 years ago — on which the city of New Orleans now rests.

Because of their mild winters, the states of the Gulf coast have long been popular with winter travelers. January mean temperatures average about 40 degrees, although the mercury does dip lower at times. Summers are a different story: Temperatures may rarely exceed 85 to 90 degrees, but the high humidity and heavy summer rains can make the summer days stifling, especially along the coasts of Louisiana and Mississippi.

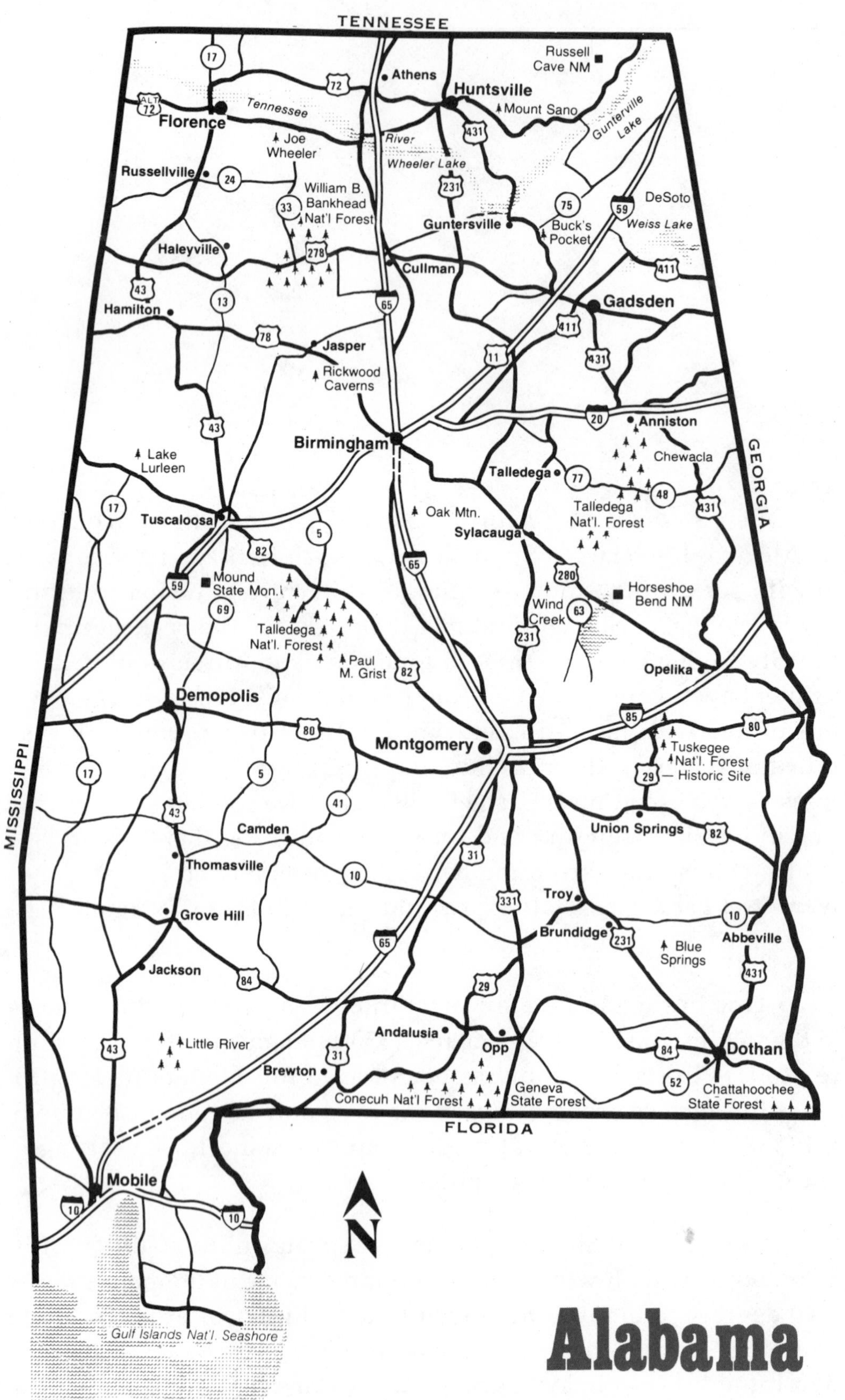

Map not to exact scale.

Alabama

Alabama has it all — relics of a prehistoric Indian culture; a Spanish and French heritage; elegant reminders of the antebellum South; rugged mountains; piney woods; moss-draped magnolias; one of the Gulf's busiest ports, Mobile; one of the nation's most important space facilities, the George C. Marshall Space Flight Center in Huntsville; and the Southern Research Institute for industrial and medical research. Best of all, Alabama has that good old-fashioned Southern hospitality.

The Spanish founded two temporary settlements in Alabama in 1559; the French occupied Alabama from 1702 to 1763; the British ruled it from 1763 to 1783; and the Spanish reigned again from 1783 to 1813. The Spanish were driven out of their base in Mobile in 1813, and the Alabama Territory was then created out of the larger Mississippi Territory.

Prior to the Civil War, Alabama became a leader in the fight for Southern and state's rights. Alabama seceded from the Union in 1861, and the Confederate government was organized and established in Montgomery, which became the "Cradle of the Confederacy." During the war, the state's soldiers distinguished themselves in battle and many of the native sons held high-ranking positions in the civil and military counsels of the Confederacy. The cost to Alabama was overwhelming, however, as losses were estimated at more than $500 million. The state was restored to the Union in 1868.

Alabama is probably the only state to have built a statue honoring a pest — the boll weevil — but that's exactly what the people of the town of Enterprise did in 1919. They decided on the statue after the boll weevil's rampage through their cotton fields turned out to be a blessing in disguise (it forced the farmers to turn to better-paying crops that weren't on the boll weevil's menu). You can see the statue, a silver-painted goddess holding the ugly little creature aloft, in the town of Enterprise, near the southern border. On

Full name: State of Alabama
Origin of name: From the Indian Alba Amo meaning "I Clear the Thicket."
Motto: *Andemus Jura Nostra Defendere* (We Dare Defend Our Rights).
Nickname: Yellowhammer State
Capital: Montgomery
Statehood: December 14, 1819, 22nd state.
Population: 3,690,000 (ranks 21st).
Major Cities: Birmingham (276,273), Mobile (196,441), Montgomery (153,345).
Bird: Yellowhammer
Flower: Camellia
Tree: Southern pine

Average daily temperatures by month

	Northern	Southern
Jan.	51.4 to 29.1	62.6 to 36.9
Feb.	55.2 to 31.3	66.2 to 39.1
Mar.	62.8 to 37.5	72.6 to 44.4
Apr.	73.9 to 47.5	81.1 to 52.0
May	81.4 to 54.6	87.2 to 58.1
Jun.	87.7 to 62.3	91.8 to 64.8
Jul.	90.1 to 66.2	92.9 to 67.9
Aug.	90.2 to 65.0	92.5 to 67.4
Sept.	85.4 to 59.4	88.4 to 63.3
Oct.	75.1 to 46.3	80.3 to 50.8
Nov.	62.9 to 36.4	70.1 to 41.5
Dec.	54.5 to 31.7	64.3 to 38.5
Year	72.6 to 47.3	79.2 to 52.1

Highlight

Statue of Vulcan

The gigantic figure of Vulcan is one of America's most remarkable monuments. This mythological god of metal-working looks down from the top of Red Mountain onto the city of Birmingham, Alabama, diversified manufacturing center of the South. The towering statue of Vulcan was the Birmingham District exhibit at the Louisiana Purchase Exposition at St. Louis in 1904. It was designed by the famed Italian sculptor, Guiseppe Moretti.

When the statue was returned to Birmingham, it ultimately was erected on top of a mountain veined with iron ore. Amid the beauty of surrounding Vulcan Park, Vulcan overlooks the long valley in which the city of Birmingham is located.

Vulcan Park recently underwent a million-dollar renovation program. Now a high-speed elevator takes you to a climate-controlled, glass-enclosed observation deck from which one can enjoy a panoramic view of the beautiful valleys below. A new concession building, formal garden and fountain grace the newly landscaped grounds.

From foot to the tip of the outstretched hand, Vulcan is 55 feet tall. The statue stands upon a pedestal 124 feet high, so the monument as a whole rises to a height of 179 feet, taller than Niagara Falls. Since Vulcan is on the crest of a mountain, he surveys the city of Birmingham from an elevation of nearly 600 feet, or just over the height of the Washington Monument, tallest shaft in America.

Vulcan is the largest iron figure ever cast. It was cast from Birmingham iron and in Birmingham foundries. Because of its weight, 120,000 pounds, it was cast in several sections. Separate molds were made of the head, arms, torso and legs, and these were welded together. Each foot is seven feet long by three feet wide and weighs about 10,000 pounds. The massive head alone required over six tons of iron. The torch which has been placed in the outstretched hand of Vulcan is a silent sentinel of safety. It burns green unless an automobile fatality has occurred; then warning red is carried that day in the hand of the mythical figure, which has become the world's largest safety reminder.

Vulcan is one of the few monuments in the world erected not to commemorate an event or to perpetuate the memory of a person, but to symbolize industry. Although the mining of coal and ore, the quarrying of limestone, the making of iron and steel and the fabrication of these materials into finished products are still important industries in the Birmingham area, its industrial complex includes the manufacture of textiles and clothing, space age components, food products, chemicals, furniture and many other products. Birmingham is also a community of science, culture and beauty as attested by its famous Medical Center, its Southern Research Institute, the Botanical Gardens, Jimmy Morgan Zoo, Art Museum, dining clubs and country clubs and attractive residential areas.

your way to and from the Boll Weevil Monument, you can also visit the Black Belt, the famous 30-mile-wide strip of rich black soil that stretches across the entire state; the George Washington Carver Museum in Tuskegee; or the De Soto caverns, the nation's oldest recorded cave.

DeSoto Falls on Little River Canyon near Fort Payne, Alabama, is one of the state's outstanding scenic attractions.

Today, Birmingham is the South's largest producer of iron and steel, and the abundant hydroelectric power provided by the Tennessee Valley Authority is a key factor in Alabama's growing industrialization. Tourism, fishing, coal mining, oil and the manufacture of textiles, paper products, chemicals and rubber products are among the state's other important activities.

Mythology's Blacksmith

Vulcan, the lame god Hesphaestus (Roman Vulcanos), was the god of fire and the forge and mythical inventor of smithing and metal working. His forges were under Mount Aetna on the island of Sicily. He was smith, architect, armorer, chariot builder and artist of all work in Olympus — dwelling place of the gods.

He built of brass the houses of the gods; he made for them the golden shoes with which they trod the air or the water, and moved from place to place with the speed of the wind or even of thought. He also shod with brass the celestial steeds, which whirled the chariots of the gods through the air or along the surface of the sea.

Vulcan was the son of Zeus and Hera. The story is that Zeus threw him out of heaven for taking part with his mother in a quarrel which occurred between them. He was lame from birth according to some stories, but others assert Vulcan's lameness was the consequence of his fall. He was a whole day falling, and at last alighted on the Island of Lemnos, which was henceforth sacred to him.

Vulcan was the architect of the palace of the sun which stood reared aloft on stones; polished ivory formed the ceilings and silver the doors. The workmanship surpassed the material, for upon the walls Vulcan had represented earth, sea and skies with their inhabitants.

With the help of Cyclops, the one-eyed giant, he made the thunderbolts of Zeus, the weapons of Hercules, and the armor of Achilles. He built the chariot of Phaeton. The axles were of gold, the spokes of silver. Along the seat were rows of chrysolites and diamonds which reflected the sun in dazzling brightness.

State Offices

Tourism
Alabama Travel Department
403 Highway Building
Montgomery, Alabama 36130
(800) 633-5761

State Police
Department of Public Safety
Montgomery, Alabama 36130
(205) 832-6735

Radio Stations

Birmingham
WERC 960 (AM)
WVOK 99.5 (FM)
Montgomery
WBAM 740 (AM)
WHHY 101.9 (FM)

Alabama Points of Interest and Attractions

Alabama International Motor Speedway. Home of NASCAR's Winston 500 and Talladega 500. Open year-round, daily (except during race week events), 8 a.m. to 6 p.m. Talladega, off US-78.

Alabama Space and Rocket Center. Experience firsthand the sights and sounds of space; try your hand at being an astronaut. Open year-round, June through August, 9 a.m. to 6 p.m.; September through May, 9 a.m. to 5 p.m. Huntsville, off US-72.

Ave Maria Grotto. A Benedictine monk spent his lifetime creating miniature religious buildings and shrines from scraps; over 150 of them are exhibited about the hillsides of this splendid park. Open year-round, 7 a.m. to sunset. Admission: fee charged. Cullman, off US-278.

Azalea Trail. A beautiful azalea-lined trail commemorating the gift of azaleas from France in 1754. Open February through March. Mobile, off Interstate 65.

Bama Scenic Rock Gardens. Impressive natural rock formations among wildflowers, ferns and wildlife. Open year-round, daily, 9 a.m. to 6 p.m. Vance, off US-11.

Battleship USS Alabama Memorial Park. Walk the decks of this historic World War II battlewagon that floats in Mobile Bay. Open year-round, daily, 8 a.m. to sunset. Mobile, off US-31.

Bellingrath Gardens and Home. World-famous gardens of every season; home filled with fine furnishings and rare art objects. Open year-round; gardens, from 7 a.m. to dusk; home, from 8:30 a.m. to 5 p.m.; last tour beginning, 4:15 p.m. Theodore (near Mobile), off US-90.

Birmingham Botanical Gardens. Seven acres of Japanese gardens; continuously changing flower show. Open year-round, daily, dawn to dusk. Free. Birmingham, off US-280.

Boll Weevil Monument. The first monument ever erected to an insect pest. Enterprise, off State Route 134.

Cheaha Mountain. The highest place in Alabama — 2,047 feet above sea level; excellent campgrounds nearby. Open year-round. Munford, in Cheaha State Park, off State Route 49.

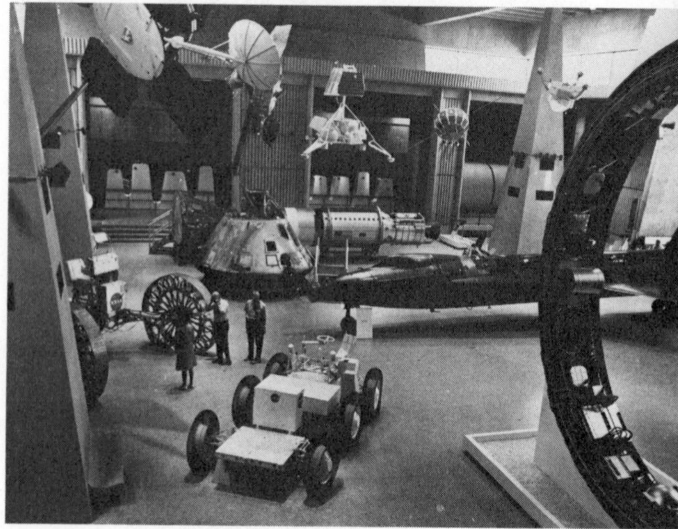

The Alabama Space and Rocket Center near Huntsville provides the setting for the world's largest display of space hardware.

Fort Gaines, on historic Dauphin Island, is a major historical landmark.

Dauphin Island. The French called this Massacre Island because the beaches were littered with bones when they landed; explore the island's incredible history. On Gulf of Mexico near Cedar Point, on State Route 163.

DeSoto Caverns. Oldest recorded caverns, rich with history and folklore; incredible natural formations. Open year-round, except December and January, daily, 9 a.m. to 6 p.m.; Sunday, 12:30 p.m. to 6 p.m.; weekends only, November, February and March. Childersburg, off State Route 76.

DeSoto Falls. Wildflower-surrounded waters cascade 110 feet into a rock basin; picnic, swim, boat, fish. Open year-round, daily, 8 a.m. to sunset. Fort Payne, in DeSoto State Park, off State Route 35.

Dismal Wonder Gardens. Mysterious twinkle-in-the-dark worms (Dismalites) and exotic plants in an enormous gulch that is anything but dismal. Open year-round, daily, 8 a.m. to sunset. Hackleburg, off US-43.

Dog Racing. Greenetrack. Luxurious clubhouse with dining facilities. Open March through November, Monday to Saturday, 8 p.m. to 11 p.m.; Saturday matinee, 1 p.m. to 4 p.m. Eutaw, off US-11.

Mobile Greyhound Park. Luxurious multi-million dollar park. Open February through December, Monday to Saturday, 6 p.m.; Saturday, noon. Mobile, off US-90.

Helen Keller's Birthplace, Ivy Green. Mementos of this great Alabama native; *The Miracle Worker* performed on the grounds each Friday night in July and August. Open year-round, daily, 8:30 a.m. to 4:30 p.m.; Sunday, 1 p.m. to 4:30 p.m. Tuscumbia, off US-72.

Horton Mill Covered Bridge. The highest covered bridge in America, 220 feet above the water, surrounded by beautiful, rugged nature trails. Near Oneonta, off US-231.

Jasmine Hill. Twelve acres of Greek sculpture, ruins, various art objects amid flowering trees and fragrant blossoms. Open year-round; December through February, weekends only; March through November, Tuesday to Sunday, 9 a.m. to 5 p.m. Wetumpka, off US-231.

Among the beautiful anti-bellum homes in Alabama is this magnificent structure which has served as the home for University of Alabama presidents.

Little River Canyon. One of the deepest gorges east of the Rockies. Open year-round, daily. Free. Fort Payne, in DeSoto State Park, off State Route 35.

Manitou Cave. A guided tour through passageways that range from nine to 90 feet high. Open year-round; summer, 7 a.m. to 7 p.m.; October through May, 8 a.m. to 5 p.m.; weekends only. Fort Payne, off State Route 275.

Natural Bridge. The longest natural bridge east of the Rockies; picnicking, nature trails. Open year-round, sunrise to sunset, daily. Haleyville, off US-278.

Noccalula Falls. Breathtaking vegetation and rock formations, spectacular falls; Indian Lover's Leap legend. Open year-round, daily. Free. Gadsden, US-431.

Point Mallard. Recreation center; swimming in the wave-pool, ice skating, nature trails, campground. Open year-round, daily, 10 a.m. to 9 p.m. Decatur, off US-31.

Rock Bridge Canyon. Intriguing rock formations, falls, massive natural bridge. Open year-round, daily. Hodges, off State Route 187.

Sequoyah Cave. Beautiful caverns with looking glass lakes; resembles an underground palace. Open year-round, 8 a.m. to 7 p.m.; holidays, 8:30 a.m. to 5 p.m. Valley Head, off US-11.

State Capitol. Numerous historical sites; a bronze star marks the spot where Jefferson Davis stood to become President of the Confederacy. Capitol building closed holidays. Montgomery, Interstate 85, Interstate 65, US-80, US-31.

Tom Mann's Fish World. Unique freshwater fish exhibit with 38,000-gallon aquarium and 10 smaller aquariums containing freshwater species of fish native to Alabama; Indian museum. Open year-round, daily; Monday to Friday, 9 a.m. to 5 p.m.; Saturday and Sunday, 9 a.m. to 9 p.m. Eufaula, off US-431.

USS Drum. Board this boat and you'll see how submarine crews lived on World War II patrols. Open year-round, daily, 8 a.m. to sunset. Mobile Bay, off US-10.

W. A. Gayle Planetarium. Lie back in one of 236 reclining seats and watch a celestial panorama on the 50-foot overhead dome; wide variety of astronomical programs. Open year-round, Monday to Friday, 8 a.m. to 5 p.m. Montgomery, off US-331.

The Governor's Mansion in Montgomery, Alabama, is one of the capitol city's showplaces, built of Greek Revival design surrounded by spacious grounds and lovely oak trees.

Alabama State Parks

Park	Location	Camping	Picnicking	Concessions	Swimming	Hiking	Boating	Fishing	Hunting	Winter Sports
Blue Springs	*Clio. Off State Route 33.*	•	•		•					
Buck's Pocket	*Groveoak. Off State Route 227.*	•	•		•	•	•	•		
Camden	*Camden. Off State Route 5.*	•	•		•		•	•		•
Chattahoochee	*Gordon. Off US-84.*	•	•			•	•	•		
Cheaha	*Lineville. Off State Route 49.*	•	•	•	•	•		•		
Chewacla	*Auburn. Off Interstate 85.*	•	•		•	•	•	•		
Chickasaw	*Gallion. Off State Route 28.*	•	•		•	•				
DeSoto	*Fort Payne. On State Route 89.*	•	•	•	•	•		•		
Gulf	*Gulf Shores. On State Route 182.*	•	•	•	•	•	•	•		
Joe Wheeler	*Towncreek. Off US-72.*	•	•	•	•	•	•	•		
Lake Guntersville	*Guntersville. On State Route 89.*	•	•	•	•	•	•	•		
Lake Lurleen	*Coker. Off State Route 21.*	•	•		•	•	•	•		
Lakepoint	*Eufala. Off State Route 165.*	•	•	•	•	•	•	•		
Monte Sano	*Huntsville. Off US-72.*	•	•			•				
Oak Mountain	*Pelham. Off State Route 43.*	•	•	•	•	•	•	•		
Paul M. Grist	*Selma. Off State Route 22.*	•	•		•	•	•	•		
Rickwood Caverns	*Warrior. Off Interstate 65.*	•	•		•	•				
Tannehill	*McCalla. Off Interstate 59.*	•	•		•	•		•		
Wind Creek	*Alexander City. Off US-280.*	•	•	•	•	•	•	•		

Alabama has no state forests. For more information on Alabama state parks, contact: *Division of State Parks, Alabama Department of Conservation and Natural Resources, 64 North Union Street, Montgomery, Alabama 36130.*

The gifted and famous Helen Keller spent her early childhood in this tiny cottage located in the charming old Southern town of Tuscumbia, Alabama, amid jasmines and magnolias. This room, along with the main Keller House, offers a display of Helen's memorabilia.

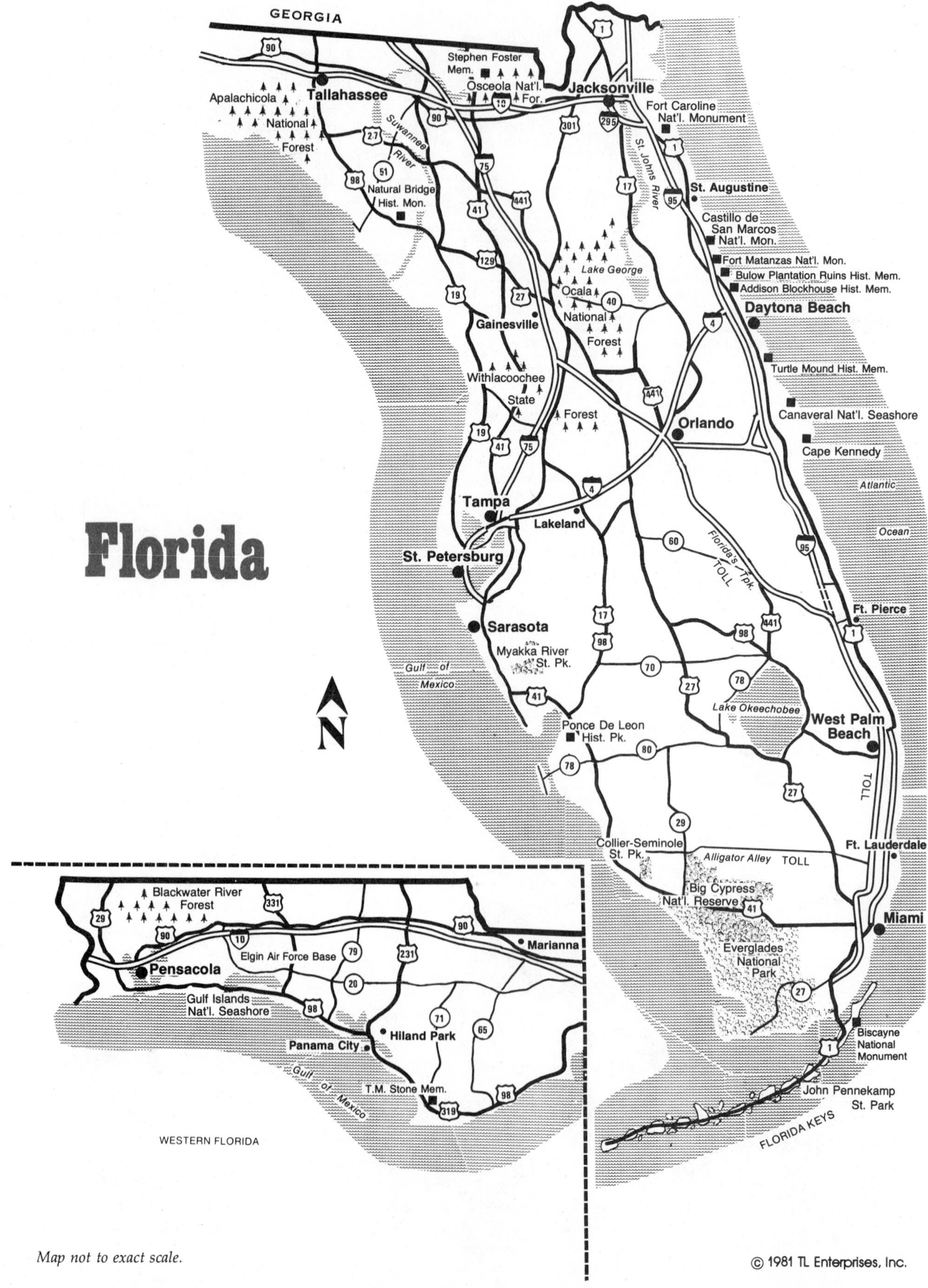

Map not to exact scale.

Florida

Tales of waters that would "maketh olde men young again" lured the first explorers to Florida's shores, but today it is the sunshine, sparkling beaches, famous resorts and an almost endless list of other attractions that entice more than 28 million visitors a year to Florida.

Juan Ponce de Leon, the Spanish explorer who was searching for the legendary Fountain of Youth, landed on the east coast of Florida in 1513, becoming the first European to set foot on its shores. Following de Leon's discovery, settlers from Spain, England and France tried to establish colonies in Florida, all without success. Florida finally became a part of the United States under the terms of the Adams-Onis Treaty negotiated February 22, 1819. Congress authorized a territorial government in 1822, and the abandoned Indian town of Tallahassee was made the capital. After two bloody wars with the Seminole Indians, development of the region progressed and Florida was admitted as a state March 3, 1845. Florida seceded from the Union in 1861, and during the war its ports were taken by Union forces and its coastline was blockaded. After the war, Florida's reentry into the Union was delayed by its failure to form a satisfactory constitution; it was readmitted as a state June 25, 1868.

Florida has a number of distinct regions with a variety of activities and attractions. Miami Beach and the numerous resorts of the east coast are familiar to everyone, as are the everglades and the Keys which stretch out into the Gulf of Mexico. Still, Florida has more to offer than those familiar attractions: In the north, you'll find moss-draped oaks and antebellum estates; St. Augustine, the oldest surviving European settlement in the United States, lies on the northeast coast; farther down the coast, you'll want to visit Cape Canaveral and the Kennedy Space Center; scattered through the north and central parts of the state are three large national forests, the Apalachicola, Osceola and Ocala; and numerous state parks, forests and lakes await the outdoor enthusiast.

Full name: State of Florida
Origin of name: From Spanish, Pascua Florida, meaning "Feast of Flowers,"
Motto: In God We Trust
Nickname: Sunshine State
Capital: Tallahassee
Statehood: March 3, 1845, 27th state.
Population: 8,452,000 (ranks eighth).
Major Cities: Jacksonville (535,030), Miami (365,082), Tampa (280,340).
Bird: Mockingbird
Flower: Orange blossom
Tree: Sabal palm

Average daily temperatures by month

	Northern	Southern
Jan.	63.7 to 42.0	76.9 to 53.7
Feb.	67.2 to 44.2	77.6 to 54.1
Mar.	73.1 to 49.3	81.2 to 57.3
Apr.	81.4 to 56.7	84.3 to 61.6
May	87.9 to 63.1	87.1 to 65.6
Jun.	91.2 to 68.8	88.7 to 69.7
Jul.	91.9 to 70.8	90.2 to 71.0
Aug.	91.8 to 70.6	90.9 to 71.4
Sept.	88.2 to 67.7	89.3 to 71.4
Oct.	80.8 to 58.0	85.6 to 67.3
Nov.	71.4 to 48.2	81.2 to 59.9
Dec.	65.5 to 43.4	77.6 to 54.6
Year	79.5 to 56.9	84.2 to 63.1

Sanibel Island

Sanibel Island, on the southwest coast of Florida, is said to be the best seashore for seashells in the Western Hemisphere, and one of the top three in the world. Many visitors to the beach keep their eyes lowered and walk in a posture called the "Sanibel Stoop." Sanibel and its sister island, Captiva, also offer great bird-watching, surf-fishing and lazy days spent in sunny seclusion.

The J.N. "Ding" Darling National Wildlife Refuge, established on Sanibel in 1945, is home to a large number of animals, from roseate spoonbills to alligators to indigo snakes. A one-lane road traverses the length of the 5,000-acre refuge.

Sanibel is about 20 miles west of Fort Myers. Highway 867 takes you to the island. For more information, write the Chamber of Commerce, Sanibel, Florida 33957.

Accounting for $5 billion in income annually, tourism ranks as Florida's number one industry. Commercial fishing is also important, as are industrial products such as chemicals, paper products, electrical equipment and fabricated metals. Of course, the state's enormous citrus industry remains an important staple of the economy, bringing income of more than $400 million annually.

The Florida landscape abounds with a number of scenic natural springs which support a wide variety of plant, animal and aquatic life.

State Offices

Tourism
Florida Department of Commerce
Collins Building
Tallahassee, Florida 32304
(904) 487-1462

State Police
Department of Public Safety
Tallahassee, Florida 32304
(904) 488-8772

Radio Stations

Ft. Lauderdale
WSHE 103.5 (FM)
WHYI 100.7 (FM)

Jacksonville
WJAX 930 (AM)
WAIV 96.9 (FM)

Miami
WWOK 1260 (AM)
WTMI 93.1 (FM)

St. Petersburg
WLCY 1380 (AM)

Tampa
WFLA 970 (AM)
WRBQ 104.7 (FM)

West Palm Beach
WIRK 1290 (AM)

Florida Points of Interest and Attractions

Aquarama Waltzing Waters. Includes a delightful sea lion and dolphin show, plus the world-famous Waltzing Waters; complete aquarama performances nightly at sundown. Open year-round. Cape Coral, off US-41.

Circus Hall of Fame. Marionette shows, magic shows, kiddie rides; circus performances during winter and summer seasons. Open year-round, daily, 9 a.m. to 5 p.m. Sarasota, off State Route 41.

Edison Home. Visit the estate of America's greatest inventor; home, botanical gardens, museum of Edison memorabilia. Open year-round, daily, 9 a.m. to 4 p.m.; Sunday, 12:30 p.m. to 4 p.m. Fort Myers, off US-41.

Everglades Wonder Gardens. Everglades wildlife, including bears, otters, panthers, deer, birds of prey, wading birds, alligators, snakes and the endangered Everglades crocodile. Open year-round, daily, 9 a.m. to 5 p.m. Bonita Springs, on US-41.

Fairchild Tropical Garden. Botanical garden with 83 acres of palms, cycads and colorful tropical plants; paths through rain forest, sunken garden, palm glade; rare-plant house. Open year-round. Miami, 10901 Old Cutler Road.

Florida Citrus Tower. A vantage point for viewing man-made and natural wonders in the beautiful highland citrus region. Open year-round, daily. Clermont, on State Route 27.

Florida Cypress Gardens. Exotic plants and flowers from around the world; electric boat tours, water-ski shows. Open year-round, daily. Cypress Gardens, off State Route 60 and US-27.

Florida's Silver Springs. Ride world-famous glass-bottom boats, take a scenic jungle cruise, see rhinoceros, giraffes, camels and other animals roaming

The John F. Kennedy Space Center displays space modules as well as multimedia exhibits.

free on the banks of the Silver River; reptile institute and deer park. Open year-round, daily, 8:30 a.m. to dusk. Silver Springs, on State Route 40.

Florida's Sunken Gardens. Thousands of tropical plants and flowers, colorful exotic birds and animals; orchid house, gift shop. Open year-round, daily, 9 a.m. to sunset. St. Petersburg, 1825 Fourth Street N.

Homosassa Springs. Walk underwater in nature's giant fishbowl, cruise tropical waterways, stroll unspoiled nature trails; see animals, orchid gardens. Open year-round, daily, 8 a.m. to 6 p.m. Homosassa Springs, off US-19.

Kennedy Space Center. Daily bus tours look at the past and future of the U.S. space program; free movies at visitors center, demonstrations, exhibits. Open year-round, daily, 8 a.m. to sunset. Kennedy Space Center, off State Route 405.

Key West Conch Train. The best way to see picturesque Key West; tour highlights all the points of interest, including

Hemingway's and Audubon's homes. Open year-round, daily, 9 a.m. to 4 p.m. Key West, 501 Front Street.

MGM's Bounty Exhibit. Walk the decks of this magnificent replica of the full-rigged ship made famous by Fletcher Christian's mutiny. Open year-round, daily, 9 a.m. to 10 p.m. St. Petersburg, 345 Second Avenue, NE.

Miami Seaquarium. Incredible "aquabatics" by killer whales; "Flipper" on stage with other performing dolphins; aquariums, scenic monorail ride. Open year-round, daily, 9 a.m. to 5 p.m. Key Biscayne, 4400 Rickenbacker Causeway.

Planet Ocean. Explores and explains the mysteries of the world's oceans; see and feel a hurricane, walk through an indoor cloud and rainstorm, listen to ships at sea, watch the birth of the oceans. Open year-round, daily, 10 a.m. to 4:30 p.m. Miami, 3979 Rickenbacker Causeway.

St. Augustine Sightseeing Trains. See the nation's oldest city on seven-mile conducted tour with stopoff privileges at attractions; board at any of 20 stops, tickets good for 24 hours. St. Augustine, State Route A1A.

Stars Hall of Fame Wax Museum. More than 200 stars of movies, TV and music presented in authentic recreations. Open year-round, daily and evenings. Orlando, 6825 Starway Drive.

Stephen Foster Center. Located on 250 acres on the Suwannee River; boat ride on the Suwannee River; animated dioramas; 200-foot carillon tower. Open year-round, daily, 9 a.m. to 5:30 p.m. White Springs, three miles off Interstate 75.

Tiki Gardens. Land of pagan customs and South Sea Island beauty; 10 gift shops, restaurant. Open year-round, daily, 9:30 a.m. to 10:30 p.m. Indian Shores, off US-41.

Vizcaya. Private palace; 50 superb rooms and acres of beautiful gardens. Open year-round, daily except Christmas. Miami, 3251 South Miami Avenue.

Wakulla Springs and Lodge. Glass-bottom boat tours over the Big Spring; jungle-boat tours down the scenic Wakulla River; abundance of wildlife; Registered Natural Landmark. Open year-round, daily; summer, 9:30 a.m. to 6:30 p.m.; winter, 9:30 a.m. to 5:30 p.m. Tallahassee, 11 miles south off US-319.

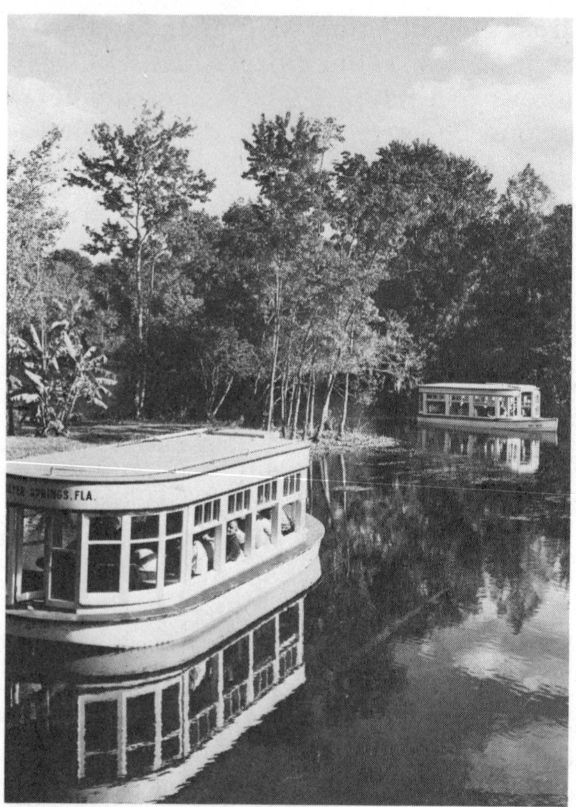

Glass-bottom boat rides take visitors on a tour of the numerous springs at Silver Springs, Florida, where the clear waters permit views of thousands of feeding fish.

Weeki Wachee Spring. Underwater mermaid show, birds of prey, river cruise, exotic birds, nature trail, petting zoo, gardens. Open year-round, daily, 9 a.m. to 5 p.m. Weeki Wachee, at US-19 and State Route 50.

Florida State Parks

Park	Location	CAMPING	PICNICKING	CONCESSIONS	SWIMMING	HIKING	BOATING	FISHING	HUNTING	WINTER SPORTS
Blackwater River	*Milton. Off US-90.*	•	•		•	•	•	•		
Blue Spring	*Orange City. Off Interstate 4 and US-17.*	•	•	•	•	•	•	•		
Caladesi Island (no vehicles)	*Dunedin (offshore). Off US-19A.*		•		•	•	•	•		
Collier-Seminole	*Naples. Off US-41.*	•	•			•	•	•		
Faver-Dykes	*St. Augustine. Off US-1.*	•	•			•	•	•		
Florida Caverns	*Marianna. Off State Route 167.*	•	•		•	•	•	•		
Fort Clinch	*Fernandina Beach. Off State Route A1A.*	•	•		•	•	•	•		
Fort Cooper	*Inverness. Off Old Floral City Road.*		•		•			•		
Highlands Hammock	*Sebring. Off US-27-98.*	•	•	•		•				
Hillsborough River	*Zephyrhills. Off US-301.*	•	•	•	•	•	•	•		
Hontoon Island (no vehicles)	*Deland. Off State Route 44.*	•	•			•	•	•		
Itchetucknee Springs	*Fort White. Off State Routes 47 and 238.*		•		•					
John Pennekamp Coral Reef	*Key Largo. Off US-1.*	•	•	•	•	•	•	•		
Jonathan Dickinson	*Stuart. Off US-1.*	•	•	•	•	•	•	•		
Lake Kissimmee	*Lake Wales. On Camp Mack Road.*		•			•	•	•		
Lake Louisa	*Clermont. On Lake Nellie Road.*		•		•			•		
Little Talbot Island	*Jacksonville. Off State Route A1A.*	•	•		•		•	•		
Manatee Springs	*Chiefland. Off US-19-98.*	•	•	•	•	•	•	•		
Mike Roess	*Keystone Heights. Off State Route 21.*	•	•	•	•	•	•	•		
Myakka River	*Sarasota. Off State Route 72.*	•	•	•		•	•	•		
Ochlockonee River	*Sopchoppy. Off US-319.*	•	•		•	•	•	•		
O'Leno	*Lake City. Off US-51.*	•	•		•	•	•	•		
Suwannee River	*Live Oak. Off US-90.*	•	•		•	•	•	•		
T.H. Stone Memorial	*Port St. Joe. Off US-98.*	•	•	•	•	•	•	•		
Tomoka	*Ormond Beach. On North Beach Street.*	•	•	•		•	•	•		
Torreya	*Bristol. Off State Route 12.*	•	•	•		•		•		
Wekiwa Springs	*Orlando. Off Interstate 4.*		•	•	•	•	•	•		

Florida State Forests

Forest	Location	CAMPING	PICNICKING	CONCESSIONS	SWIMMING	HIKING	BOATING	FISHING	HUNTING	WINTER SPORTS
Blackwater River	*Milton. Off US-90.*	•	•		•	•	•	•		
Cary	*Bryceville. Off US-301.*					•				
Pine Log	*Ebro. Off State Route 79.*	•	•				•	•		
Withlacoochee	*Tarrytown. On State Route 471.*	•	•		•	•	•	•		

For more information on Florida state parks and forests, contact: *Department of Natural Resources, Division of Recreation and Parks, Crown Building, Tallahassee, Florida 32304, (904) 488-7326.*

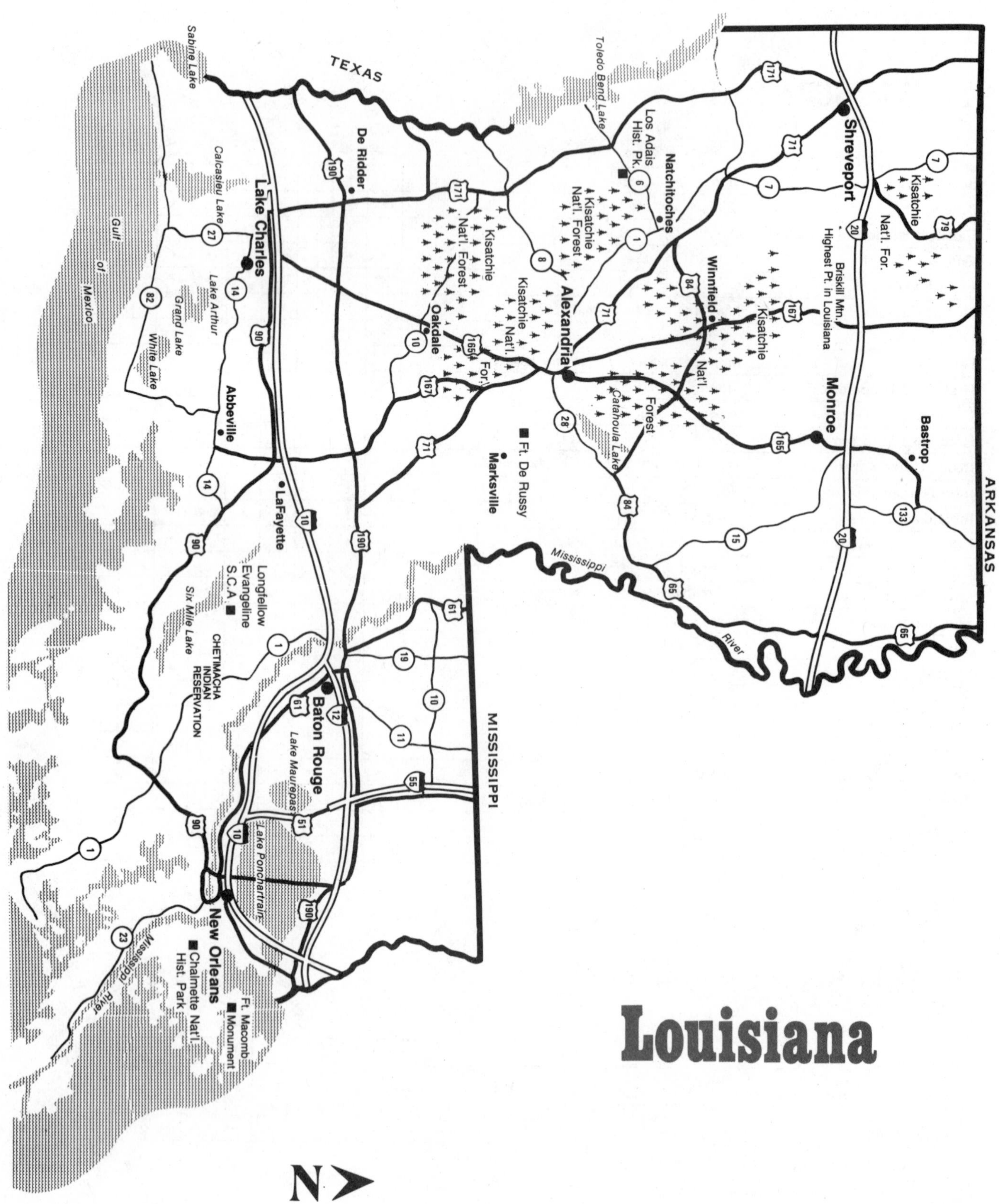

Map not to exact scale.

Louisiana

The mere mention of Louisiana brings to mind the sights and sounds of colorful New Orleans and Bourbon Street Jazz; the riotous celebration of Mardi Gras; the aroma of Creole cooking; the picture of an old stern-wheeler plying the lazy waters of the Delta; an elegant plantation high atop a rich, green, tree-studded hill. For if it is nothing else, Louisiana is a romantic state.

There were approximately 12,000 Indians living in the Louisiana region when it was first visited by Spanish explorer Cabeza de Vaca in 1530, and Hernando De Soto in 1540, when they came searching for legendary mines of precious metals. When that quest went unrewarded, the region remained largely untouched until 1682, when LaSalle traveled from Canada to the Mississippi's mouth and claimed the entire valley for Louis XIV of France, naming it "Louisiana" in his honor. Subsequent attempts by LaSalle to establish a colony in the area failed, and the first permanent settlement wasn't planted until 1699. The colony, near what is now Biloxi, Mississippi, was neglected, however, and it and several other French colonies were largely unsuccessful. The French lost control of the region in 1762, giving way to Spain, but regained possession in 1800. Three years later, Napolean Bonaparte, needing funds to support his European military campaigns, sold the territory to the United States, in the Louisiana Purchase.

Following the acquisition of the French landholdings, the boundaries of the present state were carved out and Louisiana was admitted to the Union in 1812. Despite their status as a state, the

Full name: State of Louisiana
Origin of name: In honor of King Louis XIV of France.
Motto: Union, Justice and Confidence
Nickname: Pelican State
Capital: Baton Rouge
Statehood: April 30, 1812, 18th state.
Population: 3,921,000 (ranks 20th).
Major Cities: New Orleans (559,770), Baton Rouge (294,394), Shreveport (185,711).
Bird: Brown pelican
Flower: Magnolia
Tree: Bald cypress

Average daily temperatures by month

	Northern	Southern
Jan.	57.1 to 35.0	64.3 to 43.6
Feb.	61.1 to 37.4	66.6 to 45.5
Mar.	67.9 to 43.5	72.2 to 51.4
Apr.	77.2 to 53.4	80.0 to 59.5
May	84.0 to 60.5	85.7 to 65.3
Jun.	90.6 to 68.0	90.6 to 70.9
Jul.	93.3 to 71.0	91.8 to 72.9
Aug.	93.4 to 69.6	91.6 to 72.5
Sept.	88.3 to 64.1	88.9 to 69.4
Oct.	79.5 to 52.0	82.0 to 59.3
Nov.	67.8 to 42.5	72.6 to 50.2
Dec.	59.5 to 37.2	67.7 to 45.5
Year	76.6 to 52.9	79.4 to 58.8

Louisianans were somewhat reluctant in their acceptance of the Americans — but they did unite behind Andrew Jackson to defeat the British in the legendary Battle of New Orleans. During the Civil War, Louisiana was aligned with the Confederacy, becoming the sixth state to secede. New Orleans quickly fell to the

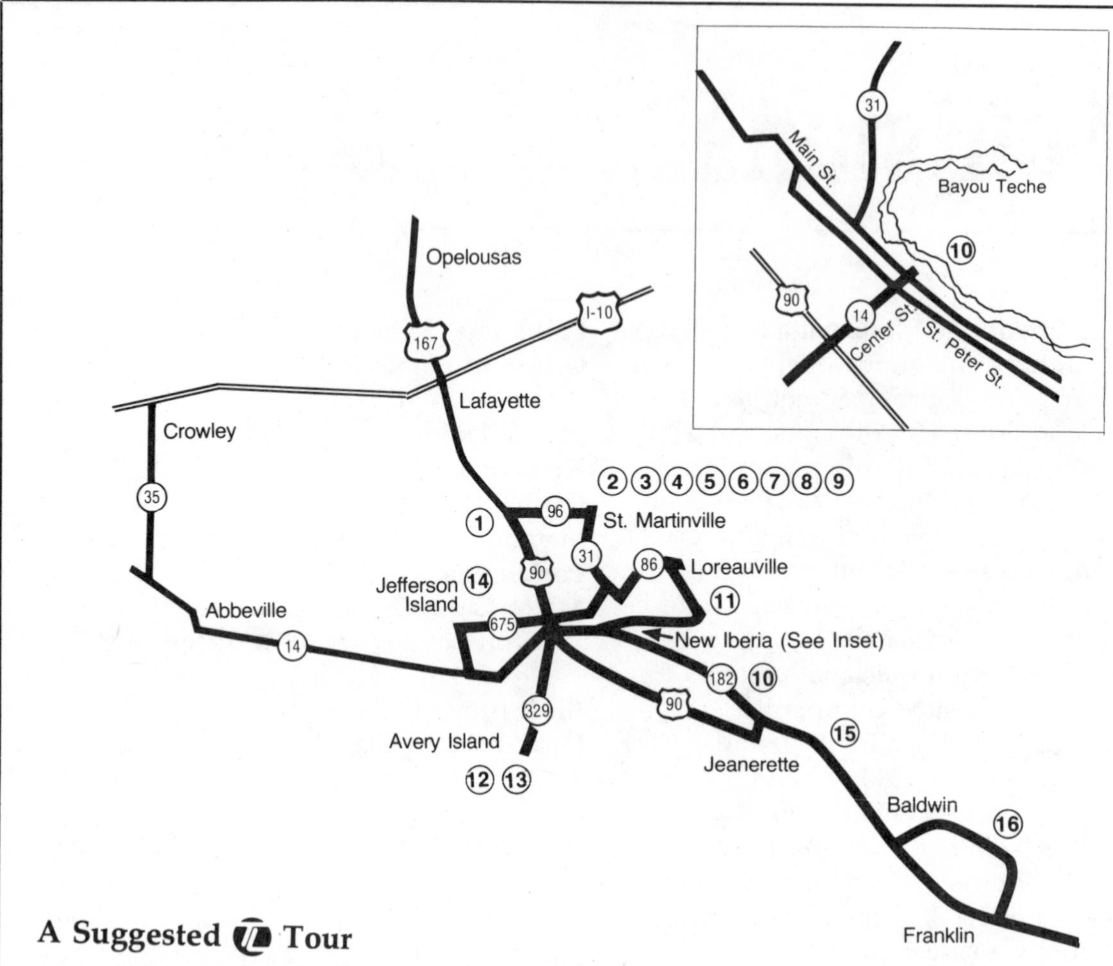

A Suggested Tour

St. Martinville and New Iberia

This outing will bring you to the cities of St. Martinville and New Iberia, both located on Bayou Teche. At the St. Martinville exit of U.S. Highway 90, you will notice the pink metal roofs of the Billeaud Sugar Mill.[1] You are now entering the heart of the south Louisiana sugarcane belt.

St. Martinville is a town with a long and fascinating history. First settled in the mid-18th century by French trappers, St. Martinville was one of the principal landing points for the Acadian refugees. After the outbreak of the French Revolution, a number of French aristocrats emigrated to St. Martinville. They re-established their courtly ceremonies, staged grand balls and operas and gave the name "Le Petit Paris" (Little Paris) to this former trapper's camp.

The focal point of St. Martinville is the square in front of the St. Martin de Tours Church.[2] St. Martin is the oldest Catholic church building in Louisiana still in use (Tours 318-394-6602). Facing the church from Main Street on the left is the "Le Petit Paris" Museum,[3] built in 1861 (318-394-6602), which features Mardi Gras costumes and personal items belonging to the early settlers of the town. To the right of the church is the handsome Greek revival Presbytere,[4] built in 1857, which is the home of the priests of St. Martin de Tours.

St. Martinville is perhaps best known as the setting of Henry Wadsworth

Longfellow's poem, *Evangeline.* The Evangeline Oak[5] marks the spot where the legendary heroine of the poem waited for her lover, Gabriel. At the rear left exterior of the Church is the tomb of Emmeline Labiche,[6] upon whose life Longfellow based his poem. The statue of Evangeline which sits atop the tomb was donated by the cast of the movie *Evangeline* which was filmed near St. Martinville. The model for the statue was the star of the movie, Dolores Del Rio.

To the north of St. Martinville is the Longfellow-Evangeline State Commemorative Area.[7] Here you will find acres thick with moss-laden oak trees on the banks of Bayou Teche. Located in the park is an Acadian Handicraft Shop[8] and the Acadian Plantation House[9] (318-394-4284), an excellent example of Louisiana's Caribbean-influenced, colonial "raised-cottage" architecture.

From St. Martinville take Highway 31 to New Iberia, the Queen City of the Teche. New Iberia is famous for its many beautiful homes, and one of these, the Shadows-on-the-Teche[10] (318-369-6446), is open to the public. Once a plantation townhouse for the Weeks family, the Shadows-on-the-Teche has been restored by the National Trust for Historic Preservation.

An alternate route from St. Martinville to New Iberia is Highway 86. This will take you to Loreauville, home of the Heritage Museum Village[11] (318-229-4740).

South of New Iberia is Avery Island,[12] which is not actually an island, but rather a salt dome. Avery Island is the home of world-famous Tabasco sauce, and the factory is open to the public (318-365-8173). Also located on the island is Jungle Gardens,[13] a 200-acre tropical garden and bird and wildlife sanctuary, which is open to the public (318-369-6243).

Jefferson Island, also a salt dome, is home of Live Oak Gardens,[14] (318-365-3631), "an English garden in a tropical setting." This former hide-out of Jean Lafitte features subtropical plantings and colorful seasonal flowers and foliage.

Further down U.S. Highway 182, known as the Old Spanish Trail, are Jeanerette and Franklin. Stately private homes line the main streets of both towns. Albania Mansion[15] (318-276-4816), on the outskirts of Jeanerette, is noted for its three-story, unsupported spiral staircase, its Louis XV, XVI and Directoire furnishings, and its doll collection. Overnight accommodations are available on the grounds. Oaklawn Manor[16] (318-828-0236), located on Irish Bend Road, is a Greek Colonial home.

Union forces, however, and the city and vital sections of the state remained in Federal hands throughout most of the war. Louisiana was readmitted to the Union in 1868.

Mardi Gras is, of course, Louisiana's most famous celebration, but the state also features more than 100 major festivals each year. There's the Crawfish Festival at Breaux Bridge, the Jambalaya Festival at Gonzales, the Corney Creek Festival at Bernice, the Cajun Festival at Mamou — the list goes on and on. Anglers will find some of the best bass, crappie, catfish and bream fishing at Toledo Bend Reservoir, and excellent saltwater angling can be found in the Gulf waters off Louisiana's coast. Along the River Road, from New Orleans to Baton Rouge, you'll see many beautiful antebellum mansions, and in just about every corner of the state you'll discover reminders of the state's colorful and cosmopolitan history.

Like many of the other Southern states, Louisiana is becoming more and more industrialized and the state is now a major producer of chemicals, petroleum and coal products, food products and fabricated metals. The Louisiana Offshore Oil Port was recently completed, allowing oil tankers too large to dock at existing ports to unload their cargo at this new superport. Not to be overlooked is the state's huge tourist industry which accounts for more than $1 billion annually.

State Offices

Tourism
Louisiana Office of Tourism
Department of Culture, Recreation and Tourism
PO Box 44291
Baton Rouge, Louisiana 70804
(504) 522-8772

State Police
Department of Public Safety
Baton Rouge, Louisiana 70821
(504) 925-6425

Radio Stations

Baton Rouge
WFMF 102.5 (FM)
WYNK 1380 (AM)
New Orleans
WWL 870 (AM)
WRNO 99.5 (FM)
WNOE 1060 (AM)
Shreveport
KEEL 710 (AM)

The *Natchez IX* (left) offers daily cruises from the Port of New Orleans. The *Delta Queen* visits New Orleans often, as part of its three-day and one-week cruises on the Lower Mississippi.

Louisiana Points of Interest and Attractions

Acadian Village and Tropical Gardens. Acadian dwellings and other antebellum structures are brought together here to represent an early Cajun bayou village; footpath winds through beautiful tropical gardens. Open year-round, daily; Memorial Day through Labor Day, 9:30 a.m. to 5:30 p.m.; 10 a.m. to 5 p.m. remainder of year. Lafayette, off State Route 342.

Acadian Park Nature Trail. A 120-acre park on the western edge of the Mississippi flood plain with 3.5-mile nature trail and interpretive center; campground. Open year-round, dawn to dusk (trail). Free. Lafayette, East Alexander Street.

Afton Villa Gardens. Majestic oak trees, Gothic gatehouse, and superb gardens on former plantation site; boxwood maze, statuary. Open March through December, daily, 9 a.m. to 4:30 p.m. Baton Rouge, north on US-61.

Brownell Carillon Tower. On the shore of Lake Palourde, situated among stand of magnificent cypress trees; beautiful music from the huge bells of the carillon; picnicking. Open year-round, daily. 9 a.m. to 5 p.m.; weekends, 9 a.m. to 7 p.m. Morgan City, on State Route 70.

Cohn Memorial Arboretum. Sixteen landscaped acres featuring more than 200 varieties of trees and shrubs native or adaptable to Louisiana. Open year-round, daily. Free. Baton Rouge, on Foster Road just off Comite Drive.

Coushatta Indian Cultural Center and Trading Post. Coushatta Indians, long famous for their basket weaving talent, maintain a museum and trading post which features basketry and other crafts. Open year-round, daily; Monday to Saturday, 8 a.m. to 5 p.m.; Sunday, 1 p.m. to 5 p.m. Elton, on US-190.

Coushatta Depot. Local arts and crafts, as well as fine wood and rock objects for sale in old train station. Open year-round, Monday to Friday, 8 a.m. to 4:30 p.m. Coushatta, on US-71.

Creole Craft House. A colonial cabin converted to quaint shop for regional books, crafts and artwork. Open year-round, daily, 9 a.m. to 5 p.m. Derry, north on State Route 1.

Delta Downs. Thoroughbred and quarterhorse racing. Season: September through March, thoroughbreds; April through June, quarter horses. Vinton, on State Route 3063. (318) 589-7441.

Evangeline Downs. Thoroughbred racing with a Cajun flair. Season: April through August, Thursday to Sunday. Lafayette, on US-167. (318) 896-6185.

Fairgrounds Racetrack. Third oldest track in America and home of the Louisiana Derby. Season: mid-November through March. New Orleans, on Gentilly Boulevard. (504) 944-5515.

Fat City. Dining, live entertainment, dancing, shopping in a unique complex of cafes, restaurants, nightclubs and shops. Open year-round. New Orleans, off Interstate 10, on North Causeway Boulevard.

Hodges Gardens. A 4,700-acre "garden in a forest" that is one of the South's most famous scenic drives and walkways; year-round blooms, waterfalls, greenhouse displays, streams and lakes; picnicking. Open January 15 through December 24, daily, 8 a.m. to sunset. Leesville, north on US-171.

Indian Trading Post. Operated by Tunica-Biloxi Indians; features fine native crafts and other unique items. "Usually" open. Marksville, one mile south on State Route 1.

Jefferson Downs. Thoroughbred racing. Season: April through mid-November, Tuesday to Friday. New Orleans, off Interstate 10.

Jubilee New Orleans. Offers the history and legends of New Orleans via fabulous displays, featuring holograms — laser projections of 360-degree moving figures — and multi-media show. Open year-round, daily, 10 a.m. to 6 p.m. New Orleans, corner of Chartres and St. Anne Streets at Jackson Square.

Jungle Gardens. Driving and walking tours of famous gardens featuring egrets, herons and 1,000-year-old Buddha; gift shop. Open year-round, daily, 9 a.m. to 5 p.m. Avery Island, on State Route 329.

Lake Charles Cruises. Cruise Lake Charles, the port and Contraband Bayou on comfortable tour boats. Open year-round, daily; several cruises each day. Lake Charles, off Interstate 10. (318) 436-9588.

Louisiana Downs. New racing facility with air-conditioned stadium and seating for 15,000. Season: July through November. Bossier City, on US-80 East. (800) 551-8622.

Louisiana Governor's Mansion. Built in 1963 as a replica of one of the state's plantation mansions; lavishly furnished. Open year-round; tours by appointment. Free. Baton Rouge, off Interstate 110 (at "Governor's Mansion" exit). (504) 387-3888.

Louisiana Hayride. Famous country music show that launched the careers of Hank Williams, Elvis Presley, Johnny Cash and many others. New auditorium, complete with restaurant that features superb barbecue dishes. Open year-round, Monday to Saturday, 5 p.m. to 10 p.m. (restaurant); live show on Saturday at 7:45 p.m. Bossier City, on State Route 3. (318) 742-7803.

Louisiana Nature Center. Trails lead through new 80-acre wooded area; research library, environmental theater. Open year-round. New Orleans, Joe Brown Park, on Lake Forest Boulevard.

Louisiana Purchase Gardens. One hundred acres of Mississippi River deltalands, featuring formal gardens, winding waterways, huge live oaks, meandering walkways and exotic animals in natural-habitat zoo. Open year-round, Friday and weekends. Monroe, south off US-165.

Louisiana Sports Hall of Fame. More than 60 of Louisiana's sporting greats (Y. A. Tittle, Joe Adcock, Billy Cannon) are honored here by portraits and memorabilia. Open year-round, Monday to Saturday, 8 a.m. to 5 p.m. Natchitoches, on campus of Northwestern State University, off State Route 1.

Louisiana Superdome. Magnificent domed stadium featuring "the largest single room in the history of man." Offers professional sports programs, exhibits, concerts and Mardi Gras parades. Open year-round, daily, tours every half-hour from 10:30 a.m. to 3:30 p.m. New Orleans, off Interstate 10, on Poydras Street.

National Fish Hatchery. Department of Interior facility responsible for stocking Louisiana's waters with striped bass, largemouth bass, catfish and other species; 20-tank aquarium. Open year-round, daily, 8 a.m. to 5 p.m. Free. Natchitoches, south on State Route 1.

State Arboretum. More than 300 acres of natural beauty, where trails lead beside some 100 species of plant life native to Louisiana. Open year-round, daily, 8 a.m. to 6 p.m. Free. Ville Platte, northwest on State Route 3042 (within boundaries of Chicot State Park).

Tubing on the Tangipahoa. Great sand beaches and inner-tube rides on the fast-flowing Tangipahoa River; campground with full hookups. Cherokee Beach, near Tickfaw, off Interstate 55, on State Route 442.

Zemurray Gardens. Rustic pathways lead around lake through 150 acres of gardens; azaleas, camellias, dogwoods and many other flowers and plants are featured. Open year-round, daily, sunrise to sunset. Tickfaw, off State Route 442.

Louisiana State Parks

Park	Location	CAMPING	PICNICKING	CONCESSIONS	SWIMMING	HIKING	BOATING	FISHING	HUNTING	WINTER SPORTS
Bogue Falaya	*Covington. Off State Route 36 (in the town of Covington).*		•		•					
Chemin-A-Haut	*Bastrop. Off State Route 139.*	•	•		•		•	•		
Chicot	*Ville Platte. On State Route 3042.*	•	•		•		•	•		
Cypremort Point	*Jeanerette. Off State Route 319.*		•		•		•	•		
Fairview Riverside	*Madisonville. On State Route 22.*	•	•				•	•		
Fontainbleau	*Mandeville. On US-90.*	•	•		•		•	•		
Grand Isle	*Grand Isle. On State Route 1.*	•	•		•		•	•		
Lake Bistineau	*Doyline. Off State Route 163.*	•	•		•	•	•	•		
Lake Bruin	*St. Joseph. Off US-65.*		•		•		•	•		
Lake Claiborne	*Homer. On State Route 146.*		•		•		•	•		
Lake D'Arbonne	*Farmerville. Off State Route 15.*		•				•	•		
St. Bernard	*Violet. On State Route 39.*	•	•				•	•		
Sam Houston	*Lake Charles. On State Route 378.*	•	•			•	•	•		

Louisiana has no state forests. For more information on Louisiana state parks, contact: *Louisiana State Parks and Recreation Commission, PO Drawer 1111, Baton Rouge, Louisiana 70821, (504) 389-5761.*

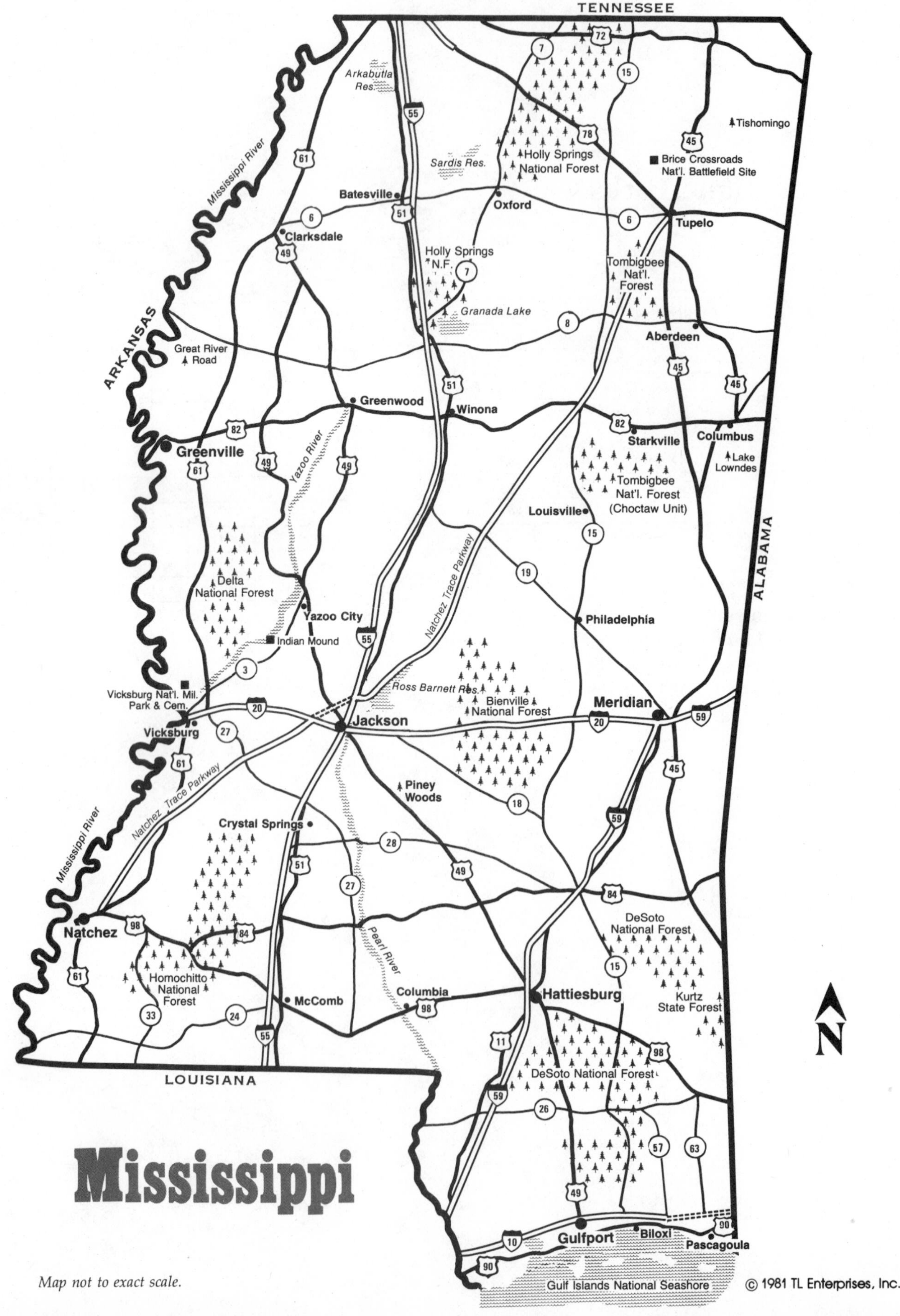

TENNESSEE
ARKANSAS
LOUISIANA
ALABAMA
Mississippi
Mississippi River
Arkabutla Res.
Sardis Res.
Holly Springs National Forest
Tishomingo
Brice Crossroads Nat'l. Battlefield Site
Batesville
Oxford
Tupelo
Clarksdale
Holly Springs N.F.
Granada Lake
Tombigbee Nat'l. Forest
Aberdeen
Great River Road
Greenwood
Winona
Starkville
Columbus
Lake Lowndes
Greenville
Yazoo River
Tombigbee Nat'l. Forest (Choctaw Unit)
Louisville
Natchez Trace Parkway
Delta National Forest
Yazoo City
Philadelphia
Indian Mound
Vicksburg Nat'l. Mil. Park & Cem.
Ross Barnett Res.
Bienville National Forest
Meridian
Jackson
Vicksburg
Piney Woods
Crystal Springs
DeSoto National Forest
Natchez
Pearl River
Homochitto National Forest
McComb
Columbia
Hattiesburg
Kurtz State Forest
Gulfport
Biloxi
Pascagoula
Gulf Islands National Seashore
N

Map not to exact scale.

Mississippi

Mississippi is a state often overlooked by travelers in spite of the fact that it has a history, beauty and hospitality unsurpassed by any other region. In Mississippi, you can travel the Natchez Trace, an 8,000-year-old path worn by buffaloes, followed by Indians, traversed by Andrew Jackson, and, in bygone days, often plagued by highwaymen. Among the state's other attractions are a number of festivals that celebrate many of the traditions of the South, Cajun cooking, scenic parks and forests, sparkling lakes, crystal-clear rivers and streams — and some of the best fishing to be found anywhere.

Mississippi was inhabited by Chocktaw, Chickasaw, Natchez and Yazoo Indians when Hernando De Soto first entered the region in 1539 during his explorations for Spain. La Salle descended the Mississippi River to its mouth and claimed possession of the entire basin for France, giving it the name Louisiana. Settlements were established by Iberville in 1699 (Biloxi) and Bienville in 1716 (Natchez). France ceded Louisiana to Spain in 1762, but Great Britain gained the portion east of the Mississippi River as a result of the Treaty of Paris in 1763. Later, during the American Revolution, the United States claimed the area in treaties with England. The Mississippi Territory was organized in 1798, and the region became a state in 1817. Mississippi sided with the Confederacy and seceded in 1861, and one of the state's leading citizens, Jefferson Davis, was elected President of the Confederacy. Because of its strategic location, Mississippi was the scene of many battles during the Civil War. The capital, Jackson, was captured in May 1863, and the remainder of the state fell in January 1864. Mississippi was readmitted to the Union February 23, 1870.

Despite the terrible destruction of the Civil War, many remnants of the antebellum days can still be found in the state, including the Governor's Mansion in

Full name: State of Mississippi
Origin of name: From the Indian, Maesi, meaning "Large," and Sipu, meaning "River."
Motto: *Virtute et Armis* (By Valor and Arms).
Nickname: Magnolia State
Capital: Jackson
Statehood: December 10, 1817, 20th state.
Population: 2,389,000 (ranks 29th).
Major Cities: Jackson (166,512), Biloxi (46,407), Meridian (46,256).
Bird: Mockingbird
Flower: Magnolia
Tree: Magnolia

Average daily temperatures by month

	Northern	Southern
Jan.	50.9 to 30.2	61.5 to 37.8
Feb.	55.0 to 32.8	65.1 to 40.3
Mar.	62.3 to 39.8	71.8 to 46.0
Apr.	73.7 to 50.6	79.9 to 54.9
May	80.8 to 57.5	85.6 to 61.2
Jun.	87.9 to 65.4	91.6 to 67.6
Jul.	90.9 to 68.5	92.7 to 70.6
Aug.	90.6 to 66.9	92.3 to 69.7
Sept.	85.4 to 61.6	88.2 to 65.3
Oct.	75.3 to 49.0	80.2 to 53.2
Nov.	62.9 to 39.1	70.0 to 44.0
Dec.	54.0 to 33.0	63.7 to 39.9
Year	72.5 to 49.5	78.6 to 54.2

A Suggested Tour

If you're looking for a camping paradise, head to Washington County, Mississippi. Here you'll find four fully developed recreation areas — Warfield Point between Greenville and the Mississippi River, Deerfield Park on Lake Lee below Highway 454, Leroy Percy State Park on Highway 12 west of the progressive community of Hollandale and Paul Love Park at the southern border of the county. These areas are all equipped with trailer pads, hookups, tables, grills, rest rooms, dump stations, playgrounds and equipment all surrounded by the peace and beauty of woodland and water.

At Warfield Point, an observation tower overlooks the majestic Mississippi River. Paul Love features its own softball field, and both parks have bath houses for swimmers. Leroy Percy offers a swimming pool, cabins, laundry facilities, a small museum, zoo and nature trails draped in Spanish moss. Rental boats and fishing can be found at Percy, Love and Deerfield.

But that's not all. For picnics and sightseeing, the Yazoo Wildlife Refuge near Leroy Percy provides thousand-year-old Indian mounds and allows hunting on a restricted basis. Winterville Mounds State Park on Highway 1 offers a museum filled with regional Indian artifacts and picnic space near the Indian mounds. Deer Creek Recreational Park off Highway 82 near Leland features picnic tables and play areas. Lake Washington presents a view of stately antebellum homes dating from 1820. Glen Allen offers a photographer's dream come true in the vined and shadowed ruins of St. John's Episcopal Church.

In between the parks and wilderness areas, stop to see a few of the millions of tons of cargo passing through the Towboat Capital of the World at Greenville. Drive down Mississippi's unofficial Antiques Avenue between Greenville and Leland on Highway 82. Time your visit to take in special events like the Greenville Arts and Crafts Fair in May or the Christmastime Bayou Floats down the road a piece in Leland.

Take your time . . . camp in the wilderness areas . . . fish in the lakes . . . talk to the people. It's Washington County . . . and it's a great place to visit.

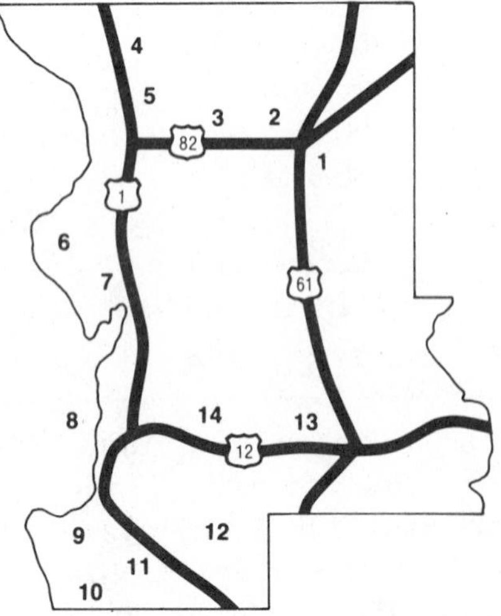

WASHINGTON COUNTY

1. Leland
2. Deer Creek Park
3. Antiques Avenue
4. Winterville Mounds State Park
5. Greenville
   Towboat Capital of the World
6. Warfield Point
7. Deerfield Park
8. Lake Lee
9. Lake Washington
10. Paul Love Park
11. Glen Allan
12. Yazoo Wildlife Refuge
13. Hollandale
14. Leroy Percy State Park

Majestic Dunleith Plantation near Natchez stands like a mighty Grecian temple above the oak-shaded lawns that fold away on every side.

Jackson which has been designated a National Historic Landmark. Another recently-named National Historic Landmark is William Faulkner's home in Oxford, which is open to visitors and serves as one of the cultural highlights of a visit to Mississippi. The state's Gulf Coast offers a total of 360 miles of shoreline dotted with bays, coves and sandy beaches, and just off the coast is the scenic Gulf Islands National Seashore Park.

In recent years, Mississippi has made a concerted effort to balance agriculture with industry. Part of this balance has been the combining of the two fields — so the state now has a large food processing industry. A major boost for the economy was the recent addition of a large shipbuilding facility at Pascagoula. Tourism brings in an additional $400 million annually for the state.

Highlight

Mississippi Crafts

Mississippi crafts stem from a varied cultural heritage; native civilizations and French, Spanish and English colonization have contributed to a growing American cultural identity. Crafts were developed to meet basic needs of survival and have been modified to include folk art and contemporary designs. Mississippians recognize the utilitarian and artistic importance of crafts by preserving traditions and encouraging new concepts. Throughout the state are living history exhibits, museums and shops where devotees can observe craftsmen in action, admire collections and purchase handmade crafts objects.

Following is a list of some of the major crafts attractions in Mississippi.

CHOCTAW CRAFTS CENTER

Contributing to Mississippi's wealthy cultural heritage is the Choctaw Crafts Center at the Pearl River community near Philadelphia. Operated by the Mississippi Band of Choctaw Indians, the center markets richly embroidered traditional clothing, unique double-weave baskets, beadwork, quilts and other handmade items. Demonstrations are available upon request.

Mississippi Band of Choctaw Indians
Tribal Office Building
Route 7, Box 21
Philadelphia, Mississippi 39350
(601) 656-5251

FLOREWOOD RIVER PLANTATION

Crafts were considered necessities in the 1850s; today they are respected as art. Daily demonstrations of traditional crafts of the mid-19th century are still a part of life at Florewood River Plantation near Greenwood.

A spinner at an antique wheel produces cotton and wool yarns using vegetables, herbs and bark for natural dyes. A potter uses Carroll County clay to create a range of pottery from bowls to wind chimes. Other artisans fashion candles and baskets, prepare old-fashioned food and demonstrate blacksmith skills. Locally-made crafts are on sale in the general store.

Florewood is operated by the State Park Commission as a living history exhibit and is open year-round for a small admission charge.

Box 680
Greenwood, Mississippi 38930
(601) 455-3821

LAUREN ROGERS MUSEUM

The Lauren Rogers Library and Museum of Art in Laurel houses a collection of outstanding Americana. More than 600 baskets representing 45 American Indian tribes are featured in the Basket Room.

In addition to other fine examples of American Indian crafts, the museum also contains famous works by European and American artists and sculptors, Japanese prints and antiques.

Box 1108
Laurel, Mississippi 39440
(601) 428-4875

MISSISSIPPI CRAFTS CENTER

Operated by the Craftsmen's Guild of Mississippi, Incorporated, the Mississippi Crafts Center on the Natchez Trace at Ridgeland offers for sale a variety of handcrafts, from cornhusk dolls to unique glass creations fashioned at the center. Guild craftsmen donate demonstration time to the center, especially on summer weekends, and three craftsmen-in-residence exhibit their skills at the center year-round. The guild also sponsors an educational program with classes in design and craft marketing, and the center is part of a pilot project by the National Park Service to market handcrafts in parks.

Box 69
Ridgeland, Mississippi 39157
(601) 856-7546

MOUNT LOCUST

Built in 1777 and used as a Natchez Trace inn, Mount Locust has been completely restored and furnished to 1820 authenticity. From March through October, craftsmen in period clothing demonstrate soap making, rail splitting, shake making for roof shingles, and the carding and spinning of cotton. Mount Locust is located on the Trace about 15 miles north of Natchez.

Route 4, Box 166
Natchez, Mississippi 39120
(601) 842-1572

TUPELO VISITORS CENTER

The Tupelo Visitors Center, at almost the mid-point on the Natchez Trace between Nashville and Natchez, features a summertime demonstration of sorghum pressing and preparation.

Natchez Trace Parkway
Route 1, NT 143
Tupelo, Mississippi 38801
(601) 842-1572

ANNUAL CRAFTS FAIRS

Crafts fairs are held year-round throughout Mississippi. Several of these have become annual events scheduled around the same time and at the same location each year. Some of the better known of these annual crafts fairs are listed below; for a more complete and current listing, write to the Mississippi Department of Tourism Development for a Calendar of Events.

Greenwood Arts Festival, March, Greenwood.
Sycamore Festival, early April, Senatobia.
Lively Arts Festival, April, Meridian.
Crosstie Festival, April, Cleveland.
Gum Tree Festival, mid-May, Tupelo.
July Crafts Jamboree, July (1st weekend), Jackson.
Great River Road Crafts Festival, October (2nd weekend), Natchez.
Chimneyville Crafts Festival, December (1st weekend), Jackson.

For information, contact: The Craftsmen's Guild of Mississippi, Incorporated, Box 22886, Jackson, Mississippi 39205, (601) 354-8884.

State Offices

Tourism
Department of Tourism and Development
Mississippi Agricultural and Industrial Board
PO Box 22825
Jackson, Mississippi 39205
(601) 354-6715

State Police
Department of Public Safety
Jackson, Mississippi 39205
(601) 982-1212

Radio Stations

Biloxi
WQID 93.7 (FM)

Jackson
WJDX 620 (AM)
WZZQ 102.9 (FM)

Mississippi Points of Interest and Attractions

Elvis Presley House. Boyhood home of the famous "King of Rock 'n Roll" in his hometown. Open year-round. Tupelo, off Natchez Trace Parkway.

Longwood. Unique octagonal house, largest and most elaborate in the nation. Open year-round. Natchez, off US-61.

Mississippi Petrified Forest. Giant stone trees dating back some 30 million years; extinct species of fir, maple, birch and sequoia; only petrified forest in Eastern U.S.; campground and hiking trails. Flora, off US-49.

Natchez Trace. Historic trail used as a trade route by the Indians as early as 8,000 years ago. From 1800 to 1820, the Natchez Trace was the most traveled road in the Southwest. Today the path is a National Parkway, crossing the state from its northeast to southwest boundary. Along the parkway you will find numerous points of interest, attractions and historic sites. Natchez to Tishomingo.

Natchez Under-the-Hill. A notorious site at the base of Natchez' high bluffs along the Mississippi, where river travelers paused to gamble. The site gained such a bad reputation in its day that one clergyman called it the "worst hell-hole on earth." Open year-round. Natchez, off US-65.

Rowan Oak. Home of William Faulkner, Nobel Prize and Pulitzer Prize-winning author, who lived here from 1930 until his death in 1962. Open year-round. Oxford, off State Route 7.

Ship Island. Boat cruises to fascinating and historic island in the Gulf of Mexico. Season: year-round. Biloxi, off Interstate 10.

U.S. Army Engineer Waterways Experiment Station. View scale models used to study flood control and navigational problems. Open year-round, Monday to Friday. Vicksburg, off Interstate 20.

Mississippi State Parks

Park	Location	CAMPING	PICNICKING	CONCESSIONS	SWIMMING	HIKING	BOATING	FISHING	HUNTING	WINTER SPORTS
Arkabutla	*Hernando. Off State Route 304.*	•	•		•		•	•		
Buccaneer	*Bay St. Louis. Off US-90.*	•	•	•	•	•		•		
Casey Jones	*Vaughan. Off Interstate 55 (exit 133).*		•	•						
Clarkco	*Meridian. Off US-45.*	•	•	•	•	•	•	•		
Florewood	*Greenwood. Off US-82.*		•	•						
Golden Memorial	*Walnut Grove. Off State Route 35.*	•	•	•	•		•	•		
Great River Road	*Rosedale. Off State Route 1.*		•	•				•		
Holmes County	*Durant. Off Interstate 55 (exit 150).*	•	•	•	•	•	•	•		
Hugh White	*Grenada. Off State Route 8.*	•	•	•	•	•	•	•		
J.P. Coleman	*Luka. Off State Route 25.*	•	•	•	•	•	•	•		
John W. Kyle	*Sardis. Off State Route 315 and Interstate 55 N (exit 61).*	•	•	•	•	•	•	•		
Lake Lowndes	*Columbus. Off State Route 69.*	•	•	•	•	•	•	•		
Leroy Percy	*Hollandale. Off State Route 12.*	•	•	•	•	•	•	•		
Nanih Waiya	*Noxapater. Off State Route 490.*	•	•			•				
Paul B. Johnson	*Hattiesburg. Off US-49.*	•	•	•	•	•	•	•		
Percy Quin	*McComb. Off Interstate 55S (exit 5).*	•	•	•	•	•	•	•		
Roosevelt	*Morton. Off State Route 13 and Interstate 20 (exit 25).*	•	•	•	•	•	•	•		
Tishomingo	*Dennis. Off State Route 25.*	•	•	•	•	•	•	•		
Tombigbee	*Tupelo. Off State Route 6.*	•	•	•	•	•	•	•		
Wall Doxey	*Holly Springs. Off State Route 7.*	•	•	•	•	•	•	•		
Yocona Ridge	*Oakland. Off State Route 32.*	•	•	•	•	•	•	•		

For more information on Mississippi state parks, contact: *Mississippi Park Commission, 717 Robert E. Lee Building, Jackson, Mississippi 39201, (601) 354-6321.*

Gulf States Calendar of Events

Spring
(March, April, May)

Alabama

Storybook Festival, Robinson Memorial Park. March, Andalusia.

Flea Market, Alabama State Fairgrounds. People from several surrounding states gather to sell items on the third weekend of every month. March through remainder of year, Birmingham.

Annual Confederate Memorial Day Services, Confederate Memorial Cemetery. March, Mountain Creek and Verbena.

Harmony Hills Annual Show. Barbershop harmony. March, Birmingham.

Rattlesnake Rodeo, Lee-Channel Stadium. Rattlesnake race, arts and crafts, air show, fried rattlesnake. March, Opp.

Jubilee Time Historic Mobile Tours. Historic residences and buildings open for tours. March, Mobile.

Annual Southeastern Livestock Exposition World Championship Rodeo, Garrett Coliseum. March, Montgomery.

Annual Heart of Dixie Old-Time Fiddlers Contest, Bell Auditorium, University of Alabama. March, Birmingham.

Heritage Week. March and April, Tuscaloosa.

Annual Historic Selma Pilgrimage. March and April, Selma.

Indian Crafts Festival, DeSoto Caverns. March, Childersburg.

Azalea Show, Jasmine Hill Garden. April, Montgomery.

Talladega College Annual Arts Festival. April, Talladega.

Annual Eufaula Pilgrimage. April, Eufaula.

Annual Arts and Crafts Festival, Ingle Park. April, Cullman.

Calico Fort Arts and Crafts Fair. April, Fort Deposit.

Annual Cahaba Horse Trails, Patchwork Farm. April, Birmingham.

Muscle Shoals Bass Rodeo, Wilson Dam Reservoir. Prizes for largest spotted, smallmouth and largemouth bass. April, Muscle Shoals.

Annual Easter Pageant, "The Road To Calvary," Mound State Park. April, Moundville.

Azalea Tours, Noccalula Falls Park. April, Gadsden.

Annual Alabama Forest Festival, Garrett Coliseum. Arts and crafts, games, contests, exhibits, sky divers, free prizes. April, Montgomery.

Annual Racing Horse Spring Warm-Up Show, Southeastern Horse Center. A full horse show with 26 classes. April, Decatur.

Annual Spring Craft Show and Sale, University of South Alabama. April, Mobile.

Honeysuckle Art Festival. April, Selma.

Annual Sunday on the Square. April, Monroeville.

Atmore Mayfest, South Eighth Avenue Park. May, Atmore.

Annual NASCAR Sportsman 300, Alabama International Motor Speedway. May, Talladega.

Annual Winston 500, Alabama International Motor Speedway. May, Talladega.

Annual International Folk Festival, Jasmine Hill Garden. May, Montgomery and Wetumpka.
Annual Montgomery Master's Track Meet. May, Montgomery.
Mountain Laurel and Magnolia Blooming Festival. May, Hodges.
Northeast Alabama Festival. Tours of places with historic interest, displays, antique show and sale, square dancing, music, barbecue dinner. May, Fort Payne.
Gem and Mineral Show, Opelika Community Center. May, Opelika.
Montgomery Jubilee Celebration. May, Montgomery.

Florida

Central Florida State Fair. March, Orlando.
Chalo Nitka Festival and Rodeo, Chalo Nitka Square. March, Moore Haven.
Florida Strawberry Festival. March, Plant City.
Medieval Fair, Ringling Museums and New College. March, Sarasota.
Tomato-Snook Festival, Community Park. March, Bonita Springs.
Azalea Festival. March, Palatka.
Annual Seminole Powwow Festival. March, Seminole.
Annual Spring Festival. March, Lake Worth.
National Tractor Pull. March, Eustis.
Fun 'N Sun Festival. April, Clearwater.
Florida State Fair, Florida State Fairgrounds. April, Tampa.
Easter Beach Run. April, Daytona Beach.
Annual Art Show of the Sarasota County Public Schools, Sarasota Art Association, Civic Center. May, Sarasota.
Annual Summer Season of Exhibitions. Art show. May, Naples.
Chiselers Annual Thieves Market, University of Tampa. May, Tampa.
Founders Day, City Hall Grounds. May, Belleview.
Dunnellon Boom Town Days. May, Dunnellon.
Annual Florida Folk Festival, Stephen Foster Center. May, White Springs.
Zellwood Sweet Corn Festival. May, Longwood.

Louisiana

Audubon Pilgrimage. March, St. Francisville.
St. Mary Parish Tour of Homes. March, Franklin.
Redbud Festival. March, Vivian.
Oyster Day. March, Amite.
Antiques Show and Sale. March, Jackson.
Strawberry Festival. March, Ponchatoula.
Azalea Trail. March, Lafayette.
Dogwood Festival. March, Bogalusa.
Arts and Crafts Festival. April, Clinton.
Jazz and Heritage Festival. April, New Orleans.
Holiday in Dixie. April, Shreveport.
New Orleans Open. PGA tournament. April, New Orleans.
Little Italy Festival. April, Independence.
Festival of Flowers. April, New Orleans.
Acadian Music Festival. April, Abbeville.
Heritage Tour. April, Baton Rouge.
Madewood Arts Festival. April, Napoleonville.
Contraband Days. May, Lake Charles.
Crawfish Festival (even numbered years only). May, Breaux Bridge.
Sawmill Days. May, Fisher.
Jazz on the Bayou. May, Slidell.
Poke Salat Festival. May, Blanchard.
Bluegrass Festival. May, St. Maurice.
Stage Coach Trail Tour. May, Gibsland.

Mississippi

Clarksdale Antique Show and Sale. March, Clarksdale.
Gum Tree Festival. March, Tupelo.
Sycamore Arts Festival. March, Senatobia.
Natchez Pilgrimage. March and April, Natchez.
Mainstream Arts and Crafts Festival. March, Greenville.
Meridian Annual Antique Show. April, Meridian.
Arts and Crafts Festival. April, Carthage.
Mississippi Arts Festival. April, Jackson.
McComb Lighted Azalea Trail. April, McComb.

Festival of Harmony. Barbershop quartet singing. May, Jackson.
Gold in the Hills. Melodrama. May, Hattiesburg.
Hattiesburg Flea Market. May, Hattiesburg.
Atwood Bluegrass Festival. May, Monticello.
Catfish Festival. May, Belzoni.

Summer
(June, July, August)

Alabama
Mountain Laurel and Magnolia Blooming Festival, Rock Bridge Canyon. June, Hodges.
Summer Flower Show, Bellingrath Gardens and Home. June, Mobile.
Annual Alabama State Square and Round Dance Convention. June, Huntsville.
Annual Appaloosa Show. June, Montgomery.
Annual Summer Dance Workshop, Ballet House and Arts Annex, University of Alabama. June, Birmingham.
Helen Keller Festival, "Ivy Green" (Helen Keller's home). July, Tuscumbia.
Summer Foliage and Alamanda Display, Bellingrath Gardens Home. July, Mobile.
Dixie Annual Art Exhibit. July, Montgomery.
Annual Fireworks Display, Opelika High School. July, Opelika.
Spirit of America Festival, Point Mallard Park. Fireworks, beauty pageant, games, music, presentation of the Audie Murphy Award for patriotism. July, Decatur.
Annual Fourth of July Celebration. July, Mobile.
Stars and Stripes Fair. July, Talladega.
Annual Alabama Shakespeare Festival, Festival Theater. July, Anniston.
Farm Market Days. July, Birmingham.
Alabama Mule Association's Mule Show and Pull. July, Decatur.
Brushy Creek Bluegrass Festival, Smith Lake. July, Arley.
Annual Arts and Crafts Show and Sale. July, Haleyville.
Annual Preservation Conference. Speakers in the field of historic preservation, workshops in archaelogy. July, Tuscaloosa.
Blessing of the Fleet, Municipal Docks. July, Bayou La Batre.
Crape Myrtle Show, Jasmine Hill Garden. August, Wetumpka.
Horse Pens Summer Old-Time Fiddlers Convention and Contest. August, Asheville-Oneonta.
Annual Arca "200" Stock Car Race, Alabama International Motor Speedway. August, Talladega.
Farm Market Days. August, Birmingham.
Summer Festival, Exhibition Hall. August, Birmingham.
Annual Lake Eufaula Summer Spectacular; boat races. August, Eufaula.
Franklin County Fair. August, Russellville.

Florida
Royal Poinciana Festival. June, Miami.
Marathon Annual Bonefish Tournament. June, Marathon.
Cross and Sword. Outdoor drama of early Florida. June through August, St. Augustine.
Silver Spurs Rodeo. July, Kissimmee.
All-Florida Championship Rodeo. July, Arcadia.
Indian Key Festival. August, Islamorada.
Days In Spain. August, St. Augustine.

Louisiana
Jambalaya Festival. June, Gonzales.
Corney Creek Festival. June, Bernice.
Peach Festival. June, Ruston.
Louisiana Cavalier. Outdoor drama. July through August, Natchitoches.
Crab Festival. July, LaCombe.
Cajun Festival. July, Mamou.
Catfish Festival. July, Des Allemands.
Oyster Festival. July, Galliano.
Soybean Festival. July, Jonesville.
Bastille Day. July, Jennings.

Creole Summer Festival. July, French Settlement.
Fine Arts Festival. July, Lafayette.
Seafood Festival. July, Lafitte.
Watermelon Festival. July, Farmerville.
Shrimp Festival. August, Delcambre.
Grand Champ Tractor Pull. August, Montpelier.
Pioneer Days. August, Greenwood.

Mississippi
Choctaw Indian Fair. June, Philadelphia.
Mississippi Deep Sea Fishing Rodeo. June, Biloxi.
Annual Blessing of the Fleet and Shrimp Festival. June, Biloxi.
Neshoba County Fair. June, Philadelphia.
Delta Jubilee, Soldiers Field. July, Clarksdale.
Fireworks Display, Beach Park. July, Pascagoula.
July Fourth Special Events, John W. Kyle State Park. July, Sardis.
Deep-Sea Fishing Rodeo, Small Craft Harbor. World's largest fishing rodeo. July, Gulfport.
Fiddle and Banjo Contest. July, Oxford.
Choctaw Indian Fair. July, Philadelphia.
Miss Mississippi Pageant. July, Vicksburg.
National Tobacco Spitting Contest, Billy John Crumpton's Pond. World championship contest, music, mule racing, bird-calling contest, food. July, Raleigh.
Neshoba County Fair. July, Philadelphia.

Fall
(September, October, November)

Alabama
September Flower Show, Bellingrath Gardens. September, Mobile.
Alabama International Billfish Tournament. September, Orange Beach.
Alabama River Raft Race. Homemade rafts, trophies for seven places. September, Selma.
Manitou Arts and Crafts Show, Manitou Cave. September, Fort Payne.
Coon Dog Cemetery Decoration and Barbecue. Labor Day celebration with country music and a liars contest to honor the 111 coon dogs buried there. September, Cherokee.
Central Alabama Hamfest. Amateur radio exhibits and displays. September, Montgomery.
Annual Festival in the Park, Oak Park. September, Montgomery.
Northwest Alabama Fair. September, Jasper.
Annual Selma Horse Show, Bloch Park. September, Selma.
Annual Montgomery Art Guild. September, Montgomery.
North Alabama County Fair. September, Muscle Shoals.
Brushy Creek Bluegrass Festival. September, Arley.
September Fest. September, Childersburg.
Annual Outdoor Arts and Crafts Show, Langan Park. September, Mobile.
Lee County Fair. October, Opelika.
Pike County Fair. October, Troy.
Fall Color Spectacular, Jasmine Hill Garden. October, Wetumpka.
Alabama's Annual Shrimp Festival. October, Gulf Shores.
Annual Tennessee Valley Old-Time Fiddlers Convention, Athens State College. October, Athens.
Annual Boaz Harvest Festival. October, Boaz.
Annual Art Show, Confederate Park. October, Demopolis.
Historic Jacksonville Tour. October, Jacksonville.
Annual Kentuck Arts and Crafts Festival, Kentuck Park. October, Northport.
Annual Rumbling Waters Arts and Crafts Show. October, Wetumpka.
Baldwin County Fair. October, Robertsdale.
Riverfront Market Days. Arts and crafts, music, food specialties. October, Selma.
Annual National Peanut Festival and Fair. October, Dothan.
Annual Montgomery Art Guild/South Alabama State Fair Art Exhibit. October, Montgomery.

Halloween Trick or Treat, Eastdale Mall. October, Montgomery.
Annual Homes Tour, Camellia Show and Antique Sale and Fair. November, Greenville.
Annual Festival of Sacred Music. November, Birmingham.
Annual Creek Indian Thanksgiving Day Homecoming Powwow. November, Poarch.
Annual Christmas Carol Service, McCoy United Methodist Church. November, Birmingham.
Christmas in the Canebrake, Bluff Hall. A 19th-century Christmas celebration. November, Demopolis.

Florida
Pioneer Day. September, Dade City.
Rattlesnake Festival and International Championship Gopher Race. October, San Antonio.
Swamp Buggy Races. October, Naples.
Destin-Gulf Coast Deep-Sea Fishing Rodeo. October, Destin.
North Florida Fair. October, Tallahassee.
Key Colony Beach Sailfish Tournament. November, Key Colony Beach.
Antique Car Meet. November, Ormond Beach.

Louisiana
Shrimp and Petroleum Festival (Labor Day Weekend). September, Morgan City.
Antiques Show and Sale. September, Thibodaux.
Bouillabaisse Festival. September, Larose.
Festivals Acadiens. September, Lafayette.
Gumbo Festival. September, Chackbay.
Sugar Cane Festival. September, New Iberia.
Toledo Fall Festival. September, Many.
Forestry Festival. September, Leesville.
Angola Prison Rodeo. October, Angola.
Acadiana Antique Show. October, Lafayette.
Art and Folk Festival. October, Columbia.
Catahoula Lake Festival. October, Pineville.
La Vie Lafourchaise Festival. October, Raceland.
Festival de Pointe Coupee. October, New Roads.
Los Islenos Spanish Festival. October, St. Bernard.
Cotton Festival. October, Ville Platte.
Dairy Festival. October, Abbeville.
Yambilee. October, Opelousas.
Historical Tour. October, Natchitoches.
Sauce Piquante Festival. October, Raceland.
Pecan Festival. November, Colfax.
Allons aux Avoyelles Tour. November, Mansura.
Hungarian Folk Festival. November, Albany.
Swine Festival. November, Basile.
Tamale Fiesta. November, Zwolle.

Mississippi
Pioneer Crafts Festival, Mississippi Crafts Center. September, Ridgeland.
National Association of Women Artists Exhibition. September, Columbus.
Folklife Festival. September, Hollandale.
Singing River Charity Classic Arabian Horse Show. September, Gautier.
Wildlife Show, Leigh Mall. September, Columbus.
Day in the Mall in the Fall, Downtown Mall. September, Laurel.
Indian Bayou Arts and Crafts Festival. September, Indianola.
Territorial Fair, Liberty Park. October, Natchez.
Autumn Feast, Wall Doxey State Park. October, Holly Springs.
Gumbo Festival of the Universe. Gumbo eating contest, Gumbo Queen contest, entertainment. October, White Cypress-Necaise Crossing.
Gateway to the Delta Arts and Crafts Festival. October, Yazoo City.
Mississippi/Alabama State Fair. October, Meridian.
Greek Festival. November, Biloxi.
Holiday Parade. November, Meridian.
Olde English Feast. November, Vicksburg.
Go-Cart Races. November, Columbus.
Opera/South. November, Jackson.

Winter
(December, January, February)

Alabama

Candlelight Christmas at Oakleigh, Oakleigh House Museum. December, Mobile.

Annual Christmas Parade. One of the largest parades in the state. December, Phenix City.

Annual Presentation of Handel's Messiah. December, Bessemer.

Annual Christmas Art and Craft Fair, Cullman Community Center. December, Cullman.

"Christmas at Arlington," Arlington Antebellum Home and Gardens. December, Birmingham.

Annual Christmas Parade. December, Rainsville.

Annual Christmas Dance. December, Fairfield.

Birmingham Symphony's Annual Free Concert, Civic Center Concert Hall. December, Birmingham.

Annual Blue and Gray All-American Football Classic, Cramton Bowl. December, Montgomery.

Hall of Fame Bowl, Legion Field. December, Birmingham.

Winter Blooming Azalea and Camellia Show, Jasmine Hill Garden. January, Montgomery and Wetumpka.

Millard Fillmore Festival. Film festival and essay contest. January, Enterprise.

Azalea Trail Queen Coronation, Ladd Memorial Stadium. January, Mobile.

Alabama Junior Miss Program. January, Montgomery.

Winter Flower Show, Bellingrath Gardens. February, Mobile.

Hobby and Ceramic Show. February, Opelika.

Annual Sweetheart Dance, Fultondale Community Center. February, Fultondale.

Mobile's Azalea Trail and Festival. A 35-mile marked route winding through the city when the azaleas are in bloom; variety of entertainments. February, Mobile.

Annual Founder's Day Celebration. February, Tuscaloosa.

Mardi Gras. Gala balls and parades held prior to Ash Wednesday. February, Mobile.

Florida

Gator Bowl. December, Jacksonville.

Orange Bowl Festival. December and January, Miami.

South Florida Fair and Exposition. January and February, West Palm Beach.

Silver Sailfish Derby. January and February, West Palm Beach.

Festival of Epiphany. January, Tarpon Springs.

Florida State Fair. February, Tampa.

Daytona 500. February, Daytona.

Louisiana

Christmas Festival. December, Natchitoches.

Camellia Show. December, Lafayette.

Christmas in the Country. December, Elizabeth.

Christmas Parades. December, Baton Rouge.

Lighting Display. December, Hodges.

Bonfires on the Levee, River Roads (Christmas Eve). December, Baton Rouge to New Orleans.

Sugar Bowl (New Year's Day). January, New Orleans.

Carnival Season begins. January, New Orleans.

Fur and Wildlife Festival. January, Cameron.

La Grand Boucherie. February, St. Martinville.

Frontier Days. February, Logansport.

Bayou Ramble Antiques Show. February, Opelousas.

Boudin Festival. February, Broussard.

Mississippi

Tour of Homes. December, Louisville.

Singing Christmas Tree, Bellhaven College. December, Jackson.

Christmas Parade. December, Inverness.

Christmas at Florewood. Events depicting life as it would have been in 1850s, Florewood River Plantation. December, Greenwood.

Luminaries on the Bayou. Spectacular Christmas Eve display consisting of 2,000 candles placed along both sides of Lake Bradley. December, Inverness.

Delta Band Festival and Winter Carnival. December, Greenwood.

Dixie National Livestock Show and Rodeo. January, Jackson.

Picayune Arts Festival. January, Picayune.

Mississippi State Fox Hunters Field Trials and Bench Show. January, Kosciusko.

Mississippi Junior Miss Pageant. February, Vicksburg.

Biloxi Mardi Gras. February, Biloxi.

ILLINOIS
The Water Tower
Buckingham Fountain
Shedd Aquarium
Picasso Statue
Chicago's John Hancock Center
Mackinac Bridge
MICHIGAN
Tulip Farm Holland Michigan
GREENFIELD VILLAGE
120
17
Greenfield Village
Ice Boating, Lake Michigan

WISCONSIN
Cedar Grove Dutch Festival
Dairy State
Lincoln Tomb—Springfield
Chicago Art Institute
Lake Geneva
Madison—State Capitol
R. McKee
Mac-O-Cheek Castle, West Liberty
OHIO
Perry's Peace Memorial
Schoenbrunn
Pioneer Village—Mitchell
Parke County Covered Bridges
INDIANA
Soldiers & Sailors Monument, Indianapolis

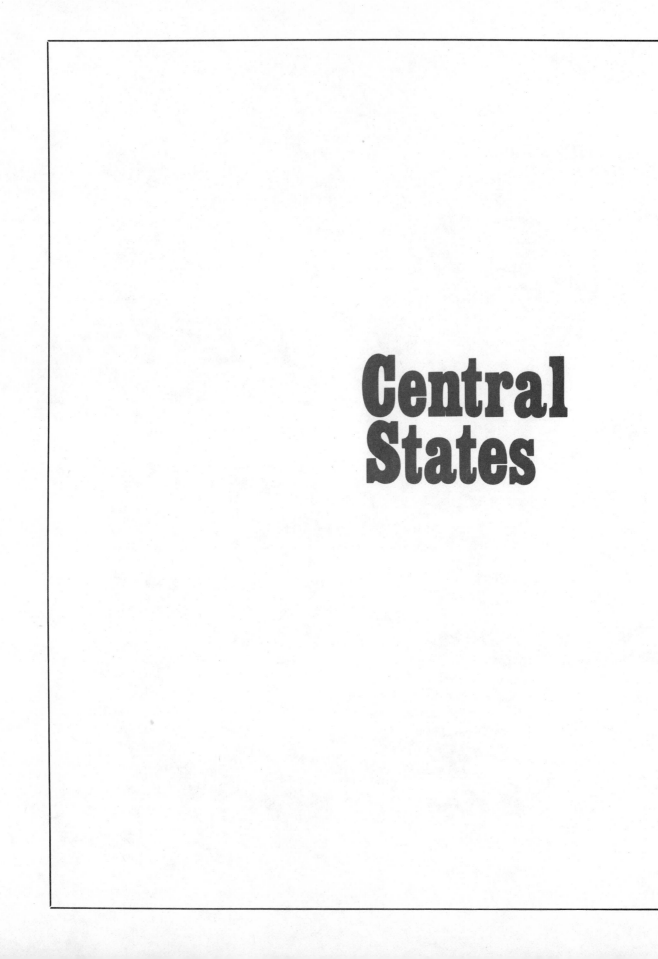

Central States

The Great Lakes are without a doubt the most dominant geographical feature of the Central states, and the single most important factor in the settlement of the region. Today, the Lakes continue their domination, supporting the key cities of Chicago, Detroit, Grand Rapids, Cleveland, Toledo and Milwaukee, as well as playing an important role in the overall economy, and even the weather, of each state. Of course, the Great Lakes have also given the region one of the richest and most scenic playgrounds to be found anywhere in America.

Covering 95,000 square miles, the Great Lakes are the largest expanse of fresh water on the face of the earth, holding enough water to cover the entire United States to a depth of 12 feet. The lakes are indeed impressive: Superior, the largest body of fresh water in the world, plunges to a depth of 1,333 feet; Lake Michigan, the only lake wholly within U.S. boundaries, has a maximum depth of 923 feet; Huron, currently the cleanest of the lakes, is 750 feet deep; and Erie, the 12th largest body of fresh water on the planet, has a relatively shallow depth of only 210 feet.

Given these awesome statistics, it's no wonder that the Great Lakes have spawned a whole body of tall tales, folklore and legends, ranging from accounts of ghost ships haunting the coastline to the whimsical tale of Paul Bunyan gouging out the Lakes to provide ponds for his sawmills. The frequent disasters befalling the ships that ply these waters have also inspired stories of sunken treasure; rich cargoes, gold coin and valuable ore are said to lie in the Lakes' cold depths.

One of the most interesting aspects of the Lakes is their role as a weather maker. Slow to react to winter cold and summer heat, the Lakes appear to exert a calming influence on the air that passes over them. Many lakeside cities, for instance, seldom see the tornado weather that is so common to the states of the heartland, yet those cities and towns that lie only a few miles farther inland are subject to weather alerts throughout tornado season.

While the Great Lakes are a good reason to visit the states that comprise this region of the country, they are by no means the area's only attractions. Throughout these states you'll find numerous points of interest, and attractions ranging from the numerous national forests and many fine state parks to the Amish settlements of Indiana and Ohio.

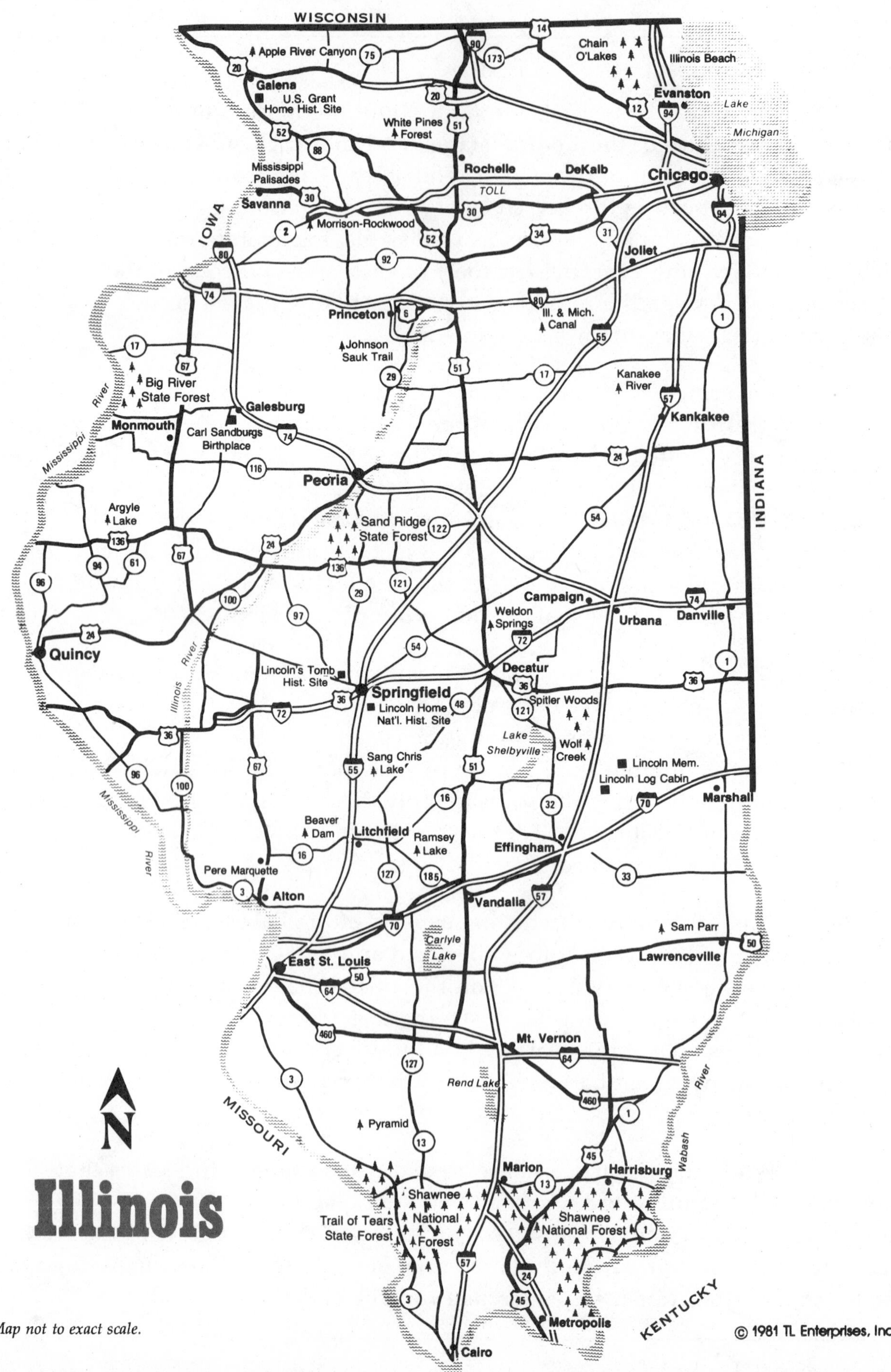

Map not to exact scale.

Illinois

Illinois is really two states in one: The north-central region, composed of gently rolling plains; and the rugged hill country of the south. Those topographical differences, along with events of the past, have combined to give the two regions distinctly different characters. The north, which includes bustling Chicago, the nation's second largest city, has a quicker pace and an identity more akin to the states of the heartland. The "downstate" region, known among the natives as "Little Egypt," has definite ties with the lifestyle and traditions of the South. It all makes for an interesting state that is often called "a land of contrasts."

The earliest inhabitants of Illinois were prehistoric Indians who left a legacy of several thousand temple and burial mounds. Jolliet and Marquette made a brief visit to the region in 1673, during their exploration of the Mississippi River. A few years later, LaSalle entered the territory and established Fort Crevecoeur, near what is now Peoria, and another fort near the present town of LaSalle. The first permanent settlement was founded in 1699 by French priests at Cahokia, a Mississippi River community that is located south of St. Louis. This settlement, through the use of large numbers of slaves, was extremely prosperous, supplying food and other staples to both New Orleans and French outposts on the Great Lakes. The Treaty of Paris transferred the Illinois territory to the British, who lost it on July 4, 1778, when George Rogers Clark took possession of Kaskaskia and other settlements. After the War of 1812, settlers began to flood into the area and Illinois was admitted to the Union on December 3, 1818. Prior to the Civil War, there were some conflicts between the interests of the northern part of the state and those in the south, because many of the southern Illinoisans were slaveholders. These problems were resolved before the outbreak of hostilities, and Illinois remained firmly tied to the Union.

Full Name: State of Illinois
Origin of name: From the Indian name meaning "The Men."
Motto: State Sovereignty — National Union
Nickname: Prairie State
Capital: Springfield
Statehood: December 3, 1818, 21st state.
Population: 11,245,000 (ranks fifth).
Major Cities: Chicago (3,099,391), Rockford (145,459), Peoria (125,983).
Bird: Cardinal
Flower: Native violet
Tree: Oak

Average daily temperature by month

	Northern	Southern
Jan.	29.7 to 12.3	43.8 to 24.3
Feb.	34.5 to 16.8	48.2 to 27.5
Mar.	44.6 to 25.8	57.4 to 35.2
Apr.	60.0 to 37.8	70.9 to 46.5
May	71.2 to 47.4	80.0 to 54.6
Jun.	81.1 to 57.6	88.6 to 63.3
Jul.	84.1 to 61.5	91.4 to 66.8
Aug.	82.7 to 60.0	90.4 to 64.4
Sept.	76.2 to 52.4	84.5 to 57.3
Oct.	65.1 to 41.6	73.3 to 45.6
Nov.	48.0 to 29.2	57.9 to 35.8
Dec.	34.8 to 18.4	46.8 to 28.4
Year	59.3 to 38.4	69.4 to 45.8

Sears Tower, the world's tallest building, dominates almost any view of Chicago's skyline including this one looking northeast toward Lake Michigan.

Illinois' most famous historic site is undoubtedly Abraham Lincoln's tomb in Springfield, but elsewhere in the state you'll find a number of other points of interest related to Lincoln and his family's residency in Illinois, including the Lincoln Heritage Trail. For scenic beauty, you shouldn't miss the Mississippi Palisades in the northwest or the rugged Shawnee Hills (Illinois Ozarks) in the south. For excitement and culture, try Chicago. And while you're there, visit the Sears Tower, the world's tallest building (110 stories). An observation deck on the 103rd floor provides a spectacular view that extends all the way to Wisconsin.

Surprisingly, southern Illinois contains about 25% of the nation's coal and the mining of that mineral is of prime importance to the state's economy. A combination of fertile soil and a long growing season also makes Illinois one of the nation's major agricultural states, with soybeans, corn and dairy products among its most important products. Manufacturing includes machinery, food products, chemicals, clothing, transportation equipment and musical instruments.

Highlight

The Windy City has a wide variety of attractions to interest travelers, but two of Chicago's best offerings are the Sears Tower and Lincoln Park.

The Sears Tower, rising 110 stories above the city, is one of the world's tallest buildings. Featured is Alexander Calder's first moving wall sculpture, *Universe,* and an observation platform on the 103rd floor that provides a commanding view of the city and beyond from a vantage point that is 1,350 feet above street level. The skydeck is open year-round, daily, 9 a.m. to midnight. Adults $1.50, children under 12 $1. Location is at Jackson and Franklin Streets.

In Lincoln Park you can visit the famed Conservatory, which offers floral shows throughout the year, take in the renowned Lincoln Park Zoo, or simply stroll through the park or sit on the beach and watch the waves of Lake Michigan lap the shores. There are numerous playgrounds for the youngsters. Open year-round, daily. Along Lake Shore Drive between North and Hollywood Avenues.

State Offices

Tourism
Illinois Department of Business and Economic Development
222 South College
Springfield, Illinois 62706
(217) 782-7500

State Police
Department of Public Safety
103 Armory Building
Springfield, Illinois 62706
(217) 782-7762

Radio Stations

Chicago
WLS 890 (AM)
WGN 720 (AM)
WXRT 93.1 (FM)
WMAQ 670 (AM)
Peoria
WIRL 1290 (AM)
Rockford
WZOK 97.5 (FM)

Illinois Points of Interest and Attractions

Adler Planetarium. Located on Chicago's lakefront near the Field Museum of Natural History and the Shedd Aquarium. Planetarium interior is on two levels; the main floor features the Sky Theater, the lower level has an exhibit area. Open year-round, except Thanksgiving, Christmas and New Year's Day. Admission charged for shows in theater. Chicago, 1300 South Lake Shore Drive.

Aldeen Nature Trail. A self-guided tour along loop trails in Reuben Aldeen Park. Open year-round; lodge open from April 1 through October 31, 8 a.m. to dusk. Rockford, 623 North Alpine Road.

Back Door Store. Store that is part of the Helen Gallagher-Foster House; actually the back door to their warehouse. More than 10,000 unique gifts to choose from. Open year-round, daily; Monday to Saturday, 9:30 a.m. to 6 p.m.; Sunday, noon to 6 p.m. Peoria, north on State Route 29.

Candy Cone. An authentic old-fashioned ice cream parlor done in the style of the

Gay '90s; sandwiches and bakery products. Richmond, 5620 Broadway.

Children's Farm. A place where children can observe and learn about farms, farm animals and animals native to the area. Attractions include wagon rides, covered bridge, numerous barns with exhibits, windmill, silo, hatchery. Open spring through fall, Monday to Saturday. Rockford, Safford Road.

Clayville Stagecoach Stop. A historic 145-year-old tavern and popular place for travelers. Abraham Lincoln is said to have been one of the guests here. Open year-round, daily. Springfield, west on State Route 125.

Engine No. 2500. A giant steam engine that pulled some of the fastest passenger trains on the Illinois Central Railroad. Huge engine weighs 225 tons. Centralia, on State Route 161 (near Fairview Park).

Garden of the Gods. A special recreation attraction in the Shawnee National Forest, featuring unique rock formations that evolved some 200 million years ago; camping, picnicking. Karbers Ridge, off State Route 34.

Garfield Park Conservatory. One of the most beautiful publicly-owned botanical gardens in the world. Extensive floral displays, large collection of exotics, 5,000 species and varieties housed in six different houses. Open year-round, daily, 9 a.m. to 9 p.m. Chicago, 300 North Central Park Boulevard.

Haeger Potteries. The largest artwares factory in the world. Open year-round, Monday to Friday; guided tours show each step in the production process. Macomb, off US-136.

Hill Nursery. Ten formal Japanese gardens, featuring an extensive collection of bonsai plants. Open year-round, daily, Elgin, at junction of State Routes 31 and 72.

Hulling Quarter Horse Ranch. View top quarterhorses in action in the "cutting pens;" 181-acre ranch also features outdoor show arenas, horseshoeing shop and several horse barns housing some of the top quarter horses in the nation. Open year-round. Smithton, off State Route 159.

Illinois Iron Furnace. The first charcoal-fired iron furnace in Illinois, operating from 1839 to 1883; now maintained by National Forest Service; information area. Open year-round. Elizabethtown, north off State Route 146.

Jade House. The only shop in the region dealing exclusively in jade; extensive selection of jewelry and gift items. Open year-round, Monday to Friday, 10:30 a.m. to 5 p.m. Chicago, 24 North Wabash, Suite 932.

John Deere Administrative Center. World headquarters for John Deere; display building contains current and historic John Deere products; unique three-dimensional mural designed by Alexander Girard. Open year-round, Monday to Friday; tours at 10:30 a.m. and 1:30 p.m. Moline, southeast off US-150.

Julia Belle Swan. Steam sternwheeler with authentic steam calliope takes visitors for cruises on Illinois River. Open May through October with cruises at regularly scheduled intervals throughout the day; moonlight cruises with live entertainment depart at 8 p.m. Peoria, Main Street Dock (at foot of Main Street).

LaGrange Lock and Dam. Excellent recreation spot on the Illinois River with camping and picnicking facilities. Open year-round, daily. La Grange, off US-67.

LaRue Pine Hills Ecological Area. Dense vegetation, towering limestone bluffs overlooking LaRue swamp; rare and abundant wildlife; campgrounds and picnic areas nearby; in the Shawnee National Forest. Open year-round. Grand Tower, off State Route 3.

Lincoln Memorial Gardens and Nature Center. A living memorial to Lincoln, featuring native Illinois landscape familiar to Lincoln; plant and animal life displays; crafts. Open year-round. Many other Lincoln attractions nearby. Springfield, off Interstate 55 on east side of Lake Springfield.

Little Grand Canyon. A natural wonder called the Grand Canyon of Illinois and the Little Grand Canyon; walls tower as high as 200 feet above canyon floor in spots. Open year-round. Murphysboro, south off State Route 127.

Little Theater on the Square. Thirteen major theater productions presented during season; children's theater. Season: April through October. Sullivan, on State Route 121.

Mary's River Covered Bridge. Built in 1854, this picturesque bridge was originally part of the toll road link between the communities of Chester and Bremen. Off State Route 150.

Morton Arboretum. Extensive collection of trees, shrubs and vines from all over the world, including the rare Ginkgo tree; five trails. Open year-round, daily, 8 a.m. to sunset. Lisle, on State Route 53.

Our Lady of Snows. Beautiful national shrine featuring picturesque landscaping, Lourdes Grotto, Annunciation Garden, Angelus Bells, reflecting pools, outdoor altar of black marble; gift shop, restaurant. Christmas is especially festive, as the shrine is lit up in commemoration of the birth of Jesus. Open year-round, daily. Belleville, off US-route 460.

Pomona Natural Bridge. One of southern Illinois' natural wonders, the bridge measures 90 feet in length, six feet wide, and nine feet thick at the narrowest point in the arch. Murphysboro, south off State Route 127.

Ripley's Believe-It-Or-Not! Museum. Galleries filled with curiosities and oddities collected from more than 200 countries around the world. Open year-round, daily, noon to midnight. Chicago, North Street and Lake Shore Drive.

Rockome Gardens. In the heart of Illinois' Amish settlement, Rockome Gardens features an extensive collection of rocks that have been fashioned into countless designs; rock shop, basket shop, Indian shop and museum. Open year-round. Arcola, off Interstate 57.

Rockton's Main Street. Main street of community of Rockton restored in the period of the early 1900s; brightly colored buildings, old-fashioned balconies. Rockton, on State Route 75.

Sinnisippi Sunken Gardens. Brilliant floral displays; roses, annuals and perennials; special shows, November, December and at Easter. Open year-round, daily, 9 a.m. to 5 p.m. Free. Rockford, east on State Route 51.

Spoon River Arts Ark. Displays of local arts and crafts in quaint old church. Open year-round. Ellisville, off State Route 9.

Tinker Swiss Cottage. A reproduction of a Swiss chalet constructed in the late 1800s on a limestone cliff along Kent Creek; the realization of the dream of Robert Hall Tinker. Open year-round, Wednesday, Thursday, Saturday and Sunday, 2 p.m. to 4 p.m. Kent, off State Route 73 and US-20, 411 Kent Street.

Thompson Mill Covered Bridge. Picturesque old bridge spanning the Kaskaskia River. Shelbyville, 10 miles south off State Route 16.

Vinegar Hill Lead Mine. The only lead mine approved by the Bureau of Mines for public tours. In the mid-1850s, the mine was producing at its height, making the region the lead mining capital of the world. Open year-round, daily, 9 a.m. to 5 p.m. Galena, six miles north on State Route 84.

Illinois State Forests

Park	Location	CAMPING	PICNICKING	CONCESSIONS	SWIMMING	HIKING	BOATING	FISHING	HUNTING	WINTER SPORTS
Argyle Lake	*Colchester. Off US-136.*	•	•	•		•	•	•	•	
Beaver Dam	*Plainview. Off State Route 4 and 108.*	•	•	•			•	•		
Cahokia Mounds	*East St. Louis. Off Interstate 55 and Interstate 64.*	•	•	•						
Cave-In-Rock	*Cave-In-Rock. Off State Route 1.*	•	•	•			•	•		
Chain O'Lakes	*Spring Grove. Off State Route 59 and US-12.*	•	•	•	•	•	•	•	•	
Delabar	*Oquawka. Off US-34.*	•	•	•			•	•		
Dixon Springs	*Brownfield. Off State Route 145.*	•	•	•						
Eagle Creek	*Findlay. Off State Route 16.*	•	•	•			•	•		
Eldon Hazlet	*Carlyle. Off State Route 127.*	•	•				•	•		
Ferne Clyffe	*Goreville. Off Interstate 57.*	•	•			•		•		
Fort Massac	*Metropolis. Off State Route 145.*	•	•				•	•		
Fox Ridge	*Charleston. Off State Route 130.*	•	•	•			•	•		
Frank Holten	*East St. Louis. Off Interstate 64.*	•	•				•	•		
Giant City	*Makanda. Off US-51.*	•	•	•		•	•	•	•	
Illini	*Marseilles. Off State Route 23.*	•	•	•			•	•		
Illinois Beach	*Zion. Off US-294.*	•	•	•	•			•		
Johnson Sauk Trail	*Kewanee. Off State Route 78.*	•	•	•		•	•	•		
Jubilee College	*Brimfield. Off US-74.*	•	•	•						
Kankakee River	*Bourbonais. Off Interstate 57.*	•	•	•			•	•		
Kickapoo	*Oakwood. Off Interstate 74.*	•	•	•		•	•	•	•	
Lake Le-Aqua-Na	*Lena. Off State Route 73.*	•	•	•			•	•		
Lake Murphysboro	*Off State Route 13 and 127.*	•	•	•			•	•		
Lincoln Trail	*Off State Route 1.*	•	•	•			•	•		
Mississippi Palisades	*Savanna. Off State Route 84.*	•	•			•	•	•		
Morrison-Rockwood	*Morrison. Off State Route 78.*	•	•	•			•	•		
Pere Marquette	*Grafton. Off State Route 100.*	•	•	•		•	•	•	•	
Prophetstown	*Morrison. Off State Route 78.*	•	•				•	•		
Pyramid	*Pinckneyville. Off State Routes 13 and 127.*	•	•			•	•	•	•	
Ramsey Lake	*Ramsey. Off US-51.*	•	•	•		•	•	•	•	
Red Hills	*Sumner. Off US-50.*	•	•	•		•	•	•	•	
Rock Cut	*Caledonia. Off US-90.*	•	•	•		•	•	•		
Sam Parr	*Newton. Off State Route 130.*	•	•			•	•	•		
Sangchris Lake	*Rochester. Off State Route 29.*	•	•				•	•		
Siloam Springs	*Clayton. Off State Route 104.*	•	•	•			•	•		
Silver Springs	*Yorkville. Off State Route 47.*		•	•			•	•		
Starved Rock	*Utica. Off Interstate 80.*	•	•	•			•	•		
Stephen A. Forbes	*Kinmundy. Off US-50.*	•	•	•		•	•	•	•	
Walnut Point	*Oakland. Off State Route 133.*	•	•	•			•	•		
Wayne Fitzgerrell	*Benton. Off Interstate 57.*	•	•			•	•	•	•	
White Pines Forest	*Mt. Morris. Off State Route 64.*	•	•	•		•		•		
Wolf Creek	*Findlay. Off State Route 32.*	•	•				•	•		

Illinois State Parks

Forest	Location	CAMPING	PICNICKING	CONCESSIONS	SWIMMING	HIKING	BOATING	FISHING	HUNTING	WINTER SPORTS
Big River	*Keithsburg. Off US-67.*	•	•				•	•	•	
Hidden Springs	*Strasburg. Off State Route 32.*	•	•			•			•	
Sand Ridge	*Forest City. Off US-136.*	•	•			•			•	
Trail of Tears	*Jonesboro. Off State Route 146.*	•	•			•			•	

For more information on Illinois state parks and forests, contact: *Department of Conservation, 405 East Washington, Springfield, Illinois 62706, (217) 782-3340.*

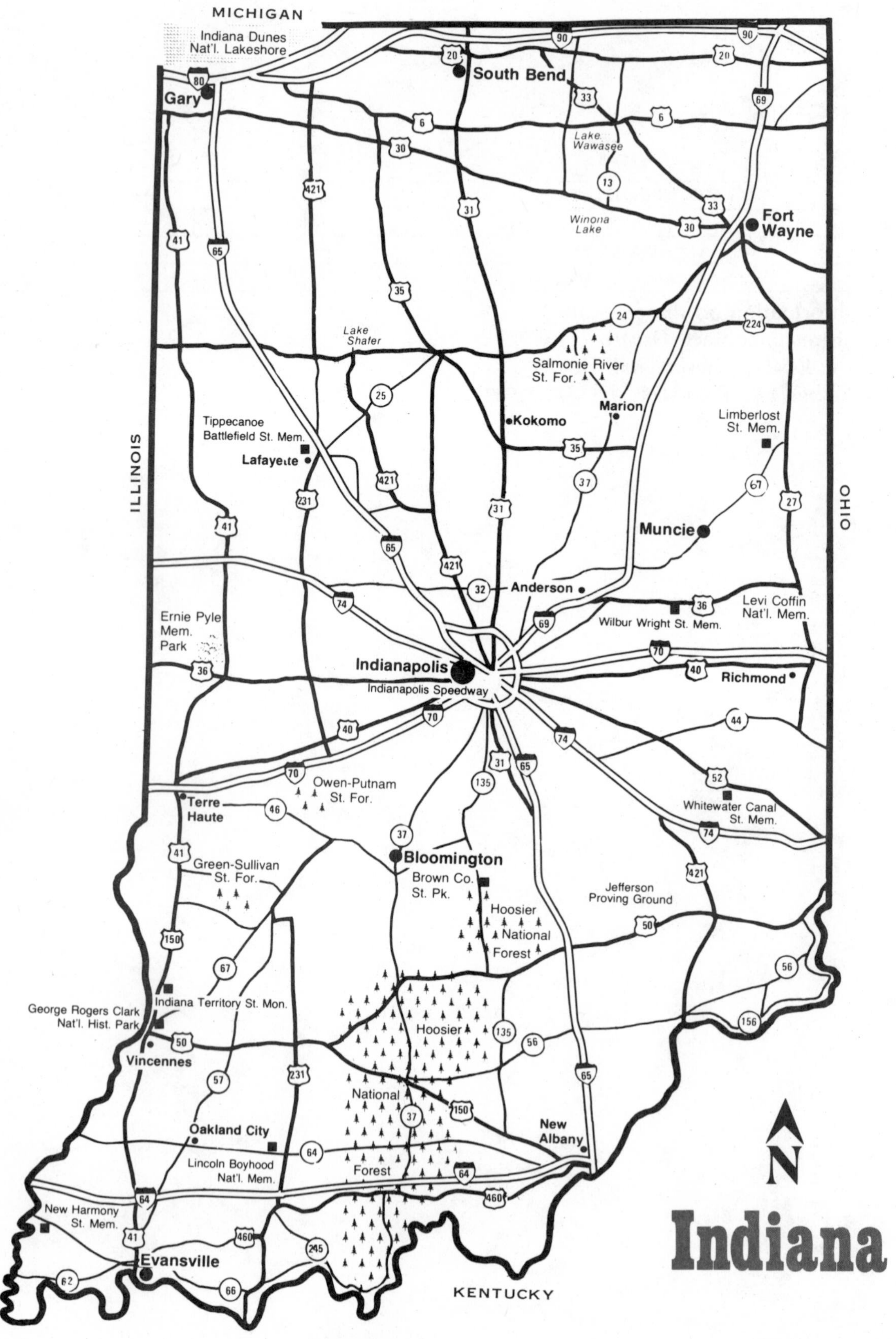

Map not to exact scale.

Indiana

Indiana is no doubt best known for its annual Memorial Day event, the Indianapolis 500; but the state's offerings go far beyond that single attraction. Indiana has something for just about everybody, at any time of year. In the north, there are hundreds of clear, picturesque lakes, the white sandy beaches and dunes that line Lake Michigan's shores and the fascinating people of Indiana's Amish country. The state's central region features the Old National Road, a pioneer highway now lined with antique shops. And in the south you'll find rolling hills, forests, caves and charming river towns. Indiana is a state blessed with a remarkable diversity — a diversity made even more remarkable by the fact that it is the smallest state west of the Alleghenies.

Indiana was originally a part of the colonial empire of France, but in 1763 the British gained control through the Treaty of Paris. The British, in turn, lost control of the region in 1783, when the Definitive Treaty of Peace made the Mississippi River the western boundary of the United States. Settlers came slowly to the region, primarily because of hostile Indians; but after Benjamin Harrison won the Battle of Tippecanoe in 1811, and defeated a combined British and Indian force in 1812, colonization began in earnest. By 1815, the territory had a population of more than 60,000, and Indiana was admitted as a state the following year.

Indiana has long been called the "Hoosier State," yet nobody seems to be able to agree on just how it got its nickname. One of the more plausible stories has it that the name can be credited to Samuel Hoosier, a contractor on the

Full name: State of Indiana
Origin of name: Denoted that state was the domain of Indians.
Motto: The Crossroads of America
Nickname: Hoosier State
Capital: Indianapolis
Statehood: December 11, 1816, 19th state.
Population: 5,330,000 (ranks 12th).
Major Cities: Indianapolis (714,878), Fort Wayne (185,299), Gary (167,546).
Bird: Cardinal
Flower: Peony
Tree: Tulip

Average daily temperature by month

	Northern	Southern
Jan.	32.9 to 15.8	40.0 to 20.1
Feb.	37.1 to 19.2	43.8 to 22.3
Mar.	47.1 to 27.3	52.7 to 30.0
Apr.	62.3 to 38.4	66.9 to 41.8
May	73.5 to 48.0	76.4 to 50.1
Jun.	83.4 to 57.2	84.6 to 59.4
Jul.	86.1 to 60.9	87.8 to 63.1
Aug.	84.6 to 58.8	87.0 to 60.7
Sept.	78.4 to 51.8	81.1 to 53.7
Oct.	66.4 to 41.7	70.2 to 41.6
Nov.	49.5 to 31.1	54.5 to 32.1
Dec.	37.1 to 21.7	43.5 to 24.4
Year	61.5 to 39.3	65.7 to 41.6

Ohio Falls Canal at Louisville, Kentucky, in 1826. Sam, it is said, preferred to hire his men from the Indiana side of the Ohio River; "Hoosier's men" soon was shortened to "Hoosiers," and the name later became a reference for the whole state. Today, Indiana's division of tourism invites you to enjoy a "Happy Hoosier Holiday," taking in such attractions as the Conner Prairie Settlement near

Noblesville, where people in authentic pioneer attire recreate the 1820s of Hoosier settlers; the Amish country of the north; the Tippecanoe Battlefield near Lafayette; the Wabash Valley Festival at Terre Haute. For the angler, some of the best fishing to be found anywhere is in the wooded lakes of the northeast.

Elkhart, Indiana, is, of course, known to most RVers as the center of production of many RV manufacturers, but other important industries include electronic equipment, chemicals, plastics, rubber, food and food products. From Indiana's rich farmlands come corn, soybeans, hogs, beef cattle and millions of turkeys.

State Offices

Tourism
Tourism Development Division
Indiana Department of Commerce
336 Statehouse
Indianapolis, Indiana 46204
(317) 633-5737

State Police
Department of Public Safety
100 North Senate Avenue
Indianapolis, Indiana 46204
(317) 633-5271

Radio Stations

Indianapolis
WNAP 93.1 (FM)
WIBC 1070 (AM)

Ft. Wayne
WOWO 1190 (AM)
WPTH 95.1 (FM)

Indiana Points of Interest and Attractions

Amish Acres. A historical farm where Amish folk adhere to the lifestyle and customs of their forefathers, who first settled here in 1850; lecture tour of 12-room Amish house; demonstration of pioneer skills; restaurant. Open year-round; May through October, Monday to Saturday, 9 a.m. to 9 p.m.; remainder of year, Saturday and Sunday, 11 a.m. to 4 p.m. Nappanee, one mile west on US-6.

Amishville. Tour an authentic Amish home and see the smoke house and old-fashioned garden; buggy rides; restaurant; campground. Open year-round, daily; Monday to Saturday 9 a.m. to 5 p.m.; Sunday, 11 a.m. to 5 p.m. Free. Berne, three miles south off US-27.

Avalon Grotto. An example of Frank Lloyd Wright's Prairie School style. South Bend, 715 West Washington Street.

Ball State University Planetarium. Astronomical shows presented in the 77-seat "sky chamber." Open September 20 through May 16; programs, 2:30 p.m. and 7:30 p.m. Saturday and Sunday. Free. Muncie, off State Route 32.

Benholzer Winecellars. Tours of wine cellar, processing center, vineyards, tasting room and art gallery; 72-acre site with 100-year-old peg and beam barn, picnic area. Open year-round, Monday to Saturday, 11 a.m. to 5 p.m. Free. Hesston, three miles east on County Road 1000 north.

Bonneyville Mill. Built in 1832, the only operating horizontal grist mill in Indiana; rich natural setting with hiking, fishing, picnicking. Open year-round, Monday to Friday. Free. Bristol 2½ miles east on County Road 131.

Boone Caverns. Spectacular subterranean world of magnificent formations, falls, rivers and world's largest travertine dam formation. Squire Boone, Daniel's brother, discovered the cave in 1790 and is buried inside. Open year-round, daily, 9 a.m. to 5 p.m. Corydon, 10 miles south on State Route 135.

Canal House. Built in 1842, this authentically restored structure served as a clearing house for the Whitewater Canal; listed on the National Register of Historic Places. Open year-round, Saturday and Sunday, 1 p.m. to 8 p.m. Connersville, 11 East Fourth Street.

Cannelton Locks and Dam. An overlook atop the locks and dam provides a vantage point for visitors to see huge barges and towboats being raised and lowered through the locks. Cannelton, three miles east on State Route 66.

Cataract Falls. Indiana's largest natural waterfall, in a scenic setting at the southern end of 1,500-acre Cataract Lake. Cloverdale, on State Route 42.

Christy Woods Arboretum and Wheeler Orchid Collection. Extensive collection of roses, woody plants and native and exotic wildflowers serving as an outdoor laboratory for Ball State University zoology and botany students. Muncie, off State Route 32, at university.

Clay City Pottery. Established in 1885 and operated continuously by members of the same family; the state's only stoneware pottery. Open year-round, Monday to Friday, 8 a.m. to 5 p.m., Saturday, 8 a.m. to 3 p.m. Free. Clay City, one block west of State Route 157.

Clegg Memorial Garden. Twenty-acre area situated along the wooded hilltops, glacier-made ridges and ravines that border Wildcat Creek. Open year-round, daily, 10 a.m. to sunset. Free. Lafayette, 1782 North County Road at 400 East.

Covered Bridge at Longwood. Built in 1884, this bridge is 97 feet long, 14 feet wide, and 12 feet, 11 inches high; it's the only remaining covered bridge in Fayette County. Connersville, on County Road 75.

Deam Oak. Preserved in the center of a small track of state-owned land, this rare hybrid oak stands as a memorial to its discoverer, Dr. Charles Deam, nationally known forester and botanist. Open year-round, daily. Free. Bluffton, two miles north on State Route 11.

Dugger Coal Mine. Features the world's second-largest dragline coal shovel, capable of scooping up 215 tons of earth at one time; electric power that runs the shovel could supply a town of 20,000 residents. Sullivan, 10 miles east on State Route 54.

Golden Rain Tree Winery. Small winery designed as a Swiss chalet; tasting room and underground wine cellar. Open year-round, Monday to Thursday, 11 a.m. to 10 p.m.; Friday and Saturday, 11 a.m. to 11 p.m. Free. Evansville, eight miles northwest on Winery Road.

Goshen Mill Race and Dam. A shady retreat featuring fishing in the Elkhart River and scenic hiking trails. Goshen, off State Route 15.

Martha A. Graham Sidewheel Ferryboat. The last of its kind on the Ohio River, this ferry runs continuously from Indiana to Kentucky. Open year-round, daily, 6 a.m. to 6 p.m. Vevay, at riverfront.

Mary Gray Bird Sanctuary. A restful scenic area of 654 wooded acres with marked foot trails, ponds, shelter house, picnic facilities, museum and library; owned by Indiana Audubon Society. Open year-round, daily, sunrise to sunset. Connersville, on outskirts at intersection of County Roads 350 and 425.

Grissom Air Force Base. An important link in the nation's air defense system, home of the 305th Air Refueling Wing of the Strategic Air Command and the 434th Tactical Fighter Wing; guided tours by prior arrangement. Open year-round. Free. Peru, eight miles south on US-31. (317) 689-2211.

Hesston Gardens. Charming garden created by Father Joseph Sokolowski over the span of 50 years; antiques for sale; special collection of icons. Open April through November, daily, 9 a.m. to 5 p.m.

Donations accepted. LaPorte, 1000 North at 215 East.

International Friendship Gardens. Dedicated to world peace and harmony, this garden features more than 200 floral specimens donated by foreign countries and planted in the garden styles of their nationality. Operettas and concerts in outdoor theater during summer months. Open year-round, daily, 9 a.m. to sunset. Michigan City, off US-12.

Kimball Piano and Organ Company. Tours of famous piano and organ manufacturing facility. Open year-round, Monday to Friday; tours at 1:30 p.m. (by appointment). French Lick, on the Boulevard. (812) 936-4522.

Oliver Winery. Indiana's oldest and largest winery; tasting and sales, picnic area. Open year-round, Monday to Saturday, 11 a.m. to 6 p.m. Free. Bloomington, seven miles north on State Route 37.

Possom Trot Vineyards and Winecellar. Vineyards and wine cellar tucked in the scenic hills and wooded countryside of Brown County; wine-tasting, picnicking. Open March through December, Monday to Saturday, 10 a.m. to 8 p.m. Free. Unionville, on Possum Trot Road.

Pretzel Factory. Hand-twisted pretzels in the tradition of the founder, Casper Gloor, a master baker from Switzerland. Open year-round, Monday to Friday, 8 a.m. to 3 p.m. Free. Tell City, 911 Fulton Street.

Purdue University. Noted for outstanding schools of agriculture and engineering, Purdue has grown from its early start as a Land Grant College in 1869 to an enrollment of more than 30,000. Information and maps available in the east front of the Memorial Union. Open year-round, daily. Free. West Lafayette, State and South Grant Streets.

Rum Village Nature Center. Natural history exhibits, nature walks, programs, 2½ miles of hiking trails. Open year-round, Sunday to Friday, 10 a.m. to 5 p.m. Free. South Bend, 112 South Lafayette Boulevard.

Sampler. Furniture crafting from southern Indiana cherry wood, narrated slide presentation, showroom. Open year-round, daily; Monday to Saturday, 9 a.m. to 5 p.m.; Sunday, 1 p.m. to 5 p.m. Free. Homer, one block north of State Route 44.

Santa Claus Land. Santa Claus is present year-round at this park with a Christmas theme; buildings of Bavarian design, historical exhibits, dolls, petting zoo, rides. Open year-round, daily. Santa Claus, seven miles south of State Route 162 off Interstate 64, on State Route 245.

Scenic Drive. Approximately 10 homes and buildings along this tree-shaded drive provide visitors with an opportunity to view examples of Greek Revival, Federal and Victorian architecture. Hagerstown, State Route 38 to stoplight, turn right on Sycamore Street for six blocks, west on Main Street, south on Perry Street five blocks to Main Street.

Schenley Distillers. Stop and observe the operations of a complete liquor distillery. Open year-round, Monday to Friday, 9 a.m. to 2:30 p.m. Free. Greendale, off US-50, on Mary Street.

Terre Haute Action Track. Site each May of the world's richest sprint car race, the "Tony Hulman Classic." Open year-round, daily, 7 p.m. to 4 p.m. Terre Haute, 817 Wabash Avenue, on Vigo County Fairgrounds.

Tobacco Auctions. The excitement and color of true-to-life barter sessions at some of the country's largest tobacco auctions; two million pounds of tobacco in each warehouse; $100,000 worth sold in an hour. Open November through April, Monday to Thursday, 9:30 a.m. to 2 p.m. Free. Madison, Hughes Tobacco Auction, Wilson Avenue; Maddox Tobacco Auctions, West and Vaugh Streets.

University of Notre Dame. View the Golden Dome, stroll the 1,700-acre campus, see the Stepan Center geodesic dome, and the 13-story marble mosaic facade of the library. Office hours are year-round, Monday to Friday, 8 a.m. to noon and 1 p.m. to 5 p.m. Free. South Bend, north on US-31 and 33 to Angela Boulevard.

Whitewater Valley Railroad. Travel over 30 miles of scenic Hoosier countryside on vintage 1920-30's steam railway equipment; longest steam railroad in the region. Open May through October; departures Saturday and Sunday at 12:01 p.m. Connersville, on State Route 121.

Wyandotte Caves. Wyandotte Cave has the largest underground room and underground mountain of any known cave in the world, and approximately 25 miles of discovered passages. In prehistoric times, the cave was used by Indians for shelter and as a burial site. Open year-round, daily, 8:45 a.m. to 3:45 p.m. Leavenworth, on State Route 62.

Zimmerman Art Glass Company. Handcrafted paperweights, vases, perfume bottles and other individually-blown glass novelties and art objects. Open year-round, Monday, Thursday, Friday and Saturday, 8 a.m. to 2 p.m.; Sunday, 9 a.m. to 3 p.m. Corydon, East Beech Street.

Highlight

Indianapolis Motor Speedway

The famous Indianapolis Motor Speedway is a 2½-mile rectangular racetrack built on 559 acres of ground located seven miles northwest of the center of the Hoosier capital. It has been the scene of the International 500-mile automobile races since 1911.

The Speedway was built in 1909 when four prominent Indianapolis businessmen — Carl G. Fisher, James A. Allison, Arthur C. Newby and Frank H. Wheeler — pooled their ideas and resources to create a "great outdoor laboratory" for the young automotive industry.

During its early years, particularly, the track gained deserved recognition as an important test course and proving grounds for such innovations as high compression engines, four-wheel brakes, experimental fuels and lubricants, front-wheel-drive and four-wheel-drive systems, low pressure tires, superchargers and hydraulic shock absorbers.

In more recent times, following the creation of private test facilities by most automobile manufacturers, the annual 500-mile events have earned a permanent place on the international

Built in 1909, the famed Indianapolis Motor Speedway draws thousands of spectators each year for the 500-mile race held on Memorial Day. The Indy Hall of Fame Museum features displays of race cars and driver memorabilia.

sports calendar largely by virtue of their highly competitive nature. In quest of victory, however, members of the racing fraternity continue to make important contributions each year to the development of spark plugs, piston rings, turbochargers, suspension systems and aerodynamic designs which have increased the safety, performance and comfort qualities of modern passenger cars.

Straightaways 50 Feet Wide

The original course in 1909, a mixture of crushed stone and tar, was designed to fit into an area one mile long and a half-mile wide, with four identical quarter-mile turns.

Two long straightaways measuring five-eighths of a mile each, and two short straightaways, one-eighth of a mile each, completed the circuit. All four straightaways were built 50 feet wide with the track broadening to 60 feet midway through each of the turns, which were banked in identical manner at nine degrees and 12 minutes.

Balloon and motorcycle contests were sponsored by the management while the finishing touches were being made to the facilities for the inaugural three-day program of auto races starting August 19.

Several drivers were clocked at slightly better than 70 miles an hour for a complete lap in competition. Barney Oldfield claimed a new world record for one mile on a closed course by averaging 83.2 miles an hour for that distance on a segment of the course which included part of the northwest turn and the main stretch.

With as many as 17 cars participating in some of the longer races, however, the track began to disintegrate. Conditions finally became so hazardous that the final day's 300-mile feature attraction was halted at 235 miles by officials of the American Automobile Association in charge of the proceedings, causing Fisher and his associates to make plans immediately to resurface the course with 3,200,000 paving bricks grouted in cement.

Work was completed in time for the scheduling of several short-distance events on December 18, but sub-freezing weather caused many entrants to withdraw. Additional race programs were held on the new course during the Memorial Day, Independence Day and Labor Day weekends of 1910 with attendance diminishing as the season progressed.

Then, after consulting with prominent drivers and interested automobile manufacturers, the decision was made to concentrate on a single major attraction each year. May 30, 1911, was chosen as the date for the first event and the distance was set at 500 miles because a contest of that length would give the spectators approximately the same amount of track action as offered during the six or seven hours required for one of the 1910 programs.

Harroun Wins First "500"

Prize money of $25,000 was posted by the speedway management and 40 entrants accepted the challenge, most of them participating as members of factory teams. Ray Harroun, driving "according to plan" on the basis of experience gained in the 1910 races on the brick surface, won at the wheel of a six-cylinder Marmon Wasp in six hours, 42 minutes and eight seconds for an average speed of 74.59 miles an hour. He and Cyrus Patschke, his replacement as driver of the Marmon for several laps near the halfway point of the event, circled the course steadily at approximately 75.5 miles an hour to conserve their tires.

Since then the prize money has increased steadily to an annual purse of more than $1 million for each of the last nine events.

Improved equipment, meanwhile, has enabled the world's outstanding drivers to set new records annually. The

winners included Bill Holland at 121.327 miles an hour in 1949, Bill Vukovich at 130.840 in 1954. Rodger Ward at 140.293 in 1962, Jim Clark of Scotland at 150.686 in 1965 and Mark Donohue at 162.962 in 1972. These "milestones" were reached despite time lost in the pits for refueling and changing tires and the necessity of running at reduced speed for brief intervals because of hazardous conditions on the course. Tom Sneva holds the one-lap and four-lap records of 203.620 and 202.156, respectively, set during the 1978 official time trials to determine starting positions.

Mauri Rose and A.J. Foyt, Jr., became three-time winners after World War II and Foyt scored an unprecedented fourth victory in 1977. Al Unser became another three-time winner in 1978.

Although the annual "500" is the only race held at the Indianapolis Motor Speedway, it is a full-time project for participants and management alike. Entries are accepted from early January until April 15, and more than 70 usually are received each year.

The Speedway's Hall of Fame

The magnificent new Hall of Fame building, replacing the smaller structure built in 1956, is located inside the track between the No. 1 and No. 2 turns. It is one of the nation's outstanding tourist attractions with a huge display area on the main floor to show approximately 60 famous cars simultaneously, including those which won 22 of the annual Indianapolis 500-mile events.

Four of them were two-time winners: The Boyle Maserati (Wilbur Shaw, 1939-40), the Blue Crown Spark Plug Special (Mauri Rose, 1947-48), the Fuel Injection Special (Bill Vukovich, 1953-54), and the Belond Special (Sam Hanks in 1957 and Jimmy Bryan in 1958).

Other winning cars on display are Ray Harroun's 1911 Marmon Wasp, Joe Dawson's 1912 National, Rene Thomas' 1914 Delage, the Duesenberg that Jimmy Murphy drove to victory in the 1921 French Grand Prix before winning the 1922 Indianapolis race in the same car with a Miller engine, Louis Meyer's 1928 Miller Special, Fred Frame's 1932 Miller-Hartz Special, George Robson's 1946 Thorne Engineering Special. Lee Wallard's 1951 Belanger Special, Bob Sweikert's 1955 John Zink Special, A.J. Foyt's 1961 Bowes Seal Fast Special, Rodger Ward's 1962 Leader Card 500 Roadster, Parnelli Jones' 1963 Agajanian Willard Battery Special, and Bobby Unser's 1968 Rislone Special.

One section of the display area also is devoted to an impressive collection of classic and antique passenger cars.

The museum is open daily throughout the year, except Christmas Day, from 9 a.m. until 5 p.m. Admission is $1 for adults with no charge for visitors under 16 years of age.

Buses are available for a ride around the track at a price of 50 cents, whenever the course is not being used for competition or test purposes. Another special attraction is the impressive Louis Chevrolet Memorial near the southwest corner of the museum.

Indiana State Parks

Park	Location	CAMPING	PICNICKING	CONCESSIONS	SWIMMING	HIKING	BOATING	FISHING	HUNTING	WINTER SPORTS
Bass Lake	*Bass Lake. On State Route 10.*	•	•		•	•	•	•		
Brown County	*Nashville. Off State Routes 135 and 46.*	•	•		•	•	•	•		
Chain O'Lakes	*Albion. On State Route 9.*	•	•	•	•	•	•	•		
Clifty Falls	*Madison. Off State Routes 107 and 56.*	•	•	•	•	•	•	•		
Indiana Dunes	*Chesterton. On US-12 and State Route 49.*	•	•	•	•	•	•	•		
Harmonie	*New Harmony. Off State Route 69.*	•	•	•	•	•	•	•		
Lincoln	*Lincoln City. Off State Route 162.*	•	•	•	•	•	•	•		
McCormick's Creek	*Spencer. Off State Route 46.*	•	•	•	•	•	•	•		
Mounds	*Anderson. Off Interstate 69.*	•	•	•	•	•	•	•		
Pokagon	*Angola. Off Interstate 69, on US-27.*	•	•	•	•	•	•	•		
Quabache	*Vera Cruz. On State Route 124.*	•	•	•		•	•	•		
Shades	*Waveland. Off State Route 234.*	•	•	•	•	•	•	•		
Shakamak	*Jasonville. Off State Routes 48 and 159.*	•	•	•	•	•	•	•		
Spring Mill	*Mitchell. On State Route 69.*	•	•	•	•	•	•	•		
Tippecanoe River	*Winamac. On US-35.*	•	•	•		•	•	•		
Turkey Run	*Marshall. Off State Route 47.*	•	•	•	•	•	•	•		
Versailles	*Versailles. On US-50.*	•	•	•	•	•	•	•		
Whitewater	*Liberty. On State Route 101.*	•	•	•	•	•	•	•		

Indiana State Forests

Forest	Location	CAMPING	PICNICKING	CONCESSIONS	SWIMMING	HIKING	BOATING	FISHING	HUNTING	WINTER SPORTS
Clark	*Scottsburg. Off US-31.*	•	•			•	•	•	•	
Ferdinand	*Jasper. On State Route 264.*									
Greene-Sullivan	*Pleasantville. On State Route 159.*	•	•			•	•	•	•	
Harrison-Crawford	*Leavenworth. Off US-460.*	•	•			•	•	•	•	
Jackson-Washington	*Brownstone. On State Route 250.*	•	•			•	•	•	•	
Martin	*Shoals. On US-50.*	•	•			•	•	•	•	
Morgan Monroe	*Martinsville. Off State Route 37.*	•	•			•	•	•	•	
Owen-Putnam	*Spencer. Off US-231.*	•	•			•	•	•	•	
Pike	*Petersburg. On State Route 364.*	•	•			•	•	•	•	
Salamonie River	*Largo. Off State Route 524.*	•	•			•	•	•	•	
Yellowwood	*Nashville. Off State Route 46.*	•	•			•	•	•	•	

For more information on Indiana state parks and forests, contact: *Indiana Department of Natural Resources, 615 State Office Building, Indianapolis, Indiana 46204, (317) 633-4294.*

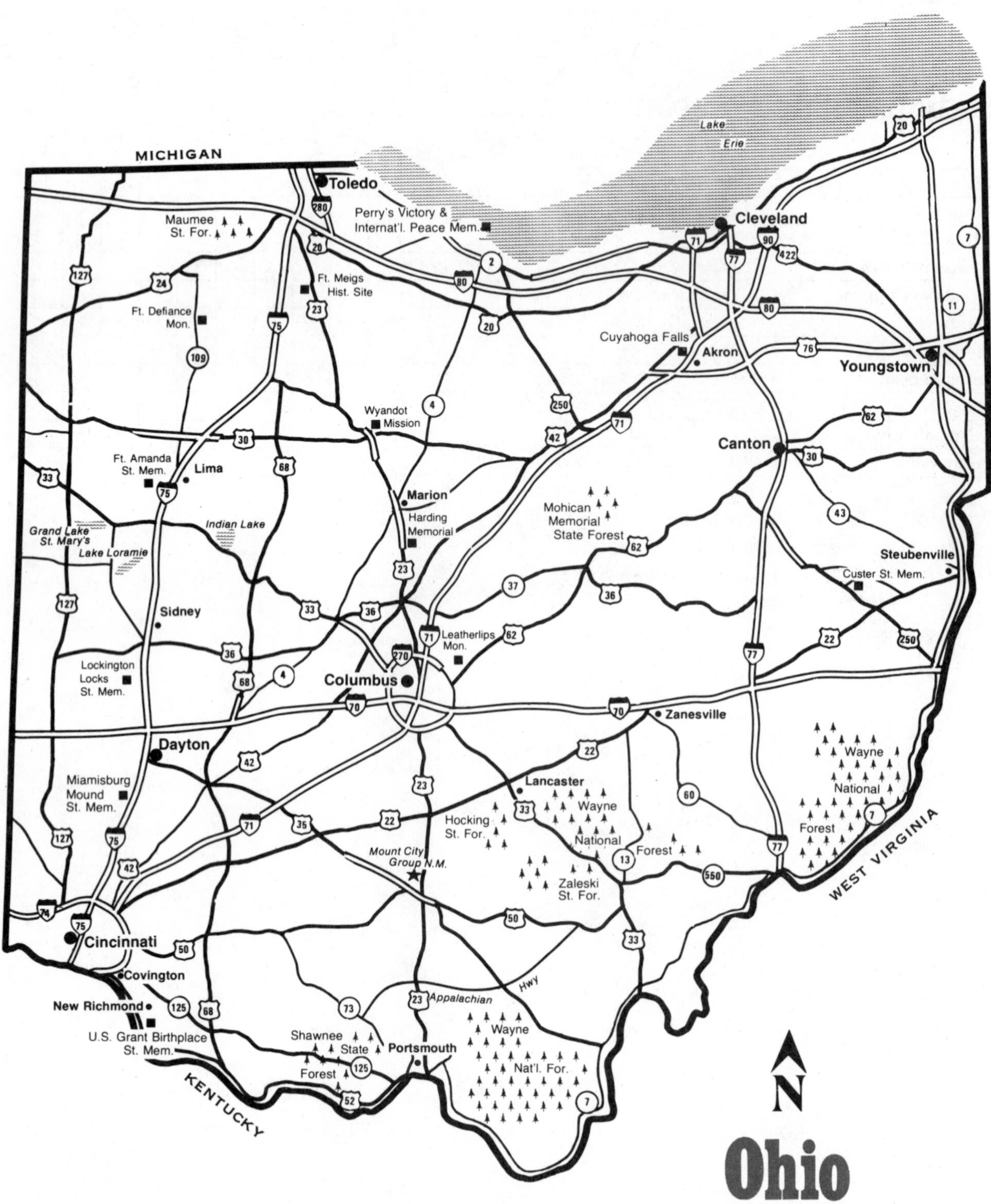

Map not to exact scale.

Ohio

By virtue of its proximity to important markets and its abundant natural resources, Ohio has grown to be the third-ranking industrial state in the nation. More than factories, though, Ohio has a rich history that stretches from prehistoric Indian mound builders to Johnny Appleseed and the Wright Brothers; it has the scenic beauty of the Wayne National Forest and the picturesque shoreline of Lake Erie; and it has the big-city attractions of Cleveland, Columbus and Cincinnati.

Surprisingly enough, Ohio has early roots in New England, as the first permanent white settlement was founded at Marietta in 1788 by a New Englander, General Rufus Putnam. These early settlers were plagued by fierce Indian resistance until 1794, when General "Mad Anthony" Wayne crushed the forces of Indian leader Little Turtle in the Battle of Fallen Timbers, near the present city of Toledo. In 1802, the western boundaries of the Ohio territory were set and a convention of 35 delegates drew up a constitution that led to Ohio's entry as a state on February 19, 1803. A spawning ground for the Abolitionist Movement prior to the Civil War, and the site of heavy participation in the Underground Railroad, Ohio contributed mightily to the Union cause and lost some 25,000 sons in battle.

The diversity of the "Buckeye State" is amazing. You can trace its New England roots in Marietta, at the Campus Martius Museum and the Putnam House; in the valleys around Sugarcreek, you can enjoy the old-world delights of the Amish settlements; or you can learn about Ohio's Swiss heritage at the Swiss Festival, also at Sugarcreek. For outdoor fun, stop for a few days at one of the excellent state parks, rent a canoe and glide down the waters of the Mohican River, or fish for muskies in Clear Fork Reservoir. There are also a number of unique attractions that you won't want to miss — so take a tour of the Smuckers factory at Orrville, where

Full name: State of Ohio
Origin of name: From Iroquois name meaning "Great."
Motto: With God, All Things Are Possible
Nickname: Buckeye State
Capital: Columbus
Statehood: March 1, 1803, 17th state.
Population: 10,701,000 (ranks sixth)
Major Cities: Cleveland (638,793), Columbus (535,610), Cincinnati (412,564).
Bird: Cardinal
Flower: Scarlet carnation
Tree: Buckeye

Average daily temperatures by month

	Northwestern	Southwestern
Jan.	33.7 to 17.5	41.2 to 21.2
Feb.	36.0 to 18.7	44.4 to 23.2
Mar.	45.0 to 26.4	53.0 to 30.7
Apr.	59.9 to 37.8	66.1 to 40.7
May	70.0 to 47.0	75.6 to 49.9
Jun.	78.5 to 56.0	83.8 to 58.6
Jul.	82.1 to 60.2	87.6 to 62.9
Aug.	80.8 to 58.5	86.8 to 61.1
Sept.	74.7 to 52.9	81.0 to 54.3
Oct.	63.9 to 42.7	70.2 to 42.8
Nov.	49.1 to 32.4	55.3 to 32.7
Dec.	37.3 to 22.4	44.5 to 25.2
Year	59.3 to 39.4	65.8 to 41.9

some of the country's tastiest jams and jellies are produced; explore the fantasy land of Kings Island amusement park; take in the Honey Festival at Lebanon; try a piece of the world's largest pumpkin pie at the Circleville Pumpkin Show . . . in Ohio, the list is almost endless.

With a foundation laid by Harvey Firestone, Akron now leads the world in the production of rubber and plastic products; Dayton is a leading center for the production of business machines; and Youngstown is a major producer of steel. The manufacture of chemicals, glass products, electronic equipment and food products are also important to Ohio's economy, as are agriculture, mining (coal, natural gas, oil) and the $3 billion-a-year tourist industry.

State Offices

Tourism
Office of Travel and Tourism
PO Box 1001
Columbus, Ohio 43216
(614) 466-8844

State Police
Department of Public Safety
Columbus, Ohio 43205
(614) 466-2660

Radio Stations

Akron
WSLR 1350 (AM)
Cincinnati
WCKY 1530 (AM)
Cleveland
WZZP 106.5 (FM)
WGAR 1220 (AM)
Columbus
WNCI 97.9 (FM)
WTVN 610 (AM)
Dayton
WONE 980 (AM)

Ohio Points of Interest and Attractions

Arawanna II. See the port of Toledo and the Maumee River aboard this popular cruise boat. Season: spring to fall. Toledo, off Interstate 280.

Black Swamp Farm. A farm operated in the manner of the early 19th century; name refers to the fact that the area of the state once had such poor drainage that it could not be farmed. Open year-round. Auglaize, off State Route 307.

Blue Bird Special. This excursion train will take you through the lush forests of northwestern Ohio and on a spectacular ride over the bridge at Grand Rapids. Season: spring through fall. Toledo, south at Waterville Station, off State Route 65.

Carillon Park. Come fly a kite and listen to the magnificent 41-bell Deeds Carillon, or take in exhibits that include a Conestoga wagon and the city's oldest building, Newcom Tavern. Open year-round. Dayton, off Interstate 75.

Dayton Air Force Museum. Exhibits range from a replica of a plane built by Dayton natives Wilbur and Orville Wright to a supersonic jet and rockets — the largest collection of aviation equipment ever displayed. Open year-round. Dayton, off Interstate 675.

Delta Queen. This famous riverboat and her sister ship, the *Mississippi Queen,* leave from port on excursions that take them all the way to Louisville and New Orleans. The *Delta Queen* is the only overnight paddle-wheeler in inland waters still carrying on the traditions of the great passenger riverboats of the 19th century. Season: spring to fall. Cincinnati, off Interstate 74 and Interstate 71.

General Harrison. Ride over a mile of the Miami and Erie Canal on a mule-drawn canal boat. Season: spring through fall. Piqua, off Interstate 75.

Glacial Grooves. Carved out by a glacier some 25,000 years ago, these grooves are the largest set of exposed glacial scratchings in the nation. Outdoor exhibits describe the history of this phenomenon; Inscription Rock, nearby, is a large boulder on which prehistoric Indians made carvings. Kelley's Island, take ferry from Marblehead, off State Route 163.

Golden Lamb. The oldest hotel in Ohio and a historic meeting place for presidents, generals and celebrities that included Charles Dickens; elegant restaurant. Open year-round. Lebanon, off Interstate 71, on US-42.

Goodtime II. A three-decker boat from which you can see the lights of Cleveland on a nighttime cruise along the Cuyahoga River. Season: spring to fall. Cleveland, off Interstate 90 and Interstate 71.

Le Boudin Vineyard. Tours of facility where table wines are made and stored in huge oak casks; tasting room, wine sales. Open year-round. Cardington, off US-42.

The Lorena. A stern-wheel riverboat whose restoration was the Bicentennial project of the community of Zanesville; rides on Muskingum River. Season: spring to fall. Zanesville, off Interstate 70, at Putnam Landing Park, south of the Sixth Street Bridge.

Mon Ami Champagne Company. Grapes used in making the wines and champagne that you will sample are grown right here on Catawba Island Peninsula. Open year-round. Catawba Island, off State Route 53.

Neil Armstrong Air and Space Museum. Extensive exhibits on Ohio's pioneers of flight; experience the Sound Tunnel, Infinity Room and Astrotheater in this museum that is located in Armstrong's hometown. Open year-round. Wapakoneta, off Interstate 75.

Professional Football Hall of Fame. Exhibits, pictures and busts honoring the great players and their teams. Open year-round. Canton, 2121 Harrison Avenue, NW

Ohio's capitol in Columbus is considered one of the purest examples of Doric architecture in the United States.

Shawnee Vineyards. Watch the pressing of wine and taste the final product. Open year-round. Circleville, off US-22.

Smuckers Jams. Tour the facilities of the famous jam, jelly and sauce maker at the "Sweetest Town in Ohio." Open year-round. Orrville, off State Route 57.

Stan Hywet Hall and Gardens. A 65-room mansion filled with priceless antiques and works of art, surrounded by beautiful gardens. Open year-round. Akron, off Interstate 77 and Interstate 76.

Sugarcreek. The graceful black buggies of the Amish scurry through the countryside surrounding this community. In each buggy you're likely to see a bearded Amish farmer and his family, reminders of the way of life that is followed throughout the Holmes County area. Sugarcreek, on State Route 39 (this route runs the entire length of the county).

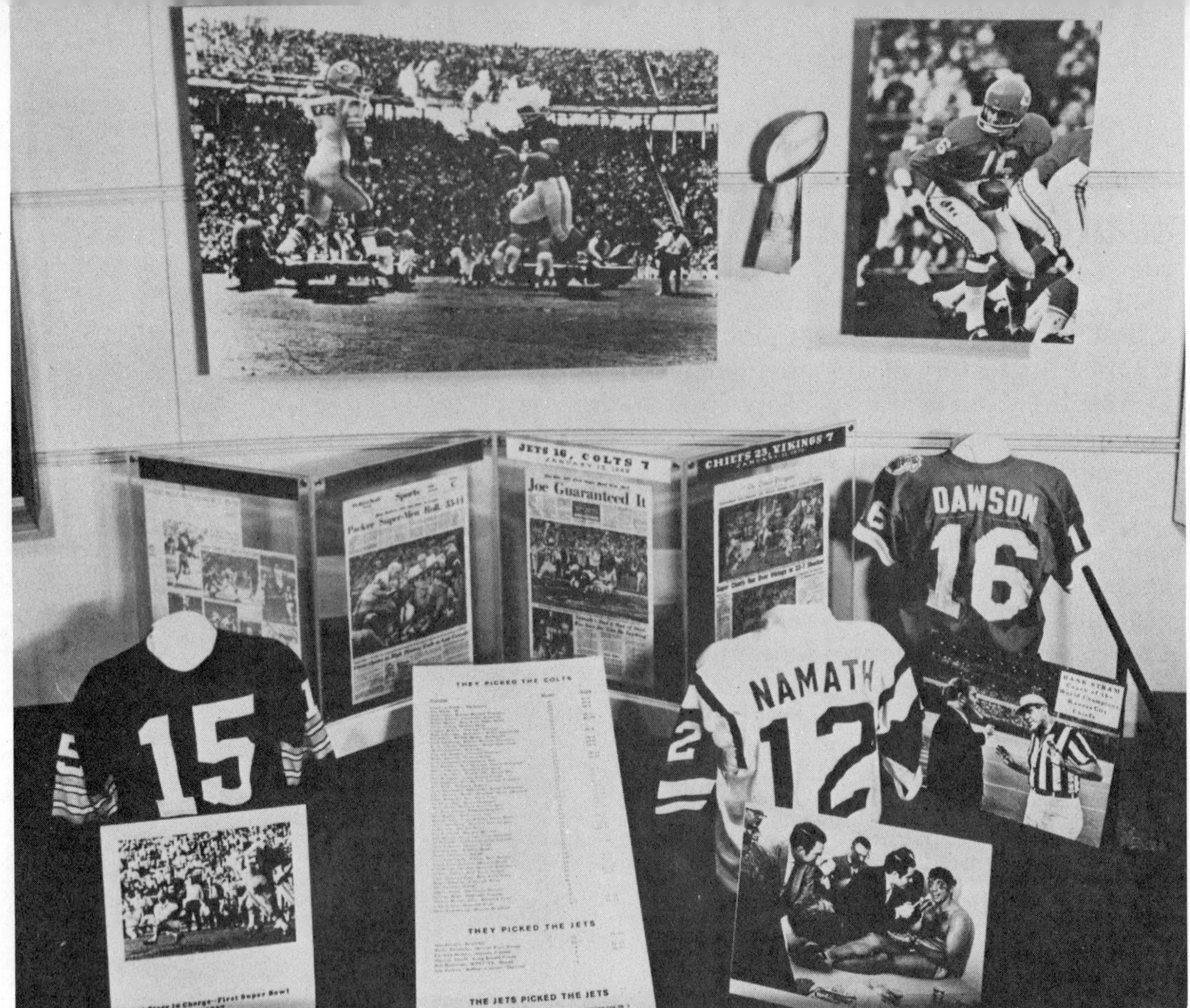

Special displays like the one shown above trace the history of pro football at the Pro Football Hall of Fame in Canton, Ohio.

The Pro Football Hall of Fame

The Pro Football Hall of Fame represents one of America's most popular sports in a great number of colorful and exciting ways. Included in the sparklingly modern three-building complex are three eye-catching exhibition areas, a football action movie theater, a research library and the twin enshrinement halls, where the greats of pro football are permanently honored.

A seven-foot bronze statue of Jim Thorpe, the legendary hero of early-day pro football, greets each guest as he enters the Hall. The visitor then follows a gently-sloping ramp to the exhibition rotunda, where pro football's history is unfolded in dramatic display form. Many priceless mementoes will capture each visitor's attention as the rotunda curves around the 52-foot, football-shaped dome that dominates the Hall and concludes with the multicolored Professional Football Today display, where every one of the 28 National Football Leagues teams is honored.

The Enshrinee Mememtoes Room, located in a second building, honors each enshrinee in picture or memento form. A third large exhibition area, the Leagues and Champions Room, graphically outlines the histories of all major leagues of professional football. Also featured in this room are display stories of the Super Bowl, the Pro Bowl and the Evolution of the Football Uniform.

Throughout the major exhibition areas, electronic devices encourage each fan to participate actively in history as he tours the Hall. Rearview movie projectors, taped voice recordings, two question-and-answer boards, and selective slide machines all play a part in telling the total story of pro football.

While the Hall is rich in the treasured relics of the past, there is also an emphasis on recent and even current-day events in pro football. Many displays are constantly being updated with significant new materials. A $625,000 expansion project in 1971 almost doubled the size of the Hall and made it possible, more than ever before, to promise something of interest to every visitor, regardless of age or favorite team.

The Hall of Heroes

As a colorful, exciting and action-punctuated sport, pro football could not be properly showcased in a Hall of Fame where a hushed and reverent atmosphere prevailed. Thus, by design, the Pro Football Hall of Fame is a shrine where happy and enthused fans are encouraged to relax and enjoy their visit.

But there is an unspoken exception to this general theme in the twin enshrinement areas, where the niches of the greats who have been bestowed pro football's highest honor are located. The impressive galleries lend themselves to moments of more somber reflection of the great stars and the outstanding contributions they made to a game they loved.

A new class of enshrinees is elected each year by a 27-man Board of Selectors, all of whom are outstanding media personnel from across the nation. There is no retirement time limit for the contributor (coach, owner, league official), but a player must have been retired five years before he can be elected.

Each niche contains a bronze bust, a brightly-lighted mural showing the enshrinee doing the thing in football he did best and a capsule biography. As you glance at each honored spot, you can be sure that the man honored there is among the very finest that any sport ever produced.

Movies

A different pro football action movie, in full color and sound, is shown every hour in the Hall's 250-seat movie theater. There is no additional charge for the movies and every visitor is welcome to stay for as many showings as he would like.

Open Memorial Day through Labor Day, 9 a.m. to 8 p.m.; remainder of the year, 9 a.m. to 5 p.m. The Pro Football Hall of Fame is closed on Christmas Day but is open every other day of the year. Admission: adults $2, children under 14 50 cents; family (parents and all dependent children), $4.50. Special group rates are also available by calling (216) 456-8207. (Prices subject to change.)

Canton, Ohio, the home of the famous Bulldogs, an early-day pro powerhouse, was selected as the site of the Pro Football Hall of Fame because the National Football League was founded there in 1920.

It proved also to be a fortunate choice geographically, for Canton is located within easy driving distances of many major cities and several transcontinental highways. The Hall is located right on Interstate 77, which intersects many principal highways within a few minutes of Canton.

—PJF

More Family Fun

Adjacent to the Pro Football Hall of Fame is a fine Canton city park which offers several unusual attractions. Located along the winding park road that leads directly from the Hall are the beautiful Stark County Garden Center, the stately McKinley Monument, the entertaining Stark County Historical Center and unique Mother Goose Land. All of these family-fun attractions are offered without charge or at minimal cost.

Highlight

Ohio's Ghosts

Every corner of the nation boasts its local legends and tales of the supernatural, but none are more fertile ground for stories of ghostly hauntings than the hills of southeastern Ohio.

"The Ghost of Moonville" is one popular tale told about a small deserted town in Zaleski State Forest. Today, all that remains of Moonville is an old railroad trestle and tunnel, but over 100 years ago Moonville was one of many small towns in the southeastern region that grew up around a booming iron furnace industry. A railroad track ran through the town, and each night a railroad man would stand along the tracks with his lantern to signal the approaching trains. One morning the man was found lying along the tracks with all the blood drained from his body. There were no clues to his mysterious death . . . but from that time forward there have been repeated reports that on certain foggy nights a lantern can be seen eerily bobbing along the deserted tracks.

There are also many legends that surround the old iron furnaces themselves. One of these involves the remains of an old furnace at Lake Hope

Ohio State Parks

Park	Location	CAMPING	PICNICKING	CONCESSIONS	SWIMMING	HIKING	BOATING	FISHING	HUNTING	WINTER SPORTS
Adams Lake	*West Union. On State Route 41.*		•		•	•	•	•		
Alum Creek	*Delaware. Off Interstate 71.*	•	•				•	•	•	
A.W. Marion	*Circleville. Off US-22.*	•	•		•	•	•	•	•	
Barkcamp	*Belmont. Off Interstate 70.*	•	•	•	•	•	•	•	•	
Beaver Creek	*Lisbon. Off US-30.*	•	•			•		•		
Blue Rock	*Philo. Off State Route 60.*	•	•		•	•	•	•		
Buck Creek	*Springfield. Off State Route 4.*		•		•	•	•	•		
Buckeye Lake	*Hebron. On State Route 79.*		•		•		•	•		
Burr Oak	*Glouster. Off State Routes 13 and 78.*	•	•	•	•	•	•	•		
Caesar Creek	*Waynesville. Off State Route 73.*		•				•	•	•	
Cowan Lake	*Clarksville. Off State Route 350.*	•	•		•	•	•	•		
Crane Creek	*Port Clinto. On US-2.*		•		•	•	•	•	•	
Deer Creek	*Mt. Sterling. On State Route 207.*	•	•		•	•	•	•	•	
Delaware	*Delaware. Off US-23.*	•	•		•	•	•	•	•	
Dillon	*Zanesville. On State Route 146.*	•	•	•	•	•	•	•	•	
East Fork	*Batavia. Off State Route 222.*	•	•			•	•	•	•	
East Harbor	*Port Clinton. Off State Route 269.*	•	•	•	•	•	•	•	•	
Findley	*Wellington. On State Route 58.*	•	•	•	•	•	•	•	•	
Forked Run	*Reedsville. On State Route 124.*	•	•	•	•	•	•	•	•	
Geneva	*Geneva-On-The-Lake. Off State Route 534.*		•		•		•	•	•	
Grand Lake St. Marys	*St. Marys. Off State Route 703.*	•	•	•	•	•	•	•	•	
Guilford Lake	*Lisbon. On State Route 172.*	•	•		•		•	•		

State Park. During the days of its operation, the furnace had to be guarded day and night for fear someone would fall into its hot, bubbling contents. So a watchman was posted to walk the ledge of the furnace. One stormy night, as he walked along the furnace's rim with his lantern, lightning struck and he fell into the molten iron. The furnace has long since closed, the town is gone and the crumbling ruins of the furnace now sit along the shores of Lake Hope. But legend has it that under similar stormy conditions, hikers have reported seeing the glow of a lantern and the outline of a man walking along the furnace ledge.

In Hocking Hills State Park, there is yet another tale of "Old Man Rowe" — a veteran of the Civil War who sought refuge in Old Man's Cave, where it was rumored he stashed large amounts of gold. When Old Man Rowe died, his body mysteriously disappeared — and so did his gold. His ghost, however, can still be seen roaming the hills of the park and his shadow can often be seen lurking just inside the cave. Or so say those who've seen him . . .

Ohio State Parks

Park	Location	CAMPING	PICNICKING	CONCESSIONS	SWIMMING	HIKING	BOATING	FISHING	HUNTING	WINTER SPORTS
Harrison Lake	*Fayette. Off US-20.*	•	•		•	•	•	•		
Houston Woods	*Oxford. Off State Routes 732 and 177.*	•	•	•	•	•	•	•		
Independence Dam	*Defiance. Off State Route 24.*	•	•		•	•	•	•	•	
Indian Lake	*Bellefontaine. Off US-33.*	•	•			•	•	•	•	
Jefferson Lake	*Richmond. Off State Route 43.*	•	•		•	•	•	•	•	
John Bryan	*Yellow Springs. Off State Routes 343 and 370.*		•		•	•		•		
Kiser Lake	*Quincy. Off State Route 235.*	•	•	•	•	•	•	•	•	
Lake Alma	*Wellston. Off State Route 349.*	•	•		•	•	•	•	•	
Lake Hope	*Zaleski. On State Route 278.*	•	•	•	•	•	•	•	•	
Lake Logan	*Logan. On State Route 664.*		•	•	•	•	•	•	•	
Lake Loramie	*Minster. Off State Route 66.*	•	•		•	•	•	•	•	
Lake White	*Waverly. Off State Route 220.*	•	•			•	•	•	•	
Madison Lake	*London. Off State Route 665.*	•	•		•	•	•	•	•	
Mohican	*Loudonville. Off State Route 3.*	•	•	•		•	•	•	•	
Mosquito Creek	*Warren. Off State Routes 46 and 305.*	•	•		•	•	•	•	•	
Mount Gilead	*Mt. Gilead. On State Route 95.*	•	•		•	•	•	•		
Paint Creek	*Hillsboro. Off US-50.*	•	•			•	•	•	•	
Pike Lake	*Morgantown. Off State Route 124.*	•	•	•	•	•	•	•	•	
Portage Lakes	*Akron. Off State Route 619.*		•		•	•	•	•	•	
Punderson	*Newbury. On State Route 87.*	•	•	•	•	•	•	•	•	
Pymatuning	*Andover. Off US-85.*	•	•	•	•	•	•	•	•	
Rocky Fork	*Hillsboro. On State Route 124.*	•	•	•	•	•	•	•	•	

Ohio State Parks

Park	Location	CAMPING	PICNICKING	CONCESSIONS	SWIMMING	HIKING	BOATING	FISHING	HUNTING	WINTER SPORTS
Salt Fork	*Cambridge. Off US-22.*	•	•	•	•	•	•	•	•	
Scioto Trail	*Chillicothe. On State Route 372.*	•	•		•	•	•	•	•	
Shawnee	*Portsmouth. On State Route 125.*	•	•	•	•	•	•	•	•	
South Bass Island	*Port Clinton. Reached by ferry.*	•	•				•	•		
Stonelick	*Edenton. On State Routes 727 and 133.*	•	•	•	•	•	•	•	•	
Strouds Run	*Athens. Off US-33.*	•	•	•	•	•	•	•	•	
Tar Hollow	*Adelphi. On State Route 327.*	•	•		•	•	•	•	•	
Tinkers Creek	*Aurora. Off State Route 43.*		•		•	•		•		
Van Buren	*Van Buren. Off US-25.*	•	•		•	•	•	•		
West Branch	*Ravenna. On State Route 5.*	•	•	•	•	•	•	•	•	
Wolf Run	*Belle Valley. Off State Route 821.*	•	•		•	•	•	•	•	

Ohio State Forests

Forest	Location	CAMPING	PICNICKING	CONCESSIONS	SWIMMING	HIKING	BOATING	FISHING	HUNTING	WINTER SPORTS
Blue Rock	*Blue Rock. Off State Route 60.*		•			•			•	
Brush Creek	*Peebles. Off State Route 73.*		•			•			•	
Chapin	*Willoughby. Off Interstate 90.*		•			•			•	
Dean	*Pedro. Off State Route 93.*								•	
Gifford	*Chesterhill. Off State Route 550.*								•	
Hocking	*Rockbridge. Off State Route 374.*	•				•			•	
Maumee	*Swanton. Off State Route 20.*					•			•	
Pike	*Latham. Off US-50.*					•			•	
Richland Furnace	*Byer. Off State Route 327.*					•			•	
Scioto Trail	*Chillicothe. Off US-23.*								•	
Shade River	*Reedsville. Off State Route 681.*								•	
Shawnee	*Friendship. Off State Route 125.*	•				•			•	
Tar Hollow	*Londonderry. Off State Route 327.*	•				•			•	
Yellow Creek	*Wellsville. Off State Route 39.*								•	
Zaleski	*Zaleski. Off State Route 278.*	•				•			•	

For more information on Ohio state parks and forests, contact: *Department of Natural Resources, Fountain Square, Columbus, Ohio 43224, (614) 466-2838.*

ONTARIO
ISLE ROYALE NAT'L PARK
Lake Superior
Marquette
Pictured Rocks Nat'l. Lakeshore
Munising
Hiawatha Nat'l. For.
Newberry
Tahquamenon St. Park
Escanaba St. For.
Hiawatha Nat'l. For.
WISCONSIN
NORTHERN MICHIGAN
Cheboygan
Lake Huron
Vanderbilt
Pigeon River St. For.
Hardwood State Forest
Atlanta
Lake Michigan
Traverse City
Au Sable State Forest
Huron National Forest
Curtisville
Fife Lake St. For.
Sleeping Bear Dunes Nat'l. Lakeshore
Higgins St. For.
Cadillac
Ogemaw St. For
Lumbermen's Mon.
Ludington
Gladwin
Manistee National Forest
Big Rapids
N
Saginaw
Muskegon
Grand Rapids
Flint
Lansing
Pontiac
Allegan St. For.
Detroit
Lake Erie
Ann Arbor
Kalamazoo
INDIANA
OHIO

Michigan

Map not to exact scale.

Michigan

Bordered by Lake Superior, Lake Michigan, Lake Huron and Lake Erie, Michigan is appropriately called the "Great Lake State." Although this state has much more to offer in its Upper and Lower Peninsulas, it is first and foremost a water wonderland, as Michigan's shoreline of more than 3,000 miles is longer than the Atlantic Coast from Maine to Florida. There are also 11,000 inland lakes in Michigan, and 36,000 miles of rivers and streams.

Michigan was populated by several Indian tribes when the French explorer, Etienne Brule, arrived in 1618. Brule was followed by other Frenchmen, including a number of intrepid Jesuit missionaries — among them Jacques Marquette — who founded the first settlement in 1668 at Sault Sainte Marie. For almost a century, the region remained in control of the French, who established several more settlements that were used mainly as fur-trading outposts. The British gained control of the region in 1763, but lost it in the settlement following the American Revolution. On July 11, 1796, the American flag was raised at Detroit, and some nine years later Michigan was officially designated a territory. The region's early growth was slow, however, due to its removal from the more settled areas of the country and because of problems with the native Indians. The completion of the Erie Canal in 1825 finally brought Michigan within reach of the westward-moving settlers, and the population grew rapidly from 1830 on. Statehood was delayed for a time, due to a boundary dispute with Ohio, but Michigan was finally admitted to the Union on January 26, 1837. Michigan's development as a state was greatly enhanced by the construction of a number of important rail lines and canals. The Republican Party was born in Jackson in 1854, and antislavery sentiments were so strong during the Civil War that Michigan contributed 100,000 troops to the Union cause.

Full name: State of Michigan
Origin of name: From Michigama meaning "Great Water."
Motto: *Si Quaeras Peninsulam Amoenam Circumspice* (If You Seek a Pleasant Peninsula, Look Around You).
Nickname: Wolverine State
Capital: Lansing
Statehood: January 26, 1837, 26th state.
Population: 9,129,000 (ranks seventh).
Major Cities: Detroit (1,335,085), Flint (174,218), Warren (172,755).
Bird: Robin
Flower: Apple blossom
Tree: White pine

Average daily temperatures by month

	Northeastern	Southern
Jan.	23.1 to 8.4	31.1 to 17.4
Feb.	24.0 to 7.4	31.9 to 16.5
Mar.	31.7 to 15.8	40.7 to 24.1
Apr.	46.4 to 29.6	55.9 to 35.5
May	59.9 to 39.3	68.1 to 46.0
Jun.	69.9 to 48.0	78.4 to 56.3
Jul.	75.6 to 53.5	83.4 to 59.9
Aug.	74.0 to 54.0	81.6 to 58.8
Sept.	64.4 to 47.1	73.0 to 51.0
Oct.	54.5 to 38.1	61.4 to 41.1
Nov.	39.6 to 26.9	45.3 to 30.5
Dec.	27.3 to 14.4	34.0 to 21.0
Year	49.2 to 31.9	57.1 to 38.2

Today, Michigan has four distinct regions — and each offers a rich variety of attractions for visitors. In the Upper Peninsula, where 90% of the land is still covered by forest, there are endless delights for outdoor enthusiasts; you can camp and hike in four million acres of public land, canoe on one of the sparkling streams, or try downhill skiing on the slopes of Iron Mountain. In the western part of the state, the emphasis is on wide-open spaces; here you'll find the longest freshwater beach in the world, or

The contrast between the old and new can be seen in the old French post of Fort Michilimackinac and the five-mile-long Mackinac Straits Bridge.

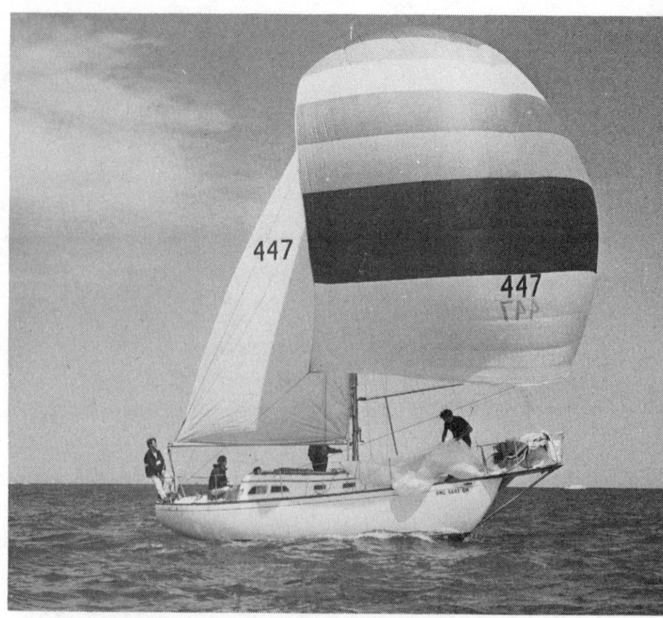

Surrounded by the waters of the Great Lakes, Michigan is a boater's paradise.

you might try rockhounding for Petoskey stones. In east Michigan, there's a country atmosphere; picturesque farms; the Au Sable River, one of the nation's premier trout streams; and, for a change of pace, you can visit the state capitol building in Lansing. Southeast Michigan boasts Detroit, the "Motor City," where more automobiles are produced than anywhere else in the world.

As vital as the automobile business is to Michigan, tourism is almost as important, as travelers spend more than one billion

STEPPING STONE FALLS

Stepping Stone Falls, featuring cascading waters over a uniquely designed section of the 1,800-foot dam which creates Mott Lake, provides viewers with a spectacularly colored light show after sunset.

A green and lush area during the daytime hours, the Falls at night are highlighted by a changing light show of dancing colors from submerged and elevated lights which create striking patterns on the rushing water.

Picnic facilities can be found in this tranquil area, which is open daily from Memorial Day weekend through Labor Day from 8 a.m. to midnight.

A modern rest room and concession building serves Stepping Stone Falls, and there is a boardwalk from the parking lot to the Falls.

The Falls are open free of charge to the public. Near Flint, north off Irish Road.

dollars a year in the state. Other major industries are mining (salt, iron, natural gas), agriculture and the manufacture of machinery, chemicals, electrical equipment and primary metals.

Michigan's capitol building, erected in 1879, features a Michigan heritage display and hosts visitor tours throughout the year.

State Offices

Tourism
Michigan Travel Commission
Law Building
PO Box 30226
Lansing, Michigan 48909
(517) 373-2090

State Police
Department of Public Safety
East Lansing, Michigan 48823
(517) 332-2521

Radio Stations

Ann Arbor
WAAM 1600 (AM)
WIQB 102.9 (FM)
Detroit
WCAR 1130 (AM)
CKLW 800 (AM)
Flint
WKMF 1470 (AM)
Grand Rapids
WJFM 93.7 (FM)
Kalamazoo
WKMI 1360 (AM)

Michigan Points of Interest and Attractions

Beaver Island. Located in Lake Michigan, this island was the home of the nation's only monarchy, ruled by Mormon King James Strang during the early 1840s. Can be reached by ferry from Charlevoix, off US-31.

"Be Good To Your Mother-In-Law." A unique 139-foot swinging bridge with an unusual name provides a breathtaking walk across the Black River. Croswell, off State Route 90.

Big Rock Point. This nuclear research and development laboratory features an information center that explains the mysteries of the atom. Open year-round, Monday to Saturday. Charlevoix, off US-131.

Brockaway Mountain. The true beauty of Keweenawland unfolds before the visitor on the drive to the top, and there is a magnificent scenic view from the summit. Harbor, off US-41.

Cascades. Illuminated falls are a spectacle of sheer beauty. Jackson, off Interstate 94.

Detroit. Within the "Motor Capital of the World" you'll find Belle Isle Park, Tiger Stadium, Ford Memorial Auditorium, Cranbrook Institute, Cobo Hall and many other sites and attractions.

Fort Wilkins. The last remaining wooden fort east of the Mississippi River, with its original buildings still standing. Open year-round. Copper Harbor, east, off US-41.

Grand Haven. The world's largest musical fountain combines music, water formations and colored lights in a constantly changing panorama. Grand Haven, off US-31.

Holland. The site of cultural and historic Windmill Island Park features a 200-year-old windmill imported from the Netherlands; residents celebrate annual Tulip Festival with brightly colored native dress. Holland, on US-31.

Irish Hills. This area is dotted with 28 lakes and surrounded by magnificent scenery. Michigan International Speedway is located nearby. Cambridge, on US-12.

Kitch-iti-ki-pi Spring. Natural spring famous for its crystal-clear waters; location often used for making underwater movies of scuba diving. Manistique, north off State Route 94, in Palms-Book State Park.

Lake of the Clouds. A lake nestled high in the Porcupine Mountains above Lake Superior. Bergland, off State Route 28.

Lumberman's Memorial. Located on the famed Au Sable River, this is a monument to the days when lumber was king in Michigan. Tawas, northeast, off State Route 65.

Mackinac Bridge. Better known as "Big Mac," the five-mile-long suspension bridge spans the Straits of Mackinac and connects Michigan's two peninsulas. Mackinaw City, on Interstate 75.

National Ski Hall of Fame. Part of the National Ski Museum, the hall of fame contains plaques commemorating feats of the world's greatest skiers, as well as a collection of historical ski equipment. Open year-round, daily. Ishpeming, off US-41.

Pictured Rocks. Unique rock formations rising from 50 to 200 feet above Lake Superior and stretching some 20 miles. Munising, off State Route 28.

Soo Locks. Opened in 1855, more tonnage passes through these locks annually than through the Panama Canal and Suez Canal combined. Sault Sainte Marie, on Interstate 75.

Upper Tahquamenon Falls. With the exception of Niagara, this is the largest waterfall east of the Mississippi River; lower falls is a series of drops divided by an island. Newberry, off State Route 123.

Michigan State Parks

Park	Location	CAMPING	PICNICKING	CONCESSIONS	SWIMMING	HIKING	BOATING	FISHING	HUNTING	WINTER SPORTS
Algonac	*Algonac. On State Route 29.*	•	•			•	•	•		
Aloha	*Aloha. On State Route 212.*	•	•		•		•	•		
Bald Mountain	*Lake Orion. Off State Route 24.*	•	•	•	•	•	•	•	•	
Baraga	*Baraga. On US-41.*	•	•		•			•		
Bay City	*Bay City. On State Route 247.*	•	•	•	•	•		•		
Bewabic	*Crystal Falls. On US-2.*	•	•		•	•	•	•		
Brighton	*Brighton. Off Interstate 96.*	•	•	•	•	•	•	•	•	
Brimley	*Brimley. Off State Route 221.*	•	•		•		•	•		
Burt Lake	*Indian River. Off Interstate 75.*	•	•	•	•	•	•	•		
Cheboygan	*Cambridge Junction. On US-23.*	•	•		•	•		•		
Clear Lake	*Atlanta. On State Route 33.*	•	•		•	•	•	•	•	
DeTour	*Detour. On State Route 134.*	•	•		•	•	•	•		
Fayette	*Garden. Off US-2.*	•	•		•	•	•	•		
Fort Wilkins	*Copper Harbor. On US-41.*	•	•			•	•	•		
Gladwin	*Gladwin. Off State Route 18.*	•	•			•	•	•		
Grand Haven	*Grand Haven. Off US-31.*	•	•		•		•	•		
Harrisville	*Harrisville. Off US-23.*	•	•		•	•	•	•		
Hartwick Pines	*Grayling. On State Route 93.*	•	•			•	•	•		
Higgins Lake	*Roscommon. Off US-27.*	•	•	•	•	•	•	•		

Michigan State Parks

Park	Location	CAMPING	PICNICKING	CONCESSIONS	SWIMMING	HIKING	BOATING	FISHING	HUNTING	WINTER SPORTS
Highland	*Highland. On State Route 59.*	•	•		•	•	•	•	•	
Holland	*Holland. Off US-31.*	•	•	•	•	•	•	•		
Holly	*Holly. Off US-23.*	•	•	•	•	•	•	•	•	
Indian Lake	*Manistique. Off US-2.*	•	•		•	•	•	•		
Ionia	*Ionia. Off State Route 21.*		•					•	•	
Island Lake	*Brighton. Off Interstate 96.*	•	•	•	•	•	•	•	•	
Lake Gogebic	*Marenisco. On State Route 64.*	•	•		•	•	•	•		
Lakeport	*Port Huron. On US-25.*	•	•	•	•	•	•	•		
Leelanau	*Northport. Off State Route 201.*	•	•					•	•	
Ludington	*Ludington. On State Route 116.*	•	•	•	•	•	•	•	•	
Maybury	*Northville. Off Interstate 96.*		•			•				
McLain	*Calumet. On State Route 203.*	•	•		•	•	•	•		
Mears	*Pentwater Village. Off US-31.*	•	•	•	•	•	•	•		
Metamora-Hadley	*Metamora. Off State Route 24.*	•	•	•	•	•	•	•	•	
Mitchell	*Cadillac. On State Route 115.*	•	•		•	•	•	•		
Muskallonge Lake	*Newberry. Off State Route 123.*	•	•		•	•	•	•		
Muskegon	*Muskegon. Off US-31.*	•	•	•	•	•	•	•		
Newaygo	*Newaygo. Off State Route 37.*	•	•			•	•	•	•	
Onaway	*Onaway. On State Route 211.*	•	•		•	•	•	•		
Orchard Beach	*Manistee. Off US-31.*	•	•		•	•		•		
Ortonville	*Ortonville. Off State Route 15.*	•	•	•	•	•	•	•	•	
Otsego Lake	*Gaylord. Off Interstate 75.*	•	•	•	•	•	•	•		
Petoskey	*Petoskey. On State Route 131.*	•	•	•	•			•		
Pinckney	*Pinckney. Off State Route 36.*	•	•	•	•	•	•	•	•	
Pontiac Lake	*Pontiac. Off State Route 59.*	•	•		•	•	•	•		
Porcupine Mountains	*Ontonagon. On State Route 107.*	•	•		•	•	•	•		
Port Crescent	*Port Austin. On State Route 25.*	•	•		•	•	•	•		
Proud Lake	*Milford. Off State Route 59.*	•	•		•	•	•	•	•	
Rifle River	*Rose City. Off State Route 33.*	•	•			•	•	•	•	
Sanilac	*Forestville. Off State Route 25.*	•					•	•		
Silver Lake	*Hart. Off US-31.*	•	•		•	•	•	•		
Sleeper	*Caseville. Off State Route 25.*	•	•		•	•	•	•	•	
Sterling	*Monroe. Off Interstate 75.*	•	•	•		•	•	•		
Straits	*St. Ignace. On US-2.*	•	•		•		•	•		
Tahquamenon	*Eckerman. On State Route 123.*	•	•			•	•	•		
Tawas Point	*East Tawas. Off US-23.*	•	•		•	•	•	•		
Traverse City	*Traverse City. On US-31.*	•	•		•	•	•	•		
Twin Lakes	*Winona. On State Route 26.*	•	•		•		•	•		
Van Buren	*South Haven. Off Interstate 196.*	•	•	•	•	•			•	
Van Riper	*Champion. On US-41.*	•	•		•	•		•		
Warren Dunes	*Bridgman. Off Interstate 94.*	•	•	•	•	•		•	•	
Waterloo	*Chelsea. Off Interstate 94.*	•	•	•	•	•	•	•	•	
Wells	*Cedar River. On State Route 35.*	•	•		•	•	•	•		
White Cloud	*White Cloud. On State Route 20.*	•	•			•		•		
Wilderness	*Mackinaw City. Off US-31.*	•	•		•	•	•	•		
Wilson	*Harrison. Off US-27.*	•	•		•		•	•		
Yankee Springs	*Hastings. Off State Route 37.*	•	•		•	•	•	•		
Young	*Boyne City. Off US-131.*	•	•	•	•	•	•	•		

Michigan State Forests

Forest	Location	CAMPING	PICNICKING	CONCESSIONS	SWIMMING	HIKING	BOATING	FISHING	HUNTING	WINTER SPORTS
Ambrose Lake	*West Branch. Off Interstate 75.*	•	•		•	•	•	•		
Avery Lake	*Atlanta. Off State Route 32.*	•	•			•	•	•		
Big Bear Lake	*Johannesburg. Off State Route 32.*	•	•	•	•	•	•	•		
Black Creek	*Sanford. On US-10.*	•	•	•		•	•	•		
Black Lake	*Onaway. Off State Route 211.*	•	•	•	•	•	•	•		
Canoe Harbor	*Grayling. Off Interstate 75.*	•	•			•	•	•		
Ess Lake	*Hillman. Off State Route 32.*	•	•		•	•	•	•		
Houghton Lake	*Houghton Lake. On US-27.*	•	•	•	•	•	•	•		
House Lake	*Skeels. On State Route 18.*	•	•		•	•	•	•		
Jackson Lake	*Atlanta. On State Route 33.*	•	•		•	•	•	•		
Jones Lake	*Frederic. Off Interstate 75.*	•	•	•	•	•	•	•		
Lake Margrethe	*Grayling. On State Route 72.*	•	•	•	•	•	•	•		
Little Wolf Lake	*Lewiston. Off State Route 32.*	•	•		•	•	•	•		
Manistee Bridge	*Grayling. On State Route 72.*	•	•	•		•	•	•		
McCullum Lake	*Curran. Off State Route 65.*	•	•	•	•	•	•	•		
Mio Pond	*Mio. Off State Route 33.*	•	•		•	•	•	•		
Munuscong River	*Sault Ste. Marie. Off Interstate 75.*	•	•		•	•	•	•	•	
Ossineke	*Ossineke. Off US-23.*	•	•		•	•	•	•		
Pigeon River	*Vanderbilt. Off Interstate 75.*	•	•	•	•	•	•	•		
Pike Lake	*Farwell. Off US-10.*	•	•	•	•	•	•	•		
Reedsburg	*Houghton Lake. On State Route 55.*	•	•			•	•	•		
Rifle River	*Rose City. Off State Route 33.*	•	•			•	•	•		
Tittabawasee River	*Gladwin. Off State Route 18.*	•	•		•	•	•	•		
Tomahawk Lake	*Onaway. Off State Route 33.*	•	•	•	•	•	•	•		
Trout Lake	*Skeels. Off State Route 18.*	•	•		•	•	•	•		
Van Etten Lake	*Oscoda. Off US-23.*	•	•		•	•	•	•		
White Pine	*Grayling. Off Interstate 75.*	•	•			•	•	•		

For more information on Michigan state parks and forests, contact: *Department of Natural Resources, PO Box 30028, Lansing, Michigan 48909, (517) 373-1270.*

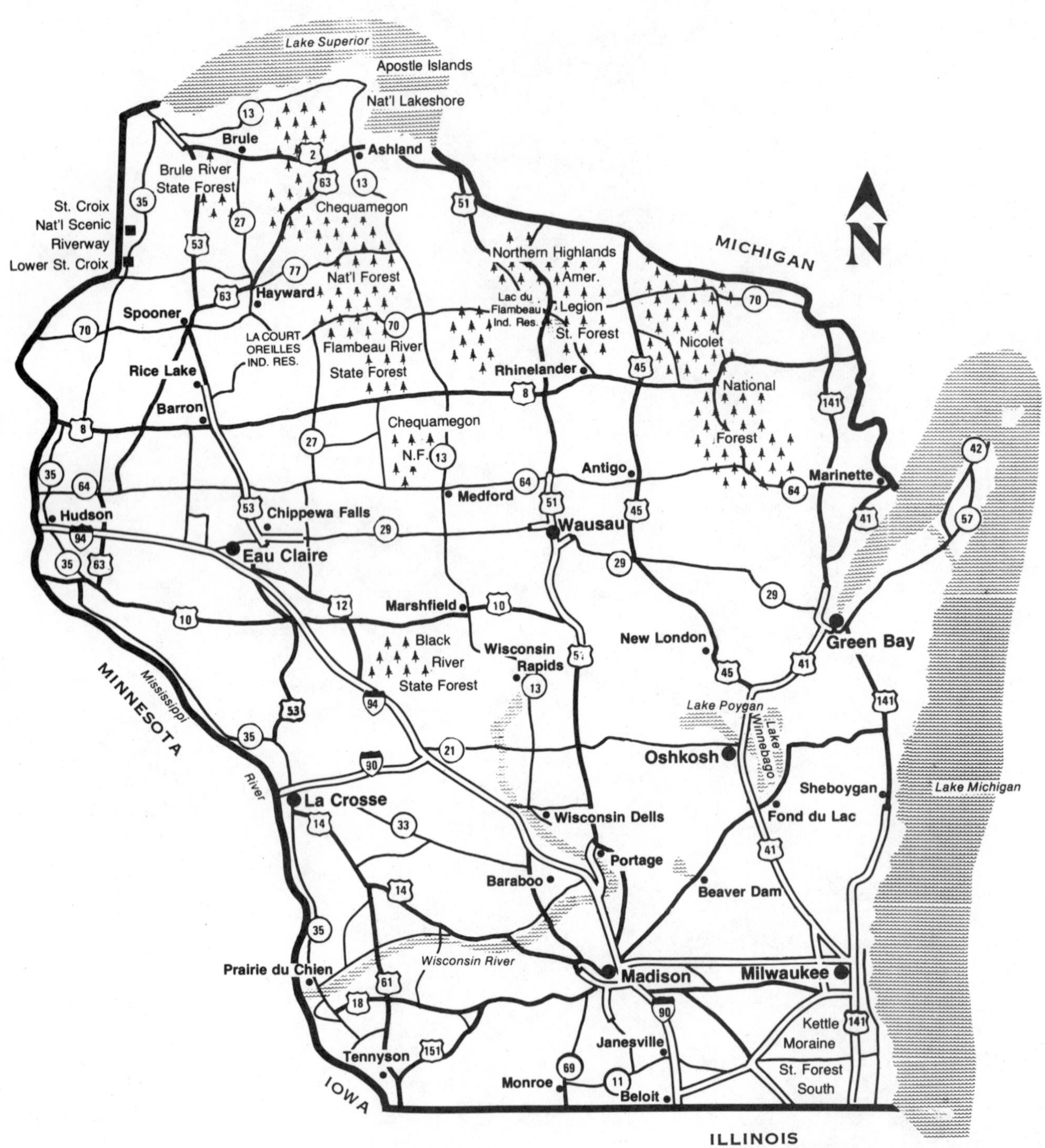

Wisconsin

Map not to exact scale.

Wisconsin

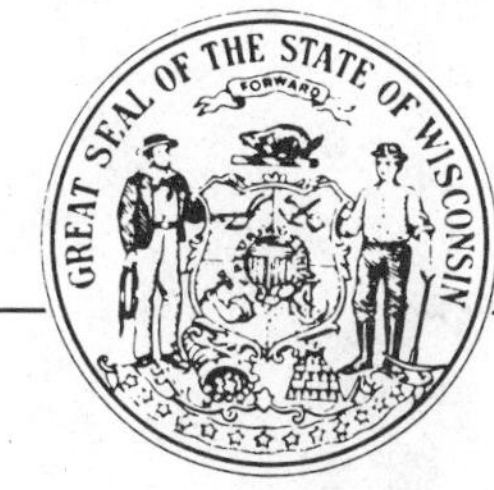

For many people, Wisconsin means cows grazing peacefully on a lush, green hillside. And this is as it should be, perhaps, for Wisconsin is indeed the nation's dairyland. But it is also a land of breathtaking scenic beauty — rolling hills, spectacular river bluffs, fertile plains, sparkling lakes. And it's a land with a rich, cosmopolitan heritage — as Swiss, Germans and Scandinavians were among the first European immigrants to this region, and their customs still linger in the small towns that dot the countryside.

Wisconsin was discovered by the French in 1634, when Jean Nicolet was sent to explore the region in an attempt to find a route to the Western ocean and the Orient. In 1671, the territory was officially annexed to France in a ceremony at Sault Sainte Marie. The French control of the region lasted for more than a century, with a number of settlements established by Jesuit missionaries. The British took possession of the area before the American Revolution, but later ceded the region to the United States in treaties that followed the war. However, the British remained in control of much of the territory until after the War of 1812, when they finally withdrew their forces from Prairie du Chien. Wisconsin became a separate territory in 1836, after several conflicts with Indians of the Winnebago tribe. Spurred by a boom in lead mining, immigration to Wisconsin increased rapidly, and by the end of 1840 the population had swelled to more than 30,000. Wisconsin joined the Union in 1848. One of the most noteworthy events in the state's history was the great Peshtigo forest fire of 1871, which killed more than 1,000 people and destroyed property valued in excess of $5 million.

Wisconsin's most famous natural attraction in undoubtedly the Dells of the Wisconsin River, where bizarre stone formations have been etched in the sheer cliffs by the river's waters. Another popular spot with vacationeers is the Door Peninsula, a 70-mile finger of land that juts

Full name: State of Wisconsin
Origin of name: Indian, meaning "gathering of the waters."
Motto: Forward
Nickname: Badger State
Capital: Madison
Statehood: May 29, 1848, 30th state.
Population: 4,651,000 (ranks 16th).
Major Cities: Milwaukee (665,795), Madison (168,196), Racine (94,745).
Bird: Robin
Flower: Wood violet
Tree: Sugar maple

Average daily temperatures by month

	Northern	Southern
Jan.	19.1 to 1.0	27.4 to 9.6
Feb.	25.0 to 3.8	32.4 to 13.9
Mar.	35.5 to 15.4	42.2 to 23.5
Apr.	51.5 to 30.7	58.9 to 36.8
May	64.1 to 41.3	70.8 to 46.7
Jun.	73.3 to 51.3	80.2 to 56.4
Jul.	77.3 to 55.9	84.2 to 60.7
Aug.	75.1 to 54.0	82.5 to 59.2
Sept.	65.4 to 45.3	75.0 to 51.5
Oct.	55.9 to 36.9	64.0 to 42.1
Nov.	37.2 to 23.0	46.2 to 29.2
Dec.	24.3 to 9.0	32.6 to 17.0
Year	50.3 to 30.6	58.0 to 37.2

This scene in Sauk County is typical of the lush countryside to be found in the dairy lands of Wisconsin.

into Lake Michigan. Sometimes called the "inland Cape Cod," the Door features a number of fine resorts, a mild climate, cherry and apple orchards and a fascinating history that draws thousands of visitors each year. Indians have played a major role in Wisconsin's past, and the state currently has five Indian reservations that welcome visitors — one of the most popular being the Lac du Flambeau, where special ceremonial dances are performed each week. The days of the "lead rush" are recalled in the old ghost towns of the era, as well as in the restorations of the Cornish miners' homes in Mineral Point.

Wisconsin may enjoy a national reputation as a dairy capital, but manufacturing actually represents its major economic activity today. Top products include machinery, paper, chemicals, lumber and food products. The state is also the nation's number-one supplier of beer, with most of the brewers concentrated in the Milwaukee area. Agriculture, including dairying and dairy products, is, of course, still important, with mining also playing a key role in Wisconsin's economic well-being.

Highlight

Wisconsin's Historical Parks

Within its superb system of state parks, Wisconsin has set aside special areas as historical, memorial and archaeological parks. For a fascinating glimpse into the state's history, take time to visit a few of these sites.

Heritage Hill State Park.
Heritage Hill State Park is located near Green Bay. This new state park provides the visitor the opportunity to view some of the oldest buildings in Wisconsin that were associated with the early history and heritage of the state. Included in the collection are the Tank Cottage built in 1776; the Cotton House built in the 1840s; three buildings of Fort Howard, where President Zachary Taylor and Confederate President Jefferson Davis both served; a trapper's cabin built about 1820; the Baird Law Office built in 1835; and many others. All historic buildings either are or will be furnished with artifacts and antiques representative of the period. Heritage Hill State Park will be open to the public from May 26 to October 31 of each year.

First Capitol State Park (Belmont). Site of the first capitol and first state supreme court. Original buildings now in a restored condition are on the site.

Nelson Dewey State Park (Cassville). Home of Governor Nelson Dewey, first governor of Wisconsin. Also the site of Stonefield Village; a reproduction of the typical Wisconsin village at the turn of the century.

Tower Hill State Park (Spring Green). Site of a "shot tower" used to produce "lead shot." Operation commenced in 1821 and terminated in 1861.

Wade House State Park (Greenbush). Site of an early Wisconsin inn.

Cushing Memorial State Park (Delafield). Birthplace of the "Three Wisconsin Cushings who won unusual distinction for bravery during the Civil War."

Brunet Island State Park (Cornell). Site of conflict between Chippewa and Wisconsin troops during the Civil War period.

Perrot State Park (Trempealeau). Site where Nicholas Perrot built a fort in 1685 while claiming the Northwest Territory for the King of France.

Aztalan State Park (Lake Mills). Site of an ancient Indian village.

Copper Culture State Park (Oconto). Burial grounds of the "Copper Culture" people estimated to have existed about 2590 B.C.

Lizard Mound State Park (West Bend). Contains Indian mounds built in shapes of birds and animals.

Natural Bridge State Park (Baraboo). Site of one of the country's largest "Natural Bridges," used for shelter purposes by many prehistoric Indian tribes.

State Offices

Tourism
Wisconsin Department of Natural Resources
Vacation and Travel Service
PO Box 450
Madison, Wisconsin 53701
(608) 266-3222

State Police
Department of Public Safety
PO Box 7912
Madison, Wisconsin 53702
(608) 266-3212

Radio Stations

Madison
WISM 1480 (AM)
Milwaukee
WFMR 96.5 (FM)
WISN 1130 (AM)

Wisconsin Points of Interest and Attractions

Apostle Islands. A group of 22 islands off the Bayfield Peninsula noted for their rough and rugged scenery; a favorite of hunters and fishermen. Bayfield, off State Route 13.

Brule River. An excellent river for trout fishing and canoeing; President Coolidge once had his "summer White House" here. Danbury, on State Route 35, and north along river to Lake Superior.

Dells. The famous Wisconsin attraction along the Wisconsin River; unique rock formations, intriguing canyons, Indian ceremonials and much more for the visitor to see. Wisconsin Dells, off Interstate 94.

Door County. Located in the northeastern corner of the state, Door County's terrain is reminiscent of that in New England; mild climate and numerous interesting craft shops are special features. Along State Routes 42 and 57.

Green Lake. Wisconsin's deepest lake, reaching 235 feet in spots, is famous for its lake trout. Princeton, south, off State Route 73.

Horicon Wildlife Refuge. A 31,000-acre refuge with a wide variety of native wildlife; autumn Canada Geese migration is an unforgettable sight. Fond du Lac, south, off US-41.

Lake Geneva. The gem of the southern lakes, offering all forms of water recreation, plus the world-famous Yerkes Observatory at Williams Bay. Observatory open year-round, Saturdays only. Lake Geneva, off US-12.

Madison. The state capital and site of the University of Wisconsin, a famous arboretum and the U.S. Forest Products Laboratories; surrounding lakes offer a wide variety of activities, as well as scenic beauty. Off Interstate 90.

Mineral Point. Town containing restorations of Cornish miners' homes, recalling state's lead mining days; numerous relics of the mining activity are present throughout the area. Off US-151, on Shake Rag Street.

Monroe. The "Swiss Cheese Capital of the U.S.," with numerous cheese factories located throughout the area open for tours. On State Routes 69 and 11.

Superior. One of Wisconsin's most famous port cities and the site of some of the world's largest ore docks and grain elevators; a major loading point for the Great Lakes' ports. On US-53 and State Route 35.

Trees For Tomorrow. A unique forest conservation camp providing fascinating demonstration forests and scenic nature trails. Near Eagle River, off US-45.

Wisconsin State Parks

Park	Location	CAMPING	PICNICKING	CONCESSIONS	SWIMMING	HIKING	BOATING	FISHING	HUNTING	WINTER SPORTS
Amnicon Falls	*Poplar. Off US-2.*	•	•					•		
Big Bay	*Bayfield. Off State Route 13.*	•	•		•		•	•		
Big Foot Beach	*Lake Geneva. Off State Route 120.*	•	•		•			•		
Blue Mound	*Blue Mounds. Off US-18.*	•	•		•	•				
Brunet Island	*Comell. Off State Route 64.*	•	•		•	•	•	•		
Cadiz Springs	*Browntown. Off State Route 11.*		•		•			•		
Copper Falls	*Mellen. Off State Route 13.*	•	•		•	•		•		
Council Grounds	*Merrill. Off State Route 107.*	•	•		•	•		•		
Devils Lake	*Baraboo. Off US-12.*	•	•	•	•	•	•	•		
Governor Dodge	*Dodgeville. Off State Route 23.*	•	•		•	•	•	•		
Harrington Beach	*Belgium. Off Interstate 43.*		•	•	•			•		
Hartman Creek	*Waupaca. Off State Route 54.*	•	•		•	•	•	•		
High Cliff	*Sherwood. Off State Route 55.*	•	•	•	•	•	•	•		
Interstate	*St. Croix Falls. Off US-8.*	•	•	•	•	•	•	•		
Lake Kegonsa	*Stoughton. Off Interstate 90.*	•	•		•	•	•	•		
Lake Wissota	*Chippewa Falls. Off State Route 29.*	•	•		•	•	•	•		
Lucius Woods	*Solon Springs. Off US-53.*	•	•		•	•	•	•		
Merrick	*Fountain City. Off State Route 35.*	•	•		•	•	•	•		
Mill Bluff	*Camp Douglas. Off Interstate 90.*	•	•		•					
Mirror Lake	*Lake Delton. Off State Route 23.*	•	•		•	•	•	•		
New Glarus Woods	*New Glarus. Off State Route 69.*	•	•		•					
Ojibwa	*Ojibwa. Off State Route 70.*	•	•			•		•		
Pattison	*Superior. Off State Route 35.*	•	•		•	•		•		
Peninsula	*Fish Creek. Off State Route 42.*	•	•		•	•	•	•		
Perrot	*Trempealeau. Off State Route 93.*	•	•			•	•	•		
Pike Lake	*Hartford. Off State Route 60.*	•	•	•	•	•		•		
Potawatomi	*Sturgeon Bay. Off State Route 57.*	•	•			•	•	•		
Rib Mountain	*Wausau. Off US-51.*	•	•							
Roche A Cri	*Friendship. Off State Route 13.*	•	•							
Rocky Arbor	*Wisconsin Dells. Off Interstate 90.*	•	•							
Terry Andrae	*Sheboygan. Off Interstate 43.*	•	•		•	•		•		
Tower Hill	*Spring Green. Off US-14.*	•	•			•	•	•		
Wildcat Mountain	*Ontario. Off State Route 131.*	•	•					•		
Willow River	*Burkhardt. Off Interstate 94.*	•	•		•	•	•	•		
Wyalusing	*Prairie Du Chien. Off State Route 18.*	•	•			•	•	•		
Yellowstone Lake	*Blanchardville. Off State Route 78.*	•	•	•	•	•	•	•		

Wisconsin State Forests

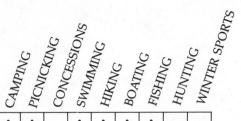

Forest	Location	CAMPING	PICNICKING	CONCESSIONS	SWIMMING	HIKING	BOATING	FISHING	HUNTING	WINTER SPORTS
Black River	*Black River Falls. Off Interstate 94.*	•	•		•	•	•	•		
Brule River	*Brule. Off US-2.*	•	•			•	•	•		
Flambeau River	*Phillips. On State Route 70.*	•	•		•	•	•	•		
Kettle Moraine (northern unit)	*Campbellsport. Off State Route 67.*	•	•		•	•	•	•		
Kettle Moraine (southern unit)	*Eagle. Off State Routes 67 and 106.*	•	•		•	•	•	•		
Northern Highland-American Legion	*Boulder Junction. On US-51.*	•	•		•	•	•	•		
Point Beach	*Two Rivers. Off State Route 52.*	•	•		•	•		•		
St.Croix River	*Grantsburg. Off State Route 70.*		•			•				

For more information on Wisconsin state parks and forests, contact: *Wisconsin Department of Natural Resources, PO Box 7921, Madison, Wisconsin 53707, (608) 266-2621.*

Central Region Calendar of Events

Spring
(March, April, May)

Illinois

Flower and Garden Show. March, Chicago.

Annual Spring Arts Festival. April, Crystal Lake.

Annual Kite Derby. April, Evanston.

"Blossoms and Wings of Spring," Mississippi Palisades Park. May, Savanna.

Renaissance Festival. April, Palos Hills.

Rend Lake Water Festival. Miss Rend Lake Pageant, parade. May, Benton.

Streator Heritage Festival. May, Streator.

Spring Festival. May, Zion.

White Squirrel Bass Fishing Derby. May, Olney.

Spring Planting, Lincoln Log Cabin State Historic Site. May, Charleston.

Annual Rose Queen Pageant. May, Roselle.

Annual Tour of Homes. May, Waukegan.

Annual Brandeis Used Book Sale. May, Wilmette.

Indiana

Election 1836. Citizens of Conner Prairie Pioneer Settlement elect community leaders in the style of 1836; visitors may cast ballots. April, Noblesville.

Romantic Festival. April, Indianapolis.

Rock and Gem Festival. April, Richmond.

Sugar Creek Canoe Race. April, Crawfordsville.

Perry County Dogwood Festival. April, Tell City, Troy and Rome.

Orleans Dogwood Festival. April, Orleans.

Sassafras Tea Festival and Boat Race. April, Vernon.

"500" Festival. A month packed with activities surrounding the Indianapolis 500 Race. April through May, Indianapolis.

Spring Blossom Festival. May, Nashville.

Bicycle Day, Eagle Creek Park. May, Indianapolis.

May Day in Metamora. May, Metamora.

Ohio River Arts Festival. May, Evansville.

Fair-On-The-Square. Arts and crafts fair on the library plaza. May, Columbus.

Spring Lake Music Festival. Traditional and bluegrass concerts in lakeside and woodland setting. May, Mooresville.

Log Cabin Tours. May, Nashville.

Spirit of Vincennes Rendezvous. May, Vincennes.

Indianapolis "500" Race. May (Memorial Day), Indianapolis.

Banks of the Wabash Festival. Arts and crafts displays, music, carnival rides. May, Terre Haute.

Michigan

Arts and Crafts Exhibit, Meridian Mall. April, Okemos.

Great Northern Oprey, Iron County Armory. April, Iron River.

Polka Jamboree, Yack Arena. April, Wyandotte.

May Festival. Music. April, Ann Arbor.

Italian Festival. April, Wyandotte.

Maple Syrup Festival. April, Vermontville.

Blossomtime Festival. April, Benton Harbor/St. Joseph.

Minstrel Show. May, Elk Rapids.

Blue Water Gem and Mineral Show, Wagenseil Community Center. May, Port Huron.
Wildflower Sunday. May, Kalamazoo.
Spring Horse Show, state fairgrounds. May, Detroit.
Festival of Wheels. May, Dearborn.
Balloon Festival. May, Carson City.
Tuliptime Festival. May, Holland.
Country Fair of Yesteryear, Greenfield Village. May, Dearborn.
Historical Homes Tour. May, Ionia.
Michigan Week. May, various locations statewide.
Mexican Festival, Yack Arena. May, Wyandotte.
Greek Festival, Hart Plaza. May, Detroit.
Highland Festival and Games. May, Alma.
Fort Michilimackinac Pageant. May, Mackinaw City.
Black River Tick Festival. May, Bessemer/Ironwood.
Brown Trout Derby, Tawas Bay. May, Tawas/East Tawas.
Pike Fishing Festival. May, St. Charles.

Ohio

Buzzard Day. Traditional return of Buzzards on March 19. Hinckley.
American-Canadian Sportsmen's Vacation and Boat Show. March, Cleveland.
Annual Arcade Art Affair. May, Newark.
Annual Spring Bluegrass Reunion. May, Ottawa.
Annual Bath Antique Show. May, Bath.
Fairfield Heritage Annual Pilgrimage. May, Lancaster.
Jewish Festival. May, Sylvania.
Dunham Tavern Museum Antique Show. May, Cleveland.
Spring Tour of Zoar Homes. May, Zoar.
Avon Festival of Flowers. May, Avon.
Central Ohio Jazz Festival. May, Columbus.
Medieval Renaissance Festival. May, Columbus.
Mad River Regional Arts and Crafts Festival. May, Dayton.
Cherry Blossom Festival. May, Barberton.
Deer Creek Dam Days Festival. May, Williamsport.

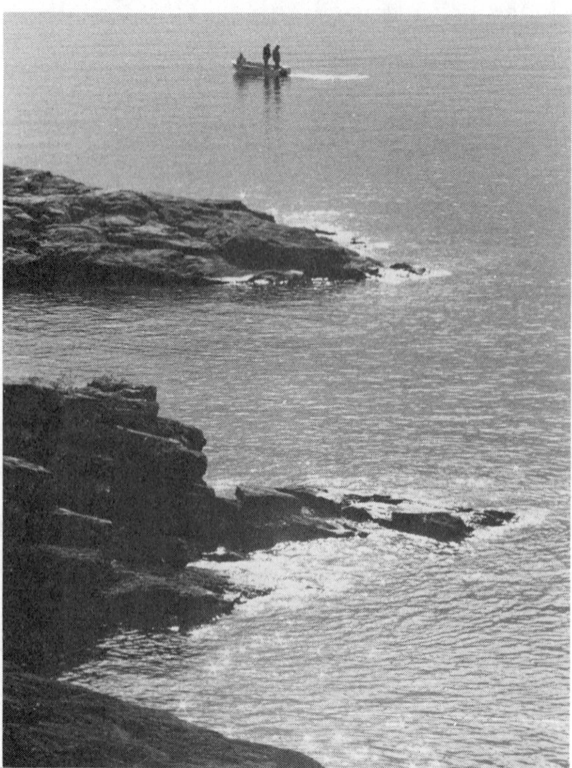

From its rugged coastline to its unspoiled stretches of forests visitors to Michigan will find the serenity and beauty of nature.

When we think of Indiana we think of boating — a most popular pastime in the Hoosier state, especially on the southern tip of Lake Michigan.

Annual Bach Festival. May, Berea.
Family Tree Festival. Displays of old genealogical records, photos, genealogy book dealers. May, Hillsboro.
Annual International Chicken Flying Festival. Feather fanciers bring their prize flyers to town in an attempt to break the world's record chicken flight of 297′2″. May, Rio Grande.
Springthing. Garden plants, solar demonstrations. May, Toledo.
Dulcimer Days. May, Coshocton.
Moonshine Festival. Moonshine still displays, moonshine pie, sno cones, arts and crafts, carnival, games, square dancing. May, New Straitsville.
Frontier Days, American Legion Grounds. May, Milford.

Wisconsin
No major spring events.

Summer
(June, July, August)

Illinois
Rose Festival Days Carnival, Turners Park. June, Roselle.
International Carillon Festival. Carilloners from a number of nations participate in this event; dancers; carillon concerts. June, Springfield.
Bluegrass Music Festival. June, Keithsburg.
Atwood Summer Festival Days, Atwood Park. June, Atwood.
Old Canal Days Festival. June, Lockport.
Midwest Music Festival. June, Plainfield.
Annual Swedish Days. June, Geneva.
Old Settlers Annual Fair. June, Metamora.
Deutschfest, Public Square. June, DuQuoin.
Annual Folk and Bluegrass Festival. June, Goodfield.
Annual Spoon River Days. June, Wyoming.
Annual Illinois Country Music Festival, Illinois Country Opry. July, Petersburg.
German Music Festival. July, Arcola.
Annual Italian Feast. July, Melrose Park.
Obon Dance Festival. July, Chicago.
Old-Time Fiddlers' Festival. July, Arcola.
Barbershop Quartet Music Festival. August, Arcola.
Folk Art Festival. August, Galesburg.
Bluegrass Festival. Lincoln Log Cabin State Historical Site. August, Charleston.
Blue Mound Fall Festival. August, Blue Mound.
Fun Days. August, Milford.
Old Settlers Days. August, Hillsboro.
Square Dancing Festival. August, Oregon.
Annual Sweetcorn Festival. Antique show and art sale, queen contest, talent show. August, Mendota.

Indiana
Camelot Wine Festival. June, Bloomington.
Hoosier Hills Festival. June, Bloomington.
Indiana Rose Festival. More than 200,000 blooms on display at Hillsdale Rose Gardens. June, Castleton.
Beanblossom Bluegrass Festival. June, Beanblossom.
Strawberry Festival. June, Indianapolis.
Carroll County Pork Festival. June, Flora.
Renaissance Fair. June, Muncie.
Jayland Bluegrass Festival. June, Portland.
Civil War Days. June, Rockville.
Mermaid Festival. June, North Webster.
Turtle Days. The sighting of a giant turtle in Fulk Lake near Churubusco in 1949 led to a frenzied but unsuccessful search for the great creature. So the "Beast of Busco" is now the subject of annual celebration. June, Churubusco.
Twelve-Mile "500" Riding Lawn Mower Race. June, Twelve Mile.
Flotilla Festival. July, Syracuse.
Three Rivers Festival. July, Fort Wayne.
Grecian Festival. July, Merrillville.
Wilderness Festival. July, New Carlisle.
Steam Harvest Days. Harvest auction, tent show melodrama. July, Rockville.
WNAP Great Raft Race. July, Indianapolis.
Corn Roast. August, Schererville.
Battle of Hesston Junction. 300 authentically-dressed Civil War soldiers set up camp on Heston Steam Grounds and conduct target practice with pistols, muskets and cannons. August, Hesston.
Popcorn Festival. August, Van Buren.

Potato Creek Festival. August, North Liberty.
Indiana State Fair. August, Indianapolis.
Founder's Festival Days. August, Connersville.
Little Italy Festival. August, Clinton.
Watermelon Festival. August, Brownstown.
Oktoberfest. August and September, Michigan City.

Michigan
Muzzle Loaders Festival, Greenfield Village. June, Dearborn.
Red Cedar Jubilee. June, Williamston.
Old-Time Summer Festival. June, Dearborn.
Seaway Festival. June, Muskegon.
Thornapple Bluegrass Music Festival. June, Hastings.
Thimbleberry Festival. June, Houghton/Hancock.
Dancing Hippopotamus Arts and Crafts Festival. June, Ocqueoc.
National Forest Festival. June, Manistee.
Arab Festival. July, Detroit.
Sauerkraut Festival. July, Bridgeport.
Blue Water Festival. July, Port Huron.
Pigeon River Festival. July, Vanderbilt.
Alpenfest. July, Gaylord.
National Blueberry Festival. July, South Haven.
Polish Festival Days. July, Bronson.
Potato Festival. July, Munger.
Medieval Festival. July, Ann Arbor.
Coast Guard Festival. July, Grand Haven.
Ingham County Fair. July, Mason.
Summer Clown Festival. August, Detroit.
Polish Polka Festival. August, Wyandotte.
Irish Festival. August, Wyandotte.
Danish Festival. August, Greeneville.
India Festival, Hart Plaza. August, Detroit.
Frog Jumping Contest. August, Springport.
U.S. Cheerleaders National Grand Championships, Civic Center, August, Lansing.
Michigan Peach Festival. August, Romeo.

The Glockenspiel Tower of Michigan's Bavarian Inn contains a 35-bell carillon which plays three melodies.

Ohio

Fairhaven Antique Festival. June, Fairhaven.

Little Miami River Canoe and Kayak Races. June, Milford.

Heritage Home Tour. June, Mount Vernon.

Super Summer Sunday Concerts. June through August, Toledo.

Annual NHRA Spring Nationals, National Trail Raceway. June, Newark.

Annual International Hummel Festival. Display of world's rare Hummel figurines. June, Eaton.

Troy Strawberry Festival. June, Troy.

Maumee Valley Frontier Day. June, Defiance.

Festival of the Fish. Boat races, parades, model boat show, fish dinners, fishing contest. June, Vermilion.

House and Garden Pilgrimage. June, Hundson.

Ohio State Trapshoot. June, Vandalia.

Mid-Ohio Bluegrass Festival. June, Reynoldsburg.

Annual Geauga County Air Show and Summer Festival. June, Middlefield.

Annual Haus and Garten Tour. June, Columbus.

Great Miami River Festival. June, Dayton.

Great Lakes Shakespeare Festival. July through September, Lakewood.

Annual Midyear Show, Butler Institute of American Art. July, Youngstown.

Huron Water Festival. July, Huron.

Annual Millionaire's Walk. Tour of old mansions. July, Warren.

Canal Days. July, Canal Fulton.

Old-Time Music Festival, Hale Farm and Village. July, Bath.

Ohio Hills Folk Festival. July, Quaker City.

Annual Roseville-Crooksville Pottery Festival. July, Crooksville.

Annual Outdoor Arts Festival. July, Willoughby.

Annual Twins Day. Entire day of activities in honor of twins; parade, art show, entertainment, games and contests. July, Twinsburg.

Dixie Days Festival. August, Mount Vernon.

Annual Ohio National Bluegrass Festival. August, Ottawa.

Ohio Shaker Festival. August, Kettering.

Inter-Lake Yachting Association Regatta. August, South Bass Island.

Grand American Trapshoot. August, Vandalia.

Annual Rio Grande Bean Dinner. August, Rio Grande.

Bratwurst Festival. August, Bucyrus.

Annual German-American Festival. August, Maumee.

Sweet Corn Festival. August, Millersport.

Wisconsin

June Sprints. Auto racing. June, Elkhart Lake.

Lakefront Festival of the Arts. June, Milwaukee.

Heidi Festival. The enchanting tales of Heidi and Wilhelm Tell are retold. June, New Glarus.

Summerfest. June, Milwaukee.

Art Fair on the Square. June, Madison.

Holland Festival. June, Cedar Grove.

Lumberjack Championships. July, Hayward.

Experimental Aircraft Association Fly-In. July, Oshkosh.

Wisconsin State Fair. August, Milwaukee.

Peninsula Music Festival. August, Fish Creek.

Fall
(September, October, November

Illinois

Grape Festival. September, Nauvoo.

Hog Capital of the World Festival. September, Kewanee.

Golden Marigold Festival. September, Golden.

Bean Days. September, Wayne City.

Homestead Festival. September, Princeton.

Annual Morton Pumpkin Festival. Giant pumpkin contest, parade. September, Morton.

Murphysboro Apple Festival. Four days of activities that include parade, band contest, tractor pull, apple core throwing. September, Murphysboro.
Summit Fireman's Annual Festival. September, Summit.
Apple and Pork Festival. September, Clinton.
Fall Craft Festival. October, Springfield.
Chrysanthemum Show. November, Chicago.
Ansar Shrime Circus. November, Springfield.

Indiana
Lake James Jazz Festival. September, Angola.
Tipton County Pork Festival. September, Tipton.
Steamboat Days Festival. September, Jeffersonville.
Canaan Fall Festival. September, Canaan.
Turkey Trot Festival. September, Montgomery.
Bed Race Festival. Bed races, tug-o-war, arts and crafts, hobby show, baking contest. September, South Whitley.
Oktoberfest. September, Terre Haute.
Johnny Appleseed Festival. September, Fort Wayne.
Cory Apple Festival. September, Cory.
Festival of the Turning Leaves. September, Thorntown.
Hope Heritage Days. September, Hope.
Westside Nut Club Festival. October, Evansville.
Orange County Pumpkin Festival. October, West Baden.
Fodder Festival and Old Settlers Days. October, Salem.
James Whitcomb Riley Festival. October, Greenfield.
Village Tour of Homes. October, Zionsville.
Feast of the Hunters' Moon. October, Lafayette.
Amish Acres Fall Craft Days. October, Nappanee.
Harvest Homecoming. October, New Albany.
Covered Bridge Festival. October, Rockville.
Fright Nights. October, Indianapolis.
Sorghum Festival. October, Leavenworth/Marengo.
Callithumpian Week. Oldest Halloween parade in Indiana. October, Decatur.
Trappers' Rendezvous. October, Fort Wayne.
Mrs. Claus' Closet. Gigantic display of Christmas gifts. November, Brownsburg.

Built by the French in 1715, Michigan's Fort Michilimackinac has been restored and designated a national historic landmark.

Michigan
Mackinac Bridge Walk. September, St. Ignace/Mackinaw City.
Old Car Festival. September, Dearborn.
Carry Nation Festival. September, Holly.
Blues Festival. September, Detroit.
Honey Harvest. September, Bloomfield Hills.
Grape and Wine Festival. September, Paw Paw.
Four Flags Area Apple Festival. September, Niles.

Ohio
River Days. September, Portsmouth.
Melon Festival. September, Milan.
Tomato Festival. September, Reynoldsburg.
Honey Festival. September, Lebanon.
Johnny Appleseed Festival. September, Lisbon.
International Mining and Manufacturing Festival. September, Cadiz.
Ohio Swiss Festival. September, Sugarcreek.
Grape Jamboree. September, Geneva.
Paul Bunyan Show. October, Nelsonville.
Holmes County Antique Festival. October, Millersburg.
Pumpkin Show. October, Circleville.
Fall Festival of Leaves. October, Bainbridge.
Dayton Holiday Festival. November to December, Dayton.
The Skies of November. November, Salt Fork State Park.

Wisconsin
Wilhelm Tell Festival. September, New Glarus.
Oktoberfest. September to October, La Crosse.
Holiday Folk Fair. November, Milwaukee.

Winter
(December, January, February)

Illinois
Poinsettia Show. December, Peoria.
Shady Lane Farm Playhouse. Last shows of season. December, Marengo.

Indiana
Christmas at the Sieberling Mansion. December, Kokomo.
Revolutionary War Christmas. December, Fort Wayne.
Christmas at the Zoo. December, Indianapolis.
Christmas Candlelight Tour. December, Indianapolis.
Winter Sports Festival. Nordic and alpine ski races, ice fishing contests. January, New Carlisle.
Winter Carnival. January, New Paris.
Winterfest. January, Bloomington and Fort Wayne.
Parke County Maple Fair. February, Rockville.

Michigan
No major winter events.

Ohio
Annual Winter Hike. January, Hocking Hills.
Winter Workshop. February, Pymatuning State Park, Andover.
Hueston Woods Maple Syrup Festival. February, Hueston Woods State Park, Oxford.

Wisconsin
World Snowmobile Championships. January, Eagle River.
American Birkebeiner. Cross-country ski race. February, Telemark to Hayward.

No visit to Springfield would be complete without a visit to the silver-domed Illinois Capitol Building.

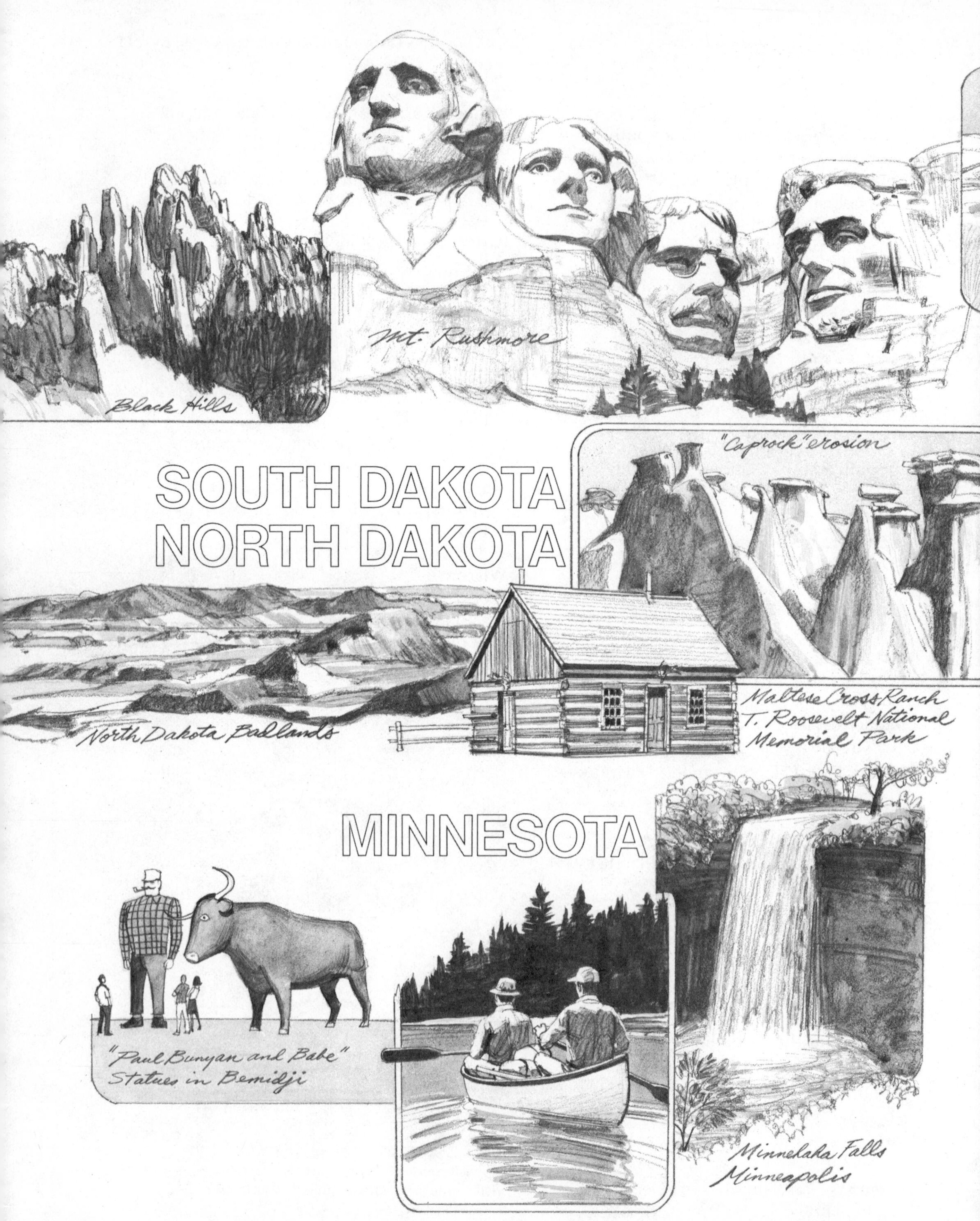
Mt. Rushmore
Black Hills
"Caprock" erosion
SOUTH DAKOTA
NORTH DAKOTA
North Dakota Badlands
Maltese Cross Ranch
T. Roosevelt National
Memorial Park
MINNESOTA
"Paul Bunyan and Babe"
Statues in Bemidji
Minnehaha Falls
Minneapolis

Mitchell Pass on the Oregon Trail
Chimney Rock Pioneer Landmark
R. McKee
NEBRASKA
Buffalo Bill's Home - North Platte
Eisenhower home, Abilene
GENERAL OUTFITTING
LONG BRANCH
DRY GOODS
CITY DRUG STORE
Front Street - Dodge City
KANSAS
MISSOURI
St. Louis
Mark Twain Home, Hannibal
Truman Library, Independence
Ragtime music
IOWA
Hog Capitol
Carver Hall - Iowa State U.
Des Moines State Capitol

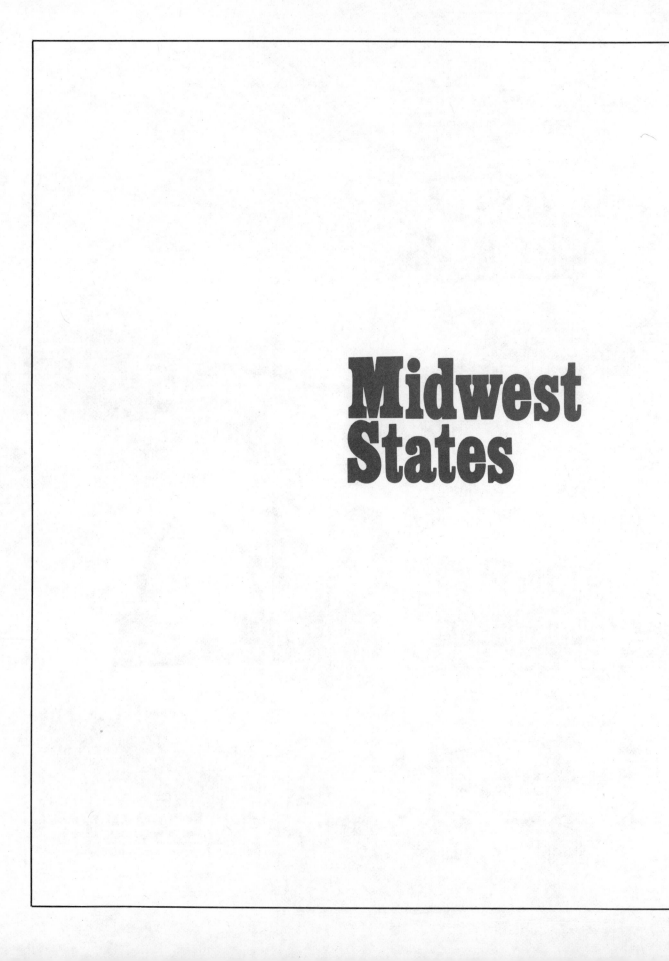

Midwest States

Bordered on the east by the Mississippi River and on the west by the Rocky Mountains, the states of America's heartland consist mainly of gently rolling plains and prairies developed into a patchwork quilt of farms and ranches. Though much of the land in this region has been claimed for practical use to meet the needs of man, there are still a great many recreation opportunities available for those who take the time to seek them out.

In Iowa, the state that is sometimes called the "biggest cornfield on earth," there are a number of backcountry towns inviting exploration and a host of colorful fairs and festivals waiting to entertain you. Throughout North Dakota and South Dakota, you'll encounter constant reminders of the region's Old West heritage, plus some of the best fishing and pheasant hunting to be found anywhere. In Kansas, among the waving fields of wheat, you'll find remnants of the Wild West days, when trailhands drove vast cattle herds through the state on their way to market, and you'll also enjoy excellent upland game shooting.

For sheer scenic beauty, few states can match Minnesota's lake and woods country, and the spectacular Boundary Waters Canoe Area Wilderness. In Missouri's Ozarks, you'll come across some sharp contrasts with the rest of the states in the area; there's a southern flavor in these rolling hills and a rich heritage of folkways and skills. Nebraska has its Sand Hills and Great Plains, as well as the cultural offerings to be found in the galleries and museums of Omaha and Lincoln; it also has excellent fishing waters and hunting for everything from pheasants and ducks to deer and elk.

So don't hurry through the Midwest . . . stop and enjoy!

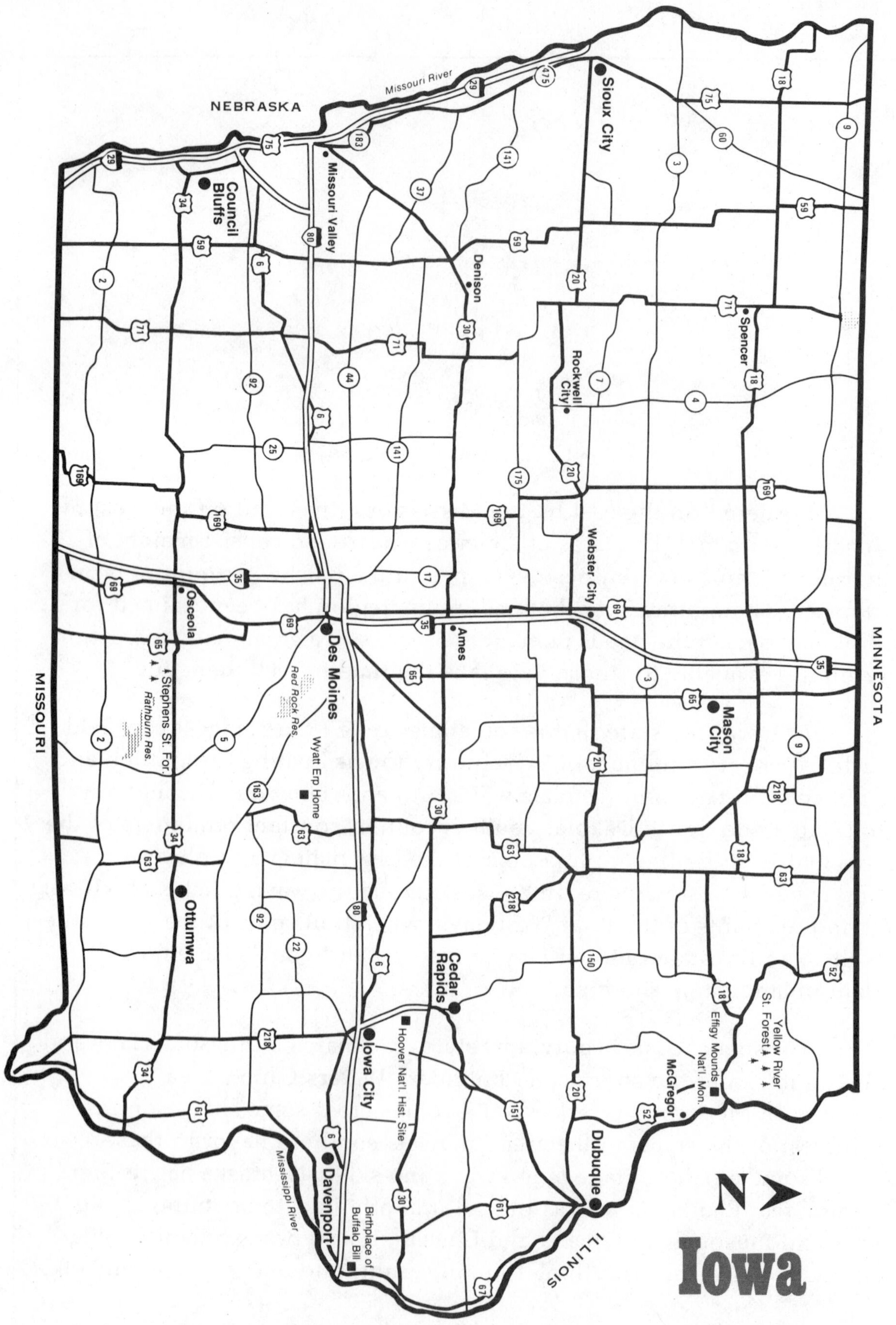
Iowa
N
NEBRASKA
Missouri River
MINNESOTA
MISSOURI
ILLINOIS
Sioux City
Council Bluffs
Missouri Valley
Denison
Spencer
Rockwell City
Webster City
Ames
Osceola
Des Moines
Mason City
Stephens St. For.
Rathburn Res.
Red Rock Res.
Wyatt Erp Home
Ottumwa
Cedar Rapids
Iowa City
Hoover Nat'l. Hist. Site
Davenport
Mississippi River
Birthplace of Buffalo Bill
Dubuque
McGregor
Effigy Mounds Nat'l. Mon.
Yellow River St. Forest

Map not to exact scale.

Iowa

With 93% of its land devoted to agriculture, Iowa has come to symbolize the nation's cornucopia heartland. However, this doesn't mean that Iowa lacks attractions for the traveler. The state offers reminders of a prehistoric Indian past, the Old World Amish, the unique Amana colonies, colorful festivals, beautiful parks, sparkling rivers and much more. In fact, Iowa's very name is an old Indian word meaning "Beautiful Land," and as you travel from the rolling hills of the east to the state's western prairies, you will find little that doesn't please the eye.

The first Europeans to visit Iowa were Louis Jolliet and Father Jacques Marquette, who came to the region in 1673 during their explorations for France. From 1673 to 1762, Iowa remained in the hands of the French, after which Spain acquired the region and divided it into three private land grants — Dubuque in 1796, Tesson in 1799 and Giard in 1800. At Napolean's command, Spain reluctantly ceded Iowa back to France, which controlled the area until it was acquired by the United States in the Louisiana Purchase. Permanent settlement in Iowa finally began in 1833, following a white victory in the Black Hawk War. Iowa was admitted to the Union on December 28, 1846.

If you want to get a closeup look at life on a farm, you might consider stopping for a time at one of Iowa's guest farms, where you'll enjoy sheer relaxation, superb food and an opportunity to pitch in with the chores if you like. If you want to sample more of the rural life, take in one of the state's many county fairs, or time your visit to coincide with the Iowa State Fair held at Des Moines in late summer. For a glimpse of small-town pageantry, visit Mason City in early June for the festivities of the North Iowa Band Festival.

Full name: State of Iowa
Origin of name: From the name of the Sioux tribe, the Ioways or Aiouez, meaning "Sleepy Ones."
Motto: Our Liberties We Prize and Our Rights We Will Maintain
Nickname: Hawkeye State
Capital: Des Moines
Statehood: December 28, 1846, 29th state.
Population: 2,879,000 (ranks 25th).
Major Cities: Des Moines (194,170), Cedar Rapids (108,998), Davenport (99,941).
Bird: Eastern goldfinch
Flower: Wild rose
Tree: Oak

Average daily temperatures by month

	Northern	Southern
Jan.	21.9 to 4.0	31.0 to 12.9
Feb.	27.7 to 9.6	37.3 to 18.6
Mar.	37.4 to 20.1	47.0 to 27.2
Apr.	56.2 to 35.0	62.8 to 40.8
May	69.3 to 46.4	74.2 to 51.6
Jun.	79.1 to 56.7	83.0 to 61.1
Jul.	82.2 to 60.7	87.1 to 65.2
Aug.	81.1 to 58.7	85.4 to 63.3
Sept.	71.8 to 48.9	77.6 to 54.8
Oct.	61.7 to 38.9	67.5 to 44.6
Nov.	43.1 to 24.6	50.1 to 30.8
Dec.	28.0 to 11.7	36.4 to 19.6
Year	55.0 to 34.6	61.6 to 40.9

Iowa is a leading producer of corn, soybeans, hogs and cattle, and only California exceeds it in total cash farm income. Manufacturing includes farm and garden equipment, meat packing, chemicals, grain processing, electrical equipment and pharmaceuticals.

State Offices

Tourism
Travel Development Division
Iowa Development Commission
250 Jewett Building
Des Moines, Iowa 50309
(515) 281-3401

State Police
Department of Public Safety
Wallace State Office Building
Des Moines, Iowa 50319
(515) 281-5114

Radio Stations

Cedar Rapids
WMT 600 (AM)
Des Moines
KIOA 940 (AM)
Sioux City
KBCM 95.5 (FM)

Iowa Points of Interest and Attractions

Amana Colonies. Seven villages with Old World charm and hospitality, founded in 1854 by an offshoot of the Lutheran Church. The 26,000-acre area includes general stores, bakeries, winery, furniture shop, woolen mill, meat shops, and many other unique craft-oriented businesses. Little Amana, off Interstate 80 (northwest of Iowa City).

Czech Village. An ethnic community featuring a charming mixture of shops, businesses and people that preserves the history, culture and traditions of the original settlers of this locality; special events throughout spring, summer and fall months. Cedar Rapids, near downtown area, off Interstate 380.

Glacial Rock. Deposited by the Wisconsin Glacier more than 50,000 years ago, this rock is the largest of its kind in the Midwest. Nashua, three miles west on State Route 54 and south three-quarters of a mile on dirt road (rock lies in middle of field on east side of road).

Old Creamery Theater Company. A repertory company of professional actors presenting five different plays during the season. Season: May through September, Thursday, Friday, Saturday, Sunday. Garrison, off US-218, on State Route 198. (319) 477-3925.

Original Delicious Apple Tree. Planted in the 1860s by Jesse Hiatt, a Quaker who came to the area in 1856; from this original tree, Stark Nurseries developed the Delicious Apple. It is estimated that some 10 million trees have come from the branches of this original tree. Peru, southeast of Des Moines, off Interstate 35.

Plow-In-Oak Park. A roadside park containing an ancient oak tree with an old iron plow embedded in it. The plow was placed against the tree by the son of a pioneer farmer; as the tree grows it engulfs more and more of the plow which no longer rests on the ground. Exira, one mile south on US-71.

Snake Alley. This unique street was featured in Ripley's "Believe-It-Or-Not" as "the crookedest street in the world." Situated on a limestone bluff, the street consists of five half-curves and two quarter-curves descending over a distance of 275 feet. The curves in the street were designed to permit horses to descend the hill at safe speeds. Burlington, on North Sixth Street, between Washington and Columbia Streets.

Spillville. A little community that claims two distinctions as home of the famous composer Antonin Dvorak and home of the Bily Clocks. Actually, Dvorak only spent one summer here with his family, but it is said he composed at least one quartette in Spillville in addition to finding the inspiration for *Humoresque.* The Dvorak house is now marked and Dvorak concerts are presented from time to time.

Bily Clocks. The Bily brothers, Frank and Joseph, built clocks of such unique design that they drew attention from all over the world. The amazing and fascinating clock collection is now on display in the Dvorak house. On State Route 325 (southwest of Decorah).

Valley Junction. An area of downtown Des Moines, the state capital, that features a number of unique antique, apparel, craft and gift shops, as well as art galleries, restaurants and specialty shops. On Fifth and Elm Streets.

Lake Okoboji in Northwest Iowa is the setting for many sailing regattas during the summer months and a popular resort area for visitors.

Highlight

Spillville

Spillville, a predominately Czech village, came into existence in 1854 when Joseph Spielman, who came from Europe in 1849 and located there, built a sawmill, subsequently adding a grist mill and other buildings that acquired the name of Spielville, later Americanized into Spillville. Many of those who followed Spielman were from Bohemia, a few were from Switzerland. They brought with them traditions of their fatherlands which are retained in part to this day, giving to this picturesque inland village a happy combination of Old World atmosphere and modern progress. Progress is expressed by numerous homes of modern equipment; the Old World atmosphere is found in the hospitality that radiates from these homes and their surroundings of neatly kept lawns and old-fashioned gardens.

Another Old World feature is the public square around which is built the business section of the town. Adorning the center of the square is a well-proportioned bandstand, built at the close of World War I in honor of American soldiers and sailors — a substantial evidence of the loyalty of Spillville to the American government and the men who defended it in the cause of liberty and equality.

With its background of gently rising hills, the village presents an inviting picture to the visitor. Its streets are lined with native elms. They are well kept, and the citizens have bent their energies toward enhancing the natural beauty of the locality.

Music has long been one of Spillville's traditions. Out of an early-day orchestra, other musical organizations developed.

The citizens of Spillville have developed one of the most inviting parks in northeastern Iowa. This park lies on the east side of the village and is bordered by the Turkey River. In its center is the Inwood Pavilion, which is surrounded by excellent picnic ground and playground facilities.

Iowa State Parks

Park	Location	CAMPING	PICNICKING	CONCESSIONS	SWIMMING	HIKING	BOATING	FISHING	HUNTING	WINTER SPORTS
Ambrose A. Call	*Algona. Off US-169.*	•	•			•				
Backbone	*Strawberry Point. Off State Route 410.*	•	•		•	•	•	•		•
Beeds Lake	*Hampton. Off State Route 3.*	•	•		•	•	•	•		•
Bellevue	*Bellevue. Off US-52.*	•	•			•				•
Big Creek	*Polk City. Off State Route 415.*		•			•	•	•		
Black Hawk Lake	*Lake View. Off State Route 175.*	•	•		•		•	•	•	•
Bob White	*Allerton. Off State Route 40.*	•	•		•	•	•	•		
Clear Lake	*Clear Lake. Off State Route 106.*	•	•		•		•	•	•	•
Dolliver Memorial	*Lehigh. Off State Route 50.*	•	•		•	•	•	•		
Echo Valley	*West Union. Off State Route 56.*		•		•	•				
Elk Rock	*Knoxville. Off State Route 14.*	•	•			•	•	•		•
Emerson Bay	*Milford. Off State Route 32.*	•	•		•		•	•		•
Fairpoint	*Muscatine. Off State Route 22.*	•	•		•		•	•		
Fort Defiance	*Estherville. Off State Route 9.*	•	•			•		•		
Geode	*Danville. Off State Route 16.*	•	•		•	•	•	•		•
George Wyth Memorial	*Cedar Falls. Off US-20.*	•	•			•	•	•		•
Green Valley	*Creston. Off State Route 25.*	•	•		•		•	•		•
Gull Point	*Milford. Off State Route 32.*	•	•		•	•	•	•		•
Honey Creek	*Moravia. Off State Route 5.*	•	•		•	•	•	•		•
Lacey-Keosauqua	*Keosauqua. Off State Route 1.*	•	•	•	•	•	•	•		•
Lake Ahquabi	*Indianola. Off State Route 349.*	•	•		•	•	•	•		•
Lake Anita	*Anita. Off Interstate 80.*	•	•		•		•	•		•
Lake Darling	*Brighton. Off State Routes 78 and 1.*	•	•		•	•	•	•		•
Lake Keomah	*Oskaloosa. Off State Route 371.*	•	•		•	•	•	•		•
Lake MacBride	*Solon. Off State Route 382.*	•	•		•	•	•	•		•
Lake Manawa	*Council Bluffs. Off State Route 192.*	•	•		•		•	•		•
Lake of Three Fires	*Bedford. Off State Route 49.*	•	•		•	•	•	•		•
Lake Wapello	*Drakesville. Off State Route 273.*	•	•		•	•	•	•		•
Ledges	*Boone. Off State Route 164.*	•	•			•		•		•
Lewis and Clark	*Onawa. Off State Route 324.*	•	•		•	•	•	•		•
Lower Gar	*Arnolds Park. Off US-71.*	•	•					•		•
McGregor Heights	*McGregor. Off US-18.*		•							
McIntosh Woods	*Ventura. Off US-18.*	•	•		•		•	•		•
Maquoketa Caves	*Maquoketa. Off US-61.*	•	•			•				
Marble Beach	*Orleans. Off State Route 276.*	•	•		•	•	•	•		•
Margo Frankel Woods	*Des Moines. Off State Route 415.*		•			•				
Nine Eagles	*Davis City. Off US-69.*	•	•		•	•	•	•		•
Okamanpedan	*Dolliver. Off State Route 9.*		•		•		•	•		
Palisades-Kepler	*Mount Vernon. Off US-30.*	•	•			•	•	•		•
Pammel	*Winterset. Off State Routes 92 and 162.*	•	•			•		•		
Pikes Peak	*McGregor. Off State Route 340.*	•	•			•				
Pilot Knob	*Forest City. Off State Route 9.*	•	•			•	•	•		•
Pilsbury Point	*Arnolds Park. Off US-71.*		•		•	•	•	•		
Pine Lake	*Eldora. Off State Route 118.*	•	•		•	•	•	•		•

Iowa State Parks

Park	Location	CAMPING	PICNICKING	CONCESSIONS	SWIMMING	HIKING	BOATING	FISHING	HUNTING	WINTER SPORTS
Prairie Rose	*Harlan. Off State Route 44.*	•	•		•		•	•		•
Preparation Canyon	*Moorhead. Off State Route 372.*		•			•				
Red Haw Lake	*Chariton. Off US-34.*	•	•		•	•	•	•		•
Rice Lake	*Lake Mills. Off US-69.*		•		•		•	•		
Rock Creek	*Kellogg. Off US-6.*	•	•		•	•	•	•		•
Sharon Bluffs	*Centerville. Off State Route 2.*		•			•				
Springbrook	*Guthrie Center. Off State Routes 25 and 384.*	•	•		•	•	•	•		•
Stone	*Sioux City. Off State Route 12.*	•	•			•		•		•
Trappers Bay	*Lake Park. Off State Route 219.*		•				•	•		•
Union Grove	*Gladbrook. Off State Route 96.*	•	•		•	•	•	•		•
Viking Lake	*Stanton. Off US-32 and US-71.*	•	•		•	•	•	•		•
Walnut Woods	*Des Moines. Off State Route 5.*	•	•			•	•	•		
Wanata	*Peterson. Off State Route 10.*		•			•				
Wapsipinicon	*Anamosa. Off US-151.*	•	•			•	•	•		•
Waubonsie	*Sidney. Off State Route 239.*	•	•			•				•
Wildcat Den	*Fairport. Off State Route 22.*	•	•			•				
Wilson Island	*Loveland. Off US-30.*	•	•			•	•	•		•

Iowa State Forests

Forest	Location	CAMPING	PICNICKING	CONCESSIONS	SWIMMING	HIKING	BOATING	FISHING	HUNTING	WINTER SPORTS
Pilot Mound	*Pilot Mound. Off State Route 329.*		•							
Stephens	*Chariton. Off US-65 and US-34.*	•	•			•	•	•		•
Shimek	*Farmington. Off State Route 2.*	•	•			•	•	•		•
Yellow River	*Waukon. Off State Route 76.*	•	•			•	•	•		•

For more information on Iowa state parks and forests, contact: *Iowa Conservation Commission, Wallace State Office Building, Des Moines, Iowa 50319, (515) 281-5886.*

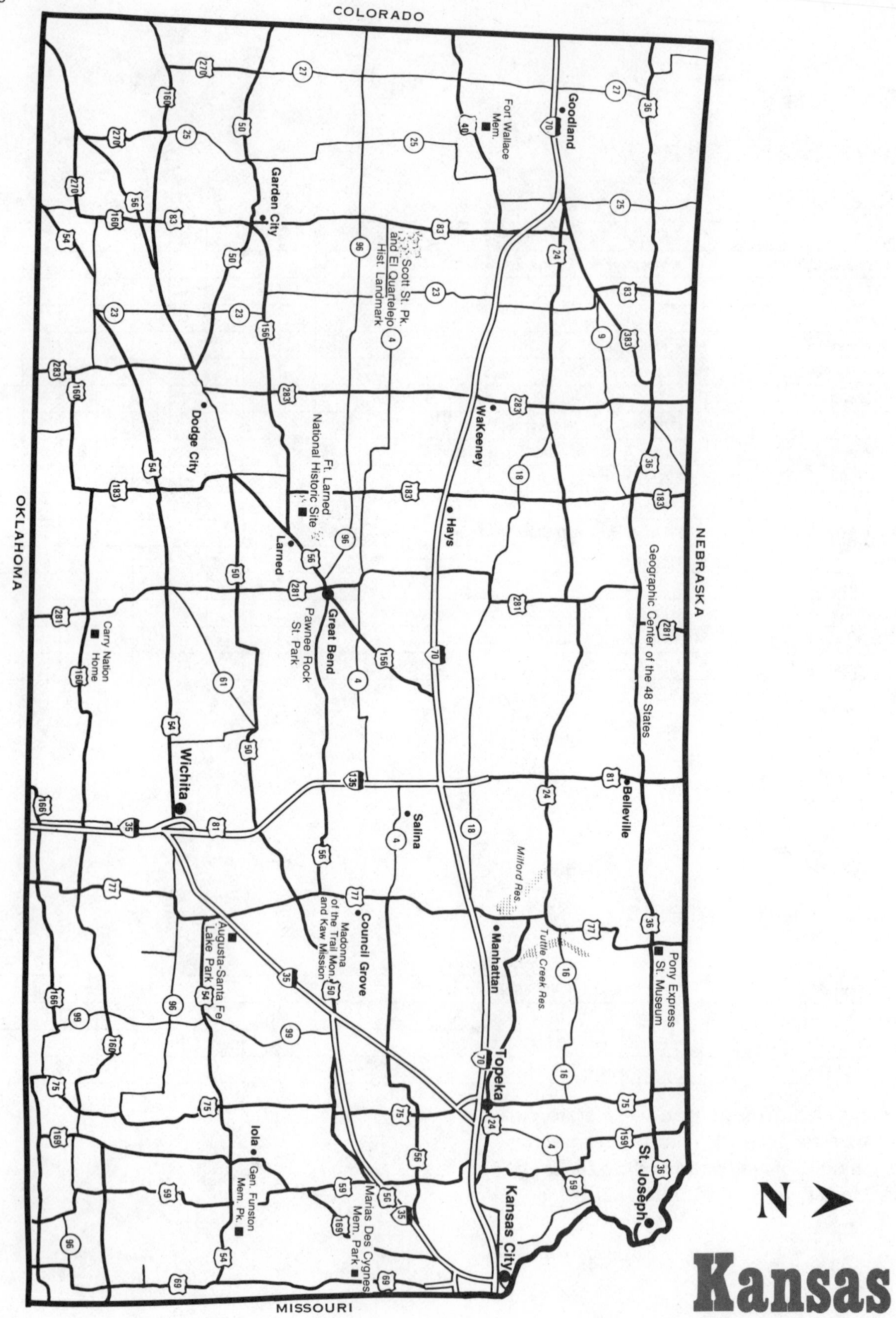
COLORADO
OKLAHOMA
NEBRASKA
MISSOURI
Goodland
Fort Wallace Mem.
Garden City
Scott St. Pk. and El Quartelejo Hist. Landmark
Dodge City
WaKeeney
Ft. Larned National Historic Site
Larned
Hays
Great Bend
Pawnee Rock St. Park
Carry Nation Home
Geographic Center of the 48 States
Wichita
Salina
Belleville
Milford Res.
Council Grove
Madonna of the Trail Mon. and Kaw Mission
Manhattan
Tuttle Creek Res.
Pony Express St. Museum
Augusta-Santa Fe Lake Park
Topeka
Iola
Gen. Funston Mem. Pk.
Marias Des Cygnes Mem. Park
Kansas City
St. Joseph
N
Kansas

Map not to exact scale.

Kansas

Travelers who follow the east-west route of Interstate 70 across Kansas may conclude that the state consists only of flat prairie land — but they'd be wrong. Kansas has an extremely varied terrain that rises from an elevation of 700 feet in the southeast to more than 4,000 feet in the northwest. And in between, there are thousands of rolling hills, lush valleys, picturesque chalk and sandstone formations and nearly a hundred small lakes.

Several Indian tribes — Kansas, Wichita, Pawnee, Comanche — inhabited the Kansas region before the Spanish explorer Francisco Vasquez de Coronado came to the area in 1541 in search of fabulous treasures. No attempts were made to establish settlements in the region, however, and even after the Louisiana Purchase, which made Kansas a part of the United States, the region was thought to be too barren for development. After 1830, the territory was designated as permanent Indian country and several tribes from the Northeastern United States were relocated there. During this period, several forts (Leavenworth, Scott and Riley) were established as outposts to protect travelers against Indian raids. With the passage of the Kansas-Nebraska Act in 1854, the territory became the scene of several bloody skirmishes between the free-state "Jayhawkers" (including abolitionist John Brown) and proponents of slavery. The Jayhawkers were ultimately victorious and Kansas was admitted to the Union in 1861 as a free state.

One of the most famous remnants of Kansas' Old West heritage is Dodge City, the legendary frontier town that was the world's largest cattle market in the 1800s. Other towns like Abilene, Hays and Wichita also preserve reminders of an era that echoed with the gunfire of western heroes like Bat Masterson and Wyatt Earp.

In recent years, more than 30 federal reservoirs have been constructed which

Full name: State of Kansas
Origin of name: From name of Sioux tribe meaning "People of the South Wind."
Motto: *Ad Astra per Aspera* (To The Stars Through Difficulties).
Nickname: Sunflower State
Capital: Topeka
Statehood: January 29, 1861, 34th state.
Population: 2,326,000 (ranks 31st).
Major Cities: Wichita (264,901), Kansas City (168,153), Topeka (119,203).
Bird: Western meadowlark
Flower: Sunflower
Tree: Cottonwood

Average daily temperatures by month

	Northern	Southern
Jan.	40.2 to 14.9	45.0 to 21.7
Feb.	46.7 to 20.4	50.9 to 26.1
Mar.	54.0 to 26.8	58.9 to 32.9
Apr.	67.9 to 39.4	71.3 to 44.9
May	77.6 to 50.6	80.4 to 54.8
Jun.	88.0 to 61.1	90.3 to 64.5
Jul.	93.3 to 66.2	94.9 to 69.0
Aug.	92.2 to 64.5	94.2 to 67.3
Sept.	82.6 to 54.2	84.9 to 59.2
Oct.	71.9 to 42.0	74.1 to 47.5
Nov.	54.8 to 28.2	58.0 to 34.0
Dec.	43.1 to 18.9	46.9 to 25.0
Year	67.7 to 40.6	70.8 to 45.6

Highlight

Atchison, Kansas, has been immortalized in the famous song that celebrates the Atchison, Topeka and Santa Fe Railroad — and deservedly so, because it is a colorful community that has a good deal to offer travelers.

Symbolic of the town's role in the history of railroading is the old locomotive that sits in a park adjoining the Union Station. Fittingly, the locomotive was a gift from the Atchison, Topeka and Santa Fe Railroad. A monument to the railroad is in front of the Memorial Hall at 819 Commercial Street.

A marker at the town's courthouse commemorates a speech which Abraham Lincoln gave there and later delivered in New York City. It is said that that speech brought Lincoln the national recognition that earned him the presidential nomination.

Atchison is also the birthplace of Amelia Earhart, and you'll find a monument to the famed aviatrix at the Amelia Earhart Memorial Airport three miles west of town.

Before you end your sojourn in Atchison, take a walk along the bluffs at Benedictine College, where there is a memorable view of the Missouri River.

now provide facilities for camping, fishing, swimming and other water sports. Kansas also has an outstanding system of roadside parks to welcome weary travelers.

Because of Kansas' strategic location in the geographical center of the continental United States, it is especially attractive to industries with nationwide distribution. A major industrial activity is the manufacture of transportation equipment — Wichita produces more than half of the nation's aircraft, while Topeka is a center for the production and repair of railroad cars. Of course, the state is also an important agricultural center and Kansas remains the leading wheat producer and flour miller. The mining of oil and natural gas are also important elements in the state's economy.

State Offices

Tourism
Kansas Department of Economic Development
122 South State Office Building
Topeka, Kansas 66612
(913) 296-3483

State Police
Department of Public Safety
200 East Sixth Street
Topeka, Kansas 66603
(913) 296-3102

Radio Stations

Topeka
KEWI 1440 (AM)
Wichita
KLEO 1480 (AM)

Kansas Points of Interest and Attractions

Agricultural Hall of Fame. Monument to the industry that was once the leader in the nation; three buildings house exhibits on the evolution of agriculture. Open year-round. Bonner Springs, off Interstate 70 (west of Kansas City).

Dalton Gang Hideout. Follow a secret escape tunnel from the house to the barn, then view the exhibits in the western museum that contains one of the finest gun collections in the nation. Meade, off US-54, on Main Street.

Eisenhower Center. Complex that includes the Eisenhower family home, presidential library and "A Place Of Meditation," Eisenhower's grave. Open year-round. Abilene, off US-40, on State Route 15.

Flint Hills. A series of grassy and scenic outcroppings that ripple across the state from Marshall County in the north to Cowley County in the south. Wildflowers dot the hills from spring through fall; in the fall you may see cattle being driven to market after grazing all summer long on the eight-foot-high bluestem grasses that are also native to the hills. From Marysville in the north to Burden in the south, roughly following the path of State Route 177.

Geographical Center. A marker denotes the geographical center of the contiguous 48 states. Near Mankato, off US-36.

"Little House On The Prairie." The childhood home of famed writer Laura Ingalls Wilder, who authored numerous stories on growing up in the Midwest and West. Open year-round, Independence, 10 miles southwest off US-75.

Monument Rocks. Carved by wind and water into unique formations, these chalk outcroppings are the first Natural National Landmark in Kansas. The formations which rise some 60 feet from the floor of the Smokey Hill River valley are made up of sedimented remains of ancient marine life. Wallace, off US-40.

Kansas State Parks

Park	Location	CAMPING	PICNICKING	CONCESSIONS	SWIMMING	HIKING	BOATING	FISHING	HUNTING	WINTER SPORTS
Cedar Bluff	*Wakeeney. Off State Route 47.*	•	•	•	•		•	•		
Cheney	*Wichita. On State Route 251.*	•	•	•	•		•	•		
Clinton	*Lawrence. On US-40.*	•	•							
Council Grove	*Council Grove. On US-56.*	•	•	•	•		•	•		
Crawford	*Girard. On State Route 7.*	•	•	•	•		•	•		
El Dorado	*El Dorado. On State Route 177.*	•	•							
Elk City	*Independence. On US-160.*	•	•		•		•	•		
Fall River	*Fredonia. On State Route 96.*	•	•		•		•	•		
Glen Elder	*Beloit. On US-24.*	•	•		•		•	•		
John Redmond	*Hartford. Off US-50.*	•	•		•		•	•		
Kanopolis	*Ellsworth. On State Route 41.*	•	•	•	•		•	•		
Kirwin	*Kirwin. On State Route 9.*	•	•				•	•		
Lovewell	*Mankato. On State Route 14.*	•	•	•	•		•	•		
Meade	*Meade. On State Route 23.*	•	•		•		•	•		
Melvern	*Lyndon. On State Route 278.*	•	•		•		•	•		
Milford	*Junction City. On State Route 57.*	•	•	•	•		•	•		
Perry	*Topeka. On State Route 237.*	•	•		•		•	•		
Pomona	*Ottawa. On State Route 368.*	•	•	•	•		•	•		
Prairie Dog	*Norton. Off US-36.*	•	•		•		•	•		
Sand Hills	*Hutchinson. Off State Route 61.*	•	•							
Scott	*Scott City. On State Route 95.*	•	•	•	•		•	•		
Toronto	*Yates Center. On State Route 105.*	•	•	•	•		•	•		
Tuttle Creek	*Manhattan. On US-24.*	•	•	•	•		•	•		
Webster	*Stockton. On US-24.*	•	•		•		•	•		
Wilson	*Wilson. Off State Route 232.*	•	•	•	•		•	•		

Kansas has no state forests. For more information on Kansas state parks, contact: *State Park and Resources Authority, 503 Kansas, PO Box 977, Topeka, Kansas 66601, (913) 296-2281.*

ONTARIO
Grand Portage Nat'l. Monument
Lake Superior
NORTH EAST MINN.
Northwest Angle State Forest
Lake of the Woods
MANITOBA
Zippel Bay
Baudette
International Falls
Voyageurs National Park
ONTARIO
Hayes Lake
Smokey Bear
Old Mill
Beltrani Island State Forest
Pine Island State Forest
Thief River Falls
Kabetogama State Forest
Red Lake
Koochiching State Forest
Nett Lake Ind. Res.
East Grand Forks
Red Lake Indian Reservation
Sturgeon River
Buena Vista
Superior National Forest
Geo. Washington State Forest
Virginia
Bemidji
Winnibigoshish Lake
Chisholm
NORTH DAKOTA
Cass Lake
White Earth
Chippewa National Forest
Grand Rapids
White Earth Indian Reservation
Paul Bunyan St. Forest
Leech Lake
Cloquet Valley State Forest
Two Inlets
Hill River
Lake Superior
Moorhead
Badoura
Land O'Lakes
Duluth
Detroit Lakes
Park Rapids
Foothills
Emily
Savannah St. For.
Cloquet
Crow Wing
River
Savannah Portage
Fond de Lac
Lyons
Wadena
Pillsbury
Mississippi
Crosby
WISCONSIN
Fergus Falls
Brainerd
Mille Lacs Lake
Moose Lake
Nemadji State Forest
St. Croix
Lake Carlos
Alexandria
Rum River
Red River
Chengwatana
Sauk Center
St. Cloud
Glacial Lakes
Upper & Lower St. Croix National Scenic Riverway
St. Croix River
Big Stone Lake
Ortonville
Sand Dunes
Appleton
Monson Lake
Wilmar
Minneapolis
Lac Qui Parle
St. Paul
Montevideo
SOUTH DAKOTA
Hastings
Minnesota
Red Wing
Marshall
Fort Ridgely Mem.
Nerstrand Woods
Richard J. Dorer Mem. Hardwood State Forest
Mississippi River
Sakatah Lake
Lake Shetek
Flandrau
Mankato
Rice Lake
Winona
Pipestone Nat. Mon.
Rochester
Blue Mounds
Worthington
Albert Lea
Helmer Myre
Austin
IOWA

Map not to exact scale.

Minnesota

Minnesota has long been known as the "Land of 10,000 Lakes." But that's not quite true. The state actually has some 11,000 lakes that were carved by giant glaciers thousands of years ago. More miles of shoreline than California and Oregon combined were left behind, creating an unmatched water wonderland for the angler and the outdoor enthusiast. Some 800,000 fishermen test Minnesota's waters each year, and thousands of canoeists and campers come annually to experience the beauty of the magnificent Boundary Waters Canoe Area Wilderness — a region of more than 1,000 miles of canoe routes and over 2,000 campsites.

The first inhabitants of Minnesota are thought to have dated from about 20,000 years ago, and Norsemen may have visited the area as early as the 14th century. The first Europeans of record were French trappers and Jesuit missionaries who came through the region between 1654 and 1660 on their voyages to the Northwest. Minnesota remained under French control until 1763, when it was ceded to the British. The British, in turn, sent several explorers into the region and developed an extensive Indian trade until 1783, when the area came under U.S. jurisdiction through the Definitive Treaty of Peace. White men in Minnesota came in contact with two Indian tribes, the Sioux and the Chippewa, and through treaties the United States purchased a large area of land from the Indians in 1837. A number of settlements were established immediately after the treaty and Minnesota Territory was established in 1849. Additional treaties with the Indians soon opened more land for settlement and the population increased rapidly, reaching more than 157,000 by 1857. Minnesota was admitted as a state on May 11, 1858.

Natives of Minnesota will tell you that one of the state's big attractions is its "theater of seasons." When summer turns to fall, the reds, yellows and oranges of the seasonal transition are simply

Full name: State of Minnesota
Origin of name: From the Sioux meaning "Sky-Tinted Water."
Motto: *L'Etoile du Nord* (The Star of the North).
Nickname: North Star State
Capital: St. Paul
Statehood: May 11, 1858, 32nd state.
Population: 3,975,000 (ranks 19th).
Major Cities: Minneapolis (378,112), St. Paul (279,535), Duluth (93,971).
Bird: Common loon
Flower: Pink and white lady's slipper
Tree: Norway pine

Average daily temperatures by month

	Northern	Southern
Jan.	15.4 to -9.4	22.9 to 2.5
Feb.	24.2 to -4.2	29.1 to 8.2
Mar.	37.0 to 9.9	39.5 to 20.1
Apr.	52.7 to 26.8	58.5 to 35.3
May	66.6 to 37.8	71.8 to 46.7
Jun.	76.0 to 48.3	81.3 to 56.8
Jul.	80.3 to 52.9	85.0 to 61.1
Aug.	78.3 to 51.1	83.3 to 58.9
Sept.	67.0 to 41.8	74.0 to 49.1
Oct.	56.6 to 33.4	63.8 to 39.3
Nov.	35.9 to 18.3	43.5 to 25.1
Dec.	21.9 to 1.1	29.0 to 11.4
Year	51.0 to 25.7	56.8 to 34.5

breathtaking. And they say that when Minnesota's waters cool down in the fall, the fish get even hungrier! When fall gives way to winter, you'll find yourself in an icy white wonderland and you'll want to try your hand at making snow sculptures, or go sledding, tobogganing, snowmobiling or snowshoeing. And to prove that there's more to Minnesota than the great outdoors, visit the Paul Bunyan Center in Brainerd; take the world's only underground mine shaft tour — and descend 2,400 feet in an elevator cage; stop off at the North West Company Fur Post at Pine City; or visit the boyhood home of famous aviator Charles A. Lindbergh, just south of Little Falls.

Agriculture is big business in Minnesota, and the state's farming industry is number one nationally in the production of sweet corn, timothy seed and non-fat dry milk. Mining is also an important industry, with about 70% of the nation's iron ore coming from Minnesota's Mesabi, Vermilion and Cuyuna ranges. Manufacturing includes machinery, electrical equipment, paper and paper products, industrial instruments and chemicals.

State Offices

Tourism
Tourism Division
Minnesota Department of Economic Development
480 Cedar Street
Hanover Building
St. Paul, Minnesota 55101
(612) 296-5027

State Police
Department of Public Safety
St. Paul, Minnesota 55155
(612) 482-5900

Radio Stations

Duluth
WEBC 560 (AM)
Minneapolis-St. Paul
KSTP 1500 (AM)
WDGY 1130 (AM)

Minnesota Points of Interest and Attractions

Ak-Sar-Ben Gardens. Two acres of formal gardens, Oriental rockwork, zoo, picnic area, trout fishing pond. Open spring through fall, daily, 9 a.m. to 7 p.m. Garrison, off US-18, on Tame Fish Road.

Brainerd. The central community in the heart of Paul Bunyan country; here you'll find the Paul Bunyan Center, where you can actually talk with the 50-foot lumberjack. Open May through September, daily. In Brainerd, you will also find the Crow Wing County Historical Museum and the Brainerd International Raceway (check schedule for auto racing events). Also nearby is the pioneer village of Lumbertown USA containing attractions for the whole family. On State Route 210.

Charles Lindbergh Home. The home of the famous aviator who made his historic transatlantic flight in 1927. Stop in at the interpretive center for highlights — in photos, slide shows and displays — of three generations of Lindberghs. Open year-round. Little Falls, on US-10.

Eloise Butler Wildflower Garden and Bird Sanctuary. A 20-acre reserve for plants native to Minnesota. Open spring through fall, daily. Minneapolis, Glenwood Avenue and Theodore Wirth Parkway.

Grand Mound Interpretive Center. Exhibits and audiovisual programs explain the early Indian cultures that built burial mounds here nearly 2,000 years ago. Grand Mound, the largest prehistoric burial mound in Minnesota, is 136 feet long, 98 feet wide and 40 feet high. International Falls, 17 miles west on State Route 11.

Hiawathaland Apple Blossom Drive. Breathtaking drive through river and valley vistas near La Crescent, the "Apple Capital" of Minnesota. In fall, several roadside stands offer apples for sale. La Crescent, off State Route 26.

Hull-Rust-Mahoning Mine. The world's largest open-pit iron mine that's almost five miles across and nearly 600 feet deep; tours. Open spring through fall. Hibbing, on US-169.

Mayo Clinic and "Mayowood." Tours of the famous medical facility are offered weekdays, and the Mayo Medical Museum is open daily. Not far away is "Mayowood," the spacious estate of Dr. Charles H. Mayo, built in 1910. Rochester, on US-63.

Murphy's Landing. A Minnesota Valley Restoration Project recreating the river town of the era 1840-1890; attractions include the cabin of fur trader Oliver Faribault, a German immigrant farm and several interesting old structures. Open spring through fall, daily. Shakopee, on US-169.

Northland Ecological Tract. A 40-acre natural tract operated by Northland Community College. Open spring through fall, daily. Thief River Falls, east on State Route 1.

Sauk Centre. The small town immortalized by Sinclair Lewis in his Pulitzer prize-winning novel, *Main Street.* Enter the town via Sinclair Lewis Avenue and you'll drive past the author's boyhood home. Museum. Open Memorial Day through Labor Day. Interstate 94 and US-71 (interpretive center and museum).

Underground Mine Shaft Tour. Take the world's only underground mine shaft tour one-half mile below the earth in Tower-Soudan State Park. Open June through September. Ely, west to park off State Route 169.

Viking Sword. A sword believed to be more than 700 years old is a remnant of Viking explorers found by a farmer plowing his field. The sword may be seen in the town museum; if you arrive on a day when the museum is closed, go to the drugstore to see about getting in. Ulen, northeast of Hawley on State Route 32.

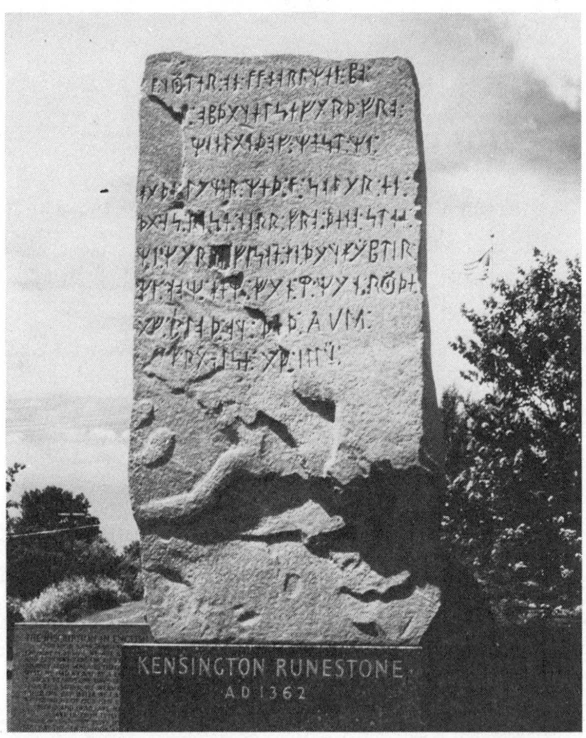

This monument is a reproduction of the famous Runestone found near Alexandria, Minnesota, which tells of explorations in 1362 by the Vikings.

This huge figure stands as a memorial to the French-Canadian explorers who opened much of the Minnesota territory in the late 1600s.

Highlight
Minnesota Industrial Tours

American Crystal Sugar Co. Highway 212, Renville 56284. Sugar beet processing. By appointment, special times and dates. Two hours. No children under 12, no cameras. Group limit 10. Contact: Pat Estes, Prairie West Publications, Wahpeton, North Dakota, (707) 642-1501.

Arctic Enterprises, Inc. Highway 32 S, Thief River Falls 56701. Snowmobiles, wetbikes and other recreational products. Groups by appointment at 10 a.m. and 2 p.m., Monday through Friday, March through November, 45 minutes. No cameras, no smoking. Children must be able to wear safety glasses. Contact: Cheryl Rugland, Public Relations, (218) 681-1147, ext. 279.

A.R. Wood Manufacturing Co. 200 E. Maple Street, Luverne 56156. Poultry brooders and confinement systems for hogs, poultry and cattle. By appointment, all year. One hour. Children under 12 to be accompanied by adult. Safety glasses provided. Contact: Darryl Steckelberg or Carl Kahler, (507) 283-4411.

Blandin Paper Co. 115 SW First Street, Grand Rapids 55744. Publication-quality coated printing papers. By appointment, 10 a.m. to 4 p.m., Monday, Wednesday and Friday, June through August. Meet behind Coast to Coast building, 109 NW Second Street, 45 minutes. Age 10 or older, ages 10-14 with adults. Contact: J. W. Reif, Industrial Relations, (218) 326-8531, ext. 276.

Hill Wood Products. Box 398, Cook 55723. Wood products. By appointment, 9 a.m. to 3 p.m., all year, 30-60 minutes. Adult supervision for children under 12. Contact: Richard Waataja or Steve Hill, (218) 666-5933.

Medtronic Inc. 6972 Old Central Avenue, NE, Fridley 55432. Biomedical engineering, pacemakers, neurological products. By appointment two weeks in advance, Monday through Thursday, 9 a.m. and 1 p.m., all year, 90 minutes. Group limit 50. High school juniors and up. No cameras. Contact: Visitor's Bureau, (612) 574-4000.

Minneapolis Grain Exchange. 150 Grain Exchange Buildings, Minneapolis 55415. Commodity trading in futures and cash markets. Monday through Friday, 8:45 and 10 a.m., also 12:30 p.m. by appointment, all year. One hour. Group limit 65. Contact: Jay Sidie or David Zarken, (612) 338-6212.

Tonka Toys. 5300 Shoreline Boulevard, Mound 55331. Toys for boys and girls. By advance registration only, Tuesday and Friday, February through November, 45 minutes. No cameras. Children must be five years or preschoolers accompanied by parent. Contact: Virginia Hedtke, (612) 472-8000.

U.S. Steel-Minnesota Ore Operations. PO Box 417, Mountain Iron 55792. Taconite mining, processing. Three observation stands. By appointment, 9:30, 10:30, 11:30 a.m. and 12:30, 1:30, 2:30, 3:30 and 4:45 p.m., May through August 20, 45 minutes. Ear plugs, eyeglasses and hard hats supplied. Contact: Ray Riley, (218) 749-7200.

Whirlpool Corp. 850 Arcade Street, St. Paul 55106. Freezers, floor care products, ice makers. By appointment, one week ahead, all year, 90 minutes. Age 16 and older. No cameras. Contact: Zora Schultz, (612) 778-2243.

Winona Knitting Mills Inc. 902 East Second Street, Winona 55987. Sweaters for men and women, factory outlet store. By appointment at 1 p.m., Monday through Friday, all year, 30 minutes. Group limit 20; larger groups split. Young children with escorts only. Contact: Sharon Rose, (507) 454-4381.

WTCN-TV, Channel 11. 441 Boone Avenue N, Golden Valley 55427. Television station. By appointment, 9 a.m. to 5 p.m., Monday through Friday, all year, 45 minutes. Group limit 20. Not suited to children under six. Audiences (group limit 40) booked for live daily broadcast of "What's New" show. Contact: Anne Birch, Director of Press and Publicity, (612) 546-1111, ext. 222.

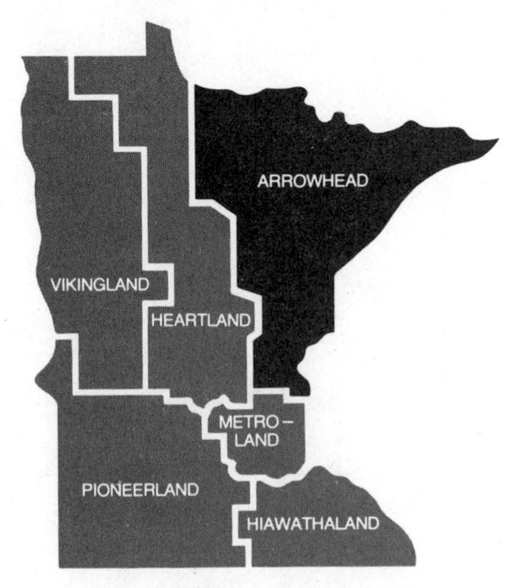

Because of the abundance of Minnesota state parks, a regional breakdown is provided. See shaded maps for reference.

Minnesota State Parks
Arrowhead Region

Park	Location	Camping	Picnicking	Concessions	Swimming	Hiking	Boating	Fishing	Hunting	Winter Sports
Banning	*Sandstone. Off Interstate 35.*	•	•			•	•			•
Baptism River	*Two Harbors. Off US-61.*		•			•		•		
Bear Head Lake	*Tower. Off State Route 169.*	•	•		•	•	•	•		•
Cascade River	*Grand Marais. Off US-61.*	•				•		•		•
Franz Jevne	*Birchdale. On State Route 11.*	•							•	
George H. Crosby Manitou	*Finland. Off State Route 1.*					•		•		
Gooseberry Falls	*Two Harbors. Off US-61.*	•	•			•		•		•
Interstate	*Taylors Falls. Off US-8.*	•	•			•	•	•		•
Jay Cooke	*Duluth. Off State Route 210.*	•	•			•		•		•
Judge C.R. Magney	*Grand Marais. Off US-61.*	•				•		•		
McCarthy Beach	*Hibbing. Off State Route 73.*	•	•		•	•	•	•		•
Moose Lake	*Moose Lake. Off Interstate 35.*		•		•	•	•	•		•
St. Croix	*Hinckley. Off State Route 48.*	•	•		•	•	•	•		•
St. Croix Wild River	*North Branch. Off State Route 95.*	•	•			•				•
Savanna Portage	*McGregor. Off State Route 65.*	•	•		•	•	•	•		•
Scenic	*Big Fork. Off State Route 38.*	•	•		•		•	•		•
Split Rock Lighthouse	*Two Harbors. Off US-61.*					•				
Temperance River	*Grand Marais. Off US-61.*	•	•			•		•		
Tower Soudan	*Soudan. Off State Route 169.*		•			•		•		•

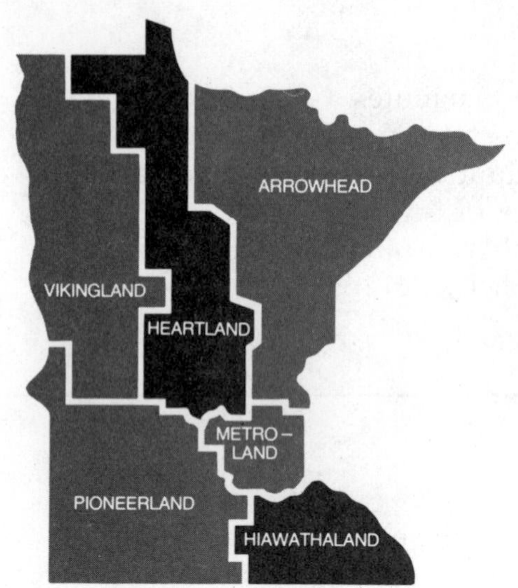

Heartland Region

Park	Location	CAMPING	PICNICKING	CONCESSIONS	SWIMMING	HIKING	BOATING	FISHING	HUNTING	WINTER SPORTS
Charles A. Lindbergh	*Little Falls. On State Route 238.*	•	•			•				
Crow Wing	*Brainerd. Off State Route 371.*	•	•			•		•		•
Father Hennepin	*Isle. Off State Route 47.*	•	•		•	•		•		
Hayes Lake	*Roseau. Off State Routes 89 and 11.*	•	•		•	•		•		•
Lake Bemidji	*Bemidji. Off US-71.*	•	•	•	•	•	•	•		•
Mille Lacs Kathio	*Onamia. Off US-169.*	•	•		•	•	•	•		•
Schoolcraft	*Deer River. Off State Route 6.*	•	•			•		•		
Zippel Bay	*Williams. Off State Route 11.*	•	•		•			•		•

Hiawathaland

Park	Location	CAMPING	PICNICKING	CONCESSIONS	SWIMMING	HIKING	BOATING	FISHING	HUNTING	WINTER SPORTS
Carley	*Plainview. Off State Route 42.*	•	•					•		•
Beaver Creek Valley	*Caledonia. Off State Route 76.*	•	•			•		•		
Forestville	*Wykoff. Off State Route 16.*	•	•			•		•		•
Frontenac	*Lake City. Off US-61.*	•	•			•		•		•
Helmer Myre	*Albert Lea. Off Interstate 90.*	•	•			•		•	•	
John Latsch	*Winona. Off US-61.*	•	•			•		•		•
Lake Louise	*Leroy. Off State Route 56.*	•	•		•	•		•		•
Nerstrand Woods	*Northfield. Off State Route 246.*	•	•			•				
Rice Lake	*Owatonna. Off State Route 14.*	•	•	•	•	•		•		•
Whitewater	*St. Charles. Off State Route 74.*	•	•		•	•		•		•

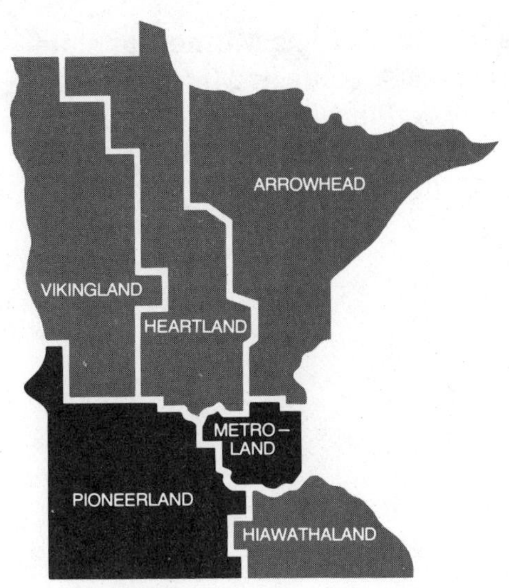

Metroland

Park	Location	CAMPING	PICNICKING	CONCESSIONS	SWIMMING	HIKING	BOATING	FISHING	HUNTING	WINTER SPORTS
Afton	*Hastings. Off US-10, on County Road 21.*					•				
Fort Snelling	*St. Paul. Off State Route 55.*		•		•	•	•	•		•
Lake Maria	*Monticello. Off Interstate 94.*		•			•	•	•		•
William O'Brien	*Stillwater. Off State Route 95.*	•	•		•	•	•	•		•

Pioneerland

Park	Location	CAMPING	PICNICKING	CONCESSIONS	SWIMMING	HIKING	BOATING	FISHING	HUNTING	WINTER SPORTS
Big Stone Lake	*Ortonville. Off US-75.*	•	•			•	•	•		•
Birch Coulee	*Morton. Off US-71.*		•			•				
Blue Mounds	*Luverne. On US-75.*	•	•		•	•		•		•
Camden	*Marshall. Off State Route 23.*	•	•		•	•		•		•
Flandrau	*New Ulm. Off State Route 15 and US-14.*	•	•		•	•		•		•
Fort Ridgely	*Fairfax. Off State Route 4.*	•	•			•				•
Kilen Woods	*Lakefield. Off State Route 86.*	•	•			•		•		•
Lac Qui Parle	*Montevideo. Off State Routes 7 and 40.*	•	•		•	•		•		•
Lake Shetek	*Slayton. Off State Route 30.*	•	•		•	•	•	•		•
Minneopa	*Mankato. On State Route 60.*	•	•			•		•		
Monson Lake	*Sunburg. Off State Routes 104 and 9.*	•	•			•		•		
Sakatah Lake	*Waterville. On State Route 60.*	•	•		•	•		•		•
Sibley	*New London. Off State Route 9 and US-71.*	•	•		•	•	•	•		•
Split Rock Creek	*Ihlen. On State Route 23.*	•	•		•	•		•		•
Traverse Des Sioux	*St. Peter. Off State Route 99.*		•			•		•		•
Upper Sioux Agency	*Granite. Off State Routes 67 and US-212.*		•			•		•		•

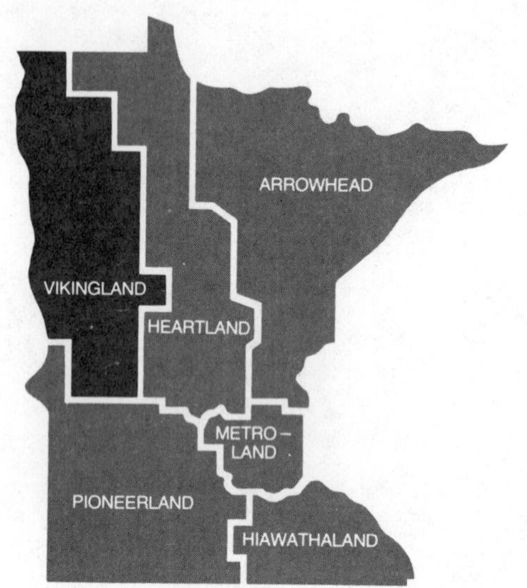

For more information on Minnesota state parks and forests, contact: *Minnesota Department of Natural Resources, Space Center Building, 444 Lafayette Road, St. Paul, Minnesota 55101, (612) 296-4776.*

Vikingland

Park	Location	CAMPING	PICNICKING	CONCESSIONS	SWIMMING	HIKING	BOATING	FISHING	HUNTING	WINTER SPORTS
Buffalo River	*Moorhead. Off US-10.*	•	•		•			•		•
Glacial Lakes	*Starbuck. Off State Route 29.*	•	•		•	•	•	•		•
Itasca	*Park Rapids. Off US-71.*	•	•		•	•	•	•		•
Lake Bronson	*Lake Bronson. Off US-59.*	•	•		•	•	•	•		•
Lake Carlos	*Alexandria. Off State Route 29.*	•	•		•	•		•		•
Little Elbow Lake	*Waubun. Off State Route 113.*	•	•					•		
Maplewood	*Pelican Rapids. Off State Route 108.*	•	•		•	•		•		•
Old Mill	*Warren. Off US-75.*	•	•		•	•		•		•

Minnesota State Forests

Forest	Location	CAMPING	PICNICKING	CONCESSIONS	SWIMMING	HIKING	BOATING	FISHING	HUNTING	WINTER SPORTS
Birch Lake	*Brainerd. Off State Route 18.*	•	•		•	•		•		•
Cloquet Valley	*Duluth. Off US-53.*	•	•		•	•	•	•		•
Crow Wing	*Brainerd. Off State Route 6.*	•	•		•		•	•		•
Finland	*Duluth. On State Route 1.*	•	•			•	•	•		•
General C.C. Andrews	*Moose Lake. Off Interstate 35.*	•	•				•	•		•
George Washington	*Hibbing. On State Route 65.*	•	•		•	•	•	•		•
Hill River	*Haypoint. On US-169.*	•	•			•	•	•		•
Huntersville	*Park Rapids. Off State Route 64 and US-71.*	•	•				•	•		•
Kabetogama	*Orr. On US-53.*	•	•		•	•	•	•		•
Land O'Lakes	*Hill City. Off State Route 6.*	•	•		•	•	•	•		•
Lyons	*Oylen. Off State Route 64.*	•	•			•		•		•
Namadji	*Moose Lake. Off State Route 23.*									•
Sand Dunes	*Cambridge. Off US-169.*	•	•		•	•				•
Savannah	*Hill City. Off State Route 65.*	•	•		•	•	•	•		•

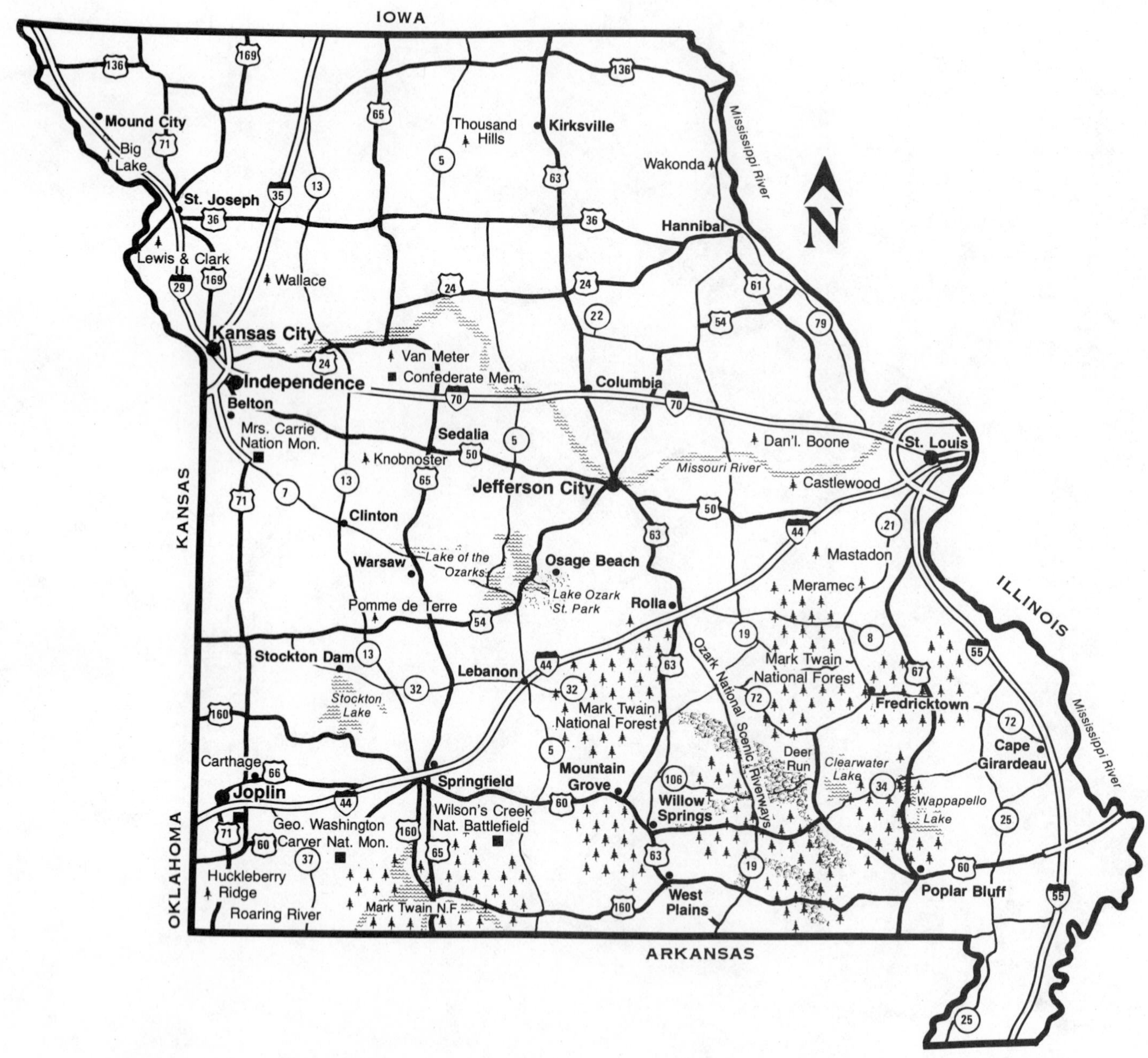

Missouri

Map not to exact scale.

Missouri

From the quaint charm of the Mark Twain region in the northeast and the majestic Gateway Arch on the banks of the Mississippi to the Lake of the Ozarks playground and the urban sprawl of Kansas City, Missouri is a state of infinite variety. One of Missouri's most unique attractions is its abundance of caves: 3,900 known caves lie beneath the state's rich soil, and 23 of them are commercially operated. Of course, you won't want to miss the famous Ozarks, a land of scenic valleys, green forests, rolling hills, sheer bluffs and sparkling, free-flowing rivers.

Mound Builders were the earliest known inhabitants of the Missouri region, but the recorded history of the area begins with the explorations of Father Jacques Marquette and Louis Jolliet, during their famous 1673 expedition by canoe down the Mississippi River from the north. Following a number of later explorations, lead mines and salt springs were discovered and made productive, and profitable fur trading was established. The first permanent settlement was St. Genevieve, established about 1735, and the second settlement was St. Louis, founded by Laclede in 1764. The region was occupied for a time by the Spanish, but there was a heavy migration of Americans to the area during the Revolutionary War and the U.S. finally took permanent possession under the Louisiana Purchase. When petitions were presented in 1818 and 1819 for Missouri's statehood, Congress engaged in a bitter debate of the slavery issue. The controversy was finally ended with the Missouri Compromise of 1820, which gave the territory the right to form a state constitution and government without a restriction on slavery. On August 10, 1821, Missouri was admitted as a state. In the years preceding the Civil War, the slavery issue created a tense political climate which erupted in the bloody Missouri-Kansas border wars. Though Missourians were sharply divided over the issue, they voted in 1861 not to secede from the Union.

Full name: State of Missouri
Origin of name: From name of Sioux tribe.
Motto: *Salus Populi Suprema Lex Esto* (Let the Welfare of the People Be the Supreme Law).
Nickname: Show-Me State
Capital: Jefferson City
Statehood: August 10, 1821, 24th state.
Population: 4,801,000 (ranks 15th).
Major Cities: St. Louis (524,964), Kansas City (472,529), Springfield (131,557).
Bird: Bluebird
Flower: Hawthorn
Tree: Flowering dogwood

Average daily temperatures by month

	Northern	Southern
Jan.	32.4 to 13.8	44.8 to 21.0
Feb.	38.2 to 19.2	49.3 to 25.0
Mar.	48.2 to 27.5	57.3 to 32.0
Apr.	63.3 to 41.1	69.6 to 43.0
May	73.8 to 51.6	77.5 to 51.6
Jun.	82.5 to 60.8	85.0 to 60.1
Jul.	87.3 to 65.0	89.4 to 64.3
Aug.	85.3 to 62.9	88.7 to 62.2
Sept.	77.4 to 54.8	81.4 to 55.3
Oct.	66.9 to 44.8	71.7 to 43.5
Nov.	50.6 to 31.2	57.3 to 32.2
Dec.	37.0 to 20.6	46.9 to 24.9
Year	61.9 to 41.1	68.2 to 42.9

If you're looking for an ideal campsite in Missouri, you might want to try one of the sections of the Mark Twain National Forest in the southwest corner of the state. Although this section of the state is popular with travelers, it still remains the most "natural," featuring open countryside, small towns and two of the state's finest rivers, the Current and Jacks Fork, which are protected in the Ozark National Scenic Riverways. For a change of pace, visit St. Louis and the 630-foot Gateway Arch, America's tallest man-made monument. And while you're in St. Louis, be sure to see the 83-acre Forest Park Zoo and the beautiful Missouri Botanical Gardens. And if historic sites excite you, Missouri offers a long list that includes the Pony Express Stables Museum in St. Joseph, the scene of the Civil War Battle of Lexington and the Harry S. Truman Library and Museum in Independence.

Tourism and sport fishing have emerged in recent years as two of Missouri's most important industries, but the state's central location also makes it popular with businesses that are seeking good transportation facilities and the availability of labor. Manufacturing includes transportation equipment, chemicals, clothing, glass products, paper and paper products, machinery and electrical equipment.

State Offices

Tourism
Missouri Division of Tourism
PO Box 1055
Jefferson City, Missouri 65101
(314) 751-4133

State Police
Department of Public Safety
Jefferson City, Missouri 65101
(314) 755-3313

Radio Stations

Kansas City
 KCMO 810 (AM)
 WHB 710 (AM)
Springfield
 KWTO 98.7 (FM)
St. Louis
 KADI 96.3 (FM)
 KSD 550 (AM)
 KMOX 103.3 (FM)
 WIL 1430 (AM)

Missouri Points of Interest and Attractions

Anheuser-Busch Brewery. Home of the world-famous Budweiser Clydesdale eight-horse hitch and a six-story brew house that dates from 1891; one-hour tour of brewery. Open year-round, Monday to Friday, 9:30 a.m. to 3:30 p.m. St. Louis, Broadway and Pestalozzi Streets.

Gateway Arch. The fourth-most-visited attraction in the world; ride to the top of the 630-foot arch in one of the special

This statue of Tom Sawyer and Huckleberry Finn sits at the foot of Cardiff Hill in Hannibal.

capsule-elevators for a spectacular view of the metropolitan area and the riverfront. Open year-round. St. Louis, off Interstate 70.

Harry S. Truman Birthplace. Harry S. Truman, 32nd President and the only Missourian ever elected President, was born here in 1884. Lamar, off US-71.

Laumier Park. A 76-acre park, one of only three sculpture-gardens in the nation. St. Louis, off Interstate 70.

Locust Creek Covered Bridge. A scenic bridge built in 1868. Laclede, on US-36 and one mile north and east on gravel road.

Mark Twain Birthplace. A shrine encloses the two-room cabin in which author Samuel Clemens (Mark Twain) was born in 1835; memorabilia and library. Perry, off State Route 104, in Mark Twain State Park. Other Mark Twain attractions can be found in Hannibal, on the Mississippi River, on US-36 and 61.

Missouri Botanical Gardens. Undoubtedly one of the most beautiful botanical gardens in the country, featuring nearly 80 acres of gardens and horticultural displays. A highlight is the geodesic dome, Climatron. St. Louis, 2101 Tower Grove Avenue (off Interstate 44).

Sandy Creek Covered Bridge. A 76-foot-long bridge constructed of white pine. Hillsboro, five miles north off US-21, on old Lemay Ferry Road.

Shepherd of the Hills Farm. A unique attraction that features a nightly outdoor pageant each summer that tells the story of frontier life in the Ozarks. Branson, on US-65.

Silver Dollar City. A recreated 1870s Ozark town, where rides and shows combine with crafts to form a complete folk entertainment center. Branson, on US-65.

Union Covered Bridge. Built in 1870, the last surviving bridge with a "Burr-arch" truss. Paris, five miles west off US-24, on Monroe County C.

Highlight

MISSOURI'S CAVES

The beauty of Missouri is more than skin deep. With about 3,000 known caves, the state is as beautiful below the ground as it is above. Most of these caves are wild caves; however, there are 23 commercially operated caves in Missouri that have been approved for safety by the Division of Mine Inspection. Each of these caves has its own history, colorful lighting and fascinating formations to make it distinctively different and uniformly lovely.

An average of 150 new caves are discovered each year in Missouri and the rate of discovery seems to be accelerating. In 1972, a total of 228 new caves were found. For those who enjoy the eerie wonder and quiet beauty of these hidden masterpieces, Missouri's caves are ideal.

Commercial Caves

Bluff Dwellers Cave, Noel
Bonne Terre Mine, Bonne Terre
Boone Cave, Rocheport
Bridal Cave, Camdenton
Cameron Cave, Hannibal
Crystal Cave, Springfield
Crystal Caverns, Cassville
Fantastic Caverns, Springfield
Fantasy World Caverns, Osage Beach
Fisher's Cave, Sullivan
Indian Burial Cave, Osage Beach
Jacob's Cave, Versailles
Mark Twain Cave, Hannibal
Marvel Cave, Silver Dollar City (Branson)
Meramec Caverns, Stanton
Onondaga Cave, Leasburg
Onyx Cave, Van Buren
Ozark Caverns, Osage Beach
Ozark Wonder Cave, Noel
Rebel Cave, Silva
Round Spring Cave, Round Spring
Talking Rocks Cave, Silver Dollar City (Branson)
Truitt's Cave, Lanagan

The School of the Ozarks

The School of the Ozarks is a unique institution established in 1906 "to provide the advantages of a Christian education for youth of both sexes, especially those found worthy, but who are without sufficient means to procure such training."

On an 1,800-acre tract on the banks of Lake Taneycomo in the heart of the Tri-Lakes area of Missouri's Ozarks, 1,200 young men and women from the hill country are now working toward a college degree. This is being made possible through the gifts and contributions of hundreds of persons willing to help worthy young persons procure a Christian education.

The institution has grown from an elementary school to the stature of an accredited four-year college. And all because its leaders had faith that there are in America men and women so grateful of what life has given them that they are willing to help these students.

Every S of O student works an average of 20 hours each week in return for tuition, board and room. Only those young persons who could not afford to go to college elsewhere are admitted. There is always a long waiting list.

The Walking Tour

A walking tour of the campus should include the **Williams Memorial Chapel and Hyer Bell Tower.** The chapel is a fine example of Neo-Gothic architecture and contains many beautiful stained glass windows. Carillion concerts are played at noon, mid-afternoon and at evening time.

Other special attractions for visitors include the **Ralph Foster Museum,** which contains hundreds of artifacts from cultures of the North and South American Indians, Rose O'Neill Kewpies, western memorabilia and a 100,000-piece collection "Monies of the World."

The **M. A. Lyons Memorial Library** contains a fine collection of library materials including books on the Ozarks.

Other Areas of Interest

The Friendship House at the entrance of the campus features a gift shop, buffet and tourist information center. The train tours (see below) begin here.

The summer stock **Beacon Hill Theater** runs from mid-June to mid-August, with plays presented nightly Wednesday through Saturday.

Memorial Fieldhouse, one of the largest in southwest Missouri, can seat 4,500 persons.

The **Edwards Mill** is a replica of a typical Ozark water mill and here corn is ground on stone buhrs. The building is a museum.

The **Clint McDade Orchid Collection** produces blossoms for retail and wholesale trade.

The **Good Memorial College Center** provides both motel rooms and a cafeteria for the public.

The **Paul M. Pfeiffer Biological Science Building** provides the finest for scientific research studies.

W. Alton Jones Dairy has the Midwest's Holstein championship herd.

Conducted Tours

The S of O Special, a miniature tour train, leaves from the Friendship House at 10 a.m., 1:30 p.m. and 3:30 p.m. Monday through Saturday, and 1:30 p.m. and 3:30 p.m. on Sundays, making stops at the W. Alton Jones Dairy, the Williams Memorial Chapel and Hyer Bell Tower and Point Lookout. The train operates from April 15 through November 1.

Chapel Services

Visitors to the area are invited to attend the worship services at 11 a.m. each Sunday. Music is by the 40-voice chapel choir.

—PJF

A fine example of neo-Gothic architecture, the Williams Memorial Chapel and Hyer Bell Tower comprise the focal point of the School of the Ozarks campus. A 96-bell carillon tolls each hour with Westminster chimes, and plays 15-minute concerts three times daily.

Missouri State Parks

Park	Location	CAMPING	PICNICKING	CONCESSIONS	SWIMMING	HIKING	BOATING	FISHING	HUNTING	WINTER SPORTS
Arrow Rock	*Arrow Rock. On State Route 41.*	•				•				
Dr. Edmund A. Babler Memorial	*Chesterfield. Off State Route 109.*	•	•		•	•				
Battle of Anthens	*Kahoka. Off State Route 81.*		•			•		•		
Bennett Spring	*Lebanon. Off State Route 64.*	•	•	•	•	•	•	•		
Big Lake	*Bigelow. Off State Routes 118 and 159.*	•	•		•		•	•		
Big Oak Tree	*East Prairie. Off State Route 102.*		•			•		•		
Confederate Memorial	*Higginsville. Off State Routes 20 and 13.*		•					•		
Crowder	*Trenton. Off State Route 128.*	•	•		•	•		•		
Cuvre River	*Troy. Off State Route 47.*	•	•		•	•	•	•		
Elephant Rocks	*Graniteville. Off State Route 21.*		•			•				
Finger Lakes	*Columbia. US-63.*		•			•		•		
Graham Cave	*Montgomery. Off Interstate 70.*	•	•			•				
Hawn	*Weingarten. Off State Route 32.*	•	•			•				
Johnson's Shut-Ins	*Middle Brook. Off State Route 49.*	•	•		•	•		•		
Knob Noster	*Knob Noster. Off US-50.*	•	•		•	•		•		
Lake of the Ozarks	*Kaiser. Off US-54.*	•	•	•	•	•	•	•		
Lake Wappapello	*Popular Bluff. Off State Route 172.*	•	•	•	•	•	•	•		
Lewis and Clark	*Rushville. Off State Route 45.*	•	•		•		•	•		
Mark Twain	*Stoutsville. Off State Route 107.*	•	•			•		•		
Meramec	*Sullivan. Off State Route 185.*	•	•	•	•	•	•	•		
Montauk	*Salem. Off State Route 119.*	•	•	•		•		•		
Pershing	*Laclede. Off US-36.*	•	•			•		•		
Pomme De Terre	*Pittsburg. Off US-54.*	•	•	•	•	•	•	•		
Roaring River	*Cassville. Off State Route 112.*	•	•	•	•	•		•		
Rock Bridge	*Columbia. Off State Route 163.*		•			•				
St. Francois	*Bonne Terre. Off US-67.*	•	•		•			•		
Sam A. Baker	*Patterson. Off State Route 143.*	•	•	•	•	•		•		
Stockton	*Stockton. Off State Route 215.*	•	•	•	•		•	•		
Table Rock	*Branson. Off State Route 165.*	•	•		•	•	•	•		
Thousand Hills	*Kirksville. Off State Route 6.*	•	•	•	•	•	•	•		
Trail of Tears	*Cape Girardeau. Off State Route 177.*	•	•			•		•		
Van Meter	*Miami. Off State Route 122.*	•	•			•		•		
Wakonda	*LaGrange. Off US-61.*	•	•					•		
Wallace	*Cameron. Off State Route 121.*	•	•		•	•		•		
Washington	*DeSoto. Off State Route 21.*	•	•	•	•	•		•		
Watkins Mill	*Lawson. Off US-69.*	•	•		•	•	•	•		

The feats of the courageous Pony Express riders are honored in a statue and museum in St. Joseph, the eastern terminus for the route that ran from Missouri to Sacramento, California.

Missouri State Forests

Forest	Location	CAMPING	PICNICKING	CONCESSIONS	SWIMMING	HIKING	BOATING	FISHING	HUNTING	WINTER SPORTS
Alley Spring	*Alley Spring. Off State Route 106.*	•	•			•		•	•	
Coldwater	*Coldwater. On US-67.*	•	•			•		•	•	
Daniel Boone Memorial	*Jonesburg. Off State Route 19.*	•	•			•			•	
Deer Run	*Ellington. Off State Route 106.*	•	•			•			•	
Huckleberry Ridge	*Pineville. Off US-71.*	•	•			•			•	
Huzzah	*Leasburg. Off Interstate 44.*	•	•			•			•	
Indian Trail	*Salem. Off State Route 117.*	•	•			•			•	
Reifsnider	*Warrenton. Off Interstate 70.*	•	•			•			•	

For more information on Missouri state parks and forests, contact: *Division of Parks and Recreation, PO Box 176, Jefferson City, Missouri 65102, (314) 751-3443.*

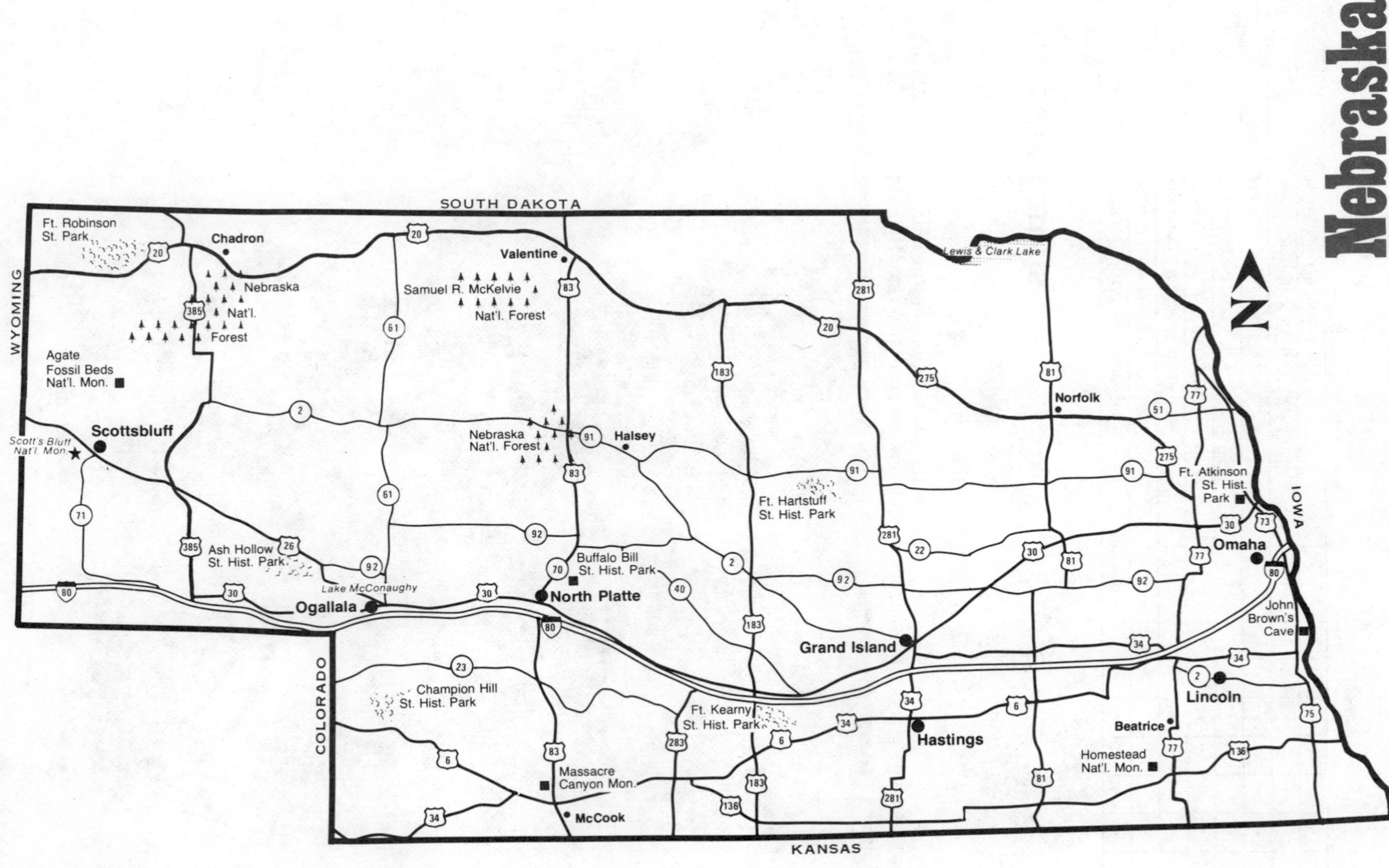

Map not to exact scale.

Nebraska

It is said that the people of this state live longer than those in any other; and if you ask a Nebraskan why, chances are he'll reply: "Because in Nebraska we have the good life." That "good life" includes an abundance of wide-open spaces, the colorful riverfront area of the "Muddy" Missouri, a rich pioneer history, some of the nation's best fishing and hunting, and an industrious and hospitable people waiting to welcome you to their state.

The name Nebraska was given to the region in 1714 by the French explorer Bourgmont, who borrowed it from the Otoe Indians. The purchase of the Louisiana Territory and the subsequent explorations of Lewis and Clark (1804-1806) awakened interest in the region, and development began with the establishment of Fort Lisa, a fur-trading post. Pioneers going west along the Oregon Trail, which followed the Platte River valley, stimulated trading and settlement. Francis Burt of South Carolina became territorial governor at Bellevue on October 16, 1854, and the first territorial legislature was assembled in Omaha a few months later on January 16, 1855. Statehood was granted in 1867. Through many of the early years the state was the scene of bitter and prolonged conflict between homesteaders and cattlemen, who wanted the land for their herds. This struggle was finally resolved by the 1904 Kincaid Act, which gave the last of the state's open range land to the homesteaders.

Today, much of Nebraska is divided into neat farms, but that doesn't mean there isn't plenty of space left for visitors. In the northeastern part of the state, you'll find

Full name: State of Nebraska
Origin of name: From Omaha Indian name for the Platte River.
Motto: Equality Before the Law
Nickname: Cornhusker State
Capital: Lincoln
Statehood: March 1, 1867, 37th state.
Population: 1,561,000 (ranks 35th).
Major Cities: Omaha (371,455), Lincoln (163,112).
Bird: Western meadowlark
Flower: Goldenrod
Tree: American elm

Average daily temperatures by month

	Western	Eastern
Jan.	41.4 to 11.7	29.3 to 9.7
Feb.	46.6 to 16.4	36.0 to 15.8
Mar.	51.3 to 21.6	44.9 to 25.2
Apr.	63.7 to 31.7	61.8 to 38.9
May	73.7 to 43.0	72.7 to 50.4
Jun.	83.4 to 52.6	81.7 to 60.7
Jul.	90.7 to 58.2	85.8 to 64.9
Aug.	89.7 to 56.0	84.3 to 62.7
Sept.	79.8 to 45.0	75.0 to 53.1
Oct.	68.9 to 33.2	66.0 to 42.1
Nov.	52.4 to 21.5	49.1 to 28.2
Dec.	42.2 to 14.1	35.9 to 16.7
Year	65.3 to 33.8	60.2 to 39.0

Niobrara State Park where you can pause to wet a line in the Niobrara River or enjoy a leisurely afternoon of boating. In Omaha, you can visit the Strategic Air Command Headquarters Museum; the Joslyn Art Museum; or Boys Town, the "City of Little Men." Out in the Sand Hills country, there's Buffalo Bill's ranch, Fort Hartstuff State Historical Park and Fort Niobrara

National Wildlife Refuge. And along the old Oregon Trail, you'll find the landmarks of the pioneers, Chimney Rock and the Scottsbluff National Monument.

Agriculture is the mainstay of the Nebraska economy, with annual harvests of corn, sorghum, wheat, oats, rye, soybeans and alfalfa. Omaha reigns as one of the nation's major livestock marketing centers, holding the title of the largest meat-packing center and the second-largest cattle market in the U.S. and the world. The manufacture of farm machinery, electrical equipment, chemicals and metal products also play a key role in the state's economy.

State Offices

Tourism
Travel and Tourism Division
PO Box 94666
Lincoln, Nebraska 68509
(402) 471-3111

State Police
Department of Public Safety
Junction US-77 and N-2
Lincoln, Nebraska 68509
(402) 477-3951

Radio Stations

Alliance
KCOW 1400 (AM)
Beatrice
KWBE 1450 (AM)
Columbus
KJSK 900 (AM)
Grand Island
KMMJ 750 (AM)
Hastings
KHAS 1230 (AM)
Kearney
KRNY 1460 (AM)
Lincoln
KBHL 95.3 (FM)
KFOR 1240 (AM)
Omaha
KEFM 96.1 (FM)
KFAB 1110 (AM)
WOW 590 (AM)

Nebraska Points of Interest and Attractions

Ak-Sar-Ben Aquarium. One of Nebraska's newest attractions (formerly Gretna Hatchery). Favorite displays include a terrarium, which features a variety of turtles, frogs and other amphibians in a natural aquatic environment; and fish displays, which hold a representative sampling of nearly all the fish native to Nebraska. Open year-round. Free. Gretna, off Interstate 80 (six miles south).

Belle of Brownville. Take a ride on the mighty Missouri River aboard this restored side-wheeler. Evening entertainment is available in the theater in Brownville, and many restored homes are open all summer. Excursion season: April 1 through November 1, Saturdays and Sundays. Adults $2.50, children $1.75. Brownville, on US-136.

Boys Town. Father Flanagan's famous community, where thousands of boys have become men. Open for tours year-round, Monday to Saturday, 8 a.m. to 4:15 p.m.; Sundays and holidays, 9 a.m. to 4:30 p.m. Free. Omaha, 8401 West Dodge Street.

Buffalo Bill's Scout's Rest Ranch. Buffalo Bill's home and Wild West Show headquarters; tours of his home and barn. Open May 15 through September 15, daily, 9 a.m. to 8 p.m. Free. North Platte, off US-83, north, on State Route 30.

Chimney Rock. On the Oregon Trail, this was one of the most significant landmarks looked for by early pioneers; interpretive center. Season: Memorial Day through Labor Day, daily, 8 a.m. to 7 p.m. Bayard, south on State Route 92.

Courthouse and Jail Rocks. Other scenic landmarks on the trail west; interpretive center. Season: Memorial Day through Labor Day, daily, 8 a.m. to 7 p.m. Bridgeport, four miles south on State Route 88.

Front Street. At the end of the Texas Trail, cowboys frequented the saloons along this street and occasionally ended up in Boot Hill. The re-created street offers family entertainment nightly. Season: April 29 through October 1, daily, 8 a.m. to 10 p.m.; western shows nightly at 7:15 and 8:30 p.m. Adults $1.75, children 75 cents. Ogallala, off Interstate 80, at 519 East First Street.

Neihardt Center. Built in honor of poet John Neihardt, the center features architectural themes from his Indian verse. Open year-round, daily; Monday to Saturday, 9 a.m. to 5 p.m.; Sunday, 1 p.m. to 5 p.m. Free. Bancroft, off State Route 51, at corner of Elm and Washington Streets.

Neligh Mills. Old flour mill with all equipment recently restored; campground nearby. Open April 1 through November 15, daily. Neligh, off US-275, at corner of "N" Street and Wylie Drive.

Omaha Old Market. A turn-of-the-century marketplace of brick streets and old buildings, featuring a variety of quaint shops and restaurants; special events and crafts fairs. Open year-round, daily. Omaha, off Interstate 80 (14th Street exit), south to 10th and Howard Streets.

State Capitol. This building, home of the nation's only unicameral legislature, is called the "Tower of the Plains" because it rises 400 feet; classic artworks depict plains life. Open year-round, daily. Free tours. Lincoln, 1445 "K" Street.

Strategic Air Command Museum. A collection of military aircraft; 34 airplanes and missiles from the B-17 to the B-36 and B-52. Located next to Offut Air Force Base, Strategic Air Command Headquarters is the nerve center for the nation's air defense. Open year-round. Bellevue, off US-34.

Nebraska is primarily an agricultural state with interest in the eastern portion focused on corn, wheat and stock-feeder operations, while the western reaches boast large cattle ranches and vast wheat fields.

Wildcat Hills Recreation Area. A beautiful and rugged area holding remnant buffalo and elk herds. Season: Easter Sunday through October 31, daily (24 hours for campground). Free. Gering, nine miles south on State Route 71.

Willa Cather Pioneer Memorial. Dedicated to the famous authoress who wrote so descriptively of the pioneers' struggle to tame the plains. Open year-round, daily. Free for center and museum; childhood home, adults $1, children 50 cents. Red Cloud, intersection of US-281 and US-136.

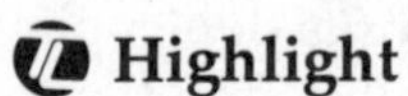

Nebraska—"The Beef State"

BEEF PRODUCTION

The livestock industry is a vital part of Nebraska's agriculture. Livestock and livestock products have accounted for over $2 billion worth of cash receipts to Nebraska farmers and ranchers annually since 1972. This is more than half of the total cash receipts of all agricultural products from Nebraska's farm and ranches.

The livestock industry is composed of several parts. The main ones are cattle, swine, sheep and poultry. The largest segment in dollar value and number is cattle. Three main components are cow-calf operations, feeding and fattening cattle and dairy cattle.

THE COW-CALF OPERATION

A cow-calf operation is typically thought of as a cow herd kept primarily for breeding purposes and raising calves to 400-600 pounds.

This is the sole enterprise on many ranches in the Sandhills area and western Nebraska, but beef cattle are found in every county of the state. Herds may be from five head, up to several thousand on some of the larger ranches.

BEEF FEEDLOTS

Cattlemen are always striving for a higher quality beef animal through research and selective breeding. Heavier weaning weights, less time in the feedlot using less feed to produce the same amount of meat are the goals of the cattlemen in producing the high quality animal.

The feeding and fattening of beef cattle take the 400-600 pound calf up to a 1,000-1,200 pound animal suitable for slaughter.

This is accomplished in some of the more than 15,000 feedlots in Nebraska, concentrated in northeast Nebraska and along the Platte River valley. These calves start on a ration composed of corn and sorghum silage, alfalfa hay and feed grain ration to product fast gain.

Nebraska feeder cattle, steaks and other beef cuts are known worldwide for their quality and desirability.

Nebraska State Parks

Park	Location	CAMPING	PICNICKING	CONCESSIONS	SWIMMING	HIKING	BOATING	FISHING	HUNTING	WINTER SPORTS
Chadron	*Chadron. Off US-385.*	•	•	•	•	•	•	•		
Fort Robinson	*Crawford. Off US-20.*	•	•	•		•	•	•	•	•
Indian Cave	*Brownville. Off State Route 67.*	•	•			•				•
Niobrara	*Niobrara. Off State Route 12.*	•	•	•	•	•	•	•		•
Ponca	*Ponca. Off State Route 12.*	•	•	•	•	•	•	•		•

Nebraska has no state forests. For more information on Nebraska state parks, contact: *Nebraska Game and Parks Commission, Box 30370, Lincoln, Nebraska 68503, (303) 234-3914.*

North Dakota

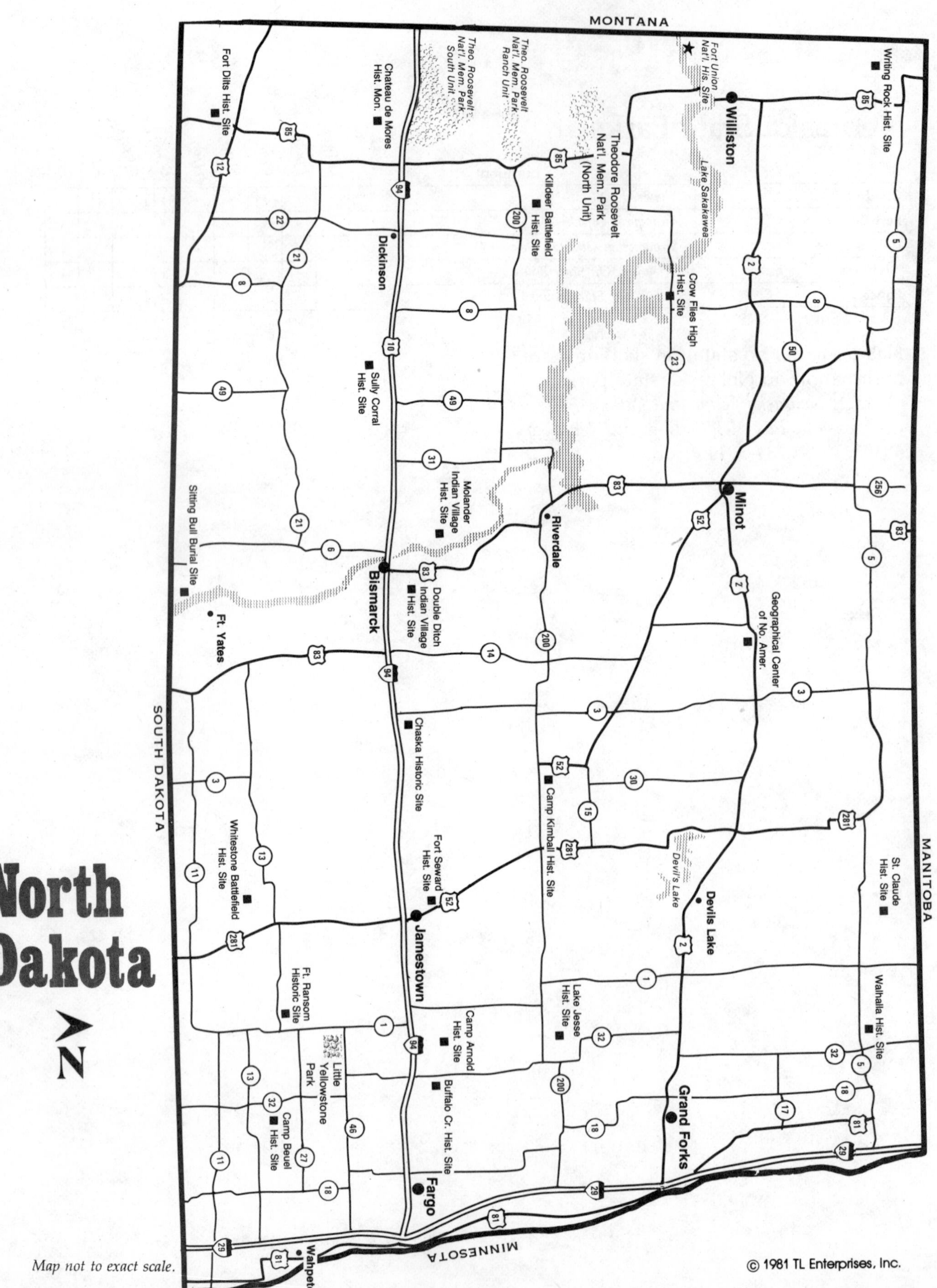

Map not to exact scale.

North Dakota

Because it's tucked away in the extreme north-central part of the nation, North Dakota is a state that might be easily overlooked. On the contrary, though, it is one state that you won't want to miss. With more than 90% of its land in farms, North Dakota is the most rural of all the states; it's a region of wide-open spaces that includes the spectacular beauty of the 70,000-acre Theodore Roosevelt National Park; the 2,300-acre Peace Garden, a monument to friendly U.S.-Canada relations; and the 178-mile-long Lake Sakakawea. And North Dakota is a state of cosmopolitan cultures; people from all over the world migrated to this area, and you can recapture their heritage in annual events like the Ukranian Days in Belfield, the Octoberfest in New Leipzig or the colorful Pioneer Days at Bonanzaville.

The first Europeans to explore what is now North Dakota were Sieur de la Verendrye and his sons, who visited the area in 1738. The first permanent settlement was established in 1812 at Pembina, in the Red River region, by a group of Scottish and Irish immigrants. Throughout the early part of its history, North Dakota was a part of South Dakota. The territory was later divided, however, and in 1889 North Dakota was admitted to the Union along with South Dakota. (The statehood papers were deliberately marked so that neither state could claim prior entry; for the record, though, North Dakota is listed as the 39th state and South Dakota as the 40th.)

Today, the spirit of the pioneers who tamed North Dakota lives on. On the farms that stretch across the landscape, modern machines have replaced the horse-drawn plow, but the people who work the land still have the same dedication, courage and hospitality of their ancestors. You can learn more about North Dakota's past by visiting Fort Mandan, winter headquarters for Lewis and Clark, from 1804 to 1805; Fort Union, a trading post built in 1829 by the American Fur Company; or the restored cowtown of

Full name: State of North Dakota
Origin of name: From the Sioux meaning "Alliance With Friends."
Motto: Liberty and Union
Nickname: Flickertail State
Capital: Bismarck
Statehood: November 2, 1889, 39th state.
Population: 653,000 (ranks 45th).
Major Cities: Fargo (56,058), Grand Forks (41,909), Bismarck (38,378).
Bird: Western meadowlark
Flower: Wild prairie rose
Tree: American elm

Average daily temperatures by month

	Northern	Southern
Jan.	11.4 to -7.9	17.5 to -3.9
Feb.	19.1 to -1.7	24.1 to 2.4
Mar.	30.7 to 11.0	35.0 to 13.8
Apr.	50.2 to 28.2	53.2 to 29.6
May	65.4 to 39.5	67.4 to 41.1
Jun.	75.4 to 50.3	76.3 to 51.7
Jul.	80.9 to 54.7	83.7 to 56.3
Aug.	79.9 to 53.0	83.6 to 54.7
Sept.	67.4 to 41.9	70.7 to 43.2
Oct.	55.6 to 31.8	59.5 to 33.4
Nov.	33.6 to 16.2	38.9 to 18.0
Dec.	19.3 to 1.3	24.6 to 4.5
Year	49.1 to 26.5	52.9 to 28.7

North Dakota's Great Way Trails

For travelers who like to retrace history, North Dakota has a system of three different well-marked routes that will lead you on an extended tour into the past.

Explorers Highroad
The Explorers Highroad is a unique international driving tour, winding through the heartland of North America. In North Dakota travel the Highroads of Interstate 29, US-2, Interstate 94 and US-85 for a safe trip.

Lewis and Clark Trail
Follow the route traveled by the American expedition of Lewis and Clark as they explored the Louisiana Purchase for Thomas Jefferson. The route generally follows Highway 1804 along the Missouri River and Highway 1806 follows their return route.

Old West Trail
The Old West Trail states each have their own legends, songs and characters. Experience North Dakota's Old West on this trail through the Badlands, on US-85 or through central North Dakota on US-2, 281, 23, 5 and 83.

North Dakota's spectacular Badlands are marked by plateaus, buttes and brilliantly colored formations that make the area a scenic wonderland.

Medora. For the sportsman, North Dakota offers some of the best fishing and hunting to be found anywhere in the nation. While you're in the northern part of the state, you might want to slip across the border into Canada to take in some of the sights the state shares along its 310 miles of border with its neighbor to the north.

Besides agriculture (wheat, barley, flax, potatoes, sugar beets), major industries in the state include petroleum, natural gas, sand and gravel. North Dakota has vast reserves of lignite coal that are currently being strip mined and burned in large electricity-generating power plants. These power plants now supply electricity for a seven-state region of the upper Midwest.

State Offices

Tourism
State Travel Division
Highway Department Building
State Capital Grounds
Bismarck, North Dakota 58505
(800) 437-2077

State Police
Department of Public Safety
Bismarck, North Dakota 58505
(701) 224-2500

Radio Stations

Bismarck
KFYR 550 (AM)
Fargo
KFGO 790 (AM)

North Dakota Points of Interest and Attractions

Bismarck-Mandan. Bismarck is the capital and third largest city in the state. At Dakota Zoo you'll find Clyde, the largest known Kodiak bear in existence. Mandan claims to be where the West begins; special features include Rawhide City and Beck's Great Plains Museum.

Bonanzaville USA. A frontier village comprised of original buildings from the Red River Valley. Attractions include an auto collection, old-fashioned general store, church and school, and some 30 other buildings. The Edward A. Mulligan Memorial American Indian Museum is an added attraction. Open year-round. West Fargo, off Interstate 94.

Burning Coal Vein. The cause of the burning coal is unknown, but it is widely believed to have been started by lightning hundreds of years ago. Juniper trees grow in a columnar shape here, and this is a phenomenon you'll see nowhere else on earth. Campgrounds nearby. Amidon, off US-85.

Fargo. North Dakota's largest city and the home of North Dakota State University, founded in 1890. The city is well-known for its cultural, recreational and shopping opportunities. On Interstate 94 and Interstate 29.

Frontier Village. Home of the world's largest buffalo, a concrete giant that weighs 60 tons and stands 25 feet tall. This reconstructed frontier town also features a museum, gift shop and snack bar. Open year-round. Jamestown, Interstate 94.

Geographical Center. The geographical center of North America lies in North Dakota and it is marked with a rock cairn; Geographical Center Museum nearby. Rugby, off US-2.

Grand Forks. North Dakota's second largest city, home of the University of North Dakota and the State Mill and Elevator. Campbell House and Myra Museum will be of interest to history buffs. Nearby (15 miles west) is the Grand Forks Air Force Base, home of the 321st Strategic Missile Wing and the 319th Bomb Wing.

International Peace Garden. A man-made botanical masterpiece covering 2,300 acres of the Turtle Mountains along the North Dakota-Manitoba border; highlights include formal gardens, 18-foot floral clock, All Faiths Peace Chapel,

International Music Camp; camping and picnicking. Dunseith, off US-281.

Medora. A reconstructed cowtown of the 1880s, featuring shops and a number of special events; camping, picnicking, horse rentals. Off Interstate 94.

Sheyenne River Valley Scenic Drive. A scenic drive along the Sheyenne River near Fort Ransom; camping and picnicking; Ransom County Historical Museum; good canoeing in early spring and summer. Near Fort Ransom and Enderlin, off State Route 46.

State Capitol. This modern 18-story building is considered to be one of the most unique and efficient capitol buildings in the nation; the view of the North Dakota countryside from the observation deck is extraordinary. Tours of the building are available. Open year-round. Bismarck, on Interstate 94.

Sully's Hill National Game Preserve. A wooded area on the south shore of Devil's Lake featuring deer, elk and buffalo in their natural habitat; picnic area. Devil's Lake, off State Route 19.

Turtle Mountains-Lake Metigoshe. The wooded Turtle Mountains provide several recreation areas; in addition to Lake Metigoshe State Park, other areas include Strawberry Lake, Twisted Oaks and Pelican Lake; camping, hiking, canoeing, picnicking. Belcourt, off US-281.

North Dakota State Parks

Park	Location	CAMPING	PICNICKING	CONCESSIONS	SWIMMING	HIKING	BOATING	FISHING	HUNTING	WINTER SPORTS
Beaver Lake	*Burnstad. Off State Route 3.*	•	•		•	•	•	•		
Fort Lincoln	*Mandan. Off State Route 1806.*	•	•	•	•	•	•	•		•
Fort Ransom	*Fort Ransom. Off State Route 27.*	•	•		•	•		•		•
Fort Stevenson	*Garrison. Off State Route 37.*	•	•		•	•	•	•		•
Icelandic	*Cavalier. Off State Route 5.*	•	•		•	•	•	•		•
Lake Metigoshe	*Bottineau. Off State Route 43.*	•	•		•	•	•	•		
Lake Sakakawea	*Pick City. Off State Route 200.*	•	•	•	•	•	•	•		•
Lewis and Clark	*Williston. Off State Route 1804.*	•	•		•	•	•	•		•
Streeter Memorial	*Streeter. Off State Route 30.*		•		•					
Turtle River	*Grand Forks. Off State Route 2.*	•	•	•	•	•	•	•		•

North Dakota State Forests

Forest	Location	CAMPING	PICNICKING	CONCESSIONS	SWIMMING	HIKING	BOATING	FISHING	HUNTING	WINTER SPORTS
Homen	*Dunseith. Off State Route 43.*	•	•			•	•	•	•	•
Turtle Mountain	*Bottineau. Off State Route 14.*	•	•			•	•	•	•	•

For more information on North Dakota state parks and forests, contact: *North Dakota Parks and Recreation, PO Box 139, Mandan, North Dakota 58554, (701) 663-9571.*

South Dakota

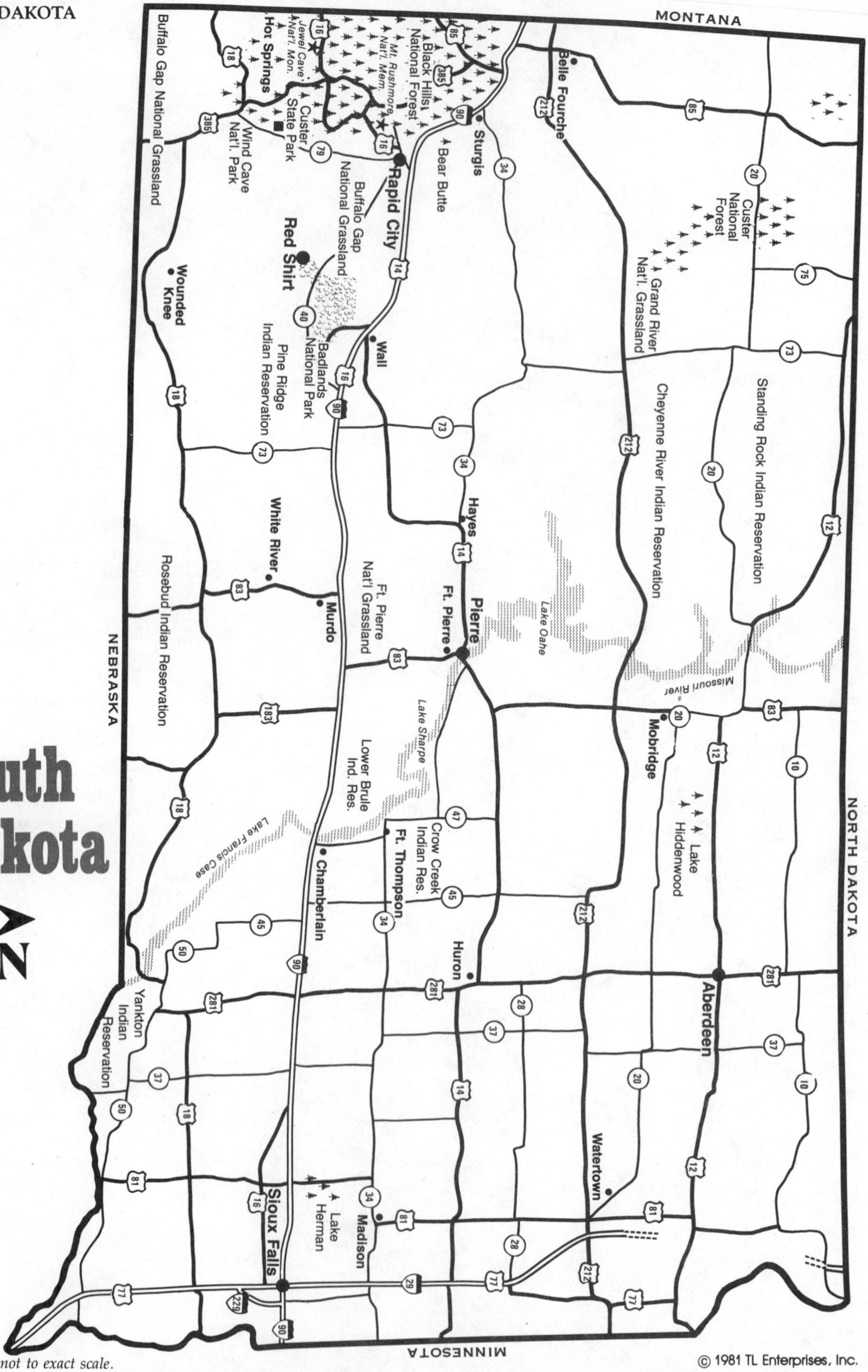
MONTANA
NORTH DAKOTA
MINNESOTA
NEBRASKA
N
Belle Fourche
Sturgis
Black Hills National Forest
Mt. Rushmore Nat'l. Mem.
Jewel Cave Nat'l. Mon.
Hot Springs
Custer State Park
Wind Cave Nat'l. Park
Buffalo Gap National Grassland
Bear Butte
Rapid City
Buffalo Gap National Grassland
Red Shirt
Wounded Knee
Wall
Badlands National Park
Pine Ridge Indian Reservation
Custer National Forest
Grand River Nat'l. Grassland
Standing Rock Indian Reservation
Cheyenne River Indian Reservation
Hayes
Lake Oahe
White River
Murdo
Ft. Pierre Nat'l Grassland
Ft. Pierre
Pierre
Missouri River
Rosebud Indian Reservation
Lake Sharpe
Lower Brule Ind. Res.
Mobridge
Lake Hiddenwood
Lake Francis Case
Chamberlain
Ft. Thompson
Crow Creek Indian Res.
Huron
Aberdeen
Yankton Indian Reservation
Watertown
Lake Herman
Madison
Sioux Falls
16
18
85
385
90
79
34
14
212
20
75
73
40
12
83
183
10
47
45
50
281
28
37
81
77
29
229

Map not to exact scale.

South Dakota

By state standards, South Dakota is just a youngster, and the memories of its heritage are still fresh — and rich with names like Lewis and Clark, Sitting Bull, Crazy Horse, George Armstrong Custer, Wild Bill Hickok and Calamity Jane. The magnificent landscape of South Dakota includes the mighty Missouri River, the sprawling cattle ranches of the high plains, the brooding beauty of the Badlands, the rugged Black Hills — and the spirit of America, carved into the craggy boulders of Mount Rushmore. In short, this is a land of big horizons and easy-going lifestyles, where a friendly people invite you to "roam free."

The first inhabitants of the region that is now South Dakota were the Mound Builders, who can be traced from about 1200 A.D. In 1600 or thereabouts, the Mound Builders were replaced by the more advanced Arikara Indians, an agricultural people who were later driven out by the Sioux. In 1682, the region was visited by Robert Cavelier Sieur de La Salle and claimed for France. The French made no attempt to develop the region, however, and in 1762 it was ceded to Spain. Napolean Bonaparte reclaimed the territory in 1800, but three years later it became a part of the U.S. under the terms of the Louisiana Purchase. Despite this, actual control of the area remained in the hands of the Sioux until 1877, when the Army avenged Custer's defeat at Little Big Horn and opened the Black Hills to white exploitation. In 1890, one year after South Dakota was admitted as a state, 3,840,000 acres of the Great Sioux Indian Reservation were opened to settlement by whites, and the Sioux were limited to five other reservations that had been previously established. Spurred by the discovery of gold and the coming of the railroad, South Dakota's growth following statehood was rapid.

While you're exploring South Dakota's Old West heritage, you won't want to miss historic Deadwood, the place where Wild Bill Hickok was gunned down by Jack

Full name: State of South Dakota
Origin of name: From the Sioux meaning "Alliance With Friends."
Motto: Under God The People Rule
Nicknames: Coyote State, Sunshine State
Capital: Pierre
Statehood: November 2, 1889, 40th state.
Population: 689,000 (ranks 44th).
Major Cities: Sioux Falls (73,925), Rapid City (48,156), Aberdeen (26,630).
Bird: Ringnecked pheasant
Flower: Pasqueflower
Tree: Black Hills spruce

Average daily temperatures by month

	Northern	Southern
Jan.	19.2 to -1.7	32.0 to 9.8
Feb.	26.1 to 5.1	38.0 to 15.2
Mar.	37.3 to 16.1	45.6 to 22.2
Apr.	55.4 to 30.6	61.4 to 34.9
May	68.3 to 41.8	72.6 to 46.7
Jun.	77.4 to 52.3	81.9 to 57.0
Jul.	84.6 to 57.2	89.7 to 62.7
Aug.	84.6 to 55.7	88.2 to 61.2
Sept.	72.5 to 44.4	77.2 to 50.4
Oct.	61.1 to 34.4	65.9 to 39.9
Nov.	40.7 to 19.3	48.5 to 25.9
Dec.	26.0 to 6.6	36.0 to 15.3
Year	54.4 to 30.2	61.4 to 36.8

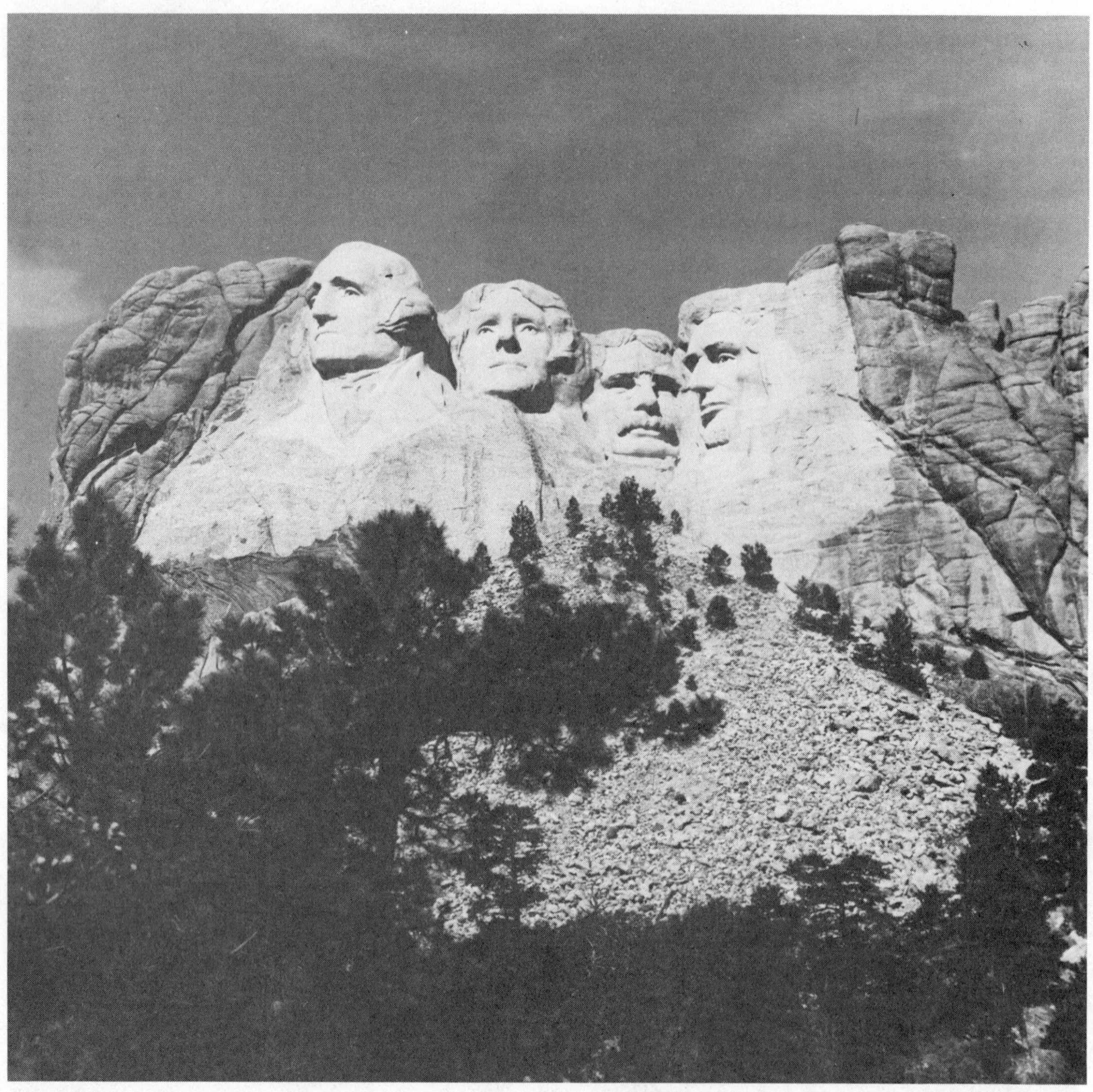

Majestically towering over the pine-covered Black Hills of South Dakota is Mount Rushmore National Memorial.

McCall, and the town where Calamity Jane settled in 1875. While you're touring the countryside, visit the 72,000-acre Custer State Park, but come prepared — the park is inhabited by a herd of hungry burros who will be looking for a handout of apples, crackers or any other snack you'd care to offer. In northeast South Dakota, you'll find a landscape dotted with lakes offering superb fishing for serious anglers — and fun for the youngsters. And there's much more: ghosts of the cavalry linger at Fort Sisseton; the world's most unique drugstore is at Wall; and one of the most unusual entertainment halls, the famous Corn Palace, can be found in Mitchell.

The mining of gold, silver and other minerals is still an important part of the South Dakota economy, and the Homestake Gold Mine in Lead is the largest producing gold mine in the country. Agriculture is another important activity in the state, as is tourism, farm equipment manufacturing, meat packing and flour and feed milling.

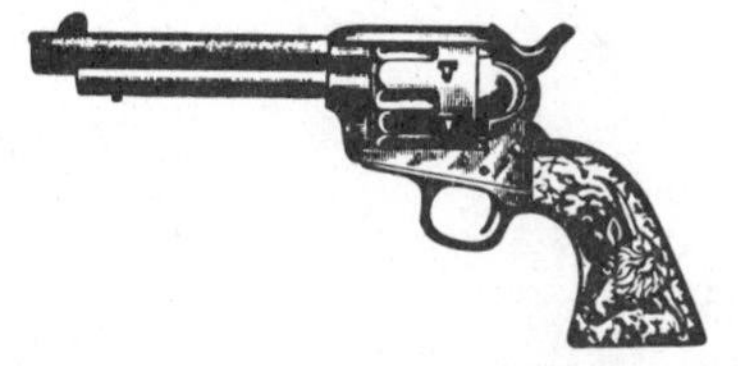

Some of the denizens of Dakota Territory

Poker Alice
As a young girl she married a rancher east of Sturgis. One winter her husband died. Legend has it that she didn't get him into town until spring for a proper burial, selling her wedding band to pay for the funeral. Broke and destitute, she went to work and became Deadwood's most notorious faro dealer. And she kept a little something going on the side: the bawdiest of bawdy houses in nearby Sturgis.

Calamity Jane
In 1875 Calamity Jane settled into Deadwood with ease. A former scout, bull-whacker and soldier, Calamity drank her whiskey neat and swore worse than the miners. She rode the pony express between Deadwood and Custer in the days when it took a sharp trigger finger and considerable skill on a horse just to stay alive. She had her tender side, too. She is said to have solicited groceries for needy families at the point of a six-shooter. During the smallpox scourge of 1878 she nursed many residents of Deadwood back to health.

Deadwood Dick
The first Deadwood Dick was Nat Love, a black cowboy who won the award for wild horse riding, pistol shooting and roping during the Deadwood celebration of July 4, 1876, an event known today as "The Days of '76." Nat dubbed himself Deadwood Dick and the legend began. Others who followed him with the name were an actor from Cheyenne who fell in love with a song-and-dance girl, and an ex-stagecoach driver.

Potato Creek Johnny
Supposedly he discovered the largest nugget of gold ever found in the Black Hills. He used to tie it in a silk kerchief and offer to show it to people for a drink. He tied about a dozen knots in the kerchief, and as he moved from table to table, it took three or four drinks to get the knots untied. He lived on Potato Creek, about 25 miles from Deadwood Gulch.

Teepees and mountain men are rare sights almost everywhere except at South Dakota's Ft. Sisseton Historical Festival. The Festival re-creates the days of cavalry men, cowboys, and homesteaders.

State Offices

Tourism
South Dakota Division of Tourism
Joe Foss Building
Pierre, South Dakota 57501
(605) 773-3301

State Police
Department of Public Safety
118 West Capitol Avenue
Pierre, South Dakota 57501
(605) 773-3105

Radio Stations

Aberdeen
KSDN 930 (AM)
KABR 1420 (AM)
KKAA 1560 (AM)
Brookings
KBRK 1430 (AM)
KESD 88.3 (FM)
KGKG 94.3 (AM)
Rapid City
KIMM 1150 (AM)
KKLS 920 (AM)
KTOQ 1340 (AM)
KOTA 1380 (AM)
KKHJ 93.9 (FM)
KGGG 100.3 (FM)
Sioux Falls
KXRB 1000 (AM)
KNWC 1270 (AM)
KLYX 1520 (AM)
KELO 92.5 (FM)
KNWC 96.5 (FM)
Yankton
WNAX 570 (AM)
KYNT 1450 (AM)
KQHU 104.1 (FM)

South Dakota Points of Interest and Attractions

Badlands Petrified Gardens. A rare display of Badlands minerals, prehistoric fossils, dinosaur tracks, fossil tree trunks and the Badland's largest petrified logs; fluorescent mineral exhibits. Open mid-April through late October, daily, 7 a.m. to 8 p.m. Kadoka, off Interstate 90.

Big Thunder Gold Mine. A tour into the past with informative guides, featuring the history of this old community and the chance to mine your own gold samples. Open May 1 through October 15, daily, 7:30 a.m. to 8:30 p.m. Keystone, on State Route 244 and US-16 Alternate.

Black Hills Central Railroad. A nostalgic ride through the gold rush country of the 1880s behind one of America's last operating steam locomotives. Open mid-June through August 29; four departures daily. Hill City, off US-16 and 385. (605) 574-2222.

Black Hills Passion Play. A cast of 250 recreates the dramatic events of the last seven days in the life of Christ in an outdoor amphitheater with a mammoth stage. Season: June 3 through September 2, Sunday, Tuesday and Thursday, 8:15 p.m. Spearfish, on US-14 and US-85.

Black Hills Petrified Forest. Guided tours through the only petrified forest in the upper Midwest; museum, fluorescent mineral display, large arrowhead collection, rock shop, gift shop. Open Memorial Day to September 15. Piedmont, off Interstate 90.

Black Hills Playhouse. Students and staff from the University of South Dakota present live musical, comedy and dramatic productions. Season: June 8 through August 26, daily, 8:30 p.m.; matinee at 2 p.m. Hermosa, in Custer State Park, off State Route 36. (605) 255-4141.

Black Hills Race Track. Greyhound racing; children permitted. Season: May 25 through September, daily, 8:10 p.m. Rapid City, on Business Loop Interstate 90.

Bobtail Placer Mine. An old gold claim where you can pan the gravel for yourself. Open May 20 through October 1, 7:30 a.m. to 6 p.m. Between Deadwood and Central City, on US-14 Alternate.

Broken Boot Gold Mine. Underground tours of this historic mine. Open May 15 to October 1, 8 a.m. to 4 p.m. Deadwood, off US-14.

Chapel in the Hills. A replica of the famous 800-year-old Stave Church in Norway; vesper worship every evening from first Sunday in June through last Sunday in August. Open May 1 through October 1, 7 a.m. to sunset. Rapid City, west on State Route 44.

Circle B Chuckwagon Suppers and Western Show. Chuckwagon supper every night at 7:30 p.m., western music by the Circle B cowboys; reservations required. Season: Memorial Day through mid-September. Rapid City, off Interstate 90 and US-14. (605) 348-7358.

Corn Palace. Thousands of bushels of natural colored corn, wheats and Sudan grass are used each year to make picture designs on the exterior of "The World's Only Corn Palace." Open "most days" from June 1 through September 1. Free. Mitchell, off Interstate 90.

Cosmos of the Black Hills. The laws of nature seem to be defied at every turn here, and the result is an experience you won't forget. Open April through mid-October, daily, 9 a.m. to 5 p.m.; summer hours, 7 a.m. to 8 p.m. Rapid City, on US-14.

Diamond Crystal Cave. A spectacular natural cavern, millions of years old, where you'll see a variety of beautiful formations; rock shop, gift shop, petrified gardens. Open May 1 through September 30, daily, 14 hours. Rapid City, three miles west on State Route 44.

Dinosaur Park. A group of life-size prehistoric reptiles reproduced in concrete; gift shop. Open May 1 to October 1, daily, 8 a.m. to 10 p.m. Rapid City, on Skyline Drive.

Evans Plunge. World's largest natural warm-water indoor swimming pool. Open year-round, daily, 8 a.m. to 6 p.m. Hot Springs, off US-18.

Homestake Gold Mine Tours. Tour the surface workings of the largest operating gold mine in this hemisphere. Open May 1 through October 31, Monday to Saturday, 8 a.m. to 4 p.m. Lead, off US-85.

Mount Moriah. See the graves of "Wild Bill" Hickok, Calamity Jane, Preacher Smith, Potato Creek Johnny and others in this old "Boot Hill" cemetery; beautiful view of surrounding countryside. Deadwood, off US-14 Alternate.

North American Bison (some 1,300 animals in all) roam free in South Dakota's Custer State Park.

Mount Rushmore. The famous massive granite sculpture that memorializes four American Presidents — George Washington, Thomas Jefferson, Theodore Roosevelt and Abraham Lincoln. Open year-round; during summer, parking is very limited — so RVers pulling trailers are asked to leave them in the campground. Near Keystone, off US-16.

The Phantom of Matthew's Opera House. A melodrama performed in an ornate turn-of-the-century opera house; two hours of laughter, spooky chills and music. Season: June 15 through August 18, Monday, Wednesday, Friday and Saturday, 8 p.m. Spearfish, on Main Street. (605) 642-2626.

Reptile Gardens. A new sky dome covers this extensive reptile collection set among tropical foliage and orchids; trained animals in the Bewitched Village; alligator wrestling. Open April 1 through

November 1, daily, 7 a.m. to 9 p.m. Rapid City, six miles south on State Route 16.

Rushmore Aerial Tramway. Take a relaxing ride to the top of the tramway for a spectacular view of Mount Rushmore and the Black Hills area; gift shop. Open May through September, daily. Keystone, on US-16 Alternate.

Rushmore Cave. Scenic tours of underground caverns and unique formations. Open May 1 through October 31. Near Keystone, off US-16.

Sitting Bull Crystal Caverns. Tours of caverns that include petrified sea-life embedded in the walls. Open May 15 through October 15, daily, 7 a.m. to 7 p.m. Rapid City, 10 miles south on US-16.

Stage Barn Crystal Cave. The largest variety of formations found in any Black Hills cave; ultra-violet displays. Open Memorial Day through Labor Day, daily, 8 a.m. to 8 p.m. Rapid City, northwest in scenic Stagebarn Canyon, off Interstate 90 (exits 46 and 48).

Story Book Island. Nursery Rhymes come to life in animated and real-life scenes. Open June 1 through weekend after Labor Day, daily, 8 a.m. to 8 p.m. Free, donations accepted. Rapid City, off Interstate 90.

Terry Peak Chair Lift. A beautiful ride to the top of the highest mountain east of the Rockies offers a five-state view below. Season: May 1 through September 20 (summer season); December 15 through April 15 (winter season). Lead, off US-85.

Thunderhead Falls. A spectacular vertical waterfall located deep inside a mountain that holds the oldest gold mine (1878) open to the public in the Black Hills area. Open April through November 1, daily, sunrise to sunset. Rapid City, west 10 miles on US-44.

Trial of Jack McCall. Reenactment of the trial for the murder of Wild Bill Hickok in Saloon No. 10, Deadwood Gold Camp, August 2, 1876. Season: June through August, nightly except Sundays, 8 p.m. Deadwood, on US-14 Alternate.

Wall Drug Store. Features a mechanical Cowboy Band, animated Chuck Wagon Quartet, 1908 Hupmobile display, four art galleries, western mall with nine shops, restaurants. Open year-round, daily. Wall, on Interstate 90.

Western Woodcarvings. The largest collection of animated wood carvings in the world; hundreds of characters come to life at the push of a button. Also, a woodcarver's studio and gift shop. Open May through September, daily, 9 a.m. to 6 p.m. Custer, off US-16.

South Dakota's Corn Palace is like no other building in the world. The exterior decorations are constructed entirely of corn and other local vegetation. Each year, local artists design new murals that reflect specific themes. The Palace also attracts big name entertainers in early fall, when it is the site of special annual performances.

Wind Cave. Tours of underground caverns; 28,000-acre wildlife park nearby; campground. Open year-round, daily. Hot Springs, 10 miles north off US-385.

Wonderland Cave. A two-level cavern, 60 million years old; gift shop, snack bar, picnic area. Open May 15 through October 15, daily, 8 a.m. to 10 p.m. Sturgis, off Interstate 90 (exit 32).

South Dakota State Parks

Park	Location	CAMPING	PICNICKING	CONCESSIONS	SWIMMING	HIKING	BOATING	FISHING	HUNTING	WINTER SPORTS
Bear Butte	*Sturgis. Off State Route 79.*	•	•		•	•	•	•		
Custer	*Custer. Off US-16 Alternate*	•	•	•	•	•	•	•		
Fisher Grove	*Redfield. Off US-212.*	•	•			•	•	•		
Hartford Beach	*Milbank. Off State Route 15.*	•	•	•	•	•	•	•		
Lake Herman	*Madison. Off State Route 34.*	•	•	•		•	•	•		
Lake Hiddenwood	*Selby. Off US-83.*		•		•	•	•	•		
Newton Hills	*Fairview. Off Interstate 29.*	•	•	•		•				
Oakwood Lakes	*Volga. Off US-14.*	•	•	•	•	•	•	•		
Palisades	*Corson. Off Interstate 90.*	•	•		•	•		•		
Roy Lake	*Lake City. Off State Route 10.*	•	•	•	•		•	•		
Sica Hollow	*Sisseton. Off State Route 10.*		•			•				
Union County	*Beresford. Off Interstate 29.*	•	•			•				

South Dakota has no state forests. For more information on South Dakota state parks, contact: *Department of Game, Fish and Parks, Pierre, South Dakota 57501, (605) 773-3482.*

Midwest States Calendar of Events

Spring
(March, April, May)

North Dakota

North Dakota Winter Show and Agriculture Fair. March, Jamestown.
Manitoba Days. May, Fargo.
State Music Festival, Bismarck Junior College. May, Bismarck.
Spring Choir Concert, Bismarck Junior College. May, Bismarck.
Fishing Tourney. May, Devils Lake.

South Dakota

Garden Show. March, Rapid City.
All-State Band Festival. March, Sturgis.
Annual Spring Sport Show. March, Sioux Falls.
South Dakota Community Theater Festival. March, Mitchell.
Schmeckfest. March, Freeman.
Annual Home Show. March, Sioux Falls.
Flea Market and Antique Sale. March, Rapid City.
Annual Flea Market. April. Geddes.
Annual Art Show. April, Mobridge.
Old-Time Fiddlers Jamboree. April, Lake Norden.
Official Opening of all State Parks and Recreation Areas. May, statewide.
Jackrabbit Stampede. May, Brookings.
Square Dance Festival. May, Freeman.
Maverick Stampede. Rapid City.

Iowa

St. Patrick's Day Celebration. March, Emmetsburg.
Special Arts Festival. Art work by the handicapped. April, Des Moines.
Images. Art exhibits. April, Cedar Rapids.
Tulip Time Festival. Thousands of multi-colored tulips fill flower beds throughout the community. May, Pella.
Special Spring Music Festival. May, Muscatine.
Spring Horse Show, Iowa Horse Show Association, Iowa State Fairgrounds. May, Des Moines.
Bluegrass Festival. May, Sigourney.

Kansas

Kansas Festival of American Community Theater. March, Wichita.
Hays City Music Festival. March, Hays.
Annual Gun, Coin and Antique Show. March, Colby.
Mid-America Farm Expo. March, Salina.
Spoonbill Snagging Contest. March, Chetopa.
Recreational Vehicle Show. March, Parsons.
Southwest Kansas Square Dance Festival. April, Dodge City.
Arts Fair. April, Lindsborg.
Annual Messiah Festival. April, Lindsborg.
Wichita Jazz Festival. April, Wichita.
Spring Arts Festival. April, Hays.
Chisholm Trail Jubilee. May, Wichita.
May Fete. May, McPherson.
Annual Art and Book Fair, Wichita Art Museum. May, Wichita.
Annual Old Fort Days and Championship Rodeo. May, Fort Scott.

Minnesota

Annual Thunderbird International Golf Tournament. March, International Falls.
Annual Nightriders Snowmobile "Snodeo and Winter Fair." March, Nay-Tah-Waush.

Annual Fantasy On Ice Show. Amateur ice production featuring 175 students in all age groups. March, Bemidji.
Annual Jaycee's Home, Sport and Travel Show. March, Bemidji.
Annual St. Urho Day Celebration. Parade, potluck dinner, dancing. March, Finland.
International Snodeo. March, International Falls.
Downhill Canoe Race. Special snow chute against the clock. March, Taylors Falls.
St. Patrick's Day Celebration. March, Maple Lake.
Miss Minnesota Universe Pageant. March, Hamel.
Minnesota's Little Miss Sweetheart. Children's pageant. March, Arden Hills.
Annual Craft Show. March, Edina.
Annual Smelt Run. Smelt spawning running on Lake Superior and in North Shore streams for two weeks. April, Duluth.
Art Fair Festival. April, Grand Rapids.
Annual Smelt Fry. April, Beaver Bay.
Syttende Mai Fest. Norwegian Independence Day celebration; carnival, flea market, folk dancing, Norwegian foods. May, Spring Grove.
Annual People's Fair. May, Mankato.
Early Settlers' Day. May, International Falls.

Missouri

St. Patrick's Day Celebration. March, Rolla.
Dogwood Festival. April, Camdenton.
Kewpiesta. Annual celebration honoring Rose O'Neill, Ozark writer, artist, sculptress and creator of the Kewpie doll. April, Branson.
Valley of Flowers Festival. May, Florissant.
Spring National Crafts Festival. May, Silver Dollar City (Branson).
Missouri State Trapshooters Championship Shoot. May, Osage Beach.

Nebraska

St. Patrick's Day Celebration. March, O'Neill.
Arbor Day Celebration. April, Nebraska City.
German Heritage Days. May, McCook.

Summer
(June, July, August)

North Dakota

Annual International Old-Time Fiddlers Contest, International Peace Garden. June, Dunseith.
Miss North Dakota Pageant. June, Bismarck.
Annual All-Arabian Horse Show; North Dakota Arabian Horse Show Association. June, Valley City.
Art Exhibit. June, Valley City.
International Music Camp and Band Concert. June, Dunseith.
Wells County Fair. June, Fessenden.
International Festival of the Arts Concert, International Peace Garden. June, Dunseith.
Roundup Days. June, Ellendale.
Miss North Dakota National Teenager Pageant. June, Jamestown.
Geographical Center Days Festival. June, Rugby.
Roughrider Days. July, Dickinson.
Annual Mandan Jaycee Rodeo. July, Mandan.
Stutsman County Fair. July, Jamestown.
North Dakota State Dairy Show. July, Jamestown.
Fireworks Display. July, Fargo.
Annual Rodeo. July, Raleigh.
Annual Fourth of July Celebration. July, Park River.
Killdeer Mountain Roundup Rodeo. July, Killdeer.
Festival in the Park. July, Minot.
Anniversary Celebration. July, Walcott.
Red River Valley Fair. July, West Fargo.
North Dakota State Fair. July, Minot.
Red River Mall Street Fair. July, Fargo.
Annual Divide County Threshing Bee and Antique Show. July, Fargo.

Annual Governor's Walleye Fishing Tourney. July, Garrison.
Crazy Days, Kirkwood Plaza. July, Bismarck.
Garden and Flower Display. August, Bismarck.
Pioneer Days, Bonanzaville USA. August, West Fargo.
Golden Valley County Fair. August, Beach.

South Dakota
Kampeska Walleye Classic. June, Watertown.
Fort Sisseton Historical Festival. June, Fort Sisseton.
Antique Auto Show. June, Sisseton.
Miss South Dakota Pageant. June, Hot Springs.
Doland Rodeo. June, Doland.
Sioux Stampede. June, Martin.
Czech Days. June, Tabor.
Bison Rodeo. June, Bison.
Gala Day and Rodeo. June, Bison.
Sitting Bull Stampede. July, Mobridge.
Annual Black Hills Roundup. July, Belle Fourche.
Fourth of July Celebration. July, Harrold.
Fourth of July Celebration. July, Sioux Falls.
Wall Roundup Days Rodeo. July, Wall.
Folk Arts Festival. July, Brookings.
Corn Palace Stampede. July, Mitchell.
Dacotah Wacipi Powwow. July, Flandreau.
Heart of the Hills Celebration. July, Hill City.
Pioneer Days. July, Dupree.
Black Hills Square Dance Festival. July, Rapid City.
Annual Gold Discovery Days Celebration. July, Custer.
Dakotah Stampede. July, Aberdeen.
Fall River County Fair and Rodeo. August, Edgemont.
Isabel Rodeo. August, Isabel.
Annual Pukwana Turkey Races. August, Pukwana.
Black Hills Motorcycle Classic. August, Sturgis.
Central States Fair. August, Rapid City.
Fine Arts Festival. August, Rapid City.
Faith Stock Show and Rodeo. August, Faith.
Sioux Empire Fair. August, Sioux Falls.
Oahe Days. August, Pierre.
Gem and Mineral Show. August, Mitchell.
Crow Creek Powwow and Fair. August, Fort Thompson.
Custer County Fair and Achievement Days. August, Hermosa.
Black Hills Steam and Gas Threshing Bee. August, Sturgis.
Frontier Days. August, White River.
Major James Stampede. August, McLaughlin.
Steam Threshing Jamboree. August, Madison.
Annual South Dakota 4-H Finals Rodeo. August, Ft. Pierre.

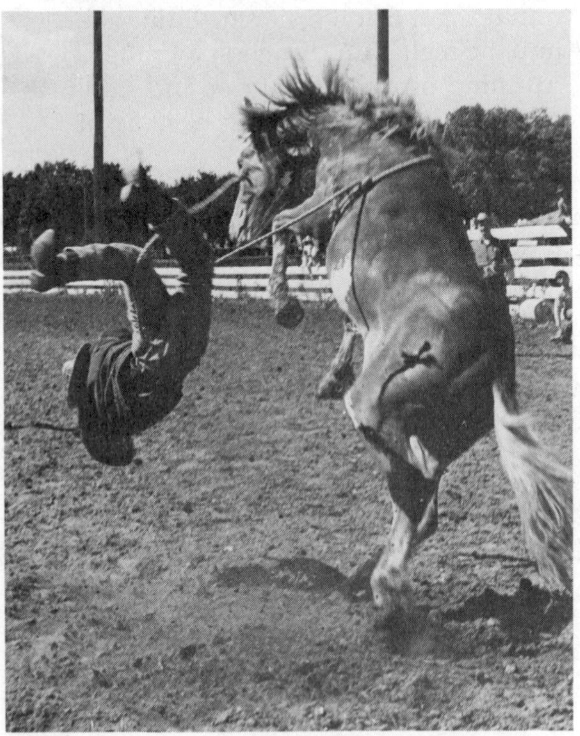

Iowa
Sidewalk Antique Fair. June, Fort Dodge.
North Iowa Band Festival. More than a hundred high school bands from northern Iowa and southern Minnesota; grand parade, floats, band competition, concert. June, Mason City.
Truck Rodeo. June, Cedar Rapids.
Outdoor Living Fair. June, Des Moines.
Horse and Buggy Days. June, Des Moines.
Civil War Days. June, Hopkinton.

Annual Flight Breakfast. June, Denison.
Annual Pork Barbecue. June, Sioux Center.
Soybean Days. June, Sheldon.
Strawberry Days. June, Strawberry Point.
International Folk Festival. June, Bettendorf.
Annual Firemen Legion. June, Preston.
Dairy Day. June, Fredericksburg.
Annual Senior Citizens Golf Tournament. June, Des Moines.
Kolach Festival. June, Cedar Rapids.
Fine Arts Festival. June, Indianola.
Annual Chuckwagon Races. June, Charles City.
Snake Alley Art Fair. June, Burlington.
Annual Scandinavian Dager Celebration. June, Eagle Grove.
Annual Bluegrass Festival. June, Charlton.
Bouton Sauerkraut Day. June, Perry.
Annual Grinnell Run. June, Grinnell.
Annual Riverboat Days Celebration. June, Clinton.
Annual Pageant of Drums. July, Clinton.
Annual Stock Car Race. July, Independence.
Old-Fashioned Fourth of July Celebration. July, Tipton.
Annual Great Canoe Race and Fourth of July Celebration. July, Bentonsport-Bonaparte.
Fourth of July Trap Shoot. July, Rock Valley.
Fun and Feed Days. July, Ankeny.
Roaring Raft Bash. July, Gray's Lake.
Tractor Pull. July, Iowa Falls.
Sauerkraut Days. July, Ackley.
Miss Forest City Pageant. July, Forest City.
Annual Vinton Invitational Swimming and Diving Meet. July, Vinton.
Annual Horse Show. July, Mallard.
Stub's Threshing Bee. July, Spencer.
Bluegrass Festival. July, Newton.
Homemade Pie Social. July, Des Moines.
Shriners Parade and Barbecue. July, Montezuma.
Grain Harvest Festival. July, Des Moines.
Fall Festival. July, Clive.
National Hobo Days. August, Britt.
Annual Scout Komallya Campout. August, Indianola.
National Dvorak Festival. August, Spillville.
U.S. National Hot-Air Balloon Championships. August, Indianola.
Firemen's Festival. August, Dawson.
Annual All-Iowa Antique Auto Show. August, Arnolds Park.
Iowa Corn Days. August, Des Moines.
Annual Cresco Fine Arts Fair. August, Cresco.
Family Arts Festival. August, Ottumwa.
Cougar National Sailing Championships. August, Clear Lake.
Watermelon Day. August, Stanhope.
Annual National Sprint Car Races. August, Knoxville.
Sweet Corn Days. August, Elkader.
Summerfest. August, Ames.
Sweet Corn Festival. August, West Point.
Annual Crawford County Old Settlers Picnic. August, Denison.
Art Fair. August, Nevada.
Wright County Shrine Sweetcorn Feed. August, Clarion.
Annual Summer Arts Festival, Charles H. MacNider Museum. August, Mason City.
Annual Regional Glider Meet. August to September, Tipton.

Kansas

Old Shawnee Days. June, Shawnee.
National Fingerpicking Championships. June, Winfield.
Miss Southern Kansas Pageant. June, Greensburg.
Annual Old-Time Traditional Bluegrass Festival. June, Wichita.
Santa Fe Trail Center Annual Dedication Celebration. June, Larned.
Frontier City Summerfest. June, Hays.
Smoky Hill River Festival. June, Salina.
Marshall Civic Band Concert. June, Topeka.
Art Festival. June, Arkansas City.
Annual Old-Fashioned Fourth of July. July, Wichita.
Miss Kansas Pageant. July, Pratt.
Sumner County Wheat Festival. July, Wellington.

Annual Potawatomie Indian Powwow. July, Mayetta.
Sunflower Rodeo. July, Russell.
Annual Threshing Days. July, Goessel.
Kickapoo Indian Powwow. July, Horton.
Annual Inter-Tribal Powwow and Arts and Crafts Fair. July, Wichita.
Annual After Harvest Czech Festival. July, Wilson.
Mitchell County Fair. July, Beloit.
Annual Cowtown and Rodeo Celebration. August, Baxter Springs.
McLouth Threshing Bee. August, McLouth.
Annual Old Settlers Picnic. August, Halstead.
Birthday Celebration and Buffalo Bill Cody Days. August, Leavenworth.
Ellsworth Cowtown Festival. August, Ellsworth.
Old Settlers Day. August, Gove.
Huff and Puff Hot-Air Balloon Races. August, Topeka.

Minnesota
Boyd Good Time Days. June, Boyd.
Huntersville Annual Spring Trail Ride. June, Huntersville.
Springtime Awakening. June, Carver.
Straight River Days. June, Medford.
Danish Day. Folk dancing, strolling musicians, prizes, clowns, pony rides. June, Minneapolis.
Pine Island Cheese Festival. June, Pine Island.
Annual Edina Art Fair. June, Edina.
Onamia Days. June, Onamia.
Hokah Fun Daze. June, Hokah.
Swedish Festival. June, Cambridge.
Janesville Hay Daze. June, Janesville.
Dairy Days. Parade, coronation, contests, dance. June, Battle Lake.
Rose Fete. June, Minneapolis.
Miss Minnesota Pageant. June, Austin.
Fiesta Days. June, Montevideo.
Scandinavian Midsummer Fest. June, Fergus Falls.

Minnesota Polka Festival. June, Mounds View.
Minnesota Sit 'N Spit Club Annual Marble Tournament. June, Mankato.
Svenskarnas Dag (Swedish Day). June, Minneapolis.
Midsummernats Fest. June, Starbuck.
Mountain Lake Powwow. June, Mountain Lake.
Spass Tag Festival. June, Waite Park.
Pioneer and Centennial Days. July, Crookston.
Fourth of July Festival. July, Apple Valley.
City Fireworks Display. July, Detroit Lakes.
Fourth of July Homecoming Event. July, Hill City.
Lumberjack Days. July, Cloquet.
Litchfield Watercade. July, Litchfield.
Faribo Festival. July, Faribault.
Northwest Water Carnival. July, Detroit Lakes.
Paul Bunyan Sweetheart Days. July, Hackensack.
Isle Fun Days. Rides, softball tourney, parade, pancake breakfast, queen contest. July, Isle.
Korn and Klover Karnival. July, Hinckley.
Duk Duk Daze. July, New Hope.
Annual Raspberry Festival. July, Hopkins.
Kelliher-Washkish Wild Rice Festival. July, Kelliher.
Sinclair Lewis Days Festival. Parades, pageants. July, Sauk Center.
Pork Days. July, Lakefield.
Edgerton Dutch Festival. July, Edgerton.
Annual Street Rod Nationals. July, St. Paul.
Song of Hiawatha Pageant. July, Pipestone.
Merrifield Fun Festival. July, Merrifield.
Leprechaun Days. Carnival and rides, parade, soap box derby, outdoor dance, fireworks, picnic, kiddie parade. July, Rosemount.
Moose Lake Agate Days. July, Moose Lake.
Civil War Weekend. July, St. Paul.
Festag Days. July, Minnesota Lakes.
River City Days. July, Chaska.
Annual Kolacky Day. July, Montgomery.
Mermaid Rock Regatta. August, International Falls.
Annual Antiques Show and Sale. August, Grand Rapids.
Lumberjack Days. August, Stillwater.
Frazee Turkey Days. August, Frazee.
Pola Czesky Days. August, Silver Lake.
Duluth Folk Festival. August, Duluth.
Remer Fall Festival. August, Remer.
Cokato Corn Carnival. August, Cokato.
Walleye Festival. August, Garrison.
Ortonville Sweetcorn Festival. August, Ortonville.
Hoghead Festival. August, Proctor.
Corn on the Cob Days. August, Plainview.
Minnesota Renaissance Festival. August, Shakopee.
Askov Rutabaga Festival and Fair. Folk dancing, farm and garden exhibits, needlework, baking. August, Askov.
Great Bed Race. August, Pipestone.
Steam Threshers Reunion. August, Rollag.

Missouri

Possum Trot Frontier Festival. June, Kansas City.
Great Meramec River Raft Float. June, St. Louis.
June Festival of Mountain Folks' Music. June, Silver Dollar City (Branson).
Ragtime Festival. June, St. Louis.
National Tom Sawyer Fence Painting Contest. July, Hannibal.
Strassenfest. July, St. Louis.
J-Bar-H Rodeo. July, Camdenton.
Ozark Empire Fair. August, Springfield.
Bootheel Rodeo. August, Sikeston.
Jour de Fete. Celebration of the founding in 1735 of Ste. Genevieve, the oldest town in Missouri. August, Ste. Genevieve.
Missouri State Fair. August, Sedalia.

Nebraska

Swedish Festival. June, Stromsburg.
Nebraskaland Days and Buffalo Bill Rodeo. June, North Platte.
Arrows to Aerospace. June, Bellevue.
Independence Day Celebration. July, Seward.
Tribal Powwows. August, Macy.

Czech Festival. August, Wilber.
Sidney Rodeo. August, Sidney.
Thunderboat Race. August, Lake McConaughy.

Fall
(September, October, November)

North Dakota
Annual Labor Day Reunion. September, Almont.
United Tribes Powwow. September, Bismarck.
Consecutive Fall Festival. September, Hebron.
Annual Central North Dakota Steam Threshers Show. September, New Rockford.
Antique Show, Kirkwood Plaza. September, Bismarck.
Gem and Mineral Show. September, Mandan.
Annual Sheyenne Valley Arts and Crafts Festival. September, Fort Ransom.
Downtown October Fest. October, Fargo.
Sauerkraut Day. October, Wishek.
Polkafest. October, Mandan.
Annual Norwegian Hostefest. October, Minot.

South Dakota
Labor Day Celebration. September, Wagner.
Annual Horse Show. September, Colton.
Annual Caravan Tour of Butte County. September, Belle Fourche.
Fall and Winter Sport and Variety Show. September, Sioux Falls.
Corn Palace Festival. September, Mitchell.
Plains Indian Crafts Expo. September, Rapid City.
Official Closing State Parks. September, statewide.
Founders Day. October, Springfield.
Pioneer Weekend. October, Yankton.
Custer Park Buffalo Auction. November, Custer State Park.
Veterans' Day Powwow. November, Wagner.
Snow Queen Contest. November, Lake Preston.
Christmas in the Hills. November, Hot Springs.

Iowa
Tri-State Rodeo. September, Fort Madison.
Mississippi Valley Arts and Crafts Fair. September, Davenport.
National Dairy Cattle Congress. September, Waterloo.
Oktoberfest. September, Amana Colonies.
Images of Art. September, Sheldon.
Fort Atkinson Rendezvous. September, Fort Atkinson.
Covered Bridge Festival. September, Winterset.
Henkle Creek Arts Festival. September, Garrison.
Fall Color-Cade. September and October, statewide.
Annual Port of McGregor Autumn Art Fest. October, McGregor.
Thieves Market. October, Iowa City.
Rebekah Craft Carnival. October, Red Oak.

Kansas
Annual Labor Day Parade and Celebration. September, Hoisington.
Fall Festival. September, Beloit.
Watermelon Festival. September, Clyde.
Mexican Fiesta. September, Garden City.
National Flatpicking Championships. September, Winfield.
Annual Flea Market. September, Lyons.
Mini-Sapa Festival. September, Oberlin.
Elsmore Bean Day. September, Elsmore.
Annual Homecoming. October, Fredonia.
Pioneer Harvest Fiesta Steam Engine Show. October, Fort Scott.
Annual Homecoming Parade. October, Fredonia.
October Fall Festival. October, Syracuse.
Annual Harvest Home Festival. October, Wichita.
Maple Leaf Festival. October, Baldwin City.
Halloween Parade and Frolic. October, Hiawatha.
Arts and Crafts Fair. November, Hays.

Proud to Be An American Celebration. November, McPherson.
Baldknobbers Hillbilly Jamboree Show. November, Fort Scott.
Annual Christmas Craft Show. November, Russell.
Community Thanksgiving Feast. November, Sterling.
Holiday Parade. November, Emporia.

Minnesota
Wild Rice Festival. September, McGregor.
Red Rooster Day. September, Midway.
Silver Bay Days. September, Silver Bay.
Lake Region Pioneer Threshermen's Association Annual Show. September, Dalton.
Defeat of Jesse James Days. Bank raid reenactment, parade, art exhibits, rides, concessions. September, Northfield.
Leech Lake Area Perch Contest. September, Walker.
Annual Arts and Crafts Festival. September, Hutchinson.
Annual Hawk Migration. September, Duluth.
Fall Festival. September, Morris.
Utschtallung. Mennonite Fair. September, Mountain Lake.
Octoberfest. September, Emily.

Missouri
Santa-Cali-Gon. Pioneer festival featuring arts and crafts, fiddlers' contest, beard and costume contests, food, games. September, Independence.
Badenfest. September, St. Louis.
Forest Park Balloon Rally. Hot-air balloons gather from around the nation. September, St. Louis.
National Crafts Festival. September, Silver Dollar City (Branson).
Bevo Day. September, St. Louis.
Cotton Carnival. September, Sikeston.
Country Club Plaza Art Fair. September, Kansas City.
Colorama Tours. Mid-October, Salem, Ava and Branson.
American Royal Rodeo. November, Kansas City.

Nebraska
Ak-Sar-Ben Livestock Exposition and Rodeo. September, Omaha.

Old-Time Christmas and Tour of Homes. November, Brownville.

Winter
(December, January, February)

North Dakota
No major winter events.

South Dakota
Holiday Tourney and Pageant. December, Huron.
Snow Queen Festival. January, Aberdeen.
Junior Miss Pageant. January, Sturgis.
Winter Ice Carnival. January, Watertown.
Miss South Dakota USA Pageant. January, Sioux Falls.
Black Hills Stock Show and Rodeo. February, Rapid City.
Farm and Home Show. February, Winner.
Winter Quarter Horse Show. February, Sioux Falls.
Miss Mitchell Pageant. February, Mitchell.
Winter Carnival. February, Deadwood.

Iowa
Iowa Winter Olympics. January, Clear Lake.

Kansas
Fort Scott Community Christmas Parade and Show. December, Fort Scott.
Santa's Arts and Crafts Show. December, Humboldt.
Christmas at Old Shawneetown. December, Shawnee.
State Piano Festival. January, Hays.
Ozarks Country Jubilee. January, Fort Scott.
String Fling. January, Manhattan.
Boat and RV Show, Expo Grounds. January, Topeka.
Kansas Day Celebration. January, Larned.
Kansas Flower, Lawn and Garden Show, February, Topeka.
Antique and Gun Show. February, Ulysses.
International Pancake Race. February, Liberal.

Minnesota
No major winter events.

Missouri
Christmas Activities, Country Club Plaza. Decorations and special events. December and January, Kansas City.

Nebraska
Christmas Pageant. Lavish display of lights, religious pageant and carillon bell concert in "The Christmas City." December. Minden.

Mt. Rushmore National Memorial, the Shrine of Democracy with the faces of George Washington, Abraham Lincoln, Thomas Jefferson and Theodore Roosevelt was carved by Gutzon Borglum (left).

COLORADO
IDAHO
Alice Lake
Boise,
State Capitol

WYOMING
Yellowstone
Arches National Monument
UTAH
R. McKee
Mormon temple
Salt Lake City
Glacier National Park
MONTANA
George Armstrong Custer

Rocky Mountain States

For the early pioneers, the Rocky Mountains were a formidable barrier on the road West. For today's traveler, however, they are an easily-explored range of backcountry villages, picturesque byways and unparalleled scenic beauty.

Besides sharing the common bond of these majestic peaks, the Rocky Mountain states all have one other thing in common — wide-open spaces. For though these states make up nearly one-fourth of the land mass of the continental United States, only three out of every 100 Americans live here — and most of them are concentrated in the region's two major cities, Denver and Salt Lake City.

In any one of these states, you'll find a rich Western heritage and constant reminders of the struggle between the white man and the Indian for domination of the territory. In each town, you'll find numerous tales recounting the lawless days of the frontier, when justice came swiftly from the barrel of a six-gun or at the base of a hanging tree. More often than not, the violence that erupted in these frontier towns had its roots in man's quest for the rich gold and silver deposits that were so prevalent here.

You'll also find limitless fishing and hunting opportunities throughout the Rocky Mountain states. There are the renowned trout waters of Flaming Gorge Reservoir and the trout and bass waters of Lake Powell. In Utah, you'll find the elk meadows of the High Uinta Primitive Area, and in Montana the big-game ranges of the Bearpaw, Swan and Mission Mountains await the sportsman.

And should you grow tired of the serenity of the wide-open spaces, you can always retreat to the cities for excitement. (Try Cheyenne in July for the festivities of Frontier Days, or Denver and Salt Lake City for a variety of special events and cultural offerings.)

Most of all, the Rocky Mountain states offer a wonderful feeling of freedom and room to roam — so they should rank high on the travel list of today's RVer.

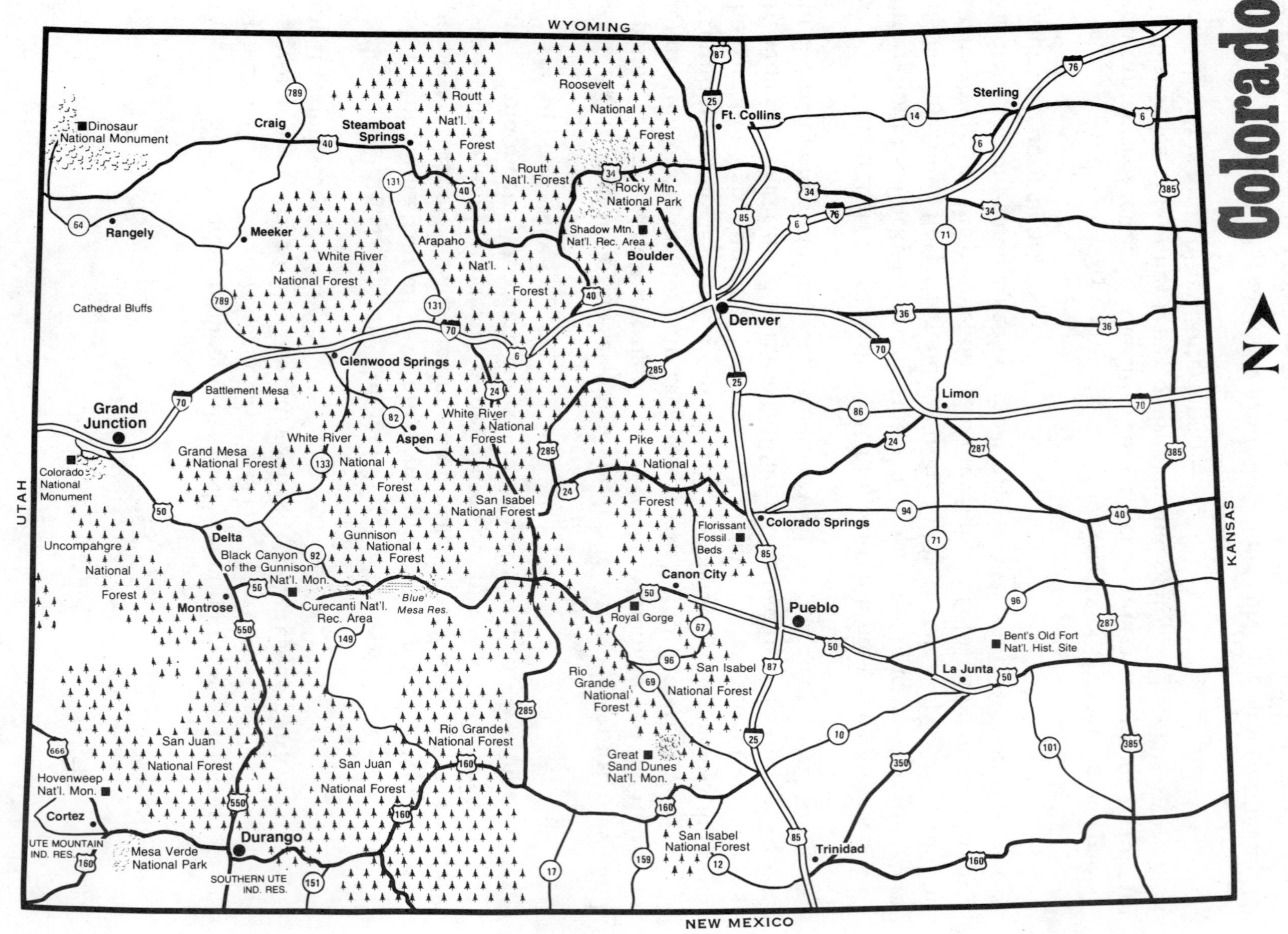
WYOMING
UTAH
KANSAS
NEW MEXICO
Dinosaur National Monument
Craig
Steamboat Springs
Routt Nat'l. Forest
Roosevelt National Forest
Ft. Collins
Sterling
Rangely
Meeker
White River National Forest
Arapaho Nat'l. Forest
Routt Nat'l. Forest
Rocky Mtn. National Park
Shadow Mtn. Nat'l. Rec. Area
Boulder
Cathedral Bluffs
Denver
Glenwood Springs
Battlement Mesa
Grand Junction
Limon
White River National Forest
Aspen
Grand Mesa National Forest
White River National Forest
Pike National Forest
Colorado National Monument
San Isabel National Forest
Colorado Springs
Florissant Fossil Beds
Delta
Gunnison National Forest
Uncompahgre National Forest
Black Canyon of the Gunnison Nat'l. Mon.
Canon City
Montrose
Curecanti Nat'l. Rec. Area
Blue Mesa Res.
Royal Gorge
Pueblo
Bent's Old Fort Nat'l. Hist. Site
San Isabel National Forest
La Junta
Rio Grande National Forest
Rio Grande National Forest
San Juan National Forest
San Juan National Forest
Great Sand Dunes Nat'l. Mon.
Hovenweep Nat'l. Mon.
Cortez
San Isabel National Forest
Trinidad
UTE MOUNTAIN IND. RES.
Mesa Verde National Park
Durango
SOUTHERN UTE IND. RES.

N ➤ **Colorado**

Map not to exact scale.

Colorado

With some 1,100 peaks rising to 10,000 feet or more, Colorado can easily lay claim to the title of the most mountainous of all the states. The Indians called this region the "Land of the Long Look," and one of the best viewpoints is from the 14,110-foot summit of Pikes Peak, which can be reached by cog railway, by climbing or in your own vehicle. By contrast, there's the scenic Royal Gorge, where you can look down on the Arkansas River from the vantage point of the world's highest, 1,053-foot suspension bridge. If you visit Colorado in the fall, head for the high country to gaze upon the fiery spectacle of the aspens, scrub oak and sumac. To make your view of magnificent Colorado even more enjoyable, the state and federal governments have set aside 13 million acres of land that includes 400 campgrounds in 11 national forests, four national monuments and two national parks.

Cliff-dwelling Indians were probably the first inhabitants of Colorado, but the first Europeans to visit the area were those who came under the banner of Spain seeking the fabled wealth of the Southwest. In 1706, Ulibarri crossed the upper Arkansas River and took formal possession of the Colorado region for Spain, calling it Santo Domingo. The eastern part of the territory, which fell under the control of France, was ceded to the United States in 1803 as part of the Louisiana Purchase. The rest of Colorado was taken by Kearny in the Mexican War of 1848. The gold rush of the late 1850s resulted in the influx of nearly 100,000 people, who were later threatened by conflicts with the Arapaho and Cheyenne Indians. After the Indians were defeated, the large population created the need for an organized government, and the Colorado Territory

Full name: State of Colorado
Origin of name: From Spanish for "Colored Red."
Motto: *Nil Sine Numine* (Nothing Without the Deity).
Nickname: Centennial State
Capital: Denver
Statehood: August 1, 1876, 38th state.
Population: 2,619,000 (ranks 28th).
Major Cities: Denver (484,531), Colorado Springs (179,584), Pueblo (105,312).
Bird: Lark bunting
Flower: Rocky Mountain columbine
Tree: Blue spruce

Average daily temperatures by month

	Northern	Southern
Jan.	30.3 to 0.7	46.7 to 21.2
Feb.	33.1 to 2.0	48.9 to 22.3
Mar.	38.0 to 7.3	53.4 to 25.1
Apr.	47.4 to 17.5	63.2 to 33.2
May	58.9 to 25.9	73.0 to 42.4
Jun.	68.7 to 31.2	83.0 to 50.7
Jul.	74.8 to 36.0	86.8 to 56.6
Aug.	73.0 to 35.6	84.6 to 55.3
Sept.	66.7 to 27.9	78.5 to 47.7
Oct.	56.4 to 20.6	68.3 to 38.1
Nov.	40.4 to 10.1	55.0 to 27.7
Dec.	31.5 to 2.3	47.9 to 22.3
Year	51.6 to 18.1	65.8 to 36.9

was created in 1861. The advent of the railroad in the 1870s further spurred growth, and Colorado was finally admitted as a state in 1876.

At Mesa Verde National Park, in the southwest corner of the state, you can start to trace the early history of the region by visiting the prehistoric cliff dwellings. Move on to the era of the gold rush with a visit to

Leadville, the first gold camp and later the silver-mining center of the state.

No visit to Colorado is complete without a stopover in the "Mile-High City," Denver, where you can visit the state capitol, stroll through historic Larimer Square, or tour the U.S. Mint that turns out 20 million coins a day. After you visit the city, you might want to embark on a tour of Denver's 27 mountain-parks, where you'll see buffalo grazing, the tomb of Buffalo Bill Cody and the unique Red Rocks Amphitheater.

With so much magnificent scenery, it's not surprising that tourism ranks as one of Colorado's most important industries. Agriculture is also one of the main industries, as is the mining of molybdenum, a metal used in rocketry. Lately, the state has also become a center for the manufacture of machinery, transportation equipment, food products and instruments.

State Offices

Tourism
Division of Commerce and Development
1313 Sherman Street
Room 500
Denver, Colorado 80203
(303) 839-3045

State Police
Department of Public Safety
4201 East Arkansas Avenue
Denver, Colorado 80222
(303) 757-9011

Radio Stations

Alamosa
- KGIW 1450 (AM)

Aspen
- KSNO 1260 (AM)

Boulder
- KADE 1190 (AM)

Colorado Springs
- KSSS 740 (AM)
- KRDO 1240 (AM)

Denver
- KOAQ 103.5 (FM)
- KERE 710 (AM)
- KVOD 99.5 (FM)
- KOA 850 (AM)
- KBNO 1220 (AM)
- KDKO 1510 (AM)

Durango
- KIUP 930 (AM)

Grand Junction
- KSTR 620 (AM)

Pueblo
- KCSJ 590 (AM)
- KIDN 1350 (AM)

Colorado Points of Interest and Attractions

Air Force Academy. Visitors are encouraged to tour this 18,000-acre campus, which sits in the shadow of the Rockies' Rampart Range. Open year-round, daily. Colorado Springs, 12 miles north on Interstate 25 (exit 150).

Bridal Veil Falls and Hanging Lake. A spectacular lake that seems to be hanging on a sheer cliff, 1,200 feet above the canyon floor; beautiful falls pour over the rock ledges; 1½-mile hike or horseback ride to top. Glenwood Springs, 10 miles east, on US-6.

Buckskin Joe. A reproduction of one of Colorado's original mining towns, using log structures that date back as early as 1859. Open April through November, daily, 8 a.m. to dusk. Adults $1.50, children $1, under 5 free. Canon City, one mile south off US-50, on Royal Gorge Road.

Central City. One of Colorado's oldest towns dating back to the 1859 gold discovery on the North Fork of Clear Creek. Today, the town is a fascinating stop for the traveler, featuring historic landmarks, galleries, gift shops, old saloons and a quaint Victorian atmosphere. Off Interstate 70, on State Route 279.

Colorado Central Narrow Gauge Railway. Departs from downtown Central City on a round-trip to Blackhawk, highlighting scenic and historic landmarks along the way. Season: June through August, daily, 10 a.m. to 5 p.m.; remainder of year, 10 a.m. to 6 p.m., Saturday and Sunday. Adults $2, children 6 to 12 $1, under 6 free.

Chamberlin Observatory. This is a University of Denver facility offering shows, films and lectures. Open year-round, Tuesday and Saturday; advance reservations required. Denver, 2930 East Warren Avenue. (303) 753-2070.

Coors Brewery. The country's fifth-largest brewery offering daily tours; floral displays. Open year-round, Monday to Saturday, 9 a.m. to 4 p.m. Free. Golden, west of Denver off Interstate 70, 13th and Ford Streets.

Cripple Creek Railroad. An interesting and educational four-mile trip on an old narrow-gauge train to an area of abandoned mines. Open June through early October, daily, 10 a.m. to 5 p.m. Adults $2.50, children 3 to 12 $1.75, under 3 free. Cripple Creek, off State Route 67, on Bennett Avenue.

Cumbres and Toltec Scenic Railway. A narrow-gauge railroad owned by the states of Colorado and New Mexico. America's last narrow-gauge luxury line, the train formerly connected Denver with the mining country of southwest Colorado. Now operates between Antonito, Colorado, and Chama, New Mexico. Season: Mid-June through mid-October, daily. Round-trip fare: adults $18, children under 12 $7; reservations advised. Antonito, junction of State Route 17 and US-285. (303) 376-5483.

Denver Botanic Gardens. A 20-acre garden featuring a domed conservatory, herbarium, library and gift shop. Open year-round, daily, 9 a.m. to 4:45 p.m. Free. Denver, 1005 York Street.

Eisenhower Tunnel. Opened in 1973, this tunnel makes it possible to drive under the Continental Divide; 1.7 miles long. Dillon, east on Interstate 70.

Estes Industries. A leading producer of model rockets; offers tours and slide show. Open year-round, Monday to Friday. Free. Canon City, 12 miles east on US-50.

Fiske Planetarium. Features a 65-foot diameter star theater, multi-media show, special programs; operated by the University of Colorado. Open year-round, Wednesday to Saturday. Adults $2, children 6 to 12 $1.50. Boulder, Folsom Street and Regent Drive. (303) 492-5001.

Garden of the Gods. A 940-acre natural park dominated by massive red sandstone rock formations; picnic areas, trails. Open year-round, daily, 9 a.m. to 11 p.m. Free. Colorado Springs, off US-24 and Interstate 25.

Heritage Square. A recreation of an 1880s Colorado town featuring crafts shops, ice-cream parlor, beer garden, dinosaur park, restaurant, opera house with old-fashioned melodramas, and rides. Open Memorial Day through Labor Day, daily, 10 a.m. to 9 p.m.; remainder of year, daily, 10 a.m. to 6 p.m. Free. Golden, off US-6, on US-40.

Magic Lantern Theater. Presenting the entertaining and authentic "Cripple Creek Story." Open year-round, daily, 10 a.m. to 6 p.m.; weekends only November through April. Adults $2, children under 16 $1.

Cripple Creek, on State Route 67 and Bennett Avenue.

Mollie Kathleen Gold Mine. Underground tours take you 1,000 feet into old gold mine. Open May through September, daily, 9 a.m. to 5 p.m. Adults $3, children under 11 $1.50. Cripple Creek, on State Route 67.

Pike's Peak Cog Railway. Train departs from Manitou Springs for 3½-hour round-trip to 14,100-foot summit of Pikes Peak (weather permitting). Season: May through October, two trips daily; reservations advised. Manitou Springs, 515 Ruxton Avenue.

Pike's Peak Highway. Highway winds 18 miles to the summit. RVers should exercise caution; trailerists should leave trailers at a campground. Season: May through October, daily (weather permitting), 8 a.m. to 4 p.m. Toll: 50 cents. Colorado Springs, 12 miles west, off US-24.

Pine Cone Players. A repertoire company offering six plays each season. Season: mid-June through mid-August, nightly. Adults $5, children under 18 $4, children under 12 $3. Grand Lake, 1120 Grand Avenue.

Redstone Castle. An English Tudor-style mansion built on a hillside above the Crystal River; tour includes library and trophy room; magnificent decor and furnishings. Open Memorial Day through September, daily, 10 a.m. to 5 p.m. Adults $3, children under 12 $1, family rate of $10. Carbondale, on State Route 133.

Ricker-Bartlett Pewter Casting Studio. Collection of pewter castings sculpted by well-known artist, Michael A. Ricker. Open year-round, Monday to Saturday. Free. Estes Park, on US-34.

Royal Gorge. Gorge with sheer cliffs rising as high as 1,200 feet features the world's highest suspension bridge, 1,053 feet above the Arkansas River. Open year-round, daily, sunrise to sunset. Admission and toll: adults $2.50, children 7 to 12 $2.25. Canon City, eight miles west on Royal Gorge Road. Royal Gorge Scenic Railway. Three-mile ride to Point Alte Vista, overlooking Royal Gorge. Season: May through mid-October, daily, 8:30 a.m. to 6 p.m. Adults $1, children under 16 50 cents.

Santa's Workshop. Chat with Santa, pet his reindeer, watch his helpers at work; magic shows, rides, gift from Santa for children. Open May through September, and December 24, daily, 10 a.m. to 5 p.m. Colorado Springs, 12 miles west, off US-24, on Pike's Peak Highway.

Scenic Drives. *Boulder:* West from US-36 to Flagstaff Highway, which winds to the summit of Flagstaff Mountain, 1,600 feet above the city. *Aspen:* Ten miles southwest, you'll find the scenic Maroon Bells; road junctions with State Route 82 one-half mile west of Aspen and follows Maroon Creek. Note: In mid-summer, drive may be restricted to bus tours due to vehicle congestion. *Glenwood Canyon:* (near Glenwood Springs). One of the state's most scenic drives takes you through a canyon cut by the Colorado River, along Interstate 70; 17 miles; picnic areas. From Gunnison, 10 miles north on State Route 135 to Almont, 22 miles northeast along Taylor River to the reservoir; campground.

The Troupe. A repertoire company noted for their versatility. Season: mid-June through August, nightly (except Tuesday); matinees, Thursday and Saturday. Admission: $5, matinees $3.50. Colorado Springs, Fine Arts Center, Cascade and Dale Streets. (303) 475-8470.

U.S. Mint. This mint stamps all denominations of U.S. coins and some foreign coins; gold depository worth several billion dollars; tours, sales room, exhibits. Open year-round, Monday to Friday; usually closed the last two weeks of June for closing of fiscal year. Denver, 320 West Colfax.

Van Briggle Pottery. Authentic pottery-making featured on tour through factory; exhibits. Open year-round, Monday to Saturday, 8 a.m. to 5 p.m. Free. Colorado Springs, off Interstate 25 (exit 156) at 1025 North Gate Road.

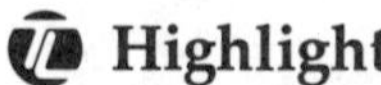

Autumn Colors

The fall color season, a most spectacular time to visit and see Colorado, begins in mid-September and runs through the month of October. The largest aspen groves generally are found between elevations of 8,000 to 10,000 feet. Colors start at the higher elevations and spread their way down as the season progresses. A bright golden yellow is the predominant color, with varying shades of brilliant reds, browns and oranges interspersed with the green of the slower changing leaves and the surrounding conifers.

To help you plan a trip to Colorado's high country during this most colorful of the seasons, we are listing some of the more dramatically colorful areas along with suggested routings.

- US-550, "Million Dollar Highway," between Durango and Ouray.
- US-160, "Navajo Trail," between Pagosa Springs and Cortez.
- Lizard Head Pass, State Highway 145 between Dolores and Telluride.
- Steamboat Springs, Elk River Country, north and Buffalo Pass, east.
- Independence Pass, State Highway 82 between Twin Lakes and Aspen.
- Maroon Bells area above Aspen.
- Cottonwood Pass, State Highway 306 between Buena Vista and Taylor Park.
- Grand Mesa, State Highway 65 east of Grand Junction and north of Delta.
- State Highway 67 between Divide and Cripple Creek.
- Platoro Reservoir, South of Del Norte and west of Conejos.
- State Highway 135 between Crested Butte and Gunnison.
- Slumgullion Pass Country, State 149 between Lake City, Creede and South Fork.
- Boreas Pass, between Como and Breckenridge.
- Flat Tops country, between Buford and New Castle.
- Cochetopa Pass between Saguache and Gunnison.
- Trail Ridge Road through Rocky Mountain National Park (US-34).
- Guanella Pass between Georgetown and Grant.
- Monarch Pass, US-50 Salida to Gunnison.
- Cucharas Pass, State 12, Trinidad to Walsenburg.

One-Day "Circle Trips" from the Denver Area

Almost anywhere you go in the mountains you'll find beautiful aspen displays; but here are two suggestions for one-day "circle trips" near the Denver area:

1. Leave Denver on U.S. Highway 40 for Bergen Park and from there follow Colorado Highways 74 and 103 to Echo Lake. Then follow Chicago Creek to Idaho Springs, and from there return to Denver.

2. Take U.S. Highway 6 from Denver to the junction at Central City-Blackhawk turnoff. Follow Colorado 119 from Blackhawk to Nederland and from there take Colorado 72 to Ward and Allenspark. From Allenspark, you may return to Nederland or continue on to Estes Park and return to Denver from Estes Park.

Colorado Mountain Peaks

14,000 feet high or more

Peak	Elevation	Peak	Elevation
Mt. Elbert	14,433	Longs Peak	14,256
Mt. Massive	14,421	Mt. Wilson	14,246
Mt. Harvard	14,420	Mt. Shavano	14,229
Blanca Peak	14,345	Mt. Princeton	14,197
La Plata Peak	14,336	Mt. Belford	14,197
Uncompahgre Peak	14,309	Mt. Yale	14,196
Crestone Peak	14,294	Crestone Needle	14,191
Mt. Lincoln	14,286	Mt. Bross	14,172
Grays Peak	14,270	Kit Carson Peak	14,165
Mt. Antero	14,269	El Diente Peak	14,159
Torreys Peak	14,267	Maroon Peak	14,156
Castle Peak	14,265	Tabeguache Mt.	14,155
Mt. Evans	14,264	Mt. Oxford	14,153
Quandary Peak	14,264	Mt. Sneffels	14,150

Colorado Mountain Passes

• Passes closed to winter travel

Pass	Elevation	Highway	Pass	Elevation	Highway
Berthoud Pass	11,314	US-40	North Pass	10,149	CO-114
Cucharas Pass	9,994	CO-12	Poncha Pass	9,010	US-285
Cumbres Pass	10,022	CO-17	Rabbit Ears Pass	9,426	US-40
Dallas Divide	8,970	CO-62	Red Hill Pass	9,993	US-285
Douglas Pass	8,268	CO-139	Red Mountain Pass	11,018	US-550
Fremont Pass	11,318	CO-91	•Slumgullion Pass	11,361	CO-149
Gore Pass	9,524	CO-134	•Spring Creek Pass	10,901	CO-149
Hoosier Pass	11,541	CO-9	Squaw Pass	9,807	CO-103
•Independence Pass	12,095	CO-82	Tennessee Pass	10,424	US-24
Kenosha Pass	10,001	US-285	•Trail Ridge High Point	12,183	US-34
La Manga Pass	10,230	CO-17	Trout Creek Pass	9,346	US-24, US-285
Lizard Head Pass	10,222	CO-145	Ute Pass	6,800	US-24
Loveland Pass	11,992	US-6	Vail Pass	10,603	US-6
McClure Pass	8,755	CO-133	Wilkerson Pass	9,507	US-24
•Milner Pass	10,759	US-34	Willow Creek Pass	9,621	CO-125
Molas Divide	10,910	US-550	Wolf Creek Pass	10,850	US-160
Monarch Pass	11,312	US-50			
Muddy Pass	8,772	US-40			
North La Veta Pass	9,413	US-160			

Mt. Democrat	14,148	Mt. Lindsey	14,042
Capitol Peak	14,130	Little Bear Peak	14,037
Pikes Peak	14,110	Mt. Sherman	14,036
Snowmass Peak	14,092	Red Cloud Peak	14,034
Windom Peak	14,087	Pyramid Peak	14,018
Mt. Eolus	14,084	Wilson Peak	14,017
Mt. Columbia	14,073	Wetterhorn Peak	14,017
Culebra Peak	14,069	North Maroon Peak	14,014
Missouri Mountain	14,067	San Luis Peak	14,014
Humboldt Peak	14,064	Huron Peak	14,005
Mt. Bierstadt	14,060	Mt. of the Holy Cross	14,005
Sunlight Peak	14,059	Sunshine Peak	14,001
Handies Peak	14,048		

Pikes Peak, America's most famous mountain, is beautifully framed by two giant sandstone monoliths in the Garden of the Gods. Once a sacred Indian ceremonial ground, this colorful area is now a favorite Colorado vacation mecca.

A Suggested Tour

Colorado's Golden Aspen Tours

The aspen becomes king of the mountains in Colorado between mid-September and the first two weeks in October. The shimmering "quakie" colors first crown the higher elevations, and then, as molten gold, slowly flow downward as the month-long season progresses.

The largest aspen groves are found between 8,000 and 10,000 feet altitude, but there are Colorado highways to take you within close viewing distance and optimum camera range.

The San Juan mountain highways of southwestern Colorado take on a special fall magic. Both the Million Dollar Highway between Durango and Ouray and the Lizard Head Pass Route 145 between Dolores and Telluride offer dramatic stands. A close neighbor of these paved roads is the Slumgullion Pass Route 149 between Lake City and Creede.

True to its namesake, the Aspen area is one of Colorado's most spectacular autumn amphitheaters. Independence Pass, Maroon Bells and the ghost town of Ashcroft, all near Aspen, present a dazzling color carnival.

Grand Mesa offers many scenic miles of aspen glory, plus the thrill of driving America's largest plateau. It is reached via State 65 east of Grand Junction and north of Delta.

There are four resplendent aspen viewing areas right in Denver's backyard. Routes 74 and 103 — winding westward from Evergreen over Squaw Pass to Echo Lake — that are popular with autumn vacationers. Less traveled, but equally awesome, is the Peak to Peak Highway from Black Hawk to Allenspark, along which the best aspen groves are between Nederland and Ward on State 72.

Superb aspen viewing awaits travelers along spectacular Trail Ridge Road, the highest continuous paved highway in the country. It reaches an altitude of 12,183 feet in its meanderings through Rocky Mountain National Park to Grand Lake.

Its southern counterpart in fall foliage is found along Highway 67 from Divide to Cripple Creek. Each autumn, Cripple Creek's Two-Mile-High Club sponsors exciting jeep trips in this famed gold mining area.

Ouray, Telluride, Gunnison, Salida and Steamboat Springs also stage fall jeep tours as part of their annual Rites of Autumn. Nature's big show usually gets under way in these mountain areas about the middle of September.

Colorado State Parks

Park	Location	CAMPING	PICNICKING	CONCESSIONS	SWIMMING	HIKING	BOATING	FISHING	HUNTING	WINTER SPORTS
Arapahoe	*Denver. Off State Route 83.*		•							•
Barr Lake	*Denver. Off Interstate 76.*		•			•				
Boyd	*Fort Collins. Off US-287.*	•	•	•	•		•	•		
Castlewood	*Franktown. Off State Route 83.*		•			•				
Golden Gate Canyon	*Blackhawk. On State Route 119.*	•	•			•				
Lathrop	*Walsenburg. Off Interstate 25, on US-160.*	•	•		•	•	•	•		
Lory	*Fort Collins. Off US-287.*	•	•		•	•	•	•		
State Forest	*Walden. On US-14.*	•	•			•	•	•		
Steamboat Lake	*Steamboat Springs. Off US-40.*	•	•	•		•	•	•		

Colorado has no state forests. For more information on Colorado state parks, contact: *Division of Parks and Outdoor Recreation, Centennial Building, Room 618, 1313 Sherman Street, Denver, Colorado 80203, (303) 839-3311.*

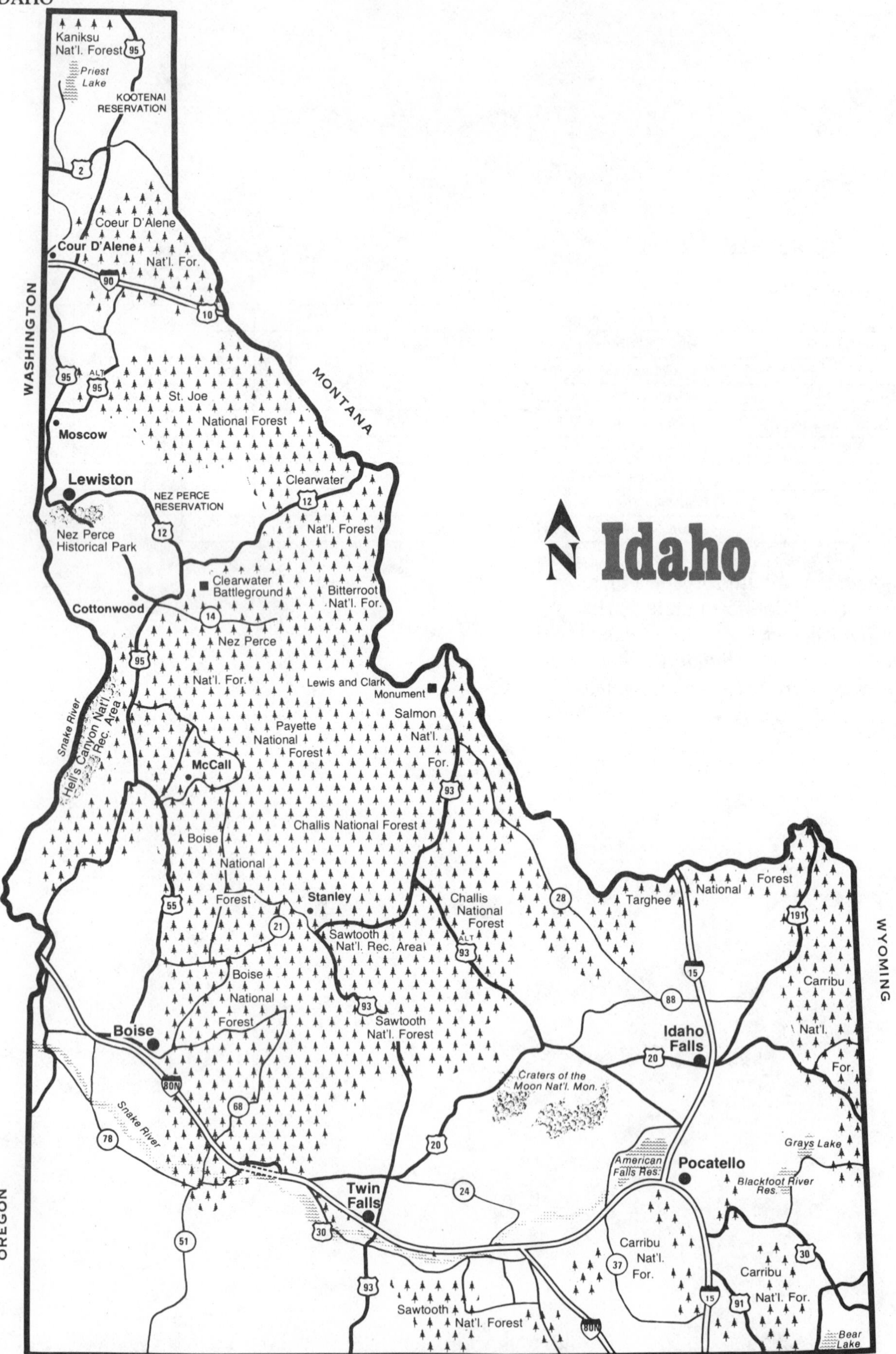

Map not to exact scale.

Idaho

When you think of Idaho, chances are you think of potatoes — or perhaps a resort, like Sun Valley. After a visit to this magnificent state, though, your thoughts will be of spectacular natural beauty — rugged mountains, deep canyons, wild rivers. Idaho is a wilderness state, as nearly 70% of it — an area larger than New York and Massachusetts combined — consists of publicly-owned lands. Much of the state is covered with mountains, and several different ranges have more than 50 peaks loftier than 10,000 feet. Idaho also boasts North America's deepest chasm, the 7,900-foot Hells Canyon, which was forged by the incessant cutting action of the Snake River. The Snake and Salmon Rivers are two of the state's major attractions, and a thrilling ride along the roaring course of either one could be the highlight of your trip to Idaho. But if your tastes run to less exciting pursuits, try exploring some of the gold rush country of the 1860s — or the stark landscape of the Craters of the Moon National Monument.

Indians are thought to have inhabited the Idaho region as early as 10,000 years ago, long before the Lewis and Clark expedition of 1805-06. During the following half century, a number of posts were established for the fur trade, along with several Mormon missions, but no attempts were made to establish permanent settlements until the 1860s gold rush. As people continued to pour into the region, the Idaho Territory was created in March of 1863. This growing white population also led to Idaho's best-known territorial event, the savage Indian wars of 1877-79, in which the U.S. Army crushed, in turn, the Nez Perce, the Bannocks and the Sheepeaters.

Full name: State of Idaho
Origin of name: From the Indian word meaning "Gem of the Mountains."
Motto: *Esto Perpetua* (It Is Forever).
Nickname: Gem State
Capital: Boise
Statehood: July 3, 1890, 43rd state.
Population: 857,000 (ranks 41st).
Major Cities: Boise (99,775), Pocatello (40,980), Idaho Falls (37,042).
Bird: Mountain bluebird
Flower: Syringa
Tree: Western pine

Average daily temperatures by month

	Eastern	Western
Jan.	28.1 to 11.1	38.6 to 22.8
Feb.	34.3 to 15.9	45.7 to 26.7
Mar.	42.9 to 21.8	54.3 to 30.5
Apr.	55.8 to 30.5	63.4 to 36.9
May	67.8 to 39.1	72.2 to 45.0
Jun.	75.5 to 45.7	79.3 to 51.8
Jul.	86.5 to 51.3	88.4 to 57.3
Aug.	84.6 to 49.7	86.3 to 55.2
Sept.	73.2 to 40.7	77.2 to 46.4
Oct.	60.5 to 31.3	65.0 to 37.1
Nov.	43.2 to 22.6	50.1 to 29.9
Dec.	30.5 to 13.4	39.9 to 24.6
Year	56.9 to 31.1	63.4 to 38.7

Today, you can bring those Indian conflicts to life with a visit to the Nez Perce National Historical Park, where the White Bird and Clearwater Battlefields are located. Preserved in Silver City, once the nation's second-largest silver-producing area, are reminders of a bloody miners' war that climaxed with a gun battle outside the old Idaho Hotel. Anglers will find extraordinary Kamloops and Dolly Varden trout in the depths of Pend Oreille Lake. And if you're a skier you'll surely want to head for one of Idaho's many fine resorts, where the winter snowfall averages 100 inches or more.

Agriculture is still Idaho's leading industry and the state produces about one-fourth of all the nation's potatoes. Manufacturing has been increasing in recent years and now includes lumber and wood products, chemicals, rubber, plastics and glass products. Mining is also important, and the Sunshine Mine near Kellogg is the nation's leading producer of silver. Tourism is on the rise, and is now the third-ranked industry with more than six million visitors to the state each year.

State Offices

Tourism
Division of Tourism and Industrial Development
State Capital Building
Boise, Idaho 83720
(208) 384-2470

State Police
Department of Public Safety
Box 34
Boise, Idaho 83731
(208) 384-2900

Radio Stations

Boise
KBOI 670 (AM)

Idaho Points of Interest and Attractions

Because so much of Idaho consists of federal lands, there are only a limited number of state attractions; see Historical Sites, National Parks, National Forests and Indian Reservations for additional Idaho attractions.

Arco. The first town in the United States to be supplied with electricity generated by nuclear power. On US-93 and US-26.

City of Rocks. Strange stone formations inscribed with the scribblings of pioneers. Burley, south off State Route 27, near town of Almo.

Craters of the Moon. Strange volcanic formations of black lava tubes, cones and trees. The area is so stark and desolate that the American astronauts trained here for the Apollo moon flights. Arco, southwest off US-93.

Empire Mine. Old gold mine located in the shadow of Mount Borah, Idaho's highest peak (12,665 feet). Mackay, off US-93.

Fossil Beds. Remains of prehistoric animals. Hagerman, west, off US-30, on US-12.

Shoshone Falls. Spectacular falls, taller than Niagara (best in spring). Twin Falls, off Interstate 86.

Soda Springs Geyser. In the 1930s, the people of Soda Springs were drilling for a water source for a town swimming pool and tapped this geyser. Off US-30, on Main Street (behind Enders Hotel).

Cataldo's Sacred Heart Mission, built by the Jesuit Missionaries and the Indians, is Idaho's oldest standing building.

Highlight

Lewiston

Historic Lewiston is located on the site of the 1805 encampment of Lewis and Clark, and was also the scene of a major gold discovery in 1860. Today the city has a number of attractions for travelers ranging from industrial tours and scenic drives to historic sites and museums.

Luna House Museum. Offers displays of Indian artifacts and other relics dating back as much as 2,000 years. Open year-round, Monday to Saturday, 9 a.m. to 5 p.m. Free. 0306 Third Street.

Potlatch Corporation. Offers guided tours of a plywood and veneer plant, tissue mill and large sawmill. Open year-round, Monday to Friday; tour hours vary. Free. Children under 8 not permitted. Off US-95.

Spalding Site. The site of the second Spalding Mission, built by the Reverend Henry H. Spalding and his wife Eliza in the mid-1800s. The site now serves as the headquarters of the Nez Perce National Historical Park and contains the graves of the Spaldings as well as a number of interesting rock formations that figured in the oral traditions of the Nez Perces. Open year-round, daily, from 8 a.m. East of city, 12 miles.

Spiral Highway. Beginning at the northern edge of the city, this route winds up Lewiston Hill for eight miles to a panoramic view of the countryside and the confluence of the Clearwater and Snake Rivers.

Idaho State Parks

Park	Location	CAMPING	PICNICKING	CONCESSIONS	SWIMMING	HIKING	BOATING	FISHING	HUNTING	WINTER SPORTS
Bear Lake	*St. Charles. Off US-89.*		•		•	•	•	•		
Black Canyon	*Emmett. On State Route 52.*		•		•		•	•		
Bruneau Dunes	*Bruneau. On State Route 51.*	•	•	•		•		•		
Farragut	*Athal. Off US-95.*	•	•		•	•	•	•		
Henry's Lake	*Macks Inn. Off US-20-191.*	•	•		•		•			
Heyburn	*Plummer. Off US-95.*	•	•		•		•	•		
Indian Creek	*Priest River. Off State Route 57.*	•	•		•	•		•		
Indian Rocks	*McCammon. Off Interstate 15.*	•	•							
Lava Hot Springs	*Lava Hot Springs. On US-30.*		•		•			•		
Lucky Peak	*Boise. Off State Route 21.*		•		•	•	•	•		
Mann Creek	*Weiser. On US-95.*	•	•		•		•	•		
Packer John's Cabin	*New Meadows. Off State Route 55.*	•	•							
Ponderosa	*McCall. Off State Route 55.*	•	•		•	•	•	•		
Round Lake	*Sandpoint. Off US-95.*	•	•		•		•	•		
Three Island	*Glenns Ferry. Off US-30.*	•	•			•	•	•		

Idaho has no state forests. For more information on Idaho state parks, contact: *Parks and Recreation Department, Statehouse, Boise, Idaho 83707, (208) 384-2154.*

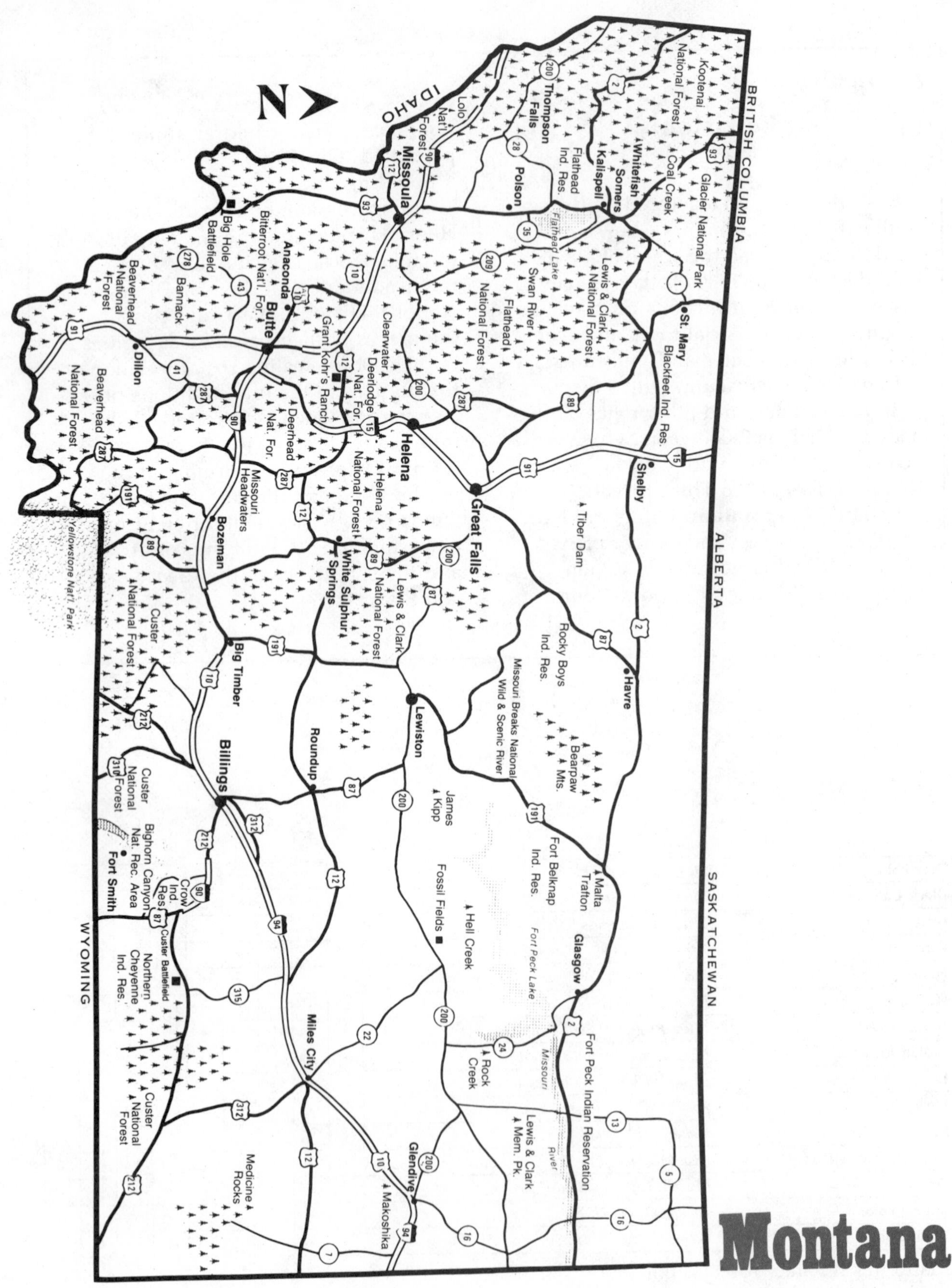

Map not to exact scale.

Montana

Montanans use the catchy phrase "the last of the big time splendors" to describe their state. And, indeed, Montana is a big land of tall mountains and rolling plains that ranks as America's fourth-largest state in area. As for splendors, there is the breathtaking beauty of Glacier National Park; the wide-open wonders of the Charlie M. Russell National Wildlife Range; the sight of a magnificent Bighorn standing proud on a mountain ledge; a herd of buffalo roaming free on a rich green prairie; and the colorful spectacle of an authentic Indian ceremony.

A number of Indian tribes were living in the Montana region at the time the eastern part became an American possession through the Louisiana Purchase; the western portion, a part of the Oregon Country, was ceded to the U.S. by Great Britain in the Oregon Treaty of 1846. The primary exploration of both regions was by Lewis and Clark, and the first activity by white men was the opening of the fur trade on the upper Missouri River in 1809 by Manuel Lisa. Later, the American Fur Company built two of Montana's earliest settlements, Fort Union (1829) and Benton (1846). Gold was discovered at Bannack in 1862, at Virginia City in 1863 and at Helena in 1864. These finds swelled the population dramatically, making a civil government necessary, and the territory of Montana was created in 1864. From 1867 to 1877, Montana was the scene of a number of Indian wars, including the famous 1876 Battle of the Little Bighorn, in which the Cheyennes and Sioux annihilated Lieutenant Colonel George A. Custer and his command of more than 200 cavalrymen.

Full name: State of Montana
Origin of name: From Spanish word meaning "Mountainous."
Motto: *Oro y Plata* (Gold and Silver).
Nicknames: Treasure State; The Big Sky Country; Land of the Shining Mountains.
Capital: Helena
Statehood: November 8, 1889
Population: 761,000 (ranks 41st).
Major Cities: Billings (68,987), Great Falls (60,868), Missoula (25,570).
Bird: Western meadowlark
Flower: Bitteroot
Tree: Ponderosa pine

Average daily temperatures by month

	Eastern	Western
Jan.	22.5 to 0.1	33.3 to 18.5
Feb.	30.7 to 7.5	41.9 to 23.2
Mar.	40.4 to 16.5	48.8 to 25.3
Apr.	56.7 to 29.9	58.9 to 31.5
May	68.9 to 41.5	69.2 to 38.5
Jun.	77.7 to 51.0	76.3 to 45.4
Jul.	85.7 to 55.6	86.6 to 48.1
Aug.	85.6 to 53.5	85.2 to 46.8
Sept.	72.6 to 42.6	74.9 to 40.0
Oct.	61.0 to 32.9	59.6 to 33.0
Nov.	41.9 to 19.8	43.1 to 26.9
Dec.	29.6 to 8.3	34.8 to 32.1
Year	56.1 to 29.9	59.4 to 33.3

Today, Montana has an Indian population of about 30,000, almost all of whom live within the boundaries of seven reservations which cover more than five million acres. To learn more about Montana's Indian past, visit the Museum of the Plains Indian at Browning (and try to take in the North American Indian Days celebration at the All-Indian Rodeo held there every July). The Big Hole National Battlefield commemorates the exodus of the Nez Perce nation across Montana in 1877, and the historic Battle of the Little Bighorn is memorialized at the Custer Battlefield National Monument. If you want to really enjoy Montana's wide-open spaces, try a float trip down the Missouri or Yellowstone Rivers, or track the backcountry on one of the many backpacking trails you'll find in Montana's 11 national forests. And if you're into rockhounding, you've come to the right place, for Montana is called "The Treasure State" because of its two natural gem stones, the sapphire and agate.

Ranching is one of Montana's most important activities, and the state is said to have over three times as many cattle and sheep as it has people. The development of coal reserves has recently taken on more significance, and the state is continuing to attract new industry to add to such current staples as lumbering, tourism, agriculture and oil products.

Montana Points of Interest and Attractions

Alder Gulch. Rich gold strikes were made here in 1863; reconstructed ghost towns, excellent rockhounding. Virginia City, off State Route 287.

Gates of the Mountains. Discovered and named by Lewis and Clark in 1805, these sheer cliffs rise 1,200 feet above the Missouri River; area has abundant wildlife, fishing and boating. Helena, off Interstate 15.

Great Falls of the Missouri River. Discovered in 1805 by Lewis and Clark, this site features the largest freshwater springs in the world. Great Falls, off US-87.

Hungry Horse Dam. A 564-foot dam that forms a reservoir surrounded by beautiful

State Offices

Tourism
Montana Highway Department
Travel Promotion Unit
Helena, Montana 59601
(406) 449-2654

State Police
Department of Public Safety
Helena, Montana 59601
(406) 449-3000

Radio Stations

Billings
KOOK 970 (AM)

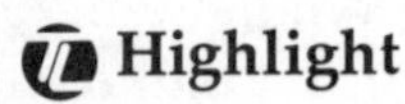

Virginia City

The site of a major gold strike in 1863, Virginia City is today one of Montana's most popular tourist attractions. Within a few weeks after gold was discovered here, the town had grown to a population of several thousand miners and outlaws. After the outlaw element had committed more than 190 murders in less than six months, the miners formed a vigilante group that captured and hung 21 of the criminals. Among those who met their fate at the end of a rope was the sheriff, who was found to be the leader of the outlaw band.

More than 20 of the original buildings have been restored; among them the state's first newspaper office, the general store, the pharmacy, the Wells Fargo Express Office and the Bale of Hay saloon. An old garage features a display of antique cars and lodging is available in some of the restored facilities. Gold panning, hunting and fishing are also offered. Open mid-June through Labor Day, daily. Off US-287, southwest of Ennis.

rugged mountains; camping, boating, fishing. Hungry Horse, off US-2.

Last Chance Gulch. Gold was discovered here on July 14, 1864. Points of interest nearby include State Capitol, Governor's Mansion. Helena, off Interstate 15.

Libby Dam. A 420-foot, 2,900-foot long dam that forms 90-mile-long Lake Koocanusa; camping, boating, fishing. Libby, off State Route 33.

Madison Canyon Earthquake Area. At 11:37 p.m. on August 17, 1959, an awesome earthquake slid half a mountain into the canyon, creating a giant dam and Quake Lake; visitors center, memorial, scenic vista. Cameron, off US-287.

National Bison Range. Large herd of bison and other species, including elk, pronghorn antelope, deer and some longhorn cattle; tours. Open June through Labor Day. Ravalli, off State Route 200.

Pompey's Pillar. On July 25, 1806, Captain William Clark carved his name on this 200-foot-high rock formation and the signature is still there; Registered National Historic Landmark. Pompey's Pillar, off Interstate 94.

Richest Hill On Earth. In this one area gold, silver, copper and zinc have been taken from mines and open pits; World Museum of Mining. Butte, off Interstate 90.

Scenic Drives. *Beartooth Pass:* A scenic switchback highway that travels to an altitude of 10,940 feet for a panoramic view of alpine lakes and the countryside below; campgrounds, fishing, hunting, winter sports. Red Lodge, south along US-212. *Pintler Scenic Route:* Take in the picturesque towns of Anaconda, Georgetown Lake, Philipsburg and Drummond; see ghost towns and the world's largest smoke stack at Anaconda smelter. Begin at Anaconda, off Interstate 90, along US-10A.

A Suggested Tour
West Yellowstone Loop
260 Miles

The most awe-inspiring country you will ever have the pleasure to visit is on the West Yellowstone Loop. There are numerous fishing access areas, campgrounds, backpacking trails and scenic wonders that defy description. To see it is to believe it.

Historic Virginia City offers rockhounding, scenic photography, sightseeing, a real glimpse into shades of the Old West. What can we say? Virginia City has something for everyone.

Take a side tour from Twin Bridges through the Jefferson Valley to picturesque Whitehall for fine dining, then on to Lewis and Clark Caverns for a few hours of cave exploration, then south again to Ennis.

Ennis is the gateway to Hebgen Dam and Quake Lake. After your stop at the Visitors Center at Quake Lake, don't miss the side trip to West Yellowstone for fun and relaxation, superb dining and a little humor thrown in.

Onward to the Red Rock Lakes, a stones-throw from the Continental Divide. Up and over Monida Pass (elevation 6,823 feet above sea level). Relax at the Clark Canyon Dam and try your favorite lure on the big ones.

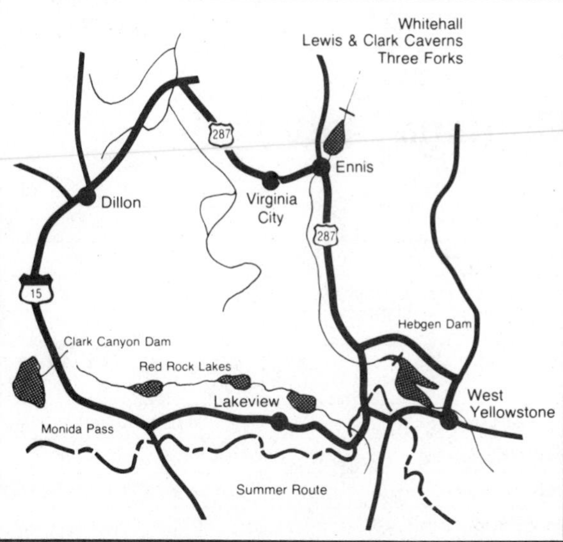

This park along the Missouri River includes one of the world's largest springs. Discovered by Lewis and Clark in 1805, the springs disgorges 388 million gallons of water every 24 hours.

Montana State Parks

Park	Location	CAMPING	PICNICKING	CONCESSIONS	SWIMMING	HIKING	BOATING	FISHING	HUNTING	WINTER SPORTS
Bannock	*Dillon. Off US-91.*	•	•							
Giant Springs	*Great Falls. Off US-87.*		•			•				
Lewis and Clark Caverns	*Three Forks. Off US-10.*	•	•			•				
Lone Pine	*Kalispell. Off US-2.*		•							
Lost Creek	*Anaconda. Off US-10A (not recommended for trailers).*	•	•			•				
Makoshika	*Glendive. Off Interstate 94.*	•	•			•				
Medicine Rocks	*Ekalaka. Off State Route 7.*	•	•							
Missouri Headwaters	*Three Forks. Off Interstate 90.*	•	•				•	•		
West Shore	*Kalispell. Off US-93.*	•	•		•	•	•	•		

Boating on Montana's Missouri River is a way to get away from it all and enjoy the quiet scenic beauty of the river.

Montana State Forests

Forest	Location	CAMPING	PICNICKING	CONCESSIONS	SWIMMING	HIKING	BOATING	FISHING	HUNTING	WINTER SPORTS
Clearwater	*Tuscor. Off US-2.*	•	•			•		•	•	
Lincoln	*Lincoln. Off State Route 200.*	•	•			•		•	•	
Stillwater	*Hamilton. Off US-93.*	•	•			•		•	•	
Sula	*Swan Lake. Off State Route 209.*	•	•			•		•	•	
Swan River	*Swan Lake. Off State Route 83.*	•	•			•		•	•	
Thompson River	*Happys Inn. Off US-2.*	•	•			•		•	•	

For more information on Montana state parks and forests, contact: *Department of Fish and Game, 1420 East Sixth Avenue, Helena, Montana 59601, (406) 449-3750.*

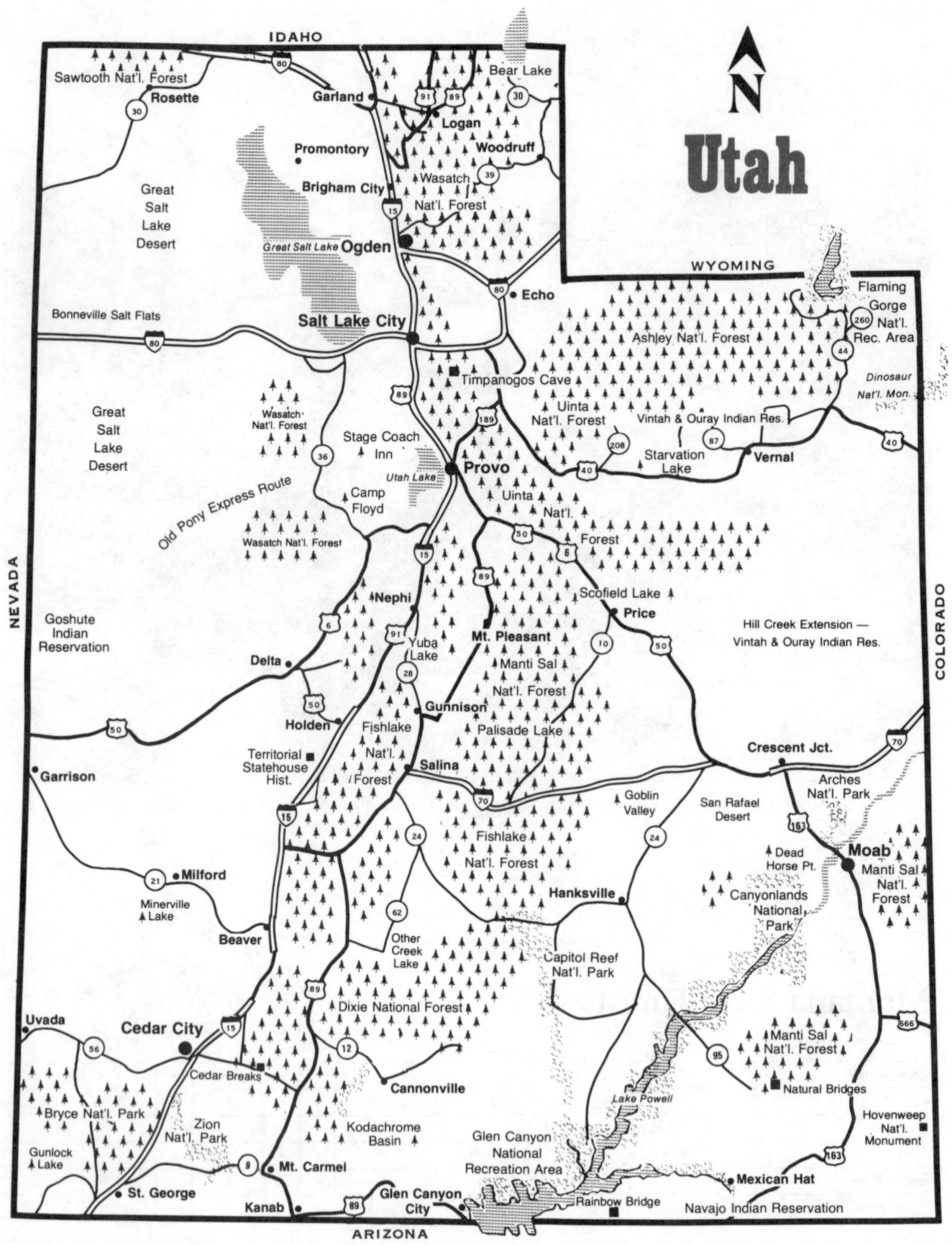
Utah
IDAHO
WYOMING
NEVADA
COLORADO
ARIZONA
Sawtooth Nat'l. Forest
Rosette
Garland
Logan
Bear Lake
Woodruff
Promontory
Brigham City
Wasatch Nat'l. Forest
Great Salt Lake Desert
Great Salt Lake
Ogden
Echo
Bonneville Salt Flats
Salt Lake City
Flaming Gorge Nat'l. Rec. Area
Ashley Nat'l. Forest
Timpanogos Cave
Dinosaur Nat'l. Mon.
Uinta Nat'l. Forest
Vintah & Ouray Indian Res.
Wasatch Nat'l. Forest
Stage Coach Inn
Starvation Lake
Vernal
Provo
Utah Lake
Old Pony Express Route
Camp Floyd
Uinta Nat'l. Forest
Wasatch Nat'l. Forest
Scofield Lake
Nephi
Price
Goshute Indian Reservation
Mt. Pleasant
Hill Creek Extension — Vintah & Ouray Indian Res.
Yuba Lake
Delta
Manti Sal Nat'l. Forest
Gunnison
Holden
Fishlake Nat'l. Forest
Palisade Lake
Territorial Statehouse Hist.
Salina
Crescent Jct.
Garrison
Goblin Valley
San Rafael Desert
Arches Nat'l. Park
Fishlake Nat'l. Forest
Dead Horse Pt.
Moab
Milford
Manti Sal Nat'l. Forest
Minerville Lake
Hanksville
Canyonlands National Park
Beaver
Other Creek Lake
Capitol Reef Nat'l. Park
Dixie National Forest
Uvada
Cedar City
Manti Sal Nat'l. Forest
Cedar Breaks
Cannonville
Natural Bridges
Lake Powell
Bryce Nat'l. Park
Zion Nat'l. Park
Kodachrome Basin
Glen Canyon National Recreation Area
Hovenweep Nat'l. Monument
Gunlock Lake
Mt. Carmel
Mexican Hat
St. George
Kanab
Glen Canyon City
Rainbow Bridge
Navajo Indian Reservation
80
30
91
89
30
39
15
80
80
260
44
89
189
208
87
40
36
40
50
6
15
89
10
6
91
50
28
50
50
70
15
70
163
24
21
24
62
89
666
15
56
12
95
9
89
163

Map not to exact scale.

Utah

Utah is a land of bustling cities and tiny hamlets, pine-studded forests and sandstone canyons, arid wasteland and verdant valleys. These startling contrasts translate into a diversity that makes Utah a state of almost endless fascination — so when you come here, plan to stay awhile. In the southeast corner of the state, nature did some of her most awesome work, creating the colorful landscape of Monument Valley and the spectacular formations of Arches National Park. A little to the north, you'll encounter the rugged canyons and recesses of Robbers Roost, the hiding place for such legendary badmen as Butch Cassidy and the Sundance Kid. In the northeast, you'll find Utah's dinosaur country and the Dinosaur National Monument, where paleontologists are still at work unearthing the bones of those prehistoric creatures. And there's much more — Salt Lake City and the Great Salt Lake, the fiery formations of Bryce Canyon, wild rivers, majestic mountains, backcountry trails . . . the offerings are truly limitless.

The early inhabitants of Utah were cave dwellers dating back about 10,000 years. Other early Indian tribes included the Anasazi, or basket makers, and, later, the Pueblos, who built cliff dwellings and granaries that still can be found partially or wholly intact in the eastern and southern parts of the state. The first white men, soldiers of Coronado, found the Ute (or Eutaw) Indians living in the region when they came in 1540, looking for the mythical Seven Cities of Gold. The first permanent settlers of the region, of course, were the Mormons who came in 1847 to escape the religious persecution they had suffered in

Full name: State of Utah
Origin of name: From the Indian tribe, Utes.
Motto: Industry
Nickname: Beehive State
Capital: Salt Lake City
Statehood: January 4, 1896, 45th state.
Population: 1,270,000 (ranks 36th).
Major Cities: Salt Lake City (169,917), Ogden (68,980), Provo (55,595).
Bird: Seagull
Flower: Sego lily
Tree: Blue spruce

Average daily temperatures by month

	Northern	Southern
Jan.	33.2 to 10.6	41.9 to 16.3
Feb.	35.5 to 10.3	46.1 to 21.0
Mar.	40.9 to 16.0	52.4 to 25.5
Apr.	52.8 to 26.1	61.0 to 32.3
May	65.3 to 34.3	71.8 to 41.0
Jun.	73.7 to 40.4	82.8 to 49.1
Jul.	83.3 to 46.6	89.7 to 57.7
Aug.	81.3 to 45.2	87.0 to 56.4
Sept.	72.3 to 36.9	79.5 to 46.7
Oct.	60.0 to 28.6	67.2 to 36.0
Nov.	44.2 to 21.1	52.4 to 25.1
Dec.	34.8 to 13.8	42.8 to 17.5
Year	56.4 to 27.5	64.6 to 35.4

Illinois. The industry of the Mormons made the desert bloom, and in 1849, they set up a provisional government and petitioned the U.S. government for admission to the Union as the State of Deseret (a book of Mormon word for honeybee, which signified their agrarian industry). The petition was denied, but Congress did act in 1850 to create the

Territory of Utah and named Brigham Young as governor.

No visit to Utah would be complete without learning something about the state's Mormon founders, and you'll find that fascinating history in Salt Lake City at Temple Square. Just a few blocks away lies the State Capitol building, and near to that is the Daughters of Utah Pioneers Museum, where you can research Utah's past and obtain more information on points of interest throughout the state.

When you're in Salt Lake City, remember that the mountains nearby offer a number of resorts with year-round activities (including a skiing season which sometimes lasts as long as five months). If you're an outdoor enthusiast, you can take a Jeep safari out of Moab into the canyon country. And if you're in Utah in the summer, stop off in Promontory for a reenactment of the ceremony that linked the transcontinental railroad in 1869. Another worthwhile trip would be to the small southeastern community of Bluff, where you can take in the Indian Days festival held each year in June.

Following its Mormon heritage, Utah still puts a good deal of emphasis on agriculture, but over the last two decades manufacturing has become increasingly vital. Leading industries now include the manufacture of food products, fabricated steel, glass products, chemicals and electrical equipment. Mining of such important minerals as oil, coal, uranium, lead, copper and zinc are also taking on increasing significance.

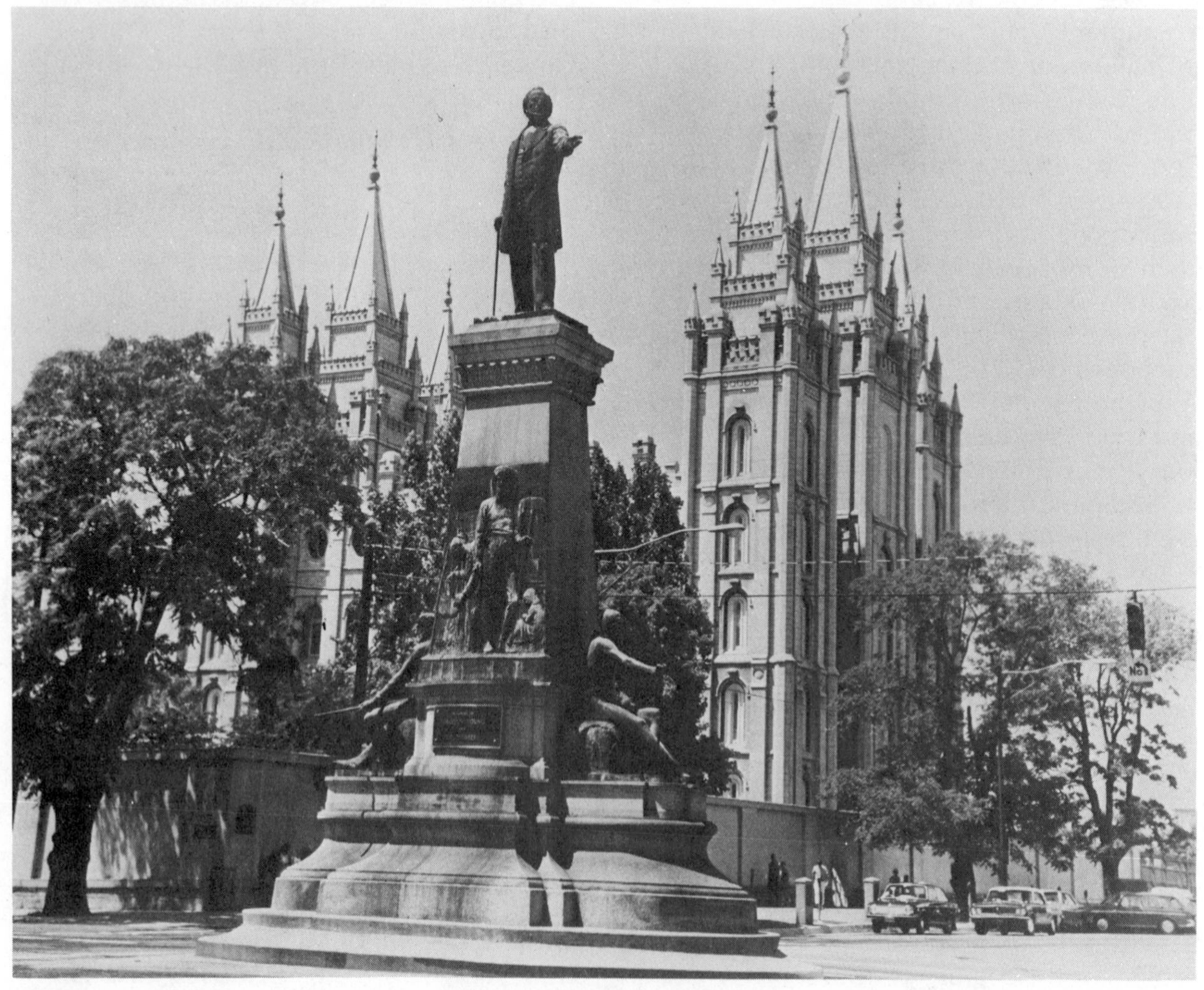

Standing near Salt Lake City's Mormon Temple is this monument honoring Brigham Young, the colonizer of Utah and the greatest of all Mormon leaders.

State Offices

Tourism
Utah Travel Council
Council Hall/Capital Hill
Salt Lake City, Utah 84114
(801) 533-5681

State Police
Department of Public Safety
Salt Lake City, Utah 84114
(801) 553-5621

Radio Stations

Salt Lake City
KRSP 1060 (AM)
KSL 1160 (AM)

Utah Points of Interest and Attractions

Bear River Migratory Bird Refuge. Nesting grounds for more than 200 different bird species and marshland wildlife; largest refuge in America. Open year-round, daily, 8 a.m. to 4 p.m. Brigham City, off Interstate 15.

Brigham Young Home. This mansion in St. George served as the winter home for Brigham Young while he directed the construction of the Mormon Temple. Open year-round. Santa Clara, off Interstate 15.

Bryce Canyon. Towering columns of orange and red sandstone arranged in thousands of magnificent formations; campgrounds. Panguitch, off US-89.

Cascade Springs. Quiet tree-lined walkways through a beautiful natural springs thick with ferns and aquatic plants. Heber City, off US-189.

Devil's Slide. Two limestone reefs, 40 feet high and 20 feet apart, plunge hundreds of feet down a sheer mountainside to the Weber River. Ogden, south, off Interstate 80N.

Great Salt Lake. America's "Dead Sea," the lake is 75 miles long and 25 miles wide — and salty enough to allow swimmers to literally float like corks. Salt Lake City, off Interstate 80 or Interstate 15.

Utah's great Salt Lake, "America's Dead Sea," is four to five times saltier than any ocean. Day use and overnight camping facilities are available on Antelope Island (above), 38 miles northwest of Salt Lake City, and on the lake's south shore, 15 miles west of city center.

Hansen Planetarium. The Space Transit Star Projector can create the sky anywhere in the Universe; star shows. Open year-round, daily, show times vary according to season. Salt Lake City, at State Street and South Temple. (801) 364-3611.

Heber Creeper. A turn-of-the-century railroad offering two trips daily through the lush Heber Valley, past Deer Creek Reservoir and down Provo Canyon to Bridal Veil Falls. Season: mid-May through September. Heber City, off US-40.

Hole In The Rock. A site used by early pioneers to cross the Colorado River; reached by gravel road from Escalante or by boat from Halls Crossing or Bullfrog Basin; guided four-wheel-drive tours in fall foliage season. Glen Canyon City, off US-89, or Hite, off State Route 95.

International Peace Gardens. Floral architecture and displays representative of the countries throughout the world. Open May through September. Salt Lake City, 1000 South 900 West.

Iron Mine and Iron Mountain. An extensive iron mining area that provides most of the iron ore for the steelworks at Geneva (north of Provo). Cedar City, off State Route 56.

Memory Grove. A carefully-groomed park in memory of Utah's war veterans; a pleasant refuge for picnicking in the heart of Salt Lake City. On State Street.

Mirror Lake. Surrounded by 12,000-foot snowcapped peaks and pine forests, this lake provides excellent fishing, camping, boating and hiking opportunities. Kamas, off State Route 150.

Scenic Drives. *Abajo Mountain Drive:* An alpine drive that is exceptionally beautiful in the fall. Between Blanding and Monticello, off US-163. *Bountiful Peak:* A 21-mile canyon loop featuring breathtaking alpine vistas and a spectacular view of the Great Salt Lake; camping, picnicking. Road open May through October. Between Bountiful and Farmington, off Interstate 15. *Clear Creek Canyon:* A beautiful canyon surrounded by rocky cliffs with a small stream running through it; cutoffs lead to historic mining sites; campground. Between Cove Fort and US-89, on old US-4. *Fisher Towers:* A scenic drive following the Colorado River to the Fisher Towers, a dazzling series of red rock spires rising 1,500 feet above the valley floor. Moab, on State Route 128. *Whiterocks Drive:* Along Whiterocks Road into beautiful Whiterocks Canyon; camping, fishing. Tridell, off State Route 121.

State Capitol. Completed in 1916, the pure Corinthian architecture of this building which overlooks Salt Lake City is very reminiscent of the U.S. Capitol. Open Memorial Day through Labor Day, Monday to Friday, 8:30 a.m. to 6 p.m.; Saturday and Sunday, 9 a.m. to 6 p.m. On State Street.

Swinging Foot Bridge. Cross the San Juan River as the Indians did; view ancient Indian ruins. Bluff, off US-163.

Temple Square. A 10-acre block that is the heart of the worldwide Mormon Church and Salt Lake City's most famous landmark. The square is completely enclosed by a 15-foot wall which surrounds the imposing granite Temple, the domed Tabernacle with its great organ, Assembly Hall, Seagull Monument, visitors center and the log remains of Salt Lake City's oldest standing home. Open year-round, daily; winter, 7 a.m. to 10 p.m.; summer, 6 a.m. to 10:30 p.m. Guided tours every half hour. Salt Lake City.

Trolley Square. Salt Lake City's shopping and entertainment center, situated within renovated 1908 trolley barns; shops, restaurants, theaters, art displays, open market. Free parking at Fifth Street South and Seventh Street East. Open year-round, day and night.

Upheaval Dome. A unique sandstone crater, 1000 feet deep. Moab, southwest off State Route 313, on gravel road.

A Suggested Tour

Zion/Cedar Breaks/ Cedar City Tour

Travelers on this tour are treated to the splendors of Zion National Park and Cedar Breaks National Monument. In addition to the striking scenery, fishing in several of the local lakes is excellent. Begin at Cedar City. Spend two days.

1. Cedar City. An ideal jumping-off point to tour the heart of Utah's Color Country. In town visit Old Main & Administration Building at Southern Utah State College.

2. Kolob Canyon. Paved road in northwest corner of Zion National Park. Striking scenery in hues of gold and red. Red canyons with deeply colored cliffs, beautifully worn by wind and water.

3. Zion National Park. Giant monoliths, massive formation. Camping, swimming, exploring. Information center.

4. **Strawberry Point.** Scenic view and camping.

5. **Navajo Lake.** Camping, fishing, picnicking.

6. **Cedar Breaks National Monument.** Brilliant wind-eroded rock formations as well as lovely forests.

7. **Brian Head Resort.** Skiing in winter and summer home area. Picnicking, camping, hiking.

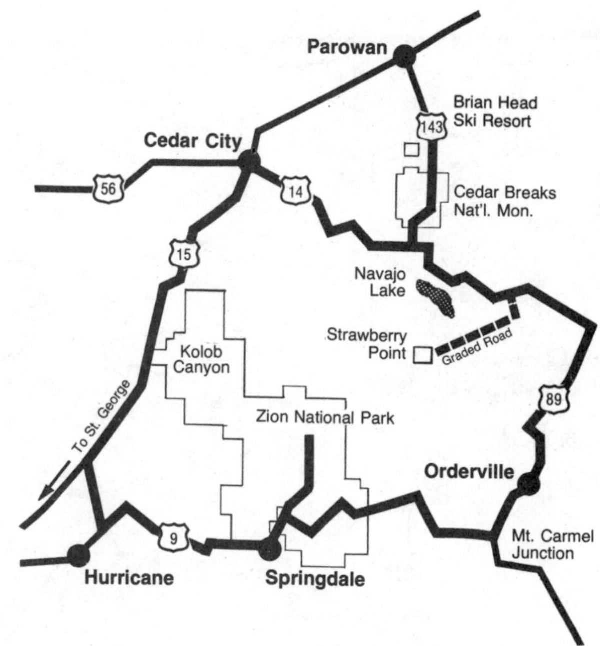

Utah State Parks

Park	Location	CAMPING	PICNICKING	CONCESSIONS	SWIMMING	HIKING	BOATING	FISHING	HUNTING	WINTER SPORTS
Dead Horse Point	*Crescent Junction. Off State Route 163.*	•	•							
Great Salt Lake (Two separate districts)	*Salt Lake City. Off Interstate 80.*	•	•		•					
Snow Canyon	*St. George. Off State Route 18.*	•	•			•				
Wasatch Mountain	*Heber City. Off US-40.*	•	•	•		•				

Utah State Forests

Forest	Location	CAMPING	PICNICKING	CONCESSIONS	SWIMMING	HIKING	BOATING	FISHING	HUNTING	WINTER SPORTS
Book Cliffs	*Green River. Off Interstate 70.*	•	•			•			•	
Flake Mountain	*Bryce. Off US-12.*	•	•			•			•	
Franklin Basin	*Logan. Off US-89.*	•	•			•			•	
Monty Cristo	*Ogden. Off State Route 39.*	•	•			•			•	
Oderville Canyon	*Glendale. Off US-89.*	•	•			•			•	
Parker Mountain	*Antimony. Off State Route 22.*	•	•			•			•	
Patmos Ridge	*East Carbon City. Off State Route 22.*	•	•			•			•	
Phil Pico	*Manila. Off State Route 43.*	•	•			•			•	
Tabby Mountain	*Fruitland. Off US-40.*	•	•			•			•	

For more information on Utah state parks and forests, contact: *State Division of Parks and Recreation, Headquarters Office Building, 1596 West North Temple, Salt Lake City, Utah 84116, (801) 533-6011.*

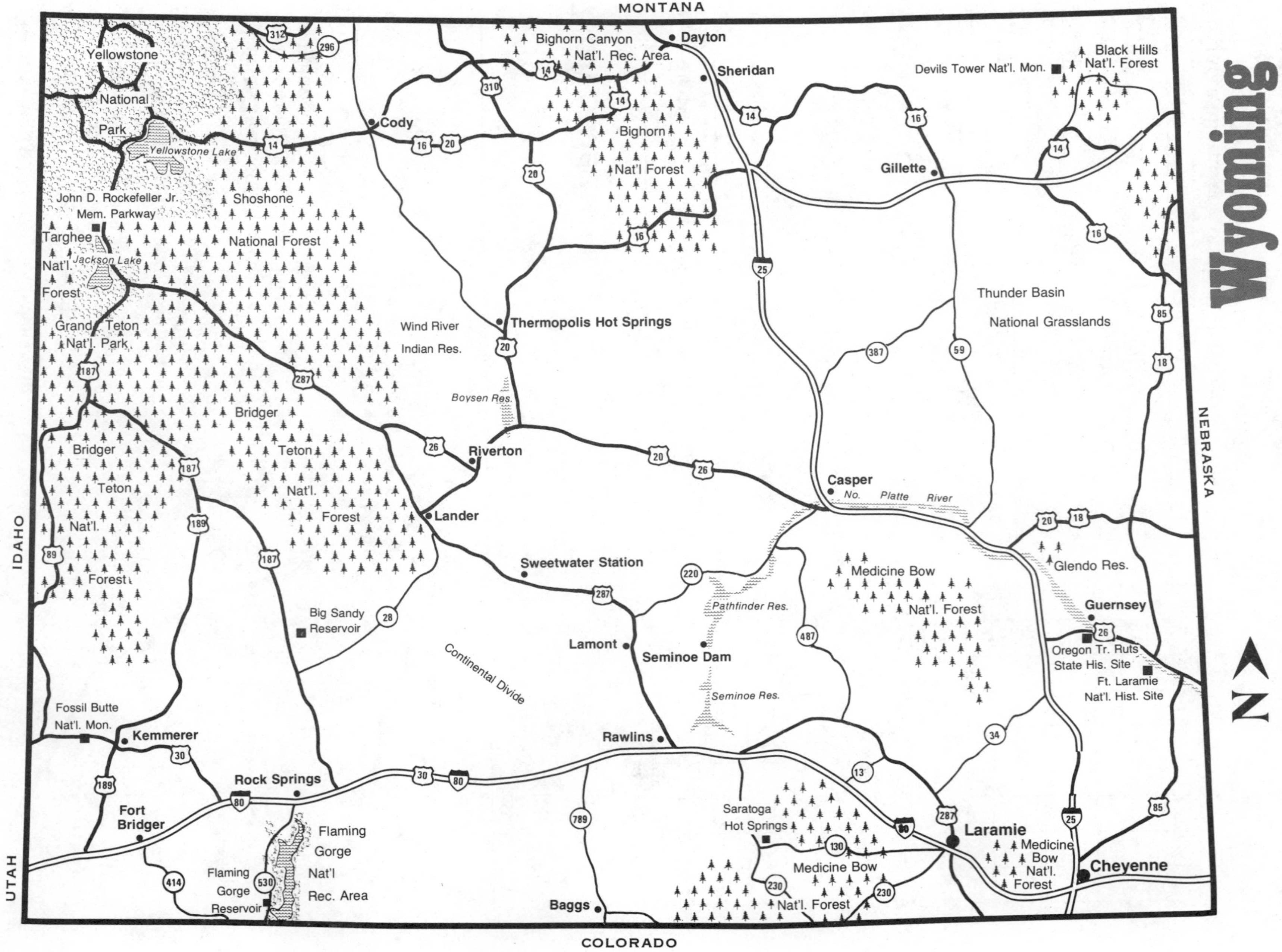

Map not to exact scale.

Wyoming

Wyoming is a state of firsts — first national park, Yellowstone; first national monument, Devils Tower; first national forest, the Shoshone; first road west, the Oregon Trail. And the list doesn't stop here, either, because Wyoming has a number of other firsts that have made it a leader in women's rights. It was the first state to grant women the right to vote, the first to elect a woman justice of the peace, the first to have a woman superintendent of schools, the first to have a woman state representative and the first to elect a woman governor. And once you've visited Wyoming, you will probably be tempted to rank it as first in scenic beauty. For Wyoming is a land of big horizons, sweeping panoramas and awesome natural splendors. Not only does it have Yellowstone, it also has the Grand Tetons, Big Horn Canyon, Flaming Gorge and the wild Snake River.

The first white man known to have entered the Wyoming region was John Colter, a fur-trapper member of the Lewis and Clark expedition. It was a number of years later, however — when pioneers began coming through the area along the Oregon Trail — before any attempts were made to establish permanent settlements. The Mormons were the first to attempt such a settlement (1853), and further immigration was spurred by the discovery of gold in South Pass in 1867. Numerous Indian tribes caused considerable trouble for settlers, raiding wagon trains and clashing repeatedly with federal troops. In the late 1860s and 1870s, all of the tribes except the Shoshone and Arapaho were relocated. The two remaining tribes were placed on the Wind River Reservation, where they remain today. Once these Indian problems were solved, the population of the state swelled dramatically, leading to Wyoming's admission to the Union on July 10, 1890.

One of Wyoming's most colorful spectacles, the Cheyenne Frontier Days held in late July, vividly recalls much of

Full name: State of Wyoming
Origin of name: Named after Wyoming Valley, Pennsylvania; Indian word meaning "Alternating Mountains and Valleys."
Motto: Equal Rights
Nickname: Equality State
Capital: Cheyenne
Statehood: July 10, 1890, 44th state.
Population: 406,000 (ranks 50th).
Major Cities: Cheyenne (46,680), Casper (41,195), Laramie (23,425).
Bird: Meadowlark
Flower: Indian paintbrush
Tree: Cottonwood

Average daily temperatures by month

	Northern	Southern
Jan.	30.2 to 5.2	32.5 to 9.3
Feb.	38.8 to 13.2	35.1 to 10.9
Mar.	47.2 to 19.9	39.3 to 15.0
Apr.	57.9 to 30.1	50.0 to 24.0
May	69.7 to 41.6	62.2 to 33.7
Jun.	79.4 to 49.7	72.6 to 41.9
Jul.	89.0 to 54.5	80.3 to 47.9
Aug.	87.0 to 51.9	78.3 to 46.2
Sept.	73.8 to 40.6	69.1 to 37.2
Oct.	62.3 to 30.2	57.8 to 27.9
Nov.	44.8 to 19.1	42.3 to 17.1
Dec.	34.0 to 9.5	34.4 to 10.7
Year	59.5 to 30.5	54.5 to 26.8

the state's Old West heritage, featuring rodeos, parades, Indian ceremonies and an abundance of tasty frontier food. If you want to get a little more involved in the Western way of life, pause for a few days at one of the fine dude ranches that are located near Jackson Hole, DuBois, Cody and Sheridan. Sportsmen will find some of the best hunting in the country within Wyoming's borders, and fishermen have more than 20,000 miles of streams and over 270,000 surface acres of lakes awaiting them.

The short, tough grass that covers much of Wyoming's terrain makes it ideal for the grazing of cattle and sheep, and the state is second only to Texas in the production of wool. Mining is now the state's number one industry, with coal and uranium being the mainstays. Today, tourism is more important than ever, and it is estimated that more than nine million people visit Wyoming annually.

State Offices

Tourism
Wyoming Travel Commission
Interstate 25 at Etchepare Circle
Cheyenne, Wyoming 82002
(307) 777-7777

State Police
Department of Public Safety
Cheyenne, Wyoming 82001
(307) 777-7301

Radio Stations

Buffalo
  KBBS 1450 (AM)
Casper
  KAWY 94.5 (FM)
Cheyenne
  KFBC 1240 (AM)
  KRAE 1480 (AM)
  KLEN 106.3 (FM)
Green River
  KUGR 1490 (AM)
Lander
  KOVE 1330 (AM)
Laramie
  KOJO 1490 (AM)
  KIOZ 102.9 (FM)
  KOWB 1290 (AM)

Wyoming Points of Interest and Attractions

Atlas Theater. Built in the 1900s, this theater has provided a variety of entertainment over the years and is now the home of the Cheyenne Little Theater Players, who provide melodramas on selected summer evenings. Cheyenne, on 16th Street between Capitol and Carey Avenues.

Ayres Natural Bridge. The cascading waters of LaPrele Creek have formed an arch 150 feet long and 50 feet high through eons of erosive action. Between Douglas and Glenrock, off Interstate 25.

Buffalo Bill Dam. The highest dam in the world at the time of its completion in 1910; the first concrete dam ever constructed. The dam backs up the waters of Shoshone River to form the nucleus of Buffalo Bill State Park. It is 328 feet high, 108 feet thick and 200 feet long at its crest. Cody, off US-20.

Castle Gardens. A formation of knobs, pinnacles and spires rising abruptly 10 to 100 feet above the prairieland. The formations contain petroglyphs, ageless artworks created in the soft sandstone. Designated a state historical monument. Riverton, 25 miles east on State Route 136.

Como Bluff Fish Hatchery. This hatchery provides trout and pike for hundreds of lakes and streams in the area; tours. Medicine Bow, 19 miles east off US-287.

F. E. Warren Air Force Base. The history of this base dates back to 1867 when it was the headquarters for cavalry troops protecting railroad workers and pioneers. The post was transferred to the air force in 1947 and was assigned to the Strategic Air Command in 1958. Guided tours during the summer, daily, at 3 p.m. Cheyenne, north off US-87.

Emigrant Springs. These springs, located on a branch of the Overland Trail, were a welcome sight to early pioneers. Opal, north at junction of US-189 and State Route 372.

Hell's Half Acre. This unusual setting of natural scenery covers approximately 320 acres and resembles the Grand Canyon of Yellowstone. Site was visited by a detachment of Captain B. L. E. Bonneville's party in July 1833, and they named it "The Burning Mountain." Casper, 44 miles west on US-20-26.

Intermittent Spring. This spring is unique for its geyser-like behavior, gushing forth a large volume of water for about 18 minutes, then entirely ceasing to flow for a like period of time. This cycle is operative for nine months of the year, from about May 15 to August 15, during the period of high water runoff. In Bridger National Forest, near Afton, off US-89.

Kendall Warm Spring. This is the only place in the world where the tiny Kendall Dace is found. Barely two inches long when fully grown, this mini-fish spends its entire life in these springs, which maintain a constant temperature of 84.4 degrees F year-round. Cora, off State Route 352.

Mormon Ferry. Along the Platte River near Fort Casper, this is the site where, in 1847, under the direction of Brigham Young, the Mormons built a ferry to enable the emigrants traveling the Oregon Trail to cross the river. The ferry operated for about 10 years until the Platte Bridge was constructed. Casper, off US-20-26.

Mother Store of J. C. Penney. One of the largest retail chains in the country was born here in 1902. J. C. Penney opened his first store, with first-day sales amounting to $466.59; the first year the store grossed $29,000. Kemmerer, on US-189.

Names Hill. This hill is sometimes called "the Calendar of the West" because it was here that most of the pioneers traveling the Sublette Cutoff of the Overland Trail carved their names or initials on the soft sandstone rock. LaBarge, five miles south on US-189, across the Green River.

Rocky Mountain Herbarium. This herbarium contains more than 300,000 plant specimens; the largest and most representative collection of Central Rocky Mountain plants anywhere. All of Wyoming's known flowering plants are represented. Open year-round. Laramie, on the third floor of the Aven Nelson Building.

Scenic Drives. *Mountain Country:* Slowly climb to, and pass among, the 12,000-foot snowcapped peaks that crown the Medicine Bow Mountain Range. The road passes numerous crystal clear mountain lakes; campgrounds, picnic areas. Between Laramie and Walcott Junction along State Route 130. *Rivers Road:* This road approaches the headwaters country of the Laramie and North Platte Rivers; it connects the town of Laramie with the resort area of Saratoga and, in between, passes through a series of picturesque mountain communities. Along State Route 230. *South Fork Drive:* An outstanding tour along the south fork of the Shoshone River. Along the route you'll find the famous TE Ranch established by Colonel Cody. Cody, southwest along State Route 291 to Valley.

Shirley Basin Uranium Fields. A deposit that is one of the largest and richest in the world; the mining operation has led to the creation of one of Wyoming's newest towns, Shirley Basin. Tours available. Medicine Bow, on State Route 487.

Highlight

Wyomingold Scenic Drives

The meaning of Wyomingold can only be realized when you begin one of Wyoming's many spectacular fall color tours. Lodging accommodations, whether hotel, motel or campground, are easily found. The weather is just right, too; moderately warm days and cool, crisp nights dominate the Wyoming highlands at this time.

Expect to see a variety of trees and foliage while on your tour. The most colorful trees are the quaking aspen, found on meadows and hillsides throughout Wyoming's mountain areas. In the autumn, the leaves turn golden or reddish-orange, contrasting beautifully with adjacent evergreens. Wyoming's state tree, the cottonwood, is somewhat taller, standing up to 60 feet. They can be found in bottomlands along major rivers at lower elevations and in valleys and along streams in the foothills of the mountains. Another handsome broadleaf is the American elm which is native only in the northeastern corner of Wyoming. The balsam poplar can be found in foothills and mountains at about 6,000 to 8,300 feet.

Two types of oak are found in Wyoming. The bur is found in northeastern Wyoming, while the smaller gambel is found along the southern border in the Sierra Madre Range.

The only native maple tree to Wyoming is the bigtooth. This western border tree is conspicuously beautiful as its leaves turn a brilliant red, producing a striking sight as it mingles among the pine, fir and aspen of the area.

The time of the fall color change in Wyoming's mountain ranges varies by both elevation and latitude. Generally speaking, however, a visitor can expect to see outstanding color displays throughout northwestern Wyoming starting in mid-September. The foothills and mountain slopes in the central and western parts of the state should exhibit their colors by the end of September while southern and eastern Wyoming will be at their best during October.

Following are a few good bets for Wyomingold viewing:

IN YELLOWSTONE try the area north from Canyon over Mt. Washburn to Tower Junction then west to Mammoth.

FOLLOW THE SNAKE RIVER Jackson Hole and Grand Teton National Park and explore along some of the major tributaries including the Buffalo Fork, the Gros Ventre and the Hoback rivers. Snake River Canyon southwest of Jackson and the region around Alta and Targhee Resort on the west slope of the Teton Range will also be rewarding.

IN THE CODY COUNTRY, drive west through Wapiti Valley toward the East Gate of Yellowstone or follow the South Fork Road into the Absaroka Range. The more adventuresome might want to take a look at Sunlight Basin to the northwest.

IN WESTERN WYOMING, try the Wind River Range east of Pinedale along the Half Moon Lake road or north along the Cora-Green River Lakes road. The Wyoming Range west of Big Piney and LaBarge also offers spectacular color displays as does the entire Star Valley north and south of Afton.

FALL COLOR IN THE BIG HORN RANGE of north-central Wyoming is a special treat for interstate highway travelers between Kaycee, Buffalo and Sheridan with side trips recommended into the Story and Dayton regions. On the west side of the Range, the riverbottoms in Bighorn Canyon National Recreation Area near Lovell as well as the foothills near Shell and Ten Sleep display brilliant colors as do the mountain meadows near the summit of the Big Horns.

CENTRAL WYOMING presents excellent viewing and photography possibilities in the South Pass and Sinks Canyon State Park areas southwest of Lander and in the Wind River Valley west of Dubois toward Togwotee Pass. Casper Mountain south of Casper comes alive with fall color and numerous access roads lead over and around the mountain.

AUTUMN COLORS IN THE LARAMIE MOUNTAINS of eastern Wyoming can be best enjoyed by traveling access roads leading south from Douglas, west from Glendo and Wheatland and along the scenic "Happy Jack" road connecting Cheyenne and Laramie.

THE SNOWY RANGE AND SIERRA MADRE MOUNTAINS in southern Wyoming feature outstanding aspen groves that can be viewed along forest highways connecting the towns of Centennial, Saratoga, Encampment and Savery. Interstate highway travelers will want to explore the north end of the Snowys near Arlington and Elk Mountain.

THE BLACK HILLS in northeastern Wyoming mix a full range of autumn colors into a kaleidoscopic display extending from Newcastle on the south through Sundance to Hulett and Aladdin on the north. A particular treat is offered in the vicinity of Devil's Tower National Monument.

Wyoming State Parks

Park	Location	CAMPING	PICNICKING	CONCESSIONS	SWIMMING	HIKING	BOATING	FISHING	HUNTING	WINTER SPORTS
Boysen	*Shoshoni. Off US-20.*	•	•	•	•	•	•	•		
Buffalo Bill	*Cody. Off US-16.*	•	•					•		
Curt Gowdy	*Cheyenne-Laramie. On Interstate 80.*	•	•			•				
Glendo	*Glendo. Off State Route 319.*	•	•	•	•	•	•	•		
Guernsey	*Guernsey. Off US-26.*	•	•		•		•	•		
Hot Springs	*Thermopolis. Off State Route 120.*	•	•		•	•				
Keyhold	*Sundance. On Interstate 90.*	•	•		•	•	•	•	•	
Seminole	*Sinclair. Off State Route 71.*	•	•			•		•		
Sinks Canyon	*Lander. Off State Route 131.*	•	•		•	•	•	•		

Wyoming has no state forests. For more information on Wyoming state parks, contact: *Wyoming Recreation Commission, Cheyenne, Wyoming 82002, (307) 777-7695.*

Rocky Mountain States Calendar of Events

Spring
(March, April, May)

Colorado

Annual Art Festival Exhibition. May, Canon City.

Annual Music and Blossom Festival. May, Canon City.

Cinco de Mayo Celebration. May, Fort Collins.

Parade of Homes. May, Grand Junction.

Mayfest Activities. May, Estes Park.

Idaho

Boise Sports and RV Show. March, Boise.

Spring Roundup, Busterback Ranch. March, Stanley.

Atom Buster Breakfast. April, Arco.

Kamloops and Kokanee Week. Fishing derby, awards, dance. May, Sandpoint.

Apple Blossom Festival and Boomerang Days. Parade, barbecue and carnival. May, Payette.

Annual Fisherman's Free Breakfast. May. St. Anthony.

Annual Blossom Festival. May, Lewiston.

Locust Blossom Festival. May, Kendrick.

Montana

Bucking Horse Show and Sale. May, Miles City.

Utah

Annual Jewelry and Small Sculpture Exhibition, Weber State College. March, Ogden.

Annual Coca-Cola/Park City Snow Sculpture Contest. March, Park City.

Utah Boat Sports and Travel Show. March, Salt Lake City.

Utah Round Dance Association Round Dance Festival. March, Salt Lake City.

Semi-Annual General Conference of the Church of Jesus Christ Of Latter-Day Saints, Temple Square. March, Salt Lake City.

Golden Spike Gem and Mineral Show. March, Ogden.

Annual Park City Clown Days. April, Park City.

Annual Jeep Safari. Guided four-wheel-drive trips for families on rugged trails into the backcountry. April, Moab.

Tri-Valley Square Dance Spring Dance. April, Salt Lake City.

Annual Concert Salt Lake Symphonic Choir, Capital Theater, Salt Lake City.

Annual May 10th Celebration, Golden Spike National Historic Site. May, Promontory.

Statewide Square Dance Spring Festival. May, Salt Lake City.

Wyoming

May Fair, Laramie County Community College. May, Cheyenne.

Platte River Valley Art Show. May, Saratoga.

Mrs. Olson's Swedish Dinner and Firemen's Ball. May, Dubois.

Ethnic Cultural Festival. May, Rock Springs.

Anniversary Square Dance. May, Laramie.

Mother's Day Fun Races. May, Riverton.

Scenic Float Trips Begin, Snake River.

Annual Car Show. May, Casper.

Wyoming Fiddlers Jam Session. May, Powell.

Annual Cowtown Hoedown. May, Sheridan.

Annual Frank Hornecker Memorial Roping. May, Lander.

Alpine Art and Craft Family Faire. May, Alpine.

Annual Old-Time Fiddlers Contest. May, Shoshoni.

Summer
(June, July, August)

Colorado

Aspen Arts Festival. June, Aspen.

Annual Strawberry Days. June, Glenwood Springs.

International White Water Boat Races. June, Salida.

Art in the Park. June, Salida.

Bluegrass-Country Festival. June, Telluride.

Aspen Music Festival. June, Aspen.

Cherry Days Festival and Parade. July, Delta.

Annual Cowboys Roundup Rodeo. July, Steamboat Springs.

Fireworks Display, Skyline Drive. July, Canon City.

Annual Buffalo Chip Throwing Contest. July, Salida.

Annual Roping Club Rodeo. July, Sugar City.

Elkhorn — Montana's persistent ghost town — fascinates tourists while it slumbers in the sun dreaming of glories past and — possibly — glories still to come.

Woodland Old-Fashioned Fourth. July, Woodland Park.
Buffalo Barbecue and Pancake Breakfast. July, Buena Vista.
Royal Gorge Rodeo. July, Canon City.
Annual Summer Arts Festival. July, Steamboat Springs.
Annual Pioneer Banquet. July, Gunnison.
Annual Horse Show, Rodeo Grounds. July, Gunnison.
Old-Time Fiddlers Contest. July, Pagosa Springs.
Annual Antique Show and Sale. July, Gunnison.
Annual Art in Legion Park Show. July, Gunnison.
Annual Kendall Mountain Summer Run. July, Silverton.
Harvest Festival. Barbecue, dance, demolition derby. August, Limon.
Larimer County Fair. August, Loveland.
Pageant Parade of the Rockies. August, Colorado Springs.
Annual Mountain Melodarama. August, Telluride.
Lincoln County Free Fair and Rodeo. August, Hugo.
Burro Race, Stagecoach Ride and Bed Race. August, Buena Vista.
Garden and Flower Show. August, Grand Junction.
Carnation Festival. August, Wheat Ridge.
Jazz Festival. August, Central City.
Annual Basalt Fair. August, Basalt.

Idaho

Gyro Lead Creek Derby Days. June, Wallace.
International Fasching Festival. June, Ketchum.
Smelterville Days. June, Smelterville.
National Old-Time Fiddlers Contest and Festival. June, Weiser.
Cherry Blossom Festival and Square Butte Rockhound Show. June, Emmett.
Jamboree. Chuckwagon feed, specialty acts, dancing. June, Rupert.
All-Girl Rodeo. July, Driggs.
Fourth of July Celebration. July, Caldwell.
Frontier Days. July, Nordman.
Border Days. July, Grangeville.
Salmon River Days. Parade, motorcycle races, demolition derby, free breakfast, fireworks. July, Salmon.
Sagebrush Days. Barbecue, parade, fireworks, dancing. July, Buhl.
Annual Pancake Breakfast. July, Stanley.
Winchester Days. July, Winchester.
Whooper Days. July, Rexburg.
Whaa-La Days. War dances and Indian games. July, Worley.
Kootenai River Days. July, Bonners Ferry.
Priest River Loggers Celebration. July, Priest River.
Old-Timers Celebration. July, Harrison.
Kooskia Days. Parade, street sports, raft races, rock and artifacts show. July, Kooskia.
Sun Dances. Religious Indian observance and buffalo feast. July, Fort Hall.
Idaho State Square Dance and Round Dance Festival. July, Moscow.
Indian Days and Plummer Festival. July, Plummer.
Friendship Festival. August, Deary.
Barbecue Day. August, Hayden Lake.
Pierre's Hole Rendezvous. August, Driggs.
Pi-Nee Waus Days. August, Lapwai.
Country-Western Jamboree. August, Burley.
Yearly Pilgrimage to Old Cataldo Mission. August, Cataldo.
Mud Springs Camp. Indian games, feast. August, Winchester.
Western Idaho State Fair. August, Boise.

Montana

North American Indian Days. Blackfoot pageant, dances, parade. July, Browning.
Custer's Last Stand. Reenactment of the Battle of the Little Big Horn. July, Crow Indian Reservation.
Last Chance Stampede. July and August, Helena.
State Fair and Rodeo. July and August, Great Falls.

Utah

Children's Festival. June, Salt Lake City.
Annual Quilt and Fiber Show. June, Springville.

Utah Pageant of the Arts. June, American Fork.

Strawberry Days. June, Pleasant Grove.

Annual Golden Spike National Old-Time Fiddlers Contest and Bluegrass Festival. June, Ogden.

Logan City Fireworks Display. July, Logan City.

Independence Day Celebration. July, Delta.

Cherry Days. July, North Ogden.

Murray Fun Day. Parade, flag-raising ceremony, breakfast, concessions. July, Murray.

"Mormon Miracle" Pageant. July, Manti.

Utah Shakespearean Festival. July, Cedar City.

Pioneer Days Celebration. July, Ogden.

Annual Bridgerland Bluegrass Festival. July, Logan.

Deseret News Marathon. A 25-mile footrace over historic pioneer trail. July, Salt Lake City.

Annual Festival of the American West. July, Logan.

Wasatch County Fair. August, Heber City.

Utah Industrial Convention. Parades, art show, flower show, talent show, races, ball games, speakers, fashion shows, contests. August, Roosevelt.

Annual Highland Fling. August, Highland.

Railroaders Folk Festival. August, Promontory.

Homecoming Day. August, Oak City.

Midway Swiss Days. August, Midway.

Alpine Days. August, Alpine.

Wyoming

Dairy Days. June, Afton.

White Water Float Trips Begin, Snake River. June, Jackson.

Spring Fling, Jackson Lake Lodge. June, Grand Teton National Park.

Annual Craftsmen Exhibit. June, Cheyenne.

All-Girl Rodeo. June, Douglas.

Mountain Dewers Square Dance. June, Encampment.

Roundup Days. June, Pinedale.

The Obon Festival is celebrated every year in Salt Lake City, Utah.

Woodchoppers Jamboree. Timber carnival. June, Encampment.

Mustang Days. June, Lovell.

Wild Wild West Flaming Gorge Days. June, Green River.

Cowboy Days. June, Gillette.

Annual Mini-Marathon. An 8.5-mile footrace. June, Powell.

Fish Derby. June, Pinedale.

Wyoming State Trap Shoot. June, Laramie.

Annual Steer Roping and Fun Days. June, Dixon.

Newcastle Night Rodeo. July, Newcastle.

Lander Pioneer Days. July, Lander.

Cody Stampede. July, Cody.

Annual Big Horn Festival of the Arts. July, Greybull.

Old-Timers Reunion, Rodeo and Barbecue. July, Guernsey.

Chuckwagon Days. July, Big Piney.

Independence Day Parade. July, Afton.

Red, White and Blue Parade and Fireworks. July, Saratoga.

Green River Rendezvous. July, Pinedale.

Medicine Bow Days. July, Medicine Bow.

Laramie Jubilee Days. July, Laramie.

Fair in the Square. July, Jackson.

Annual Fish Tagging Party, Boysen Reservoir. July, Shoshoni.

Annual Winchester Gun Show. July, Cody.

Wyoming Fiddlers Jam Session. July, Byron.

Grand Teton Music Festival. July, Teton Village.
Annual $10,000 Boysen Pike Derby, Boysen Lake. July, Shoshoni.
Cheyenne Frontier Days. Rodeos, parade, live entertainment; Wyoming's biggest annual celebration. July, Cheyenne.
Shoshone Tribal Sun Dance. July, Fort Washakie.
All-American Indian Days. July, Sheridan.
Wind River Valley Artists Guild National Art Show. July, Dubois.
Cody Western and Wildlife Art Classic. July, Cody.
Central Wyoming Fair and Rodeo. July, Casper.
Teenage Jackpot Rodeo and Trail Days. August, Pine Bluffs.
King Coal Day. August, Hanna.
Arapahoe Tribal Powwow. August, Arapahoe.
Gift of the Waters Pageant, Hot Springs State Park. August, Thermopolis.
Moonlight Tour. August, Fort Laramie.
Annual Firemen's Buffalo Barbecue. August, Dubois.
Bean Festival. August, Basin.
Wyoming State Fair. August, Douglas.
Sheridan Art Festival. August, Sheridan.
Wyoming Governor's Cup and Down River Race, Snake River. August, Jackson.

Fall
(September, October, November)

Colorado
Horse Show Fun Day. September, Estes Park.
Buffalo Barbecue, Soda Springs Park. September, Manitou Springs.
Arvada Harvest Festival and Parade. September, Arvada.
Octoberfest at Briarhurst. September, Manitou Springs.
Annual Culinary Arts Fair. September, Ouray.
Alferd Packer Fall Banquet. September, Lake City.
Fall Color Week. September, Ouray.
Aspenfest. September, Estes Park.
Golden Octoberfest. September, Golden.
Octoberfest at Larimer Square. September, Denver.
Penrose Apple Day. September, Penrose.
Annual Pioneer Day Celebration. September, Norwood.
Annual Ruggerfest. September, Aspen.
Coloride Weekend Fall Tours. September, Telluride.
Potato Day. Carnival, barbecue, games. October, Carbondale.
Korean National Folk Festival. October, Fort Collins.
Rockhounders Rendezvous Mineral Show. October, Silverton.
Hunters Ball. October, Lake City.

Idaho
Labor Day Festival. September, Bellevue.
Eastern Idaho State Fair. September, Blackfoot.
Payette River Cattlemen's Annual Barbecue. September, Garden Valley.
Paul Bunyan Days. September, St. Maries.
Old-Timers Picnic. September, Spirit Lake.
Wagon Days. September, Ketchum.
Air Force Appreciation Day. September, Mountain Home.
Annual Barbecue. September, Mackay.
Idaho Annual Spud Day. Parade, free baked potato, fishing derby, Little League football, bands. October, Fort Hall.
Fiddlers Jamboree. October, Riggins.
Lemhi County Fair. October, Salmon.
Thanksgiving Day Celebration. November, Lapwai.
Saint Andrews Annual Dinner. November, Twin Falls.
Christmas City Opening. Bands, parade, Santa comes to town. November, Weiser.
Christmas Parade. November, Boise.

Montana
No major fall events.

Utah
Iron County Fair. September, Parowan.

Annual Peach Days Art Festival. September, Brigham City.

Utah State Fair. September, Salt Lake City.

Wasatch Gem and Mineral Show, Murray Armory. September, Salt Lake City.

Annual Melon Days. September, Green River.

Bonneville Nationals Speed Trials for Cars and Motorcycles. September, Bonneville Salt Flats.

Annual Show of Gems and Minerals, National Guard Armory. September, Tooele.

Annual Convention for the National Society of the Daughters of Utah Pioneers. October, Salt Lake City.

Semi-Annual Conference of the Church of Jesus Christ of Latter-Day Saints, Temple Square. October, Salt Lake City.

Annual Art Auction. October, Ogden.

Annual Oktoberfest. October, Snowbird.

Squararama, Ogden Area Square Dance Association's Annual Square Dance Festival. November, Ogden.

Fall Festival of the Arts and Photo Contest. November, St. George.

Tri-Valley Square Dance Fall Dance. November, Salt Lake City.

Christmas Parade. November, Salt Lake City.

Wyoming

No major fall events.

Winter
(December, January, February)

Colorado

Annual Christmas Walk in Larimer Square. December, Denver.

Outdoor Christmas Market. December, Georgetown.

Civic Center Christmas Display. December, Denver.

Annual New Year's Eve Fireworks Display. January, Pikes Peak.

National Western Rodeo. January, Denver.

Idaho

Christmas Gift Show. December, Boise.

Annual Basque Sheepherders Ball. December, Boise.

Festival of the Trees. December, Idaho Falls.

Christmas Tree Lane. December, Rexburg.

Christmas Eve at Sun Valley. December, Sun Valley.

Mighty-Mite Race. Children's ski race. January, Kellogg.

Winter Carnival. January, Priest Lake.

Schweitzer Winter Ski Carnival. January, Schweitzer.

Silver Valley Winter Festival. January, Kellogg.

Busterback Stampede. Cross-country ski race. January, Busterback Ranch.

Kanganark Mushers Preston Sled Dog Race. February, Preston.

Winter Carnival. February, McCall.

Sno-Mobile Club Oval Race. February, Lava Hot Springs.

Gem Show, Western Idaho Fairgrounds. February, Boise.

Montana

No major winter events.

Utah

Annual Youth Songfest. December, Salt Lake City.

Christmas Eve Torchlight Parade. December, Alta.

Community Christmas Celebration. December, Park City.

New Year's Eve Torchlight Parade. December, Alta.

Festival of Trees, Salt Palace. December, Salt Lake City.

Annual Winter Carnival. January, Park City.

Winterskol. January, Snowbird.

Scottish Tartan Ball. January, Salt Lake City.

Annual Statewide College Art Students Traveling Exhibition, Brathwaite Fine Arts Gallery. February, Cedar City.

Wyoming

No major winter events.

ARIZONA
"White Dove of the Desert"
Sedona
Kachina Dolls
Taos Pueblo
NEW MEXICO
Carlsbad Caverns

Grand Canyon Country
Desert View Watch Tower
"Old Tucson" Stage
Oral Roberts University Tower Tulsa
OKLAHOMA
Will Rogers Museum – Claremore
Oklahoma City State Capitol
TEXAS
Big Bend National Park
The Alamo San Antonio
State Capitol Austin

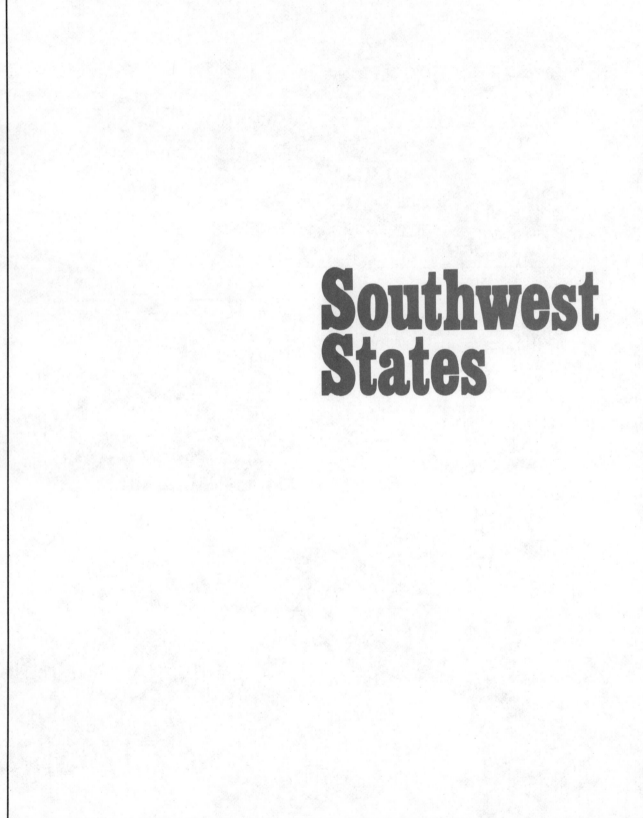

Southwest States

The Southwest is a sparsely populated (only 15 people per square mile) region of varied landscapes — prairies, plains, mountains and deserts — offering a variety of recreation opportunities.

In Texas alone, which sprawls 750 miles in length and breadth, you'll find the scenic, cool highlands of the Rockies and Guadalupe Mountains, the oil well-dotted plains and Gulf Coast and the stark deserts of the central lowlands. Two of Texas' most interesting regions are the Big Bend wilderness in the west along the Rio Grande, and the Big Thicket area along the eastern border. The rugged Big Bend country has an awesome, austere beauty featuring spectacular sunrises and sunsets and temperatures that can vary as much as 50 degrees in a single day. Despite these extremes, the Big Bend is home to an amazing variety of wildlife and is a birdwatcher's paradise. In sharp contrast, the Big Thicket is a timber-rich region of scattered black swamps and black-water sloughs that were once the home of bears, panthers and wolves, and the refuge of desperadoes and moonshiners. Today, the bears and panthers have gone the way of the desperadoes, but there's still an abundance of wildlife and a host of friendly natives who will be happy to regale you with wondrous tales of the old days.

In Arizona, New Mexico and Oklahoma, the traveler will find much the same varied landscape and many sites of equal interest. Of course, nothing can match the splendor of Arizona's Grand Canyon, but no visit to that state would be complete without a drive through a few of the other scenic areas, like Sedona and Oak Creek Canyon, Saguaro National Monument and the Coronado Trail, or the rapidly growing urban centers of Phoenix and Tucson. In New Mexico, you'll find similar scenic wonders, in addition to dozens of Indian Pueblos where you can watch silver artisans and other craftsmen at work. Oklahoma also has its Indian craftsmen, as well as bustling cities, oil wells, legends of the Old West and scenic wonders like Turner Falls, Ouachita Mountains and the rugged Wichita Mountains National Wildlife Refuge.

With such a rich variety, the states of the Southwest have something to offer everybody.

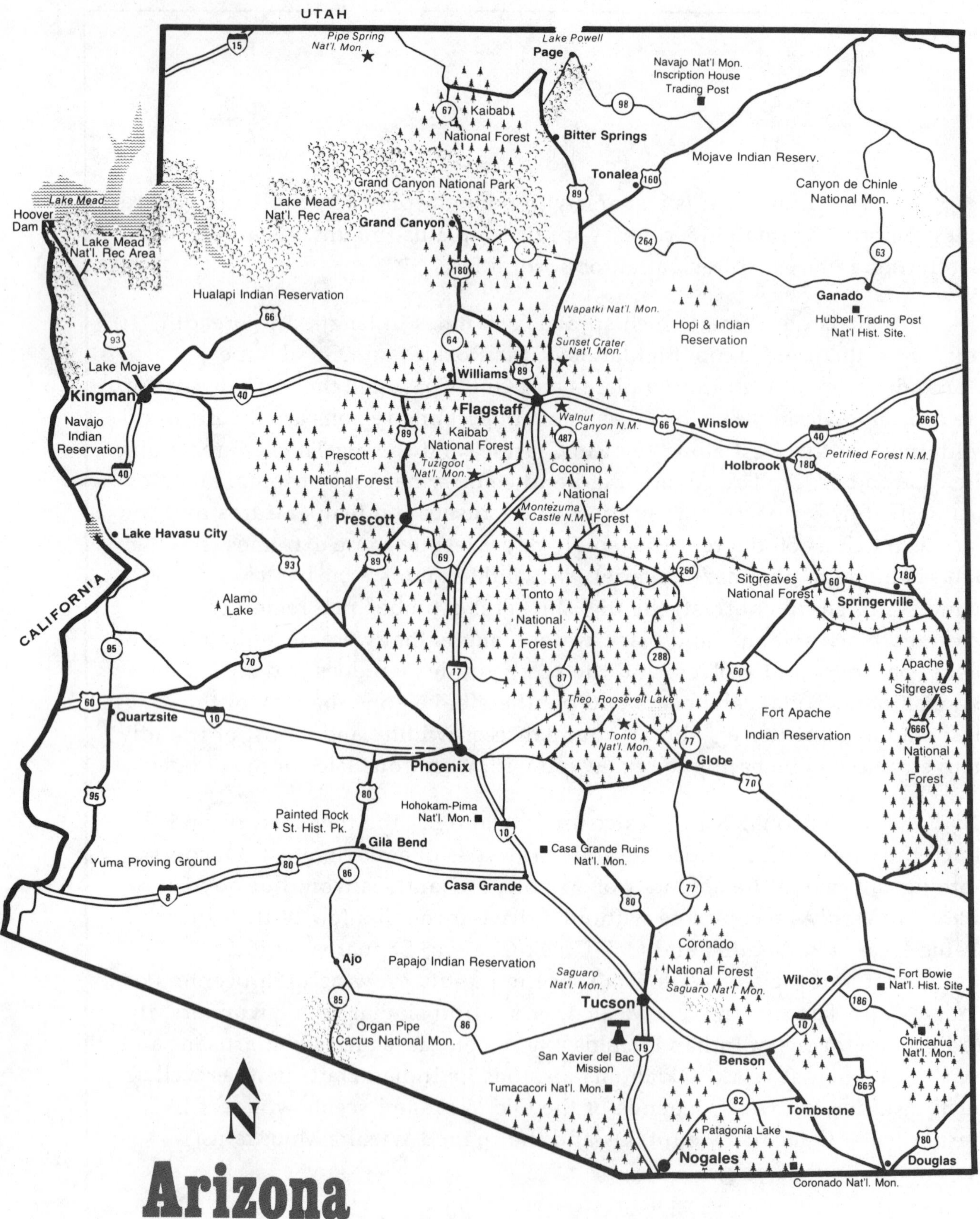

Map not to exact scale.

Arizona

Arizona is made up of three distinct regions: the Sonoran Desert of the southwest, the central highlands and the high country of the northwest Colorado Plateau. The varied climate offered by these regions makes Arizona an ideal year-round vacation spot. In summer, the high country is the most pleasant, with daytime temperatures rarely hitting 90 and nighttime temperatures falling into the 50s. In winter, the warmth of the southern regions provides a perfect escape for those who live in colder climates, and the state's popularity as a winter retreat has earned it the nickname "Florida of the West." The state's most famous attraction is, of course, the Grand Canyon, but other scenic areas like Oak Creek Canyon, colorful Indian pageants, excellent dude ranches and superb skiing are just a few of the things that await the visitor to Arizona.

Mummies and other ancient relics found in Arizona have led archeologists to conclude that several Indian cultures may have lived in the region as long ago as 25,000 to 10,000 B.C. Some of the oldest human habitations in the United States can be found in Arizona, such as the Hopi Indian community of Oraibi, which was built more than 1,000 years ago. Historians are not certain who the first white visitors were; padres Juan de la Asuncion and Pedro Nazal are said to have reached the region in 1538, and it is certain that Coronado crossed the territory in 1540 in his search for the Seven Cities of Gold. For about 200 years, beginning in 1629, the Jesuits and Franciscans worked as missionaries among the Indians of the area, establishing a number of missions. From 1821 to 1856, the Mexicans controlled the region and established two tenuous settlements in the Santa Cruz Valley, Tucson and Tubac. Following the Mexican War, the United States gained a part of Arizona, but the Treaty of Guadalupe Hidalgo left nearly all of the area south of the Gila Valley as part of the Mexican state of Sonora. Later, under the terms of the Gadsden Purchase (1853), the remainder of

Full Name: State of Arizona
Origin of name: From the Indian, Alek-zon, meaning "Small Spring."
Motto: *Ditat Deus* (God Enriches).
Nickname: Grand Canyon State
Capital: Phoenix
Statehood: February 14, 1912, 48th state.
Population: 2,296,000 (ranks 32nd).
Major Cities: Phoenix (664,721), Tucson (296,457), Mesa (99,043).
Bird: Cactus wren
Flower: Saguaro cactus
Tree: Paloverde

Average daily temperatures by month

	Northern	Southern
Jan.	39.5 to 20.6	67.7 to 33.4
Feb.	42.7 to 22.6	72.0 to 36.2
Mar.	48.6 to 26.3	77.2 to 40.0
Apr.	59.1 to 32.9	86.0 to 45.7
May	70.5 to 42.2	95.5 to 54.0
Jun.	81.2 to 52.1	104.5 to 63.4
Jul.	86.9 to 58.5	107.3 to 74.5
Aug.	83.4 to 56.5	104.0 to 72.9
Sept.	76.2 to 50.2	100.9 to 64.7
Oct.	63.8 to 40.2	90.3 to 52.2
Nov.	48.6 to 28.7	76.6 to 40.8
Dec.	39.6 to 21.4	67.9 to 34.2
Year	61.7 to 37.7	87.5 to 51.0

the present state was acquired from Mexico. The federal Territory of Arizona was established by Congress on February 24, 1863, and nearly 50 years later, on February 14, 1912, Arizona was admitted to the Union as the 48th state.

Naturally, if you're traveling to Arizona, you'll want to visit the Grand Canyon. From the rim, you will gaze down nearly a mile to the boiling Colorado River as it continues its carving of the canyon, carrying away 80,000 tons of silt a day — and from the rim, it's only a short drive to Hoover Dam and the fishing and boating fun of the Lake Mead Recreation Area. If you're traveling southeast from the canyon, stop off at the state's most mysterious wonder, Meteor Crater, the 60-story-deep crater blasted by a meteor which fell to earth some 20,000 years ago. In Flagstaff, you can enjoy cool July weather while you take in the All-Indian Powwow that features a rodeo, colorful ceremonial dances and a crafts bazaar.

Tourism plays a key role in Arizona's economy, but as a result of a number of recent defense contracts the state's leading industry is manufacturing, with items like electronic equipment, aircraft engines and machinery heading the list. Arizona's mining industry also produces a number of metals, including molybdenum and the majority of the nation's copper.

State Offices

Tourism
Arizona Department of Economic Planning and Development
1645 West Jefferson Street
Phoenix, Arizona 85007
(602) 255-3618

State Police
Department of Public Safety
PO Box 6638
Phoenix, Arizona 85005
(602) 262-8011

Radio Stations

Phoenix
KBBC 98.7 (FM)
KNIX 1580 (AM)
Tucson
KWFM 92.9 (FM)
KTKT 990 (AM)

Arizona Points of Interest and Attractions

Cave Creek Canyon. This scenic canyon features rugged, towering cliffs of red rhyolite; campgrounds, hiking trails. Portal, off US-80.

Colossal Cave. One of the nation's scenic wonders; spectacular underground formations. Open year-round. Tucson, off Interstate 19.

Davis Dam. Built to harness the lower Colorado River, this dam is 67 river-miles below Hoover Dam and 32 miles west of Kingman. Its reservoir, Lake Mohave, has a capacity of 1,890,000-acre-feet; campgrounds, boating, fishing. Bullhead City, off State Routes 68, 95 and 163.

Desert Botanical Garden. A 150-acre garden devoted exclusively to desert plants. The height of the blooming season is late March through May, and an annual cactus show is held each March. Open year-round, daily, 9 a.m. to sunset. Adults $1.50, children 5 to 12, 50 cents. Phoenix, 1201 North Galvin Parkway.

Glen Canyon Dam. Located on the Colorado River at the lower margin of the Upper Colorado Basin, this 700-foot-high dam stores the erratic flows and assures a steady release of water to the Lower Colorado River Basin. Page, off US-89.

Grace H. Flandrau Planetarium. A University of Arizona facility that includes science halls and exhibits on astronomy and space exploration. A 16-inch telescope is available for night viewing in the public observatory. Open year-round, Tuesday to Sunday, 7 p.m. to 10 p.m. Free. Tucson, University Boulevard at Cherry Avenue.

Grand Canyon Caverns. A 21-story elevator descent takes you to these caverns which display colorful rock formations in a temperature that remains at 56 degrees F throughout the year. Open year-round, daily, 8 a.m. to 5 p.m. Adults $5.50, children 6 to 14, $3.50. Nelson, on US-66.

Hoover Dam. The largest of all federal reclamation projects, and one of the greatest feats of mankind, this dam is 727 feet high, 115 miles long, covers 227 square miles and has a storage capacity of 30,500,000 acre-feet. Kingman, 72 miles north to Boulder City, off US-93.

Inspiration Consolidated Copper Company. A mining operation that offers tours of the open pit area, smelter, leaching plant and electrolyte process. Visitors must use their own vehicles for touring, but motorhomes are not permitted. Open year-round, Monday to Friday. Free. Miami, on US-60.

Kaibab Trail. A steep, 6½-mile trail to the Colorado River Suspension Bridge; recommended for rugged hikers only. An alternative trail leads from the head of the Kaibab Trail to Cedar Ridge and a Fossil Fern Exhibit (1½ miles). Be sure to carry plenty of water as none is available on any of the trails. Grand Canyon Village, 3½ miles east, near Yaki Point.

London Bridge. The famed London Bridge that was transplanted to the desert shores of Arizona. Lake Havasu City, off State Route 95.

Lowell Observatory. One of the leading observatories in the United States; the planet Pluto was discovered from here in 1930. Lecture and slide show each Friday evening in the summer. Open year-round, Monday to Friday. Free. Flagstaff, one mile west via Santa Fe Avenue.

Mormon Flat Dam. A part of the Salt River Irrigation Project, this dam forms Canyon Lake. Tortilla Flat, on State Route 88.

Navajo Bridge. Seven miles below historic Lee's Ferry, this bridge is 467 feet above the water level of the Colorado River with a span of 616 feet in length. Marble Canyon, off US-89A.

Visitors at Arizona's Old Tucson fun park and motion picture studio often have a chance to watch an actual movie or television filming. Shown in the foreground here, they watch actor Cameron Mitchell at work.

Old Tucson. A reconstructed village showing Tucson as it was in the middle 1800s. More than 60 motion pictures have been filmed here. Tucson, 13 miles southwest, off Interstate 10.

Painted Desert. Nature has painted the landscape here in a variety of brilliant hues. May be viewed from US-66, US-89 and US-160 (east of Flagstaff).

Salt River Canyon. A spectacular Gorge with scenic approaches and lookout points. Globe, north on US-60.

Scenic Drives. *Apache Trail:* This famous trail winds through gorgeous mountain scenery to Globe. Highlights include the dams and lakes on the Salt River. Begin at Apache Junction, 34 miles east of Phoenix, off State Route 88. *Pinal Pioneer Parkway:* A 30-mile billboard-free passage north on US-80-89 from Oracle Junction through one of the state's most attractive Sonoran Desert areas; rest areas, signs identify major plants. *Schulz Pass Road:* A scenic dirt-road drive through Schulz Pass between San Francisco Peaks and Elden Mountains; north off US-180 and northeast of US-89, north of Flagstaff. Check locally for road conditions.

A Suggested Tour

Sedona and Oak Creek Canyon

This arts and crafts vacation center sits amid some of the most dramatically colored, beautiful scenery in the country. US-89A curls for some 12 miles through the gorge, part of a natural recreation area. Sedona has long been favored as a Hollywood and TV movie background. In and just out of town, see the Arts Center; the Mexican village replica of craft shops, galleries and restaurants called Tlaquepaque; modernistic Chapel of the Holy Cross; Shrine of the Red Rocks; the scenic drive up Schnebly Hill; former movie sets; and spectacular backcountry jeep tours. For information, contact: Sedona-Oak Creek Chamber of Commerce, PO Box 478, Sedona, Arizona 86336. (602) 282-7722.

Tour 1. Jerome, Douglas Mine State Park and Tuzigoot National Monument. Drive west on Highway 89A through Cottonwood. Two miles before you reach Clarkdale is the ancient Tuzigoot National Monument, a pre-Columbian ruin dating about 1300 A.D. Continue on west to Jerome, the largest and liveliest ghost town in America. This billion-dollar copper camp once reached a 15,000 population before the mines were shut down. Jerome is picturesquely located on a steep mountainside at an elevation of about 7,200 feet. There are good restaurants for lunch. The famous Douglas Mine State Park Museum is a treasure-house of archaeological, mining and historical lore of this area. Don't miss the Old Schoolhouse with its many shops under one roof. Return to Sedona for excellent meals.

Tour 2. Oak Creek Canyon, Flagstaff, Lowell Observatory, Walnut Canyon National Monument, Wapatki National Monument, and Sunset Crater National Monument. Drive north through scenic Oak Creek Canyon to Indian Gardens, Slide Rock, Old Mayhew Lodge, View Point and into Flagstaff. There are two excellent museums, Pioneer Historical and the Museum of Northern Arizona. Don't miss the famous Lowell Observatory. Take Highway 89 north to Wupatki National Monument to see the prehistoric Indian ruins. Next stop is Sunset Crater National Monument, a cone-shaped crater of volcanic cinder. During the winter months visit the Snow Bowl for winter sports or during the balance of the year, travel south to Walnut Canyon National Monument. Here you may view from the Visitors Center or hike down a paved foot trail to see the many Indian cliff dwellings. Continue your drive along the shores of Lake Mary to Mormon Lake. Return to Sedona in beautiful red rock country.

Tour 3. Montezuma Castle and Well, Fort Verde Historic Park and Arcosanti. Down Highway 179 to Montezuma's Well, a cup-shaped lake 78 feet below the surrounding terrain, 1.750 feet in diameter and fed by springs. Continue south on Highway 17 to Montezuma's Castle National Monument. The castle's history is shrouded in the mist of centuries, yet is one of the best preserved prehistoric Indian structures in the Southwest. It is perched high in a limestone cliff on the north side of Beaver Creek. Farther down Highway 17 we discover Camp Verde and close by

Built by the Salado Indians, these prehistoric cliff dwellings contain the remains of a two-story adobe and rock house built in a natural cave.

Fort Verde Historic Park. This United States military garrison began in 1865 at the request of settlers who were having troubles with Indian uprisings. Our last stop south is just east of Cordes Junction. Arcosanti, a small new city of the future designed by Paolo Soleri. Hundreds of students and professionals have come each year since 1970 to work on the city and attend seminars conducted by Soleri. Now a beautiful drive back to Sedona via Highway 279 through Cottonwood and the Verde Valley.

Tour 4. Grand Canyon — Kaibab National Forest — Tusayan Ruin Museum — Little Colorado River Gorge. Get an early start for this beautiful drive via Oak Creek Canyon Highway 89A to Flagstaff. North on Highway 180 past the twin peaks of Mt. San Francisco (12,670 feet — highest point in Arizona) and through Kaibab National Forest. View the grandeur and the many vistas of Grand Canyon from the south rim, one of the world's great scenic wonders. You will have time to spend in the museum, Visitors Center and the shopping district. After lunch, drive east on Highway 64 to the Tusayan Ruin Museum and Desert View. Continue east to Highway 89 through the Little Colorado River Gorge and then return to friendly Sedona.

Shrine of St. Joseph. A small chapel with scenes of the Last Supper, Garden of Gethsemane and the Way of the Cross. Open year-round, daily, 6 a.m. to 6 p.m. Donations asked. Yarnell, off US-89.

Southwestern Arboretum. A unique wonderland of plant life founded by the late William Boyce Thompson. Open year-round, daily. Florence Junction, east off US-60.

Superstition Mountains. Named for the many legends that surround them, this range is said to hold the secret of the Lost Dutchman Gold Mine. It is not known for certain whether the mine ever really existed, but at least eight men have died because of it and many others have perished in the search. Apache Junction, east off State Route 88 and US-89.

Taliesin West. The architectural school and offices of Frank Lloyd Wright. Open year-round, daily, except holidays, 9 a.m. to 10 p.m. Adults $3, under 12 free. Scottsdale, 108th Street, north of East Shea Boulevard. (602) 948-6670.

Tonto Natural Bridge. This natural formation reaches a height of 183 feet with the opening beneath measuring 150 feet in width and 400 feet in length. Open year-round, daily (weather permitting). Adults $1.50, children 7 to 17, $1.

Watchtower. This tower offers views of the Grand Canyon, Painted Desert, and Kaibab National Forest; base of the tower is Indian motif with pictographs and symbolic paintings. Open year-round, daily. Admission 25 cents. Grand Canyon Village, 25 miles east off State Route 64.

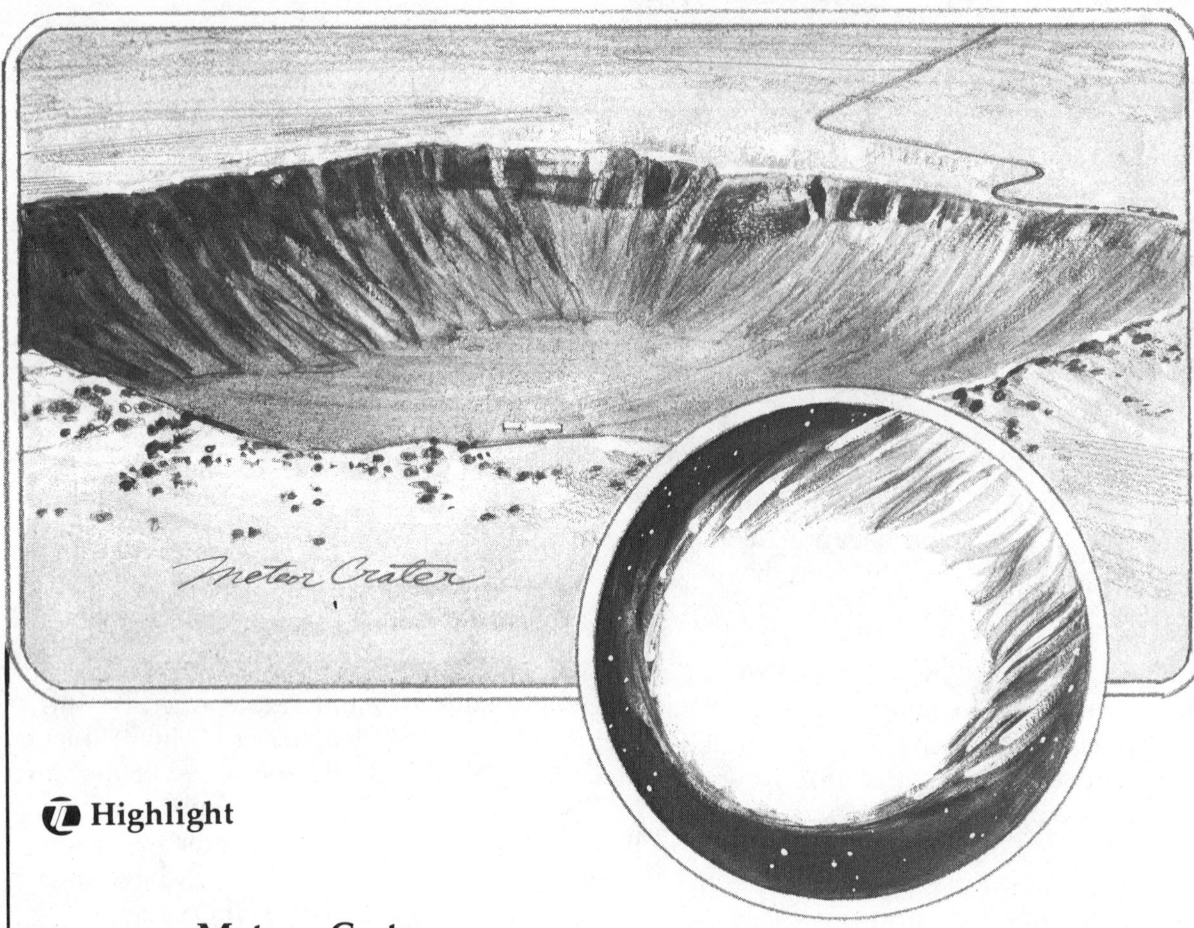

Highlight

Meteor Crater

The world's best preserved and first proven meteorite crater is 4,150 feet from rim to rim, three miles in circumference and 570 feet deep. The meteoritic mass from interplanetary space that gouged out Meteor Crater, 92% iron, 7% nickel, traveling at 30-33,000 miles per hour, struck the earth here with a force of a multi-megaton bomb, splashing nearly half a billion tons of rock from the crater and probably destroying all plant and animal life within a 100-mile area.

Meteor Crater has been used extensively by NASA for the training of American astronauts. Simulating lunar walks, they rehearsed the techniques of sampling the local stratification and were taught the transformations that took place under high velocity impact. The crater itself closely approximates many structures that scar the surface of the moon.

A lecture at the Museum of Astrogeology describes the crater, its history and geological importance. A high-powered telescope, located on the highest point of the crater's rim, provides a view of the surrounding points of interest — the many-hued Painted Desert, the towering San Francisco Peaks and the Hopi Mesas.

The museum and crater grounds are open to the visitor from 8 a.m. to sunset, 365 days year. Meteor Crater is easily reached by an all-weather, paved road from Interstate 40, between Flagstaff and Winslow, Arizona, and is centrally located amid Northern Arizona's other great scenic wonders including the mighty Grand Canyon to the north.

Highlight

The Arizona-Sonora Desert Museum

This unique museum is a combination of zoo, aquarium, botanical garden and natural history museum which tells the ecological story of the Sonoran Desert region, including Sonora and Baja California, Mexico and Arizona. You'll see over 300 kinds of plants and over 200 different animals of this rugged and beautiful country, along nature paths winding through several acres of indoor and outdoor displays.

TRAVELERS' TIPS

- Pets are *not* allowed on the museum grounds and at the present time no facilities are available for them.
- Be sure to bring your camera equipment. There are unusual photographic opportunities at the Desert Museum because many animals are displayed in modern naturalistic settings. Also, various Sonoran Desert plants border the museum's nature paths providing numerous close-up possibilities.
- An average Desert Museum tour takes 1½ to two hours, although some people spend much longer depending on individual interest.

Open every day from 8:30 a.m. until sundown. Adults $2.50, juniors (13-17) $1.50, children (6-12) 50 cents — (under 6) free.

For additional information on the Arizona-Sonora Museum, write to PO Box 5607, Tucson, Arizona 85703.

Arizona State Parks

Park	Location	CAMPING	PICNICKING	CONCESSIONS	SWIMMING	HIKING	BOATING	FISHING	HUNTING	WINTER SPORTS
Alamo Lake	*Wenden. Off US-60-70.*	•	•	•	•	•	•	•		
Boyce Thompson	*Superior. On US-60.*		•			•				
Buckskin	*Parker. Off State Route 95.*	•	•		•	•	•	•		
Cattail Cove	*Lake Havasu City. Off State Route 95.*	•	•	•	•	•	•	•		
Dead Horse	*Cottonwood. Off US-89A.*	•	•			•		•		
Fort Verde	*Camp Verde. Off Interstate 17.*		•							
Lost Dutchman	*Apache Junction. On State Route 88.*		•			•				
Lyman	*St. Johns. Off US-666.*	•	•	•	•	•	•	•		
McFarland	*Florence. On US-89.*		•							
Patagonia	*Nogales. On State Route 82.*	•	•	•	•	•	•	•		
Picacho Peak	*Tucson. Off Interstate 10.*	•	•		•	•	•	•		
Pittsburg Point	*Lake Havasu City. Off State Route 95.*	•	•	•	•		•	•		
Roper Lake	*Safford. Off US-666.*	•	•		•	•	•	•		
Tombstone	*Tombstone. On US-80.*		•							
Tubac	*Tubac. Off Interstate 19.*		•							
Yuma	*Yuma. Off Interstate 8.*		•							

Arizona has no state forests. For more information on Arizona state parks, contact: *Arizona State Parks, 1688 West Adams, Phoenix, Arizona 85007, (602) 271-4174.*

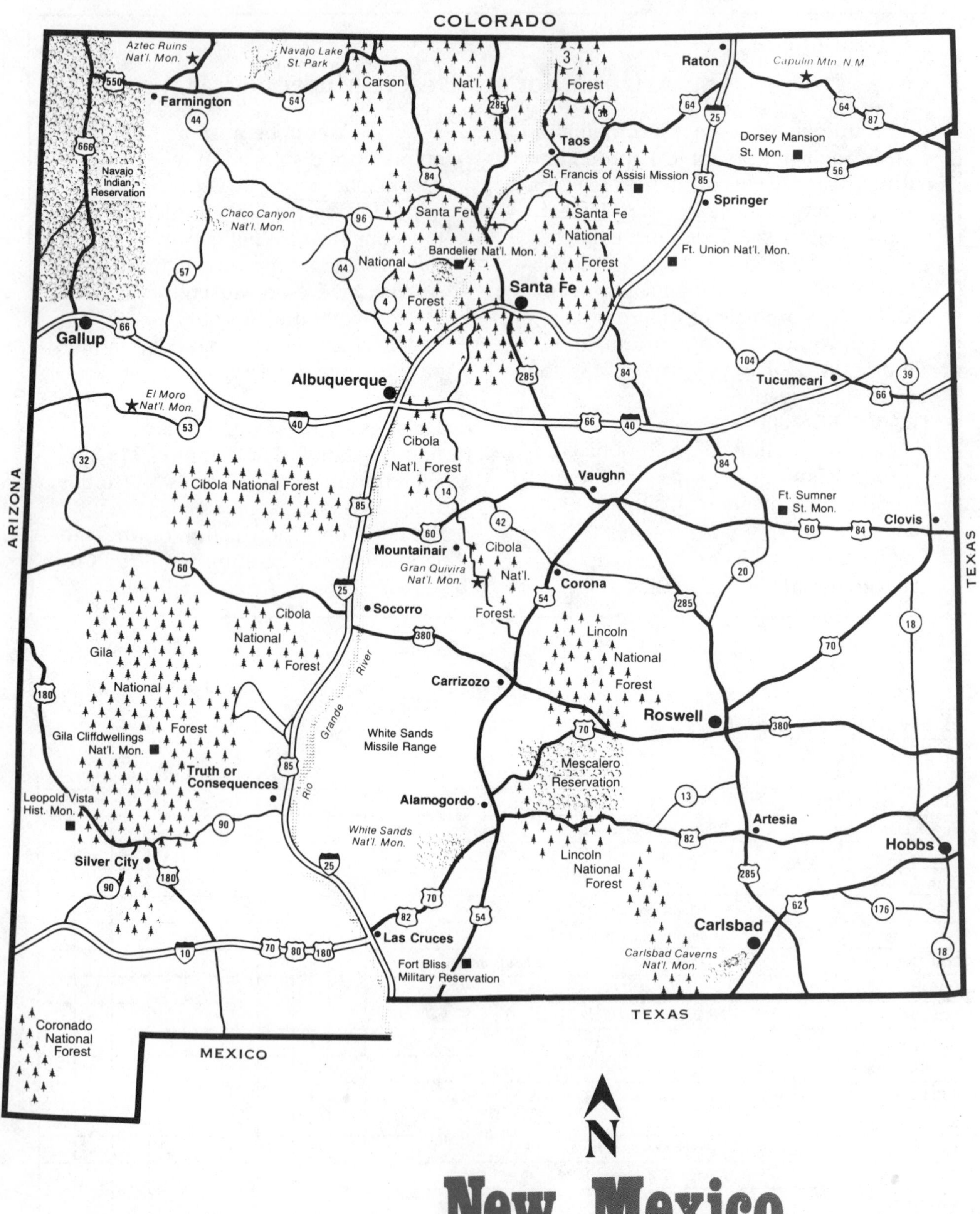

Map not to exact scale.

New Mexico

New Mexico has long been known as the "Land of Enchantment" — an apt name for a state of such remarkable diversity. The enchantment can be seen in a landscape that ranges from shifting desert sands and spectacular mountain ranges to lush forests and awesome caverns. The enchantment can be found in remnants of an advanced Indian culture that simply vanished and the awakening of the atomic age with an explosion of the first hydrogen bomb at Alamagordo. And then there is the enchantment of the four seasons — warm, dry summers; fall's blazing colors in the high country; a winter that contrasts snowcapped peaks with the Indian summer of the lowlands; and a spring that brings forth desert blooms, rivers and streams swollen with snowmelt, while Albuquerque skies fill with brightly-colored hot-air balloons.

A cave in the Sandia Mountains, east of Albuquerque, has yielded evidence of the presence of prehistoric man in New Mexico more than 22,000 years ago. But the first record of exploration by Europeans dates back to 1540, and Coronado's explorations in search of the mythical cities of gold. After a number of subsequent explorations by Spanish soldiers and missionaries, Juan de Onate entered the region and established the first settlement, San Juan de los Caballeros. The Spanish control, which lasted for several years, was briefly interrupted in 1680 by an Indian rebellion that forced most of the Spaniards out of the territory. Control was re-established in 1692, but was intermittently threatened by attacks from the Navajo, Ute, Apache and Commanche. Spanish rule gave way in 1821, when Mexico declared its independence; however, Mexican rule of the region remained weak and New Mexico guided its own destiny until the Americans, led by General Kearny, captured the territory in 1846. Four years later the Territory of New Mexico was established, and statehood was attained in 1912.

Full name: State of New Mexico
Origin of name: From the Aztec, Mexitli, meaning "War God."
Motto: *Crescit Eundo* (It Grows As It Goes).
Nickname: Land of Enchantment.
Capital: Santa Fe
Statehood: January 6, 1912, 47th state.
Population: 1,190,000 (ranks 37th).
Major Cities: Albuquerque (279,400), Santa Fe (44,940).
Bird: Road runner
Flower: Yucca
Tree: Pinon or nut pine

Average daily temperatures by month

	Northern	Southern
Jan.	46.5 to 18.7	57.1 to 27.5
Feb.	49.3 to 20.7	61.1 to 30.4
Mar.	54.6 to 25.0	67.6 to 36.3
Apr.	63.2 to 32.6	77.8 to 43.8
May	72.2 to 41.6	87.0 to 52.0
Jun.	81.0 to 49.6	95.7 to 61.7
Jul.	83.1 to 54.7	95.3 to 65.4
Aug.	80.8 to 53.0	92.7 to 63.7
Sept.	76.0 to 46.1	88.1 to 57.5
Oct.	67.4 to 36.4	77.9 to 46.1
Nov.	54.5 to 25.2	65.7 to 34.0
Dec.	47.4 to 19.4	57.1 to 27.7
Year	64.7 to 35.3	76.9 to 45.5

New Mexico has an abundance of national parks and national monuments; among the more interesting are Carlsbad Caverns, the largest known underground caverns featuring countless curious formations; Gila Cliff Dwellings, inhabited about 100 to 1300 A.D.; Chaco Canyon, the site of a lost pre-Colombian civilization. In Albuquerque and Silver City, the Cinco de Mayo (May 5) festivals held each year are colorful celebrations of the state's Mexican heritage. In Albuquerque, which has recently become the hot-air ballooning capital of the world, various ballooning events fill the skies with these colorful crafts. For the angler, Ute and Alamagordo Reservoirs provide unsurpassed fishing.

Ranching is still New Mexico's chief industry, but the state remains in the forefront of energy research and development. At the Los Alamos and Sandia Laboratories, important research continues in the nuclear, solar and geothermal fields, while manufacturing is centered around food processing, stone, clay and glass products, chemicals and electronic equipment.

New Mexico Points of Interest and Attractions

Bradbury Science Hall. Exhibits on the history of nuclear energy research, computers, laser science, radiation therapy and energy production. Open year-round, daily, except holidays. Free. Los Alamos, one-quarter mile south of Los Alamos Canyon Bridge, on Diamond Drive.

Cumbres and Toltec Railroad. A narrow-gauge line that offers four eight-hour trips per week. Open June through October 15. Adults $20, children under 12, $8; reservations required. Chama, on State Route 17. (505) 756-2151.

Frontiertown. A reproduction of a western town of the 1890s. Open June through August, daily, noon to 6 p.m. Adults 50 cents, children under 13,

State Offices

Tourism
Tourist Division
Department of Development
113 Washington Avenue
Santa Fe, New Mexico 87503
(505) 827-5571

State Police
Department of Public Safety
PO Box 1628
Santa Fe, New Mexico 87501
(505) 827-2551

Radio Stations

Albuquerque
KRKE 610 (AM)
KOB 770 (AM)

---

25 cents; rides not included in entrance fee. Albuquerque, 11 northeast off Interstate 40.

Ghost Ranch. Operated by the National Forest Service, this facility stresses conservation education with live exhibits of native animals and plants; exhibits include miniature forest, geology and paleontology displays. Open Memorial Day through Labor Day, 8 a.m. to 6 p.m. Abiquiu, 14 miles northwest on US-84.

Harwood Foundation. Featuring exhibits by early Taos artists, Persian miniatures, Indian and Spanish art objects. Open year-round, Monday to Saturday. Free. Taos, Ledoux Street.

Rio Bravo River Tours. Float trips of one-half to one full-day duration on the Rio Grande River; hike and lunch included in fare. Open mid-May to mid-September, daily; reservations required. Fare: $40. Santa Fe, PO Box 524. (505) 988-1153.

Sandia Peak Tram. A year-round attraction that is also a ski lift from approximately Thanksgiving through Easter. Spectacular views from Summit of Sandia Peak (10,378 feet). Albuquerque, off Interstate 25 at Tramway Road exit, and east off US-66.

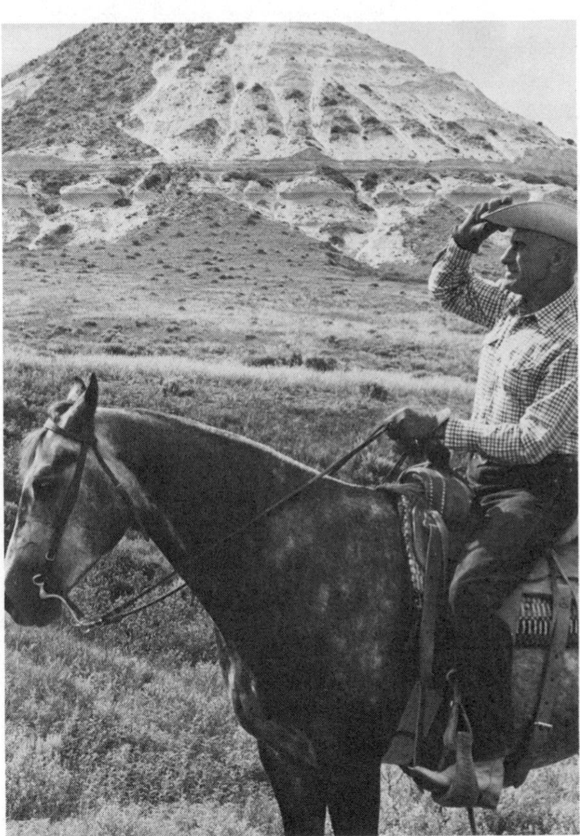

Santuario de Chimayo. A farmer working the land here is said to have been instructed by a vision to dig beneath his plow for earth that had healing powers. In digging, he unearthed a cross and a piece of cloth that had belonged to two priests who were martyred at the site. A chapel was constructed in 1816 to house the cross, and today many pilgrims come to the area to partake of the purported curative powers of the earth found in a pit inside the chapel. Open year-round. Chimayo, at east end of town.

Sierra Blanca Gondola. A gondola ride (30 minutes round-trip) to an 11,400-foot peak; restaurant. Open June through Labor Day, daily. Fare: $2.50.

Highlight

For the Sportsman . . .

More than 32 million acres of public lands, hundreds of miles of flowing water, blue jewels of trout lakes and great reservoirs beckon the outdoorsman and his family. Whether you're looking for the delight that comes to a child's face when he hooks a bluegill or planning a high-country stalk for elk, you'll find New Mexico's hunting and fishing opportunities run the full gamut.

The State Game Commission sets season dates as far in advance as is practicable, making your planning easier. Big game seasons are set in early February, and hunting information sheets are available by April 1. Bird seasons are set in August and September. Species hunted in New Mexico include mule and white-tailed deer, elk, antelope, bear, Barbary, Rocky Mountain and desert bighorn sheep, javelina, mountain lion, oryx, ibex, squirrel, turkey, grouse, prairie chicken, quail, pheasant, dove, sandhill crane, snipe, rails, gallinules and waterfowl, including a wide variety of duck and geese species.

Trout of several varieties swim New Mexico waters: rainbow, brown, brook, native or cutthroat and Dolly Varden are here, and plantings of kokanee salmon have proven successful in some waters. Warm-water fish include black bass, white bass, walleye, crappie, catfish, northern pike and sunfish.

New Mexico State Parks

Park	Location	CAMPING	PICNICKING	CONCESSIONS	SWIMMING	HIKING	BOATING	FISHING	HUNTING	WINTER SPORTS
Bluewater Lake	*Grants. Off State Route 12.*	•	•		•		•	•		
Bottomless Lakes	*Roswell. Off State Route 409.*	•	•		•		•	•		
Caballo Lake	*Hatch. Off Interstate 25.*	•	•	•	•		•	•		
Chicosa Lake	*Roy. Off State Route 120.*	•	•							
City of Rocks	*Deming. Off State Route 61.*	•	•							
Clayton Lake	*Clayton. Off State Route 370.*	•	•		•		•	•		
Conchas Lake	*Tucumcari. Off State Route 104.*	•	•	•	•		•	•		
Coronado	*Bernalillo. On State Route 44.*	•	•							
Coyote Creek	*Mora. Off State Route 38.*	•	•				•			
Elephant Butte Lake	*Truth or Consequences. Off Interstate 25.*	•	•	•	•		•	•		
El Vado Lake	*Tierra Amarilla. Off State Route 112.*	•	•	•	•		•	•		
Heron Lake	*Tierra Amarilla. Off State Route 95.*	•	•				•	•		
Hyde Memorial	*Santa Fe. Off State Route 475.*	•	•							•
Indian Petroglyph	*Albuquerque. Off Interstate 40 and Interstate 25.*						•	•		
Kit Carson Memorial	*Taos. Off State Route 68.*		•							
Leasburg Dam	*Las Cruces. Off US-85.*	•	•				•	•		
Manzano	*Montainair. Off State Route 14.*	•	•							
Oasis	*Clovis. Off State Route 467.*	•	•					•		
Pancho Villa	*Deming. Off State Route 11.*	•	•							
Percha Dam	*Truth Or Consequences. Off Interstate 25.*	•	•					•		
Red Rocks	*Gallup. Off State Route 566.*	•	•							
Rio Grande Gorge	*Taos. Off State Route 68.*	•	•					•		
Rock Hound	*Deming. Off State Route 11.*	•	•							
San Gabriel	*Albuquerque. Off Interstate 40 and Interstate 25.*		•							
Sumner Lake	*Fort Sumner. Off State Route 203.*	•	•		•		•	•		
Storrie Lake	*Las Vegas. Off State Route 3.*	•	•		•		•	•		
Ute Lake	*Logan. Off State Route 540.*	•	•	•	•		•	•		
Valley of Fires	*Carrizozo. Off US-380.*	•	•			•				
Villanueva	*Las Vegas. Off Interstate 25.*	•	•					•		

New Mexico has no state forests. For more information on New Mexico state parks, contact: *State Park and Recreation Commission, 141 East De Vargas, Santa Fe, New Mexico 87503, (505) 827-2726.*

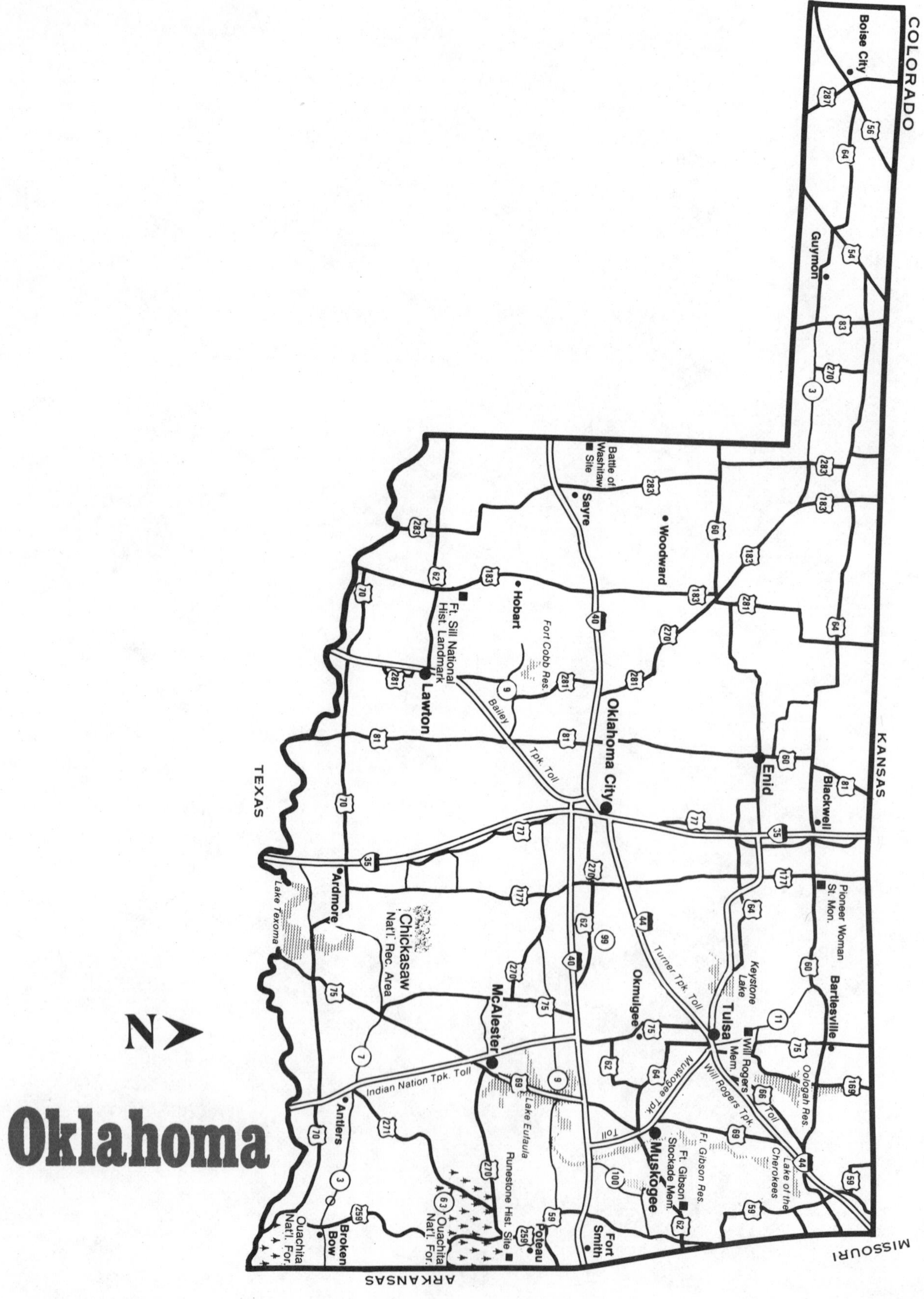

Map not to exact scale.

Oklahoma

Oklahoma's name is derived from two Choctaw words: "Okla," meaning people, and "humma," meaning red. Literally, Oklahoma means red people and, indeed, in the 19th century the region was the reservation for a number of tribes uprooted from their homelands in the East. Today, Oklahoma is the home for more than 120,000 Indians of 35 tribes — the largest Indian population of any state in the nation. You can't travel far in Oklahoma without finding some reminder of the state's Indian and Old West heritage. There's the American Indian Exposition in Anadarko and the Cowboy Hall of Fame in Oklahoma City; the Cherokee National Museum in Tahlequah; the Chisholm Trail along the route of US-81; the Tom Mix museum in Dewey; and in Claremore you'll find the memorial and museum that commemorates the state's most famous native son, Western humorist Will Rogers.

Various bands of Indians inhabited the Oklahoma region before the first Europeans — soldiers of Coronado's expedition — crossed into the area in 1541. That expedition gave Spain a claim to the territory, but no attempt was made to establish settlements and the claim was lost to France through the later explorations of Jolliet and LaSalle. In 1803, most of Oklahoma was acquired through the Louisiana Purchase. American explorers made repeated visits to Oklahoma following its purchase, and in 1824 Colonel Matthew Arbuckle established Forts Gibson and Towson. During this time, the U.S. government designated most of Oklahoma "Indian Territory," and used it for the forcible resettlement of what were called the Five Civilized Tribes (Choctaw, Cherokee, Creek, Chickasaw, Seminole). Many of these Indians, who had been living in close contact with white men for nearly 100 years, took up farming — and some even followed the Southern tradition of maintaining slaves. The Civil War shattered Indian unity, however, for although they fought for both sides, they

Full name: State of Oklahoma
Origin of name: From Choctaw meaning "Red People."
Motto: *Labor Omnia Vincit* (Labor Conquers All).
Nickname: Sooner State
Capital: Oklahoma City
Statehood: November 16, 1907, 46th state.
Population: 2,811,000 (ranks 27th).
Major Cities: Oklahoma City (365,920), Tulsa (331,730), Lawton (76,420).
Bird: Scissortailed flycatcher
Flower: Mistletoe
Tree: Redbud

Average daily temperatures by month

	Northern	Southern
Jan.	47.3 to 23.0	55.1 to 28.7
Feb.	53.2 to 27.5	60.7 to 33.0
Mar.	61.1 to 34.6	68.5 to 40.4
Apr.	72.9 to 46.3	78.3 to 51.2
May	81.9 to 56.1	85.1 to 59.3
Jun.	91.6 to 65.6	93.1 to 67.3
Jul.	96.4 to 70.4	98.2 to 71.0
Aug.	95.1 to 68.6	98.4 to 69.7
Sept.	86.2 to 60.5	90.1 to 62.8
Oct.	75.8 to 49.1	79.6 to 51.8
Nov.	60.0 to 35.7	65.9 to 39.6
Dec.	49.4 to 26.7	57.4 to 31.8
Year	72.6 to 47.0	77.5 to 50.6

were largely identified as sympathetic to the Confederate cause. After the war, the federal government used the wartime disloyalty of some tribal leaders as a pretext to seize the western region so that other tribes from both sides of the Mississippi River could be resettled there. Although a number of laws and treaties existed that prohibited white encroachment on the Oklahoma region, settlers continued their migration and the Oklahoma Territory was created in 1890. In 1907, the Indians petitioned to have the region admitted to the Union as the state of Sequoyah, but the petition was denied and their region was merged with the territory and was admitted as a single state.

Though many of Oklahoma's attractions are tied to its Indian history, the state does have other offerings for visitors. You'll find a number of excellent state parks throughout Oklahoma, many located on large man-made lakes where you can pursue a variety of water sports. In Comanche County, the Wichita Mountains Wildlife Refuge preserves the natural environment of prairie dogs, deer, elk, bison and Texas longhorns. Of course, Oklahoma also offers some superb scenery — pine forests, sweeping plains, rolling prairies and rugged canyons.

In recent years, tourism has grown to be one of Oklahoma's major industries, but for now oil is the economic mainstay. The principal crop is wheat, and manufacturing includes machinery, rubber and plastics and electronic equipment.

Oklahoma Points of Interest and Attractions

Antiques Incorporated. An extensive exhibit of American and foreign antique cars, all in running condition. Open year-round, daily, 10 a.m. to 5 p.m.; closed some holidays. Adults $2.50, children 6 to 16, $1.25. Muskogee, on US-62.

State Offices

Tourism
Tourism Promotion Division
Oklahoma Tourism and Recreation Department
500 Will Rogers Building
Oklahoma City, Oklahoma 73105
(405) 521-2406

State Police
Department of Public Safety
3600 North Eastern Avenue
Oklahoma City, Oklahoma 73111
(405) 424-4011

Radio Stations

Oklahoma City
KATT 100.5 (FM)
KOMA 1520 (AM)
Tulsa
KMOD 97.5 (FM)

Indian City USA. A fascinating re-creation of villages common to the Kiowa, Caddo, Comanche, Wichita, Pawnee, Apache and Navajo tribes; museum, campground, tours, tribal ceremonies. Open year-round, daily. Adults $3, children 6 to 11, $1.50. Anadarko, on State Route 8.

National Cowboy Hall of Fame. A center honoring the men and women who made important contributions to the development of the West. Displays include memorial busts, art and animated relief map that provides a historical perspective of the Westward movement. Open year-round, daily, except for Thanksgiving, Christmas and New Year's Day. Adults $2, children 6 to 12, $1. Oklahoma City, 1700 NE 63rd Street.

National Softball Hall of Fame. Pays tribute to the great players and coaches of this popular amateur sport; exhibits on the history of the game; library. Open year-round, daily, except some holidays. Adults 50 cents, children 6 to 11, 25 cents. Oklahoma City, off Interstate 35, at 2801 NE 50th Street.

Oklahoma Heritage Center. The former home of Judge R. A. Hefner, State Supreme Court Justice and Mayor of Oklahoma City, features elegant furnishings, antiques and Oklahoma Hall of Fame exhibit. Open year-round, daily, 9 a.m. to 5 p.m.; Sundays, 1 p.m. to 5 p.m. Adults $2, children under 12, $1.50. Oklahoma City, 201 NW 14th Street.

Oral Roberts University. A famous center of higher education that features a 200-foot glass and steel prayer tower, six-story hexagonal library, modern sports center, symphony hall, carillon and chapel. Open year-round, daily, 8:30 a.m. to 5:30 p.m.; tours originate at Prayer Tower. Free. Tulsa, off Interstate 44, at 7777 South Lewis Avenue.

Pensacola Dam. A dam that forms Grand Lake, spanning the river between Disney and Langley; spillway and dam are 6,565 feet in length; lookout house; tours. Open year-round, Wednesday to Sunday, 8 a.m. to 4:30 p.m. Free. Grand Lake, off Will Rogers Turnpike.

Robert S. Kerr Environmental Water Research Agency. Facility conducts research into the problems of water pollution; tours. Open year-round, daily. Free. Ada, off State Route 3.

University of Oklahoma. A 3,000-acre campus with more than 300 buildings, including extensive laboratory and research facilities. Open year-round, Monday to Saturday; tours on weekdays at 2 p.m.; Saturday, 9:30 a.m. Free. Norman, 407 West Boyd Street.

Wichita Mountains Wildlife Refuge. Harbors buffalo, elk, deer, longhorn cattle, wild turkey and many other species; campgrounds; hiking and fishing nearby. Lawton, 12 miles west off US-62, on State Route 115.

Will Rogers Memorial. A ranch-house museum on the site where Will Rogers planned to build his home, featuring art exhibits, memorabilia, diorama, library. Rogers' tomb is located in a small garden in front of the museum. Open year-round, daily, 8 a.m. to 5 p.m. Claremore, on State Route 88.

The Will Rogers Memorial houses an extensive collection of memorabilia in honor of Oklahoma's most famous native son.

Highlight

TALIMENA SKYLINE DRIVE

Stretching across the top of the Ouachita Mountains is Talimena Skyline Drive, which runs from just east of Talihina, Oklahoma, to Mena, Arkansas.

"Breathtaking" understates the beauty and magnitude of this magnificent highway, as it gives RVers a spectacular view of the Ouachita Mountains that also gave the forest its name.

Smokish haze dominates the skyline as the highway oscillates up and down mountainsides. Highway turnouts are popular spots for photographers. Information centers are at both ends of the drive.

HEAVENER RUNESTONE

A few miles north of the drive is Heavener Runestone, a 12-foot-high slab of stone on which eight characters from an early-day alphabet provide a time-link back nearly 1,000 years.

For the inscription has been translated as the date November 11, 1012 A.D., which is considered proof that Vikings visited the area some 500 years before Columbus.

The stone is the central attraction in the Heavener Runestone State Park. An Interpretive Center is built around the slab.

Highlight

Oklahoma City's 45th Division Museum

The displays of this museum tell the story of the 45th Infantry Division, the Oklahoma National Guard and the earlier Oklahoma Militia. However, the story it tells could be repeated, with variations, in relating the experiences of all who have served our nation's Armed Forces in times of peace and war.

The story began not long after the arrival of the Five Civilized Tribes in Indian Territory in the 1830s. Each of these tribes appointed a police force to keep order in their territories. These police units operated as the militia for their respective tribes until statehood in 1907.

The Oklahoma Territorial Militia was loosely organized in 1890 and was officially reorganized as the Oklahoma Territorial National Guard on March 8, 1895. The first National Guard consisted of infantry companies, cavalry troops and artillery batteries. Its total strength in peacetime was limited to 500 men.

After the sinking of the Battleship *Maine* on February 15, 1898, relations between the United States and Spain deteriorated until war was declared by both sides. Congress passed a volunteer bill allowing National Guard units to serve in the regular army as state units with the approval of their governors. The first United States volunteer cavalry was commanded by Colonel Leonard Wood, with Lieutenant-Colonel Teddy Roosevelt as his assistant. Members were mustered from New Mexico, Arizona, Oklahoma and the Indian Territories. The public promptly named them the Rough Riders because of their cowboy backgrounds. After a brief period in Texas for training, the Rough Riders left Tampa, Florida, for Cuba on June 13, 1898. Three cavalry troops of the First Territorial Regiment were part of the Rough Riders. One was from Oklahoma Territory and two were from Indian Territory. Of all the actions the Rough Riders engaged in during the three months war, the most famous was the charge on San Juan Hill.

The Territorial Militia grew in the years following the Spanish-American War. Federal allotments to support the troops doubled and the territorial legislature voted to expand support in money and men. Statehood, in 1907, ended the territorial status of the Oklahoma National Guard.

In 1916, when trouble broke out on the Mexican border and war threatened, the Oklahoma National Guard, then known as the First Oklahoma Infantry, was called to active duty and sent to the border near San Benito. The guardsmen spent nearly a year on the border, but saw no combat. They returned to Oklahoma to be discharged just in time to be called up again for World War I.

In World War I, Oklahoma National Guardsmen were divided, but most of the units were combined with the Texas National Guard into the 36th Infantry Division, which saw combat in the Battle of the Meuse-Argonne. Some of the small units became part of the Rainbow Division, and conscripts went to the 90th (Texas-Oklahoma) Infantry Division. All three of these divisions saw combat in France.

Following the war, the National Defense Act of 1920 created the right to form the 45th Infantry Division from among four states — Oklahoma, Colorado, Arizona and New Mexico. This division became fully organized by

1923 and camped together for the first time at Fort Sill in 1924.

In August 1940, the 45th Division was ordered into federal service for one year to engage in a training program. By the end of that period, America was faced with World War II.

At this point, the combat history of the 45th Division began. The Thunderbirds landed in Sicily in July 1943, in the first major amphibious combat landing on a European continental area. This began 70 continuous days of combat and the Sicilian victory, which resulted in Italy being eased out of the war.

Next was a landing at Salerno, Italy, moving up toward Cassino. Then in January 1944, it was another amphibious landing, this time in Anzio, where the Thunderbirds faced elements of seven German divisions in what German Field Marshal Kesselring called "an epic of American arms."

After assisting in the capture of Rome, the 45th made its fourth combat amphibious landing, this time in southern France. After that it was the march to Alsace, into the Rhineland and breaking the Siegfried Line; then Nurnberg, the shrine city of Nazidom. A week before V-E day, the 45th marched into Munich. The division then had 511 combat days on the line — one of the best records of World War II. It had taken 126,000 prisoners and suffered 28,000 casualties. It was General George S. Patton, Jr. who said, "The 45th is one of the best, if not actually the best division in the history of American Arms."

Following World War II, the 45th Division became an all-Oklahoma organization and reverted to National Guard status. In 1950, at the beginning of the Korean War, the 45th was one of the first two divisions to be called into active duty. It trained at Camp Polk, Louisiana, and on the island of Hokkaido, Japan. In December 1951, it was the first National Guard division to see action in Korea, relieving the First Cavalry Division. It served in the Yonchon-Chorwon area, and then fought in the crucial sector fronting Old Baldy, Pork Chop Hill, Heartbreak Ridge and Luke's Castle. In late 1953, the division returned to the States and was disbanded. Meanwhile, however, Oklahoma Guardsmen, who had returned on rotation, had already reformed a 45th National Guard division in 1952. The Oklahoma division accepted the colors which had remained with the 45th in Korea.

It has been said of the 45th Division, "Whatever destiny may hold in store for our great country and however long that country's military history may continue, readers in the future will search long before finding a chapter more brilliant than that written by the quill which was dipped into the blood of the Thunderbird."

And if that sounds like extravagant praise, you owe yourself a visit to the fighting 45th's museum.

—PJF

The 45th Infantry Museum is located at 2124 NE 36th Street, Oklahoma City, Oklahoma 73111. (405) 424-5313. Open free to the public — 9 a.m. to 5 p.m. daily and 1 p.m. to 5 p.m. Sunday (closed Monday).

Oklahoma State Parks

Park	Location	CAMPING	PICNICKING	CONCESSIONS	SWIMMING	HIKING	BOATING	FISHING	HUNTING	WINTER SPORTS
Alabaster Caverns	*Freedom. Off State Route 50.*	•	•		•					
Arrowhead	*Eufaula. Off US-69.*	•	•	•	•	•	•	•		
Beaver	*Beaver. Off US-270.*	•	•			•				
Beaver's Bend	*Broken Bow. On State Route 259.*	•	•		•	•	•	•		
Black Mesa	*Boise City. Off US-287.*	•	•			•	•	•		
Boiling Springs	*Woodward. On State Route 50B.*	•	•		•	•	•	•		
Fort Cobb	*Fort Cobb. On State Route 9.*	•	•		•		•	•		
Foss	*Clinton. On State Route 73.*	•	•		•		•	•		
Fountainhead	*Checotah. Off State Route 150.*	•	•	•	•	•	•	•		
Great Salt Plains	*Cherokee. Off State Routes 38 and 11.*	•	•		•	•	•	•		
Greenleaf	*Muskogee. Off State Route 10.*	•	•		•	•	•	•		
Heavener Runestone	*Heavener. Off US-59.*		•			•				
Keystone	*Tulsa. On State Route 51.*	•	•			•	•	•		
Little River	*Norman. On State Route 9.*	•	•		•	•	•	•		
Locust Grove	*Locust Grove. On US-33.*		•							
Murray	*Ardmore. On US-77.*	•	•	•	•	•	•	•		
Osage Hills	*Pawhuska. On US-60.*	•	•		•		•	•		
Quartz Mountain	*Mangum. On State Route 44A.*	•	•	•	•	•	•	•		
Red Rock Canyon	*Hinton. On State Route 2.*	•	•		•	•		•		
Robber's Cave	*Wilburton. On State Route 2.*	•	•		•	•		•		
Rocky Ford	*Tahlequah. On State Route 82.*		•							
Roman Nose	*Watonga. On State Route 8.*	•	•		•	•	•	•		
Sequoyah	*Wagoner. On State Route 51.*	•	•	•	•	•	•	•		
Talimena	*Talihina. On State Route 1.*	•	•							
Tenkiller	*Gore. On State Route 100.*	•	•	•	•	•	•	•		
Walnut Creek	*Tulsa. Off State Route 99.*	•	•	•	•		•	•		

Oklahoma has no state forests. For more information on Oklahoma state parks, contact: *Oklahoma Department of Tourism and Recreation, 504 Will Rogers Building, Oklahoma City, Oklahoma 73105, (405) 521-2646.*

With more than 65 tribes living in Oklahoma, colorful Indian events and ceremonies can be viewed throughout much of the year. The American Indian Exposition held each August in Anadarko is one of the largest festivals.

Performed each year from mid-June through late August, "Dust On Her Petticoats" is an outdoor drama that depicts the role of the pioneer woman in the settling of the Oklahoma Territory. This and other productions can be seen at the Discoveryland Amphitheater in Tulsa (opposite page, bottom).

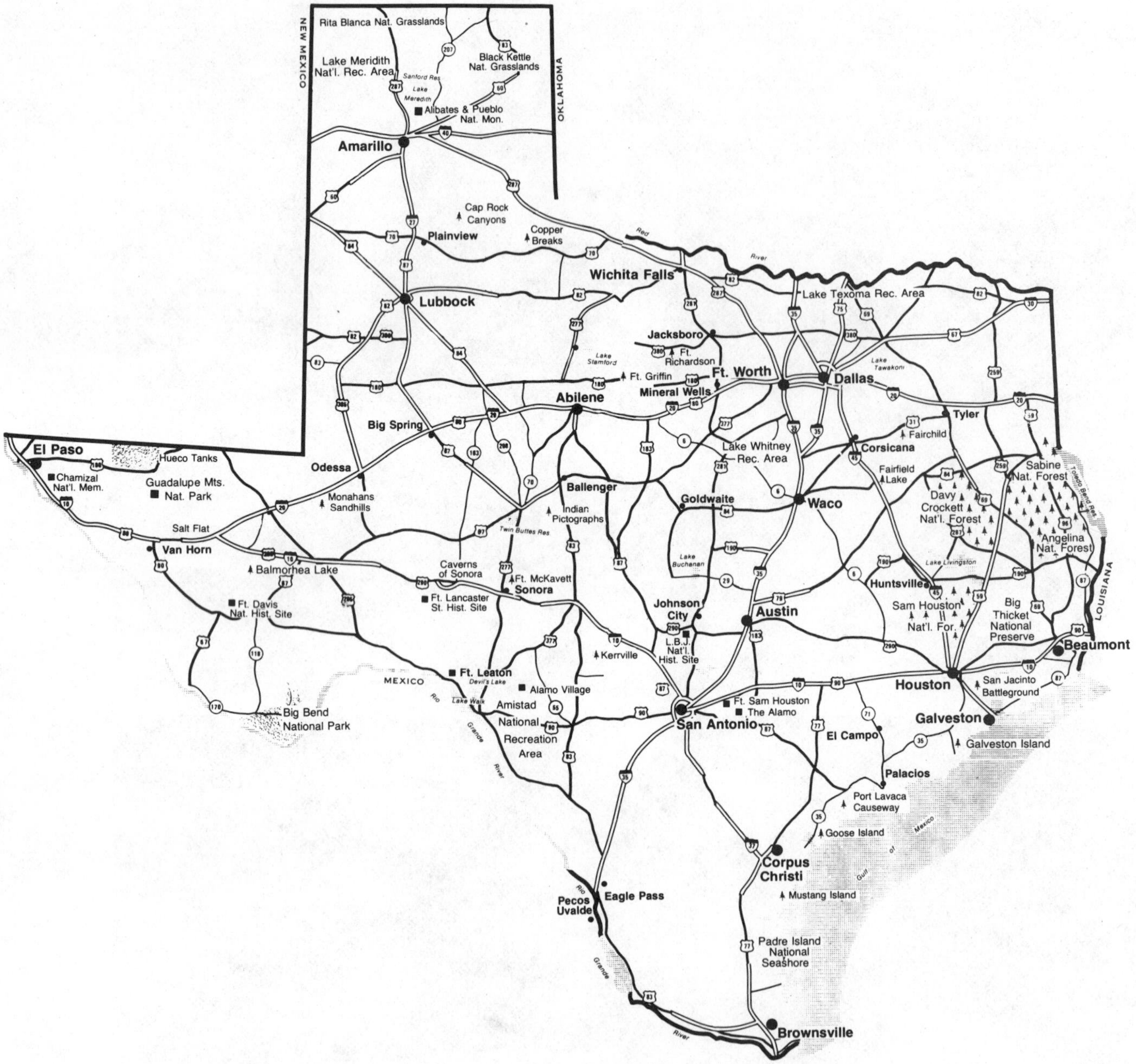

NEW MEXICO
OKLAHOMA
LOUISIANA
MEXICO
Rita Blanca Nat. Grasslands
Lake Meridith Nat'l. Rec. Area
Sanford Res
Lake Meredith
Black Kettle Nat. Grasslands
Alibates & Pueblo Nat. Mon.
Amarillo
Cap Rock Canyons
Copper Breaks
Plainview
Red River
Wichita Falls
Lubbock
Lake Texoma Rec. Area
Jacksboro
Ft. Richardson
Lake Stamford
Ft. Griffin
Ft. Worth
Mineral Wells
Dallas
Lake Tawakoni
Abilene
Tyler
Big Spring
Fairchild
El Paso
Hueco Tanks
Chamizal Nat'l. Mem.
Guadalupe Mts. Nat. Park
Odessa
Monahans Sandhills
Lake Whitney Rec. Area
Corsicana
Fairfield Lake
Sabine Nat. Forest
Toledo Bend Res
Ballenger
Indian Pictographs
Twin Buttes Res
Goldwaite
Waco
Davy Crockett Nat'l. Forest
Angelina Nat. Forest
Salt Flat
Van Horn
Balmorhea Lake
Lake Buchanan
Caverns of Sonora
Ft. McKavett
Sonora
Ft. Lancaster St. Hist. Site
Lake Livingston
Huntsville
Ft. Davis Nat. Hist. Site
Johnson City
Austin
Sam Houston Nat'l. For.
Big Thicket National Preserve
Beaumont
L.B.J. Nat'l. Hist. Site
Kerrville
Ft. Leaton
Devil's Lake
Lake Walk
Alamo Village
Amistad National Recreation Area
Houston
San Jacinto Battleground
Ft. Sam Houston
The Alamo
San Antonio
Galveston
Big Bend National Park
El Campo
Galveston Island
Palacios
Rio Grande River
Port Lavaca Causeway
Goose Island
Gulf of Mexico
Corpus Christi
Eagle Pass
Pecos
Uvalde
Mustang Island
Padre Island National Seashore
Brownsville

N

Texas

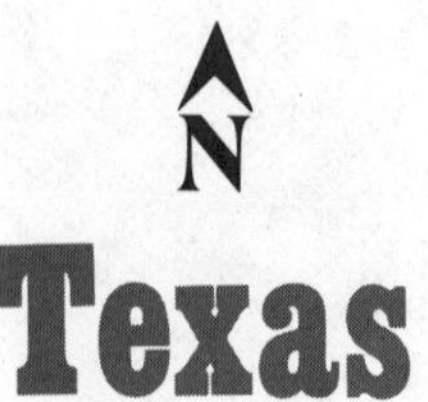

Map not to exact scale.

Texas

The admission of Alaska may have cost Texas its title as the largest state in the Union, but it still can claim the distinction of being the largest — 267,339 square miles — in the contiguous 48 states. For travelers, Texas' wide horizons translate into a state of almost limitless opportunities. The southernmost tip of the state, the Lower Rio Grande Valley, is a perfect hideaway for winter sun seekers; in the frontier country of west Texas lie some of the state's most beautiful and serene vistas; east Texas offers the Big Thicket country, a land of lakes and piney woods; and in the state's midsection you'll find reminders of Texas' rich Old West history.

Indians probably inhabited what is now Texas as early as 20,000 years before the first visit by Spanish explorer Alonso de Pineda in 1519. After this initial visit, other Spanish explorers traversed the area over the next 150 years, eventually establishing a settlement at Ysleta (near present-day El Paso). In 1685, France attempted to claim a portion of the area, and even established a short-lived colony near Matagorda Bay. The presence of the French stimulated Spain's efforts to control the territory, and the Spaniards established a number of missions and military outposts during the next century. With the Louisiana Purchase, Spanish rule was once again challenged as Americans began moving across the border to establish settlements.

With the Mexican Independence of 1824, control of Texas shifted to Mexico and the Mexicans immediately moved to curb the influx of Americans. The result was a number of minor clashes between American dissidents and Mexican troops, with the pivotal confrontation coming on March 6, 1836, when Mexican dictator Antonio Lopez de Santa Anna launched his legendary assault on the Alamo. Emboldened by his victory at the Alamo, Santa Anna then moved quickly to crush the rest of the American forces. But on April 21, a Texas army under the command of Sam Houston surprised Santa Anna's numerically superior force at San

Full name: State of Texas
Origin of name: From the Indian meaning "Friends" or "Allies."
Motto: Friendship
Nickname: Lone Star State
Capital: Austin
Statehood: December 29, 1845, 28th state.
Population: 12,830,000 (ranks third).
Major Cities: Houston (1,326,810), Dallas (812,800), San Antonio (773,250).
Bird: Mockingbird
Flower: Bluebonnet
Tree: Pecan

Average daily temperatures by month

	Northern	Southern
Jan.	53.0 to 25.4	67.4 to 47.4
Feb.	57.3 to 28.8	69.8 to 50.9
Mar.	64.9 to 34.3	74.4 to 55.9
Apr.	74.5 to 44.4	80.4 to 63.0
May	82.1 to 54.3	85.9 to 69.1
Jun.	91.4 to 63.6	90.5 to 74.0
Jul.	92.4 to 66.5	93.5 to 74.6
Aug.	91.7 to 65.8	93.8 to 74.5
Sept.	84.4 to 58.4	90.1 to 71.4
Oct.	74.8 to 47.5	84.5 to 64.5
Nov.	62.4 to 33.3	73.8 to 54.3
Dec.	54.7 to 27.3	68.8 to 49.5
Year	73.6 to 45.8	81.1 to 62.4

Jacinto, routed the Mexicans, took Santa Anna prisoner and ended the brief but bloody war. With the Mexicans driven out of the territory, Texas was declared an independent republic and Houston was named to the presidency. Texas remained a separate nation for nearly 10 years, until financial problems and internal conflicts brought about a petition for annexation to the U.S. Statehood, which came in 1845, was not without controversy because Texas was admitted as a slave state. It was that slave-holding status, combined with fierce states' rights views, that led to Texas' secession in 1861. After the Civil War, Texas was ruled by a sometimes chaotic reconstruction government until it regained its full status as a state in 1876.

To help you get a start on seeing their vast state, Texans maintain 11 different tourist bureaus where counselors will provide you with up-to-date travel information. If you're into amateur archaeology, you might want to visit Monahans Sandhills State Park, near Odessa, where a number of Indian relics and prehistoric animal bones have been found. In Big Bend National Park, you'll find a variety of unusual rock formations as well as three scenic canyons carved by the Rio Grande. Of course, Big Texas is also synonymous with Big Oil; and if you want to get some idea of how extensive the commitment to oil can be, visit Kilgore, in the eastern part of the state. Here, more than 300 working wells are spaced throughout the town. And if you're curious about what happens to that oil after it leaves the ground, stop off at one of the state's many refineries and take a guided tour.

Cattle and oil are the two things most responsible for the economic development of Texas, but the state is diversifying into other forms of industry. Cotton, wheat and corn are important crops, and manufacturing includes machinery, motor vehicles, ships and chemicals. In recent years, Houston has become famous for the Lyndon B. Johnson Space Center, which serves as control headquarters for the space shots launched from Cape Canaveral.

Highlight

The Alamo

When his makeshift fort was besieged by a Mexican army of 3,000 men, Colonel William Travis issued a terse communique to his Commander-in-Chief: "Do hasten on aid to me as rapidly as possible," he urged Sam Houston, "as from the superior number of the enemy, it will be impossible for us to keep them out much longer. Give me help, oh my Country!"

But help never came. And on the 13th day of siege — March 6, 1836 — General Antonio Lopez de Santa Anna hurled 1,800 men against the Alamo's 183 defenders. Twice the Mexicans charged; twice the Texans sent them reeling. But now Santa Anna unleashed his reserves — some 1,000 grenadiers and *Zapadores* — and to the assassin call of *Dequello,* they stormed the Alamo's northern postern, breached the southwest palisade, then poured into the plaza, where they rampaged room-to-room until the last Texan had fallen.

"It was but a small affair," Santa Anna would say, as he strolled through the smoking plaza searching for the body of William Travis. But he was wrong. Texas had a war cry now — and it would crush him six weeks hence at San Jacinto.

—PJF

Open year-round, Monday to Saturday and holidays, 9 a.m. to 5:30 p.m.; Sunday, 10 a.m. to 5:30 p.m. Free. San Antonio, off Interstate 37.

State Offices

Tourism
Texas Tourist Development Agency
Box 12008
Capital Station
Austin, Texas 78711
(512) 475-4326

State Police
Department of Public Safety
Austin, Texas 78773
(512) 452-0331

Radio Stations

Amarillo
KIXZ 940 (AM)
KPUR 1440 (AM)
Dallas
KLIF 1190 (AM)
KMGC 102.9 (FM)
El Paso
KHEY 690 (AM)
KINT 97.5 (FM)
Fort Worth
WBAP 820 (AM)
KTXQ 102.1 (FM)
Houston
KULF 790 (AM)
KXYZ 1320 (AM)
KLOL 101.1 (FM)
KRYL 93.7 (FM)

Texas Points of Interest and Attractions

Alamo Village Vacationland and Movieland. A replica of San Antonio during the Battle of the Alamo in 1836, constructed for the motion picture *The Alamo.* Attractions include stagecoach and horseback rides, live entertainment. Open June through September, daily, 9 a.m. to 8 p.m. Adults $3, children 6 to 11, $2. Brackettville, north off US-90.

Amarillo Garden Center. Gardens featuring a variety of floral displays and shows; peak bloom time is May through October. Open year-round, Monday to Friday, 9 a.m. to 5 p.m. Amarillo, off Interstate 40 (exit 65), at Coulter Drive.

Astrodome. The prototype for the modern domed stadium, featuring a span of 642 feet, maximum height of 218 feet, seating for up to 66,000 spectators; tours. Open year-round, daily, 9 a.m. to 5 p.m. Admission: $2.50 for everyone over seven years of age; parking $2. Houston, at junction of Interstate 610 and Kirby Drive.

Botanic Gardens. Plants include a variety of flowers, roses and shrubs; greenhouses. Open year-round, Monday to Friday, 8 a.m. to 4 p.m., 7:30 a.m. to sunset. Free. Fort Worth, off Interstate 20, at 3220 Botanic Garden Drive.

Brazos Queen. An old-fashioned sternwheeler offering two-hour narrated excursions on the Brazos River; dinner and evening cruises. Season: April through September 5, daily. Waco, off Interstate 35 at Fort Fisher exit. (817) 752-5800.

Cascade Caverns. Caverns approximately one-third of a mile in length, 140 feet below the surface; waterfall, fascinating rock formations, excellent lighting effects. Open April through September, daily, 9 a.m. to 6 p.m.; remainder of year, 9 a.m. to 5 p.m. Adults $3.50, children 6 to 12, $1.75. Boerne, off Interstate 10, on Cascade Caverns Road.

Caverns of Sonora. Colorful and unusual rock formations viewed from a one-mile trail; tours, campground. Open year-round, daily, 8 a.m. to 6 p.m. Adults $4, children 6 to 11, $3. Sonora, off Interstate 10, on Cavern Road.

Dallas Theater Center. The only theater building designed by Frank Lloyd Wright, housing a repertory company and student groups from Trinity University graduate school; tours. Open year-round, daily, except Wednesday. Dallas, 3636 Turtle Creek Boulevard.

Don Harrington Discovery Center. A multi-media planetarium with changing presentations and exhibits. Open year-round, daily, 9 a.m. to 3 p.m. Adults

$1.50, students $1. Amarillo, off US-66 and Interstate 40 Business Loop.

Douglas MacArthur Academy. A 3,500-square-foot mural and large electric map of MacArthur's Pacific campaigns highlight this facility, which also presents exhibits depicting the evolution of Western Civilization; guided tours. Open year-round, daily; closed during school vacation period. Free. Brownwood, on Howard Payne University campus, at Austin and Coggin Streets.

Greer Island Nature Center. A wildlife refuge and nature center featuring several nature trails. Open year-round, daily. Free. Fort Worth, off State Route 199.

Houston Arboretum. A 265-acre arboretum and botanical gardens with numerous species of shrubs and trees; hiking trails, botanical hall. Open May through September, daily, 8:30 a.m. to 8 p.m.; remainder of the year, 8:30 a.m. to 6 p.m. Houston, in Memorial Park at 4501 Woodway Drive.

Heritage Garden Village. A living museum of pioneer life, featuring an extensive collection of pioneer artifacts, original buildings and a mantel clock five stories high. Open year-round, daily, 9 a.m. to 6 p.m. Adults $1.50, children 6 to 12, 75 cents. Woodville, 1¾ miles west on US-190.

Inner Space Cavern. A cave discovered in 1963 during the construction of Interstate 35; special sound and light effects, display of prehistoric relics taken from the cavern. Open Memorial Day through Labor Day, daily, 9 a.m. to 6 p.m. Adults $5, children 5 to 12, $2.50. Georgetown, on Interstate 35.

International Helium Centennial Time Columns Monument. A 60-foot stainless steel structure commemorating the discovery of helium in 1868; exhibits feature the uses of helium. Open year-round, daily. Amarillo, Interstate 40 at Nelson Street.

John Fitzgerald Kennedy Memorial. A white concrete cenotaph erected by the people of Dallas in tribute to the President who was slain in 1963. Designed as a place of meditation, it has walls to shut out the outside world, but is open at the top. Dallas, Main and Market Streets.

King Ranch. Visitors may tour the headquarters area of the famous King Ranch, an 823,400-acre operation that is the home of Santa Gertrudis cattle — the first species to originate in the United States; feeding pens, show pens, auction ring, quarterhorses. Open year-round, daily. Free. Kingsville, off State Route 141.

Lyndon B. Johnson Space Center. A research and development center for the National Aeronautics and Space Administration, this is the focal point for the country's manned space flight program. Information center includes displays of craft that have flown in space, photos, paintings, moon rocks, lunar rover and lunar module. Open year-round, daily, 9 a.m. to 4 p.m. Free. Houston, off Interstate 45, on NASA Road.

Lone Star. An outdoor drama based on the battle led by Sam Houston that won Texas' independence from Mexico. *Annie Get Your Gun* is performed on alternate nights. Season: Memorial Day through Labor Day, Tuesday to Sunday, 8:30 p.m. Admission: reserved seats $4 and $5, general admission $3, children 2 to 12, $2. Galveston, 12 miles southwest on Seawall Boulevard, in amphitheater. (713) 737-3442.

Lone Star Brewery. Tours of brewery include the Buckhorn Hall of Horns. Open year-round, Monday to Thursday. San Antonio, 600 Lone Star Boulevard.

Municipal Rose Garden. One of the largest rose gardens in the country. Open year-round, daily, 8 a.m. to 5 p.m. Free. Tyler, West Front Street.

Natural Bridge Caverns. This cave features a number of noteworthy formations, such as the "fried eggs" and "king's throne."

Open year-round, daily, 10 a.m. to 4 p.m. Adults $3.50, children 3 to 11, $2.50. San Antonio, off Interstate 35, on Natural Bridge Caverns Road.

Paseo Del Rio. This river walk provides a pleasant stroll past craft shops, art galleries and restaurants along an area that has been transformed by urban renewal into a prime attraction. Open year-round, daily. San Antonio, off Commerce and Market Streets.

Pearl Brewery. This brewery doesn't offer plant tours, but it does feature an Old West room that is a replica of Judge Roy Bean's Jersey Lily Saloon, complete with a collection of Bowie knives and Winchester rifles. Open January 1 through October, Monday to Friday, 10 a.m. to 4 p.m. San Antonio, on Pearl Parkway.

Sierra de Cristo Rey. A shrine on the Mexican border that includes a huge statue of Christ and a footpath with 14 stations of the cross that will take you up the mountainside to the summit. *NOTE:* Climb is steep and requires at least one hour. Open year-round. El Paso, off Interstate 10 (Anapra exit).

Tramway. This tram provides a scenic ride to the 5,622-foot summit of Mount Franklin's Ranger Peak, from which you can view Mexico and three states. Open year-round, daily, noon to 6 p.m. Adults $1.50, children under 12, 75 cents. El Paso, at Alabama and McKinley Streets.

Treasure Isle Tour Train. A tour of the major points of interest in Galveston in an open-car train; 17 miles, 1½ hours. Season: year-round, daily (weather permitting). Galveston, Seawall Boulevard and 21st Street. Adults $2.50, children 3 to 12, $1. (713) 765-9564.

USS Texas. A veteran of two world wars, this famous battlewagon now welcomes tourists aboard. Open year-round, daily, 10 a.m. to 5 p.m. Port Arthur, southwest, off State Route 87, in San Jacinto Battleground Park.

Viva! El Paso! A musical history of El Paso and its four cultures — Mexican, Spanish, Indian and Western. Season: July through August, Wednesday to Saturday, 8:30 p.m. Adults $2, children under 12, $1. El Paso, 2½ miles north in McKelligon Canyon.

Highlight

San Marcos

San Marcos calls itself "the most exciting river city in Texas," and most visitors agree that it lives up to its billing. For in and around San Marcos you'll find Aquarena Springs, Wonder World, the clear waters of the San Marcos River and mammoth Canyon Lake — a paradise for water skiers, sailors and fishermen. San Marcos is also the home of Southwest Texas State University (the alma mater of Lyndon B. Johnson), and hosts the annual Chilympiad, Texas' own state chili cookoff, which draws huge crowds on the third weekend in September.

Aquarena Springs. An oasis for family recreation, this unique attraction features a Submarine Theater with regular underwater shows, glass-bottom boats, the 250-foot Gyro Tower Swiss Sky Ride, Hanging Gardens and Texana Village, a re-created old western town. An excellent inn and restaurant adjoin the park.

Wonder World. A spectacular underground cavern is the central attraction of this complex, which includes a 7½-acre Wildlife Park, a bewildering Anti-Gravity House, a rock shop and the Texas Tower, which offers a panoramic view of the surrounding hill country.

—PJF

For more information on the fun to be had in San Marcos, write: Tourist Development Department, PO Box 2310, San Marcos, Texas 78666.

Texas State Parks

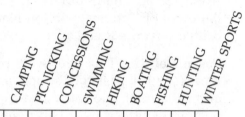

Park	Location	CAMPING	PICNICKING	CONCESSIONS	SWIMMING	HIKING	BOATING	FISHING	HUNTING	WINTER SPORTS
Abilene	*Abilene. Off US-84.*	•	•		•	•		•		
Atlanta	*Atlanta. Off US-59.*	•	•		•	•	•	•		
Balmorhea	*Balmorhea. Off US-290.*	•	•		•					
Bastrop	*Bastrop. Off State Route 21.*	•	•	•	•			•		
Bentsen—Rio Grande Valley	*Mission. Off US-83.*	•	•		•					
Blanco	*Blanco. Off US-281.*	•	•		•			•		
Bonham	*Bonham. Off State Route 78.*	•	•		•		•	•		
Brazos Island	*Brownsville. Off State Route 48.*	•	•		•			•		
Buescher	*Smithville. Off State Route 71.*	•	•					•		
Caddo Lake	*Marshall. Off State Route 43.*	•	•			•	•	•		
Cleburne	*Cleburne. Off US-67.*	•	•		•	•	•	•		
Daingerfield	*Daingerfield. On State Route 49.*	•	•	•	•	•	•	•		
Davis Mountains	*Fort Davis. Off State Route 118.*	•	•		•	•				•
Eisenhower	*Denison. Off State Route 75A.*	•	•	•	•	•	•	•		
Falcon	*Falcon. Off US-83.*	•	•	•	•	•	•	•		
Fort Griffin	*Albany. Off US-180.*	•	•			•		•		
Galveston Island	*Galveston. On US-75.*				•		•	•		
Garner	*Concan. Off US-83.*	•	•	•	•	•	•	•		
Goose Island	*Rockport. Off State Route 35.*	•	•		•		•	•		
Huntsville	*Huntsville. Off Interstate 45.*	•	•	•	•	•	•	•		
Indianola	*Port Lavaca. Off State Route 316.*	•	•		•	•	•	•		
Inks Lake	*Burnet. Off State Route 29.*	•	•	•		•	•	•		
Kerrville	*Kerrville. Off State Route 16.*	•	•		•	•	•	•		
Lake Arrowhead	*Wichita. On US-281.*		•		•	•	•	•		
Lake Brownwood	*Brownwood. Off State Route 279.*	•	•	•	•	•	•	•		
Lake Colorado City	*Colorado City. On Interstate 20.*	•	•		•	•	•	•		
Lake Corpus Christi	*Mathis. Off State Route 359.*	•	•		•	•	•	•		
Lake Somerville	*Brenham. On State Route 36.*	•	•		•		•	•		
Lake Whitney	*Whitney. Off State Route 22.*	•	•	•	•		•	•		
Lockhart	*Lockhart. Off US-183.*	•	•	•	•			•		
Lyndon B. Johnson	*Johnson City. Off US-281.*		•			•		•		
Mackenzie	*Lubbock. Off US-82.*	•	•	•	•			•		
Martin Dies, Jr.	*Woodville. On US-190.*	•	•	•	•		•	•		
Meridian	*Meridian. Off State Route 22.*	•	•		•	•		•		
Monahans Sandhills	*Monahans. Off US-80.*	•	•	•		•				
Mother Neff	*Moody. On State Route 236.*	•	•			•		•		
Palmetto	*Luling. Off US-183.*	•	•			•		•		
Palo Duro Canyon	*Canyon. Off US-87.*	•	•	•		•				
Possum Kingdom	*Caddo. Off US-180.*	•	•		•	•	•	•		
Stephen F. Austin	*Sealy. Off Interstate 10.*	•	•	•		•	•	•		
Tyler	*Tyler. Off State Route 64.*	•	•	•	•	•	•	•		

Texas State Forests

Forest	Location	CAMPING	PICNICKING	CONCESSIONS	SWIMMING	HIKING	BOATING	FISHING	HUNTING	WINTER SPORTS
Fairchild	*Rusk. Off US-84.*	•	•		•			•		
Jones	*Conroe. Off Interstate 75.*	•	•		•	•		•		
Siecke	*Kirbyville. Off US-96.*	•	•			•		•		

For more information on Texas state parks and forests, contact: *Parks and Wildlife Department, 4200 Smith School Road, Austin, Texas 78744, (512) 475-4888.*

Southwestern Region Calendar of Events

Spring
(March, April, May)

Arizona

Annual Scottscale "Arts Festival 10." March, Scottsdale.
Tombstone Heritage Days. March, Tombstone.
Annual "Jailbird" Square and Round Dance Festival. March, Yuma.
Stagecoach Days. March, Maricopa.
Annual Winter Arts and Crafts Fair. March, Tucson.
"Where the Hell is Benson?" Days. Rodeo. March, Benson.
Butterfield Stage Days. March, Gila Bend.
Aerospace and Arizona Days, Davis Monthan Air Force Base. March, Tucson.
Tucson Festival. April, Tucson.
Annual Plant Sale, Desert Botanical Gardens. April, Phoenix.
Annual Whoopee Daze. April, Tolleson.
Fiesta de los Ninos. April, Tucson.
Frontier Town Celebration. Rodeo, parade. April, Cave Creek/Carefree.
Annual Arizona Bluegrass Festival. April, Phoenix.
Annual Boyce Thompson Arboretum Plant Sale. April, Superior.
Celebration of Spring. April, Sedona.
Annual Open Rodeo. April, Superior.
Fiesta de la Placita. April, Tucson.
Canyon Day All-Indian Rodeo. April, Whiteriver.
Hiking Day. April, Chiracahua National Monument.
Desert Caballeros Trail Ride. Men only. April, Wickenburg.
London Bridge Regatta. April, Lake Havasu City.
Annual Two Flags Festival of the Arts. April, Douglas.
Annual Pioneer Day Celebration and Barbecue. April, Peoria.
Annual Old Congress Days. April, Congress.
Western Swing Festival. May, Old Tucson.
Loggers Festival. May, Alpine.
Cinco de Mayo Celebrations. May, Phoenix, Tucson, Scottsdale and border towns.
Zonta Home Tour. May, Prescott.
Greek Festival. May, Phoenix.
Old Miner's Day. May, Chloride.
Fiesta Days Parade. May, Maryvale.
Annual Airstream Caravan. May, Globe.
Wild Burro Barbecue Days. May, Bullhead City.
Annual Yarnell Daze. May, Yarnell.
Trout Days, Sunrise Lake. May, McNary.

New Mexico

Annual San Felipe Feast Day. May, San Felipe Pueblo.
Coming of the Rivermen. May, Cochiti Pueblo.
Annual Rose Festival. May, Tularosa.
Annual Spring Arts and Crafts Fair. May, Farmington.
Annual Ralph Edwards Fiesta and Sheriff's Posse Arena Suicide Race. Old-time fiddlers contest. May, Truth Or Consequences.
Annual El Cinco de Mayo Festival. May, Las Vegas.
Annual San Ysidro Fiesta. May, Taos Pueblo.

Annual Memorial Day Square Dance. May, Red River.

Annual Gila-Fort Bayard Open Trail Run. May, Bayard.

Annual May Fair Arts and Crafts Festival. May, Cloudcroft.

Annual Four Corners Hot-Air Balloon Rally, La Plata Canyon. May, Farmington.

Annual Santa Rosa Day Celebration. Arts and crafts, Little Miss Rosebud contest, street dance, stock car show, barbecue, fishing contests. May, Santa Rosa.

Annual Open Gymkana. Equestrian track and field events. May, Silver City.

Oklahoma

Soul Bazaar. Exhibits, fashion shows, baby contest, queen pageant. March, Oklahoma City.

Waurika Rattlesnake Hunt. April, Waurika.

Azalea Festival. April, Muskogee.

Cimarron Territory Celebration. World Champion Cow Chip Throwing Contest; rodeo. April, Beaver.

Eighty-Niner Day Celebration. Celebration of the land run of 1889. April, Guthrie.

Pioneer Day Celebration. April, Okemah.

Mangum Rattlesnake Derby. Prizes for the longest, shortest and fattest snakes; carnival, flea market. April, Mangum.

Waynoka Rattlesnake Hunt. April, Waynoka.

Oklahoma City Festival of the Arts. April, Oklahoma City.

Kolache Festival. Czechoslavakian celebration. April, Prague.

No Man's Land Pioneer Days Celebration. April, Guymon.

Canton Lake Walleye Rodeo. May, Canton.

Strawberry Festival. May, Stilwell.

Rooster Day Celebration. May, Broken Arrow.

Durant Western Days. May, Durant.

Bigheart Day. Parade, barbecue, fiddlers contest. May, Barnsdall.

Italian Festival. May, McAlester.

Santa Fe Trail Daze. Annual pioneer festival that includes a tour of the Black Mesa area. May, Boise City.

Texas

Historic Homes Tour. March, Brenham.

Recreational Vehicle Show. March, Corpus Christi.

Home and Garden Pilgrimage. March, San Antonio.

Tyler County Dogwood Festival. March, Woodville.

Bluebonnet Days. April, Kenedy.

East Texas Country Fair. Crafts, chili cookoff. April, Nacogdoches.

Miss Waxahachie Pageant. April. Waxahachie.

Rattlesnake Roundup. April, Freer.

Winedale Spring Festival and Craftsman's Exhibit. April, Round Top.

Dogwood Fiesta. Arts and crafts, barbecue, trail ride. April, Quitman.

Fine and Folk Arts Festival. April, Athens.

Spring Pilgrimage. Homes tours. April, Calvert.

Prairie Dog Chili Cookoff. April, Grand Prairie.

Azalea Trail. April, Jasper.

Recreational Vehicle Show and Flea Market. April, Jasper.

San Jacinto Week. April, Pasadena.

Flower Show and Garden Pilgrimage. April, Chappell Hill.

Junior Rodeo. April, Bridgeport.

Fiesta San Antonio. Band concert, barbecue, parade. April, San Antonio.

Reeking Regatta on Buffalo Bayou. April, Houston.

Strawberry Festival. April, Poteet.

Neches River Festival. April, Beaumont.

Spring Festival. Exhibits, shows, tours. April, Weatherford.

Sylvan Beach Festival. April, La Porte.

Wildflower Trails. Foods, crafts, country store. April, Avinger/Hughes Springs/Linden.

State Festival of Ethnic Cultures. April, Ballinger.

Ham Radio Swap Meet. April, Brownfield.

Blessing of the Fleet. April, Freeport.

Home Beautiful Tour. April, Port Arthur.
Bluebonnet Trails, April, Brenham.
Cinco de Mayo Celebration. May, Del Rio.
Little Britches Rodeo. May, Cleburne.
Cinco de Mayo Celebration. May, Hondo.
Strawberry Festival. Foods, crafts, plants. May, Dickinson.
National Polka Festival. May, Ennis.
Fish Day. May, Seymour.
Chisholm Trail Roundup. May, Lockhart.
Pioneer Roundup. May, Plainview.
Community Barbecue. May, Bellville.
Powwow Festival. May, Port Neches.
Magnolia Homes Tour. May, Columbus.
Laguna Gloria Art Fiesta. May, Austin.
Bromeliad Flower Show. May, Houston.
Annual Folk Festival. May, Kerrville.
Old Fiddlers Reunion. May, Athens.

Summer
(June, July, August)

Arizona

Annual White Mountain Standard Quarterhorse Show. June, Show Low.
Cedar Creek All-Indian Powwow and Rodeo. June, Cedar Creek.
Annual Sheriff's Posse Roundup. June, Globe.
Mayer Days. Parade, barbecue, western events. June, Mayer.
Annual Old-Timers Picnic. June, Casa Grande.
Mile-High Square Dance Festival. June, Prescott.
Fiesta de los Flores. June, Morenci.
Western Trail Days. June, Sedona.
Indian and Antique Festival. June, Payson.
Big Innertube Race. June, Parker.
Old-Time Country Music Festival. June, Payson.
Seven-Mile All-Indian Rodeo. June, Whiteriver.
Fiesta de los Artes. June, Sedona.
Founder Days Rodeo. June, Taylor.
Cha-Be-Tooe Roundup and Indian Dances. June, Whiteriver.
Hopi Indian Craftsmen's Show. June, Flagstaff.
Annual All-Indian Powwow. Parade, dances, rodeos. June, Flagstaff.
All-Western Day. July, Patagonia.
Fourth of July Community Celebration. July, Yuma.
Cedar Creek Memorial Rodeo. July, Cedar Creek.
White Mountain Square Dance Festival. July, Show Low.
Pioneer Days. July, Lakeside.
Canyon Day All-Indian Rodeo. July, Canyon Day.
Annual Sawdust Festival. July, Payson.
Annual Ceremonial Dances. August, Hopi Indian Reservation (dates and locations are announced about 10 days prior to ceremony; photos not permitted.)
Annual Mountaineers Square and Round Dance Festival. August, Flagstaff.
All-Police Rodeo. August, Prescott.
Cucumber Festival Parade and Rodeo. August, Taylor.

New Mexico

Annual June Music Festival. June, Albuquerque.
Annual Miss Hobbs Beauty Pageant. June, Hobbs.
Annual Craft Exhibition. June, Tucumcari.
Annual Pioneer Days and Rodeo. Parade, beauty pageant. June, Clovis.
San Antonio Feast Day. June, Sandia/San Ildefonso, Santa Clara/Taos.
Annual Old Fort Days. June, Fort Sumner.
Annual Angel Fire Regatta. June, Eagle Nest.
Annual Indian Capital Amateur Rodeo. June, Gallup.
Annual New Mexico Arts and Crafts Fair. June, Albuquerque.
Annual San Juan Feast Day. June, San Juan/Taos Pueblos.
Annual San Pedro Feast Day. June, San Felipe/Acoma Pueblos.
Annual July Show. June to July, Silver City.
Annual Torrance County Sheriff's Posse Ride. June, Albuquerque.
Bluegrass Festival. June, Red River.
Annual Summer Exhibition. July, Albuquerque.

Annual Fourth of July Rodeo and Barbecue. July, Clayton.
Annual Maverick Rodeo. July, Cimarron.
Annual Fourth of July Fiesta. Music, parade, fireworks. July, Las Vegas.
Annual Aztec Fiesta Days. Old-time carnival, mariachi band, parade, sidewalk sale, burning of Old Man Gloom. July, Aztec.
Annual Miss New Mexico Beauty Pageant. July, Hobbs.
Annual Rodeo de Santa Fe. July, Santa Fe.
Annual Fiesta de Taos. July, Taos.
Annual Tri-State Arts and Crafts Exhibit. July, Carlsbad.
Annual Summer Exhibition. August, Albuquerque.
Annual Arts Festival, Fuller Lodge. August, Los Alamos.
Annual Santo Domingo Feast Day. Big celebration with more than 500 dancers. August, Santo Domingo Pueblo.
Lea County Fair and Rodeo. August, Lovington.
Annual Old-Timer's Day and Rodeo. August, Melrose.
Annual San Antonio Feast Day. August, Laguna Pueblo.
Anniversary Bosque Farms Fair. Parade, rodeo, games. August, Belen.
Annual Hot-Air Balloon Festival. August, Eagle Nest.
Annual Connie Mack World Series Baseball Tournament, Ricketts Park. August, Farmington.
Annual Santa Fe Rose Show. August, Santa Fe.
Annual Socorro Fair and Rodeo. August, Socorro.

Oklahoma

Love County Frontier Days. June, Marietta.
Sequoyah Intertribal Powwow. June, Elk City.
Wagoner Lake Festival. June, Wagoner.
Belle Starr Festival. June, Wilburton.
Hub City Powwow. Indian dance ceremonies, authentic arts and crafts. June, Clinton.
Pioneer Reunion and Rodeo. July, Mangum.
Shawnee Old Santa Fe Days. July, Shawnee.
Tulsa Powwow. July, Tulsa.
Round Spring Park Bluegrass Festival. July, Disney.
Oklahoma City Indian Hills Powwow. July, Oklahoma City.
All-Night Singing Under the Stars. Gospel singers serenade from 7 p.m. to early morning. July, Holdenville.
Huckleberry Festival. July, Jay.
Oklahoma Steam Threshers Association Show. August, Pawnee.
Peach Festival. August, Porter.
Kihekah Steh Powwow. August, Skiatook.
Watermelon Festival. August, Rush Springs.
American Indian Exposition. August, Anadarko.
World Championship Watermelon Seed Spitting Contest. August, Weatherford.
Frontier Days Celebration. August, Cache.
Oklahoma State Prison Rodeo. Professional cowboys and prison inmates perform. August, McAlester.

Texas

Leather Tom-Tom Festival and Rodeo. June, Yoakum.
Cavalcade of Wheels. Custom car show. June, Victoria.
Big Thicket Day. June, Saratoga.
Annual Gingerbread Trail. June, Waxahachie.
Hardcourt Tennis Tourney. June, Corpus Christi.
Bach Festival Week. June, Victoria.
Championship Muzzle Loaders Rifle Meet. June, Brady.
Ye Olde Summertime Fair. June, Odessa.
Houston County Birthday Party. June, Crockett.
Rodeo Week. June, Gladewater.
Jazz Festival. June, Houston.
Cowboy Reunion and Rodeo. June, Big Spring.
Fort Griffin Fandangle. June, Albany.

Petticoat Fishing Tourney. June, Port Aransas.
Kerr County Fair. June, Kerrville.
July Jubilee. June to July, Brady.
Shakespeare Festival. June, Odessa.
Jim Bowie Days Rodeo and Celebration. June, Bowie.
Watermelon Thump. June, Luling.
Fishing Fiesta and Shrimp Festival. June, Freeport.
Championship Pinto Bean Cookoff. June, Kingsville.
Texas Championship Billfish Tourney. June, Port Aransas.
Independence Day Festival. July, Odessa.
Cowboy Reunion and Rodeo. July, Stamford.
Old-Time Fiddlers Contest. Fireworks. July, Amarillo.
Lake Meredith Festival. Swimming, musket shoot. July, Borger.
Fourth of July Celebration. July, Hempstead.
International Music Festival. July, Round Top.
Market Day. July, Wimberley.
Annual Jazz Festival. July, Corpus Christi.
Shakespeare Festival. July, Dallas.
Old Settlers Reunion Rodeo. July, Seymour.
Jubilee Week. July, Wylie.
Old Settlers Rodeo. July, Childress.
Black-Eyed Pea Jamboree. July, Athens.
National Texas-Style Domino Tourney. July, Big Spring.
Peach and Melon Festival. July, De Leon.
Annual Deep-Sea Roundup. July, Port Aransas.
International Armadillo Confab and Exposition. August, Victoria.
Blessing of the Shrimp Fleet. August, Seabrook.
Pioneers and Old Settlers Reunion. Parade, music show, fiddlers contest. August, Alvarado.
Prazka Pout. Czech homecoming celebration. August, Praha/Flatonia.
Turtle Derby and Carnival. August, Freeport.
Forest Festival. Arts, crafts, home tours. August, Atlanta.
Gillespie County Fair. August, Fredericksburg.
St. Louis Day Celebration. Alsatian food. August, Castroville.
Bluegrass Festival. August, Kerrville.
Oatmeal Festival. Barbecue, variety show, parade, foods, contests, dinner, gospel singing. August, Oatmeal/Bertram.

Fall
(September, October, November)

Arizona

Brewery Gulch Days. Fair and mine tours. September, Bisbee.
Labor Day Square Dance. September, Show Low.
Annual Mexican Independence Day Celebration. September, Phoenix/Tucson/border towns.
White Mountain Fall Festival. September, Pinetop/Lakeside.
White Mountain Apache Cowboy Association Rodeo. September, Whiteriver.
Indian Days. September, Parker.
Annual Arts, Crafts and Antique Show. September, Pinetop.
Annual Hays Ranch Calf Sale and Barbecue. September, Peeples Valley.
Arizona Old-Time Fiddlers Contest and Festival. September, Payson.
Western Navajo Fair. October, Tuba City.
London Bridge Square and Round Dance. October, Lake Havasu City.
Autumn Arts Festival. October, Sedona.
Fiesta Del Tlaquepaque. October, Sedona.
London Bridge Days. October, Lake Havasu City.
Annual Grand Canyon Bicycle Tour. October, Flagstaff.
Annual Mohave Gemstoners Gem and Art Show. October, Kingman.
London Bridge Marathon Boat Races. October, Lake Havasu City.
Annual "Helldorado Days" Celebration. October, Tombstone.
Scandinavian Day. October, Mesa.
Annual Harvest Time Arts and Crafts Fair. October, Tucson.

Annual Old Pueblo Lapidary and Gem Show. October, Tucson.

Annual Cowboy Artists of America Exhibition. October, Phoenix.

Annual Halloween Carnival. October, Buckeye.

Arizona State Fair. November, Phoenix.

Annual Papago Tribal Rodeo and Fair. November, Sells.

Annual Huachuca Mineral and Gem Club Fall Show. November, Sonoita.

Annual Festival of Thanksgiving. November, South Phoenix.

Annual Thunderbird Invitational Hot-Air Balloon Races. November, Glendale.

Annual Arizona Mobile Home and Travel Trailer Show. November, Phoenix.

Fall Festival. November, Cave Creek.

Havasu Gem Festival. November, Lake Havasu City.

Blessing of the Harvest Festival. November, Pioneer.

New Mexico

Annual Vaquero Days. Hot-air balloon race, arts and crafts, chili cookoff, beard growing contest, barbecue, fair, parade. September, Las Cruces.

Annual Chili Festival. September, Hatch.

Annual Pioneers Picnic. September, Bloomfield.

Annual Curry County Fair. September, Clovis.

Annual Art-In-The-Park. Flea market. September, Silver City.

Annual Northern Navajo Fair and Rodeo. September, Farmington.

Annual New Mexico State Fair. September, Albuquerque.

Annual Fiesta de Santa Fe. September, Santa Fe.

Annual LULAC Fiesta. Coronation, dancing, barbecue. September, Deming.

Annual Wildflower Show. September, Silver City.

Annual San Jose Feast Day. September, Laguna Pueblo.

Annual St. Elizabeth Feast Day. September, Laguna Pueblo.

Annual Ranch Fall Bird Migration Weekend. Warblers, sparrows, wrens, humming birds. September, Silver City.

Annual San Geronimo Feast Day. September, Taos Pueblo.

Annual Aspencade Festival. September, Red River.

Annual Taos Festival of the Arts. October, Taos.

Annual Greek Festival. October, Albuquerque.

Annual Mule-O-Rama. Mule races, barn dance, fiddlers contest, aspencade, parade, chuckwagon dinner. October, Ruidoso.

Annual International Hot-Air Balloon Fiesta. Over 200 balloons. October, Albuquerque.

Annual Klobase Barbecue. Bohemian sausage, cotton bale auction. October, Deming.

Annual St. Margaret Mary Feast Day. October, Laguna Pueblo.

Annual Doll and Miniature Fair. October, Albuquerque.

Oklahoma

KRMG Great Raft Race. Homemade rafts challenge a nine-mile course on the Arkansas River. September, Sand Springs/Tulsa.

Cattle Trails Festival. September, Elk City.

State Fair of Oklahoma. September, Oklahoma City.

Czech Festival. October, Yukon.

World's Richest Roping and Western Art Show. October, Chelsea.

National Finals Rodeo. November, Oklahoma City.

Texas

Fiesta de las Flores. September, El Paso.

Kimble Kounty Kow Kick. Arts and crafts, foods, fiddlers contest, chili cookoff. September, Junction.

Saltwater Fishing Rodeo. September, Port Arthur.

Labor Day Cowboy Horse Races. September, Bracketville.

Gem and Mineral Show. September, Houston.

Cotton Festival. September, Miles.
Septemberfest. September, Midland.
Town and Country Days Fair. September, Karnes City.
Pecan Festival. September, Groves.
International In-the-Water Boat Show. September, Seabrook.
Shrimporee and Benefit Auction. September, League City.
Sports, Camping and Vacation Show. September, Houston.
Community Fall Fair. September, Dublin.
Fiesta de la Paloma. September, Coleman.
Fall Festival on the Strand. September, Galveston.
Renaissance Festival. September, Magnolia.
State Fair of Texas. October, Dallas.
Texas Rose Festival. October, Amarillo.
Air Show. October, Harlingen.

Winter
(December, January, February)

Arizona
Annual Christmas Show. December, Cottonwood.
Here Comes Santa Claus Parade. December, Page.
Gomper's Winter Festival. December, Phoenix.
Annual Lighting of the Courthouse. December, Prescott.
Annual Verde Valley Christmas Invitational Exhibition and Sale. December, Jerome.
Annual Holiday Arts and Crafts Fair. December, Tucson.
Annual St. Francis Xavier Feast Day Celebration. December, Tucson.
Annual Festival of the Christmas Trees. December, Phoenix.
Annual Santa's Christmas Parade. December, Bullhead City.
Santa's Water Lane Parade. December, Bullhead City.
Fiesta del Sol Rodeo. December, Mesa.
Annual Rough Stock Calcutta. December, Wickenburg.
Fiesta Bowl Parade. December, Phoenix.
Festival of the Lights. December, Sedona.
Annual Hot-Air Balloon Races. January, Casa Grande.
Annual Apache Junction Gem and Mineral Show. January, Mesa.
Southern Arizona Square and Round Dance Festival. January, Tucson.
Annual Copper World Classic. January, Phoenix.
Ground Hog Breakfast. February, Snowflake.
Annual Gem and Hobby Powwow and Barbecue. February, Quartsite.
Annual Tucson Gem and Mineral Show. February, Tucson.
Alpine Sled Dog Races. February, Alpine.
Annual "CB" Radio Jamboree. February, Yuma.
Spring Rendezvous. February, Pioneer.
Dog Sled Races. February, Greer.

New Mexico
No major events.

Oklahoma
International Finals Rodeo. January, Tulsa.

Texas
Fat Stock Show and Rodeo. January, Fort Worth.
Citrus Fiesta. January, Mission.
Livestock Show and Rodeo. February, Houston.
Charro Days. Four-day pre-Lenten fiesta. February, Brownsville.

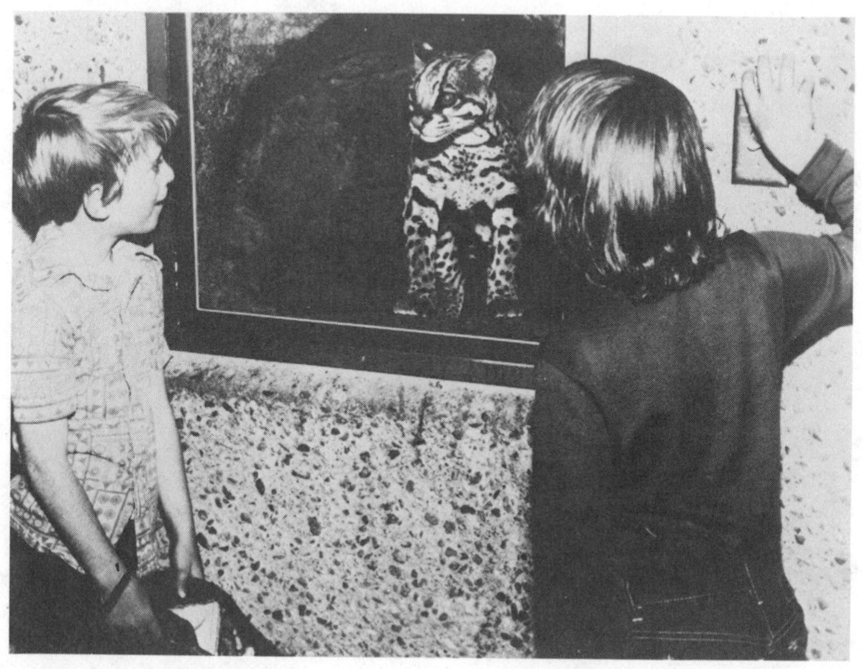

Visitors to the Arizona-Sonoma Desert Museum in Tucson view wild animals in their naturalistic habitats.

Tucson, Arizona's, Mission San Zavier Del Bac is known as the White Dove of the Desert (left) and has been in continual use since 1629. Old Tucson (above) captures the feeling of the Pioneer West with a stagecoach ride through the streets of the town.

Seattle
WASHINGTON
La Conner Washington
OREGON
Mt. Hood
Port Townsend Victorian Homes
NEVADA
Wheeler Peak
GAMBLING
CASINO
ASINO
Las Vegas and Reno
Bristlecone Pine

Fisherman's Wharf
GOLDEN GATE
CALIFORNIA
Knotts Berry Farm
Disneyland
Mission San Diego
San Simeon
Yosemite Half Dome
ALASKA
R. McKee
Mt. McKinley
Northern Lights
HAWAII

Western States

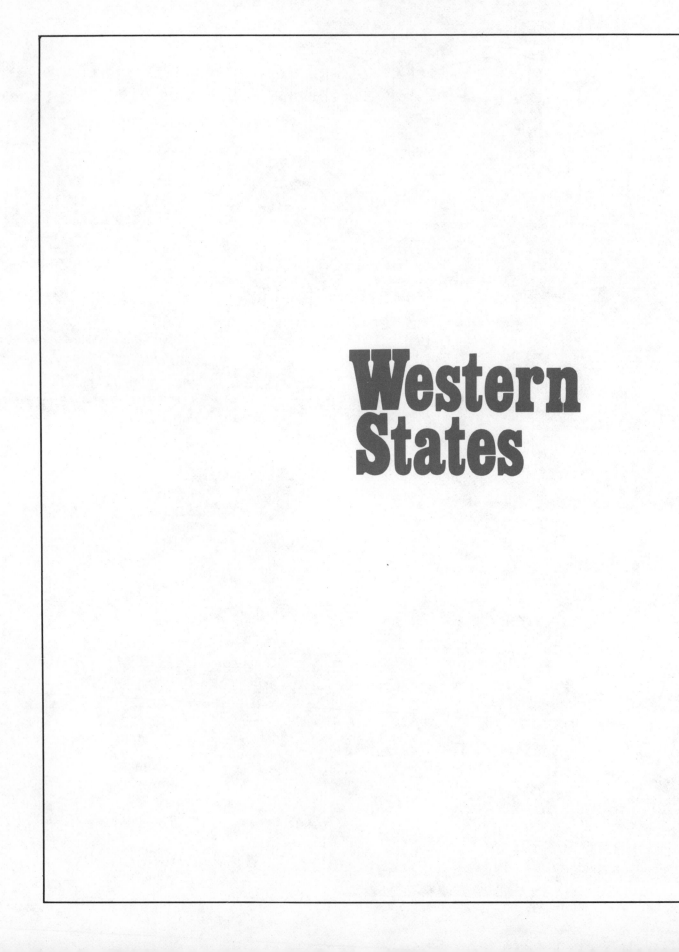

All but one of the states in this region are lapped by the waters of the Pacific Ocean, and each of the five states touched by the sea has a coastline that offers some of the most spectacular scenery to be found anywhere in the nation. In the Pacific Northwest, you'll find Oregon's rugged, cliff-lined coast and a Washington shore that offers a mixture of broad beaches, rocky outcroppings and the turbulent waters of the Columbia Bar. California's coastline stretches for nearly 1,300 miles, taking in the sandy beaches of the south, the breathtaking beauty of the Monterey Peninsula and the misty shores of redwood country. The Hawaiian coast is unmatched for its verdant, tropical splendor and the awesome surf to be found in areas like the Bonzai Pipeline. Alaska's shores are more forbidding than any of these, but one has only to travel the Inland Passage to discover that Alaska has one of the most beautiful coastlines in all of the Western states.

Inland, each of the Western states offers mountains to be admired and explored, and attractions as diverse as the Alaskan wilderness and the hills of Hollywood. For the sportsman, this region is a veritable paradise: Hunters will find excellent upland game shooting in the broad valleys, and a wide variety of big game can be stalked in the mountains and foothills; anglers can go after the big ones in ocean waters, or challenge the wily trout in clear mountain streams.

For those who like their excitement a little more civilized, there's much to be said for such cultural and entertainment centers as Seattle, Portland, San Francisco, Los Angeles and San Diego. And if it's "action" you crave, try the glittering cities of Nevada — Las Vegas, Reno, Tahoe — with their spectacular live shows and myriad games of chance.

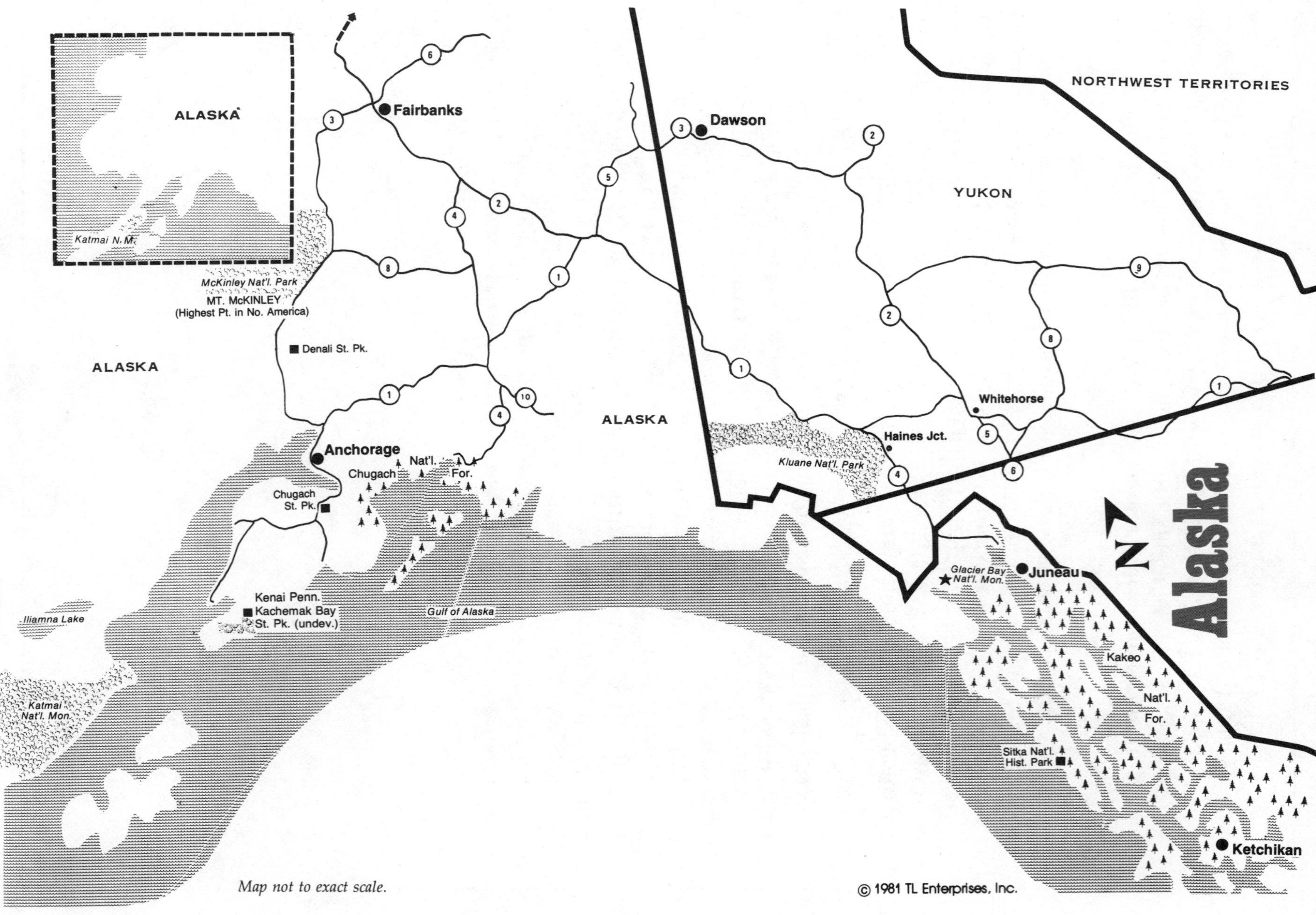

Alaska
ALASKA
Katmai N.M.
NORTHWEST TERRITORIES
Fairbanks
Dawson
YUKON
McKinley Nat'l. Park
MT. McKINLEY
(Highest Pt. in No. America)
Denali St. Pk.
ALASKA
ALASKA
Whitehorse
Haines Jct.
Kluane Nat'l. Park
Anchorage
Chugach Nat'l. For.
Chugach St. Pk.
Kenai Penn.
Kachemak Bay St. Pk. (undev.)
Gulf of Alaska
Iliamna Lake
Katmai Nat'l. Mon.
Glacier Bay Nat'l. Mon.
Juneau
Kakeo Nat'l. For.
Sitka Nat'l. Hist. Park
Ketchikan
Map not to exact scale.
© 1981 TL Enterprises, Inc.

Alaska

Alaska gets its name from the Eskimo word "Alayeska," meaning "The Great Land"—and never was a title more apt. For with 586,412 square miles of area (375 million acres), it is by far the largest state in the Union—so large, in fact, that it covers as many time zones as the lower 48 states; its 33,000-mile coastline is longer than that of the continental U.S.; its tallest mountain, 20,320-foot Mt. McKinley, is the highest peak in North America; and its Malaspina Glacier, alone, is nearly equal in size to the state of Rhode Island.

Commissioned by Russian Czar Peter the Great, Vitus Bering, a Danish sea captain and explorer, was the first white man to set foot on Alaskan soil, landing there on July 16, 1741. Though Bering perished on the return trip, his crew managed to reach Petropavlovsk with a valuable cargo of furs, including pelts of the sea otter, previously unknown in Asia or Europe. The rich fur trade prompted Russian colonization of Alaska and cruel exploitation of its resources and native Eskimos. For nearly a century the Russians, Americans and Europeans carried on a lively and highly profitable fur trade in Alaska, but by 1861 the cost of maintaining the Russian colony in Alaska began to outstrip the profits. For the Russians, the logical solution appeared to be the sale of the territory to the United States, and negotiations with U.S. Secretary of State William H. Seward finally led to a treaty for the purchase of Alaska in 1867 for $7,200.

At the time, the acquisition of Alaska was derisively termed "Seward's folly" and "Seward's icebox," as very few people recognized the economic and strategic value of the region. Within a few years, however, Alaska had a prosperous fishing industry,

Full name: State of Alaska
Origin of name: From Aleutian word "Alayeska."
Motto: North to the Future.
Nickname: The Great Land.
Capital: Juneau
Statehood: January 3, 1959 (49th state).
Population: 405,000 (ranks 49th).
Major Cities: Anchorage (161,020), Fairbanks (30,130).
Bird: Willow ptarmigan
Flower: Forget-Me-Not
Tree: Sitka spruce

Average daily temperatures by month

	Northwestern	Southeastern
Jan.	3.2 to -10.6	34.6 to 23.0
Feb.	3.3 to -11.8	39.6 to 27.0
Mar.	8.1 to - 9.1	41.8 to 27.5
Apr.	22.3 to 3.7	47.3 to 31.7
May	37.8 to 23.7	53.2 to 37.3
Jun.	49.6 to 37.3	57.1 to 43.4
Jul.	58.7 to 47.1	60.5 to 47.9
Aug.	55.9 to 45.4	61.5 to 48.5
Sept.	46.5 to 35.7	58.2 to 44.0
Oct.	28.7 to 18.5	50.5 to 37.4
Nov.	13.4 to 2.0	42.6 to 31.4
Dec.	2.6 to -10.3	37.7 to 27.6
Year	27.5 to 14.2	48.7 to 35.6

and the discovery of gold on Klondike Creek in 1896 led to a gold rush across Alaska. A favorable homestead act was passed by Congress in 1903, but development of the territory was hampered by conservation policies that prohibited the use of much of Alaska's resources. Ten years later, a new federal policy of leasing lands for exploitation eased the problem somewhat, and development proceeded at a more rapid pace. By World War II, when Japanese forces seized three of the Aleutian Islands, the strategic value of the territory became fully appreciated, and Alaska's isolation was ended by the army's construction of the Alaskan Highway and several airports. After the war, Alaskan voters declared in favor of statehood, but almost 15 years passed before Alaska was finally admitted as the 49th state on January 3, 1959.

Today, the discovery of oil on the North Slope and the Alaskan pipeline has spurred new growth for the state, but Alaskans have taken great pains to assure that this growth allows the preservation of much of Alaska's natural beauty. The state remains a vacation paradise, with 126 million acres recently set aside for 13 national parks, 21 wildlife refuges, two national forest wilderness areas and 112 wild and scenic rivers. In Alaska you'll find unsurpassed fishing and hunting, breathtaking scenery, remnants of the Russian occupation in towns like Sitka, and the fascinating culture and traditions of the native Indian tribes.

Oil, of course, has become Alaska's biggest industry in recent years, but fishing for salmon, shrimp, herring and halibut is still a significant part of the state's economy. Other important activities include coal mining, wood processing, military and government operations and a growing tourist trade.

State Offices

Tourism
Alaska Division of Tourism
Department of Economic Development
Pouch E-907
Juneau, Alaska 99811
(907) 465-2010

State Police
Alaska State Troopers
Juneau, Alaska 99811
(907) 465-4305

Radio Stations

Anchorage
KFQD 750 (AM)
KANC 1080 (AM)
KGOT 101 (FM)
Fairbanks
KFAR 660 (AM)
KIAK 970 (AM)
Juneau
KJNO 630 (AM)
KINY 800 (AM)

Alaska Points of Interest and Attractions

Alaskaland. A city-operated outdoor park featuring historical exhibits and artifacts from all over Alaska and wildlife native to the region. Fairbanks, on Airport Way between Peger Road and Moore Street.

Alaska Repertory Theater. Alaska's first performing arts organization. Plays are produced in both Anchorage and Fairbanks, and the company tours annually throughout Alaska. Anchorage, West Eighth Avenue.

Alaska Show and Sourdough Buffet. Entertainment in the Alaska Room, Anchorage-Westward Hilton, featuring Robert Service's most famous poems, together with films and songs that recall the pioneer gold rush days. Dinner show about $21 per person, show only, $8 per person. Anchorage, West 12th Avenue. (907) 278-3831.

Alaska Story. A multi-media, giant-screen presentation of the history of Alaska. Season: June through September, daily, 6:30 p.m., 8:30 p.m., 10:15 p.m. Juneau, Baranof Hotel.

Alaska Wild Berry Products. Jams, jellies, juices, sauces and syrups prepared from the wild berries of the Kenai Peninsula; tours of kitchen and processing plant. Open May 31 through September 6. Homer, in center of town.

Highlight

Alaska State Ferry

The state of Alaska operates a fleet of nine ferryliners that transport passengers and vehicles within southeast Alaska and within certain portions of central and southwest Alaska. The system also connects the Inside Passage communities of southeast Alaska with British Columbia and the state of Washington.

There are two separate route systems of the Alaska Marine Highway and they do not interconnect. The Southeast System operates from the two southern gateways of Seattle, Washington, and Prince Rupert, British Columbia. This system makes port calls on various Inside Passage communities, principally Ketchikan, Wrangell, Petersburg, Sitka, Juneau, Haines and Skagway, as well as several smaller communities via shuttle-service ferries. The Southwest System operates in Prince William Sound and in Cook Inlet. Service is also provided to seaside communities on the Kenai Peninsula and to Kodiak Island. Ferries on both the southeast and southwest systems operate year-round, with 25% discount in the "off-season," October through April.

The 1,130-mile voyage from Seattle through the Inside Passage to the northern turnaround port of Skagway takes four days. Express service between Seattle and Haines-Skagway is offered twice a week by the *M.V. Columbia* and the *M.V. Matanuska*. Other Southeast System ferries, among them the *M.V. Aurora, Chilkat, Le Conte, Malaspina* and *Taku* operate within the Alaska portion of the Inside Passage and connect with Prince Rupert, B.C., the other southern gateway city.

Travel by ferry is less costly than travel by cruise ship and allows greater flexibility in selecting an itinerary. There is no charge for stopping over in port while en route; you merely leave one ferry and board the next ferry sailing in the direction you wish to travel. You can travel as a foot passenger or drive aboard with your camper or motorhome. Most ferries have cabins which can be rented for the duration of the voyage. If you do not take cabin space, you can rest overnight in comfortable reclining deck chairs at no additional cost. Meals are available from either fast food service counters or from the ship's cafeteria. Many of your fellow passengers will be Alaskans, who take advantage of this economical way to travel within their home state.

Glacier-bound waterways host Alaska's three modern ferry vessels and provide motoring access to the state's "Panhandle" region. Schedules include stops at island communities and storied Gold Rush towns. As an added travel bonus, Alaska visitors may now elect to parallel much of Canada's Alaska Highway and cruise the Marine Highway route.

Burnt Paw Northland Specialties. Featuring sled dogs and dog mushing equipment; visitors are invited to view and photograph the various dogs and sleds used for freighting, trapping and racing. Other attractions include wildlife displays, furs, gifts, native crafts and paintings. Open year-round, daily, except Sunday. TOK, at mile 1314 off Alaska Highway.

Captain Cook Recreation Area. Offers fishing, waterfowl viewing, beachcombing and camping. Kenai, on North Kenai Road; access by vehicle or float plane. Leave the Sterling Highway at Soldotna and take the Kenai Spur Road to Kenai, then drive the North Kenai Road to the end.

Fur Seal Rookeries. The Pribilof Islands in the Bering Sea are breeding grounds for the largest herd of Pacific northern fur seals in the world (over 1¼ million), as well as a sanctuary for more than 100 million birds of 190 species. Pribilof Islands, reached by boat from several coastal points.

Gold Creek Salmon Bake. Alaska salmon barbecued over open alder-wood fire, salads, relish, bread, and beer, lemonade or coffee. All you can eat for $10 served every night from 5:30 p.m. to 9 p.m. Open June 1 through September 7. Juneau, by free bus from Baranof Hotel at 6 p.m., to Basin Road.

Gold Rush Minstrel Show. A cabaret-type dinner show, in the Latchstring Restaurant of the Baranof Hotel. Dinner served from 6 p.m. to 8 p.m.; show begins at 8:30 p.m.; reservations required. Approximately $16 per person, tax and tip included. Baranof Hotel, Juneau, Franklin Street. (907) 586-2660.

Independence Mine. This mine was the second-largest gold mine in Alaska, established in 1897 and closed in 1950; slated to become an Alaska State Historical Park. Palmer, located on Mile 23 of the Fishhook Road, northwest of Palmer.

Last Chance Players. The farcical melodrama *Delila's Dilemma* staged nightly in the Last Chance Opera House. Season: June 8 through September 4. Adults $4, children $2. Juneau, Basin Road. (907) 789-0123.

McNeil River State Bear Sanctuary. A controlled-access area and one of the most famous locations in North America for photographing brown/grizzly bear. Permits required for photographing bears may be obtained from Area Biologist, Alaska Division of Game, Box 37-DOT, King Salmon, Alaska 99613. (907) 246-3340. Located at mouth of McNeil River on west coast of Cook Inlet, 230 air miles southwest of Anchorage.

Naval Arctic Research Laboratory. Run by the University of Alaska, this facility also features native handicrafts, artifacts and scientific specimens. Barrow, four miles north.

New Orpheum Theater. Showings of award-winning Alaskan films by Juneau

A quiet cove, vast forests and magnificent snowcapped peaks are typical of the awesome beauty to be found in our 49th state.

An excursion boat gives visitors a closeup look at one of the massive ice floes that drift along the Alaskan coast.

film makers. Open May through September, daily, film at 2:15 p.m. Juneau, Marine Way.

"Northpole Alaska." A small community on the Richardson Highway (Alaska Route 4), about 14 miles east of Fairbanks, that specializes in Christmas gifts available at Santa Claus House. (907) 488-2200.

Old St. Nicholas Russian Orthodox Church. Vestments and icons in this chapel were brought to Alaska from the Soviet Union during the 1920s. Anchorage, 25 miles north, on Eklutna Village Road.

Portage Glacier. A daily tour bus will take you to the glacier where U.S. Forest Service naturalists interpret the features of Portage Valley, which includes four other glaciers; hiking trails, wildlife and hundreds of species of wildflowers. Season: May through September. Anchorage, 55 miles southeast, on Seward Highway.

Riverboat Discovery I and II. Authentic Alaskan stern-wheelers which make four-hour narrated cruises on the Chena and Tanana Rivers; Season: mid-May to mid-September, departure each afternoon. Fairbanks. (907) 497-6673.

Saint Nicholas Russian Orthodox Church. Built in 1894 and restored in 1977, this church is one of the oldest log buildings in Southeast Alaska and the first church built in Juneau. Church contains numerous artifacts and many interesting icons. Open May through September, daily. Juneau, 326 Fifth Street.

Skagway In The Days of '98. Historical comic-drama covering Skagway's early history; gambling for an Alaskan souvenir and dancing to '90s music. Open year-round, daily, 8 p.m. Adults $6, children $2. Skagway, in the Eagles Hall. (907) 983-2545.

Stern-wheeler Nenana. The last steamboat to offer passenger and freight service along the Yukon, Kuskokwim and Tanana Rivers, now restored and remodeled into a restaurant and Little Theater. Fairbanks.

Totem Bight. A community house and totem park with 13 totems situated on a point overlooking Tongass Narrows and reached by a short trail from the parking area. Open May through September, daily. Ketchikan, north, about 25 minutes on paved highway.

Selected Ferry Tariffs

FROM	Passenger	Average Size Car	Four-Berth Stateroom*	Travel Time/ Nautical Miles
Seattle to Skagway	$109.00	$374.00	$112.00	60 hrs/1090 mi
Prince Rupert to Ketchikan	15.00	46.00	31.00	6 hrs/103 mi
Prince Rupert to Juneau	54.00	149.00	59.00	24 hrs/354 mi
Prince Rupert to Skagway	71.00	187.00	69.00	33 hrs/453 mi
Ketchikan to Juneau	39.00	112.00	46.00	18 hrs/250 mi
Juneau to Haines	11.00	38.00	31.00	6½ hrs/77 mi
Juneau to Skagway	17.00	44.00	33.00	7½ hrs/94 mi
Seattle to Ketchikan	73.00	257.00	87.00	40 hrs/740 mi
Whittier to Valdez	27.00	51.00	not available	7 hrs/90 mi
Homer to Kodiak	22.00	66.00	38.00	11½ hrs/155 mi

*Staterooms are sold as a unit, not on a per-person basis. Hence the cost to each of four persons sharing a four-berth stateroom is $28 for the duration of the voyage.

Rates shown above were in effect during the summer of 1979 and are subject to change.

Ice floes are sculpted into a variety of shapes by the springtime sun that warms the Alaskan landscape.

Alaska State Parks

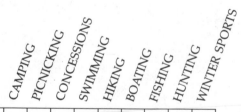

Park	Location	CAMPING	PICNICKING	CONCESSIONS	SWIMMING	HIKING	BOATING	FISHING	HUNTING	WINTER SPORTS
Byers Lake	*Cantwell. On State Route 3.*	•	•		•	•	•	•		
Chilkat	*Haines. On Haines Highway.*	•	•			•	•	•		
Denali	*Cantwell. On State Route 3.*	•	•							
Eagle River	*Eagle River. Off Alaska Parks Highway.*	•	•				•	•		
Kachemak Bay	*Seldovia. Off Sterling Highway on Kenai Peninsula.*	•	•				•	•		
Wood-Tikchik	*Dillingham. Must be reached by air.*	•	•				•	•		

Alaska has no state forests. For more information on Alaska state parks, contact, *Department of Natural Resources, Division of Parks, 619 Warehouse Avenue, Anchorage, Alaska 99501, (907) 274-4676.*

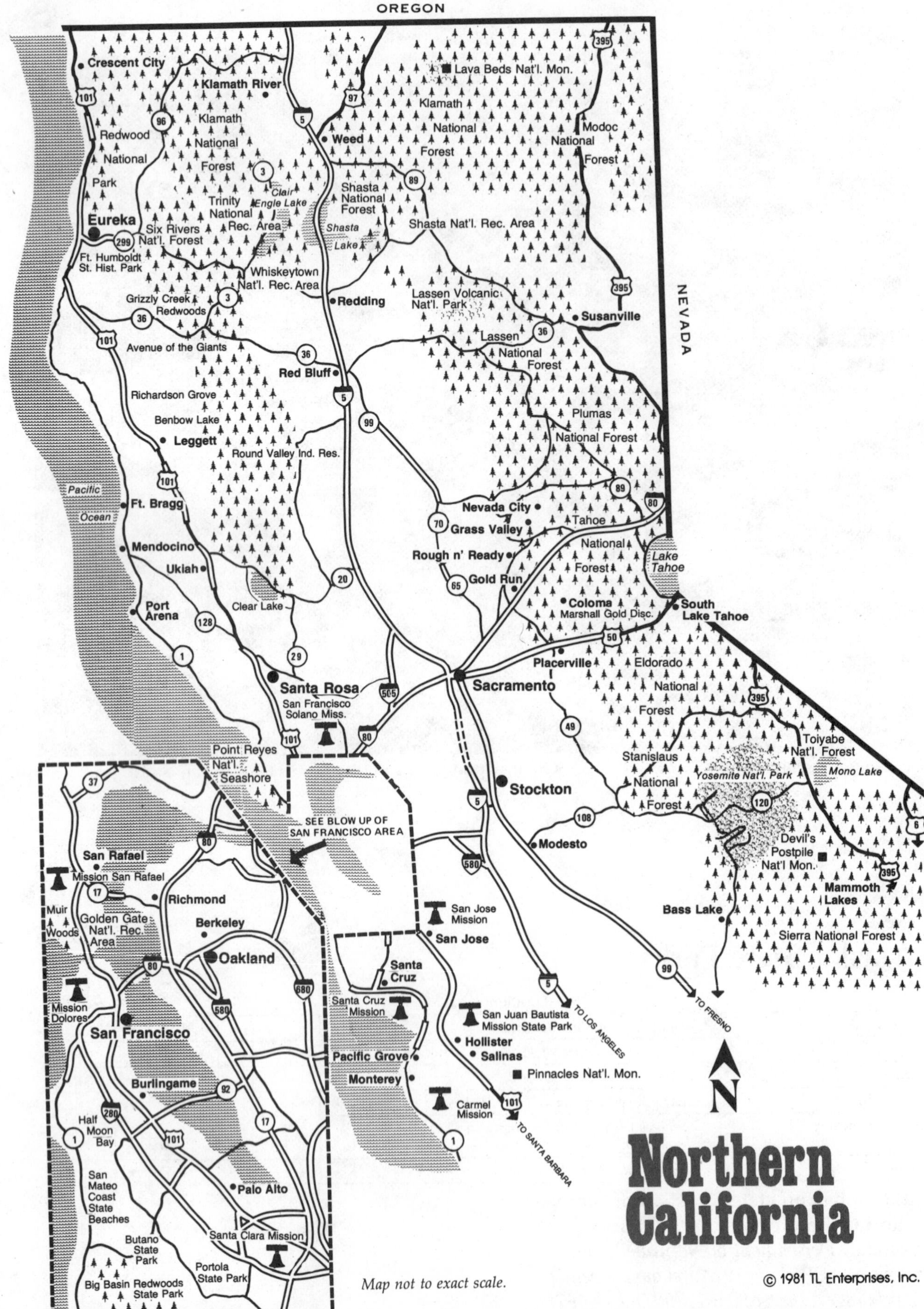
OREGON
NEVADA
Crescent City
Klamath River
Lava Beds Nat'l. Mon.
Klamath National Forest
Modoc National Forest
Weed
Redwood National Park
Klamath National Forest
Trinity National Rec. Area
Clair Engle Lake
Shasta National Forest
Shasta Lake
Shasta Nat'l. Rec. Area
Eureka
Six Rivers Nat'l. Forest
Ft. Humboldt St. Hist. Park
Whiskeytown Nat'l. Rec. Area
Redding
Lassen Volcanic Nat'l. Park
Susanville
Grizzly Creek Redwoods
Lassen National Forest
Avenue of the Giants
Red Bluff
Richardson Grove
Benbow Lake
Leggett
Round Valley Ind. Res.
Plumas National Forest
Pacific Ocean
Ft. Bragg
Nevada City
Grass Valley
Tahoe National Forest
Mendocino
Rough n' Ready
Lake Tahoe
Ukiah
Gold Run
Port Arena
Clear Lake
Coloma
Marshall Gold Disc.
South Lake Tahoe
Placerville
Eldorado National Forest
Santa Rosa
Sacramento
San Francisco Solano Miss.
Point Reyes Nat'l. Seashore
Toiyabe Nat'l. Forest
Stanislaus National Forest
Yosemite Nat'l. Park
Mono Lake
Stockton
SEE BLOW UP OF SAN FRANCISCO AREA
Modesto
Devil's Postpile Nat'l Mon.
Mammoth Lakes
San Rafael
Mission San Rafael
Richmond
San Jose Mission
Bass Lake
Muir Woods
Golden Gate Nat'l. Rec. Area
Berkeley
San Jose
Sierra National Forest
Oakland
Santa Cruz
Santa Cruz Mission
Mission Dolores
San Francisco
San Juan Bautista Mission State Park
TO LOS ANGELES
TO FRESNO
Hollister
Salinas
Pacific Grove
Pinnacles Nat'l. Mon.
Monterey
Burlingame
Carmel Mission
TO SANTA BARBARA
N
Half Moon Bay
Northern California
San Mateo Coast State Beaches
Palo Alto
Santa Clara Mission
Butano State Park
Portola State Park
Big Basin Redwoods State Park
Map not to exact scale.
© 1981 TL Enterprises, Inc.

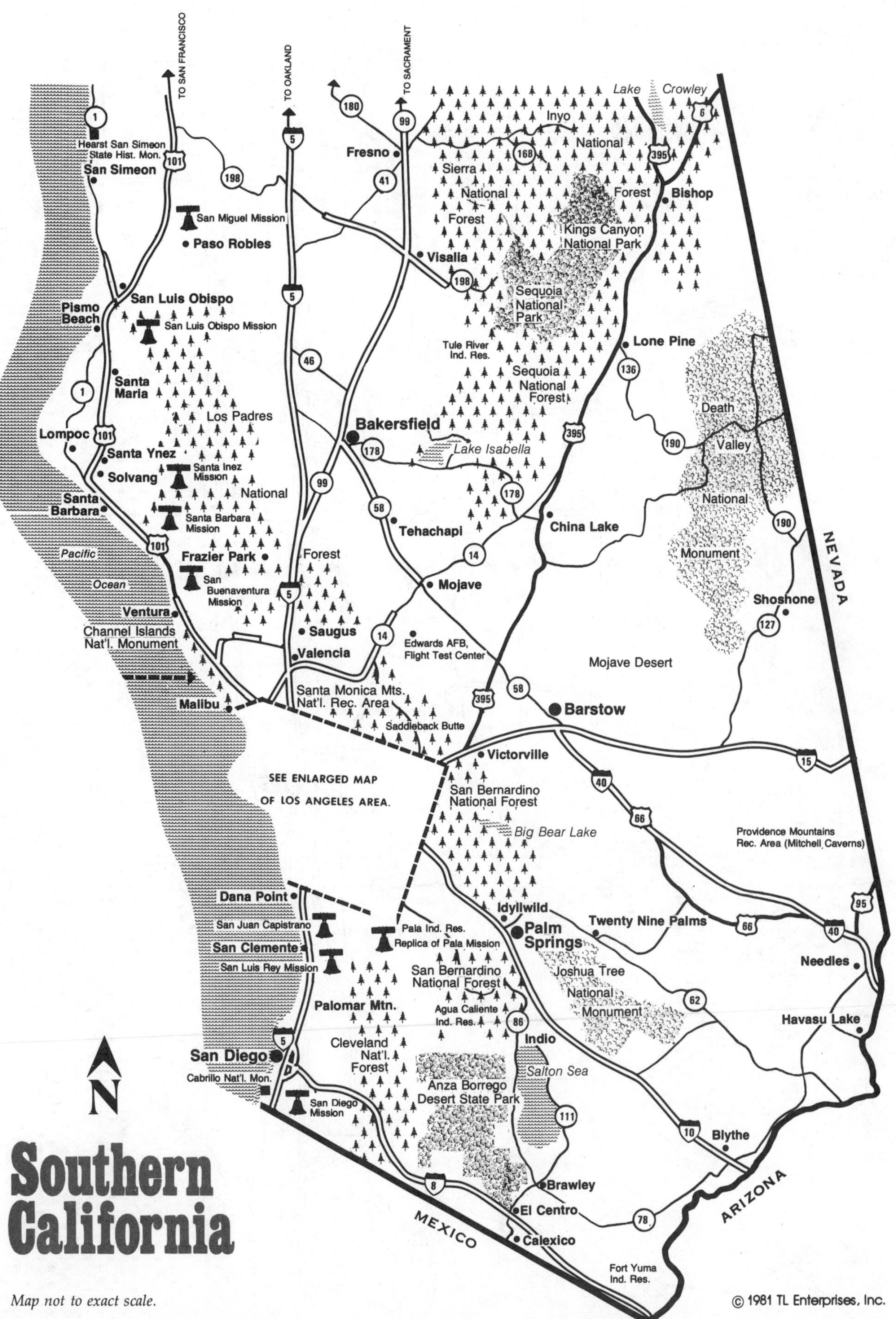

Southern California

Map not to exact scale.

Los Angeles Area

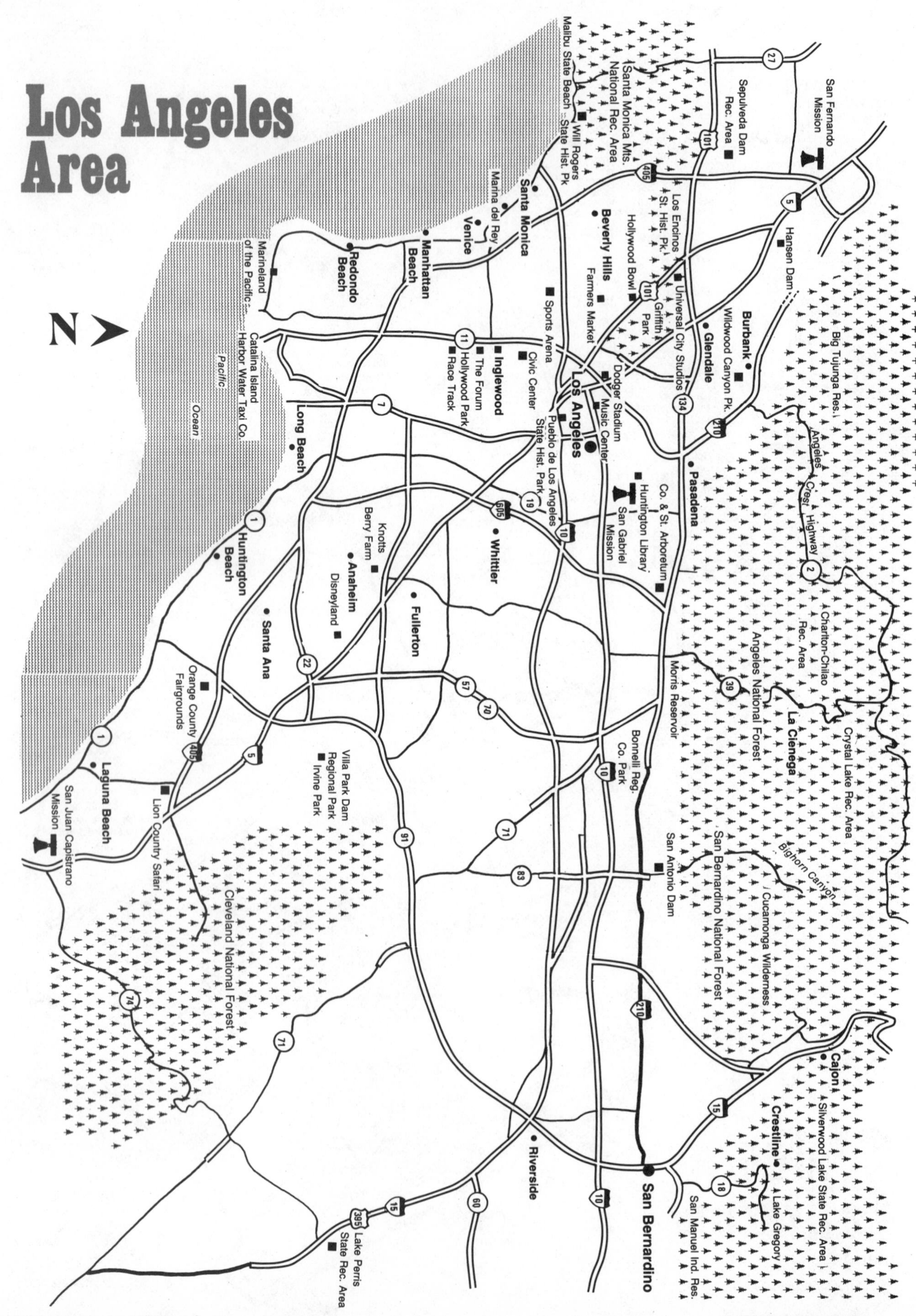

Map not to exact scale.

California

California, the most populous of the states and the third largest in area, is a place of remarkable diversity and unsurpassed beauty. Blessed by a mild climate, it is an ideal year-round vacationland offering virtually unlimited outdoor recreation opportunities from the Pacific shores and desert floors to the trails and slopes of the High Sierras. And as if that wasn't enough, California also has two of the nation's most exciting cities: San Francisco, "the city by the bay," has its cable cars, opera, ballet, superb restaurants and Chinatown, plus a unique charm unmatched by any other city; and Los Angeles, a city that is at once both fast-paced and relaxed, sprawls across the Southern California landscape and offers attractions that range from the make-believe world of the Hollywood studios and nearby Disneyland to the ethnic centers of Little Tokyo and Olvera Street.

The early exploration of California was carried out by Juan Rodriguez Cabrillo, a Portugese in the employ of the Spanish conqueror Cortez, who led an expedition along the coast in 1542. In 1579, Sir Francis Drake also explored the region and claimed it for Queen Elizabeth I; but it was the Spaniards who established the first permanent settlements — a string of 21 missions that spread from San Diego to Sonoma. In 1822, after Mexico gained its independence from Spain, California became a province of the Republic of Mexico, and in 1841, the first group of American settlers moved into California. Within a few years, the United States made an offer to buy the territory. Mexico refused to sell, however, and it wasn't until the Treaty of Guadalupe Hidalgo, which ended the Mexican War in 1848, that sovereignty over California was transferred to the United States.

The single most important happening in the history of California was the discovery of gold at Sutter's Mill near Coloma in 1849 — an event that inspired an influx of "get rich quick" immigrants that saw the

Full name: State of California
Origin of name: From an imaginary island in a 16th-century Spanish romance.
Motto: *Eureka* (I Have Found It).
Nickname: The Golden State
Capital: Sacramento
Statehood: September 9, 1850, 31st state.
Population: 22,295,000 (ranks first).
Major Cities: Los Angeles (2,727,405), San Diego (773,998), San Francisco (664,525).
Bird: California Valley quail
Flower: Golden poppy
Tree: California redwood

Average daily temperatures by month

	Northern	Southern
Jan.	44.2 to 22.6	65.2 to 38.5
Feb.	49.0 to 25.4	69.7 to 42.3
Mar.	52.1 to 26.8	74.1 to 45.6
Apr.	60.4 to 30.2	81.3 to 52.2
May	69.8 to 36.4	89.2 to 59.1
Jun.	78.5 to 42.6	98.4 to 66.8
Jul.	87.6 to 45.8	104.4 to 76.0
Aug.	86.1 to 44.2	102.7 to 74.9
Sept.	80.5 to 39.0	98.4 to 67.0
Oct.	68.4 to 33.2	87.5 to 56.4
Nov.	53.8 to 28.6	74.3 to 46.1
Dec.	46.0 to 24.4	66.2 to 39.3
Year	64.7 to 33.3	84.3 to 55.4

Surging surf churns on the Sonoma Coast of the Redwood Empire.

population jump from 15,000 to almost 300,000 in less than seven years. With the discovery of $450 million in gold, and a steadily increasing population, California was quickly admitted to the Union as a free state under the terms of the Compromise of 1850.

Today, many reminders of the state's gold rush days can still be found in the small towns that line the aptly-named State Route 49. Besides taking travelers on a historical tour of California's Gold Country, this route, which hugs the foothills of the Sierras, also passes through some of California's most scenic country. For sheer beauty, though, nothing can match a trip along State Route 1, the highway that follows the California coastline from Morro Bay in the south to the small community of Rockport in the north. Travel this route and you'll find the awesome majesty of Big Sur, the magnificent Point Lobos Reserve, the white sandy beaches of the Monterey Peninsula, the charming seaside community of Carmel, and the splendor of Point Reyes National Seashore. Elsewhere, there's even more to see: the stately redwoods, the wine country of Napa and Sonoma Counties, Death Valley, Yosemite, Joshua Tree National Monument — in California, the list goes on and on.

In addition to leading all the states in population, California also leads the nation in agriculture and is the second most important industrial state (aerospace, oil, transportation equipment, chemicals, fishing, motion pictures, tourism).

State Offices

Tourism
State Office of Visitor Services
PO Box 1499
Sacramento, California 95805
(916) 322-2881

State Police
Department of Public Safety
Sacramento, California 95804
(916) 445-1564

Radio Stations

Fresno
- KFRE 940 (AM)

Los Angeles
- KMPC 710 (AM)
- KFI 640 (AM)
- KFWB 980 (AM)
- KIIS 102.7 (FM)
- KLOS 95.5 (FM)
- KWST 105.9 (FM)
- KRTH 101 (FM)
- KGIL 1260 (AM)

San Bernardino
- KMEN 1290 (AM)
- KCKC 1350 (AM)

San Diego
- KFSD 94.1 (FM)
- KCBQ 1170 (AM)

San Francisco
- K101 101.3 (FM)
- KKHI 1550 (AM)
- KMEL 106.1 (FM)

Sacramento
- KRAK 1140 (AM)
- KWOD 106.5 (FM)

California's Missions

Ostensibly established as Christian seminaries and training centers for the native Indians, California's missions were also the means by which Spain maintained its colonial influence in California.

In the late 1760s, King Charles III of Spain granted permission to the Franciscan Order to develop missions in the unknown lands of Alta (Upper) California. The plan for each mission called for 10 years of training by the priests to educate and Christianize the natives. As soon as the acquisition of an education and necessary agricultural skills permitted the Indians to become self-sufficient, the mission lands and improvements were to be turned over to them to become self-governing Spanish subjects.

Under the direction of Father Junipero Serra, the first of these missions was founded in San Diego. Between 1769 and 1823, a total of 21 missions were built. The missions, spaced about a day's horseback ride apart, eventually extended from San Diego to San Francisco, linked by the El Camino Real or King's Road. At the height of their operation, the missions had in residence more than 21,000 natives, and by 1846 it is estimated that the total number of baptisms had reached 98,000. The decline of the mission system began under Mexican rule when laws provided for the mission property to pass into the hands of secular owners.

Under the large landowners, the mission properties fell into a general state of decay, but the influence of the missions was indelibly imprinted on the California landscape and culture. The location and names of many of the state's major cities were directly determined by the mission sites. The original mission trail, El Camino Real, later became US-101, the state's primary highway. The vast California agriculture industry blossomed from the nucleus of the mission farms. The influence of the Spanish architecture, with its heavy adobe walls, central plazas, red-tiled roofs and extensive overhangs, can be seen in homes and shopping plazas in California cities from San Diego to San Francisco.

Today, happily, all of the missions have been restored. A trip through the state would be incomplete without a visit to at least one mission site. The following is a geographic listing of all 21 missions with a notation of its founding date.

San Diego de Alcala (1769), San Diego.
San Luis Rey de Francia (1798), Oceanside.
San Juan Capistrano (1776), San Juan Capistrano.
San Gabriel Arcangel (1771), San Gabriel.
San Fernando Rey de Espana (1797), San Fernando.
San Buenaventura (1782), Ventura.
Santa Barbara (1786), Santa Barbara.
Santa Ines (1804), Solvang.
La Purisima Concepcion (1787), Lompoc.
San Luis Obispo de Tolosa (1772), San Luis Obispo.
San Miguel Arcangel (1797), San Miguel.
San Antonio de Padua (1771), King City.
San Carlos Borromeo (1770), Carmel.
Nuestra Senora de la Soledad (1791), Soledad.
San Juan Bautista (1797), San Juan Bautista.
Santa Cruz (1791), Santa Cruz.
Santa Clara de Asis (1777), Santa Clara.
San Jose (1797), Fremont.
San Francisco de Asis/Delores (1776), San Francisco.
San Rafael Arcangel (1817), San Rafael.
San Francisco Solano (1823), Sonoma.

 Look for this symbol on the State Maps.

Highlight

Hollywood Show Tickets

For network radio and television show ticket information, address your request well in advance to "Tickets" (include name of show) at the following: ABC, 4151 Prospect, Hollywood 90027; CBS, 6121 Sunset Boulevard, Los Angeles 90049; NBC, 300 West Alameda, Burbank 91505.

Universal Studios Tour, in Universal City, invites visitors to survive an airplane crash as part of the Screen Test Theatre.

Highlight

Walking Tours in San Francisco

Chinatown. From Union Square, east on Post to Grant, north two blocks to tiled Chinatown gateway. Continue north to Broadway, discovering blocks adjacent to Grant (especially Jackson, Clay, Washington, Sacramento). Look for Bufano's statue of Sun-Yat Sen (St. Mary's Parkway), historic Portsmouth Square (Robert L. Stevenson monument), Tien How Temple (Waverly Place), Chinese Historical Society (Adler Place), Cultural Center (Holiday Inn), 1851 Kong Chow Temple (855 Stockton), Old St. Mary's Church, pagoda roofs, decorated balconies. *Distance: 29 blocks; 2½ to 3½ hours.*

Golden Gate Promenade. Called "the most spectacular walk in the world," the promenade takes in 3½ miles of San Francisco's northern shoreline from Aquatic Park to historic Fort Point, under south anchorage of Golden Gate Bridge. Once "off-limits" areas were opened to public by Golden Gate National Recreation Area in 1975. Blue and white signs mark route (Municipal Pier, Fort Mason-GGNRA Headquarters, Marina Green, Crissy Field in the Presidio, Fort Point). Picnic, recreation spots at water's edge. Start from either end or in the middle. MUNI Bus No. 28 to Toll Plaza, or any GG Bus north to Toll Plaza, cross viewing plaza to path leading down to Fort Point.

North Beach, Fisherman's Wharf. Kearny Street bus to Broadway and Grant. Walk north three blocks on Grant (once "beatnik" row), west one block to Washington Square, heart of Italian neighborhood (Saints Peter and Paul Church, North Beach, music, Italian delicatessens, coffee houses, statue to firebuff Lillie Coit). Follow Columbus Avenue to Taylor, five blocks to Wharf (net menders, fishing boats, shops, cafes, new Pier 39 complex, sailing-ship museum — *Balclutha,* take tours of harbor, Alcatraz). Westward, walk aboard old ships at Hyde Street Pier, see Maritime and Wine museums, the Cannery, Ghirardelli Square before boarding Powell-Hyde Cable Car back to Union Square. *Distance: 28 blocks; 3½ to 5 hours.*

California Points of Interest and Attractions

Alcatraz Island. Formerly a federal prison site, this island, located in San Francisco Bay, is now open for tours. Open year-round, daily, 9 a.m. to 5 p.m.; reservations recommended. San Francisco, Red and White Fleet Pier. (415) 546-2805.

Azalea Reserve. Beautiful gardens with peak blooms in June and July. Open year-round, daily, sunrise to sunset. Arcata, off US-101.

Balboa Park. A 1,158-acre center that was the former site of the 1915-16 Panama-California Exposition; many of the exhibit halls still remain and others have been restored. Facilities included in the park are the Old Globe Theater, site of San Diego's Shakespeare Festival; Natural History Museum; San Diego Museum of Art; San Diego Zoo, and the Spanish Village Arts and Crafts Center. Check with individual attraction for hours and admission fees. At northeast edge of the city's business district, off Interstate 5, on State Route 163.

Berkeley Municipal Rose Garden. Especially beautiful late spring and early summer, this garden contains more than 4,000 varieties of roses. Open year-round, daily, sunrise to sunset. Berkeley, Euclid Avenue and Bayview Place.

Bishop Creek Canyon. A magnificent canyon where walls rise as much as 1,000 feet from the canyon floor. A series of dams impound Bishop Creek and generates an enormous amount of power for the towns of Riverside and San Bernardino. Bishop, on State Route 168.

Botanic Garden. A 65-acre site devoted to native California trees, flowers, shrubs and cacti. Open year-round, daily, 8 a.m. to sunset. Free. Santa Barbara, 1212 Mission Canyon Road.

Boyden Cavern. Featuring unique rock formations in a cave that lies within the Sequoia National Forest. Open May through October, daily, 10 a.m. to 5 p.m. Adults $2, children 6 to 12, $1. Grant Grove, on State Route 180.

Jaunty little San Francisco cablecar mounts steep Hyde Street hill, while grim Alcatraz Island and its former federal penitentiary looms in the background.

Butterfly Trees. Between late October and March, these pine trees are covered with Monarch butterflies. Pacific Grove, on Lighthouse Avenue.

California Alligator Farm. Featuring alligators, snakes and one of the largest crocodiles in captivity. Open year-round, daily; July and August, 10:30 a.m. to 8 p.m.; remainder of year, 10:30 a.m. to 5 p.m. Adults $4, children 5 to 14, $2. Buena Park, 7671 La Palma Avenue.

California Almond Growers Exchange. Films and exhibits on the growing, harvesting and processing of almonds; tours. Open year-round, Monday to Friday, from 10 a.m. Sacramento, 1802 C Street.

Chinatown. More Chinese live in this 16 square-block area than in any other place outside of China or Singapore; unique shops, tearooms and temples. San Francisco, bounded by Broadway, Bush, Kearny and Stockton Streets.

Chinese Culture Center. Located within Chinatown, the center presents artifacts documenting Chinese-American history as well as displays of Chinese art and other exhibits. Open year-round, Tuesday through Saturday, 10 a.m. to 5 p.m. Free. San Francisco, 750 Kearny Street (on third floor of Holiday Inn).

Daffodil Hill. From late March to mid-April, this area, located in the heart of the state's Gold Rush country, is covered with daffodils originally planted in the 1850s. Volcano, three miles north, off State Route 49.

Descanso Gardens. These magnificent gardens contain some 100,000 camellias from throughout the world as well as fuchsias, roses, begonias and other blooms; art exhibits in Hospitality House; Japanese Tea Gardens. Open year-round, daily, March through Labor Day, 11 a.m. to 4 p.m.; remainder of year, Tuesday to Sunday. Adults 50 cents, children 5 to 17, 25 cents. La Canada, off Foothill Boulevard, at 1418 Descanso Drive.

Dos Pueblos Orchid Company. One of the nation's most extensive collections of orchids, located within boundaries of the historic 4,500-acre Rancho Dos Pueblos; peak bloom in spring. Open year-round, Monday to Friday, 8 a.m. to 4 p.m. Goleta, on US-101.

Downieville. A quaint Gold Country village that was once the center of exceptionally rich diggings. The town retains much of its earlier atmosphere in the narrow, tree-lined main street that is flanked by brick and stone buildings and wooden sidewalks. Off State Route 49.

Feather River Hatchery. This facility stocks Northern California streams with about 10 million salmon and one million steelhead each year. Open year-round, daily, sunrise to sunset. Oroville, 5 Table Mountain Road.

Fisherman's Village. Colorful Cape Cod-style buildings along the waterfront providing specialty shops and restaurants; harbor cruises depart from nearby docks; boat rentals. Open year-round, daily, from 10 a.m. Marina Del Rey, 13755 Fiji Way.

Golden Gate Bridge. One of the longest single-span suspension bridges in the world — 8,981 feet in length, with a main span length of 4,200 feet; 220-foot clearance permits passage of the largest ocean-going vessels. The bridge, which has a toll on the southbound side, connects San Francisco with Marin County and the Redwood Highway, US-101.

Golden Gate Park. Covering some 1,000 acres, this park has many miles of roads, bridle paths and foot trails as well as attractions that include the Asian Art Museum, Morrison Planetarium and the California Academy of Sciences. Open year-round, daily; check individual facility for hours and admission charges. San Francisco, bordered by Fulton and Stanyan Streets, Lincoln Way and the Great Highway.

Griffith Park. One of the largest city parks in the nation (4,063 acres), Griffith Park offers bridle paths, hiking trails, scenic roadways and attractions that include the Los Angeles Zoo, Griffith Park Observatory, Travel Town, Hall of Science, and train and carousel rides. Open year-round, daily; check individual attractions for hours and fees. Los Angeles, at Los Feliz Boulevard and Riverside Drive.

Hollywood Bowl. A natural amphitheater in the Hollywood foothills, this facility has seating for 17,599 and hosts concerts by the Los Angeles Philharmonic and numerous other special events. Open year-round, daily; concert season, July 4 to September 17. Adults $1 to $16.50, student and senior citizen discounts available. Hollywood, off Highland Avenue.

Humboldt Bay Harbour Cruises. A 75-minute tour of the scenic harbor area. Season: May through October, daily.

Adults $3, children 12 to 17, $2, 6 to 11, $1.50. Eureka, at the foot of C Street.

Huntington Library, Art Gallery and Botanical Gardens. This cultural center houses one of the world's most valuable collections of rare books and manuscripts, including the Gutenberg Bible, Ellesmere Chaucer, and Benjamin Franklin's autobiography written in his own hand. The art gallery features many valuable paintings, tapestries, procelains and sculptures, and the gardens boast a number of unusual trees and shrubs. Open year-round, except October, Tuesday to Sunday, 1 p.m. to 4:30 p.m. Free. San Marino, 1151 Oxford Road.

Hurd Beeswax Candle Factory. Handcrafted candles turned out by skilled workers in the quaint setting of a turn-of-the-century building. Open year-round, daily, 10 a.m. to 5:30 p.m. St. Helena, on State Route 29, at 3020 St. Helena Highway North.

Hyde Street Pier. The berth of five historic ships, including the *Balclutha,* an old iron-hulled sailing ship; guided and self-guided tours. Open year-round, daily, 10 a.m. to 5 p.m. Free. San Francisco, at the foot of Hyde Street.

Japan Center. A center for Japanese stateside government and several commercial and cultural attractions. A Peace Pagoda, a gift of the Japanese people, stands in the central plaza. Open year-round, daily. Free. San Francisco, bounded by Post, Geary, Laguna and Fillmore Streets.

Aerial view of the Golden Gate Bridge, main unit in the Redwood Empire's highway system. Construction of the bridge, with the second-longest single span of any bridge in the world, is considered one of the outstanding engineering feats of all time.

Lake Shasta Caverns. Well-lighted caves featuring spectacular formations; tours. Open year-round, daily (weather permitting), 9 a.m. to 5 p.m. Adults $5, children 5 to 15, $3.

Lawrence Livermore Laboratory Visitors Center. Exhibits and multi-media presentations on research into new energy sources; tours. Open year-round, daily; Monday to Friday, 9:30 a.m. to 5 p.m.; Saturday and Sunday, noon to 5 p.m. Free. Livermore, off Greenville Road.

Leonis Adobe. A restored adobe furnished in the late 19th-century period. Open year-round, Wednesday, Saturday, Sunday and holidays, 1 p.m. to 4 p.m. Free. Calabasas, off US-101, at 23537 Calabasas Road.

Lick Observatory. A division of the University of California at Santa Cruz, the observatory offers fascinating exhibits and shows; tours. Open year-round, daily, 1 p.m. to 5 p.m. Free. San Jose, on the summit of Mount Hamilton, on Mount Hamilton Road.

Little Tokyo. Center for Japanese culture in Los Angeles; shops, restaurants. Los Angeles, bounded by First, Los Angeles, Third and Alameda Streets.

Los Angeles Mormon Temple. One of the largest Mormon Temples in the nation; features a 15-foot statue of Angel Moroni atop the temple's 257-foot tower; tours. Open year-round, daily, 9 a.m. to 10 p.m. Los Angeles, 10777 Santa Monica Boulevard.

Los Angeles State and County Arboretum. A horticultural research center with 127 acres of trees, shrubs and floral displays; library, bird sanctuary, walking tours. Open year-round, daily, 9 a.m. to 4:30 p.m. Adults $1, children 5 to 17 and senior citizens, 50 cents. Arcadia, 301 North Baldwin Avenue.

Luther Burbank Memorial Gardens. Splendid gardens that also house the grave of the famed horticulturist who lived and worked here for 50 years; guided tours. Open year-round, daily, 24 hours. Adults 50 cents, children 9 to 17, 10 cents. Santa Rosa, at Santa Rosa Avenue and Sonoma Avenue.

The "Carson Mansion" in Eureka is now a private club. Built in 1884-86, it is one of the most photographed houses in America.

Mercer Caverns. Limestone formations in unique caverns; guided tours. Open year-round, daily, 9 a.m. to 5 p.m. Adults $2.50, children 5 to 11, $1.25. Murphys, off State Route 49.

Moaning Cave. Discovered by miners in 1851, this cave has one of the largest single-room caverns of any cave in California. Open year-round, daily, 9 a.m. to 5 p.m. Adults $3, children 6 to 12, $1.50. Vallecito, off State Route 49.

Moorten Botanical Garden. These gardens feature desert plants and cactus displays arranged to represent different regions throughout the world where cactus grows. Open year-round, daily, 9 a.m. to 5 p.m. Adults $1, children 7 to 17, 50 cents.

Mount Shasta State Fish Hatchery. Some 5-10 million trout are produced annually in this hatchery for replenishment of Northern California streams. Open year-round, daily, 7:30 a.m. to 3:30 p.m. Free. Mount Shasta, off Interstate 5.

Mount Whitney. The highest mountain (14,495 feet) in the contiguous 48 states; summit may be reached by a 10.7-mile foot trail from the end of Whitney Portal Road; obtain wilderness permit at Forest Ranger Station in Lone Pine. Lone Pine, off US-395.

Movieland-Of-The-Air. Features one of the largest collections of antique aircraft in the country; more than 50 planes. Open year-round, daily, 10 a.m. to 5 p.m. Adults $2.25, children 12 to 17, 75 cents. Santa Ana, off Interstate 5, at Orange County Airport.

Municipal Rose Garden. More than 5,000 plants; peak bloom in May and June. Open year-round, daily. Free. San Jose, on Nagle Avenue.

Music Center. A three-building complex consisting of the Dorothy Chandler Pavilion, Mark Taper Forum and the Ahmanson Theater hosting comedy, drama, ballet, opera and symphonic productions; tours. Los Angeles, First Street and Grand Avenue. (213) 972-7485 for schedule of events.

Mystery Spot. A section of redwood forest where the laws of gravity seem to be defied; guided tours. Open year-round, daily, 9:30 a.m. to 5 p.m. Adults $2, children 5 to 11, $1. Branciforte Drive, Santa Cruz.

Newport Harbor Showboat Cruises. Tours the scenic harbor and oceanfront along picturesque Newport Beach. Open year-round, daily. Newport Beach, 700 East Edgewater Avenue. (714) 673-0240, for schedule.

Old Governor's Mansion. An ornate and elegantly furnished Victorian mansion, built in the late 19th century. Open year-round, daily, 10 a.m. to 4:30 p.m. Adults 50 cents, children under 18, free. Sacramento, 16th and H Streets.

Old Lighthouse. This lighthouse still contains the original light as well as a museum, a collection of antique clocks and photographs of shipwrecks. Open March through November, Wednesday to Sunday, 10 a.m. to 4 p.m. Adults 50 cents, children under 12, free. Crescent City, on Battery Point at the end of A Street.

Old U.S. Mint. This restored facility has old assaying equipment, scales, presses, exhibits, gold bullion, national medals and coin displays; tours. Open year-round, Tuesday to Saturday, 9 a.m. to 4 p.m. San Francisco, Fifth and Mission Streets.

Olvera Street. One of Los Angeles' oldest streets, restored in 1930 as a Mexican marketplace featuring arts and crafts and restaurants that serve native Mexican dishes; Mexican Christmas festival held in December. Open year-round, daily, 10 a.m. to 8 p.m. Los Angeles, between North Main and Alameda Streets.

Palm Springs Aerial Tram. This tram transports passengers 2½ miles to an 8,516-foot mountain peak for spectacular views of Palm Springs and the rugged San Jacinto Mountains; restaurant, cocktail lounge, snack bar, picnic area. Open year-round (except 10 days after Labor Day), daily, 10 a.m. to 9 p.m. Adults $4.95, children 12 to 17, $3.95, 4 to 11, $2.25. Palm Springs, off State Route 111.

Palomar Observatory. A five-dome observatory that houses the 200-inch Hale Telescope; museum, gallery. Open year-round, daily, 9 a.m. to 5 p.m. Free. Palomar Mountain, off State Route 79.

Pixie Woods Wonderland. A children's playland featuring recreations of scenes from popular children's stories and legends; theater. Open March through October, Wednesday to Sunday, 11 a.m. to 6 p.m. Adults 30 cents, children under 12, 25 cents.

Ports O'Call Village. A complex of quaint shops and restaurants that recalls life in a mid-19th-century seaport. Open year-round, daily, 11 a.m. to 9 p.m. Free. San Pedro, off Harbor Freeway.

Queen Mary. This retired luxury liner features exhibits, a museum, an aquarium, restaurants and live entertainment; guided tours. Open year-round, daily, 10 a.m. to 5 p.m. Adults $6, children 5 to 11, $2.50. Long Beach, off Long Beach Freeway.

Ramona Pageant. An annual dramatization of Helen Hunt Jackson's novel, presented in the Ramona Bowl. Season: April through early May, Saturday and Sunday afternoons. Hemet, off Interstate 10.

Rancho Santa Ana Botanic Garden. Features an excellent collection of native California plants and flowers; peak bloom February through June. Open year-round, daily, 8 a.m. to 5 p.m. Free. Claremont, 1500 North College Avenue.

Rim of the World Drive. A winding 40-mile road at elevations of 5,000 to 7,200 feet, offering spectacular panoramic views. San Bernardino, on State Route 18, leading to Lake Arrowhead, Big Bear Lake and other resorts.

Ripley's Believe It Or Not Museum. Displays of the bizarre and unusual, based on Ripley's famous *Believe It Or Not* comic strips. Open year-round, daily, 9 a.m. to 11 p.m. Adults $4, children 4 to 12, $2. San Francisco, on Fisherman's Wharf.

Palomar Observatory, a huge dome on Palomar Mountain, lies 65 miles north of San Diego and houses America's largest telescope. The giant 200-inch mirror enables scientists to explore an area one billion light-years away.

Roaring Camp and Big Trees Narrow-Gauge Railroad. An 1880 steam train that makes a six-mile round-trip from Roaring Camp Station into the redwoods of Santa Cruz County. Open year-round, daily, departures at 11 a.m., 12:15 p.m., 1:30 p.m., 2:45 p.m. and 4 p.m. Adults $5.95, children 3 to 11, $3.95. Felton, off US-101.

Santa Catalina Island. Twenty-two miles from the California mainland, this island is 21 miles long and eight miles wide, and the town of Avalon is its principal population center. Attractions include a museum and inland and harbor area tours. (Visitors may also rent open cars for self-guided tours of the island.) Access: year-round, by plane or boat from Long Beach, Los Angeles, San Pedro and Santa Ana Harbors. (213) 510-1520.

Santa's Village. A children's attraction featuring a gingerbread house, puppet theater, sleigh, monorail and burro rides. Open year-round (except December 25), daily, 10 a.m. to 5 p.m. Adults $4.75, children 3 to 4, $4.25; includes all rides and attractions. Skyforest, on State Route 18.

San Onofre Nuclear Generating Station. Displays and exhibits illustrating the conversion of the atom to electricity; film. Open year-round, daily, 9 a.m. to 4:45 p.m. Free. San Clemente, off Interstate 5, at Basilone Road.

Sebastian's General Store. A state historical landmark originally built in 1852 and still operating as a general store. Open year-round, daily, 8:30 a.m. to 5:30 p.m. San Simeon, off State Route 1.

Sequoia Park. A 52-acre grove of virgin redwoods that also includes a duck pond and deer and elk paddocks. Open year-round, daily, 9 a.m. to dusk. Free. Eureka, Glatt and W Streets.

Seventeen-Mile Drive. A spectacularly scenic drive between the communities of

Pacific Grove and Carmel. Points of interest include Seal Rock, Cypress Point and the famous Pebble Beach golf course, scene of the annual Bing Crosby Pro-Am Tournament. Toll: $4.

Shields Date Gardens. Displays of several varieties of dates; 25-minute slide show on the cultivation and history of dates. Open year-round, daily, 8 a.m. to 6 p.m. Free. Indio, off Interstate 10.

South Coast Botanic Garden. Over 2,000 plant species featured; tram tours. Open year-round, daily, 9 a.m. to 5 p.m. Adults $1, children 6 to 17, 50 cents. Palos Verdes Peninsula, 26300 Crenshaw Boulevard.

Squirrel. An open-end sightseeing bus that takes visitors on a seven-hour tour of the Northern California redwood country. Season: June 15 through September 15, Monday, Wednesday, Friday and Saturday. Adults $12, children 2 to 12, $6.

Subway Cave. A lava tube, four to 17 feet high, that winds 1,300 feet through the lava flow that covered Hat Creek Valley less than 2,000 years ago; lantern or flashlight needed. Lassen National Forest, off State Route 89.

Table Mountain. A split lava cap that is covered with wildflowers and waterfalls during spring and early summer; abandoned mines, museum, ghost town, picnic area nearby. Oroville, on Cherokee Road, via Table Mountain Boulevard.

Telegraph Hill. This landmark site is topped by a park and the Coit Memorial Tower, built to memorialize the city's volunteer firemen. Open year-round, daily, 9 a.m. to 4:30 p.m. San Francisco, off Stockton and Broadway Streets.

Torrey Pines State Preserve. This is the natural habitat of the Torrey Pine, which you'll find twisted into unique shapes by the Pacific winds; nature walks, museum. Open year-round, daily, 9 a.m. to 5 p.m. Admission: $1.50 per vehicle. Del Mar, on North Torrey Pines Road.

Tucker Wildlife Sanctuary. A sanctuary noted for an abundance of hummingbirds; observation porch. Open year-round, daily, 9 a.m. to 4 p.m. Admission: 50 cents. Orange, 28322 Modjeska Canyon Road.

Undersea Caverns. Live sea plants, animals and fish viewed through underwater windows; scuba diving shows. Open May through September, daily, 9:30 a.m. to 5:30 p.m. Adults $2.50, children 12 to 17, $1.75, 6 to 11, $1.50. Crescent City, off US-101, at Anchor Way.

Watts Towers. Three webb-like towers of concrete-coated steel rods encrusted with tile, glass chips and shells; 33 years in the making. Open year-round, daily, 10 a.m. to dusk. Free. Los Angeles (Watts), 1765 East 107th Street.

Wayfarer's Chapel. Designed by Lloyd Wright, son of Frank Lloyd Wright, this unique "Glass Church" is surmounted by a 50-foot stone campanile which can be seen from both sea and land. Open year-round, daily, 11 a.m. to 4 p.m. Palos Verdes Peninsula, 5755 Palos Verdes Drive.

Winchester Mystery House. World-famous house designed by Winchester Arms heiress Sarah Winchester in an effort to baffle the evil spirits that supposedly haunted her. The house has 160 rooms with 2,000 doors, 13 bathrooms, 10,000 windows, 47 fireplaces, blind closets, secret passageways and 40 staircases. Open year-round, daily, 9 a.m. to 6 p.m. Adults $4.95, senior citizens $3.95, children 5 to 12, $3.25. San Jose, near junction of Interstate 280 and State Route 17.

Whittier Narrows Nature Center. A wildlife and plant sanctuary; trails. Open year-round, daily, 9 a.m. to 5 p.m. El Monte, 1000 North Durfee Avenue.

Highlight

Point Lobos State Reserve

Point Lobos State Reserve, which the National Park Service designated a Registered Natural Landmark in 1968, is an area of 1,250 acres located in Monterey County along the south shore of Carmel Bay. The reserve derives its name from its colonies of California and Steller's sea lions. The sound of their hoarse barking carries inland from the offshore rocks at Punta de los Lobos Marinos, Point of the Seawolves.

Scientific interest centers here because of the two species of sea lions that live at Point Lobos, and because this is the northernmost breeding place of the California brown pelican. Also, many forms of land and marine life remain here free from encroachment.

Sometimes visitors can glimpse the California sea otter offshore diving for food or floating on its back in the kelp beds. Driven to the brink of extinction by the fur trade many years ago, the otters are now under strict protective laws and today number about 1,000 in California.

In November, the California gray whale begins to migrate to breeding and calving areas in Lower California, returning to the feeding grounds in the Bering Sea each spring. This large mammal, up to 40 tons and 50 feet long, can be seen as it travels close to shore on its 12,000-mile migration. A whaling station was located here in Whaler's Cove between 1861 and 1884.

Monterey Cypress

Another outstanding feature of the reserve is its grove of Monterey cypress. In earlier geological times the Monterey cypress was widely distributed. Now it is making a last stand in the Monterey region. Clinging to the cliffs above the surf, distorted by wind and weather, sometimes shrouded in drifting fog, the trees tell of the never-ending conflict between sea and land. The still-living trees are rich green with foliage; the dead are stark in silhouette, their bleached and twisted branches red with algae.

Almost miraculously, Point Lobos escaped destruction as it passed from one owner to another in years past. Once, in the free and easy days of the Mexican regime, it changed hands in a game of cards. Site of a whaling station, shipping point for a coal mine, proposed as a townsite, grazed over by cattle, and occasionally burned, it finally was acquired by an owner who appreciated its unique qualities. When it passed into the trusteeship of the state of California in 1933, it had somehow managed to retain most of its essential, primitive character. And it is still unspoiled. Roads through the park have been kept to a minimum. The finer areas of the reserve can be seen only on foot over unobtrusive trails that lead to its greatest features of beauty and interest.

Point Lobos is a unique outdoor museum. Large flocks of cormorants, pelicans, gulls and other waterfowl interest the visitor. Over 300 plant and 250 bird and animal species have been identified. From early spring until fall, acres of wildflowers transform the meadows, the shaded Monterey pine woods and the seacoast into a variegated pattern of color.

Interesting offshore formations include Sea Lion Rocks, home of the noisy sea lions; Bird Island, sanctuary for thousands of shore and water birds;

and the Pinnacles, where the dramatic action of the waves is a grand and never-ending spectacle.

In 1960, 750 acres of submerged land were added to the reserve to create the first underwater reserve in our nation. Intertidal and subtidal marine plant and animal species are fully protected so that the normal balance of conditions favorable to the survival of each plant and animal can remain undisturbed. By permit, underwater studies are conducted by individuals, universities and private research groups.

Guided Tours

Visitors are offered guided tours twice daily during the summer and on a reduced schedule during the off season. One can visit six different areas: the cypress grove, the pine wood, Bird Island, the North Shore trail, Whaler's Cove or the sea lion area. There is also a tidepool walk held early on summer mornings when the weather and tide table permit.

Point Lobos State Reserve
Route 1, Box 62
Carmel, California 93921
(408) 624-4909

A solitary Monterey cypress surveys the sea from atop a crag in Pebble Beach, California — a common sight along Seventeen Mile Drive, one of America's most famous scenic roads.

California State Parks

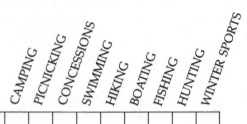

Park	Location	CAMPING	PICNICKING	CONCESSIONS	SWIMMING	HIKING	BOATING	FISHING	HUNTING	WINTER SPORTS
Angel Island	*San Francisco. In San Francisco Bay, by ferry from San Francisco, Berkeley or Tiburon.*		•	•		•				
Annadel	*Santa Rosa. On Channel Drive.*					•		•		
Anza-Borrego Desert	*San Diego. 85 miles northeast off Interstate 8.*	•	•			•				
Big Basin	*Santa Cruz. Off State Route 1.*	•	•	•		•				
Border Field	*San Diego. Off Interstate 5.*				•	•		•		
Bothe-Napa Valley	*St. Helena. On State Route 29.*	•	•		•	•				
Butano	*Pescadero. On Cloverdale Road.*	•	•			•				
Calaveras Big Trees	*Arnold. On State Route 4.*	•	•		•	•		•		
Castle Crags	*Dunsmuir. On Interstate 5.*	•	•		•	•		•		
Castle Rock	*Aptos. Off State Route 9.*	•	•			•				
Caswell Memorial	*Ripon. On Austin Road.*	•	•		•	•		•		
Clear Lake	*Kelseyville. On Soda Bay Road.*	•	•		•	•		•		
Cuyamaca Rancho	*San Diego. On State Route 79.*	•	•			•		•		
D.L. Bliss	*Tahoe City. On State Route 89.*	•	•		•			•		
Donner Memorial	*Truckee. On State Route 40.*	•	•		•	•		•		
Dry Lagoon	*Eureka. On US-101.*		•					•		
Emerald Bay	*Tahoe City. On State Route 89.*	•	•		•	•		•		
Forest of Nisene Marks	*Aptos. On Aptos Creek Road.*		•			•				
Fremont Peak	*San Juan Bautista. Off US-101.*	•	•							
Gaviota	*Santa Barbara. On US-101.*	•		•	•	•		•		
Grizzly Creek Redwoods	*Garberville. On State Route 36.*	•	•		•	•		•		
Grover Hot Springs	*Markeleville. On Hot Springs Road.*	•	•		•	•		•		
Hendy Woods	*Boonville. Off State Route 128.*	•	•	•	•	•		•		
Henry Cowell Redwoods	*Santa Cruz. On State Route 9.*	•	•	•	•	•		•		
Henry W. Coe	*Morgan Hill. Off US-101.*	•	•	•		•		•		
Humboldt Redwoods	*Eureka. Off US-101.*	•	•		•	•		•		
Jedediah Smith Redwoods	*Crescent City. On State Route 199.*	•	•		•	•		•		
Julia Pfeiffer Burns	*Carmel. Off State Route 1.*		•			•				
MacKerricher	*Fort Bragg. On State Route 1.*	•	•			•		•		
Malibu Creek	*Calabasas. Off US-101, on Las Virgenes Road.*					•		•		
McArthur-Burney	*Burney. On State Route 89.*	•	•	•	•	•		•		
Mendocino Headlands	*Mendocino. Off State Route 1.*					•		•		
Montana de Oro	*Los Osos. Off State Route 1.*	•	•		•	•		•		
Morro Bay	*Morro Bay. Off State Route 1.*	•	•	•	•	•		•		
Mount Diablo	*Danville. Off Interstate 680.*	•	•			•				
Mount San Jacinto	*Idyllwild. On State Route 243.*	•	•	•		•				
Mount Tamalpais	*Mill Valley. On Panoramic Highway.*	•	•		•	•				
Palomar Mountain	*Escondido. On State Route S6.*	•	•		•	•				
Patrick's Point	*Eureka. On US-101.*	•	•			•		•		
Pfeiffer Big Sur	*Carmel. On State Route 1.*	•	•	•	•	•		•		
Plumas-Eureka	*Blairsden. Off State Route 89.*	•	•			•		•		
Point Mugu	*Oxnard. On State Route 1.*	•	•		•	•		•		
Portola	*Portola. Off State Route 35.*	•	•			•		•		

Peaceful and picturesque, the Redwood Empire town of Mendocino, Mendocino County, perches on a bluff overlooking the far reaches of the Pacific Ocean, a rendezvous for sportsmen, artists and vacationers.

California State Parks

Park	Location	CAMPING	PICNICKING	CONCESSIONS	SWIMMING	HIKING	BOATING	FISHING	HUNTING	WINTER SPORTS
Prairie Creek Redwoods	*Eureka. On US-101.*	•	•			•		•		
Richardson Grove	*Garberville. On US-101.*	•	•	•	•	•		•		
Robert Louis Stevenson	*Calistoga. On State Route 29.*		•			•				
Russian Gulch	*Mendocino. On State Route 1.*	•	•			•		•		
Saddleback Butte	*Lancaster. On Avenue J.*	•	•			•				
Salt Point	*Jenner. On State Route 1.*	•	•			•		•		
Samuel P. Taylor	*San Rafael. On Sir Francis Drake Boulevard.*	•	•		•	•		•		
Sugarloaf Ridge	*Santa Rosa. Off State Route 12.*	•	•			•				
Sugar Pine Point	*Tahoe City. On State Route 89.*	•	•		•	•		•		
Van Damme	*Mendocino. On State Route 1.*	•	•			•		•		
Wilder Ranch	*Santa Cruz. On State Route 1.*	•	•					•		

California State Forests

Forest	Location	CAMPING	PICNICKING	CONCESSIONS	SWIMMING	HIKING	BOATING	FISHING	HUNTING	WINTER SPORTS
Boggs Mountain	*Lower Lake. Off State Route 53.*	•	•			•		•	•	
Jackson	*Fort Bragg. Off State Route 1.*	•	•			•		•	•	
LaTour	*Shingletown. Off Interstate 5.*	•	•			•		•	•	
Mountain Home	*Springville. Off State Route 190.*	•	•			•		•	•	

For more information on California state parks and forests, contact: *Department of Parks and Recreation, PO Box 2390, Sacramento, California 95811, (916) 445-4624.*

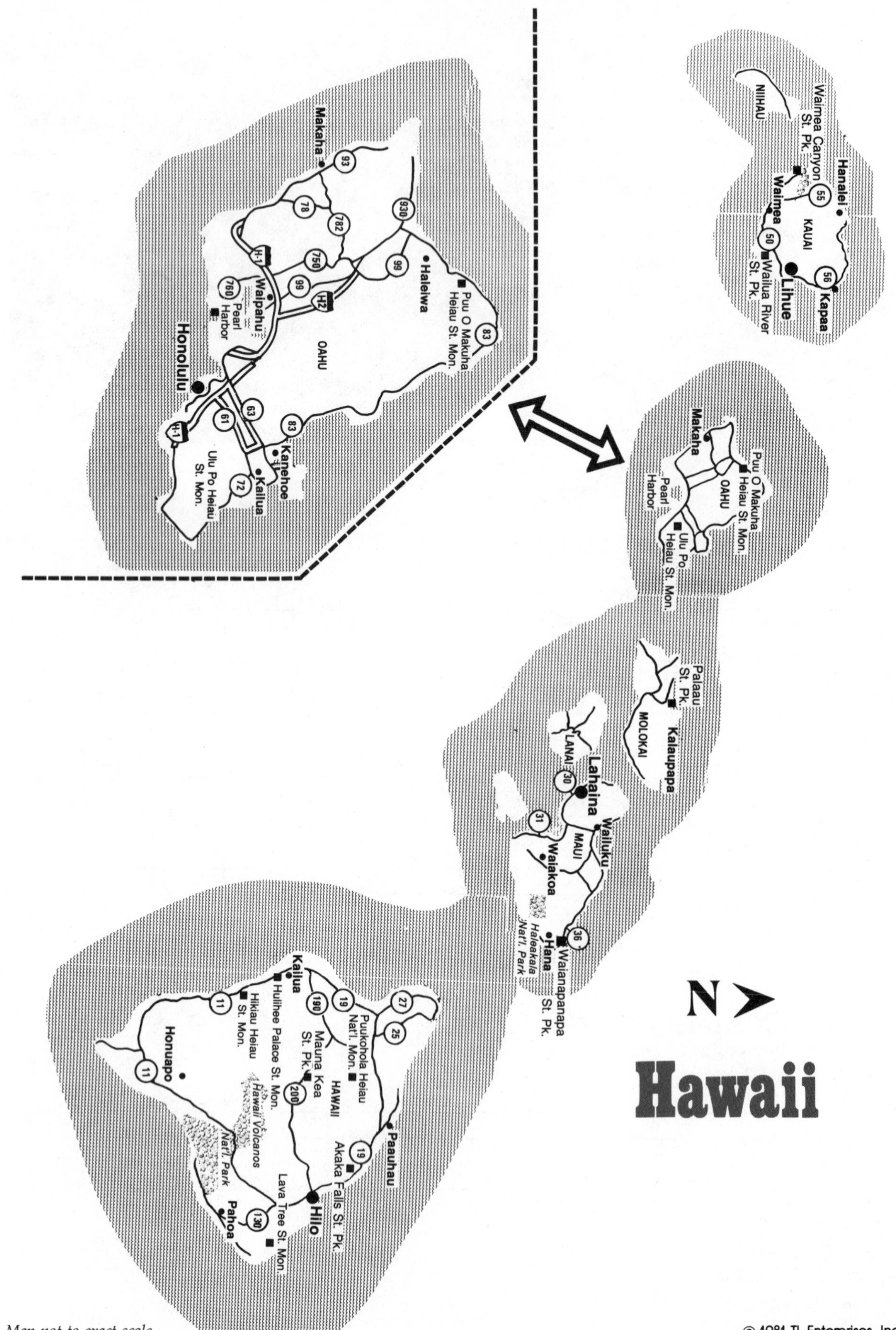

Map not to exact scale.

Hawaii

For obvious reasons, Hawaii is often overlooked by RVers. But just because you can't reach the islands with your rig doesn't mean that our 50th state isn't RV territory. Indeed, for your next vacation you might want to consider flying to Hawaii and renting an RV from one of the many rental agencies scattered throughout the islands. Once you're behind the wheel — if you're on the "Big Island," Hawaii — you might want to head for scenic State Route 137 and a shoreside drive that will take you through the lush countryside that still abounds in the less-crowded areas of the islands. Then drive from Keaau to Pahoa along State Route 130 — a road that is lined with yellow ginger and fields of wild orchids. On Kauai, you won't want to miss the beautiful Kalalau Valley; and on Molokai, follow the coast road to Halawa Bay, where the twin falls drop into a verdant valley. If you *really* want to get away from it all, go to the tiny island of Lanai, where you can walk the beaches for miles at a time and not see another soul.

When British explorer Captain James Cook landed on the islands of Hawaii in 1795, he found a Polynesian population with a well-developed feudal form of government and a religion that included human sacrifice and idolatry. Soon after Cook's discovery of the area, which he called the Sandwich Islands in honor of the Earl of Sandwich, yankee fur traders from the Pacific Northwest began visiting the islands. By the early 1800s, missionaries became active on the islands; and by 1840, increased trade and growing sugar and pineapple industries led to the adoption of the first constitution. As the islands continued to prosper, American growers began to demand annexation to the U.S. in order to protect their interests. Finally, in 1900, Hawaii became a full-fledged territory with American citizenship bestowed on all its citizens.

The attack by the Japanese on Pearl Harbor, and the war that followed, had a

Full name: State of Hawaii
Origin of name: Perhaps from the native name of the Polynesians' original home.
Motto: *Ua Mau Ke Ea O Ka Aina I Ka Pono* (The Life of the Land is Perpetuated in Righteousness).
Nickname: Aloha State
Capital: Honolulu
Statehood: August, 21, 1959
Population: 895,000 (ranks 40th).
Major Cities: Honolulu (705,385), Hilo (29,000).
Bird: Hawaiian goose
Flower: Hibiscus
Tree: Kukui

Average daily temperatures by month

	Mountains	Coast
Jan.	74.3 to 56.8	79.6 to 62.8
Feb.	73.5 to 56.4	79.4 to 62.6
Mar.	73.4 to 57.2	78.8 to 63.3
Apr.	73.7 to 58.5	79.8 to 64.6
May	74.8 to 59.4	81.3 to 65.6
Jun.	76.4 to 60.4	82.7 to 66.5
Jul.	77.0 to 61.4	83.0 to 67.5
Aug.	77.6 to 62.0	83.5 to 68.2
Sept.	78.3 to 61.1	83.6 to 67.6
Oct.	77.9 to 60.8	83.2 to 66.7
Nov.	75.6 to 59.9	81.3 to 65.6
Dec.	74.1 to 58.1	79.4 to 63.7
Year	75.6 to 59.3	81.3 to 65.4

Iolani Palace, one of Honolulu's historic sites, houses the only throne room under the American flag. Hawaiian Royalty once lived in the Palace and until recently the Hawaii State Legislature convened each year in its downstairs galleries.

tremendous impact on the islands, for it wrought vast economic and social changes. At the peak of hostilities, Hawaii was also host to about 250,000 American troops — and this seemed to make the islands an even more integral part of the U.S. Accordingly, President Truman announced in favor of statehood in 1946, and after a number of long delays, Congress passed the statehood bill in 1959.

While you're in Hawaii, you may be treated to the spectacle of lava erupting from the steaming volcano, Pele. If it starts to rain while you're viewing the volcano, simply slip into your rig and head for another part of the island; chances are you'll drive out of the rain just a few miles away. Of course, no visit to Hawaii would be complete without participating in a luau and watching some of the native dances — and because these spectacles are such a major part of the charm of the islands, you'll have ample opportunity to do both.

Today, tourism ranks as one of the state's major revenue sources; the pineapple and sugar industries are still strong, but they have declined somewhat in recent years under pressure from foreign competition. Since the islands remain strategically important to the nation's defense, military and government operations also play a key role in Hawaii's economy.

State Offices

Tourism
Hawaii Visitors Bureau
2270 Kalakaua Avenue
Honolulu, Hawaii 96815
(808) 923-1811

State Police
Hawaii does not have a state police department; each island maintains a separate police force which reports to the mayor of that island.

Radio Stations

Hilo
KPUA 970 (AM)
Honolulu
KORL 650 (AM)
KGU 760 (AM)
KQMQ 93 (FM)
KHSS 97 (FM)
Kailua
KLEI 1130 (AM)
Wailuku
KAOI 95 (FM)
Waipahu
KULA 92 (FM)

Hawaii Points of Interest and Attractions

HAWAII

Kaimu Black Sand Beach. This unique beach is made up of pulverized lava, fringed by towering coconut palms. Kalapana, in the Puna District, off State Route 130.

Kamehameha Statue. This statue was originally lost at sea during shipment to Hawaii but was later recovered after a replica had been made and erected in Honolulu. Kohala, off State Route 270.

Laupahoehoe. A scenic and historic spot whose name translates as "leaf of lava." Ookala, off State Route 19.

Lava Flows. The flows that have surged down the mountains of Mauna Loa and Kilauea since prehistoric times are marked on the island by Warrior signs. On State Routes 11, 19 and 190.

Painted Church. The oldest Catholic church on the island, constructed in 1875, and featuring brilliantly hued murals depicting biblical scenes on the interior walls. Honaunau, off State Route 11.

Parker Ranch. The second-largest cattle ranch in the United States, located at the foot of Mauna Kea. Waimea-Kamuela district, off State Route 190.

Puna Lava Flow. One of the most recent lava flows, still exuding heat and steam. Apua Point, off State Route 130.

Rainbow Falls. One of Hawaii's most beautiful waterfalls. Hilo, on State Route 130.

KAUAI

Botanical Gardens. Abounding in natural vegetation, Kauai also has five botanical gardens — Olu Pua Gardens at Kalaheo; Menehune Gardens in Nawiliwili; Paradise Pacifica at Wailua; Plantation Gardens in Poipu; and Pacific Tropical Botanical Garden in Lawai. Each of these gardens offers an unusual assortment of flowers, shrubs, cacti and other magnificent species of plant life.

Swaying hips and lovely hula hands are basic to any dancer of the Hawaiian hula. This pretty Hawaiian girl dressed in a ti leaf skirt demonstrates the gracefulness of her art.

Fern Grotto. A hauntingly beautiful cave festooned with growing ferns. Near Wailua Marina, off State Route 56.

Kalalau Lookout. A magnificent viewpoint that was once occupied by preening peacocks and terraces of taro. North of Kekaha, on State Route 55.

Lumahai Beach. Probably the most photographed beach on Kauai — and the location for the Nurses' Beach in *South Pacific.* Haena Point, off State Route 56.

Menehune Ditch. Only small portions remain of this aqueduct, which is thought to have been built long before the Hawaiians came, possibly by the Menehune. Waimea, off State Route 50.

Menehune Fish Pond. The remarkable stone walls that enclose this fish pond are said to have been built in one night by the Menehune. The pond they enclose is still in use. Puhi, off State Route 50.

Opaekaa Falls. The Wailua River makes a dramatic plunge over a high cliff; the name of the falls means "rolling shrimp" and dates from the days when swarms of shrimp were seen rolling in the turbulent waters at the base of the falls. Wailua, off State Route 56.

Paradise Pacifica. A 23-acre field with gardens, lagoons, exotic birds and unique narrated train rides that meander through a rain forest, a Polynesian village, Japanese island, a Filipino village and other interesting and colorful exhibits. A 75-minute extravaganza is performed nightly in the lagoon, featuring dances and music of Japan, Hawaii, the Philippines and Tahiti. Wailua, off State Route 56.

Sprouting Horn. When the tide is running high here, waves pressured through lava tubes are forced through a hole in coastal rocks, then burst noisily into fantastic fountains of salt spray and foam. Koloa, off State Route 53.

Waimea Canyon. This is more than just a view, it is an experience you won't soon forget — for the grandeur of this canyon's scenery and jewel-tone colors is simply awesome. North of Kekaha, on State Route 55.

Waipahee Slippery Slide. Accessible only by a canefield road and trail, these falls form a natural rock slide and pool. Anahola, off State Route 56.

Wet and Dry Caves of Haena. These eerie caverns, one dry, the other filled with limpid green water, are where chiefs are said to have gathered in ancient times. Haena Point, off State Route 56.

MAUI

Banyan Tree. Planted in 1873, this magnificent tree is said to be the largest banyan tree in all of Hawaii. Lahaina, off State Route 30.

Kanaha Bird Sanctuary. Each winter, migratory birds from the northwest make this park their island home. Kahana, off State Route 30.

Ohe'o Stream (Seven Pools). A series of crystal pools, part of the largest of many beautiful streams found along the east Maui coast. Kaupo, off State Route 36.

Puaa Kaa Park. A gorgeous park whose name means "the place of the rolling pigs" — referring to days gone by when plump wild pigs were said to have rolled down the slick, steep, grassy hills in this area. Nahiku, off State Route 36.

Waianapanapa Caves. Strong swimmers and scuba divers may dive into this pool and swim underwater to reach a big inner cave that was a legendary trysting place for lovers of old. Kapukaulua Point, off State Route 36.

Wailua Lookout. Visitors have a choice view of the entire Keanae Peninsula and its spectacular coastline from this vantage point. Nahiku, off State Route 36.

MOLOKAI

Halawa Valley. A road zigzags down the ridge into the valley, and a fork in the road takes you to the shore, where you can swim in the bay and at the mouth of the stream. Another road goes a short way into the valley, where you can pick up a foot trail that will take you to Moaula Falls (about an hour's hike). Pohakuloa, off State Route 45.

Kalaupapa. A low tableland of 4½ square miles where sufferers of leprosy or Hansen's disease were once banished to live out their lives. Transportation to the village is made by a mule ride down the steep pali, via small plane. Off State Route 47.

Kalaupapa Overlook. A walk through a trail carpeted with ironwood needles leads to a view of Kalaupapa, the wharf, churches, lighthouse, landing field and crater below. Off State Route 47.

Kapuaiwa Grove. One thousand coconut trees cover 10 acres along a beach park said to have been planted by King Kamehameha V in the 1860s. Kaunakakai, on State Route 46.

Lanikaula Grove. This sacred grove of kukui trees is the burial place of Lanikaula, a famous Molokai prophet; on private land, but can be seen from the road. Near Cape Halawa, on State Route 45.

Moanui Sugar Mills. The ruins and smokestack remain of a sugar mill that was run between 1870 and 1900 by Norwegian Tollifson. Kaunakakai, off State Route 45.

Octopus Stone. This stone, painted white, stands at the edge of the highway where the road takes a sharp turn inland. Legend has it that this is the rocky remainder of a cave where a supernatural octopus lived, and the stone is thought to still have special powers. Opposite Kupeke Fishpond, on State Route 45.

Ualapue Fishpond. One of the many ancient fishponds to be found along the Molokai coast. Between Pohakuloa and Kaunakakai, along State Route 45.

Waialua. Where Kamehameha nui was raised solely on taro leaves — so fishbones would not choke him. His giant *awa* cup is found by the stream. A rock by the road is said to have had an ear that could hear an enemy approaching. The taro patch is right off the road. Off State Route 45.

Wailau Trail. A difficult trail on private property and the only access to a hidden valley on the northern side of the island — a former population center for ancient Hawaiians. Pukoo, off State Route 45.

Waikolu Valley. A lookout in this valley offers views of an inaccessible valley which opens to the north side of the island; picnic area. Kualapuu, off State Route 47.

OAHU

Aloha Tower. A familiar landmark in Honolulu, offering an excellent view of the harbor area. Open year-round, daily. Honolulu, off H-1.

Aquarium. A top attraction for visitors, this aquarium contains an extensive collection of brilliantly colored tropical fish. Open year-round, daily. Waikiki, on Kalakaua Ave., across from Kapiolani Park.

Hawaii's Royal Fishponds

Hawaii's ancient people depended to a great extent on fishing for subsistence. Fishing was also enjoyed as a sport by royalty and commoner alike, and the more highly skilled were held in great esteem.

Fish were caught with nets, hooks and lines, spears, traps, poisons, as well as by hand. They were also captured in hundreds of fishponds that at one time dotted the coastlines of all the islands. The fishponds belonged exclusively to the kings and chiefs of the inlands. The commoners, though they constructed, maintained and stocked the ponds, could fish the sea only beyond the ponds.

The fishponds were constructed in shallow offshore areas and at the mouth of natural inlets by building stone walls. A type of sluice gate, called *makaha,* was used to allow small fish to enter and prevent large fish from leaving. The shallow ponds, usually no deeper than three to four feet, permitted sunlight to penetrate the water, encouraging the growth of microscopic foods for the fish to feed upon.

Although the ruins of fishponds may be found throughout the Hawaiian Islands, the largest concentration is found on Molokai. At one time the coast of Molokai had 58 ponds ranging up to 2,000 feet long.

Most of the ponds may be seen on Molokai along Route 45, the coastal drive toward Halawa. Two of the largest, Keawanui and Ualapue ponds, have been made a part of a National Historic Landmark. Keawanui pond covers 54½ acres and is enclosed by a 2,000-foot wall.

USS Arizona Memorial

This battleship took five direct hits during the Japanese attack on Pearl Harbor on December 7, 1941; the bodies of most of the 1,177 crewmen who perished in that infamous assault are still entombed in the sunken hull. A memorial walkway that now spans the vessel lists the names of the *Arizona's* Navy and Marine Corps dead. Near Honolulu, off H-1; reached by launch.

National Memorial Cemetery of the Pacific

Punchbowl or Puowaina, literally translated "Hill of Sacrifice," is the final resting place of thousands of World War II, Korean and Vietnam war veterans. Open seven days a week, it overlooks the vast expanse of Pearl Harbor, Honolulu and Waikiki.

Blow Hole. Here the sea is forced through a tiny hole in a lava ledge, blowing miniature geysers into the air. Near Koko Head, off State Route 72.

Chinatown. This downtown section of Honolulu is an exciting blend of shops, restaurants and markets displaying Chinese wares and foods — as well as goods from the countries of origin of Hawaii's early immigrants. Off H-1.

Coral Gardens. Coral growing in unique and spectacular shapes can be seen from glass-bottom boats. Kaneohe, off State Route 83.

Diamond Head. The world-famous landmark that bounds Waikiki Beach on the south. An extinct volcano, it is said to have once been the home of Pele, the Fire Goddess.

Foster Botanic Garden. Remarkable botanical displays, including a photogenic orchid section, in a 20-acre section in downtown Honolulu. Off H-1.

Hanauma Bay. A delightful sea cove in Koko Head Park, the rugged grandeur of this area was created by volcanic action more than 10,000 years ago. A favorite spot for swimming and picnicking. Off State Route 72.

Kahana Beach. Here breadfruit, Hawaiian bamboo and mango trees mark what was once a well-settled, old Hawaiian community. Between Kaaawa Park and Punaluu Park, off State Route 83.

Kahuku Sugar Mill. For many years an actual sugarcane processing plant, the mill today is an entertaining cultural attraction, offering visitors a multi-media presentation about former plantation life and a plant tour that explains the process of sugar-making. Kahuku, off State Route 83.

Kaneana Cave. The formations in this cave are both volcanic and coral. Kaneana, the sharkman deity, is supposed to have made

Although it appears to be lost in some remote setting, lovely Rainbow Falls is located just a few minutes from the port town of Hilo on the Big Island of Hawaii.

his home in the cave. Makua, just before the end of the Farrington Highway.

Kewalo Basin. Sampans and other fishing boats moor in this small boat harbor, which is also the departure point for Pearl Harbor curises. Honolulu, off H-1.

Makaha Beach. Site of international surfing meets, on the leeward side of the island, near Nanakuli and Waianae; also a popular sport fishing and picnic spot. Off State Route 930.

Nuuanu Pali. Oahu's scenic masterpiece, where Kamehameha the Great defeated the Oahuans in a bloody battle in 1795, thus adding Oahu to his realm. Thousands of the defeated warriors were forced over the precipice to meet death on the jagged rocks below. Near Honolulu, at the head of Nuuanu Valley, on State Route 61.

Paradise Park. This park is an extensive tropical exhibit set amidst varied gardens, mountain streams and waterfalls. Hundreds of tropical birds inhabit the park, which features an entertaining demonstration of trained birds. Stroll along trails through bamboo forests and Hau jungle growth. Honolulu, off State Route 61.

Rabbit Island. One of the many interesting islets that border Oahu, the island is shaped like a rabbit's head, and was once overrun by them. Near Waimanalo, off State Route 72 (reached by boat).

Hawaii State Parks

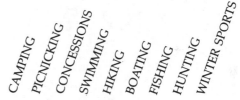

Park	Location	CAMPING	PICNICKING	CONCESSIONS	SWIMMING	HIKING	BOATING	FISHING	HUNTING	WINTER SPORTS
Aina Moana	*Honolulu. Off Route H-1. (Oahu)*		•		•					
Akaka Falls	*Honomu. Off Route 19. (Hawaii)*		•							
Kahana Valley	*Honolulu. On Route 83. (Oahu)*		•		•					
Kokee	*Kekaha. On Route 50. (Kauai)*	•	•	•	•	•	•	•	•	
Mackenzie	*Pahoa. Off Route 130. (Hawaii)*	•	•					•		
Mauna Kea	*Hilo. Off Route 137. (Hawaii)*		•			•				
Na Pali Coast	*Near Polihale Landing. (Kauai)*	•	•			•	•	•		
Palaau	*Kualapuu. Off Route 47. (Molokai)*	•	•							
Polihale	*Bonham Air Force Base. Five miles north off Route 50. (Kauai)*		•		•					
Waianapanapa	*Hana. Off Route 30. (Maui)*	•	•					•		
Wailua	*Lihue. On Route 56. (Kauai)*	•	•		•			•		
Wailuku	*Hilo. On Route 130. (Hawaii)*		•							
Waimea Canyon	*Kekaha. On Route 55. (Kauai)*		•			•				

Hawaii has no state forests. For more information on Hawaii state parks, contact: *Department of Land and Natural Resources, Division of Parks, Outdoor Recreation and Historical Sites, 1151 Punchbowl Street, Honolulu, Hawaii 96813, (808) 548-7455.*

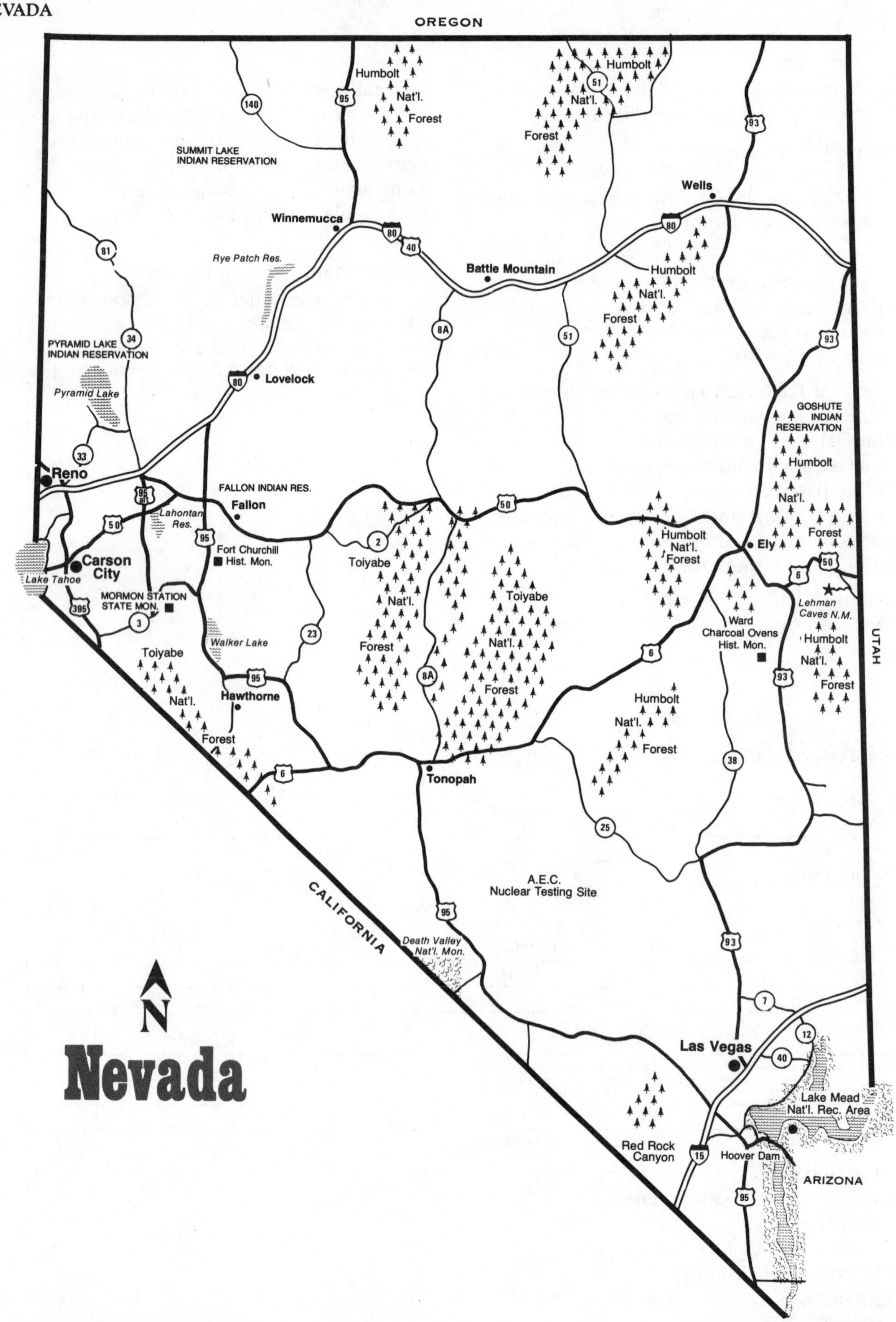

Map not to exact scale.

Nevada

Mention Nevada to most people and they immediately think of the glitter, glamour and gaming tables of Las Vegas, Reno and Tahoe. While gambling and live-entertainment are undoubtedly the state's biggest attractions, Nevada really has much more to offer travelers. For once you're beyond the lights of the gambling centers, you'll discover a landscape that is just about evenly divided between desert and mountains; and within those two extremes you'll find some surprisingly beautiful scenery, a number of picturesque old ghost towns, some of the best fishing waters in all of the West and excellent big-game hunting.

Nevada was claimed by the Spaniards in 1776 after a Spanish missionary named Francisco Garces passed through the region on his way to the West Coast. Despite the Spanish claim, the area lay unexplored until John C. Fremont and Kit Carson searched the area between 1843 and 1845. Following the Mexican War, the United States gained possession of the area, and the first settlement, a Mormon trading post, was established at what is now the town of Genoa. With the discovery of the Comstock Lode at Virginia City in 1859, large numbers of Californians settled in Carson County. Not wishing to be under Mormon rule, the settlers petitioned Congress to create the Nevada Territory out of western Utah, and Nevada became a separate territory in 1861. Three years later, amid the turmoil and politics of the Civil War, Nevada was admitted as a state.

While you're in Nevada, you're bound to see a great deal of money change hands, but chances are it won't equal the amount

Full name: State of Nevada
Origin of name: From Spanish meaning "Snow-Clad."
Motto: All for Our Country.
Nickname: Silver State
Capital: Carson City
Statehood: October 31, 1864, 36th state.
Population: 633,000 (ranks 46th).
Major Cities: Las Vegas (146,036), Reno (78,098).
Bird: Mountain bluebird
Flower: Sagebrush
Tree: Single-leaf pinon

Average daily temperatures by month

	Northern	Southern
Jan.	37.7 to 17.9	57.1 to 28.7
Feb.	41.7 to 21.6	62.6 to 32.5
Mar.	45.0 to 23.0	68.2 to 36.5
Apr.	54.0 to 30.0	76.5 to 43.5
May	64.2 to 37.7	85.8 to 51.4
Jun.	73.2 to 44.0	95.6 to 59.5
Jul.	85.4 to 51.3	102.1 to 67.2
Aug.	83.3 to 49.8	99.7 to 65.8
Sept.	74.1 to 40.3	92.9 to 57.1
Oct.	63.0 to 31.8	80.7 to 46.9
Nov.	48.0 to 25.2	66.0 to 36.3
Dec.	39.2 to 18.8	57.6 to 29.4
Year	59.1 to 32.6	78.7 to 46.2

produced by the Carlin Mine, the second-richest gold mine in the nation. So if you want to get an idea of what a $100,000 gold bar looks like, stop off at the mine; its off Interstate 80, just north of Carlin. Southeast of Las Vegas, you'll find Hoover Dam and the massive Lake Mead. Take a tour of the dam and then head for the lake for a houseboat sojourn or a few days of superb angling.

Ever since the legalization of gambling in 1931, tourism has been Nevada's main industry, but the mining of copper, gold, silver, zinc, lead, tungsten and magnesium also plays an important role in the economy. Because of the state's dry climate (annual rainfall of only 3.73 inches), agriculture is limited; however, there is a limited amount of sheep and cattle ranching.

Las Vegas is only one of Nevada's three major gambling centers, offering round-the-clock entertainment and excitement.

State Offices

Tourism
Department of Economic Development
Blasdel Building
Carson City, Nevada 89701
(702) 882-7478

State Police
Department of Public Safety
Carson City, Nevada 89711
(702) 885-5440

Radio Stations

Las Vegas
KDWN 720 (AM)
KENO 1460 (AM)

Garnet Hill

Dark red garnets are still plentiful on Garnet Hill near Ely in spite of rather heavy collections in recent years. A few of these garnets are of gem value, but most of them have flaws and are valuable primarily as souvenirs or for "rockhound" collections. A long search may be required to find a crystal of quality and size suitable for use in jewelry, but naturally faceted stones of much interest can be found at the rate of a dozen per hour in better places.

The garnets may be found by breaking up the pinkish rhyolite where they were formed in quartz vugs. Best luck is usually reported by those who carefully search the surface of the soil for dark spots which are caused by the reddish crystals that have weathered from the rock through centuries.

These garnets have been identified by the Nevada Bureau of Mines as a deep red variety of spessartite, manganese-aluminum garnet.

Kennecott Open-Pit Mine

Nearly 1,400 men and women are engaged in recovering copper from open-pit mines at Kennecott Copper Corporation's Eastern Nevada operations.

Each day some 22,000 tons of ore and 80,000 tons of waste must be removed at Kennecott's five-pit mining operation at Ruth, Nevada, just west of Ely. The ore is sent by railroad to a concentrator-smelter complex at McGill, 12 miles north of Ely. Here the mineral is crushed and ground and chemically treated to produce a copper concentrate which in turn is smelted to produce 140 tons of blister copper.

The company provides free tours of the mill and smelter Monday through Friday, from June 15 to September 1. A lookout point is provided year-round for the visitors at the Ruth Pit.

Nevada Points of Interest and Attractions

Atmospherium and Planetarium. This facility presents programs of the night skies and changing shows depicting astronomical events of the past, present and future; exhibits. Open year-round, daily, except major holidays. Adults $2.50, children under 13, $1.50; museum admission free. Reno, on North Virginia Street, at northern edge of University of Nevada campus.

Beatty. A picturesque mining town at the Nevada approach to Death Valley National Monument. On US-95.

Chollar Mine. A gold and silver mine of the Comstock era, featuring an original structure of square-set timbers; tours. Open April through October, daily, 11 a.m. to 6 p.m. Adults $2, children 6 to 16, $1.

Goldfield. A famous mining camp and the site of one of the West's richest gold deposits. Mining operations have recently been resumed. In the early 1900s, the town was also the setting for the renowned 42-round Gans-Nelson lightweight world boxing championship. On US-95.

Harrah's Automobile Collection. Exhibits of antique, vintage and classic automobiles, as well as motorcycles, boats, airplanes and railroad cars. Visitors may also view restorations in progress. Open year-round, daily, 9 a.m. to 6 p.m. Adults $4, children over 13, $2, 5 to 12, $1.50. Sparks, off Glendale Road.

Virginia and Truckee Railroad. A restored standard-gauge railroad that offers excursions between Virginia City and Gold Hill. Open mid-May through September, daily, 10:30 a.m. to 6 p.m. Adults $1.85, children 5 to 12, $1. Virginia City, off US-50.

Westworld. An entertainment complex featuring western characters, an old fort and the home movies of Elvis Presley. Open year-round, daily. Free; rides extra. Henderson, on Boulder Highway.

Nevada State Parks

Park	Location	CAMPING	PICNICKING	CONCESSIONS	SWIMMING	HIKING	BOATING	FISHING	HUNTING	WINTER SPORTS
Beaver Dam	*Caliente. Off US-93. (Trailers not permitted)*	•	•			•		•	•	
Berlin-Ichthyosaur	*Gabbs. Off State Route 23.*	•	•			•				
Cave Lake	*Ely. Off US-93.*	•	•		•		•	•		
Fort Churchill	*Silver Springs. Off US-95.*	•	•			•				
Lahontan	*Fallon. Off US-50.*	•	•		•		•	•		
Lake Tahoe—Nevada	*Incline Village. On State Route 28.*		•			•	•	•		
Mormon Station	*Genoa. Off US-395.*		•							
Rye Patch	*Lovelock. Off Interstate 80.*	•	•		•		•	•		
Spring Valley	*Ursine. Off US-93.*	•	•		•	•	•	•		
Valley of Fire	*Moapa. Off Interstate 15.*	•	•			•				
Ward Charcoal Ovens	*Ely. Off US-6 and US-50.*		•							
Washoe Lake	*Reno. Off US-395.*	•	•		•	•		•		

Nevada has no state forests. For more information on Nevada State parks, contact: *Department of Conservation and Natural Resources, State Park System, 201 South Fall Street, Carson City, Nevada 89701, (702) 885-4384.*

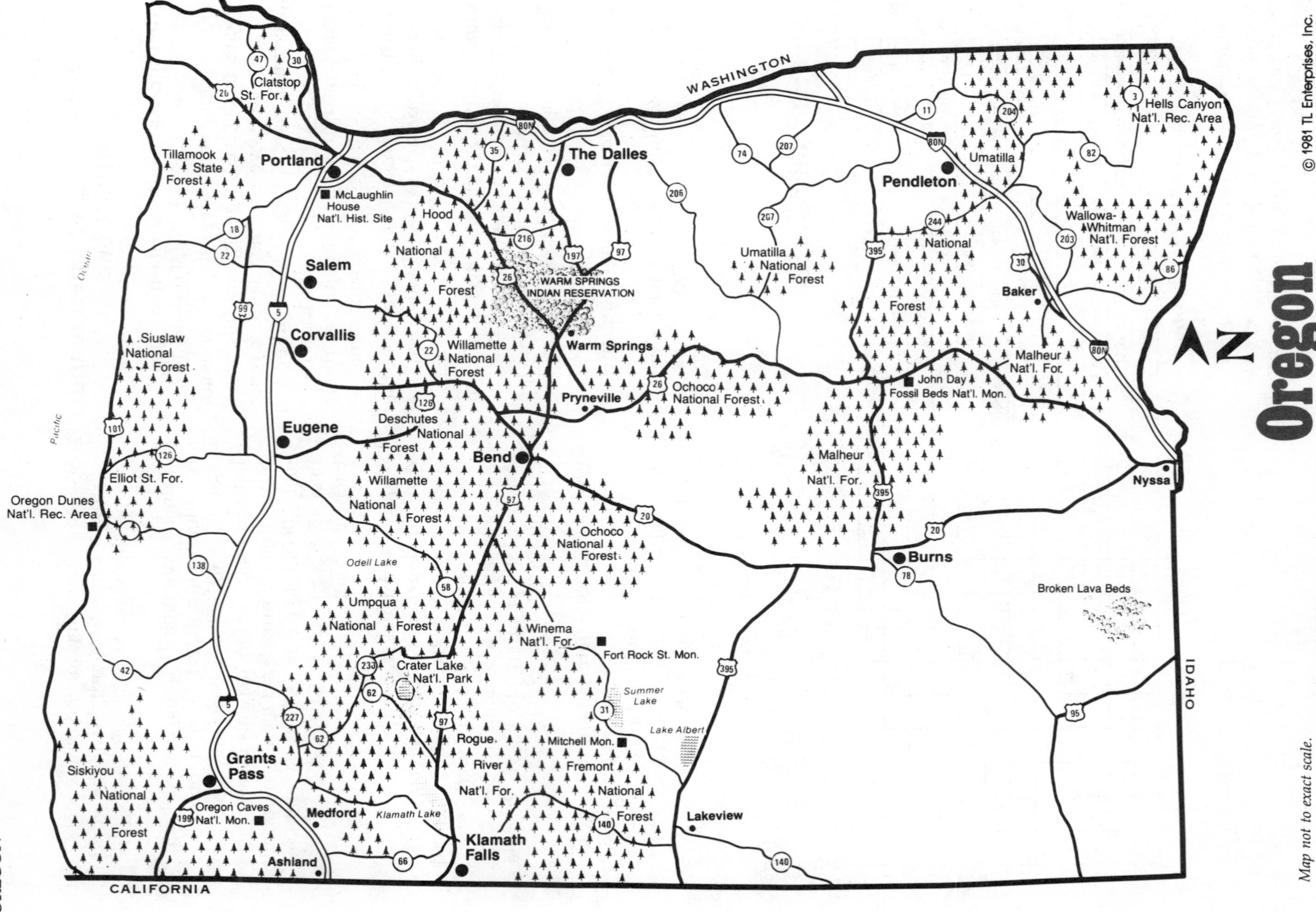

Map not to exact scale.

Oregon

Oregon and trees are nearly synonymous — and with more than 30 million acres (more than half the state's total area) in forest lands, it's not surprising that Oregon is the nation's leading lumber state. Combine those lush forests with the state's other natural resources — snowcapped peaks, verdant valleys, rich plains, and nearly 400 miles of Pacific coastline — and it's also not surprising that Oregon is one of the most scenic of all the 50 states.

The first European known to have sighted the Oregon coast was Sir Francis Drake in 1577. Following Drake's visit, little exploration of the area was done until the Spanish launched an expedition in 1774, followed by Captain Cook and Captain George Vancouver in 1776 and 1792, respectively. The first exploration by Americans was that of Lewis and Clark from 1804 and 1806. Within a few years (1811) the Pacific Fur Company established a post at the mouth of the Columbia River and development spread gradually, first with missions for the Indians and later with scattered colonization. In the early 1840s, settlement increased dramatically as large numbers of pioneers poured into the region over the Oregon Trail. No legal title to the land was possible at that time, however, as the territory was jointly occupied by Great Britain and the United States.

Finally, the Oregon Treaty of 1846 settled the problem, as Britain and the U.S. agreed to the 49th parallel for the US-Canadian border west of the Rockies. The territory thus established included not only the present state of Oregon but Washington, Idaho and Montana, as well.

Full name: State of Oregon
Origin of name: Probably from "Ouragan," the Indian name for the Columbia River.
Motto: The Union.
Nickname: Beaver State.
Capital: Salem
Statehood: February 14, 1859, 33rd state.
Population: 2,376,113 (ranks 30th).
Major Cities: Portland (356,372), Eugene (92,511), Salem (78,168).
Bird: Western meadowlark
Flower: Oregon grape
Tree: Douglas fir

Average daily temperatures by month

	Northeastern	Southwestern
Jan.	37.9 to 22.8	47.9 to 34.2
Feb.	43.5 to 26.1	54.0 to 36.0
Mar.	49.0 to 28.1	57.6 to 36.3
Apr.	57.8 to 32.6	63.8 to 38.8
May	66.6 to 38.7	70.3 to 43.6
Jun.	73.8 to 44.8	76.5 to 49.3
Jul.	84.7 to 48.9	84.2 to 52.3
Aug.	83.0 to 47.6	83.2 to 51.9
Sept.	74.8 to 41.0	78.5 to 47.5
Oct.	62.6 to 33.9	66.6 to 42.9
Nov.	47.8 to 28.8	54.3 to 39.3
Dec.	39.3 to 24.0	48.4 to 35.6
Year	60.1 to 34.8	65.4 to 42.3

Washington was later separated in 1853, Idaho in 1863 and Montana in 1864. Prior to these divisions, Oregon — with its capital at Oregon City — was recognized as a territory in 1849. Ten years later, at the same time that the discovery of gold in the

Cascades inspired Oregon's gold rush, the territory was granted statehood.

Today, Oregon remains one of America's wilderness strongholds, and it offers almost limitless outdoor recreation. You won't want to miss the magnificent coastal region, where you'll find attractions such as Gold Beach, Oregon Dunes National Recreation Area and Cape Kiwanda. Inland, along the Willamette Valley — the site of the original settlements — there is the bustling city of Portland, the nearby Columbia Gorge, the Columbia River Highway and Mount Hood. Southern Oregon offers Crater Lake National Park, Oregon Caves National Monument and the famous Rogue River. And once you've seen these sights, you've sampled only a fraction of what Oregon has to offer, as there's much remaining to explore on the east side of the Cascades, in the region known as the Columbia Plateau.

Besides lumber, tourism plays an important role in Oregon's economy, and manufacturing includes food products, primary metals and paper products. Agriculture also has a key role, with wheat, potatoes, hay and grass seed among the chief crops.

Oregon Points of Interest and Attractions

Astoria Column. This 125-foot high column was erected in 1926 in commemoration of the discovery, exploration and settlement of the Northwest around Astoria. Located on a hill 700 feet above the Columbia River, the site provides an excellent vantage point for viewing the nearby mountains, ocean and river. Open June through Labor Day, daily, 8 a.m. to sunset. Free. Astoria, off US-30.

Bonneville Lock and Dam. This lock and dam, separated by Bradford Island, creates a deep lake which extends upstream for 50 miles. Visitors may watch the upstream

State Offices

Tourism
Oregon Department of Transportation
Travel Information Section
State Transportation Building
Salem, Oregon 97310
(503) 378-3438

State Police
Department of Public Safety
Salem, Oregon 97310
(503) 378-3720

Radio Stations

Eugene
KUGN 590 (AM)
KZEL 96.1 (FM)
Portland
KGW 620 (AM)
KINK 101.9 (FM)

An exciting way to take to the air in northern Oregon is a gondola ride from Wallowa Lake (4,400-foot elevation) to the summit of Mount Howard, nearly 8,200 feet high. Wallowa Lake and the Wallowa Valley can be seen in the distance.

Oregon's Hot Springs

Hot springs oases ranging from full-service luxury resorts to rustic cabin complexes and secluded forest waysides are among Oregon's endless variety of travel destinations. Invigorating springs offer a bonus for many of the state's visitors and residents, whether at the end of 18 holes of play on a plush, green resort golf course or as a part of a quiet mountain hike.

The following is a directory to the state's hot springs sites (there is a charge for use unless otherwise noted):

Austin Hot Springs — 35 miles southeast of Estacada in Mount Hood National Forest. Take Forest Service Road No. S-46 off Oregon Highway 224 and follow approximately seven miles to hot pools in Clackamas River. Free day-use is maintained by Portland General Electric Company.

Facilities: Picnic area.

Accommodations: None. Nearest Forest Service campgrounds (tent camping only) are four miles west of springs.

Bagby Hot Springs — 40 miles southeast of Estacada in Mount Hood National Forest. Take Forest Service Road No. S-46 off Highway 224 to Riverford Campground, then follow Forest Service S-63 along Collawash River, and then S-70 to Bagby Hot Springs parking area. A 1½-mile hiking trail leads to the springs.

Hunter's Lodge — 1½ miles north of Lakeview on site of Old Perpetual Geyser, reported to be only continuous spouting geyser in nation.

Facilities: Parking area and viewpoint for viewing geyser.

Accommodations: Motel units and restaurants; water heated by geyser.

Jackson Hot Springs — Two miles north of Ashland off Highway 99.

Facilities: Swimming pool (lukewarm) for seasonal use, year-round private mineral baths.

Accommodations: Cabins, trailer park, tent campsites. Reservations recommended. (503) 482-3776.

Kah-Nee-Ta Vacation Resort — On Warm Springs Reservation, 114 miles east of Portland off U.S. Highway 26. Full-service luxury vacation resort with mineral-heated pools.

Facilities: Mineral springs-heated pools and mineral baths at Village area; heated pool and saunas at Lodge.

Accommodations: Cottages, trailer campground and "tepee" camping shelters at Village; luxury units at Lodge. Reservations recommended. Call toll-free (800) 452-1138.

Radium Hot Springs Park — 12 miles north of Baker, one mile north of Haines on Oregon Highway 30. Site of old sanatorium.

Facilities: Large hot swimming pool, picnic area (open mid-April to mid-September).

Accommodations: Tent camping site.

Ritter Hot Springs — 51 miles north of John Day and 25 miles north of Long Creek (make left turn after crossing bridge over middle fork of John Day River). Year-round hot springs resort.

Facilities: Hot mineral baths, swimming pool (covered in cool weather).

Accommodations: Hotel rooms, cabins and trailers with kitchen facilities. Reservations recommended. (503) 421-3841.

spawning migration of fish through underwater viewing windows. Peak migration: March to November. Open year-round, daily, during daylight hours. Free. Bonneville, on Interstate 84 and US-30.

Dalles Dam. Visitors are invited to tour this facility, which is a vital link in the development of the Columbia River and the Pacific Northwest. Open year-round, 8 a.m. to 4 p.m.; train ride open May 15 to September 15, daily, 10 a.m. to 5:30 p.m. Free. The Dalles, off Interstate 84.

Enchanted Forest. Storybook characters are featured in a woodland setting. Open March through September, daily. Adults $2.25, children 3 to 12, $1.50. Salem, off Interstate 5 (exit 248), on Enchanted Way.

Hoyt Arboretum. A 213-acre facility containing 650 varieties of trees; trails, guided tours. Open year-round, daily, 5 a.m. to midnight. Free. Portland, Burnside Road.

Ira's Fountain. One square block of waterfalls, pools, streams, trees and grass. Fountain has an output of 13,000 gallons-per-minute. Operates year-round, Thursday through Tuesday, 8:30 a.m. to 11 p.m. Portland, Third and SW Clay Streets.

Lava Cast Forest Geological Area. At this unique site you will find the molds of pine trees which were engulfed by slow-moving lava; self-guided trails. Open year-round, daily. Bend, south on US-97.

Malheur Cave. A one-half mile deep lava tube offering self-guided exploration; lantern needed. Open year-round, except last two weeks in August, daily. Burns, off State Route 78.

Marine Science Center. Aquarium and museum exhibits in Oregon State University facility. Open June 11 through September 8, daily, 10 a.m. to 6 p.m.; remainder of year, 10 a.m. to 4 p.m. Free. Newport, on Yaquina Bay.

Mary's Peak. The highest peak in the Pacific Coast Range (4,097 feet) offering spectacular views of the ocean and Cascade Mountains; campground, picnic areas. Corvallis, off State Route 34.

Newberry Crater. An old volcano crater divided into two parts and forming East Lake and Paulina Lake; excellent fishing. Bend, 24 miles south, off US-97.

Otter Crest Wayside. A flat-topped rock rising 453 feet above the tide which offers excellent views of a rocky seashore that is inhabited by several species of birds, sea lions and seals. Otter Rock, off US-101.

Petersen's Rock Gardens. Several acres of colorful bridges, terraces and replicas of historic structures built of petrified wood and rock; picnic area.Open year-round, daily, 7 a.m. to sunset. Redmond, off US-97.

Prehistoric Gardens. Life-sized replicas of dinosaurs and other prehistoric beasts in forest setting. Open year-round, daily, 8 a.m. to sunset. Adults $2.50, children 12 to 18, $2, 5 to 11, $1.25. Port Orford, on US-101.

Round Butte Dam. A hydroelectric project located on the Deschutes River featuring geological, wildlife and artifact displays; picnic area. Open Memorial Day through Labor Day, Wednesday to Sunday, 10 a.m. to 6 p.m. Free. Madras, off US-97.

Scenic Drives. *Cascade Lakes Highway:* A magnificent 76-mile drive that takes you through the Deschutes National Forest, to Elk Lake, Crane Prairie Reservoir and Pringle Falls. Bend, southwest to US-97. *Columbia River Highway:* From Portland to the west or east, this route takes you through some of the most scenic country in all of Oregon. On the eastward leg you'll see the spectacular Columbia River Gorge, with unique rock formations and cliffs rising as high as 2,000 feet, together with a number of beautiful waterfalls. *Mount Emily:* This road is best traveled by vehicles with high ground clearance, as it is a rugged route that winds 10 miles to the top of Mount Emily overlooking the Grand Ronde Valley. Near LaGrande, off Interstate 84. *Mount Hood Highway:* This loop road passes through historic Bennett Pass and crosses the White River Glacier, providing a view of a glacial stream near its source. In Mount Hood National Forest, between Sandy and Gateway. *Palmer Butte Overlook:* This route rises to an elevation of 2,000 feet to provide scenic panoramas of the coastal mountains, the ocean and the community of Brookings. Brookings, east on Chetco River Road. *Rim Drive:* This 35-mile-long route runs one-way around the rim of Crater Lake; from various points along the road, you'll have beautiful views of the lake and surrounding landscape. Open July 4 through September 25 (weather permitting). In Crater Lake National Park, from Cleetwood Cove.

Undersea Gardens. View marine plants and animals in their natural habitat; scuba diving shows. Open year-round, daily, 10 a.m. to sunset. Adults $3, children 12 to 17, $2, 5 to 11, $1. Newport, 267 SW Bay Boulevard.

Yaquina Bay Lighthouse. This interesting structure is furnished in the period of its construction, the late 1800s. Open June through mid-September, Thursday to Monday, 12:30 p.m. to 7:30 p.m. Adults 50 cents, children under 6, free. Newport, in Yaquina Bay State Park, on US-101.

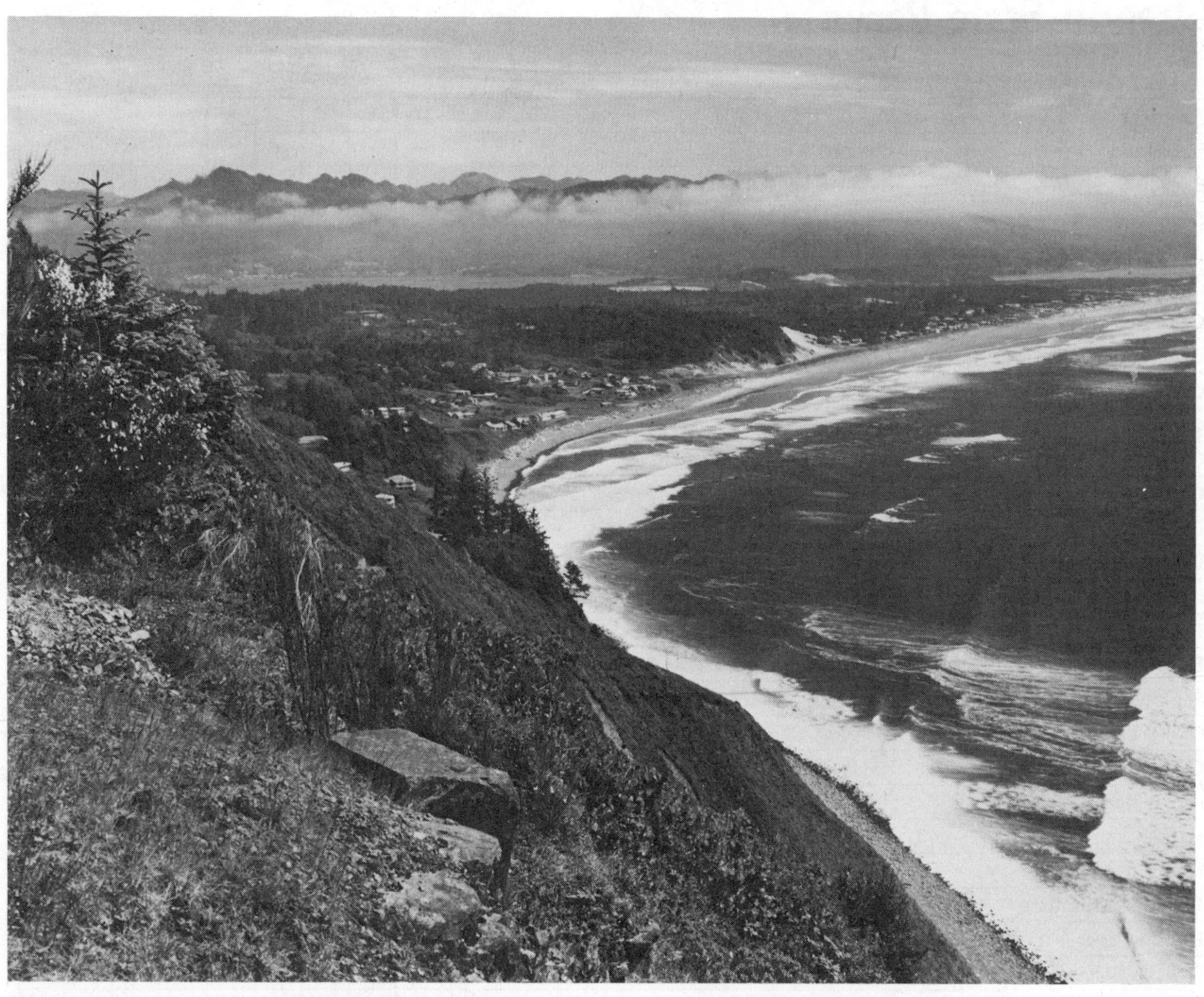

Neahkahnie Mountain rises above the pounding surf at Oswald West State Park on the northern Oregon Coast. The mountain has been the scene of frequent searches for treasure supposedly hidden by the crew of a wrecked Spanish galleon.

Oregon State Forests

Forest	Location	Camping	Picnicking	Concessions	Swimming	Hiking	Boating	Fishing	Hunting	Winter Sports
Diamond Mill	*Tillamook. Off State Route 6.*	•	•					•		
Elk Creek	*Forest Grove. Off State Route 6.*	•	•					•		
Gales Creek	*Forest Grove. Off State Route 47.*	•	•			•		•		
Jones Creek	*Tillamook. Off State Route 6.*	•	•					•		
Nehalem Falls	*Mohler. Off US-101.*	•						•		

Oregon State Parks

Park	Location	Camping	Picnicking	Concessions	Swimming	Hiking	Boating	Fishing	Hunting	Winter Sports
Armitage	*Eugene. Off Interstate 5.*	•	•		•	•	•	•		
Beachside	*Waldport. On US-101.*	•	•		•	•		•		
Benson	*Portland. Off Interstate 84.*		•		•		•	•		
Beverly Beach	*Newport. On US-101.*	•	•		•			•		
Bullards Beach	*Bandon. Off US-101.*	•	•		•	•	•	•		
Cape Arago	*Charleston. Off US-101.*		•		•	•		•		
Cape Blanco	*Port Orford. Off US-101.*	•	•		•	•		•		
Cape Lookout	*Tillamook. Off US-101.*	•	•		•	•		•		
Carl G. Washburne Memorial	*Florence. Off US-101.*	•	•		•	•		•		
Cascadia	*Sweet Home. On US-20.*	•	•		•	•		•		
Casey	*Medford. On State Route 62.*		•				•	•		
Collier Memorial	*Klamath Falls. On US-97.*	•	•			•		•		
Dabney	*Portland. On US-30.*		•		•			•		
Deschutes River	*The Dalles. Off Interstate 80N.*	•	•					•		
Detroit Lake	*Detroit. On State Route 22.*	•	•		•		•	•		
Devil's Lake	*Lincoln City. On US-101.*	•	•				•	•		
Farewell Bend	*Huntington. Off Interstate 84.*	•	•			•		•		
Fogarty Creek	*Depoe Bay. On US-101.*		•		•	•		•		
Goose Lake	*Lakeview. Off US-395.*	•	•		•		•	•		
Governor Patterson Memorial	*Waldport. On US-101.*	•	•		•		•	•		
Harris Beach	*Brookings. On US-101.*	•	•		•	•		•		
Hat Rock	*Umatilla. Off US-730.*		•		•	•	•	•		
Hendricks Bridge	*Eugene. On US-126.*		•		•	•	•	•		
Humbug Mountain	*Port Orford. On US-101.*	•	•		•	•		•		
Illinois River	*Cave Junction. Off US-101.*		•		•			•		
Jackson F. Kimball	*Fort Klamath Junction. On State Route 232.*		•					•		
Jessie M. Honeyman Memorial	*Florence. Off US-101.*	•	•		•	•	•	•		
Joseph H. Stewart	*Medford. Off State Route 62.*	•	•		•	•	•	•		

Oregon State Parks

Park	Location	Camping	Picnicking	Concessions	Swimming	Hiking	Boating	Fishing	Hunting	Winter Sports
Lake Owyhee	*Nyssa. Off State Route 301.*	•	•		•		•	•		
Lewis and Clark	*Troutdale. Off Interstate 84.*		•		•		•	•		
Leob	*Brookings. Off US-101.*	•	•		•			•		
Mayer	*The Dalles. Off Interstate 84.*		•		•		•	•		
Milo McIver	*Estacada. Off State Route 211.*	•	•		•	•	•	•		
Muriel O. Pansler Memorial	*Florence. On US-101.*		•		•			•		
Nehalem Bay	*Manzanita Junction. Off US-101.*	•	•		•		•	•		
Neptune	*Yachats. On US-101.*		•		•			•		
North Santiam	*Mill City. Off State Route 22.*		•		•	•		•		
Ochaco Lake	*Prineville. On US-26.*	•	•		•	•	•	•		
Ona Beach	*Newport. On US-101.*		•		•		•	•		
Oswald West	*Manzanita. On US-101.*	•	•		•	•		•		
Prineville Reservoir	*Prineville. Off US-26.*	•	•		•		•	•		
Rooster Rock	*Portland. Off Interstate 84.*		•		•		•	•		
Samuel H. Boardman	*Brookings. On US-101.*		•			•	•	•		
Sarah Helmick	*Monmouth. On US-99W.*		•		•			•		
Sunset Bay	*North Bend. Off US-101.*	•	•		•	•		•		
Susan Creek	*Roseburg. On State Route 138.*	•	•					•		
Tou Velle	*Medford. Off State Route 62.*		•		•		•	•		
Tumalo	*Bend. Off US-20.*	•	•		•	•		•		
Unity Lake	*Unity Junction. On State Route 7.*	•	•		•		•	•		
Valley of the Rogue	*Rogue River. Off Interstate 5.*	•	•		•		•	•		
Wallowa Lake	*Joseph. On State Route 82.*	•	•	•	•	•	•	•		
William M. Tugman	*Coos Bay. On US-101.*	•	•		•		•	•		
Yaquina Bay	*Newport. On US-101.*		•		•			•		

For more information on Oregon state parks and forests, contact: *State Parks and Recreation Branch, 525 Trade Street, SE, Salem, Oregon 97310, (503) 378-6305.*

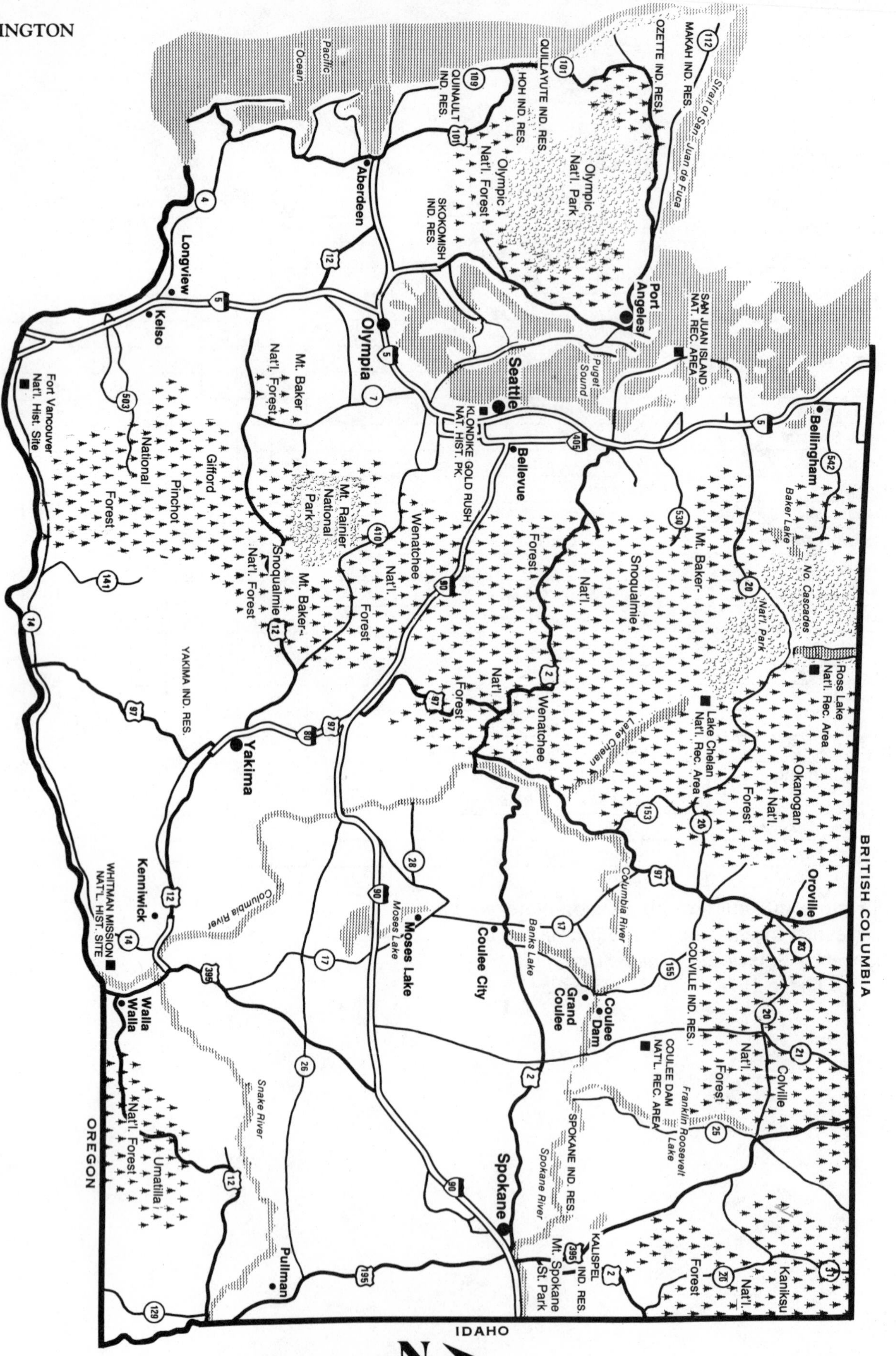

N

Map not to exact scale.

Washington

Washington

Like the other Western states, Washington is a paradise for outdoor lovers. Heavy rains might discourage some activities during the winter months, but summers are generally dry and sunny — ideal for a day of fly-fishing on the Stittagaumish River; clamming on the ocean beaches of Carkeek, Lincoln and Alki; backpacking along the trails of the Cascade and Olympic mountains; or simply relaxing in your national forest or state park campsite.

Spanish explorer Juan Perez, discoverer of Nootka Sound and Mount Olympus in 1774, led the European exploration of the region now known as Washington state. British and Americans — Captain Cook and Lewis and Clark — followed in quick succession, and by the early 1800s those two nations were engaged in a race for the possession of the region. In 1811, John Jacob Astor of the American Fur Company founded Astoria, which was taken over by the British in 1812, but restored to the Americans in 1818. That same year, the United States and Britain entered into an agreement to jointly occupy the territory, but American settlers continued to move into the region in large numbers, thus pressuring the English to relinquish their claim to the lands that lay below the 49th parallel. In 1853, Washington Territory was created from the Oregon Territory, and for the next 30 years Washington's development was spurred by mining booms and the attendant population influx. A petition for statehood was finally granted in 1889.

With an abundance of state parks, six national forests and three national parks, you won't have to search very far for a scenic campsite — and near that campsite you'll find countless opportunities for fishing, boating and swimming, as well as attractions like Snoqualmie Falls and Grand Coulee Dam. For the history buff there's Fort Simcoe, a 200-acre state historic park that contains one of the two U.S. Army posts established in the Washington territory, or Whitman Mission,

Full name: State of Washington
Origin of name: In honor of George Washington.
Motto: *Alki* (By and By).
Nickname: Evergreen State.
Capital: Olympia
Statehood: November 11, 1889, 42nd state.
Population: 3,658,000 (ranks 22nd).
Major Cities: Seattle (487,095), Spokane (173,698), Tacoma (151,267).
Bird: Willow goldfinch
Flower: Western rhododendron
Tree: Western hemlock

Average daily temperatures by month

	Eastern	Western
Jan.	31.4 to 19.2	43.6 to 33.0
Feb.	37.4 to 22.5	47.0 to 34.5
Mar.	47.0 to 29.1	51.3 to 36.2
Apr.	58.6 to 35.9	58.2 to 40.1
May	69.3 to 43.1	65.6 to 45.3
Jun.	74.5 to 49.3	69.9 to 49.7
Jul.	85.6 to 55.4	75.6 to 54.1
Aug.	83.0 to 52.9	74.6 to 53.6
Sept.	74.7 to 47.0	69.3 to 50.5
Oct.	60.1 to 38.0	60.3 to 44.4
Nov.	42.9 to 28.5	49.6 to 38.1
Dec.	35.9 to 24.2	45.9 to 35.7
Year	58.4 to 57.1	59.2 to 42.9

Washington state operates a fleet of ferry boats that cruise the Puget Sound from Tacoma to the San Juan Islands year-round, transporting cars and recreational vehicles to the islands. The San Juan Islands comprise a partially submerged archipelago between the Washington mainland and Vancouver Island, British Columbia, and enjoy a milder climate than the rest of western Washington.

a 98-acre site established in 1836 by Dr. Marcus Whitman and his wife. And while those winter rains may deter some forms of recreation, they mean snow for the high country — as much as 200 inches on some peaks — and this translates into some of the best skiing and winter sports in the Western U.S.

Agriculture occupies about 40% of Washington's total land area, and Washington leads the nation in the production of apples. Other important crops include cherries, peaches, plums, pears, hops, potatoes, lettuce and asparagus. In recent years, Washington has moved to diversify its industry, with less dependency on federal defense contracts. Tourism now occupies an important place in the overall economic picture and the manufacture of chemicals, wood products and primary metals is taking a more important place.

State Offices

Tourism
Department of Commerce and Economic Development
Travel Development Division
General Administration Building
Olympia, Washington 98404
(206) 464-6282

State Police
Department of Public Safety
Olympia, Washington 98504
(206) 753-6540

Radio Stations

Seattle
KOMO 1000 (AM)
KVI 101.3 (FM)
KZAM 1540 (AM)

A Suggested Tour

Oregon Border to British Columbia Border Via US-395

Beginning where the Columbia River turns north, US-395 crosses the Snake River, then angles northeast to join with Interstate 90 into Spokane. From there it turns north through Panorama Land, crosses Roosevelt Lake and proceeds north to the Canadian border. This 260-mile stretch of highway can be driven in 6½ hours — and these will be your signposts:

- Oregon Border
- Junction of US-395 and US-12 leading east to Walla Walla and Clarkston.
- PASCO. The earliest descriptions of the area are found in the journals kept by the Lewis and Clark Expedition as they came westward in 1805. The first settlers were cattlemen arriving about 1871. The climate is desert-like with an average of 300 days of sunshine per year. Richland (Pasco, Kennewick and Richland form the Tri-Cities) is the site of the Hanford Atomic Research Center, thus the very modern originated in one of the older settlements of the Northwest. Proceed northeast on US-395 through expanded farm lands brought to life through irrigation to . . .
- Junction of Interstate 90 and US-395.
- SPOKANE. Center of the Inland Empire and home of the 1974 Expo '74 World's Fair, this city was founded by mining interests and now is the economic hub of eastern Washington, northern Idaho and western Montana. There is a fine Indian interpretive center here, and the memorabilia of Bing Crosby may be seen at Gonzaga University. From Division Street and Second Avenue, head north on US-395. A short trip can be made to the Spokane House and the Indian rock paintings looping back to US-395. US-2 leads east to the Rocky Mountains, four miles north of Spokane. Proceeding north to . . .
- CHEWELAH. Just a short side trip to 49 Degrees North ski area. US-395 heads up the Colville River valley and flanks the Huckleberry Mountains. Proceed north to . . .
- COLVILLE. A brawling frontier town 100 years ago, it has now quieted down and reflects the peacefulness of the area known as Panorama Land. The town is named after the Colville Indians. State Route 20 goes east from Colville to Newport and joins US-2 at the Idaho border. North to . . .
- KETTLE FALLS. Near the confluence of the Columbia and Kettle Rivers. The town had to be relocated due to the rising waters on the river caused by construction of Grand Coulee Dam. Continue to . . .
- Junction of State Route 20 leading west to the Okanagan Valley and the North Cascade Highway. Proceed north to . . .
- The British Columbia border.

Washington Points of Interest and Attractions

Bill Speidel Underground Tours. Walking tours that take in the 19th-century storefronts in Seattle's Pioneer Square area. Tours include subterranean streets and storefronts created when street levels were raised eight to 35 feet following a fire in 1889; flashlight needed and comfortable shoes advised. Open year-round, daily, 9 a.m. to 5 p.m.; reservations required. Adults $2.50, children 6 to 12, $1.25. Seattle, off Interstate 5. (206) 682-4646.

Dry Falls. Sheer, curving cliffs where the prehistoric Columbia River plunged 400 feet from the upper Grand Coulee on its erosive course to the sea; interpretive center. Open May through September, Wednesday to Sunday, 10 a.m. to 6 p.m. Free. Coulee City, off State Route 17.

Dungeness State Salmon Hatchery. Thousands of salmon are detoured to this hatchery each year on their fall run to their spawning area. Best time for adult salmon run is late October to early November. Open year-round, daily, 8 a.m. to 4 p.m. Free. Sequim, off US-101, on Taylor Cutoff Road.

Evergreen Point Floating Bridge. The world's longest floating pontoon bridge (7,578 feet) made up of 33 separate pontoon units. Seattle, three miles north, off Interstate 5.

Fire Station No. 4. At this station you can board some of the world's largest fireboats. Open year-round, daily, 1 p.m. to 4 p.m. Free. West Seattle, 2550 26th Avenue, SW.

Gardner Cave. Unique rock formations in 875-foot passageway; guided tours, picnicking. Open year-round, Wednesday to Sunday, 10 a.m. to 3 p.m. Free. Metaline Falls, north, in Crawford State Park.

Grand Coulee Dam. This dam, one of the largest concreted dams in the world, has tamed the Columbia River for irrigation, power and flood control. The dam is 550 feet high, 500 feet wide at the base, and 5,223 feet long. Self-guided tours are offered and an information center is on the west riverbank below the dam. Open year-round, daily (weather permitting). Coulee City, off State Route 155.

Hanford Science Center. Exhibits, displays, models and library devoted to energy. Open year-round, daily, 9 a.m. to 5 p.m. Richland, 825 Jadwin.

Japanese Tea Garden. A beautifully landscaped garden in the University of Washington Arboretum, designed by Japanese landscape architects. Open year-round, daily, 10 a.m. to sunset. Free. Seattle, off Washington Boulevard.

Kingdome. A new domed stadium that houses sporting events, trade shows and concerts; tours. Open year-round, daily. Adults $1.50, children 6 to 12, 75 cents. Seattle, Second Avenue and King Street.

Lacey V. Murrow Floating Bridge. A floating bridge, more than a mile in length, consisting of 10 standard and 15 special sections that are anchored to the lake bottom. Free. Seattle, on Interstate 90, spanning Lake Washington via Mercer Island.

Lake Whatcom Railway. Take a scenic 1½-hour trip through the Washington countryside on steam-powered trains. Season: June through September 7, Tuesday, Saturday and Sunday, 1 p.m. and 3 p.m. Adults $4, children under 18, $2. Park, on State Route 9. (206) 595-2218.

Leavenworth Salmon Hatchery. A large hatchery that was built as part of the Grand Coulee Dam project. Open year-round, daily, 7:30 a.m. to 4 p.m. Free. Leavenworth, two miles south, on US-2.

Loboland. A facility that houses several species of wolves. Open year-round, daily, 10 a.m. to sunset. Adults $2.50, children 4 to 12, $1. Gardiner, on US-101.

Mayfield Dam. This dam forms a 13-mile-long lake on a gorge in the Cowlitz River; boating, fishing, picnicking, camping. Mossyrock, six miles west, on US-12.

Narrows Bridge. One of the largest suspension bridges in the world, center span is 188 feet high and 2,800 feet long. Tacoma, on State Route 16.

Pacific Science Center. Exhibits include space technology displays, Indian artifacts and films on aviation. Open year-round, daily, 10 a.m. to 5 p.m. Adults $2.50, children 5 to 17, $1. Seattle, at Seattle Center, off State Route 99.

Puget Sound and Snoqualmie Valley Railroad. An operating railroad museum running a seven-mile round-trip to Snoqualmie, Snoqualmie Falls and North Bend. Antique streetcars and steam engines are among the equipment displayed. Open June through August, Saturday and Sunday, 11 a.m. to 5 p.m. Adults $3, children 4 to 10, $1.65, senior citizens over 62, $2.35. Snoqualmie, off State Route 202. (206) 888-0373.

Seattle Center. Located on the site of the former world's fairgrounds, this center now hosts civic and cultural functions. Seattle, off State Route 99, near Elliott Bay. For information on functions, telephone (206) 625-4234.

Skagit Hydroelectric Project Tours. A four-hour tour that includes a ride on an incline lift, a boat excursion to Ross Dam and a tour of the Ross Powerhouse, followed by a family-style meal. Open mid-June through Labor Day, tours by reservation. Adults $10, children 4 to 11, $7. Diablo, on State Route 20. (206) 625-3030.

Space Needle. This 605-foot tower provides a panoramic view of Seattle from its observation platform. A restaurant at the top of the needle rotates one full circle every hour. Open year-round, daily, 11 a.m. to midnight. Admission to observation deck: Adults $1.75, children 6 to 12, 75 cents. Seattle, in Seattle Center, off State Route 99.

A youngster playing on a Washington State beach examines new treasure — a fisherman's glass float. Carried across the Pacific by the Japanese Current and brought to shore by a summer squall, the float becomes a child's link to the Orient.

Stonehenge. A replica of the 4,000-year-old English Stonehenge, situated on a cliff overlooking the Columbia River. Open year-round, daily. Maryhill, off State Route 14.

USS Missouri. On September 2, 1945, the "Mighty Mo" was the site where the Japanese signed the formal surrender document that ended hostilities in the Pacific in World War II. The battleship is now anchored adjacent to the naval shipyard in Bremerton. Open year-round, daily, 10 a.m. to dusk. Off State Route 16.

Washington State Parks

Park	Location	CAMPING	PICNICKING	CONCESSIONS	SWIMMING	HIKING	BOATING	FISHING	HUNTING	WINTER SPORTS
Alta Lake	*Pateros. Off US-97 and State Route 53.*	•	•		•		•	•		•
Battle Ground Lake	*Vancouver. Off State Route 503.*	•	•	•	•	•	•	•		•
Bay View	*Bellingham. Off Interstate 5.*	•	•			•		•		
Beacon Rock	*Bonneville Dam. On State Route 14.*	•	•		•	•	•	•		
Belfair	*Belfair. Off State Route 300.*	•	•		•			•		
Birch Bay	*Blaine. Off Interstate 5.*	•	•		•	•		•		
Bogachiel	*Bogachiel. On US-101.*	•	•			•		•		
Bridgeport	*Bridgeport. Off State Route 17.*	•	•					•		
Brooks Memorial	*Goldendale. Off US-97.*	•	•			•				
Camano Island	*Camano Island. Off State Route 532.*	•	•		•	•	•	•		
Central Ferry	*Pomeroy. On State Route 127.*	•	•		•		•	•		
Conconully	*Conconully. Off US-97.*	•	•		•		•	•		•
Crow Butte	*McNary Dam. On State Route 14.*	•	•		•		•	•		
Curlew Lake	*Republic. On State Route 21.*	•	•			•	•	•		
Dash Point	*Tacoma. Off Interstate 5.*	•	•		•	•		•		
Deception Pass	*Mt. Vernon. Off State Route 20.*	•	•		•	•	•	•		
Dosewallips	*Brinnon. Off US-101.*	•	•			•		•		
Fay Bainbridge	*Winslow. On State Route 305.*	•	•		•		•	•		
Fields Spring	*Anatone. Off State Route 129.*	•	•			•				
Fort Canby	*Ilwaco. Off US-101.*	•	•		•	•	•	•		
Horsethief Lake	*Lyle. On State Route 14.*	•	•		•	•	•	•		
Illahee	*Bremerton. On State Route 306.*	•	•		•	•	•	•		
Jarrell Cove	*Shelton. Off State Route 3.*	•	•			•	•	•		
Kitsap Memorial	*Poulsbo. Off State Route 3.*	•	•		•	•		•		
Kopachuk	*Tacoma. Off Interstate 5.*	•	•		•	•		•		
Lake Chelan	*Chelan. Off US-97.*	•	•	•	•	•	•	•		
Lake Cushman	*Hoodsport. Off US-101.*	•	•		•	•	•	•		
Lake Easton	*Easton. Off Interstate 90.*	•	•		•	•	•	•		
Lake Sammamish	*Issaquah. Off State Route 203.*		•		•	•	•	•		
Lake Sylvia	*Montesano. Off US-12.*	•	•	•	•	•	•	•		
Lake Wenatchee	*Leavenworth off State Route 207.*	•	•	•	•	•	•	•		
Larrabee	*Bellingham. On State Route 11.*	•	•		•	•	•	•		
Lewis and Clark Trail	*Long. On US-12.*	•	•			•		•		
Lyon's Ferry	*Washtucna. Off State Route 260.*	•	•	•	•	•	•	•		
Maryhill	*Goldendale. On US-97.*	•	•	•	•	•	•	•		
Millersylvania	*Olympia. Off Interstate 5.*	•	•		•	•	•	•		
Moses Lake	*Moses Lake. Off Interstate 90.*		•	•	•			•		
Mount Spokane	*Spokane. Off US-2 and State Route 206.*		•	•	•					
Ocean City	*Ocean City. Off State Route 109.*	•	•		•	•		•		
Old Fort Townsend	*Port Townsend. Off State Route 113.*	•	•		•	•		•		
Osoyoos Lake	*Oroville. On US-97.*	•	•		•		•	•		
Paradise Point	*Vancouver. Off Interstate 5.*	•	•		•	•	•	•		
Pearrygin Lake	*Winthrop. Off State Route 153.*	•	•		•	•	•	•		
Pend Oreille	*West Branch. Off US-2.*	•	•			•				

Washington State Parks

Park	Location	CAMPING	PICNICKING	CONCESSIONS	SWIMMING	HIKING	BOATING	FISHING	HUNTING	WINTER SPORTS
Penrose Point	*Long Branch. off State Route 16.*	•	•	•		•	•	•		
Potholes	*Moses Lake. Off Interstate 90.*	•	•		•	•	•	•		
Potlatch	*Hoodsport. Off US-101.*	•	•		•			•		
Rainbow Falls	*Chehalis. On State Route 6.*	•	•		•	•		•		
Riverside	*Spokane. On State Route 291.*	•	•			•		•		
Rockport	*Rockport. Off State Route 20.*	•	•			•		•		
Saltwater	*Des Moines. Off State Route 509.*		•	•	•		•	•		
Scenic Beach	*Bremerton. Off State Route 16.*	•	•		•			•		
Schafer	*Satsop. Off US-12.*	•	•		•	•		•		
Sequim Bay	*Sequim. Off US-101.*	•	•		•	•	•	•		
Steamboat Rock	*Grand Coulee. On State Route 155.*	•	•	•	•	•	•	•		
Sun Lakes	*Coulee City. On State Route 28.*	•	•	•	•	•	•	•		
Twanoh	*Union. On State Route 106.*	•	•	•	•	•	•	•		
Twenty-Five Mile Creek	*Chelan. Off US-97.*	•		•	•	•	•	•		
Twin Harbors	*Westport. On State Route 105.*	•	•		•	•		•		
Wanapum	*Vantage. Off Interstate 90.*	•	•		•			•		
Wenberg	*Marysville. Off Interstate 5.*	•	•		•	•	•	•		
Yakima Sportsmen's	*Yakima. Off State Route 24.*	•	•					•		

Washington has no state forests. For more information on Washington state parks, contact: *State Parks and Recreation Commission, 7150 Cleanwater Lane, Olympia, Washington 98504, (206) 753-5755.*

Western States Calendar of Events

Spring
(March, April, May)

Alaska

Iditarod Trail Race. Annual marathon sled dog race. March, Wasilla.

Cross-Country Snow Machine Race. April, Kotzebue.

Ketchikan Salmon Derby. May, Ketchikan.

Little Norway Festival. Annual event that coincides with Norwegian National Independence Day. May, Petersburg.

California

Camellia Festival. Parade. March, Sacramento.

Annual Kite Festival. March, Ocean Beach.

International Orchid Show. March, Santa Barbara.

St. Patrick's Day Parade. March, San Francisco.

Swallows Return to Mission San Juan Capistrano. March, San Juan Capistrano.

National Orange Show. March, San Bernardino.

Hangtown Motocross. March, Sacramento.

Cherry Trees in Bloom, Golden Gate Park. March, San Francisco.

Colgate-Dinah Shore Winners Circle LPGA Golf Tourney. March, Palm Springs.

Daffodil Hill in Bloom. March and April, Amador County.

Annual Bay Area Science Fair. March, San Francisco.

Apple Blossom Festival. April, Sebastapol.

Pegleg Liars Contest. April, Borrego Springs.

Crew Classic. April, San Diego.

Fisherman's Festival. April, Bodega Bay.

Cherry Blossom Festival. Parade. April, San Francisco.

Pan American Festival. April, Lakewood.

Annual American Indian and Cowboy Art Exhibit. April, Los Angeles.

Annual Rhododendron Festival. April, Eureka.

Cinco de Mayo Fiestas. May, statewide.

Spring Art Show, Folsom Prison. May, Folsom.
Annual World Championship Cribbage Tournament. May, Quincy.
Hi Desert Escapade. May, Ridgecrest.
Fireman's Muster. May, Columbia.
Conejo Valley Days. Parades, rides, chili cookoff. May, Thousand Oaks.
Rhododendron Festival. May, Fort Bragg.
Annual Mount Whitney 50-Mile Endurance Horse Race. May, Lone Pine.
Mother Lode Roundup. May, Sonora.
Calaveras County Fair and Jumping Frog Jubilee. May, Angels Camp.
Kingsburg Swedish Festival. May, Fresno.
La Purisma Mission Fiesta. May, Lompoc.
Bay to Breakers Race. May, San Francisco.
West Coast National Fly-In. May, Watsonville.
Jazz Festival, Old Sacramento. May, Sacramento.

Hawaii
St. Patrick's Day Parade. March, Waikiki.
Miss Aloha Hawaii Pageant. March, Hilo.
Buddha Day. April, throughout all islands.
Merrie Monarch Festival. Sports events, dance contest to commemorate the days of King Kalakaua. April, Hilo.
Lei Day. May, Honolulu.
Annual Golden Goddess Jackpot Women's Fishing Tournament. May, Kailua-Kona.
Miss Kauai Filipina Pageant. May, Lihue.
All-Girls Rodeo. May, Waimea.
State Fair. May, Honolulu.

Nevada
Carson Valley Days. March, Minden and Gardnerville.
Miss Nevada Pageant. March, Reno.
Antique Show. March, Virginia City.
Miss Winnemucca Pageant. April, Winnemucca.
Cabin Fever Reliever Square Dance. April, Elko.
Pioneer Arts and Crafts Festival. May, Elko.

Oregon
All-Northwest Barbershop Ballad Contest and Gay '90s Festival. March, Forest Grove.
Oregon Shakespeare Festival. May through October, Ashland.
Grande Ronde River Rally and Raft Race. May, La Grande.
May Day Activities. May, Newberg.
International Festival. May, Corvallis.
Oregon State Old-Time Fiddlers Contest. May, Bend.
Hell's Canyon Rodeo. May, Halfway.
Central Oregon Timber Carnival. May, Prineville.
Azalea Festival. May, Brookings-Harbor.
All-Indian Rodeo. May, Klamath Falls.
Strawberry Festival. May. Lebanon.

Washington
Apple Blossom Festival. May, Wenatchee.

Among the attractions of Las Vegas' nightlife are the extravagant productions in the tradition of the Folies Bergere and Lido de Paris.

Summer
(June, July, August)

Alaska

Midsummer Festival. June, Palmer.
Golden Days Celebration. July, Fairbanks.
Alaska State Fair. August, Palmer.
"Cry of the Wild Ram." August, Kodiak.
Golden North Salmon Derby. August, Juneau.
Gold Rush Days. Relives the lusty days of the quest for gold with parades, can-can girls, games and casino night. August, Valdez.
Silver Salmon Derby. August, Valdez.

California

Riverside Napa 400. June, Riverside.
Bluegrass Festival. June, Grass Valley.
Anniversary of Sir Francis Drake's California Landing. June, Point Reyes National Seashore.
Lompoc Valley Flower Festival. June, Lompoc.
Secession Day Celebration. June, Rough and Ready.
Annual Frontier Days. July, Willits.
Annual Grand Prix Bicycle Races. July, Manhattan Beach.
Fifty-Mile Horse Ride. July, Ebbetts Pass.
Mission San Luis Rey Fiesta. July, San Luis Rey.
Bach Festival. July, Carmel.
Feast of Lanterns. July, Pacific Grove.
Mother Lode Fair. August, Sonora.
Old Spanish Days Fiesta. August, Santa Barbara.
California State Fair. August, Sacramento.
Renaissance Pleasure Faire and Half Penny Market. August, Marin County.
Score Offroad National Races. August, Riverside.

Hawaii

King Kamehameha Celebration. One of Hawaii's brightest state holidays featuring parades, dances, exhibits. June, Oahu and Hawaii.
Fiesta Filipina. June, Honolulu.
Victoria to Maui Yacht Race. June, Maui.
Annual Hilo Orchid Society Flower Show. July, Hilo.
Allison Tuna Tournament. July, Waianae Coast, Oahu.
International Festival of the Pacific. July, Hilo.
Annual Maui Jaycees Carnival. July, Kahului.
Annual Maui Sauza Cup Regatta. July, Lahaina.
Annual Ukulele Festival. July, Waikiki.
Obon Odori Festival. August, Haleiwa.
Hula Festival. August, Waikiki.
Annual Hawaiian International Billfish Tournament. August, Kailua-Kona.
Annual Macadamia Nut Augustfest. August, Honokaa.

Nevada

Annual Art Fair. June, Lamoille.
International Festival. Music, dance, foods of the world. June, Las Vegas.
Annual Celebration of Winnemucca Basque Club. June, Winnemucca.
Annual National Basque Festival. July, Elko.
Ely Festival. July, Ely.
Pony Express Days. August, Ely.
Basque Celebration. August, Reno.

Oregon

Troy Days. June, Troy.
Portland Rose Festival. June, Portland.
Philomath Western Frolic. June, Philomath.
Anniversary Celebration of Sir Francis Drake's Landing, Cape Arago. June, Coos Bay.
Tie and Ride Race. June, Sunriver.
Phil Sheridan Days. June, Sheridan.
Pioneer Day. June, Jacksonville.
Annual Rose Show. June, Grants Pass.
Doll Show. June, Grants Pass.
Summer Solstice Wine Festival, Amity Vineyards Winery. June, Amity.
Buckeroo Square Dance Roundup. June, Roseburg.
Scandinavian Festival. June, Astoria.
Molalla Buckeroo. June, Molalla.
Sumpter Valley Days. July, Sumpter.

Hillsboro Happy Days, Washington County Fairgrounds. July, Hillsboro.
Bohemia Mining Days. July, Cottage Grove.
Caledonian Games. July, Athena.
Bluegrass Festival. July, Hillsboro.
Jefferson Mint Festival. July, Jefferson.
Old-Fashion Days. July, Newberg.
Wood'n Nickel Days. July, Myrtle Creek.
Renaissance Feast. July, Ashland.
Broiler Festival. July, Springfield.
Miss Oregon Pageant. July, Seaside.
Turkey Rama. July, McMinnville.
Catherine Creek Stampede. July, Union.
Japan Nite Obon Festival. July, Ontario.
Sandcastle Building Contest. July, Lincoln City.
Thunderegg Days. August, Nyssa.
Applegate Traildays Festival. August, Veneta-Elmira.
Boones Ferry Days. August, Wilsonville.
Warm Springs Huckleberry Feast. August, Warm Springs Reservation.
Scandinavian Festival. August, Junction City.
Seaside Beach Run. August, Seaside.
Dufur Threshing Bee. August, Dufur.
Blackberry Festival. August, North Bend.
Great Oregon Rallye. August, Forest Grove.
Astoria Regatta. August, Astoria.

Washington

Old-Fashioned Fourth of July and Logging Show. July, Forks.
Fiddle Tunes Festival. July, Port Townsend.
Fireworks Display. July, Tacoma.
Summer Festival. July, Everson.
Skagit River Raft Race. July, Mount Vernon.
Jazz Festival. July, Port Townsend.
Startup Loggers Days. July, Startup.
Square Dance Festival. July, Mount Vernon.
Bluegrass Celebration. July, Darrington.
Annual Logging Show. July, Cathlamet.
Whaling Days. July, Silverdale.
Harvest Days. July, Battle Ground.

Western states play host to a number of rompin', stompin', ride 'em cowboy rodeos guaranteed to have never a dull moment.

McCleary Bear Festival. July, McCleary.
Downtown Bellingham Festival Days. July, Bellingham.
Annual Kettle River Raft Race. July, Orient to Barstow.
Ano-Chords Annual Barbershop Concert and Salmon Barbeque. July, Anacortes.
Old-Fashioned Days. July, Anacortes.
Biking-Canoeing-Running Relay Races. August, Anacortes.
Annual Arts and Crafts Festival. August, Anacortes.
Loggers Playday. August, Hoquiam.
Threshing Bee. August, Lynden.
Omak Stampede and Suicide Race. August, Omak.
Sumner Summer Festival. August, Sumner.
Kalispel Salish Fair. August, Usk.
Columbia Gorge Flower Show. August, White Salmon.
Spokane Indian Festival. August, Wellpinit.

Fall
(September, October, November)

Alaska

Alaska Festival of Music. September, Anchorage.

Alaska Day. October, Sitka.

California

Scottish Gathering and Games. September, Santa Rosa.

National Begonia Festival. September, Santa Cruz.

Lodi Grape Festival and National Wine Show. September, Lodi.

California State Fair Horse Show. September, Sacramento.

Monterey Jazz Festival. September, Monterey.

Los Angeles County Fair. September, Los Angeles.

Annual Danish Days. September, Solvang.

Cabrillo Festival. September, San Diego.

National Raisin Festival. September, Dinuba.

Cabrillo Landing Pageant. October, San Pedro.

Corcoran Cotton Festival. October, Corcoran.

Sandcastle and Sand Sculpture Contest. October, Newport Beach.

Annual Desert Festival. October, Borrego Springs.

Annual Dodger Stadium RV Show. November, Los Angeles.

Festival of the Masks. November, Los Angeles.

National Amateur Horse Show. November, Santa Barbara.

Santa Claus Lane Parade. November, Hollywood.

California Wine Festival. November, Monterey.

Hawaii

Annual Rough Water Swim. September, Waikiki.

Hawaii County Fair. September, Hilo.

Chieftan's Night. September, Honolulu.

Aloha Week Festivals. September and October, all islands.

Makahiki Festival. October, Waimea Falls Park.

Annual Orchid Plant and Flower Show. October, Honolulu.

Na Mele O Maui. November, Lahaina.

Kona Coffee Festival. November, Kailua-Kona.

Hawaiian Pro-Surfing Championships. November and December, Oahu.

Nevada

National Championship Air Races. September, Reno.

Oregon

Oregon State Fair. September, Salem.

Fun Festival. September, Coos Bay.

Alpenfest. September, Wallowa Lake.

Fall Festival, Central Park. September, Corvallis.

Wintering-In Harvest Festival. September, Portland.

Greek Festival Bazaar. October, Portland.

Yachats Kite Festival. October, Yachats.

Home Tour. October, Jacksonville.

Oakridge Tree Planting. October, Oakridge.

Kraut and Sausage Feed and Bazaar. November, Verboort.

Veteran's Day Parade. November, Albany.

Santa's Arrival, Water Street Station. November, Albany.

Christmas Green Show. November, Salem.

Washington

Methow Mule Days Rodeo. September, Winthrop.

Fire Department Chicken and Spaghetti Feed. September, Ford.

Old-Fashioned Ice-Cream Festival. September, Northwest Trek.

Annual Prosser States Day Celebration. September, Prosser.

Vancouver Sausage Fest. September, Vancouver.

Alpine Days. September, North Bend.

Annual Salmon Derby. September, Key Center.
Huckleberry Festival. September, Bingen and White Salmon.
Pioneer Fall Festival. September, Waitsburg.
Wooden Boat Festival. September, Port Townsend.
Annual Sausage Fest. September, Richland.
Gold Bar Nugget Festival. September, Gold Bar.
Autumn Leaf Festival. September, Leavenworth.
Hearts of Gold Festival and Junior Rodeo. September, Spokane.
Everett Sausage Fest. October, Everett.
Octoberfest. October, Tacoma.
Marcus Cider Festival. October, Marcus.
International Folkdance Festival. October, Richland.
Apple Squeeze Festival. October, Steilacoom.
Scandinavian Festival. October, Tacoma.
Annual Rock and Gem Show. November, Mount Vernon.

Winter
(December, January, February)

Alaska

Anchorage Fur Rendezvous. February, Anchorage.
Iceworm Festival. February, Cordova.
Valdez Winter Carnival. Snowmobile races, dogsled races, snowshoe softball, Miss Valdez Pageant. February, Valdez.

California

Annual Festival of the Trees. December, San Rafael.
Los Posados. December, Los Angeles.
Dickens Christmas Fair. December, San Francisco.
Annual Tournament of Roses Parade and Football Game. January, Pasadena.
Bob Hope Desert Golf Classic. January, Palm Springs.
San Francisco Sports and Boat Show. January, San Francisco.
Holtville Carrot Festival. January, Holtville.
California Junior Miss Pageant. January, Santa Rosa.
California Gray Whale Watch. February, Coastal Counties.
Chinese New Year Celebration. February, San Francisco.
National Date Festival. February, Indio.
World Championship Crab Races and Crab Feed. February, Crescent City.

Hawaii

Annual Honolulu Marathon. December, Honolulu.
Kailua Madrigal Singers Annual Christmas Concert. December, Kailua.
Annual Rainbow Classic. Basketball tournament. December, Honolulu.
Hula Bowl Game. January, Aloha Stadium, Oahu.
Narcissus Festival. January, Honolulu.
Cherry Blossom Festival. January, Honolulu.
Punahou Carnival. February, Honolulu.
Miss Koreana Pageant. February, Honolulu.
Chinese New Year. February, Honolulu.
Haleiwa Sea Spree. February, Haleiwa.
Annual Carole Kai Bed Race. February, Waikiki.

Nevada

No major events.

Oregon

Christmas Parade. December, Springfield.
Annual Swine Day. December, Corvallis.
Winter All-Breed Pigeon Show. December, Portland.
Rickreall Christmas Pageant. December, Rickreall.
Winter Solstice Wine Festival. December, Amity.
Snowflake Classic Car Show. December, Salem.

Washington

Christmas Lighting. December, Leavenworth.
Christmas Around the World. December, Seattle.

National Forests

The National Forests are publicly owned lands managed for the sustained production of various products and services. They provide not only an important part of the Nation's recreation areas, but also produce vital quantities of water for domestic and industrial purposes, 30% of the nation's softwood sawtimber harvest, and substantial forage crops sustaining more than 7.2 million head of livestock and a large part of the wildlife in American. They also contain outstanding examples of our nation's previous wilderness heritage.

These forest resources are managed by the Forest Service under a coordinated system of multiple use. Multiple use means that National Forests support and supply several different crops and services simultaneously. Thus on large forest areas, timber harvesting, livestock grazing, various uses of water, recreation, hunting and fishing, berrypicking, and similar activities may be carried on at the same time. Adjustment of activities prevents measurable interference with each other. Here and there, one resource use may be so important as to be given top priority to exclude other uses. The multiple-use plan provides for this. The objective is to maintain a coordinated pattern of use which will produce the largest net total of public benefits, now and in the future.

In addition to their value for recreation, National Forest lands contribute to other areas of American life. Sales of National Forest timber for lumber and pulp, plus fees for various other uses of timber and National Forest land, bring in more than $300 million a year to the U.S. Treasury. One-fourth of this income is returned to the states from which it came for use on schools and roads in the counties having National Forest land. An additional 10% is used to build roads and trails within the National Forests. The benefits of multiple-use management extend from beautiful forests and plentiful resources to the jobs and industries in the rural areas of our country.

You can enjoy your vacation in a superlative setting of scenic charm and natural beauty in one of the more than 160 National Forests managed by the Forest Service of the United States Department of Agriculture. The choice of the outing is yours: Rough it on a sylvan trail or relive the days of the pioneer by adventuring in remote stretches of comparatively untouched America, either on horseback or by toting a backpack into the wilderness. Or perhaps you'd rather take a leisurely drive to a nearby woods for a picnic outing or an extended weekend.

Whatever you desire, your quest for fun and excitement can be easily satisfied. You'll find a National Forest vacation spot within a day's drive of almost any point in the U.S. (except in Hawaii and Alaska). The nearly 200 million acres in the National Forest System offer an endless variety of vegetation, scenery, climate and topography: cypress swamps and sand pines in the south; alpine meadows and great fir forests in the Rocky Mountains of the West and the Cascade Range or Oregon and Washington; spreading hardwoods in the Midwest and Appalachians; Giant Sequoias in California's Sierras; lush greenery and verdant slopes in the New England states; semi-desert landscapes in Utah.

Alabama

Conecuh National Forest. Located 50 miles from the Gulf of Mexico in the flat coastal plain of southern Alabama; lush pine forests and semitropical vegetation; five-mile hiking trail. 85,000 acres.

Talladega National Forest. At the southern tip of the Appalachian Mountains; rugged country, heavily wooded hillsides and several scenic trails. 360,000 acres.

Tuskegee National Forest. Between the mountains and the coast in the rolling hills of the piedmont; one of the smallest of the National Forests, consisting chiefly of large stands of southern pine; William Bartram Recreation Trail. 11,000 acres.

William B. Bankhead National Forest. Located in northern Alabama and intersected with beautiful streams and dotted with several lakes which are lined with picturesque bluffs. Within the forest, the Bee Branch research area harbors the state's last stand of virgin hardwoods. 181,000 acres.

Alaska

Chugach National Forest. Undoubtedly one of the most beautiful of all the National Forests; rugged mountains, glaciers and sparkling rivers and streams. The Resurrection Trail leads to Kenai Lake and has several Forest Service cabins along its route. 4,723,000 acres.

Tongass National Forest. A huge forest featuring a rain forest of Sitka spruce and western hemlock, low marshy bogs and the great Mendenhall Glacier. 16,001,000 acres.

Arizona

Apache National Forest. A mixture of semi-desert, rich conifer forests and scrub vegetation of timberline, this forest runs along the Arizona-New Mexico border, with part of the northern segment spilling into New Mexico. 1,732,891 acres.

Coconino National Forest. This forest surrounds the city of Flagstaff and includes the San Francisco Mountains, whose slopes are covered with ponderosa pines. Within this forest is the popular and scenic Oak Creek Canyon. 1,800,738 acres.

Coronado National Forest. A vast forest just north of the Mexican border that includes desert lands and mountain peaks. Many scenic roads throughout the area provide access to numerous points of interest and campgrounds. 7,790,935 acres.

Kaibab National Forest. The Kaibab surrounds the Grand Canyon and also takes in about 8,000 acres of the Sycamore Canyon Wilderness. 1,720,285 acres.

Prescott National Forest. Consisting of two sections that run parallel to each other in central Arizona, the Prescott takes in two mountain chains that feature beautiful scenic drives and a mild climate. 1,247,572 acres.

Sitgreaves National Forest. Located in the high country of central Arizona, this forest includes vast areas of giant ponderosa pine and the historic route along the Mogollon Rim. 807,833 acres.

Tonto National Forest. This forest offers an exceptional variety of recreation opportunities with six man-made lakes totaling more than 30,000 acres of water and the scenic Beeline Highway and Apache Trail. 2,898,118 acres.

Arkansas

Ouachita National Forest. Encompassing the mountain ranges of the Ouachita, Kiamichi and Winding Stair, this forest also includes eight major artificial lakes and numerous smaller lakes. 1,575,291 acres.

Ozark National Forest. Divided into five sections, the main body of this forest lies northeast of Fort Smith and due north of Russellville — and takes in the Boston Mountains and large stands of oaks. 1,110,890 acres.

St. Francis National Forest. This forest, which takes its name from the St. Francis River, contains every species of hardwood found in Arkansas and features the fertile bottomlands of the Mississippi delta and the highlands of Crowley's Ridge. 20,946 acres.

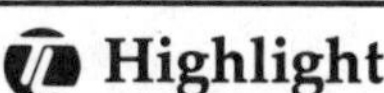

Arkansas' Blanchard Springs Caverns

The Dripstone Trail

The Dripstone Trail winds through the uppermost level of the caverns for about 0.7 miles. The walking surface is a smooth, paved trail with ramps at inclines. Approximately 50 stair steps must be negotiated if the tour is taken in its entirety. Visitors can avoid these steps by taking other routes which bypass only two formations. These routes are available for those unable to climb steps.

The features along the trail are lighted with white or pastel lights to bring out natural color, form and texture.

Forest Service guides accompany each tour to provide an interpretation of the features, and of the biological and geological processes of the caverns.

From the Dripstone Trail, you can enjoy practically every type of calcite formation found in limestone caves. The trail takes you through two major rooms in the upper level of the cavern system. These rooms remain at a temperature of approximately 57 degrees F all year. The relative humidity is always near 100%.

The Discovery Trail

The Discovery Trail passes through typical passages found in most limestone caves. By elevator, visitors descend 216 feet to the underground lobby. From this point they travel a bit more than a mile underground. The trip has a total elevation difference of 476 feet and is more strenuous than the Dripstone Trail. This trail has approximately 600 steps to climb or descend and is not recommended for persons with walking difficulties or heart or respiratory ailments.

Limestone walls formed by the solutioning process eons ago are lighted with the natural colors of the cave's formations. Geological deposits are unique and spectacular.

Forest Service guides explain the caverns to tour groups. These groups are limited in number to assure each visitor the opportunity to hear and to ask questions.

The Discovery Trail travels through the lower levels of Blanchard Caverns, passing near the underground stream. Temperatures vary only near the caverns' natural entrance, which is a 70-foot vertical passage.

California

Angeles National Forest. Consisting mostly of chaparral-covered mountain slopes of the San Gabriels, this forest lies along the north side of Los Angeles. The forest is bisected by the scenic Angeles Crest Highway, and also includes the 36,000-acre San Gabriel Wilderness. 691,000 acres.

Calaveras Big Tree National Forest. The smallest of all National Forests, the Calaveras consists of a grove of giant sequoias that lie within the boundaries of the Stanislaus National Forest. 300 acres.

Cleveland National Forest. Located near San Diego, the Cleveland is divided into three sections consisting of topography that varies from chaparral-covered hills to lofty peaks covered with lush forests. 385,531 acres.

Eldorado National Forest. This forest contains the Desolation Wilderness, a popular backpacking area, and the Crystal Basin recreation area, which harbors two large reservoirs and numerous RV campgrounds. 665,083 acres.

Inyo National Forest. This long, narrow forest takes in the Sequoia, Kings Canyon and Yosemite National Parks along the eastern slope of the Sierra Nevada Mountains. Elevations range from 4,000 feet to the summit of Mount Whitney (14,494 feet), the tallest mountain in the contiguous 48 states. 1,776,951 acres.

Klamath National Forest. Located in Northern California, just below the Oregon border, the Klamath includes great stands of sugar, white, Jeffrey and ponderosa pines, as well as red, white and Douglas firs. The Klamath, Scott and Salmon Rivers provide excellent fishing within the forest's boundaries. 1,671,078 acres.

Lassen National Forest. The Lassen consists of a region of former volcanic activity and includes within its boundaries Lassen Volcanic National Park. Within the forest are numerous lakes, the 15,000-acre Thousand Lakes Wilderness and the unique Subway Cave, a 1,300-foot lava tube. 1,056,258 acres.

Los Padres National Forest. Divided in two sections, the Los Padres stretches along the Pacific Coast from Carmel to Ojai. Within the forest are two condor sanctuaries and the San Rafael and Ventana Wilderness areas. 1,750,229 acres.

Mendocino National Forest. An important lumbering region, the Mendocino also offers excellent recreation opportunities on its lakes and rivers and in the 108,000-acre Yolla Bolly-Middle Eel Wilderness area. 873,113 acres.

Modoc National Forest. In the extreme northeastern corner of the state, the Modoc is a mixture of pine forests, scenic meadows and open rangeland. Summit Trail traverses the backbone of the mountains that run through the area, running 27 miles from Patterson Meadow to Porter Reservoir. 1,633,148 acres.

Plumas National Forest. A forest rich in lakes and streams, Plumas features the deep canyons and mountain valleys of the Feather River drainage basin — the most important water supply source in California. 1,154,754 acres.

San Bernardino National Forest. A prime recreation area in Southern California, featuring nearly 1,200 campsites and five winter sports areas. Included in the region is the 9,000-acre Cucamonga Wilderness and the 11,485-foot-high Mount San Gorgonio. 627,133 acres.

Sequoia National Forest. Within this forest are groves of the majestic redwoods that give it its name. There are 37 groves in all, with the largest tree being the Boole Tree, standing 269 feet high and having a girth of 90 feet. 1,119,487 acres.

Shasta-Trinity National Forest. Within these combined forests are three large lakes — Shasta, Whiskeytown and Clair Engle — and the scenic Trinity Alps Wilderness. 2,064,435 acres.

Sierra National Forest. Situated between Yosemite and Kings Canyon national parks, the Sierra includes a number of lakes, rivers and streams and features many well-marked backpacking trails. 1,285,877 acres.

Six Rivers National Forest. This forest lies in the heart of California's Bigfoot country and takes its name from the six major rivers, which cut through the forest on their way to the Pacific. 968,792 acres.

Stanislaus National Forest. A major lumbering area, the Stanislaus lies on the edge of California's gold country and takes in the Emigrant Basin Wilderness area and several major winter sports areas. 985,921 acres.

Tahoe National Forest. The main feature of this forest is huge Lake Tahoe, but within its boundaries are other smaller lakes, numerous trails and a number of popular winter recreation areas. 747,626 acres.

Colorado

Arapaho National Forest. A forest of tall mountains, excellent winter sports areas and spectacular vistas from numerous scenic routes, the Arapaho also includes the Gore Range-Eagle Nest Primitive Area, a favorite of backpackers. 993,469 acres.

Grand Mesa-Uncompahgre National Forest. Two combined forests consisting of a 10,500-foot mesa and a rolling plateau that is part of the San Juan Mountains. Within the forests' boundaries are excellent hunting and fishing opportunities. 1,290,001 acres.

Gunnison National Forest. Featuring 27 peaks that rise to 12,000 feet or more, the Gunnison lies in the heart of the Colorado Rockies in an area that is famous for its trout fishing. 1,663,269 acres.

Pike National Forest. Within the Pike are attractions like Pikes Peak, the Cripple Creek gold fields and the Lost Creek scenic

Scores of the giant sequoias have been preserved for present and future generations to enjoy in state and federal parks, especially in California's Mendocino, Humbolt and Del Norte Counties.

area, as well as several winter sports areas. 1,104,908 acres.

Rio Grande National Forest. This forest contains the headwaters of the Rio Grande River, as well as a number of historical sites from Colorado's gold rush days. 1,850,212 acres.

Roosevelt National Forest. An important watershed forest, the Roosevelt also contains the 27,000-acre Rawah Wilderness and surrounds the scenic Rocky Mountain National Park. 781,637 acres.

Routt National Forest. Three major recreation areas lie within the boundaries of this forest that also includes the 74,000-acre Mount Zirkel Wilderness and Buffalo Hot Springs, where the water rises from the earth at a temperature of 150 degrees F. 1,125,145 acres.

San Isabel National Forest. This forest takes in Mount Elbert (14,433 feet), the highest peak in Colorado, and includes a number of routes that wind through high mountain passes. Also included in the forest's boundaries are a number of winter sports areas and old mining towns. 1,107,291 acres.

San Juan National Forest. An area of large stands of spruce and pine trees, the San Juan also harbors sites like Treasure Falls, Chimney Rock and Dolores River Canyon. 1,867,018 acres.

White River National Forest. This forest encompasses three wilderness areas — Flat Tops Primitive Area, Snowmass-Maroon Bells Wilderness and the Gore Range-Eagle Nest Primitive Area — and is home to a number of peaks that are popular with climbers. 1,939,348 acres.

Highlight

Selected Trails in Georgia's Chattahoochee National Forest

CHATTOOGA RIVER TRAIL (10 MILES). *Tallulah Ranger District.* The Chattooga River Trail begins (northern end) at the Bartram Trail at Dick's Creek Road and continues south along the west bank of the Chattooga River. The trail is entirely within the boundaries of the Chattooga Wild and Scenic River corridor.

Take US-76 east from Clayton for nine miles to Chattooga River, where trail begins.

THREE FORKS TRAIL (5.5 MILES). *Tallulah Ranger District.* The Three Forks Trail begins at the summit of Rabun Bald at 4,696 feet elevation, and ends in a small clearing on a bluff above the west fork of the Chattooga River at an elevation of 2,060 feet. Some steep descents mark portions of the trail. It follows Hale Ridge Road (Forest Service Road 7) for about 1½ miles before continuing on an old woods road.

Take Warwoman Road (County road) east from Clayton for 16 miles to Overflow Road (Forest Service Road 86). Turn left (northwest) for four miles to John Teague Gap, where trail crosses.

HOLCOMB CREEK TRAIL (1.3 MILES). *Tallulah Ranger District.* Holcomb Creek Trail makes a short loop off Forest Service Road 86, the Overflow Creek Road. It begins at the intersection of this road with Hale Ridge Road (Forest Service Road 7) and ends on Overflow Creek Road about 1½ miles north of the beginning. The trail takes the hiker to Holcomb Creek Falls and Ammons Creek Falls where an observation deck has been constructed.

Take Warwoman Road (County road) east from Clayton for 10 miles. Turn left (north) on Forest Service Road 7 (Hell Ridge Road) for nine miles. Trail begins at intersection of Forest Service Road 7 and Forest Service Road 86.

Florida

Apalachicola National Forest. Besides vast stands of southern pine and cedar, this forest also contains groves of hardwoods and unusual hardwood swamps. 557,229 acres.

Ocala National Forest. This forest consists of deep, coarse, porous sand that supports large numbers of sand pines — the only trees capable of growing in this type of soil. Within the forest is the Ocala Trail, which leads to some of the most beautiful spots in the area. 367,283 acres.

Osceola National Forest. In northern Florida, near the Georgia border, the Osceola is a forest of moss-draped cypress dotted with ponds, sinks and swamps. 157,230 acres.

Georgia

Chattahoochee National Forest. With altitudes ranging from 1,000 to nearly 5,000 feet, this forest features a diverse terrain that includes mountain slopes, piedmont plateaus and river valleys that support a wide variety of hardwood species. 739,252 acres.

Oconee National Forest. Divided by Interstate 20, the Oconee consists of dense stands of pine and hardwoods, and is dotted with small lakes. Within the forest are the remains of the historic village of Scull Shoals and the Scull Shoals Indian Mounds. 103,808 acres.

Idaho

Boise National Forest. The vast Boise forest features excellent hunting and fishing opportunities, plus the Sawtooth Wilderness and Idaho Primitive Area. Popular ski areas include the Bogus Basin, Brundage Mountain and Payette Lakes. 2,642,453 acres.

Caribou National Forest. In the southeastern corner of Idaho, this forest consists of high mountain peaks covered with dense stands of aspen, Douglas fir and lodgepole pine. A number of historical sites lie within or near the forest, including Fort Hall and a section of the Oregon Trail. 980,539 acres.

Challis National Forest. Located in the center of the state, this forest is made up of the Salmon River, Lost River and the Lemhi mountain ranges. In the 1800s, the region was a rich source of furs and gold. 2,459,431 acres.

Clearwater National Forest. An important timber area in the state's panhandle, the Clearwater has vast stands of hemlock, spruce and lodgepole pine. In 1877, Chief Joseph of the Nez Perce Nation led his people through the region after fighting the U.S. forces at Stites and Whitebird. 1,823,492 acres.

Coeur d'Alene National Forest. This is an important winter sports region featuring many miles of snowmobile trails and the major ski areas of Silverhorn, Kellogg and Lookout Pass. A 3,600-acre experimental forest is maintained by the Forest Service near the city of Coeur d'Alene. 724,322 acres.

Kaniksu National Forest. Once the center of fur-trading and logging operations for the laying of the tracks for the Northern Pacific Railroad, the Kaniksu is now managed carefully to control its lumber yield. Recreation opportunities include excellent fishing and numerous hiking and backpacking trails. 1,455,676 acres.

Nez Perce National Forest. This forest was originally the ancestral land of the Nez Perce Indians and now includes thriving lumber operations and recreation areas like the 130,000-acre Hells Canyon Wilderness and the Salmon River Breaks Primitive Area. 2,205,742 acres.

Payette National Forest. Located in central Idaho, the Payette is a rugged and wild region consisting of steep mountains and roaring rivers; the forest has more than 150 lakes and some 1,500 miles of fishing streams within its boundaries. 2,307,276 acres.

Salmon River National Forest. The middle fork of the Salmon River is one of the main attractions of this wild forest where big-game hunters can pursue a variety of quarry that includes deer, bighorn sheep, elk and Rocky Mountain goat. 1,769,544 acres.

St. Joe National Forest. Named for the St. Joe River, which is the main artery of this forest, the St. Joe extends from the slopes of the Bitteroot Range to the Palouse Plateau. 862,915 acres.

Sawtooth National Forest. This forest includes the jagged peaks of the Sawtooth range, as well as those of the White Cloud, Boulder and Pioneer Mountains. In the 1860s, the Sawtooth region was the site of considerable gold mining activity, and it later served as one of the West's most important sheep-grazing ranges. 1,799,665 acres.

Targhee National Forest. This forest touches the border of both Yellowstone and Grand Teton National Parks and extends to the headwaters of the Snake River in eastern Idaho and western Wyoming. In winter, the trumpeter swan makes its home on the spring-fed waters of the Henry's Fork River. 1,642,417 acres.

Illinois

Shawnee National Forest. Located in the southern part of the state, this forest takes in the rugged Shawnee Hills and attractions like the Garden of the Gods and the LaRue-Pine Hills Ecological Area. 255,984 acres.

Indiana

Hoosier National Forest. A forest of rolling hills and sharp ridges, the Hoosier includes a number of lakes and streams that offer excellent fishing. Vast stands of hardwoods are intersected with a number of scenic hiking trails. 179,349 acres.

Kentucky

Daniel Boone National Forest. A forest that consists primarily of hardwoods, this region includes numerous natural stone arches and waterfalls, as well as the scenic Red River Gorge. 648,000 acres.

Louisiana

Kisatchie National Forest. A land of swamps and bayous made up of loblolly, slash and longleaf pines and moss-draped magnolias. Within the forest, which is separated into eight different districts, the rugged Kisatchie Hills form one of the most interesting areas. 595,361 acres.

Michigan

Hiawatha National Forest. The Hiawatha stretches for more than 125 miles across Michigan's Upper Peninsula and includes a number of scenic drives, together with excellent hunting and fishing areas. 863,859 acres.

Huron National Forest. One of the Huron's chief features is the famed Au Sable River, a scenic waterway that is a great favorite among fly-fishermen. Within the forest, 4,100 acres have been set aside as a habitat for the rare Kirtland's warbler. 417,088 acres.

Manistee National Forest. The Manistee offers year-round recreation on its rivers, trails and mountain slopes. The forest also touches the shores of Lake Michigan, where sandy beaches provide a water playground. 496,875 acres.

Ottawa National Forest. This forest is noted for an abundance of rivers and more than 30 waterfalls. Within its boundaries is the 21,000-acre Sylvania recreation area, which provides a number of campgrounds, beaches, lakes and clear rivers that are a favorite with canoeists. 918,00 acres.

Highlight

Bald Eagle in Minnesota's Chippewa National Forest

The best estimate of the number of eagles alive today in the United States (exluding Alaska) is about 600 breeding pairs. Numbers have dwindled rapidly in recent years. Some populations in the East have disappeared entirely. The Chippewa is unusual in that a large number of eagles continue to breed with fair reproductive success. The 1½ million-acre Chippewa National Forest has about 150 nest sites. Surveys indicate that in any one year about 70% of the nests are occupied by breeding adults. Thus, the breeding population is estimated at about 105 pairs, plus an unknown number of immatures and transients. Eagles are found regularly on the Chippewa from about March 15 through November 30. Their wintering ground is unknown at the present time.

The bald eagle with a wingspan of over seven feet is the largest bird of prey in this area. The adult eagle is readily identified by its immaculate white head and tail. The sub-adults do not have a white head and tail and are often mistaken for "hawks" or golden eagles. Adult plumage is not attained until the fourth or fifth year of life.

The osprey and turkey vulture are the only other birds on the Chippewa approaching the bald eagle in size. They can be distinguished at a distance by their manner of soaring; the bald eagle with flat wings, the turkey vulture with upswept wings; the osprey with a kink or crook in its wings.

Ranger District personnel assist in maintaining an inventory of eagle nests in the National Forest. Annual appraisals are made of nesting activity and success.

Special buffer zones are established around each nest site to limit activity and prevent disturbance of nesting eagles. No timber cutting or other management is permitted within 330 feet of any nest. Another zone of 650 feet from the nest is established where activity is permitted, but not during the time of year eagles are nesting. An effort is also made to preserve old-growth trees in the vicinity for roosting and alternate nest sites.

Banding of young eagles will help to answer many questions concerning the eagle's life history and status. Some eagles have been banded on the Chippewa, but there is a great need for additional effort.

Bald eagles are protected by federal and state laws. Severe fines can be imposed for destruction of birds and their nests. Malicious killing is nevertheless an important reason for the decline of the bald eagle. Help us to protect this vanishing species. Enjoy the eagles on the Chippewa National Forest, but watch at a distance and do not disturb or harm the nesting birds.

Minnesota

Chippewa National Forest. The Chippewa encompasses vast stands of pines and more than 1,300 lakes. With so much water, it's not surprising that boating, canoeing, swimming and other water sports are this forest's most popular pastimes. 656,645 acres.

Superior National Forest. The main attraction of this forest region is the 747,000-acre Boundary Waters Canoe Area, a unique wilderness area that has been called the finest canoe region in the country. Naturally, fishing is also popular here, and winter sports include skiing and snowmobiling. 2,058,337 acres.

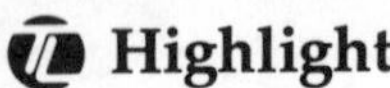

Boundary Waters Canoe Area

Geology

The BWCA is a part of the Laurentian upland or, more commonly, the Canadian Shield. It is some of the oldest and toughest rock known. About 700 million years ago, the area was the scene of extensive volcanic activity during which tremendous volumes of granitic lava were expelled. Gradually, the forces of nature created land forms similar to that of Kentucky and Tennessee today. Streams and tributaries were common, lakes rare.

Subsequent sheets of glacial ice covered the land at least four times in the last million years. The ice plowed up whole forests, leveled rocky outcrops and stripped land of soil. Massive rocks were picked up and served to file, groove and polish the bare rock as the ice ground relentlessly forward.

The retreat of the last glacier left a stark, barren landscape. Boulders of incredible size were scattered over the area. Earlier drainage patterns were altered as meltwater filled depressions. In the wake of the retreating glacier, the myriad lakes now found in the BWCA were formed.

Slowly, vegetation began to stake a new claim. Gradually, the limited amount of soil now covering the rocks formed. Decaying aquatic plants collected in shallow lakes to form present-day bogs and swamps. These processes continue today.

As you travel through the area, note the smooth, polished and grooved surfaces on the exposed ledgerock. Observe how little soil is found on some areas and recall that it took 11,000 years to form. Plant cover is all that holds this soil in place; that is why we must take special care not to harm the vegetation.

Birds

A host of birds make the BWCA home during the summer. These range from the tiny ruby-throated hummingbird to the great bald eagle. Included are some 150 other species of which the state bird of Minnesota, the common loon, is one.

Trees

The land areas are almost completely forested. The principal conifers are the pines — jack, white and red. White and black spruce, balsam fir, northern white cedar and tamarack are also common. The principal broad-leaved trees are quaking aspen and paper birch.

Wild Flowers

A great variety of flowers, including many sub-arctic species, can be found here. The cool climate is especially suitable to orchids, of which there are close to 30 native species. The pink-and-white lady slipper, Minnesota's state flower, is one.

Wildlife

The wildlife of the BWCA, too, is unique. It is the haunt of the last substantial population of timber wolves in the contiguous United States.

Mississippi

Bienville National Forest. A forest of ash, hickory, poplar, pine and oak, the Bienville offers excellent fishing opportunities and a number of fine campsites. 177,040 acres.

Delta National Forest. The Delta includes the 1,700-acre Greentree Reservoir, a popular spot with hunters, and stands of cypress, cottonwood, gum, tupelo and elm. Rivers within the Delta offer excellent fishing for bass, bream and catfish. 59,159 acres.

De Soto National Forest. The De Soto is divided into several sections throughout the southeastern part of the state and includes many scenic rivers, streams and lakes. The Tuxachanie Trail provides access to scenic bottomlands and beautiful pine woods. 499,863 acres.

Holly Springs National Forest. Located in northern Mississippi, along the Tennessee border, Holly Springs is a mixture of pines and hardwoods. The forest is popular with hunters, offering excellent deer, squirrel, quail and turkey hunting in the fall. 145,121 acres.

Homochitto National Forest. The Homochitto is a timber region with only limited recreation opportunities. Principal attractions include the Homochitto River and Clear Springs Lake. 189,439 acres.

Tombigbee National Forest. A small forest of hardwoods and pines located southwest of Tupelo, this region includes the historic Owl Creek Indian Mounds and the 200-acre Davis Lake. 65,367 acres.

Missouri

Mark Twain National Forest. This forest is divided into several sections that are scattered throughout the southern part of the state, and consists of rolling hills, deep hollows, steep gorges and vast stands of hardwoods. Two scenic hiking routes — the Cane Ridge and Victory Trails — wind through dense woodlands and across the steep ridges. 1,434,330 acres.

Montana

Beaverhead National Forest. The Beaverhead lies in a great valley at the foot of the Madison, Beaverhead, Anaconda and Tobacco Root mountain ranges.

The fisher, a furbearer once thought close to extinction in the United States, is now common in the BWCA. Other mammals found here include white-tailed deer, moose, black bear, otter, weasel, mink, coyote, muskrat, beaver, fox, and a variety of squirrels and other rodents.

Fish

The principal native game fish are walleye, northern pike and lake trout. Some lakes have small-mouth bass. Bluegills and crappies are occasionally taken but they are not widely distributed. Rainbow and brook trout have been stocked in a few lakes.

Cooking Tip

There is a variety of light-weight, freeze-dried and dehydrated foods available to make your meals in the BWCA easy to plan and prepare.

Travel Permits

• Travel permits must be obtained before entering the BWCA. These are available without charge from ranger stations in Cook, Isabella, Tofte, Grand Marais and the Voyageur Visitor Center in Ely. *Travel permits must be in possession while in the BWCA.*

• There are limits on the number of travel permits available during the summer for overnight use. Information on how to reserve a travel permit in advance may be obtained by writing the Forest Supervisor, PO Box 338, Duluth, Minnesota 55801.

Within the forest are a number of scenic drives and numerous campgrounds. 2,114,577 acres.

Bitterroot National Forest. The Bitterroot is a wild forest with few roads, making it a prime area for big-game hunters who come here to stalk elk, moose, mountain goats, bighorn sheep and deer. Included in its boundaries are three wilderness areas and many fine hiking trails. 1,650,325 acres.

Custer National Forest. The Custer has a varied terrain of rugged mountains, timbered slopes and rolling prairie in its various divisions that stretch across the southern part of Montana. Extensive snowmobile trails make this a popular winter sports area. 1,113,892 acres.

Deerlodge National Forest. This forest, made up of large stands of lodgepole pine, straddles the Continental Divide and features excellent hiking and backpacking trails as well as fine fishing opportunities at Georgetown Lake. 1,185,084 acres.

Flathead National Forest. Much of this forest is devoted to the Bob Marshall and Mission Mountains Wilderness Areas, but the North Fork of the Flathead River and the Swan River Valley offer spectacular scenic drives. 2,363,392 acres.

Gallatin National Forest. The earthquake that struck the Gallatin in 1959 had a major impact on this region, reshaping part of the landscape and creating a new lake. The forest includes information on the quake at the Madison Earthquake Area. 1,726,707 acres.

Helena National Forest. This forest surrounds the city of Helena, a former mining town that grew to become the state capital. The Gates of the Mountain Wilderness offer exceptional hiking along scenic trails. 972,408 acres.

Kootenai National Forest. The Kootenai includes three mountain ranges — the Cabinets, Flatheads and Purcells — and offers scenic drives along the Yaak River and along the shores of Lake Kookanusa. Native wildlife includes the grizzly. 1,779,932 acres.

Lewis and Clark National Forest. A rugged and wild forest, the Lewis and Clark has the distinction of once being one of the world's leading producers of sapphires (the famous Tollgate Sapphire Mines at Yogo Gulch produced more than $10 million worth of fine gemstones). 1,835,264 acres.

Lolo National Forest. This forest lies on the eastern slopes of the massive Bitterroot Range, surrounding the town of Missoula. The streams within the forest provide excellent trout fishing and big-game hunters can stalk elk, deer, bear and mountain goats. 2,091,043 acres.

Nebraska

Nebraska National Forest. The Nebraska has the distinction of containing the only completely man-made forest in the nation. The remainder of the region is composed of prairie grasslands and rolling sand hills. 256,921 acres.

Nevada

Humboldt National Forest. The vast Humboldt is primarily an area of sagebrush and sand scattered with jagged peaks that bring water to the thirsty desert. Within the forest's many sections there are rich mineral deposits and large expanses of grazing land for several thousand head of sheep and cattle. 2,528,076 acres.

Toiyabe National Forest. This forest is divided into four distinct regions, encompassing the heavily forested slopes of the eastern side of the Sierra Nevadas and the desert landscape of the central part of the state. 3,375,482 acres.

New Hampshire

White Mountain National Forest. The dense hardwood stands of the White Mountains provide a blazing show of

Highlight

Camping in New Hampshire's White Mountain National Forest

Before setting out on a trail, have a good idea where you will spend the night. Study the Restricted Use Areas on the Forest Service map. Don't spoil your trip to the mountains by arriving at a hut for the night only to discover you need a reservation.

OVERNIGHT ALTERNATIVES INCLUDE:

AMC Huts. The huts are a series of eight mountain hostels located about one day's hike apart. Operated by the AMC on a reservation basis, each has a staff providing food, lodging and information on hiking and the mountain environment. Huts vary in capacity from 36 to 90 persons. *No camping is permitted around the huts.*

Cabins. Ten cabins are scattered throughout the forest offering a more primitive experience. There are no cooking facilities, so bring your own stove. Each cabin accommodates around a dozen people. Again, there is no camping permitted directly around the cabins. Due to heavy use, don't count on space being available. Be sure and bring along a tent, and if you have to use it, go at least one-fourth mile from the cabin and well off the trail.

Shelters/Tent Platforms. "Adirondack" shelters with adjacent camping and tent platform sites are two of the improved types of campsites in the Forest. They include privies and fireplaces. Tent platforms allow more concentrated use of an area with less soil compaction. Hikers must bring a tent because space within the shelter is limited. Dead and "downed" wood is scarce, so bring a stove. At some sites, a caretaker is present and a fee charged. Sites are administered by the Forest Service, AMC and other cooperators.

Designated Campgrounds. The Forest Service and the state of New Hampshire operate a number of roadside campgrounds. Each have carefully marked campsites, tables, fireplaces, running water and toilet facilities. They can accommodate trailers and tent campers. All operate on a first-come, first-served basis, and a fee is charged. Special areas for large group camping exist at Campton Group Area and Barnes Field at Dolly Copp Campground.

Forest Camping. There are thousands of acres in the White Mountain National Forest where you can camp outside of designated camping areas. Getting off the trail and pitching a tent can be an enjoyable experience, but it should be done in such a way as not to infringe on other Forest users. In most RUA's, you must camp 200 feet from the trail, but outside of RUA's, the 200-foot rule is not mandatory. However, it is a good rule to follow as it keeps the trail from being scarred with hardened campsites. Keep well below timberline and away from surface water. *The entire Presidential Range region is an RUA.* Remember, there is no camping in the Cutler River Drainage, except at shelters. This includes Huntington and Tuckerman Ravines.

In general, if you want to camp overnight, keep in mind the following:

- Make sure your campsite is 200 feet away from the trail.
- Camp below timberline.
- Camp outside state park boundaries and one-fourth mile away from a hut or cabin.
- Camp one-fourth mile away from most roads. (Check the map; in some areas, the distance may differ.)

colors during the fall and a prime recreation area year-round. There are a number of scenic drives within the forest and viewpoints that offer spectacular vistas of the forest region. 683,944 acres.

New Mexico

Carson National Forest. The mountains of the Carson contain extensive stands of lush pine forests, but the landscape in the lower elevations consists mainly of the red rock formations and sandy desert that is so prevalent throughout New Mexico. Scenic drives through this forest will take you past many remainders of the state's Old West heritage. 1,390,800 acres.

Cibola National Forest. This was the region where Francisco Coronado searched for the legendary Seven Cities of Gold — and it is here that archaeologists have found traces of civilization dating back thousands of years. 1,616,496 acres.

Gila National Forest. The Gila is a remote region consisting of rugged desert and pine, spruce and aspen-covered mountain slopes. Within the forest, the Gila Wilderness and Gila Primitive Area combine to produce a wild area of more than 560 acres. 2,704,724 acres.

Lincoln National Forest. This is the forest that produced the legendary Smokey Bear, a young cub found badly burned in a fire that swept through the forest in 1950. This is a popular winter sports area, as well as an excellent hunting and fishing region. 1,103,270 acres.

Santa Fe National Forest. The Santa Fe contains the Los Alamos atomic research center, but it also offers more than 1,000 miles of excellent hiking trails, 400 miles of fishing streams and countless scenic drives. 1,580,969 acres.

North Carolina

Croatan National Forest. This forest takes its name from the word "Croatan" — the only sign left by the lost colony of Roanoke Island. The forest itself is a combination of swampland and forests of loblolly and longleaf pine. 308,226 acres.

Nantahala National Forest. Once the home of the Cherokee Nation, the Nantahala now offers a wide variety of recreation opportunities, numerous campsites and the virgin timber of the Joyce Kilmer Memorial Forest. 456,890 acres.

Pisgah National Forest. The Pisgah, once owned by industrialist George Vanderbilt, is the first forest in the U.S. to have been managed on a sustained yield basis. The year-round beauty of this forest includes brilliant wildflower displays in the spring and blazing colors in the fall. 482,370 acres.

Uwharrie National Forest. This is a small forest offering excellent fishing in the Uwharrie River and Badin Lake. The forest has no developed campgrounds. 45,760 acres.

Ohio

Wayne National Forest. The Wayne is a restored forest area reclaimed in 1951 from land that had been misused for nearly 200 years. Today, the region offers good bass fishing, hunting for deer and wild turkey and several scenic drives. 166,035 acres.

Oregon

Deschutes National Forest. The Deschutes rests on the eastern slope of the Cascades, taking in areas of old volcanic activity, three wilderness areas and 40 miles of the Oregon Skyline Trail, a segment of the Pacific Crest Trail. 1,600,616 acres.

Fremont National Forest. The Fremont contains towering stands of pine, traces of old volcanic activity and a number of unique geologic formations. The forest is named for Captain John C. Fremont, who led one of the first explorations of southern Oregon. 1,195,031 acres.

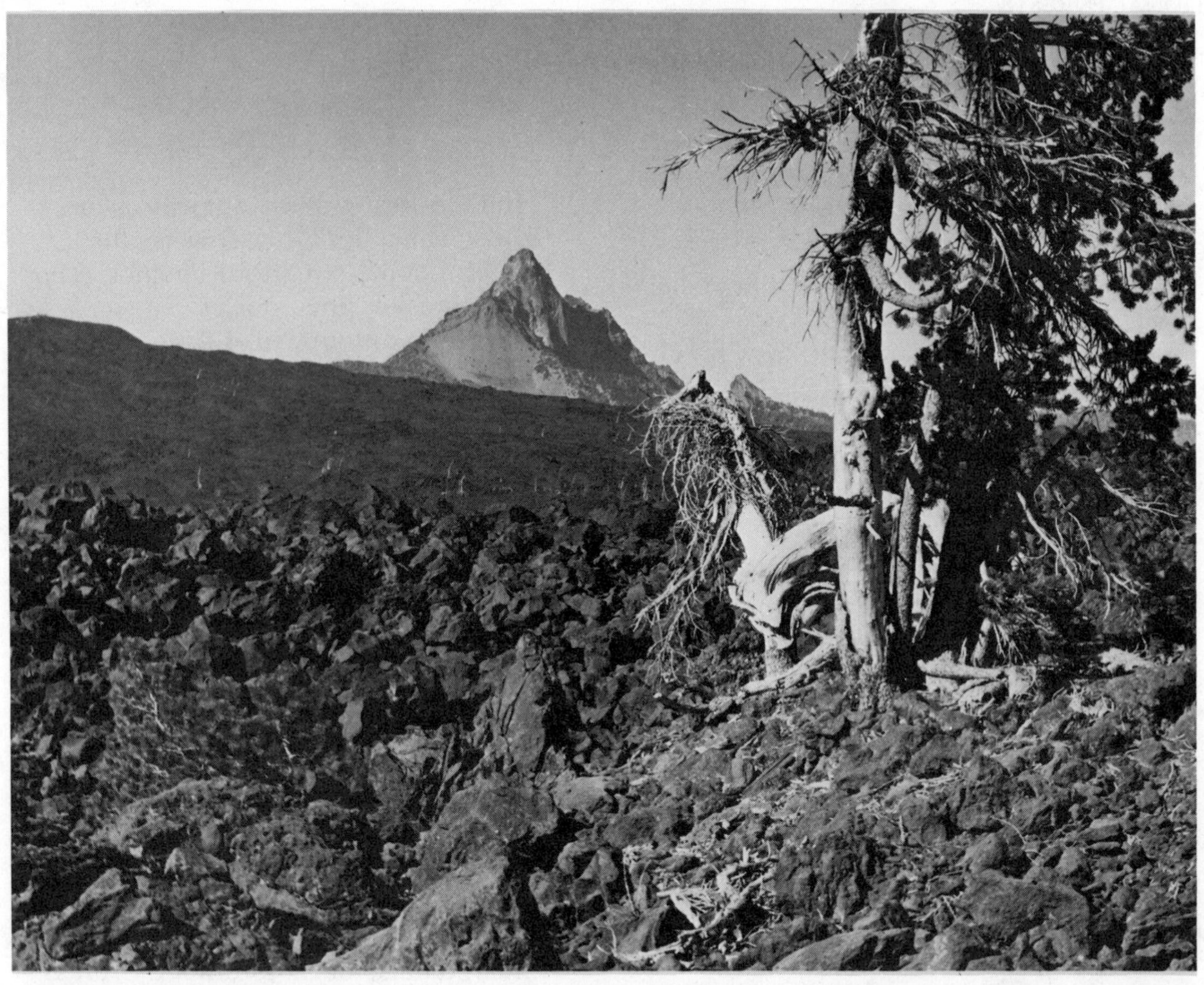

Astronauts destined for the moon came to practice on these lava fields off McKenzie Pass in Oregon's Cascade Mountains. The most extensive fields in the state, they cover a nine-square-mile area east of Eugene and west of Sisters on Oregon State Highway 242. To the north, volcanic Mount Washington rises 7,794 feet.

Malheur National Forest. The Malheur combines the arid country of Oregon's high desert and the ponderosa pine forests of the Blue Mountains. Within the forest's boundaries, the 33,000-acre Strawberry Mountain Wilderness contains a number of glacial lakes and thousands of acres of alpine and subalpine flora. 1,457,457 acres.

Mount Hood National Forest. This forest begins at the south shore of the scenic Columbia River and extends south to embrace snowcapped Mount Hood. An outstanding scenic drive here is the one that takes you through the Columbia Gorge. 1,059,240 acres.

Ochoco National Forest. This forest is the center of the rockhound area that includes Prineville, "America's Agate Capital." Besides excellent rockhounding opportunities, the forest also offers superb hunting and excellent fishing in several lakes. 843,694 acres.

Rogue River National Forest. This forest surrounds the headwaters of the Rogue River and encompasses part of Crater Lake National Park. The Mount Ashland Ski Area is a popular winter sports center. 583,885 acres.

Siskiyou National Forest. The Siskiyou hosts large numbers of fishermen and white-water enthusiasts who are drawn to the forest each year by the turbulent Rogue River. Besides being an excellent steelhead and salmon stream, the Rogue offers some of the most scenic white-water stretches in the nation. 1,057,691 acres.

Siuslaw National Forest. Located along Oregon's rugged north coast, the Siuslaw contains a lush green rain forest and sharply contrasting stretches of sand dunes. 622,963 acres.

Umatilla National Forest. Stretching across the northern end of Oregon's Blue Mountains, the Umatilla spills over into Washington, east of Walla Walla. The forest offers a variety of year-round activities including fishing, hunting, white-water rafting, skiing and snowmobiling. 1,079,074 acres.

Umpqua National Forest. This dense forest takes its name from the scenic Umpqua River, which begins here in the snowmelt of the Cascades. The forest offers outstanding fishing for brook and rainbow trout and steelhead. 988,309 acres.

Wallowa-Whitman National Forest. This forest, which was once the homeland of the Nez Perce Nation, includes the 220,000-acre Eagle Cap Wilderness, the famed Hells Canyon and the Seven Devils scenic area. 2,246,771 acres.

Willamette National Forest. The densely wooded Willamette produces about 10% of the timber cut in the national forests and is also a valuable watershed for the cities of the Willamette Valley. 1,667,821 acres.

Winema National Forest. This forest encircles the vast Klamath Marsh that was once the home and hunting grounds of the Klamath Indians. The 23,071-acre Mountain Lakes Wilderness is a region of exceptional scenic beauty, containing a number of alpine lakes. 907,929 acres.

Pennsylvania

Allegheny National Forest. Established in 1923, the Allegheny is a superb hardwood forest reclaimed from land that had been stripped by early settlers. The Allegheny and Clarion Rivers provide good bass fishing and hunters should have good luck here pursuing bear, deer and turkey. 506,381 acres.

Grey Towers

In the forested hills of northeastern Pennsylvania lies Grey Towers, the beautiful home of Gifford Pinchot, who was a forester, governor of Pennsylvania, founder of American conservation and first chief of the U.S. Forest Service.

Tour Schedule: Daily, from 9 a.m. to 3 p.m., every hour on the hour. Groups of 30 or more, please call for reservations. (717) 296-6401.

Location: In Milford, Pennsylvania, 45 miles east of Scranton on Route 209, just off exit 10 of Interstate 84.

South Carolina

Francis Marion National Forest. It was here that General Francis Marion, "The Swamp Fox," used guerilla warfare to harass British troops during the American Revolution. This is a dense swamp-forest with large tracts of moss-draped cypress and gum trees. 249,401 acres.

Sumter National Forest. Divided into three distinct regions, the Sumter encompasses the Blue Ridge Mountains and mixed forests of pines and hardwoods. A number of historical sites are found within the Sumter's boundaries, as well as several scenic drives. 357,424 acres.

South Dakota

Black Hills National Forest. The scenic and rugged Black Hills is a dense forest covering an ancient mountain range that is older than the Rockies or the Swiss Alps. Once the home of great herds of buffalo, the forest has also been the site of a number of gold discoveries and several Indian battles. 1,055,631 acres.

Tennessee

Cherokee National Forest. Divided in two

sections, the Cherokee follows the backbone of the Appalachian Range. Visitors will find a number of scenic routes winding through the mountain backcountry of dense pine and hardwood forests. 620,350 acres.

Texas

Angelina National Forest. A forest of mixed pine and hardwoods, the Angelina surrounds the excellent fishing waters of the Sam Rayburn Reservoir. 154,703 acres.

Davy Crockett National Forest. A forest of shortleaf and loblolly pine and hardwoods in the river bottoms. Largely undeveloped, the region offers only two campgrounds. 161,578 acres.

Sabine National Forest. The Sabine is located on the border of Texas and Louisiana, along the shores of the Toledo Bend Reservoir. There is excellent fishing for catfish, bass and bream. 186,689 acres.

Sam Houston National Forest. This forest consists of dense stands of shortleaf and loblolly pines, and large groves of hardwoods growing in the riverbottoms. A number of small lakes and streams also make for good fishing here. 158,648 acres.

Utah

Ashley National Forest. A thick pine forest lying across the eastern half of the Uintas Mountains, the Ashley includes the scenic Flaming Gorge National Recreation Area and Sheep Creek Canyon, an area of spectacular geologic formations. 1,405,604 acres.

Cache National Forest. Straddling the Utah-Idaho border, the Cache is a valuable watershed area for nearby communities, as well as a region of scenic wonders. 679,503 acres.

Dixie National Forest. The Dixie is a region of strange and colorful rock formations that offers almost limitless scenic drives. Deer and elk hunting is good here, and so is the trout fishing in the numerous lakes and streams. 1,885,632 acres.

Fishlake National Forest. Located in central Utah, this forest takes its name from the scenic Fish Lake. The aspen-lined lake supports a large population of trout and provides some of the best fishing in the state. 1,423,900 acres.

Manti-La Sal National Forest. The Manti-La Sal combines lush forests and unique geologic formations that offer endless scenic delights. Hunting, fishing and hiking are popular pursuits and the region is also a popular ski area. 1,238,151 acres.

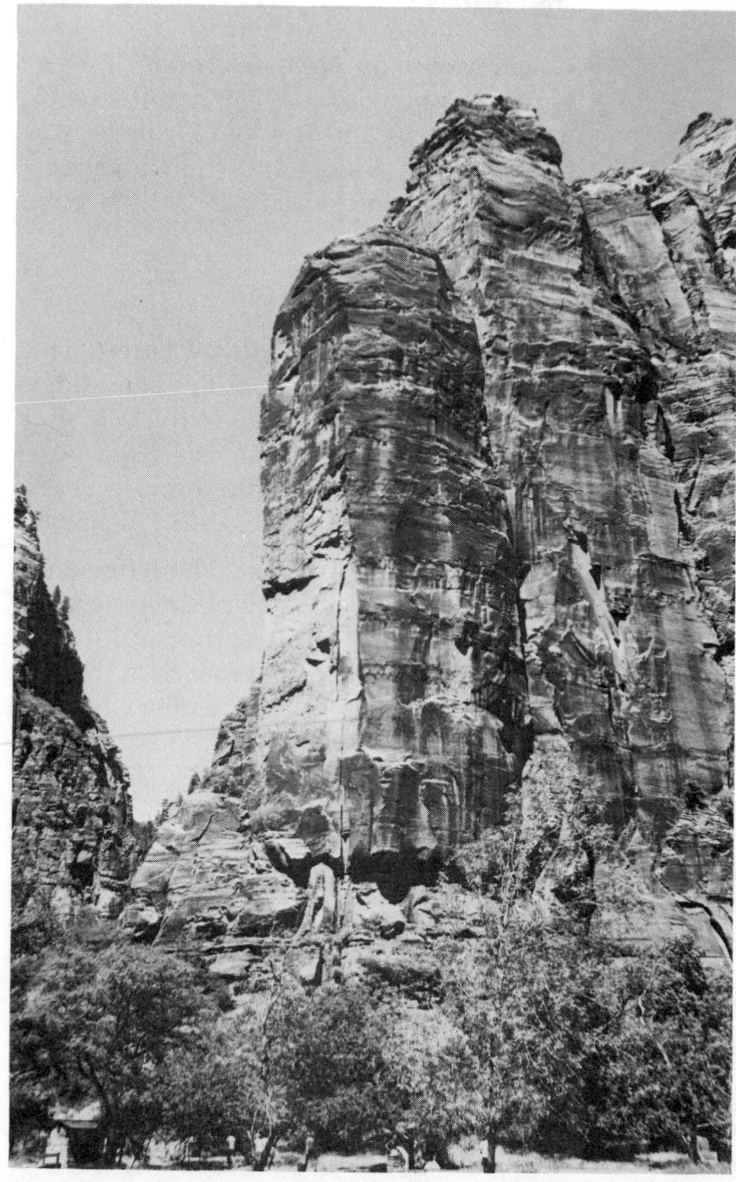

Uinta National Forest. A major lumber producer, the Uinta provides more than three million board-feet of lumber each year, but the forest is most valuable as a watershed for nearby cities and towns. Hikers and backpackers will find more than 2,000 miles of trails here. 812,865 acres.

Wasatch National Forest. This forest lies right in the backyard of Salt Lake City and serves as a busy recreation area for the nearby residents. Trout fishing is excellent and hunting for mule deer, elk and moose is rated as good. 848,672 acres.

Vermont

Green Mountain National Forest. This scenic New England forest is dotted with quaint villages and is noted for its beauty in all seasons. Skiing and snowmobiling are popular winter pastimes. 261,591 acres.

Virginia

George Washington National Forest. This forest lies on the slopes of the Blue Ridge Mountains, on either side of the beautiful Shenandoah Valley. Some 864 miles of trails take hikers deep into the forest's hardwood-covered slopes. 943,174 acres.

Jefferson National Forest. The Jefferson is a year-round scenic showplace, covered with wildflowers in the spring and summer and brilliant red foliage in the fall. One of the most popular pastimes here is horseback riding along the many trails that wind into the backcountry. 670,779 acres.

Washington

Colville National Forest. The Colville is a little-used forest that hosts a number of lakes, streams and scenic drives. This forest is especially noted for its mushroom and huckleberry picking. 943,793 acres.

Gifford Pinchot National Forest. Drenched by heavy annual rain and snowfalls, the Pinchot consists of dense conifer forests and sparkling rivers and streams. Wild blackberries and huckleberries abound. 1,251,051 acres.

Mount Baker-Snoqualmie National Forest. These combined forests of dense fir and spruce lie on the western slopes of the Cascades in a region of fairly recent volcanic activity. More than 2,500 miles of trails wind through the forest and seven ski areas host winter sport enthusiasts. 2,512,735 acres.

Okanagan National Forest. Situated on the eastern slopes of the Cascades, the Okanagan is a ponderosa pine forest popular with hikers and backpackers. 1,499,428 acres.

Olympic National Forest. The Olympic combines lush vegetation, abundant wildlife and spectacular mountain scenery to create one of the most beautiful forests in the nation. It's not surprising that this forest contains such lush vegetation when you consider that it receives about 144 inches of rain annually. 651,347 acres.

Wenatchee National Forest. The Wenatchee River, a roaring, white-water stream, gives this forest its name. More than 1,900 miles of trails extend into the scenic backcountry. 1,614,520 acres.

West Virginia

Monongahela National Forest. The Monongahela covers both the Appalachian and Allegheny Mountain ranges along the West Virginia-Virginia border. Like many of the forests of this region, the Monongahela is a reconstructed forest rebuilt on land that was once an eroding eyesore. 841,700 acres.

Wisconsin

Chequamegon National Forest. This is a thick pine, spruce and hardwood forest dotted with hundreds of backcountry lakes. Because these lakes are fished only

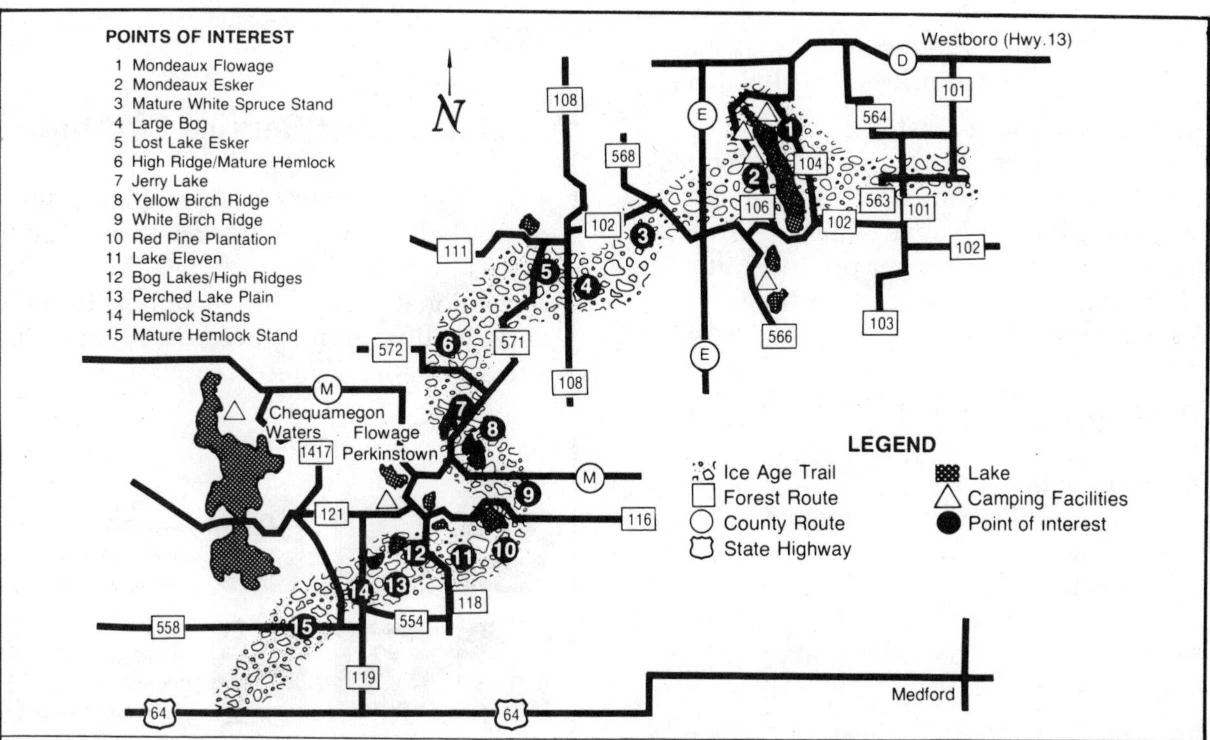

The Ice Age Trail

A scenic segment of the Ice Age Trail runs diagonally across the Medford Ranger District on the Chequamegon National Forest. It is approximately 40 miles long and available for year-round use.

Traversing eskers and moraines, around kettle lakes and kettle holes, the Ice Age Trail gives the hiker intimate contact with the land forms that were created when the last glacier covered Wisconsin. Many lakes, streams and bogs in various stages of succession offer a variety of scenic qualities to the area. These include the Yellow River, Jerry Lake and Lake Eleven. The trail also runs adjacent to Mondeaux Flowage, a man-made lake constructed by the Civilian Conservation Corps in the 1930s. The numerous bodies of water provide good fishing.

Many varieties of trees and other plants provide variety and a feeling of solitude along the trail. Although the tree species include aspen, birch, white spruce, balsam fir, swamp conifers and northern hardwoods such as maple, yellow birch and ash, the most majestic are the white pine and hemlock. Many species of wild flowers are present, including an abundance of trillium in the hardwood areas in the spring.

Wildlife that can be observed from the trail include deer, porcupine, skunk, squirrel, ruffed grouse, waterfowl, and numerous species of hawks and songbirds. Sometimes, pine snakes and other reptiles can be observed. Occasionally, a bear, coyote or bald eagle may be seen. In addition to the natural features, there are many forest management activities including wildlife openings, hunter walking trails, tree plantations, water impoundments and recreation areas.

Developed campsites and drinking water near the trail are available on the Mondeaux Flowage. Camping is also allowed at Jerry Lake and Lake Eleven and at least 50 feet back from other portions of the trail. There are many access points on the trail for those who wish to hike only for short distances. Developed parking facilities are available at the Mondeaux Flowage and off Forest Route #571 at Jerry Lake.

moderately, they produce trophy-sized bass, walleye and muskies. 840,189 acres.

Nicolet National Forest. The Nicolet extends along the border near Michigan's Upper Peninsula and contains thick stands of birch, pine and sugar maples. Although the area is a major lumber producer, it still offers excellent hunting and fishing. 651,721 acres.

Wyoming

Bighorn National Forest. This forest takes in the rugged Bighorn Mountains, a formidable wall of peaks rising to altitudes of 12,000 feet and more. One of the major attractions is the Cloud Peak Primitive Area, containing 256 fishing lakes and 49 miles of fishing streams. 1,107,342 acres.

Bridger-Teton National Forest. These two regions combine to make a vast forest that covers the mountain ranges from the Continental Divide to the state's western border. The region is noted for its excellent trout waters. 3,400,549 acres.

Medicine Bow National Forest. This forest is broken into four divisions in the southeastern part of the state. Each section offers a variety of recreation opportunities and excellent scenic drives. 1,093,177 acres.

Shoshone National Forest. This forest takes in the wild Absaroka Range and the Beartooth Plateau on the east side of Yellowstone National Park. Four separate wilderness areas provide excellent backcountry opportunities for backpackers and hikers. 2,431,948 acres.

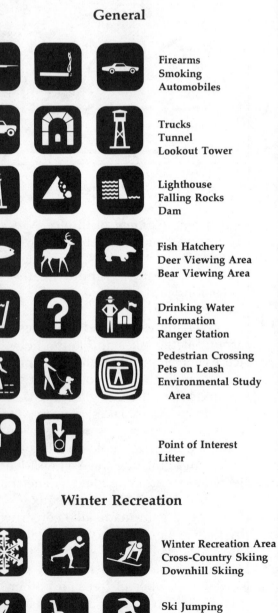

U.S. Forest Service Symbols

The Forest Service has designed a series of symbols to convey information without words on signs in U.S. Forest Service recreational areas. These symbols locate and identify services, accommodations and items of general interest.

General

Firearms
Smoking
Automobiles

Trucks
Tunnel
Lookout Tower

Lighthouse
Falling Rocks
Dam

Fish Hatchery
Deer Viewing Area
Bear Viewing Area

Drinking Water
Information
Ranger Station

Pedestrian Crossing
Pets on Leash
Environmental Study Area

Point of Interest
Litter

Winter Recreation

Winter Recreation Area
Cross-Country Skiing
Downhill Skiing

Ski Jumping
Sledding
Ice Skating

Ski Bobbing
Snowmobiling
Snow Shoeing

Accommodations and Services

Lodging
Food Service
Grocery Store

Men's Restroom
Restrooms
Women's Restroom

First Aid
Telephone
Post Office

Mechanic
Handicapped
Airport

Lockers
Bus Stop
Gas Station

Vehicle Ferry
Parking
Showers

Viewing Area
Sleeping Shelter
Campground

Picnic Shelter
Trailer Sites
Trailer Sanitary Station

Campfires
Trail Shelter
Picnic Area

Kennel
Laundry
Spelunking

Land Recreation

Recreation Vehicles
Hiking Trail
Playground

Amphitheater
Tramway
Hunting

Stable
Interpretive Trail
Interpretive Auto

Rock Climbing
Climbing
Rock Collecting

Horse Trail
Trail Bike Trail
Bicycle Trail

Water Recreation

Marina
Launching Ramp
Motorboating

Sailboating
Rowboating
Water Skiing

 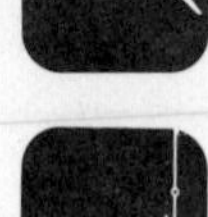 

Surfing
Scuba Diving
Swimming

Diving
Fishing
Canoeing

Boat Tours
Wading

Symbol with red slash mark indicates activity is prohibited.

National Forests

State	Forest	CAMPING	PICNICKING	CONCESSIONS	SWIMMING	HIKING	BOATING	FISHING	HUNTING	WINTER SPORTS
Alabama	Tuskegee	•	•	•		•		•	•	
	William B. Bankhead	•	•		•	•		•	•	
	Conecuh	•	•	•	•	•	•	•	•	
	Talladega	•	•	•	•	•	•	•	•	
Alaska	Chugach	•	•	•	•	•		•	•	•
	Coconino	•	•	•		•	•	•	•	•
	North Tongass	•	•	•	•	•	•	•	•	•
	South Tongass	•	•	•	•	•	•	•	•	•
Arizona	Apache	•	•	•		•	•	•	•	
	Coronado	•	•	•	•	•	•	•	•	•
	Kaibab	•	•	•		•	•	•	•	•
	Prescott	•	•	•		•	•	•	•	•
	Sitgreaves	•	•	•		•	•	•	•	
	Tonto	•	•	•	•	•	•	•	•	
Arkansas	Ouachita	•	•	•	•	•	•	•	•	
	Ozark	•	•	•	•	•	•	•	•	
	St. Francis	•	•			•				
California	Angeles	•	•	•	•	•	•	•	•	•
	Cleveland	•	•	•	•	•		•	•	•
	Eldorado	•	•	•	•	•	•	•	•	•
	Inyo	•	•	•	•	•	•	•	•	•
	Klamath	•	•	•		•		•	•	•
	Lassen	•	•	•	•	•	•	•	•	•
	Los Padres	•	•	•	•	•		•	•	•
	Mendocino	•	•	•	•	•	•	•	•	
	Modoc	•	•	•	•	•	•	•	•	
	Plumas	•	•	•	•	•	•	•	•	
	San Bernardino	•	•	•	•	•		•	•	•
	Sequoia	•	•	•	•	•	•	•	•	•
	Shasta	•	•	•	•	•	•	•	•	•
	Sierra	•	•	•	•	•	•	•	•	•
	Six Rivers	•	•	•	•	•	•	•	•	
	Stanislaus	•	•	•	•	•	•	•	•	•
	Tahoe	•	•	•	•	•	•	•	•	•
	Trinity	•	•			•		•	•	
Colorado	Arapaho	•	•	•		•	•	•	•	•
	Grand Mesa	•	•	•	•	•	•	•	•	•
	Gunnison	•	•	•	•	•	•	•	•	•
	Pike	•	•	•		•	•	•	•	•
	Rio Grande	•	•	•		•	•	•	•	•
	Roosevelt	•	•	•		•	•	•	•	•
	Routt	•	•	•		•	•	•	•	•
	San Isabel	•	•	•	•	•	•	•	•	•
	San Juan	•	•	•	•	•	•	•	•	•
	Uncompahgre		•			•		•	•	
	White River	•	•	•	•	•	•	•	•	•

National Forests

State	Forest	CAMPING	PICNICKING	CONCESSIONS	SWIMMING	HIKING	BOATING	FISHING	HUNTING	WINTER SPORTS
Florida	Apalachicola	•	•		•	•	•	•	•	
	Ocala	•	•	•	•	•	•	•	•	
	Osceola	•	•	•	•	•	•	•	•	
Georgia	Chattahoochee	•	•	•	•	•	•	•	•	•
	Oconee	•	•	•	•	•		•	•	
Idaho	Boise	•	•	•	•	•	•	•	•	•
	Caribou	•	•	•	•	•	•	•	•	•
	Challis	•	•	•	•	•	•	•	•	
	Clearwater	•	•	•	•	•	•	•	•	
	Coeur d'Alene	•	•			•	•	•	•	•
	Nez Perce	•	•	•	•	•	•	•	•	
	Payette	•	•	•	•	•	•	•	•	•
	Salmon	•	•	•	•	•	•	•	•	•
	Sawtooth	•	•	•	•	•	•	•	•	•
	St. Joe	•	•	•	•	•	•	•	•	•
	Targhee	•	•	•	•	•	•	•	•	•
Illinois	Shawnee	•	•	•	•	•	•	•	•	
Indiana	Hoosier	•	•	•	•	•	•	•	•	•
Kentucky	Daniel Boone	•	•	•	•	•	•	•	•	
Louisiana	Kisatchie	•	•	•	•	•	•	•	•	
Maine	White Mountain	•	•	•		•	•	•	•	•
Michigan	Hiawatha	•	•	•	•	•	•	•	•	
	Huron	•	•	•	•	•	•	•	•	•
	Manistee	•	•	•	•	•	•	•	•	•
	Ottawa	•	•	•	•	•	•	•	•	•
Minnesota	Chippewa	•	•	•	•	•	•	•	•	•
	Superior	•	•	•	•	•	•	•	•	•
Mississippi	Bienville	•	•		•	•	•	•	•	
	Delta	•	•	•		•	•	•	•	
	De Soto	•	•	•	•	•	•	•	•	
	Holly Springs	•	•	•	•	•	•	•	•	
	Homochitto	•	•	•	•	•	•	•	•	
	Tombigbee	•	•		•	•	•	•	•	
Missouri	Mark Twain	•	•	•	•	•	•	•	•	•
Montana	Beaverhead	•	•		•	•	•	•		
	Bitterroot	•	•	•	•	•	•	•	•	•
	Deerlodge	•	•	•	•	•	◦	•	•	•
	Flathead	•	•	•	•	•	•	•	•	•
	Gallatin	•	•		•	•		•	•	
	Helena	•	•	•		•	•	•	•	•
	Kootenai	•	•	•		•	•	•	•	•
	Lewis and Clark	•	•	•	•	•		•	•	•
	Lolo	•	•	•	•	•		•	•	•
Nebraska	Nebraska	•	•	•	•	•	•	•	•	
Nevada	Humboldt	•	•	•		•	•	•	•	•
	Toiyabe	•	•	•	•	•	•	•	•	•

National Forests

State	Forest	CAMPING	PICNICKING	CONCESSIONS	SWIMMING	HIKING	BOATING	FISHING	HUNTING	WINTER SPORTS
North Carolina	Croatan	•	•	•	•	•	•	•	•	
	Nantahala	•		•	•	•	•	•	•	
	Pisgah	•	•	•	•	•	•	•	•	•
	Uwharrie	•	•	•	•	•	•	•	•	•
New Mexico	Carson	•	•	•		•		•	•	•
	Cibola	•	•	•	•	•		•	•	•
	Gila	•	•			•	•	•	•	
	Lincoln	•	•	•		•	•	•	•	•
	Santa Fe	•	•	•		•		•	•	•
Ohio	Wayne	•	•	•	•	•	•	•	•	•
Pennsylvania	Allegheny	•	•	•	•	•	•	•	•	•
South Carolina	Francis Marion	•	•	•		•	•	•	•	
	Sumter	•	•	•	•	•	•	•	•	
South Dakota	Black Hills	•	•	•	•	•	•	•	•	•
	Custer	•	•	•	•	•	•	•	•	
Oregon	Deschutes	•	•	•	•	•	•	•	•	•
	Fremont	•	•	•	•	•	•	•	•	•
	Malheur	•	•	•	•	•	•	•	•	•
	Mount Hood	•	•	•	•	•	•	•	•	•
	Ochoco	•	•	•	•	•	•	•	•	•
	Rogue River	•	•	•	•	•	•	•	•	•
	Siskiyou	•	•	•	•	•	•	•	•	
	Siuslaw	•	•	•	•	•	•	•	•	•
	Umatilla	•	•	•	•	•	•	•	•	
	Umpqua	•	•	•		•		•	•	•
	Wallowa-Whitman	•	•	•	•	•	•	•	•	•
	Willamette	•	•	•	•	•	•	•	•	•
	Winema	•	•		•	•	•	•	•	
Tennessee	Cherokee	•	•	•	•	•	•	•	•	
Texas	Angelina	•	•	•	•	•	•	•	•	
	Davy Crockett	•	•		•	•	•	•	•	
	Sabine	•	•	•	•	•	•	•	•	•
	Sam Houston	•	•	•	•	•	•	•		
Utah	Ashley	•	•	•	•	•	•	•	•	•
	Cache	•	•	•		•	•	•	•	•
	Dixie	•	•	•	•	•	•	•	•	•
	Fishlake	•	•	•	•	•	•	•	•	
	Manti-La Sal	•	•	•		•	•	•	•	•
	Uinta	•	•	•	•	•	•	•	•	
	Wasatch	•	•	•	•	•	•	•	•	•
Virginia	George Washington	•	•		•	•	•	•	•	
	Jefferson	•		•	•	•	•	•	•	
Vermont	Green Mountain	•	•	•	•	•	•	•	•	•
Washington	Colville	•	•	•	•	•	•	•		•
	Gifford Pinchot	•	•	•	•	•	•	•	•	•
	Kaniksu	•	•	•	•	•	•	•	•	•

National Forests

State	Forest	CAMPING	PICNICKING	CONCESSIONS	SWIMMING	HIKING	BOATING	FISHING	HUNTING	WINTER SPORTS
Washington	Mount Baker	•	•	•	•	•	•	•	•	•
	Okanagan	•	•	•		•	•	•	•	•
	Olympic	•	•	•	•	•	•	•	•	•
	Snoqualmie	•	•	•	•	•	•	•	•	•
	Wenatchee	•	•	•	•	•	•	•	•	•
Wisconsin	Chequamegon	•	•	•	•	•	•	•	•	•
	Nicolet	•	•	•	•	•	•	•	•	
West Virginia	Monongahela	•	•	•	•	•	•	•	•	
Wyoming	Bighorn	•	•	•		•	•	•	•	•
	Bridger	•	•	•	•	•	•	•	•	•
	Medicine Bow	•	•	•		•	•	•	•	•
	Shoshone	•	•	•		•	•	•	•	•
	Teton	•	•	•	•	•	•	•	•	•

For more information on National Forests and National Parks, contact:

Forests

U.S. Department of Agriculture
U.S. Forest Service
Washington, D.C. 20250

Parks

North Atlantic Regional Office

National Park Service
15 State Street
Boston, Massachusetts 02109
Phone: (617) 223-0058

Mid-Atlantic Regional Office

National Park Service
143 South Third Street
Philadelphia, Pennsylvania 19106
Phone: (215) 597-7018

National Capital Regional Office

National Park Service
1100 Ohio Drive, SW
Washington, D.C. 20242
Phone: (202) 426-6700

Southeast Regional Office

National Park Service
75 Spring, SW
Atlanta, Georgia 30303
Phone: (404) 221-3471

Midwest Regional Office

National Park Service
1709 Jackson Street
Omaha, Nebraska 68102
Phone: (402) 221-3471

Rocky Mountain Regional Office

National Park Service
PO Box 25287
Denver, Colorado 80225
Phone: (303) 234-3095

Southwest Regional Office

National Park Service
Old Santa Fe Trail
PO Box 728
Sante Fe, New Mexico 87501
Phone: (505) 988-6375

Western Regional Office

National Park Service
450 Golden Gate Avenue
Box 36063
San Francisco, California 94102
Phone: (415) 556-4122

Pacific Northwest Regional Office

National Park Service
Room 931, Fourth and Pike Building
1424 Fourth Avenue
Seattle, Washington 98101
Phone: (206) 442-0170

National Parks

The National Park System of the United States, now in the early years of its second century, comprises nearly 320 areas covering some 76 million acres in 49 states, the District of Columbia and several of the U.S. possessions. The areas within this system are of such national significance as to justify special recognition and protection.

On March 1, 1872, Congress passed an act establishing Yellowstone National Park in the Territories of Montana and Wyoming "as a public park or pleasuring ground for the benefit and enjoyment of the people" and placed it "under the exclusive control of the Secretary of Interior." In the years following the establishment of Yellowstone, the United States authorized additional parks and monuments, most of them carved from the federal lands of the West. Many of these were administered by the Department of Interior, but others were administered as separate units under several other federal agencies. Finally, in 1916, Congress established the National Park Service in the Department of Interior and charged it with the responsibility for regulating these national areas.

Additions to the National Park System are now generally made through acts of Congress, and national parks can be created only through such acts. But the President has authority, under the Antiquities Act of 1906, to proclaim national monuments on lands already under federal jurisdiction.

Park Service Designations

The diversity of the parks is reflected in the variety of titles given them. The following definitions will help explain some of the distinctions.

National Park. Contains a variety of resources and encompasses sufficient land or water to ensure adequate protection of the resources.

National Monument. Usually smaller than a national park and lacks the diversity of attractions.

National Preserves. Established primarily for the protection of certain resources; activities such as hunting and fishing or the extraction of minerals and fuels may be permitted if they do not jeopardize the area's natural values.

National Lakeshores and National Seashores. Established for the preservation of natural values in shoreline and offshore island areas, while at the same time providing for water-oriented recreation.

National Rivers and Wild and Scenic Riverways. Ribbons of land bordering on free-flowing streams which have not been dammed, channelized or otherwise altered by man are maintained. Besides preserving rivers in their natural state, these areas provide opportunities for outdoor activities such as hiking, canoeing and hunting.

National Historic Site. This is the designation for small areas of historic significance.

Teddy Roosevelt's Maltese Cross Ranch Cabin is located at the entrance to Theodore Roosevelt National Park, Medora, North Dakota.

National Military Park, National Battlefield Park, National Battlefield Site, National Battlefield. Areas associated with American military history.

National Monuments and National Historical Park. Areas of historical significance that may also include features associated with military history.

National Historical Parks. Areas of greater size and complexity than national historical sites.

National Memorial. The designation given to areas that are primarily commemorative.

National Recreation Areas. Originally the designation given to areas surrounding reservoirs built by federal agencies, this title has been expanded to encompass other lands and waters set aside for recreational use by Congress.

National Parkways. Encompass ribbons of land flanking roadways that offer an opportunity for leisurely driving through areas of scenic interest.

Sites for the Performing Arts. Currently, only two areas hold this designation — Wolf Trap Farm Park for the Performing Arts in Virginia and the John F. Kennedy Center for the Performing Arts in Washington, D.C.

Backpackers in Arkansas explore the "Goat Trail" located high above the Buffalo National River.

Alabama

Horseshoe Bend National Military Park. General Andrew Jackson's forces broke the power of the Creek Indian Confederacy and opened Alabama and other parts of the Old Southwest to settlement after fierce fighting here on March 27, 1814, in the battle on the Tallapoosa River. 2,040 acres.

Russell Cave National Monument. An almost continuous archaeological record of human habitation from at least 7000 B.C. to about A.D. 1650 is revealed in this cave. 310.45 acres.

Tuskegee Institute National Historic Site. Booker T. Washington founded this college for black Americans in 1881. Preserved here are the brick buildings the students constructed themselves, Washington's home, and the George Washington Carver Museum. An antebellum mansion serves as park headquarters and visitors center. 74 acres.

Alaska

Aniakchak National Monument. The Aniakchak Caldera, covering some 30 square miles, is one of the great dry calderas in the world. Located in the volcanically active Aleutian Mountains, the Aniakchak last erupted in 1933. The crater includes lava flows, cinder cones and explosion pits, as well as the aptly named Surprise Lake, which cascades through a 1,500-foot gash in the crater wall. *No federal facilities.* 364,000 acres.

Bering Land Bridge National Monument. Located on the Seward Peninsula in northwest Alaska, the monument is a remnant of the land bridge that once connected Asia with North America more than 13,000 years ago. Paleontological and archaeological resources abound; large populations of migrating birds nest here. Ash explosion craters and lava flows, rare in the Arctic, are also present. *No federal facilities.* 2,848,000 acres.

Cape Krusenstern National Monument. Archaeological sites located along a succession of 114 lateral beach ridges illustrate Eskimo communities of every known cultural period in Alaska, dating back some 4,000 years. Older sites are located inland, along the foothills. The monument includes a representative example of the Arctic coastline along the Chukchi Sea. *No federal facilities.* 677,000 acres.

Denali National Monument. Adjacent to Mount McKinley National Park, this monument includes the southern flanks of the mountain with its massive glaciers, the beautiful Cathedral Spires and critical wildlife habitats. "Denali" is the ancient Athapascan Indian name for the mountain, meaning "the great one." 3,993,000 acres.

Gates of the Arctic National Monument. Lying entirely north of the Arctic Circle, the monument includes a portion of the Central Brooks Range, the northernmost extension of the Rocky Mountains. Often referred to as the greatest remaining wilderness in North America, the monument, which is the nation's second largest unit of the National Park System, is characterized by jagged peaks, gentle arctic valleys, wild rivers and numerous lakes. The forested southern slopes contrast to the barren northern reaches of the monument at the edge of Alaska's "north slope." *No federal facilities.* 9,432,000 acres.

Glacier Bay National Monument. Great tidewater glaciers, a dramatic range of plant communities from rocky terrain recently covered by ice to lush temperate rain forest, and a large variety of animals, including brown and black bear, mountain goats, whales, seals and eagles can be found within the park. Also included are Mount Fairweather, the highest peak in southeast Alaska, and the U.S. portion of the Alsek River. 3,355,269 acres.

Katmai National Monument. Variety marks this vast land: lakes, forests, mountains and marshlands all abound in wildlife. The Alaska brown bear, the world's largest carnivore, thrives here, feeding upon red salmon which spawn in the monument's lakes and streams. Wild rivers and renowned sport fishing add to the attractions of this subarctic environment. Here, in 1917, Novarupta Volcano erupted violently, forming the ash-filled "Valley of Ten Thousand Smokes" where steam rose from countless fumaroles in the ash. Today, only a few active vents remain. 4,293,125 acres.

Kenai Fjords National Monument. The monument, within 20 miles of Seward, includes one of the four major ice caps in the U.S., the Harding Icefield. Glaciers radiating from the 700-square-mile icefield continue to cut deep glacial valleys, many ending at tidewater. The coastal fjords and associated offshore islands are remnants of "drowned" mountains. Here, a rich varied rainforest is home to sea lions, sea otters, seals and tens of thousands of breeding birds, including puffins, murres and auklets. *No federal facilities.* 672,000 acres.

Klondike Gold Rush National Historical Park. Historic buildings in Skagway and portions of Chilkoot and White Pass Trails, all prominent in the 1898 gold rush, are included in the park. *Limited federal facilities.* 13,270 acres.

Kobuk Valley National Monument. Embracing the central valley of the Kobuk River, the monument, located entirely north of the Arctic Circle, includes a blend of biological, geological and cultural resources. Here, in the northernmost extent of the boreal forest, a rich array of Arctic wildlife can be found, including critical caribou migration routes, grizzly and black bear, wolf and fox. The 25-square-mile Great Kobuk Sand Dunes rise 100 feet above the surrounding Arctic terrain, just south of the placid Kobuk River. Archaeological sites revealing more than 10,000 years of human occupation, are among the most significant sites known in the Arctic. 1,764,000 acres.

Lake Clark National Monument. Located in the heart of the Chigmit Mountains along the western shore of Cook Inlet, the park contains great geologic diversity, including jagged peaks, granite spires, glaciers and two symmetrical active volcanoes. More than a score of glacial carved lakes rim the mountain mass. More than 40 miles long, Lake Clark is not only the largest lake here, but it is also the headwaters for the most important spawning ground in North America. Merrill and Lake Clark Passes cut through the mountains and are lined by dozens of glaciers and hundreds of waterfalls which cascade over rocky ledges. While there are no federal facilities, this area, which is across Cook Inlet from Anchorage, provides major recreation potential and is already popular with summer hikers and fisherman. 2,930,000 acres.

Mount McKinley National Park. Mount McKinley, at 20,320 feet, is the highest mountain in North America. Large glaciers of the Alaska Range, caribou, Dall sheep, moose, grizzly bears, timber wolves, and other wildlife are highlights of this national park. 1,939,492 acres.

Noatak National Monument. The Noatak River basin is the largest mountain-ringed river basin in the nation still virtually unaffected by man. The monument includes landforms of great scientific interest, including the 65-mile-long Grand Canyon of the Noatak, a transition zone and migration route for plants and animals between subarctic and Arctic environments, and an array of flora which is among the most diverse anywhere in the earth's northern latitudes. Hundreds of archaeological sites and rich wildlife populations add to the significance of the area. 5,800,000 acres.

Sitka National Historical Park. The site of the 1804 fort and battle which marked the last major Tlingit Indian resistance to Russian colonization is preserved here. Tlingit totem poles are exhibited. 107 acres.

Wrangell-St. Elias National Monument. The Chugach, Wrangell and St. Elias mountain ranges converge here in what is often referred to as the "mountain kingdom of North America." The largest unit of the National Park System, and a day's drive east of Anchorage, the monument includes the continent's largest assemblage of glaciers and the greatest collection of peaks above 16,000 feet, including Mount St. Elias. At 18,008 feet, it is the second highest peak in the U.S. Adjacent to Canada's Kluane National Park, the monument is characterized by its remote mountains, valleys and wild rivers, all rich in their concentrations of wildlife. 11,923,000 acres.

Yukon-Charley National Monument. Located along the Canadian border in central Alaska, the monument preserves 115 miles of the 1,800-mile Yukon River and the entire 88-mile Charley River basin. Numerous old cabins and relics are reminders of the importance of the Yukon River during the 1898 gold rush. Paleontological and archaeological sites here add much to our knowledge of man and his environment thousands of years ago. Peregrine falcons nest in the high bluffs overlooking the river, while the rolling hills that make up the monument are home to a rich array of wildlife. The Charley, clean and clear, is considered by many to be the best white-water river in Alaska. 2,520,000 acres.

Arizona

Canyon de Chelly National Monument. At the base of sheer red cliffs and in caves in canyon walls are ruins of Indian villages built between A.D. 350 and 1300. Modern Navajo Indians live and farm here. 83,840 acres.

Casa Grande National Monument. Perplexing ruins of a massive four-story building, constructed of high-lime desert soil by Indians who farmed the Gila Valley 600 years ago, raise many unanswered questions for modern man. 472.5 acres.

Chiricahua National Monument. The varied rock formations here were created millions of years ago by volcanic activity, aided by erosion. 11,088 acres.

Coronado National Monument. Our Hispanic heritage and the first European exploration of the Southwest, by Francisco

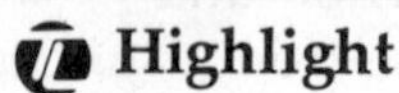

Petrified Forest National Park

The most spectacular display of petrified wood known in the world, as well as some of the most colorful parts of the Painted Desert, are included in Petrified Forest National Park in northeastern Arizona. Unique in its vivid and varied colors, the petrified wood of this area has long attracted visitors from all parts of the world. Within the monument are six separate "forests" with giant logs of agate lying on the ground and numerous broken sections and smaller chips and fragments forming a colorful ground cover.

The area is part of the Painted Desert of northern Arizona, a region of banded rocks of many hues carved by wind and rain into a landscape of fantastic color and form. Here and there are beds of shale containing perfectly preserved fossil leaves of plants of a remote age. Occasionally, the bones of giant amphibians and reptiles are washed from their burial places in the soft rock.

Many Indian ruins and petroglyphs are found, evidence of Indians who lived in this area long before America was discovered.

Travel Information

Petrified Forest National Park is open during daylight hours every day of the year.

Excellent paved highways make the area easily accessible by car. US-66 crossing the area near the Painted

Vasquez de Coronado in 1540-42, are commemorated here, near the point where Coronado's expedition entered what is now the United States. 4,674 acres.

Fort Bowie National Historic Site. Established in 1862, this fort was the focal point of military operations against Geronimo and his band of Apaches. The ruins can be reached only by trail. 1,000 acres.

Desert is the approach from the east. Travelers from the southeast, south and west enter by way of US-180. The park road connects these two main highways and leads through the more interesting parts of the area.

History

The first known report of the "stone trees" was by Lieutenant Sitgreaves, an army officer who explored parts of northern Arizona in 1851, soon after Arizona was acquired by the United States from Mexico.

The petrified forests remained almost unknown, however, until the settlement of northern Arizona began in 1878 and the Atlantic and Pacific (now the Sante Fe) Railway was completed across northern Arizona in 1883. During the following years, the existence of the petrified forests was threatened by souvenir hunters, gem collectors, commercial jewelers and manufacturers of abrasives. Entire logs were blasted to obtain the quartz and amethyst crystals often found within the logs, and much agate was carried away for making jewelry. The erection of a stamp mill near the forests to crush the petrified logs into abrasives offered the most serious threat. Alarmed, the citizens of Arizona, through their territorial legislature, petitioned Congress to make the area a national reserve so that "future generations may enjoy its beauties, and study one of the most curious . . . effects of nature's forces."

Grand Canyon National Park. The park, focusing on the world-famous Grand Canyon of the Colorado River, encompasses the entire course of the river and adjacent uplands from the southern terminus of Glen Canyon National Recreation Area to the eastern boundary of Lake Mead National Recreation Areas. The forces of erosion have exposed an immense variety of formations which illustrate vast periods of geological history. 1,218,375 acres.

Hohokam Pima National Monument. Preserved here are the achaeological remains of the Hohokam culture. Hohokam is a Pima Indian word meaning "those who have gone." *Not open to the public.* 1,690 acres.

Hubbell Trading Post National Historic Site. This still-active trading post illustrates the influence of reservation traders on the Indians' way of life. 160 acres.

Montezuma Castle National Monument. One of the best-preserved cliff dwellings in the United States, this five-story, 20-room castle is 90% intact. Montezuma Well is also of archaeological and geological interest. 849 acres.

Navajo National Monument. Betatakin, Keet Seel and Inscription House are three of the largest and most elaborate cliff dwellings known. 360 acres.

Organ Pipe Cactus National Monument. Sonoran Desert plants and animals found nowhere else in the United States are protected here, alongside traces of a historic trail, Camino del Diablo. 330,688 acres.

Petrified Forest National Park. Trees that have petrified, or changed to multi-colored stone, Indian ruins and petroglyphs, and portions of the colorful Painted Desert are features of the park. 93,492 acres.

Pipe Spring National Monument. The historic fort and other structures, built here by Mormon pioneers, memorialize the struggle for exploration and settlement of the Southwest. 40 acres.

Saguaro National Monument. Giant saguaro cactus, unique to the Sonoran Desert of southern Arizona and northwestern Mexico, sometimes reach a height of 50 feet in this cactus forest. 83,576 acres.

Sunset Crater National Monument. Its upper part colored as if by sunset glow, this volcanic cinder cone with summit crater was formed just before A.D. 1100. 3,040 acres.

Tonto National Monument. These well-preserved cliff dwellings were occupied during the 13th and 14th centuries by Salado Indians who farmed in the Salt River Valley. 1,120 acres.

Tumacacori National Monument. This historic Spanish Catholic mission building stands near the site first visited by Jesuit Father Kino in 1691. 16 acres.

Tuzigoot National Monument. Ruins of a large Indian pueblo which flourished in

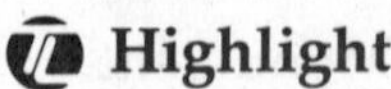

Tuzigoot National Monument

Tuzigoot National Monument preserves the excavated ruins of a prehistoric pueblo which flourished between A.D. 1100 and 1450. A visitors center houses the entire collection of artifacts recovered from the site during the excavations of 1933-34.

The ruin is strategically located on the end of a long limestone ridge that rises 120 feet above the Verde River near Clarkdale, Arizona.

Tuzigoot is a typical hilltop pueblo of 110 clustered rooms. It covers the summit of the ridge and is terraced part way down the slopes. Two-storied in part, the pueblo is about 500 feet long and 100 feet across at its greatest width. An open plaza separates an outlying unit from the main body of the pueblo — an unbroken mass of rooms 325 feet long. Many rooms are quite large; the average being 12 by 18 feet.

The pueblo was entered by means of ladders to the rooftops and from there into the rooms through roof hatchways.

Rediscovery

For five centuries, Tuzigoot pueblo lay forgotten and undisturbed, its rooms obscured under fallen material from the ruined upper floors and roofs. In 1933 and 1934, complete excavation of the site was carried out by the University of Arizona. Federal relief funds and the cooperation of the Phelps Dodge Corporation, which donated the land, helped to make this project possible.

Through the interest of public-spirited local citizens, the entire hill of Tuzigoot, with museum and complete collection, was donated to the federal government, and on July 25, 1939, Tuzigoot National Monument, a tract of 43 acres, was established by presidential proclamation.

About Your Visit

The ruins and visitors center are open between 8 a.m. and 5 p.m. During this time, a ranger is on duty to assist you and provide additional information.

A nominal entrance fee is charged all adult visitors. Children under 12 and school groups are admitted free if accompanied by an adult responsible for their orderly conduct.

There are no accommodations in the monument, but nearby are several small towns where meals and lodging can be obtained.

the Verde Valley between A.D. 1100 and 1450 have been excavated here. 848 acres.

Walnut Canyon National Monument. These cliff dwellings were built in shallow caves under ledges of limestone by Pueblo Indians about 800 years ago. 2,249 acres.

Wupatki National Monument. Ruins of red sandstone pueblos built by farming Indians about A.D. 1065 are preserved here. The modern Hopi Indians are believed to be partly descended from these people. 35,253 acres.

Dwarfed by the massive bluffs that line Arkansas' Buffalo National River, anglers try their luck for large- and small-mouth bass.

Arkansas

Arkansas Post National Memorial. On this site the first permanent French settlement in the lower Mississippi Valley was founded in 1686. 389 acres.

Buffalo National River. Offering both swift-running and placid stretches, the Buffalo is one of the few remaining unpolluted, free-flowing rivers in the Lower 48 states. It courses through multi-colored bluffs and past numerous caves and springs along its 132-mile length. 94,146 acres.

Fort Smith National Historic Site. One of the first U.S. military posts in the Louisiana Territory, the fort was a center of authority for the untamed region to the west from 1817 to 1890. 63 acres.

Hot Springs National Park. More than a million gallons of water a day flow from 47 hot springs here, unaffected by climate or seasonal temperatures. Persons suffering from illness or injury often seek relief in the ancient tradition of thermal bathing. 5,826 acres.

Pea Ridge National Military Park. The Union victory here on March 7-8, 1862, in one of the major engagements of the Civil War west of the Mississippi, led to the Union's total control of Missouri. 4,300 acres.

California

Cabrillo National Monument. Juan Rodriguez Cabrillo, Portuguese explorer who claimed the West Coast of the United States for Spain in 1542, is memorialized here. Gray whales migrate offshore during the winter. 143 acres.

Channel Islands National Monument. The monument, with large rookeries of sea lions, nesting sea birds and unique plants and animals, consists of Anacapa and Santa Barbara Islands. San Miguel Island, owned by the United States Navy, is managed jointly by the Navy and the Park Service (permit required to visit San Miguel). 18,399 acres.

Arkansas' Hot Springs National Park, renowned for its modern spa treatment facilities, also boasts the new Mid-America Center Museum, featuring exhibits demonstrating the principals of life, energy and matter.

Highlight

Hot Springs National Park

Hot Springs National Park has long been regarded as one of the world's leading and most modern spa treatment centers. Physical medicine in Hot Springs rates among the best, and its health facilities are the only ones in the nation under federal regulations.

Even the Caddo and Quapaw Indians knew the value of these thermal waters long before 1541, when Hernando De Soto became the first European to discover the steaming springs. This ground was sacred to Indians of all tribes, and here they gathered in peace to bathe their sick and injured. Perhaps it was the stories about these waters that led Ponce de Leon to search for the Fountain of Youth.

As early as 1832, the Congress of the United States recognized the therapeutic value of the hot springs waters and did something about preserving them for the benefit of all humanity. Ambrose H. Sevier, Arkansas' first U.S. Senator, was author of the bill (HR 274) that created the Hot Springs Reservation, which included the 47 hot springs and four square miles of surrounding land.

Today Hot Springs has over 70 physicians who have been approved by the United States government to prescribe the famous thermal water treatments at 10 hydrotherapy institutions, the Libbey Memorial Physical Medicine Center and the Leo N. Levi Memorial National Arthritis Hospital. These physicians are found qualified by the Federal Registration Board of Physicians, which also acts in an advisory capacity to the National Park Service. All personnel in the entire thermal water industry must qualify under the federal regulations.

More than 200,000 thermal baths are given annually to visitors from every state in the nation and several foreign countries — some of them returning once or twice a year. The famous thermal baths, which have been known to help so many physical disorders, are also wonderfully relaxing and serve greatly to ease tension and occupational fatigue, and many have found that, though not actually sick, the benefits derived from a few baths make such a big difference in the way they feel that the time spent taking the baths becomes a sort of health insurance.

The advantages of water for the application of thermal stimulation are well known. Thermal water is a good conductor of heat. It eliminates the force of gravity to some extent. Immersion in the water has a great potential for relieving muscle spasm. It stimulates cutaneous and venous circulation and produces a good psychological effect on the bather.

An innovation being tried includes three types of bath — the standard, the stimulating and the sedative, attuned to the individual requirements of the bather. Accompanying massage is keyed to match the bath.

The extended bathing hours at Health Services are: Monday to Friday, 4:30 p.m. to 7:30 p.m.; Saturdays and half-holidays, 2 p.m. to 5:30 p.m.; Sunday and whole holidays, 8 a.m. to 11 a.m.

Chemical Analysis of Thermal Waters at Hot Springs National Park (Milligrams per Liter)

Silica (SiO_2)	42.0
Calcium (Ca)	45.0
Magnesium (Mg)	4.8
Sodium (Na)	4.0
Potassium (K)	1.5
Bicarbonate (HCO_3)	165.0
Sulfate (SO_4)	8.0
Chloride (Cl)	1.8
Fluoride (F)	0.2
Oxygen (O)	3.0
Free Carbon Dioxide (CO_2)	10.0

Radioactivity Analysis By University of Arkansas

Radioactivity through radon gas emanation is 0.81 millimicrocurie per liter.

(Water comes from 47 hot springs along the lower slopes of Hot Springs Mountain. At its source, the water averages 143° Fahrenheit.)

Death Valley National Monument. This large desert, nearly surrounded by high mountains, contains the lowest point in the Western Hemisphere. The area includes Scotty's Castle, the grandiose home of a famous prospector, and other remnants of gold and borax mining activity. 2,067,795 acres.

Devils Postpile National Monument. Hot lava cooled and cracked some 900,000 years ago to form basalt columns 40 to 60 feet high, resembling a giant pipe organ. The John Muir Trail between Yosemite and Kings Canyon National Parks crosses the monument. 798 acres.

Fort Point National Historic Site. This classic brick and granite mid-19th-century coastal fortification is the largest on the West Coast of North America. 29 acres.

Golden Gate National Recreation Area. The park encompasses shoreline areas of San Francisco and Marin Counties, including ocean beaches, redwood forests, lagoons, marshes, ships of the National Maritime Museum, historic military properties, a cultural center at Fort Mason, and Alcatraz Island, site of a famous penitentiary. 38,676 acres.

John Muir National Historic Site. The home of John Muir and adjacent Martinez Adobe commemorate Muir's contribution to conservation and literature. 8 acres.

Joshua Tree National Monument. A representative stand of Joshua trees and a great variety of plants and animals, including the desert bighorn, exist in this desert region. 559,959 acres.

Kings Canyon National Park. Two enormous canyons of the Kings River and the summit peaks of the High Sierra dominate this mountain wilderness. General Grant Grove, with its giant sequoias, is a detached section of the park. 460,136 acres.

Lassen Volcanic National Park. Lassen Peak, a recently active volcano in the coterminous United States, erupted intermittently from 1914 to 1921. 106,372 acres.

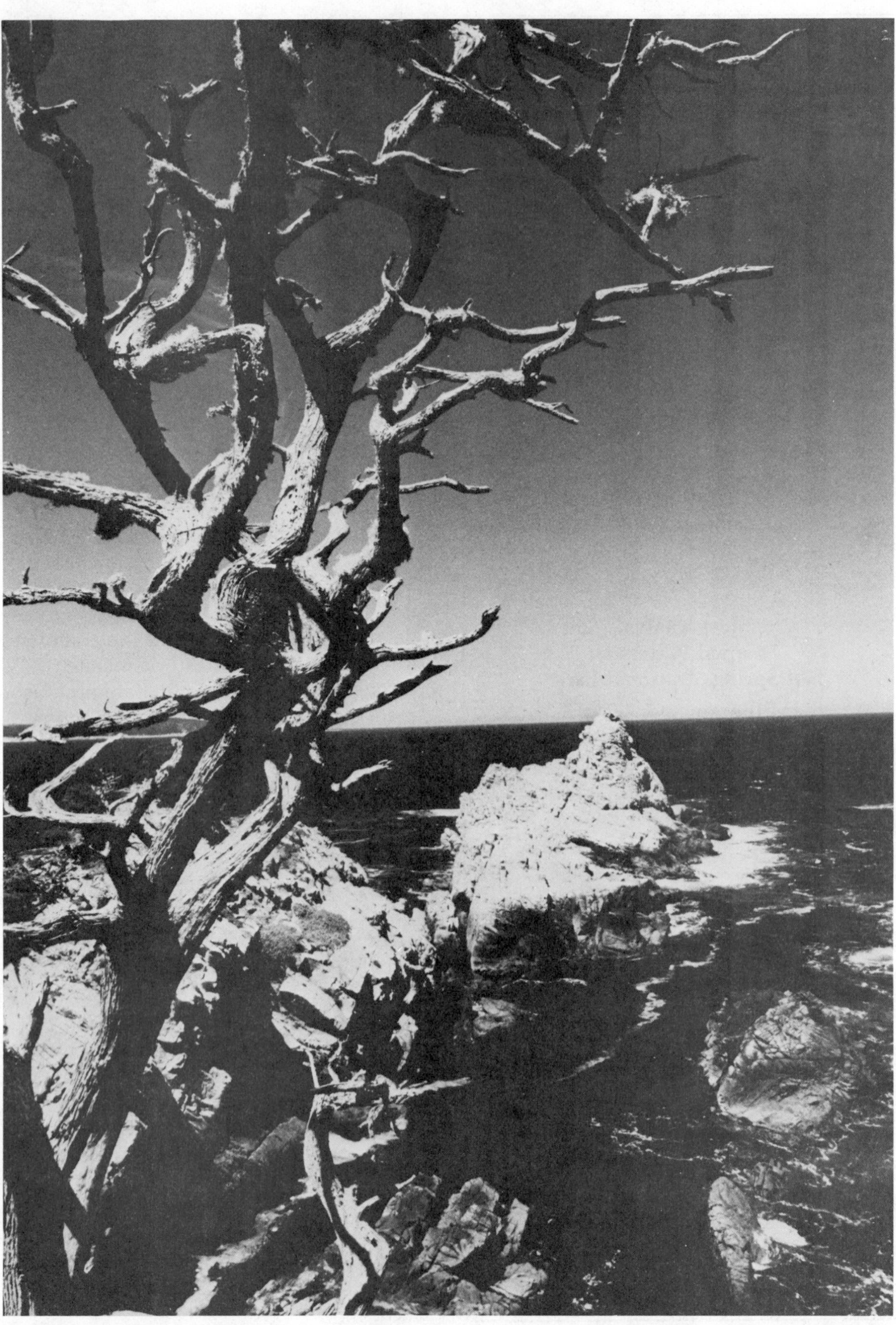

Lava Beds National Monument. Volcanic activity spewed forth molten rock and lava here, creating an incredibly rugged landscale — a natural fortress used by the Indians in the Modoc Indian War, 1872-73. 46,821 acres.

Muir Woods National Monument. This virgin stand of coastal redwoods was named for John Muir, writer and conservationist. 553 acres.

Pinnacles National Monument. Spirelike rock formations 500 to 1,200 feet high, with caves and a variety of volcanic features, rise above the smooth contours of the surrounding countryside. 16,221 acres.

Point Reyes National Seashore. This peninsula near San Francisco is noted for its long beaches backed by tall cliffs, lagoons and esteros, forested ridges, and offshore bird and sea lion colonies. Part of the area remains a private pastoral zone. 67,265 acres.

Redwood National Park. Coastal redwood forests with virgin groves of ancient trees, including the world's tallest, live in a mixture of sun and fog. The park includes 40 miles of scenic Pacific coastline. 109,026 acres.

Santa Monica Mountains National Recreation Area. This park is a large, rugged landscape, covered with chaparral, fronting on the sandy beaches north of Los Angeles. The area will provide recreational opportunities within easy reach of millions in Southern California. 150,000 acres.

Sequoia National Park. Great groves of giant sequoias, the world's largest living things, Mineral King Valley, and Mount Whitney, the highest mountain in the U.S. outside of Alaska, are spectacular attractions here in the High Sierra. 403,023 acres.

Whiskeytown-Shasta-Trinity National Recreation Area. Whiskeytown Unit with its mountainous backcountry and large reservoir provides a multitude of outdoor recreation opportunities. Shasta and Clair Engle Units are administered by Forest Service, U.S. Department of Agriculture. 42,497 acres.

Yosemite National Park. Granite peaks and domes rise high above broad meadows in the heart of the Sierra Nevada; groves of giant sequoias dwarf other trees and tiny wildflowers; and mountains, lakes and waterfalls, including the nation's highest, are found here. 760,917 acres.

Colorado

Bent's Old Fort National Historic Site. As a principal outpost of civilization on the Southern Plains in the early 1800s and rendezvous for Indians, the post became the center of a vast fur-trading empire in the West. 800 acres.

Black Canyon of the Gunnison National Monument. Shadowed depths of this sheer-walled canyon accentuate the darkness of ancient rocks of obscure origin. 13,672 acres.

Colorado National Monument. Sheer-walled canyons, towering monoliths, weird formations, dinosaur fossils and remains of prehistoric Indian cultures reflect the environment and history of this colorful sandstone country. 20,449 acres.

Curecanti National Recreation Area. Three lakes — Blue Mesa, Morrow Point and Crystal — extend for 40 miles along the Gunnison River. When full, Blue Mesa Lake, with a surface area of 14 square miles, is the largest lake in Colorado. 42,114 acres.

Dinosaur National Monument. Spectacular canyons were cut by the Green and Yampa Rivers through upfolded mountains. A quarry contains fossil remains of dinosaurs and other ancient animals. 211,060 acres.

Florissant Fossil Beds National Monument. A wealth of fossil insects, seeds and leaves of the Oligocene Period are preserved here in remarkable detail.

Here, too, is an unusual display of standing petrified sequoia stumps. 5,998 acres.

Great Sand Dunes National Monument. Among the largest and highest in the United States, these dunes were deposited over thousands of years by southwesterly winds blowing through the passes of the lofty Sangre de Cristo Mountains. 38,951 acres.

Hovenweep National Monument. Pre-Columbian Indians built these six groups of towers, pueblos and cliff dwellings. 785 acres.

Mesa Verde National Park. These pre-Columbian cliff dwellings and other works of early man are the most notable and best preserved in the United States. 52,085 acres.

Rocky Mountain National Park. The park's rich scenery, typifying the massive grandeur of the Rocky Mountains, is accessible by Trail Ridge Road, which crosses the Continental Divide. Peaks towering over 14,000 feet shadow wildlife and wildflowers in these 412 square miles of the Rockies' Front Range. 263,790 acres.

Yucca House National Monument. Ruins of these large prehistoric Indian pueblos are as yet unexcavated. *Not open to the public.* 10 acres.

Connecticut

Appalachian National Scenic Trail. (See Maine.)

District of Columbia

Chesapeake and Ohio Canal National Historical Park. (See Maryland.)

Ford's Theatre National Historic Site. On April 14, 1865, President Lincoln was shot while attending a show here. He was carried across the street to the Peterson house, where he died the next morning. The theater contains the Olroyd Collection of Lincolniana.

Frederick Douglass Home. From 1877 to 1895, this was the home of the nation's leading 19th-century black spokesman. He was U.S. minister to Haiti, 1889.

John F. Kennedy Center for the Performing Arts. Cultural events are presented in this structure designed by Edward Durell Stone. The building contains the Eisenhower Theater, a concert hall, an opera house and the Terrace Theater.

Lincoln Memorial. This classical structure of great beauty contains a marble seated statue 19 feet high of the Great Emancipator by sculptor Daniel Chester French. Architect of the building was Henry Bacon.

Lyndon Baines Johnson Memorial Grove on the Potomac. A living memorial to the 36th President, the park overlooks the Potomac River vista of the capital. The design features 500 white pines and engravings on Texas granite. 17 acres.

National Capital Parks. The park system of the nation's capital comprises parks, parkways and reservations in the Washington metropolitan area, including such properties as the Battleground National Cemetery, the President's Parks (Lafayette Park north of the White House and the Ellipse south of the White House), the parks flanking the Great Falls of the Potomac, a variety of military fortifications and green areas. 6,469 acres.

National Mall. This landscaped park, extending from the Capitol to the Washington Monument, was envisioned as a formal park in the L'Enfant Plan for the city of Washington. 146 acres.

National Visitor Center. The National Visitor Center encompasses a diverse complex of programs and facilities to welcome visitors to the nation's capital. Conversion of Washington's Union Station for this purpose began in 1974.

Rock Creek Park. One of the largest urban parks in the world, this wooded preserve contains a wide range of natural, historical and recreational resources in the midst of metropolitan Washington, D.C. 1,754 acres.

Sewall-Belmont House National Historic Site. Rebuilt after fire damage from the War of 1812, this red brick house is one of the oldest on Capitol Hill. It has been the National Women's Party headquarters since 1929 and commemorates the party's founder and women's suffrage leader, Alice Paul, and associates.

Theodore Roosevelt Island. On this wooded island sanctuary in the Potomac River, trails lead to an imposing statue of Roosevelt, the conservation-minded 26th President. His tenets on nature, manhood, youth and the state are inscribed on tablets. 88 acres.

Thomas Jefferson Memorial. This circular, colonnaded structure, in the classic style introduced in this country by Jefferson, memorializes the author of the Declaration of Independence and President from 1801 to 1809. The interior walls present inscriptions from his writings, and the heroic statue was sculptured by Rudolph Evans.

Washington Monument. A dominating feature of the nation's capital, this 555-foot obelisk honors the country's first President, George Washington. 106 acres.

White House. The White House has been the residence and office of the Presidents of the United States since November 1800. The cornerstone was laid October 13, 1792, on the site selected by George Washington and included in the L'Enfant Plan; renovations were made 1949-52.

Florida

Big Cypress National Preserve. Adjoining the northwest section of Everglades National Park, this large area provides a freshwater supply crucial to the park's survival. Subtropical plant and animal life abounds in this ancestral home of the Seminole and Miccosukee Indians. 570,000 acres.

Biscayne National Monument. Most of the park is reef and water, but within its boundaries about 25 keys, or islands, form a north-south chain, with Biscayne Bay on the west and the Atlantic Ocean on the east. 103,642 acres.

Canaveral National Seashore. Immediately north of the famed Kennedy Space Center, the seashore offers a great variety of wildlife, including many species of birds, on a segment of largely undeveloped wild lands. The area includes a portion of 140,393-acre Merritt Island National Wildlife Refuge, administered by Fish and Wildlife Service, U.S. Department of the Interior. 57,627 acres.

Castillo de San Marcos National Monument. Construction of this oldest masonry in continental United States was started in 1672 by the Spanish to protect St. Augustine, first permanent settlement by Europeans in continental United States (1565). The floorplan is the result of "modernization" work done in the 18th century. 20 acres.

De Soto National Memorial. The landing of Spanish explorer Hernando De Soto in Florida in 1539 and the first extensive organized exploration of what is now the southern United States by Europeans are commemorated here. 30 acres.

Everglades National Park. This largest remaining subtropical wilderness in the coterminous United States has extensive fresh- and saltwater areas, open Everglades prairies and mangrove forests. Abundant wildlife includes rare and colorful birds. 1,398,800 acres.

Fort Caroline National Memorial. The fort overlooks the site of a French Huguenot colony of 1564-65, the second French attempt at settlement within the present United States. Here, the French and Spanish began two centuries of European colonial rivalry in North America. 138 acres.

Fort Jefferson National Monument. Built in 1856 to help control the Florida Straits, this is the largest all-masonry fortification in the Western world; it served as a federal military prison during and after the Civil War. The bird refuge and marine life here are features. 47,125 acres.

Fort Matanzas National Monument. This Spanish fort was built in 1740-42 to protect St. Augustine from the British. 298 acres.

Gulf Islands National Seashore. Offshore islands and keys have both sparkling white sand beaches and historic ruins. Mainland features of this unit, which is located near Pensacola, Florida, include the Naval Live Oaks Reservation, beaches and ruins of military forts. All areas are accessible by car. 65,816 acres.

Mar-A-Lago National Historic Site. This private mansion is representative of the affluent society's way of life in the 1920s. *Not open to the public.* 17 acres.

Georgia

Andersonville National Historic Site. This Civil War prisoner-of-war camp commemorates the sacrifices borne by American prisoners, not only in the 1861-65 conflict, but in all wars. Site includes Andersonville National Cemetery which has 15,591 interments, 1,041 unidentified. 478 acres.

Chattahoochee River National Recreation Area. A series of sites along a 48-mile stretch of the Chattahoochee River, extending into Atlanta, will be preserved for public enjoyment of scenic, recreational and historical values. 8,514 acres.

Chickamauga and Chattanooga National Military Park. This park includes the Civil War battlefields of Chickamauga, Orchard Knob, Lookout Mountain and Missionary Ridge. 8,098 acres.

Cumberland Island National Seashore. Magnificent and unspoiled beaches and dunes, marshes and freshwater lakes make up this largest of Georgia's Golden Isles. Accessible by tour boat only. 36,544 acres.

Fort Frederica National Monument. General James E. Oglethorpe built this British fort in 1736-48, during the Anglo-Spanish struggle for control of what is now Southeastern United States. 214 acres.

Fort Pulaski National Monument. Bombardment of this early 19th-century fort by federal rifled cannon in 1862 first demonstrated the ineffectiveness of old-style masonry fortifications. 5,615 acres.

Kennesaw Mountain National Battlefield Park. Two engagements took place here between Union and Confederate forces during the Atlanta Campaign, June 20 to July 2, 1864. 2,884 acres.

Ocmulgee National Monument. The evolution of the Indian mound-builder civilization in the Southern United States is represented in the remains of mounds and villages. 683 acres.

Guam

War in the Pacific National Historical Park. This park will provide an opportunity to interpret events in the Pacific theater of World War II. It includes major historic sites associated with the 1944 battle for Guam, an example of our island-hopping military campaign against the Japanese. 1,923 acres.

Hawaii

Haleakala National Park. The park preserves the outstanding features of Haleakala Crater on the island of Maui and protects the unique and fragile ecosystems of Kipahulu Valley, the scenic pools along Oheo gulch, and many rare and endangered species. 28,655 acres.

Hawaii Volcanoes National Park. Active volcanism continues here, on the island of Hawaii, where at lower elevations luxuriant and often rare vegetation provides food and shelter for a variety of animals. 229,177 acres.

Kaloko-Honokohau National Historical Park. Park is intended to preserve native culture of Hawaii. This was the site of important Hawaiian settlements before arrival of European explorers. It includes three large fishponds, house sites and other archaeological remnants. 1,310 acres.

Pu'uhonua o Honaunau National Historical Park. Until 1819, vanquished Hawaiian warriors, noncombatants and kapu breakers could escape death by reaching this sacred ground. Prehistoric house sites, royal fishponds, coconut groves and spectacular shore scenery comprise the park. 181 acres.

Puukohola Heiau National Historic Site. Ruins of Puukohola Heiau ("Temple on the Hill of the Whale"), built by King Kamehameha the Great during his rise to power, are preserved. 76 acres.

Idaho

Craters of the Moon National Monument. Volcanic cones, craters, lava flows and caves make this an astonishing landscape. 53,545 acres.

Nez Perce National Historical Park. The history and culture of the Nez Perce Indian country are preserved, commemorated and interpreted here. Four federally-owned sites are administered by the National Park Service, and 20 sites through cooperative agreements. 2,109 acres.

Illinois

Lincoln Home National Historic Site. Abraham Lincoln left his house here in 1861 to accept the presidency. It was the only home he ever owned.

Indiana

George Rogers Clark National Historical Park. This classic memorial, near the site of old Fort Sackville, commemmorates the seizure of the fort from the British by Lieutenant Colonel George Rogers Clark, February 25, 1779. 24 acres.

Indiana Dunes National Lakeshore. Magnificent dunes rise as high as 180 feet above Lake Michigan's southern shore. Other natural features include beaches, bogs, marshes, swamps and prairie remnants; historic sites include an 1822 homestead and 1900 family farm, both restored. 12,534 acres.

Lincoln Boyhood National Memorial. On this southern Indiana farm, Abraham Lincoln grew from youth into manhood. 197 acres.

Iowa

Effigy Mounds National Monument. The monument contains outstanding examples of prehistoric burial mounds, some in the shapes of birds and bears. 1,474 acres.

Herbert Hoover National Historic Site. The birthplace, home and boyhood neighborhood of the 31st President, 1929-33; the gravesites of President and Mrs. Hoover, and the Hoover Presidential Library and Museum, which is administered by the National Archives and Records Service, General Services Administration, are within the park. 186 acres.

Kansas

Fort Larned National Historic Site. The fort protected traffic along the Santa Fe Trail, was the key military base in the Indian war of 1868-69, and served as an Indian agency. 718 acres.

Fort Scott National Historic Site. The reconstructed 19th-century fort commemorates historic events of the Civil War period. 6 acres.

Kentucky

Abraham Lincoln Birthplace National Historic Site. An early 19th-century

Kentucky cabin, symbolic of the one in which Lincoln was born, is preserved in a memorial building at the site of his birth. 116 acres.

Cumberland Gap National Historical Park. This mountain pass on the Wilderness Road, explored by Daniel Boone, developed into a main artery of the great trans-Allegheny migration for settlement of "the Old West" and an important military objective in the Revolutionary and Civil Wars. 20,273 acres.

Mammoth Cave National Monument. This series of underground passages — with beautiful limestone, gypsum and travertine formations, deep pits and high domes, and an underground river — has been explored and mapped for 194 miles, making this the longest recorded cave system in the world. 52,128 acres.

Louisiana

Jean Lafitte National Historical Park and Preserve. The park preserves significant examples of natural and historical resources of the Mississippi Delta. It includes the Chalmette Unit, where American forces were victorious in the Battle of New Orleans in the War of 1812. Chalmette Unit includes Chalmette National Cemetery, 15,219 interments, 6,773 unidentified; grave sites not available. 20,000 acres.

Maine

Acadia National Park. The sea sets the mood here, uniting the rugged coastal area of Mount Desert Island (highest elevation on the eastern seaboard), picturesque Schoodic Peninsula on the mainland, and the spectacular cliffs of Isle au Haut. 38,523 acres.

Appalachian National Scenic Trail. Approximately 2,000 miles of this scenic trail follow the Appalachian Mountains from Mount Katahdin, Maine, through New Hampshire, Vermont, Massachusetts, Connecticut, New York, New Jersey, Pennsylvania, Maryland, West Virginia, Virginia, Tennessee and North Carolina, to Springer Mountain, Georgia. The trail is one of the two initial units of the National Trail System. 52,034 acres.

Saint Croix Island National Monument. The attempted French settlement of 1604, which led to the founding of New France, is commemorated on Saint Croix Island in the Saint Croix River on the Canadian border. 35 acres.

Maryland

Antietam National Battlefield. General Robert E. Lee's first invasion of the North was ended on this battlefield in 1862. Antietam (Sharpsburg) National Cemetery — 5,032 interments, 1,836 unidentified — adjoins the park. 3,300 acres.

Assateague Island National Seashore. This 37-mile barrier island, with sandy beach, migratory waterfowl and wild ponies, includes 9,021-acre Chincoteague National Wildlife Refuge, administered by the Fish and Wildlife Service, U.S. Department of the Interior. 39,630 acres.

Catoctin Mountain Park. Part of the forested ridge that forms the eastern rampart of the Appalachian Mountains in Maryland, this mountain park has sparkling streams and panoramic vistas of the Monocacy Valley. 5,768 acres.

Chesapeake and Ohio Canal National Historical Park. The park follows the route of the 184-mile canal along the Potomac River between Washington, D.C., and Cumberland, Maryland. The canal was built between 1828 and 1850. 20,781 acres.

Clara Barton National Historic Site. This 38-room home of the founder of the American Red Cross was for seven years headquarters of that organization.

Fort McHenry National Monument and Historic Shrine. Successful defense of this fort in the War of 1812, September 13-14, 1814, inspired Francis Scott Key to write *The Star Spangled Banner.* 43 acres.

Fort Washington Park. This fort across the Potomac from Mount Vernon, built to protect Washington, D.C., was begun in 1814 to replace an 1809 fort destroyed by the British. Recreational facilities are included in the park. 341 acres.

Greenbelt Park. Just 12 miles from Washington, D.C., this woodland park offers urban dwellers access to many forms of outdoor recreation. 1,166 acres.

Hampton National Historic Site. This is a fine example of the lavish Georgian mansions built in America during the latter part of the 18th century. 59 acres.

Monocacy National Battlefield. In a battle here, July 9, 1864, Confederate General Jubal T. Early defeated Union forces commanded by Brigadier General Lew Wallace. Wallace's troops delayed Early, however, enabling Union forces to marshal a successful defense of Washington, D.C. 1,220 acres.

Piscataway Park. The tranquil view from Mount Vernon of the Maryland shore of the Potomac is preserved as a pilot project in the use of easements to protect parklands from obtrusive urban expansion. 4,217 acres.

Thomas Stone National Historic Site. "Habre-de-Venture," a Georgian mansion built in 1771 near Port Tobacco, Maryland, was the home of Thomas Stone, 1771-87. A signer of the Declaration of Independence, Stone was a delegate to the Continental Congress, 1775-78 and 1783-84. *Not open to the public.* 322 acres.

Massachusetts

Adams National Historic Site. The home of Presidents John Adams and John Quincy Adams, of U.S. Minister to Great Britain Charles Francis Adams, and of the writers and historians Henry Adams and Brooks Adams, this house at 135 Adams Street reflects the influence of each of these distinguished men. The park also

For those seeking the delights of outdoor recreation, from hiking and backpacking to cross-country skiing, Acadia National Park on the Maine coast has it all.

includes, at 133 and 141 Franklin Street, two other houses — the birthplaces of the two Presidents.

Appalachian National Scenic Trail. (See Maine.)

Boston National Historic Park. This park includes Faneuil Hall, Old North Church, Old State House, Bunker Hill, Old South Meeting House, Charlestown Navy Yard, berth for *USS Constitution,* Paul Revere House and Dorchester Heights. 40 acres.

Cape Cod National Seashore. Ocean beaches, dunes, woodlands, freshwater ponds and marshes make up this park on outer Cape Cod. The area preserves notable examples of Cape Cod homes, an architectural style founded in America. 44,596 acres.

John Fitzgerald Kennedy National Historic Site. This house is the birthplace and early boyhood home of the 35th President.

Longfellow National Historic Site. Poet Henry Wadsworth Longfellow lived here from 1837 to 1882 while teaching at Harvard. The house had been General Washington's headquarters during the siege of Boston, 1775-76.

Lowell National Historic Park. America's first planned industrial community is commemorated by this park at the heart of the city. Elements of Lowell's factories, canal system, and the lifestyle of its people will be preserved and interpreted here. 134 acres.

Minute Man National Historic Park. Scene of the fighting on April 19, 1776, that opened the American Revolution, the park includes North Bridge, Minute Man statue, four miles of Battle Road between Lexington and Concord, and "The Wayside," Nathaniel Hawthorne's home. 745 acres.

Salem Maritime National Historic Site. During the Revolution, this was the only major port never occupied by the British. Later, it was one of the nation's great mercantile centers. Structures of maritime significance include the Custom House where Nathaniel Hawthorne worked, Derby Wharf, the Bonded Warehouse and the West India Goods Store.

Saugus Iron Works National Historic Site. This reconstruction of the first integrated iron works in North America, begun in 1646, includes the ironmaster's house, furnace, forge, and rolling and slitting mill.

Springfield Armory National Historic Site. Over a span of 200 years, this small-arms manufacturing center produced such weapons as the 1795 flintlock and the 1883, 1903, M-1 and M-14 rifles. The largest collection of Confederate and other small arms is maintained here. 55 acres.

Michigan

Isle Royale National Park. The largest in Lake Superior, this forested island is also distinguished for its wilderness character, timber wolves and moose herd, and pre-Columbian copper mines. 571,796 acres.

Pictured Rocks National Lakeshore. Multi-colored sandstone cliffs, broad beaches, sand bars, dunes, waterfalls, inland lakes, ponds, marshes, hardwood and coniferous forests, and numerous birds and animals comprise this scenic area on Lake Superior. This was the first national lakeshore. 70,807 acres.

Sleeping Bear Dunes National Lakeshore. Beaches, massive sand dunes, forests and lakes are outstanding characteristics of the Lake Michigan shoreline and two offshore islands. 71,105 acres.

Minnesota

Grand Portage National Monument. This nine-mile portage was a rendezvous for traders and trappers on a principal route of Indians, explorers, missionaries and fur traders into the Northwest. The Grand Portage post of the North West Company has been reconstructed here. 709 acres.

Pipestone National Monument. From this quarry Indians obtained materials for making pipes used in ceremonies. 281 acres.

Voyageurs National Park. Beautiful northern lakes, once the route of the French-Canadian voyageurs, are surrounded by forest in this land where geology and history capture your imagination. 219,128 acres.

Mississippi

Brices Cross Roads National Battlefield Site. The Confederate cavalry was employed with extraordinary skill here during the battle of June 10, 1864.

Gulf Islands National Seashore. Sparkling beaches, historic ruins and wildlife sanctuaries, accessible only by boat, can be found on the offshore islands of this unit, located near Pascagoula and Biloxi, Mississippi. On the mainland, there's an urban park with a nature trail, picnic area and a campground at Ocean Springs. 73,958 acres.

Natchez Trace Parkway. This historic route generally follows the old Indian trace, or trail, between Nashville, Tennessee, and Natchez, Mississippi. (Of the estimated 448 miles, 333 are completed.) 48,370 acres.

Tupelo National Battlefield. Here, on July 13-14, 1864, Lieutenant General Nathan Bedford Forrest's cavalry battled a Union force of 14,000 sent to keep Forrest from cutting the railroad supplying Major General William T. Sherman's march on Atlanta.

Vicksburg National Military Park. Fortifications of the 47-day siege of Vicksburg, which ended July 3, 1863, are remarkably well preserved here. Victory gave the North control of the Mississippi River and cut the Confederacy in two. Vicksburg National Cemetery — 18,207 interments, 12,954 unidentified — adjoins the park. 1,740 acres.

Missouri

George Washington Carver National Monument. Existing landmarks at the birthplace and childhood home of the famous black agronomist include a spring, a grove of trees and the graves of the Moses Carver family. 210 acres.

Jefferson National Expansion Memorial National Historic Site. This park on St. Louis' Mississippi riverfront memorializes Thomas Jefferson and others who directed territorial expansion of the United States. Eero Saarinen's prize-winning, stainless steel gateway arch commemorates westward pioneers. Visitors may ascend the 630-foot-high arch. In the nearby courthouse, Dred Scott sued for freedom in the historic slavery case. 90 acres.

Ozark National Scenic Riverways. For about 140 miles, the Current and Jacks Fork Rivers flow through a quiet world of nature. Notable features include huge freshwater springs and numerous caves. 79,587 acres.

Wilson's Creek National Battlefield. The Confederate victory here on August 10, 1861, was the first major engagement west of the Mississippi. It culminated in severe losses on both sides, yet Union troops were able to retreat and regroup. 1,749 acres.

Montana

Big Hole National Battlefield. Nez Perce Indians and U.S. Army troops fought here in 1877 — a dramatic episode in the long struggle to confine the Nez Perce, and other Indians, to reservations. 655 acres.

Bighorn Canyon National Recreation Area. Bighorn Lake, formed by Yellowtail Dam on the Bighorn River, extends 71 miles, including 47 miles through spectacular Bighorn Canyon. The Crow Indian Reservation borders a large part of the area. 120,157 acres.

Custer Battlefield National Monument. The famous Battle of the Little Big Horn between 12 companies of the 7th U.S. Cavalry and the Sioux and Northern Cheyenne Indians was fought here on June 25-26, 1876. Lieutenant Colonel George A. Custer and about 268 of his force were killed. Custer Battlefield National Cemetery, with 4,487 interments, 277 unidentified, is included within the park. 765 acres.

Fort Benton. Founded in 1846, this American Fur Company trading post was an important river port from 1859 through the Montana gold rush of 1862, until rail service surpassed river cargo transport.

Glacier National Park. With precipitous peaks ranging above 10,000 feet, this ruggedly beautiful land includes nearly 50 glaciers, many lakes and streams, a wide variety of wildflowers, and wildlife such as bighorn sheep, bald eagles and grizzly bears. 1,013,594 acres.

Grant-Kohrs Ranch National Historic Site. This was the home ranch area of one of the largest and best known 19th-century range ranches in the country. 1,527 acres.

Nebraska

Agate Fossil Beds National Monument. These renowned quarries contain numerous, well-preserved Miocene mammal fossils and represent an important chapter in the evolution of mammals. 3,055 acres.

Homestead National Monument of America. One of the first claims under the Homestead Act of 1862 was filed for this land; includes Freeman School. 194 acres.

Scotts Bluff National Monument. Rising 800 feet above the valley floor, this massive promontory was a landmark on the Oregon Trail, associated with overland migration between 1843 and 1869 across the Great Plains. 2,987 acres.

Highlight

Scotts Bluff National Monument

Scotts Bluff is a massive promontory rising 800 feet above the valley floor and 4,649 feet above sea level. Named for Hiram Scott, a fur trapper who died in the vicinity about 1828, the bluff is an ancient landmark and was noted by the earliest tribes whose records have been preserved. To the Indians of the Plains, Scotts Bluff was Me-a-pa-te, or "the hill that is hard to go around."

The bluff was once part of the ancient High Plains. Erosion over long periods has cut down the surrounding valleys to their present level, leaving Scotts Bluff and the adjoining hills as remnants of the unbroken plains which now lie farther to the west.

The North Platte Valley, of which Scotts Bluff is the dominant natural feature, has been a human migration corridor for centuries. Some stone artifacts found here indicate that man has been here for more than 10,000 years. When white men first arrived, they found that this area was a favorite hunting ground of Sioux, Cheyenne and Arapaho Indians, for here vast herds of buffalo came to water.

The first white men to see Scotts Bluff were Robert Stuart and his companions, who in 1812-13 passed by carrying dispatches to John Jacob Astor from his new fur post in Oregon. In the years that followed, trappers and traders saw it when they brought their beaver pelts down the Platte River to settlements farther east; and explorers and missionaries passed the bluff on their way from advance posts of civilization into the western wilderness.

In 1843, the vanguard of a great pioneer army passed Scotts Bluff in the first large migration to Oregon. Four years later, Brigham Young led the first group of his followers past the bluff on the north side of the Platte, a route later famous as the Mormon Trail. The two years following the discovery of gold in California in 1848 saw more than 150,000 men, women and children traveling through the area.

In 1860-61, Pony Express riders galloped through Mitchell Pass. They were followed shortly by the first transcontinental telegraph. The Overland Mail, Pony Express, Pacific Telegraph and Overland State built stations near Scotts Bluff. In 1864, Fort Mitchell was established 2½ miles to the northwest to protect stagecoaches and wagon trains on the Oregon Trail. The following year, the North Platte Valley was considered as a possible route for the Union Pacific, then building westward to link up with the Central Pacific to form the first transcontinental railroad, but a line through Cheyenne was chosen instead. The completion of the railroad in 1869 marked the decline of the Oregon Trail, although it continued in use locally for many years.

In the late 1870s and early 1880s, Scotts Bluff was the geographical center of the open-range cattle industry, the last great romantic episode of the frontier. With the arrival of the first homesteaders in the North Platte Valley in 1885, the local frontier disappeared and Scotts Bluff became a symbol of the nation's past.

ABOUT YOUR VISIT

Scotts Bluff National Monument adjoins the south bank of the North Platte River three miles west of Gering via Neb-92, which bisects the area from east to west. The monument is five miles southwest of the town of Scottsbluff via US-26, which connects with Neb-92 north of the river. From US-30, it is 42 miles to the monument via Neb-71.

The visitors center contains exhibits telling the story of the westward migration and recalling Scotts Bluff's role as a landmark on the Oregon and Mormon Trails. Paintings by William Henry Jackson, the famous pioneer photographer and artist who followed the Oregon Trail as a bullwhacker in 1866, are also displayed.

POINTS OF INTEREST

The Summit Self-guiding Trail, extending to the north and south overlooks from the summit parking area, is 0.6 of a mile long, hard-surfaced and an easy grade. The trail guide booklet, keyed to 17 numbered posts along the trail, explains the natural and historical features of the monument. From the north overlook there is a panorama of the North Platte Valley, highlighted by several famous landmarks: Chimney Rock, 25 miles to the east, and Laramie Peak, 100 miles to the west. From the south overlook, you look down on the Oregon Trail approach to Mitchell Pass. The summit trail offers other grand vistas.

Oregon Trail. Except for intermittent stretches of cultivation or where modern roads have been superimposed, the trough of the old trail, ground down by the passage of a million emigrants, can still be seen from the transmonument road south of the east entrance, across from the visitors center, and in Mitchell Pass. From the visitors center, you can walk along the Oregon Trail to the site where William H. Jackson camped in 1866.

Nevada

Lake Mead National Recreation Area. Lake Mead, formed by Hoover Dam, and Lake Mohave, by Davis Dam, on the Colorado River comprise this first national recreation area established by an act of Congress. 1,496,600 acres.

Lehman Caves National Monument. Tunnels and galleries decorated with stalactites and stalagmites honeycomb these caverns of light-gray and white marble. 640 acres.

New Hampshire

Saint-Gaudens National Historic Site. This memorial to sculptor Augustus Saint-Gaudens contains his home, "Aspet," and his studios and gardens. 149 acres.

New Jersey

Edison National Historic Site. Buildings and equipment used by Thomas A. Edison for many of his experiments are here, as are his library, papers and models of some of his inventions. The site also includes Glenmont, Edison's 23-room home, with original furnishings. 21 acres.

Gateway National Recreation Area. The narrow Sandy Hook Peninsula offers bathing beaches, interesting plant and animal life, and historic structures, including the Sandy Hook Lighthouse, reputed to be the oldest in the United States (1764). 4,675 acres.

Morristown National Historical Park. For two winters during the Revolution — 1777 and 1779-80 — the Continental Army established winter headquarters here. Washington's headquarters, Ford Mansion, is included in the park. 1,677 acres.

New Mexico

Aztec Ruins National Monument. Ruins of this large Pueblo Indian community of 12th-century masonry and timber buildings have been largely excavated and stabilized. The ruins, misnamed by settlers, are unrelated to the Aztecs of Mexico. 27 acres.

Bandelier National Monument. On the canyon-slashed slopes of the Pajarito Plateau are the ruins of many cliff houses of 15th-century Pueblo Indians. 36,971 acres.

Capulin Mountain National Monument. This symmetrical cinder cone is an interesting example of a geologically recent, extinct volcano. 775 acres.

Carlsbad Caverns National Park. This series of connected caverns, the largest underground chambers yet discovered, has countless magnificent and curious formations. 46,755 acres.

Chaco Canyon National Monument. The canyon, with hundreds of smaller ruins, contains 13 major Indian ruins unsurpassed in the United States, representing the highest point of Pueblo pre-Columbian civilization. 21,509 acres.

El Morro National Monument. "Inscription Rock" is a soft sandstone monolith on which are carved hundreds of inscriptions, including those of 17th-century Spanish explorers and 19th-century American emigrants and settlers. The monument also includes pre-Columbian petroglyphs. 1,278 acres.

Fort Union National Monument. Three U.S. Army forts were built on this site — a key defensive point on the Santa Fe Trail — and were occupied from 1851 to 1891. Ruins of the last fort, which was the largest military post in the Southwest, have been stabilized. 720 acres.

Gila Cliff Dwellings National Monument. These well-preserved cliff dwellings in natural cavities on the face of an overhanging cliff were inhabited from about A.D. 100 to 1300. 533 acres.

Gran Quivira National Monument. Perched high atop a limestone ridge, Pueblo de las Humanas was occupied from about A.D. 900 through the 1670s. Two 17th-century Franciscan mission churches, 21 Pueblo Indian apartment complexes and 16 kivas are elements of the massive archaeological remains of a settlement which once housed 2,000 Pueblo Indians. 610 acres.

Pecos National Monument. Foundations of a 17th-century mission, ruins of an 18th-century church, ancient Pueblo structural remains and restored kivas comprise the park. This site was once a landmark on the Santa Fe Trail, ruts of which are still in existence. 364 acres.

White Sands National Monument. The park contains the world's largest gypsum dunefield covering nearly 230 square miles. The glistening white dunes rise 60 feet high. Small animals have adapted to this harsh environment by developing light, protective coloration. Plants also have adapted extending root systems to remain atop the ever-shifting dunes. 144,419 acres.

New York

Castle Clinton National Monument. Built 1808-11, this structure served successively as a defense for New York harbor, a promenade and entertainment center, and an immigration depot through which more than eight million people entered the United States from 1855 to 1890. It is located in Battery Park, Manhattan.

Eleanor Roosevelt National Historic Site. Mrs. Roosevelt used her "Val-Kill" estate as a personal retreat from her busy life. The pastoral setting of the cottage, built for her by her husband in 1925, includes fields, trees, swamps and ponds. She also used the estate to entertain friends and dignitaries and to promote the many causes which interested her. *Not open to the public.* 179 acres.

Federal Hall National Memorial. This graceful building is on the site of the original Federal Hall where the trial of John Peter Zenger, involving freedom of the press, was held in 1735; the Stamp Act Congress convened, 1765; the Second Continental Congress met, 1785; Washington took the oath as first U.S. President, and the Bill of Rights was adopted, 1789. Present building was completed in 1842 as a federal customs house.

Fire Island National Seashore. This barrier island off the south shore of Long Island possesses opportunities for beach-oriented recreation and ecological observations. 19,578 acres.

Fort Stanwix National Monument. The American stand here in August 1777 was a major factor in repulsing the British invasion from Canada. The fort was also the site of the treaty of Fort Stanwix with the Iroquois on November 5, 1768. 15 acres.

Gateway National Recreation Area. With beaches, marshes, islands and adjacent waters in the New York harbor area, this park offers urban residents a wide range of recreational opportunities. 21,497 acres.

General Grant National Memorial. This memorial to Ulysses S. Grant, the Union commander who brought the Civil War to an end, includes the tombs of General and Mrs. Grant. As the President of the United States (1869-77), Grant signed the act establishing the first national park, Yellowstone, on March 1, 1872. The memorial is on Riverside Drive near West 122nd Street.

Hamilton Grange National Memorial. "The Grange," named after his grandfather's estate in Scotland, was the home of Alexander Hamilton, American statesman and first Secretary of the Treasury.

Home of Franklin D. Roosevelt National Historic Site. This was the birthplace, lifetime residence and "Summer White

House'' of the 32nd President. He entertained many distinguished visitors here. The gravesites of President and Mrs. Roosevelt are in the Rose Garden. 263 acres.

Martin Van Buren National Historic Site. Lindenwald estate, south of Albany, was the home of the eighth President — a leader in the emergence of Jacksonian Democracy — for 21 years until his death in 1862. 40 acres.

Sagamore Hill National Historic Site. This estate was the home of Theodore Roosevelt from 1885 until his death in 1919. Used as the ''Summer White House,'' 1901-08, it contains original furnishings. The Old Orchard Museum is on the grounds. 85 acres.

Saratoga National Historical Park. The American victory here over the British in 1777 was the turning point of the Revolution and one of the decisive battles in world history. Major General Philip Schuyler's country home is nearby. 2,455 acres.

Statue of Liberty National Monument. The famous 152-foot copper statue bearing the torch of freedom was a gift of the French people in 1886 to commemorate the alliance of the two nations in the American Revolution. The monument includes the American Museum of Immigration, in the base of the status, and Ellis Island, an immigration port from 1892 to 1954. 58 acres.

Theodore Roosevelt Birthplace National Historic Site. The 26th President was born in a four-story, brownstone house here on October 27, 1858. Demolished in 1910, it was reconstructed 1921-23, following TR's death.

Theodore Roosevelt Inaugural National Historic Site. Theodore Roosevelt took the oath of office as President of the United States on September 14, 1901, here in the Ansley Wilcox House, after the assassination of President William McKinley.

Upper Delaware Scenic and Recreational River. The Park Service will acquire numerous access sites along 100 miles of this free-flowing fishing stream between Hancock and Sparrow Bush, New York, along the Pennsylvania border.

Vanderbilt Mansion National Historic Site. This palatial mansion is a fine example of homes built by 19th-century millionaires.

North Carolina

Blue Ridge Parkway. Following the crest of the Blue Ridge Mountains, this scenic parkway averages 3,000 feet above sea level, embracing several large recreational areas and preserving mountain folk culture and scenic resources. First national parkway. 81,536 acres.

Cape Hatteras National Seashore. Beaches, migratory waterfowl, fishing and points of historical interest, including the Cape Hatteras Lighthouse overlooking the ''graveyard of the Atlantic,'' are special features of the first national seashore. 30,318 acres.

Cape Lookout National Seashore. This series of barrier islands extends for 58 miles along the lower Outer Banks embracing beaches, dunes, salt marshes and historic Portsmouth Village. 28,400 acres.

Carl Sandburg Home National Historic Site. ''Connemara'' was the farm home of the noted poet-author for the last 22 years of his life. During his residence here, several of his books were published. 247 acres.

Fort Raleigh National Historic Site. The first English settlement in North America was attempted here (1585-87). The fate of Sir Walter Raleigh's ''Lost Colony'' remains a mystery. 157 acres.

Guilford Courthouse National Military Park. The battle fought here on March 15, 1781, opened the campaign that led to Yorktown and the end of the Revolution. 220 acres.

Moores Creek National Military Park. The battle on February 27, 1776, between North Carolina Patriots and Loyalists, is commemorated here. The Patriot victory notably advanced the revolutionary cause in the South. 86 acres.

Wright Brothers National Memorial. The first sustained flight in a heavier-than-air machine was made here by Wilbur and Orville Wright on December 17, 1903. 431 acres.

North Dakota

Fort Union Trading Post National Historic Site. The trading post that stood here was the principal fur-trading depot in the Upper Missouri River region from 1829 to 1867. Located at the confluence of the Missouri and Yellowstone Rivers, Fort Union served the Dakotas, Montana and the Prairie Provinces. 436 acres.

Knife River Indian Villages National Historic Site. Remnants of historic and prehistoric Indian villages, last occupied in 1845 by the Hidatsa, contain an array of artifacts of Plains Indian culture. 1,291 acres.

Theodore Roosevelt National Park. The park includes scenic badlands along the Little Missouri River and part of Theodore Roosevelt's Elkhorn Ranch. 70,344 acres.

Ohio

Cuyahoga Valley National Recreation Area. This recreation area links the urban centers of Cleveland and Akron, preserving the rural character of the Cuyahoga River Valley and such historic resources as the century-old Ohio and Erie Canal system. 32,460 acres.

Mound City Group National Monument. Twenty-three burial mounds of Hopewell Indians (200 B.C. — A.D. 500) yielded copper breastplates, tools, obsidian blades, shells, ornaments of grizzly bear teeth, and stone pipes carved as birds and animals.

These provide insights into the ceremonial customs of these prehistoric people. 67 acres.

Perry's Victory and International Peace Memorial. Commodore Oliver H. Perry won the greatest naval battle of the War of 1812 on Lake Erie. The memorial — the world's most massive Doric column — was constructed in 1912-15 "to inculcate the lessons of international peace by arbitration and disarmament." 25 acres.

William Howard Taft National Historic Site. This house was the birthplace and boyhood home of the only man to serve both as President and Chief Justice of the United States — 27th President, 1909-13; U.S. Chief Justice, 1921-30.

Oklahoma

Chickasaw National Recreation Area. The man-made Lake of the Arbuckles provides water recreation for an extensive Midwest area, and numerous cold mineral and freshwater springs, including bromide waters, surface here. 9,500 acres.

Oregon

Crater Lake National Park. This unique, deep blue lake lies in the heart of Mount Mazama, an ancient volcanic peak that collapsed centuries ago. The lake is encircled by multi-colored lava walls reaching 500 to 2,000 feet above the lake waters. 160,290 acres.

Fort Clatsop National Memorial. The Lewis and Clark Expedition camped here in the winter of 1805-06. 130 acres.

John Day Fossil Beds National Monument. Plant and animal fossils show five epochs, from Eocene to the end of Pleistocene. 14,100 acres.

Oregon Caves National Monument. Ground water dissolving marble bedrock formed these cave passages and intricate flowstone formations. 473 acres.

Pennsylvania

Allegheny Portage Railroad National Historic Site. Traces of the first railroad crossing of the Allegheny Mountains can still be seen here. An inclined plane railroad, it permitted transportation of passengers and freight over the mountains, providing a critical link in the Pennsylvania Mainline Canal system and with the West. Built between 1831 and 1834, it was abandoned by 1857. 1,476 acres.

Delaware National Scenic River. This park contains the portion of the Delaware River which lies within the boundaries of Delaware Water Gap National Recreation Area. The free-flowing stream offers swimming, canoeing and fishing opportunities. 2,750 acres.

Delaware Water Gap National Recreation Area. This scenic area preserves relatively unspoiled land on both the New Jersey and Pennsylvania sides of the Middle Delaware River. The river segment flows through the famous gap in the Appalachian Mountains. The park sponsors an "Artist-in-Residence" program and three environmental education centers. 71,000 acres.

Edgar Allan Poe National Historic Site. The life and work of this gifted American author are described in exhibits in this house at 530 North Seventh Street where Poe lived from 1844-45.

Eisenhower National Historic Site. This was the home and farm of President and Mrs. Dwight D. Eisenhower. *Not open to the public.* 688 acres.

Fort Necessity National Battlefield. Colonial troops commanded by Lieutenant Colonel George Washington, then 22 years old, were defeated here in the opening battle of the French and Indian War on July 3, 1754. The park includes the nearby monument to Major General Edward Braddock and the early 19th-century Mount Washington Tavern and Jumonville Glenn, site of the first skirmishing of the French and Indian War, May 28, 1754. 900 acres.

Friendship Hill National Historic Site. Stone and brick home on the Monongahela River near Point Marion, Pennsylvania, belonged to Albert Gallatin, Secretary of the Treasury, 1801-13, under Presidents Jefferson and Madison. *Not open to the public.* 675 acres.

Gettysburg National Military Park. The great Civil War battle fought here July 1-3, 1863, repulsed the second Confederate invasion of the North. Gettysburg National Cemetery — 7,036 interments, 1,668 unidentified — adjoins the park. President Lincoln delivered his Gettysburg address here in dedicating the cemetery November 19, 1863. 3,862 acres.

Hopewell Village National Historic Site. This is one of the finest examples of a rural American 19th-century ironmaking village. The buildings include the blast furnace and auxiliary structures. 848 acres.

Independence National Historic Park. The park includes structures and properties in old Philadelphia associated with the American Revolution and the founding and growth of the United States — Independence Hall, the Liberty Bell, Congress Hall, old City Hall, the First and Second Banks of the United States, Franklin Court and Deshler-Morris House in Germantown. 36 acres.

Johnstown Flood National Memorial. The tragic Johnstown Flood of 1889 caused by a break in the South Fork Dam is memorialized here. 175 acres.

Thaddeus Kosciuszko National Memorial. The life and work of this Polish-born patriot and hero of the American Revolution are commemorated at 301 Pine Street, Philadelphia.

Valley Forge National Historical Park. Site of the Continental Army's bitter winter encampment, 1777-78, the park contains General Washington's headquarters, a variety of monuments and markers, and re-creations of log buildings and cannon used by colonial troops. 2,466 acres.

Puerto Rico

San Juan National Historic Site. These massive masonry fortifications, oldest in the territorial limits of the United States, were begun by the Spanish in the 16th century to protect a strategic harbor guarding the sea lanes to the New World. 53 acres.

Rhode Island

Roger Williams National Memorial. This memorial is in honor of the founder of the Rhode Island colony and a pioneer in religious freedom.

South Carolina

Congaree Swamp National Monument. Located on an alluvial flood plain 20 miles southeast of Columbia, the park contains the last significant tract of virgin, southern bottomland hardwoods in the Southeastern United States. 15,200 acres.

Cowpens National Battlefield. Brigadier General Daniel Morgan won a decisive Revolutionary War victory here over British Lieutenant Colonel Banastre Tarleton on January 17, 1781. 842 acres.

Fort Sumter National Monument. The first engagement of the Civil War took place here on April 12, 1861. The park also embraces Fort Moultrie, scene of the patriot victory of June 28, 1776 — one of the early defeats of the British in the Revolutionary War. The fort has been restored to reflect 171 years of seacoast defense. 64 acres.

Kings Mountain National Military Park. American frontiersmen defeated the British here on October 7, 1780, at a critical point during the Revolution. 3,945 acres.

Ninety Six National Historic Site. This important colonial backcountry trading village and government seat after 1769 was held briefly by the British during the Revolutionary War and is the scene of Nathanael Greene's siege in 1781. The site contains earthwork embankments of a 1759 fortification, the remains of two historic villages, a colonial plantation complex and numerous prehistoric sites. 1,115 acres.

South Dakota

Badlands National Park. Carved by erosion, this scenic landscape contains animal fossils of 40 million years ago. Prairie grasslands support bison, bighorn sheep, deer and antelope. 243,302 acres.

Jewel Cave National Monument. Caverns, in limestone formation, consist of a series of chambers connected by narrow passages, with many side galleries and fine calcite crystal encrustations. 1,274 acres.

Mount Rushmore National Memorial. Colossal heads of Presidents George Washington, Thomas Jefferson, Abraham Lincoln and Theodore Roosevelt were sculptured by Gutzon Borglum on the face of a granite mountain. 1,278 acres.

Wind Cave National Park. These limestone caverns in the scenic Black Hills are decorated by beautiful boxwork and calcite crystal formations. Elk, deer, pronghorn, prairie dogs and bison live in the park. 28,292 acres.

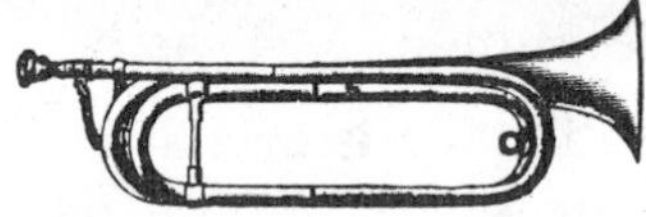

Tennessee

Andrew Johnson National Historic Site. The site includes two homes and the tailor shop of the 17th President, who served from 1865 to 1869, and the Andrew Jackson National Cemetery, where the President's burial site is one of 741 interments. 16 acres.

Big South Fork National River and Recreation Area. The free-flowing Big South Fork of the Cumberland River and its tributaries pass through scenic gorges and valleys containing a wide range of natural and historical features. The U.S. Army Corps of Engineers is coordinating planning and development of the area. 122,960 acres.

Fort Donelson National Military Park. The first major victory for the Union Army in the Civil War occurred here in February 1862 under the leadership of Ulysses S. Grant. Fort Donelson (Dover) National Cemetery — 1,197 interments, 512 unidentified — adjoins the park. 543 park acres.

Great Smoky Mountains National Park. Loftiest range east of the Black Hills, and one of the oldest uplands on earth, the Smokies have a diversified and luxuriant plantlife, often of extraordinary size. The park has been selected for International Biosphere Reserve status. 517,368 acres.

Obed Wild and Scenic River. The Obed River and its two main tributaries, Clear Creek and Daddy's Creek, cut into the Cumberland Plateau of East Tennessee, providing some of the most rugged scenery in the Southeast. Elevations range from 900 to 2,900 feet above sea level. 5,250 acres.

Shiloh National Military Park. The bitter battle fought here April 6-7, 1862, prepared the way for Major-General U.S. Grant's successful siege of Vicksburg. Well-preserved prehistoric Indian mounds overlook the river. Shiloh (Pittsburg Landing) National Cemetery — 3,761 interments, 2,370 unidentified — adjoins the park. 3,761 park acres.

Stones River National Battlefield. The fierce midwinter battle, which began the Federal offensive to trisect the Confederacy, took place here December 31, 1862 to January 2, 1863. Stones River (Murfreesboro) National Cemetery — 6,831 interments, 2,562 unidentified — adjoins the park. 330 park acres.

Texas

Alibates Flint Quarries National Monument. For more than 10,000 years, pre-Columbian Indians dug agatized dolomite from quarries here to make projectile points, knives, scrapers and other tools. 1,332 acres.

Amistad National Recreation Area. Boating and watersports highlight activities in the U.S. section of Amistad Reservoir on the Rio Grande. 62,451 acres.

Big Bend National Park. Mountains contrast with desert in this great bend of the Rio Grande, where a variety of unusual geological formations are found. 708,118 acres.

Big Thicket National Preserve. This unique ecosystem is a mingling of diverse plant associations resulting in a large variety of plant species found in close proximity. Study and research opportunities are excellent. 84,550 acres.

Chamizal National Memorial. The peaceful settlement of a 99-year boundary dispute between the United States and Mexico is memorialized here. The Chamizal Treaty, ending the dispute, was signed in 1963. An amphitheater and 500-seat auditorium are used by theatrical groups from both nations. 54 acres.

Fort Davis National Historic Site. A key post in the west Texas defensive system, the fort guarded emigrants on the San Antonio-El Paso road from 1854 to 1891. 460 acres.

Guadalupe Mountains National Park. Rising from the desert, this mountain mass contains portions of the world's most extensive and significant Permian limestone fossil reef. Also featured are a tremendous earth fault, lofty peaks, unusual flora and fauna, and a colorful record of the past. 76,293 acres.

Lake Meredith National Recreation Area. Man-made Lake Meredith on the Canadian River is a popular water-activity center in the Southwest. 44,994 acres.

Lyndon B. Johnson National Historic Site. The birthplace, boyhood home and ranch of the 36th President, 1963-69, and his grandparents' old ranch make up the park. 225 acres.

Padre Island National Seashore. Noted for its wide sand beaches, excellent fishing, and abundant bird and marine life, this barrier island stretches along the Gulf Coast for 80.5 miles. 133,918 acres.

Palo Alto Battlefield National Historic Site. The park contains the site of the first of two important Mexican War battles fought on American soil. General Zachary Taylor's victory here made invasion of Mexico possible. 50 acres.

Rio Grande Wild and Scenic River. A 191.2-mile strip on the American shore of the Rio Grande in the Chihuahuan Desert protects the river. It begins in Big Bend National Park and continues downstream to the Terrell-Val Verde County Line. 9,600 acres.

San Antonio Missions National Historical Park. Four Catholic frontier missions, part of a system that stretched across the Spanish Southwest in the 18th century, are commemorated here. Included in the park are a related historic dam and aqueduct system. Missions open to the public. 2,500 acres.

Utah

Arches National Park. Extraordinary products of erosion in the form of giant arches, windows, pinnacles and pedestals change color here constantly as the sun moves overhead. 73,378 acres.

Bryce Canyon National Park. In horseshoe-shaped amphitheaters along the edge of the Paunsaugunt Plateau in southern Utah stand innumerable, highly colored and bizarre pinnacles, walls and spires, perhaps the most colorful and unusual erosional forms in the world. 35,835 acres.

Canyonlands National Park. In this geological wonderland, rocks, spires and mesas rise more than 7,800 feet. Here, too, are petroglyphs left by Indians about 1,000 years ago. 337,570 acres.

Capitol Reef National Park. Narrow, high-walled gorges cut through a 60-mile uplift of sandstone cliffs with highly colored sedimentary formations. Dome-shaped, white-cap rock along the Fremont River accounts for the name. 241,904 acres.

Cedar Breaks National Monument. A huge amphitheater has eroded into the variegated Pink Cliffs (Wasatch Formation), which are 2,000 feet thick at this point. 6,154 acres.

Glen Canyon National Recreation Areas. Lake Powell, formed by the Colorado River, stretches for 186 miles behind one of the highest dams in the world. 1,236,880 acres.

Golden Spike National Historic Site. Completion of the first transcontinental railroad in the United States was celebrated here where the Central Pacific and Union Pacific Railroads met in 1869. 2,203 acres.

Natural Bridges National Monument. Three natural bridges, carved out of sandstone, are protected here. The highest is 220 feet above the streambed, with a span of 268 feet. 7,779 acres.

Rainbow Bridge National Monument. Greatest of the world's known natural bridges, this symmetrical arch of salmon-pink sandstone rises 290 feet above the floor of Bridge Canyon. 160 acres.

Timpanogos Cave National Monument. This colorful limestone cavern on the side of Mount Timpanogos is noted for helictites — water-created formations that grow in all directions and shapes, regardless of the pull of gravity. 250 acres.

Zion National Park. Colorful canyon and mesa scenery includes erosion and rock-fault patterns that create phenomenal shapes and landscapes. Evidence of former volcanic activity is here, too. 146,546 acres.

Vermont

Appalachian National Scenic Trail. (See Maine.)

Virginia

Appomattox Court House National Historical Park. Here on April 9, 1865, General Robert E. Lee surrendered the Confederacy's largest field army to Lieutenant General Ulysses S. Grant. 1,318 acres.

Arlington House, The Robert E. Lee Memorial. This antebellum home of the Custis and Lee families overlooks the Potomac River and Washington, D.C.

Booker T. Washington National Monument. This site was the birthplace and early childhood home of the famous black leader and educator. 223 acres.

Colonial National Historic Park. This park encompasses most of Jamestown Island, site of the first permanent English settlement; Yorktown, scene of the culminating battle of the American Revolution in 1781; a 23-mile parkway connecting these and other colonial sites with Williamsburg; and Cape Henry Memorial, which marks the approximate site of the first landing of Jamestown's colonists in 1607. Yorktown National Cemetery, containing Civil War gravesites — 2,183 interments, 1,434 unidentified — adjoins the park. 9,833 park acres.

Fredericksburg and Spotsylvania County Battlefields Memorial National Military Park. Portions of four major Civil War Battlefields — Fredericksburg, Chancellorsville, the Wilderness, Spotsylvania Court House — Chatham Manor, and several smaller historic sites comprise the park. The battles occurred between 1862 and 1864. 5,888 park acres.

George Washington Birthplace National Monument. Birthplace of the first U.S. President, the park includes a memorial mansion and gardens, and the tombs of his great-grandfather, grandfather and father. 538 acres.

George Washington Memorial Parkway. This landscaped riverfront parkway links many landmarks in the life of George Washington. It connects Mount Vernon and Great Falls on the Virginia side of the Potomac and Great Falls with Chain Bridge on the Maryland side. The parkway includes natural, historical and recreational areas. 7,141 acres.

Maggie L. Walker National Historic Site. The brick house at 110-A East Leigh Street, Richmond, was the home of the daughter of an ex-house slave who became the first woman president of an American financial institution.

Manassas National Battlefield Park. The Battles of First and Second Manassas were fought here July 21, 1861, and August 28-30, 1862. The 1861 battle was the first

Eighteenth century Williamsburg, Virginia, returns to life in front of the Palace of the Royal Governors with its authentic furnishings and formal gardens.

test of Northern and Southern military prowess. Here, Confederate Brigadier General Thomas J. Jackson acquired his nickname "Stonewall." 3,108 acres.

Petersburg National Battlefield. The Union Army waged a 10-month campaign here 1864-65 to seize Petersburg, center of the railroads supplying Richmond and General Robert E. Lee's army. Also includes City Point in Hopewell, Virginia, where Ulysses S. Grant made his headquarters at Appomattox Manor for the final 10 months of the war. Poplar Grove (Petersburg) National Cemetery — 6,315 interments, 4,110 unidentified — is near the park. 1,536 park acres.

Prince William Forest Park. In this forested watershed of Quantico Creek, pines and hardwoods have replaced worn-out farmland. 18,571 acres.

Richmond National Battlefield Park. The park commemorates several battles to capture Richmond, the Confederate capital, during the Civil War. 769 acres.

Shenandoah National Park. Skyline Drive winds through hardwood forests along the crest of this outstanding portion of the Blue Ridge Mountains, with spectacular vistas of historic Shenandoah Valley and the Piedmont. 194,327 acres.

Wolf Trap Farm Park for the Performing Arts. At this first national park for the performing arts, Filene Center can accommodate an audience of 6,500, including 3,000 on the sloping lawn in a setting of rolling hills and woods. The stagehouse is 10 stories high and the stage 100 feet wide by 64 feet deep. 130 acres.

Virgin Islands

Buck Island Reef National Monument. Coral grottoes, sea fans, gorgonias and tropical fishes — along an underwater trail — make this one of the finest marine gardens in the Caribbean. The island is a rookery for frigate birds and pelicans and the habitat of green turtles. 880 acres.

Christiansted National Historic Site. Colonial development of the Virgin Islands is commemorated by 18th- and 19th-century structures in the capital of the former Danish West Indies on St. Croix Island. Discovered by Columbus in 1493, St. Croix was purchased by the United States in 1917. 27 acres.

Virgin Islands National Park. The park covers about three-fourths of St. John Island and Hassel Island in St. Thomas harbor and includes quiet coves, blue-green waters, and white sandy beaches fringed by lush green hills. Here, too, are early Carib Indian relics and the remains of Danish colonial sugar plantations. 14,708 acres.

Washington

Coulee Dam National Recreation Area. Formed by Grand Coulee Dam (part of the Columbia River Basin project), 130-mile-long Franklin D. Roosevelt Lake is the principal recreation feature here. 100,059 acres.

Logging is a way of life in the lush forests of Washington state (above).

Pleasure boats cruise the waters of Lake Chelan National Recreation Area in the beautiful Stehekin Valley of Washington state.

Fort Vancouver National Historic Site. As the western headquarters of Hudson's Bay Company, 1825 to 1849, this was the hub of political and fur-trading activities. A U.S. military reservation — Vancouver Barracks established in 1849 — took over the fort in 1860, remaining active until 1949. 208 acres.

Klondike Gold Rush National Historical Park. The park orientation center is at 117 South Main Street in Seattle's Pioneer Square area.

Lake Chelan National Recreation Area. Here the beautiful Stehekin Valley, with a portion of fjordlike Lake Chelan, adjoins the southern unit of North Cascades National Park. 61,889 acres.

Mount Rainier National Park. This greatest single-peak glacial system in the United States radiates from the summit and slopes of an ancient volcano, with dense forests and subalpine flowered meadows below. 235,404 acres.

North Cascades National Park. High, jagged peaks intercept moisture-laden winds, producing glaciers, icefalls, waterfalls and other water phenomena in this wild alpine region where lush forests and meadows, plant and animal communities thrive in the valleys. 504,780 acres.

Olympic National Park. This mountain wilderness contains the finest remnant of Pacific Northwest rain forest, active glaciers, rare Roosevelt elk and 50 miles of wild, scenic ocean shore. 908,720 acres.

Ross Lake National Recreation Area. Ringed by mountains, this reservoir in the Skagit River drainage separates the north and south units of North Cascades National Park. 117,574 acres.

San Juan Island National Historical Park. This park marks the historic events on the island from 1853 to 1871 in connection with final settlement of the Oregon Territory's northern boundary, including the so-called Pig War of 1859. 1,751 acres.

Whitman Mission National Historic Site. Dr. and Mrs. Marcus Whitman ministered to spiritual and physical needs of the Indians here until slain by a few of them in 1847. The mission was a landmark on the Oregon Trail. 98 acres.

West Virginia

Chesapeake and Ohio Canal National Historical Park. (See Maryland.)

Harpers Ferry National Historical Park. Because of its strategic location at the confluence of the Shenandoah and Potomac Rivers, this town changed hands many times during the Civil War. John Brown's raid took place here in 1859. 1,909 acres.

New River Gorge National River. A rugged, white-water river, flowing northward through deep canyons, the New is among the oldest rivers on the continent. The free-flowing, 66-mile section from Hinton to Fayetteville is abundant in natural, scenic, historic and recreational values. 62,024 acres.

Wisconsin

Apostle Island National Lakeshore. Twenty picturesque islands and an 11-mile strip of adjacent Bayfield Peninsula along the south shore of Lake Superior comprise this northern park. 42,009 acres.

Lower St. Croix National Scenic River. Recreational opportunities for much of the upper Midwest are provided here along this 27-mile segment of the St. Croix River, a component of the Wild and Scenic Rivers System. 8,679 acres.

St. Croix National Scenic River. About 200 miles of the beautiful St. Croix River and its Namekagon tributary make up this area, an initial component of the National Wild and Scenic Rivers System. 62,695 acres.

Highlight

Harpers Ferry National Historical Park

Harpers Ferry, situated on a point of land at the confluence of the Shenandoah and Potomac Rivers and dominated by the Blue Ridge Mountains, was a beckoning wilderness in the early 1700s. By mid-19th century, it was a town of some 3,000 inhabitants, an important arms-producing center, and a transportation link between east and west. John Brown's raid in 1859 and the Civil War thrust the town into national prominence. The destruction wrought by the war and repeated flooding was responsible for the town's eventual decline.

The first settler on this land was Peter Stephens, a trader, who came here in 1733 and set up a primitive ferry service of the two rivers. Fourteen years later, Robert Harper, a millwright and the man for whom the town is named, settled here, taking over Stephens' ferry operation. Seeing the waterpower potential, he later built a mill. The ferry and the mill have long since disappeared.

Within a century, Harpers Ferry developed from a tiny village into an industrialized community. The town received its first real impetus in the 1790s when President George Washington urged Congress to establish a national armory here along the Potomac. The armory supported the economy of the town and encouraged the establishment of small industries on adjacent Virginius Island. The arrival of the Chesapeake and Ohio Canal and the Baltimore and Ohio Railroad in the 1830s assured Harpers Ferry of the economic success it was to enjoy well past mid-century.

Then came disaster. In October 1859, John Brown's raid jarred the peaceful town, and the Civil War that followed 17 months later was to leave a path of destruction that wrecked the town's economy. The armory and arsenal buildings were burned in 1861 to keep them from falling into Confederate hands. Because of the town's geographical location and its railway system, Union and Confederate troop movements through Harpers Ferry were frequent, and soldiers of both armies occupied the town intermittently throughout the war. The largest military operation against Harpers Ferry occurred prior to the Battle of Antietam in September 1862, when General Thomas J. "Stonewall" Jackson's Confederate corps seized the town and captured the 12,700-man Union garrison commanded by Colonel Dixon Miles.

Discouraged by continual war damage and the lack of employment, many townspeople moved away. When some of these returned after the war to begin life anew, any hopes they might have had for the town's economic revival were dashed by a series of devastating floods in the late 1800s. For years following, empty buildings stood in silent desolation and once-active industrial sites were slowly reclaimed by nature.

The one bright hope in the story of Harpers Ferry after the Civil War was the establishment of a normal school for the education of freed blacks. The first classroom of what was to become Storer College was located in the Lockwood House, an abandoned armory dwelling above the town. The college remained in operation until 1955.

John Brown (1800-1859)

John Brown, whose raid brought Harpers Ferry to national attention, was a native of Connecticut, had been an abolitionist all his life, and in 1855-56 had been a leader in the bloody sectional strife in Kansas. Of stern religious bent, ardent to the point of fanaticism, he had conceived a plan to liberate slaves by violence and set up a free-Negro stronghold in the mountains of Maryland and Virginia.

He fixed upon Harpers Ferry as the starting point for the insurrection, apparently because the town was near the Mason-Dixon line and the surrounding mountains were suitable for guerilla warfare. Further, capture of the thousands of arms stored in the arsenal of the U.S. Armory at the ferry could equip a formidable army.

Brown and his 18-man "army of liberation" attacked Harpers Ferry on the night of October 16, 1859, seizing the armory and several other strategic points before the startled townspeople realized their purpose. When the alarm spread and local citizens and state militia converged on the town, the raiders barricaded themselves in the armory fire engine and guard house ("John Brown's Fort"). They were captured when a contingent of marines commanded by Colonel Robert E. Lee and Lieutenant J.E.B. Stuart stormed the building on the morning of October 18. Brought to trial for murder, treason and conspiring with slaves to create insurrection, Brown was found guilty and subsequently hanged at nearby Charles Town on December 2, 1859.

The day of his execution, Brown wrote a last (and prophetic) message to the world and handed it to his jailor. In clear but slightly unsteady handwriting, it said: "I, John Brown, am now quite certain that the crimes of this guilty land will never be purged away but with blood. I had, as I now think, vainly flattered myself that without very much bloodshed it might be done."

Sixteen months later, on April 12, 1861, the war that John Brown seemed to foretell began at a place called Fort Sumter in Charleston Harbor, South Carolina.

Wyoming

Devils Tower National Monument. A fur-trade post once stood here, but the surviving buildings are those of a major military post that guarded covered-wagon trails to the West, 1849-90. 856 acres.

Fossil Butte National Monument. An abundance of rare fish fossils, 40-65 million years old, is evidence of former habitation of this now semiarid region. 8,198 acres.

Grand Teton National Park. The most impressive part of the Teton Range, this series of blue-gray peaks rising more than a mile above the sagebrush flats was once a noted landmark of Indians and "Mountain Men." The park includes part of Jackson Hole, winter feeding ground of the largest American elk herd. 310,515 acres.

John D. Rockefeller, Jr. Memorial Parkway. Linking West Thumb in Yellowstone with the South Entrance of Grand Teton National Park, this scenic 82-mile corridor commemorates Rockefeller's role in aiding establishment of many parks, including Grand Teton. 23,777 acres.

Yellowstone National Park. Old Faithful and some 10,000 other geysers and hot springs make this the earth's greatest geyser area. Here, too, are lakes, waterfalls, high mountains and the Grand Canyon of the Yellowstone — all set apart in 1872 as the world's first national park. It is the largest park in the National Park System. 2,219,822 acres.

Affiliated Areas of the National Park Service

Affiliated Areas of the National Park System

Benjamin Franklin National Memorial. In the Rotunda of the Franklin Institute the colossal seated statue of Franklin, by James Earle Fraser, honors the inventor-statesman. Philadelphia, Pennsylvania 19103.

Cherokee Strip Living Museum. This privately run museum near the Oklahoma border commemorates the opening of the "Indian Territory" to settlement. Arkansas City, Kansas 67005.

Chicago Portage National Historic Site. A portion of the portage discovered by French explorers Jacques Marquette and Louis Joliet is preserved here. Used by pioneers as a link between the Great Lakes and the Mississippi, the portage was one of the economic foundations of Chicago. 91 acres. River Forest, Illinois 60305.

Chimney Rock National Historic Site. As they traveled west, pioneers camped near this famous landmark, which stands 500 feet above the Platte River along the Oregon Trail. 83 acres. Gering, Nebraska 69341.

Ebey's Landing National Historical Reserve. An area of central Whidbey Island encompassing the community of Coupeville, the reserve will protect important natural and historic values. 8,000 acres. Seattle, Washington 98101.

Eugene O'Neill National Historic Site. Tao House, near Danville, California, was built for Eugene O'Neill, who lived here from 1937 to 1944. Several of his best known plays, including *The Iceman Cometh* and *Long Day's Journey Into Night*, were written here — now a memorial to the playwright and a future park for the performing arts. 14 acres. Alamo, California 94507.

Father Marquette National Memorial. The memorial to Father Jacques Marquette, French priest and explorer, is to be built in Straits State Park near St. Ignace, Michigan, where he founded a Jesuit mission in 1617 and was buried in 1678. 52 acres. Lansing, Michigan 48909.

Gloria Dei (Old Swedes') Church National Historic Site. This the second-oldest Swedish church in the United States was founded in 1677. The present structure, a splendid example of early Swedish church architecture, was erected about 1700. Philadelphia, Pennsylvania 19106.

Ice Age National Scientific Reserve. This first national scientific reserve contains nationally significant features of continental glaciation. State parks in the area are open to the public. 32,500 acres. Madison, Wisconsin 53701.

Iditarod National Historic Trail. One of the Alaska Gold Rush Trails, this 2,037-mile trail extends from Seward to Nome and is composed of a network of trails and side trails developed during the gold rush era at the turn of the century. Anchorage, Alaska 99501.

International Peace Garden. Peaceful relations between Canada and the United States are commemorated here. North Dakota holds the 888-acre U.S. portion for International Peace Garden, Incorporated, which administers the area for North Dakota and Manitoba. The National Park Service has assisted in the master plan. 2,330 acres. Dunseith, North Dakota 58637.

Authentic demonstrations of a soldier's life during the Revolutionary War are given regularly at Saratoga National Historic Park, New York (above). Medieval dancers entertain 20th-century pleasure seekers at the annual Renaissance Faire in California's Santa Monica Mountains National Recreation Area.

Jamestown National Historic Site. Part of the site of the first permanent English settlement in North America (1607) is on the upper end of Jamestown Island, scene of the first representative legislative government on this continent, July 30, 1619. 20 acres. Richmond, Virginia 23220.

Lewis and Clark National Historic Trail. Designates the 3,700-mile route over land and water of the 1804-06 expedition exploring the Louisiana Purchase from Wood River, Illinois, to Fort Clatsop, Oregon. Denver, Colorado 80225.

McLoughlin House National Historic Site. Dr. John McLoughlin, often called the "Father of Oregon," was prominent in the development of the Pacific Northwest as chief factor of Fort Vancouver. He lived in this house from 1847 to 1857. Oregon City, Oregon 97045.

Mormon Pioneer National Historic Trail. This 1,300-mile trail follows the route over which Brigham Young led the Mormon adherents from Nauvoo, Illinois, to the site of modern Salt Lake City, Utah, in 1847. Denver, Colorado 80225.

Oregon National Historic Trail. The 2,000-mile trail took pioneers westward from Independence, Missouri, to the vicinity of modern Portland, Oregon, 1841-48. Among 482 historic places en route, many — including several segments of original trail — have potential for visitor use development. Seattle, Washington 98101.

Pennsylvania Avenue National Historic Site. This site includes a portion of Pennsylvania Avenue and the area adjacent to it between the Capitol and the White House encompassing Ford's Theatre National Historic Site, several blocks of the Washington commercial district and a number of federal structures. Washington, D.C. 20004.

Pinelands National Reserve. The largest essentially undeveloped tract on the Eastern seaboard, exceeding one million acres, the area is noted for its massive water resources with myriad marshes, bogs and ponds, and the dwarfed pines from which it gets its name. The reserve concept envisions close, cooperative preservation efforts among federal, state and local governments and private property owners. Philadelphia, Pennsylvania 19106.

Roosevelt Campobello International Park. President Franklin D. Roosevelt was stricken here at his summer home in New Brunswick, Canada, at the age of 39 by poliomyelitis. This is the first international park to be administered by a joint commission. 2,721 acres. Lubec, Maine 04652.

Saint Paul's Church National Historic Site. This 18th-century church is significant because of its connection with events leading to the John Peter Zenger trial involving freedom of the press, and because of its place in American architectural history and the Revolution. Mount Vernon, New York 10550.

Touro Synagogue National Historic Site. One of the finest examples of colonial religious architecture, this synagogue is the present-day place of worship of Congregation Jeshuat Israel. Designated March 5, 1946; owned by Congregation Shearith Israel, New York City. National Park Service lends technical assistance for preservation of the building under a cooperative agreement with the two congregations. Newport, Rhode Island 02840.

USS Arizona Memorial. This memorial floats over the battleship *USS Arizona*, sunk in Pearl Harbor by Japanese attack, December 7, 1941. It is owned and administered by the U.S. Navy. When shoreside visitor facilities are completed, the National Park Service will administer the site under cooperative agreement with the U.S. Navy. Honolulu, Hawaii 96850.

Wild & Scenic Rivers System

Allagash Wilderness Waterway. Including the Allagash and several interconnected lakes in northern Maine, this is a major recreation resource. 22,840 acres. Augusta, Maine 04333.

American River, North Fork. A fairly inaccessible river flowing through deeply-incised canyons, northeast of Sacramento, California, preserves spectacular Sierra mountain scenery. 13,430 acres. Nevada City, California 95959.

Chattooga River. Passing through a primitive setting in North Carolina, South Carolina and Georgia, this is one of the few remaining free-flowing streams in the Southeast. 16,424 acres. Gainesville, Georgia 30501.

Clearwater River, Middle Fork. Part of the exploration route of Lewis and Clark, most of this river lies in northern Idaho's primitive wilderness. 55,651 acres. Orofino, Idaho 83544.

Eleven Point River. This spring-fed stream meanders past limestone bluffs and crystal springs in Missouri's Ozark hills. 14,195 acres. Rolla, Missouri 65401.

Feather River, Middle Fork. This generally inaccessible fishing stream in Northern California features Feather Falls, the third-highest waterfall (640 feet) in the United States. 19,873 acres. Quincy, California 95971.

Flathead River. Coursing the western boundary of Glacier National Park, Montana, this is a noted spawning stream. 57,400 acres. Kalispell, Montana 59901.

Little Beaver Creek. This stream system and surrounding valley near the Pennsylvania border contain some of

Ohio's wildest lands. 2,637 acres. Columbus, Ohio 43224.

Little Miami River. Flowing through a deep gorge, wooded bluffs and rolling farmlands, this popular Ohio stream is easily reached from Cincinnati or Dayton. 3,202 acres. Columbus, Ohio 43224.

Lower St. Croix River. The northern portion of the lower St. Croix is a unit of the National Park System. The southern portion, jointly administered by the states of Minnesota and Wisconsin, is a wide, gently flowing river which ends in the Mississippi River. 6,065 acres. St. Paul, Minnesota 55155.

Missouri River. A spectacular Montana valley with striking rock formations and diverse flora and fauna, this river corridor also includes numerous historical and archaeological sites. 131,838 acres. Billings, Montana 59107.

Missouri River. This stretch of the "Big Muddy" from Gavins Point Dam, near Yankton, South Dakota, to Ponca, Nebraska, is still semi-wild. 14,941 acres. Omaha, Nebraska 68102.

New River, South Fork. The ancient, northward-flowing New River passes through valleys and bottomlands in western North Carolina. 1,900 acres. Roaring Gap, North Carolina 28668.

Pere Marquette River. Wandering gently through overhanging bluffs and across the grassy floodplains of central Michigan, this is one of the finest trout streams of the Midwest. Cadillac, Michigan 49601.

Rapid River. A part of the Forest Service — adminstered by Hells Canyon National Recreation Area in Idaho — this river's white-water harbors an important salmon hatchery. 8,382 acres. Baker, Oregon 97814.

Rio Grande. Challenging white-water enthusiasts, this rugged stretch of the upper Rio Grande roars through a deep canyon in northern New Mexico. 16,880 acres. Big Bend National Park, Texas 79834.

Rogue River. Emerging from the western slope of Oregon's Cascade Mountains, the Rogue winds across farmlands and orchards before passing through wilderness to the Pacific Ocean. 25,999 acres.Portland, Oregon 97208.

Saint Joe River. This central Idaho river offers outstanding scenery, good fishing and plenty of wildlife. 21,803 acres. Coeur d'Alene, Idaho 83814.

Salmon River, Middle Fork. Churning through central Idaho's wilderness, this river remains as primitive as it was during the explorations of the Lewis and Clark expedition. 32,000 acres. Challis, Idaho 83226.

Skagit River. The Skagit and its Cascade Sauk and Suiattle tributaries feed into Puget Sound in northern Washington. The area features rugged canyons, glacier-clad mountains and densely forested slopes. 34,650 acres. Seattle, Washington 98101.

Snake River. Traversing Hells Canyon, the deepest gorge on the North American continent, the Snake is famed for white-water boating and fishing. 17,546 acres. Baker, Oregon 97814.

Wolf River. Noted as one of the most scenic and rugged rivers in the Midwest, the Wolf flows through the Menominee reservation. Keshena, Wisconsin 54135.

National Trail System

Continental Divide National Scenic Trail. In close proximity to the Continental Divide, the trail extends from the Canadian border in Glacier National Park, Montana, through Idaho, Wyoming, Colorado, and New Mexico to Mexico. 3,100 miles. Washington, D.C. 20013.

Pacific Crest Trail. Extending from the Mexico-California border northward along the mountain ranges of California, Oregon and Washington, the trail reaches the Canadian border near Ross Lake, Washington. 2,600 miles. Washington, D.C. 20013.

The spectacular rock formations of the Garden of the Gods are just a few attractions of southern Illinois' 257,000-acre Shawnee National Forest.

MEXICO
Acapulco Bay
Taxco Hillside
Stone Heads of La Venta

Chichen Itza
(Mayan)
Morelia
Toltec Statues
El Toro!
Column of Independence
Mexico City
R. McKee
Lake Patzcuaro butterfly fishermen

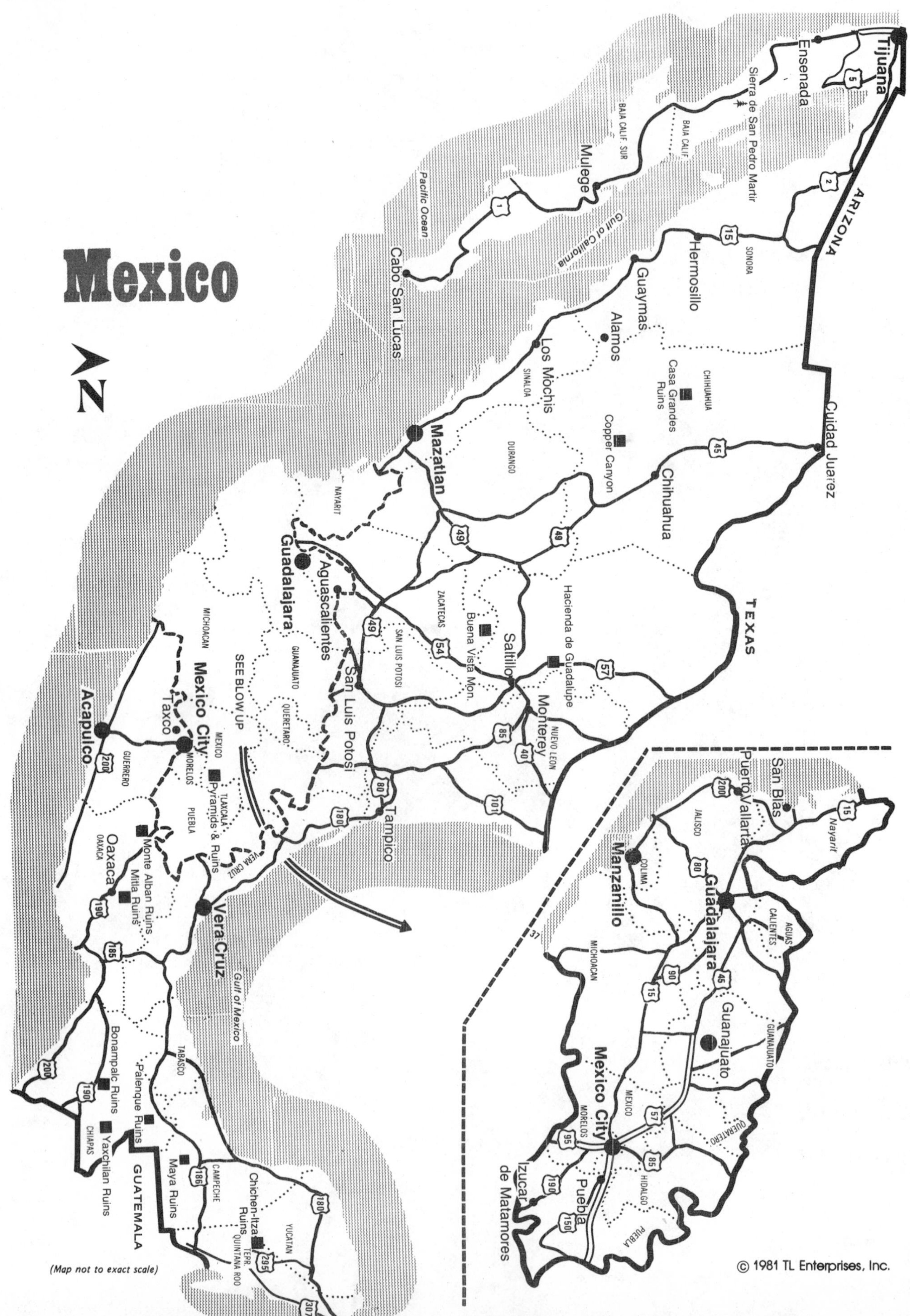

Mexico
N
Tijuana
Ensenada
Sierra de San Pedro Martir
BAJA CALIF.
BAJA CALIF. SUR
Mulege
Pacific Ocean
Gulf of California
Cabo San Lucas
ARIZONA
SONORA
Hermosillo
Guaymas
Alamos
Los Mochis
SINALOA
CHIHUAHUA
Casa Grandes Ruins
Copper Canyon
DURANGO
Cuidad Juarez
Chihuahua
Mazatlan
NAYARIT
Guadalajara
Aguascalientes
ZACATECAS
Buena Vista Mon.
Hacienda de Guadalupe
Saltillo
TEXAS
SAN LUIS POTOSI
San Luis Potosi
GUANAJUATO
QUERETARO
MICHOACAN
SEE BLOW UP
Mexico City
Taxco
Acapulco
GUERRERO
MEXICO
MORELOS
Pyramids & Ruins
TLAXCALA
PUEBLA
Monterey
NUEVO LEON
Tampico
Oaxaca
OAXACA
Monte Alban Ruins
Mitla Ruins
VERA CRUZ
Vera Cruz
Gulf of Mexico
TABASCO
Palenque Ruins
Bonampak Ruins
CHIAPAS
Yaxchilan Ruins
GUATEMALA
Maya Ruins
CAMPECHE
Chichen-Itza Ruins
YUCATAN
QUINTANA ROO
TERR.
(Map not to exact scale)
San Blas
Puerto Vallarta
Nayarit
JALISCO
Manzanillo
COLIMA
AGUAS CALIENTES
MICHOACAN
Guanajuato
GUANAJUATO
QUERETARO
MEXICO
MORELOS
HIDALGO
Puebla
PUEBLA
Izucar de Matamores
5
2
1
15
45
49
54
57
85
40
101
80
180
200
190
185
186
295
307
90
95
150
37
© 1981 TL Enterprises, Inc.

Mexico

Mexico is a fascinating blend of modern cities, luxurious coastal resorts, remote villages, lively fiestas and friendly people — all with a rich Indian and Spanish heritage.

The first Indian inhabitants of Mexico are thought to have come to the region via the land bridge that once joined Asia and Alaska. The country's first civilization was developed along the Veracruz coast by the prehistoric Olmec Indians. The Olmec, who have left behind relics that include colossal heads and rare jade artifacts, later spawned the Mayan civilization that evolved into a highly civilized culture in the Yucatan. The Mayans established cities at Palenque, Chichen Itza, Uxmal and Tulum and began construction on pyramids near Mexico City. At its height, the Mayan Empire stretched throughout Mexico and much of Central America, with at least one city having a population of nearly 125,000.

The Mayan culture declined around 900 A.D., probably as a result of a series of calamities — hurricanes, earthquakes, agricultural disasters, invasions by hostile tribes — that occurred within a short period of time. The Mayans were followed by the militaristic reign of the Toltecs, who later gave way to the Aztecs. The Aztec culture produced a highly complex and contradictory society that included a government supported by taxes, remarkable engineering feats, well-planned cities and a harsh, barbaric religion which worshipped deities with offerings of human hearts that were torn, still beating, from their victims' chests. The religion also called for other forms of human sacrifice, such as the decapitation of women, the drowning of children and the flaying of captives — all in the belief that such acts would ensure the continuance of the Aztec world.

Spanish interest in the region that is now Mexico began in the early 1500s with the explorations of Francisco Hernandez de Cordoba. Actual exploration of the interior came in 1519, when Hernan Cortez landed in the harbor of Veracruz and moved inland to the Aztec capital. With the aid of Indian allies who were enemies of the Aztecs, Cortez conquered the Aztecs and established a Spanish colony at the present location of Mexico City. Spanish rule of Mexico continued for nearly 300 years, until a revolution led to the declaration of Mexican independence in 1813. Despite independence from Spain, Mexico was plagued by internal strife and endured a number of revolutions throughout the 1800s. Finally, in 1910, a revolution led by Francisco I. Madero produced a number of reforms that helped to calm the country — and later allowed it to emerge as a politically and economically stable land that now plays an increasingly important role in world affairs.

Full name: United Mexican States.
Capital: Mexico City
Population: 65,835,000
Major Cities: Mexico City (8,591,750), Guadalajara (1,560,805), Monterey (1,049,958), Cuidad Juarez (520,540).
Official language: Spanish
Currency: Peso (at presstime, the current rate of exchange is 1 peso = 4 cents).

Sunny sands of Acapulco lure sun worshipers to enjoy boating, beach and bathing in this tropical setting.

A large labor pool and widespread oil reserves are currently Mexico's most important assets, but progress in industry and agriculture is also contributing to the development of a stronger Mexican economy. Important products include chemicals, coffee, cotton, grains, lead, salt, sugar, sulfur, shrimp, vegetables, zinc and textiles.

Tourist Regulations for Visitors to Mexico

U.S. citizens are not required to have passports to visit Mexico, but must have proof of citizenship (such as birth certificates, voter's registration, passport, etc.). Naturalized U.S. citizens must carry naturalization certificates or U.S. passports. Alien residents in the U.S. should consult nearest Mexican Consulate or Mexican Government Tourist Office. All persons regardless of age must carry the 180-day (free) tourist card obtainable at the border or from any Mexican Consulate or Mexican Government Tourist Office in the United States or Canada.

A smallpox vaccination certificate is no longer required when entering Mexico or returning to the United States, unless you have traveled in Central America or Europe.

Car permits are obtainable at the border upon presentation of proof of ownership, registration, certificate of title or a notarized affidavit that the applicant is the owner or drives with the permission of the owner. These permits must be turned in to the Mexican customs at the border on returning to the United States. Canadian and American insurance is not valid in Mexico. Short-term tourist insurance is available at most ports of entry. Border town visits of less than 72 hours do not require the tourist card, passport or car permit.

Gasoline is readily available on main highways. On other roads fill tank often.

The use of citizen band radios is forbidden in Mexico. Tourists visiting Mexico need no longer remove them before entering the country, but it is recommended that you inquire locally since this policy may vary.

It is against the law to take firearms to Mexico, except on trips exclusively for hunting, in which case the interested party should contact in advance the nearest Mexican Consulate for details.

Each U.S. resident may bring into the United States free of duty articles purchased in Mexico for personal or household use and not intended for resale to an aggregate fair retail value of $100 if he has not claimed the exemption during the preceding 30 days. Make local inquiry for further exemptions.

Correct at date of publication, but subject to change.

Driving In Mexico

The poor quality of Mexican roads has long been a problem for RVers traveling in Mexico, but a massive road-building program is now adding a number of superhighways to the Mexican landscape and bringing vast improvements to older routes. Even so, travelers are advised to use caution in driving through Mexico; the roads are not as clearly marked as those in the United States; lanes and shoulders are narrow, and road surfaces may be uneven.

To make your travels trouble-free, here are some additional safety tips:

• Avoid driving after dark. In addition to reduced visibility, there is a constant hazard from vehicles that are not equipped with headlights.

• Since most highways are not fenced, there is always the danger that livestock will appear unexpectedly on the road. So

Tourism Offices

Address requests for tourist cards and information to **Mexican National Tourist Council:**

Peachtree Center
Cain Tower
Atlanta, Georgia 30303

John Hancock Center
Chicago, Illinois 60611

Two Turtle Creek Village
Dallas, Texas 75219

633 17th Street
First Denver Plaza
Denver, Colorado 80202

9701 Wilshire Boulevard
Los Angeles, California 90212

100 North Biscayne Boulevard
Tower Building
Miami, Florida 33132

One Shell Square Building
New Orleans, Louisiana 70130

3443 North Central Avenue
Phoenix, Arizona 85012

304 North St. Mary's Street
San Antonio, Texas 78205

San Diego Federal Building
600 B Street
San Diego, California 92101

50 California Street
San Francisco, California 94111

2744 East Broadway
Tucson, Arizona 85716

1156 15th Street, NW
Washington, D.C. 20005

exercise extra caution when driving in the country.

• The maximum speed limit is about 60 miles per hour on the highway and 18 to 25 miles per hour in villages and cities — and you are expected to drive accordingly.

• Read street signs carefully. Most cities have many one-way streets and signs at each intersection will indicate traffic direction. Two-way streets have an arrow with two points. Red arrows are stop signs. Green arrows facing you indicate that you have the right-of-way if you are on a one-way street.

• Signs saying *Bordos, Tumulor* or *Topes* serve as warnings that bumps have been built into the road to slow traffic.

• Don't park on curves and pull off the roadway completely when stopping, even if it is for a brief time.

• Exercise extreme caution when approaching bridges. At narrow, one-lane bridges, the first driver to flick his lights has the right-of-way.

• RVers should always check backroad routes with local residents before proceeding, as many country routes are not suitable for RV travel.

• Do not camp along the highway and *never* park in isolated areas.

• Always lock your rig when it is left unattended.

Emergency Road Service

For RVers who may experience a mechanical failure on one of Mexico's main highways, the Mexican Ministry of Tourism maintains the "Green Angels" — those familiar green and orange vehicles that cruise the main tourist thoroughfares from 8 a.m. to 9 p.m. daily. Each of these radio-equipped vehicles is manned by two English-speaking mechanics who are carefully picked for their knowledge of first-aid, geography, history and the facilities along their assigned routes. You will be charged for the cost of parts and for gasoline and oil, but labor charges are free. Routes that offer these patrols are generally marked.

Mexico Points of Interest and Attractions

The Alameda. A beautiful central park established in 1592 — and the site of burnings during the Inquisition. Many of the eucalyptus, ash and elm trees are between 200 and 300 years old. Mexico City, between Juarez and Hidalgo Avenues.

The Barranca. A deep gorge cut by the Santiago and Verde Rivers featuring spectacular colors and tropical fruit vegetation. Guadalajara, off Highway 15.

Cacahuamilpa Caves. These magnificent caves include huge chambers and dramatically lighted rock formations. Open year-round, daily, 10 a.m. to 5 p.m. Admission charged. Cacahuamilpa, at the intersection of Highways 166 and 55.

Cacalotenango Falls. A majestic site near the grave of Cuauhtemoc, the last Aztec emperor. Near Taxco, west on rocky road to Ichcateopan. A taxi and guide are recommended for this trip.

Chipinque Mesa. Here you will find an inspiring view of the Monterrey Valley; picnicking. Monterrey, 17 kilometers southwest of the Saltillo Highway.

Cocona Caves. Features many unique formations and a sinkhole that drops into an underground stream. Open year-round, daily, 9 a.m. to 6 p.m. Admission charged. Teapa, east on a narrow, unpaved road. Road is too narrow for RVs; take a taxi from Teapa's main plaza.

Desert of the Lions. A national park that contains the ruins of Santo Desierto, a Carmelite monastery; picnicking. Open year-round, daily, 1 p.m. to 5:30 p.m. Villa Obregon, 24 kilometers northwest on the road to Toluca, off Highway 15.

Horsetail Falls. A 1.25-kilometer path leads to this scenic falls atop a mountain on the Hacienda Vista Hermosa. Visitors may walk or hire horses, burros, horse-drawn carts or jeeps with drivers. Fee for parking at base of path. Near El Cercado.

Hot Spring. The waters here were noted for their curative value long before the coming of the Spanish. Apache Indians from the United States are said to have come here to bathe in the sulfurous waters. Near Camargo.

Jesus Nazareno Hospital. The oldest functioning hospital in the Americas, founded in 1527 by Cortez; contains relics and personal files of the conquistador. Mexico City, Calle Republica del Salvador 117 at Pino Suarez.

Juanacatlan Falls. At full volume (usually from June through September), this is the largest waterfall in Mexico. Guadalajara, 23 kilometers southeast, off Highway 44.

Lakes of Zempoala. Seven lakes — Zempoala, Compela, Tonatihagua, Quila, Hueyapan, La Seca and Ocoyotonga — situated 2,900 meters above sea level, offering fishing and camping. Cuernavaca, 21.75 kilometers north off old Highway 95, on a narrow, winding road. Pay toll at ranger station.

Latino-Americana Tower. A 44-story skyscraper that rests on floating piers sunk deep into underlying clay. Open year-round, daily, 10 a.m. to midnight. Admission charged. Mexico City, Madero and San Juan de Letran Avenues.

Lecuona Garden. More than 200 varieties of orchids and displays of gardenias, azaleas and camellias. Open year-round, daily. In the town of Banderilla, near Jalapa.

Mandinga Lagoon. A mangrove-hidden lake that offers good fishing for bass and perch; boats and motors available. Veracruz, off the Anton Lizardo route.

Market Hill. A hill of high-content iron ore that is one of the largest single iron deposits in the world. Durango, north of the city.

Tipping In Mexico

Many people in Mexico depend on tips for their livelihood, since their salaries — if they do receive a salary — are far below the equivalent paid in the United States. The following will serve as a guide to tipping in Mexico:

- In restaurants, tip at least 15% of the bill — and 20% if you have received excellent service.
- Taxi drivers do not expect tips in Mexico, but it is considered a nice gesture to leave the driver the remainder of your change to the nearest five pesos.
- In hotels, you should tip bellhops about 10 to 20 pesos per bag. Chambermaids should be left 25 pesos for two or three nights and 50 pesos for a stay of a week *if you have received good service.*
- Gas station attendants in Mexico expect a tip, even if they don't clean your windshield or check under the hood. A few pesos is adequate.
- Throughout Mexico, you will often be approached — accosted may be more accurate — by a stranger offering to clean your windshield, guard your RV or perform other special services. If you do not want these services you should say no immediately, otherwise you might end up having to pay a few pesos to get rid of the person.
- If you park your RV or tow vehicle in a garage or parking lot, the parking attendant will expect a tip upon its return.
- Tips of 15% to 20% are customary in barbershops and beauty shops.
- Ushers in theaters and motion picture houses should be given a couple of pesos when they.show you to your seat.
- At the border, the Mexican official who signs your tourist card and issues your RV permit will expect a tip of 10 to 20 pesos.

National Observatory. This well-equipped observatory features a Schmidt camera that is capable of 20-minute exposures covering a distance of 300 million light-years; exhibits and shows. Open year-round. Tonantzintla.

The Pantheon. A catacombs lined with about 100 well-preserved mummies, some with shoes and hair, having escaped decomposition because of the exceptionally dry climate. A Spanish-speaking guide is available. Guanajuato, 1.5 kilometers southwest of the main plaza.

Plaza of the Americas. Mexico's centennial exposition grounds, featuring a domed auditorium, a historical museum and the School of Popular Arts. Open year-round, Monday to Saturday. Puebla, on De los Fuertes Avenue.

Presa Rodrigo Gomez. A man-made lake that is a popular spot for fishing, boating, swimming and water skiing. El Cercado, 3.25 kilometers north.

Royal Chapel. Originally built for defensive purposes, this unique chapel has seven naves and 49 domes. Open year-round, daily. Cholula.

San Anton Falls. A scenic falls featuring a walkway that has been carved into the rock behind the cascade. On a ledge above the falls is the tiny potters' village of San Antonio, home of the famous Cuernavaca pottery. Cuernavaca, 1.5 kilometers south, off Highway 95D.

Tule Tree. A giant ahuehuete that is thought to be from 2,000 to 3,000 years old; measuring 50 meters high and 49 meters around at the base. In the village of El Tule, near Oaxaca, on Highway 190.

Tuxpango Reservoir. Near this impounded lake you'll find a cable railway that drops along a 70-degree grade to the small village of Tuxpanga. Open year-round, daily, 6:30 a.m. to 7 p.m. (hours may be irregular). For a few coins, the boys from the village will entertain visitors by sliding down the cable rails on a tire-rim. The boys' descent takes about one minute; the cable car about 10 minutes. Orizaba, off Highway 150.

Valenciana Mine. Discovered in 1760, this is one of Mexico's richest silver mines. It was reactivated about 10 years ago and now produces lead and nickel ore, as well as silver. Open year-round. Guanajuato, off Highway 110, across from the Church of La Valenciana.

Highlight

The Corrida de Toros

Hemingway once said that there are two types of spectators at the *corrida de toros:* those who identify with the matador and those who identify with the bull. If you are among the latter group, you probably shouldn't attend a bullfight. However, if you can appreciate the traditions of the arena, you will probably enjoy the pageantry of this Sunday afternoon spectacle.

Bullfighting is thought to have originated on the Isle of Crete in the Mediterranean, more than 2,000 years before the birth of Christ. It was carried to Spain by the Moors in the 12th

Museums and Historical Sites

Alhondiga de Granaditas. A massive structure that now houses a museum. During the War for Independence, the royalists of Guanajuato held out here until the door was set afire and the building was overrun by revolutionaries. Open year-round, Tuesday to Sunday, 9 a.m. to 2 p.m. and 4 p.m. to 7 p.m. Guanajuato, Mendizabel and Cinco de Mayo.

Anahuacalli. A black-lava building that houses more than 50,000 items of pre-Hispanic art, representing the various cultures of Mexico. Open year-round, Tuesday to Saturday, 10 a.m. to 1 p.m. and 3 p.m. to 6 p.m. Mexico City, at Calle Tecuila 150, off Division del Norte.

Archaelogical and Historical Museum of Yucatan. This museum features a fine collection of Mayan relics. Open year-round, Monday to Saturday, 8 a.m. to 2 p.m. Merida, on Paseo de Montejo.

---

century, and the Spaniards in turn brought it to Mexico, holding the first bullfight in 1529. Originally the province of the aristocracy, bullfighting was taken over by professionals in the 18th century following a series of tragic accidents.

The customs and traditions of bullfighting have changed little over the years. The prologue to the bullfight begins with the formal seating of the official in charge, who then raises his hand to signal the start of the pageant. As the music rings out, the *alguacil,* or constable of the ring, rides to the official, removes his hat and seeks permission for the fight to begin. He then withdraws, leaving the arena to the richly garbed *matadores,* who parade into the ring followed by a retinue of *banderilleros, picadores* and ring attendants. After doffing their hats before the official, the participants form a semicircle at the edge of the arena. Then, with great ceremony, the matadors remove their elegant capes and fling them to friends in the first row, who drape them over the railing of the arena.

Following these opening ceremonies, the bullfighting begins with the first of the *tercios.* This consists of the passing of the bull by enticing him with the cape, and the work of the picadores, who prick the bull with a long pole. The second tercio involves the placing of the banderillas — short lances decorated with brightly colored paper. The purpose of this is to weaken the muscles that support the bull's head, forcing him to keep his head lowered and thus facilitating the kill. The final tercio, and the most important, consists of passing the bull with the *muleta,* a red cloth mounted on a stick, over the sword. During this phase of the fight, the matadors perform some of their most artistic maneuvers, usually concluding with a chest pass, when the bull's horns almost scrape the chest of the matador. When the bull appears to be slowing down, the matador moves in for the kill.

At the end of a good fight, the matador will be called to the center of the ring for a bow. If the matador has shown great skill and daring, he may receive one or both of the bull's ears as a token of approval. For an exceptional performance, the matador may receive both ears and a tail. When the triumphant matador makes his tour of the ring, it is customary to throw flowers, wine flasks, jackets and hats to him. (Never throw a seat cushion; it is an insult and illegal.)

A typical corrida consists of six bullfights, with each of three matadors fighting two bulls. Bullfights are scheduled on Sundays and holidays during a season that runs from November through March. Less experienced *toreros* take part in bullfights that are held the remainder of the year.

Bello Museum. Houses ornate furniture, paintings, ironwork, glassware and gold and silver artifacts. Open year-round, daily, 10 a.m. to 5 p.m. Puebla, on Avenue 3.

Buena Vista Battlefield. At this site, on February 22, 1847, a U.S. force under the command of General Zachary Taylor crushed the army of Mexico's dictator, Santa Anna. Near Saltillo.

Chapultepec Castle. Standing on a hill that was once the seat of government for the Aztec emperors, this castle was completed in 1840 and made the home of Mexico's Military College. The Americans seized it in an attack in 1847, and Maximilian chose it as his royal residence in 1866. Now a museum, the castle contains relics of Maximilian, including magnificent tapestries and furnishings. Other historic points of interest and memorials are a part of the castle, which also served as the site of the Inter-American Conference on Problems of War and Peace, in 1945. Open year-round, Monday and Wednesday to Saturday, 9 a.m. to 5:30 p.m.; Sunday, 10 a.m. to 1:30 p.m. Mexico City, in Chapultepec Park, on Paseo de la Reforma.

Convent of St. Matthew. Built in 1678 on the ruins of an ancient temple, this structure has been restored and converted to a museum containing colonial art and coaches. Open year-round, Tuesday to Sunday, 10 a.m. to 5 p.m. Churubusco.

Cuicuilco Pyramid. Constructed more than 2,500 years ago, this pyramid is 118 meters in diameter and 18 meters high; small museum nearby. Open year-round, daily, 9 a.m. to 5 p.m. Tlalpan, 2.5 kilometers west.

Frida Kahlo Museum. The home of artist Frida Kahlo and her muralist husband, Diego Rivera, from 1929 until their deaths in the 1950s. Museum now displays the works and personal effects of both artists. Open year-round, daily, 10 a.m. to 6 p.m. Coyoacan, Londres 127 at Calle Allende.

Government Palace. This Spanish baroque building, built in 1643, was the site of Hidalgo's decree abolishing slavery. It now houses murals by Orozco and a number of artifacts. Guadalajara, facing the Plaza Mayor.

Monastery of San Agustin Acolman. This fortress-like structure contains frescoes depicting the life of St. Augustine and a small state museum. Open year-round, daily (except Friday), 10 a.m. to 5 p.m. Acolman.

National Museum of Natural History. Made up of 10 enormous interconnecting domes that include exhibits on geology, astronomy, biology and the origins of life; electronic guide system. Open year-round, Tuesday to Sunday, 9 a.m. to 4 p.m. Mexico City, in southwest section of Chapultepec Park, off Paseo de la Reforma.

National Palace. Built on the site of Mayan Emperor Montezuma's palace by Cortez, formerly the official residence of the viceroys until the establishment of the Republic. The palace now contains murals by Diego Rivera, Mexico's Independence Bell and many furnishings from the reign of Maximilian. Open year-round, Tuesday to Sunday, 9 a.m. to 5 p.m. Mexico City, on east side of the Zocalo, on Moneda Zapata.

Quinta Luz. A 50-room mansion that was the home of Pancho Villa, outlaw — hero of the Mexican Revolution. The home is now a museum that contains Villa memorabilia, including the bullet-riddled car in which he was ambushed and killed. Open year-round, Monday to Saturday, 10 a.m. to 2 p.m. and 4 p.m. to 6 p.m. Chihuahua, at Calle 10 Norte 3014.

San Francisco Cathedral. One of the oldest churches in Mexico, founded in 1529 by Cortez. Open year-round, daily. Cuernavaca, on Avenida Morelos.

San Francisco Church and Convent. Built in 1629, this building is an excellent example of colonial architecture. Open year-round, daily. Celaya.

Tenayuca Pyramid. Originally part of the Chichimec Empire, this site was later occupied by Alcolhuas, Tepanecs and Aztecs. The 52 plumed serpents that adorn the three sides of the pyramid's base correspond to the Aztec cycle of 52 years. Some experts believe that the pyramid was used as an astronomical observatory. Open year-round, daily, 8 a.m. to 6 p.m. Tlalnepantla, 3.3 kilometers east.

Tepozteco Pyramid. Reached by a rather difficult climb on a steep path, this pyramid, built by the Tlahuica Indians, honors Tepoztecatl, the god credited with creating *pulque,* a fermented drink. Tepozotlan.

Teopanzolco Pyramid. Probably built by the Aztecs, this pyramid was discovered during the Mexican Revolution of 1910 when a large hill on the outskirts of Cuernavaca was used as an artillery base for attacks on that city. Vibrations from the gunfire shook away some of the earth, exposing the pyramid. Open year-round, daily. Cuernavaca.

Tepanapa Pyramid. The scene of active archaeological diggings, this pyramid measures 402 meters at the base and contains more than eight kilometers of lighted tunnels. Views from the top of the pyramid site are excellent. Guides available. Open year-round, daily, 9 a.m. to 1 p.m. and 2 p.m. to 4 p.m. Cholula.

Viceregal Museum. This museum in a Jesuit seminary houses three centuries of colonial and religious art. Treasures include rare 16th-century vestments, altar hangings from the National Cathedral and a painting of the Blessed Virgin attributed to Murillo. Open year-round, Tuesday to Sunday, 10 a.m. to 6 p.m. Tepotzotlan.

Ruins

Casas Grandes Ruins. First explored in the 1880s, this site contains traces of the Pueblo culture of the Rio Grande Valley and the Mesoamerican culture of the Central Mexican Plateau. The last inhabitants of the area were the Paquime Indians, from 1300 to 1500 A.D. Open year-round, daily, 9 a.m. to 5 p.m. Nuevo Casas Grandes, 7.25 kilometers south.

Chichen Itza Ruins. The remains of a great Mayan City and one of the archaeological wonders of the world, these ruins contain richly carved pyramids, shrines and temples covering a 9.75-kilometer area. This city was probably founded between 360 and 435 A.D., and is thought to have fallen to the Toltecs about 900 A.D. The Toltecs abandoned it in 1200 A.D. The central feature is the Great Plaza Castle, a nine-level stepped-pyramid topped by a temple. Within this Toltec shell is an older Mayan pyramid that houses the famous limestone jaguar with jade eyes and a Chac Mool. East of the castle is the Court of the Thousand Columns and the Temple of the Warriors. Allow at least two days for a complete tour of the ruins. Guides for tours may be hired in Merida, 121 kilometers west on Highway 180. Open year-round, daily, 6 a.m. to 6 p.m. Admission charged, fee for parking. Chichen Itza, off Highway 180.

Chicomoztoc Ruins. Partially restored, these ruins reveal the narrow streets and foundations of the homes and temples of the Nahuatlacas Indians who occupied this valley in 1170 A.D. Open year-round, daily, 9 a.m. to 5 p.m. Zacatecas, off Highway 54.

Mitla Ruins. Elaborate cut-stonework ruins built by the Zapotecs and later occupied by the Mixtecs. Featured is the Hall of Columns that has six enormous columns, each fashioned from a single stone. Open year-round, daily, 9 a.m. to 5 p.m. Mitla, about 0.75 kilometers north of the town plaza.

Monte Alban Ruins. Once a major religious city built between 800 B.C. and 1500 A.D. by the Zapotec Indians. The site contains the Great Plaza, about 297 meters long and 198 meters wide, and includes terraces, ballcourts, dwellings, tombs and giant staircases. Open year-round, daily, during daylight hours. Oaxaca, 8.75 kilometers southwest on a narrow, winding road.

Palmillas Ruins. Consisting of two unreconstructed pyramids of river boulders. At the base of the pyramids, there is a ground-hugging weed called vergonzosa — "The Bashful" — that folds its green, fernlike leaves at the slightest touch. Open year-round, daily. Cuitlahuac, off Highway 150.

Tulum Ruins. The remains of a Mayan city that flourished in the 14th century containing 60 well-preserved buildings. Open year-round, daily. On the Quintana Roo mainland across from Cozumel Island.

Uxmal Ruins. Ruins that include buildings adorned with elaborate stone carvings, the Governor's Palace, the House of Nuns and El Adivino Pyramid. The city is believed to have been founded about 1007 A.D. as part of the Mayan culture. Open year-round, daily, 6 a.m. to 6 p.m. Uxmal, off Highway 261.

Xochicalo Ruins. Covering a 15.5-kilometer area, these ruins are believed to have been an important ceremonial center about 500 years before the Spanish occupation. Artwork on the structures gives evidence of Toltec, Mayan and Zapotecan influence. One of the chambers contains a "telescope" orifice through which the astrologer-priests were able to determine the arrival of the summer solstice. Open year-round, daily, sunrise to sunset. Cuernavaca, 37 kilometers southwest, off Highway 421, on a paved road that winds to the top of the mountain.

Zaachila Ruins. This site is the first capital city of the Zapotecan Empire, built between 700 and 1050 A.D. Guides available in Oaxaca. Open year-round, daily, sunrise to sunset. Oaxaca, across the Atoyac River, via the Monte Alban Road.

Zempoala Ruins. A former Totonac ceremonial center that houses six main structures including the Great Pyramid, made of river stones, and the Temple of the Chimneys. Open year-round, daily. Zempoala, on the north edge of the town.

Mexico's Calendar of Events

Spring
(March, April, May)

Holy Week. March or April, celebrated throughout Mexico.

Annual Strawberry Fair. Fireworks, crowning of festival queen, bullfights, exhibits. March, Guanajuato.

Festival of San Idelfonso. Fireworks, serenades, games. April, Izamal, Yucatan.

Fair of St. Mark. One of the most important religious festivals in the country. April, Aguascalientes.

Annual Flower Festival. April, Veracruz.

Festival of the Holy Christ. April, Chumayel, Yucatan.

Labor Day, May 1, celebrated throughout Mexico.

Feast of the Holy Cross. Native dances. May, Valle de Bravo.

Prayers for Rain and Good Harvest. May, Ozumba.

Day of San Isidro. Patron saint of rain and livestock. May, celebrated throughout Mexico.

Spring Festival. May, Juchitan, Oaxaca.

Festival of the Hammocks. May, Tecoh, Yucatan.

In December, all Mexico comes alive in a blaze of festive lights to celebrate the feast of Our Lady of Guadalupe.

Summer
(June, July, August)

Navy Day. June, celebrated in various ports.
Corpus Christi Day. June, celebrated throughout Mexico.
Festival of St. Fermin. July, Comitan, Chiapas.
St. Mary Magdalen Festival. Native dances, parades. July, Uruapan, Michoacan.
Grape Fair. August, celebrated throughout Mexico.
Dances on Cuauhtemoc. August, Mexico City.
Festival of St. Augustine. August, Puebla.
Festival of La Morisma. Reenactment of battles between the Moors and Christians. August, Zacatecas.

Fall
(September, October, November)

Native Dances. September, Atlixco.
Independence Day. September, celebrated throughout Mexico.
Annual Cotton Fair. October, Ciudad Delicias, Chihuahua.
Fiesta of Our Lady of the Rosary. October, Alvarado, Veracruz.
Columbus Day. October, Guadalajara and Zapopan.
All-Souls Day. November, celebrated throughout Mexico.
Native Dancing. November, Texcoco.

Winter
(December, January, February)

Fiesta of Our Lady of Health. December, Patzcuaro, Michoacan.
Feast of Our Lady of Guadalupe. December, celebrated throughout Mexico.
Christmas Week Celebrations. December, Mexico City, Oaxaca, San Miguel de Allende.
Day of the Three Kings. Mexican children receive their Christmas presents on this day, which is celebrated with native dances and other special events. January, throughout Mexico.
Celebration of the Virgin of Buctozotz. January, Temax.
St. Anthony's Day. Children all over Mexico take their animals to church to be blessed. January.
Fiesta of Santa Prisca. Fairs, dancing. January, Taxco.
San Sebastian Day. Fairs and folk dances. January, Chiapa del Corzo, Leon, Guanajuato.
Carnaval. February or March, Mazatlan, Merida, Veracruz.
Dia de la Candelaria. February, celebrated throughout Mexico.

CANADA
VICTORIA R.I.
Victoria B.C.
7
"Calgary Stampede"
Saskatchewan Grain Elevators
Alert Bay, British Columbia

Chateau Frontenac
Quebec city
R. McKee
Changing the Guard on Parliament Hill-Ottawa
St. Joseph's Oratory-Montreal
Charlevoix Windmill
Toronto City Hall

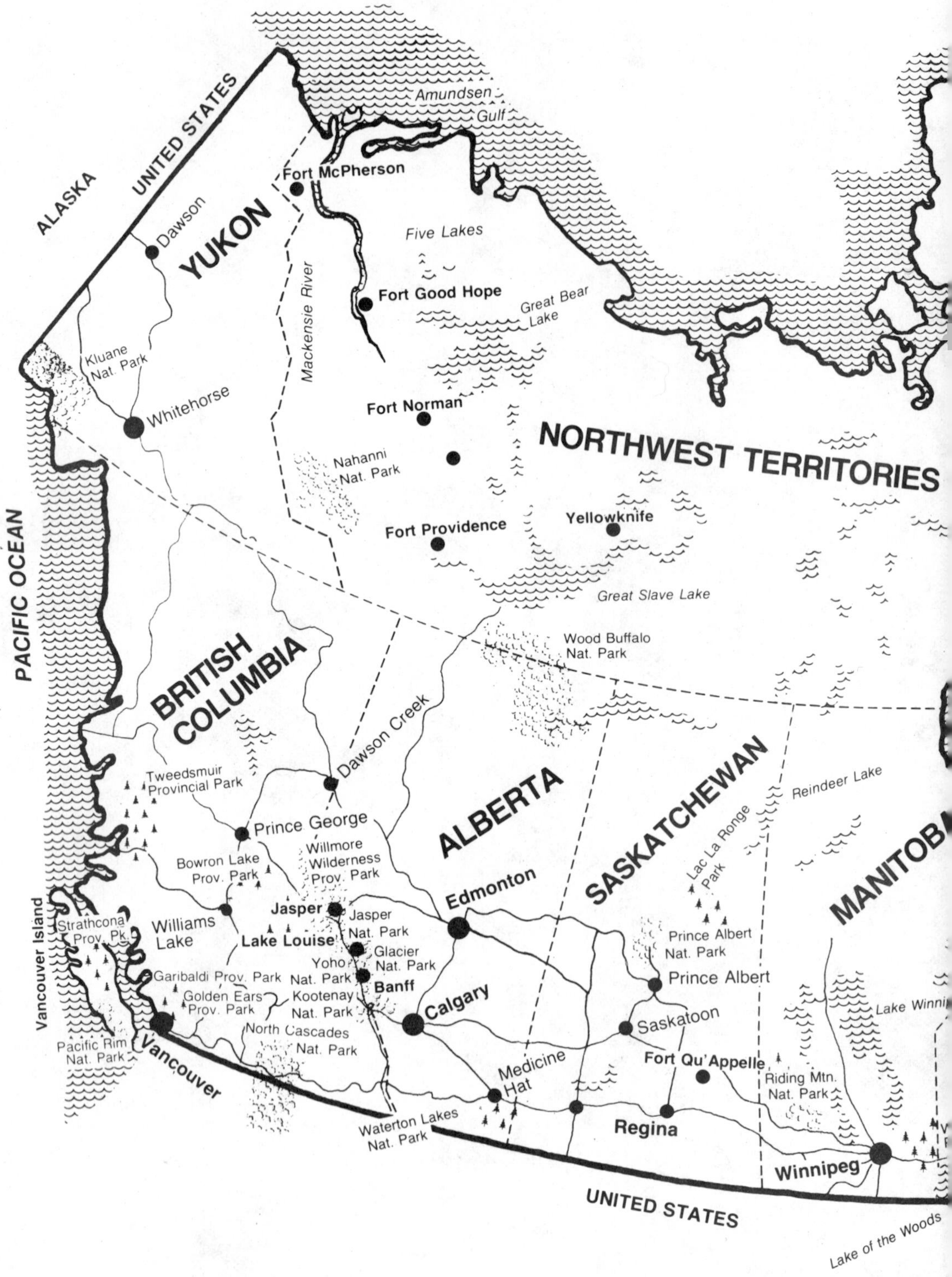

Map not to exact scale.

Hudson Strait
Labrador Sea
Ungava Bay
Hudson Bay
Goose Bay
NEWFOUNDLAND
St. Anthony
St. Johns
QUEBEC
James Bay
Port Cartier
Sept-Iles Park
Anticosti Island
St. Lawrence River
Gulf of St. Lawrence
Chibougamau Reserve
Haute Mauricie Res.
Laurentide Park
Chicoutini Park
Prince Edward Island
Cape Breton Highlands Nat. Park
Sydney
NEW BRUNSWICK
NOVA SCOTIA
Fundy Nat. Park
Halifax
Fredrickton
Kejimkujik Nat. Park
TARIO
Lake Nipigon
De La Verendrye Res.
Quebec
Lake Superior Prov. Park
Pukaskwa Nat. Park
North Bay
Ottawa
Montreal
Sault Ste. Marie
Lake Superior
Algonquin Prov. Park
UNITED STATES
ATLANTIC OCEAN
Lake Huron
Toronto
Sarnia
London
Lake Ontario
Lake Erie
N

Canada

Canada

Touring Canada by RV is a convenient, comfortable and enjoyable way to discover everything there is to see and do across this magnificent land. Whether you drive the paved highways or venture off the beaten path to explore the unspoiled backcountry, you're sure to find superb scenery and fascinating landmarks at almost every turn, together with a friendly people who are anxious to help you enjoy your visit.

The 10th-century Norseman Leif Ericsson was probably the first white man to set foot on Canadian soil, briefly establishing a settlement at the tip of Newfoundland's great northern peninsula. With the Norse eventually driven out by hostile Indians, several hundred years elapsed before other Europeans — John Cabot, Jacques Cartier, Henry Hudson — returned to explore the region. But it wasn't until the initial explorations in 1604 of Samuel de Champlain that serious efforts were again made to colonize Canada.

After enduring a number of hardships and returning to France to report his discoveries, Champlain came back to Canada in 1608 to establish the first permanent settlement at Quebec. More hardships followed, including a major setback at the hands of the British, but Champlain's colony prospered and in 1634 a large group of settlers arrived at "New France."

With the settlement of Quebec firmly established, a number of other French explorers came to map the interior and establish fur trading posts throughout the Canadian West. Before long, France had firmly established its claim to all of

Capital: Ottawa
Population: 23,632,000
Major Cities: Toronto (2,849,200), Montreal (2,809,900), Vancouver (1,172,200). (Population figures are for entire metropolitan area.)
Official languages: English and French
Currency: Canadian dollar (at presstime the current rate of exchange is $1.14 = $1 in U.S. currency).

Canada. But by 1749, the French presence in North America was leading to friction with the British colonists, and in that year the French and Indian War broke out. That war was to later become part of the larger European conflict between the French and British, the Seven Years War (1756-1763). By the time those hostilities had ended, the British had defeated the French in North America and replaced the French rule in Canada.

With the outbreak of the American Revolution, the colonists tried unsuccessfully to enlist the support of the French Canadians. The Canadians, however, chose to remain neutral and this, combined with the large numbers of British Loyalists who fled to Canada during the Revolution, helped cement the allegiance to the British crown. After the British defeat in the Colonies, the U.S. government tried to stir unrest in Canada in an effort to annex that nation. For more than a century, a small band of maverick Americans tried everything from guerilla warfare to threats and invitations in an effort to unite the two countries. The few vestiges of anti-Americanism that may be left in Canada today are largely a result of those actions.

Canada's emergence as a major force in world politics began with the completion of the Canadian Pacific Railway in 1885 and the confederation of the provinces. Spurred by an abundance of natural resources, Canada's economy began to boom, and following the industrialization during the World War I years, Canada gained worldwide recognition as an emerging power. In 1931, Canada was granted independence within the British Commonwealth of Nations. Despite some setbacks during the depression of the 1930s, Canada has continued to prosper and today it has one of the world's strongest economies.

Geographically, Canada can be divided into five regions — the West, the Prairie Region, Ontario, Quebec and Atlantic Canada. Within each of these regions you'll find a wide variety of offerings.

The West

British Columbia, the Yukon Territory, the Northwest Territories and Alberta want you to see firsthand the bounty of this region. British Columbia is 366,000 square miles of beautiful, natural attractions and offers mountains, valleys, rivers and the sea. Alberta stretches over 246,000 square miles, an interesting province of mountains and prairie. The Yukon Territory (208,000 square miles), a land first opened to settlement as a result of gold-seekers and would-be prospectors, is still a challenging frontier. The Northwest Territories cover more than 1,300,000 square miles. The roads to adventure in Canada's virgin Northwest Territories lead to unique forts and towns, and to great unspoiled wilderness.

The Prairie

Canada's "bread basket" region stretches through Alberta, Saskatchewan and Manitoba. Alberta (246,000 square miles), is known as the country's energy province because of its vast quantities of oil. Saskatchewan, the province in which the buffalo once roamed freely and where the mounted police brought peace to the West, is an ideal destination for vacationers interested in excellent campsites and abundant provincial and national parkland. Saskatchewan's 252,000 square miles accommodates parks like Prince Albert National Park: prairie grasslands and boreal forest with swimming, boating, nature tours, campfire talks and paddle-wheeler rides.

Manitoba (251,000 square miles), is the friendly province. The International Peace Garden, shared by Manitoba and North Dakota, symbolizes the friendship between Canada and the United States and the general spirit of the province.

Ontario

A place to grow. Ontario's 413,000 square miles is a treasure box of events, attractions, great restaurants, interesting cities and fun things to do both indoors and outdoors. The province's cities — Thunder Bay, London, Sault Ste. Marie, Kingston, Ottawa, Hamilton, Toronto, Stratford — serve up an extensive variety of activities like a well-planned menu. Ontario's recreational facilities are staggering: water-skiing, boating and swimming, numerous lakes, as well as great camping in large, well-organized parks like Algonquin Provincial Park, a wilderness park also offering excellent fishing and canoeing. Art and culture are revered throughout the province's exceptional theater centers and museums. Ontario's highway system is excellent, leading you in and out of cities and towns that testify to the region's thriving industry and superlative facilities.

Quebec

The province with flair and spirit. Throughout this region's 595,000 square miles, you'll discover a curious mixture of old and new. Here lies part of the province's charm. Montreal, Canada's second-largest metropolitan center, which is located on the shore of the St. Lawrence River, is the city which hosted the international Expo '67 and 1976 Olympic Games and one in which you can travel by subway or horse-drawn *caleche.* Vibrant and "vivant," Quebec is a must if your interests include theater, handicrafts, fine cuisine, great camping and fishing, historic attractions or simply a good time.

Atlantic Canada

The tang of salt air lets you know that you've reached Canada's Atlantic coast. Nova Scotia, New Brunswick, Prince Edward Island and Newfoundland await you. They're accessible but not spoiled and welcome you with down-east hospitality. Atlantic Canada is not large — Nova Scotia, 21,000 square miles; New Brunswick, 28,000 square miles; Prince Edward Island, 2,200 square miles; and Newfoundland, 151,000 square miles — but its potential to please is enormous. If you'd like to scuba dive, play a few rounds of golf, take the children to historic forts and villages, sail the ocean blue or feast on seafood delicacies, this is the region for you.

Tourism Office

Canadian Government Office of Tourism
235 Queen Street
Ottawa, Ontario, Canada K1A OH6

General Weather Information and Seasons

Vacation seasons

Spring — Mid-March to mid-May
Summer — Mid-May to mid-September
Autumn — Mid-September to Mid-November
Winter — Mid-November to mid-March

Note: *During winter months, all main highways are snowplowed and usually free of snow.*

Month	Weather and Suggested Clothing
January and February	General winter temperatures. Winter apparel (overcoat, hat, footwear, gloves). Snow in most provinces. Excellent months to enjoy winter activities. Motorists should ensure cars are winterized.
March	Moderate temperatures. Winter apparel with some mediumweight wear. Snow begins to disappear; however, in main winter vacation areas, winter activities may still be enjoyed. Cars should still be winterized.
April	Days become milder but evenings cool. Mediumweight apparel including topcoat. Snow disappears — however, some of the higher mountainous areas still offer spring skiing.
May	Warmer in daytime — cool at night. Mediumweight and summer apparel. Enjoyable period for those who prefer spring travel. The country is green again and spring flowers are in bloom by middle of the month.

June Warm temperatures. Summer clothing with some mediumweight wear as a precaution against cool evenings. Ideal for summer travel. All summer outdoor activities.

July and Aug. Normally warmest months of summer. Summer clothing. Ideal for summer travel. Summer activities in all areas.

Sept. Days warm with evenings cool. Summer clothing along with mediumweight wear. Ideal for autumn travel. In most areas, foliage takes on fall coloring around September 20. Ideal for color photography.

Oct. Cool temperatures. Mediumweight apparel including topcoat. Excellent weather for autumn vacation. Leaves and other foliage in full autumn color during early part of this month. Many wonderful opportunities for color photography.

Nov. Cool — frosty. Mediumweight apparel including topcoat. First signs of winter. Late season travel usually good. Motorists should have cars winterized. First snow generally appears.

Dec. Winter temperatures. Winter apparel as in January. Winter season. Under normal conditions, first heavy snows arrive around December, usually the start of winter sports activities. Motorists should ensure cars are winterized.

Some important traffic signs

Most traffic signs in Canada are easy to understand from their inscriptions. Others are self-explanatory. Examples:

Drive on the right — No left turn — Children at play — School — Winding road — Right turn — Railway crossing — Sharp turn

Canadian road speed limits are posted in kilometers per hour (km/h). Note the following examples:

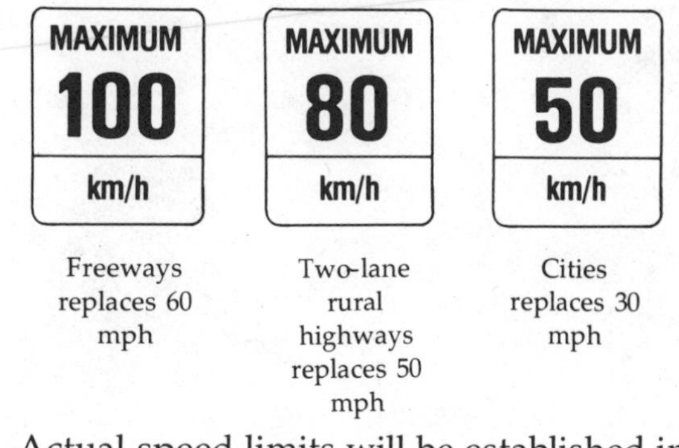

Freeways replaces 60 mph — Two-lane rural highways replaces 50 mph — Cities replaces 30 mph

Actual speed limits will be established in accordance with local regulations.

Entry Into Canada

Citizens or permanent residents of the United States can cross the U.S.-Canada border either way, usually without difficulty or delay. They do not require passports or visas. However, to assist officers of both countries in speeding the crossing, native-born U.S. citizens should carry some identifying paper such as a birth, baptismal or voter's certificate which shows their citizenship. Proof of residence may also be required. Naturalized U.S. citizens should carry a naturalization certificate or some other evidence of citizenship, in case they are asked for it. Permanent residents of the United States who are not American citizens are advised to have their Alien Registration Receipt Card (U.S. Form 1-151 or Form 1-551).

Insurance-Vehicle

U.S. motorists planning to travel in Canada are advised to obtain a Canadian Non-Resident Inter-provincial Motor Vehicle Liability Insurance Card which provides evidence of financial responsibility by a valid automobile liability insurance policy. This card is available only in the United States through U.S. insurance agents. All provinces in Canada require visiting motorists to produce evidence of financial responsibility should they be involved in an accident. Financial responsibility limits vary by province.

Information and advice regarding automobile insurance may be obtained from the Insurance Bureau of Canada, 181 University Avenue, Toronto, Ontario, Canada, M5H 3M7.

New Brunswick's capital, Fredericton, stands on the site of an old French village that later became a settlement for Loyalists who fled the U.S. at the end of the Revolutionary War.

Returning to the United States

After less than 48 hours

Residents of the United States visiting Canada for less than 48 hours may take back, for personal or household use, merchandise to the fair retail value of $10 free of U.S. duty and tax. Any or all of the following may be included, so long as the total value does not exceed $10: 50 cigarettes, 10 cigars (non-Cuban in origin), 224 gm (eight ounces) of manufactured tobacco, 112 ml (four ounces) of alcoholic beverages, or 112 ml (four ounces) of alcoholic perfume. However, if 112 ml (four ounces) of alcoholic perfume are purchased, no tobacco or alcoholic beverages may be included.

If any article brought back is subject to duty or tax, or if the total value of all articles exceeds $10, no article may be exempted from duty or tax. Members of a family household are not permitted to combine the value of their purchases under this exemption.

After more than 48 hours

United States residents returning from Canada may take back, once every 30 days, merchandise for personal or household use to the value of $100 free of United States duty and tax, provided they have remained in Canada 48 hours. The exemption will be based on the fair retail value of the article acquired.

The Skylon Tower in Calgary, Alberta (above), is a 520-foot tower with a revolving restaurant on top and glass highspeed elevators. (Right) The Provincial Archives in New Brunswick offers an ideal starting place for RVers searching for their family roots. Archives contain hundreds of records and geneological aids.

Goods must accompany the resident upon arrival in the United States. Members of a family household traveling together may combine their personal exemptions — thus a family of five could be entitled to a total exemption of $500. Up to 100 cigars (non-Cuban in origin) per person may be imported into the United States by U.S. residents. One quart, 910 ml (32 ounces U.S.) of alcoholic beverages may be imported if the resident has attained the age of 21 years. There is no limitation on the number of cigarettes that anyone, regardless of his age, may import for his personal use. If, however, the state laws of residence prohibit importation of any such goods, U.S. Customs will not clear them.

Boats and Recreational Vehicles

Under a permit issued by Canada Customs, visitors to Canada may temporarily import boats, motors, trailers, etc., for personal use for the duration of their visit, on the condition that all such articles will be re-exported at the conclusion of the visit or at the end of the season. A boat, motor or tracked snow vehicle may be retained in Canada beyond the normal period of use only when legitimate repairs or maintenance work is to be undertaken by a bona fide marina or service depot during the off-season. Under this procedure, the owner must provide a copy of the work order or a written statement from the individual or firm who will be effecting the repairs, indicating a description of the article, the name and address of the owner, the type of repair work to be done, as well as the time and location at which the work will be effected.

Pets

Dogs and cats from the United States must be accompanied by a certificate, signed by a licensed veterinarian of

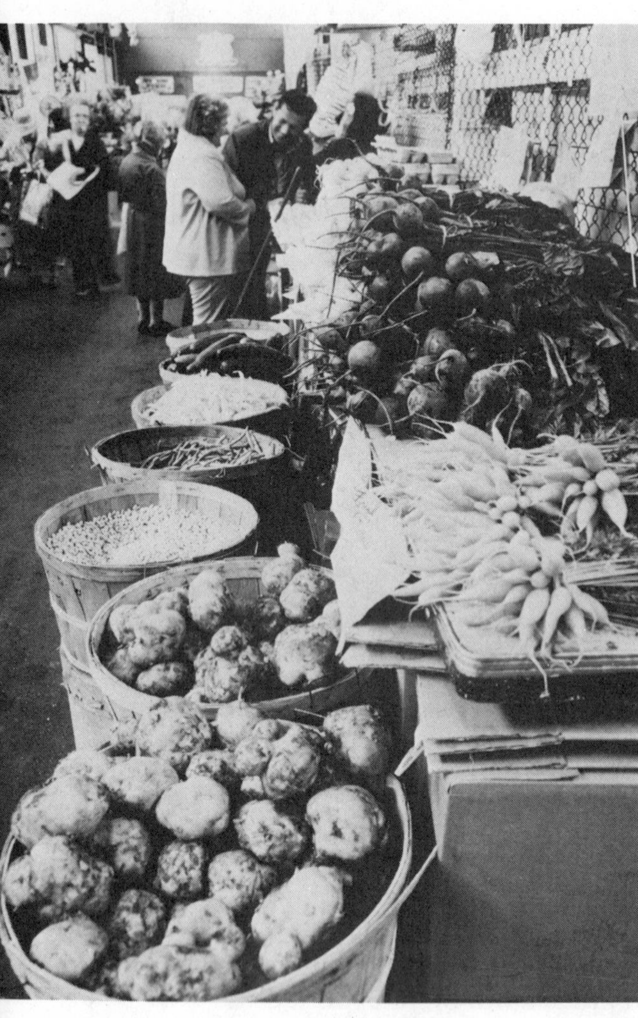

Loyalist City Market in St. John, New Brunswick, is Canada's oldest common law market privilege, where local farmers come to sell their wares.

Canada or the United States, certifying that the dog or cat has been vaccinated against rabies during the preceding 36 months. Such a certificate shall carry an adequate and legible description of the dog or cat and date of vaccination and shall be initialled by the inspecting official at the Customs port-of-entry and returned to the owner. Puppies or kittens from the United States under three months of age may be imported into Canada without a rabies vaccination.

Metric Conversions

(km) kilometer	=	0.62 (mi) mile
(m) meter	=	1.09 (yd) yard
(m) meter	=	3.28 (ft) foot
(cm) centimeter	=	0.39 (in) inch
(sq km) square kilometer	=	0.386 (sq mi) square mile
(ha) hectare	=	0.405 (ac) acre
(t) metric ton	=	1.10 (tn) ton
(kg) kilogram	=	2.2 (lb) pound
(1) liter	=	0.88 (qt) Canadian quart
(1) liter	=	0.22 (gal) Canadian gallon
(1) liter	=	0.264 (gal) American gallon
(mi) mile	=	1.61 (km) kilometer
(yd) yard	=	0.914 (m) meter
(ft) foot	=	0.304 (m) meter
(in) inch	=	2.45 (cm) centimeter
(sq mi) square mile	=	2.59 (sq km) square kilometer
(ac) acre	=	0.405 (ha) hectare
(tn) ton	=	0.91 (t) metric ton
(lb) pound	=	0.454 (kg) kilogram
(qt) Canadian quart	=	1.14 (1) liter
(gal) Canadian gallon	=	4.55 (1) liter
(gal) American gallon	=	3.7 (1) liter

Canada Points of Interest and Attractions

Alberta

Calgary Centennial Planetarium. Shows on the solar system; lectures, slides, films. Open year-round, daily, 10:30 a.m. to 10 p.m. Admission $1.50 (afternoon show), $2.50 (evening show). Calgary, 11th Street and Seventh Avenue, Southwest.

Calgary Tower. An observation tower that provides a panoramic view of the city and nearby Rocky Mountains; restaurant. Open year-round, daily, 8 a.m. to 11 p.m. Adults $1.50, children 6 to 12, 75 cents. Calgary, Ninth Avenue at Center Street, South.

Calgary Zoo and Dinosaur Park. An extensive collection of mammals, birds and reptiles; children's zoo, dinosaur replicas. Open year-round, daily, 9.a.m. to 5 p.m. Adults $1.50, children 12 to 17, 75 cents, under 12, 25 cents. Calgary, Memorial Drive and 12th Street, East.

Frank Slide. Site of a disaster that struck the community in 1903, when a gigantic wedge of rock crashed down from nearby Turtle Mountain. More than 90 million tons of rock swept over 1.5 kilometers, destroying much of the town and killing 70 of the residents. Frank, on the east side in the Crowsnest Pass.

Jasper Sky Tram. Carries passengers up Whistler's Mountain in enclosed aerial cars; nature trails, observation platform, restaurant at top. Operates mid-May to Thanksgiving, daily, 8 a.m. to 9 p.m. Adults $4.25, children 6 to 14, $1.75. In Jasper National Park, off Highway 93 and Whistler Mountain Road.

Rocky Mountain Raft Tours. Scenic two-hour raft trips on the Athabasca River. Operates June 21 through September 20, from 9:30 a.m. Adults $15, children $7.75. Obtain tickets at Jasper Park Lodge in Jasper National Park.

Tar Island River Cruises and Camps. Overnight cruises to an island in the Peace River that includes accommodations and meals; wildlife, fishing. Operates June through September, daily, at 2:30 p.m. Adults $45, children 6 to 12, $30, under 6, $20. Peace River, 10004 100th Street (Shell Gas Station).

British Columbia

Butchart Gardens. Features a sunken garden, English Rose Garden, Japanese Garden, Italian Garden; live entertainment, light displays. Open spring through fall, daily. Adults $4.50, children 13 to 17, $2.25, 5 to 12, $1. Victoria, 22 kilometers north.

Chinatown. Features unique oriental shops, sidewalk markets and special events. Open year-round, daily. Vancouver, East Pender Street.

Flintstones Bedrock City. A theme park featuring characters from the Flintstones cartoon and comic strip; rides, movies, miniature golf, picnic area. Open May 15 through September, daily, 9 a.m. to 7 p.m. Adults $3.45, children 3 to 12, $2.45, students and senior citizens, $2.75. Kelowna, on Highway 97 and 990 McCurdy Road.

Glass Castle. Constructed of more than 180,000 bottles; stream, bridge, fishpond. Open year-round, daily, dawn to sunset. Adults $1.50, students and senior citizens $1, children under 12, 50 cents. Duncan, on Trans-Canada Highway 1.

Glass House. A six-room house built of more than 500,000 bottles. Open May through October 15, daily, 8 a.m. to 8 p.m. Adults $1.25, students $1, children under 12, 75 cents. Boswell, on Highway 3A.

Japanese Friendship Gardens. Beautiful gardens featuring scenic pathways and cherry trees that were a gift from the people of Moriguchi, Japan. Open year-round, daily. New Westminster, on Royal Avenue.

Ksan Indian Village. An authentic Gitksan Indian Village featuring four communal houses and a carving house decorated in the style of the West Coast Indians. Open May through October 15, daily, 9 a.m. to 6 p.m. Adults $2, students 13 to 18, $1, children 6 to 12, 50 cents. Hazelton, off Highway 16.

Lava Beds and New Aiyansh Indian Village. Lava beds created by the eruption of a volcano some 300 to 400 years ago; trail leads to top of volcano. Indian village features totems and council hall. Open during summer, daily. Terrace, off Highway 16, on Col-Nell Nass Road (use caution, as road requires careful driving because of numerous turns).

Manitoba

Souris Gravel Pits. Contain large deposits of agate, jasper, dendrite, petrified wood and epidote; registration required at Rock Shop. Open May 15 through September 15, daily, 9 a.m. to 6 p.m. Admission: $2.50 per family. Souris, 206 Dickson Street.

Mennonite Village Museum. Features a replica of a Mennonite village with all buildings completely furnished; garden, stock pens, steam engine, antiques, manuscripts. Open June through September, daily, 9 a.m. to 9 p.m.; afternoons on Sunday. Adults $2, senior citizens $1, children 75 cents. Steinbach, on Highway 12.

Paddlewheel Riverboats. Offer sightseeing and dinner-dance cruises on the Red River; live entertainment. Operates May through October, daily, from 2 p.m. Fare: $3.95 to $4.95. Winnipeg, on Main Street at Redwood Avenue Bridge.

New Brunswick

Animaland. Sculptured animals in their natural settings; live animals, playground, aquarium, picnic area. Open May 15 to October 15, daily, 8 a.m. to sunset. Adults $2, children 8 to 12, $1. Sussex, on Trans-Canada Highway 2.

Opus Craft Village. A working craft village where you watch artisans demonstrate their skills; sales. Open year-round, daily during summer, 9 a.m. to 5 p.m.; remainder of year by appointment. Admission: $1. Fredericton, off Trans-Canada Highway 2 (exit 274). (506) 363-3845.

Reversing Falls Rapids. At low tide, the St. John River descends into the ocean at the bottom of a wide gorge. For a few minutes at half tide, the waters are quiet; then, with the incoming tide, the ocean waters rush upstream. In order to fully appreciate this phenomenon, you should try to see it at high, slack and low tides. Tourist office with lounge and restaurant is nearby. Open May 17 through October 15, daily, 9 a.m. to 9 p.m. Free. Saint John, off Highway 100.

Village Historique Acadien. A historic center that features some 40 buildings devoted to the Acadians, French-speaking inhabitants of New Brunswick who were expelled from the area in 1755 by the British; craft demonstrations, period costumes. Open June through August, daily, 10 a.m. to 6 p.m. Adults $3, senior citizens and children 6 to 16, $1.50. Caraquet, west on Highway 11.

Woolastock Wildlife Park. A wide variety of animals and birds native to the Atlantic region; nature trails, picnic area. Open May 15 through October 15, daily, 8 a.m. to 9 p.m. Adults $2.25, children 5 to 15, $1.25, family rate $7. Fredericton, west on Highway 2.

Newfoundland

L'Anse Aux Meadows. This area is believed to have been the site of a Viking settlement about 1000 A.D. Stories surrounding the region tell of numerous attacks on the settlement by Indians, forcing the Vikings to finally withdraw to Greenland. Open June 15 through Labor Day, daily, 9 a.m. to 8 p.m. Free. At the tip of Newfoundland's great northern peninsula.

Newfoundland Museum. Houses relics of the Beothuck Indians and plans of early French forts; paintings. Open year-round, daily, except Monday, 10 a.m. to 6 p.m. Free. St. John, on Duckworth Street.

Northwest Territories

Wood Buffalo National Park. One of the many Canadian National Parks featuring spectacular scenery, a wide variety of wildlife, boating and camping areas and several miles of hiking trails. On the border of Alberta and the Northwest Territories, off Highway 5.

A Suggested Tour

Nova Scotia's Lighthouse Route

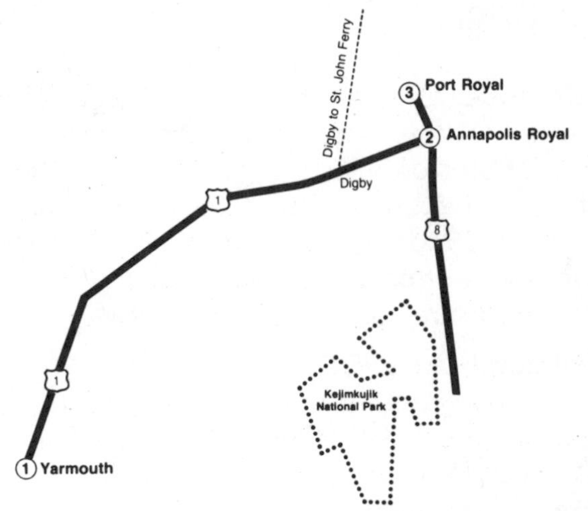

Including the famous Yarmouth Light, this tour takes you through two restored 17th-century forts and one of Canada's most productive fruit-growing regions to Digby — home of the salt herring, "Digby chicks."

1. Yarmouth. Terminal point for ferry service from Portland and Bar Harbour, Maine. Dates from 1761 when it was settled by New Englanders from Massachusetts.

Fishing is an important industry.

Yarmouth Light (lighthouse) has a striking offshore location.

Visit Yarmouth County Historical Museum, including nautical displays dating back to the Norse explorations of 1000 A.D. and the Firefighters' Museum of Nova Scotia.

Event: Western Nova Scotia Festival (July).

Contact: County Tourist Association, Yarmouth Tourist Bureau, Main Street, Yarmouth, Nova Scotia, B5A 4B1.

En route: Digby, on the Annapolis Basin, is a popular summer resort area. See the Loyalist Church of St. Edward (1784) at Clementsport.

Note: From Digby, an optional tour is available on Digby Neck to Brier Island — approximately 129 kilometers (80 miles) for the round trip.

Ferry service is available from Digby to Saint John and New Brunswick.

2. Annapolis Royal. Dating back to 1635 and overlooking Annapolis Basin.

Fort Anne National Historic Park contains 28 acres and is the site of an early Acadian settlement and a British garrison. Well-preserved earthworks, fortifications, museum and historic library are there.

Contact: Superintendent, Fort Anne National Historic Park, Annapolis Royal, Nova Scotia, B0S 1A0.

3. Port Royal. See the replica of the original Port Royal Habitation built by Champlain and De Monts in 1605.

Port Royal National Historic Park is a re-creation of the first permanent Canadian settlement including the governor's residence, guardroom, chapel, kitchen, bakery, blacksmith shop and traders' room; audio-visual presentation depicts fort life; guides.

Contact: Superintendent, Port Royal National Historic Park, PO Box 73, Granville Ferry, Annapolis Royal, Nova Scotia, B0S 1A0.

4. Kejimkujik National Park. A 140-square-mile area of lakes, forest and streams, once the winter home of Micmac Indians.

An interpretive program, including hikes, is conducted by a resident naturalist. Camping facilities year-round. Interesting plant, animal and bird life.

Contact: Superintendent, Kejimkujik National Park, Nova Scotia.

Nova Scotia

Alexander Graham Bell National Historic Park. Features displays, papers, diagrams and photos of Bell's inventions during the time he lived here. Open May 20 through October 15, daily, 9 a.m. to 9 p.m.; from October 16 through May 19, daily, 9 a.m. to 5 p.m. Free. Baddeck, on Highway 205.

Balmoral Grist Mill. One of the oldest water-powered mills in the province; flour may be purchased. Open May 15 through October 15, daily, 9:30 a.m. to 5:30 p.m. Free. Tatamagouche, off Highway 311.

Birds Islands. A 2½-hour boat ride takes visitors to these islands inhabited by seals and wildfowl. Operates May 15 through September 15, daily, from 10 a.m. Adults $6, children under 10, $3. Big Bras D'or, off Trans-Canada Highway 105.

Public Gardens. One of the finest gardens in all of Canada offering gravel walkways winding through acres of flowers and shrubs; lily ponds. Open May through October, daily, 8 a.m. to sunset. Free. Halifax, on South Park Street.

Storybook Village. Features re-creations of fairy tales and Mother Goose settings. Open mid-June through Labor Day, 9 a.m. to 7:30 p.m. Adults $1.75, children 3 to 12, $1.25. New Glasgow, 39 Bell Street.

Ontario

African Lion Safari and Game Farm. Features more than 1,000 animals and birds roaming free in a drive-thru park; no pets allowed, but free kennels are available. Open year-round, daily, 10 a.m. to 4:30 p.m. Adults $4.75, children 13 to 17 and senior citizens $3.50, 3 to 12, $2.25. Rockton, off Highway 52.

Bell Homestead. The home of Alexander Graham Bell and the site of the invention of the telephone; period furnishings, exhibits. Open year-round, Tuesday to Sunday, 10 a.m. to 6 p.m. Free. Brantford, 94 Tutela Heights Road.

Canadian Football Hall of Fame. Exhibits highlighting popular figures in Canadian football. Open year-round, daily, 9 a.m. to 5 p.m. Adults $1, senior citizens and students, 50 cents, children 6 to 14, 25 cents. Family rate $2.50. Hamilton, in City Hall Plaza.

Cobalt's Northern Ontario Mining Museum. Features exhibits tracing the history of silver mining in the area, re-creation of early prospector's camp, silver displays. Open May through October, daily 9 a.m. to 5 p.m. Adults $1, children and senior citizens, 50 cents. Cobalt, 24 Silver Street.

Crystal Beach Amusement Park. Features 30 major rides, 10 kiddie rides and games, shooting gallery, swimming, refreshment stands. Open June through September, Tuesday to Sunday, from 11 a.m. Adults $6.75, children 4 to 11, $4.75. Fort Erie, on Regional Road 28.

Floral Clock. Made up of thousands of colorful blooms; keeps accurate time and chimes every 15 minutes. Open year-round, daily. Free. Niagara Falls, at Sir Adam Beck-Niagara Generating Station.

Fort George. This was the principal British outpost in the region until its capture by the Americans in 1813; officer's quarters, barracks, kitchen. Open mid-May through October, Monday to Friday, 8 a.m. to 4:30 p.m. Adults $1, children 7 to 12, 50 cents. Niagara-On-The-Lake, at south edge of town.

Hockey Hall of Fame. Exhibits and photos featuring the greats of hockey. Open year-round, daily, 10:30 a.m. to 5 p.m. Free. Toronto, in Exhibition Place.

International Hockey Hall of Fame. More exhibits and displays on figures in the sport of hockey. Open year-round, daily, 1 p.m. to 6 p.m. Adults $1, children 12 to 15, 50 cents. Kingston, at York and Alfred Streets.

Old Fort Erie. Originally built in 1764, this fort was the scene of several disasters as

Highlight

Canada's Capital

At the junction of the Rideau and Ottawa Rivers stands Canada's capital. On Parliament Hill, the guard changes at 10 a.m. on summer mornings (weather permitting), in the shadow of the three Gothic stone Houses of Parliament.

Ottawa's downtown is a cornucopia of major attractions including Sparks Street Mall. Several major museums, including the Bytown and Canadian War Museums, The Royal Canadian Mint, Laurier House and Rideau Hall, are open for inspection.

Thousands of people pass daily through the National Gallery of Canada and the National Film Board to view the painting and photography of Canada.

Every evening the National Arts Center features a special performance.

Ottawa boasts acres of beautiful parkland — for strolling, playing and loafing in summer, or cross-country skiing, snowshoeing and ice skating in winter. (The Rideau Canal is one of the longest ice rinks anywhere.)

On the outskirts of the city lie excellent golfing facilities and fascinating, rugged scenery.

well as an attack by American forces led by General Jacob Brown. Now completely restored, the fort features relics of the War of 1812 and guards in period uniforms. Open mid-May to mid-October, daily, 9:30 a.m. to 6 p.m. Adults $1.25, children under 13, 50 cents.

Parliament Buildings. Three Gothic structures atop Parliament Hill; tours, changing of the guard ceremony. Open year-round, daily, 9 a.m. to 4:30 p.m. Free. Ottawa.

Royal Botanical Gardens. Features a number of floral gardens, a marsh and game preserve; nature trails, interpretive center. Open year-round, Saturday and Sunday, 10 a.m. to 4:30 p.m. (Interpretive Center); park open daily, dawn to dusk. Hamilton, on western edge of the city.

Scenic Caves. Features an Ice Cave and unique formations in caverns that were once used by the Huron Indians. Open May 15 through October, daily, 8:30 a.m. to sunset. Adults $2.50, children 6 to 14, $1.25. Collingwood, on Scenic Caves Road.

Shakespeareland. Features scale replicas of 60 buildings from Stratford-On-Avon, England; fishing and boating, zoo. Open May through September, daily, 9 a.m. to 6 p.m. Adults $2.25, senior citizens and students $1.75. Stratford, on Romeo Street, North.

Prince Edward Island

Fairyland. Molded displays of children's narrated nursery rhymes spaced through a scenic pine grove; picnic area. Open June 15 through September 15, daily, 9 a.m. to sunset. Adults $2.50, children 2 to 12, $1.25. Bonshaw, on Trans-Canada Highway 1.

Green Gables. House immortalized in *Anne of Green Gables;* part of national park interpretive program. Open May 15 through September 15, daily, 9 a.m. to 9 p.m. Free. Cavendish, off Highway 6.

House of International Dolls. Features more than 1,000 dolls in national and provincial costumes. Open June 15 through September 15, daily, 9 a.m. to 9 p.m. Adults $1.25, children 12 to 18, 80 cents, under 12, 50 cents. Bonshaw, on Trans-Canada Highway 1.

Jewell's Gardens and Pioneer Village. A country gardens with structures reminiscent of a pioneer village; museum. Open June through October 15, daily, 9 a.m. to sunset. Adults $2.50, children under 14, $1.25. Charlottetown, off Highways 2 and 25.

Rainbow Valley. An amusement area that features a children's farm, boating lake and fantasy area. Open June 15 through September 15, daily, 9 a.m. to sunset. Cavendish, on Highway 6.

Quebec

Albert Gilles Copper Shop. Features a set of 50 panels depicting the life of Christ on silver plating executed by the French sculptor Albert Gilles. Open year-round, daily, 8 a.m. to 7 p.m. Free. Chateau Richer, on Highway 138.

Maison De Radio-Canada. Headquarters for the Canadian Broadcasting Company's French TV and radio studios; puppet theater, tours. Free. Montreal, 1400 Boulevard Dorchester, East.

Montmorency Park. On the site of the first Canadian parliament building. Open year-round, daily. Free. Quebec, on Rue Fort-Dauphin.

Olympic Park. The site of the 1976 summer Olympic Games; guided tours. Open year-round, daily, 9 a.m. to 5 p.m. Adults $3, children 7 to 16, $1. Montreal, in eastern part of the city.

Parc Safari Africain. A 400-acre wild animal park featuring a variety of African, North American and European animals; dolphin shows. Open May 10 through October 15, daily, 10 a.m. to 5 p.m. Adults $4.95, children 4 to 14, $3.95. Hemmingford, on Highway 202.

Quebec Zoo. Features more than 350 species of mammals and birds. Open year-round, daily, 10 a.m. to sunset. Adults $1, children 6 to 13, 25 cents. Quebec, off Highway 73.

Saskatchewan

Prairie Wildlife Center. Exhibits on the wildlife, plants and climate of Canada's vast prairie lands; self-guided trails. Open June through September, daily, 9 a.m. to 9 p.m. Free. Swift Current on Highway 1.

Royal Canadian Mounted Police Barracks. Western headquarters for the famed police force; parade daily at 1 p.m. Open year-round, daily, 8 a.m. to 5 p.m. Free. Regina, at west edge of city.

Western Development Museum. Features exhibits on pioneer life, as well as displays of automobiles, agricultural machinery and household items. Open year-round, daily, 9 a.m. to 5 p.m. Adults $1.50, children under 16, 50 cents, family rate $4. North Battleford, at junction of Highways 16 and 40.

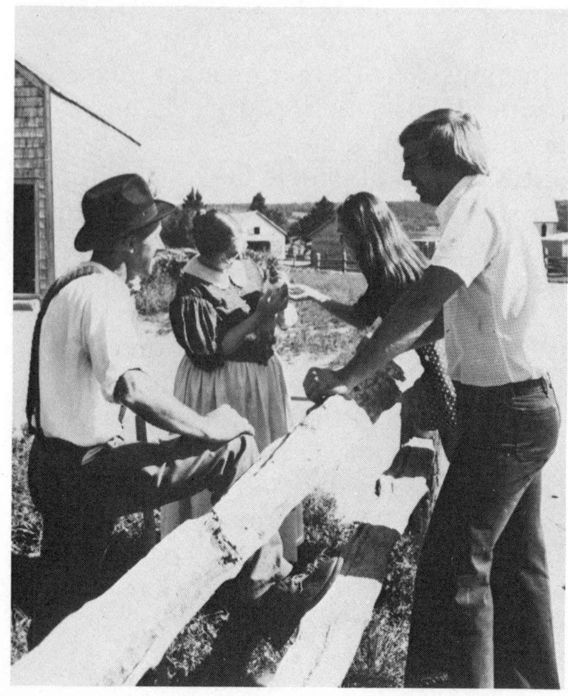

A Suggested Tour

South Shore

As with the previous tour, the South Shore tour provides an opportunity to enjoy the scenic Richelieu Valley country. But you also have the added attractions of the South Shore of the St. Lawrence River, an area of old seigniories, manors and churches.

1. Montreal.

En route: At Boucherville the manor of Pierre Boucher (1672), Lafortune House and La Chaumiere are of interest; the church here was originally built in 1801.

2. Varennes.

Attractions: Le calvaire, Beauchemin House (1770), Beauchamp House and Chaput House.

See also two procession chapels dedicated to Sainte-Anne and Saint-Joachim and the sanctuary to Mere Marguerite d'Youville, founder of the Soeurs Grises (Gray Nuns).

Contact: Hotel de Ville de Varennes, 175 Sainte-Anne, PO Box 800, Varennes, Quebec, J0L 2P0.

En route: Vercheres, a resort and farming area in a beautiful setting; see a 19th-century church and an old windmill. Contrecoeur. Tracy, where you can make an appointment to tour a Hydro-Quebec power plant; other industrial visits are available.

3. Sorel. At the mouth of the Richelieu River, Sorel is an important port, remembered for its shipbuilding during World War II.

Attractions: Chateau des Gouverneurs, former summer residence of Canada's governors-general and visiting princes; Church of Saint-Pierre (1826-30) and Christ Church.

Visit the monument at the site of Fort Saurel, and the tricentennial monument and cenotaph in carre Royal (Royal Square).

Cruises among the Iles de Sorel and the chenail du Moine.

Contact: Hotel de Ville de Sorel, 71 Charlotte Street, Sorel, Quebec, V3P 5N6.

4. Saint-Hyacinthe. Where the Market Place in the center of town is interesting.

College (1813), courthouse and cathedral form an interesting architectural setting.

See the monument to Hyacinthe Simon de Lorme.

Tours to the organ factory are available.

Event: Agricultural Fair (August).

Contact: Saint-Hyacinthe Chamber of Commerce, PO Box 217, Saint-Hyacinthe, Quebec, J2S 7B4.

History, resorts and cruises

En route: Returning to Montreal, visit Mont-Saint-Hilaire, where points of interest include a bird sanctuary and nature conservation center, Campbell Manor (the only Tudor-style residence in Canada), an 1837 church with unique frescoe done by Quebec artist, Ozias Leduc. Go to Beloeil, where you can visit Lanctot House (1792) in the cultural park and Longueuil, where you get a magnificent view of Montreal; tour the fine old buildings including the convent and Maison des Oeuvres (1815).

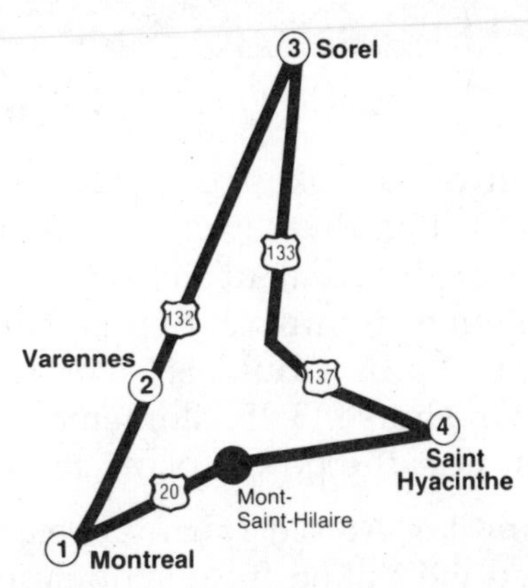

Yukon Territory

M. V. Schwatka. Takes passengers on a two-hour Yukon River excursion that passes through turbulent Miles Canyon. Operates June 15 through September 15, daily, from 2 p.m. Adults $8, children 6 to 11, $4. Whitehorse, 3.25 kilometers southeast near the power plant and dam.

S.S. Klondike. An old stern-wheeler that once plied the Yukon from Whitehorse to Dawson; tours. Open June through Labor Day, daily, 9 a.m. to 6 p.m. Whitehorse, on Second Avenue.

White Pass and Yukon Railway. A narrow-gauge railroad that winds from Whitehorse through White Pass to Skagway along an exceptionally scenic route. Operates spring through fall, daily, from Whitehorse at 9 a.m. and Skagway at 5 p.m. Fare: One-way, $49, children half-fare. (403) 667-7617.

Highlight

Gold In The Klondike

"There's gold in the Klondike!"

It was a message to lighten the heart of a world weary with economic depression. The message fell on ears deadened by the din of daily labors; on ears numbed by the nagging of wives no longer young and desirable; on ears which were always cocked to the prospect of profit to be fairly, or unfairly, gained. They say butchers dropped their aprons on the spot; druggists ground their last prescriptions; clerks tallied up their final bill of sale, or didn't tally it, depending on how strong the urge was to head for the Klondike.

Meanwhile, men who made a career of gold-digging were packing up their gold pans in camps scattered across Alaska, the Caribou country in British Columbia and the western states. The Klondike was a magnet drawing miners and non-miners from everywhere. Few of them suspected that staking along the Klondike creeks was well underway before anyone south of 60° had ever heard of the place.

By 1898, the rush was a frenzy. Half the fun was getting there — at least you'd think it was fun the way the city dudes clambered over the Chilkoot Pass with no more worry than if it had been a pile of sand. Only the most faint-hearted were daunted by the prospect of lugging the required 2,000 pounds of food and mining supplies over the 3,000-foot summit. When they reached Bennett Lake, and the challenge of building a boat to carry them to Dawson, greenhorns and able carpenters worked side by side competing with whip saws and against time to be ready to sail across Bennett as soon as the ice was out.

Down the river in droves they came, squealing with fright at the Whitehorse Rapids where 150 boats were torn by the currents in 1898 alone. With a hunger unimaginable they persisted, on to Dawson, to the Klondike . . . to gold!

In the early days of the rush, the Klondike capital was a scraggly settlement of tents and miners' shacks, but by 1900 Dawson was the largest, swankiest and sassiest burg west of Winnipeg. Gold dust spilled onto the shavings on every barroom floor and janitors got rich panning the night's sweepings. Arizona Charlie Meadows built the Palace Grand Theater in a style finer than any expected that boom town of boasting. There was a bar on every corner, and, inside, men wheeled and dealed with claims and nuggets freely as though there weren't already enough broken hearts and busted bank accounts to tell the tale. The ladies of the night were confined to Lousetown, a respectable distance from the town proper.

But one lady was welcome anywhere. She was Klondike Kate, the blue-eyed darling of the miners. Her red-gold hair and her sweet songs stood her in high stead among the usual run of dance hall girls who were called, with affectionate disrespect, names like Nellie the Pig and the Oregon Mare.

By 1903, over $96 million in gold had been taken from the richest creeks, Eldorado and Bonanza, and from the other, less prosperous areas like Hunker, Bear and Dominion. Most of the gold seekers had left with empty pockets; some lay in cold graves along the Yukon River and among the coiled gravel of the tailings from the sluice boxes. A few millionaires reigned from mansions in Seattle; the prospectors who always roamed for gold and always would had moved on to new finds in Nome.

The Klondike Valley was falling back to sleep again after a dream, or a nightmare, that hadn't lasted 10 years. The rush was over.

Highlight

Robert Service — the 'Bard of the Yukon'

If there ever was one individual who was able to incorporate into his poetry all of the elements for which the north is famous, it was Robert William Service.

Service's poetry has an incomparable meter which rolls easily off the tongue. It not only lends itself to recital, but invites it. His poetry bubbles with humor, is flourished with description and seeths with adventure. It also instills an underlying mystic philosophy; a law of the north which encourages the reader to "do his own thing," and "stand on his own two feet," virtues by which Service and his fellow pioneers had lived.

The "Bard of the Yukon" as he was called, produced such favorite poems as: *The Spell of the Yukon, The Shooting of Dan McGrew,* and *The Cremation of Sam McGee* — verse which has permeated the English-speaking world and is still much recited.

Robert Service was born January 16, 1874, in Preston, England. He attended school in Glasgow, Scotland, but withdrew in his early teens to apprentice with the Commercial Bank of Scotland.

When he was 21, he migrated to Canada, where he roamed working as a ranch hand, bookkeeper, farmer and newsman, from British Columbia to Mexico.

Service gained employment with the Canadian Bank of Commerce in the fall of 1903, and in less than a year the bank had transferred him to Whitehorse, then a small community at the terminus of the White Pass and Yukon Railroad in the Yukon Territory.

The bank clerk was greatly impressed with the northern frontier. And since people and their actions make history, the rough and ready personalities of these northern individuals were perfect for characterization in his poetry. This exposure to northern people and their ways inspired Service's first book of verse, *Songs of a Sourdough,* which he published in 1907.

Shortly afterward, Service was transferred to Dawson City, where he became cashier at the Dawson City branch of the Bank of Commerce, which today utilizes the same building where the famous poet had worked.

In Dawson, Service lived in a small cabin which has since become a major tourist attraction. He continued his writing, often pinning the verse on the cabin wall to work it and re-work it.

The turning point in Service's career came when he left Canada to become a war correspondent for the *Toronto Starr* in the Balkan War and in World War I. He joined the Canadian Ambulance Corps as a driver and wrote the gripping *Rhymes of a Red Cross Man* in 1916. This was followed by *Ballads of a Bohemian* in 1920 and *The Roughneck* in 1923.

After the war, Service took up residence in France where he married a French girl and settled down to raise a family. There he remained until the Nazi invasion in 1940, when he moved with his wife and daughter to Hollywood,

California; they lived there during the war years and then returned to France.

Service died in France on September 11, 1958. He had written thousands of lines of verse and a number of novels, many of which are now out of print.

Whether Service's writing was describing the awe-inspiring country and moods of the north, or telling about its people and their struggle to survive, it has a simple and time-tested appeal and is written in a language which everyone can understand.

Excerpt from Service's *Cremation of Sam McGee:*

There are strange things done
in the midnight sun
By the men who moil for gold;
The Arctic trails have their secret tales
That would make your blood run cold;

The Northern Lights have seen queer sights,
But the queerest they ever did see
Was that night on the marge of Lake Lebarge
I cremated Sam McGee.

Highlight

The Yukon's Chilkoot Trail

Tens of thousands of gold-crazed stampeders challenged the Chilkoot Pass in 1898. It was the most popular route to the rich gold fields of the Klondike, although it defeated many of those intent on making a fast fortune.

Each stampeder was required by Canadian law to carry 2,000 pounds of provisions up over the 3,000-foot summit and across the U.S./Canadian border. Sometimes 30 trips had to be made up a 45-degree slope in an unending human chain. No man could stop to rest for fear that it would take several hours to get back into line.

Today, hikers on the Chilkoot Trail can retrace the footsteps of these early gold seekers with only a fraction of the hardship and effort. The trail is well marked and patrolled by Canadian and U.S. guides.

The trail begins at Dyea near Skagway, Alaska, and ends at Lake Bennett in British Columbia, a distance of approximately 32 miles, which takes an average of 2½ to 3½ days to hike.

The terrain ranges from lush rain forest to subalpine and alpine regions. Here and there along the way, there remains evidence of the early stampeders — a discarded shoe, a rusted horse's bit or the remnants of old log shelters.

Today's hiker also has a choice of carrying his or her own tent for overnighting or staying in one of the new log shelters especially designed for this purpose.

From Bennett, the hiker can catch the narrow-gauge White Pass and Yukon Railway which runs between Skagway and Whitehorse, to complete the trip in comfort.

Chilkoot Trail:

Other Hiking Areas

Kluane National Park

Kluane National Park is relatively new, and due to its remoteness, is lacking established hiking trails. Some hiking is possible in the park, but hikers are advised to make arrangements with the Information Centers or Warden Services to obtain current information on conditions, along with further details on the areas they intend to hike.

Whitehorse Area

There are three popular trails near Whitehorse ranging from a short seven-mile walk to a two-day hike.

Whitehorse to Canyon City hike: A very scenic walk that may be undertaken by inexperienced hikers which follows a well-defined path as far as the site of abandoned Canyon City.

Grey Mountain Hiking Trail: A well-marked trail, approximately 15 miles long, which passes several old cabins. This trail may be walked in one day.

Stoney Creek Hike: A scenic trail that rises to a small subalpine lake and a moorland campsite. At certain times of the year, berries are profuse and the entire area offers pleasant tramping above timber. A two-day hike.

Canada's Calendar of Events

Spring
(March, April, May)

Greater Moncton Music Festival. March, Moncton, New Brunswick.
Paddyfest. March, Listowel, Ontario.
Figure Skating Carnival. March, Wainwright, Alberta.
Ice Carnival. March, Maidstone, Saskatchewan.
Snowmobile Racing. March, Meadow Lake, Saskatchewan.
Annual Music Festival. April, Balcarres, Saskatchewan.
Dance Festival. April, North Battleford, Saskatchewan.
Spring Musical. April, High River, Alberta.
Mennonite Festival of the Arts. April, Waterloo, Ontario.
Blossom Festival. May, Niagara Falls, Ontario.
Festival of Spring. May, Ottawa, Ontario.
Shaw Festival. May to October, Niagara-On-The-Lake, Ontario.
Ukrainian Dance Festival. May, Fort Saskatchewan, Alberta.
Sundown Day. May, Banff, Alberta.
Spring Square Dance Festival. May, Fredericton, New Brunswick.

Summer
(June, July, August)

Heritage Week. June, All Provinces.

Salmon Festival. June, Campbellton, New Brunswick.

Charlottetown Summer Festival. June, Charlottetown, Prince Edward Island.

Flin Flon Trout Festival. June, Flin Flon, Manitoba.

Annual Highland Games. June, Whitehorse, Yukon.
Frantic Follies. June to September, Whitehorse, Yukon.
Annual Midnight Golf Tournament. June, Yellowknife, Northwest Territories.
International Folk Festival. June, Red Deer, Alberta.
Williams Lake Stampede. June, Williams Lake, British Columbia.
St. John's Summer Festival. July, St. John, Newfoundland.
Seafood Days. July, All Provinces.
Seafood Square and Round Dance Festival. July, Clementsport, Nova Scotia.
Highland Games. July, Antigonish, Nova Scotia.
Quebec Summer Festival. July, Quebec, Quebec.
National Ukrainian Festival. July, Dauphin, Manitoba.
Morris Stampede. July, Morris, Manitoba.
Pioneer Days. July, Saskatoon, Saskatchewan.
Calgary Stampede. July, Calgary, Alberta.
Sea Festival. July, Vancouver, British Columbia.
Peach Festival. July, Penticton, British Columbia.
Transarctic Games. July, Inuvik, Northwest Territories.
Discovery Days. August, Dawson City, Northwest Territories.
B. C. Summer Games. August, Kelowna, British Columbia.
Icelandic Festival. August, Gimli, Manitoba.
Ontario Summer Games. August, Peterborough, Ontario.
Acadian Festival. August, Caraquet, New Brunswick.
Oyster Festival. August, Tyne Valley, Prince Edward Island.

Fall
(September, October, November)

Niagara Grape and Wine Festival. September, St. Catharines, Ontario.
Fisheries Exhibition and Reunion. September, Lunenburg, Nova Scotia.
Sussex Fall Fair. September, Sussex, New Brunswick.
Annual Fall Fair. September, Calgary, Alberta.
Harvest Festival. September, Outlook, Saskatchewan.
Harvest Ball and Demolition Derby. October, Frontier, Saskatchewan.
Moose Jaw Arts and Crafts Festival. October, Moose Jaw, Saskatchewan.
Oktoberfest. October, Red Deer Alberta.
Harvest Fest. October, Rycroft, Alberta.
Friendship Festival. October, Rivere du Portage, New Brunswick.
Carnival. November, Frontier, Saskatchewan.
Royal Agricultural Winter Fair. November, Toronto, Ontario.
Stockade Roundup. November, Lloydminster, Alberta.

Winter
(December, January, February)

Polar Picnic. December, Mirror Lake, Alberta.
Twilight Twinkle Hour. December, Lloydminster, Alberta.
Community Carol Festival. December, Humboldt, Saskatchewan.
Snow Show Days. January, Oxbow, Saskatchewan.
Sno-Mo Days. February, Norquay, Saskatchewan.
Snofest. February, Lacombe, Alberta.
Annual Alberta Snowmobile Association Jamboree. February, Sylvan Lake, Alberta.
Banff Winter Festival. February, Banff, Alberta.
North American International Snowmobile Races. February, Wetaskiwin, Alberta.

Canada's National Parks

Canada's National Parks are special places set aside for the benefit, education and enjoyment of visitors — and to preserve unique samples of Canada's heritage.

Canada's constantly expanding National Parks System includes parks in every province and territory.

This National Parks System is administered by Parks Canada, part of the Department of Indian Affairs and Northern Development.

Parks are open year-round and activities include camping, hiking, swimming, fishing, boating, nature study, photography, sightseeing and picnicking. Types of recreation vary according to the park and the season.

All except the most remote parks maintain excellent campgrounds, hiking and riding trails and driveways leading through scenic areas.

Programs presented by park naturalists, including illustrated talks and conducted outings, as well as exhibits and displays, will make your visit even more enjoyable.

Parks Canada has five regional offices, in Calgary, Winnipeg, Cornwall, Quebec City and Halifax. If you have any questions about Canada's National Parks, you can write directly to the park or regional office.

Canals and Waterways

Parks Canada maintains the St. Peters Canal in Nova Scotia; the Carillon, Sainte Anne, Saint Ours and Chambly Canals in Quebec; the Rideau Canal and the Trent-Severn Waterway in Ontario.

Information Available

Pamphlets describing Canada's National Parks, Historic Parks and Sites and Historic Canals and Waterways are available from: Parks Canada, Ottawa, Ontario K1A 0H4.

Canoeists enjoy the peaceful waters of Astotin Lake in Elk Island National Park in Alberta (above) while RVers enjoy the great outdoors in a number of Canada's forest campgrounds (left).

Trailriding in Alberta's beautiful Canadian Rockies is a popular vacation adventure, from the tranquil beauty of Waterton Lakes National Park through Banff and Jasper.

Western Region

Pacific Rim. Fabulous Long Beach is a major feature of this park on the west coast of Vancouver Islands, currently in the planning state. The park will include a historic Lifesaving Trail and the Broken Island Group. The park, accessible by highway, features an interpretive program and sea lion viewing. 389 square kilometers. PO Box 280, Ucluelet, British Columbia, V0R 3A0. (604) 726-7721.

Mount Revelstoke. Rolling mountaintop on the west slope of the Selkirk Mountains provides colorful alpine meadows, sparkling lakes and an interpretive program, all accessible by Trans-Canada Highway. Accommodations are available in the nearby town of Revelstoke; picnic facilities in the park. 263 square kilometers. PO Box 350, Revelstoke, British Columbia, V0E 2S0. (604) 837-5155.

Glacier. This rugged alpine region in the Selkirk Mountains offers towering peaks, rushing streams, avalanche slopes, over 100 glaciers and an interior western forest of large hemlock and cedar. Area is accessible by the Trans-Canada Highway, with nearby hotels and campgrounds available. 1,349 square kilometers. PO Box 350, Revelstoke, British Columbia, V0E 2S0. (604) 837-5155.

Yoho. Lofty peaks, glaciers, waterfalls and lakes are all found on the west slope of the Rocky Mountains. An interpretive program explains the natural history of the Yoho and Kicking Horse Valleys, accessible by Trans-Canada Highway. Lodges, chalets and campgrounds provide nearby accommodations. 1,313 square kilometers. PO Box 99, Field, British Columbia, V0A 1G0. (604) 343-6324.

Kootenay. There is much to see in this spectacular area on the west slope of the Rockies, including two river valleys of different character, high glaciers and deep canyons, icy alpine lakes and hot springs. Campgrounds in the area provide for RVs. 1,406 square kilometers. PO Box 220, Radium Hot Springs, British Columbia, V0A 1M0. (604) 347-9615.

Waterton Lakes. The Canadian section of Waterton-Glacier International Peace Park offers colorful mountain scenery with charming lakes and many breathtaking vistas. An interpretive program points out the striking contrasts between the mountain and grasslands areas. RV accommodations nearby as well as hotels, motels and chalets. 526 square kilometers. Waterton Park, Alberta, T0K 2M0. (403) 859-2262.

Banff. Canada's oldest national park is noted for its ice-capped peaks, deep valleys, glaciers and lakes. Within the park are the well-known resorts of Banff and Lake Louise, featuring the famous ski center, mineral hot springs and a park museum. Park is accessible by rail and the Trans-Canada Highway, and offers all

A Suggested Tour

Stampede City and Fort Whoop-Up

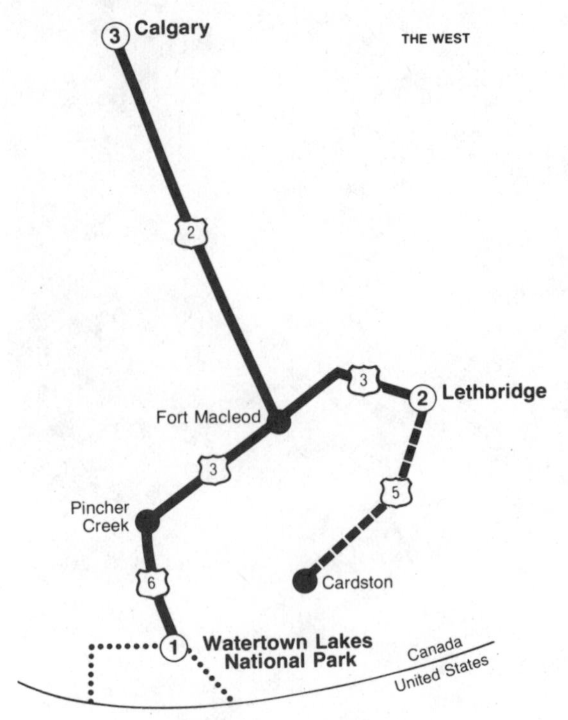

1. Waterton Lakes National Park. Extends over 203 square miles along the eastern slope of the Rocky Mountains.

With Glacier National Park in the United States, it forms Waterton-Glacier International Peace Park; headquarters at Waterton Park townsite on Emerald Bay. The park features a chain of lakes, the largest of which is Upper Waterton. Boat cruises are available to Goat Haunt, Montana, as well as shoreline cruises.

Park is in the transition zone between prairie and mountain.

Activities: Educational displays with walks conducted by park naturalists, campfire talks in an outdoor amphitheater, nature trails, boating, golf, tennis and swimming.

Ample campground and commercial accommodations are available.

Contact: Superintendent, Waterton Lakes National Park, Waterton Park, Alberta T0K 2M0.

En route: Pincher Creek, and Fort Macleod, location of the first North West Mounted Police post in Western Canada, incorporating Fort Macleod Museum.

2. Lethbridge. Surrounded by over one million acres of irrigated land, it is a distribution center for a rich agricultural and ranching region.

Henderson Lake Park includes camping facilities, a swimming pool, lake stocked annually with rainbow trout, picnic areas, golf course and Nikka Yuko Japanese Gardens.

Attractions: Fort Whoop-Up, Indian Battle Park, Galt Gardens, Sir Alexander Galt Museum, Canada Agricultural Research Station, High Level Bridge and St. Mary Dam, southwest of Lethbridge.

Event: Whoop-Up Days Exhibition and Rodeo (July) is a lively event.

Contact: Lethbridge Chamber of Commerce, 817 Fourth Avenue South, Lethbridge, Alberta, T1J 0P3.

Option: Cardston, where the temple of the Church of Jesus Christ of Latter Day Saints is of interest.

3. Calgary. "Stampede City" in southern Alberta's Rocky Mountain foothills amid ranching country; oil drilling and processing are important.

Visit Glenbow Alberta Institute, Centennial Planetarium, Sam Livingstone Fish Hatchery and Rearing Station, and Fort Calgary Interpretive Center. Heritage Park recaptures the setting and atmosphere of a historic pioneer settlement. Visitors can ride a steam railroad or ride on the stern-wheeler *SS Moyie.*

Calgary Zoo and Natural History Park on St. George's Island include a zoo, prehistoric museum, aviary and children's playland, as well as a special children's zoo where youngsters can play with small animals under supervision; the island also features life-size replicas of reptiles that roamed the area 20 million years ago.

types of modern accommodations and campgrounds. 6,641 square kilometers. Banff, Alberta, T0L 0C0. (403) 762-3324.

Jasper. The famous resort town of Jasper is situated within the striking alpine landscape, featuring ice-capped mountain peaks, icefields, beautiful lakes and a noted ski area. The area is accessible by rail and highway. 10,878 square kilometers. Jasper, Alberta, T0E 1E0. (403) 852-4401.

Elk Island. The rolling landscape of aspen and spruce forest contrast with the surrounding flat farmlands near Edmonton. The area features numerous small lakes, supports a large bison herd and offers a beach area accessible by highway. The park offers campground accommodations. 194 square kilometers. Site 4, RR No. 1, Fort Saskatchewan, Alberta, T8L 2N7. (403) 998-3781.

Prairie Region

Kluane. In the southwest corner of the Yukon Territory are located Canada's highest mountains, featuring extensive icefields and glaciers, fine wildlife populations and an interpretive program currently in the planning stages. Accessible by highway, the park offers nearby accommodations. 22,014 square kilometers. Haines Junction, Yukon Territory, Y0B 1L0. (403) 634-2251.

A river rafting tour in Alberta's Canadian Rockies is a novel way to see some spectacular mountain scenery (left).

A Suggested Tour

Saskatchewan's Qu'Appelle Valley

Enjoy the fine swimming, fishing and boating in the Qu'Appelle Valley's seven lakes, cradled within the gently contoured hillsides, and see the deep-rutted wagon trails used by pioneers.

1. Regina.
Options: Last Mountain House Historic Park; Rowan's Ravine Provincial Park; Earl Grey, where you can visit Earl Grey Centennial Museum, and Echo Valley Provincial Park, where you can camp for the night.

2. Fort Qu'Appelle. Established in 1864 as a fur-trade post and later a North West Mounted Police post.

A 48-kilometer (30-mile) chain of beautiful lakes. See the restored Hudson's Bay Company trading post.
Attractions: Hansen Pottery Center, Indian Handcrafts Co-operative and Echo Lake Provincial Fish Station.

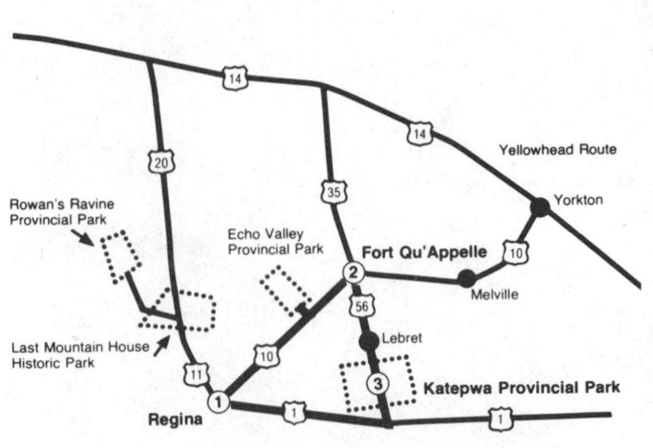

En route: At Lebret visit the tiny chapel on a hill; the Stations of the Cross lead up a steep slope from the village.

3. Katepwa Provincial Park. On the eastern shore of Katepwa Lake in the Fishing Lakes region, the park offers swimming, a boat launching ramp, picnic sites, golf and a forest.

Just outside the park are commercial campgrounds.
Contact: Sask Travel, 1825 Lorne Street, Regina, Saskatchewan, S4P 3N1.
En route: Returning to Regina visit Indian Head, with an important Dominion Experimental Farm and Nursery; provincial government information center at McLean Trans-Canada Campground.

Nahanni. This wilderness area along the South Nahanni River, in the southwestern corner of the Northwest Territories, offers deep river canyons and spectacular Virginia Falls, as well as numerous hot springs and interesting flora. The park is currently in the planning state and is not accessible by highway. 4,766 square kilometers. Postal Bag 300, Fort Simpson, Northwest Territories, (403) 872-2349.

Wood Buffalo. Canada's largest national park is an immense area of the Great Plains, butting up against the Canadian Shield. Some interesting geographical points of interest include flood plains, plateaus, gypsum and limestone karst features in the north, the Peace-Athabasca Delta in the south. Resources include the largest herd of free-roaming bison, staging ground for North America's four major waterfowl flyways and nesting ground of the last wild flock of whooping cranes. Canoeing and hiking are also popular in this area accessible by highway and campground accommodations are available. 44,807 square kilometers. Box 750, Fort Smith, Northwest Territories, X0E 0P0. (403) 872-2349.

Prince Albert. This forested region is dotted with lakes and interlaced with streams, providing an interesting transition between northern forests and prairie grassland. An interpretive center provides an interesting program describing the park's many natural features. Accessible by highway, the area contains many hotels, motels, bungalows and campgrounds. 3,875 square kilometers. Box 100, Waskesiu Lake, Saskatchewan S0J 2Y0. (306) 663-3511.

Riding Mountain. On the summit of a Manitoba escarpment lies this gentle blend of northern and eastern forest with western grasslands and fine lakes. The park, with its lodges, motels, bungalows, campgrounds and interpretive center, is accessible by highway. 2,976 square kilometers. Wasagaming, Manitoba, R0J 2H0. (204) 848-2811.

Ontario Region

Pukaskwa. Situated along the northern shore of Lake Superior in the wilderness area of northern Ontario, this rugged terrain contains many lakes and rivers and a wide variety of wildlife. The park, still under development, is not yet accessible by highway. Commercial accommodations are nearby. 1,878 square kilometers. Box 550, Marathon, Ontario, P0T 2E0. (807) 229-0801.

Georgian Bay Islands. Some 40 picturesque islands form a varied landscape of glacier-scraped rock, weathered pine and dense maple-beech-oak woodland. The area boasts the remarkable rock pillars on Flowerpot Island; islands are accessible by boat from nearby mainland points, where accommodation is also available. Campgrounds are located on Beausoleil Island. 14 square kilometers. Honey Harbor, Ontario, P0E 1E0. (705) 756-2415.

Point Pelee. Canada's most southern mainland is a birdwatcher's paradise on two major migration flyways. The area offers a large cattail marsh, rare forest, 23 kilometers of beach and an interpretive center and program accessible by highway. Accommodations at Leamington and vicinity. 16 square kilometers. Leamington, Ontario, N8H 3V4. (519) 326-3204.

St. Lawrence Islands. Captivating scenery, ideal for all water sports, is available in this group of 18 heavily-treed islands and 80 rocky islets in the famous Thousand Islands region. The mainland is accessible by highway, the islands by boat, with accommodations in nearby communities, and campgrounds at Mallorytown Landing and on Grenadier Island. Four square kilometers. PO Box 469, RR No. 3, Mallorytown, Ontario, K0E 1R0. (613) 923-5241.

Quebec Region

La Mauricie. This heavily wooded, largely unspoiled section of the Laurentian Mountains in Grand-Mere and Shawinigan is almost equidistant between Montreal and Quebec, with its numerous lakes and interpretive program. Accessible by highway, the area is still under development; offers nearby accommodations and campgrounds. 544 square kilometers. PO Box 758, Shawinigan, Quebec, G9N 6V9. (819) 536-2638.

Auyuittuq. This arctic area with fjords and deeply-carved mountains resides on the Cumberland Peninsula of Baffin Island and its numerous glaciers extend from massive icecaps, supporting many forms of arctic wildlife. Currently in the planning stage, the park is accessible by air from Montreal. 21,471 square kilometers. Pangnirtung, Northwest Territories, X0A 0R0. (819) 437-9962.

Forillon. The development of this park, on the scenic tip of Forillon Peninsula on the Gulf of St. Lawrence, reflects both the unique coastal environment and rich human history of the famous Gaspe region. Accessible by highway, the park offers an interpretive center and program, campgrounds and other accommodations nearby. 240 square kilometers. PO Box 1220, Gaspe, Quebec, G0C 1R0. (418) 368-5505.

Atlantic Region

Kouchibouguac. Kouchibouguac Bay, along the northern section of Northumberland Strait, has as its most outstanding feature the 25-kilometer sweep of offshore sandbars. Quiet lagoons and bays provide excellent protected swimming. Campgrounds in the area are accessible by highway. 225 square kilometers. Kouchibouguac, Kent County, New Brunswick, E0A 2A0. (506) 876-3973.

Fundy. This park is a fine example of the

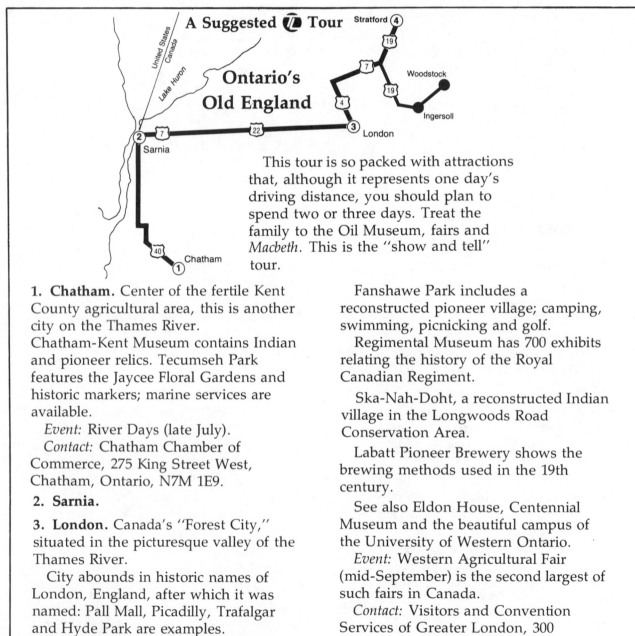

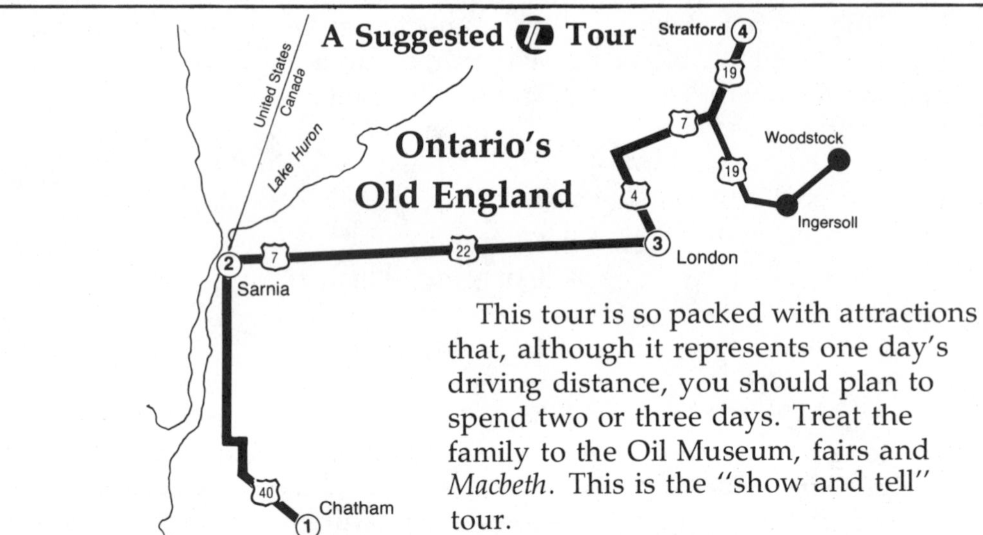

This tour is so packed with attractions that, although it represents one day's driving distance, you should plan to spend two or three days. Treat the family to the Oil Museum, fairs and *Macbeth*. This is the "show and tell" tour.

1. Chatham. Center of the fertile Kent County agricultural area, this is another city on the Thames River. Chatham-Kent Museum contains Indian and pioneer relics. Tecumseh Park features the Jaycee Floral Gardens and historic markers; marine services are available.

Event: River Days (late July).

Contact: Chatham Chamber of Commerce, 275 King Street West, Chatham, Ontario, N7M 1E9.

2. Sarnia.

3. London. Canada's "Forest City," situated in the picturesque valley of the Thames River.

City abounds in historic names of London, England, after which it was named: Pall Mall, Picadilly, Trafalgar and Hyde Park are examples.

Springbank Park has a zoo, Storybook Gardens, miniature train, recreational and picnic facilities.

Fanshawe Park includes a reconstructed pioneer village; camping, swimming, picnicking and golf.

Regimental Museum has 700 exhibits relating the history of the Royal Canadian Regiment.

Ska-Nah-Doht, a reconstructed Indian village in the Longwoods Road Conservation Area.

Labatt Pioneer Brewery shows the brewing methods used in the 19th century.

See also Eldon House, Centennial Museum and the beautiful campus of the University of Western Ontario.

Event: Western Agricultural Fair (mid-September) is the second largest of such fairs in Canada.

Contact: Visitors and Convention Services of Greater London, 300 Dufferin Avenue, London, Ontario, N6A 4L9.

En route: Elginfield.

Bay of Fundy's rugged shoreline, with its sandstone cliffs, coves, inlets and the highest tides in the world. This is the area of rolling, forested landscape with waterfalls, streams and small lakes, dotted by motels, chalets and campgrounds, all accessible by highway. 206 square kilometers. Alma, New Brunswick, E0A 1B0. (506) 887-2000.

4. Stratford. "Canada's Festival City" where the Stratford Shakespearean Festival has become a major cultural event; there is also a season-long program of musical events at the Festival and Avon theaters.

Stratford is known for its beautiful parks system with Queen's Park surrounding Victoria Lake.

The Gallery, an attractive building in a semi-rural setting, features international exhibits of modern art and sculpture, as well as films, lectures and concerts.

Shakespeareland contains 60 authentic, large-scale replicas of well-known buildings in Stratford-On-Avon, England.

Minnie Thomson Memorial Museum displays pioneer household effects, cars, trucks and agricultural implements.

See Fryfogel's Inn and Museum, 12.9 kilometers (eight miles) east on Highway 8. Farmers' Market is held each Saturday morning. Wildwood Dam area, 9.7 kilometers (six miles) from Stratford, offers swimming, fishing, sailing and camping facilities.

Event: The Western Ontario Antique Show and Sale (August) is a week-long event.

Contact: Stratford Chamber of Commerce, 38 Albert Street, Stratford, Ontario, N5A 3K3.

On the way back to Chatham, visit Woodstock, where the Oxford Museum in the historic City Hall is of interest; Ingersoll and Thamesville.

Prince Edward Island. This coastal strip 40 kilometers long on the Gulf of St. Lawrence is a scenic area of dunes, cliffs, salt marshes and fine bathing beaches. Lodges, bungalows and campgrounds are all accessible by highway. 18 square kilometers. PO Box 487, Charlottetown, Prince Edward Island, C1A 7L1. (902) 672-2211.

Kejimkujik. A superb example of inland Nova Scotia is this area of rolling landscape, numerous lakes and countless islands and bays. Indian petroglyphs (rock carvings) are described in a detailed interpretive program. Campgrounds are found in the park, all accessible by highway. 382 square kilometers. PO Box 36, Maitland Bridge, Nova Scotia, B0T 1N0. (902) 242-2770.

Cape Breton Highlands. This huge tableland rises to 515 meters above sea level, offering a rugged Atlantic coastline with forested hills and fine seascapes from the Cabot Trail. Campgrounds are found in the park, other accommodations are available in adjacent communities. 951 square kilometers. Ingonish Beach, Nova Scotia, B0C 1L0. (902) 285-2270.

Gros Morne. Newfoundland's western coast contains the most spectacular section of the Long Range Mountains, which rise dramatically and abruptly from the low coastal plain. The area contains fjord-like lakes, dense forests, rugged seacoast and beautiful beaches. The park, still under development, is accessible by highway. 1,943 square kilometers. PO Box 130, Rocky Harbor, Bonne Bay, Newfoundland, A0K 4N0.

Terra Nova. This rugged, deeply indented coastline with its spectacular inlets boasts a typical boreal forest of spruce and bogs, and icebergs offshore in spring. Bungalows, campgrounds are accessible by Trans-Canada Highway. 397 square kilometers. Glovertown, Newfoundland, A0G 2L0. (709) 533-2291.

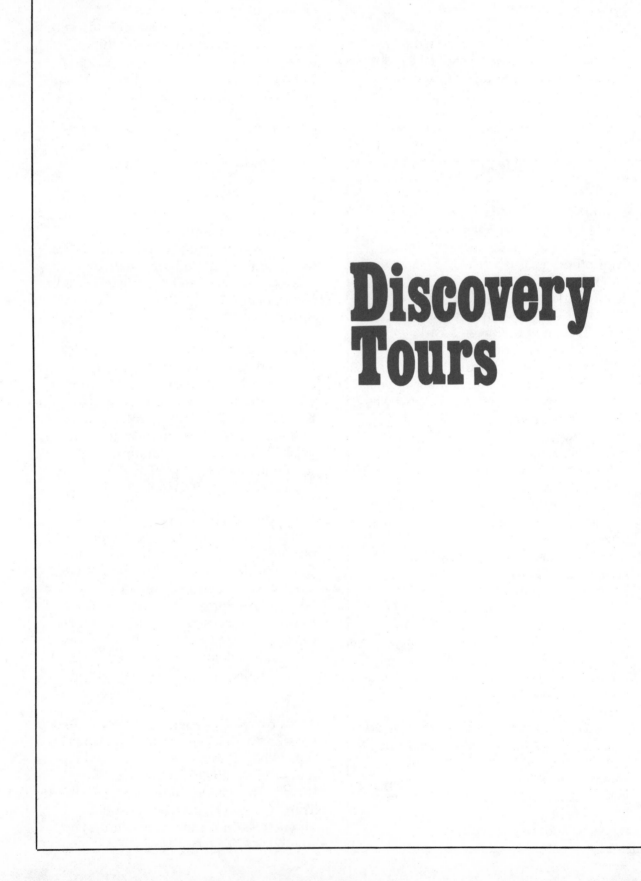

Discovery Tours

Travel should be more than going from one point to another; it should be a time of discovery, an exploration of the new worlds that you find along the road. In the following pages you'll find a guidebook for your explorations — a listing of historical sites and museums, an introduction to the Indian and Amish cultures, and a comprehensive guide to California's Wine Country, among others.

In facilities as lavish as New York's Whitney Museum of American Art or as simple as Kadoka, South Dakota's Prairie Homestead, you'll find the history and culture of the nation preserved for your enjoyment and enlightenment. If your journey takes you cross-country you can relive the westward migration in museums along the way. If your travels are narrower in scope, what better way to discover the essence of the region you're in than through a visit to the local museums and historical sites?

For anyone interested in discovering the nation's past, an exploration of Indian history is essential. Facilities like the Cochise Visitor Center in Wilcox, Arizona, and sites like the Puye Cliff Dwellings in Espanola, New Mexico, provide fascinating exhibits on the Indian peoples of the West. But don't forget the tribes of the East; their history can be traced with a visit to the Oconaluftee Indian Village in Cherokee, North Carolina, the New Echota Historic Site at Calhoun, Georgia, or one of the many fine museums found throughout Eastern U.S.

There are countless other worlds to explore, many more historical and cultural attractions than could ever be listed in the pages of any one book — in the U.S. alone there are more than 6,000 museums — so let these pages help you chart the paths to your own discoveries.

The Brooks Grove Methodist Church in Genesee Country Village still graces Mumford, New York (above right). Historical marker in Greenville, Ohio, commemorates famous sharp-shooter Annie Oakley (below right). Modern-day Seventh Cavalry parades in formation in North Dakota as it once rallied around General George A. Custer (below).

Historical Sites & Museums

The following listing highlights some of the more significant state historical sites and museums (see the National Parks section for a detailed listing of the points of interest that have been designated as national historic sites, monuments, battlefields, memorials and historic parks).

Alabama

Arlington Antebellum Home. Dating from 1822, Arlington is a fine example of old Alabama mansions; antiques, gardens on grounds. Open year-round, Tuesday to Sunday, 9 a.m. to 5 p.m. Adults $2, children 12 to 18, $1, 4 to 11, 75 cents. Birmingham, 331 Cotton Avenue, SW.

Army Aviation Museum. Contains an extensive collection of U.S. Army aircraft and features numerous exhibits on the evolution of the helicopter. Open year-round, daily, 10 a.m. to 5 p.m. Free. Ozark, off US-231.

Ceremonial Indian Mound. One of the greatest mounds in the Tennessee Valley, dating back to pre-Columbian era; museum of Indian artifacts nearby. Open year-round, Tuesday to Saturday, 9 a.m. to noon and 1 p.m. to 4 p.m. Adults $1, children under 18, 25 cents. Florence, on South Court Street.

First White House of the Confederacy. The home of Jefferson Davis and his family when Montgomery was the capital of the Confederacy; exhibits and memorabilia. Open year-round, daily, 8 a.m. to 5 p.m. Free. Montgomery, on Washington Avenue.

Fort Toulouse. Dates back to 1717 when it was first built by the French; rebuilt and occupied by Andrew Jackson in 1814. Open year-round, daily, 8 a.m. to 5 p.m. Adults 50 cents, children under 12, 25 cents. Wetumpka, off US-231.

Alaska

Anchorage Historical and Fine Arts Museum. Exhibits of artifacts dealing with native Alaskan cultures; contemporary arts and crafts. Open year-round, Monday to Saturday, 9 a.m. to 6 p.m. Free. Anchorage, 121 West Seventh Avenue.

Trail of '98 Museum. Features Tlingit Indian artifacts and exhibits on Alaskan history and native cultures. Open May through September, daily, 8 a.m. to 8 p.m. Adults $1, children under 12, 50 cents. Skagway, between Seventh and Eighth Avenues.

Arizona

Arizona History Room. Exhibits on the life and culture of the Indians, Spaniards, Mexicans and Americans who have occupied the state of Arizona; mineral displays. Open year-round, Monday to Friday, 10 a.m. to 3 p.m. Free. Phoenix, 100 West Washington, in the First National Bank Plaza.

Arizona Museum. Indian artifacts, exhibits on state history; gun and mineral displays. Open November 1 through May, Wednesday to Sunday, 2 p.m. to 5 p.m. Free. Phoenix, 1002 West Van Buren.

Boothill Graveyard. Contains the graves of nearly 200 notorious Old West figures. Open year-round, daily, 8 a.m. to 6 p.m. Donation asked. Tombstone, off US-80.

Cochise Visitor Center and Museum. Exhibits on the Apache Indians and a history of the American military in the area; costumes, saddles and other memorabilia donated by Western star Rex Allen. Open year-round, Monday to Friday, 8 a.m. to 5 p.m. Free. Willcox, off state route 186 and Interstate 10.

Heard Museum. Anthropological and primitive art exhibits; Indian artifacts and Eskimo exhibits, Kachina dolls. Open year-round, daily, 10 a.m. to 5 p.m. Adults $1.50, children 50 cents. Phoenix, 22 East Monte Vista Road.

OK Corral. The site of the famous shootout between the Earp brothers, Doc Holliday and the Clantons; life-size figures of the principals are featured. Open year-round, daily, 8:30 a.m. to 5 p.m. Adults $1, children under 12, 50 cents. Tombstone, on Allen Street, between Third and Fourth Streets.

Phoenix Art Museum. Features works of the medieval, Renaissance and French Baroque periods, as well as exhibits of contemporary paintings, sculptures and graphic arts. Open year-round, Tuesday to Sunday, 10 a.m. to 5 p.m. Free. Phoenix, 1625 North Central Avenue.

Tusayan Ruin and Museum. This facility traces the development of early man at the Grand Canyon; guided walks. Open year-round, daily, 8 a.m. to 5 p.m. Free. Grand Canyon Village, 22 miles east, off East Rim Drive.

California

Angels Camp Museum. Contains exhibits and artifacts of the Gold Rush era. Open year-round, Thursday to Monday, 11 a.m. to 5 p.m. Adults 50 cents, children 6 to 12, 25 cents. Angels Camp, on State Route 49.

Burton's Tropico Gold Mine and Museum. Features a mine shaft, gold mill, gold camp and museum of mining relics; gold-panning championship held every March. Open year-round, Thursday to Monday, 10 a.m. to 4 p.m. Adults $2, children 5 to 11, $1.50. Rosamond, on Mojave Tropico Road.

La Brea Tar Pits. One of the richest sources of Ice Age fossils in the country, these sticky pits entrapped a wide variety of prehistoric plant and animal species; museum nearby. Open year-round, daily; tours 11 a.m. to 4:30 p.m. Free. Los Angeles, Wilshire Boulevard and Curson Avenue.

Los Angeles County Museum of Art. Houses a number of outstanding collections of period and contemporary art; theater and outdoor cafe, changing exhibits. Open year-round, daily, 10 a.m. to 5 p.m. Adults $1, children 5 to 17, 50 cents. Los Angeles, on Wilshire Boulevard.

Marshall Gold Discovery Site. Here is where the Gold Rush of 1849 began at Sutter's Mill. A replica of the mill is located on the original discovery site and a museum, monument and other historical buildings are nearby. Open year-round, daily, 10 a.m. to 5 p.m. Coloma, on State Route 49.

National Maritime Museum. Features ship models, artifacts and photos; several historic ships nearby. Open year-round, daily, 10 a.m. to 6 p.m. Free. San Francisco, at the foot of Polk Street, in Aquatic Park.

Norton Simon Museum of Art. Features works by Impressionists and exhibits of tapestries, sculptures and paintings; meditation garden. Open year-round, Wednesday to Sunday, noon to 5 p.m. Adults $1, children under 12, free. Pasadena, 411 West Colorado Boulevard.

San Diego Museum of Art. Works by European masters from early Renaissance to contemporary; sculptures, Asian arts.

Open year-round, Tuesday to Sunday, 10 a.m. to 5 p.m. Adults $1, children under 16, 50 cents. San Diego, on north side of El Prado, in Balboa Park.

San Simeon State Historical Monument. The famed castle of William Randolph Hearst, consisting of 123 acres overlooking San Simeon and the Pacific Ocean. The main residence, La Casa Grande, houses a portion of the $50 million Hearst collection of art treasures and antiques. The magnificently landscaped grounds are studded with pools, fountains and statuary. Open year-round, daily, for tours only from 8 a.m. to 4 p.m. Adults $5, children 6 to 17, $2.50. San Simeon, off State Route 1.

Scripps Aquarium-Museum. Features specimen tanks, oceanography exhibits and an onshore tide pool; a branch of the University of California. Open year-round, daily, 9 a.m. to 5 p.m. Free. La Jolla, 8602 La Jolla Shores Drive.

Whittier Mansion. The northern headquarters of the California Historical Society, where information on other points of interest in the state can be obtained. The splendid mansion dates from 1896; tours. Open year-round, Wednesday, Saturday and Sunday, 1 a.m. to 5 p.m. Adults $1, children 12 to 17, 50 cents. San Francisco, 2090 Jackson Street.

Colorado

Colorado Heritage Center. Exhibits on the history of the state, featuring the "Coloradoans," a multi-unit display on Colorado history. Open year-round, daily, 9 a.m. to 5 p.m. Free. Denver, 1300 Broadway.

Colorado Railroad Museum. Steam locomotives and old railroad cars on display, along with records and artifacts of the early narrow-gauge railroads of Colorado. Open year-round, daily, 9 a.m. to 5 p.m. Adults $1.50, children 75 cents, family rate $3.50. Golden, on State Route 58, at 17155 West 44th Avenue.

Denver Art Museum. Extensive display of historical art; costumes, textiles, quilts. Open year-round, Tuesday to Saturday, 9 a.m. to 5 p.m. Free. Denver, at the south end of the Civic Center.

Healy House. A restored house that offers exhibits of the 1870 to 1880 gold rush era; Dexter Cabin nearby, finished inside with fine woodwork and hardwood floors. Open May 15 through September, daily, 9 a.m. to 4:30 p.m. Adults $1.50, children under 16 and senior citizens, 75 cents. Leadville, 912 Harrison Avenue.

Old Baca House and Museum. An adobe house built in 1869 by a prosperous rancher; museum depicts the active days of the Santa Fe Trail. Open June 1 through August, daily, 10 a.m. to 4 p.m. Adults $1.50, children 5 to 15, 75 cents. Trinidad, Main Street.

Overland Trail Museum. Exhibits of historical artifacts and fossils from northeastern Colorado; picnic area. Open May through September, daily, 9 a.m. to 5 p.m. Free. Sterling, on US-6.

Connecticut

Barnum Museum of Science and History. A museum of circus artifacts and historical items housed in a Byzantine-style building donated in 1893 by P. T. Barnum. Open year-round, Tuesday to Sunday, noon to 5 p.m. Donation asked. Bridgeport, 820 Main Street.

Henry Whitfield State Historical Museum. Believed to be the oldest house in New England, this building was restored in the 1930s and now contains exhibits of 17th- and 18th-century furniture, as well as other articles of the Colonial period. Open year-round, Wednesday to Sunday, 10 a.m. to 5 p.m. Adults 50 cents, children 6 to 18, 25 cents. Guilford, Whitfield Street.

Mark Twain Memorial. An 18-room house that was occupied by Mark Twain for many years; superb interior decor by Louis

Tiffany. Open year-round, daily, 10 a.m. to 4:30 p.m. Adults $3.50, children 6 to 15, $1.75. Hartford, 351 Farmington Avenue.

Mystic Seaport Museum. A re-creation of the homes, shops and lofts of a New England seaport of the mid-19th century; wooden sailing ships on the waterfront, ship models in museum, demonstration of shipbuilding methods, rigging and sail setting. Open year-round, daily, 9 a.m. to 5 p.m. Adults $6, students and senior citizens $5.25, children 6 to 11, $3. Mystic, off Interstate 95 along the Mystic River.

Tale of Whale Museum. Depicts the history of whaling in exhibits that include artifacts of the whaling industry; housed in a Greek Revival structure built in 1832. Open year-round, Tuesday to Sunday, 1 p.m. to 5 p.m. Adults 50 cents, children 6 to 16, 35 cents. New London, on Huntington Street.

Webb-Deane Stevens Museum. This museum complex consists of three restored 18th-century houses furnished with Colonial antiques and collections of Early American art. The Yorktown campaign of the Revolutionary War was planned here in 1781. Open year-round, daily, 10 a.m. to 4 p.m. Adults $1.50, children under 16, 50 cents. Wethersfield, off Interstate 91 (exit 26).

Delaware

Delaware Art Museum. Features a collection of English pre-Raphaelite paintings and works by American artists Thomas Pyle, Winslow Homer, the Wyeths and Thomas Eakins; lectures. Open year-round, daily, 10 a.m. to 5 p.m. Adults $1, students 50 cents, senior citizens free. Wilmington, Kentmere Parkway at Woodlawn Avenue.

Delaware Museum of Natural History. Nature's creations displayed in a natural setting; includes the largest known bird's egg collection of extinct New Zealand birds. Open year-round, Wednesday to Sunday, 9 a.m. to 4 p.m. Adults $2, children under 16, $1. Wilmington, on State Route 52.

Hagley Museum. A 200-acre complex located on the site of the original Du Pont black powder works; contains restored mills and exhibits on the industrial development of the region. Open year-round, Tuesday to Saturday, 9:30 a.m. to 4:30 p.m.; Sunday, 1 p.m. to 5 p.m. Adults $2.50, students $1, senior citizens $1.25. Wilmington, on State Route 141.

Henry Francis Du Pont Winterthur Museum. Contains the largest and richest collection of Early American interior architecture, furniture and accessories arranged in more than 100 rooms. Open year-round, Tuesday to Sunday, from 10 a.m.; reservations required to see some of the exhibits. Admission varies according to season; no children under 12 permitted. Wilmington, on State Route 52. (302) 656-8591.

Old Town Hall. Contains Colonial and Revolutionary War relics and a library of maps, newspapers and manuscripts pertaining to the history of Delaware. Open year-round, Monday to Saturday, noon to 4 p.m. Free. Wilmington, 512 Market Street.

Florida

Ernest Hemingway Home and Museum. A Spanish colonial mansion owned by the late Nobel Prize-winning author from 1931 to his death in 1961. Among the works he wrote here are *For Whom the Bell Tolls* and *A Farewell To Arms.* Open year-round, daily, 9 a.m. to 5 p.m. Adults $1.50, children 6 to 12, 50 cents. Key West, on US-1 at 907 Whitehead Street.

Florida State Museum. Exhibits of Indian artifacts, native birds and relics of Florida history. Open year-round, Monday to Saturday, 9 a.m. to 5 p.m.; Sunday, 1 p.m. to 5 p.m. Gainesville, on University of Florida campus, on Museum Road.

Kingsley Plantation State Historic Site. A complex of historic structures; tours. Open year-round, daily, tours from 9 a.m. Adults 50 cents, children under 6, free. Fort George Island, on State Route A1A.

Marjorie Kinnan Rawlings State Historic Site. The restored home of the Pulitzer Prize-winning author of *The Yearling*. Open year-round, daily, 9 a.m. to 5 p.m. Adults 50 cents, children under 6, free. Cross Creek, on State Route 325.

Ringling Museums. A complex of museums of art, the circus and a theater of the 68-acre estate of the late John Ringling. Open year-round, daily, from 9 a.m. Adults $3.50, children under 12, free. Sarasota, on US-41.

U.S. Naval Aviation Museum. Traces the development of American naval aviation through exhibits of more than 75 aircraft. Open year-round, daily, 9 a.m. to 5 p.m. Free. Pensacola, off Interstate 10.

Georgia

Atlanta Historical Society. Features archives, an auditorium and museum of Atlanta's history, architecture, art and music. Open year-round, Tuesday to Sunday, 10:30 a.m. to 4:30 p.m. Adults $3, children 6 to 17, $1.75. Atlanta, nine miles north at 3099 Andrews Drive.

Fort Benning Infantry Museum. Traces the evolution of the U.S. Army infantry from the French and Indian War to the present; weapons, uniforms, artifacts, medals and battle flags on display. Open year-round, daily, 10 a.m. to 4:30 p.m. Free. Columbus, on Ingersoll Street, Building 1234.

New Echota Historic Site. The site of the last capital of the Cherokee Nation in Georgia; the treaty which moved the Cherokee west was signed here. Open year-round, Tuesday to Saturday, 9 a.m. to 5:30 p.m.; Sunday, 2 p.m. to 5:30 p.m. Free. Calhoun, on State Route 225.

Oak Hill and Martha Berry Museum. The former plantation home of Martha Berry, founder of Berry College, includes a formal gardens and museum. Open year-round, daily, 10 a.m. to 5 p.m. Donations asked. Rome, on US-27.

Washington-Wilkes Historical Museum. A museum of the Confederacy featuring relics of the period and antique furnishings. Open year-round, Tuesday to Sunday, 9 a.m. to 5 p.m. Donations asked. Washington, on US-78.

Hawaii

Carthaginian II. A ship that now serves as a whaling museum; several whaling-era buildings are located nearby. Open year-round, daily, 9 a.m. to 5 p.m. Admission charged. Lahaina, Maui.

Hulihee Palace. A royal retreat in the 1800s, this coral and lava structure now serves as a Hawaiian historical museum. Open year-round, daily, 10 a.m. to 6 p.m. Free. Kailua-Kona, Hawaii.

Kauai Museum. Features the "Story of Kauai," a permanent historical exhibit. Open year-round, daily. Free. Lihue, Kauai.

Polynesian Cultural Center. Consists of authentic replicas of Polynesian villages and contains demonstrations of Polynesian arts, crafts and music. A nighttime music and costume show is featured. Open year-round, daily. Admission charged. Laie, Oahu.

Puako Petroglyphs. The largest — and perhaps the oldest — collection of petroglyphs on the islands. Open year-round, daily. Free. Hapuna Beach, Hawaii.

Idaho

Bannock County Historical Museum. Includes exhibits on the Old Oregon Short Line Railroad, fur trading and the Bannock and Shoshone Indian tribes. Open year-round, Monday to Saturday, 2 p.m. to 5 p.m. Free. Pocatello, at Center and Garfield.

Blaine County Historical Museum. Contains exhibits of early pioneer relics and features an extensive collection of American political memorabilia. Open June 15 through September 15, daily, except Tuesday, 10 a.m. to 5 p.m. Adults 50 cents, children under 12, free. Hailey, on North Main Street.

Old Idaho Penitentiary. Features tours of the former state prison grounds. Open year-round, daily, noon to 4 p.m. Adults $1.50, children 6 to 13, $1. Boise, five miles east on Penitentiary Road.

Illinois

Art Institute of Chicago. Houses famous paintings and watercolors ranging from the 13th century to the present; outstanding exhibit of miniature famous rooms; plays, lectures. Open year-round, daily, 10:30 a.m. to 5 p.m. Adults $2, students and senior citizens $1, free on Thursday. Chicago, Michigan Avenue at Adams Street.

Field Museum of Natural History. One of the foremost museums of natural sciences, established in 1893. Exhibits include the cultures of the American Indian and the civilizations of China and Tibet. Open year-round, daily, 9 a.m. to 6 p.m. Adults $1.50, students 50 cents, senior citizens 35 cents. Chicago, in Grant Park on Lake Shore Drive.

Fort Kaskaskia State Historic Site. A wooden stockade built by the French in 1736; Garrison Hill Cemetery. Open year-round, daily. Free. Chester, off State Route 3.

Hull House. The home of Jane Addams, pioneer social worker and first American woman to win the Nobel Prize for Peace. Open year-round, Sunday to Friday, 10 a.m. to 4 p.m. Free. Chicago, 800 South Halsted Street.

Highlight

Conner Prairie Pioneer Settlement

Conner Prairie, a 55-acre, 25-building open-air museum, brings the past alive — and you become a part of the experience. The year 1836 is re-created, not just with buildings and artifacts, but with carefully trained men and women who portray the occupations, the chores and the everyday lives of early Indiana settlers.

Well-worn paths lead you through the village where you can savor the scents of open-hearth cooking. You chat with the blacksmith over the sparks and ringing as he forges the villagers' wares. You chant the sing-song lessons in the one room "loud" school, and even risk a scolding if you dawdle on the path to learning.

Hours: Conner Prairie Pioneer Settlement is open from April 3 to December 16, 10 a.m. to 5 p.m., Tuesdays through Sundays. The Settlement is closed on Mondays, Easter and Thanksgiving.

Admission: Adults $3.50, senior citizens (age 60 and over), $2.75; children 6 through 18 and students with school I.D., $1.50. No charge for children 5 and under when they are part of a family group. Discount rates are available for groups of 15 or more by advance reservations, (317) 773-3633. No group rates offered on Sundays.

Visitors Center: The Prairie Inn cafeteria serves lunch and snacks daily. Special sit-down meals for groups may be arranged. Picnic facilities are also located on the grounds. The Trading Post gift shop sells many items handcrafted by Conner Prairie artisans.

Location: Conner Prairie is located six miles north of the Allisonville Road exit of Interstate 465, and four miles south of Noblesville, Indiana.

Highlight

Children's Museum

The Children's Museum of Indianapolis beckons children of all ages to its colorful and educational galleries full of treasures from other times, other places. Selected traveling exhibits reflecting international art and culture also will be shown at the museum during the Year of the Child celebration.

Step back through time to another world as you walk into the museum's realistic gallery settings. Explore an authentic 1800s log cabin nestled in an autumn woods diorama. Learn how other Americans lived in igloos and tepees.

Imagine yourself growing up in a Victorian nursery surrounded by a rocking horse, puzzles, games and toys.

Tour a railroad caboose hitched to a 55-ton locomotive at a re-created turn-of-the-century depot. Or go spelunking in the twisting passages of a simulated Indiana limestone cave.

During your excursions through time, you'll meet some of the museum's famous inhabitants. Replicas of a Tyrannosaurus Rex dinosaur and a Pteranodon flying reptile dominate the Story of Our Earth gallery. Two giant polar bears guard the entrance to the Eskimo gallery, while Wenuhotep, a 3,000-year-old mummy, lies in state inside the re-creation of an Egyptian tomb room.

The joy of being a child is captured in the exhibits on the museum's top level. During special hours, visitors can ride one of the 42 handcarved wooden animals on a turn-of-the-century carousel. Goats, reindeer, giraffes, horses, a lion and a tiger go up, down and around to the accompaniment of a real carousel band organ.
Nearby, toy trains zoom through villages and towns on a never-ending journey. And a changing exhibit of toys and dolls from the past 150 years is guaranteed to delight both young and young-at-heart.

The world's largest children's museum also houses the Lilly Theater, the only theater in Indiana which regularly presents touring programs for children. Puppets, plays, music, drama, dance and films entertain audiences in several theater seasons throughout the year.

Carousel

The carousel operates on school days from 2 p.m. to 5 p.m., on Saturdays and school holidays from 10 a.m. to 5 p.m. and on Sundays from 1 p.m. to 5 p.m. The cost is 25 cents for the public and free for members upon showing their membership cards.

Refreshments

A sandwich and ice-cream shop is located on the second level of the museum. No facilities are available for sack lunches. A variety of other restaurants can be found within 10 blocks of the building.

Hours

The Children's Museum is open Tuesday through Saturday from 10 a.m. to 5 p.m. and Sunday from 1 p.m. to 5 p.m. The museum is closed Monday.

Holiday Hours.

The museum is closed New Year's Day, Thanksgiving and Christmas. It is open from 1 p.m. to 5 p.m. Memorial Day, July Fourth and Labor Day, even if these holidays fall on a Monday.

Admission

Admission to the museum is always free.

Location

Indianapolis, between Meridian and Illinois Streets on 30th Street.

Highlight

Iowa's Living History Farms

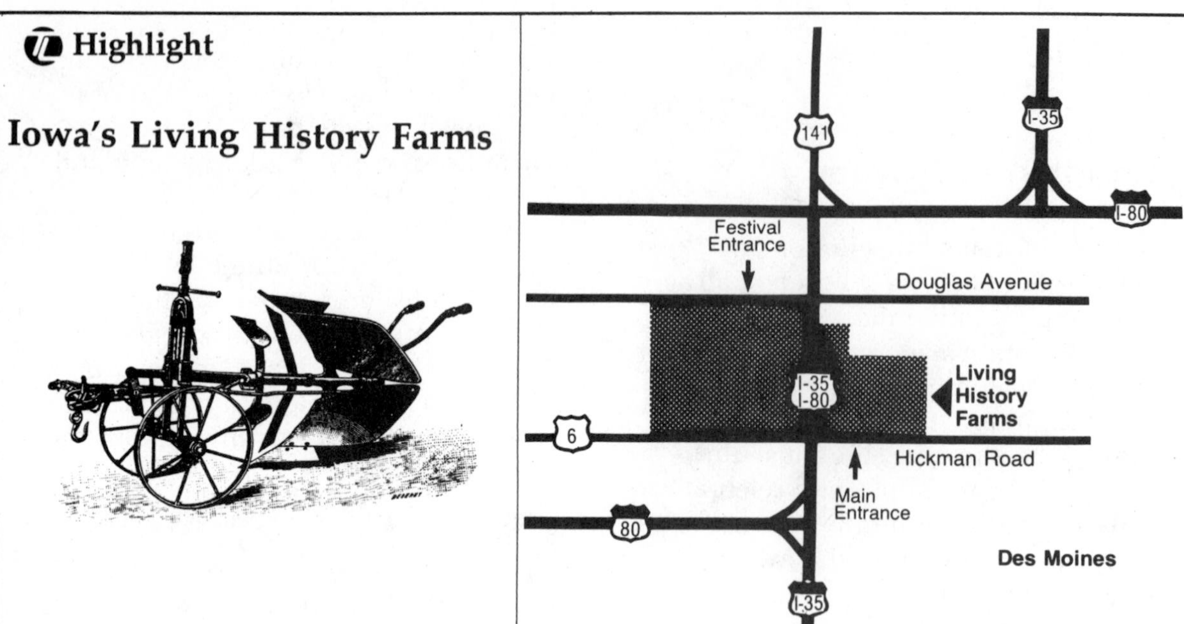

1840's Pioneer Farm

This area includes the Pioneer Farm in addition to the Oak Grove Stage Station. Oxen help with the heaviest work such as plowing and hauling while hand labor is used to plant and harvest. An endless round of gardening, cooking at the open hearth, making butter, cheese and soap, washing, sewing and mending fill the daylight hours and provide the family with basic needs.

Walnut Hill — 1870

By 1870, Iowa farmers could visit rural communities like Walnut Hill for most of their necessary goods and services. Along with a potter and blacksmith, carpenter shop, schoolhouse, general store, veterinary infirmary and a neighboring Victorian home, this area includes the main entrance, food and rest room facilities, a textile exhibit, craft gallery and business offices.

1900 Farm

The 1900 farmer relies upon horse-drawn equipment to plow, plant and cultivate his fields. Crops of corn, hay and oats feed the livestock and also provide some produce for the market. Housework centers around the noon meal cooked on the woodburning range. Washing and ironing, sewing and mending, cleaning and baking complete the farm wife's weekly schedule.

Location

West of Des Moines at exit #125 (Hickman Road) on the combined Interstates 35 and 80. Main entrance is from Hickman Road. Use Douglas Avenue entrance west of the Interstate for Corn and Grain Harvest Festivals.

Hours

Open daily, 9 a.m. to 5 p.m., April through October.

Admission

Adults $4, senior citizens $3, children 4 to 16, $2. Group rates available. For arrangements call (515) 278-5286.

Lincoln Log Cabin State Historic Site. Contains the reconstructed cabin of Thomas and Sarah Bush Lincoln, the President's father and stepmother. Open year-round, daily, 8 a.m. to 5 p.m. Free. Charleston, off State Route 16.

Lincoln's New Salem State Historic Park. An authentic restoration of the old town of New Salem, where Lincoln lived from 1831 to 1837. The original Onstot Cooper Shop, where Lincoln studied at night, is still standing; museum. Open year-round, daily, 8:30 a.m. to 5 p.m. Free. Petersburg, on State Route 97.

Ulysses S. Grant Home. Presented by the people of Galena to General Grant upon his return from the Civil War in 1865; contains many of Grant's personal possessions. Open year-round, daily, 9 a.m. to 5 p.m. Free. Galena, Bouthillier and Fourth Streets.

Indiana

Abraham Lincoln Library and Museum. Features an extensive collection of paintings and original photos of Lincoln and his family; library, archives. Open May through November, Monday to Saturday 8 a.m. to 4:30 p.m. Free. Fort Wayne, 1300 South Clinton Street.

Auburn-Cord-Duesenberg Museum. Features classic cars in the original factory showroom of the Auburn Automobile Company, erected in 1930. Open year-round, daily, 9 a.m. to 7 p.m. Adults $2, senior citizens and students $1, children under 6, free. Auburn, off Interstate 69, at 1600 South Wayne Street.

Children's Museum. Exhibits on natural history, science, American Indians and cultures of other lands; antique automobiles, 3,000-year-old mummy, carrousel, nature hikes. Open year-round, Tuesday to Saturday, 10 a.m. to 5 p.m.; Sunday, 1 p.m. to 5 p.m. Free. Indianapolis, between Meridian and Illinois Streets on 30th Street.

Home of James Whitcomb Riley. The home of the famous Indiana poet, preserved as it was when he lived there. Open year-round, Tuesday to Sunday, 10 a.m. to to 4 p.m. Adults $1, children 12 to 16, 25 cents. Indianapolis, 528 Lockerbie Street.

Tippecanoe Battlefield State Memorial. Marks the site of the 1811 battle in which General William Henry Harrison defeated the Indians led by Prophet, the brother of Tecumseh; museum. Open year-round, daily. Adults 25 cents, children 15 cents. LaFayette, off State Route 43.

Iowa

Amana Home. A 117-year-old home that features artifacts and furnishings of the early Amana settlement. Open April through November, Monday to Saturday, 10 a.m. to to 5 p.m.; Sunday, noon to 5 p.m. Adults 75 cents, children under 10, 25 cents. Amana Colonies, on US-6.

Cedar Rapids Art Center. Changing art exhibits, lectures, films and tours. Open year-round, Tuesday to Sunday, 10 a.m. to 5 p.m. Free. Cedar Rapids, 324 Third Street.

Des Moines Art Center. Exhibits include works of Rodin, Goya and several contemporary artists; building won international acclaim for its design. Open year-round, Tuesday to Sunday, 11 a.m. to 5 p.m. Free. Des Moines, Grand Avenue at 45th Street.

Grout Museum of History and Science. Indian culture and historical exhibits; blacksmith and apothecary shops. Open year-round, Tuesday to Saturday, 1 p.m. to 4:30 p.m. Free. Waterloo, off US-218.

Museum of Amana History. Features family heirlooms, original tools, industrial artifacts, art, photos and books related to the early settlers of the Amana Colonies. Open April 15 to November 15. Adults $1, children under 12, 50 cents. Amana Colonies, on State Route 220.

Kansas

Boot Hill and Front Street. A complex that contains a replica of the historic cemetery, six museums, the jail, and a replica of Front Street as it appeared in the 1870s. Open year-round, daily, 9 a.m. to 5 p.m.; hours extended in summer. Adults $1.50, children 6 to 11, $1. Dodge City, on Spruce, between Fourth and Fifth Avenues.

Dickinson County Historical Museum. Exhibits highlighting the life of pioneers; display of telephone equipment. Open year-round, daily, 10 a.m. to 4:30 p.m. Free. Abilene, 412 South Campbell Street.

Fort Dodge. Was one of the most important military posts in the late 1800s; established to protect the Santa Fe Trail from Indians. Open year-round, daily, during daylight hours. Free. Dodge City, on US-154.

Fort Leavenworth. A 7,000-acre facility that is one of the oldest army posts in the United States; museum. Open year-round, daily, from 10 a.m. Free. Lawrence, on US-73.

Fort Riley. Established in 1853 to safeguard travelers on the Santa Fe Trail; Old Trooper Statue and U.S. Cavalry Museum. Open year-round, Tuesday to Sunday, 10 a.m. to 5 p.m. Free. Fort Riley, off Interstate 70 (exit 299).

Pioneer Museum. Exhibits on pioneer life, Indian artifacts, musical instruments and aerobatic airplanes. Open year-round, daily, 10:30 a.m. to 6 p.m. Donation asked. Ashland, on US-160.

Kentucky

Fort Boonesborough. A replica of the fort built by Daniel Boone in 1775; crafts demonstrations. Open April through October, daily, 10:30 a.m. to 6:30 p.m. Adults $2, children 7 to 12, $1. Boonesboro, off State Route 388.

Headley Whitney Museum. Collections of

Louisiana's Longfellow-Evangeline State Commemorative Area

If you listen carefully, Acadian storytellers say, you can hear the whispering of Evangeline and Gabriel beneath the ancient oak tree near Acadian House. Of course, it may be only the gentle breeze from Bayou Teche stirring the lacy moss in the trees. But then again, it could be the famous lovers.

Visitors to this charming area are always captivated by the lifestyle of the inhabitants as well as the natural beauty of the land chosen by Acadian settlers for their new home. It was around the unhappy sequence of events during the first half of the 18th century that Henry Wadsworth Longfellow wrote his famous poem *Evangeline.* The work became his most famous literary contribution and helped earn for him a place in Poet's Corner, Westminster Abbey.

Interestingly enough, when Longfellow first heard the story of a young Acadian couple separated by the British in 1755, he suggested to his friend and fellow writer Nathaniel Hawthorne that Hawthorne use the material in his writings, but the latter replied that the story did not suit his style. Thereafter, Longfellow wrote the poignant love story in rich, gentle verse.

The poem is taken from the story of Emmeline Labiche and Louis Arceneaux, who, according to Acadian legend, became separated during their journey from Canada and were finally reunited beneath the Evangeline Oak in St. Martinville, Louisiana. The reunion was not a happy one, however, because Louis had fallen in love with and married another. This tragic news drove Emmeline into insanity and she died shortly thereafter.

Longfellow's account includes the separation of Evangeline and her lover Gabriel, but has Evangeline searching for him in vain for many years. As an old woman, she goes to Philadelphia and there, serving in a hospital during an epidemic, she finally finds her Gabriel barely alive, a patient in the hospital. He cannot even utter her name, but his eyes tell of his love, and as she kisses him, he dies in her arms.

The Acadian house, legendary home of Gabriel, is now a museum depicting the typical plantation-type dwelling of the 17th and 18th centuries. It was built around 1765 by Magdeleine Victoire Petit de la Houssaye, wife of a French military officer. The structural timbers are fastened with wooden pegs, as nails were not in common use at that time. Walls are made of moss, mixed adobe and brick, with heavy shutters on the windows. Furnishings are much as they were at the time the house was built, and you'll find many fine examples of early Louisiana pieces made of cypress. There is a kitchen-garden outside.

Near the museum is an Acadian Craft Shop, where one may examine and purchase authentic items made exactly as they were in the 18th century. Included are woven articles, examples of palmetto work, basketry and other genre arts.

As befits an area famous for its provincial cooking, a replica of an Acadian kitchen is available to visitors. Only the ancient cooking utensils and furnishings are on display, however. The visitor must journey to nearby restaurants for crawfish dishes and other local delicacies.

Museum Hours

9 a.m. to 5 p.m. Mondays through Saturdays; 1 p.m. to 5 p.m. Sundays. Closed on Christmas, New Year's Day and Thanksgiving holidays.

jewelry; shells and porcelains by George Headley; Whitney dollhouses. Open year-round, Wednesday to Sunday. Adults $2, students $1. Lexington, 4435 Old Frankfort Pike.

Mary Todd Lincoln House. The childhood home of Abraham Lincoln's wife; features memorabilia and Georgian furnishings. Open April through December, Tuesday to Saturday, 10 a.m. to 3 p.m. Adults $3, children 6 to 12, $1. Lexington, 578 West Main Street.

Perryville Battlefield State Shrine. The site of Kentucky's bloodiest Civil War battle; 22,000 Union troops clashed here in 1862 with 17,000 Confederates, with the Union forces emerging as the victors; museum. Open year-round, daily, 9 a.m. to 5 p.m. Perryville, off US-68.

Louisiana

Historic New Orleans Collection. Consists of 11 galleries featuring displays on early life along the Mississippi River. Open year-round, Tuesday to Saturday, 10 a.m. to 5 p.m. Adults $1, children under 13, 50 cents. New Orleans, 533 Royal Street.

Longfellow-Evangeline State Commemorative Area (PO Box 497, St. Martinville, Louisiana 70582, (318) 394-3754) is located within the city limits of St. Martinville in St. Martin Parish on La-31, along the banks of Bayou Teche. Development is centered around an Acadian house of the late 18th century and its kitchen-garden. Also of note is the Acadian craft shop, an accurate wood and mud replica of an old Acadian cottage. The 157-acre park and its structures interpret the history of the early French settlers of Louisiana.

Louisiana Historical Association Confederate Museum. Features relics and documents of the Civil War. Open year-round, Monday to Saturday, 10 a.m. to 4 p.m. Adults 50 cents, students under 12, 25 cents. New Orleans, 929 Camp Street.

New Orleans Museum of Art. Houses displays of ancient glass and pottery, paintings, sculpture, coins and needle work. Open year-round, daily, 10 a.m. to 5 p.m. Adults $1, students 50 cents. New Orleans, in City Park on center of traffic circle.

Old Cemeteries. Scattered throughout the city of New Orleans are a number of cemeteries that contain tombs of solid masonry 100 or more feet long and four tiers high, placed above ground because of the moist soil.

Maine

Bath Marine Museum. Exhibits on local shipbuilding families and traditions, along with small boatbuilding yard; boat ride. Open year-round, daily, 10 a.m. to 5 p.m. Adults $3, children under 16, $1. Bath, 963 Washington Street.

Nordica Homestead Museum. The birthplace of American singer Lillian Nordica; displays feature her costumes, jewelry and other mementos of her career. Open June through Labor Day, Tuesday to Sunday, 10 a.m. to 5 p.m. Adults $1, children 6 to 18, 50 cents. Farmington, off State Route 4.

Wadsworth-Longfellow House. The childhood home of Henry Wadsworth Longfellow, containing the furnishings and artifacts of the Wadsworth and Longfellow families. Open June through October, Monday to Friday, 9:30 a.m. to 4:30 p.m. Adults $1, children under 12, 25 cents. Portland, 487 Congress Street.

Maryland

Baltimore Museum of Art. Highlights include 19th- and 20th-century French art objects, as well as contemporary art and American decorative arts. Open year-round, Tuesday to Sunday, 11 a.m. to 5 p.m. Free. Baltimore, on Art Museum Drive.

Cross Manor. Said to be the oldest house in the state, built about 1643 by Thomas Cornwalleys. Open only in May during the Maryland House and Garden Pilgrimage. St. Inigoes, off State Route 5.

Peale Museum. Contains prints and historical portraits, many by the founder, Rembrandt Peale. Open year-round, Tuesday to Sunday, 10:30 a.m. to 4:30 p.m. Free. 225 North Holiday Street.

Highlight

Hubbarton Battlefield and Museum

On July 7, 1777, Colonel Seth Warner and the Green Mountain Boys with Colonial troops from Massachusetts and New Hampshire, fought at Hubbarton, the only battle on Vermont soil during the American Revolution. The British and Germans were hotly pursuing the main American Army on its retreat from Fort Ticonderoga. Detached to hold back these forces, Colonel Warner and the Vermonters helped perform one of the most successful rear-guard actions in the annals of American military history. They inflicted so many casualties on the enemy that the attacking forces turned around and limped across country back to Fort Ticonderoga. Thus, the British strategy to seize stores and property at Castleton and Rutland and to wreak havoc on the main American army ahead was completely upset. Though a short battle involving no more than 2,000 men, its significance was quite out of proportion to its size. The first successful resistance to Burgoyne, it forged the first link in a chain of military events leading to the capitulation of his once splendid Royal Army at Saratoga, two months later.

Open late May through mid-October, daily. Admission charged. East Hubbarton, Vermont, seven miles off US-4.

St. Mary's Square Museum. Consists of two buildings containing exhibits of historical and local interest. Open May through October, Saturday and Sunday, 10 a.m. to 4 p.m. Free. St. Michaels, at St. Mary's Square.

Massachusetts

Bunker Hill Monument. On Breed's Hill at the site of the battle of Bunker Hill on June 17, 1775. Open year-round, daily. Boston, Monument Square.

Common. This is the oldest public park in the country, set aside in 1634 for common use as a "cow pasture and training field." The Puritans had stocks and pens in the park for the punishment of those who profaned the Sabbath. The British mustered here before the battle of Bunker Hill. Boston, bounded by Beacon, Charles, Tremont, Park and Boylston Streets.

Faneuil Hall. Given to the city of Boston by Peter Faneuil, this building served as a meeting place during the revolutionary movement; paintings of famous battles, library, military museum. Open

Highlight

Detroit's Science Center

The Detroit Science Center is a new science museum located on eight acres of land in Detroit's Cultural Center, just two miles north of downtown. It's not an ordinary museum, however. It's 36,250 square feet of mind-expanding space, where you can experience firsthand the marvels of science and technology. There are no "hands-off" signs here. Over 50 exhibits invite you to use your muscles and intellect to discover a scientific principle for yourself. Visitors of all ages push buttons, pull levers and turn knobs to make the exhibits work for them. There are no guided tours as such. Science Center visitors are encouraged to explore the exhibit hall at their own pace. Demonstrator-hosts and hostesses are always available, however, if you find an exhibit that puzzles you. In addition to the Center's permanent exhibits, special temporary exhibits on loan from such sources as the American Medical Association and NASA are on display from time to time.

A demonstration theater in the exhibit hall features live demonstration programs on a wide variety of science topics ranging from chemistry to lasers to space exploration.

The Detroit Science Center consists of three basic floor levels: ground, plaza and exhibit floor. Visitors enter the building on the plaza level. It serves as a waiting and reception area where visitors purchase admission tickets and gather material for their visit. From here, take an elevator to the exhibit hall or an escalator down to the space theater. The ground floor is the site of administrative offices, work shop, visitor service areas, an orientation area for group tours and the space theater. All public areas of the building are easily accessible to the handicapped.

Hours

The Science Center is open year-round. Call (313) 833-1892 for a current listing of hours.

Admission

Visitors 6 years and older, $2; $1 for visitors 5 years and younger. There are no group rates. Admission includes a visit to the exhibit hall and one space theater show.

How to Get There

The Science Center is easily accessible from Detroit's major freeways. It's located at the corner of John R Street and E. Warren Boulevard — just one block east of Woodward Avenue in the heart of the Detroit Cultural Center.

year-round, daily, 9 a.m. to 5 p.m. Free. Boston, Faneuil Hall Square at Merchants Row.

House of Seven Gables. This home, built in 1668, was the inspiration for Nathaniel Hawthorne's novel, *The House of the Seven Gables*. On the grounds are several other historic structures. Open year-round, daily, 9:30 a.m. to 6:30 p.m. Adults $2, children 5 to 12, 50 cents. Salem, 54 Turner Street.

Lexington Green. The site of the first skirmish of the American Revolution, April 19, 1775, between Patriots and Concord-bound British troops. Open year-round, daily. Lexington, Massachusetts Avenue and Bedford Street.

Museum of Fine Arts. Features American, European, Classical, Egyptian and Asiatic paintings and sculptures. Open year-round, Tuesday to Sunday, 10 a.m. to 5 p.m. Adults $1.75, children under 17, free. Boston, at Huntington Avenue and the Fenway.

Museum of Science. Offers displays and exhibits on natural history, physical science, medicine and astronomy. Open year-round, daily, 9 a.m. to 5 p.m. Adults $3.50, children 5 to 16, $2.25. Boston, at Science Park.

Old North Church. The oldest church in Boston, built in 1723; from the window of the steeple, lanterns flashed the signal of the approaching British. Open year-round, daily, 9 a.m. to 5 p.m. Boston, 193 Salem Street.

William Cullen Bryant Home. The poet and editor of the *New York Evening Post* was born here in 1794; original furnishings. Open year-round, Friday to Sunday and holidays, 1 p.m. to 5 p.m. Adults $1.25, children under 15, 50 cents. Cummington, off State Route 9, 1½ miles south on State Route 112.

Michigan

Call of the Wild Museum. Featured displays on more than 150 lifelike North American wild animals and birds in their natural settings. Open year-round, daily, 8 a.m. to 6 p.m. Adults $2, children 13 to 17, $1.50, 5 to 12, 75 cents. Gaylord, off Interstate 75.

Detroit Historical Museum. Displays trace the development of Detroit's growth from Indian times to the present. Open year-round, Tuesday to Sunday, 9:30 a.m. to 5 p.m. Donations asked. Detroit, Woodward and Kirby.

Detroit Institute of the Arts. Exhibits on the development of the arts from ancient to modern times; collections of armor, African art and Impressionists. Open year-round, Tuesday to Sunday, 9:30 a.m. to 5:30 p.m. Donations asked. Detroit, Woodward and Kirby.

Old Fort Mackinac. Features 14 original buildings preserved as a museum; costumed guides; Indian museum. Open May 15 through October 15, daily, 9 a.m. to 6 p.m. Adults $2.50, children 13 to 17, $1.50. Mackinac Island, accessible by boat from St. Ignace or Mackinaw City.

Minnesota

Mayo Medical Museum. Extensive exhibits include life-size anatomical models of the human body, the "Transparent Man" demonstration and illustrations of standard surgical procedures. Open year-round, daily, 9 a.m. to 5 p.m. Free. Rochester, in Damon Parkade.

Minnesota Museum of Art. Features contemporary and Asian art, crafts and sculptures. Open year-round, Monday to Friday, 11 a.m. to 5 p.m. Donations asked. St. Paul, Kellogg Boulevard and St. Peter Street.

Sibley House. Built in 1835, this is the first stone house in Minnesota, constructed by pioneer fur-trader Henry Sibley. The house has been restored and features fine furnishings. Open May through October, daily, 10 a.m. to 5 p.m. Adults $1.50, children 12 to 17, 50 cents, 6 to 11, 25 cents. Mendota, off Interstate 35.

Walker Art Center. Features displays of 20th-century American and European art; paintings, sculptures and prints from the last two decades of American art. Open year-round, Tuesday to Sunday, 10 a.m. to 5 p.m. Free. Minneapolis, Hennepin Avenue and Vineland Place.

Mississippi

Beauvoir. The last home of Jefferson Davis, President of the Confederacy. Features a beautiful home and gardens maintained as a Confederate shrine; many furnishings are original. Open year-round, daily, 8:30 a.m. to 5 p.m. Adults $3, children 8 to 16, $1, senior citizens and military $2. Biloxi, on US-90.

Jimmie Rodgers Memorial Museum. A museum devoted to the "father of country music," with exhibits of his guitars, music and correspondence. Open year-round, daily, 10 a.m. to 4 p.m. Adults $1, children under 10, free. Meridian, about three miles northwest in Highland Park.

Merriwether Lewis Site. A tribute to the Western explorer, Captain Meriwether Lewis; museum. Open year-round, daily, 8 a.m. to 5 p.m. Hohenwald, 7½ miles east, at junction of State Route 20 and Natchez Trace Parkway.

Missouri

Battle of Lexington State Historic Site. The site of the Civil War battle popularly called the "Battle of the Hemp Bales," so named for the movable breastworks used by the Confederates; museum nearby. Open year-round, daily. Lexington, off US-24.

Jefferson Memorial. Headquarters for the Missouri Historical Society, featuring relics portraying the history of Missouri and St. Louis. Open year-round, daily, 9:30 a.m. to 4:45 p.m. Free. St. Louis, in Forest Park.

Kansas City Museum of Science and History. Offers more than 60,000 exhibits on natural history and regional history. Open year-round, Tuesday to Saturday, 9:30 a.m. to 4:30 p.m. Adults $1, students 50 cents, children under 6 not admitted. Kansas City, 3218 Gladstone Boulevard.

Liberty Jail. Mormon prophet Joseph Smith was confined here for four months in 1838 and 1839; it is said that Smith received several revelations during his incarceration. Open year-round, daily, 8 a.m. to 6 p.m. Free. Liberty, in the museum, one block north of the square.

Pony Express Stables Museum. This site was the eastern terminus for the service which originated in California. On April 3, 1860, riders from Sacramento, California, completed the 1,966-mile trip in 10 days. Open year-round, daily, April through September, 9 a.m. to 5 p.m.; weekends only during October. Adults 50 cents, children 25 cents. St. Joseph, 914 Penn Street.

Montana

Museum of the Plains Indian. Exhibits of historic and contemporary Indian arts; audiovisual presentations, special exhibits, dioramas. Open year-round, daily, 9 a.m. to 5 p.m. Free. Browning, at junction of US-2 and US-89.

Central Montana Museum. Features Indian artifacts and early photos of the area. Open year-round, Monday to Friday, 8 a.m. to 5 p.m. Free. Lewistown, 408 Northeast Main Street.

C. M. Russell Museum. Contains the watercolors, models, notes and letters of famed Western artist Charles M. Russell; studio nearby. Open year-round, daily, 10 a.m. to 5 p.m. Adults $1, students

50 cents, children under 12, free. Family rate $2. Great Falls, 12th Street and Fourth Avenue.

Nebraska

Harold Warp Pioneer Village. Features more than 30,000 historic items depicting America's development from 1830; wood-burning locomotives, antique autos, Indian fort, original pony express station, general store. Open year-round, daily, 8 a.m. to sunset. Adults $3, children 6 to 15, $1 (admission valid for two days). Minden, off Interstate 80, on US-6 and US-34.

Joslyn Art Museum. Includes exhibits of contemporary American art, Nebraska artists and Indian art; lectures, films. Open year-round, daily, 10 a.m. to 5 p.m. Adults 75 cents, children under 12 and senior citizens, 25 cents. Omaha, 2200 Dodge Street.

Stuhr Museum of the Prairie Pioneer. A two-story museum featuring exhibits on pioneer life in Nebraska. The museum sits on an island in the middle of a man-made lake; grounds include a re-created railroad town of the 1860s. Open year-round, daily, 9 a.m. to 6 p.m. Adults $1, children 7 to 15, 50 cents. Grand Island, at junction of US-34 and 281.

Union Pacific Museum. Exhibits on the development of the railroad; pioneer and Indian artifacts, personal papers of Abraham Lincoln. Open year-round, Monday to Saturday, 9 a.m. to 5 p.m. Free. Omaha, 1416 Dodge Street.

Nevada

Hamilton. A ghost town that was a booming mining town between 1866 and 1876; mines produced $9 million of silver ore. Open year-round, daily. Free. Ely, 45 miles west, off US-50.

Ward Charcoal Ovens Historic State Monument. Six 30-foot high, stone "beehive" ovens constructed during the mining boom. Open year-round, daily. Free. Ely, 12 miles southeast, off US-50.

New Hampshire

Daniel Webster Birthplace. The restored home that features antiques and relics of the period. Open late June through Labor Day, Wednesday to Sunday, 9 a.m. to 6 p.m. Adults 50 cents, children under 18, free. Franklin, 3½ miles south, off State Route 127.

John Paul Jones House. The home of naval hero John Paul Jones while his ship, the *Ranger,* was being built; personal items, portraits. Open May 15 through October 15, Monday to Saturday, 10 a.m. to 4 p.m. Adults $1.50, children 6 to 14, 50 cents. Portsmouth, Middle and State Streets.

Mystery Hill. Consists of prehistoric stone structures believed to be the oldest of their kind on the North American continent. Research indicates that ancient Celts from the Mediterranean may have lived in the area between 800-300 B.C. Open April through December, daily, 9:30 a.m. to 5:30 p.m. Adults $3, students and senior citizens $2.50, children 6 to 12, $1. North Salem, off State Route 111, on Haverhill Road.

Old Fort Number Four. A reconstructed fort originally built in 1746; period furnishing and craft demonstrations. Open May 15 through October 17, daily, 10 a.m. to 5 p.m. Adults $2.50, children 7 to 13, $1. Charlestown, on State Route 11.

New Jersey

Grover Cleveland Birthplace. The house in which Cleveland, President of the United States from 1885 to 1889 and 1893 to 1897, was born in 1837; contains many personal items. Open year-round, daily, 10 a.m. to 6 p.m. Admission 25 cents. Caldwell, 207 Bloomfield Avenue.

Johnston National Scouting Museum. A museum on the grounds of the national headquarters of the Boy Scouts of America featuring exhibits and artifacts relating to scouting. Open year-round, Tuesday to Sunday, 9 a.m. to 4:30 p.m. Free. New Brunswick, south of junction of US-1 and US-130.

Smithville. A restoration of a historic 18th-century southern New Jersey community featuring some 45 buildings and several commercial shops. Open year-round, daily, 11 a.m. to 9 p.m. in summer; 11 a.m. to 6 p.m. in winter. Free. Smithville, at junction of US-9 and Country Route 561A.

Walt Whitman Home. The famed poet lived here from 1873 until his death in 1892; features original furnishings and many mementos. Open year-round, Wednesday to Sunday, 9 a.m. to 5 p.m. Admission 50 cents. Camden, 330 Mickle Street.

New Mexico

Albuquerque Museum. Features exhibits reflecting the history, art and science of the Rio Grande Valley. Open year-round, Tuesday to Sunday, 10 a.m. to 5 p.m. Free. Albuquerque, 2000 Mountain Road.

Indian Pueblo Cultural Center. Features a museum depicting the history and traditions of the Pueblo Indians; crafts and fine arts, restaurant, crafts market. Open year-round, daily, 9 a.m. to 6 p.m. Free. Albuquerque, off Interstate 40 at 12th Street exit.

Puye Cliff Dwellings and Communal House Ruins. Remnants of the ancient Pajaritan Indians featured in cave dwellings hollowed out of the soft stone cliff. Open year-round, daily, 8 a.m. to 6 p.m. Adults $1, children 50 cents. Espanola, 11 miles west.

New York

Adirondack Museum. Features exhibits on the Adirondacks from the colonial period on; museum houses special exhibits, photos, dioramas, railroad equipment. Open June 15 through October 15, daily, 10 a.m. to 5 p.m. Adults $4, children 7 to 15, $2.25. Blue Mountain Lake, on State Routes 28 and 30.

Albright-Knox Art Gallery. Houses a notable art collection and features the "Mirrored Room," a full-size room, table and chair made completely of mirrors. Open year-round, Tuesday to Sunday, 10 a.m. to 5 p.m. Donations asked. Buffalo, at junction of State Route 198 and Elmwood Avenue.

Millard Fillmore Cabin. A replica of the cabin in which the 13th President of the United States was born. Open May 15 to October 16, daily, 8 a.m. to 10 p.m. Free. Moravia, on State Route 38.

Museum of Modern Art. Houses an outstanding collection of modern sculpture, design, drawings, prints, photos, films and paintings; movies shown at intervals throughout the week. Open year-round, daily, except Wednesday, 11 a.m. to 6 p.m. Adults $1.50, children under 16 and senior citizens, 55 cents. New York City, 11 West 53rd Street.

Thomas Paine Cottage. Former home of Revolutionary War activist Thomas Paine; features personal mementos. Open year-round, Tuesday to Sunday, 2 p.m. to 5 p.m. Free. New Rochelle, North and Paine Avenues.

Washington's Headquarters State Historic Site. Was Washington's headquarters from April 1, 1782 to August 19, 1783; paintings, period furnishings and historical relics. Open year-round, Wednesday to Sunday and holidays, 9 a.m. to 5 p.m. Free. Newburgh, Liberty and Washington Streets.

Whitney Museum of American Art. An extensive collection of contemporary American paintings and sculptures housed in a unique building. Open year-round, Tuesday to Sunday, 11 a.m. to 6 p.m. Free. New York City, 945 Madison Avenue.

North Carolina

Bath. The oldest incorporated town in the state, founded in 1705, and the first official port of entry for the colony; tours. Open year-round, daily 9 a.m. to 5 p.m. Adults $1, children under 12, 50 cents. Bath, on State Route 92.

Museum of the Cherokee Indian. Features displays on the history of the Cherokee Indians; crafts, clothing, weaponry. Open year-round, daily 9 a.m. to 5:30 p.m. Adults $2.50, children 6 to 13, $1.25. Cherokee, on US-441.

Oconaluftee Indian Village. A Cherokee Indian center where Indians practice the crafts of their ancestors; huts contain articles as old as 200 years. Open mid-May through late October, daily, 9 a.m. to 5:30 p.m. Adults $3.50, children 6 to 12, $2. Cherokee, off US-441.

Tryon Palace Restoration Complex. The home of William Tryon, constructed in 1770, once considered the finest government building in colonial America; antique furnishings, gardens. Open year-round, Tuesday to Sunday, 9:30 a.m. to 4 p.m. Adults $2, students $1. New Bern, on George Street.

North Dakota

Beck's Great Plains Museum. Features historical exhibits, antiques and Indian artifacts; replica of pioneer town. Open May 15 to October 15, daily, 11 a.m. to 6 p.m. Adults $1.75, children 6 to 16, 75 cents, family rate $5. Mandan, on State Route 1806.

Bonanzaville USA. Consists of a pioneer village, Indian Museum and the Regional Museum of the Red River and Northern Plains. Open year-round, daily, 9:30 a.m. to 5 p.m. Adults $2, children 2 to 16, $1. Fargo, six miles west on US-10.

State Historical Museum. On the state capitol grounds; features historical exhibits and Indian artifacts. Open year-round, daily, 9 a.m. to 5 p.m. Free. Bismarck, on North Sixth Street.

Ohio

Cincinnati Art Museum. Displays of paintings, prints and sculptures representing great civilizations. Open year-round, Tuesday to Sunday, 10 a.m. to 5 p.m. Free. Cincinnati, off US-22 in Eden Park.

Cleveland Museum of Art. Collections representing a wide variety of cultures and periods; concerts, lectures, films. Open year-round, Tuesday to Sunday, 10 a.m. to 5 p.m. Free. Cleveland, 11150 East Boulevard.

Cleveland Museum of Natural History. Displays interpret early man and the natural history of the region; 70-foot dinosaur, planetarium. Open year-round, daily, 10 a.m. to 5 p.m. Adults $1.50, senior citizens and children 6 to 18, 50 cents. Cleveland, on Wade Oval in University Circle.

Lawnfield. The restored home of James Garfield, 20th President of the United States; mementos, library, campaign office. Open year-round, Tuesday to Sunday, 9 a.m. to 5 p.m. Adults $1.50, students 12 to 18, $1, under 12, free. Mentor, 8095 Mentor Avenue.

Ohio Historical Center. The headquarters of the Ohio Historical Society housing historical, archaeological material, library and transportation exhibit. Open year-round, Monday to Saturday, 9 a.m. to 5 p.m.; Sunday 10 a.m. to 5 p.m. Free. Columbus, at junction of Interstate and 17th Avenue.

Highlight

Oklahoma's Pioneer Woman Museum

The Pioneer Woman Museum, Ponca City, Oklahoma, was dedicated on September 16, 1958, the 65th anniversary of the opening of the Cherokee Strip for settlement. The museum's geographical location in this historical pioneering area, once a part of Indian Territory, embraces the boundless horizons of the prairie as a tribute to the pioneer woman's endless faith and dreams for the future of her family. The sweeping forceful winds of the Plains symbolize the resistance of hardships and struggle that challenged this pioneer helpmate in changing the wilderness and prairies of Oklahoma into thriving towns and productive farms.

The Pioneer Woman Museum houses exhibits of household furniture, equipment, costumes and memorabilia of family life in the pioneer era. Originally, some of the artifacts were in use in nearby log cabins in wooded areas or sod houses built by the pioneers of the plains area where there was a scarcity of trees. Artifacts and photographs of regional oil and ranching developments, with emphasis on the famous 101 Ranch, are also preserved.

Hours: Monday through Saturday, 9 a.m. to 5 p.m. Open until 7 p.m. each day during Daylight Savings Time. Admission is free.

Oklahoma

Cherokee Strip Historical Museum. Depicts pioneer life on the Cherokee Strip; furnished one-room schoolhouse, farm machinery. Open year-round, Tuesday to Sunday, 9 a.m. to 5 p.m. Free. Perry, off Interstate 35 (Fir Avenue exit).

Fort Chickamauga. A functional cavalry post built in the style of the 1860s; troops perform in authentic uniforms. Open February 15 through January 15, daily, 9 a.m. to 5 p.m. Adults $1.50, children 6 to 16, 75 cents. Cookson, on State Route 82.

Fort Reno. A frontier fort of the 1870s. Open year-round, Monday to Friday, 9 a.m. to 5 p.m. Free. El Reno, off US-66.

Fort Washita. An early Indian Territory Fort built in 1842; last occupied during the Civil War. Open year-round, daily, 9 a.m. to 5 p.m. Free. Madill, on State Route 199 East.

Oregon

Butler Museum of American Indian Art. Houses a number of art objects of various North American tribes; tours. Open year-round, Tuesday to Saturday, 10 a.m. to 5 p.m. Adults $1.50, children 12 to 18, 75 cents, under 12, 25 cents. Eugene, 1155 West First Street.

Oregon Historical Society. A museum and library that includes exhibits of historical and archaeological artifacts; miniature wagon collection. Open year-round, Monday to Saturday, 10 a.m. to 4:45 p.m. Free. Portland, 1230 SW Park Avenue.

Portland Art Museum. Contains a wide variety of American and European art, as well as a number of Indian art objects. Open year-round, Tuesday to Sunday, noon to 5 p.m. Adults $1, students 50 cents, children under 13 and senior citizens, free. Portland, 1219 SW Park Avenue at Jefferson.

Pennsylvania

Brandywine Battlefield Park. Encompasses 50 acres and takes in the site of the Battle of the Brandywine, where American forces were defeated by the British on September 11, 1777; exhibits. Open year-round, daily 9 a.m. to 5 p.m. Donations asked. Chadds Ford, on US-1.

Currier and Ives Antiques Gallery. Exhibits original lithographs published by Currier and Ives; prints, antiques. Open year-round, Monday to Friday, 10 a.m. to 3 p.m. Adults $1.50, children under 12, free. York, 43 West King Street.

Fort Ligonier. A wooden fort established in 1758, now restored and furnished with period artifacts; museum. Open April 15 through November 15, daily, 9 a.m. to sunset. Adults $2.75, children 6 to 13, $1.50, senior citizens $2. Ligonier, at junction of US-30 and State Route 711.

Pennsylvania Military Museum. Depicts the history of Pennsylvania military from the Revolution through present; uniforms, equipment displayed. Open year-round, Tuesday to Sunday, 10 a.m. to 4:30 p.m. Adults $1, children under 12, free. Boalsburg, on US-322.

William Penn Memorial Museum and Archives Building. Houses art exhibits, historic documents and a mural depicting the state's history; natural history exhibits. Open year-round, daily 9 a.m. to 5 p.m. Free. Harrisburg, on Third Street.

Rhode Island

Hunter House. A restored home that offers an outstanding example of Colonial architecture and features fine paneling, furniture and paintings. Open May through October, daily, 10 a.m. to 5 p.m. Adults $2.50, children 6 to 12, $1.25. Newport, 54 Washington Street.

Museum of Art. Houses collections of classical art, European porcelains and Oriental works, as well as works of American artists. Open year-round, Tuesday to Sunday, 11 a.m. to 4:30 p.m. Adults $1, children 5 to 18, 25 cents. Providence, 224 Benefit Street.

Slater Mill Historic Site. Restored mill that depicts the development of factory processes and life in a 19th-century industrial village; demonstrations. Open March through December, Tuesday to Sunday, 10 a.m. to 5 p.m. Adults $2, children 6 to 14, 75 cents, senior citizens $1.25. Pawtucket, on Roosevelt Avenue.

South Carolina

Charleston Museum. One of the country's oldest museums, featuring a superb collection of furniture, textiles, arts and crafts. Open year-round, daily, 9 a.m. to 5 p.m. Adults $1, children 6 to 18, 50 cents. Charleston, 121 to 125 Rutledge Avenue.

Heyward-Washington House. Built in 1770, this historic structure was the home of Thomas Heyward, Jr., a signer of the Declaration of Independence. Open year-round, daily, 10 a.m. to 5 p.m. Adults $1.75, children 6 to 18, 50 cents. Charleston, 87 Church Street.

Magnolia Plantation and Gardens. A magnificent plantation dating from the late 1600s; the 400-acre grounds contain some 950 varieties of camellias and 250 types of azaleas. Open year-round, daily, 8 a.m. to dusk. Adults $4, children 12 to 19, $3, 4 to 11, $2. Charleston, off US-17, on Ashley River Road.

South Dakota

Call of the Wild Museum. Extensive exhibits on North American wildlife. Open year-round, daily, 9 a.m. to 5 p.m. Adults $2, children 6 to 15, $1. Hill City, on Main Street.

Prairie Homestead. An original homesteaders dwelling built of sod and logs. Open June through September 15, daily, 9 a.m. to 5 p.m. Adults $1.50, children 11 to 17, $1. Kadoka, off Interstate 90 (exit 131).

South Dakota Memorial Art Center. Features paintings of artist Harvey Dunn and works of other artists. Open year-round, daily, 8 a.m. to 5 p.m. Free. Brookings, Medary Avenue at Harvey Dunn Street.

Tennessee

Casey Jones Home and Railroad Museum. The home of legendary railroad hero John Luther "Casey" Jones; museum nearby contains the sister engine and tender to his "Old 382." Open year-round, daily, 8 a.m. to 5 p.m. Adults $1, children 6 to 12, 50 cents. Jackson, 211 West Chester Street.

The Hermitage. The estate of Andrew Jackson containing many of the original furnishings and fixtures, as well as personal effects of the President and Mrs. Jackson. Open year-round, daily, 8 a.m. to 6 p.m. Adults $3, children 6 to 13, $1. Nashville, off US-70 and Interstate 40.

James K. Polk Ancestral Home. Contains the original furnishings, portraits and personal items of the Polk family. Open April to October, Monday to Saturday, 9 a.m. to 5 p.m. Adults $1.50, children 12 to 18, 50 cents, under 12, 25 cents. Columbia, on US-43.

Museum of Appalachia. Features an extensive collection of frontier artifacts; reconstructed log cabins. Open year-round, daily, 8 a.m. to dusk. Adults $1.75, children 6 to 12, $1. Norris, on State Route 61.

Texas

Bayou Bend. The former home of Miss Ima Hogg containing some of the finest American furniture from the early 17th, 18th and 19th centuries; tours by reservation only. Open year-round, Tuesday to Saturday. Houston, at 1 Westcott Street. (713) 529-8773.

Confederate Air Force Flying Museum. The world's most extensive collection of World War II aircraft maintained in flying condition; air shows. Open year-round, daily 9 a.m. to 5 p.m. Adults $3, children 6 to 14, $1.50. Harlingen, in Harlingen Industrial Park.

Magoffin Home State Historic Site. A restored adobe home originally built in 1875; period furnishings. Open year-round, Wednesday to Sunday, 9 a.m. to 4 p.m. Adults 50 cents, children under 12, 25 cents. El Paso, 1120 Magoffin Avenue.

Panhandle Plains Historical Museum. Features exhibits on the development of the Great Plains region; Indian artifacts. Open year-round, daily, 9 a.m. to 5 p.m. Canyon on State Route 217.

Spanish Governor's Palace. Restored structure contains furnishings imported from Spain. Open year-round, daily, 9 a.m. to 5 p.m. Adults 40 cents, children 7 to 13, 15 cents. San Antonio, on Military Plaza.

Utah

Daughters of Utah Pioneers Museum. Extensive exhibits on the development and history of the state. Open year-round, Monday to Friday, 9 a.m. to 5 p.m. Free. Springville, 175 South Main Street.

Iron Mission State Historical Monument. The site of the first pioneer foundry west of the Mississippi; stagecoach and surrey collection, farm machinery and industrial vehicles. Open year-round, daily, 9 a.m. to 5 p.m. Free. Cedar City, on State Route 91.

The Oregon Trail

The Diary of a Pioneer

Many pioneers recorded their impressions along the Oregon Trail in personal diaries. Most would never find the inspiration they had found on the trail to write again, but their memories live on. The following includes excerpts from the diary of Enoch W. Conyers who traveled the Oregon Trail in 1852.

April 20, 1852 — It was an ideal spring morning, the sun shining its very brightest . . . when about 10 o'clock our long journey across the plains was commenced. Our wagon, secured especially for the trip, was light and of the very best material; our team consisted of four yoke of cattle, none over four years of age . . . We parted with our nearest and dearest relatives and friends, who had accompanied us thus far and wished us God-speed and a safe journey to the new Eldorado. Then it was that we realized that we were gone from those who we would never see again and were left to propel our "prairie schooner" something over 2,000 miles through the wilderness by ox power. Our load, consisting of bedding, clothing and provisions for a six-month journey, weighed about 1,600 pounds. . . .

April 27 — Weather good, roads drying up. We had to cross several narrow and very sidling ridges on our way today, but drove over all of them safely, nothing unusual happening. . . .

May 7 — Tonight we are camped at Fort Kearny. The fort is built from the land . . . sod and adobe. They tell us the earth walls are warm in the winter and cool in the summer, but they don't hold out the rain. We fixed our wagons as well as we could, and stocked up on flour and bacon. The road ahead follows the Platte River and the next military outpost is Fort Laramie some 300 miles away. . . .

May 19 — A wagon fell off the ferry while crossing the river today, rolling and bobbing as the current carried it away. Finally, it brought up on a sand bar. None that witnessed the accident believed it possible that either of the occupants would be found alive, but, to the great surprise and joy of all, the young man extricated himself from under the contents and then brought his sister alive to the surface.

May 26 — More wagon trains on the road now. It is quite amusing to note the different mottos on the wagon covers, such as, "From Danville, Illinois, and Bound for Oregon," or, "Bound for California or Bust." Saw one wagon with, "Root, Little Hog, or Die," scrawled on both sides. Observed a splendid four-horse coach in which was seated four richly dressed young ladies and two young girls. A few minutes later our captain rode by saying, "The emigrants ahead are having trouble with the Indians. Be ready boys, that they do not take us by surprise." We see a lot of Indians along the road, all dressed up in war paint, their hair cut short except for a small bunch on the top of their heads which is stuck full of quills. Their quivers are full of arrows all ready for use. We came another six miles without incident. . . .

June 5 — Several of our party have symptoms of cholera brought on, as I verily believe, by drinking water from the well we dug last night, it being strongly impregnated with alkali.

June 12 — We came 15 miles today and camped at Ash Hollow. The road today has been exceedingly rough; scarcely a foot of anything like a piece of level road and the word "steep" does not begin to describe the final descent into the Hollow. We had to rough-lock the wheels for the first time and several times I felt sure that the wagon would tip over on the tongue yoke of cattle. This afternoon I saw our first buffalo. Some emigrants, some afoot and others on horseback, were in hot pursuit. We heard several shots fired, but they did not bring him down. Both buffalo and men very soon passed out of sight beyond the hills . . . fresh graves line the sides. . . .

June 16 — We came in view of Courthouse Block and Chimney Rock about noon today while crossing the ruins of the "ancient bluffs." We have a splendid view of those noted rocks from our camp tonight which brings to mind some verses composed by "The Platte River Poet," one of which runs thus:

"The next we came to was Platte River
Great sights were there to see.
There was Courthouse Block and Chimney Rock
And, next, Fort Laramie."

June 18 — We started at 6 a.m. and came 12 miles and stopped for lunch near Scott's Bluffs on the Platte River. It commenced raining and blowing a perfect hurricane, and we were obliged to form a corral with our wagons for the purpose of preventing a stampede of cattle. The storm had spent its force in about 25 minutes without any damage being done. Grazing is very good here, but could find no "buffalo chips" for fuel. . . .

June 22 — We passed Fort Laramie yesterday and obtained several little articles needed in camp. At this camp, an emigrant, who, with his wife, was traveling with another family, murdered the other man and his wife. He then took possession of the man's team and provisions, and he and his wife started the return trip to the Missouri River, reporting that they had become discouraged and would go no farther. Within a day, the dead bodies of the murdered couple were discovered and the officers at Fort Laramie notified. We heard that they were apprehended, tried at Fort Laramie at the charge of murder, convicted and hanged. We did not learn their names. . . .

June 26 — Today we camped near the "natural bridge" and laid by to wash and rest our cattle. We noticed that it has become general for the stock to begin to suffer and lag with the increasing roughness of the country. It is more noticeable among the horses than with the cattle. We saw several bands of buffalo today but got no meat. Grass is scarce and seems to be getting more and more scarce the farther we go, having been used up by those ahead of us. We were obliged to drive our cattle three miles from camp tonight to obtain any grass whatever for them. . . .

July 2 — We are camped tonight on the "Sweetwater," on the east side and near by the "Independence Rock." Why this stream is called Sweetwater, I don't know, but after being obliged to drink alkali water or the roily water from the River Platte most all the way, it certainly causes this pure mountain water to taste very sweet indeed . . . Most of our company visited the summit of Independence Rock, which was reached with much difficulty but without accident. We found the rock literally covered with the names of emigrants. Some of these names were written with chalk; some were cut with a cold chisel, whilst others were written with tar. From the numerous names, one would naturally suppose that every man, woman and child that ever passed this way succeeded in writing or having their names written on this rock. Beyond stands "Devil's Gate" which is something grand — perpendicular rocks of granite formation towering 400 feet high on either side of the river, the Sweetwater tunneling between having cut its way through. . . .

July 4 — Sunday — Yesterday the boys who went hunting returned, some loaded with antelope, some with sagehens, and some with jackrabbits. Others brought a huge snowball, inserting a pole through the center the easier to carry it . . . This Independence Day was ushered in with the booming of small arms. Although the noise was not so great as that made by a cannon, it was the best we could do, so far from civilization. We raised our 40-foot flagstaff with Old Glory nailed fast to the top after which our company circled around and sung *The Star Spangled Banner.* Then all gathered around the tables loaded with refreshments and enjoyed a feast of antelope, sagehen, jackrabbit, potatoes, beans, breads, cakes and pies fresh from the oven. The snowball was brought into use in making a fine lot of Sweetwater Mountain ice cream.

July 10 — We have traveled 22 miles over a very rocky and mountainous road. Heretofore the dust was from four to six inches deep, and almost unbearable; but today it has been too rocky to raise a dust. We are now on the first bench of the Rocky Mountains and are camped on a small fork of the Sweetwater. About 50 yards from camp is a snowbank five feet deep. Tonight we are supposed to be about three-fourths of a mile from the summit of the South Pass of the Rocky Mountains.

July 12 — Yesterday we crossed the "roof of the Continent" and entered into "Oregon Country." We passed Pacific Springs, which consists of nothing but tough sod that has grown over the water, but the water does flow to the west for the first time. We have shortened our wagon bed by cutting off two feet. This lightens up our load by about 100 pounds yet we have about 1,200 pounds left, consisting of bedding and provisions. We passed the junction of "Sublette's Cutoff" this afternoon and came on down the Salt Lake Road to camp on the Little Sandy. . . .

July 14 — We came to the lower crossing of the Green River, which is about 75 yards wide, and crossed over about noon. The charge for ferrying was $3 per wagon and we swam our cattle. We traveled about one mile after crossing the river to the forks in the road. Here our train separated, part of the train going to California and part to Oregon. One might imagine that it was quite easy for us to part company, yet it was quite the reverse. I do not believe that there was a man, woman or child in the company but what shed tears . . . We had traveled so far together that we had become attached almost as one family. . . .

Salt Lake Art Center. Features works by regional artists. Open year-round, Tuesday to Sunday, noon to 5 p.m. Free. Salt Lake City, 20 Southwest Temple Street.

Vermont

Home of Calvin Coolidge. The birthplace, boyhood home and grave of the 30th President of the United States; original furnishings. Open Memorial Day through mid-October, daily 9:30 a.m. to 5:30 p.m. Adults $1, children under 14, free. Plymouth, off State Route 100A.

Hubbarton Battlefield and Museum. The site of a Revolutionary War battle; diorama. Open mid-May to mid-October, daily, 9 a.m. to 5 p.m. Free. Castleton, off US-4.

Museum of American Fly Fishing. Displays of fishing equipment, including the tackle of Presidents Herbert Hoover and Dwight Eisenhower. Open year-round, daily 9 a.m. to 5 p.m. Free. Manchester, on US-7, in the Orvis Company.

Shelburne Museum. An outdoor museum of early New England life featuring more than 35 buildings on 45 acres; blacksmith shop, jail, meeting house, stagecoach inn. Open May 15 to October 15, daily, 9 a.m. to 5 p.m. Adults $5, students $2.50. Shelburne, on US-7.

Virginia

Historic Mitchie Tavern Museum. A famous tavern whose guests included Jefferson, Madison, Monroe, Jackson and Lafayette; other historic buildings on site. Open year-round, daily, 11:30 a.m. to 3 p.m. Adults $2, children 6 to 12, $1.50. Charlottesville, on State Route 20, off Interstate 64.

James Monroe Museum and Memorial Library. Features mementos of the President and Mrs. Monroe, as well as

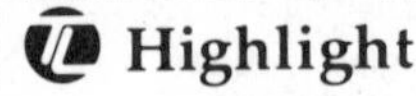

Historic Bethlehem, Pennsylvania

Bethlehem was founded in 1741 by the Moravians, middle-European Protestants known also as the Unity of the Brethren. They served as missionaries to other Germanic settlers and to the Indians and brought order, industry, music and education to the Pennsylvania wilderness.

One of the unique aspects of 18th-century Bethlehem was the complex of crafts, trades and industries which made the community nearly self-supporting. By 1747, there were 32 industries located along the Monocacy Creek, many of them using the most advanced technology of the time to produce a variety of high-quality products.

By the middle of the 19th century, however, most of the early industries had ceased operation. The buildings were torn down or used for other purposes and, by the middle of the 20th century, the whole area had become an automobile junkyard. But in the 1960s, the city of Bethlehem rescued the area from its blight and turned the nine-acre tract over to Historic Bethlehem Incorporated, a voluntary, non-profit, community educational organization.

Historic Bethlehem's current efforts are centered on preserving and restoring this 18th-century industrial area. To describe and interpret this heritage, there are tours by guides in colonial Moravian dress, sight-and-sound displays, exhibits of goods and tools, and demonstrations of colonial crafts.

Open year-round, Tuesday to Saturday, 10 a.m. to 4 p.m. Adults $1.25, children 75 cents. Bethlehem, off Interstate 78.

A few of Bethlehem's historic attractions . . . .

Site of 1761 Tanner's Work House. Raw animal hides were prepared for the tanning process here. They were washed in the creek, soaked in lime and water, and scraped to remove the hair.

Foundations of 1753 Butchery and Site of Butcher's Stable and Corral. Here animals were slaughtered to provide meat for Bethlehem's residents. The hides went to the Tanner's Work House and Tannery.

Foundations of 1771 Dye House and Dwelling. Here craftsmen used animal and plant dyes to color woolen and linen cloth until 1835. The building was partially demolished in 1893.

Site of 1751 Grist Mill and Fulling Mill. In this limestone building, a waterwheel powered beaters to shrink and clean, or full, woolen cloth and also turned stones to grind grain. When the complex burned in 1869, the present Luckenbach Mill was built on its foundation.

1830s Grist Miller's House. The lower, stone portion of this building was constructed in 1782 to house the miller and his family. The upper, brick section was added in the 1830s.

Foundation of 1749 Pottery. In this two-story limestone building, potters made redware bowls, dishes, pie plates, pipe heads and tile stoves. Stocking weavers worked on the second floor.

Site of 1750 Forge Complex. In this two-story limestone structure, the blacksmith, locksmith and nailsmith plied their trades.

Restored John Sebastian Groundie House. John Sebastian Groundie was a prominent Moravian brewer. His house, built in the Federal architectural style about 1810, was probably the first brick residence in Bethlehem. The north rooms have been restored and furnished as a period dining room and kitchen.

furnishings originally used in the White House. Open year-round, daily, 9 a.m. to 5 p.m. Adults $1, students 40 cents. Fredericksburg, 908 Charles Street.

Mary Washington House. The home of George Washington's mother, who lived here until her death in 1789; English garden. Open year-round, daily, 9 a.m. to 5 p.m. Adults $1, students 50 cents. Fredericksburg, Charles and Lewis Streets.

Monticello. The home of Thomas Jefferson from 1772 until his death in 1826; personal effects. Open year-round, daily, 8 a.m. to 5 p.m. Adults $2, children 6 to 11, 50 cents. Charlottesville, on State Route 53.

Museum of the Confederacy. On the grounds of the Confederate White House; features exhibits, artifacts and paintings of the Confederacy. Open year-round, daily, 9 a.m. to 5 p.m. Adults $1, children 7 to 12, 50 cents. Richmond, at 12th and Clay Streets.

Williamsburg. A colonial restoration project that features 88 18th-century structures; exhibits, shops, special events. Open year-round, daily. Williamsburg, off US-60 on Lafayette Street and Francis Street.

Washington

Hovander Homestead. A restored home that is part of a large park encompassing a barn, milk house, gardens and children's farm zoo; antique furnishings and farm equipment. Open year-round, Monday to Friday, 10 a.m. to 6 p.m.; Saturday and Sunday 10 a.m. to 8 p.m. Donation 50 cents. Ferndale, off Interstate 5.

Pioneer Village and Willis Carey Historical Museum. Features the history of the Columbia River Indians and rebuilt pioneer structures. Open April through

September, Wednesday to Sunday, 10 a.m. to 4:30 p.m. Cashmere, off US-2.

Seattle Art Museum. Houses an outstanding collection of Oriental art, as well as selected American paintings, prints and sculpture. Open year-round, Tuesday to Sunday, 10 a.m. to 5 p.m. Adults $1, students and senior citizens 50 cents. Seattle, in Volunteer Park.

Washington State Historical Society Museum. Natural history displays and exhibits on Indian and pioneer life. Open year-round, Tuesday to Sunday, 9 a.m. to 5 p.m. Free. Tacoma, 315 North Stadium Way.

West Virginia

Campbell Mansion. The former home of Alexander Campbell, founder of Bethany College; period furnishings. Open April through November, Tuesday to Sunday, 10 a.m. to 5 p.m. Adults $1, students 50 cents. Bethany, on State Route 67.

Huntington Galleries. Features an extensive collection of paintings, prints, carvings, ceramics, firearms and Georgian Silver. Open year-round, Tuesday to Sunday, 10 a.m. to 4 p.m. Huntington, Eighth Street Road.

Pocahontas County Historical Museum. Located in an old house featuring documents, implements, clothes, gadgets and toys that depict the history of the county. Open June through Labor Day, daily, 11 a.m. to 5 p.m. Adults 50 cents, children 12 to 18, 25 cents. Marlinton, on US-219.

Wisconsin

Galloway House and Village. A restored 30-room Victorian mansion and gardens; grounds include one-room school, gazebo, print shop, blacksmith shop. Open Memorial Day through September, daily, 1 p.m. to 5 p.m. Adults $2, children under 19, 50 cents. Fond Du Lac, on US-41.

Milwaukee Art Center and War Memorial. Houses exhibits of paintings, sculptures, prints and decorative arts; tours. Open year-round, Tuesday to Sunday, 10 a.m. to 5 p.m. Adults $1, senior citizens and students 50 cents, under 12, free. Milwaukee, 750 North Lincoln Memorial Drive.

Milwaukee Public Museum. Displays on state's history and history of Indians in the region; plant and animal exhibits. Open year-round, daily, 9 a.m. to 5 p.m. Adults $2, children under 18, 75 cents. Milwaukee, 800 Wells Street.

National Railroad Museum. Exhibits of railroad equipment dating back to 1880; train rides. Open year-round, daily, 9:30 a.m. to 5 p.m. Adults $2.50, children 5 to 12, $1.25. Green Bay, 2285 South Broadway.

Surgeon's Quarters. A restored building built about 1828 on the original site of old Fort Winnebago; period furnishings, historic documents. Open May through October, daily 9 a.m. to 5 p.m. Adults $2, children 4 to 14, 50 cents. Portage, on State Route 33.

Wyoming

Buffalo Bill Historical Center. Displays depicting Old West history and the life of Buffalo Bill Cody. Open year-round, daily, 8 a.m. to 5 p.m. Adults $2.50, children 6 to 15, $1. Cody, on US-14.

Cheyenne Frontier Days Old West Museum. Features displays of Sioux Indian artifacts and a collection of horse-drawn vehicles. Open year-round, daily, 9 a.m. to 5 p.m. Adults $1, children under 12, free with adult. Cheyenne, adjacent to Frontier Park.

Fort Bridger State Historic Site. Fort established in 1842 by Jim Bridger; many of original buildings still standing; museum. Open year-round, daily, 8 a.m. to 6 p.m. Free. Fort Bridger, on US-30.

Stagecoach Museum. Features displays of relics of pioneer and Indian life; an original stagecoach. Open May 15 through October, daily, 10 a.m. to 5 p.m. Adults 50 cents, children 12 to 15, 25 cents. Lusk, on US-85.

Highlight

Where East Met West

Just outside of Corinne, Utah, at Promontory Summit, the first transcontinental railroad was completed. This important moment in history is recaptured in a museum sponsored by the Sons of Utah Pioneers at Corinne, Utah. Located approximately 55 miles north of Salt Lake City and a mere four miles off Interstate 15 is the Railroad Village Museum featuring vintage engines, rail cars, tools and a typical western rail station, including many pioneer antiques and art objects.

A mural depicts the Central Pacific's engine, Jupiter, meeting nose to nose with the Union Pacific's No. 119, just prior to the driving of the Golden Spike.

Two vintage steam engines donated by the railroads are on exhibit. The Union Pacific engine No. 6254 was built in 1907 by the Baldwin locomotive works in Philadelphia at an initial cost of $17,032. A giant in its day, it has eight drive wheels, is capable of carrying 7,000 gallons of water and 14 tons of coal. It weighs more than 186 tons. The Central's No. 1744 is a smaller six-wheeler. Both are open daily, 10 a.m. to 5 p.m. for close-hand inspection by the public.

Museum is open March through September, Monday to Saturday, 10 a.m. to 5 p.m. Adults 50 cents, children under 12, 25 cents.

Highlight

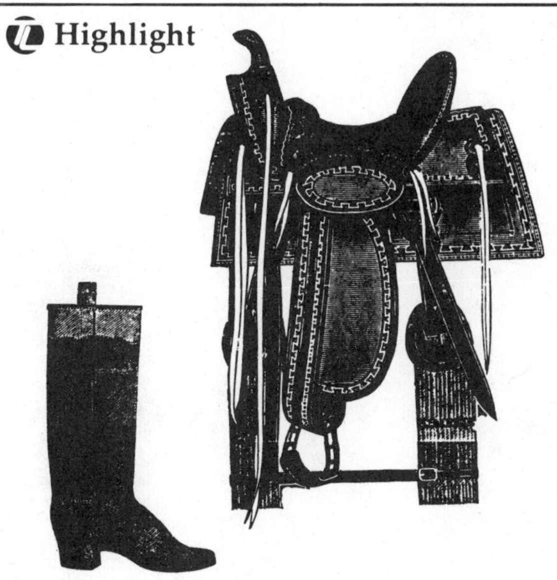

Cowboy Gear

The cowboy's dress evolved from functional needs. His trousers were worn tight to avoid being caught in the brush; the chaps were added for protection from thorns and branches. The vest with deep pockets held tobacco and incidentals; this sleeveless garment provided warmth and ease of movability. The broad-brimmed hat shielded eyes from the sun, wind or rain; it could be used to send messages, fan a fire or direct a herd of cattle. The ornamental bandanna was a breathing mask to keep out trail dust; the yellow slicker functioned as the oiled canvas raincoat for the trail. The high-heeled boots were a point of ethnic pride for the man who was seldom on foot; the heel gave him a hold in the stirrup while the pointed toe helped him slip easily into the stirrup or slip free if thrown. The saddle was the cowboy's most prized personal possession and varied in value and style. Today's cowboy still selects his boots and hats with discriminatory care and wears the denim shirts, jackets and trousers, referred to as "jeans." This western wear is popular with many in occupations unrelated to cattle or horses.

Arizona's Hopi Indian culture is preserved nearly unchanged at this village known as Walpi atop First Mesa.

The unique craftsmanship of Hopi basketry is part of the endless variety of Indian artistry abounding in Arizona (above). Life continues at its slow pace at a Tsa-La-Gi Indian village in Oklahoma (right).

Tracing Our Indian History

They came to North America some 30,000 to 50,000 years ago across an ice bridge that stretched from Siberia to Alaska. Thus, the Indians became the first immigrants to the New World, settling in its mountains and valleys and eventually ranging over the entire continent.

As the Indians — or native Americans, as they now like to be called — spread out across North America, they developed diverse cultures with as many as 200 distinct languages and dialects. To a great extent, those cultures were shaped by the land on which the Indians lived. Those who settled in regions where game was plentiful became hunters. The tribes that settled along seashores, lakes or rivers became primarily fishermen. Where the land was rich and fertile, the tribes took to agriculture. And, for those who lived in more arid regions, foraging became a way of life.

Whichever way of life the Indians followed, they prospered; and by the time the first Europeans arrived in the New World, vast numbers of Indians populated the continent from the north to the south and from coast to coast. Contrary to popular belief, the Indians were generally a peace-loving people, and they greeted the white man accordingly. But as more and more immigrants came, the inevitable struggle for dominion began. For several hundred years, with few exceptions, the Indians were repeatedly driven from their lands — through duplicity and slaughter — until their numbers were so decimated that they had little choice but to accept the reservations to which they were assigned.

Though the Indian population has been greatly reduced, there are still nearly a million Indians of various tribes living all across the United States, mostly on reservations. In every state in the union you'll find remnants of past Indian cultures, and in many states, there are reservations that welcome visitors. If you do visit a reservation, remember you are a guest in the Indians' houses; always ask permission to take pictures and respect those areas that may be off limits. It is also customary, when taking pictures, to offer some compensation; exactly how much to offer will depend on the situation.

The following will serve as a guide for those who wish to learn more about the rich culture and history of the Indians. At the end of each state you will also find a list of the tribes that are currently active there. For more information on Indian reservations, attractions and special events, contact:

Bureau of Indian Affairs
U.S. Department of the Interior
Washington, D.C. 20245.

Alabama

Indian Mound and Museum, Florence.
Mound State Monument, Moundville.
Russell Cave National Monument, Northwest of Bridgeport.

Alaska

Alaska State Museum, Juneau.
Sitka National Monument, Sitka.
Tongass Historical Society Museum, Ketchikan.
University Museum, University of Alaska, Fairbanks.

Tribes: Eskimo, Aleut, Tlingit.

Arizona

Besh-Ba-Gowah, South of Globe.
Canyon de Chelly National Monument, near Chinle.
Casa Grande Ruins National Monument, Coolidge.
Colorado River Tribes Indian Museum, Parker.
Gila River Indian Museum, Sacaton.
Grand Canyon National Park, South Rim, North Rim.
Kinishba Pueblo, West of Whiteriver.
Montezuma Castle National Monument, South of Flagstaff.
Museum of Northern Arizona, Flagstaff.
Navajo National Monument, Northwest of Tuba City.
Navajo Tribal Museum, South of Window Rock.
Oraibi Pueblo, southeast of Tuba City.
Pueblo Grande Museum, Phoenix.
Tonto National Monument, northwest of Globe.
Tuzigoot National Monument, northwest of Cottonwood.
Walnut Canyon National Monument, southeast of Flagstaff.
Walpi Pueblo, southeast of Tuba City.
Wupatki National Monument, northeast of Flagstaff.

Tribes: Cocopah, Havasupai, Hualapai, Hopi, Mohave-Apache, Maricopa, Navajo, Papago, Yavapai.

Arkansas

Caddo Burial Mounds, west of Murphreesboro.
Henderson State University Museum, Arkadelphia.
University of Arkansas Museum, University of Arkansas, Fayetteville.

California

Antelope Valley Indian Research Museum, near Lancaster.
Big and Little Petroglyph Canyons, near China Lake.
Calico Mountains Archaeological Project, northeast of Barstow.
California State Indian Museum, Sacramento.
Catalina Island Museum, Santa Catalina Island.
Clarke Memorial Museum, Eureka.
Indian Grinding Rock State Historical Monument, Pine Grove.
Joshua Tree National Monument, Twenty-nine Palms.
Los Angeles County Museum of History and Science, Los Angeles.
Lowie Museum of Anthropology, University of California, Berkeley.
Oakland Museum, Oakland.
Pioneer Museum and Haggin Galleries, Stockton.
Riverside Municipal Museum, Riverside.
San Bernardino County Museum, Badlands.
San Diego Museum of Man, San Diego.
Santa Barbara Museum of Natural History, Santa Barbara.
Southwest Museum, Los Angeles.
Tulare County Museum, Visalia.

Tribes: Chemehuevi, Chukchansi, Hoopa, Maidu, Mission, Mi-Wok, Paiute, Pomo, Wailaki, Yuma, Yurok.

Colorado

Colorado State Museum, Denver.
Denver Museum of Natural History, Denver.
Koshare Indian Kiva Museum, La Junta.
Lowry Pueblo Ruins, National Historic Landmark, northwest of Cortez.
Mesa Verde National Park, east of Cortez.
Pioneers Museum, Colorado Springs.
University of Colorado Museum, Boulder.
Ute Indian Museum, south of Montrose.

Tribe: Ute.

Connecticut

Peabody Museum of Natural History, Yale University, New Haven.
Tantaquidgeon Indian Museum, Uncasville.

Tribe: Pequot.

Delaware

Island Field Archaeological Museum and Research Center, South Bowers.

Tribe: Nanticoke.

Florida

Florida State Museum, University of Florida, Gainesville.
Museum of Florida History, Tallahassee.
Seminole Museum, West Hollywood.
Southeast Museum of the North American Indian, Marathon.
Temple Mound Museum and Park, Fort Walton Beach.

Tribe: Seminole.

Georgia

Creek Museum, Indian Springs.
Etowah Mounds Archaeological Area, Cartersville.
Kolomoki Mounds State Park, north of Blakely.

Idaho

Nez Perce National Historical Park, Spalding.

Tribes: Bannock, Coeur D' Alene, Kootenai, Nez Perce.

Illinois

Cahokia Mounds State Park, East St. Louis.
Dickson Mounds Museum of the Illinois Indian, outside Lewistown.
Field Museum of Natural History, Chicago.
Illinois State Museum, Springfield.

Indiana

Angel Mounds State Memorial, near Evansville.
Mounds State Park, east of Anderson.
Museum of Indian Heritage, Indianapolis.

Iowa

Effigy Mounds National Monument, north of McGregor.

Tribes: Sauk and Foxes, Winnebago.

Kansas

El Quartelejo Indian Kiva Museum, Scott City.
Fort Larned National Historic Site, Larned.
Indian Burial Pit, near Salina.
Inscription Rock, Lake Kanpolis State Park, southeast of Ellsworth.
Kansas Sac and Fox Museum, Highland.
Pawnee Indian Village Museum, northwest of Belleville.

Tribes: Kickapoo, Sauk and Foxes, Pottawatomi.

Kentucky

Adena Park, north of Lexington.
Ancient Buried City, southeast of Cairo.
Museum of Anthropology, University of Kentucky, Lexington.

Louisiana

Louisiana State Exhibit Museum, Shreveport.
Marksville Prehistoric Indian Park State Monument, Marksville.

Tribes: Chittimacha, Coushatta.

Maine

Robert Abbe Museum of Stone Age Antiquities, Bar Harbor.

Tribes: Passamaquoddy, Penobscot.

Maryland

Baltimore Museum of Art, Baltimore.

Massachusetts

Fruitlands Museum, Harvard University, Cambridge.
Memorial Hall, Deerfield.
Robert S. Peabody Foundation for Archaeology, Phillips Academy, Andover.
Peabody Museum, Salem.
Peabody Museum of Archaeology and Ethnology, Harvard University, Cambridge.
Plimoth Plantation, Inc., Plymouth.
Springfield Science Museum, Springfield.

Michigan

Chief Blackbird Home Museum, Harbor Springs.

Fort Wayne Military Museum, Detroit.
Grand Rapids Public Museum, Grand Rapids.
Great Lakes Indian Museum, Cross Village.
Kingman Museum of Natural History, Battle Creek.
Norton Mounds, south of Grand Rapids.
University of Michigan Exhibit Museum, Ann Arbor.
Wayne State University Museum of Anthropology, Detroit.

Tribes: Chippewa, Potawatomi.

Minnesota

Crow Wing County Historical Society, Brainerd.
Mille Lacs State Indian Museum, Mille Lacs.
Pipestone National Monument, south of Pipestone.
The Science Museum of Minnesota, St. Paul.

Tribes: Chippewa, Menominee, Munsee, Oneida.

Missouri

Cherokee Museum, St. Louis.
Ralph Foster Museum, School of the Ozarks, Point Lookout.
Graham Cave, Graham Cave State Park, Interstate 70 near Danville.
Kansas City Museum of History and Science, Kansas City.
Lyman Archaeological Research Center and Hamilton Field School (Utz Site), northwest of Marshall.
Missouri State Museum, Jefferson City.
Museum of Anthropology, University of Missouri, Columbia.
Museum of Science and Natural History, St. Louis.

Tribes: Sauk and Foxes.

Mississippi

Emerald Mound, northeast of Natchez
Natchez Trace Visitor Center, north of Tupelo.

Montana

Chief Plenty Coups Museum, Pryor.
Custer-Sitting Bull Battlefield Museum, Crow Agency.
Museum of the Plains Indians, Browning.
Poplar Indian Arts and Crafts Museum, Poplar.

Tribes: Assiniboine, Atsina, Blackfeet, Chippewa, Crow, Cree, Cheyenne, Flathead, Kootenai, Sioux.

Nebraska

Fort Robinson Museum, Nebraska State Historical Society, Fort Robinson.
Fur Trade Museum, Chadron.
University of Nebraska State Museum, Lincoln.

Nevada

Lost City Museum of Archaeology, near Lake Mead.

Tribes: Paiute, Shoshone.

New Hampshire

Dartmouth College Museum, Hanover.

New Jersey

Newark Museum, Newark.
New Jersey State Museum, Trenton.

New Mexico

Acoma Pueblo, south of Casa Blanca.
American Indian Arts Museum, Santa Fe.
Anthropology Museum, Eastern New Mexico University, Portales.
Aztec Ruins National Monument, Aztec.
Bandelier National Monument, Los Alamos.
Chaco Canyon National Monument, Bloomfield.
Coronado State Monument, Bernalillo.
El Morro National Monument, west of El Morro.
Gallup Museum of Indian Arts, Gallup.
Gila Cliff Dwellings National Monument, Gila Hot Springs.
Gran Quivira National Monument, south of Mountainair.
Jemez State Monument, southwest of Los Alamos.

Jicarilla Apache Tribal Museum, Dulce.
Kwilleylekia Ruins Monument, Cliff.
Laguna Pueblo, west of Albuquerque.
Maxwell Museum of Anthropology, University of New Mexico, Albuquerque.
Palace of the Governors, Santa Fe.
Pecos National Monument, Pecos.
Picuris Pueblo, southwest of Taos.
Puye Cliff Ruins, Santa Clara Indian Reservation, southwest of Espanola.
Salmon Ruins Museum, three miles west of Bloomfield.
Sandia Man Cave, northeast of Albuquerque.
San Juan Pueblo, north of Espanola.
Santa Clara Pueblo, northwest of Santa Fe.
Taos Pueblo, Taos.
Zia Pueblo, north of Santa Ana.
Zuni Pueblo, southwest of Gallup.

Tribes: Apache, Navajo, Pueblos, Zuni.

New York

American Museum of Natural History, New York.
Buffalo and Erie County Historical Society, Buffalo.
Buffalo Museum of Science, Buffalo.
Canandaigua Historical Society Museum, Canandaigua.
Castile Historical Society Museum, Castile.
Cooperstown Indian Museum, Cooperstown.
Fort Plain Museum, Fort Plain.
Fort William Henry Restoration and Museum, Lake George.
Mohawk-Caughnawaga Museum, Fonda.
Museum of the American Indian, Heye Foundation, New York.
New York State Museum and Science Service, Albany.
Owasco Indian Village, Owasco.
Oysterponds Historical Society, Orient.
Rochester Museum and Science Center, Rochester.
Six Nations Indian Museum, Onchiota.
Yager Museum and Library, Oneonta.

Tribes: Cayuga, Mohawk, Onondaga, Seneca, Tuscarora.

North Carolina

Museum of the American Indian, Boone.
Museum of the Cherokee Indian, Cherokee.
Oconaluftee Indian Village, Cherokee.

Tribe: Cherokee.

North Dakota

Affiliated Tribes Museum, Newtown.
Lewis and Clark Trail Museum, Alexander.
Slant Indian Village, Fort Lincoln State Park, south of Mandan.

Tribes: Arikara, Chippewa, Gros Ventre, Mandan, Sioux.

Ohio

Allen County Museum, Lima.
Cleveland Museum of Art, Cleveland.
Cleveland Museum of Natural History, Cleveland.
Fort Ancient State Memorial, southeast of Lebanon.
Indian Museum, Piqua.
Johnson-Humrickhouse Memorial Museum, Coshocton.
Miamisburg Mound State Memorial, Miamisburg.
Mound City Group National Monument, Chillicothe.
Ohio State Museum, Columbus.
Seip Mound, east of Bainbridge.
Serpent Mound State Memorial, northeast of Peebles.
Story Mound, Chillicothe.

Oklahoma

Andarko Museum, Andarko.
Cherokee Center, Tahlequah.
Cherokee History Museum, Tahlequah.
Creek Indian Museum, Okmulgee.
Five Civilized Tribes Museum, Muskogee.
The Thomas Gilcrease Institute of American History and Art, Tulsa.
Indian City, U.S.A., Andarko.
Kerr Museum, Poteau.
Museum of the Great Plains, Lawton.
Oklahoma Historical Society, Oklahoma City.
Osage Tribal Museum, Pawhuska.

Ottawa County Historical Society, Miami.
Philbrook Art Center, Tulsa.
Ponca City Indian Museum, Ponca City.
Sequoyah's Home, Sallisaw.
Southeastern Plains Indian Museum, Andarko.
J. Willis Stovall Museum, University of Oklahoma, Norman.
Tsa-La-Gi Indian Village, Tahlequah.
Woolaroc Museum, southwest of Bartlesville.

Tribes: Apache, Arapaho, Caddo, Cherokee, Cheyenne, Chickasaw, Choctaw, Creeks, Comanche, Delaware, Iowa, Kickapoo, Kiowa, Peoria, Ponca, Seminole, Seneca, Shawnee, Sauk and Foxes, Tonkawa, Wichita, Wyandotte.

Oregon

Collier State Park, north of Klamath Falls.
Coos-Curry Museum, North Bend.
Horner Museum, Corvallis.
Klamath County Museum, Klamath Falls.
Museum of Natural History, University of Oregon, Eugene.

Tribes: Cayuse, Grand Ronde, Klamath, Modoc, Paite, Snake, Walla Walla, Wasco.

Pennsylvania

American Indian Museum, Harmony.
American Indian Museum, Pittsburgh.
Hershey Museum, Hershey.
Indian Steps Museum, east of York.
E. M. Parker Indian Museum, Brookville.

Tribe: Seneca.

Rhode Island

The Museum of Natural History, Roger Williams Park, Providence.
Tomaquag Indian Museum, Exeter.

Tribe: Narraganset.

American Indian Hall of Fame

Long before Columbus left Europe, the North American Indian had evolved a complex culture. Skillful leadership was required to preserve and develop that culture against the changing fortunes of time.

Through the years, great Indian statesmen, innovators and warriors emerged, each leaving significant contributions both to his own people and to modern America.

The National Hall of Fame for Famous American Indians is a sculpture garden honoring many of those leaders. Likenesses of Sequoyah, Hiawatha, Pocahontas and other Native Americans are displayed in a beautiful outdoor setting.

Located on US-62, east of Anadarko, Oklahoma, the Hall of Fame is open free of charge during daylight hours, seven days a week.

A new visitor information center includes descriptive literature on the Hall of Fame and other Indian attractions in Anadarko, "the Indian Capital of the World."

Be sure to stop at the Southern Plains Indian Museum, next door to the Hall of Fame, and see its collection of Indian arts and crafts. Indian City, just south of town on State Highway 8, features reconstructed Plains Indian dwellings and a new museum.

The American Indian Exposition, held in August, is the largest gathering of native Americans in the world. Its week-long activities include pageants, ceremonials and Indian dance competitions.

The Wichita Mountains Wildlife Refuge near Lawton contains one of the world's only surviving buffalo herds. The Museum of the Great Plains and the Fort Sill Museum, also in Lawton, are well worth a visit.

South Dakota

Badlands National Monument, southeast of Rapid City.
Buechel Memorial Sioux Indian Museum, St. Francis.
Indian Arts Museum, Martin.
Land of the Sioux Museum, Mobridge.
Red Cloud Indian Museum, Kadoka.
Robinson Museum, Pierre.
Mari Sandoz Museum, Pine Ridge Reservation.
Sioux Indian Museum, Rapid City.
Sioux Land Heritage Museum, Pettigrew Museum, Sioux Falls.

Tribe: Sioux.

Tennessee

Chucalissa Indian Town and Museum, Memphis.
Shiloh Mounds, Shiloh National Military Park, Savannah.

Texas

Alabama-Coushatta Indian Museum, Livingston.
Alibates Flint Quarries National Monument, Sanford.
Dallas Museum of Fine Arts, Dalls.
El Paso Centennial Museum, University of Texas, El Paso.
Fort Concho Preservation and Museum, San Angelo.
Fort Worth Museum of Science and History, Fort Worth.
Indian Museum, Harwood.
Museum of Texas Tech University, Lubbock.
Museum of the Big Bend, Alpine.
Museum of the Department of Anthropology, University of Texas, Austin.
Panhandle-Plains Historical Museum, Canyon.
Texas Memorial Museum, University of Texas, Austin.
The Wilderness Park Museum, El Paso.

Tribes: Alabama, Coushatta.

Utah

Anasazi Indian Village State Historical Site, east of Escalante.
Anthropology Museum, Brigham Young University, Provo.
Canyonlands National Park, southwest of Moab.
Hovenweep National Monument, at Utah-Colorado border northwest of Cortez, Colorado.
Natural History State Museum, Vernal.
Newspaper Rock, Indian Creek State Park, northwest of Monticello.
Utah Museum of Natural History, University of Utah, Salt Lake City.

Tribes: Gosiute, Paiute, Ute.

Virginia

Hampton Institute Museum, Hampton.
Valentine Museum, Richmond.

Tribes: Mattapony.

Washington

Eastern Washington State Historical Society, Spokane.
Lelooska's, Ariel.
North Central Indian Museum, Wenatchee.
Pacific Northwest Indian Center, Spokane.
Roosevelt Petroglyphs, east of Roosevelt.
Seattle Art Museum, Seattle.
State Capitol Museum, Olympia.
Wanapum Tour Center, Wanapum Dam.
Washington State Historical Museum, Tacoma.
Washington State Museum, University of Washington, Seattle.

Tribes: Chehalis, Colville, Hoh, Lummi, Makah, Quileute, Quinault, Salish, Shoalwater, Snohomishu, Swinomishi, Spokane.

West Virginia

Archaeology Museum, West Virginia University, Morgantown.
Grave Creek Mound State Park (Mammoth Mound), Moundsville.

Custer's Last Stand

General George Armstrong Custer — his name and his deeds grace the pages of history books with the infamy of a man who sought his own vain glory and ended in bloody defeat.

The lowest in his West Point class in 1861, Custer became a nationally known Civil War hero seeking to regain his good name after his suspension on the grounds of presenting damaging evidence about the secretary of war.

On June 22, 1876, Custer led his Seventh Cavalry into Sioux Territory, bent on attack. Ignoring the advice of his Indian scouts, he led over 200 exhausted troopers to a bloody death at the hands of the Sioux and northern Cheyenne who had joined forces to protect their hunting grounds.

Custer's spectacular death has made him a controversial figure, and to this day he is still the subject of much dispute over his actions and character.

Wisconsin

Aztalan State Park, Aztalan.
Kenosha Public Museum, Kenosha.
Logan Museum of Anthropology, Beloit College, Beloit.
Milwaukee Public Museum, Milwaukee.
Museum of Anthropology, Wisconsin State University, Oshkosh.
Ojibwa Nation Museum, Hayward.
Sheboygan Mound Park, south of Sheboygan.
State Historical Society of Wisconsin, Madison.
Winnebago Indian Museum, Wisconsin Dells.

Tribes: Chippewa, Menominee, Munsee, Oneida, Stockbridge.

Wyoming

Arapaho Cultural Museum, Ethete.
Buffalo Bill Museum and Plains Indian Museum, Cody.
Colter Bay Indian Arts Museum, Colter.
Fort Casper Museum and Historic Site, Casper.
Fort Laramie National Historic Site, Fort Laramie.

Tribes: Arapaho, Shoshone.

The Battle of the Big Hole: One Tribe's Long Journey to Surrender

In the summer of 1877, a small group of Nez Perce Indians began a journey along the route from the tip of western Oregon, through the Idaho Territory, and over the Bitterroot Mountains into Montana Territory, stopping finally at Bear Paw Mountain just south of Canada. Five Nez Perce bands were involved in this venture — about 800 people, including 125 warriors — and they were herding more than 2,000 horses and carrying whatever possessions they could manage. Yet they made this long and difficult trek in less than four months — for they were fleeing from the U.S. Army, which was under orders to place them on a reservation in western Idaho Territory.

Although these Indians hoped to escape from the Army peaceably, they were forced to stop and face their pursuers nearly a dozen times. In the Big Hole Valley, the two forces met in one of the major battles of this epic journey, a journey now called the Nez Perce Indian War of 1877.

By tracing the events that led up to their retreat and those that happened along the way, another tragic episode unfolds in that long struggle to confine the Indians to ever-diminishing reservations.

1855
The First Treaty

The traditional homeland of the Nez Perce was that place where Oregon, Washington and Idaho meet. Mistakenly called Nez Perce (pierced nose) by French-Canadian trappers, possibly because a few Indian women were wearing nose ornaments, these peaceful, semi-nomadic people grazed horses on the valley grasslands, gathered edible roots and bulbs on the prairies, fished the streams, and hunted buffalo east of the mountains.

But in the mid-1800s, settlers, stockmen and gold miners began moving into their lands. Desiring peace, the Nez Perce agreed to a treaty in 1855 that confined them to a reservation. They were content with this agreement; the reservation included much of their ancestral land, and the treaty promised that non-Indians could live on the reservation only with the Indians' consent.

1863
The Second Treaty

Settlers and miners, wanting more of the Nez Perce land, forced a new treaty in 1863 which reduced the spacious Nez Perce reservation to one-fourth its original size. Those chiefs whose lands lay within the diminished reservation signed; however, a third of the Nez Perce lived outside the new boundaries and refused to participate in the talks or to sign the new treaty.

Furthermore, they declared that no other Nez Perce could sign for them, because they had never recognized a single leader or council who could speak for the entire tribe. These Indians who refused to participate are known as the "non-treaty" Nez Perce.

1877
Capitulation and Conflict

The non-treaty bands remained in their homeland for several years. Increasing demands for settlement and mining continued, however, and in 1877, political pressure forced the Indian Bureau to order the various bands of Nez Perce to move onto the smaller reservation. The Army command of General O. O. Howard was ordered to support the local Indian agent. At first, the Indians questioned Howard's authority to tell them where to live. He was adamant, however, and in mid-May issued an ultimatum that the Nez Perce must be on the reservation within 30 days.

Chief Joseph, one of the non-treaty spokesmen, probably reflected the general reaction of most of the non-treaty Nez Perce in saying:

"My people have always been friends of white men. Why are you in such a hurry? I cannot get ready to move in 30 days. Our stock is scattered and Snake River is very high. Let us wait until fall, then the river will be low."

The appeal was unheeded, and General Howard threatened to use force if necessary:

"The soldiers will be there to drive you onto the reservation, and all your cattle and horses outside the reservation at that time will fall into the hands of the white man."

Somehow the non-treaty chiefs persuaded their people to obey the ultimatum. They rounded up as many of their far-ranging livestock as they could, took all the possessions they could pack, struggled across the flooded Snake River, and made their way to a camp within a few kilometers of the reservation.

Though reluctantly, the Nez Perce had almost met the 30-day deadline when, on June 15, three young warriors seeking revenge attacked a group of white settlers who earlier had cheated or killed older members of their families. Four settlers were killed. Believing that the Army surely would retaliate for these rash acts, most of the non-treaty Nez Perce fled to White Bird Canyon.

In recalling the event two years later, Chief Joseph said:

"I said in my heart that, rather than have war I would give up my country . . . I would give up everything rather than have the blood of white men upon the hands of my people . . . . I blame my young men and I blame the white man . . . . My friends among the white men have blamed me for the war. I am not to blame. When my young men began the killing, my heart was hurt. Although I did not justify them, I remembered all the insults I had endured, and my blood was on fire. Still I would have taken my people to the buffalo country without fighting, if possible.

"I could see no other way to avoid war. We moved over to White Bird Creek 16 miles away, and there encamped, intending to collect our stock before leaving; but the soldiers attacked us and the first battle was fought."

June 17, 1877
White Bird Canyon

General Howard had indeed sent a force to quell the uprising, but it was beaten by the poorly armed and smaller band of non-treaty warriors. Flanked on all sides, the U.S. Army force was routed and suffered heavy losses.

July 11 and 12, 1877
Clearwater

During the following month, the Indians moved east from White Bird Canyon, their journey marked by only minor encounters and skirmishes involving individuals and scouting parties.

General Howard, under increasing criticism from local residents and from newspapers throughout the country, summoned troops from up and down the West Coast to begin an encircling movement to trap the elusive Nez Perce.

Then on July 11, Howard's forces met the Nez Perce near the Clearwater River, and they fought for two days with neither side winning. Finally, the Nez Perce withdrew, once again evading capture by a much stronger force.

Exodus

It was now clear to the non-treaty Nez Perce that they could not escape from the Army in Idaho Territory. In council, the five bands agreed to follow the leadership of Chief Looking Glass, who persuaded them to turn their backs on their homeland and head east to join the Crow Tribe in buffalo country. They would follow the Lolo Trail, which Nez Perce hunters had used for centuries, and join the Crows in Montana Territory. The Nez Perce wished only to find a place where the Army would leave them alone and where they would be far enough from settlements to avoid further clashes.

Chief Joseph's important task in this effort was to shepherd the Nez Perce dependents along the way; his hope was to bring them back home again when things settled down.

By early August, the Indians had crossed the mountains and reached the Bitterroot Valley in Montana. They were among friendly Montana settlers, and General Howard was far behind. But a second force, under Colonel John Gibbon, who commanded the 7th U.S. Infantry in the western part of Montana Territory, had entered the valley in pursuit.

Chief Looking Glass, unaware of Gibbon's forces, slowed the pace of travel even though some of the chiefs and warriors urged haste.

August 9 and 10, 1877
Battle at the Big Hole

On the western side of the Big Hole Valley, Ruby Creek joins Trail Creek to form the north fork of the Big Hole River; the steep slopes of Battle Mountain merge with the willow-dotted marsh that stretches to the riverbed. But the east bank of the valley is grassy, and when the Indians arrived there on the morning of August 7, for the first time since leaving Clearwater, they could set up their tepees. They cut trees to replace lost or worn-out poles and put up 89 tepees. When camp work was done, they played games, sang, danced and told stories long into the night. Looking Glass, believing that they were at last out of danger, did not post guards. Life was almost normal again.

But by the next afternoon, August 8, Colonel Gibbon's advance party had found the Nez Perce camp. Shortly before dawn on August 9, Gibbon's men, joined by civilian volunteers, crept through the darkness to the west bank of the Big Hole River, preparing for a surprise attack on the Nez Perce camp. The attack began prematurely, and the attackers crossed the river firing on the sleeping Nez Perce, some of whom scattered quickly, while others were slow to awaken. The soldiers soon occupied the camp, but the Nez Perce warriors found sniping positions and with deadly accurate shooting forced Gibbon's men back across the river. There the soldiers dug in and were pinned down all that day and night and the next day. Under this protection, Chief Joseph gathered his people together and hurriedly led them southward. Once more they were on the move, trying to avoid conflict.

Aftermath of Big Hole

The Nez Perce had escaped again, and in a military sense had won the battle. In many ways, however, the "victory" was devastating. They had lost approximately 40 women, children and old people in the early morning attack, and about 30 warriors in the fighting — staggering losses to such a small band. Even more shattering was the final realization that the Army was not going to leave them in peace.

Chief Looking Glass, the day-to-day leader, had refused to put out sentries, and Colonel Gibbon was thus able to make the surprise attack. After the battle, the council of chiefs gave leadership to Chief Lean Elk, who urged a hasty retreat. The Nez Perce now decided to go to Canada and join Sitting Bull — an idea that had been considered and rejected earlier, when the Indians still had hope of returning to their homeland.

In contrast, the Army was elated after the Battle of Big Hole. The command was trying to make up for the disastrous loss of Custer and his 7th Cavalry at the Little Bighorn in June the year before. The Army was hungry for a victory of any kind. The military counted 29 dead and 40 wounded, but they knew that they had inflicted great damage to the fighting ability of the Nez Perce. The strategy of encircling the Nez Perce with various commands approaching from different directions was working. Furthermore, the 7th Infantry had not been forced to retreat as other units of infantry and cavalry had been in the past. Because the infantry held its ground and fought valiantly, seven enlisted men were awarded the Congressional Medal of Honor, and those officers who survived received brevet promotions. Unfortunately for the Army, Gibbon's command was out of action. General Howard continued the chase.

After Big Hole, the harried Nez Perce had a few skirmishes with the Army. Following Indian hunting trails, they headed toward Yellowstone National Park. To the south was Shoshone country where they hoped to pick up warriors to replace those lost at the Big Hole. Then they visited the Crow Nation to seek help and possible allies. But they were rejected by both the Shoshone and the Crow, who wished to avoid trouble with the Army.

October 5, 1877
Surrender at Bear Paw Mountain

Finally, on September 30, in the Bear Paw Mountains of Montana, just south of the Canadian border, the Nez Perce were surprised by Army troops under the command of Colonel Nelson A. Miles. The chiefs rallied their followers, but after five days of fighting and intermittent negotiations, they finally surrendered to Miles — more from exhaustion than from defeat.

Of the 800 non-treaty Nez Perce who had started the trek to Canada, some had been killed in battles or skirmishes en route, some had succeeded in reaching Canada, some were hiding in the hills and others had found sanctuary with other tribes. Only 480 were left to surrender, and they had traveled almost 2,720 kilometers (1,700 miles) only to be stopped 48 kilometers (30 miles) short of sanctuary. In the end, it was the loss of fighting men, as well as the emotional blow at Big Hole, that broke the Nez Perce power to resist.

Their desperation is echoed in the statement of Chief Joseph to Colonel Miles:

"Tell General Howard I know his heart. What he told me before I have in my heart. I am tired of fighting. Our chiefs are killed. Looking Glass is dead. Too-hul-hul-sote is dead. The old men are all dead.

"It is the young men who say yes or no. He who led the young men is dead. It is cold and we have no blankets. The little children are freezing to death. My people, some of them, have run away to the hills, and have no blankets, no food; no one knows where they are – perhaps freezing to death. I want to have time to look for my children and see how many of them I can find. Maybe I shall find them among the dead. Hear me, my chiefs. I am tired; my heart is sick and sad. From where the sun now stands I will fight no more forever."

What to See and Do at Big Hole National Battlefield

Visitor Center

Stop first at the visitor center for basic orientation through an audiovisual program and exhibits, including the original mountain howitzer from the battle. National Park Service employes there will help you plan your visit.

Touring the Battlefield

A short drive to the lower parking area connects with a foot trail to the Siege Area and the Howitzer Capture Site.

Siege Area

Within this wooded area, the soldiers were besieged for more than 36 hours starting at 8 a.m. on August 9, 1877.

Howitzer Capture Site

Take the trail up the hill to the site where the soldiers positioned the mountain howitzer, and where it was then captured by the Nez Perce. The walk takes about 20 minutes.

Picnicking and Camping

There are several picnic tables in the Battle Area near the lower parking area. No camping or overnight facilities are provided in the park, but several campgrounds are nearby. Ask at the visitor center for details.

Fishing and Hunting

You can fish within the national battlefield and the national forest as provided by Montana law.

No hunting is allowed within the national battlefield; Montana laws apply in the adjacent national forest. Fishing and hunting on private land is by permission only.

Your Trip — How To Get There

Big Hole National Battlefield is 19.2 kilometers (12 miles) west of Wisdom, Montana, on Mont-43. From Butte, Montana, take Interstate 15 southwest to Divide, then to Wisdom on Mont-43; from the west, Mont-43 intersects US-93 at the state line, between Salmon, Idaho, and Hamilton, Montana.

Services

Facilities such as gasoline stations, grocery stores, restaurants and lodging — although limited — can be found in Wisdom, Montana. There are more complete services in Butte, Montana, to the northeast, and Hamilton, Montana, or Salmon, Idaho, to the west.

Members of Sioux Indian tribe entertain visitors to their South Dakota village with traditional native dances.

Discovering the Amish

The Amish are a branch of the Mennonites who broke with the parent sect in 1609 to follow the sterner leadership of Jacob Ammann from whom the sect derives its name. The Amish started immigrating to this country from their native Germany and Switzerland in 1754 to escape religious persecution. The sect settled first in rural Pennsylvania where William Penn had promised them freedom to worship God in their own way. Moving into Ohio in the early 1820s, the Amish settled first in Holmes and Tuscarawas counties because this region of rolling farmland most closely resembed the agricultural areas of Pennsylvania.

The church dictates the pattern of existence of its members, including the clothes that must be worn. The women wear long dresses of plain-colored fabric and black bonnets or prayer caps. The men wear plain homemade suits and broad-brimmed black hats and let their beards grow after marriage. The children look like carbon copies of their elders. Hooks and eyes and pins are used as fasteners instead of buttons, since buttons suggest military uniforms and the Amish are pacifists.

Only the barest essentials in material possessions are allowed, and no adornment of person or home is permitted. The Amish will neither own nor drive automobiles (although most of them have no objection to riding in one), and they insist on operating their farms and homes without benefit of electricity. They are also opposed to other than an elementary education, contending that too much schooling would make their children worldly and lure them from the Amish way of life.

In spite of their occasional conflicts with the outside world, the Amish are a highly contented people. They keep to themselves most of the time, intermarry and live a 19th-century type of American farm life.

The Amish are one of Ohio's most unique travel attractions. Motorists are lured to the land of the "plain" people because they find the Amish way of life an interesting contrast to their own jet-propelled world.

Visitors driving through Amish country will get the feeling they have stepped back into the 19th century when they encounter a bearded, brim-hatted man driving a horse and buggy. Sometimes they will see Amish children, dressed in period clothes, walking along the road on their way to their private, one-room school.

As motorists travel farther through the lush, rolling farmland, they may notice the two-story farmhouses (some with a single blue curtain draped to one side at each window) and a smaller house nearby where the elderly parents live. In the tightly-knit rural communities of the agrarian Amish, there are hitching posts for horses and buggies, stores that cater to the Amish trade, restaurants that specialize in Amish-style cooking and such rarities as blacksmith shops and a buggy factory.

Total Amish population residing in Ohio today numbers approximately 20,000. About a two-hour drive south of Cleveland takes you to the largest Amish settlement in the world. Centered in Holmes County (Millersburg, the county seat), it spreads into adjoining counties of Wayne (Kidron), Tuscarawas (Sugarcreek) and Coshocton (New Bedford) for a total population of 13,000. Second in size is Geauga County, southeast of Cleveland, around Burton and Middlefield. The other two major Amish settlements are in Madison County near Plain City, northwest of Columbus, and Stark County, north of Canton.

Guided tours of Ohio's Amish Country originate in the Berlin area. Contact: The Amish Farm, Box 335, Berlin, Ohio 44610, (216) 893-2614; or Amish Hayride Tours, Box 226, Berlin, Ohio 44610, (216) 893-2700.

You'll also find Amish settlements in Pennsylvania, Indiana and Iowa; contact the tourism offices within those states (listed elsewhere in this book) for the exact locations of the colonies and a list of the attractions that are open to the public.

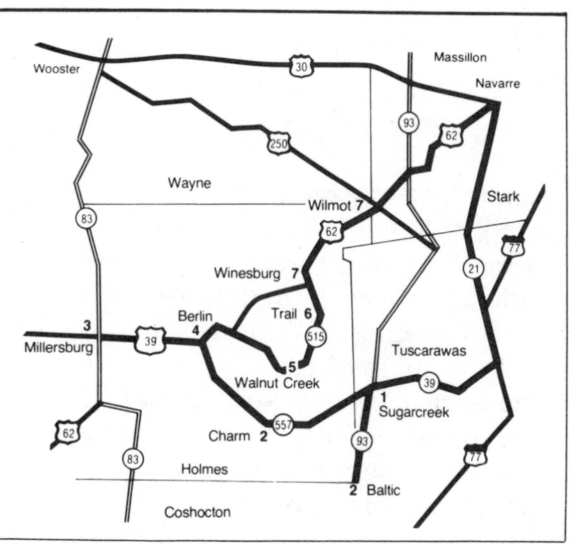

A Suggested Tour

Discovering the Amish

Here is a self-conducted auto tour of the interesting Swiss-Amish region of Ohio. When you see a sign that reads, "Enter Horse-Drawn Vehicle Area," you'll know you're in the right territory. Drive carefully, and be on the lookout for Amish buggies on the road. Also remember to exercise restraint in snapping photographs in the area; the strict Amish believe that picture-taking violates the graven image commandment and frown on it.

1. SUGARCREEK

This tour is about a two-hour drive south of Cleveland. Pick up State Route 21 below Massillon to Dover, and turn west on State Route 39 to the Swiss community of Sugarcreek where the business district resembles an Alpine Village. Many of the early settlers in the Sugarcreek area were Swiss immigrants who learned the art of cheesemaking in their native homeland and began making cheese here as a means of earning a living.

Tour Mueller's Cheese House where Swiss cheese is made in huge copper kettles; the Swiss Village Country Store, specializing in Swiss imports; The Budget which prints a weekly newspaper serving Amish-Mennonite communities throughout the world; and the Swiss Hat Restaurant which serves good food in a Swiss-style building. Also check out the municipal horse and buggy parking lot to the rear of the business district which is designed to accommodate the Amish "carriage trade."

Each fall (fourth weekend after Labor Day), the Ohio Swiss Festival is held, a colorful event highlighting yodeling contests, Swiss costume judging, Old World music and Swiss food.

2. BALTIC AND CHARM

Pick up State Route 93 south. At Baltic is Miller's Dutch Kitch'n. Closed Sunday.

Return to Sugarcreek and turn west onto State Route 557 and proceed to Charm, where approximately half the population is Amish. Retired Amish farmers lounging around the square are friendly if approached.

The Amish Corners Restaurant at Charm has Amish cooks and waitresses. House specialties are date pudding and peanut butter pie. Closed Sunday.

Guggisberg's Doughty Valley Cheese Factory, home of Ohio Baby Swiss, is located on State Route 557, north of Charm and three miles south of Berlin. If you stop before 1 p.m., you can observe cheesemaking in progress from a big show window. See a three-dimensional mural with horse-drawn wagon that actually moves. On the grounds is an exact replica of a "Little Swiss House," surrounded with beautiful shrubs and flowers. Closed Sunday.

3. MILLERSBURG

From Charm, continue to State Route 62 where you can go west to Millersburg, a county seat and trading center for the Amish. Of particular interest is the hitching rail, complete with parking meters, located along the east side of the courthouse to which the Amish farmers tie their horses while shopping.

During the first weekend in October, Millersburg stages the Holmes County Antique Festival. An antique auction and show plus a flea market offer plenty of opportunities for collectors to part with their money.

4. BERLIN

From Millersburg, return on State Route 62 and go east five miles to Berlin, another Amish trading center. Nearby (1½ miles west of Berlin) is the Rastetter Woolen Mill. It is one of only two remaining mills of its type in the United States and the last one in Ohio that does custom washing and carding of raw wool. Two sales showrooms offer a fine selection of hand-woven rugs, blankets, robes, goose-down comforters, down feather pillows, sportswear, afghans and coverlets. Closed Sunday and Monday.

In Berlin is the Helping Hands Quilt Shop where local Amish and Mennonite women can be seen practicing the "art of quilting," usually the last Tuesday of the month. The Quilt Shop does custom quilting and has finished quilts, quilt tops, quilting and embroidery supplies, quilt frames and handmade craft items for sale. All proceeds from the shop are used for charitable purposes. Closed Sunday.

Across from the Quilt Shop is Boyd & Wurthmann Restaurant and next to it an old-fashioned grocery store. Both are closed Sunday.

At the corner of State Routes 39 and 62, in Berlin, is the Berlin House Restaurant with a menu that emphasizes "homemade" ice cream and baked goods. A gift shop has Amish-made crafts and quilts. Open daily and Sunday. Amish hayride tours originate here. Another eating place is Mrs. Miller's, State Route 39, two miles east of Berlin. Food is prepared and served in her Amish home for groups by reservation only. Write: Mrs. Roman H. Miller, RD 4, Box 171, Millersburg, Ohio 44654.

About a mile north of Berlin, off US-62 at Bunker Hill Village, is Heini's Place Cheese House. Here you'll see the world's largest wheel of cheese and a huge mural which depicts the evolution of cheesemaking from early days to present time. If you arrive before noon, you can see the cheesemaking process from a glass-enclosed observation room while a guide explains the proceedings. There's a snack shop and sales room on the premises; open daily, including Sunday.

Nearby is the Dutch Country Peddler, an authentic old-fashioned country store featuring Amish goods, quilts, candy, groceries and souvenirs. Tourist information is available. Closed Sunday.

A "Pioneer Days" celebration is held in Berlin in late July. Demonstrations of old-time crafts, tours of Amish farms, Amish buggy rides and Amish foods.

5. WALNUT CREEK

On the Public Square (State Routes 15 and 39) is Der Dutchman Restaurant, where people come from miles around to order the roast beef, pan-fried chicken and oatmeal pie prepared by Amish cooks. Closed Sunday. Next door to the restaurant is a gift shop called Das Schmoke Hause with Swiss cowbells and homemade gift items for sale. Closed Sunday.

Also in the Walnut Creek area (on State Route 39, one-half mile southeast of State Route 515) is Der Candlemaker. Here, visitors can watch a candlemaker mold special candles inlaid with photos, birth or marriage certificates. Children can help make their own candles and receive a certificate designating them "Junior Candlemaker." Closed Sunday.

6. TRAIL

At the Walnut Creek square, turn north on State Route 515 which takes you to Trail (if you blink you won't see it). This village of less than 100 is the home of that famous Holmes County specialty, Trail Bologna. The product, now being made by the fourth generation of the Troyer family, is smaller than bologna we know and usually more spicy. While there are no longer tours of the factory, visitors may shop next door in the Troyer's General Store. Closed Sunday.

7. WINESBURG AND WILMOT

Continue on State Route 515 north and rejoin US-62. Continue north to the hilltop village of Winesburg, another Amish settlement. If you are ready for a meal stop, there's the Winesburg Restaurant featuring Swiss cooking. Closed Monday.

After leaving Winesburg, continue on US-62 to the Alpine-Alpa Cheese House (2½ miles south of Wilmot), which makes two tons of cheese a day. Nearby Amish farmers provide the milk for the cheesemaking. The plant is designed so visitors can watch cheese being made from a glass-enclosed viewing room. Most activity takes place between 11 a.m. and 3 p.m., Monday to Saturday. The sales room is open daily, including Sunday.

On the "cuckoo clock terrace," there is a gift shop with more than 300 cuckoo clocks on the walls and hundreds of specialty gift items. Also on the terrace is the "world's largest cuckoo clock" with a five-piece figurine band and a pair of dancers. Admission: 25 cents. Full course meals available in the dining room featuring Swiss motif.

The Amish Door Restaurant is located on US-62 at the south edge of Wilmot and features Amish-style cooking in a Swiss-style house. Chicken and dressing and date pudding are specialties. Closed Sunday.

Pick up State Route 21 at Navarre for your trip home.

California's Wine Country

California is the classic wine land. Its long, gentle, sunlit seasons nurture the world's great wine grapes. Its fabled vineyards and wineries combine tradition with modern science to produce wines for every taste, occasion and pocketbook. Each wine possesses its own proud merits and characteristics.

Throughout the United States, and in other countries as well, there is a growing appreciation and interest in the wines of California. They are gaining ever-greater recognition for their excellence and value and are assuming their place as a natural and moderate part of good eating and gracious living in the everyday lives of Americans. Each year, a growing number of Americans visit the California wine regions to learn firsthand how the wines are grown and to taste them in the vinous atmosphere of the winery.

The yellows and light greens of spring-fresh young vines thriving in rich, brown earth, the mellow hues of vineyards under summer's blue skies, the golds, scarlets, purples and greens of ripe fruit before the harvest, weave a tapestry of color only nature could conceive. In this tapestry, which unfolds over a half-million acres, are California's famed and storied wineries.

Some of them are small family operations, while others are large enterprises which distribute their wines throughout the United States and in many other countries.

At each winery open to visitors, guests are welcomed by hospitable men and women who devote their lives to the wine and cask.

Although each wine community and individual winery offers visitors unusual and varied pleasures, the actual process of winemaking, a time-honored art, does not vary greatly regardless of the locale. The visitor is told that wine is made only by nature and that man, for all his scientific knowledge, is relegated to the role of helper. The devoted winemaker merely guides nature with enthusiasm, patience and care.

California's vineyard acreage is planted in the design typical of wine regions throughout the world. In these vineyards grow the quality grapes from which California wines are made.

Aristocratic wine grapes of the *Vitis vinifera* family were introduced into the U.S. from the famed wine districts of the Old World during the last two centuries. Because of climatic conditions, they are grown in this country almost exclusively in California. Here we find more than 125 principal varieties thriving today and new varieties are constantly being developed.

In late August, heavy-hanging clusters of grapes are ready to be picked. The ripe fruit is then quickly transported to the winery, where it is gently crushed, and the process of fermentation begins.

The crushed grapes and their juices are pumped into large fermenting vats within the winery. During fermentation, the natural grape sugar is transformed by action of wine yeasts into carbon dioxide and wine alcohol. Complete fermentation, which converts all of the grape sugar and makes the wine "dry," is accomplished within varying periods, from a few days to a few weeks. When some sweetness is desired, fermentation is stopped and the proper proportion of grape sugar remains. Red wine is fermented with the pulp and skins of the grapes the natural skin

pigment giving the wine its color. White wine is made from the fermentation of the juice alone, drawn off the grapes immediately after crushing. Rosé wines are made by allowing the juice to ferment with the grape skins for a short time.

The new wine, after fermentation, goes immediately into cooperage to begin the steps of perfection and aging. (The term "cooperage" applies traditionally to storage in wooden casks, vats or barrels. However, the visitor will see that glass-lined concrete and metal tanks are also used now, especially for white and rosé wines.)

During the aging process, which may take months or years depending upon the wine type and the taste desired, the wine develops smoothness, mellowness and character. Only when it meets the exacting standards of the winemaker is it bottled.

Wine is the only beverage which continues to "grow" in quality after bottling. Many red wines continue to improve and distinguish themselves over several years, some for a decade or longer, before reaching their peak. Most white and rosé wines require only a short aging period and are generally preferred young.

For different wine types there are variances in production methods, and each winemaker has his own individual approach to his wines.

Many wineries offer their wines for sale and visitors, having become fully aware of the steps from vine to wine, may handpick a selection of the vintner's wares to take home.

Tasting rooms, where the wines are sipped, are often the showplace of the winery.

Excellent freeways, highways and roads make the wineries and vineyards easily accessible. Restaurants, drive-ins, hotels and motels are plentiful. California's countryside provides excellent sites for picnic lunches, and some of the wineries also have picnic and barbecue facilities.

A trip to the wine country may be a brief visit or an entire tour planned to include numerous wineries as well as historical landmarks. Because of the perennial nature of winemaking, there is always something for the visitor to see regardless of the time of year.

The winemaker's work is never finished. As one vintage year ends, another begins. But he always welcomes the opportunity and privilege of being host to visitors to America's wine land.

California Wineries Open to Visitors

The wineries listed by county on the following pages have stated that they are open to the public as shown. Their facilities for visitors are indicated by the following symbols noted in parentheses after the winery's name and nearest town:

P — Picnic facilities available
R — Retail sales and wine tasting at winery
TR — Tasting and retail sales outlet only (not a winery)

Many of the wineries sell wine-related gifts and accessories. Data relative to individual wineries was correct at presstime but is subject to change. Visitors planning tours in advance are advised to call wineries to avoid delay or disappointment. Large groups should always be booked in advance. *Some wineries close on certain major legal and religious holidays and not others. Visitors should check with wineries as to holiday hours.* It is strongly suggested that visitors obtain a current California state road map to supplement individual winery directions.

Alameda County

Brookside Winery, Hayward (TR) — 374 Jackson Street, daily, 11 a.m. to 6 p.m. (415) 881-9404.

Brookside Winery, Oakland (TR) — 6839 Foothill Boulevard, daily, 10 a.m. to 6 p.m. (415) 568-9223.

Richard Carey Winery, San Leandro (R) — 1695 Martinez Street, off Davis Street, directly across from the San Leandro BART Station. Friday 11 a.m. to 6 p.m., Saturday 11 a.m. to 4 p.m. (415) 352-5425.

Concannon Vineyard, Livermore (R) — From Highway 580, South on Vasco, three miles to Tesla Road, turn right, Monday to Saturday, 9 a.m. to 4 p.m.; Sunday noon to 4:30 p.m. Tours (on the hour), Monday to Friday, 9 a.m. to 3 p.m., Saturday and Sunday, noon to 3 p.m. (415) 447-3760.

Oak Barrel Winery, Berkeley (TR) — University Avenue, one block east of San Pablo Avenue, Monday to Saturday, 10 a.m. to 6:30 p.m. (415) 849-0400.

Rosenblum Cellars, Oakland — 1775 16th Street, tours and tasting by appointment only. (415) 834-6067.

Stony Ridge Winery, Pleasanton (R,P) — From Highway 680 to Sunol Boulevard toward Pleasanton to Vineyard Avenue. Right to 1188 Vineyard Avenue. Tuesday to Sunday, 11 a.m. to 5 p.m. (415) 846-2133.

Veedercrest, Emeryville (R) — 1401 Stanford Avenue, 100 yards; southwest corner of Hollis and Stanford. Visitors by appointment only. Days (415) 652-3103; evenings and weekends, (415) 849-3303.

Weibel Champagne Vineyards, Mission San Jose (R,P) — 1.1 miles south from Highway 680, 0.5 mile left on private road; daily, 10 a.m. to 4 p.m. (415) 656-9914.

Wente Bros., Livermore (R) — From Highway 580, south on Vasco, three miles to Tesla Road, turn right, Monday to Saturday 9 a.m. to 4:30 p.m., Sunday 11 a.m. to 4:30 p.m. Touring weekdays only 10 a.m. to 3:30 p.m. Picnic facilities limited. (415) 447-3603.

Wine and the People, Berkeley (TR) — 907 University Avenue. Hours Monday to Saturday 10 a.m. to 6 p.m., Sunday 11 a.m. to 5 p.m. (415) 549-1266.

Amador County

Argonaut Winery, Ione (TR) — Route 1, five miles northeast of Ione on Willow Creek Road. Tours by appointment only, write Box 612, Ione 95640.

D'Agostini Winery, Plymouth (R) — Eight miles northeast of Plymouth on Shenandoah Road. Daily, 9 a.m. to 4:30 p.m. Large groups by appointment only. (State Historical Landmark #762.) (209) 245-6612.

Montevina, Plymouth — Three miles northeast of Plymouth on Shenandoah School Road. Tours by appointment only. (209) 245-3412.

Stoneridge, Sutter Creek (R) — 2.2 miles east of junction of Highway 49 and Ridge Road on Ridge Road. Open Saturday 2 p.m. to 5 p.m., or by appointment. (209) 223-1761. (Route 1, Box 36B, Sutter Creek.)

Calaveras County

Chispa Cellars, Murphys — 425 Main Street. By appointment only. (209) 728-2106 or (209)728-3492.

Stevenot Winery, Murphys — Three miles north of Murphys on San Domingo Road. Tours by appointment only. (209) 728-3793.

Contra Costa County

Brookside Winery, Richmond (TR) — 12967 San Pablo Avenue, daily, 11 a.m. to 7 p.m. (415) 232-9912.

Brookside Winery, Walnut Creek (TR) — 2724 North Main Street, daily, 11 a.m. to 6 p.m. (415) 934-9863.

J. E. Digardi Winery, Martinez (R) — 2.3 miles southeast on Pacheco Boulevard, Monday to Friday, 9 a.m. to 3 p.m. Tours and tasting by appointment. (415) 228-2638.

Conrad Viano Winery, Martinez (R) — One mile east of VA Hospital on Highway 4, one mile north of Morello Avenue, daily, 9 a.m. to noon, 1 p.m. to 5 p.m. (415) 228-6465.

El Dorado County

Boeger Winery, Placerville (R,P) — 1709 Carson Road. Open Wednesday to Sunday 10 a.m. to 5 p.m. Closed Monday and Tuesday. (916) 622-8094.

Eldorado Vineyards, Camino (P) — Located at 3551 Carson Road. Highway 50 at Camino turnoff, four miles east of Placerville. Wine tasting and tours September to February, daily, 10 a.m. to 6 p.m., or by appointment. (916) 644-3773.

Sierra Vista Winery, Placerville — Located at end of Leisure Lane off Pleasant Valley Road in Pleasant Valley. Tours by appointment only. (916) 622-7221.

Fresno County

B. Cribari & Sons Winery, Fresno (R) — From Highway 99, at Jensen Avenue exit, east to first signal, left to Church Avenue, right to 3223 East Church Avenue, daily, 10 a.m. to 5 p.m. Large groups welcome. (209) 485-3080.

Farnesi Winery, Sanger (R) — 2426 Almond Avenue, Jensen Avenue exit from Highway 99. Retail sales only, Monday to Friday, 8 a.m. to 5 p.m.; Saturday 8 a.m. to noon. (209) 875-3004.

Mont La Salle Vineyards (Mt. Tivy Winery), Parlier — 8418 South Lac Jac. (209) 638-3544.

A. Nonini Winery, Fresno (R) — 7.5 miles west of Highway 99 on McKinley, 0.5 mile north on Dickenson Avenue, Monday to

Saturday 8 a.m. to 5 p.m. Closed Sunday. (209) 264-7857.

Villa Bianchi Winery, Fresno (R) — 13 miles west on Shaw Avenue, from Highway 99, Monday to Friday 9 a.m. to 4 p.m. (209) 846-7356.

Humboldt County

Dean Williams Winery, McKinleyville — 1904 Pickett Road; visitors by appointment only. (707) 839-3373.

Kern County

LaMont Winery, Di Giorgio (R) — Near Di Giorgio Road and Comanche Road. Located 10 miles east of Highway 99, five miles south of Highway 58. Tasting room open Tuesday to Saturday, 10 a.m. to 5 p.m. (805) 845-2231.

A. Perelli-Minetti & Sons Winery, Delano (P,R) — Adjacent to freeway at Pond Road and Highway 99. Three miles south of Delano and 28 miles north of Bakersfield. Open daily from 10 a.m. to 5 p.m. (805) 792-3162.

Lake County

Konocti Cellars Winery, Kelseyville (R) — 4350 Thomas Drive, Highway 29, three miles north of Kelseyville, three miles south of Lakeport. Group tours by appointment. (707) 279-8861.

Lower Lake Winery, Lower Lake — Highway 29, 1.2 miles south of Lower Lake on Barranca Ranch property. Appointment only. (707) 994-4069.

Los Angeles County

Ahern Winery, San Fernando — 715 Arroyo Avenue. Visitors by appointment only. (213) 361-0349 (days); (213) 989-3898 (evenings).

Barengo Vineyards, Los Angeles (TR) — Farmers Market, 6333 West Third at Fairfax, daily, 9 a.m. to 7 p.m. (213) 937-1225.

Barengo Vineyards, Santa Fe Springs (TR) — Carmenita exit off Highway 5 at 13410 Firestone Boulevard, daily, 10 a.m. to 6 p.m. (213) 921-1175.

Brookside Winery, Agoura (TR,P) — 28650 West Canwood Road, Kanan Road offramp from Ventura Freeway, daily, 10 a.m. to 6 p.m. (213) 889-9090.

Brookside Winery, Glendale (TR) — 1101 Air Way, San Fernando Road at Grandview. Monday to Saturday 10 a.m. to 7 p.m., Sunday 10 a.m. to 6 p.m. (213) 956-9406.

Brookside Winery, Long Beach (TR) — 4515 East Pacific Coast Highway, Monday to Saturday 10 a.m. to 7 p.m., Sunday 10 a.m. to 6 p.m. (213) 597-9043.

Brookside Winery, Marina Del Rey (TR) — 13490 Maxella Avenue, Monday to Saturday 11 a.m. to 7 p.m., Sunday 11 a.m. to 6 p.m. (213) 823-9600.

Brookside Winery, Pasadena (TR) — 3589 East Colorado Boulevard, two blocks off Rosemead, daily, 10 a.m. to 6 p.m. (213) 578-9317.

Brookside Winery, San Pedro (TR) — Berth #77, Ports of Call Village, daily, 11 a.m. to 9 p.m. (213) 548-9895.

Brookside Winery. Santa Monica (TR) — 2635 Wilshire Boulevard at Princeton, Monday to Saturday 11 a.m. to 7 p.m., Sunday 11 a.m. to 6 p.m. (213) 828-9976.

Brookside Winery, Torrance (TR) — 25352 Crenshaw Boulevard in Rolling Hills Plaza Shopping Center, Monday to Saturday 10 a.m. to 7 p.m., Sunday 11 a.m. to 5 p.m. (213) 326-9870.

Brookside Winery, Van Nuys (TR) — 6100 Sepulveda Boulevard between Burbank and Victory Boulevards, daily, 10 a.m. to 7 p.m. (213) 997-9848.

J. Filippi Vintage Co., El Monte (TR) — 9613 Valley Boulevard, one block west of Temple City Boulevard, daily, 10 a.m. to 6 p.m. (213) 442-8955.

J. Filippi Vintage Co., Hawthorne (TR) — 5107 El Segundo Boulevard, one block east of San Diego Freeway, daily, 10 a.m. to 6 p.m. (213) 644-4297.

J. Filippi Vintage Co., Pico Rivera (TR) — 8447 Rosemead Boulevard, one block north of Telegraph Road, daily, 10 a.m. to 6 p.m. (213) 869-9672.

J. Filippi Vintage Co., Sun Valley (TR) — 8522 Sunland Boulevard, between San Fernando Road and Golden State Freeway, daily, 10 a.m. to 6 p.m. (213) 767-3646.

The Martin Winery, Culver City (R) — 11800 West Jefferson from San Diego Freeway. Tasting daily, 11 a.m. to 8 p.m., also deli-cafe. No tours. (213) 390-5736.

Villa Bianchi Winery Museum and Tasting Room, Long Beach — Located at 1119 Queen's Highway, Mary's Gate Village. Take Southdown and Long Beach Freeway and follow signs to Queen Mary. Open daily at 11 a.m. (213) 437-8868.

Madera County

Coarsegold Wine Cellar, Coarsegold (R) — On Highway 41, three miles south of Coarsegold. Tasting daily, 10 a.m. to 5 p.m. (209) 683-4850.

Papagni Vineyards, Madera — Six miles south on Highway 99 and Avenue 9, southeast corner. Tours by appointment only. (209) 674-5652.

Quady Winery, Madera — 13181 Road 24. By appointment only. Call evenings (209) 674-8606.

Marin County

Grand Pacific Vineyard Company, San Rafael (R) — Highway 101 north from San Francisco to Freitas Parkway exit, approximately one-half mile on frontage road to 134 Paul Drive, #9, Northgate Industrial Park, daily, 10 a.m. to 5 p.m. (415) 479-WINE or (415) 457-6545.

Sonoma Vineyards (Tiburon Vintners), Tiburon (TR) — Highway 101 north from San Francisco at Tiburon-Belvedere exit, four miles to 72 Main Street, Sunday to Thursday 10 a.m. to 6 p.m., Friday and Saturday 10 a.m. to 8 p.m. (415) 435-3113.

Woodbury Winery, San Rafael (R) — Highway 101 north from San Francisco to Francisco Boulevard exit, one mile to 32 Woodland Avenue. By appointment only. (415) 454-2355.

Mendocino County

Cresta Blanca, Ukiah (R,P) — From Highway 101 at Lake Mendocino exit, right one mile to winery. Guided weekday tours, tasting room, daily, 9 a.m. to 5 p.m. Groups welcome. (707) 462-0565.

Dach Vineyards, Philo (R) — Five miles north on Highway 128 from Philo (due west of Ukiah on road map). By appointment only. (707) 895-3245.

Edmeades Vineyards, Philo (R) — 5500 Highway 128, three miles north of Philo. Tours by appointment only. Daily, 10 a.m. to 6 p.m. (707) 895-3232.

Fetzer Vineyards, Hopland (TR) — Highway 101 at Hopland, tours by appointment only. (707) 744-1737.

Fetzer Vineyards, Redwood Valley — Three miles northwest of Calpella, tours by appointment only. (707) 485-8998.

Husch Vineyards, Philo (R) — Five miles northwest of Philo on Highway 128. Open daily for retail sales, 10 a.m. to 5 p.m. (707) 895-3216.

Navarro Vineyards, Philo — 5601 Highway 128, three miles north of Philo. Tours by appointment. (707) 895-3686.

Parducci Wine Cellars, Ukiah (R,P) — Two miles north on Highway 101, right on Lake Mendocino Drive, left to 501 Parducci

Road, daily, 9 a.m. to 6 p.m. Tours 10 a.m. to 4 p.m. on the hour. (707) 462-3828.

Weibel Champagne Vineyards, Redwood Valley (R,P) — 7051 North State Street, Redwood Valley, from Highway 101, north of Highway 20, daily, 9 a.m. to 6 p.m. (707) 485-0321.

Monterey County

Bargetto's Santa Cruz Winery, Soquel (R) — 3535 North Main Street, Highway 1, four miles east of Santa Cruz. Left from Capitola-Soquel offramp, north 100 yards to Main Street. Follow Main Street to Winery. Open daily, 9 a.m. to 5:30 p.m. (408) 475-2258.

Chalone Vineyard, Soledad — By appointment only. (415) 441-8975.

Durney Vineyard, Carmel Valley — Star Route at Cachagua Road. Tours by appointment only. (408) 659-2690.

Gifts from Bacchus, Carmel (TR) — Tasting room for Monterey Peninsula Winery. One block off Ocean Avenue on Sixth between Dolores and Lincoln. Open daily, 11 a.m. to 7 p.m. (408) 625-2434.

Jekel Vineyard, Greenfield (R,P) — Walnut Avenue between 12th and 13th Streets, one mile west of Highway 101 (use Walnut Avenue offramp). Tasting, 10 a.m. to 5 p.m. Tours by appointment. (408) 675-5522.

Paul Masson Pinnacles Vineyard, Soledad — Metz Road on road to Pinnacles National Monument east of Highway 101. Tours by appointment only. Contact Paul Masson Vineyards, Saratoga. (408) 257-7800.

Mirassou Vineyards, Soledad — Arroyo Seco Road, three miles west of Highway 101, daily (vineyards only). Appointment only. (408) 675-2324.

The Monterey Vineyard, Gonzales (R,P), — Highway 101 at south edge of Gonzales. Tours daily, 10 a.m. to 5 p.m. Groups by appointment. (408) 675-2326.

Monterey Peninsula Winery, Monterey (R,P) — Corner of Monterey-Salinas Highway 68 and Canyon Del Rey Highway 218. Open daily, 10 a.m. till dark. Tours by appointment only. (408) 372-4949.

Rapazzini's Stage Coach Cellars, Aromas (TR) — Highway 101, 15 miles north of Salinas, daily, 9 a.m. to 8 p.m. (summer); 10 a.m. to 6 p.m. (winter). (408) 422-3732.

Ventana Vineyards Winery, Soledad — 5.8 miles southwest of Soledad. Take Arroyo Seco exit off Highway 101, three miles, left at Los Coches Road for one mile. Tours and tastings by appointment. (408) 678-2306.

Napa County

Alatera Vineyards, Napa — Four miles north of Napa, two miles south of Yountville on Highway 29 (Solano Avenue). Tours and sales by appointment only. (707) 944-2914.

Beckett Cellars, Napa — One mile south of entrance to Silverado Country Club at 1055 Atlas Peak Road. By appointment only. (415) 452-4592 or (707) 224-2022.

Beringer Vineyards, St. Helena (R) — Left off Highway 29 just north of St. Helena. Daily, 9 a.m. to 4:45 p.m. Guided tours 9:30 a.m. — last tour 3:45 p.m. Group tours by appointment. (707) 963-7115.

Burgess Cellars, St. Helena (R,P) — 1108 Deer Park Road, 3.4 miles east from Highway 29. Retail sales, picnic area. Tours by appointment. (707) 963-4766.

Cakebread Cellars, Rutherford — One mile south of Rutherford on Highway 29, by appointment only. (415) 835-WINE or (707) 963-9182.

Cassayre-Forni Cellars, Rutherford — One-half mile south of Rutherford at 1271 Manley Lane off Highway 29. By appointment only. (707) 944-2165 or (707) 255-0909.

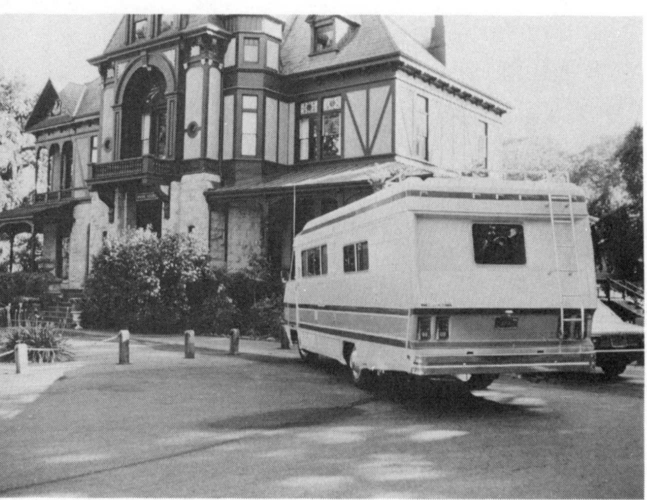

The magnificent Beringer Winery is only one of the fascinating stops in California's Napa Valley wine country.

Caymus Vineyards, Rutherford — 8700 Conn Creek Road. Retail sales and visitors by appointment only. (707) 963-4204.

Chateau Chevalier Winery, St. Helena — Two miles Northwest Madrona and Spring Mountain Road. By appointment only; no visitors Sundays and holidays. (707) 963-2342.

Chateau Montelena Winery, Calistoga (R) — 1429 Tubbs Lane. Tours and tasting by appointment only. (707) 942-5105.

The Christian Brothers Mont La Salle Vineyards and Winery, (R) — Eight miles northwest of Napa on Redwood Road, off Highway 29; daily, 10:30 a.m. to 4 p.m. Groups weekdays by appointment only. (707) 226-5566.

The Christian Brothers Wine and Champagne Cellars, St. Helena (R) — One-quarter mile north of St. Helena on Highway 29, daily, 10:30 a.m. to 4 p.m. Groups weekdays by appointment only. (707) 963-2719.

Clos du Val, Napa (R,P) — 5330 Silverado Trail, five miles north of Napa. Retail sales. No tasting. By appointment only, Monday to Friday 8 a.m. to 5 p.m. (707) 252-6711.

Conn Creek Vineyards, St. Helena — 8761 Silverado Trail (intersection of Route 128 and Silverado Trail). No tasting. Retail sales and winery tour by appointment only. (707) 963-9100 or (707) 963-3945.

Cuvaison, Calistoga (R,P) — 4550 Silverado Trail, just south of Dunaweal Lane, six miles north of St. Helena, Thursday to Monday 10 a.m. to 4 p.m. Tours by appointment. (707) 942-6266.

Domaine Chandon, Yountville (R) — Exit Highway 29 at Yountville, go west on California Drive toward Veterans Home, turn right into winery after crossing railroad tracks. Tours, (paid) tasting of sparkling wines daily, 11 a.m. to 5:30 p.m., except Monday and Tuesday. Restaurant open for lunch and dinner daily, except Monday and Tuesday. Reservations advised, (707) 944-2467. For visitor information and group tours, call (707) 944-2280 or (707) 944-8844.

Franciscan Vineyards, Rutherford (R) — One mile north on Highway 29 at Galleron Road. Tasting, tours daily, 10 a.m. to 5 p.m. (707) 963-7111.

Freemark Abbey Winery, St. Helena (R) — One mile north of St. Helena on Highway 29. Sales daily, 11 a.m. to 5 p.m.; tours daily at 2 p.m. No tasting. Restaurant for lunch and dinner. Winery (707) 963-9694; restaurant (707) 963-2706.

Grgich Hills Cellar, Rutherford — 1829 St. Helena Highway, 0.2 miles north of Rutherford on Highway 29. Retail sales 10 a.m. to 4 p.m.; tours by appointment only. (707) 963-2784.

Heitz Wine Cellars, St. Helena — Sales room at 436 St. Helena Highway, 0.5 mile southeast on Highway 29. Open daily, 11 a.m. to 4:30 p.m. No facilities for bus groups. (707) 963-3542.

Hanns Kornell Champagne Cellars, St. Helena (R) — Three miles north of St. Helena on Highway 29, one-quarter mile east on Larkmead Lane. Open daily, 10 a.m. to 4 p.m. (707) 963-2334.

Robert Keenan Winery, St. Helena — From Highway 29, five miles west on

Spring Mountain Road #3660. Visitors by appointment only. (707) 963-9177.

Charles Krug Winery, St. Helena (R) — Highway 29, just north of St. Helena. Open daily, 10 a.m. to 4 p.m. (707) 963-2761.

Long Vineyards, St. Helena — By appointment only. Write Box 50, St. Helena, or call (707) 963-2496 for appointment and directions.

Markham Winery, St. Helena (R) — Highway 29, 1¼ miles north of St. Helena at Deer Park Road. Retail sales. Tours and tasting by appointment. (707) 963-9577.

Louis M. Martini, St. Helena (R) — Highway 29, 1½ miles south of St. Helena, daily, 10 a.m. to 4 p.m. (707) 963-2736.

Mayacamas, Napa (R) — Take Highway 29 north, left on Redwood Road, West four miles, then four miles up Mt. Veeder to Lokoya. Visitors by appointment only. Open Monday to Friday by appointment only. Closed weekends. (707) 224-4030.

Robert Mondavi Winery, Oakville (R) — Highway 29, 12 miles north of Napa. Open daily, 10 a.m. to 4:30 p.m. Pre-arranged group lunches and dinners catered by appointment. (707) 963-7156.

Napa Vintners, Napa — 1721C Action Avenue East, in city limits. Retail sales. (707) 255-9463.

Nichelini Vineyard, St. Helena (R) — From Highway 29 at Rutherford, east 11 miles on Highway 128. Winery on right. Saturday, Sunday, 10 a.m. to 6 p.m. (707) 963-3357.

Niebaum-Coppola Estate, Rutherford — Visitors by appointment only. (707) 963-9435.

Robert Pecota Winery, Calistoga — 0.4 mile north on Bennett Lane. Visitors by appointment only. (707) 942-6625.

Joseph Phelps Vineyards, St. Helena (R) — 200 Taplin Road, off Silverado Trail, one mile south of St. Helena. Retail sales Monday to Saturday, 9 a.m. to 4 p.m. Tours by appointment. (707) 963-2745.

Pope Valley Winery, St. Helena (R,P) — Highway 29 north to Deerpark Road, 12 miles east of St. Helena. Open daily, 10:30 a.m. to 6 p.m., by appointment only. (707) 965-2192.

Raymond Vineyard and Cellar, St. Helena — 849 East Zinfandel Lane, south of St. Helena, three miles. Visitors by advance appointment only. (707) 963-3141.

Round Hill Vineyards, St. Helena — One mile north of St. Helena on Lodi Lane. By appointment only. (707) 963-2228.

Rutherford Hill Winery, Rutherford — Two miles east of Rutherford on Silverado Trail. By appointment only. (707) 963-7105.

Rutherford Vintners, Rutherford (R,P) — One mile north of Rutherford on west side of Highway 29. Open daily 10 a.m. to 4:30 p.m. Group tours by appointment. (707) 963-4117.

V. Sattui Winery, St. Helena (R,P) — Two miles south on Highway 29 at White Lane. Cheese shop and gourmet deli, gift shop. Tasting and informal tours. Daily, 9:30 a.m. to 6 p.m. (707) 963-7774.

Schramsberg Vineyards, Calistoga — Five miles north of St. Helena on Highway 29; no tasting. Retail sales and winery tours by appointment. (707) 942-4558.

Silver Oak Cellars, Oakville — One mile east of Highway 29 at 917 Oakville Crossroad. By appointment only. (707) 944-8866.

Spring Mountain Vineyards, St. Helena — One mile Northwest Madrona and Spring Mountain Road. By appointment only. (707) 963-4341.

St. Helena Wine Co., St. Helena — One mile north of St. Helena, corner Lodi Lane and Silverado Trail. By appointment only. (707) 963-7108 or (707) 963-3208.

Stag's Leap Wine Cellars, Napa (R) — 5766 Silverado Trail, six miles north of Napa. Tours by appointment only. Open seven days a week. (707) 942-5151.

Sterling Vineyards, Calistoga (R) — From Highway 29, seven miles north of St. Helena, east 0.5 mile on Dunaweal Lane. May 1 through October 31. Open daily, 10:30 a.m. to 4:30 p.m.; closed Monday and Tuesday, November 1 through April 30. (707) 942-5151.

Stonegate, Incorporated, Calistoga (P) — 1¼ miles south of Calistoga on Highway 29 at 1183 Dunaweal Lane. Retail sales. Tours by appointment only. 10 a.m. to noon, 1 p.m. to 4 p.m. (707) 942-6500.

Stony Hill Vineyard, St. Helena — Two miles west of Highway 29 on Lyman Canyon Road; no tasting. By appointment only. (707) 963-2636.

Sutter Home Winery, St. Helena (R) — 0.3 mile south on Highway 29, sales daily, 9 a.m. to 5 p.m.; tasting, 10 a.m. to 4:30 p.m. (707) 963-3104.

Trefethen Vineyards, Napa — Three miles north of Napa on Highway 29. Tours by appointment only. (707) 255-7700.

Tulocay Winery, Napa — 1426 Coombsville Road, 0.9 mile east of Silverado Trail, by appointment only. (707) 255-4699.

Villa Mt. Eden Winery, Oakville — North from Napa on Highway 29, two miles east of Oakville on Oakville Crossroads. By appointment only. (707) 944-8431.

Orange County

Brookside Winery, Anaheim (TR,P) — 711 S. Brookhurst Street between Lincoln and Ball, Monday to Saturday 9:30 a.m. to 6:30 p.m.; Sunday 11 a.m. to 6 p.m. (714) 778-9933.

Brookside Winery, Costa Mesa (TR) — 2925 Bristol Street, daily, 10 a.m. to 6 p.m. (714) 754-9270.

Brookside Winery, Dana Point (TR) — 24292 Del Prado, Monday to Saturday 9:30 a.m. to 6:30 p.m.; Sunday 10 a.m. to 6 p.m. (714) 496-9025.

Brookside Winery, La Habra (TR) — 2050 West Lambert Road at Beach Boulevard, Monday to Friday 9 a.m. to 6 p.m.; Saturday and Sunday 10 a.m. to 6 p.m. (213) 697-9054.

Brookside Winery, Mission Viejo (TR) — 24012 Alicia Parkway. (To be opened shortly.)

J. Filippi Vintage Company, Garden Grove (TR) — 12872 South Harbor Boulevard, between Chapman and Garden Grove Boulevard, daily, 10 a.m. to 6 p.m. (714) 534-7990.

Riverside County

Callaway Vineyard and Winery, Temecula/Rancho California — 31 miles south of Riverside on Highway 15E. Take Rancho California Road offramp, travel east approximately four miles to winery. Open daily, 11 a.m. to 4 p.m. Winery tours hourly; no tasting. Special group tours and tastings by appointment only. (714) 676-4001.

Cilurzo and Piconi Winery, Temecula (R) — Between San Diego and Riverside on Highway 15. Exit at Rancho California Road, east six miles, right on Calle Contento one-quarter of a mile. By appointment only. (704) 676-5350.

Galleano Winery, Incorporated, Mira Loma (R) — One mile east of Milliken, one-half mile south on Wineville Road. Open Monday to Saturday 8 a.m. to 6 p.m. (714) 685-5376.

GlenOak Hills Winery, Temecula — By appointment only. Directions given by winery. (714) 676-5831.

Mount Palomar Winery, Temecula (R,P) — Between San Diego and Riverside on Highway 15. Exit at Rancho California Road, then six miles east to winery. Deli, picnic facilities. Open daily, 9 a.m. to 5 p.m. (714) 676-5047.

Opici Winery, Alta Loma (R) — Five miles from Highway 10 on Haven Avenue offramp, north to Highland. Open daily, 10 a.m. to 6 p.m. (714) 987-2710.

Sacramento County

Brookside Winery, Sacramento (TR,P) — 4½ miles northeast on Highway 50, 9910 Folsom Boulevard, daily, 10 a.m. to 7 p.m. (916) 366-9959.

Brookside Winery, Sacramento (TR) — 2734 Auburn Boulevard, east on Highway 80, daily, 10 a.m. to 6 p.m. (916) 481-9556.

Brookside Winery, Sacramento (TR) — 4631 Freeport Boulevard, daily, 11 a.m. to 6 p.m. (916) 453-9197.

Coloma Cellars, Old Sacramento (TR) — 130 "K" Street, Sacramento, daily, 10 a.m. to 5 p.m. (916) 446-5775.

Jas. Frasinetti & Sons, Florin/Sacramento (R) — Highway 99 to Florin Road, east to Frasinetti Road to winery. Open Monday to Saturday 9 a.m. to 6 p.m.; Sunday 11 a.m. to 6 p.m. (916) 383-2444.

Gibson Wine Company, Elk Grove (TR) — Highway 99 at Grant Line Road, three miles south of Elk Grove. Tasting daily, no tours. (916) 685-9594.

San Benito County

Almaden Vineyards, Pacheco Pass Highway (TR) — Six miles north of Hollister, 12 miles east of Gilroy at Routes 152-156. Open daily, 10 a.m. to 5 p.m. (408) 637-7554.

Calera, Hollister (P) — 11300 Cienega Road, 11 miles south of Hollister. Tours and sales only each Saturday at 11 a.m. By appointment only. (408) 637-9170.

Cygnet Cellars, Hollister (R,P) — 11736 Cienega Road, 12 miles south of Hollister. By appointment only. (408) 733-4276 (office); (408) 637-7559 (winery).

Enz Vineyards, Hollister — 16 miles south of Hollister on Limekiln Road. By appointment only. (408) 637-3956.

San Benito Vineyards, Hollister (R) — Highway 156, one mile west of Highway 152-Highway 156 junction. Tours by appointment. (408) 637-3992.

San Bernardino County

Brookside Winery, Colton (TR,P) — 22900 Washington Avenue off Riverside Freeway. Open Monday to Saturday 9 a.m. to 7 p.m.; Sunday 9 a.m. to 6 p.m. (714) 825-9265.

Brookside Winery, Guasti (R,P) — Guasti Road at Archibald Avenue off San Bernardino Freeway, daily, 8 a.m. to 7 p.m. (714) 986-9377.

Louis Cherpin Winery, Fontana (R) — 15567 Valley Boulevard, Fontana on Highway 10 between Cherry and Citrus. Daily, 8 a.m. to 5 p.m. (714) 822-4103.

Cucamonga Vineyard Company, Cucamonga (R,P) — Two miles north of San Bernardino Freeway, 10013 East Eighth Street, between Archibald and Turner Avenues. Daily, 8 a.m. to 7 p.m. (714) 987-1716.

J. Filippi Vintage Company, South Fontana (R,P) — 1¼ miles south of San Bernardino Freeway on Etiwanda Avenue. Open daily, 9 a.m. to 6 p.m. (714) 984-4514.

Thomas Vineyards, Cucamonga (R,P) — 8916 Foothill Boulevard (Highway 66), 0.5 mile west of Cucamonga on Foothill Boulevard and Vineyard Avenue. Daily, 8 a.m. to 6 p.m. (State Historical Landmark #490.) (714) 987-1612.

San Diego County

Bernardo Winery, Escondido (R,P) — Pomerado Road off Route 15 (Highway 395), seven miles south of Escondido. Antiques, silversmith, mosaics, macrame and art studio. Deli at winery site. Daily, 7 a.m. to 6 p.m. (714) 487-1866.

Brookside Winery, Bonita (TR,P) — 3901 Bonita Road in Chula Vista area, daily, 9 a.m. to 7 p.m. (714) 422-9984.

Brookside Winery, El Cajon (TR) — 707 Arnele Street, near Arnele and Johnson. Open Monday to Saturday 10 a.m. to 7 p.m.; Sunday 10 a.m. to 6 p.m. (714) 440-9480.

Brookside Winery, Escondido (TR,P) — 2402 South Escondido Boulevard, Highway 395 exit at Felicita Road, turn east to South Escondido Boulevard. Daily, 9 a.m. to 6 p.m. (714) 743-9875.

Brookside Winery, San Diego (Pacific Beach) (TR) — 4730 Mission Bay Drive. Daily, 9 a.m. to 9 p.m. (714) 273-9512.

Ferrara Winery, Escondido (R) — 1120 West 15th Avenue, west on Felicita Avenue from Centre City, Parkway, right on Redwood Avenue to 15th Avenue. Daily, 9 a.m. to 6:30 p.m. Self-conducted tours. (714) 745-7632.

J. Filippi Vintage Company, Vista (TR) — 840 East Vista Way, on road to Fallbrook, daily, 10 a.m. to 6 p.m. (714) 724-0225.

San Pasqual Vineyards, San Diego — 13455 San Pasqual Road, three miles south of Escondido on Highway 395. Take Via Rancho Parkway turnoff, then east approximately one mile to San Pasqual Road. Open house Saturday 10 a.m. to 4 p.m. Tours by appointment only. (714) 741-0855.

San Francisco County

Brookside Winery, San Francisco (TR) — 2725 Geary Boulevard, daily, 11 a.m. to 6 p.m. (415) 929-9726.

Cannery Wine Cellars, San Francisco (TR) — 2801 Leavenworth Street, daily, 9:30 a.m. to 6:30 p.m. (415) 673-0400.

Sonoma Vineyards, (Epicurean Union), San Francisco (TR) — Wine tasting and gourmet cookware. Corner of Union Street and Fillmore at 2191 Union. Sunday to Thursday 10 a.m. to 6 p.m.; Friday and Saturday 10 a.m. to 7 p.m. (415) 567-0941.

The Wine Museum, San Francisco — Presenting The Christian Brothers Collection of Wine in the Arts. 633 Beach Street (opposite the Cannery, near Fisherman's Wharf). Tuesday to Saturday 11 a.m. to 5 p.m.; Sunday noon to 5 p.m. Closed Monday. Free. (415) 673-6990.

San Joaquin County

Barengo Vineyards, Acampo (R,P) — Winery location in Acampo, one mile west of Highway 99 at Acampo offramp. Tasting room open daily, 9 a.m. to 5 p.m.; tasting, retail sales. (209) 369-2746.

Cadlolo Winery, Escalon (R) — 1124 California Street, approximately 12 miles east of Manteca on Highway 120 in Escalon. Open Monday to Saturday 8 a.m. to 5:30 p.m. (closed December 1). (209) 838-2457.

Coloma Cellars, Escalon — "Old Winery Complex," McHenery Avenue at Escalon. Tuesday through Sunday 10 a.m. to 5 p.m. Tasting and sales. (209) 838-7060.

Delicato Vineyards, Manteca (R) — From Highway 99, 4.2 miles north of Manteca, one-quarter mile south of French Camp Road. Daily, 9 a.m. to 5 p.m., group winery tours by appointment. (209) 239-1215 or (209) 982-0679.

Franzia Brothers Winery, Ripon (R,P) — Six miles east of Manteca on Yosemite Avenue (Highway 120). Daily, 10 a.m. to 5 p.m. (209) 599-4251.

Guild's Central Cellars, Lodi (R,P) — One-half mile east of Highway 99 on Highway 12, left on Myrtle Avenue to One Winemasters' Way. Open daily, 10 a.m. to 5 p.m. Large groups welcome. Luncheon and dinner catering facilities available. Summer concert series. Display vineyard. (209) 368-5151.

Lucas Home Wine, Lodi — Highway 99 west on Turner, or Interstate 5 east on Turner, to North Davis Road. North on Davis 600 yards. Visits by appointment only. Retail sales October 1 through December 20, 9 a.m. to 6 p.m. (209) 368-2006.

San Luis Obispo County

Coloma Cellars, Cayucas (TR) — The Way Station, Highway 1, Cayucas. Tuesday to Sunday, 10 a.m. to 5 p.m.

Estrella River Winery, Paso Robles — Six miles east of Paso Robles on Highway 46. Group tours by appointment only. (805) 238-6300.

Hoffman Mountain Ranch Vineyards, Paso Robles (R) — Winery, by appointment only, (805) 238-4915. (TR) Black Oak Corner in Paso Robles, just west of Highway 101 on 24th Street. Monday to Thursday, 11 a.m. to 5 p.m.; Friday to Sunday, 10:30 a.m. to 6:30 p.m. Summer hours (June to September) daily, 10:30 a.m. to 6:30 p.m. (805) 238-6266.

Las Tablas Winery, Templeton (R) — Three miles west of Highway 101 on Winery Road between Vineyard Drive and Las Tablas Road. Open Monday to Saturday 9 a.m. to 6 p.m., Sunday 10 a.m. to 5 p.m. (805) 434-1389.

Pesenti Winery, Templeton (R) — Three miles west of Highway 101 on Vineyard Drive. Open Monday to Saturday 8 a.m. to 6 p.m., Sunday 10 a.m. to 6 p.m. (805) 434-1030.

York Mountain Winery, Templeton (R) — York Mountain Road, off Highway 46, nine miles west of Highway 101 or 12 miles east of Highway 1. Daily, 10 a.m. to 5 p.m. (805) 238-3925.

San Mateo County

Brookside Winery, Belmont (TR) — 1645 El Camino Real, daily, 10:30 a.m. to 6:30 p.m. (415) 592-9894.

Brookside Winery, Daly City (TR) — 2179 Junipero Serra Boulevard, daily, 11 a.m. to 6 p.m. (415) 755-9927.

Obester Winery, Half Moon Bay — Located one mile east of the city of Half Moon Bay on Highway 92. Open weekends 9 a.m. to 5 p.m. Informal tours. (415) 726-6465.

Woodside Vineyards, Woodside — 1.4 miles west of Woodside Town Center on Kings Mountain Road. Open Saturday and Sunday by appointment. (415) 851-7475.

Santa Barbara County

Carey Cellars, Solvang (R,P) — 1711 Alamo Pintado Road, approximately two miles north of Highway 246 on Alamo Pintado; or three miles south of Highway 154 through Los Olivos on Grand Avenue to Alamo Pintado. By appointment only. (805) 688-8554.

The Firestone Vineyard, Los Olivos (R) — One-quarter mile north of junction Highway 154 and Highway 101, go 2½ miles east on Zaca Station Road. Tours daily, 10 a.m. to 4 p.m. Closed Sunday. (805) 688-3940.

Rancho Sisquoc Winery, Santa Maria (R,P) — 18 miles east of Santa Maria on Foxen Canyon Road. From Highway 101 take Sisquoc offramp east to Foxen Canyon Road. By appointment only. (805) 937-3616.

Sanford and Benedict Vineyards, Lompoc — Nine miles west of Buellton on Santa Rosa Road. By appointment only. (805) 688-8314.

San Martin Winery, Solvang (TR) — 475 Alisal Road, from Highway 101 (or Highway 154) via Highway 246 to Solvang. Open Monday to Thursday 9:30 a.m. to 6 p.m., Friday to Sunday 9:30 a.m. to 7 p.m. (805) 688-7217.

Santa Barbara Winery, Santa Barbara (R) — One block east of State Street, two blocks north of ocean on Anapaca Street. Tasting daily, 10 a.m. to 5 p.m. Self-conducted tours. Group tours by appointment. (805) 963-8924.

Santa Ynez Valley Winery, Santa Ynez (R) — 365 North Refugio Road, approximately one mile south of Highway 246 between Santa Ynez and Solvang on Refugio Road. By appointment only. (805) 688-8381.

Santa Clara County

Almaden Vineyards, San Jose — From north, Highway 101 or Highway 280 to Highway 17, exit at Los Gatos-Santa Cruz, continue to Camden Avenue exit, left four miles to Blossom Hill Road, exit to Highway 82, one-half mile to Blossom Hill exit, one mile west to winery. Weekdays only, 10 a.m. to 3 p.m.; tours only, no sales. (408) 269-1312.

Bertero Winery, Gilroy (R,P) — From Highway 101, four miles west on Highway 152, daily, 9 a.m. to 5 p.m. (408) 842-3032.

Brookside Winery, Mountain View (TR) — 200 East El Camino Real, daily, 10 a.m. to 7 p.m. (415) 967-9865.

David Bruce, Los Gatos — 21439 Bear Creek Road, exactly five miles west of Highway 17, by appointment only, Saturday, 11 a.m. (408) 354-4214.

Casa de Fruta, Hollister (TR,P) — Highway 152, 17 miles east of Gilroy, daily, 8 a.m. to 8 p.m. (summer); 9 a.m. to 6 p.m. (winter); 24-hour restaurant, gourmet deli, recreational facilities, trailer park, motel. (408) 842-9316.

Congress Springs Vineyards, Saratoga (R) — Approximately 3½ miles from village of Saratoga on Highway 9 (Congress Springs Road). Address on mailbox on left side of road. Tasting and retail sales by appointment only. (408) 867-1409.

Fortino Winery, Gilroy (R,P) — From Highway 101, Watsonville Road at Morgan Hill to Hecker Pass Highway, approximately five miles west on Highway 152. Tours, tasting, daily, 9 a.m. to 6 p.m. Picnic facilities for small groups. (408) 842-3305.

Gemello Winery, Mountain View (R) — 2003 El Camino Real, 0.8 mile south of San Antonio Road. Tasting and tours Saturday, noon to 4 p.m. (415) 948-7723.

E. Guglielmo Winery (Emile's Wines), Morgan Hill (R,P) — 1½ miles east on Main Avenue from Monterey Street (El Camino). Picnic facilities. Parties and tours for small groups by appointment. (408) 779-2145.

Hecker Pass Winery, Gilroy (R) — Highway 152, five miles west of Gilroy, daily, 9 a.m. to 6 p.m. Group tours by appointment. (408) 842-8755.

Kirigin Cellars (formerly Bonesio Winery), Gilroy (R,P) — 11550 Watsonville Road, from Highway 101, five miles southwest on Watsonville Road, or two miles north of Highway 152 on County Road G8. Tasting daily, 9 a.m. to 6 p.m. Groups and tours by appointment. Picnic facilities. (408) 847-8827.

Thomas Kruse Winery, Gilroy (R,P) — From Highway 101 at Morgan Hill, Watsonville Road to Hecker Pass Highway. Tasting daily, noon to 6 p.m. (408) 842-7016.

La Purisima Winery, Sunnyvale (R) — From Highway 85, two miles east on El Camino Real, corner of El Camino and Sunnyvale-Saratoga Road. Open Tuesday to Friday 11 a.m. to 2 p.m. and 4:30 p.m. to 6:30 p.m.; weekends, 11 a.m. to 6 p.m. Group tours by appointment. (408) 738-1011.

Live Oaks Winery, Gilroy (R,P) — From Highway 101 west on First Street, 4½ miles west (look for sign on right), daily, 8 a.m. to 5 p.m. Close to Mt. Madonna Park. Tasting for groups 40 to 50 people, by appointment no later than 3 p.m. Picnic facilities include barbecue pit, 31 inches wide by 45 inches long, adjustable higher or lower levels. (408) 843-2401.

Llords and Elwood Winery, Fremont and San Jose — By appointment only. Contact Beverly Hills office, (213) 553-2368.

Martin Ray, Saratoga — Directions given by winery. By appointment only. (415) 321-6489.

Paul Masson Champagne and Wine Cellars, Saratoga (R) — From Highway 280, three miles southwest on Saratoga Avenue, daily, 10 a.m. to 4 p.m. Concerts of classical and jazz music during summer. Outdoor luncheons for groups of 50 or more by advance reservation, summer only. Group tours by appointment. (408) 257-7800.

Mirassou Vineyards, San Jose (R) — Capitol Expressway, east from Highway 101, turn right on Aborn Road for two miles. Open Monday to Saturday 10 a.m. to 5 p.m., Sunday noon to 4 p.m. Facilities for private lunches and dinners with tastings and group tours by appointment. (408) 274-4000.

Mount Eden Vineyards, Saratoga (R) — Directions given by winery. By appointment only, two-week advance notice. (408) 867-5783.

Novitiate Wines, Los Gatos (R,P) — Highway 17 to East Los Gatos turnoff, turn right on Los Gatos Boulevard (becomes Main Street), turn left at College Avenue to Prospect Avenue. Turn right into Jesuit Center Property. Tours Monday to Friday 1:30 p.m. and 2:30 p.m.; Saturday 10 a.m. and 11 a.m. Retail and tasting room, Monday to Saturday 9 a.m. to 4 p.m. Facilities for private picnics, lunches, and dinners, with tastings and group tours. By appointment. Closed Sunday. (408) 354-6471.

Page Mill Winery, Los Altos Hills — 0.7 mile west of Highway 280 on Page Mill Road. By appointment only. (415) 948-0958.

Pedrizzetti Winery, Morgan Hill (R,P) — 1½ miles from Highway 101 on San Pedro Avenue. Group tours by appointment only. Tasting room in Madrone, Highway 101 north of Morgan Hill, daily, 9 a.m. to 7 p.m. (408) 779-7774.

Rapazzini's Los Altos Winery, Gilroy (R) — Three miles south of Gilroy on Highway 101, daily, 9 a.m. to 7 p.m. (June 1 to September 15); 9 a.m. to 6 p.m. (September 16 to May 31). No tours. (408) 842-5649.

Richert & Sons Winery, Morgan Hill (R) — 1840 West Edmundson Avenue, from Highway 101. Open Monday to Friday by appointment; weekends 11 a.m. to 4 p.m. (408) 779-5100.

Ridge Vineyards, Incorporated, Cupertino (R) — 17100 Monte Bello Road, 4.4 miles from Stevens Creek Reservoir. Tasting, Saturday 11 a.m. to 3 p.m.; sales, Wednesday and Saturday 11 a.m. to 3 p.m. (408) 867-3233.

San Martin Winery, Gilroy (TR) — 4210 Monterey Highway at Bloomfield. Open daily, 9 a.m. to 8 p.m. (June to September), 9 a.m. to 6 p.m. (October to May). (408) 842-7741.

San Martin Winery, Morgan Hill (TR) — — (Vintage 1892) at 1110 San Pedro Avenue.(408) 779-8424.

San Martin Winery, San Martin (R,P) — Highway 101 to San Martin (between Gilroy and Morgan Hill). Winery tours by appointment only. (408) 683-4000.

Sherrill Cellars, Palo Alto — Approximately one mile south of Alpine intersection on Skyline Boulevard (Highway 35) at 1185 Skyline. By invitation and appointment only. Mail: PO Box 4155, Woodside, California 94062. (415) 941-6023.

Sommelier Winery, Mountain View (R) — 2560 Wyandotte Avenue, Section C. Take San Antonio Road to Middlefield, south on Middlefield, veer left onto Old Middlefield, left on Independence, left on Wyandotte Avenue, right into complex at 2560 Wyandotte. Sales and tasting by appointment only. (415) 969-2442.

Sycamore Creek Vineyards, Morgan Hill (R,P) — From Highway 101 at Morgan Hill, 3.9 miles on Watsonville Road to 12775 Uvas Road. (Winery is located on the corner of Uvas Road and Watsonville Road, between Uvas Meadows Park and Oak Dell Park.) Tasting Saturday and Sunday, noon to 6 p.m., or by appointment. (408) 779-4738.

Turgeon and Lohr Winery, San Jose (R) — Off Alameda, one-quarter mile south of Highway 17 at 1000 Lenzen Avenue. Tasting, tours daily, 10 a.m. to 5 p.m. Private group tours, tastings and gourmet dinners by special arrangement. (408) 288-5057.

Santa Cruz County

Ahlgren Vineyard, Boulder Creek (R) — Telephone or write in advance for appointment and directions. PO Box 931; (408) 338-6071.

Bargetto's Santa Cruz Winery, Soquel (R) — 3535 North Main Street. Highway 1, four miles south of Santa Cruz, left from Capitola-Soquel offramp. Daily, 9 a.m. to 5:30 p.m. (408) 475-2258.

Felton-Empire Vineyards, Felton — 0.2 mile from Highway 9 on Felton-Empire Road. Tours by appointment, Thursday and Sunday afternoons. (408) 335-3939.

Michael T. Parsons Winery, Soquel — 170 Hidden Valley Road, Soquel. By appointment only. (408) 475-6096.

River Run Vintners, Watsonville — 65 Rogge Lane, by appointment only. (408) 722-7520.

Roudon-Smith Vineyards, Santa Cruz (R) — Six miles north of Santa Cruz, off Mountain View Road. By appointment only. (408) 427-3492.

Santa Cruz Mountain Vineyard — Eight miles north of Santa Cruz. By appointment only. Write 2300 Jarvis Road, Santa Cruz, California 95065 for directions and appointment.

P and M Staiger, Boulder Creek (R) — Directions given by winery. By appointment only, two weeks advance notice. (408) 338-4346.

Sunrise Winery, Santa Cruz (R,P) — 16001 Empire Grade, Santa Cruz 95060. Write or call for appointment. (408) 423-8226 or (408) 286-1418.

Solano County

Cadenasso Winery, Fairfield (R) — Off Highway 80 at Fairfield-Rio Vista exit, daily, 8 a.m. to 5 p.m. (707) 425-5845.

Diablo Vista, Benicia (R) — 674 East H Street. Retail sales and tours by appointment. (415) 837-1801.

Wooden Valley Winery, Suisun City (R) — 4½ miles northwest on Suisun Valley Road, exit at Highway 80. Daily, 9 a.m. to 5 p.m.; closed Monday. No tours. (707) 864-0730.

Sonoma County

Alexander Valley Vineyards, Healdsburg (R) — 8644 Highway 128, eight miles east of Healdsburg. Tours, tasting and sales, 10 a.m. to 5 p.m., weekdays; noon to 5 p.m., weekends. (707) 433-6293.

Bandiera Wines, Cloverdale — Highway 101 at Cloverdale Boulevard, two blocks west at 155 Cherry Creek Road. Retail sales daily, 1 p.m. to 6 p.m. Winery tours. Wine museum and unique wine artifacts. (707) 894-2352.

Buena Vista Winery-Haraszthy Cellars, Sonoma (R,P) — End of Old Winery Road, one mile east of Sonoma, daily, 10 a.m. to 5 p.m. Picnic facilities for retail sales patrons only. (State Historical Landmark #392.) (707) 938-1266.

Bynum Winery, Healdsburg (R) — Take Westside Road from Healdsburg west eight miles to winery at 8075 Westside Road. Daily, 9 a.m. to 5 p.m. Tours by appointment. (707) 433-5852.

Cambiaso Vineyards, Healdsburg — 1½ miles southeast of Healdsburg, Freeway N to Healdsburg Avenue offramp, turn east on Grant Avenue to end. Open Monday to Saturday 10 a.m. to 4 p.m. Closed Sunday. Retail sales; no tasting. (707) 433-5508.

Chateau St. Jean, Kenwood (R,P) — Highway 12, eight miles east of Santa Rosa, daily, 10 a.m. to 4:30 p.m. Tours by appointment only. Tasting, retail sales and picnic area. (707) 833-4134.

Clos du Bois, Healdsburg — 36 Mill Street. No tasting. By appointment only. (707) 433-9383.

Dry Creek Vineyard, Healdsburg (R,P) — 3.2 miles northwest on Dry Creek Road. Exit from Highway 101. Daily, 10 a.m. to 5 p.m. (707) 433-1000.

Field Stone Winery, Healdsburg (P) — 10075 State Highway 128, corner of Chalk Hill and Highway 128, halfway between Healdsburg and Calistoga. Daily, 9 a.m. to 5 p.m. Retail sales but no tasting. (707) 433-7266.

Foppiano Vineyards, Healdsburg (R) — 12707 Old Redwood Highway, two miles south of Healdsburg, west of Highway 101. Daily, 10 a.m. to 4 p.m. (707) 433-1937.

Geyser Peak Winery, Geyserville (R,P) — Highway 101 at Canyon Road overpass. Daily, 10 a.m. to 5 p.m.; tours by appointment; tasting. Picnic area and choice of hillside or river walking trails. (707) 433-6585.

Grand Cru Vineyards, Glen Ellen (R,P) — Highway 12, Dunbar Road exit (two miles north of Glen Ellen), west on Henno. Weekends, 10 a.m. to 5 p.m. Group tours by appointment only. (707) 996-8100.

Gundlach-Bundschu Winery, Sonoma (R,P) — 3775 Thornsberry Road. Open noon to 5 p.m., Friday, Saturday and Sunday; or by appointment. From Sonoma Plaza, go east on Napa Street to Old Winery Road — turn left; right on Lovall Valley Road, right on Thornsberry Road. (707) 938-5277.

Hacienda Wine Cellars, Sonoma (R,P) — 1000 Vineyard Lane, private road exit off Castle Road, 1½ miles northeast of Sonoma Plaza, in historic Buena Vista Vineyards. Daily, 10 a.m. to 5 p.m. Tours by appointment. (707) 938-3220.

J. J. Haraszthy & Son, Glen Ellen — 14301 Arnold Drive in London Glen Village, one-half mile south of Glen Ellen. By appointment only. (707) 996-3040.

Hop Kiln Winery and Vineyards, Healdsburg (R,P) — 6½ miles southwest of Healdsburg at 6050 Westside Road. Open Saturday and Sunday 10 a.m. to 5 p.m., weekdays noon to 5 p.m., and by appointment. Picnic facilities for retail patrons. (State Historical Landmark #893.) (707) 433-6491.

Iron Horse Vineyards, Sebastopol — 9786 Ross Station Road. Tours and tasting by appointment only. (707) 887-1909.

Johnson's Alexander Valley Wines, Healdsburg (R,P) — Highway 128, 1¾ miles south of Jimtown Store in Alexander Valley. Open daily, 10 a.m. to 5 p.m. (707) 433-2319.

Kenwood Vineyards, Sonoma (R) — Eight miles north of Sonoma, on Highway 12, daily, 9 a.m. to 5 p.m. (707) 833-5891.

Korbel Champagne Cellars, Guerneville (R) — Three miles north of Santa Rosa on Highway 101, 14 miles west on River Road. Tours daily, 9:45 a.m. to 3:45 p.m. Group tours by appointment. Retail sales, 9 a.m. to 5:30 p.m. (707) 887-2294.

Lambert Bridge, Healdsburg — 3½ miles west on Dry Creek Road to Lambert Bridge Road, left to West Dry Creek Road, left one-half mile to winery. By appointment only. (707) 433-5855.

Landmark Vineyards, Windsor (R,P) — Highway 101 north of Santa Rosa, exit at Windsor, continue straight, crossing Old Redwood Highway onto Los Amigos Road (freeway frontage road) for one-quarter mile. Wednesday and Friday noon to 5 p.m., Saturday and Sunday 10 a.m. to 5 p.m., informal tours, retail sales. (707) 838-9466.

Lytton Springs Winery, Healdsburg — From Highway 101, one mile west on Lytton Springs Road. Monday to Friday 8 a.m. to 5 p.m., tours by appointment only. (707) 433-7721.

Mark West Vineyards, Forestville — 7000 Trenton-Healdsburg Road, Highway 101 north of Santa Rosa to River Road, 5½ miles west to Trenton-Healdsburg Road, right one-half mile to winery. By appointment only. (707) 544-4813.

Martini and Prati Wines, Incorporated, Santa Rosa (R) — Highway 101 at Guerneville Road, 8.1 miles northwest on Laguna Road. Open Monday to Friday 9 a.m. to 4 p.m. No tours. (707) 823-2404.

Matanzas Creek Winery, Santa Rose — 6097 Bennett Valley Road. Highway 101 north to Highway 12 east to Bennett Valley Road, five miles to winery. Tours by appointment only. Tastings by invitation to mailing list customers. (707) 542-8242.

Mill Creek Vineyards, Healdsburg — One mile west of Healdsburg on Westside Road. Retail sales. (707) 433-5098.

Nervo Winery, Geyserville (R,P) — Highway 101, Independence Lane East, four miles north of Healdsburg. Daily, 10 a.m. to 5 p.m. Picnic area. (707) 857-3417.

Pastori Winery, Geyserville (R) — Canyon Road exit to Geyserville Avenue, north one mile. Daily, 9 a.m. to 5 p.m. (707) 857-3418.

J. Pedroncelli Winery, Geyserville (R) — Highway 101, one mile north of Geyserville, one mile west on Canyon Road. Open daily, 10 a.m. to 5 p.m. (707) 857-3619.

A. Rafanelli, Healdsburg — Exit from Highway 101 on Dry Creek Road; 3½ miles northwest on Dry Creek Road to Lambert Bridge Road. Left to West Dry Creek Road, then left 400 yards. By appointment only. (707) 433-1385.

Sebastiani Vineyards, Sonoma (R) — Fourth Street East at Spain Street intersection, daily, 10 a.m. to 5 p.m. (State Historical Landmark #739.) (707) 938-5532.

Simi Winery, Incorporated, Healdsburg (R,P) — Dry Creek exit off Highway 101, east to Healdsburg Avenue, north one mile. Open daily, 10 a.m. to 5 p.m. Groups by appointment. (707) 433-6981.

Sonoma Vineyards (Windsor Vineyards), Windsor (R,P) — Highway 101 north of Santa Rosa to Windsor exit, three miles on Old Redwood Highway. Daily, 10 a.m. to 5 p.m. Luncheons and dinners for groups of 20 and more, by advance reservation only. Winery features concerts and cultural events during summer. (707) 433-6511.

Sotoyome Winery, Healdsburg — On Limerick Lane, 1½ miles south off Old Redwood Highway. Visits by appointment only. (707) 433-2001.

Souverain Cellars, Geyserville (R) — Highway 101 to Independence Lane/Souverain Road exit to winery, five miles north of Healdsburg. Tours and tasting daily, 10 a.m. to 4 p.m. Summer theater, art shows and other events throughout the year. (707) 433-6918. Souverain Restaurant at the winery open for lunch and dinner, reservations advised. Hours vary depending upon season. (707) 857-3789.

Robert Stemmler Winery, Healdsburg — 3.4 miles northwest on Lambert Bridge Road off Highway 101 to 3805 Lambert Bridge Road. Visits and sales by appointment only. (707) 433-6334.

Trentadue Winery, Geyserville (R) — Four miles north of Healdsburg on Highway 101 to Independence turnoff to 19170 Redwood Highway. Tasting daily, 10 a.m. to 5 p.m. No tours. Gift shop. (707) 433-3104.

Valley of the Moon, Glen Ellen (R) — Off Highway 12 on Madrone Road, daily, 8 a.m. to 5 p.m., except Thursday. No tours. (707) 996-6941.

Vina Vista, Geyserville — North on Highway 101, exit at Canyon Road, then 1.9 miles north on Chianti Road. Tours by appointment only. (415) 967-1824.

Stanislaus County

Pirrone Wine Cellars, Salida (R) — From Highway 99, 6½ miles north of Modesto on Pirrone Road. Open Monday to Friday 9 a.m. to 5 p.m. (209) 545-0704.

Tehama County

Barengo Vineyards, Red Bluff (TR) — Highway 5 at Motel Orleans, daily, 9 a.m. to 5 p.m. (916) 527-4112.

Tulare County

California Growers Winery, Incorporated, Yettem (R) — Approximately one-half mile west of Yettem, east on Avenue 384 from Highway 99. Monday to Friday, 1 p.m. to 4 p.m. Tours by appointment only. (209) 528-3033.

Tuolumne County

Gold Mine Winery, Columbia (TR) — Four miles north of Sonora near entrance to Columbia State Park, daily, 10 a.m. to 5 p.m. (209) 532-3089.

Yankee Hill Winery, Columbia (R,P) — Three-quarters of a mile east of Columbia-Yankee Hill Road. Daily, sunup to sundown. Personalized tours and tastings. Scenic picnic area. (209) 532-3015.

Ventura County

Brookside Winery, Ventura (TR,P) — 6580 Leland Street, on Highway 101, daily, 9 a.m. to 6 p.m. (805) 642-9867.

Dining Discoveries

By Elmer Dills

Too many travel guides cover where to stay and what to see in depth — while all but ignoring where to dine along the way. Since dining out is an important part of any vacation or travel adventure, here's a select list of restaurants for RVers on the go. As you'll see, these are not the big-name places in the cities we've covered; instead, they are restaurants that offer local specialties at reasonable prices, plus a warm welcome for our kind of people.

THE WEST

Washington — To visit Washington and not try some of the great seafood speciality restaurants would be like visiting Rome and ignoring St. Peters. And Washington produces some fine wines. Try something from the Ste. Michelle winery. I particularly recommend their Chenin Blanc. In Seattle, try the MERCHANT'S CAFE for lunch or dinner. It's at 109 Yesler Way and is open daily except Sunday. Order their cioppino or any of the fresh fish of the day. IVAR'S SALMON HOUSE at 401 NE Northlake Way is housed in a re-creation of an Indian house on Lake Union. Order salmon prepared Indian-style over alderwood fires. A treat for the eyes and the taste buds. Lunch and dinner daily.

Oregon — In Portland, you'll want to seek out DAN & LOUIS OYSTER BAR at 208 SW Ankeny Street. Great clam chowder, crab and oyster stews and a fine shrimp Louis. Skip the fried seafood dishes. JAKE'S FAMOUS CRAWFISH at 401 SW 12th Avenue in Portland is another good idea. Outstanding chowders and fresh seafood dishes. Dinner for two here under $15. If you're from back east and would give anything for a New York-style deli, try ROSE'S at 315 NW 23rd in Portland. For breakfast or lunch, drop in at the ORIGINAL PANCAKE HOUSE at 8601 SW 24th Street in Portland. It is not part of a chain and the pancakes are outstanding. Prices are rock bottom, too.

California — A state as vast and varied as California should and does offer a tremendous variety of restaurants of every description. There are hundreds and hundreds of little bargain restaurants to pick and choose from — but far more than can be listed here. So if you're planning to spend any time at all in the state, you should purchase one or both of the following books: *Best Restaurants Of San Francisco And Northern California* ($2.95) and *Best Restaurants Of Los Angeles And Southern California* ($3.95). Your local bookstore either has a copy or can obtain one for you. You can also write to: 101 Publications, 834 Mission, San Francisco, California 94103. Add 50 cents for each book ordered. These books also include informative sections on California wines.

Here are some of my own suggestions for bargain dining up and down the state:

In San Francisco, there's a small Italian spot called CAFFE SPORT & TRATTORIA at 547 Green Street. Lots of hearty homemade pasta dishes, and I suggest one made with pesto (basil) or the calamari fritta. A very unusual spot is the DIAMOND SUTRA at 737 Diamond Street. The menu is truly international, with dishes from China, South America, Poland, Greece, Morocco and India — to name but a few of the culinary areas covered. Most dinners are in the $5 range, which is good news for bargain hunters. If you get to Macy's on Union Square, you're in for a surprise. There's a little restaurant in Macy's basement called MAMA'S and for lunch you get some of the best Italian food and prices in town. It's worth a trip to Macy's just to lunch here. For something unusual, try the SWAN OYSTER DEPOT at 1517 Polk Street. You'll eat at a counter and the atmosphere is ground zero, but if you love fresh oysters this is the place to be between 8 a.m. and 5:30 p.m. any day but Sunday.

In Monterey, try ABALONETTI'S on Fisherman's Wharf and order their calmari (squid). They prepare it a variety of different ways and all are superior. If you're lucky, you'll sit by the window and watch the seals play a few feet below you in the bay. This is the best of the wharf restaurants. Most are disasters and overpriced. In nearby Carmel, spend some time at LE COQ D'OR at Mission and Fifth. Despite the fancy name, it really is a modestly-priced French restaurant well within modest budget limitations.

In the state capital at Sacramento, the place to be for lunch is in the patio of the FIREHOUSE COURTYARD in Old Town. Sit under the trees by a fountain and order a Hangtown Fry or Captain John Sutter's devil bee bones. If you find yourself in North Lake Tahoe in the summer, stop for lunch at the SQUIRREL'S NEST at 5405 West Lake Boulevard in Homewood. Great soups, sandwiches and salads under the trees.

In the winter, you might be skiing at Mammoth. If so, stop in at the MOGUL STEAK HOUSE where you cook your own steaks over charcoal. Quantity and quality at bargain prices is what you'll find here and few leave hungry or unhappy.

Moving south along the coast to Santa Barbara, you'll find the best and least expensive seafood served in the ENTERPRISE FISH COMPANY at 225 State Street, near the Amtrack station. Look at the chalkboard to see what's fresh that day and also check out the daily specials, which are always reasonable. If you journey over to the Danish community of Solvang, you'll find plenty of lunch bargains in the Scandinavian smorgasbords served at most of the restaurants. The DANISH INN, at 1547 Mission Drive, does one of the best in town — and at lunchtime the price is right.

Los Angeles, like San Francisco, is a restaurant world unto itself. There are hundreds and hundreds of little places for bargain dining out with new ones popping up every week while other disappear. In Hollywood, a dandy place is the LITTLE PRAGUE, at 5626 Hollywood Boulevard. This tiny spot is open for dinner nightly and for lunch on Monday and Tuesday. They serve the dishes of Germany and Czechoslovakia at truly bargain prices. Their house speciality is one-half of a roast duck with homemade dumplings and sauerkraut for under $6. For under $5, you can have one of the best Wienerschniztels I've come across and chef Maria's meatloaf is well worth ordering. (Save room for her homemade fruit dumplings for dessert.)

In the mid-city area, you'll find two bargain restaurants side by side. One is ORZA'S RUMANIAN RESTAURANT, at 448 North Fairfax. The dish to order here is the mixed grill for two at $12, which is a huge wooden board covered with steak, pork, spicy Rumanian sausage, chicken and sweetbreads. Wash it all down with a chilled bottle of Rumanian white wine, and dinner will still be in the under $16-$18 category. Next door is the FAIRFAX

YUGOSLAVIAN, where for $5 or $6 you can order a dinner that includes appetizer, soup, salad, the entree and dessert. Talk about bargains!

For Italian food, I like ANNA MARIA'S at 1356 South La Brea — just a few minutes north of the Santa Monica Freeway and easy to find. They have a charming outdoor patio, complete with umbrellas and cheerful waitresses. The secret here is not to order from the menu, but to ask owner Dan Dinardo to prepare some of his special dishes. Most are under $5, so don't worry about the cost. In Pasadena, there's a very unusual Middle Eastern restaurant called BURGER CONTINENTAL at the corner of Lake and California. They serve breakfast, lunch and dinner at unbelievable prices. Complete dinners are well under $5, and on some days they offer free refills on beer and wine and soft drinks. This is a paradise for the dedicated bargain hunter. Out in the San Fernando Valley, you should know about MOTHER'S CARVERY at 13807 Roscoe Boulevard. Every night of the week they offer a $6.95 all-you-can-eat buffet that is a winner. Turkey, ham, beef, oysters, ribs and on and on. As a bonus on Friday, Saturday and Sunday, there's a magician to entertain you.

In San Diego, I like the CAFE DEL REY MORO in Balboa Park, a treat for the eyes as well as the pocketbook. Come for lunch and sit out on the patio and enjoy one of their famous Giant Margarita Olympica's and a Mexican salad. They also have a nice Sunday champagne brunch. If you enjoy natural dishes, and a restaurant that allows no smoking, the GATEKEEPER at Interstate 8 and Waring Road is for you. Orange juice is made when you order it, salads are ultra-fresh and crispy, and their breads are their own. In the Old Town section, you'll find lots of shops and restaurants. HAMBURGUESA is one of the best and serves hamburgers in dozens of different ways. In La Jolla, I'm a fan of a German place called the RHEINLANDER at 2182 Avenida del la Playa. Sit out in the beer garden, order a beer (naturally), and try the rouladen or sauerbraten. The price is right.

BAJA, MEXICO

Although Mexico certainly doesn't represent the travel and dining out bargain paradise as in former times, there are still places where you can dine — and dine well — without spending too many pesos.

Tijuana — Not my favorite city by far, but there are some surprisingly good restaurants here. VICTOR'S STEAK HOUSE, right across the road from the race track, is exactly what the name implies — a steak house, and a good one at that. GUILLERMO'S, across from the Jai Alai Palace, serves much better than average Mexican fare, plus Spanish paella. The best bargain of all, though, is about a 45-minute drive from Tijuana along the coast highway to a little village called Puerto Nuevo (Newport). You'll know you're there when you see a low white building to your left with a sign reading "Newport — Lobster." This is a tiny little fisherman's village with some of the homes converted into makeshift restaurants. They serve the day's lobster catch at about half of what you would pay in Los Angeles or San Diego. They're even cheaper if you just buy the lobster and do your own cooking. I cannot recommend any particular restaurant here as the idea is to go from place to place, looking at what is fresh, and making your best deal. (If you hear at one place that no one has fresh lobster, don't believe it. Keep moving around and there's a good chance someone will have been lucky and pulled in some big ones that are just hours from the sea.)

Mexicali — The dining room of the HOTEL LUCERNA is the best choice in town. They often have quail, pheasant, fresh shrimp, venison and other local specialties. Most entrees are in the $6-$8 range. For Mexican specialties at very modest prices, the locals go to

CENADURIA SELECTA at Selecta 1510. It's been there for 30 years and is one of my favorites because it is spick-and-span clean and almost everything is carefully and slowly made-by-hand to your order.

Ensenada — In Ensenada, you should have one meal at the 30-year-old EL REY SOL. It is not the least-expensive place in town, but it is one of the best. They make their own breads and pastries, and I always order their sausage platter. For seafood, both the CAS MAR and the CAS MAR #2 are worth checkout out. The MESON SANTA TOMAS offers fresh quail in a brandy sauce that I really enjoy for about $8.

To watch the sun set while sipping a margarita and enjoying fresh abalone steak, there is the CUEVA DE LOS TIGRES (Cave of the Tigers). It's about a 15-minute drive south out of town and along the beach, but the way is well marked and it would be hard to miss it. And while you're in Ensenada you'll certainly want to head for HUSSONGS. It's been there for longer than anyone can remember (and looks like it), but it's a famous place where you should at least enjoy a brew or two.

THE GREAT SOUTHWEST

Arizona — Steaks and Mexican food are the popular items in this state, and that's what you should concentrate on. In Yuma, stop at the OLD WESTERN BAR B QUE at 2400 East 16th Street. Try their house specialty called the "Smokey Pig Platter" or any of the rib dishes. Popular with the locals, but not located in the best part of Yuma. But if you want great barbecue and great prices, this is the place to go. For Mexican-Arizona specialties in Scottsdale, visit GARCIA'S DEL ESTE RESTAURANT at 7633 East Indian School Road. Try the chimichangas and the margaritas. In Apache Junction, there's a place called SUPERSTITION SKIES at 3068 East Scenic Drive with a great view of the Superstition Mountains. Western dishes are served at very modest prices. If you get to Carefree, try the Sunday Champagne Brunch at the ELBOW BEND at 7210 East Elbow Bend Road. For Mexican dishes in Phoenix, there's GEORGE'S OLE at 7330 North Dreamy Draw Drive and it's open for lunch and dinner every day of the week. For fun and music and fair prices, try CRAZY ED'S at 1926 West Deer Valley Road in Phoenix.

Nevada — Las Vegas and Reno are no doubt Nevada's two most famous — and most expensive — cities, but you can still find some bargains. In Las Vegas there's a hotel called the EL CORTEZ in the downtown section that offers a complete one-pound steak dinner for $5.95, 24 hours a day. The steak is excellent, though the hotel itself leaves something to be desired. A fun place that offers lots of food, all the wine you can drink and even some songs by the owner is BATTISTA'S HOLE IN THE WALL, just off the strip. Dinners here go from under $10 to about $18, but if you stick to the less expensive items you can't go wrong for the money. In Reno, one of the best bargains is THE BASQUE RESTAURANT at 235 Lake Street in the Santa Fe Hotel. You'll sit family-style at long tables and they'll keep the food coming out of the kitchen until you yell for help. The price was $5 for more food than you can believe the last time we were there, but even if the prices go up, this place will remain one of Nevada's great bargains. In Elko, there's another good bet called the BASQUE RESTAURANT on 246 Silver Street in the Star Hotel. All you want to eat at modest prices is the policy here, too.

New Mexico — Like Arizona, New Mexico is big on Mexican dishes and the American steak. The two main cities are Santa Fe and Albuquerque, and both offer some interesting bargain-dining possibilities. In Albuquerque, try LA HACIENDA for local Mexican specialties in what was once an actual hacienda. In Santa Fe,

LA TERTULIA offers Mexican and New Mexico specialties at fair prices. In Las Cruces, LA POSTA is one of the state's best-known and most popular restaurants. (The outstanding patio here reminds us of Mexico City's famed San Angel Inn.) And if you end up in Carlsbad, the spot to try is the CORTEZ CAFE for local Mexican specialties.

Oklahoma — This is a rough and tumble cowboy state, but it has a polish and veneer all its own. In Oklahoma City, the CATTLEMAN'S CAFE at 1309 South Agnew in Stockyard City is where the the cowpokes gather — and for good reason — lots of hearty good chow at modest prices. There's also the QUEEN ANNE CAFETERIA in the United Founders Life Tower building. It's more than a cafeteria and definitely worth a visit for bargain hunters.

Texas — Like California, Texas is so huge and complicated as to boggle the imagination. Accordingly, the same company that publishes the excellent restaurant guides for California also publishes one for Texas. It's called *Best Restaurants Of Texas* and it's $2.95 plus 50 cents for postage and handling. It covers Houston, Dallas, Fort Worth, Austin and San Antonio and is indispensable for anyone traveling to this part of the world. Here are a few bargain hints taken from the book. In Austin, THE BROWN BAG at 2330 South Lamar is considered the best barbecue experience at the best price. Sit on the patio, where there's often live music. In Dallas, NOPALITOS at 2818 Harry Hines Street is a great local favorite for inexpensive Mexican dishes. The house specialty is baby goat. For barbecue, SONNY BRYAN'S at 2202 Inwood Road is considered one of the world's best. For lunch, try GENNIE'S BISHOP GRILLE at 308 North Bishop Avenue in Oak Cliff. Chicken, fried steak and all the rest of the best of the South at very modest prices. In Houston, check out FAT ERNIE'S at 1 Allen Center, which features dishes from around the world at local prices.

ROCKY MOUNTAIN AREA

Colorado — Denver is the main city of note, and it offers some fine dining out discoveries. THE HUNGRY FARMER at 6925 West Alameda in the Lakewood section serves farm food in what used to be a barn. Lots and lots of hearty fare at modest prices. For something really different, head for the OPEN SEASON at 3333 Quebec Street near the airport. Wild pheasant, boar, buffalo and even rattlesnake are often on the menu. This place is for the truly adventurous. For a fun place, try THE BRATSKELLER at 1430 Larimer Street, which offers patio dining with German and American specialties and lots of happy people. Moderate prices.

MIDWEST

Kansas — Beef and lots of it is what you'll find in Kansas. The trouble is, it isn't inexpensive. But here are some places you can still sample the local specialties without destroying the travel budget: In Kansas City, the locals swear by JESS AND JIM'S at 135th and Locust. Great steaks, cottage fries, chicken and slaw. Usually a wait, since they take no reservations. LEONA YARBROUGH'S at 2800 West 53rd Street offers home-style meals with very modest prices. In Wichita, there's BROWN'S GRILL EAST at 545 North Hillside, where the specialty is family-style cooking.

Minnesota — The twin cities of Minneapolis-St. Paul offer some inexpensive dining establishments. For German food, those in the know head for the BLACK FOREST at 1 East 26th Street in Minneapolis. (In the summer, there's an outdoor beer garden here.) Dinner for two: well under $15, lunch even less. BECKY'S CAFETERIA at 1934 Hennepin Avenue in Minneapolis goes several steps beyond normal cafeteria food. Economy, quality and ambience all combine here. In St. Paul, the BOCA CHICA at 11 Concord Street offers inexpensive Mexican fare and a great Sunday morning breakfast feast.

Missouri — In St. Louis, you wouldn't want to miss CROWN'S CAFETERIA at Jefferson and Martin Luther King Drive for barbecue, ham hocks, chicken, greens, cobblers and cornbread beyond belief. PELICAN'S, at 2256 South Grand Boulevard, offers Creole dishes like catfish, turtle soup and gumbo. Nothing fancy here — just good food at honest prices. For more German food, there's also EBERHARD'S at 117 North Main in nearby Columbia, Illinois.

THE CENTRAL STATES

Wisconsin — You have to find a German restaurant in Milwaukee to really get the flavor of the city. The best is probably KARL RATZSCH'S at 320 East Mason, but it is also the most expensive, although you can stay on your budget here at lunch. Less expensive is the GOLDEN ZITHER at 4928 West Vliet and, yes, they do have real zither music and singing many nights of the week. The hassenpfeffer is particularly recommended. On Whitefish Bay, head for PANDL'S WHITEFISH BAY INN at 1319 East Henry Clay Street — and do order the local whitefish.

Illinois — Chicago has many fine restaurants — and prices to match. But the NEW LITTLE BOHEMIA at 2700 South Christiana Avenue is not at all expensive and offers fine atmosphere and German/Czech-style dishes. Try their sauerbraten. ADOLPH'S at 845 North Rush offers A-Z complete dinners with staggering portions, including oysters and clams to start off with, for under $10. A real bargain for really hungry RVers.

Indiana — In Fort Wayne, budget-hunters go to the HERITAGE HOUSE SMORGASBORD at 4747 Luna Road. Great for families with kids in tow. In Indianapolis, SAM'S ATTIC at 28th and Meridian offers a local institution with lots of atmosphere. Spareribs are the best bet there. Also, try SHAPIRO'S on 808 South Meridian, an excellent cafeteria with deli-type dishes at very modest prices. Best bet here? The shortribs.

Michigan — Detroit is the main attraction here, and it is definitely a meat-and-potatoes city. The BRAU HAUS at 1977 East Woodbridge serves first-class German fare at second-class prices. AL'S LOUNGE at 7940 South Street gives you basic Hungarian fare at basic prices. Try the Friday fish-fry for a real bargain. Another good ethnic spot is the POLISH EAGLE at 1415 Parker. Stuffed cabbage, duck soup and other Polish dishes make this interesting as well as inexpensive.

Ohio — Lots of interesting ethnic restaurants in Cleveland offer some real dining bargains. A good example is the BALATON at 12521 Buckeye Road, which offers strolling musicians, lots of ambience and gobs of good food at very modest prices. Try the Hungarian platter with a bit of everything that's good at this restaurant on one plate. Desserts extraordinary. KIEFER'S, at 2519 Detroit Avenue, serves German fare in pleasant surroundings and at surprisingly inexpensive prices. In Cincinnati, THE CRICKET at Sixth and Vine has a huge menu with very moderate prices. Try the seafood bisque and whatever fresh fish is available on the day you're there. In Sandusky, try BETTY'S HOME COOKING at 325 West Market Street. Her braised shortribs are tops.

THE GULF STATES

Louisiana — Of course, New Orleans comes immediately to mind when Louisiana restaurants are the topic of conversation. And while the big name places like Antoine's and Brennan's are known around the world, there are some small and inexpensive specialty restaurants you should know about. Two of these, FELIX'S at 739 Iberville Street and the ACME OYSTER HOUSE at 724 Iberville are famed for fresh oysters. They'll shuck them while you belly up to the bar and keep opening those little delights until you call a halt. Don't miss either of these places. I also recommend PASCAL'S MANALE at 1838 Napolean Avenue for seafood and barbecued shrimp. Another good possibility for seafood lovers on a budget is the LAKEVIEW SEAFOOD RESTAURANT at 7400 Hayne Boulevard. The seafood boat is what to order here, plus local fresh shrimp and oysters. Very low prices considering what you get.

Florida — Seafood is king in Florida — and the choice is truly impressive. If you're going to spend any time in Florida, a copy of *Best Restaurants Of Florida* ($2.95), available from the same company listed earlier, should be in your RV. In Miami, the PORT OF CALL at 14411 Biscayne Boulevard is a good place for fresh seafood of every description. JOE'S STONE CRAB, at 227 Biscayne Street in Miami Beach, is a must. And although it is usually more expensive than the regular seafood items, do try the dish that made this place a landmark — the stone crabs. DURTY NELLY'S CRAB HOUSE AND PUB, at 18101 Southwest 98th Court, Perrine, Miami, is another place with excellent seafood and lots of character. And since there are now so many Cubans in Miami, try EL SEGUNDO VIAJANTE at 2846 Palm Avenue, right across from famed Hialeah race track. In Sarasota, locals head for WALT'S FISH MARKET RAW OYSTER BAR AND RESTAURANT at 560 North Washington Boulevard. This place is very popular, so come early to avoid the dinner rush.

THE SOUTH

Virginia — If you find yourself in Petersburg, you should try what many consider to be the finest barbecue in a state famed for its hickory-smoked specialties — KING'S BAR B QUE at 2629 Boulevard, Route 301. For complete directions, phone (804) 526-0166. In Fredericksburg, ALLMAN'S PIT COOKED BAR-B-QUE is also recommended.

South Carolina — Two fairly inexpensive seafood restaurants that a good friend recommends highly are the TRAWLER, at Mt. Pleasant, and the LORELEI, in Shem Creek, both in the Charleston area. In Myrtle Beach, good things are said about MAMMY'S KITCHEN and JUEL'S HURRICANE SEAFOOD HOUSE.

Georgia — Atlanta is where it happens in Georgia, though many who live away from this thriving center would disagree. AUNT FANNY'S CABIN, at 375 Campbell Road in Smyrna, is both picturesque and inexpensive. Fried chicken is what to order. Not fancy, but popular with the locals, is MARY MAC'S TEA ROOM at 224 Ponce de Leon Avenue, NE. Try the chicken and dumplings and the "Jimmy Carter Custard" (if it is still on the menu). One place you should not miss if you don't mind early dining is MA HULL'S, at 122 Hurt, NE and Edgewood. They serve boardinghouse meals, the cost is minimal, the quality high and the portions huge. A passing era still alive and well in Atlanta.

THE EAST

New York City — This is another city that only a book would do justice to — so do yourself a favor and buy a copy of Myra Waldon's restaurant guide. Restaurants come and go so quickly in this city that only a local expert such as Myra could keep you posted.

Pennsylvania — Both Philadelphia and Pittsburgh offer some good dining opportunities in our price range. In Philadelphia, try the SANSON STREET OYSTER BAR at 1516 Sanson Street. Great fresh seafood with goodies from both the Delaware and Chesapeake Bays on the menu at very modest prices. At nearby Hatfield, try GEORGE AND EDDIE'S COVENTRY INN at 3120 Penn Avenue, just off Route 309. Lots of character and atmosphere at very fair prices. In Pittsburg, WIEGAND'S CAFE at 422 Forland Street serves German specialties you'd expect to pay twice as much for elsewhere. Pittsburgh has a large Middle East community, and their favorite is SAMRENY'S at 4808 Baum Boulevard in Oakland. Informal and inexpensive.

New Jersey — Atlantic City is the big destination for RVers today, and if it's yours, try ABE'S OYSTER HOUSE, DOCK'S OYSTER HOUSE and THE SAND CASTLE for local seafood specialties at moderate prices. If you go all the way to the end of the state, and end up in Cape May, try the LOBSTER HOUSE there.

Maryland — Seafood is outstanding in Maryland, as it is in most of the states up and down this part of the country. For what has to be one of the greatest crab feasts in the world, head for GORDON'S in Baltimore. Another good crab spot is OBRYCKI'S OLDE CRAB HOUSE at 1729 East Pratt, but they are open only in the fresh crab season (April to November). In Annapolis, the OLDE TOWNE SEAFOOD SHOPPE, despite this too-cute name, is good for fresh seafood.

Washington, D.C. — The old joke used to be if you wanted a good meal in Washington, you had to drive to Baltimore. But this is no longer true. A real tradition is HARVEY'S at 1001 18th Street, NW, and while it isn't really the cheapest place in town, for what they give you it is well worth a visit. Bargain hunters will also like ANNA MARIA'S at 1737 Connecticut Avenue. In nearby Silver Springs, another favorite is CRISFIELD'S at 8012 Georgia Avenue. Great fresh seafood at modest prices with a fine raw-bar. For excellent Greek food at modest prices, try the menu at the ASTOR, 1813 M Street, NW. Finally, for seafood on the waterfront, there's the FLAGSHIP at 900 Water Street, SW. It's big and noisy, but they really care about what comes out of their kitchen.

NEW ENGLAND

From Maine to Connecticut, the watchword is seafood. Magnificent fresh lobster, scrod, perch, bass, clams, oysters — the full bounty of the sea is always ready for your table in New England. Sure, you can order steak — but why bother when this cornucopia of seafood delights is available every place you stop to dine?

Maine — In Bangor, head for the PILOT'S HOUSE for lobster. In Bar Harbor, it's the FISH NET on the Municipal Pier. If you find yourself in Sandy Point, don't miss the DOWNEASTER on Route 1, several miles north of Stockton Springs. The lobster stew and corn fritters here are sensational. In Freeport, you'll want to try the RED BARN for clambake dinners.

Massachusetts — The UNION OYSTER HOUSE at Union Street in Boston gives the best of the area's seafood without charging tourist prices. In Cambridge, the same can be said for the LEGAL SEA FOODS INC., at 237 Hampshire Street. In Hyannis, the HEARTH & KETTLE at Main Street is a 24-hour coffee shop-type operation — but with better than average seafood specialties at very low prices. (Come between noon and 6 p.m. and you'll really save.)

Vermont — In Bennington, the best bet is the inexpensive HERITAGE HOUSE, where clams and roast turkey are among the house specialties. In Manchester, the QUALITY RESTAURANT has an original Normal Rockwell painting and offers great platters of reasonably-priced food prepared by folks who have an abundance of New England pride.

Connecticut — In Hartford, the HONISS OYSTER HOUSE at 44 State Street offers fresh seafood at modest prices. In Mystic, you can enjoy locally famous shore dinners with a visit to SAILOR ED'S. In New London, a good tip is the WHALER RESTAURANT on Captain's Walk. Fast and inexpensive but good. In Westport, there's a restaurant in an old barn called, you guessed it, THE RED BARN. It's right on the Merrit Parkway, and it's well worth the drive.

Rhode Island — In Providence, or rather in nearby Bristol, is the LOBSTER POT, where delicious shore dinners are the specialty.

Elmer Dills is a renowned restaurant critic whose regular column, *Dining Out,* has appeared in *Motorhome Life* magazine since 1977. His knowledge of fine dining is compiled in several highly-acclaimed restaurant guide books, and he currently is heard weekly on KABC Talkradio in Los Angeles.

Travel Adventures

Fresh horizons often bring the opportunity to discover new pursuits, the chance to rekindle the pioneer spirit that lies deep within all of us, maybe the chance to challenge our own limits.

If your pioneer spirit includes a taste for the daring, you might want to test your courage by plunging through the white water of a wild and scenic river, or by diving off a cliff or out of an airplane with nothing more than a few yards of fabric to see you safely back to earth. Perhaps you'd like to test your stamina by climbing a mountain trail with a 40-pound pack on your back; the experience may strain your physical limits, but the sense of accomplishment and the magnificent view from the top will be ample reward.

Maybe your spirit is less daring, but no less adventurous. In that case, you might want to try your luck at panning for gold in a backcountry stream or search for rare minerals, rocks and fossils at the foot of a river bluff. At night you can turn your eyes to the heavens and gaze into the depths of space in search of an unnamed comet. If you'd like to recapture the essence of the Old West or get a taste of life down-on-the-farm, try a respite at a dude ranch or guest farm. And if you like relaxing exploration, take a Camp-A-Float tour of the hidden coves of the Sacramento Delta.

We are fortunate to have such a wide variety of choices, and even more fortunate that we, as RVers, can take full advantage of all those opportunities.

River Running

There's only one way to get acquainted with a wild river, and that is to meet it head on. The only way to learn the complexity of its personality — the angry forces of the thunderous white water and the serenity of its tree-shaded shallows — is to climb into a rubber raft or kayak and sample the river's many moods.

Thousands of people each year leave the security of home and hearth — and, yes, the comforts of their RVs — to experience the "high" of river running. Certainly, plummeting down a raging stretch of white water has its challenges, but there is more to it than mere thrills. There is no better way to leave the cares of civilization behind and witness the full beauty of nature's offerings than on a ride down an untamed river. Give yourself to the river and along the way you'll see, touch and feel all those things the wilderness has to offer — the sunlight spilling across the bluffs and dancing along the water, the cold spray in your face, the scented woodlands, abundant wildlife. At night you'll have the camaraderie of your fellow travelers as you share your experiences around the campfire. And, later, the unceasing sound of the waters will lull you to sleep.

Of course, you don't have to challenge the roaring rapids to experience all the joys of river running. An afternoon of drifting lazily down a quiet river in a canoe or even an old inner tube can often provide nearly the same sense of satisfaction and discovery as a roller coaster ride through rampaging white water.

Before Getting Underway

Canoes, kayaks and inflatable rafts have very different handling characteristics. However, all these craft have one thing in common; they easily capsize if they are overloaded or improperly loaded. All weight should be stowed as low in the center of the boat as possible. Stow all gear in the boat while it is beached. Never carry heavy loads aboard with you. If you change position in the boat, stay low and center your weight. Always make sure your craft is trim and "seaworthy."

Know Your Water!

Most accidents occur when boatmen attempt water more demanding than their skills, knowledge and experience can justify. The following is a recommended guide to water and experience established by the American White Water Affiliation. Never overestimate your ability or underestimate the water.

Class I. *Very Easy* (practiced beginner)
Waves small, regular; passages clear, sandbanks, some artificial difficulties like bridge piers; riffles.

Class II. *Easy* (intermediate)
Rapids of medium difficulty, with passages clear and wide; low ledges; spraydeck useful.

Class III. *Medium* (experienced)
Waves numerous, high, irregular; rocks; eddies; rapids with passages that are clear though narrow, requiring expertise in maneuvering; inspection usually needed; spraydeck needed.

Class IV. *Difficult* (Highly skilled with several years experience with organized group)
Long rapids, waves powerful and irregular; dangerous rocks; boiling eddies; passages difficult to reconnoiter; inspection mandatory first time; powerful and precise maneuvering required; spraydeck essential.

Class V. *Very Difficult* (teams of experts)
Extremely difficult, long and very violent rapids following each other almost without interruption; riverbed extremely obstructed; big drops, violent current, very steep gradient; reconnoitering essential but difficult.

Class VI. *Extremely Difficult* (teams of experts)
Difficulties of Class V carried to the extreme of navigability. Nearly impossible and very dangerous. For teams of experts only at favorable water

levels and after close study with all precautions.

Generally, Class I and II rivers can be run in open canoes. Some Class III rivers are suitable for open canoes if time is allowed for emptying water from the boat. *A class of river may change according to the amount of river runoff and the depth of water at a given point. Remember, very cold water does not have to be fast to be fatal!*

Emergency Procedures

If your boat capsizes, stay on the *upstream* side, preferably the end of the craft. This allows better visibility to enable you to swim your boat to shore. More importantly, it prevents the possibility of being pinned against obstacles.

Hold on to your boat unless you can increase your safety by abandonment. If rescue is not imminent and water is intolerably cold or perilous rapids are near, swim with the river current to the nearest landing. If you find yourself in the water alone, float downstream feet first. This will enable you to fend off from rocks and other obstacles.

Required and Recommended Safety Devices

All canoes and kayaks as well as inflatable rafts must carry a Coast Guard approved personal flotation device for each person aboard. Common sense demands that everyone wear their flotation device whenever afloat. Protective foot gear is always advisable and a crash helmet is recommended in swift rapids. Have a bailer handy at all times.

New and unfamiliar equipment should first be tested in calm water. The craft should be controlled by strong and adequately sized paddles or oars and spares should be readily available in case of loss. An emergency kit should include: flashlight, map, compass, first-aid equipment and waterproof matches. Obtain maps of unfamiliar areas.

For the inexperienced river runner, the best way to get your first taste of white water is through a professional outfitter and guide. Contact the following outfitters for further information on river expeditions in your area.

Alaska

Alaskan Rivers Touring Company
PO Box 1884
Anchorage, Alaska 99510
(907) 333-6390

Sourdough Outfitters
Bettles, Alaska 99723
(807) 692-5252

Arizona

Arizona Raft Adventure
PO Box 697
Flagstaff, Arizona 86002
(602) 774-4538

Wild and Scenic, Incorporated
PO Box 23-A
Marble Canyon, Arizona 86036
(602) 355-2222

California

Adventours — Wet and Wild, Incorporated
Box B
Woodland, California 95695
(916) 662-6824

American River Touring
1307 Harrison Street
Oakland, California 94612
(415) 465-9533

Mother Lode Trips
PO Box 30
Columbia, California 95310
(209) 532-7900

Colorado

Adventure Bound, Incorporated
6179 South Adams Drive
Box S
Littleton, Colorado 80121
(303) 771-3752

Rocky Mountain River Expeditions
PO Box 1394
Denver, Colorado 80201
(303) 289-5959

Royal Gorge Rafting
45045 U.S. Highway 50 West
Canon City, Colorado 81212
(303) 275-5161

Georgia

Southeastern Expeditions, Incorporated
1955 Cliff Valley Way, NE
Suite 220-B
Atlanta, Georgia 30329
(404) 329-0433

Idaho

Idaho Adventures, Incorporated
PO Box 834-CO
Salmon, Idaho 83467
(208) 756-2986

Wild Rivers Idaho
PO Box 3417-A
Boise, Idaho 83703
(208) 343-7728

Maine

Eastern River Expeditions
Box 1173
Greenville, Maine 04441
(207) 695-2411

Maine Whitewater, Incorporated
Suite 454G
Bingham, Maine 04920
(207) 622-2260

Montana

Double Arrow Outfitters
Drawer E
Seeley Lake, Montana 59868
(406) 677-2204

Missouri River Outfitters
Box 1212-A
Fort Benton, Montana 59442
(406) 622-3295

New Hampshire

Saco Bound/Northern Waters
Box 113
Center Conway, New Hampshire 03813
(603) 447-2177

North Carolina

Nantahala Outdoor Center
Star Route, Box 68
Bryson City, North Carolina 28713
(704) 488-2175

Oregon

Hells Canyon Guide Service
PO Box 165
Oxbow, Oregon 97840
(503) 785-3305

Osprey River Trips, Incorporated
6109G Fish Hatchery Road
Grants Pass, Oregon 97526
(503) 479-4215

Pennsylvania

Canyon Cruises
The Antlers Inn
RD 4
Wellsboro, Pennsylvania 16901
(814) 435-6300

Pocono Whitewater Rafting Center
Route #903
Box 44
Jim Thorpe 43, Pennsylvania 18229
(201) 774-6965

South Carolina

Wildwater Limited
Long Creek, South Carolina 29658
(803) 647-5336

Tennessee

Sunburst Wilderness Adventures
PO Box 238A
Ocoee, Tennessee 37361
(615) 338-8388

Texas

Far Flung Adventures
Box 31
Terlingua, Texas 79852
(915) 371-2489

Utah

Adventure River Expeditions, Incorporated
4211 Mars Way
Salt Lake City, Utah 84117
(801) 564-3648

Fastwater Expeditions
Box 365
Boulder City, Nevada 89005
(702) 293-1406

Outlaw Trails, Incorporated
PO Box 336-F
Green River, Utah 84525
(800) 453-1402

Washington

Four Seasons Outfitters and Guide Service
PO Box 149
Mazama, Washington 98833
(206) 827-1044

Rivers Northwest
141 Eagle Avenue, NE
Winslow, Washington 98110
(206) 842-5144

West Virginia

Appalachian Wild Waters
PO Box 126
Albright, West Virginia 26519
(304) 329-1665

Wisconsin

Roaring Rapids Raft Company
Star Route, Box 53
Athelstane, Wisconsin 54104
(714) 757-3300

Wyoming

Platte River Outfitters
PO Box 875
216 East Walnut
Saratoga, Wyoming 82331
(307) 326-5426

CANADA

British Columbia

Canadian River Expeditions, Limited
845 Chilco Street
Vancouver, British Columbia, Canada
(604) 926-4436

Manitoba

North Country River Trips
Berens River, Manitoba, Canada ROB 0A0
(204) 382-2284

Ontario

Wilderness Tours
Box 661
Pembroke, Ontario, Canada K8A 6X9
(613) 582-3351

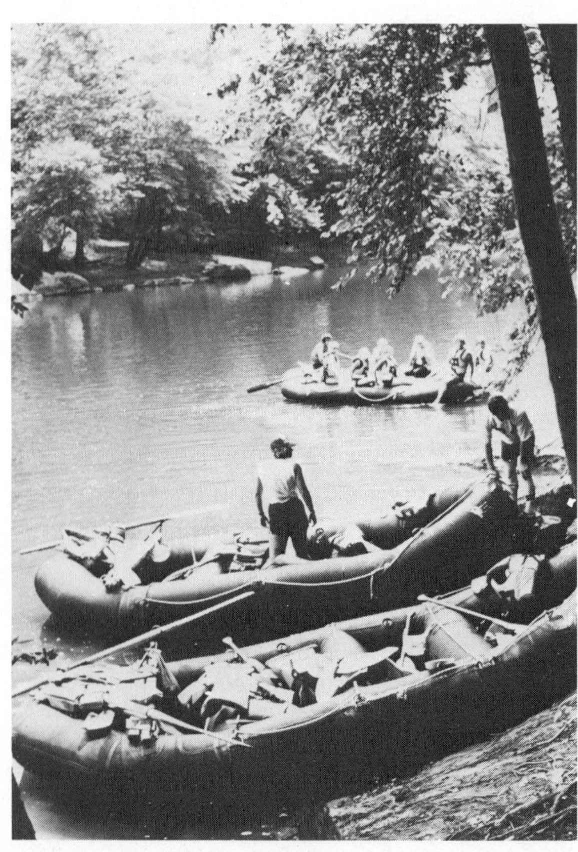

Backpacking

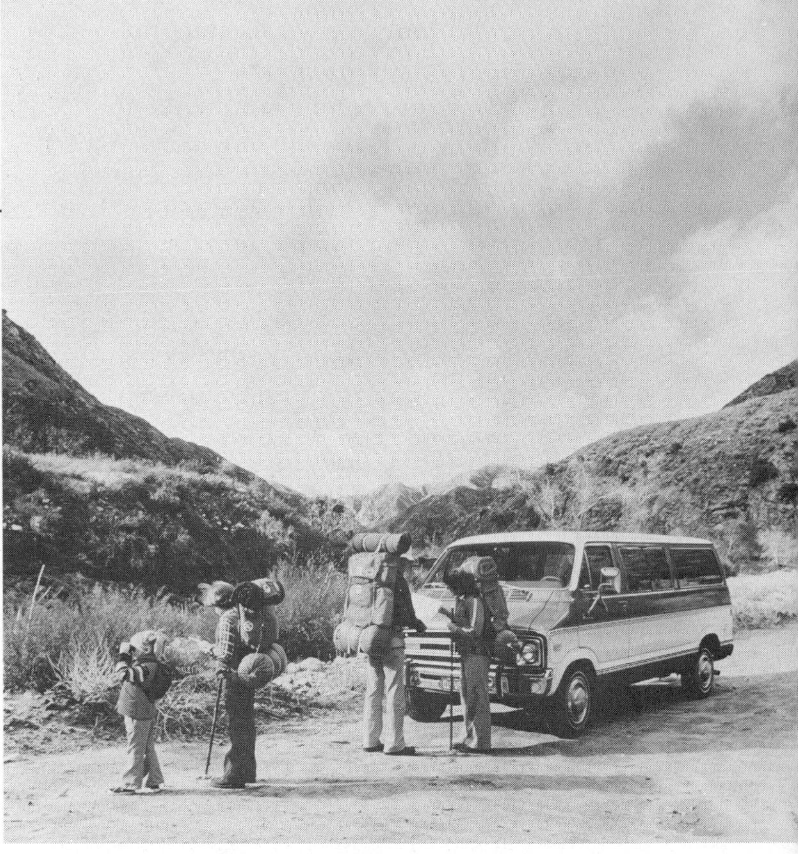

Hiking To A Spiritual High

Use your rig as a base camp and discover the quiet world beyond the road.

Why backpack? Why give up the comforts and convenience of your RV to plod along some endless trail under the weight of a 40-pound pack? Some of the answers are obvious: Backpacking is still the best way to really beat the crowds and at the same time get a truly unspoiled view of the backcountry. But, as any dedicated backpacker will tell you, there's considerably more to it than that. There are the almost undefinable benefits for those who seek to meet the wilderness on its own terms — the nourishment of the soul, the revitalization of the spirit.

James Russell Lowell, the 19th-century poet and essayist, came close to putting it in words when he wrote, "Solitude is as needful to the imagination as society is wholesome for the character." But, not surprisingly, it was John Muir, the legendary naturalist and undisputed elder of the backpacking tribe, who offered the closest definition of the backpacking mystique. "In God's wilderness," Muir wrote in his diary, ". . . the great fresh, unblighted, unredeemed wilderness — the galling harness of civilization drops off, and the wounds heal ere we are aware."

As RVers, most of us chose our rigs because we wanted to be able to get off the beaten path and find a respite from "the galling harness of civilization," so backpacking is merely a logical extension of those activities. The next time you head off into the backcountry, go with the thought of strapping on a pack and hitting that trail that you find at the end of the road. You already have a big advantage in that you have the perfect base camp. With your RV you can drive to the trailhead the night before, prepare your gear and set out the next morning fortified with a good night's sleep. And, when you return, be it from an overnight hike or an extended trek, it's great to be able to raid the refrigerator for something cold and refreshing, wash the trail dust off with some soothing hot water, and stretch out on a soft bed while you relax those tired muscles.

Besides being an ideal pursuit for the RVer, backpacking is also an ideal activity for the whole family. If you have small children, you may have to limit your trips to within one or two miles of your base, but even in that short a distance you'll still be able to get into the spirit of the wilderness. A good many people may try to tell you that small children and backpacking are just not compatible, but kids are a lot more adaptable than adults and most youngsters will greet the experience with great enthusiasm. The main thing to keep in mind with children is that they do have limitations, and if you try to force them beyond their capabilities you could end up turning them against backpacking and hiking forever.

Whatever age you start at, no one should take up backpacking without first working into it gradually. The best way to start, and the way to find out if you are really going to like it, is to buy or borrow a small day pack, toss in a sandwich and a canteen, and set out on a short, unhurried day hike. If you find the experience to your liking, you can then increase the distance, eventually starting out at dawn and returning at dusk. This kind of preparation will not only let you work into backpacking gradually, it will also get you in shape for carrying larger and heavier loads. Chances are after a few extended day hikes you will find it harder and harder to leave those inviting spots that would make perfect backcountry campsites.

Once you decide you are ready to hit the trail in earnest, it is important to remember that backpacking does carry with it certain responsibilities. It has been estimated that more than 20 million people have tried backpacking and, though the real dedicated backpackers probably represent only a fraction of that number, it is obvious that none of our wilderness areas can stand that kind of pressure for very long without some careful consideration by those who use them for recreation. Gone are the days when we can afford to — for that matter, need to — cut pine boughs for beds or have a roaring campfire at the end of each day. Some wilderness areas, such as the John Muir Trail in California and parts of the Appalachian Trail in the East, are already showing signs of overuse, so those who are just discovering the joys of backpacking must approach the pastime with a strong concern for maintaining the wilderness for future generations. A few of the basics: Always stick to established trails. Be sure to pack out what you pack in; don't bury cans, foil wrappers, disposable diapers, etc. If you must have a campfire, use only dead wood that is on the ground and bury the ashes and dismantle the fire ring before you move on. A good thing to keep in mind is the Forest Service's slogan, "Take only memories, leave only footprints."

One of the biggest mistakes novices make is approaching backpacking as a competitive sport. A basic flaw of man seems to be the need to constantly outshine his peers; consequently, many beginners approach backpacking as an endurance contest in which the ultimate objective is to see how much they can carry over a given distance in a given time. One of the fastest ways to alienate your backpacking compatriots is to hit the trail with that kind of attitude. If you are going to race up the trail oblivious of the beauty of the wilderness around you, what's the point in going at all?

When you do get started, remember that backpacking is a cooperative effort. With your backpacking partners you should plan your trips carefully in advance, making sure that there is an even distribution of the food and shelter necessities. And, for the good of the group and the safety of each individual, you should always stay together on the trail. No one should ever start backpacking by going solo and the ideal is to have at least three people in your party; that way if one person is injured or becomes ill there is always someone with them while the other member of the group goes for help.

Of course, the biggest question in the mind of the novice is going to be, "What equipment do I need?" Remember that in selecting your equipment you will want to carry as little weight as possible; therefore, the most important thing in buying gear is not necessarily price. With the modern materials now available, going light is relatively easy as long as you resist the temptation to stuff your pack with luxuries, or several of those interesting gadgets you'll find lining the shelves of the backpacking shops. It may take you a few trips to find out what you can handle comfortably, but for your initial outing trim the weight as much as possible and add weight as your proficiency grows. As a rule most backpackers can comfortably carry a load that is equal to about one-third of their bodyweight; but no matter what your weight you should try to limit your load to not more than 40 to 45 pounds for an extended trek. On weekend outings you should be able to go considerably lighter than that.

It can be said that, like an army, the backpacker marches on his stomach; therefore, the fuel you select for your personal furnace is of utmost importance. Again, as far as weight goes anyway, this task has been made fairly simple by the wide variety of prepackaged freeze-dried foods now on the market. A few words of warning: There are a number of dehydrated food brands and they can differ greatly in quality and methods of preparation. Be sure to read the labels carefully before you buy. Also, you will undoubtedly find that some of the offerings are not suited to your palate, and you will probably have to do some experimenting before you hit upon those that meet your taste requirements. The biggest drawback to dry-type foods is the cost, and once you have a pretty good idea of exactly what your food requirements are you will find that you can substitute some of the prepackaged supermarket dinners for the more expensive dehydrated offerings. When planning the rations for your trip, you should figure on about two pounds of food per day for the average-sized adult, and try to select a menu that is heavy on carbohydrates and protein.

For some people, particularly residents of the Midwest, finding a suitable place to backpack and determining when to go is going to present some difficulty. Unfortunately, Midwesterners do not have an abundance of trails from which to choose. If you do live in the Midwest, be assured that there *are* trails suitable for backpacking; it might require some careful research to find them, but you might be surprised by your discovery. The best way to locate the trails in your state is to contact the Forest Service and request information for your region, or contact your state department of parks and recreation or department of conservation. A couple of books that you may find useful are, *Mid-America Trips and Trails* by Bill Thomas, published by Stackpole Books, and *Hiking Trails in the Midwest* by Sullivan and Daniel, Great Lakes Living Press. If all else fails, try planning your next vacation around a backpack tour of one of the mountain areas in the East or West.

There are few wilderness areas throughout the country that haven't been detailed by some sort of hiking guide. Again, the best place to start for general information is the U.S. Forest Service. For more detailed information on a given area, you can obtain topographical maps from the U.S. Geological Survey office, 1200 South Eades Street, Arlington, Virginia 22202, or Federal Center, Denver, Colorado 80225. If you live in a large metropolitan area, there may be a local Geological Survey office; however, mail service is only available at the two addresses listed. Topographical maps are extremely detailed maps of an area which depict the contour of the land and illustrate trails and various landmarks.

Summer backpacking in a great many areas of the country can be almost unbearable due to heat, humidity and high insect populations. If you live in an area that fits this description, don't attempt to start backpacking until these conditions moderate. If you return from your first trip hot, tired, thirsty and with a mass of mosquito bites, you'll probably want to hang up your pack forever. For those who may want to plan mountain excursions, you can generally figure that most mountain areas will be passable from May to October, though some of the higher elevations may be snowbound as late as July.

If you are one of those people who is still reluctant to try backpacking because you are concerned about safety, rest assured that it is actually one of the safest pastimes anyone can take up. Probably the biggest hazard you will ever encounter in the wilderness is yourself. It is a good bet that if you check closely into those news stories that recount the sad fate of some backcountry wanderer, you will find that the person was ultimately either a victim of ill preparation or of plain stupidity. It is a virtual certainty that you will have nothing to fear from any of the wildlife you are likely to encounter on your trek. It is a sad commentary on our times that bears have been driven out of most wilderness areas by the constant pressure of man. If you do venture into bear country, a little common sense and precautions with your food stock will just about guarantee that you will have no problems with the furry critters.

As long as you maintain a healthy respect for the wilderness; plan your trips carefully; carry a map, compass and the basic necessities of first aid and survival you needn't be overly concerned for your safety or survival if an emergency should arise. The most important thing to remember is to check in with the ranger or park representative in charge of the area you plan to backpack and leave an itinerary which lists the date of your departure and the date of your return. When you do return be sure to let the ranger know you concluded your trip safely.

Though you may return from your first backpacking trip with tired, aching muscles, you will also return with a greater sensitivity to the wilderness and a deeper appreciation for its myriad offerings. And, you'll know exactly what John Muir meant when he advised, "Climb the mountains and get their good tidings. Nature's peace will flow into you as sunshine flows into the trees. The winds will blow their own freshness into you, and the storms their energy, while cares will drop off like autumn leaves."

HYPOTHERMIA

Hypothermia. All hikers must be alert to the conditions that cause hypothermia and its symptoms.

What Is It? A lowering of the body temperature. A drop of only five degrees is very serious. Few people whose body temperature drops more than 10 degrees survive. Hypothermia can occur in air temperature as high as 41 degrees F (5 degrees C).

How Does It Happen? Being cold, wet and exhausted are contributing factors. Many people have died of hypothermia because they thought they could keep warm by moving and not stopping to take the necessary precautions such as adding a sweater or putting on raingear.

What Are the Symptoms?
Early — shivering. Continued shivering means continued seriousness.
Serious Symptoms — slurred speech, impaired judgment, weakness, loss of coordination.
Final Symptoms — unconsciousness.

What Can I Do? Get the victim into warm clothes. Make him rest. Give him hot drinks and food. If his condition is very serious, put him in a sleeping bag with another person. Make a fire. Put up a tent or make a shelter for the victim. As soon as the patient is able, get him to a hospital for further treatment. Never think that you can continue your trip after one of your party has had hypothermia — go home, return another time.

Wet clothes can lead to heat loss and increase your chances of hypothermia. Remember, wool retains its insulating qualities when it is wet, cotton does not.

Among backpacking's many rewards is the opportunity to confront Nature at her finest in such places as the awesome glacial terrain of Montana.

Gearing Up For The Trail

Perhaps the most difficult and confusing task facing the beginning backpacker is the selection of the basic equipment necessary to keep body and soul together on the trail. Because of the recent popularity of backpacking and the tremendous interest in outdoor recreation in general, there is currently an abundance of innovative, quality gear on the market. While the availability of all this quality equipment presents some obvious advantages for outdoor enthusiasts, it can be a mixed blessing since such a wide selection can be confusing for the novice. Further complicating matters is the sudden flood in the last couple of years of cheap imitations that may approximate the higher price equipment in design, but actually fall far short in performance.

The selection of good quality gear, especially the basics, is of utmost importance. There really are no bargains when it comes to the purchase of the four equipment basics — boots, pack, sleeping bag and tent. Remember, not only is your comfort going to depend on how well your equipment performs, in adverse conditions your life may literally depend on the gear you select. Your best assurance of getting reliable equipment is to purchase it at a backpacking or mountaineering specialty shop in your area, or through one of the many reputable mail-order equipment suppliers.

Probably the best way to learn about the equipment you will need, and get a general idea of what you will have to spend, is to send off for several catalogs. The catalogs can provide an excellent education on outdoor gear and, since you can study them at home in your leisure, you should read them carefully. You may be shocked at first by some of the prices, but you can take consolation from the fact backpacking gear in general has a long life and your investment now should not have to be repeated for many years.

A final warning: At the specialty shops you may get stuck with a salesperson who is an equipment snob; there are quite a few of them out there. While it is true that there are some old established brands that have a deserved reputation for reliability, there are also some excellent new manufacturers just entering the market. In some cases this new equipment is better than the old standbys as it may feature innovations that bring considerable improvements to old designs. The point is, don't be stampeded into buying something simply because it is the brand "everybody buys."

The following tips should be of some assistance when you actually start shopping for the basics.

Boots

Most experienced backpackers will tell you that a pair of boots is the single most important piece of equipment you will select. To the uninitiated, one pair of boots may look just like the next; actually there are vast differences. Boots for backpacking come in three basic types: light-, medium- and heavyweight. The vast majority of beginning backpackers should select a mediumweight boot as it will provide the best foundation for hiking with medium to heavy loads, and also provide adequate ankle support and protection from rocks.

There is currently some controversy about the lug-type sole that has been the standard for hiking boots for many years. Though this type of sole offers excellent traction when hiking over rocks and rugged terrain, some Forest Service personnel and conservationists are claiming that the heavy lugs on the soles cause excessive wear to trails and promote and hasten erosion. A few boots with alternative soles are just now appearing on store shelves and you might want to take a look at these. Bear in mind that traction is of extreme importance, so make sure you pick a boot with good soles that will continue to provide traction even after they start to wear. Since most sales people in the specialty shops are specially trained in fitting trail boots, you should rely on their judgment and recommendations when you make your selection. If you are forced to order your boots by mail, an outline of your feet included with your order will help assure a proper fit.

Pack

A pack and packframe is the second major purchase for the beginning backpacker. There are many different models and styles to choose from, but for carrying loads for trips of any duration the only type of pack to have is one with some type of frame. A few years ago the selection was really limited to those packs that feature an external tubular metal frame, generally made of aluminum or an aluminum alloy. The frame is important in that it allows the backpacker to carry heavy loads without the necessity of forward lean, and it also makes it possible for the load to ride high, in line with a person's vertical walking axis. Practically all backpacks that are designed for heavy loads also have a waist belt (look for one that is padded) which, when cinched tight over the hips, helps distribute and support the load.

Recently, a number of spacious, well-designed internal frame packs have appeared in the backpacking shops and they might be worth considering if you don't plan to embark on trips of more than three- to four-day duration, or carry excessively heavy loads. Generally, though, it is best for the beginning backpacker to stick to an external frame pack as it will probably offer the most comfort and convenience in the long run. Don't try to save money on a pack by purchasing one of the discount store specials. The cheap packs may look adequate, but they are really not up to handling even moderate loads for very long, and you could find yourself several miles into the backcountry with a deteriorating pack, facing the prospect of a long hike home juggling your gear all the way.

Sleeping Bag

A sleeping bag's obvious function is to maintain your body temperature at a comfortable level while you are sleeping. It performs this function by placing a layer of insulation between you and the cold outside air. The two most common types of insulation used in sleeping bags today are goose down or synthetic fibers. Each of these insulators performs well and offers certain advantages, though we still favor down as being the best and most efficient of the two. The major drawbacks to down are the high price and the fact that it does lose its insulating properties when wet. If you live in an area of high humidity or heavy rainfall, you may want to consider a synthetic fill over down. Good quality synthetic insulated bags are very attractively priced; however, more synthetic fill is required to provide the same warmth as down, therefore, synthetic fill bags tend to be heavier. Another problem we have noted with these bags is the tendency to lose their loft (flatten out) after a time, thus losing some of their insulating properties. Some of the loft might return when the bag is laundered but, in our experience at least, the fill never returns to its original thickness. When choosing a sleeping bag, select one that has at least five to six inches of total loft, as that is about the minimum insulation necessary to keep you warm in cool to moderately cold temperatures.

Tents

There are still a few unreconstructed veterans out there who look on the use of a tent as somehow being a denial of our wilderness heritage. However, a tent can be a tremendous asset to your outing since not only will it provide shelter from the elements and protection from invading insects, it will also keep you warmer in cold weather and provide a clean, dry place to store your gear.

Today's backpacking tents are made of light, durable materials (usually ripstop nylon) which make them both easy to carry and to maintain. The best type to select is the two-man size which will probably weigh somewhere between five to eight pounds, complete with tent, poles and stakes. There are some larger three- to four-man tents available that are suitable for families but these tents usually start at weights of about 10 pounds and can go up to as high as 15 pounds. If your group includes three to four people, your best bet is to consider the purchase of a couple of two-man tents rather than one large one, as this will help distribute the pack loads among the group more evenly and actually provide more comfort in the long run. When you do set out to buy a tent look for one that is of double-wall construction; that is, one that has a urethane-coated nylon fly that fits over the top of the tent for rain protection. With this type of shelter the main canopy can "breathe," wicking off water vapor while you sleep and thus preventing condensation and the prospect of waking up in the morning in a cold, wet sleeping bag.

In selecting the four basics or other items of outdoor equipment, your task might be made easier if there is a mountain shop in your area that rents equipment. If there is such a shop convenient to you, by all means take advantage of the opportunity before you make a permanent investment.

Although buying backpacking gear may seem complicated, it's not as bad as it sounds. For the average person planning ordinary outings, there is a wide selection of brands and types of equipment that will serve quite well.

Some of the better-known suppliers of backpacking equipment are listed below; if none are handy to you, send for their annual catalogs and shop by mail:

Eddie Bauer
Third and Virginia
PO Box 3700
Seattle, Washington 98130
(800) 426-8020

L.L. Bean, Incorporated
Freeport, Maine 04033
(207) 865-3161

Camp Trails
4111 West Clarendon Avenue
Phoenix, Arizona 85019
(602) 272-9401

Country Ways Kits, Incorporated
3500 Highway 101 South
Winnetonka, Minnesota 55343
(612) 473-4334

Frostline Kits
Dept. C. Frostline Circle
Denver, Colorado 80241
(303) 451-5600

Holubar Mountaineering
PO Box 7
Boulder, Colorado 80306
(303) 442-8413

Eastern Mountain Sports
Vose Farm Road
Peterborough, New Hampshire 03458
(603) 924-7276

Granite Stairway Mountaineering
3040 State Street
Santa Barbara, California 93105
(805) 682-2591

The North Face
1234 Fifth Street
Berkeley, California 94710

Recreation Equipment, Incorporated
PO Box C-88125
Seattle, Washington 98188
(800) 426-4840

Early Winters
110 Prefontaine Place, South
Seattle, Washington 98104
(206) 622-5203

Stephenson's Warmlite Equipment
RFD 4, Box 398
Gilford, New Hampshire 03246

Tough Traveler
1328 State Street
Schenectady, New York 12304

For more information on organized backpacking excursions, contact:

Alaska

Alaska Discovery, Incorporated
PO Box 26
Gustavus, Alaska 99826
(907) 697-3431

Sourdough Outfitters
Bettles, Alaska 99726
(907) 692-5252

Arizona

Grand Canyon Trail Guides
PO Box 2997
East Flagstaff, Arizona 86003
(602) 526-0924

California

Mountain Travel, Incorporated
1398 Solano Avenue
Albany, California 94706
(415) 527-8100

Pacific Adventures
Box 5041
Riverside, California 92517
(714) 684-1227

Colorado

Colorado Alpine Adventures
2424 South Columbine
Denver, Colorado 80210

Trailhead Ventures
PO Box CC
Buena Vista, Colorado 81211
(303) 395-8001

Georgia

Wilderness Southeast
Route 3
Box 619-L
Savannah, Georgia 31406
(912) 355-8008

Idaho

EE-DA-HOW Mountaineering
PO Box 207
Ucon, Idaho 83454
(208) 523-9276

Iowa

Mid-America River Voyageurs
Box 125
Spencer, Iowa 51301
(712) 262-5630

Louisiana

Pack & Paddle, Incorporated
601 Pinhook Road, East
Lafayette, Louisiana 70501
(318) 232-5854

Minnesota

Bear Track Outfitting Company
Box 51
Grand Marais, Minnesota 55604
(218) 387-1162

Montana

Lone Mountain Ranch
Box 145
Big Sky, Montana 59716
(406) 995-4644

North Carolina

Folkstone Lodge Guide and Outfitting Service
Route 1, Box 310
West Deep Creek Road
Bryson City, North Carolina 28713
(704) 488-2730

Oregon

Johann Mountain Guides, Incorporated
PO Box 2334
Lincoln City, Oregon 97367
(503) 996-3232

Utah

Hondoo Rivers and Trails
Rim Rock Resort
Torrey, Utah 84775
(801) 425-3843

Vermont

Killington Adventure
Killington, Vermont 05751
(802) 422-3333

Washington

Brad's Tours
401 East Mercer #31
Seattle, Washington 98102
(206) 329-0227

Four Seasons Outfitters and Guide Service
PO Box 149
Mazama Trading Post
Mazama, Washington 98833
(509) 996-2361

CANADA

Alberta

Canatrek Mountain Expeditions, Limited
PO Box 1138
Banff, Alberta, Canada T0L 0C0
(403) 678-5255

British Columbia

Arnica Adventure, Limited
RR 1
Nelson, British Columbia, Canada V1L 5P4
(604) 825-9351

Ontario

Willard's Backpacking Expeditions
107 Dunlop Street, East
Barrie, Ontario, Canada L4M 1A6
(705) 737-1881

Aero Sports

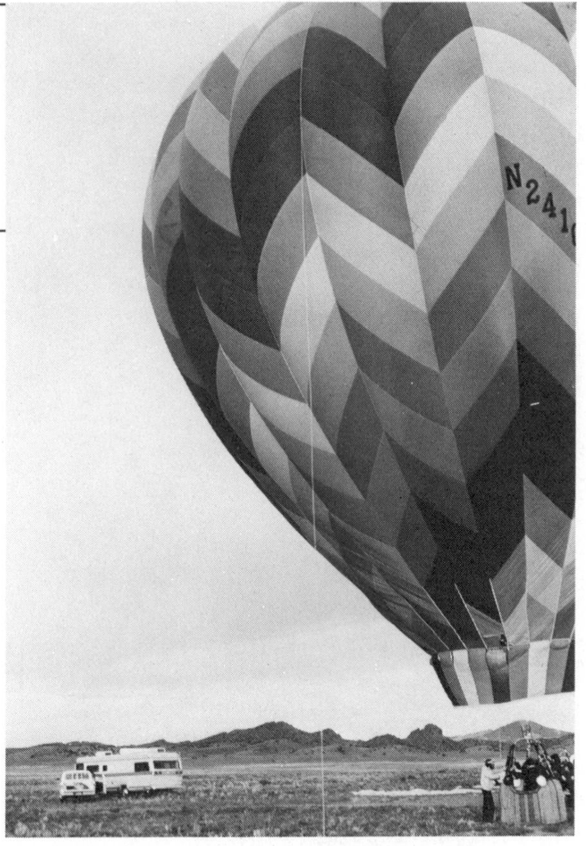

From the mythical Icarus and Leonardo da Vinci's first experiments with winged craft, to the Wright Brothers' historic flight, man has exhibited a continued fascination with overcoming what John Gillespie McGee called the "surly bonds of earth." Nowhere is that fascination more in evidence than in the wide variety of recreational crafts that man now uses in his leisure to take to the skies — balloons, hang-gliders, parachutes, sailplanes. And while each of these pastimes requires a certain degree of skill, none are beyond the reach of the individual who is willing to try anything at least once.

Ballooning

Two French brothers, Jacques and Joseph Montgolfier, started it all back in 1783. It was in that year that they built and flew the first hot-air balloon. Because the materials and the heat sources for hot-air balloons were far less than adequate, they soon gave way to gas balloons which were filled with either cooking gas or hydrogen. The modern rebirth of hot-air ballooning started some 20 years ago when it was realized that new flame-resistant fabrics and reliable propane heat sources could be used. Today, hot-air ballooning is among the fastest growing aviation activities and boasts an impressive safety record. Present-day balloon flights and balloon pilots are regulated by the federal government. All balloon pilots must have earned an FAA balloon pilot license and all balloon makers are regulated in the same fashion as the manufacturers of other aircraft.

Hang-Gliding

In hang-gliding, the pilot is suspended beneath a framed wing by means of a harness, and he achieves sustained flight by stepping off a cliff or high bluff and riding the air currents. Hang-gliding owes its existence to Francis M. Rogallo, inventor of the flexible wing deltoid glider. The superb aerodynamics of the Rogallo wing make it easy to handle and remarkably maneuverable; control is merely a matter of shifting one's weight. Of all the aerosports, hang-gliding is probably the most risky, and it should never be attempted without special instruction. Lessons cost from $30 to $100, including equipment, and for the higher rate you are usually covered by insurance, as well.

Skydiving

To step into space at altitudes of several thousand feet and entrust your life to a delicate nylon canopy requires a special kind of courage. Yet, many who have taken to the even riskier sport of skydiving have sworn that they would never parachute from an airplane in any other way. Dedicated skydivers have become enamored of the sport because of the exhiliration and serenity of the free-fall — which many liken to an almost mystical experience. The sport today is highly sophisticated and divers are able to maintain considerable control over their descent; so much so, in fact, that pinpoint landings are a rule rather than an exception. Learning to skydive also requires instruction, but only a few hours of lessons will generally be enough to send you up for your first jump. Cost of that first jump will probably be less than $100, including lessons, gear and plane rental.

Soaring

In soaring, your sailplane is launched into free flight by means of a powered tow plane or an automobile. Once you're aloft, you ride the air currents (like the hang-glider) across the sky, controlling your flight by moving from updraft to updraft and maneuvering the plane's controls much like the pilot of a power craft. Because the sport calls for riding thermal air currents, many soaring centers are located along mountain ranges or in the desert. Soaring usually requires several weeks of instruction and a license is required before you solo. But you can experience the thrill of soaring — right now — by simply going to a sailplane center in your area and paying for your first flight as a passenger.

For more information on these travel adventures, contact:

Ballooning

Arizona

Cat Balloon, 2911 East Sherran Lane, Phoenix, Arizona 85016, Attention: Jim Kitchell, (602) 279-4906.

California

Aerial Advertising, 2543 West Winston Avenue, Anaheim 92686, (714) 761-0340.

Aerostat Renaissance, PO Box 3536, Napa, California 94558, Attention: Robert Pierce, (707) 255-6356

Balloon Excelsior, Incorporated, 1241 High Street, Oakland, California 94601, Attention: Brent Stockwell, (415) 261-4222.

Cloud Pleasers Balloon Company, 816 Colusa, Berkeley, California 94707, Attention: Don Wilson, (415) 524-3953.

Daedalus School of Free Ballooning, Menlo Oaks Balloon Field, Box 2247, Menlo Park, California 94025, Attention: Deke Sonnichsen, (415) 323-2757.

Don Piccard Balloons, Incorporated, PO Box 1902, Newport Beach, California 92663, Attention: Don Piccard, (714) 646-1568 or 642-5307.

Eagle Flights, 2459 Oakleaf Canyon Road, Walnut California 91789, Attention: Ed Johnson, (714) 595-0867.

Farnham Enterprises, 1033 Cranberry Drive, Cupertino, California 95014, Attention: Captain Mick Farnham, (408) 253-1031

Hot Air Unlimited, 137 East Hamilton Avenue, Suite 206, Campbell, California 95008, Attention: Stan Finberg, (408) 379-2122.

Return in Time Ballooning, PO Box 1389, Redwood City, California 94064, Attention: Ken Frank, (414) 366-5167.

Scorpion Productions, Box 1147, Perris, California 92370, Attention: Fred Krieg, (714) 657-6930.

Sunrise Balloon, PO Box 6757, Santa Rosa, California 95406.

Colorado

The Balloon Ranch, Star Route, Box 41, Del Norte, Colorado 81132, Attention: David Levin, (303) 754-2533 or 754-3474.

Iowa

American Balloon Services, Incorporated, 113 Park Avenue, Muscatine, Iowa 52761, Attention: Tom Oerman, (319) 264-1878.

Michigan

Cameron Balloons U.S., 3600 Elizabeth Road, Ann Arbor, Michigan 48103, Attention: Bruce Comstock, (313) 995-0111.

Captain Phogg's International School of Ballooning, PO Box 3039, Flint, Michigan 48502, Attention: Captain Phogg, (313) 767-2120.

Minnesota

Wiederkehr Balloons International, Incorporated, (1323), 1604 Euclid Street, St. Paul, Minnesota 55106, Attention: Matt or Bobbie Wiederkehr, (612) BALLOON or 774-5208.

New Jersey

Sky Promotions, 20 Nassau Street, Princeton, New Jersey 08540, Attention: Bob Waligunda, (609) 921-6636.

New Mexico

World Balloon Corporation, 4800 Eubank, NE, Albuquerque, New Mexico 87111, (505) 293-6800.

North Carolina

Balloon Ascensions, Limited, Route 11, Box 97, Statesville, North Carolina 28677, Attention: William S. Meadows, (704) 876-1236

Virginia

Blue Ridge Balloonport, 11010 Bristow Road, Bristow, Virginia 22013, Attention: Michael J. Kohler, (703) 631-0423 or 361-1690.

Hang-Gliding

U.S. Hang-Gliding Association, Box 66306, Los Angeles, California 90066.

Skydiving

Arizona

Arizona Parachute Ranch, PO Box 1807, Coolidge, Arizona 85228, (602) 723-5336.

California

Perris Valley Parachute Center, 2091 Goetz Road, Perris, California 92370, (714) 657-3904 or 657-8727. Perris Valley Airport.

Pope Valley Parachute Center, 1996 Pope Canyon Road, Pope Valley, California 94567, (707) 965-3400. Pope Valley Airport.

Florida

Deland Sport Parachute Center, Incorporated, 1360 Flightline Boulevard, Deland, Florida 32720, (904) 736-3131. Deland Municipal Airport.

Paragators, Incorporated, Star Route, Box 1462, Eustis, Florida 32726, (904) 357-7800. Mid-Florida Airport.

Skydive, Incorporated, 28700 SW 217th Avenue, Homestead, Florida 33030, (305) 759-3483. Homestead General Aviation Airport.

Hawaii

Jump Hawaii, 206 Lagoon Drive, Honolulu, Hawaii 96819, (808) 836-2427. Dillingham Airfield.

Illinois

Archway Parachute Center, Hunter Field, Sparta, Illinois 62286, (618) 443-9020 or 443-2091. Hunter Field-City Airport.

Indiana

Parachute and Associates, PO Box 65, Mooresville, Indiana 46158, (317) 831-5023. Kelly Airport.

Kentucky

Greene County Sport Parachute Center of Kentucky, Route 2, Box 140, Bardstown, Kentucky 40004.

Maryland

Southern Cross Parachute Center, PO Box 366, Williamsport, Maryland 21795, (301) 223-7541. Southern Cross Airport.

Massachusetts

Orange Sport Parachuting Center, Incorporated, PO Box 96, Orange, Massachusetts 01364, (617) 544-6911. Orange Municipal Airport.

New Jersey

Parachute Associates, Incorporated, Box 811, Lakewood, New Jersey 08701, (201) 367-7773.

Ripcord Paracenter, Incorporated, Burlington County Airport, Medford, New Jersey 08055, (609) 267-9897.

New York

Albany Skydiving Center, PO Box 131, Duanesburg, New York 12056, (518) 895-8140. Duanesburg Airport.

Drop Zone Parachute Club, PO Box 88, Gloversville, New York 12028, (518) 762-4900. Fulco Airport.

North Dakota

Valley Parachuting, Incorporated, 630 Seventh Street, West, West Fargo, North Dakota 58078, (701) 282-5072. Kindred Airport.

Ohio

Greene County Sport Parachute Center of Gallipolis, PO Box 91, Bidwell, Ohio 45614, (614) 245-5011.

Pennsylvania

Maytown Sport Parachute Club, 722 Bosler Avenue, Lemoyne, Pennsylvania 17043, (717) 763-8828. Elizabethtown-Marietta Airport.

Texas

Denton Skydiving Center, 5301 Parkland Avenue, Dallas, Texas 75235, (214) 824-3540 or (817) 566-1811. Hartlee Field, Denton, Texas.

Utah

Ogden Sky Knights, PO Box 9343, Ogden, Utah 84409, (801) 773-3554 or 392-4166. Ogden Airport.

Wisconsin

Para-Naut, Incorporated, 6096 Highway 21, Omro, Wisconsin 54963, (414) 685-5995.

Soaring

California

Calistoga Soaring Center, 1546 Lincoln Avenue, Calistoga, California 94515, (707) 942-5592. Calistoga Airpark. All year, daily. Thirteen sailplanes, instruction, four towplanes. Thermal, ridge and wave soaring.

Great Western Soaring School, Box 189, Pearblossom, California 93553, (805) 944-2920. Crystalaire Airport, five miles east of Pearblossom. All year, daily. Fourteen sailplanes, instruction, four towplanes. Thermal, ridge and wave soaring.

Sailplane Enterprises, PO Box 1650, Hemet, California 92343, (714) 658-6577. Hemet-Ryan Airport. All year, daily. Eleven sailplanes, instruction, four towplanes. Thermal, ridge and wave soaring.

Skylark North Gliderport, PO Box 918, Tehachapi, California 93561, (805) 822-5267. Fantasy Haven Airport. All year, daily except Tuesday. Ten sailplanes, instruction, three towplanes. Thermal, ridge, wave and shearline soaring.

Colorado

Black Forest Gliderport, 9990 Gliderport Road, Colorado Springs, Colorado 80908, (303) 495-4144. Seven miles northeast of Colorado Springs. All year, daily. Fourteen sailplanes, instruction, four towplanes. Thermal and wave soaring.

The Cloud Base, Incorporated, Airport Road, Boulder, Colorado 80301, (303) 530-2208. Boulder Municipal Airport. All year, daily except Tuesday. Five sailplanes, instruction, two towplanes. Thermal, ridge and wave soaring.

Florida

Lenox Flight School, Route 4, Box 4639, Arcadia, Florida 33821, (813) 494-3921. Arcadia Municipal Airport. All year, daily by appointment. Seven sailplanes, instruction, two towplanes. Thermal soaring.

The Soaring School, PO Box 566, Indiantown, Florida 33456, (305) 597-3228. Circle T Ranch Airport. All year, daily except Tuesday. Seven sailplanes, instruction, one towplane. Thermal soaring.

Soaring Seminoles, Incorporated, Route 1, Box 475, Oviedo, Florida 32765, (305) 365-3201. Flying Seminole Ranch Airport. All year, daily. Four sailplanes, instruction, two towplanes. Thermal soaring.

Hawaii

Honolulu Soaring Club, Incorporated, Box 626, Waialua, Hawaii 96791, (808) 623-6711. Dillingham Airfield, five miles west of Waialua. All year, daily, four sailplanes, instruction, two towplanes. Ridge and thermal soaring.

Illinois

Hinckley Soaring, Incorporated, Hinckley Airport, U.S. Highway 30, Hinckley, Illinois 60520, (815) 286-7200. April to November, daily except Monday. Six sailplanes, instruction, two towplanes. Thermal soaring.

Massachusetts

Yankee Aviation, Incorporated/Gliding Club, Plymouth Airport, Plymouth, Massachusetts 02360, (617) 746-7337. All year, daily. Six sailplanes, instruction, two towplanes. Thermal soaring.

Michigan

Benz Aviation, Incorporated, 3148 South State Road, Ionia, Michigan 48846, (616) 527-9070 or 527-0979. Ionia County Airport, three miles south of Ionia on Highway 66. May to November, daily except Monday; weekends only April and November. Seven sailplanes, instruction, three towplanes. Thermal soaring.

Nevada

Desert Soaring, 1499 Nevada Highway, Boulder City, Nevada 89005, (702) 293-4577. Boulder City Airport. All year, daily except Monday. Six sailplanes, instruction, two towplanes. Thermal, ridge and wave soaring.

Soaring — Rides, Instruction, Rentals, PO Box 60036, Reno, Nevada 89506, (702) 972-7757. Reno/Stead Airport. All year, Thursday to Monday. Six sailplanes, instruction, one towplane. Thermal and wave soaring.

New Hampshire

Northeastern Light Aircraft, Incorporated, Box 252, Lynn, Massachusetts 01903 — mail address. (603) 898-7919 or (617) 581-1030. Northeastern Gliderport, Salem, New Hampshire. March to December, daily. Twenty-one sailplanes, instruction, three towplanes.

New York

Schweizer Soaring School, Box 147, Elmira, New York 14902, (607) 739-3821, extension 10. Chemung County Airport, 10 miles northwest of Elmira. May to October, daily. Ten sailplanes, instruction, three towplanes. Thermal and ridge soaring.

Wurtsboro Flight Service, Incorporated, Wurtsboro Airport, Wurtsboro, New York 12790, (914) 888-2791. All year, daily. Twelve sailplanes, instruction, five towplanes. Thermal, ridge and wave soaring.

Pennsylvania

Kutztown Aviation Service, Incorporated, Route 1, Box 1, Kutztown, Pennsylvania 19530, (215) 683-3821 or 683-8389. Kutztown Airport. All year, daily. Fourteen sailplanes, instruction, three towplanes. Thermal and wave soaring.

Posey Aviation, Incorporated, PO Box 41, Erwinna, Pennsylvania 18920, (215) 847-2770. Van Sant Airport. All year, daily. Ten sailplanes, instruction, three towplanes. Thermal and wave soaring.

South Carolina

Bermuda High Soaring, Incorporated, PO Drawer 809, Chester, South Carolina 29706, (803) 385-6061. Chester Airport. All year, daily except Monday. Ten sailplanes, instruction, two towplanes. Thermal and wave soaring.

Tennessee

Chilhowee Gliderport, 15 Fairhills Drive, Chattanooga, Tennessee 37405, (615) 338-2000 or 266-1767. Chilhowee Airport, five miles north of Benton on Highway 411. All year, seven days. Five sailplanes, instruction, two towplanes. Thermal, ridge and wave soaring.

Texas

Windermere Soaring School, Route 2, Box 491, Spicewood, Texas 78669, (512) 693-4663 or 327-3230. Windermere Gliderport. All year, daily except Tuesday and Wednesday. Six sailplanes, instruction, two towplanes. Thermal soaring.

Utah

Heber Valley Flying Service, Route 1, Box 443A, Heber City, Utah 84032, (801) 654-2061. Heber Valley Airport. All year, daily except Monday. Four sailplanes, instruction, two towplanes. Thermal, ridge and wave soaring.

Virginia

Warrenton Soaring Center, Incorporated, PO Box 185, Warrenton, Virginia 22186, (703) 347-0054. Warrenton Airpark (January to April, Orange County Airport, Orange). All year, Saturday and Sunday. Summers, Wednesday only. Six sailplanes, instruction, three towplanes. Thermal and wave soaring.

Washington

Soaring Unlimited, Incorporated, PO Box 548, Kirkland, Washington 98033, (206) 454-2514. Seattle Skyport, one mile west of Issaquah on Interstate 90. March to November, daily; weekends only December to February. Ten sailplanes, instruction, three towplanes. Thermal, ridge and wave soaring.

Commonly Asked Questions About Ballooning

How Does the Pilot Control the Flight of the Balloon?

The only direct control over the movement of the balloon available to the pilot is up and down. Still on most days the pilot actually has a great deal of indirect control of the horizontal movement of the balloon. It is not at all unusual to see directly opposite winds within a thousand feet of the surface. Thus controlling the movement of the balloon is not unlike sailing a boat but in three dimensions.

What Makes a Hot-Air Balloon Go Up and Down?

Warm or hot air is lighter than cool air. By heating the air inside a balloon it can be made to lift itself and the attached basket into the air. Controlling the rate of ascension and the altitude is a matter of regulating the temperature inside the balloon. Modern-day technology has developed burner systems which are easy to operate, safe and reliable. Present-day balloons are constructed of flame resistant materials to add further to safety.

Why Are Most Balloon Baskets Constructed of Wicker?

There are several reasons why wicker is most commonly used in the building of balloon baskets. Wicker is the traditional material, it is quite strong relative to its weight, it has flexibility and shock absorbing qualities. Most modern balloons have steel cables woven through the wicker. These cables support the floor and attach to the balloon itself, providing a very strong structure for the passengers to ride in. The entire balloon is built in accordance with strict FAA standards and each balloon is inspected when it is first constructed and on a regular basis during its entire time in service to ensure safety.

Of What Material is the Balloon Envelope Constructed?

The balloon envelope or bag is most usually made of nylon cloth. The actual load is carried by heavy nylon bands called load tapes. Nylon is used because of its flame-resistant qualities as well as its very high strength-to-weight ratio.

What Happens if for Some Reason the Heat Source Stops?

This is extremely unlikely but if it should happen, the balloon will slowly settle back to earth very much like a parachute. This is possible because the bottom of the balloon is open to catch the air and control the descent.

Are There Different Kinds of Balloons?

Yes. There are several balloon manufacturers and there are many differences in these balloons. Most of these differences are not easily noted by the non-balloonist and they would be similar to differences in automobiles. Most modern hot-air balloons are built either in the United States or England.

When Is the Best Time to Make a Balloon Flight?

Most balloon flights are made in very light winds or near-calm conditions. This is most common in the morning, and thus, most balloon flights are conducted in the early hours of the morning.

Do Balloon Pilots Need a Pilot's License?

Once again the answer is yes. The Federal Air Regulations require balloon pilots to qualify for and hold a valid balloon pilot license. This requires flight training under the direction of a qualified instructor and passing both a written and flight test on flying balloons. This is a separate rating from an airplane pilot license. The balloon pilot must operate his balloon in accordance with the same air regulations as pilots of other types of aircraft.

How Long Is a Typical Balloon Flight?

Typical flights last approximately one hour. Much longer flights or shorter flights can be arranged. Intermediate landings for the purpose of changing passengers usually can be arranged as well.

How Many People Can a Balloon Carry?

This depends upon the size or volume of the balloon. On an average, most balloons carry two, three or four people including the pilot. For example, a balloon of 77,000-cubic-foot volume is usually able to carry four people, while one of 56,000 cubic feet will carry three. Factors such as the air temperature and altitude also affect the number of people a balloon can carry.

Who Can Fly in a Balloon?

Almost anyone can enjoy the thrill of a balloon flight. Young children and seniors alike find ballooning a most enjoyable activity. As there is little or no motion and only the speed of the balloon drifting with the wind over the ground, there is no reason for motion sickness often associated with other forms of flight. The same lack of motion usually prevents a feeling of insecurity normally associated with heights.

Where Can You Fly Balloons?

Most areas, especially open rural areas, are suitable for balloon flying. While balloons are FAA certificated aircraft and thus subject to FAA operating rules similar to other types of aircraft, these regulations provide for safety in the operation of the balloon and not undue restrictions.

Where Do Balloons Land?

Any small open space the size of an average city lot is usually suitable for landing a balloon at the end of the flight. Balloons usually do not operate to or from airports as the space needed for a balloon is less than the space required for airplanes. This provides much more freedom in flying the balloon.

Do You Land the Balloon Where You Took Off From?

As a general rule you do not land where you took off from. Horizontal movement is controlled by selecting winds that blow in different directions. This indirect control will occasionally allow the pilot to bring the balloon back to the launch area, but most often this is either not desired or simply impossible. A ground crew is always provided. The ground crew is available to assist with inflating the balloon and to help put it away and provide transportation at the end of the flight. Two people make an ample crew.

We are grateful to Adventure Guides, Incorporated, 36 East 57th Street, New York, New York 10022, for supplying the listings for Backpacking, River Running, Ballooning, Hang-Gliding, Skydiving and Soaring. For more detailed information of outfitters for these sports consult: *Adventure Travel*, by Pat Dickerman, Adventure Guides, Incorporated.

Bicycling

BICYCLING

In an effort to conserve fuel, many RVers have taken to carrying a bicycle as an alternative source of transportation for running quick errands around the campground. While that bicycle may be a great utilitarian gas-saver, it can also enhance your RV travels.

Your bicycle offers you an opportunity to exit the cocoon of your RV and take to the backcountry roads where you can really experience the world around you — ride into the picture-postcard scenery of a country lane, feel the sun on your face and the wind in your hair, smell the new-mown fields, and the autumn fragrance of burning leaves. And, as a bonus, you'll get some invigorating exercise in the process.

In the last decade, the bicycle has enjoyed a resurgence in popularity — partly in response to the need for energy conservation, but mostly because of its rediscovered recreational value. Bicyclists received a big boost in 1976 with the opening of the Bicentennial Trans-America Trail, and state and local governments have responded by setting aside a number of areas for the exclusive use of cyclists. Many of these bike trails wind through exceptionally scenic areas where comfortable rest stops, picnic facilities and even campgrounds are provided for cyclists. In many cities, you can find an extensive system of bike routes marked along city streets which permit travel through heavy traffic areas in relative safety. Maps of bike trails and bike routes can usually be obtained in advance from the state's tourism office. You'll find the address for that office listed in the state sections.

For information on organized cycling events, contact:

California

Pacific Adventures
Box 5041
Riverside, California 92517
(714) 684-1227

Maine

Overland Rolls
1 Center Street
Brunswick, Maine 04011
(207) 725-5119

Michigan

Michigan Bicycle Touring
738 Griswold
Department AG
Jackson, Michigan 49203
(517) 784-2029

New Hampshire

The Biking Expedition
Box 547
Henniker, New Hampshire 03242
(603) 428-7500

North Carolina

Nantahala Outdoor Center
Star Route, Box 68
Bryson City, North Carolina 28713
(704) 488-2175

Vermont

Vermont Bicycle Touring
RD 3H
Bristol, Vermont 05443
(802) 388-4011

CANADA

Alberta

O.A.R.S./Sobek
PO Box 67-G
Angels Camp, California 95222
(209) 736-2661

Rocky Mountain Cycle Tours
Box 895
Banff, Alberta, Canada T01 0C0
(403) 762-3477

How To Select The Right Bicycle

You should exercise almost as much care in the selection of a bicycle as you did in choosing your RV. Much like RVs, there are a number of bicycle brands on the market; some are excellent, some are good and some are junk, dumped on the market to take advantage of the bicycle's increasing popularity.

There's no question but that you can go down to the local discount store and find a fancy looking, off-brand, 10-speed for at least half of what a similar bike of good quality would cost. But is it worth the savings when the bike breaks down 500 miles from home and you find that there are no parts available? More importantly, consider the fact that those bikes are usually unassembled, so you will either have to pay extra to have it put together or try putting it together yourself. Bear in mind that a bike assembled by a non-professional will have more potential for mechanical troubles; worse yet, it can be downright dangerous.

If you decide to buy a bicycle but you don't, for one reason or another, want to spend the money it will take to buy a quality machine, then you should seriously consider scanning the want ads for a good used bike. Chances are a used bike with a reliable reputation will give you better service and less trouble in the long run than a $79 discount special.

Another advantage of buying a quality bike, be it new or used, is that if you decide at a later date that bicycling is not for you, you can recoup a good deal of your investment by selling the bike. Poor quality bikes, even those purchased new, not only have a short life expectancy, they also have very little resale value.

You may now be convinced of the value of buying quality, but what if you are a novice? Let's assume that is the case and you know nothing about bicycles: How do you determine whether a bike is of sound construction or a rolling disaster? One of the best ways is to obtain bicycle brochures that list the prices of the bikes. Choose several bikes of various brands of the type you want to buy, but are of a higher price than what you intend to pay. Note the construction features and components of those bikes; then when you set out to shop for your bike, try to come close to duplicating or approximating those features, while still staying within your price range.

Of course, in order to make any kind of comparison, and in order to set your price range, you are going to have to have a pretty firm idea of what kind of bike you want. If you are going to take a bike along merely for alternative transportation to pedal around the campground and run errands to the corner market, you don't need to invest a lot of money in a glittering five- or 10-speed model. On the other hand, if you want the bike for both utility and recreation, i.e. sightseeing and light touring, then you shouldn't consider anything less than a five-speed.

Once you have made that decision, it is then easy to set your budget, figuring that a good one- to three-speed is going to cost between $70 to $120, and a five- to 10-speed will run about $115 to $195.

How do you determine whether you need a bike with gears? The following breakdown of the various gearing systems and how they apply to different cycling conditions should give you a better idea of what gears are all about.

- *Single Speed* — Best suited for level ground and rides of only short distances.
- *Three-Speed Hub* — Ideal for short rides on uneven terrain that is no more than moderately hilly.
- *Five-Speed Derailleur* — Allows touring of moderate distances and will permit the cyclist to negotiate most slopes.
- *Ten-Speed Derailleur* — Will handle all touring conditions and allow the rider to travel longer distances with less effort. With a 10-speed you should be able to negotiate hills without having to vary your pace.

Basically, gearing is a combination of chainwheel, sprocket and rear wheel action that enables you to coordinate the number of back wheel revolutions to your pedaling. Derailleur gearing literally means gear-changing by derailment. As you change gears, the chain, guided by the gear arm, is forced to run on any of a combination of chainrings and sprockets. This type of gearing lets the cyclist shift rapidly while maintaining a steady pace. With derailleur gears, you must keep the pedals turning when shifting from one position to another and you can't shift going uphill. Also, you must not put too much pressure on the pedals or you could damage the gears.

A new system of gearing has come on the scene in the last couple of years; called the front freewheeling system, it makes shifting much easier as it allows the gears to be changed without pedaling and permits shifting even when going uphill. With this system, if you haven't selected the proper gear by the time you hit the hill, you can simply shift again and don't have to get off and walk your bike.

The heart of any bicycle, and the single most important part, is the frame. Manufacturers attempt to produce bikes with light, but rigid, frames that are strong and easy to ride. To do this they utilize different alloys and different construction methods. When talking to salesmen about the various bikes, you will be deluged with terminology describing the different types of frame construction — butted tubes, forged frames, lugged and brazed. Butted tubes are frame pieces that have thicker walls at each end where they will be welded or brazed to other tubes; forged frames have an overall smooth appearance, and lugged frames use a lug (sleeve) at each frame joint to distribute the stresses. Lugged and brazed frames are generally the strongest, and most expensive, type of frame.

As for the other parts of the bike such as wheel rims, tires, brakes, crank, derailleurs, etc., explain to your dealer the type of riding you will be doing, and tell him that you want a quality bike within the budget you have set. Most bike shops are equipped to deal with customers who range from the casual rider to the fanatical cyclist.

When you actually start looking at the bikes in the shop, the first thing you will notice is that the majority of them have drop-style handlebars. For all-round cycling this is the best type of handlebar to have. These handlebars may look uncomfortable at first, but if you give them a try you may be surprised at just how comfortable they really are. It is a proven fact that riding with drop handlebars produces less pressure on your back and, therefore, gives you a more comfortable and less fatiguing ride. If you just can't adapt to this style of handlebar, there are some fine bikes with standard or touring-style bars. The only drawback is that your general selection is not going to be as varied.

Once you have settled on the style of bike you want, you must find one that fits. Proper fit is extremely important as it can ultimately determine whether you will become a dedicated cyclist or put your bike in the corner to gather dust.

Your proper frame size can be determined by finding the largest frame (men's diamond style) which you can straddle comfortably with both feet flat on the ground. Women who want to buy a ladies' frame can use a man's frame to determine the size that is right for them, but don't feel that you have to buy a ladies' frame just because it is the traditional thing to do. Except for the ladies' Mixte-style frame, men's frames are generally stronger, and there is no logical reason why a woman can't use this type of frame.

If you are selecting a bike for a youngster, don't try to buy a bike that you think he can grow into. It just doesn't work, and the child will be as miserable as you would be with the wrong size bike. Also, it is extremely dangerous, as the child will not have control of the bike.

After you have found the proper frame size, the next step is to adjust the seat to its proper height. The most efficient and comfortable pedaling is accomplished when the rider's leg, when he or she is seated on the bicycle, is slightly bent when the ball of the foot is on the pedal, and the pedal is at the bottom position.

Next, ask the dealer if you can ride the bike. Try to ride it over different road surfaces, up and down hills and around corners. Check the gears and brakes. If the gears shift easily and smoothly, the brakes are responsive, the bike tracks smoothly and the overall feeling is good, then buy it. Remember, don't be too critical because any bike will take some getting used to.

If you are buying bikes for the whole family, an important thing to keep in mind is that all members of the family should have bikes that are similar in quality and design. If one member of the group has a top-notch 10-speed and others have three-speeds, or the scrambler styles that are now so popular with younger riders, you can't possibly ride as a group, and your bicycling efforts will only become frustrating and unpleasant experiences.

Finally, after you have made your purchase you will need to take some steps to protect your investment. Because bicycles are popular, and quality bikes are expensive, they are a common target of thieves. If a professional thief wants your bike, he will be able to get it no matter what precautions you take. However, with the selection of a good quality lock and cable or chain, you can slow the professional down, and keep the casual thief from getting your bike. Bikes on the back of cars and RVs are especially vulnerable, so take care to buy a lock that will make it possible to lock both the frame and wheels of all bikes. A good lock and cable will probably cost about $12, and your dealer should be able to recommend several that are reliable.

With a little care and the help of a reliable dealer, you should be able to find the right two-wheelers for yourself and the other members of your family. And, once you have made your selections, you will be happy that you decided to add cycling to your leisure-hour activities.

RVing the Dude Ranches

It's great to get out in the wide-open spaces, breathe some good clean air, fish your favorite stream, hike an unfamiliar trail or just sit back and take it easy. For most RVers, that is what RVing is all about — the freedom of getting out and getting away from it all.

Now and then, though, most of us like a little departure from the traditional RVing activities; perhaps an opportunity to indulge in a little luxury, sit down to a gourmet meal, stretch out on a full-size mattress and enjoy some of the more pleasant offerings of civilization. Of course, that usually means giving up the wide-open spaces, leaving the van or truck in the driveway and heading off to someplace where you have to elbow through crowds. That's what we used to think anyway, until we discovered dude ranching, a unique vacation experience that allowed us to combine RVing and luxury living with the freedom and solitude to be found in several thousand acres of isolated Arizona countryside.

For those who have never stayed at a dude ranch, or may not have been to one recently, it is important to note that it is not merely a place where a bunch of soft suburbanites gather to dress up in western clothes and play cowboy. In fact, most ranch owners and operators now prefer the term "guest ranch" as a more accurate description of the type of ranch operation that is prevalent today. As Ed Cheek, manager of the Wickenburg Inn, an Arizona guest ranch, explained, "Basically, a dude ranch only has horses, but a guest ranch has other things. Dude ranches are dying out; within the last five or six years, the horse ranch operations have started to decline quite a bit." Replacing these are facilities that are moving more and more toward luxury while expanding on the basic concept of the dude ranch. "People are now more exercise and sports minded," Cheek added, "and guest ranches offer an opportunity to enjoy a number of activities — horseback riding, tennis, golf, arts and crafts, jogging and hiking — in one centralized location."

Of particular interest to RVers is the fact that the relaxed atmosphere and location of most ranches will still allow you to get out and use your van or truck. While most ranches don't provide hookups, campsites or other direct accommodations for RVs, your camping vehicle can be a real asset to your ranch vacation as the ranch usually makes an excellent base from which you can tour the countryside, perhaps explore some old ghost towns or maybe get in a little fishing and hunting.

All ranches do have a few common denominators, most noticeably an isolated country atmosphere where guests can unwind and roam at their leisure in the wide-open spaces; but there is actually a considerable difference in the types of accommodations and activities offered. There are still a number of working cattle ranches where guests can go to experience the atmosphere and activities of real ranch life. At those ranches the approach is usually very informal, with rustic lodgings, family-style meals and most activities geared to the outdoors, and perhaps even directly contributing to the ranch operations.

Next are the facilities that were former working ranches, or are currently scaled versions of previously active operations, where guests are treated to a variety of activities ranging from horseback riding

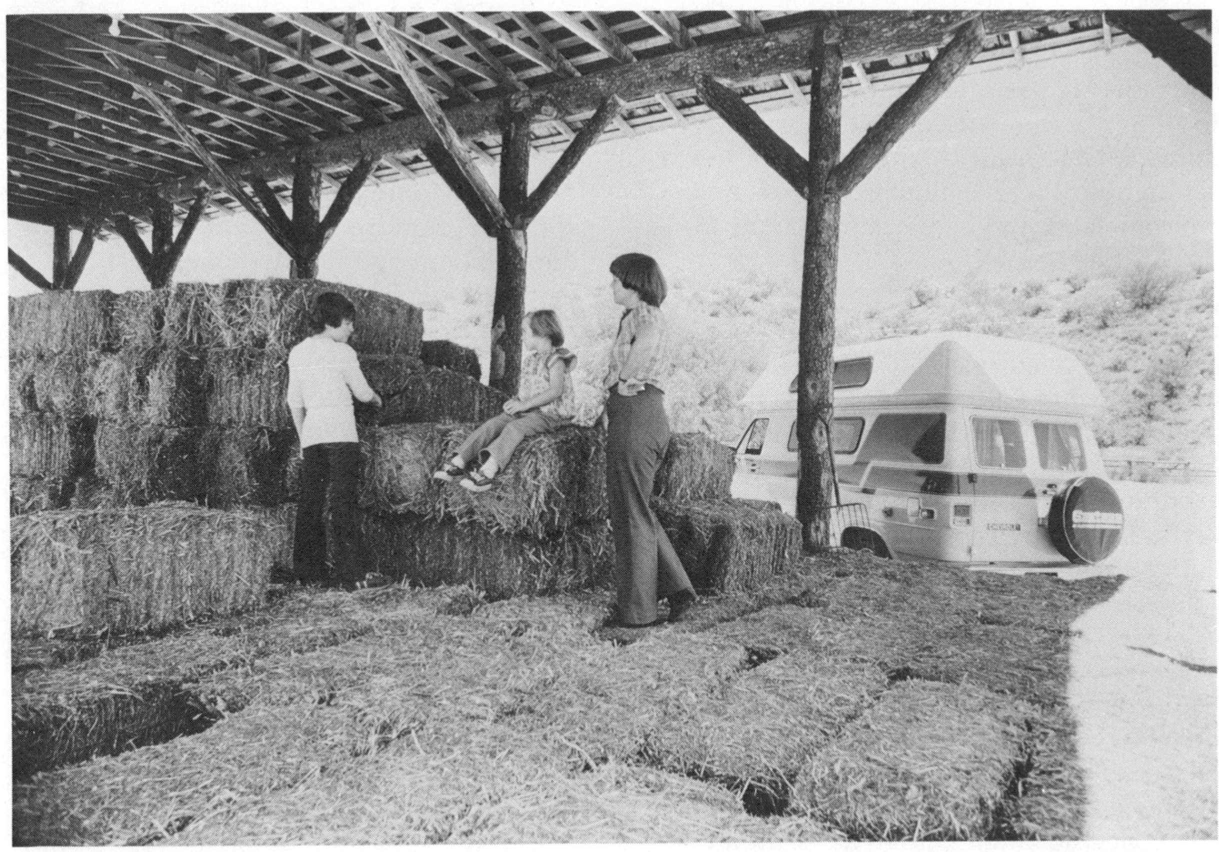

and backcountry pack trips, to tennis and golf. Here the accommodations will most likely include a few more comforts and perhaps a more formal dining atmosphere.

At the other end of the spectrum are the modern guest ranches that have no direct link to traditional ranching and may resemble posh resorts more than a ranch. Many of these may emphasize one activity such as tennis or golf, although most also offer a number of other diversions, including horseback riding, cookouts and barbecues, that are designed to create a more informal atmosphere and provide a range of activities that will appeal to all members of the family. At these ranches you will generally find luxurious accommodations, ranging from comfortable lodge rooms to individual bungalow suites, all with full maid service. Food service may still be relaxed and informal, but may also include some gourmet offerings.

Because the author and editor of this book were looking for a real change of pace, we decided to choose a ranch in the latter category — one that would allow us to experience the outdoor life, but also give us an opportunity to relax in a little luxury. After leafing through a number of brochures and calling a few ranches to ask some questions about accommodations, we settled on the Wickenburg Inn, a guest ranch located in the heart of the semi-desert Arizona region once known as "The Dude Ranch Capital of the World."

When we arrived at the ranch entrance and drove through the gate, it looked as though we were traveling on a road to nowhere; for more than a mile of dirt road the only thing we could see were vast expanses of open, rolling landscape. Then, rounding a bend, the ranch proper was spread out below in a random scattering of neat adobe buildings which included the main lodge and dining room, a number of private bungalows, an arts and crafts center, and, off in the distance, the stables, with horses grazing peacefully in the surrounding pastures. Once we had pulled to a stop in the parking lot, we were immediately struck by the silence of the setting; but the overall stillness was a welcome and noticeable change from the din of the city.

When we checked in, we were greeted by the manager who made sure all our immediate needs were attended to and invited us to join the other guests for an evening hayride and cookout. Since no motor vehicles are allowed on the ranch grounds, a staff member was assigned to drive us, in an electric cart, to our hilltop bungalow.

Inside our casita we found a luxurious, deluxe suite furnished in a rustic decor and featuring a massive stone fireplace fronted by a large sofa which converted to a king-size bed. Off of the living room was a kitchenette area with a wet bar, icemaker, small electric range and an adjacent alcove with a spiral staircase leading to a private rooftop sundeck that also included a built-in firepit. The huge, beamed-ceiling master bedroom included a king-size bed, color TV and large double doors that opened out onto a private side patio. In the bath we found a built-in Jacuzzi and a separate dressing and mirrored makeup area. All in all, the accommodations were so inviting that we were almost tempted to settle in and forget about the other offerings of ranch life.

In the evening we strolled down to the lodge where a large, hay-filled flatbed truck waited to take us and other guests on a ride into the backcountry where ranch hands were already at work on a hilltop cookout that included barbecued chicken, steaming kettles of fresh vegetables and a mountainous dessert of fresh strawberry shortcake. After the meal all the guests moved into a circle around the open campfire and, as the sun set over the desert hills, we were treated to an entertaining hour of live country-western music.

After a night of complete relaxation, we rose at dawn to join a few of the other guests on a sunrise horseback ride across a desert landscape dotted with the silhouettes of countless, ancient saguaro cactus. When we returned to the stables, we were more than ready to head for the dining room and a hearty breakfast of flapjacks, sausage, hot buttered biscuits and fresh-squeezed orange juice.

Though it would have been possible to spend several days within the confines of the ranch without becoming bored, we decided to use our RV to do a little exploring in the immediate area. We spent part of one day touring some of the historic sites that abound in the Wickenburg area and another day was spent on a drive up into the Prescott National Forest, where we found a number of good campgrounds and promising fishing spots that we plan to try the next time we return to the area.

If a ranch vacation does sound inviting, and you think you might want to work a ranch stay into your next outing, there are a few things you should know.

It is difficult to find a comprehensive list of all the ranches located throughout the West as there is no central ranch association. However, you may be able to find individual state organizations which will be able to provide you with a complete list of the ranches within that state. Your best bet might be to contact the department of tourism of the state in which you plan to travel and obtain a ranch listing from that office. After you have perused some brochures and settled on a few choices, call the ranch and ask for more details about the accommodations. There are a number of good ranches to be found but, like everything else, there are also some which are blatant ripoffs or dying ranches that will not provide adequate accommodations or service. Once you have made your final choice, it might not hurt to make another call to the local chamber of commerce to assure that the facilities are indeed as they are represented.

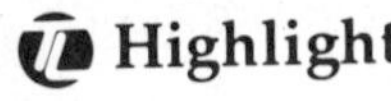 Highlight

Dude Ranch Do's and Don'ts

Visiting a working farm or ranch — an experience similar to staying with your own country cousins — is a new kind of vacation for many people. For that reason, a set of guidelines may be in order.

Do be willing to fit into the farm routine rather than expecting your hosts to adjust to yours. Part of the fun is adapting to a different lifestyle.

Do go with the idea of learning a lot from a family that has a lot to teach you — if you'll let them.

Do pitch in with bed-making and some kitchen chores if your hostess has no extra help — and if she'll let you.

Do try to adapt to your host's house rules. They are worked out for everyone's benefit.

Do check on who supplies the linens and towels when you reserve a housekeeping cabin.

Do ask about the water supply before filling a tub or taking a long shower. In some areas water is scarce during a dry spell.

Do take along shoes that thrive on mud — and extra pairs for children who like to slosh in puddles or feed troughs or other fun places.

Do be friendly, give a little, take a little, as you'd like guests to do in your own home.

Don't take a pet along unless you first ask if it will be welcome.

Don't permit your children to go near farm machinery without the host's permission — and be sure they understand that riding the horses or ponies is done only with supervision.

Don't take your children to a farm if you can't control them.

Don't forget to ask about riding if that is a special interest. Are there enough horses so that you can ride every day? Are some gentle and other spirited? Or is "riding" intended for children who will love the old gray mare in the barnyard?

Don't keep the farm folks up too late. You're the ones on vacation, not they. On most working farms and ranches, it's still "early to bed, early to rise . . . ."

Don't be surprised if your bedroom and bath in the old farmstead are on different floors. Be grateful both are indoors.

Don't forget that farm children may be earning funds for college or a 4-H project. If they do extra work to make your visit enjoyable, a bonus will be appreciated.

Don't expect the service which you receive in a resort hotel. At a ranch or farm your relationship to the hosts is more like that of friend to friend in a private home — a special hospitality that cannot be bought.

Of course, a major factor in your decision is going to be the cost. You will find that there is a considerable variation in the rates, as some ranches are on the full American plan, while others may be on a modified American plan or some other payment schedule. Further complicating the rate structure is the fact that most ranches have prices that vary according to season. Generally, you will find that rates are higher in the Northwestern states during the summer months, and lower in the Southwest. In the winter the reverse will hold true, although many ranches in Montana and Wyoming may close completely for the winter season. It is important to note that the rates are not always a reflection of the quality of accommodations; with some ranches you don't always get what you pay for. The mere fact that a ranch's rates may be high does not necessarily guarantee luxury accommodations. Finally, before you write a check for reservations, ask about the refund policy on deposits, and don't send anything more than the minimum amount.

Among the other things that we have mentioned, one thing you will find that all ranches have in common is a general cordiality on the part of the staff and a country hospitality that will add greatly to the enjoyment of your stay. Given the relaxed atmosphere and pleasant environment, staff members and ranch hands really seem to enjoy their jobs. An especially memorable part of our stay at the Wickenburg Inn was the contact with the staff members who were universally courteous, friendly and willing to go out of their way to make a guest feel right at home.

If you have never had the pleasure of a relaxing ranch holiday, or if you've thought of including a ranch vacation in your RVing activities, by all means give it a try. As Ed Cheek suggests, "A ranch could be a really nice place for a couple of days respite from camping, or a few days stopover en route to or from some other place."

For more information on dude ranches and guest farms, contact:

Arizona

Kay El Bar Guest Ranch
PO Box 2419
Wickenburg, Arizona 85358
(602) 684-7593

Lazy K Bar Ranch
Route 9, Box 560
Tucson, Arizona 85704
(602) 297-0702

Price Canyon Ranch
PO Box 1065
Douglas, Arizona
(602) 558-2383

Wickenburg Inn and Guest Ranch
PO Box P
Wickenburg, Arizona 85358
(602) 684-7811

Arkansas

Scott Valley Dude Ranch
RVG 2
Mountain Home, Arkansas 72653
(501) 425-5136

California

Circle Bar B Guest Ranch
Route 1, Box 258
Goleta, California 93017
(805) 968-1113

Coffee Creek Ranch
Trinity Center, California 96091
(916) 266-3343

Flying H Ranch
PO Box 95
Paso Robles, California 93446
(805) 238-5534

Rocking R Ranch
Moffett Creek Road
Fort Jones, California 96032
(916) 468-2393

Colorado

Arapaho Valley Ranch
Box 142
Granby, Colorado 80446
(303) 887-3495

The Balloon Ranch
Star Route Box 41
Del Norte, Colorado 81132
(303) 754-2533

Trails End Ranch
Collbran, Colorado 81624
(303) 487-3338

Wilderness Trails Ranch
Route 1, Box F
Bayfield, Colorado 81122
(303) 884-2581

Connecticut

Constitution Oak Farm
Beardsley Road
Kent, Connecticut 06757
(203) 354-6495

Florida

DeHaan Farm
Route 1, Box 355
Lutz, Florida 33549
(813) 949-4004

Idaho

Bar BQ Ranch
Box 173
Harrison, Idaho 83833
(208) 689-3528

Iowa

Little House In The Woods
RR 1, Box 204-F
Elkader, Iowa 52043
(319) 783-7774

Kansas

Thurlow Vacation Farm
Wakefield, Kansas 67487
(913) 461-5596

Kentucky

Walnut Springs Farm
Box 9
Dry Ridge, Kentucky 41035
(606) 824-4007

Maine

Oakland House
Sargentville 12
Maine 04673
(207) 359-8521

Maryland

Hidden Hollow Farm
Route 8, Box 103
Leitersburg, Maryland
(301) 733-4637

Michigan

Double H Ranch
Pecos River Trail
Brevort, Michigan 49760
(906) 292-5454

Montana

Blacktail Ranch
Wolf Creek, Montana 59648
(406) 235-4330

Canyon Ranch
RR 1
White Sulphur Springs, Montana 59647
(406) 547-3502

Hell Creek Guest Ranch
Box 325
Jordan, Montana 59337
(406) 557-2224

Nebraska

Pine Hills Ranch
Route 1, Box 30
Rushville, Nebraska 69360
(308) 327-2762

New Hampshire

Inn at East Hill Farm
Troy, New Hampshire 03465
(603) 242-6495

New Mexico

Los Pinos Ranch
Route 3, Box 8
Tererro, New Mexico 87573
(505) 757-6213

New York

All Breeze Guest Farm
Barryville, New York 12719
(914) 557-6167

Little Texas Ranch
Box 36
Obernburg, New York 12767
(914) 482-5759

North Carolina

Pisgah View Ranch
Route 1
Chandler, North Carolina 28715
(704) 667-9100

North Dakota

Hansen Family Farm
Route 2
Oakes, North Dakota 58474
(701) 783-4410

Oregon

Bar M Ranch
Route 1
Adams, Oregon 97810
(503) 566-3381

Hurtley Quarter Horse Ranch
Star Route, Highway 126
Sisters, Oregon 97759
(503) 548-3487

Pennsylvania

Chestnut Hill Ranch
RD Box 77
Shinglehouse, Pennsylvania 16748
(814) 698-3571

Texas

Weaver Ranch
Route 1
Wortham, Texas 76693
(817) 765-3489

Utah

Navajo Cliffs Ranch
Box 698
Kanab, Utah 84741
(801) 644-2125

Washington

Flying L Ranch
Route 2
Glenwood, Washington 98619
(509) 364-3488

Wisconsin

Vacationland Farm
Sister Bay, Wisconsin 54234
(414) 854-2525

Wyoming

Bill Cody's Ranch Inn
PO Box 1390-R
Cody, Wyoming 82414
(307) 587-2097

Diamond Seven Bar Ranch
Alva, Wyoming 82711
(307) 467-5612

Grizzly Ranch
North Fork Route F
Cody, Wyoming 82414
(307) 587-3966

Dude ranch and guest farm listings courtesy of Adventure Guides, Incorporated, 36 East 57th Street, New York, New York 10022. For more information, see *Farm and Ranch Country Vacations*, by Pat Dickerman, Adventure Guides, Incorporated.

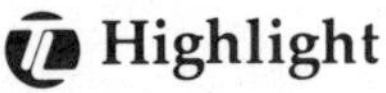

Highlight

Camp-A-Float Vacations

Just as there is no more relaxing way to travel the open road than in the comfort of your RV, there's no better way to take to the water than in your RV, too. And if that sounds downright impossible, you don't know about Camp-A-Float.

Camp-A-Float is a unique vacation opportunity that allows you to turn your RV into a houseboat for a relaxing sojourn on a quiet lake or river retreat at one of five locations across the country. And, best of all, it's all done at a fraction of the cost of a regular houseboat.

Turning your RV into a houseboat really isn't all that difficult with the Camp-A-Float system. First, your vehicle is loaded onto a pontoon cruiser at parking lot level. Then it is fastened safely and securely to the substructure, hooked into the boat's 100-gallon freshwater tank and 100-gallon holding tank, and lowered into the water via a gently sloping ramp. With all the preliminaries completed, you're ready to take the helm and literally become the captain of your ship, plying the open waters at speeds up to 12 mph.

Camp-A-Float vacations are currently available on the Kissimee Waterways, Florida; Lake Havasu, Arizona; Lake Texoma, Oklahoma/Texas; Lake Ouachita, Arkansas; and the Sacramento Delta in California. For more information, contact: Camp-A-Float, 101 South 30th Street, Phoenix, Arizona 85034. Toll-free (800) 528-8114; in Arizona or Canada call collect (602) 244-9831.

Prospecting for Gold

With great anticipation you watch the swirling water as it separates the gravel and sand, washing the particles back and forth in the bottom of the shallow pan. The water and some of the gravel is poured out and new water is taken in, as the washing process is repeated again and again. Finally, a quick dip of the pan allows most of the gravel and larger grains of sand to spill out until little is left but a layer of black silt. Then, as the water swirls once more, there it is, that unmistakable flash of yellow — "color" as the old-timers used to say — and you have panned your first gold.

While you may not have struck it rich, the chances are, at that moment, you will feel some of that same rush of excitement that must have gripped the early miners who hit paydirt more than 100 years ago on this same stream. It's a feeling that is really hard to surpass. Even Jerry Keene, president of Keene Engineering, the world's largest manufacturer of placer gold recovery equipment, concurs. "I've done a lot of things in my life," says Keene, "but I can't think of anything more exciting than looking into your gold pan or sluice box and finding gold that you have mined yourself." What's more, no matter how many times you might repeat that find, the excitement never seems to diminish.

Mention prospecting to most people and it generally brings to mind visions of a grizzled old desert rat leading a burro laden with pick, shovel, battered gold pans and assorted supplies. But, contrary to what most might think, prospecting is neither an activity that died with the last frontier, nor is it a solitary and Spartan pursuit engaged in only by society's dropouts.

Today there are thousands of "weekend prospectors" who enjoy mining as a pleasant recreational pastime. Most don't harbor any illusions of instant riches, and, in fact, many wouldn't even think of selling the gold they find. As one prospector put it, "It would be like a sport fisherman selling the fish he caught." For the majority of those who have been bitten by the prospecting bug (perhaps infected with a mild case of gold fever), gold hunting is simply another way of enjoying the outdoors, a relaxing and interesting hobby.

As for the Spartan existence that was followed by the prospectors of days gone by, you would be hard pressed to find any latter day gold seekers eating beans and hardtack and curling up in a wool blanket by an open campfire. The majority of prospecting enthusiasts have turned to some type of RV in order to more effectively pursue their hobby. With your prospecting gear packed in your RV, you can easily set up camp and work an area, quickly moving on if it is unproductive. Since a good deal of prospecting may involve working in chilly water, having a warm retreat at the end of the day can be most welcome.

Because prospecting can be an ideal family hobby, it can be an especially enjoyable vacation activity. Many of the campgrounds in the prime gold areas become small scale gold rush camps in the summer as vacationers from all over the country come to try their luck in the fresh mountain air. One native of California's Mother Lode country who has a claim along the North Yuba River, explained, "I've got one family from the Midwest that comes out every summer to work my claim. They park their trailer down by the river for three weeks, work the claim, fish, hike and just take it easy. I get 20% of whatever they take out, and they usually end up making enough each year to pay for their vacation.''

So prospecting can be profitable too. While it is true that some amateurs have hit upon some exceptionally rich finds, it is more likely that most of the enrichment is going to be for the soul. But, like everything else, you will ultimately end up getting out of prospecting what you are willing to put into it. If you are willing to spend a little time doing a little research and learning some of the finer points of gold seeking, you will probably find small amounts fairly consistently.

Veteran amateurs and the few full-time professionals will readily admit that there is far more gold still awaiting discovery than was ever found during the gold rush eras. One California geologist estimates that some of the rivers in Northern California still have a potential yield of more than $1 million worth of gold per mile. ''I think it is fair to say that with a good dredge I could find $50 to $100 worth of gold a day,'' Keene said, acknowledging that he has had considerable experience. ''And anyone who has done their homework should be able to do that much. With just a sluice box and gold pan, most anybody should be able to find $5 to $10 a day.

''I have been amazed at the amount of gold that some people have brought in,'' Keene went on. ''Two years ago a fellow bought one of our six-inch dredges and went to a river up north. The first year he made about $2,000 during the summer. The second year he filled a card tabletop with gold; he had one nugget the size of a potato that weighed about a pound and a half, and which later sold for $22,000.''

Though a nugget of that size and value is a rare find, it is not at all uncommon for smaller, but still valuable, nuggets to be uncovered quite regularly. One such small find little more than a year ago started a small gold rush in Downieville, California. John Wilburn, a prospector from Arizona, was mining a stretch along the North Yuba when he decided to cool off with a swim. When he dove in he discovered a handful of gold nuggets nestled in rocks beneath the surface of the water. Wilburn then brought in his gold dredge and word of his ''gold strike'' soon spread. Downieville officials promptly moved to close down mining operations within the city limits.

Despite the growing popularity of prospecting, there have been few formal efforts, such as those in Downieville, to restrict the activities of amateur prospectors. Gold can be found in some 35 states throughout the country, including the South, Midwest and a few Eastern states; however, none of these states has regulations that would present barriers to anyone wanting to hunt gold. Regulations that do exist generally affect only those working with more sophisticated equipment such as a dredge. In California, for instance, dredging is regulated by the Department of Fish and Game and a would-be dredger must obtain a permit which merely requires the completion of a form and payment of a five-dollar fee. No fee or permit is required for use of a pan or sluice box.

To find out about gold deposits in your state, check with your state's department of the interior, bureau of mines or other appropriate agency; you may find that there are old gold fields only a short distance from your home. Once you have gotten some general information you can probably learn more about the exact location of the gold areas, when they were last mined and other important data by consulting mining journals found in your public library.

You also need to know a little basic geology, including something about the properties of gold, and a little bit about the type of mining you are going to be doing. Fortunately, you can learn most of this on your own in a very short time by browsing through a few of the inexpensive and excellent books and pamphlets that are offered through the various mining equipment suppliers. More detailed information can be gathered as you go along and, if you really get hooked, you will find a number of sources where you can get the advanced technical data that may lead you to that big strike.

Basically, there are two types of mining: lode and placer. Lode mining is done at the source of the gold deposits, in the quartz veins within the gold-bearing rock, and requires digging tunnels or shafts along the vein to extract the gold ore. Placer mining, which is much easier and much more suitable as a recreation activity, is simply the process of removing gold from deposits of loose rock and gravel. Surface placers are the easiest to work and are usually found along streams and rivers or nearby banks and hills.

Because gold is a heavy metal, nearly eight times heavier than the rocks and gravel in which it is found, it can be easily separated in the mining process. It is this property that also provides the clue to where gold is likely to be found. As a stream or river winds through its channel, sand, rocks and (hopefully) gold are being washed into the water and carried downstream. At various times of the year, such as spring or during heavy rains, this erosion process is increased. If gold deposits should be uncovered during the heavy runoff, the gold will be carried downstream as long as the flow is unobstructed. However, as soon as an obstruction — a bend in the channel or large rock — is encountered, the gold tends to be filtered out of the other deposits and sinks to the bedrock. Since this process goes on constantly, year after year, deposits in many areas can be replenished. That accounts for the consistent finds of one prospector who returns to the same spot on a stream each year. "Every spring, without fail, I can put my dredge into that one spot on the stream," he reports, "and take out at least three ounces of gold."

Your search should begin at those spots where there is a bend, large rock, fallen tree, beaver dam or any other obstruction that slows the normal flow of water long enough for gold to settle to the bottom. However, pools below waterfalls or holes that have a smooth bottom will most likely prove unproductive as gold falling into these areas would be ground into tiny flakes.

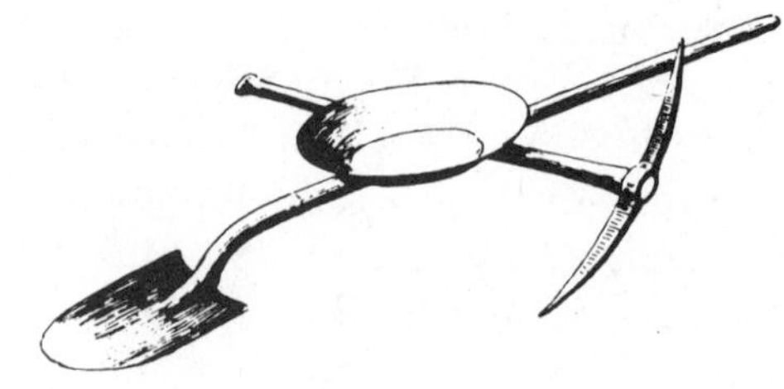

Don't Be Fooled

Remember: "All that glitters is not gold." While that is a tired old adage, it is a literal fact for the beginning prospector and something that should be kept constantly in mind. As you work your way along a stream you will probably find quite a few bright, shiny yellow flakes, either in the streambed or perhaps floating on or near the surface.

Technically known as iron pyrite, these particles are also called fool's gold and they may have duped more than one amateur into thinking they have struck it rich. Fool's gold is much lighter than real gold and will normally be on top of black sand and other gold-bearing material. A simple test to determine whether you have found gold or iron pyrite can be made by trying to cut the particle in question with a knife blade; if it shatters, it is fool's gold. Once you find your first piece of genuine gold, you won't be fooled again.

Once you've learned a few of the basics you will be ready to start gathering your gear. And one of the most pleasant aspects of this hobby is that very little investment is required to outfit yourself and the other members of your family as you prepare to seek your fortune in the gold fields.

Your basic equipment should consist of a gold pan, small shovel, bucket, crevice tool (a screwdriver with the point bent down at a 90-degree angle will do), tweezers and some old medicine bottles for storing flakes and nuggets. This array of gear can probably be gathered for less than $10. You will also want an old pair of boots that you won't mind getting wet or, better yet, a pair of hip waders.

No matter how advanced your prospecting becomes, the gold pan will remain one of your most important pieces of equipment. The average price of a gold pan, depending upon what size you select, will run between three to five dollars. The gold pan is a shallow pan about 10 to 18 inches in diameter and two to 2½ inches deep with sides having a 30-degree slope. Until recently gold pans were constructed of heavy gauge steel, but within the last few years the move has been to a new material that is a strong but light plastic. These newer pans are generally black or dark green, to aid in sighting gold, and have small ridges, called "cheater riffles," designed into the slope to assist in separating and retaining the gold during the washing process. If you purchase a plastic pan you may use it right away, whereas a steel pan will have to have the oils burned off its surface and should be blackened over a campfire and slightly rusted to roughen the surface. Plastic pans are now fairly plentiful and are now generally the first choice of knowledgeable amateurs and professionals.

After you have worked with a gold pan for a while and are having fairly consistent success in locating some gold, you will undoubtedly want to think about moving up to a sluice. A professional gold panner can process anywhere from one-half to one cubic yard of material a day; with a small sluice the average inexperienced prospector can process nearly 10 times that

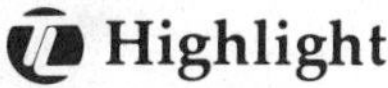

A Gold Panning Primer

Before you start to pan in earnest, you should practice along a streambed, in your backyard or, if possible, at a commercial mine. If you practice in the backyard, fill a tub or small plastic swimming pool with a good quantity of water. Fill your gold pan about half full with gravel and sand, then drop in some lead chips or buckshot to simulate gold.

Once you are set up, dip enough water into the pan to cover the gravel and sand, and hold the pan on each side so that the weight is evenly balanced. Using quick jerks, move the material in the pan so that it separates enough to start the heavy material settling to the bottom. After doing this several times, tip the pan away from you and dip the edge far enough into the water to let some of the particles float out of the pan.

Lift the pan slightly and then dip again to pour off most of the surplus water. Once again, dip the pan to get a small quantity of clean water; then use a rotating motion to swirl the water and material in the pan and separate more of the light and heavy particles. Repeat the process of dipping, separating and floating until you have relatively clean sand and gravel. At this state the larger rocks should be removed by hand, washed and inspected for small deposits of ore.

As you get down to the finer particles, you will be able to inspect the deposits, lifting out the nuggets (lead or buckshot) with tweezers and removing the finer flakes with a wet wooden matchstick. In the actual panning process, you may want to use a gold magnet which will help you sort out the gold by removing the magnetic particles around it.

Use of a sluice box can yield up to 10 times as much gold as panning. (Top, left to right) Sluice is positioned in the stream so natural flow can be used to wash ore from the gravel. When a large quantity of gravel is processed through the sluice, it is removed to the bank where the material can be finely processed in the gold pan. (Below, left to right) The prospector checks for color. With a sluice box and perseverance, the amateur prospector should be able to hit paydirt.

amount. A sluice is a long narrow box with a "riffle" grate built into the bottom. Modern mini-sluices are usually not more than a yard long with a riffle grate that is hinged and can be lifted up easily so that you can get to the gold-bearing material that is collected under the grate on a piece of indoor-outdoor carpeting. Gravel is shoveled into the upper part of the sluice while a current of water flows through it. As the gravel is carried down through the sluice, the riffles create currents resembling miniature whirlpools that allow the gold to drop down and be trapped in the bottom. After a large quantity of material has been run through the sluice, it can be moved to the stream bank where the material can be more finely processed with the use of the gold pan. Price of a good factory-made sluice varies from $20 to $35. You can find plans for sluice construction in many books dealing with gold hunting; however, a sluice made of wood has a relatively short lifespan unless it is heavily waterproofed.

If you are uncertain about what equipment to buy and would like to be assured of having adequate gear that will promise a reasonable chance of success, you might want to take advantage of one of the package deals offered by some of the mining equipment suppliers. For example, Keene Engineering offers a "Prospector's Special" which provides you with all the basic tools, gold pan, sluice and instruction book for only $35.95.

If you really get interested in prospecting and find that you are having good luck with some of the more basic equipment, you are definitely going to want to invest in one of the small portable dredges that are on the market. With a dredge you can greatly increase your productivity and, therefore, your chances of finding gold. Dredges for amateur prospectors vary in size from 1½ to six inches, a figure which refers to the inside diameter of the suction hose that goes up to the back of the sluice box.

All modern dredges work on a suction principle where water is drawn into the intake of a centrifugal pump, which is driven by a lawnmower-type gasoline engine. With the water as the carrying agent, gravel, sand and rocks are brought up the suction hose, sent through a "baffle box," which slows the solid material, so that it can then flow over and settle into the riffles of the sluice box. With a dredge you will be able to process more gold-bearing material in one hour than a professional can process with a gold pan in a whole day. A 2½-inch dredge seems to be the most popular size among amateurs as it is easily portable, can be operated by one person with no difficulty, and can be purchased for under $300.

While some prospectors choose to hang on to the gold they find, you may wish to convert yours into cash. At this writing the market value of refined gold has just hit $650 an ounce, but though you are no longer restricted to selling gold to a narrowly defined list of licensed buyers, you may have some trouble finding a buyer who knows the real value of your gold. Many buyers may try to offer you a standard 10% off the market price, based on the refined weight, but, because placer gold can vary in value, it is best to shop around. The fact is that placer or specimen gold can sell for much higher prices — at least four times the market price — and some high quality nuggets can go for as much as $1,200 an ounce. Sometimes nuggets can have added value due to an unusual shape. One such nugget weighing only about one-third of an ounce recently sold for $2,500.

Before you begin prospecting, there are a few things you should note. As the value of gold increases and its pursuit becomes more popular, more and more claims are being formally registered. It is a good idea to check an area for claim markers or signs before proceeding. Most claimholders won't mind if you work their claim as long as you ask permission first and make arrangements to give them a percentage of whatever you find. Also, if you plan to work an area on private land, it is always a good idea to ask permission. One good way to learn the etiquette of prospecting, as well as the mechanics, is to go on an outing with a prospecting club. Most of these clubs are also made up of RVing enthusiasts and many have their own claims where club members can prospect without worrying about infringing upon someone else's claim. The Gold Prospectors Association of America, 2605 Buena Rosa, Fallbrook, California 92028, phone (714) 728-6620, should be able to put you in touch with a club in your area.

If you have been looking for an unusual and challenging hobby to combine with your other RVing activities, prospecting might be just the answer. Remember there is a lot of gold out there waiting to be found and you just might be able to turn your next weekend sojourn or summer vacation into a profitable, as well as pleasurable, outing.

For more information on prospecting and equipment, contact:

Keene Engineering
9330 Corbin Avenue
Northridge, California 91324

Gold Divers
913 West 223rd Street
Torrance, California 90502

Oregon Gold Dredge Limited
50 Grimes Road
PO Box 10214
Eugene, Oregon 97401

Fiedler Equipment Company
Route 5, Box 85
Brunswick Road
Grass Valley, California 95945

Rockhounding

Rockhounds are an ever-increasing breed of travelers who collect vintage rocks and rare minerals for the same reasons that others collect antiques or stamps. Rockhounding is an inexpensive hobby an entire family can enjoy, and one that will arouse the curiosity of young and old alike. Collecting and examining age-old rocks and fossils is like opening a musty old family picture album and peering into the past. And collecting rocks that can be turned into something of beauty can provide a sense of satisfaction for years to come.

Rocks

Rocks are mixtures of one or more minerals that are classified according to their composition and physical properties — properties that can commonly be tested by simple methods such as hardness, color, crystal form and sometimes more sophisticated techniques like chemical analysis.

Minerals

Minerals are made up of one or more distinct elements in a definite chemical combination. For example, quartz is a combination of a definite amount of silicon and oxygen. The elements that make up a mineral are the same no matter where that mineral is found.

Fossils

Fossils are plants and animals that once lived on the earth and whose remains, either partial or complete, have been preserved in sediments.

If you plan to do some rockhounding while you're traveling, you should first do a little research into the types of rocks, minerals and fossils that you are likely to find. An excellent guide for beginners is the *Golden Guide to Rocks and Minerals* published by Golden Press of New York ($1.95). The information contained in this little book should provide you with all you need to know for your first few excursions into the field. As for equipment, your initial needs will also be simple: a small shovel or spade, a geologist's or other type of hammer, a sifting screen and a chisel should be adequate at the beginning.

In all the states through which you will be traveling, you can obtain information on good rockhounding areas from local chambers of commerce, gem shops or local mineral and lapidary clubs. The annual issue of *Lapidary Journal* provides an extensive list of gem and mineral clubs and bulletins; the journal also has a list of a variety of books on rockhounding for sale. For further information, contact: *Lapidary Journal*, PO Box 80937, San Diego, California 92138.

Rockhound Rules

The following suggestions should make your rock hunting easier, safer and more enjoyable.

1. *Always* obtain permission to enter private property! And whether the land is private or public, treat it with care. Don't litter and be careful with fire.

2. Be careful in all mines, quarries and pits. Most have hazardous locations you should stay clear of.

3. Never throw rocks over cliffs — you may endanger persons below.

4. Proper tools and equipment are important. You should have a pair of sturdy hiking boots and a rock hammer or masonry hammer. A small shovel for breaking through topsoil and a pocket knife for testing for hardness would also be useful. And when breaking rocks *be sure* to wear safety glasses.

5. Remember that rocks and mineral specimens are a non-renewable resource. Do not take more specimens than you will need; conserve the supply for those who will follow you. Give the younger generation of rockhounds something to look for so that this enjoyable and rewarding hobby will not diminish.

RVing the Universe

Space — the final frontier. It's the largest of all wilderness areas, said to be reserved for exploration by only a select few; certainly it's beyond the reach of the earthbound wanderings of the RVer. Or is it?

You may not be one of those selected for the next space shot (the chances are probably pretty good you don't want to be anyway), but the exploration of many of the mysteries that lie beyond the earth's atmosphere is possible for you, and just about anyone else, through the world of amateur astronomy. The requirements are simple, as the only essential is a good viewing site. And that is where the RV owner has a real edge. "As amateur astronomers, RVers have a real advantage," notes veteran amateur, Jim Somers, "because they can get away in comfort to a remote country, mountain or desert retreat where the viewing conditions are ideal. With your telescope set up in the backcountry," says Somers, who is past president and a member of the Southern California-based Polaris Astronomical Society, "you will be able to see a whole new world; you can see galaxies, nebulae and many of the other wonders of our solar system that are just too faint to be seen from inside the city where all the stray light obliterates much of the view."

Quite some time ago, amateur astronomers discovered that the RV was an invaluable addition to their pastime. "A lot of telescope owners," says Somers, "found that they could go out in an RV, sleep for a few hours, then awake refreshed and ready to really observe what's out there." Of course, those with large telescopes and other bulky equipment also turned to the RV for its use as the perfect utility vehicle. And, like other RV enthusiasts, it didn't take long for the stargazers to come up with rigs, tailored to their hobby.

It's probably safe to say that just about every RVer, at one time or another, has looked up from his campsite at the sparkling night sky and wondered about some of the mysteries of the heavens. Well, the step from idle curiosity to more serious galaxy-gazing is not really a big one and, what's more, it doesn't require a great deal of expense to get started. In fact, according to Dr. Edwin Krupp of the Griffith Observatory in Los Angeles, "The best way to get started is without a telescope, by first learning to recognize the constellations, the patterns of the stars and the brighter planets." Both professional and amateur astronomers agree that the biggest mistake the beginner can make is to buy a telescope and aim it at the sky with the expectation of being able to see all the planets and stars in vivid detail. They usually come away disappointed because they aren't able to recognize what they were viewing.

Regardless of whether you're observing the sky with the naked eye or a telescope, a basic understanding of what you're looking at is absolutely essential if you are going to get the maximum of enjoyment from your viewing hours. As Dr. Krupp notes, "The more you learn, the more you'll see."

As an amateur, how much can *you* expect to see? The possibilities are as limitless as the boundaries of space itself. Except for the stars, whose study is far too detailed and expensive for the amateur, a dedicated, serious amateur can observe many of the phenomena seen from the big observatories. In many cases, the serious amateur even stands a good chance of making a significant contribution to the world of astronomy. Despite the fact that we live in a fairly sophisticated world in which most of the sciences have advanced far beyond the level of the amateur, astronomy remains one of the few sciences where an amateur can make valuable discoveries. Because of the vastness of the universe, it is simply impossible for the professional astronomer to monitor the entire sky, and with thousands of amateurs peering into the depths of space it is not uncommon for an amateur to be the first to stumble onto something new.

The amateur field that is probably the most wide open — and the most popular — is comet hunting. Like much of astronomy, comet hunting demands patience and perseverance; but the reward can be more than just the thrill of discovery — it can also mean the prestige of having a comet named after you. Be forewarned, though, that comet hunting doesn't come easy, and most advanced amateurs who stick to this field spend an average of 1,000 hours searching before making a discovery.

For the vast majority of astronomers, however, astronomy is not nearly so demanding. In fact, some stargazers do not even use a telescope, and are content to merely learn the constellations and study the stars and planets unisolated from their surroundings. Others may view the universe as a sidelight to their real hobby of handcrafting telescopes. "But for most," Dr. Krupp says, "amateur astronomy involves observation of the details of the moon, clouds of stars and gases, the rings of Saturn, the polar cap on Mars and the other more readily identifiable objects that can be viewed with a small telescope."

Since most amateurs start out by looking at the moon, Somers offers some tips on how to get the most out of your observations. "A lot of people look at the moon when it is full," Somers explained, "and think that is the best time to look at it; actually, it is the worst time because the shadows are not placed properly and you get a washed-out effect. It's much like looking at a textured wall with a light source aimed right at it; you can't tell its texture. So with the moon, the best time to look is when it is in what is called the first quarter phase or the last quarter phase, because at that time the light is coming in perpendicular to the mountains and the craters so you can pick up all the details of those objects very nicely at that time."

Just a little celestial homework inside your RV can prepare you for an evening of entertainment under the stars.

With even the smallest of telescopes, you should be able to identify many of the moon's spectacular features. You should be able to see many of the craters and the central peaks that are inside some of the craters . . . depressions on the surface that look much like dried riverbeds . . . and the large smooth areas, called Maria, that are believed to be large lava flows that took place nearly three billion years ago. You won't be able to see the U.S. flag that was planted by the Apollo astronauts, but if you pick up a good moon map (about $1), you will be able to zoom into the various landing sites with the high-power eyepiece on your telescope.

As far as viewing the planets is concerned, the ones that are of the most interest are Jupiter and Saturn. Jupiter is probably the most interesting because it is the largest, and when you look at it through your telescope you should be able to see the bands that run across it, and its great red eye. If you continue to look for several hours, you will actually see those features appear to move across the surface because Jupiter rotates at the fairly rapid rate of once every 10 hours and 50 minutes. Of additional interest are the four moons — Lo, Europa, Ganymede and Callisto — which were originally discovered by Galileo. With careful observation you should be able to pick out the moons of Jupiter and even observe changes in their positions as they circle the planet.

Consult one of the amateur trade journals like *Sky and Telescope* or *Astronomy* magazines, or one of the sky guides you'll find in your local bookstore or library. These can be valuable sources of information to find some of the other interesting deep-sky objects such as the Pleiades, the Double Cluster, the Great Cluster in Hercules, the Great Nebula in Orion, the Ring Nebula, the Crab Nebula, the Great Galaxy in Andromeda, or any of the other fascinating subjects awaiting discovery by the amateur astronomer.

While astronomy certainly has to rank among the safest of all pastimes for the RVer or anybody else, there is one danger that all potential observers should be aware of — the sun. You should never look at the sun through your telescope, as the magnification of the sun's rays can almost instantaneously damage your eyes, causing partial or total blindness. If your telescope comes with a sun filter, the best thing to do, according to Jim Somers, is throw it away. Most inexpensive filters that are sold with beginner's telescopes cannot stand up to the heat of the sun and it could crack while you are viewing. As you become more advanced you can purchase filters that will effectively protect you from the sun's rays; they are fairly expensive, however. In the final analysis, the best advice for beginners is . . . forget the sun.

Perhaps one of the best ways to learn more about amateur astronomy, and just what there is to see and do in pursuit of that pastime, is to look up some members of a local amateur astronomy club. You should be able to find them by contacting the nearest observatory or a local telescope dealer. The chances are they will be more than happy to invite you to their next outing, or "star party," and will be delighted to introduce you to the sparkling mysteries of the nighttime sky.

For more information on astronomy, check the individual state listings for planetariums that offer sky shows and exhibits for amateur stargazers.

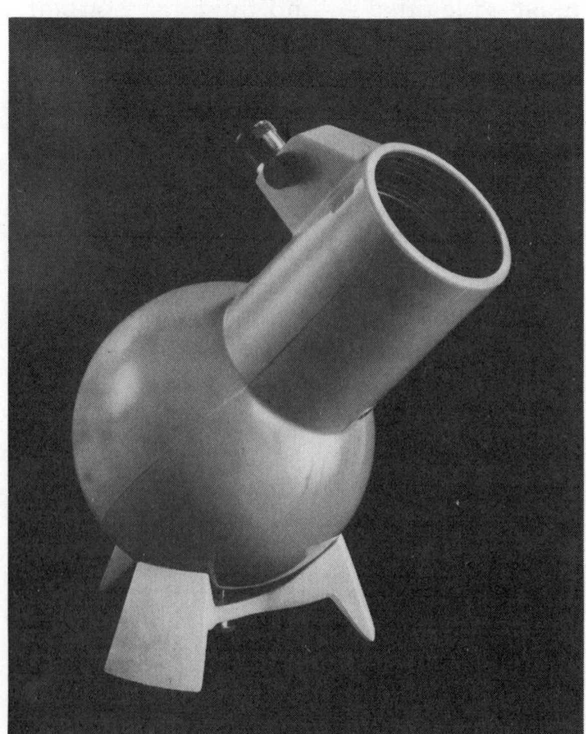

The Astroscan 2001 from Edmund Scientific is recommended by many professionals as the best scope for beginners.

Hunting and Fishing

Nowhere on the globe will sportsmen find the variety of hunting and fishing opportunities that are available on the North American continent. From the coastal ranges of the Pacific and the Maine wilderness to the rolling sagebrush flats of Mexico to Alaska's rugged Kenai National Moose Range and the arctic reaches of Canada's Northwest Territories, hunters can stalk game as diverse as the elusive woodcock and the massive grizzly. Saltwater anglers will find a number of challenging game fish in both the Atlantic and Pacific, as well as the tropical waters of the Gulfs of Mexico and California. And all across the continent you'll never be far from a lake, rolling river, clear mountain stream or massive impoundments like Lake Mead and Toledo Bend Reservoir where you can pursue everything from the ubiquitous and scrappy bluegill to lunker bass and the wily trout.

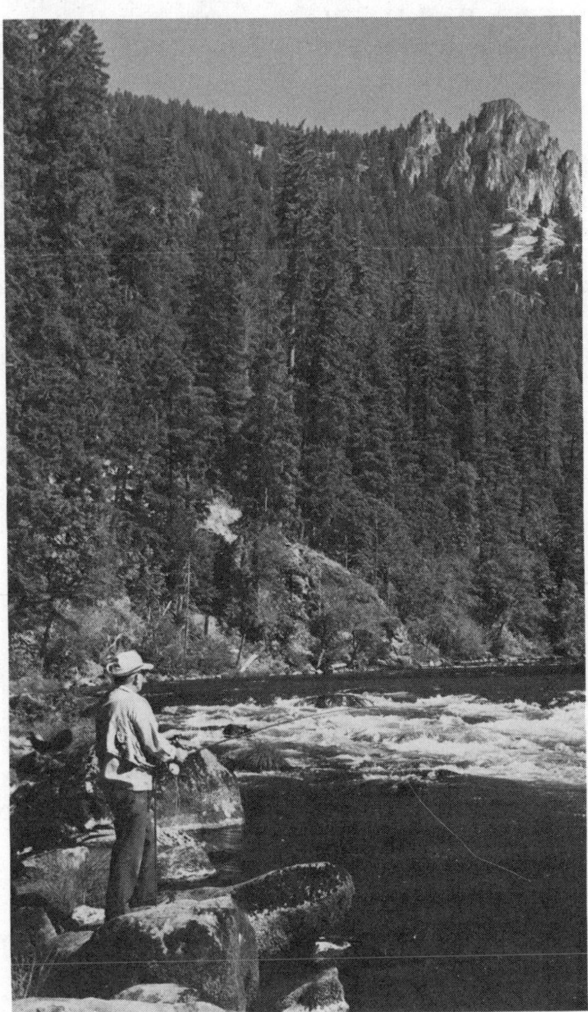

It really *is* a sportsman's paradise, this continent of ours — so when you take to the open road, be sure to pack your favorite gun and plenty of tackle. . . .

First-Aid For Tackle Troubles

An indispensible item for the angler's tackle box or fly vest is a small tackle repair kit that will allow quick emergency repairs in the field. Putting together your own tackle first-aid kit requires only a little time and very little money, but it can provide you with some invaluable angling insurance — and this will assure that your day of fishing won't be cut short by unexpected tackle troubles.

Before you start to gather items for your own repair kit, you should first review your tackle carefully, noting the model numbers on the reels and rods so you can obtain the proper spare parts from your tackle dealer. Bear in mind that you are aiming primarily at the most common problems that occur in the field, such as broken rod tips and guides, lost drag knobs, broken bail springs, cracked spools, etc. Also remember that you are not going to make permanent repairs, but only the repairs necessary in order for you to complete your day's fishing.

If you do a lot of fishing of various kinds, you may wish to make up one kit for spin fishing and bait casting, and another for fly or saltwater fishing. One important thing to remember is to make it a point to replace parts and other items as you use them. As you make a quick inventory of your tackle before you leave on your trip, also check the tackle repair box to make sure you have all the items you may need.

The following list should serve as a guide for the items to include; you may wish to make some substitutions or additions to fit your particular needs. Many of the items, especially the tools, can probably be found around the house, so your cash outlay will be minimal.

Plastic Box. A container about six inches long, four inches wide, and one to two inches deep will be about the right size to hold everything you need. A non-compartmented box is most desirable as many items will be odd-sized and difficult to fit into a container that is sectioned off. The best place to find this kind of box is at a specialty shop such as a hobby store, although your tackle shop may stock something suitable. The cost is between 69 and 99 cents.

Guides. Fly fishermen should include about four snake guides (10 to 20 cents each) of various sizes, and a couple of tip guides (50 cents each in No. 5½ and No. 6). Two stripper guides (50 cents each), about No. 8, should also be included. For spinning rods, three line guides (50 cents to $1 each) of various sizes, up to No. 24, should suffice, and two or three tip guides (50 cents to $1.50 each) should be included. Since guide repairs will be temporary, you needn't choose guides made of special alloys or expensive ceramic lined guides. After you return home, you can cut the temporary guide off and either have a permanent guide mounted or mount it yourself.

Assortment of Screws. Check your reels to determine the various sizes and types of screws you will need, and then pick up a couple of each kind so you can replace a lost screw should the need arise.

Bail Springs. A broken bail spring is a common affliction for a spinning reel, so it is important to be prepared for this occurrence, especially if your reel has been in service for a few years. Trying to get by with a reel that has a broken spring is a handicap, to say the least, but replacement in the field is a relatively easy task — if you're prepared. Cost: 25 to 50 cents each.

Extra Reel Handle. An extra handle for your spinning or bait casting reel is an item that you should include, since a lost or broken handle is one of the most common angling troubles. Since these can take up considerable room in the kit, and cost between $2 and $5, you may want to keep just one replacement for your favorite reel.

Drag Knobs. Spinning reel drag knobs are easily lost or broken and having a couple of extras on hand is always a good idea. Replacement knobs sell for $1.50 to $3.

Extra Spools. Chances are you have an extra spool for your reel in your tackle box or fly vest. If you can fit an extra spool in the kit, it is a good idea. Cost is between $2.50 and $3.50.

Extra Line. A full or partial spool of extra line may be too bulky for the kit, but if you can find something on which to store several yards of extra line, you may find that you will be congratulating yourself on your foresight when you're faced with cutting a damaged line off the reel.

Other Materials and Tools

Ferrule Cement. Marketed by Gudebrod, this cement is a waterproof, fast drying, plastic resin-base compound that was developed especially for assembling and repairing glass fishing rods. It can be used to re-cement loose ferrules and glue tip guides. To use, it has to be heated with a match and then applied hot to the rod. The great advantage to this adhesive is that it does not deteriorate with age or clog in the tube. It can be left in the box for a long period of time and still be good. Cost is a mere 60 cents.

Clear Nail Polish or Fly Tying Head Cement. This will provide a quick-drying, waterproof seal to temporary guide wraps, allowing you to resume fishing within a few minutes after it is applied. Price: 59 to 95 cents.

Waterproof Matches. You will need these to melt the ferrule cement. You can buy an inexpensive match holder (about 95 cents), or purchase the wax-coated matches that come in a book. Incidentally, having a supply of dry matches can also be great insurance should you ever become stranded or lost in the backcountry.

Wax. If you have a problem with sticky or frozen ferrules, apply a little wax once they are loosened and it will assure that the rod can be broken down with ease.

Line Cleaner. If you are a fly-fisherman, it is quite likely that you have some line cleaner in your vest. If not, put a small tin in your repair kit for maintenance of your fly line. Price is 25 to 85 cents.

Thread. One spool of Size A black nylon thread (25 cents) will handle a number of temporary guide wraps.

Leader Material. Some anglers prefer to make temporary guide wraps with monofilament leader, and if you wish you can include this instead of thread. Since the leader is heavier and stronger than thread, it can also be used to wrap broken rod sections. If leader is used, it should be coated with nail polish or cement just as any temporary guide wrap.

Vinyl Electrical Tape. In addition to temporarily mounting bent reels or replacing broken reel seats, tape can be used to join broken rod sections or to mount guides. A small spool (about 59 cents) will go a long way and take up little room in the kit box.

Combination Screwdriver. A small screwdriver with a regular and phillips head will be needed for reel repairs. Your tackle shop may have one, but an electronics store is your best bet for locating the precision type that you will need. We found a screwdriver set that included two regular and two phillips heads, that fits nicely in a little case, for only $2.25.

Hemostat or Clamp Tweezers. Originally a surgical instrument, hemostats are becoming increasingly popular with anglers because they are very effective at dislodging the hook from the mouth of a fish. They are especially effective because they can be clamped and locked shut, and that is precisely what makes them so effective for repairs. A hemostat can serve as a vice for repairing flies and lures, and for holding screws and small reel parts. Most tackle shops and mail order tackle suppliers are now stocking these, but with a starting price of about $5 they are not cheap. A pair of $2 clamp tweezers can serve as a substitute, though they are not nearly as effective.

Folding Scissors. We have included these on the list primarily because they are so compact and easily stored. Besides cutting thread, leader and tape, you will probably find a number of other uses for them. You can pick up a pair at your local tackle shop for about $2.95.

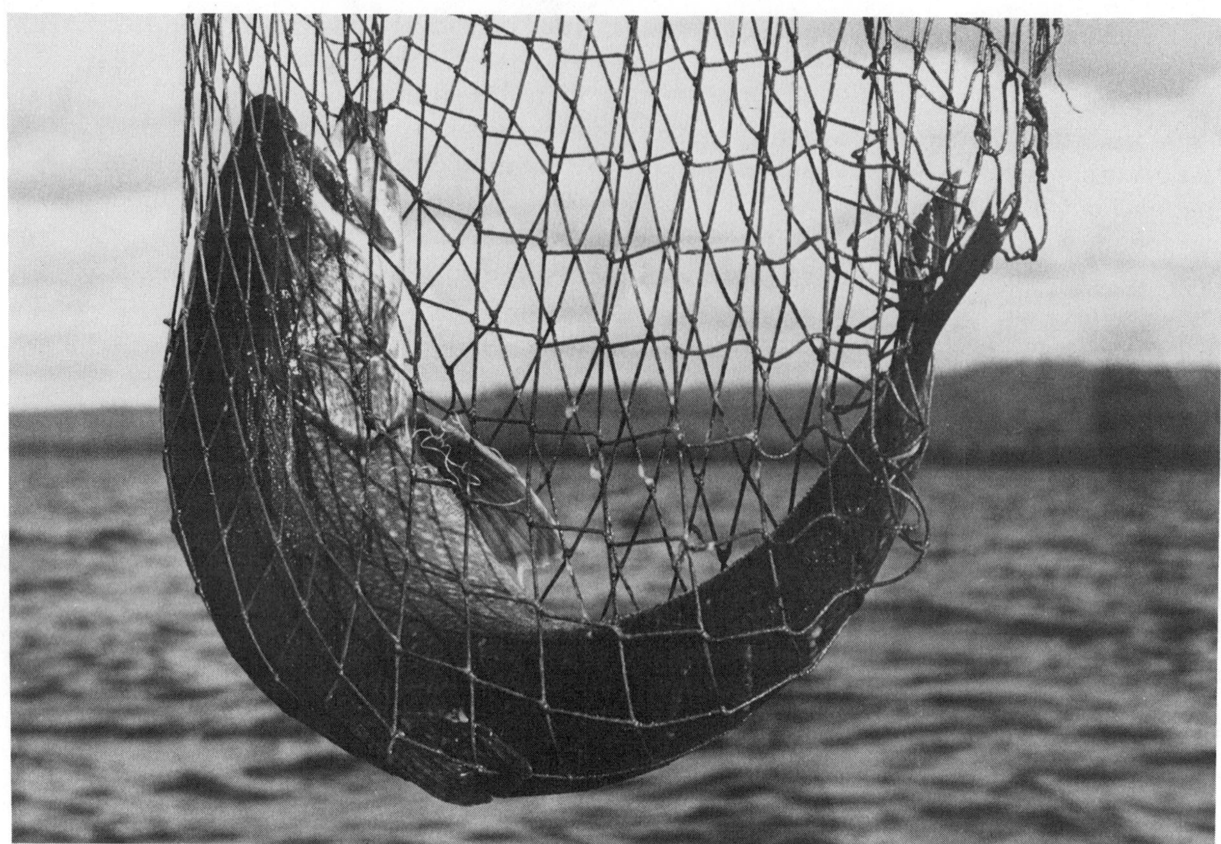

Multi-Use Knife. These knives, commonly known as Swiss army knives, contain a number of useful gadgets that may come in handy for some repair jobs. These knives may also serve as a substitute for the screwdriver set and scissors, but the tools are generally not delicate enough to handle small reel repairs. Unless you already own one, we wouldn't recommend buying one just for the kit, since they range from $10 to $25.

Pocket Flashlight. A small penlight will fit easily into the kit and come in handy even in the daytime for illuminating the dark recesses of reel mechanisms. You should be able to pick one up for no more than $1.50.

Magnifying Glass. The compact folding type is best and is invaluable for locating trouble spots in delicate, smaller reels. This is one of those items that is not absolutely necessary, but at a price of under $2 it is worth including.

Oil and Graphite. The graphite, of course, is used for lubricating reel parts after the reel has been cleaned or worked on. The oil can also be used for reels and is especially helpful when trying to separate stubborn ferrules. If you want to include either oil or graphite, pick the oil. Cost: lest than $1 for a supply of either one.

As most anglers tend to be gadget lovers, chances are good that you already have many of the items listed. Remember, the list is intended only as a guide. If you have other tools and materials that will substitute for those mentioned, by all means use them. The important thing is to gather them together into one compact kit so everything will be at hand when it is needed. The total cost for assembling the kit, including the container, should not exceed $10, and that is cheap insurance by anybody's standards.

TOP FISHING KNOTS

Knot Tying Do's and Don'ts

Hurried, careless or sloppy knot tying can weaken the strongest of knots. A few basic rules can assure that knots will deliver their full potential in holding power.

Where turns are required around the standing line, keep them separated, then pull them together in a neat spiral when tightening the knot.

Such knots hold best in low-pound test lines. Increased line diameters make it difficult to pull coils tight. Don't expect full rated strength from knots like the Improved Clinch in lines over 20-pounds test.

When double lines are used, as in the Palomar or Spider Hitch, keep them as parallel as possible. Avoid twisting as the knot is being tied.

Always pull knots up as tightly as possible with even, steady pressure. Knot slippage under pressure can cut the line.

Knots to hold terminal tackle

These are vital connections between line, hook, lure or special rig. Of many knots used for this purpose, we've selected three that our tests show can help win the battle.

Improved Clinch Knot

An old standby. Pass line through eye of hook, swivel or lure. Double back and make five turns around the standing line. Hold coils in place; thread end of line through first loop above the eye, then through big loop, as shown.

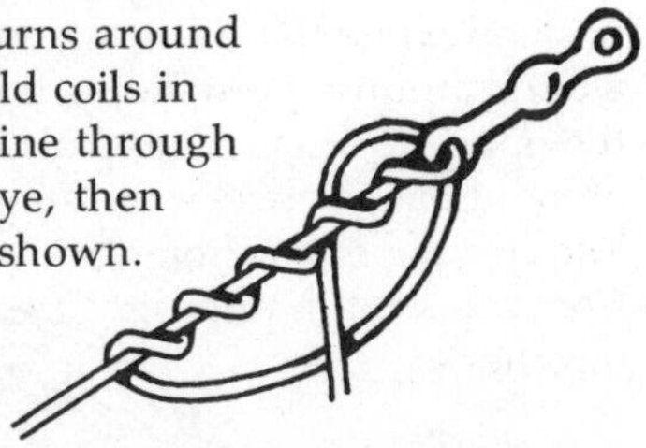

Hold tag end and standing line while coils are pulled up. Take care that coils are in spiral, not lapping over each other. Slide tight against eye. Clip tag end.

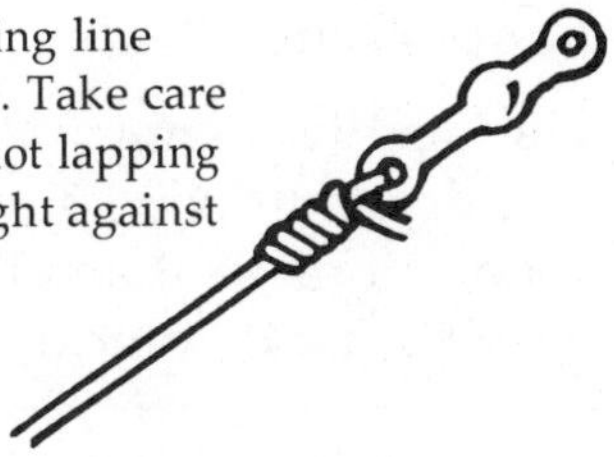

Palomar Knot

Easier to tie right, and consistently the strongest knot known to hold terminal tackle. Double about 4″ of line and pass loop through eye.

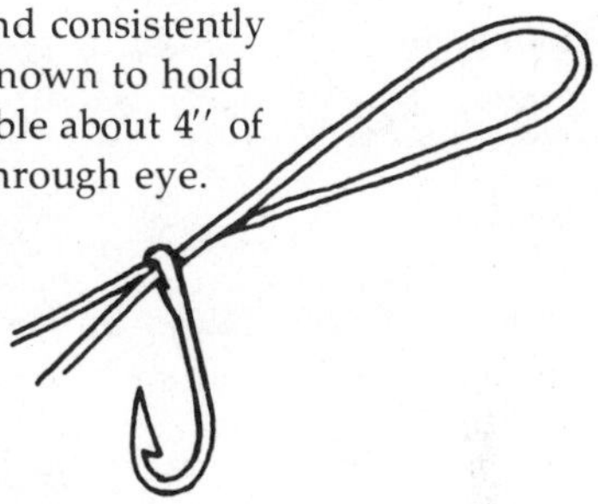

Let hook hang loose and tie overhand knot in doubled line. Avoid twisting the lines and don't tighten knot.

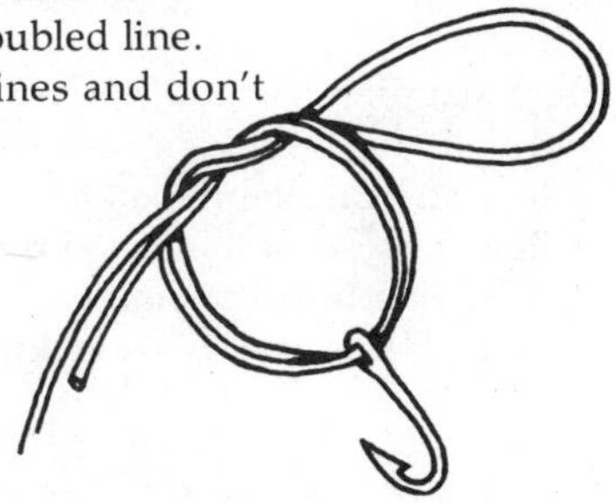

Pull loop of line far enough to pass it over hook, swivel or lure. Make sure loop passes completely over this attachment.

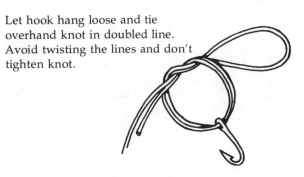

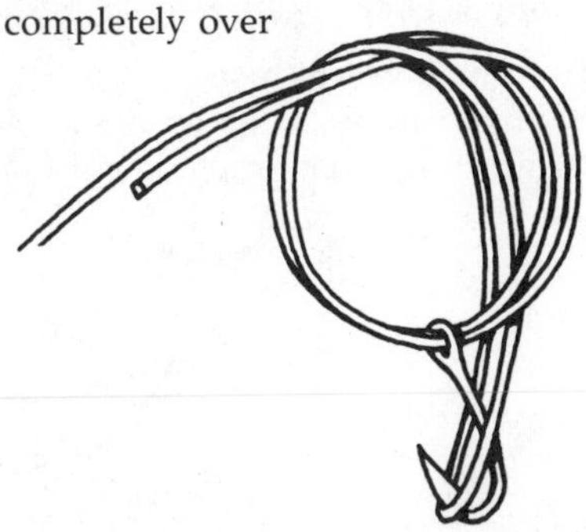

Pull both tag end and standing line to tighten. Clip about 1/8″ from knot.

Loop knots

The next two knots, surgeon's end loop and dropper loop, provide loop connections to attach leaders or other terminal tackle quickly.

Surgeon's End Loop

Double end of line to form loop and tie Overhand Knot at base of double line.

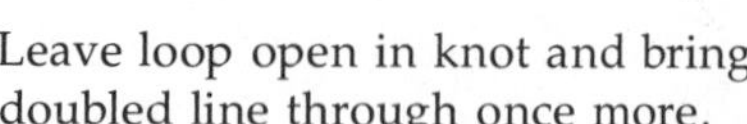

Leave loop open in knot and bring doubled line through once more.

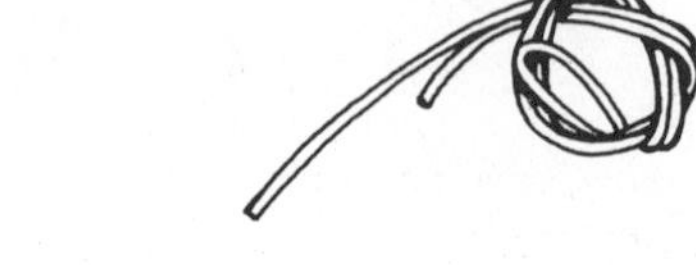

Hold standing line and tag end and pull loop to tighten knot. Size of loop can be determined by pulling loose knot to desired point and holding it while knot is tightened. Clip end 1/8″ from knot.

Dropper Loop

To form loop which stands out from line above sinker or other terminal rig. First form a loop in the line.

Pull one side of the loop down and begin taking turns with it around the standing line. Keep point where turns are made open so turns gather equally on each side.

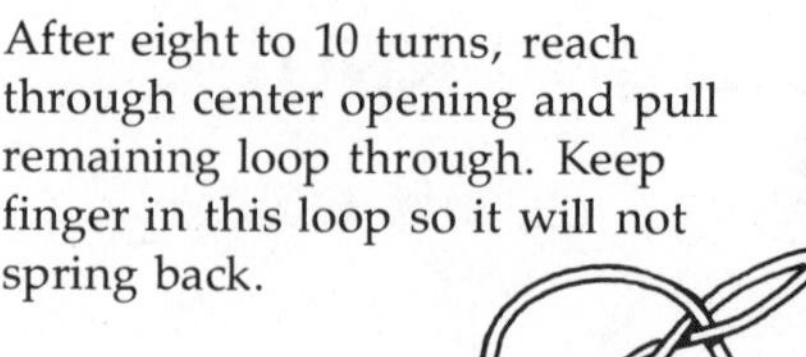

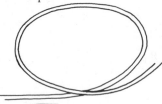

After eight to 10 turns, reach through center opening and pull remaining loop through. Keep finger in this loop so it will not spring back.

Hold loop with teeth and pull both ends of line, making turns gather on either side of loop.

Set knot by pulling lines as tightly as possible. Tightening coils will make loop stand out perpendicular to line. Not a strong knot but serviceable for pan fish and small saltwater species where such rigs are used.

Knots to tie line to line — Line to leader

The two most often used knots to join line. The Blood Knot for two lines of about the same diameter — the Surgeon's Knot to join a leader to line where the diameters vary considerably.

Blood Knot

Lay ends of lines alongside each other, lapping about 6″ of line. Hold lines at midpoint. Take five turns around standing line with tag end and bring end back between the two strands, where they are being held.

Hold this part of the knot in position while the other tag end is wound around the standing line in the opposite direction and also brought back between the strands. The two tag ends should protrude from the knot in opposite directions.

Pull up slowly on the two standing lines, taking care that the two ends do not back out of their positions. Turns will gather into loops as they come together.

Pull turns up as tightly as possible and clip ends close to the knot.

Surgeon's Knot

Lay line and leader parallel, lapping 6″ to 8″ of the two strands.

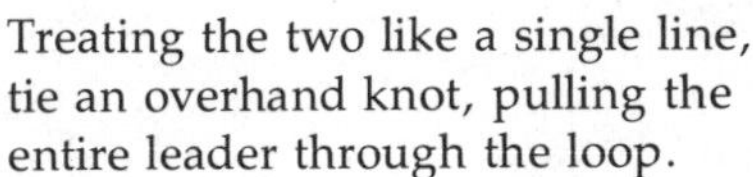

Treating the two like a single line, tie an overhand knot, pulling the entire leader through the loop.

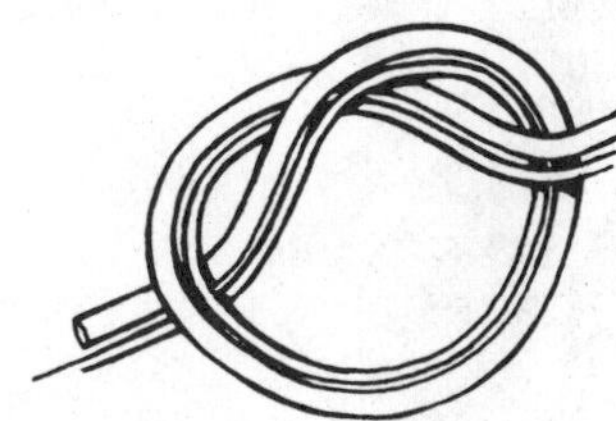

Leaving loop of the overhand open, pull both tag end of line and leader through again.

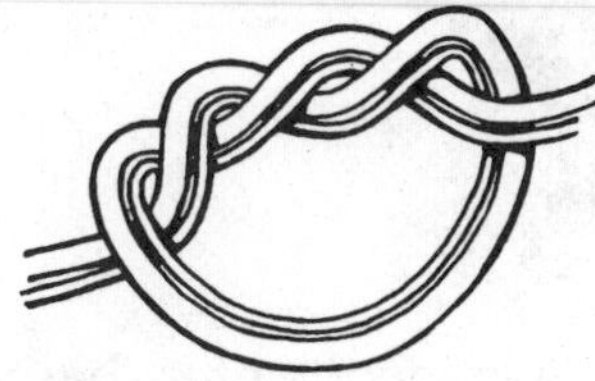

Hold both lines and both ends to pull the knot tight. Clip ends close to avoid foul-up in rod guides.

The uni-knot system

A single basic knot can be varied to meet virtually every knot-tying need. This is called the "uni-knot system." Two applications of the knot are shown here.

1. Tying to terminal tackle

Run line through eye of hook, swivel or lure at least 6″ and fold to make two parallel lines. Bring end of line back in a circle toward hook or lure.

Make six turns with tag end around the double line and through the circle. Hold double line at point where it passes through eye and pull tag end to snug up turns.

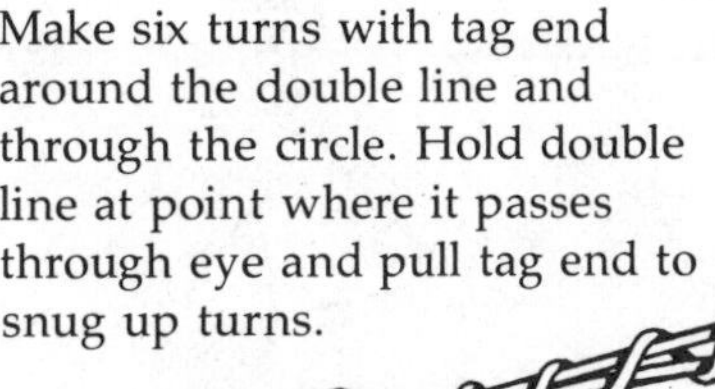

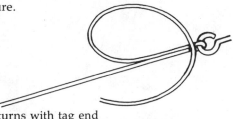

Now pull standing line to slide knot up against eye.

Continue pulling until knot is tight. Trim tag end flush with closest coil of knot. Uni-Knot will not slip.

2. Loop connection

Tie same knot to point where turns are snugged up around standing line. Slide knot toward eye until loop size desired is reached. Pull tag end with pliers to maximum tightness. This gives lure or fly natural free movement in water. When fish is hooked, knot will slide tight against eye.

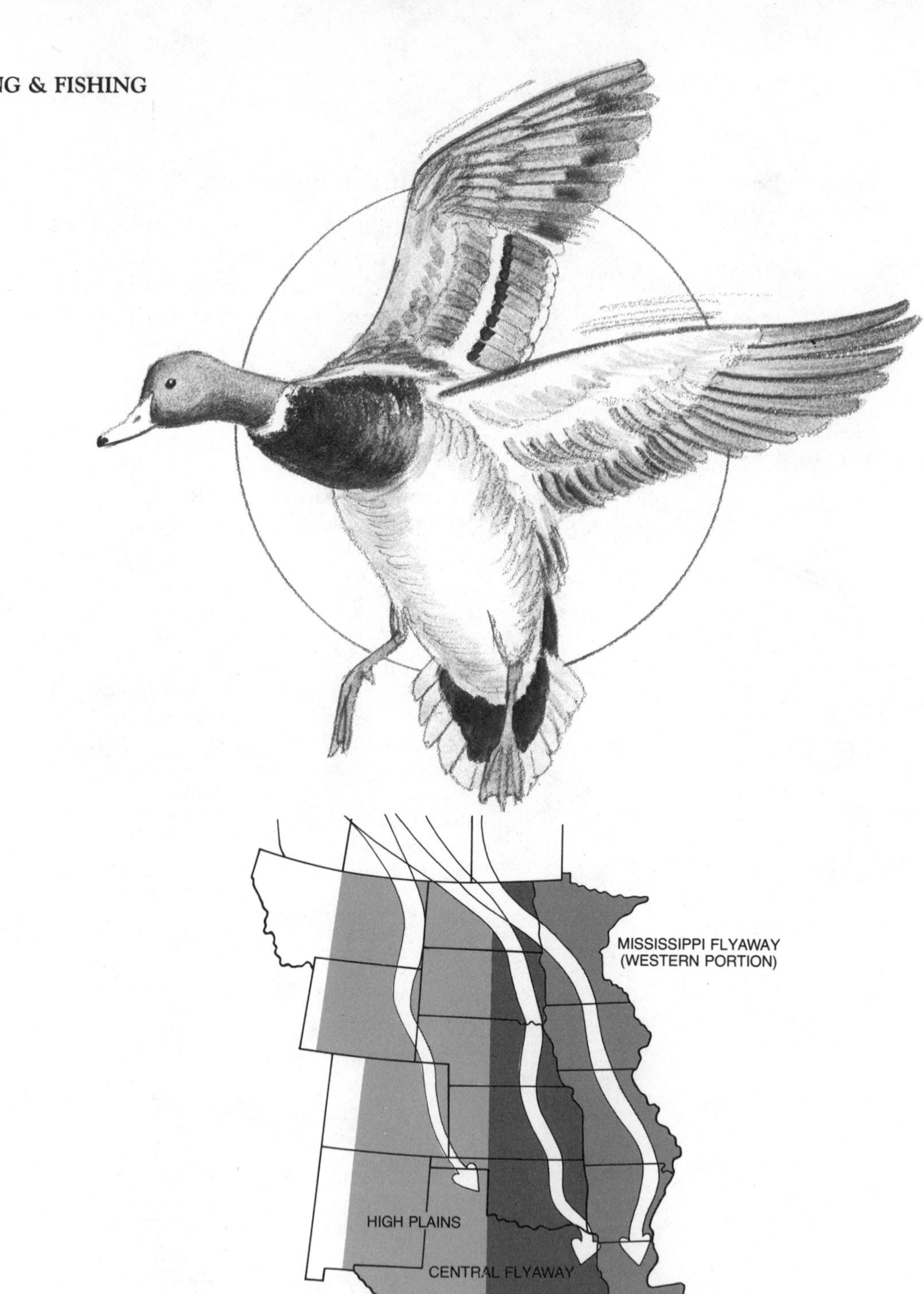

Migration Routes of Winter Banded Mallards

Recoveries of winter-banded mallards have provided survival information, defined generalized migration routes, and in part justified the inception of the late season in the High Plains portion of the Central Flyway. Routes shown are not actual migration paths but an averaged center, based on band return sites scattered on either side. Mallards are banded in mid-winter at their southernmost point of migration. Band recovery data such as this aids biologists in more precise management of mallard populations.

Courtesy: *Nebraskaland* Magazine.

United States Hunting & Fishing Regulations

New England States

State	Address	FISHING	HUNTING
Connecticut	*Department of Environmental Protection, State Office Building, Hartford, Connecticut 06115, (203) 566-5599.*	***Resident:*** $4.35; $6.35 incl. hunting ***Non-Res:*** $3.85; 3 day. $8.35; $17.35 incl. hunting	$4.35; $6.35 incl. fishing. spec. deer $10; archery $5 $13.35; $17.35 incl. fishing. spec. deer $30; archery $5.
Maine	*Department of Fisheries and Wildlife, 284 State Street, Augusta, Maine 04333, (207) 289-3651.*	***Resident:*** $7.50 or $12.50 incl. hunting. ***Non-Res:*** Jr. $4. $7.50-3 day; $15.50-15 day; $22.50 annual	$7.50; $12.50 incl. fishing; archery $7.50 $60.50; small game. $30.50; archery $60.50
Massachusetts	*Division of Fisheries and Wildlife, 100 Cambridge Street, Boston, Massachusetts 02202, (617) 727-3151.*	***Resident:*** $8.25 ***Non-Res:*** $8.25–7 day; $14.25 annual	$8.25; $1.25 state duck stamp $20.25 small game; $35.25 big game; $1.25 st. duck stamp
New Hampshire	*Fish and Game Department, 34 Bridge Street, Concord, New Hampshire 03301, (603) 271-3512.*	***Resident:*** $9.25 or $14 incl. hunting ***Non-Res:*** $7.75–3 day; $11–7 day; $16–15 day; $21 annual	$8.25; $14 inc. fishing $56 small game $31; $13–3 day
Rhode Island	*Division of Fish and Wildlife, Veterans Memorial Building, Providence, Rhode Island 02903, (401) 277-2784.*	***Resident:*** $3.25; $5.25 incl. hunting ***Non-Res:*** $3.25–3 Day; $7.25 Annual	$3.25; $5.25 incl. fishing $10.25
Vermont	*Vermont Fish and Game Department, Montpelier, Vermont 05602, (802) 828-3371.*	***Resident:*** $4 or $8 incl. hunting ***Non-Res:*** $4.75–3 day; $12.25 annual; $8.75–14 day $45.75 incl. hunting	$5; $8 incl. fishing; $4 archery spec. license (deer) $40.75–3 day; $12.25 annual; $8.75–14 day; $45.75 incl. hunting

Eastern States

State	Address	FISHING	HUNTING
Delaware	*Division of Fish and Wildlife, Dover, Delaware 19901, (302) 678-4431.*	***Resident:*** $4.20; $2.10 Trout Stamp ***Non-Res:*** $9.50 annual; $3.20–7 day; $5.25 trout stamp	$5.20 $40.25; $3 shooting preserve
Maryland	*Department of Natural Resources, Wildlife Administration, Tawes State Office Building, Annapolis, Maryland 21401, (301) 269-3195.*	***Resident:*** $4.50; $1 senior citizen; $2.50 trout stamp ***Non-Res:*** $4.50–7 day; $10.50 annual (residents of D.C., Va. and W. Va. $4.50 on Potomac R.	$8: $2.50 under 16 yrs., $1.25 Sr. citizen; $5.50 special deer & turkey stamp $30.50 min., or reciprocal with resident state; under 16 yrs. $5, $5.50 special deer and turkey stamp
New Jersey	*Department of Fish, Game and Shellfisheries, PO Box 1809, Trenton, New Jersey, 08625, (609) 292-2965.*	***Resident:*** $7.25; $4 trout stamp ***Non-Res:*** $5.25–3 day; $12.25; $8 trout stamp	$10.25 annual firearm; $10.25 archery reciprocal with $25 min.

Eastern States

		FISHING	HUNTING
New York	*Department of Environmental Conservation, 50 Wolf Road, Albany, New York 12233, (518) 457-5861.*	***Resident:*** $6.25 or $11.25 incl. hunting ***Non-Res:*** $10.25–7 day; $17.25 annual; $5.50–3 day	$6.25 small game; $5.25 big game; $11.25 incl. fishing; $4.25 bow hunting stamp $32.50 small game; $52.50 big game (additional for deer & bear); $4.25 bow hunting stamp
Pennsylvania	*Fish and Game Commission, Harrisburg, Pennsylvania 17120, (717) 787-6487.*	***Resident:*** $7.25; $2.25–65 yrs. ***Non-Res:*** $7.75–7 day; $12.75 annual	$8.25; $5.25 Jr., $3.25 Muzzleloader Deer; $2.20 archery license; $5.25–65 Yrs. & over. $40.35 hunting only; $40 trapping only

Southern States

		FISHING	HUNTING
Arkansas	*Arkansas Game and Fish Commission, No. 2 Capitol Mall, Little Rock, Arkansas 72201, (501) 371-1025.*	***Resident:*** $7.50; $3 trout permit req. ***Non-Res:*** $7.50–14 Day; $10.30 annual; $3 trout permit req.	$5; $5 archery permit $25; $10–5 day small game; $15 deer, turkey tags; $15 archery license and permit
North Carolina	*Wildlife Resources Commission, Raleigh, North Carolina 27611, (919) 733-7123.*	***Resident:*** $7.50 annual; $10 incl. hunting; $3.50 county; $3–3 day; $3.25 season trout ***Non-Res:*** $5.50–3 day; $12.50 annual–$6.25 season trout	$7.50 annual; $10 incl. fishing; $3.50 county; $3.50 big game; $8 game lands use permit $20–6 day; $25 annual; $5 big game; $10 shooting preserve; $50 sportsman; $8–game lands use permit
South Carolina	*Department of Wildlife and Marine Resources, Dutch Plaza, PO Box 167, Columbia, South Carolina 29202.*	***Resident:*** Fishing statewide $5.25; $2.25–14 day ***Non-Res:*** $4.25–10 day; $11.25 annual	$3.25 county; $6.25 state; $10.25 incl. fishing; $4.25 G.M.A. $20.25 game management area; $12.50–3 day; $22–10 day; $42.50 annual
Georgia	*Department of Natural Resources, 270 Washington Street, SW, Atlanta, Georgia 30334, (404) 393-7263.*	***Resident:*** $3.25 or $7.25 incl. hunting; $2.25 trout stamp ***Non-Res:*** $3.25–5 day; $10.25 annual; trout stamp, season $10.25; $3.25–5 day trout stamp	$4.25 or $7.25 incl. fishing; $3.25 big game; archery $3.25 $15.25–10 day; $25.25 annual; $25.00 big game; archery–annual $25.25; 10 day $12.50
Kentucky	*Department of Fish and Wildlife Resources, Capitol Plaza, Frankfort, Kentucky 40601, (502) 564-4336.*	***Resident:*** $5; $9 incl. hunting; $2.25 trout stamp ***Non-Res:*** $2.50–3 day; $4–15 day; $10–annual; $2.25 trout stamp	$5; $9 incl. fishing; $10.50 deer permit $27.50; $10–3 day, small game; $10.50 deer permit
Tennessee	*Tennessee Wildlife Resources Agency, PO Box 40747, Nashville, Tennessee 37204, (615) 741-1512*	***Resident:*** $7.50 incl. hunting; $1.50–2 day; $3–10 day; $3 trout license ***Non-Res:*** $30 incl. hunting; $5–10 day; $3–3 day; $5 trout license	$7.50 incl. fishing; $7.50 big game stamp; $2 archery stamp $8–3 day small game; $5 archery stamp; annual (comb.) $30; $7.50 big game stamp
Virginia	*Commission of Game and Inland Fisheries, PO Box 11104, Richmond, Virginia 23230, (804) 257-1000.*	***Resident:*** County $5 (incl. hunting); state $5 fish only; trout stamp $3 ***Non-Res:*** $3–5 day; $10 annual; trout stamp $7.50	$5; bear–deer–turkey $5 $20; bear–deer–turkey $20

Southern States

		FISHING	HUNTING
West Virginia	*Department of Natural Resources, Division of Wildlife Resources, 1800 Washington Street, East Charleston, West Virginia 25305, (304) 348-2771.*	***Resident:*** $6 or $10 incl. hunting; $3 trout stamp, $1 in nat'l forests ***Non-Res:*** $5–6 day. Plus $5 trout stamp; $20 annual; $1 nat'l forest; $3–in state forest & or state park; $.50 ea. add. member of family)	$6 or $10 incl. fishing; $1 in nat'l forests; $4 bear stamp $40 firearm; $15 archery; $1 in nat'l forests; $4 bear stamp; $8–6 day small game

Gulf States

		FISHING	HUNTING
Alabama	*Alabama Department of Conservation and Natural Resources, 64 North Union Street, Montgomery, Alabama 36130, (205) 832-6300.*	***Resident:*** $1.25 pole & line; $3.25 rod & reel ***Non-Res:*** $4.25–7 day; $10.25 annual	$2.75 county; $5.25 state; sr. over 65–40¢; special deer & turkey $3.15 Annual all game $50.25; small game $15.25; 5 day trip all game $25.25; small game $10.25; special deer and turkey license $3.15
Florida	*Game and Fish Commission, Tallahassee, Florida 32403, (904) 488-1960.*	***Resident:*** $3 ***Non-Res:*** $5–5 day; $7–14 day; $10 annual; fresh water	$2 County; $7.50 State; Other than home co. $4.50 $15.50–10 day; $50.50 annual; alien $50
Louisiana	*Department of Wildlife and Fisheries, 400 Royal Street, New Orleans, Louisiana 70130, (504) 568-5612.*	***Resident:*** $2 ***Non-Res:*** $3–7 day; $6 annual	$5; $5 additional for big game $10–3 day; $25 annual; $20 additional for big game
Mississippi	*Mississippi Game and Fish Commission, PO Box 451, Jackson, Mississippi 39205, (601) 354-7333*	***Resident:*** $3 or $6.50 incl. hunting; $1–3 day ***Non-Res:*** $3.00–3 day; $12 annual	$5 or $6.50 incl. fishing; $3 deer and turkey $15 small game; $25 all game; $5 deer & turkey tag; $10–7 day; $6–3 day small game

Central States

		FISHING	HUNTING
Illinois	*Division of Wildlife Resources, 100½ East Washington Street, Springfield, Illinois 62706, (217) 782-6384.*	***Resident:*** $2.25 ***Non-Res:*** $4.25–10 day; annual; reciprocal ($6.25 min.)	$3.25 Reciprocal with other states; min. $10.50–5 day; $15.50 season
Indiana	*Division of Fish and Wildlife, 607 State Office Building, Indianapolis, Indiana 46204, (317) 633-7696.*	***Resident:*** $5.25 incl. hunting & trapping; $3.50 (fishing only); $2.25 trout-salmon stamp ***Non-Res:*** $3.25–14 day; $7.50 annual; $2.25 trout-salmon stamp	$5.25 incl. fishing & trapping, $3.25 hunting & trapping only; $5.75 deer; $5.25 turkey $20.25 small game; $25.25 incl. fishing; $30.75 deer; $5.25–5 day; $25.25 trapping
Michigan	*Department of Natural Resources, PO Box 30028, Lansing, Michigan 48909, (517) 373-1220.*	***Resident:*** $22.50 sportsman's; $.75, 65 yrs. or older; $5.25 special trout & salmon stamp ***Non-Res:*** $1 per day up to 15 days; $10.25 annual; $5.25 special trout & salmon stamp	$5 small game; $7.50 deer; $7.50 archery; $1 sr. citizen deer, sportsman's $22.50 $25 small game; $40 deer; $20 archery; $25 bear

Central States

		FISHING	HUNTING
Ohio	*Division of Wildlife, Building C, Fountain Square, Columbus, Ohio 43224, (614) 466-7313.*	***Resident:*** $4.50 ***Non-Res:*** $7.50–7 day; $14.50 annual	$4.50; $10.50 turkey permit, $10.50 deer permit $30.50; $10.50 turkey permit; $10.50 deer permit
Wisconsin	*Department of Natural Resources, PO Box 7921, Madison, Wisconsin 53702, (608) 266-3696.*	***Resident:*** $4.25; $7.50 (husband & wife) ***Non-Res:*** $18 family (husband, wife and child under 18); $12.50 annual; $7.50–15 day individual; $5.50–4 day individual	$5.25 small game; $7.25 deer; $7.25 bear; $6.25 archery $100.50 general, big game & small game; $25.50 archery; $50.50 small game; $70.50 deer & bear only

Midwestern States

		FISHING	HUNTING
North Dakota	*Game and Fish Department, 2121 Lavett Avenue, Bismarck, North Dakota 58505, (701) 224-2180.*	***Resident:*** Family $5; $4; Senior Citizen $1 ***Non-Res:*** $2–7 day tourist; $6 annual	$3 small game; $7 big game General hunting $.50; small game $35; big game $51; big game archery $25; $5 state waterfowl stamp
South Dakota	*Department of Fish, Game and Parks, Pierre, South Dakota 57501, (605) 773-3482.*	***Resident:*** $4 ***Non-Res:*** $5–5 day; $15 annual	$1 general hunting, $3 small game; $12 big game; $2 turkey; $1 waterfowl $2 general hunting; $30 small game; $50 big game; $25 predator; $5 turkey; $30 waterfowl
Iowa	*Iowa Conservation Commission, Wallace State Office Building, Des Moines, Iowa 50319, (515) 281-5918.*	***Resident:*** $4; combination $8; trout stamp $5; sr. cit. $1.25; $2.50 incl. hunting ***Non-Res:*** $1–1 day; $5–6 day; $10 annual; not reciprocal with other states	$5 annual; $10 deer; $1 state waterfowl stamp, sr. cit. $1.25; $6 lifetime Not reciprocal with other states; $25 fee; $1 state waterfowl stamp
Kansas	*Kansas Fish and Game Commission, Box 54A, Route 2, Pratt, Kansas 67124, (316) 672-5411.*	***Resident:*** $5 or $10 incl. hunting ***Non-Res:*** $5–10 day; $10 annual	$5 or $10 incl. fishing; $15 special deer, antelope & turkey permits $25
Minnesota	*Division of Fish and Wildlife, 390 Centennial Building, St. Paul, Minnesota 55155, (612) 296-3325.*	***Resident:*** $5 (husband & wife $8) ***Non-Res:*** $10; $5–3 days (husband & wife $15)	$7 small game; $10 deer; $7.50 bear only Archery (deer) $25; Firearms $60; $27 small game; $25.25 bear only
Missouri	*Department of Conservation, 2901 North Ten Mile Drive, Jefferson City, Missouri 65101, (314) 751-4115.*	***Resident:*** $5.50 or $10 incl. hunting; $3–3 day ***Non-Res:*** $5–14 day; $7.50 annual; $3–3 day	$5.50 or $10 incl. fishing; $5.50 trapping $25 small game; $50 big game–$20 archery
Nebraska	*Game and Parks Commission, PO Box 30370, Lincoln, Nebraska 68503, (402) 464-0641.*	***Resident:*** $7.50; $13.50 incl. hunting ***Non-Res:*** $15–5 day; $30 annual; $10–3 day	$6.50 small game; $13.50 incl. fishing; $7.50 habitat stamp, $15 deer & antelope; $15 turkey $30 small game; $50 deer & antelope; $35 turkey

Rocky Mountain States

		FISHING	HUNTING
Colorado	*Division of Wildlife, 6060 Broadway, Denver, Colorado 80216, (303) 825-1192.*	***Resident:*** $7.50 or $10 incl. small game	$5 bird & small game; $10 incl. fishing; $13 deer; $16 elk; mtn. lion $25; $10 bear
		Non-Res: $10–5 day; $25 annual	$90 deer; $135 elk; $25 bird & small game; $50 bear; $200 mountain lion
Idaho	*Idaho Department of Fish and Game, 600 South Walnut, Box 25, Boise, Idaho 83707, (208) 384-3700.*	***Resident:*** $6 or $10 incl. game	$5 or $10 incl. fishing
		Non-Res: $3–1 Day; $7–7 day; $20 annual	$50 annual; deer & elk tags limited
Montana	*Department of Fish and Game, Helena, Montana 59601, (406) 449-3089.*	***Resident:*** $5	$4 bird; $8 elk; $7 deer; $25 moose; $15 goat; $25 sheep; $6 black bear; $5 mt. lion
		Non-Res: $2–1 day; $10–6 day; $20 annual	$225 big game, birds & fish; $30 bird; antelope $50 blk. bear; $125; Grizzly; $25 trophy fee grizzly bear; $25 mt. lion
Utah	*Division of Wildlife Resources, 1596 West North Temple, Salt Lake City, Utah 84116, (801) 533-9333.*	***Resident:*** $8–$18 incl. hunting; 12 thru 15–$3.50	Small game $6; big game $7; $18 incl. fishing
		Non-Res: $2–1 day; $7.50–5 day; $25 annual	Small Game $20; Big Game $75
Wyoming	*Department of Fish and Game, Communications Branch, Cheyenne, Wyoming 82002, (307) 777-7735.*	***Resident:*** $5; $2 resident youth	$5 birds; $10 deer; $15 elk & bk. bear; $30 bighorn sheep; $25 moose; $3 small game
		Non-Res: $5–5 day; $25 annual; $2 non-resident youth	$10 small game; $125 elk & fish; $25 birds; $50 deer; $50 Antelope; $125 moose; $150 bighorn sheep

Southwestern States

		FISHING	HUNTING
Arizona	*Department of Fish and Game, 2222 West Greenway Road, Phoenix, Arizona 85023, (602) 942-3000.*	***Resident:*** $4 annual; $3–1 day; $12–comb. fishing & hunting	$7 general game; $12 incl. fishing; big game tags additional
		Non-Res: $3–1 day; $8–9 day; $6–5 day; $12 annual; $45 incl. hunting	General hunting $30; $45 incl. fishing; big game tags additional
New Mexico	*Department of Fish and Game, State Capital, Villagra Building, Santa Fe, New Mexico 87503, (505) 827-2143.*	***Resident:*** $7.50 or $21 incl. hunting; $3.25–1 day; $2.25 to $4.25 trout stamp	$8.50 small game; $12.50 big game; $15.50 general hunting; $21 incl. fishing
		Non-Res: $3.25–1 day; $8–5 day; $15.50 annual; $2.25 to $5.25 trout stamp	$91 big game; $31 deer bow; $26 small game
Oklahoma	*Department of Wildlife Conservation, 1801 North Lincoln Boulevard, Oklahoma City, Oklahoma 73105, (405) 521-3855.*	***Resident:*** $5 or $9 incl. hunting	$5 or $9 incl. fishing plus $5 for deer
		Non-Res: $9.25 annual; $4.75–10 day	$30–small game; $50–deer
Texas	*Department of Parks and Wildlife, 4200 Smith School Road, Austin, Texas 78744, (512) 475-4907.*	***Resident:*** $4.50 annual; $1.25–3 day saltwater	$5.25
		Non-Res: $1.25–3 day saltwater; $4.50–5 day; $10.50 annual	$10.25–5 day migratory bird; $5 shooting resort; $100.75 all game in season; $37.75 small game

Western States

		FISHING	HUNTING
Alaska	*Department of Fish and Game, Subport Building, Juneau, Alaska 99801, (907) 465-4112.*	***Resident:*** $10, or $22 incl. hunting ***Non-Res:*** $15–10 day; $30 annual; $90 incl. hunting	$12 or $22 incl. fishing $200 hunting & trapping; $60 annual; $90 incl. fishing
California	*Department of Fish and Game, Resources Building, 1416 Ninth Street, Sacramento, California 95814, (916) 445-3531.*	***Resident:*** $4 ocean, warm water $2 extra; trout $3 extra ($9 total, all fish); $2–3 day (ocean license) ***Non-Res:*** $5–10 day ocean license; $15 annual ocean license, special inland water stamps required	$10; bear tag $1; deer tag $3 $35; bear tag $1; deer tag $25
Hawaii	*Division of Fish and Game, Honolulu, Hawaii 96813, (808) 548-4002.*	***Resident:*** $3.75 (includes armed forces and families) (freshwater sport fishing); $1.50 minors ***Non-Res:*** $3.75–30 day; $7.50 annual (freshwater sport fishing)	$7.50 (includes armed forces & families); sr. cit. free incl. fishing $15
Nevada	*Department of Fish and Game, 1100 Valley Road, Reno, Nevada 89520, (702) 784-6214.*	***Resident:*** $10 annual; $2–Jr. ***Non-Res:*** $10–10 day; $20 annual; $7.50–3 day; $5–Jr.	$7; deer tag $8; $2–Jr. $40; $50 deer tag; some game species closed to nonresidents; others on quota basis, subject to drawing
Oregon	*Department of Fish and Wildlife, 506 SW Mill Street, Portland, Oregon 97208, (503) 229-5403.*	***Resident:*** $2.50–1 day; $9 or $15 incl. hunting (salmon & steelhead $2 additional) ***Non-Res:*** $2.50–1 day; $10–10 days; $25 annual (salmon & steelhead $2 additional)	$7 or $15 incl. fishing plus $4 for deer; $15 for elk $75 general, tags extra
Washington	*Department of Fish and Game, 600 North Capitol Way, Olympia, Washington 98504, (206) 753-5700.*	***Resident:*** State $8.50; $14 incl. hunting; County $7; $9 incl. hunting; plus $3 steelhead permit ***Non-Res:*** $7.25–7 day; $24 annual; plus $3 steelhead permit	County $9 incl. fishing; state $7.50; $14 incl. fishing; plus add. fees for other game $60 plus $42 for elk; $42 for mtn. goat; $42 for mtn. sheep

		FISHING	HUNTING
District of Columbia	*No license is required for fishing in Washington, D.C., and no hunting is permitted.*	***Resident:*** ***Non-Res:***	
Mexico	**FISHING:** *Direccion General de Pescas, Departmento de Pesca Deportiva, Secretaria de Industria y Comercio, Cuauhtemoc 80, Sexto Piso, Mexico City, Mexico.* **HUNTING:** *Mexican Government of Tourism, Mariano Escobedo 726, Mexico City, Mexico.*	***Non-Resident:*** $1.25 per day to $5 per year Approximately $16; permits may be difficult to obtain and regulations vary from state to state. Permit applications must be accompanied by a character reference from your local police, a detailed request for permission to take firearms into the country, and five passport photos.	

Canada

Because hunting regulations and license fees change frequently, not all provinces were able to supply information on hunting licenses. Hunters should also note that all provinces charge substantial fees for the taking of big game. For information on those fees and for current fees and regulations, contact the appropriate province at the address listed below.

Canada

		FISHING	HUNTING
Alberta	*Fish and Wildlife Division, 18th Floor Centennial Building, 10015 103rd Avenue, Edmonton, Alberta, Canada T5J OH1*	***Resident:*** $4; $5 for trophy lake license	N/A
		Non-Res: $12; $4–3 day; $5 for trophy lake license	N/A
British Columbia	*Fish and Wildlife Branch, Parliament Buildings, Department of Recreation and Conservation, 400, 1019 Wharf Street, Victoria, British Columbia, Canada V8W 2Z1.*	***Resident:*** $5 fishing; $3 steelhead	$7
		Non-Res: $15; $6–3 day; $10 steelhead	$25; $75–all game
Manitoba	*Department of Mines and Natural Resources, Environmental Management, 989 Century Street, Winnipeg, Manitoba, Canada R3H OW4.*	***Resident:*** $3.30	$4 game birds; $8.50 deer; $16 moose.
		Non-Res: $11; $5.50–3 day	$40 game birds; $60 deer; $150 moose.
New Brunswick	*Fish and Wildlife Branch, Department of Natural Resources, Fredericton, New Brunswick, Canada E3B 5C3.*	***Resident:*** $10	N/A
		Non-Res: $75; $35–7 day; $25 for all species except salmon; $10–3 day.	N/A
Newfoundland	*Director of Wildlife, Department of Tourism, St. John's, Newfoundland, Canada A1A 1P9.*	***Resident:*** $5	$20 caribou; $20 moose; $15 bear; $2 grouse, ptarmigan; $2 rabbit.
		Non-Res: $5 trout; $10 two weeks; $15 season.	$500 caribou; $250 moose; $50 bear; $10 grouse, ptarmigan; $10 rabbit.
Northwest Territories	*Fish and Marine Service and Wildlife Service, Box 2310, Yellowknife, Northwest Territories, Canada X1A 2L9.*	***Resident:*** $3	N/A
		Non-Res: $10	N/A
Nova Scotia	*Department of Environment, Fisheries and Marine Service, PO Box 550, Halifax, Nova Scotia, Canada.*	***Resident:*** $3; $2 national parks.	$10; small game $7.
		Non-Res: $15; $2 national parks	$50; $25–small game
Ontario	*Fish and Wildlife Division, Ministry of Natural Resources, Whitney Block, Queen's Park, Toronto, Ontario, Canada M7A 1W3.*	***Resident:*** $6	$15 deer and bear; $5 small game.
		Non-Res: $15; $8–4 day	$80 deer and bear; $10 game birds.
Prince Edward Island	*Fish and Wildlife Division, PO Box 2000, Charlottetown, Prince Edward Island, Canada C1A 7N8.*	***Resident:*** $2	N/A
		Non-Res: $15	N/A

Canada

		FISHING	HUNTING
Quebec	*Fish and Game Branch, Department of Tourism, Parliament Building, Quebec City, Quebec, Canada G1A 1R4*	***Resident:*** $3.25; $5.25 salmon	N/A
		Non-Res: $10.50; $25.50 salmon	N/A
Saskatchewan	*Department of Tourism and Renewable Resources, PO Box 7105, Regina, Saskatchewan, Canada S4P 3N1.*	***Resident:*** $3	N/A
		Non-Res: $10	N/A
Yukon Territory	*Department of Fisheries, 1100 A First Avenue, Whitehorse, Yukon Territory, Canada Y1A 2C6.*	***Resident:*** $3	N/A
		Non-Res: $10; $3.50–5 day	N/A

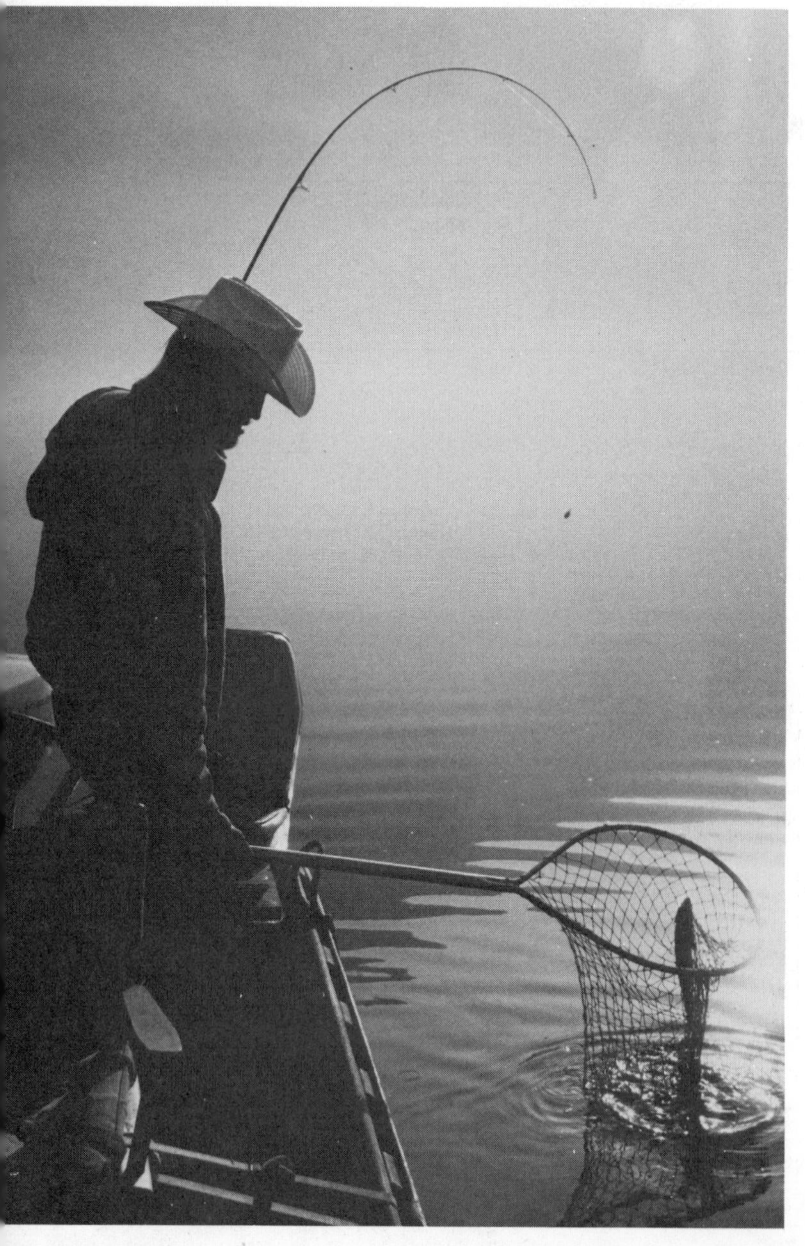

A Note to Hunters and Anglers Traveling in Canada

A visitor does not require a federal permit to possess rifles, shotguns or fishing tackle in Canada. He must provide Canada Customs with a description of such equipment and serial numbers of firearms so that the articles may be readily cleared on their return. Such permission does not give the right to hunt or fish. Two hundred rounds of ammunition per person are admitted duty-free. Revolvers, pistols and fully-automatic firearms are prohibited.

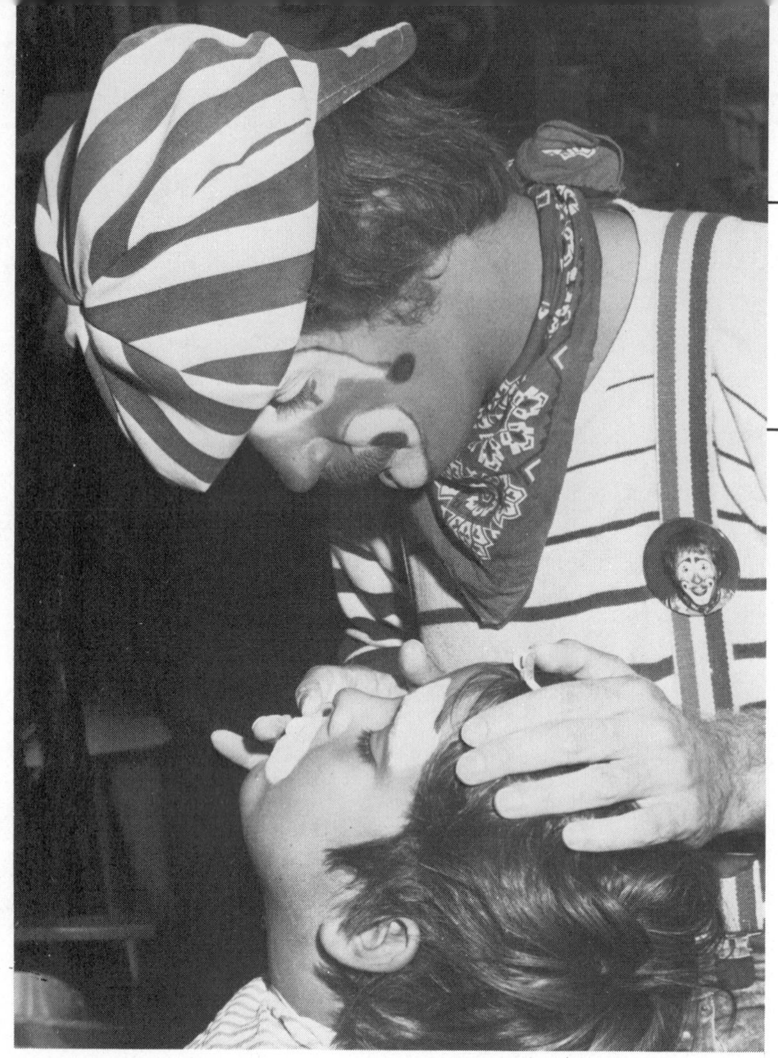

America's

Amusement Parks, Zoos, Wild Animal Parks

"Gray skies are gonna clear up, put on a happy face . . ." and join the millions of Americans who have escaped, if only for an afternoon, to the pleasure parks of America. It's fun for the whole family — guaranteed to bring back memories of a happy childhood for Mom and Dad.

Lose yourself in the fantasy world of Walt Disney, experience the toe-tapping enthusiasm of Nashville's Opryland, plunge down the steep drops of Six Flags' awesome Colossus roller coaster, take an armchair safari in the comfort of your RV — or simply stroll arm and arm past the arcades, shooting galleries and concessions where the smell of cotton candy hangs sweet on the summer air. All this and more awaits when you pass through the gates of America's amusement parks.

As you tour the country in your RV, don't miss the opportunity to sample the fun and frolic of roller coasters and merry-go-rounds. The listing that follows is a perfect way to map your amusement adventures state by state. So hold on tight!

Alabama

Alabama Space and Rocket Center. Features the Saturn V rocket and simulated flights in the Lunar Odyssey; restaurant, exhibits, picnic area. Open year-round, daily, 9 a.m. to 5 p.m. Huntsville, off Interstate 65.

Birmingham Zoo. One of the south's largest zoos; animals displayed in natural settings. Open year-round, daily, 9:30 a.m. to 5 p.m. Adults $2, children 2 to 17 and senior citizens, $1.

Fair Park Kiddieland. Features several major rides and kiddie rides; arcade, refreshments, picnic area. Open year-round, daily. Birmingham, on Bessemer Road. Admission: free.

Alaska

Alaska Children's Zoo. Set in a natural wooded area, housing numerous species of animals and birds. Open year-round, daily, except Tuesday, 10 a.m. to 5 p.m.; weekends only, October through April 15. Adults $1.50, children 3 to 12, 75 cents. Anchorage, off State Route 1.

Totem Town Amusement Park. Has seven major rides and three kiddie rides; picnic area, refreshments. Open year-round, daily. Admission: free. Anchorage, 100 Fireweed Lane.

Amusements

Arizona

Legend City. Features rides, boat rides and western stunt show; restaurant, shops, petting zoo, refreshments. Open March through December, daily. Admission: adults 50 cents, children under 13, 25 cents; rides extra. Tempe, off US-80, US-60, US-89 and Interstate 17.

Old Tucson. A western theme park with rides, exhibits and gunfights; restaurants, ice-cream parlor, picnic facilities, arcade. Open year-round, daily. Admission charged. Tucson, off US-80-89, Interstate 10, on Kinney Road.

Phoenix Zoo. Exhibits of more than 1,200 species of mammals, birds and reptiles; special feature is Arizona exhibit. Open year-round, daily. Adults $2, children 4 to 14, 75 cents. Phoenix, 5810 East Van Buren, in Papago Park.

Rawhide. A small park featuring kiddie rides; refreshment stands, museum, stage shows. Open year-round, daily. Admission: free. Scottsdale, 23023 North Scottsdale Road.

Arkansas

Animal Wonderland. Offers dolphin and exotic bird shows and animal training demonstrations; petting zoo, aviary. Open Memorial Day through Labor Day, daily, 10 a.m. to 5 p.m. Adults $3.50, children 2 to 11, $1.50. Hot Springs, two miles west, on US-270.

Arkansas Alligator Farm. Alligator exhibits and shows. Open year-round, daily, 9:30 a.m. to 4 p.m. (weather permitting). Adults $1.25, children 3 to 11, 75 cents. Hot Springs, 847 Whittington Avenue.

Dogpatch USA. This 1,000-acre park features many of the characters from the famous L'il Abner comic strip; rides, musical entertainment, animal shows, craft exhibits. Open May through September, daily, 9 a.m. to 6 p.m. Adults $7.95, children 4 to 12 and senior citizens, $6.95. Dogpatch, one mile north off State Route 7.

Magic Springs Family Fun Park. Features several rides and kiddie rides; shows, arts and crafts, refreshment stands. Open Memorial Day through Labor Day, daily, 10 a.m. to 8 p.m. Adults $6.50, children 3 to 11, $5.50, senior citizens $4.50. Hot Springs, on US-70, at 2001 Highway 70E.

California

Disneyland. More than 50 major attractions in the various "kingdoms;" kiddie rides and shows; restaurants, refreshment stands, shops, holiday theme celebrations. Open year-round; mid-June through Labor Day, daily, 9 a.m. to midnight; remainder of year, Wednesday to Sunday, 9 a.m. to 6 p.m. General admission: adults $6, children 12 to 17, $5, 3 to 11, $3; ticket books may be purchased to include admission to a certain number of rides and attractions. Anaheim, off Interstate 5.

Frontier Village. Offers 15 major rides and three games; restaurant, refreshment stand, picnic area, petting zoo, arcade. Open year-round, daily. Admission charged. San Jose, 4885 Monterey Road.

Knotts Berry Farm. An Old West theme park that features a number of major rides, kiddie rides and live entertainment; restaurants, refreshment stands, shops. Open Memorial Day through Labor Day, Tuesday to Sunday, 9 a.m. to 1 a.m.; remainder of year, Monday, Tuesday, Friday and Saturday, 10 a.m. to midnight. General admission: adults $6.95, children 3 to 11, $4.50. Buena Park, off Interstate 5, at 8039 Beach Boulevard.

Lion Country Safari. Offers the opportunity for eyeball-to-eyeball confrontations with free-roaming wild African, Asian and American animals while you drive your RV through the park. Open year-round, daily. Admission charged. Irvine, off Interstate 5.

Los Angeles Zoo. This 113-acre facility features five continental areas with more than 2,000 mammals, birds and reptiles in natural settings. Open year-round, daily, 10 a.m. to 5 p.m. Adults $2, children 5 to 15, $1. Los Angeles, near the junction of the Golden State and Ventura Freeways.

Marineland. Aquatic shows featuring killer whales, sea lions and dolphins; aquarium exhibits, entertainment featuring Hanna-Barbera cartoon characters. Open year-round, daily, 10 a.m. to 7 p.m. Adults $5.95, children 3 to 11, $3.95. Palos Verdes Peninsula, on Palos Verdes Drive.

Marine World — Africa USA. Features major rides and kiddie rides as well as animal exhibits and shows; refreshment stands, shops. Open year-round, daily; weekends only from Labor Day to Memorial Day. Redwood City, on Marine World Parkway.

Marriott's Great America. Features more than 20 major rides, kiddie rides and games; refreshment stands, restaurants, arcades, miniature golf, stage shows, music. Open year-round, daily; weekends only from October 5 to May 26. Adults $10.95, children 4 to 11, $9.95, senior citizens $8.50. Santa Clara, at junction of Great America Parkway and US-101.

San Diego Wild Animal Park. An 1,800-acre wildlife preserve associated with the world-famous San Diego Zoo. Visitors view more than 2,000 different species from a tram that circles the park; restaurant, shops, refreshment stands. Open year-round, daily. Admission charged. Escondido, on State Route 78.

San Diego Zoo. This is one of the largest zoos in the world, featuring more than 5,000 animals of some 1,600 species in displays that depict their native habitats. Open year-round, daily, 9 a.m. to 7 p.m. Adults $3, under 16 free if accompanied by an adult. San Diego, in Balboa Park.

Sea World. An oceanarium and marine life center offering shows of killer whales, sea lions and dolphins, plus exhibits of other aquatic life; restaurant, refreshment stands, shops. Open year-round, daily, 9 a.m. to sunset. Adults $7.95, children 4 to 12, $4.95. San Diego, in Mission Bay Park.

Six Flags Magic Mountain. A 200-acre amusement park and entertainment complex featuring major rides that include the huge Colossus roller coaster and the Revolution; restaurants, refreshment stands, crafts demonstrations, live entertainment. Open year-round, daily (in summer), 9 a.m. to midnight; remainder of year, weekends and holidays. Valencia, off Interstate 5.

Universal Studios. A two-part tour that includes self-guided tours of the Entertainment Center and tram tours featuring live shows and demonstrations. Open year-round, daily, 10 a.m. to 3 p.m. Adults $7.50, children 3 to 11, $5.50. Universal City, off Hollywood Freeway.

Universal Studios, California's backlot entertainment center, is the home of the silver screen's most famous and frightening movie monsters.

Colorado

Denver Zoo. Offers an extensive collection of mammals, birds and reptiles in natural habitat displays. Open year-round, daily, 10 a.m. to 5 p.m. Adults $1.50, children 6 to 16, 25 cents. Denver, in City Park, between 17th and 23rd Avenues.

Elitch Gardens. Features 17 major rides and 12 kiddie rides; refreshment stands, restaurant, arcade, miniature golf, stage shows, picnic area. Open May through September 14, daily. Admission charged. Denver, 4620 West 38th Avenue.

Fun Junction Amusement Park. Features 10 major rides, kiddie rides and games; refreshment stand, picnic area. Open April through September, daily. Grand Junction, 2878 North Avenue.

Lakeside Amusement Park. Features 26 major rides, 16 kiddie rides, games and fun house; refreshment stands, restaurant, arcade, picnic area. Open year-round, daily. 4601 Sheridan Boulevard.

Connecticut

Lake Quassapaug Amusement Park. Features 10 major rides, kiddie rides and games; arcade, miniature golf, refreshment stands, restaurant, picnic area. Open April through September, daily. Admission free. Middlebury, off State Route 64.

Ocean Beach Park. Features 13 major rides and kiddie rides; refreshment stands, restaurant, arcade, miniature golf, picnic area. Open Memorial Day through Labor Day. New London, off Interstate 95.

Willington Wild Animal Farm. Features one of Connecticut's largest wildlife displays. Open year-round, daily, 10 a.m. to 6 p.m. Adults $2.25, children under 11, $1.25. Willington, off Interstate 86E.

Delaware

Funland. Features four major rides and eight kiddie rides; arcade, refreshment stand. Open May through September 10, daily. Admission free. Rehoboth Beach, Delaware Avenue and Boardwalk.

Florida

Busch Gardens. Features six major rides and kiddie rides with several bird and animal exhibits; restaurant, refreshment stands, stage shows, crafts. Open year-round, daily. Admission charged. Tampa, 3000 Busch Boulevard.

Lion Country Safari. A drive-thru wild animal park that also offers rides; refreshment stand, restaurant, picnic area. Open year-round, daily. Loxahatchee, on State Route 80.

Marineland of Florida. Killer whale, sea lion and dolphin shows with several marine exhibits; swimming beach, picnic area. Open year-round, daily. Admission charged. St. Augustine, on State Route 1.

Miracle Strip Amusement Park. Features 16 major rides, 10 kiddie rides and three fun houses; refreshment stands, restaurant, arcade, miniature golf, swimming beach, shops. Open year-round, daily. Panama City, 12001 West Highway 98.

Sea World of Florida. Aquatic shows and exhibits; restaurants, refreshment stands, gift shops, live entertainment. Open year-round, daily. Admission charged. Orlando, 7007 Sea World Drive.

Walt Disney World. Features more than 150 rides in a 3,000-acre complex; restaurants, refreshment stands, arcades, swimming, picnic area, campground, live entertainment. Open year-round, daily, 9 a.m. to 7 p.m. Adults $9.50, children 12 to 17, $8.50, 3 to 11, $7.50, under 3 free. Lake Buena Vista, on US-192.

Georgia

Holiday Beach. Features 12 major rides, kiddie rides and games; refreshment stands, picnic area, ski shows, live entertainment, swimming. Open year-round, daily. Admission charged. Douglas, on Highway 158 West.

Kingdoms 3. Features 15 major rides, kiddie rides, games and fun house; refreshment stands, restaurants, drive-thru animal park, zoo, picnic area. Open year-round, daily. Admission charged. Stockbridge.

Six Flags Over Georgia. A 300-acre park offering nearly 50 rides and a number of games; refreshment stands, restaurants, arcades, exhibits, stage shows, fireworks, picnic area. Open year-round, daily, 9 a.m. to 6:30 p.m. (until midnight in summer). Admission: $7.95. Atlanta, off Interstate 20.

Stone Mountain. A 3,200-acre park that is one of the state's most popular attractions. A huge sculpture of Civil War heroes carved on the face of the mountain is the park's most outstanding feature; restaurants, refreshment stands, swimming, picnic area, campground. Open year-round, daily, 10 a.m. to 5:30 p.m.; until 9 p.m. in summer. Adults $7.95, children 4 to 11, $4.95.

Hawaii

Paradise Park. A 15-acre park that features a number of gardens, hundreds of colorful birds and a variety of shows and exhibits; restaurant, refreshment stand, gift shop. Open year-round, daily, 9:30 a.m. to 5:30 p.m. Adults $3.95, children 4 to 12, $2.25. Honolulu, on Manoa Road. (Oahu)

Sea Life Park. Aquatic exhibits and whale and dolphin shows in one of Hawaii's most popular parks; restaurant, refreshment stand, shops, crafts. Open year-round, daily, from 9:30 a.m. Waimanalo, on State Route 72. (Oahu)

Idaho

Funtasia. Features six major rides, kiddie rides and games; refreshment stand, arcade, swimming, picnic area. Open May through September, daily. Lava Hot Springs, off Interstate 15.

Ross Park Pleasureland. Features 10 rides and games; refreshment stand, swimming, arcade, miniature golf, zoo. Open May through September, daily. Pocatello, off Interstate 15.

Illinois

Adventure Land. Features 25 major rides, 12 kiddie rides and 15 games; refreshment stands, stage shows, arcade, picnic area. Open May through Labor Day, daily. Addison, on State Route 20.

Marriott's Great America. Features 31 major rides and games; restaurants, refreshment stands, shops, arcade, crafts, stage shows. Open April through mid-October, daily. Adults $9.90, children 4 to 11, $8.80. Gurnee, off Interstate 94.

Old Chicago. A 57-acre facility that offers puppet and magic shows in a 19th-century setting; shops, craft displays. Open year-round, daily, 11 a.m. to 9 p.m.

Adults $5.75, children 3 to 11, $4.75. Bolingbrook, at junction of Interstate 55 and State Route 53.

Lincoln Park Zoo. A world-famous zoo noted for its lion, reptile, bird and monkey houses. Open year-round, daily, 9 a.m. to 5 p.m. Free. Chicago, off Lake Shore Drive.

Playland. Features 18 major rides, 15 kiddie rides and several games; refreshment stands, arcade, picnic area. Open April through October, daily. Admission charged. Willow Springs, 79 LaGrange Road.

Indiana

Adventureland. Features 10 major rides, kiddie rides and games; refreshment stand, restaurant, arcades, petting zoo, picnic area. Open year-round. Admission charged. North Webster, on US-13.

Enchanted Forest. Features 16 major rides, kiddie rides, games and fun house; restaurant, refreshment stand, arcades, gift shop, picnic area. Open May through Labor Day, daily. Admission charged. Chesterton, at US-20 and State Route 49.

Indiana Beach. Features 18 major rides, eight kiddie rides and games; restaurant, refreshment stands, arcade, swimming, miniature golf, bands, fireworks, picnic area. Open May through September, daily. Monticello, 306 Indiana Beach Road.

Mesker Zoo. Animals displayed in natural habitats; monkeys live on a concrete replica of the *Santa Maria* in the center of a lake. Open year-round, daily, 9 a.m. to 5 p.m. Adults $1.50, children under 14, 75 cents; free for everyone from October 15 through April 15. Evansville, on St. Joseph Avenue.

Iowa

Adventureland. Features 16 major rides, kiddie rides and games; refreshment stands, arcade, swimming, musical entertainment, picnic area, camping. Open Memorial Day through Labor Day, daily. Admission charged. Des Moines, off Interstate 80.

Des Moines Children's Zoo. More than 150 mammals, birds and reptiles; elephant and burro rides. Open Memorial Day through September, 10 a.m. to 9 p.m. Adults 50 cents, children 25 cents. Des Moines, 7401 SW Ninth Street.

Lake Okoboji Amusement Park. Features 12 major rides, kiddie rides, games and fun house; restaurant, refreshment stands, arcades, stage shows, musical entertainment, picnic area. Open May through September, daily. Admission free. Arnolds Park, off US-71.

Kansas

Joyland. Features 12 major rides, kiddie rides and games; refreshment stands, picnic area, arcade, roller rink, stage shows, puppet shows. Open March 15 through October 15, daily. Admission charged. Wichita, 2801 South Hillside.

Joyland Park. Features 10 major rides and kiddie rides; refreshment stand, arcade, miniature golf. Open March through September, daily. Admission free. Topeka, 27th and California Avenues.

Topeka Zoological Park. Offers animal and reptile exhibits and features an enclosed tropical rain forest. Open year-round, daily, 9 a.m. to 5 p.m. Adults $1, children 4 to 16, 25 cents. Topeka, in Gage Park, at Sixth and Gage Streets.

Kentucky

Beach Bend Park. Features 25 major rides, kiddie rides, games and fun house; restaurants, refreshment stands, swimming, arcade, miniature golf, roller rink, picnic area, camping. Open Easter through October, daily. Admission charged. Bowling Green, off Interstate 65.

Louisville Zoological Gardens. Offers a large display of mammals, birds and reptiles plus a children's zoo; train rides. Open year-round, daily, 10 a.m. to 6 p.m.; winter months Tuesday to Sunday. Adults $1.50, children 4 to 12, 50 cents, senior citizens 75 cents. Louisville, six miles southeast at 1100 Trevillian Way.

Noble Park Funland. Features 11 major rides, kiddie rides, games and fun house; refreshment stands, picnic area, swimming, fireworks. Open April through September, daily. Admission free. Paducah, off Interstate 24.

Louisiana

Thunderbird Park. Features eight major rides and four kiddie rides; restaurant, refreshment stands, arcade, swimming, miniature golf, crafts, picnic area, camping. Open year-round, daily. Admission charged. Denham Springs, on State Route 1019.

Pontchartrain Beach. Features 18 major rides, seven kiddie rides and games; restaurant, refreshment stands, arcade, shooting gallery, magic show, diving show, gift shop. Open March through Labor Day, daily; weekends only March to Memorial Day. New Orleans, Elysian Fields Avenue and Lakeshore Drive.

Maine

Animal Forest. Features eight major rides, kiddie rides and zoo; refreshment stands, arcade. Open Memorial Day through Labor Day, daily. Admission free. York Beach, off State Route 1.

Palace Amusement Park. Features 12 major rides, kiddie rides, fun house and games; refreshment stands, arcade, shooting gallery. Open Memorial Day through Labor Day, daily. Admission free. Old Orchard Beach, off State Route 1.

Maryland

Baltimore Zoo. Offers animal and bird exhibits and reptile house; Safari tour train. Open year-round, daily, 10 a.m. to 4:30 p.m. Adults 75 cents, children under 14, 25 cents. Baltimore, in Druid Hill Park.

Playland Amusement Park. Features 12 major rides, kiddie rides and games; restaurant, refreshment stands, miniature golf, picnic area. Open April 30 through September 15, daily. Admission charged. Ocean City, off US-50.

Spectacular Rides. Features 15 major rides, four kiddie rides and games; refreshment stands, picnic area, arcade. Open May through Labor Day, daily. Bryans Road, on State Route 1.

Trimper Rides. Features 14 major rides, 12 kiddie rides, games and fun house; restaurant, refreshment stands, swimming. Open year-round, daily. Admission free. Ocean City, on Boardwalk at Division Street.

Massachusetts

Lincoln Park. Features 24 major rides, 25 kiddie rides, fun houses and games; restaurant, refreshment stands, arcade, roller rink, miniature golf, zoo, picnic area. Open May through September, daily. Admission free. North Dartmouth, on State Road.

Paragon Park. Features 27 major rides, kiddie rides and games; restaurant, refreshment stands, arcade, miniature golf, live entertainment, picnic area. Open April through Labor Day, daily. Admission free. Hull, 175 Nantasket Avenue.

Riverside Park. Features 50 major rides, kiddie rides and games; restaurant, refreshment stands, arcade, miniature golf, live entertainment, picnic area. Open May through September, daily. Admission charged. Agawam, on Main Street.

Sealand of Cape Cod. Dolphin shows and aquatic exhibits; refreshment stand, gift shop. Open May through September, daily. Admission charged. Brewster, off State Route 6A.

Michigan

Bob-Lo Island. Features 30 major rides, 11 kiddie rides, fun house and games; restaurant, refreshment stands, arcade, roller rink, zoo, picnic area. Open March 15 through Labor Day, daily. Admission charged. Detroit, at Michigan Avenue and State Route 18.

Detroit Zoo. Mammal, bird and reptile exhibits grouped by continent in surroundings that approximate the natural habitat; miniature railway. Open year-round, daily, 10 a.m. to 5 p.m. Adults $2, children 6 to 12, 75 cents, senior citizens and handicapped free. Near Detroit at Royal Oak, off State Route 1.
Edgewater Park. Features 23 major rides, six kiddie rides, fun house and games; restaurant, refreshment stands, arcade, roller rink, miniature golf, picnic area. Open April through Labor Day, daily. Admission charged. Detroit, 23500 West 7 Mile Road.

Minnesota

Minnesota Zoological Gardens. Mammals, birds and reptiles; refreshment stands, exhibits. Open year-round, daily. Admission charged. Apple Valley, 12101 Johnny Cake Ridge Road.

Valleyfair. Features 12 major rides, four kiddie rides, fun house and games; restaurants, refreshment stands, arcade, zoo, puppet show, picnic area, camping. Open Memorial Day through Labor Day, 10 a.m. to 10 p.m. Adults $7, children 4 to 11, $6, senior citizens $6. Shakopee, on State Route 101.

Mississippi

Biloxi-Gulfport Amusement Park. Features seven major rides, six kiddie rides and games; refreshment stand, swimming, fireworks, picnic area. Open year-round, daily. Admission free. Biloxi, 3315 West Beach Boulevard.

Missouri

Fairyland Park. Features 26 major rides, 10 kiddie rides, fun house and games; restaurant, refreshment stands, arcade, shooting gallery, swimming, live entertainment, picnic area. Open year-round, daily, from May through September; weekends, remainder of year. Admission charged. Kansas City, 7501 Prospect Avenue.

St. Louis Zoo. One of the most famous zoos in the world offering a large variety of mammals, birds and reptiles in natural habitat areas; chimpanzee shows, train rides. Open year-round, daily, 9 a.m. to 5 p.m. Free. St. Louis, in Forest Park.

Six Flags Over Mid-America. Features 28 major rides, kiddie rides, fun houses and games; restaurants, refreshment stands, ice-cream parlors, live entertainment, picnic area. Open mid-May through October, daily, 10 a.m. to 10 p.m. Admission: All-In-One Ticket $8.50, two-day ticket $12.75, children under 3 free. Eureka, off Interstate 44 (west of St. Louis).

Worlds of Fun. A theme park featuring a wide variety of rides and attractions including the Singapore Sling, Screamroller and Viking Voyager Flume; restaurants, refreshment stands, live entertainment, shops, picnic area. Open Memorial Day through Labor Day, daily, 10 a.m. to 10 p.m. Adults $8.50, children 3 to 11, $7.50. Kansas City, off Interstate 435.

Montana

Frontier Town. A western theme town featuring a museum, exhibits and gift shop. Open May through September, daily. Admission charged. Helena, off US-12.

Nebraska

Peony Park. Features 12 major rides, kiddie rides and games; refreshment stands, arcade, miniature golf, swimming. Open May through September, daily, 2 p.m. to 10 p.m. Admission: $6.50, or general admission with individual ride tickets. Omaha, off Interstate 680 at Dodge Street exit.

Nevada

Old Nevada Enterprises. A western theme facility featuring exhibits, arcades and stage shows; restaurants, refreshment stands. Open year-round, daily. Admission charged. Bonnie Springs.

New Hampshire

Canobie Lake Park. Features 17 major rides, 12 kiddie rides and games; restaurant, refreshment stands, arcade, roller rink, miniature golf, lake cruises, live entertainment, picnic area. Open May through Labor Day, daily. Admission charged. Salem, on North Policy Street.

Enchanted Forest. Features five major rides, kiddie rides and fun house; refreshment stand, miniature golf, arcade, zoo, picnic area. Open June 15 through Labor Day. Admission free. Laconia, off US-3.

New Jersey

Bertrand Island Park. Features 18 major rides, kiddie rides, fun house and games; restaurant, refreshment stands, arcade, miniature golf, picnic area. Open May through Labor Day, daily. Admission charged. Mount Arlington, off Interstate 80.

Casino Pier and Pool. Features 26 major rides, 20 kiddie rides, fun house and games; restaurants, refreshment stands, arcade, shooting gallery, miniature golf. Open May 15 through September 15, daily. Admission free. Seaside Heights, Grant and Boardwalk.

Great Adventure. Features 29 major rides, seven kiddie rides and games; restaurants, refreshment stands, arcade, shooting gallery, live entertainment, picnic area. Open May through September, daily; weekends April and October. Admission charged. Jackson, on State Route 528.

Sportland Pier. Features 16 major rides, six kiddie rides and games; restaurant, refreshment stands, swimming, slides. Open year-round, daily. Admission free. Wildwood, 23rd and Boardwalk.

New Mexico

Carlsbad Living Desert Zoological Park. Features native wildlife exhibits and several thousand varieties of cactus and other southwest vegetation. Open year-round, daily, 8 a.m. to sunset. Adults $1, children 7 to 17, 50 cents. Carlsbad, on US-285.

Uncle Cliff's Familyland. Features 11 major rides, nine kiddie rides and games; refreshment stands, arcade, miniature golf, picnic area. Open April through October 15, daily. Admission charged. Albuquerque, off Interstate 40 and Interstate 25.

New York

Bronx Zoo. Offers a large collection of mammals, birds and reptiles, as well as a children's zoo; animal rides, train rides. Open year-round, daily from May 1 through October, 10 a.m. to 5:30 p.m.; Friday to Monday remainder of year. Adults $1.50, children 6 to 12, 75 cents.

The Bronx, Fordham Road and Southern Boulevard.

Crystal Beach Amusement Park. Features 26 major rides, kiddie rides and games; refreshment stands, tavern, restaurant, arcade, shooting gallery, picnic area. Open May through Labor Day, daily. Admission charged. Buffalo, off State Route 5.

Fantasy Island. Features 14 major rides, 10 kiddie rides and games; restaurants, refreshment stands, arcade, shooting gallery, miniature golf, petting zoo, puppet shows, fireworks. Open June 25 through Labor Day, daily. Admission charged. Grand Island, 2400 Grand Island Boulevard.

New York Aquarium. Aquatic exhibits, dolphin shows; refreshment stands, restaurant. Open year-round, daily, 9 a.m. to 4 p.m. Admission charged. Brooklyn, Boardwalk at West Eighth Street.

Storytown USA. Features 17 major rides, kiddie rides and games; restaurants, refreshment stands, arcade, shooting gallery, zoo, thrill show, western shows, picnic area. Open Memorial Day through October, daily. Admission charged. Lake George, off Interstate 87.

Westchester Playland. Features 28 major rides, 19 kiddie rides and games; restaurant, refreshment stands, shooting gallery, swimming, fishing, picnic area. Open May 22 through Labor Day, daily. Admission free. Rye, off Interstate 95.

North Carolina

Asheville Recreation Park and Zoo. Features 10 major rides, kiddie rides, games and zoo; refreshment stand, arcade, shooting gallery, picnic area. Open Memorial Day through Labor Day, daily. Admission free. Asheville, on Old Swannanoa Road.

Carowinds. Features 20 major rides and kiddie rides; restaurants, refreshment stands, arcade, shooting gallery, live entertainment. Open Memorial Day

through Labor Day, daily. Admission charged. Charlotte, off Interstate 77.

Frontierland. Features 11 major rides and kiddie rides; restaurant, refreshment stand, arcade, stage shows, picnic area. Open Memorial Day through Labor Day, daily. Admission free. Cherokee, on US-19.

North Dakota

Rough Ride Country. Features trail rides through the badlands and several exhibits; restaurant, miniature golf, zoo, stage shows. Open Memorial Day through Labor Day, daily. Admission free. Medora, off Interstate 94.

Ohio

Americana. Features 27 major rides, 12 kiddie rides, fun house and games; restaurants, refreshment stands, arcade, shooting gallery, miniature golf, zoo, picnic area. Open May through Labor Day, daily. Admission charged. Middletown, 5757 Hamilton-Middletown Road.

Cincinnati Zoo. Features six major rides, kiddie rides and mammal, bird and reptile exhibits; restaurant, refreshment stands, arcade, shooting gallery, picnic area. Open year-round, daily. Admission charged. Cincinnati, 3400 Vine Street.

Geauga Lake. Features 32 major rides, 20 kiddie rides and games; restaurants, refreshment stands, arcade, shooting gallery, miniature golf, picnic area. Open May 1 through September 15, daily. Admission charged. Aurora, 1060 Aurora Road.

Sea World of Ohio. Aquatic shows and exhibits; restaurants, refreshment stands, deer park, Japanese Pearl Divers, penguin shows. Open Memorial Day through Labor Day, daily. Admission charged. Aurora, 1100 Sea World Drive.

Oklahoma

Spring Lake. Features 17 major rides, eight kiddie rides, fun house and games; restaurant, refreshment stands, arcade, miniature golf, circus acts, picnic area. Open year-round, daily. Admission charged. Oklahoma City, 1800 Springlake Drive.

Oregon

Oaks Amusement Park. Features 17 major rides, kiddie rides and games; refreshment stands, arcade, roller rink, picnic area. Open Memorial Day through Labor Day, daily; remainder of year, weekends. Admission free. Portland, off Interstate 5.

Oregon Undersea Gardens. Underwater aquarium, scuba diving shows. Open year-round, daily. Admission charged. Newport, 267 Southwest Bay Boulevard.

Pennsylvania

Dorney Park Coaster. Features 25 major rides, kiddie rides and games; restaurant, refreshment stands, arcade, shooting gallery, stage shows, zoo, picnic area. Open year-round, daily; weekends only September 15 through April. Admission free. Allentown, 3830 Dorney Park Road.

Conneaut Lake Park. Features 26 major rides, 12 kiddie rides and games; restaurants, refreshment stands, arcade, miniature golf, zoo, picnic area. Open Memorial Day through Labor Day, daily. Admission free. Conneaut Lake, off US-6-322.

Kennywood Park. Features 38 major rides, 15 kiddie rides and games; restaurant, refreshment stands, miniature golf, shooting gallery, picnic area. Open mid-May through September, daily. Admission charged. West Mifflin, 4800 Kennywood Boulevard.

Magic Valley. Features 10 major rides and kiddie rides; restaurant, refreshment stands, arcade, shooting gallery, zoo, ice skating rink, ski slopes, picnic area. Open Memorial Day through Labor Day, daily; Labor Day to November, weekends only. Admission charged. Bushkill, off US-209.

Philadelphia Zoo. Wide variety of mammals, birds and reptiles, plus a children's zoo; animal shows, refreshment stands. Open year-round, daily. Admission charged. Philadelphia, on Girard Avenue.

Rhode Island

Rocky Point Park. Features 29 major rides, 12 kiddie rides, fun house and games; restaurants, refreshment stands, arcade, shooting gallery, swimming, miniature golf, zoo, aquarium, live entertainment. Open April through September, daily. Admission charged. Warwick, on Rocky Point Road.

South Carolina

Grand Strand Amusement Park. Features 11 major rides and kiddie rides; refreshment stands, arcade, swimming, live entertainment. Open year-round, daily. Admission free. Myrtle Beach, 408 South Ocean Boulevard.

Myrtle Beach Pavilion and Amusement Park. Features 15 major rides, kiddie rides and fun house; restaurants, refreshment stands, arcade, miniature golf, picnic area. Open year-round, daily. Admission free. Myrtle Beach, off US-17.

South Dakota

Story Book Island. Children's fairy-tale theme park; picnic area. Open Memorial Day through Labor Day, daily. Free. Rapid City, Sheridan Lake Drive.

Tennessee

Chilhowee Park. Features 14 major rides, 12 kiddie rides, fun house and games; refreshment stands, arcade, roller rink, miniature golf, picnic area. Open year-round, daily. Admission free. Knoxville, on Magnolia Avenue.

Opryland USA. One of the South's most popular theme parks featuring 15 major rides, kiddie rides and fun house; restaurants, refreshment stands, arcade, shooting gallery, zoo, live entertainment. Open year-round, daily, 10 a.m. to 10 p.m. Admission: $9.75 includes all attractions, children under 3 free. Nashville, on Briley Parkway.

Texas

Astroworld. Features 26 major rides, 12 kiddie rides and games; restaurants, refreshment stands, arcades, shooting gallery, zoo, picnic area. Open mid-March through Thanksgiving, daily. Admission charged. Houston, 90001 Kirby Drive.

Six Flags Over Texas. A popular and large amusement park featuring 33 major rides, kiddie rides and games; restaurants, refreshment stands, arcade, shooting gallery, live entertainment, picnic area. Open mid-March through November, daily. Admission: $7.95 for all attractions, children under 3 free. Arlington, off Dallas-Fort Worth Turnpike.

Zoo World. Animal exhibits, plus amusement park attractions featuring 10 major rides, kiddie rides and games; refreshment stands, restaurant, swimming, picnic area. Open March through November, daily. Admission free. Abilene, in Nelson Park.

Utah

Lagoon. Features 24 major rides, 10 kiddie rides, fun house and games; restaurant, refreshment stands, arcade, shooting gallery, miniature golf, picnic area. Open mid-April through October, daily. Admission free. Salt Lake City, off Interstate 80 and Interstate 15.

Vermont

Steamtown. Features a large collection of steam locomotives and tours aboard a 70-year-old steam train; refreshment stands, exhibits, picnic area. Open Memorial Day to mid-October, daily, 9 a.m. to 6 p.m. Admission: adults $5.95, children 3 to 11, $3.25. Bellows Falls, on US-5.

Virginia

Busch Gardens. Features 14 major rides, kiddie rides and fun house; refreshment stands, restaurant, arcade, shooting gallery, zoo, picnic area. Open April through October, daily. Admission charged. Williamsburg, on US-60.

Kings Dominion. Features 26 major rides, kiddie rides and a zoo-preserve; restaurants, refreshment stands, arcade. Open Memorial Day through Labor Day, daily. Admission charged. Doswell, north of Richmond on Interstate 95.

Washington

Fun Forest. Features 16 major rides and six kiddie rides; refreshment stands, arcades, miniature golf. Open March through November, daily. Admission free. Seattle, 370 Thomas Street.

West Virginia

Camden Park. Features 11 major rides, kiddie rides and games; restaurant, refreshment stands, arcade, shooting gallery, roller rink, miniature golf, zoo, picnic area. Open year-round, daily; October through April, weekends only. Admission charged. Huntington, on US-60 West.

Wisconsin

Bay Beach Amusement Park. Features seven major rides and kiddie rides; restaurant, refreshment stands, wildlife sanctuary, picnic area. Open April through Labor Day, daily. Admission free. Green Bay, on East Shore Drive.

Riverview. Features 12 major rides and 14 kiddie rides; refreshment stands, arcade, shooting gallery, miniature golf, stage shows, picnic area. Open mid-May through Labor Day, daily; weekends only until October 15. Admission free. Wisconsin Dells, on US-12 and US-23.

Ron and Judy's Amusement Park. Features 15 major rides, kiddie rides and fun house; refreshment stands, arcade, shooting gallery, miniature golf, stage shows, picnic area. Open May 15 through Labor Day, daily. Admission free. Wisconsin Dells, on US-12.

Wyoming

Playland. Features five major rides, kiddie rides and games; cafe, refreshment stands, miniature golf, picnic area. Open mid-May through Labor Day, daily. Admission free. Cheyenne, in Lions Park.

The miniature bi-planes of Opryland's Barnstormer soar above Eagle Lake suspended from a 100-foot tower. There are nineteen rides at Tennessee's Opryland that range in thrills from a gently rocking train ride around the park, to the terrifying corkscrew loops of the Wabash Cannonball, to the plane ride shown here, where cables drop twelve Waldo Pepper-vintage planes in a rotating, stomach-grabbing free fall.

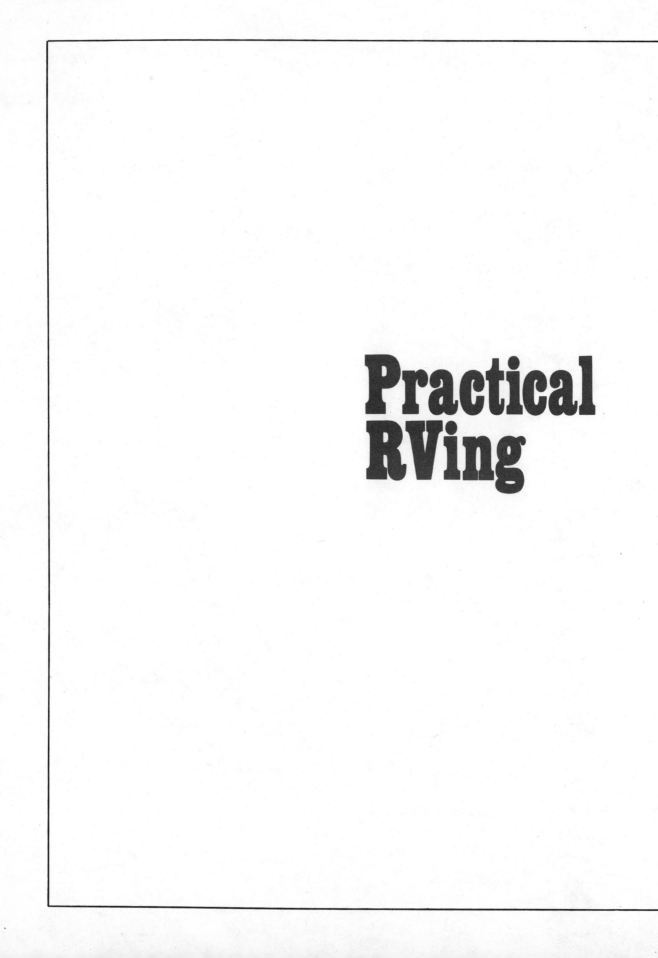

Practical RVing

While travel provides an opportunity for a respite from the ordinary concerns of everyday life, it also has its practical side. In the pages that follow you will find a wide variety of information; a practical guide for the RVer that will help you get the most out of your RV travel experience.

Fuel conservation is the prime consideration of every traveler today, and to help you stretch your fuel dollar we offer *Tips for Conserving Energy on the Road.* In this list compiled by RV experts you'll find tips that will help you put your rig in shape for fuel efficient travel, as well as provide you with information on how to conserve energy at home while you are traveling.

You'll also find here a list of *Foul Weather Driving Tips* to assure your safety in bad weather, guidelines for driving defensively, suggestions on how to deal with driving emergencies, and tips for troubleshooting on-the-road breakdowns. CBers can turn to the handy *Ten Codes* reference list for guidance in communicating with their good buddies, and amateur meteorologists will find enough basic weather information to allow them to predict weather changes with reasonable accuracy.

If you're traveling with children, your hours on the road can be much more enjoyable if you follow some of the handy hints outlined in our *Traveling With Children* section. And for your personal well-being we suggest that you consider adopting an exercise program such as that outlined in *Shape Up.* Good physical conditioning can go a long way towards relieving the effects of long hours on the road and can assure that you'll have the energy to get the maximum enjoyment out of your travels.

Finally, to help you guard against unscrupulous repair facilities as well as potential thieves we have included a comprehensive section on *Avoiding Highway Robbery* and *Deterring the RV Thief.* Although the chances of your being victimized are relatively small, an ounce of prevention just may mean the difference between a vacation cut short and one that is enjoyed to its fullest.

Driving Tips

It's probably safe to say that RVers are better than average drivers; pulling a trailer or maneuvering a motorhome requires a bit more skill than driving an automobile. Like the truck driver who must periodically sharpen his driving know-how, RVers need to review the techniques of safe driving from time to time. The following driving tips should help you hone your skills.

One of the most effective techniques that should be learned and practiced to perfection by the defensive driver is communication with other drivers by the use of lights, horn, hand and body signals.

Frequently accidents are caused by the things that happen during lane changes and left turns. These accidents occur even though one gives the proper signals. When turning or changing lanes, follow these procedures: First check your rearview mirror, then your left mirror, right mirror, then your left again. Quickly peek over your left shoulder to see that a motorcyclist or small car is not in your blind spot. If all is clear, indicate that you are going to make a left turn by activating your left turn signal. Then drift to the left an inch or two, but do not cross the center line. This will warn any driver behind that you are going to turn left and make your flashing left turn light visible to cars farther back. Finally, tap your brake pedal several times in rapid succession. Take one last quick look in the mirror and if it's clear, complete your turn.

Danger Warnings

If there is an emergency situation in your lane, you must get your own vehicle under control and then be concerned that following vehicles do not surprise you and rear-end your RV. To warn them rapidly, pump your brakes not only to stop your vehicle but also warn the drivers behind you that something is wrong. Even after you are stopped, continue pumping your brake pedal, turn on your emergency flashers, even roll down your window and wave your arms in a flag-down motion until you have a buffer of several vehicles behind you.

If a truck or car approaches you and is flashing its lights, slow down and prepare to make an emergency stop. This is the signal that some truckers use to warn of trouble ahead. On the other hand, if you observe an accident in the opposite lanes, give oncoming drivers this warning by flashing your own lights.

The lure of the road and the escape from the city are unmistakable; safe driving only adds to the further enhancement of getting away from it all.

Passing Language

Most RV drivers stay well within the speed limit. Although you may be driving at or near the speed limit, if a faster driver is attempting to pass, even if he is breaking the law, you should make every effort to assist him in passing your rig. To put the drivers behind you at ease, let them know that you see them and will assist them. Glance in the rearview mirror, wave and drift slightly to the right. The driver attempting to pass will be able to see approaching traffic in your lane much clearer and also should understand that you are going to help him pass.

If it appears to be unsafe after you drift to the right, move back to your original track so the following driver does not misinterpret your signal to mean that it's clear. When it is safe to pass, however, more over to the right and allow the vehicle to pass.

If you are traveling in a convoy, leave passing room between vehicles. Several slow-moving vehicles in a row can create an exceptionally hazardous situation. If you travel well below the speed limit, it may be wise to avoid freeways and travel on secondary roads, and if traffic is jamming up behind you, be sure to pull off and allow the faster cars to get by.

How to Get Out

One of the most frustrating driving experiences is to be trapped on a side street waiting to get onto the highway. One effective technique of getting onto the highway is to ask for assistance of highway traffic. Look an approaching driver directly in the eye, smile and wave; often a helpless shrug of the shoulders will convey your message. Seldom will more than a few cars pass before someone will slow down and motion you onto the highway. This kindness deserves another smile, a wave or a friendly toot of the horn.

Never let yourself get trapped in a situation where you don't have an out. Never drive in the pack — a group of vehicles rolling down the freeway where all lanes are full, leaving you no room to maneuver in case of an emergency. If you find yourself in a pack, pull off the road at the first opportunity and let them pass. There is usually a pack, a lot of scattered cars, then another pack. Whenever you observe any of the danger signals or become involved in a dangerous situation, be prepared to stop and always protect yourself from the front and rear. Check on the distance between you and the following vehicle; warn those behind you that something is wrong up ahead by tapping on your brakes rapidly. If necessary, bring your vehicle to a stop, turn on your flashers, but leave room for the driver behind you to stop. Hug the right side of the road as much as possible to allow following cars to see what's ahead and also give you escape room.

One skill that is essential to the defensive driver is eye tracking. The defensive driver is constantly switching his focal point, visually sweeping the road ahead like radar. He looks a half-mile, even a mile ahead to see what's going on, then he sweeps the road from a distance to a near point. Not only does he pay particular attention to his own lane, but also closely observes all other lanes including the shoulder; also, he constantly checks what is going on behind his rig. Thus he can spot danger signals and dangerous situations long before they happen.

Your ears are also important. Although you are often listening to the radio, tape deck or CB, you'd better keep your ears tuned for environmental sounds, horns, train whistles, fast approaching vehicles, etc. More than one RVer has been warned first by his ears before he saw the danger and got on the brakes, often just in time to avoid an accident.

Even your sense of smell can be important. The odors of burning rubber, hot oil and other unusual odors could be a warning that something on the vehicle is not right and should be investigated.

Tips for Conserving Energy

- Start by planning your packing. Put everything you can inside your vehicle. If you put extras like chairs or grills, bikes or boxes, on the outside of your RV, they will offer wind resistance. You'll be bucking the wind and using more fuel to keep up the speed you want.
- When you move out on the road, be sure you have left your fixed home in a "down" condition on energy use. Set the heating — or cooling — system at the minimum while you are away. Turn off the gas appliances not in use during your absence. Make sure there is no running water left behind, and no dripping connection to waste the water supply.
- Know where you are going, even if you intend to wander. Get maps for any area you will cover and pick routes where you won't waste time and energy finding your way or doubling back on a misstep. Planning ahead adds to the joy of the trip.
- Be a weight-watcher. For every 100 pounds of weight, there is a penalty of one percent on your fuel use. Don't carry what you don't really need. Travel light. Remember that water is heavy: A gallon weighs over eight pounds; a 60-gallon tank can hold 500 pounds of water. Carry only enough water for on-the-road use and fill up when you stop. You can get water at any campground. Dump your waste before leaving camp; don't put that extra weight on the road. Keep only what is needed.
- Start off early in the day. There's always less traffic then, and it's cooler in the summertime, so you use your air-conditioning less during the day's trip. Work out your journey to avoid city rush hours; they're just a waste of fuel to you.
- Avoid making a number of different stops or detours for supplies. If you can, pick up your food and drinks, take on water, get fuel, repressure your tires, or refill your LP tank, all in one trip, all at one location or in one small area. Cruising around to different places is wasteful.

Shape Up

Making sure that your RV is in top shape before you start out is part of planning ahead. There is a lot to look for:

- Is the timing on your motor set correctly?
- Is your ignition system working right?
- Is your battery weak or strong? Are the terminals clean and the cells filled?
- Are your wheels balanced and aligned?
- Is your air filter clean?
- Have you had a recent oil change and lubrication?
- Do your tires carry the correct air pressure? Are they in good shape? Do you have a spare and equipment to change a tire if needed?
- Do you have the right tires for the trip? Remember that snow tires add friction and should be on your vehicle only when there is a real need for them. Remember, also, that radial tires give better gas mileage than other types.

All of this adds up to efficiency — and energy saving — before you even start.

Road Sense

- Speed is a gas hog. Be like the turtle: slow and steady wins the race. For each five mph over 50 mph, you drop one mile per gallon. The national speed limit of 55 mph makes sense — to you.

- Get out of town and onto the highway by the most direct route. Stop-and-start city traffic wastes fuel and tries your patience.
- Don't jackrabbit. Fast getaways, skidding stops, bursts of speed and panic braking don't make sense with an RV. Get to your cruising speed, set your cruise control (if you have one), and relax; you're being efficient.
- Pace yourself for red stoplights, hills and other spots where you may have to stop, slow down or accelerate to make a steep upgrade.

Stretch Your Dollars

- Consider the fuel cost of short runs with your RV. Instead of going around the corner, or down the road, for some small item, think of adding a light bicycle — or even a mo-ped — to your standard equipment; it may pay for itself. Either can be equipped with a basket, or saddlebags, for carrying things you buy. If not this, a string bag or light backpack for hand carry can be almost as useful and a lot better exercise. Many campgrounds have a general store where you can buy what you need in one place.
- Turn off your RV's LPG appliances when they are not needed. When there is no work to be done by them, save the energy for some other time and cut your expenses.
- Use your electrical hook-up or your batteries where possible. Generators consume about three-fourths of a gallon of gas per hour.
- Turn off your refrigerator on the way to camp, and on the way home. Its insulation will keep things cool.

Foul Weather Driving Tips

* When driving in fog, slow down, turn your lights and wipers on, use your defroster to cut condensation on the inside of your windshield and remain alert for other cars. If you should have to stop in fog, pull well off the road and be sure to turn on your emergency flashers.

* If you are driving in rain, decrease your speed to avoid hydroplaning. If you feel the front wheels of your rig starting to hydroplane, or "drift," take your foot off the gas and let your rig slow of its own accord. Don't apply the brakes, however, as this may cause you to spin.

* In the rain, allow more space between your RV and the vehicle in front of you.

* In light, misting rain, use your windshield washers to clean the window before you turn on your wipers.

* If you drive through deep water, go slowly; otherwise, splashing water could short out your ignition system.

* After going through deep water, pump your brakes a few times to make sure you haven't lost braking power. If your brakes have faded, shift into low gear and lightly hold the brakes on while you drive. This will help dry them within a short distance.

* Remember to clean your headlights and taillights frequently in bad weather to make sure you'll have adequate lighting power on the road.

Avoiding Highway Robbery

In a recent report to the Senate's subcommittee on commerce, Joan Claybrook, head of the National Highway Traffic Safety Administration, told legislators that an estimated $10 billion is spent annually by motorists for fraudulent, incompetent or unnecessary repairs. If only one-half of that figure is accounted for in fraudulent and unnecessary repairs, the total is still staggering. And it is all too clear that commercial thievery — literally highway robbery — is a big and profitable business.

While no statistics are available to indicate how many victims of dishonest repair shops are RVers, it is safe to assume that RV owners pay a high percentage of these fradulent charges. Because of the nature of their travels and the complexity of their rigs and tow vehicles, RVers are particularly vulnerable and need to be especially wary of the rip-off artists who prey on unsuspecting and trusting motorists.

Currently, tires seem to be the most popular target for roadside fraud. Since a tire's state of wear and potential for trouble is something that can be open to speculation, a dishonest service station attendant — if he doesn't sabotage the tire outright — knows he has a good chance of talking you into buying replacement tires if he can prey upon your concern for the safety and well-being of your passengers. And, since the tires he sells you will most likely have an exorbitant markup, he stands to make a tidy profit off your fears.

While vacationing in the West, one Pennsylvania RVer found out just how effective, and expensive, the typical tire scam can be. After towing his trailer through heavy winds and threatening weather for several miles, the RVer pulled into a service station to fill up and check one tire that seemed a little low on his late-model pickup. That was all it took to give the fast-talking attendant an opening to tell the RVer that none of his tires looked safe enough to withstand the rigors of towing a trailer through bad weather. Unconvinced, the RVer was reluctant to accept the attendant's word; but when he left to use the restroom the attendant told his wife that the condition of their present tires meant that they were almost certain to have an accident. The spiel was so convincing and frightening that by the time he got back to his rig his wife begged him to buy the tires. Caving in to the attendant's high-pressure pitch and his wife's pleas, he had four new tires mounted on the pickup — at a cost of $850. Later, he found he could have purchased the same tires from any number of sources for less than half the amount he was charged at the service station.

Though it may be startling to see how easily this ploy works, what is worse is the tragic effect it can have on a vacation that you may have waited 50 weeks to enjoy.

Think it can't happen to you? Most of us would like to think we aren't that gullible. However, we had an occasion to learn first-hand just how convincing these sharp operators can be when we pulled into a station in Utah and made the mistake of leaving the car while the attendant filled the tank and checked under the hood. When we came back he pointed to some drops of oil running down the shocks, telling us that the shocks were bad and could be extremely dangerous on the rough roads that lay ahead. Since the car was new, with only 5,000 miles on the odometer, we were sure we were being conned. But when he began to elaborate on the dire consequences we faced, a small nagging doubt began to grow. Common sense finally overcame our fears, but if we had been a little less certain — if the car had been a little older — we might have ended up taken for a hefty chunk of cash to buy something we really didn't need.

The fact is many of these unscrupulous station owners and attendants, mechanics and tow truck operators are highly skilled professional con men. Jim Gusea, Wyoming's assistant attorney general for consumer protection, reports there is growing evidence that these people work a circuit in which they follow the peak tourist activity throughout the nation. Gusea said that dishonest garage owners and station operators hire these con artists on a straight commission basis in which they are given a 50% cut of all tires, batteries and other accessories they sell. With most items marked up more than 100% above normal retail, it is not unusual for a crooked attendant to clear more than $100 a day.

Though it is impossible to list all of the ploys, and variations thereof, employed by these retail road agents, some of the more common ones include:

- Pointing to simple weather checking as a sure sign that a tire is about to give out; using an ice pick, or a tire gauge with a point filed on it, to puncture the sidewall of a tire; or running a razor blade between the tread, and then telling you that the tread is starting to separate. If you have radial tires, the attendant may try to convince you that a sidewall puncture cannot be repaired (which is true). But what he won't tell you is that a tube can be put in a radial which will at least allow you to get to an outlet where tires are more reasonably priced.
- When checking under the hood, attendants have been known to cut the fan belt. This can work two ways: He may cut the belt all the way through and sell you a new one on the spot; or he may cut it part way, let you leave, and then send a tow truck out which will "just happen along" when you break down.
- Another ploy is sprinkling metal filings on and around the alternator. The attendant will then tell you the alternator is "throwing out" shavings and should be replaced.
- An old but still popular ruse is dropping an Alka Seltzer in the battery cells and claiming that the battery is going "bad" or is about to "explode."
- A little oil squirted on the shocks is probably as popular a trick as some of the cons used to sell tires. The simple fact is shocks do not leak in that fashion, so don't be fooled.
- Oil is also often squirted on the outside of the master cylinder or the inside of the wheels to supposedly indicate that the master cylinder or the brake lines are leaking and you are in danger of losing your brakes.
- While the attendant checks your radiator, he may also use an ice pick to puncture it. Again, he may point out the leak right away, or he may let you leave and send a tow truck out to be around when you boil over.

Since an encounter with a dishonest tow truck operator can also leave you with an empty wallet, you should exercise some caution if you do find yourself in need of a tow. Beware of the tow truck driver who tells you there is only one place in town equipped to handle your problem; in some small communities that may be true, but check it out for yourself.

In addition to staying aware of some of the dishonest devices and techniques used to dupe travelers, there are a few things you can do to decrease your chances of being unnecessarily separated from your cash.

- Before you leave on your vacation have your RV thoroughly serviced. Have your local mechanic or service station operator check for any wear or defects in the tires, belts, etc. And if you are unfamiliar with the mechanical operation of your vehicle, make a point to learn a little of the basics (a few of which are covered in this section) so that you will be able to make an intelligent decision about a proposed repair.
- Check on the prices and labor charges (these will vary from area to area) for the repair and replacement of some of the more common equipment on your rig — tires, battery, alternator, fuel pump, water

pump, etc. — so that you will have some knowledge of exactly how much an item or repair should cost.

- Beware of overeager service station attendants, especially in self-service stations, or high pressure sales tactics where the attendant warns of grave danger if you don't buy something.
- Never leave your rig unattended in a service station; this is an open invitation for the dishonest attendant to sabotage your rig.
- Don't allow anyone to check under the hood unless you are by their side. This especially holds true for self-service operations where the attendant comes out to "help you out" while you are busy filling the tank.
- If you find yourself faced with the purchase of parts and/or repairs, pay with an oil company credit card if possible. If a dispute arises later over the cost, you may be able to recover some of your money, as the oil company can usually charge any overcharge back to the station or garage. If you pay with cash or another type of credit card, the oil company supplying the station cannot legally force the dealer to refund your money and your only recourse may be the courts.

Of course, knowledge of the various tactics and a few defensive measures are no guarantee that you aren't going to be faced with repairs or replacement of some of your rig's equipment when you are on the road. If you do find yourself faced with an unexpected problem, use your common sense and don't be stampeded into making a decision because of scare tactics or seemingly sincere promises that the work can be done in only a short time.

Remember that anyone who travels is bound to have legitimate repair problems at one time or another. If you do have a breakdown, you can rest assured that the majority of service station operators, attendants and mechanics are honest and sincerely interested in getting you back on the road with the minimum of delay and expense. But, if you do run across the interstate bandits, don't just chalk it up to experience — you have a right to complain to the state's consumer affairs office, the local better business bureau, chamber of commerce and, if the rip-off is especially blatant, the local police. You may be surprised how much you can do for yourself and others if you stand up for your rights.

Deterring the RV Thief

- Always take your keys with you whenever you leave your rig, and lock the doors and windows no matter how long you intend to be gone.
- Try to park your RV in a well-lighted and secure area. However, don't be lulled into a false sense of security by thinking you needn't take any other precautions to protect your rig. Many professional thieves like to operate in areas where people wouldn't think of questioning their presence.
- In the driveway, park your vehicle with the nose toward the street so anyone tampering with the engine can be seen more easily.
- Replace standard door lock buttons with the slim, tapered kind. They're almost impossible to pull up with a wire.
- Install different locks for the doors and ignition. Then a thief who gets your door key still won't be able to turn the ignition switch.
- Don't hide spare keys on the outside of your RV. The best place to put a spare set of keys is in your wallet.
- Place some identifying mark on the various components in your RV so they can be linked to you if they are stolen.
- Record all the serial numbers on the various components in your rig and keep the list in a safe place in your home or in a safe deposit box.

Driving Emergencies

Sooner or later, everyone encounters emergency situations where extreme defensive measures are needed to avert disaster. Knowing what to do in these emergencies can often turn a potential tragedy into nothing more than a close call. Here are some suggestions to help you deal with emergencies:

* **Avoiding a head-on collision.** If another vehicle suddenly swerves into your lane of traffic, the best defensive maneuver is to swerve your rig to the right. Even if you hit something on the roadside or the vehicle in the next lane, the effects of those collisions will be far less severe than that of a head-on crash. Never swerve to your left, however, as the other driver may suddenly try to correct back into his lane.

* **If your brakes fail.** First, pump the brake pedal to try to restore the brake pressure. If that doesn't work, slowly apply the parking brake and, if you're pulling a trailer, you might try to manually activate the trailer brakes. If those two measures fail to produce results, shift into a lower gear to slow your vehicle. And if all else fails, ease your RV into a guardrail, soft shoulder, curb or even other parked vehicles. Again, you may end up with a damaged rig — but that's better than risking a much more serious collision.

* **If your accelerator is stuck.** First, simply try to free it by lifting it with the toe of your shoe. This usually does the trick; but if it remains stuck, stay calm, keep your eyes on the road and have one of your passengers try to free the pedal. If these two simple measures fail, shift into neutral and brake slowly until you can pull to a stop, out of the lanes of traffic. You should not try turning off the ignition, as this may cause you to lose your power brakes and steering.

* **If you have a blowout.** If the blowout occurs on one of the front tires, your rig will be pulled sharply in the direction of the blown tire. Don't panic, and don't slam on the brakes, as either action could cause you to lose control completely. Lift your foot off the accelerator and grip the wheel tightly to keep your RV in its proper lane. Let the rig gradually slow down of its own accord until you can safely pull off the road. If the rear tire blows, the back of your rig will weave sharply back and forth, but will probably not cause the severe control problems encountered with a front-end blowout. Handle the problem in the same way.

* **If you start to skid.** Again, don't slam on the brakes; that will cause you to lose control completely. Ease your foot off the gas and turn your wheel into the skid and your rig should straighten out. If it starts to overcorrect and begins to skid in the other direction, turn the steering wheel in that direction to regain control.

* **If you are involved in an accident.** Stop as near to the scene as you can, but try to get your rig out of the line of traffic. Give your name, address and license number to those who are also involved. If possible, you should also notify the police and fill out an accident report, as this may help with your insurance claim.

* **If you are the first to arrive at the scene of an accident.** First, take precautions to assure that you won't cause a second accident by pulling beyond the scene and parking ahead of the wreck. Turn on your emergency flashers. If it is safe to do so, turn the ignitions off in the wrecked vehicles, as this will reduce the chance of fire. Try to assist the victims with some basic first-aid techniques as needed. *Don't attempt to move any of the victims* unless it is absolutely necessary for their immediate safety. Call for help from a nearby telephone or with your CB, or send someone else to call. Also, search the immediate area for other victims who may have been thrown from the vehicles.

First Aid for RVing Emergencies

Regardless of whether your travels are limited to the fringes of civilization or frequent forays into the backcountry, an indispensible item for every RV is a well-equipped first-aid kit that will allow you to deal effectively with most travel and camping emergencies. You can purchase a ready-made kit from a drugstore or camping specialty shop, but before you do you might want to analyze your RVing habits to make sure the kit you select will permit you to treat all the minor emergency situations you might encounter. Once you have identified your needs, you may find it necessary to buy some supplementary items for the commercially-prepared kit, or you may decide that preparing your own kit is the best approach.

"The most common type of camping and RVing accidents and emergencies," says William Forgey, MD, a specialist in emergency medicine, "are from burns, blisters and small cuts. Treatment of these injuries is very similar and any kit you buy or put together yourself should contain a good supply of items to at least treat these basic injuries." For dealing with minor emergencies, Dr. Forgey recommends that any good first-aid kit you purchase or assemble include the following:

- Booklet with instructions on how to treat the common medical emergencies likely to be encountered in the field
- Splinter forceps (tweezers)
- No. 10 scalpel
- Butterfly closures (for sealing cuts)
- Eye pads
- Roll of ½-inch tape
- Gauze pads; four each of two x two-inch and three x three-inch
- Two-inch gauze roll
- Three-inch Ace bandage

- Selection of adhesive bandages
- Small plastic vials for storing an emergency supply of regularly needed prescription drugs.

In addition to these basics, Dr. Forgey suggests that you include a special antibiotic ointment, known either as triple antibiotic ointment or by one of several brand names such as Neosporin or Bacitracin. "This ointment can be obtained without a prescription," he explained, "and it is ideal for small lesions because it offers the protection of three broad-spectrum antibiotics — Neomycin, Polymyxin B and Bacitracin — that pretty well combat every type of common bacteria." For first-aid use, try to get the ointment in individual-use foil packets as it is much more efficient.

For cleansing and treating cuts and abrasions, as well as providing antibacterial action, Dr. Forgey recommends your kit include Povidone-Iodine prep pads that are also available in individual-use, sealed packets containing pads saturated with the iodine compound. Povidone-Iodine is a non-stinging and non-staining iodine preparation that is effective in combatting a host of bacteria types, fungi, viruses and other organisms.

"One thing that every emergency medical kit should definitely have is something for pain and headache," Dr. Forgey emphasizes. "The best medication you can obtain for that, without a prescription, is a compound known as Percogesic. You may have trouble obtaining it at some pharmacies," he added, "because some pharmacists may try to tell you it isn't available without a prescription. If that is the case simply shop around until you find a drugstore that does sell it over the counter." Percogesic is a mixture of Tylenol and a muscle relaxer that, according to Dr. Forgey, is extremely safe and effective for the treatment of fever, headaches, muscle aches, pain associated with injury, and is exceptionally good for tension headaches which, believe it or not, can occur quite often while traveling or camping.

RVers are reminded, of course, that mixing medications can be dangerous. If you're already taking medication for any condition, check with your doctor before using Percogesic or any other medicine.

Once you have assembled or purchased your RV first-aid kit, remember that most all the ingredients in the various compounds and ointments (even aspirin) will lose their effectiveness with age. Though the rate at which the different substances deteriorate can vary greatly, it might be a good idea to replace all the items on a regular schedule based upon the first expiration date of the various items. To keep track of the expiration dates, prepare a card that will fit inside the kit that notes the manufacturer's suggested date for discard. In a commercially prepared first-aid kit, the dates will most likely be stamped on the individual items; for those compounds you may buy in bulk, you should be sure to note the discard dates before throwing the outer carton away.

For further information on ready-made first-aid kits or to obtain supplies for the preparation of your own kit, contact: Indiana Camp Supply, Incorporated, PO Box 344, Pittsboro, Indiana 46167; Eddie Bauer, Incorporated, 1737 Airport Way South, Seattle, Washington 98134; Recreational Equipment, Incorporated, PO Box C-88125, Seattle, Washington 98188.

On the Road Repair Tips

More often than not, breakdowns are the result of minor problems that can be easily remedied if you know what to look for. Furthermore, troubleshooting doesn't require a lot of expensive tools or a great deal of mechanical skills. Here are a few of the more common on-the-road problems and their solutions:

• **Engine overheating.** Look for a water leak in the radiator or the radiator and heater hoses. If you find that a hose is leaking, wait until the engine cools, then wrap some duct tape around the hose, loosen the radiator cap to relieve pressure and drive to the nearest RV repair facility for a replacement hose. If the problem is a leak in the radiator, add water and keep an eye on your temperature gauge as you drive to the nearest town for repairs. If the problem is a broken fan belt, let the engine cool, then drive slowly until the warning light comes on again, stop, and repeat the procedure. This may be a slow process, but it will allow you to travel far enough to get help.

• **If your brake warning light comes on,** don't panic; test your brakes and, if they still work, drive slowly to the nearest repair facility. On all late-model autos, trucks and motorhomes, there are two separate hydraulic systems — one for the front brakes and one for the rear — so the chances of completely losing your brakes are remote.

• **Oil level low?** Stop immediately and check the oil level with the dipstick. If the level is indeed low, don't move your rig until you have added oil. If the warning light is just flickering, it could mean (1) your oil is getting too thin or (2) your vehicle is idling too slow. Above all, if the oil light remains on, don't drive any farther — you could seriously damage your engine.

• **Engine overheats in heavy traffic.** First, turn off your air-conditioner if it is running, then put the transmission in neutral and rev the engine; the temperature should drop. If this doesn't work, try turning on the heater to release some of the built-up heat. To avoid overheating problems in traffic, it is always a good idea to turn off your air-conditioner right away.

• **Your ignition is turned on but nothing happens.** First, switch on your headlights; if they go on and do not dim when you turn the ignition switch, you may have trouble with the "neutral" switch in your automatic transmission. Try jiggling the lever back and forth while you turn the key. If the headlights dim when you turn the ignition, you probably have corroded battery terminals or a loose cable connection. You will be able to solve this problem easily by simply removing the cables from the battery terminals, cleaning the contact points and then refastening the cables securely. When removing the cables, always take off the ground first — and when replacing them, attach the ground last. After you've followed these steps, if your lights still dim when the ignition is turned on, you probably have a low battery. Or, if your lights did not come on at all, the battery is probably dead or disconnected completely. If it's dead, you'll need a jump start to get you to the nearest garage.

• **The engine turns over but doesn't catch.** Either you have a problem in the gas line or you're not getting spark. If you have a strong gasoline smell after cranking for a few seconds, your engine is flooded. Look under the hood; if there is gas on the engine block, get help. If not, try starting the engine — but this time hold the gas pedal on the floor for several seconds. If it still doesn't start, tap the carburetor near the gas line and try it again.

To check for spark, remove one of the spark plug wires, pull open a paper clip and push it firmly into the end of the wire connector. Wrap a rag or piece of paper around the back of the spark plug wire and position the paper clip slightly above a nut or bolt on the engine block. Have someone else crank the engine while you watch for a spark to arc from the end of the paper clip. If you don't see a spark, you should call for help.

The problem could also be that your engine is not getting enough gas in the first place. To check for this, remove the top of the air cleaner and see if the choke valve is stuck in the open position. If it is, push it shut and try to start the engine. If that isn't the case, hold the choke valve open and look inside while someone pumps the gas pedal. If no gas is visible, you could have a more serious problem and you should probably call for help.

• **If your alternator light comes on,** don't stop or turn the engine off as you may not get it started again. Do keep driving until you reach the nearest repair facility; however, keep your eye on the other gauges for additional signs of trouble.

• If you're a motorhome owner, you may want to invest in Chrysler Corporation's *Motorhome Chassis Service Guide* ($5). It contains a number of valuable tips on preventive maintenance and troubleshooting. Contact: Manager, Technical Service, Chrysler Corporation, Service and Parts Division, PO Box 1718, Detroit, Michigan 48288. For the ultimate in RV repair guidance, order *Trailer Life's RV Repair & Maintenance Manual* ($12.98). Contact: Patrick J. Flaherty, Vice President, Book Division, TL Enterprises, Incorporated, 29901 Agoura Road, Agoura, California 91301.

Some Common CB 10-Codes

10-2 — receiving your signals perfectly.
10-3 — channel in use.
10-4 — roger; all right.
10-5 — pass a message along to another CBer.
10-6 — too busy to talk.
10-7 — going off-the-air.
10-8 — resuming service after a prolonged period off-the-air.
10-9 — repeat your last transmission.
10-13 — requesting report on conditions ahead; specifically weather.
10-14 — requesting approximate time.
10-20 — present location.
10-23 — stand by.
10-26 — disregard last transmission.
10-33 — a message with high priority.
10-34 — need help.
10-37 — send tow truck.
10-38 — medical emergency; send ambulance.
10-42 — traffic accident.
10-50 — break.
10-70 — fire in progress.

Traveling With Children

Traveling with children can be a rewarding experience, but it does require extra preparation. So to make your travels more enjoyable for you and your children, consider the following:

- Travel at a leisurely pace. Don't try to cover too much distance in a day and allow time for periodic stops. At each stop, give your children ample time for physical activity as this will help them burn off some of the energy they have stored up while riding.
- If you're traveling during peak vacation periods and plan to stay in a particular park, write ahead for reservations and make sure that the park accepts children.
- Stop early. Even with an RV, it takes some time to set up camp, and stopping early will give you the time you need to get your chores out of the way — and to explore your overnight spot with your children.
- If your RV is not self-contained, take a Porta-Potti for those middle of the night necessities.
- Take a few favorite toys, books and puzzles along to keep your youngsters occupied while traveling.
- Make up a "surprise sack" before you leave and hide it somewhere inside the rig. About every third day, when the old toys and games have become tiresome, pull out one of the surprise items for each child. These items need not be expensive, and you can start collecting them several months ahead of your trip during your normal shopping routine. Reserve these items strictly for driving days.
- Take advantage of each camp stop to explore the surroundings with your children. The educational opportunities are unlimited: take walks, collect shells, pine cones, unusual rocks, and acquaint them with the native plant and animal life.
- Plan your sight-seeing excursions to include places of interest for the children. Involve the children in the planning so they have something to look forward to.
- Don't fill every waking hour with plans; leave some room for unexpected side trips to points of interest you'll no doubt discover along the way.

Safety Tips

Traveling with children often calls for a few extra safety precautions — especially if the youngsters are of preschool age. As you would with your home, childproof your rig by storing matches, medicines, cleaning compounds and other toxic substances out of the reach of small hands.

- While you're cooking in the RV, let the children play outdoors, or keep them occupied as far away from the range as possible.
- Turn all of the handles to the rear of the cooktop.
- Keep an eye on children when they are playing near heater grills or electrical outlets and appliances. It might be a good idea to buy a few of the commonly available outlet covers if your children are small, because the limited dimensions of an RV can bring a child into contact with wall sockets more frequently than a home environment.
- Carry records with you that detail your child's medical history — immunization dates, allergies, special medications needed, etc.
- Don't leave small children alone in the RV for any length of time, particularly when they are sleeping.
- Be sure to lock the doors of your rig at night so your children can't wander out while you are sleeping.
- Formulate a plan of what the children should do in the event they become lost. Establish a central meeting place so they will know where to go to meet you if you become separated.

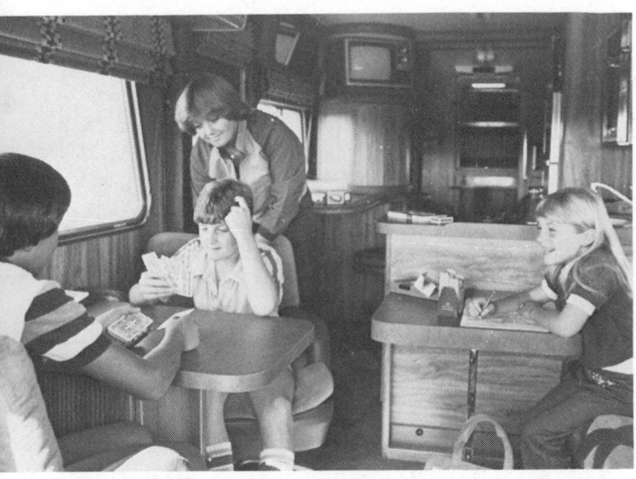

Tips for Good Pictures

Half the fun of any trip is the "remembering" — so here are a few hints that will help you take memorable pictures the next time you, and your camera, go on vacation:

- For sharp pictures, hold your camera steady and gently s-q-u-e-e-z-e the shutter release. With an adjustable camera, use a shutter speed of at least 1/125 second. If your subject is moving, use a faster shutter speed, such as 1/250 or 1/500 second.
- Always keep your camera with you and keep it loaded with film.
- Personalize your vacation pictures by including your family and friends.
- Take close-up pictures — of your family, flowers and interesting details on monuments and memorials.
- For bright pictures with an adjustable camera, follow the exposure suggestions on the film instruction sheet. The instruction sheet or film carton also gives the film-speed number to set on exposure meters and some automatic cameras.
- Take several pictures of each monument and famous building from different points of view. Walk around the subject and look for interesting angles and viewpoints.
- Add interest to your pictures by including people or hanging tree branches in the foreground.
- Hold your camera level so the subject won't appear to be sliding out of the picture.
- To get clear pictures, keep the camera lens clean. When necessary, breathe on the surface and wipe it gently with a clean, soft, lintless cloth.
- Indoors, use flash and move in close to your subject. If you stand too far away when using flash, the picture will be very dark. Check your camera instruction manual for the appropriate distances with your camera.
- Small, lightweight cameras are very popular with tourists. You can carry the camera and a day's supply of film in a sportscoat pocket or a handbag.
- Make title pictures for your slide show, movie or photo album by photographing signs of important landmarks.
- Use fresh film (check the date on the box) and have it processed promptly.
- Heat spoils pictures. Never store your film or camera in the glove compartment, trunk or on the rear-window shelf of your RV. Store it out of direct sunlight, in a well-ventilated area.
- Bad weather can mean good pictures if you have an adjustable or automatic camera. Fog, rain or dark clouds can provide unusual lighting effects and moods.
- Read the information folders available at most monuments, memorials, museums and historic sites so that you will appreciate what you are photographing. Use this information to write captions in your photo albums.

Shape-Up Exercise Program

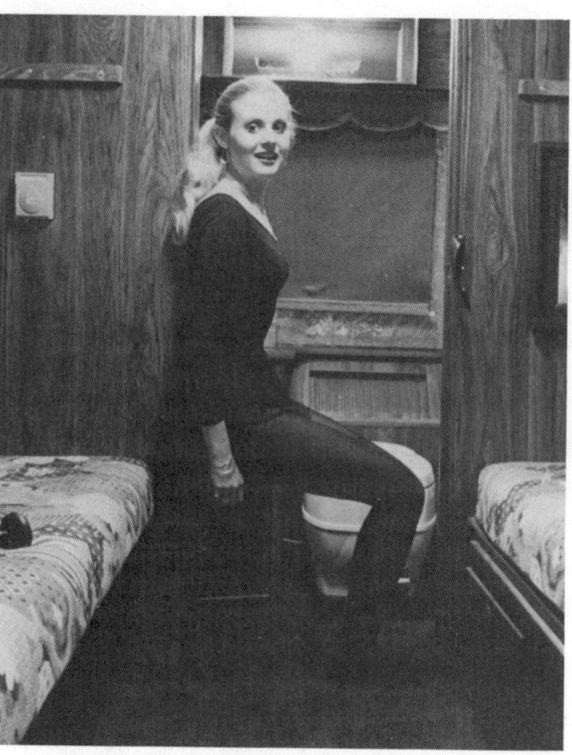

A good exercise for increasing leg strength, and one that is a lot tougher than it looks, can be done by resting your back against a wall or doorjam and bending your knees so that most of your weight is supported by your legs. Hold this position for as long as you can, gradually increasing the time.

By now, the importance of physical fitness and the value of exercise is recognized by just about everyone. With the current jogging craze and the results of several studies which point to the dangers of the sedentary life, scarcely a day goes by that we aren't reminded of both the need and benefits of regular exercise. As a group, RVers probably lead a more active life than others who follow more static pastimes and, therefore, may have less need to be concerned about a good many of the risks of inactivity. However, there are a few things you should be aware of.

Whenever you set out on a trip, be it for a long weekend, two-week vacation or even longer, the disruption of your normal daily routine can place added stress on your body. "A sudden change in your eating and sleeping habits, as well as your general level of activity can aggravate any existing health problems, or sometimes precipitate illness if you aren't in good physical condition," warns Glen Winn, MD, an RVer and North Hollywood, California, specialist in family practice. Dr. Winn also noted that hospital emergency room physicians throughout the nation report a marked increase in the treatment of out-of-state patients during the summer months for maladies that can be directly linked to vacation stress.

In order to head off some of these potential problems there are a few general things you can do. "As a rule Americans tend to have too much fat and sugar in their diets," Dr. Winn said, "But when you are traveling it is easy to fall into the trap of increasing this consumption of fats and sugar even more by eating too many sweets and junk food. While you are on the road," he added, "try to limit the intake of fast foods, and turn to more wholesome foods such as fresh fruits for snacks. Also, add more protein to your diet and, as added insurance, it might be a good idea to take a good multi-vitamin once a day."

Another problem that faces travelers, and may affect RVers to a greater extent over a long period of time, is the effect of long hours on the road. As several studies have indicated, long sedentary hours increase the risks of heart trouble. For instance, in one study, conductors on London trolley cars who walked up and down stairs and back and forth on the double-decker buses were found to have fewer heart attacks than the drivers who remained seated during their jobs. "When you sit for a long time, whether driving or as a passenger, you tend to have a pooling of the blood in your legs," Dr. Winn explained. "This can increase the risks of circulatory system problems in general. Your legs act almost like ancillary hearts in that they are pumps which drive the blood back up through the veins to the heart, so it is very important to exercise your legs periodically while traveling." To do this Dr. Winn recommends that, instead of driving three to four hours at a time between gas stations, you should stop about every hour and get out and walk around. Of course, if you are a passenger in a motorhome or camper you can get up and stretch your legs but, for the sake of the driver, try to set a routine that allows a respite from the road now and then.

While those are some of the special problems that are of particular interest to RVers, and a few suggestions for avoiding the more obvious problems that befall the frequent traveler, the best defense is still a good offense. Embarking on a good program of regular exercise during the winter months, and maintaining that program throughout the year, even while traveling, will vastly increase your chances of avoiding problems and put you in a much better condition to deal with any health problems that might occur. In addition, you will find that with an increased level of fitness comes an increased awareness and enjoyment of your RVing hours.

Of course, before anyone undertakes any type of exercise program they should first have a thorough checkup by their family physician. There is probably no one who could not indulge in, or benefit from, some type of exercise program; however, your doctor is probably the only person who can advise you on exactly how strenuous a routine you should undertake. Dr. Winn says, "I don't recommend a program of strenuous exercise for an older person, or anybody else for that matter, if they haven't exercised much in the past. For people 40 or older, especially for men, and for men and women both if they are smokers, the checkup should include a treadmill test." The treadmill test monitors blood pressure, pulse rate, oxygen consumption and the heart's electrical activity as you exercise on a treadmill or other device. Not only is this test good for detecting cardiovascular problems, it is also a good indicator of your present level of fitness.

Incidentally, once you do begin your program, a good way to monitor your progress and improve cardiovascular condition is to take your pulse for one minute while you are resting in order to determine your normal pulse rate. Then, within 15 seconds after exercising heavily, take your pulse again to obtain a peak reading, then take it again in three minutes. If after 10 minutes of exercise you have gotten your pulse rate up to about 140 beats per minute, and it drops back to normal within three minutes, you are in good physical condition. Bear in mind that the figure of 140 beats per minute is merely an example. Other factors besides general physical condition, such as age or certain medications, must be considered in determining the threshold range of an individual's heart rate. If you are under 30, for instance, your heart rate may climb to 165 or more beats per minute following strenuous exercise, while the rate of most persons over 65 may not, and probably should not, exceed 140. Your doctor can provide you with an optimum pulse rate for exercising.

In beginning your exercise routine try to aim for a balanced program that includes some static exercises such as isometrics and mild weight lifting, which will increase muscle tone and strength, combined with rhythmic exercises, such as some calisthenics, walking, jogging, bicycling or swimming, which give the cardiovascular system a good workout. Also, as an RVer, you should try to select a number of exercises that can be done within the confines of your RV. Whatever exercises you select, Dr. Winn recommends that the program be at least 20 minutes a day, either in one session or two 10-minute sessions, one in the morning and one in the evening. If you

A regular program of exercise will prepare you for your RV travels, and improving your physical condition will make your leisure hours more enjoyable.

prefer exercising every other day that's all right, and if you skip a day now and then, don't worry about it unless it gets to be a habit. You may want to increase the time as you progress, as the more you exercise, the better you'll feel and the more you may want to exercise. Whatever routine you set, start out slowly. If you have trouble disciplining yourself to a routine at the beginning, you might want to join an exercise class at the local "Y" or, better yet, organize one yourself with your RVing friends. If you are over 60 you might want to look into classes that may be offered by your local chapter of the National Association for Human Development. You can find them in your phone book, and if they don't now offer classes they may help you get one started. Naturally, you can always go to a commercial health club if you wish, but use some caution as you might end up spending a lot of money on a membership that you really don't need.

It is impossible here to list all the individual exercises and the benefits of each; if you are having trouble determining what type of routine is best for you, there are a number of good exercise books available at your bookstore, local sporting goods store or health food store.

Since jogging is the current craze, a few words about its exercise benefits seem in order. Some of the devotees of jogging have raised it almost to the level of religion and extoll its virtues so vehemently that it might seem like it is the only viable way to fitness. There is no question that jogging does have considerable value, but it is not for everyone. In fact, it can be harmful for those who have leg or back problems or other conditions which could be aggravated by the jolting running.

Also, while we are at it, a few words about exercise devices may be appropriate. There are a number of devices currently on the market which are advertised as producing remarkable results with little or no effort on the part of the user. The vast majority of these are gimmicks that are just plain rip-offs, and the only benefits will be to the bank account of the manufacturer. Probably one of the biggest rip-offs currently making the advertising rounds are the "vapor barrier garments" (rubberized suits, pants, shorts, etc.) which are supposed to produce remarkable weight loss for the user. If any weight loss does occur during use it is only temporary due to dehydration. Any weight dropped will be quickly regained as soon as the water level in your body is returned to normal. The best devices on the market are still the simple ones, such as cast iron dumbbells, interchangeable weight sets, ankle weights that attach with Velcro strips, and expanding cable or spring exercisers (the rubber cable ones are the safest) with which you can do exercises that will work all parts of the body.

It is important to note that for many years most fitness experts have harbored a good deal of prejudice against weight lifting as exercise. Most of us have heard the old wives' tales that weight lifting only builds muscles, will make you "muscle bound" and doesn't really build endurance or adequately exercise the cardiovascular system. Though there may still be a few diehards who might try to tell you differently, it has been pretty much proven in the last couple of years that weight lifting, when done with moderate weights and with a proper routine, is one of the best forms of exercise for the cardiovascular system.

An exercise program that might serve as a guide for those who want to get started might include:

A brief warm-up period of two to five minutes, followed by some calisthenics for stretching and further warm-up; then some selected routines with small weights or a cable exerciser, topped off with about 25 situps. After you have finished this routine you might want to go for a brisk walk, short jog, bike ride or swim.

W. C. Fields once said, "I get the urge to exercise every now and then, and whenever the urge strikes me I lie down until it passes." If you are waiting for the urge to pass, get up before it does and start your shape-up now.

Winter Travel

For a good many people, RVing is a strictly seasonal activity. After Labor Day, when the youngsters are back in school, and the temperatures begin to drop, the gear is unloaded from the RV and stowed to await the arrival of spring. It's an almost automatic response; most have never really considered an alternative, others may have considered it but just as quickly dismissed the notion, thinking that there were few places to go and too many discomforts to endure.

The fact is, winter RVing can open up whole new horizons. For many years, more and more of us have been enjoying winter RVing, and look forward with great anticipation to the onset of the cool fall weather that brings both beautiful landscapes and uncrowded campgrounds. In the fall and winter months, areas that have become uninterestingly familiar can take on a whole new aspect, and opportunities to sample new types of recreation are almost limitless.

Of course, winter RVing can be more demanding, and it does require that the traveler plan trips with more foresight and care. And because winter traveling and winter camping also require a willingness to accept a few discomforts and inconveniences, it is something that should only be undertaken after careful thought, and with the total agreement of everyone in your party. One thing to bear in mind, though: Few people are more ideally equipped for the rigors of winter travel, and its various adversities, than the RV owner. Ideally equipped, that is, with care taken to prepare the RV and its occupants for all contingencies.

Systematic Preparation

Before setting out on any winter outing, carefully check the various systems on your vehicle. First check your RV or tow vehicle to make sure the battery is fully charged; make sure there is fresh antifreeze in the radiator; check the water hoses for leaks or weak spots; make sure your windshield wipers are in good condition; check all lights to see that they are working, and make sure headlights are clean and aimed properly; run the heater and defroster to make sure both are in good working order; and test your brakes for proper adjustment. Tires are very important in winter driving and all your tires should have adequate tread. If you plan to do a lot of driving in snow, the ideal combination is snow tires on the rear and tires with good, deep tread on the front.

A thorough check of your vehicle's exhaust system is of primary importance. Since winter travel always brings with it the possibility that you may be stranded for a time, it is imperative that your vehicle's exhaust be unobstructed and free of leaks. This is especially important for camper owners, as the National Highway Traffic Safety Administration reported four deaths from carbon monoxide poisoning last year in camper units. The apparent cause was the fact that the standard exhaust pipes on the trucks did not extend all the way out from under the truck bodies and thus allowed exhaust fumes to seep up into the camper body.

Once you are satisfied that the vehicle is ready for winter driving, you can turn your attention to the RV systems. Check the propane tank to make sure it is full, and examine the lines to make sure they are clear and leakfree. Many vans and campers do not have the heavy insulation that is found in more sophisticated RVs, so

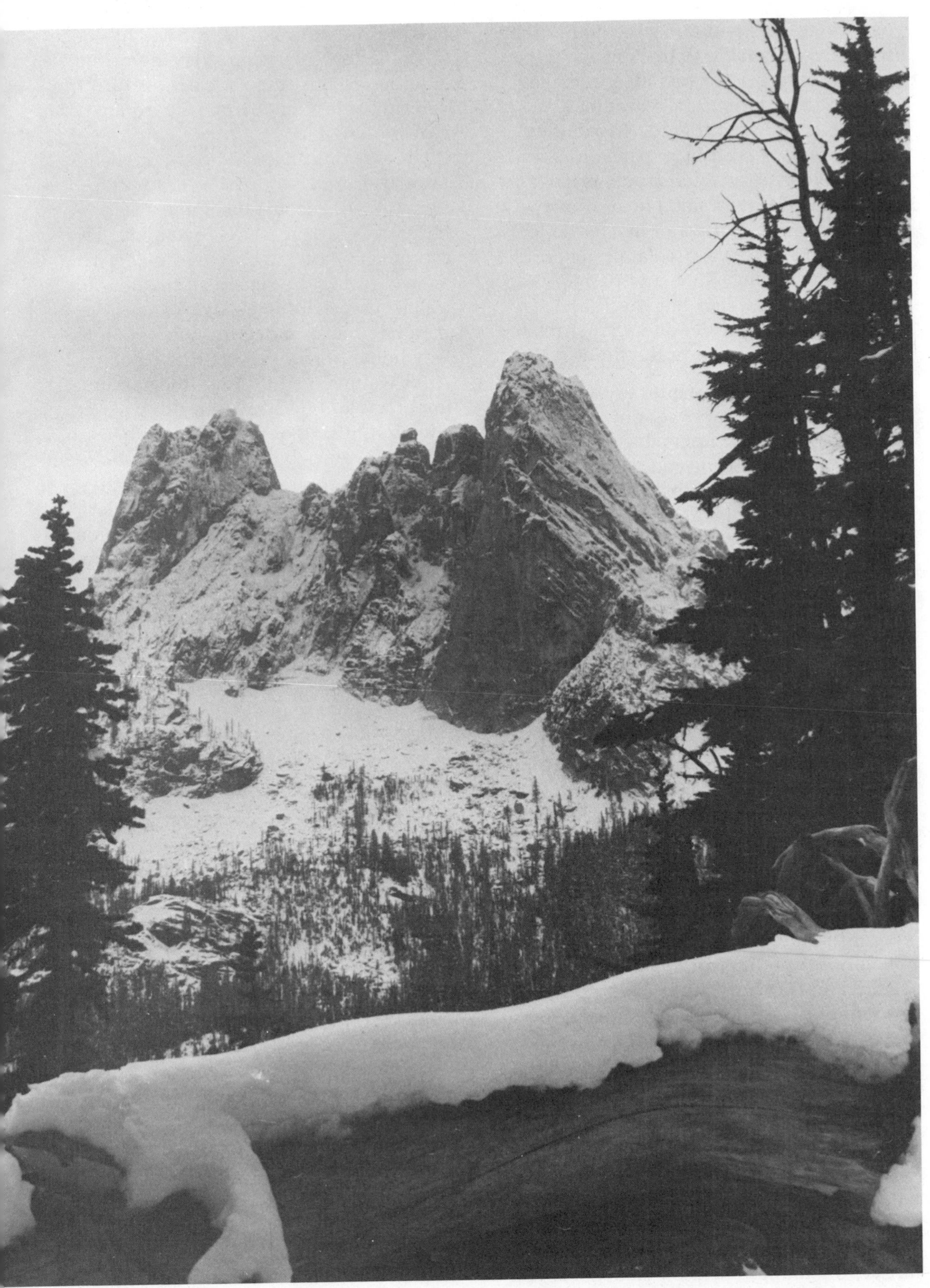

your water lines and tanks are going to be especially vulnerable to freezing temperatures. It is a good idea to make sure that your water tanks are not completely full so if they do freeze they will not be damaged by expansion. Because your freshwater supply is likely to freeze, it is always a good idea to carry a secondary supply of water inside the RV. Also, if you have a recirculating toilet, keep the water level low, and perhaps add a de-icer to the water; but check the chemical content of the de-icer first to make sure it won't harm the fittings.

Never leave on any winter trip without a full gas tank, and never set out without carrying a few basic items that will be invaluable in the event you become stuck or stranded by the weather. Though you may want to include other items, the following should be considered necessities: tire chains, sand or traction mats, small snow shovel, ice scraper, snow brush, flares and a flashlight with spare batteries. Even if you are only planning a day's outing, you should always leave sleeping bags or warm bedding packed in the RV; they could literally save your life if you are trapped in a bad storm.

Winter driving always brings with it the threat of getting stuck in snow or ice. If you do get stuck, try these tactics. Turn your wheels from side to side to clear the snow away. Keep a light foot on the gas and ease forward. Gentle rocking might help; but don't force it, as you could end up getting more deeply mired. For better traction, try putting rock salt, sand or traction mats (made out of old strips of carpeting) under the wheels. Unless you have four-wheel-drive, chains are usually the best bet for extricating yourself from snow and ice.

Storm Sense

If you find yourself trapped by a winter storm — a severe blizzard or ice storm that makes visibility so bad that it is impossible to drive — stay put and wait for help to arrive, or summon help on your CB. If you need to run your engine for warmth or to keep the fuel lines from freezing up, make sure the exhaust pipe is clear, or turn the vehicle so the fumes from the exhaust blow downwind.

Unless you can see a house or shelter, never get out and try to walk for help. It's very easy to become disoriented in a blizzard, and landmarks, even your RV, can quickly become obscured by blowing snow. During the severe storms that hit California's mountains last winter, five men became stranded in their car on the way home from a neighboring community. After waiting a short time, they became impatient and decided to try to walk to shelter. Outside of the safety of their car, they were quickly engulfed in the whiteout created by the driving snow; soon they were unable to find even their car, let alone any other shelter. The car was found the next morning by a snowplow operator; their bodies were found five months later after the spring thaw.

It is nearly impossible for even the strongest man to walk in a blizzard. If you are not swallowed in the whiteout, the fatigue is sure to get you — the mere process of dragging yourself through a foot or two of snow can sap your strength amazingly fast.

If you do have to get out of your RV, or think that you may have a good chance of getting to a nearby house to summon help, tie a length of cord or rope to the door handle and let it play out behind you as you walk. If you find that you can't make it, you will at least be able to follow the cord back to the safety of your RV. Tragically, people have perished within a few yards of their vehicle because they were unable to find it after walking just a short distance.

Though most commercial campgrounds in areas of severe weather close by late fall, many federal and state campgrounds are open year-round. In most of these campgrounds you are welcome to camp free of charge as long as access is possible. Remember, though, it is not a wise idea to park in remote sections of these areas as it may make it more difficult to get out should you awaken to find a foot or more of snow has fallen overnight. As an added precaution when traveling during the winter, always carry a weather radio that allows you to tune into broadcasts of the National Weather Service and get updated weather information before it is available on the standard radio bands. Also, before leaving on your trip, leave a list with a friend or relative of the campgrounds you may be staying at, an itinerary of other spots you intend to visit, and the approximate date and time you expect to return home.

Late fall travelers in the Southwest may not have to deal with snow and ice, but they can fall victim, if they fail to take the proper precautions, to flash floods. When a violent thunderstorm breaks over the mountain and desert regions, runoff from the torrential rains can cascade into steep canyons in a matter of minutes. A wall of water, sometimes as high as 10 to 30 feet, swirls through the canyons and arroyos, picking up mud, boulders, trees and other debris, and developing a tremendous force as it moves along. The big problem in flash floods is that they can result from thunderstorms centered over mountains many miles away, making it possible for them to strike swiftly and without warning.

To protect yourself against flash floods:

- Keep an eye on the sky, and listen frequently to weather reports.
- Camp on high ground, but not on top of exposed peaks or ridges.
- Avoid deep canyons and dry washes during stormy or threatening weather. If a thunderstorm strikes, move to high ground immediately. Do not attempt to outrun a flash flood with your RV.
- Follow the instructions of local authorities. If you are asked to leave an area, leave immediately. Many people have lost their lives needlessly because they failed to heed the warnings of police, rangers and other officials.

For up-to-date information on traveling conditions be sure to contact your local office of the highway patrol or state police, and for more information on winter travel and driving tips contact: National Safety Council, 444 North Michigan Avenue, Chicago, Illinois 60611; American Automobile Association, 8111 Gatehouse Road, Falls Church, Virginia 22042, or National Highway Traffic Safety Administration, Traffic Safety Programs (NTS-10), 400 Seventh Street, Washington, D.C. 20590.

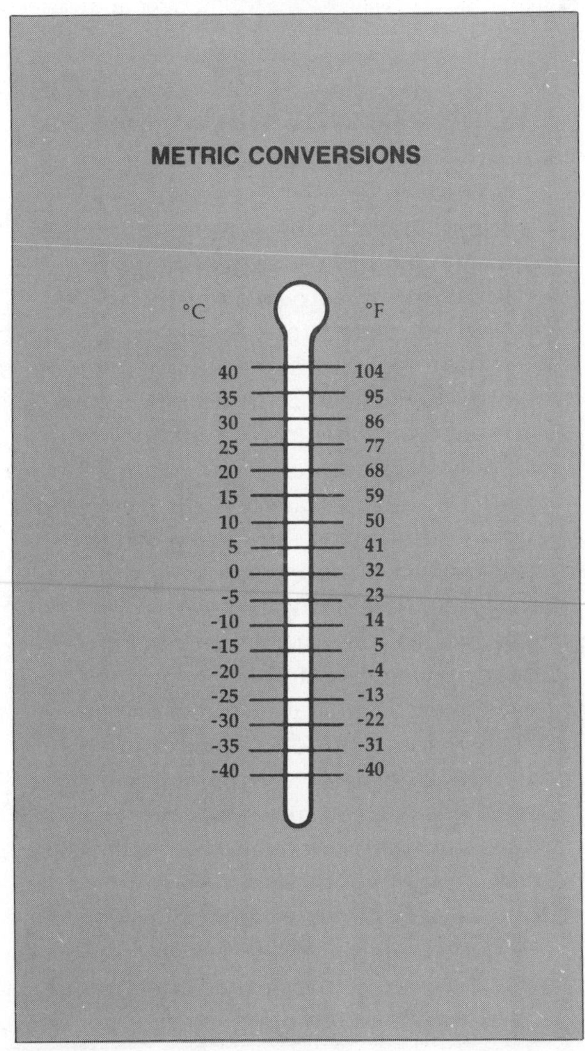

A variety of driving aids, such as these heavy-duty traction racks, make winter RVing safer and easier.

Winter Driving: Safe As You Make It

Safe winter driving is more than good equipment properly adjusted; it's a driver with attitude and reactions properly adjusted for the season.

Attitude preparation is knowledge of what to expect, what to do and when, and just as important — what *not* to do.

The general winter driving rule is *slow down.* Decreased traction calls for longer stopping distances, longer passing distances, and more time required to recognize developing danger. Complicating the problem even more is lessened visibility due to snow and mist-covered windows, wind-driven snow, fog and the decreased hours of daylight, and head and taillights partially obscured by snow and ice. Some say winter driving is the same as good, safe, smooth summer driving done in extreme slow motion.

Smooth might be just the word to describe good winter driving technique. Avoid erratic movement; excessive acceleration or braking can precipitate a skid. Remember braking transfers weight forward, and with the lessened traction of icy pavement, it's extremely easy for wheels to lock up totally. A locked, sliding front wheel will continue its forward motion no matter which direction the steering wheel is pointed. The word on braking is smooth and light.

On going into an icy turn, or down a grade that requires braking, start the braking far in advance of the point at which it would be required on dry pavement. That, of course, means greatly reduced speeds. The best winter drivers negotiate terrain as though they had no brakes, relying almost entirely on engine braking and careful gear selection and early assessment of the road conditions ahead to avoid obstacles that require braking effort. It makes sense; the problems — and the accidents — in snow and ice driving aren't usually encountered while running straight ahead with the throttle down, but stopping at lights, intersections and starting up at same.

Route planning can be one way to ensure trouble-free winter travel. Avoid whenever possible, even if it means traveling slightly farther, the steeper grades, left turns at traffic-clogged intersections and other accident-prone locations. If an alternate route gives stoplights as opposed to stop signs, chose the route with the stoplights; they may be green, especially if you time your driving to hit them properly. Coincidentally, the more heavily traveled route will have more snow plowed away, and sanding will probably begin earlier on main routes than secondary boulevards.

A trip driven at slower speeds will take longer. Start earlier if on-time arrival is a must. A 15-minute summertime commute may take 45 minutes or longer in winter blizzard conditions.

Vehicle Condition Important

Certain aspects of a vehicle's mechanical condition are especially critical to winter handling. Uneven braking forces at the wheels can be compensated for on dry roads, but will start spins and skids in winter. Glazed or oil contaminated linings, uneven rotors or out-of-round brake drums, worn shoes, partially inoperative wheel cylinders or maladjusted brakes are hazards.

Wheels only provide braking force, or traction, when they're in contact with and rolling on the roadway. Any wheel that shimmies, bounces or wobbles due to imbalance, bad shocks or poor alignment is obviously doing only a portion of the job it's designed to do.

Bigger tires and wheels decrease braking efficiency. It's a simple matter of leverage. An 11-inch brake in the middle of a 30-inch wheel is obviously better equipped to stop the rolling mass of that wheel, and the mass of everything attached to it (the truck) than the same 11-inch brake attached to the center of a 35-inch wheel. There's more tire, more rubber . . . but it's the brake that stops the wheel. The phenomenon is there; if you've larger wheels, you should at least be aware of it.

Weighty Problems

Weight distribution is more critical in winter driving. Weigh the rig, and strive for close to an even distribution of weight front to rear. Full fuel tanks usually help, and prevent water condensation as well. Whenever possible, move weight around to where it's needed. Bags of sand or rock salt are ideal ballast for winter. They provide weight where needed, and, spread under wheels, the material can pull you out of a wheel spinning situation.

With you and your RV properly prepped, you're ready to get out and enjoy the world of winter RVing.

Gearing Up for Cold Weather

While cold weather RVing is going to require more care in the preparation of your rig, it is also going to require a reevaluation of your personal outdoor gear. Sleeping bags that are more than adequate for three-season camping may be woefully inadequate during the winter months. And winter garments must be selected with care to make sure that they provide comfort for all the weather conditions you may encounter.

Generally, for sleeping in cold weather, even within the shelter of your RV, each person should have a sleeping bag or comforter that provides at least three inches of single-layer loft. Down is by far the best insulator, but down is getting exorbitantly expensive and the quality, in some cases, is beginning to suffer. If you don't want to invest in expensive, high-quality down bags or comforters, there are many fine-quality synthetic-fill sleeping bags and comforters on the market that are more reasonably priced but capable of providing you with ample

Garments constructed with Thinsulate insulation from the 3M Company are said to provide twice the warmth of any standard insulation — including down — when equal thicknesses are compared.

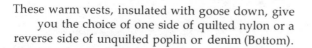

These warm vests, insulated with goose down, give you the choice of one side of quilted nylon or a reverse side of unquilted poplin or denim (Bottom).

protection from the elements. The big problem with these is that they tend to be bulkier than the down gear and, therefore, more difficult to store within the confines of your RV.

With the high interest in year-round activities, especially backpacking and alpine and nordic skiing, cold-weather apparel has seen some remarkable advances. Winter campers now have a large selection of well-constructed down and synthetic-fill jackets and parkas to choose from, as well as other garments such as wind shells and vests. Again, the best insulator for most winter conditions is probably down; however, down can quickly lose its insulating properties if it becomes wet, so you might want to look for one of the synthetic fills (Fiberfill II, Hollofil II, Thinsulate, Dacron 88) if you plan to do much camping in wet conditions. Certainly, these synthetic fills will be more suitable for children who are almost certain to get wet. Also, they're more reasonably priced — which is no small consideration when you're outfitting growing youngsters.

Thinsulate, the newest of the synthetics, deserves some special mention because of its remarkable qualities. Manufactured by 3M Company, Thinsulate is a combination of conventional polyester fibers and extremely fine polyolefin fibers. It is these minute fibers, 3M claims, that allow the material to insulate very efficiently without being bulky. These microfibers apparently trap more dead air in a given space than the larger, more widely spaced fibers of conventional synthetic fills, or even down. At any rate, Thinsulate garments are exceptionally warm without being excessively bulky, a factor that has allowed garment makers to produce fashionable clothing that is also warm.

A relatively new laminated fabric called Gore-Tex is also worthy of special mention, as its appearance in the last few years has wrought some major changes in the outdoor garment industry. The beauty of Gore-Tex is that it offers protection against moisture, even driving rain, while still allowing the garment to "breathe," which permits perspiration and water vapor to wick away.

In selecting winter apparel it is a good idea to shop carefully, since much of the clothing that was originally designed to be functional and warm has suddenly become fashionable, and many of the items now offered actually provide poor protection. Probably the best place to buy is in a specialty shop or through one of the reputable mail-order outfitters.

Finally, if you really want to beat the high cost of outdoor garments and gear, but don't want to sacrifice quality, you might want to look into sew-it-yourself kits. These kits produce marked savings because you supply the labor in the construction of the parka, vest, wind shell, sleeping bag, etc. The kit instructions are generally easy to follow and the contents can be put together by those with little or no sewing experience.

Here is a listing of some of the mail-order firms that supply quality ready-made or kit items:

Altra Kits, Incorporated
5541 Central Avenue
Boulder, Colorado 80301

Early Winters, Limited
110 Prefontaine, South
Seattle, Washington 98104

Eastern Mountain Sports
Vose Farm Road
Peterborough, New Hampshire 03458

Eddie Bauer
Fifth and Union
PO Box 3700
Seattle, Washington 98124

Frostline Kits
Frostline Circle
Denver, Colorado 80241

L. L. Bean
Freeport, Maine 04033

Winter Checklist

The following will serve as a quick checklist of those items that should be considered in preparing for winter travel emergencies.

- Flares
- Sturdy snow shovel
- Sand, traction mats (old pieces of carpet)
- Flashlight, spare batteries
- Windshield de-icer
- A couple hundred yards of rope or sturdy cord to assist you in finding your RV again if you decide to look for landmarks
- CB radio
- Compass
- Tarp or plastic sheet to seal off the engine from blowing snow
- Emergency rations, including foods that have a high carbohydrate content
- Winter-weight sleeping bags and warm blankets
- Warm clothing, including sweaters, parkas, mittens, socks, waterproof boots, scarf or ski mask to protect against wind-blown snow and ice
- Snowshoes
- Extra prescription drugs for those who may be taking important medications such as insulin or other life-supportive drugs

Weather Lore

A red dawn is a sign of rain and storm.

A red sunset is a sign of fine weather.

Brilliant Northern Lights foretell a fine day and then storm.

Hoar frost in autumn is a sign of south wind and rain.

When gulls fly high, stormy weather may be expected.

When goats come home from the hills expect rain soon.

When distant hills appear near, rainy weather is coming.

Rote from the shore on a calm night indicates wind from that direction the following day.

When wild animals take on a thick coat of fur in autumn, it is a sign of a severe winter.

After the sun crosses the line in September, watch the wind and weather for the following days. Each day is said to forecast the weather for the individual months ahead.

When the wind shifts against the sun,
Trust it not for back 'twill run.
When the wind is in the East
'Tis neither good for man or beast.
Mackerel sky and mares' tails
Make the sailor furl his sails.

Watch the new moon. If you can hang a powder horn on the lower rim of the crescent, it is a sign of stormy weather.

The following are common signs of rain: Soot falling to the ground, dogs sleeping through the day, spiders very active, rheumatic pains with elderly people.

To dream of horses is a sign with sailormen that storms will come.

When cats are very playful, they are said to "gale up the weather."

Keeping An Eye on the Weather

In your RV travels you're probably not going to be very far from your radio and the latest weather forecast. Nevertheless, that's not going to guarantee that your plans won't literally be dampened by an unexpected change in the weather. The problem is, the latest forecast might not always apply to your immediate area of travel and, at best, forecasts only have about an 80% accuracy rate.

Of course, you can't do anything about the weather — but you can keep alert to sudden changes by keeping an eye on the changing cloud formations. Here are some of the more common cloud formations and what they can tell you.

Cumulus. These are fair weather, puffy cauliflower-like clouds that form constantly changing shapes as they move through the sky. They mean fair weather unless they begin to pile up into *cumulonimbus* thunderheads.

Stratus. These are the dull-gray clouds that make for heavy laden skies. When they darken, it is a sign that they are about to drop their moisture — usually only a fine drizzle.

Cirrus. Thin, wispy and feathery, these clouds are formed of ice crystals high in the atmosphere where the temperature is always far below freezing. While they appear in fair weather, they can be a signal of an approaching storm.

Nimbostratus. The true rain clouds, they have a dark, wet look with streaks of rain often extending to the ground.

Stratocumulus. Irregular masses of clouds that are dark and puffy. They do not produce rain, but may change into nimbostratus rain clouds.

Cumulonimbus. The big thunderheads whose bases almost touch the ground; they contain violent updrafts that may carry their tops as high as 75,000 feet. It is these clouds which, in their most violent form, produce tornadoes.

A Weather Tip

You can judge the distance of an approaching thunderstorm by timing how long it takes the thunder to reach you after you see a lightning flash. Since sound travels at the speed of one mile in just under five seconds, simply count the seconds from the time you see the flash and hear the thunder.

A thunderstorm also signals its approach by the fact that cold air generally flows forward about three miles in front of the storm. A sudden rush of cold air should alert you that a storm is on its way.

TRIP DIARY

Date	Departed From	Arrived At	Mileage	Tolls	Gas	Oil	Misc.

TRIP DIARY

Date	Departed From	Arrived At	Mileage	Tolls	Gas	Oil	Misc.

TRIP DIARY

Date	Departed From	Arrived At	Mileage	Tolls	Gas	Oil	Misc.

TRIP DIARY

Date	Departed From	Arrived At	Mileage	Tolls	Gas	Oil	Misc.

TRIP DIARY

Date	Departed From	Arrived At	Mileage	Tolls	Gas	Oil	Misc.

TRIP DIARY

Date	Departed From	Arrived At	Mileage	Tolls	Gas	Oil	Misc.

TRIP DIARY

Date	Departed From	Arrived At	Mileage	Tolls	Gas	Oil	Misc.

TRIP DIARY

Date	Departed From	Arrived At	Mileage	Tolls	Gas	Oil	Misc.

Department of the Army
Office of the Chief of Engineers
Civil Works Directorate
Washington, D.C. 20314